THE CAMBRIDGE HANDBOOK OF CLINICAL ASSESSMENT AND DIAGNOSIS

AF765717

This *Handbook* provides a contemporary and research-informed review of the topics essential to clinical psychological assessment and diagnosis. It outlines assessment issues that cross all methods, settings, and disorders, including (but not limited to) psychometric issues, diversity factors, ethical dilemmas, validity of patient presentation, psychological assessment in treatment, and report writing. These themes run throughout the volume as leading researchers summarize the empirical findings and technological advances in their area. With each chapter written by major experts in their respective fields, the text gives interpretive and practical guidance for using psychological measures for assessment and diagnosis.

MARTIN SELLBOM is a Professor in the Department of Psychology at the University of Otago, New Zealand. He has received several awards for his scholarly accomplishments, including the American Psychological Foundation's Theodore Millon Award, American Psychology–Law Society's Saleem Shah Award, and the Society for Personality Assessment's Samuel and Anne Beck Award.

JULIE A. SUHR is Professor of Psychology and Director of Clinical Training in the Department of Psychology at Ohio University, USA. She is also a Fellow of the National Academy of Neuropsychology and the American Psychological Association.

THE CAMBRIDGE HANDBOOK OF CLINICAL ASSESSMENT AND DIAGNOSIS

Edited by
Martin Sellbom
University of Otago
Julie A. Suhr
Ohio University

CAMBRIDGE
UNIVERSITY PRESS

CAMBRIDGE
UNIVERSITY PRESS

University Printing House, Cambridge CB2 8BS, United Kingdom

One Liberty Plaza, 20th Floor, New York, NY 10006, USA

477 Williamstown Road, Port Melbourne, VIC 3207, Australia

314-321, 3rd Floor, Plot 3, Splendor Forum, Jasola District Centre, New Delhi - 110025, India

79 Anson Road, #06-04/06, Singapore 079906

Cambridge University Press is part of the University of Cambridge.

It furthers the University's mission by disseminating knowledge in the pursuit of education, learning and research at the highest international levels of excellence.

www.cambridge.org
Information on this title: www.cambridge.org/9781108415910
DOI: 10.1017/9781108235433

© Cambridge University Press 2020

This publication is in copyright. Subject to statutory exception and to the provisions of relevant collective licensing agreements, no reproduction of any part may take place without the written permission of Cambridge University Press.

First published 2020

A catalogue record for this publication is available from the British Library

Library of Congress Cataloging in Publication data
Names: Sellbom, Martin, editor. | Suhr, Julie A., editor.
Title: The Cambridge handbook of clinical assessment and diagnosis / edited by Martin Sellbom, University of Otago, Julie A. Suhr, Ohio University.
Description: Cambridge, United Kingdom ; New York, NY : Cambridge University Press, 2020. | Series: Cambridge handbooks in psychology | Includes bibliographical references and index.
Identifiers: LCCN 2019037676 (print) | LCCN 2019037677 (ebook) | ISBN 9781108415910 (hardback) | ISBN 9781108235433 (epub)
Subjects: LCSH: Mental illness – Classification. | Mental illness – Diagnosis. | Psychiatric social work. | Social service.
Classification: LCC RC455.2.C4 C36 2020 (print) |
LCC RC455.2.C4 (ebook) | DDC 616.89–dc23
LC record available at https://lccn.loc.gov/2019037676
LC ebook record available at https://lccn.loc.gov/2019037677

ISBN 978-1-108-41591-0 Hardback
ISBN 978-1-108-40249-1 Paperback

Cambridge University Press has no responsibility for the persistence or accuracy of URLs for external or third-party internet websites referred to in this publication, and does not guarantee that any content on such websites is, or will remain, accurate or appropriate.

Contents

Figures

Tables

Contributors

Thomas M. Achenbach, Department of Psychiatry, University of Vermont, USA
F. Taylor Agate, Department of Psychology, University of Victoria, Canada
Teresa Allan, School of Psychology, University of Ottawa, Canada
Kaley Angers, Department of Psychology, Ohio University, USA
R. Michael Bagby, Departments of Psychology and Psychiatry, University of Toronto, Canada
William Barr, Department of Neurology, NYU Langone Health, USA
Christopher T. Barry, Department of Psychology, Washington State University, USA
Philip Batterham, Centre for Mental Health Research, Australian National University, Australia
Amanda Beltrani, Department of Psychology, Fairleigh Dickinson University, USA
Yossef S. Ben-Porath, Department of Psychology, Kent State University, USA
Rachel Brand, Centre for Mental Health, Swinburne University of Technology, Australia
Keila Brockveld, Centre for Emotional Health, Department of Psychology, Macquarie University, Australia
Danielle Burchett, Department of Psychology, California State University, Monterey Bay, USA
Alison Calear, Centre for Mental Health Research, Australian National University, Australia
Natacha Carragher, Consultant, World Health Organization, Australia
Lee Anna Clark, Department of Psychology, University of Notre Dame, USA
Christopher C. Conway, Department of Psychology, Fordham University, USA
Lisa Whipple Drozdick, Pearson Inc., USA
Chloe M. Evans, Department of Psychology, University at Buffalo, The State University of New York, USA
G. Cynthia Fekken, Department of Psychology, Queen's University, Canada
Mauricio A. Garcia-Barrera, Department of Psychology, University of Victoria, Canada
Jeffrey L. Goodie, Department of Medical and Clinical Psychology, Uniformed Services University, USA
Sarah A. Griffin, Department of Psychological Sciences, University of Missouri, USA
Seth Grossman, The Millon Personality Group, USA
Jordan P. Harp, College of Medicine, University of Kentucky, USA
Ashley C. Helle, Department of Psychological Sciences, University of Missouri, USA
Ronald R. Holden, Department of Psychology, Queen's University, Canada
John Hunsley, School of Psychology, University of Ottawa, Canada
Masha Y. Ivanova, Department of Psychiatry, University of Vermont, USA
Veronica I. Johnson, Department of Counselor Education, University of Montana, USA

Zornitsa Kalibatseva, Department of Psychology, Stockton University, USA
Jennifer Braden Kirkpatrick, Department of Disability and Psychoeducational Studies, University of Arizona, USA
Sarah E. Kleiman, VA Boston Healthcare System, USA
Laura Grofer Klinger, TEACCH Autism Program, Department of Psychiatry, University of North Carolina, USA
Linda K. Knauss, Widener University, USA
Robert F. Krueger, Department of Psychology, University of Minnesota, USA
James Langenbucher, Center of Alcohol Studies, Graduate School of Applied and Professional Psychology, Rutgers, The State University of New Jersey, USA
Daniel J. Lee, National Center for PTSD, VA Boston Healthcare System and Boston University School of Medicine, USA
Frederick T. L. Leong, Department of Psychology, Michigan State University, USA
Rebecca A. Lindsey, Department of Psychology, Washington State University, USA
Benjamin J. Lovett, Teacher's College, Columbia University, New York, USA
P. Priscilla Lui, Department of Psychology, Southern Methodist University, USA
E. Hale Martin, Graduate School of Professional Psychology, University of Denver, USA
Nancy Mather, Department of Disability and Psychoeducational Studies, University of Arizona, USA
Morgan N. McCredie, Department of Psychological and Brain Sciences, Texas A&M University, USA
Lauren F. McLellan, Centre for Emotional Health, Department of Psychology, Macquarie University, Australia
Gregory J. Meyer, Department of Psychology, University of Toledo, USA
Joni L. Mihura, Department of Psychology, University of Toledo, USA
Leslie C. Morey, Department of Psychological and Brain Sciences, Texas A&M University, USA
Greg Murray, Centre for Mental Health, Swinburne University of Technology, Australia
Jason M. Nelson, Regents' Center for Learning Disorders, University of Georgia, USA
Alyssa A. Neumann, Department of Psychology, Washington State University, USA
Mia Pellizzer, School of Psychology, Flinders University, Australia
Lorna Peters, Centre for Emotional Health, Department of Psychology, Macquarie University, Australia
Jennifer Puig, Pearson Inc., USA
Amanda L. Reed, John Jay College of Criminal Justice, The City University of New York, USA
Leslie A. Rescorla, Department of Psychology, Bryn Mawr College, USA
Maegan Rides At The Door, Department of Counselor Education, University of Montana, USA
Lilian Salinas, Department of Neurology, NYU Langone Health, USA
David P. Salmon, Department of Neurosciences, University of California, USA
Rachel Sandercock, TEACCH Autism Program, Department of Psychology and Neuroscience, University of North Carolina, USA
Deborah Anne Schneider, Department of Educational Technology, University of Arizona South, USA
Martin Sellbom, Department of Psychology, University of Otago, Dunedin, New Zealand
Leonard J. Simms, Department of Psychology, University at Buffalo, The State University of New York, USA
Shauna Solomon-Krakus, Clinical Laboratory for Personality, Psychopathology, and Psychodiagnostics, University of Toronto, Canada
John Sommers-Flanagan, Department of Counselor Education, University of Montana, USA
Julie A. Suhr, Department of Psychology, Ohio University, USA

Matthew Sunderland, The Matilda Centre for Research in Mental Health and Substance Use, University of Sydney, Australia
Jane L. Swanson, Department of Psychology, Southern Illinois University, USA
Neil Thomas, Centre for Mental Health, Swinburne University of Technology, Australia
Timothy J. Trull, Department of Psychological Sciences, University of Missouri, USA
Tracey Wade, School of Psychology, Flinders University, Australia
Frank W. Weathers, Department of Psychology, Auburn University, USA
Jennifer White, Department of Disability and Psychoeducational Studies, University of Arizona, USA
Kevin Wilfong, Department of Medical and Clinical Psychology, University of North Carolina, USA
Lindsey Williams, TEACCH Autism Program, Department of Psychiatry, University of North Carolina, USA
Trevor F. Williams, Department of Psychology, University at Buffalo, The State University of New York, USA
Dustin B. Wygant, Department of Psychology, Eastern Kentucky University, USA
Patricia A. Zapf, Palo Alto University, USA

Acknowledgments

We would like to thank several people who have been instrumental in this project. We are grateful to Scott Lilienfeld for his initial support for this overall project and helpful feedback at the early stages. Madeline Dykes provided very helpful clerical support. We would also like to express our significant gratitude to our managing editor Stephen Accera and editorial assistant Emily Watton at Cambridge University Press for their patience, support, and prompt and clear guidance as we completed this handbook.

1 Introduction to the Handbook of Clinical Assessment and Diagnosis

JULIE A. SUHR AND MARTIN SELLBOM

OVERVIEW

This handbook provides up-to-date summaries and applied recommendations for psychological assessment and diagnosis. The comprehensive compilation of chapters written by experts in their respective fields should guide graduate-level teaching/training and research as well as serve as an update on assessment for behavioral health service providers. Each chapter presents major theoretical, empirical, methodological, and practical approaches used in psychological assessment and diagnosis across different assessment methods, varied psychological disorders/ presentations, and unique assessment settings. As will be seen when reading the chapters, a major theme for empirically based assessment is that test users must "read well beyond the manual" to decide whether to use and how to interpret any psychological test or measure (Holden & Fekken, Chapter 23, this volume, p. 322).

We believe this handbook will appeal to three primary audiences. The first is academicians, including professors/ instructors and graduate students completing training in psychological assessment. The chapters provide updated and empirically supported recommendations consistent with the competency-based training model of the American Psychological Association (2006). The chapters include valuable coverage of foundational assessment topics as well as more advanced training in the application of assessment skills in clinical practice. However, the handbook should also be valuable to professional psychologists (and related mental health professionals) by providing a current, updated coverage of assessment topics, consistent with ethical practice guidelines. Finally, researchers of applied psychological assessment as well as those who wish to include clinically meaningful measures in their research should benefit from this comprehensive handbook.

STRUCTURE OF THE HANDBOOK

Part I of the handbook (Chapters 2 through 9) outlines major issues that cross all psychological assessment methods, settings, and disorders. Chapter 2 provides coverage of contemporary psychometric topics relevant to both researchers and clinicians who conduct assessments. Chapter 3 provides a conceptual and empirical presentation of multicultural assessment issues, which are critical to test development and test interpretation/use. Chapter 4 discusses common ethical issues that arise in psychological assessment. Chapter 5 presents information on contemporary diagnosis, including review of the most common approaches as well as presentation of new approaches and their empirical bases. Chapter 6 presents a critical topic often neglected in existing assessment tests: noncredible responding and performance and the importance of taking validity of patient/participant response into account when interpreting assessment results in both clinical and research contexts. Chapter 7 focuses on empirical review of a new assessment technology with growing use in both research and clinical settings: ambulatory assessment, which serves as a foundational example of our intent to consider technological advances in the field of psychological assessment across methods, diagnoses, and settings. Chapter 8 considers a key development in the integration of psychological assessment and intervention, the Therapeutic Assessment (e.g., Finn, 2007) approach, providing practical recommendations for the delivery of assessment feedback and also its use as an intervention in its own right. Chapter 9 reviews critical elements of the psychological report. In each of the chapters in Part I, the authors provide interpretive and practical recommendations and discuss frequent misuses or misunderstandings of the assessment methods/ approaches presented.

Part II of the handbook (Chapters 10 through 20) covers specific assessment methods, including interviewing; use of collateral reports; intellectual assessment; achievement assessment; vocational assessment; neuropsychological assessment; omnibus personality and psychopathology instruments, including the Minnesota Multiphasic Personality Inventory-2-Restructured Form (MMPI-2-RF; Ben-Porath & Tellegen, 2008), the Personality Assessment Inventory (PAI; Morey, 2007), and the Millon Clinical

Multiaxial Inventory-IV (MCMI-IV; Millon et al., 2015); the psychometric status of various specific-construct self-report instruments (e.g., Beck Depression Inventory [Beck, Steer, & Brown, 1996]; Depression, Anxiety, Stress Scales [Lovibond & Lovibond, 1993]); and performance-based instruments (e.g., Rorschach Inkblot Method [Rorschach, 1942]; Thematic Apperception Test [Murray, 1943]). Within each chapter, the authors discuss psychometrics of the tests and measures they review and offer practical recommendations for their selection and use. In addition, when making recommendations to the reader, the authors take into consideration diversity issues and research findings on the use of psychological instruments in diverse populations. Further, authors also review the degree to which the instruments of focus assess for noncredible report/responding. Finally, the authors present any upcoming technologies and assessment advances in their area of focus and critically consider the degree to which they are ready to be implemented in clinical assessment practice or research.

Part III of the handbook (Chapters 20 through 31) covers various forms of psychopathology and cognitive dysfunctions commonly encountered in clinical practice (or as areas of research focus) across the life span, including neurodevelopmental disorders, disruptive behavior disorders, depression, anxiety, trauma, psychosis, eating disorders, substance use disorders, personality disorders, dementia, and traumatic brain injury. Within each chapter, the authors provide a contemporary, evidence-based conceptualization of the constructs and disorders of focus. In addition, all authors consider the cross-cutting issues (as reviewed in Part I), including a critical psychometric review of instruments presented, use of the instruments in diverse populations, consideration of noncredible presentation/report in assessment of the respective construct/disorder, and unique ethical and practical issues. Finally, if there are emerging techniques and technologies unique to the assessment of their construct/disorder of focus, those are also critically examined.

Part IV, the final section of the handbook (Chapters 32 through 35), consists of chapters covering assessment in four particularly unique clinical settings – integrated primary care, forensic practice, neuropsychological settings, and school-based assessment – which often warrant special procedural considerations beyond what would be expected in "typical" assessments conducted in mental health settings. Within these chapters, the authors continue to consider the critical assessment issues presented in Part I by addressing general assessment considerations unique to their setting, cultural/diversity issues specific to their setting, consideration of the importance of assessment for noncredible presentation/report in their setting, psychometrics of any tests and measures unique to their setting, unique ethical/practical issues in the setting of focus, and presentation of any emerging techniques and technologies unique to their setting.

WHAT IS A GOOD CLINICAL PSYCHOLOGICAL ASSESSMENT?

Cross-Cutting Handbook Themes

One of the holistic goals for this handbook is to provide resources necessary to gain a comprehensive understanding of what constitutes a good clinical assessment. In this introductory chapter, we provide guidance on some broad and important domains that go into such evaluations and how the chapters that follow broadly reflect on them.

The referral question. The key consideration up front for any assessment is the reason the person is being seen. In a general mental health assessment, the patient will often be self-referred or referred by a general practitioner or psychiatrist for the purpose of determining a diagnosis and/or obtaining treatment recommendations. But there are several settings in which standard recommendations presented throughout various chapters might not always apply. Part IV of the handbook covers four unique types of settings: primary care (Chapter 32), forensic (Chapter 33), neuropsychology (Chapter 34), and school (Chapter 35) (but see also Chapter 14 for the vocational counseling context), in which special considerations in light of referral are often necessary to structure the evaluation. For instance, Zapf, Beltrani, and Reed (Chapter 33) note that, in many forensic evaluations, the person being evaluated is not the actual client, which has significant implications for informed consent and confidentiality but also the structure of the evaluation itself. More generally, psychologists who conduct psychological assessments in any setting should be aware of the many ethical issues (see Chapter 4) that pertain specifically to assessment prior to starting an evaluation.

Another setting in which the referral question (and thus approach to assessment) is quite unique is when quick treatment decisions must be made in the primary care setting (Chapter 32) or in crisis management (e.g., risk for self-harm). Psychometric issues with screening instruments are discussed in Chapter 2. The use of screening measures in clinical practice and the differences between screening and comprehensive assessment are discussed in Chapters 13, 19, 23, 25, 29, 31, and 32.

Sources of information/methodology. Psychological assessments are often tailored to individual referral questions and various chapters raise a number of different issues relevant to both the assessment for specific mental disorders and the broader areas of functioning (e.g., intelligence [Chapter 12], achievement (Chapter 13), neurocognitive [Chapters 15, 31, 34], and vocational [Chapter 14]). Virtually all psychological assessments will require a good clinical interview (Chapter 10) and many chapters discuss specific structured interviews for different types of mental disorders (Chapters 5, 10, 22–29). Structured clinical interviews can be particularly important if a specific diagnostic decision must be made (e.g., post-traumatic stress disorder [PTSD] for an insurance claim) and reliability of decision-making is a key issue.

Furthermore, across the parts and chapters, readers will find comprehensive coverage of self-report instruments commonly used in both clinical and research settings as well as instruments that are relatively unique to assessment of specific disorders/constructs or in specific assessment settings. These can be useful for obtaining corroborating quantitative information about an individual's standing on a construct of interest; if the assessment is ultimately for treatment, such measures can also be used to track outcome. Readers will also find comprehensive coverage of cognitive tests commonly used in both clinical and research settings (e.g., Chapters 12, 13, 15, 21, 30, 31, 32, 34, 35). Finally, collateral reports (see Chapters 11, 21, 22, 33) can be useful in many assessments, particularly in cases in which individuals might not have sufficient ability to self-report (e.g., children) or have motivation to present themselves in an accurate light; Achenbach, Ivanova, and Rescorla (Chapter 11) provide useful guidance on how to integrate information across various methods and measures in assessment.

Another major theme that emerges across the chapters herein is the importance of the overall assessment progress beyond the use of specific tests or measures/methods. For example, in several chapters (Chapters 8, 10, 14, 21, 25–28), the importance of a good working relationship with the person being assessed is emphasized. In Chapters 8, 10, and 14, the importance of assessment for beginning the therapeutic process is also emphasized. Further, Chapter 13 reminds readers of the importance of careful administration and scoring to the overall assessment process. Finally, regardless of the assessment circumstances, a basic risk assessment for harm to self or others is always imperative (Chapters 23, 27, 33).

Differential diagnosis. Mental health evaluations frequently require an element of differential diagnosis to guide formulation, treatment recommendations, and goal-setting (e.g., Sellbom, Marion, & Bagby, 2013). It is therefore important that a clinician undertaking a psychological assessment is aware of both contemporary thinking about psychopathology generally (see Chapter 5) and current models of common mental health problems as they select the most appropriate assessment tools to evaluate competing hypotheses. Indeed, an entire section (Part III: Assessment and Diagnosis of Specific Mental Disorders) is devoted to the evaluation of assessment methods and tests for common forms of psychopathology, including depression, anxiety and obsessive-compulsive disorders, PTSD, psychosis and bipolar disorders, eating disorders, substance use disorders, and personality disorders in adulthood as well as autism spectrum disorders, attention-deficit/hyperactivity disorder (ADHD), and other disruptive behavior disorders in childhood. Particularly impressive is that most of these chapter authors provide summative and evaluative lists of measures for each, so readers can compare which instruments seem to have the best psychometric support for what purpose and with what population.

It is important to keep in mind, however, that single-construct measures (both interviews and self-report inventories) are often limited to that construct only and do not measure noncredible responding. In many circumstances, the diagnostic picture might be more opaque. The inclusion of established omnibus inventories that assess for a range of constructs, such as the MMPI-2-RF (Chapter 16), PAI (Chapter 17), MCMI-IV (Chapter 18), or performance-based methods (e.g., the Rorschach Inkblot Method; Chapter 20), might be particularly useful to assist the clinician with a broader picture for both diagnostic decision-making and broader clinical formulation.

Noncredible responding. Many individuals undergoing psychological evaluations have an incentive to misrepresent themselves. Such responding can be intentional or unintentional but nevertheless will affect the ultimate clinical formulation if undetected and if not considered when interpreting test results. This issue is so critical to clinical practice that we have devoted a whole chapter to it (Chapter 6). Readers will also see the growing understanding of the importance of considering noncredible report and behavior in interpreting both self-report and cognitive test results, including areas in which these measures have been well developed, as well as domains where much more work is needed to develop and use such measures. Of course, it is important that readers be aware that *any* report (i.e., self- [both interview and questionnaire] and informant reports) is potentially vulnerable to noncredible responding. Although in extreme cases noncredible reporting might invalidate an entire assessment (e.g., feigning mental illness during a criminal responsibility evaluation), in many mental health evaluations it can also serve as useful information in understanding clients (e.g., extreme symptom exaggeration as an indication of an extremely negativistic perceptual style or significant minimization of obvious problems as an extreme tendency toward social desirability across contexts). In any instance, clinicians should be careful not to interpret either self-report or collateral measures or performance on tests as valid if invalidity measures, or other indicators, suggest caution in interpretation.

Clinical formulation. Every good psychological assessment ultimately needs a formulation of some kind on which any opinions and/or recommendations are ultimately based (e.g., Chapters 8, 9, 10, 18, 25, 26, 27, 34). Such a formulation is often based on a particular theoretical perspective (e.g., Eells, 2007), such as a cognitive behavioral model (e.g., Persons, 2008) or psychodynamic perspective (e.g., McWilliams, 1999), especially if treatment recommendations follow. But it is not required, and sometimes not even appropriate, given the referral question at hand. For instance, judges would likely not care about competency to stand trial being formulated from a cognitive behavioral therapy (CBT) or any particular theoretical perspective; it is a capacity-based question. Individuals undergoing neuropsychological evaluations are best formulated from a biopsychosocial perspective (see Chapters 14, 31, and 34) that emphasizes the contributions of brain processes, sociocultural influences, and individual difference factors in patient presentation and interpretation of test results.

We do not advocate for a particular theoretical perspective here and it would be far beyond the scope of this chapter, or even the handbook, to do so. Rather, we make some broader recommendations for formulations that readers might want to keep in mind. First, we believe it is a good idea that *any* clinical formulation considers a developmentally informed biopsychosocial approach at minimum (Campbell & Rohrbaugh, 2006; Suhr, 2015; see also Chapters 14, 31, 32, and 34). Thus, regardless of theoretical perspective, humans are influenced by their biology, psychological processes, and external circumstances in a dynamic fashion throughout their development. These should all be emphasized in any clinical formulation. Furthermore, chapter authors also remind readers that assessment data should speak to issues beyond specific symptoms and maladaptive traits, such as assessing for evidence of functional impairment (Chapters 15, 21, 22, 25, and 31–35), measuring contextual factors that may maintain/exacerbate presenting problems or be protective (Chapters 13,17, 22, and 27), and assessment of comorbidities (Chapters 21, 24, and 25). In fact, a major theme emerging from the chapters is that assessment should capture the unique presentation for each person (see Chapter 22 as a particularly good example), given the heterogeneity of presentations for individuals with any given psychological diagnosis.

Considerations of diversity issues. It is critical that clinicians consider a range of multicultural and other diverse characteristics about their clients undergoing assessments. Although this field continues to be woefully understudied with respect to the great number of diversity issues to which clinicians need to be attuned (e.g., LGBTQIA+, physical disability, diversity within nonmajority cultures), progress has been made in the multicultural domain. In Chapter 3, Leong, Lui, and Kalibatseva discuss important threats to cultural validity in assessment practice, educate the readers broadly on how to address these threats, and also provide indications of best practices. But this handbook goes beyond one important chapter. Indeed, throughout almost every chapter, the need to continue to address the validity of both self-report measures and cognitive tests in diverse populations is emphasized. In recent decades, much work has been done in this area, as presented in the chapters herein, which present data on translations of tests for different languages and cultures, statistical analysis for bias in test interpretation, and norms for diverse populations. However, the reader will recognize across the chapters that more work is clearly needed and hopefully the information presented in the chapters can serve as a good starting point to inspiring more research in this important area of assessment.

Treatment implications/recommendations. For many clinical assessments, the goal is to both generate a broad understanding about the implications of the assessment findings for treatment and articulate specific recommendations. Depending on context, therapeutic goal-setting could be considered at this stage as well. Various treatment implications are considered across many chapters, including guiding treatment decisions (Chapters 5, 8, 17, 18, 22, 25, 31, 32, 34), identifying patient characteristics likely to affect therapeutic alliance (Chapters 13,17, 22, 23, 26), predicting treatment outcome (Chapters 17, 24), and tracking treatment outcome over time (Chapters 2, 13, 23, 24, 25, 26, 32, 34). A thorough assessment of stages of change (Prochaska and DiClemente, 1983) as a treatment-choice determinant can be useful in many contexts (see Chapter 28). Moreover, specific treatment recommendations should naturally flow from the conceptual formulation and should consider the type of treatment (if any), including modality (e.g., individual, group, family), and whether referral to a psychiatrist for psychotropic medications would be warranted. In more rare circumstances, individuals undergoing assessments might require acute care and/or be heavily monitored for risk to self and/or others.

Report writing. Most psychological assessments culminate in a psychological report and we have a chapter dedicated to this topic (Chapter 9); report writing is also discussed in Chapter 33, which specifically covers forensic settings. Chapter 9 provides a recommended structure of a psychological report (see Table 9.2), which includes a biographical sketch of the report author, identifying information and referral question, sources of information, informed consent, presenting problem(s) and symptoms(s) and/or background situation, psychosocial background, mental status and behavioral observations, evidence-based psychological tests, clinical interview results, case formulation, recommendations, and summary and conclusions. Not surprisingly, these sections map onto our own recommendations on what constitutes a good psychological evaluation. Furthermore, Zapf et al. (Chapter 33) remind us that reports in the forensic context differ in important ways from those conducted in a therapeutic context, in that the sources, methodology, and reporting of findings are directly tailored to addressing a particular psycho-legal question for the Court.

FUTURE DIRECTIONS OF CLINICAL ASSESSMENT

Virtually all chapters provide directions for future developments for their particular area. One of the areas we asked chapter authors to consider in their respective areas of expertise was technological advancements; and, while some chapters (e.g., Chapter 7 on ambulatory assessment) specifically highlighted a general method moving the whole field forward in this regard, many authors discussed other technological advances that either have some preliminary support or are important future directions for the field. For example, some authors (Chapters 19, 29) discuss the potential benefits of computer adaptive testing (CAT) in both symptom and personality trait assessment, which is possible given the increasing emphasis on using item response theory (IRT; see Chapter 2) in scale construction. CAT provides for the potential benefit of significant time savings in assessment and increased precision of scores given reliance on latent modeling techniques. We note, though, that the CAT concept in personality assessment has been a target for quite some time (e.g., Forbey & Ben-Porath, 2007; Roper, Ben-Porath, & Butcher, 1991) and we hope for future investment in this important area. Similarly, in the context of achievement testing (Chapter 13), authors highlight information and computer technology (ICE), which represents a digital method for the administration, scoring, and interpretation of educational achievement testing. Finally, some chapter authors (Chapters 8, 24) call for consideration of virtual reality in the context of therapeutic assessment, building on important gains in the treatment for particular disorders (e.g., exposure disorder for phobia; see Powers & Emmelkamp, 2008). Other chapters consider the implementation of today's technology (internet, smartphone, video-chat capabilities) for the assessment context, such as the use of smartphones to gather ambulatory data (Chapter 14) and telepsychology (Chapter 34).

In sum, we believe that further development of assessment methods to reach geographically or otherwise physically disadvantaged individuals through various computer and internet-based technology is a very important direction for the field. We hope that psychological assessment scholars continue to innovate and bring some of our more archaic techniques into the twenty-first century. We hope that such innovation will not come at the cost of careful psychometric validation for these instruments, which is critical in aiding assessors in determining what measures/tests are most valid for a particular person in a particular setting to answer a particular assessment question.

REFERENCES

American Psychological Association. (2006). *APA task force on the assessment of competence in professional psychology: Final report*, October 2006. www.apa.org/ed/resources/competency-revised.pdf

Beck, A. T., Steer, R. A., & Brown, G. K. (1996). *Manual for the Beck Depression Inventory- II*. San Antonio, TX: Psychological Corporation.

Ben-Porath, Y. S., & Tellegen, A. (2008). *MMPI-2-RF, Minnesota Multiphasic Personality Inventory-2 Restructured Form: Manual for administration, scoring and interpretation*. Minneapolis: University of Minnesota Press.

Campbell, W. H., & Rohrbaugh, R. M. (2006). *The biopsychosocial formulation manual*. New York: Routledge.

Eells, T. D. (Ed.). (2007). *The handbook of psychotherapy case formulation* (2nd ed.). New York: Guilford Press.

Finn, S. E. (2007). *In our clients' shoes: Theory and techniques of therapeutic assessment*. Mahwah, NJ: Lawrence Erlbaum Associates.

Forbey, J. D., & Ben-Porath, Y. S. (2007). Computerized adaptive personality testing: A review and illustration with the MMPI-2 computerized adaptive version. *Psychological Assessment, 19*(1), 14–24.

Lovibond, S. H., & Lovibond, P. F. (1993). *Manual for the Depression Anxiety Stress Scales (DASS)*. University of New South Wales: Psychology Foundation Monograph.

McWilliams, N. (1999). *Psychoanalytic case formulation*. New York: Guilford Press.

Millon, T., Grossman, S., & Millon, C. (2015). *Millon Clinical Multiaxial Inventory-IV manual*. Minneapolis, MN: Pearson Assessments.

Morey, L. C. (2007). *Personality Assessment Inventory professional manual* (2nd ed.). Lutz, FL: Psychological Assessment Resources.

Murray, H. A. (1943). *Thematic Apperception Test manual*. Cambridge, MA: Harvard University Press.

Persons, J. B. (2008). *The case formulation approach to cognitive-behavior therapy*. New York: Guilford Press.

Powers, M. B., & Emmelkamp, P. M. (2008). Virtual reality exposure therapy for anxiety disorders: A meta-analysis. *Journal of Anxiety Disorders, 22*(3), 561–569.

Prochaska, J. O., & DiClemente, C. C. (1983). Stages and processes of self-change of smoking: Toward an integrative model of change. *Journal of Consulting and Clinical Psychology, 51*, 390–395.

Roper, B. L., Ben-Porath, Y. S., & Butcher, J. N. (1991). Comparability of computerized adaptive and conventional testing with the MMPI-2. *Journal of Personality Assessment, 57*(2), 278–290.

Rorschach, H. (1942). *Psychodiagnostics: A diagnostic test based on perception*. Bern: Verlag Hans Huber.

Sellbom, M., Marion, B. E., & Bagby, R. M. (2013). Psychological assessment in adult mental health settings. In J. R. Graham & J. A. Naglieri (Eds.), *Handbook of psychology. Vol. 10: Assessment psychology* (pp. 241–260). New York: Wiley.

Suhr, J. A. (2015). Using a developmentally informed biopsychosocial lens in assessment. In J. A. Suhr (Ed.), *Psychological assessment: A problem-solving approach*. New York: Guilford Press.

PART I

GENERAL ISSUES IN CLINICAL ASSESSMENT AND DIAGNOSIS

2 Psychometrics and Psychological Assessment

JOHN HUNSLEY AND TERESA ALLAN

The measurement of psychological characteristics has long been a cornerstone of psychological research. Psychometrics, the science of psychological measurement, is comprised of concepts, principles, and statistical procedures designed to ensure that the measurement of any psychological characteristic is as accurate and relevant as possible. In the realm of applied psychology, psychometrics has been described as being one of the "great ideas" of clinical science (Wood, Garb, & Nezworski, 2006). Simply put, without attention to psychometrics and psychometric evidence, it is not possible for psychological assessment to be scientifically based or to meet professional standards for conducting such assessments. This applies to the full range of psychological instruments, including performance tests (e.g., measures of memory, intelligence, and cognitive functioning), diagnostic interviews, observational coding systems, self-report personality tests, projective personality tests, and measures of psychosocial functioning based on self-report or the report of other informants.

In this chapter, we address the key psychometric concepts of standardization, reliability, validity, norms, and utility. We focus primarily on classical test theory (CTT), which disaggregates a person's observed score on an instrument into true score and error components, because it is the psychometric framework most commonly used in the clinical assessment literature. Given its limited use in the clinical assessment literature, we do not review generalizability theory (Cronbach et al., 1972) but we do present basic aspects of item response theory (IRT) because of its growing use with psychological instruments (e.g., Reisse & Revicki, 2015). In contrast to CTT, which assumes that all items on an instrument are equally relevant in evaluating a person's true score, IRT assumes that some items are more relevant than others to evaluating a person's true score and that the extent to which an item accurately measures a person's ability can differ across ability levels. Following a presentation of the central aspects of CTT and IRT models, we conclude the chapter with a discussion of the need to consider cultural/diversity issues in the development, validation, and use of psychological instruments.

STANDARDIZATION

Standardization is an essential aspect of any psychological instrument. It implies consistency across assessors and evaluation occasions in the procedures used to administer and score a test, self-report measure, semi-structured interview, or observational coding system (Anastasi & Urbina, 1997). Without standardization, it is virtually impossible for assessors to replicate the information gathered in an assessment. Further, without standardization, results are likely to be highly specific to the unique aspects of the evaluation situation and are unlikely to provide data that can be generalized to evaluations conducted by another professional or to other situations in the life of the person being evaluated.

Standardization is therefore the first psychometric element necessary to ensure that assessment results are generalizable and could be replicated by another assessor. Accordingly, efforts must be made to minimize the influence of unique aspects of both the evaluation situation and the assessor. To this end, developers of performance tests typically provide detailed instructions regarding the nature of the stimuli, administrative procedures, time limits (if relevant), and the types of verbal probes and responses to the examinee's questions that are permitted. For all psychological instruments, scoring instructions must be provided. For many instruments, especially self-report measures, only simple addition of responses is required to obtain a score; some instruments, such as performance tests and projective tests, have complex scoring rules that are mastered through extensive training and supervision. Unfortunately, with some instruments, assessors may disregard the use of complex scoring criteria in favor of nonstandardized, personally developed approaches to scoring. This can only result in data of unknown scientific or clinical value. For example, the Thematic Apperception Test (a projective test in which respondents provide stories to pictures presented by the clinician) has been used clinically for many decades despite the lack of consensus on how to administer, score, and interpret responses to pictures (Teglasi, 2010).

RELIABILITY

Reliability is the next psychometric element to be considered in evaluating an instrument. It refers to the consistency of a person's score on a measure (Anastasi & Urbina, 1997; Wasserman & Bracken, 2013), including whether (1) all elements of a measure contribute in a consistent way to the data obtained (i.e., internal consistency), (2) similar results would be obtained if the measure was used or scored by another assessor (i.e., inter-rater reliability), or (3) similar results would be obtained if the person being evaluated completed the measure a second time (i.e., test-retest reliability or test stability). Standardization of stimuli, administration, and scoring are necessary, but not sufficient, to establish reliability.

According to CTT, part of the variance in a set of scores on an instrument is explained by the characteristic measured by the instrument (i.e., the true score). Reliability estimates based on a set of scores indicate the proportion of variance in the scores that is explained by the true score itself and therefore express the degree of consistency in the measurement of test scores. Score reliability is critical to the determination of a measure's merit, as a measure cannot be scientifically sound if it lacks evidence of reliability. Additional variability in a set of test scores may be due to other influences such as sampling or measurement error. For example, a self-report personality test may consist of some components that are influenced by ephemeral characteristics of the person being evaluated or by contextual characteristics of the testing (including demand characteristics associated with the purpose of the testing and the behavior of the assessor). Alternatively, variability due to measurement error may stem from scoring criteria being overly complex or insufficiently detailed to ensure reliable scoring by different assessors. This appears to be the case with some instruments commonly used to assess sex offenders' risk for reoffending, as the inter-rater reliability estimates derived from forensic evaluations are much lower than those reported in the manuals for the instruments (Miller et al., 2012; Smid et al., 2014).

Reliable results are necessary if we wish to generalize the test results and their psychological implications beyond the immediate assessment situation. That being said, it is important to bear in mind that reliability estimates are always conditional, based on the characteristics of the assessment activity, the context of the assessment, and the nature of the sample of individuals who completed the test (Haynes, Smith, & Hunsley, 2019). In other words, a measure can produce reliable scores in one study and unreliable scores in another study with different participants, as reliability can be influenced by the composition and variability of the sample (e.g., age, ethnicity, socioeconomic status) and the sample size. Many researchers and clinicians erroneously believe that reliability is a property of an instrument and that, once an instrument is found to be "reliable," this status is unchangeable. However, a measure in itself is neither reliable nor unreliable, as reliability is a property of the scores obtained by a certain sample on the measure (Rousse, 2007; Vacha-Haase, Henson, & Caruso, 2002).

Determining Reliability Estimates

The most straightforward way to establish the reliability of scores on instrument A is to develop two instruments, A and B, that are intended to measure the same construct. Correlating scores obtained on these alternate test forms provides an indication of the reliability of the score on instrument A, with a correlation of 1.0 indicating perfect reliability. However, as there is always some error associated with any measurement, no instrument can yield scores that are perfectly reliable.

In its purest sense, alternate forms reliability assumes that one form is completed immediately after the other, with minimal time between administrations. In test-retest reliability (or temporal stability), the time between administrations is increased so that the focus is on the correlation between scores obtained at different assessment occasions (i.e., the same instrument is administered at two or more distinct time points and the correlation of scores between time points is determined). If this type of reliability is estimated, there is an assumption that the behaviors or traits being assessed are truly stable over the time of the two (or more) test administrations. Test-retest reliability values will be influenced by both the temporal nature of the construct being assessed (i.e., is it transitory, state-like, or trait-like?) and the time interval chosen to calculate the reliability value.

Inter-rater reliability can be determined for scores on instruments that require coding/rating by judges/observers. In this case, all judges observe the same behavior for each individual and then code the behavior using the same instrument: The degree to which judges agree in their ratings reflects inter-rater reliability. Behaviors can be observed live, via recordings, or via a completed test protocol (such as a completed test of intelligence). Thus inter-rater reliability can be determined for data from observational coding systems, semi-structured interviews, behavior checklists, or performance tests. There are two important caveats to consider when calculating inter-rater reliability. First, evidence for inter-rater reliability should only come from data generated within the same class of judges; estimates of cross-informant agreement, such as between parent and teacher ratings, are not indicators of reliability. Second, the method used to evaluate inter-rater reliability can affect the resulting reliability estimate. For example, Chmielewski and colleagues (2015) reported much lower reliability estimates when diagnoses were made on the basis of separate semi-structured interviews conducted by clinicians than when made on the basis of clinicians listening to an audio recording of a single diagnostic interview.

The most common way that score reliability is assessed is by examining the internal consistency of scores on an instrument (Hogan, Benjamin, & Brezinski, 2000). This form of reliability evaluates the degree of consistency of scores on the items or elements within an assessment instrument. Coefficient α is the most widely used index of internal consistency (Streiner, 2003a). Coefficient α is essentially the average of all possible split-half correlations (i.e., randomly dividing items from a measure into two sets and then correlating scores on one set with the other set) and is, therefore, influenced by the number of items in a measure. Although there have been repeated calls to abandon the use of coefficient α in favor of either simpler forms of internal consistency such as the average inter-item correlation or more robust and accurate alternatives such as versions of omega (e.g., Dunn, Baguley, & Brunsden, 2014; Revelle & Zinbarg, 2009), it is rare to find alternative internal consistency coefficients used in the clinical assessment literature.

Reliability and the Standard Error of Measurement

A question that typically arises in both clinical and research situations is how reliable scores on an instrument should be. As Hogan (2014) has suggested, this is similar to asking how high a ladder should be – the answer in both cases is that it depends on the purpose you have in mind. Owing to the reduction in precision, the use of measures with low reliability estimates can be detrimental for both research (e.g., Rodebaugh et al., 2016; Stanley & Spence, 2014) and clinical purposes (e.g., Brooks et al., 2009; Morash & McKerracher, 2017). Nevertheless, there is a clear consensus that the level of acceptable estimates of reliability for instruments used for clinical purposes must be greater than it is for instruments used for research purposes. The main reason that high reliability is so important for clinical purposes is that reliability estimates reflect how much error there is in scores on a measure. This can be extremely important in clinical contexts where precise cutoff scores are frequently used to make diagnostic and treatment decisions. It should be noted, however, that it is possible for internal consistency to be too high, as a value close to unity typically indicates substantial redundancy among items and, therefore, limited breadth of construct coverage (see Streiner, 2003a; Youngstrom et al., 2017).

In considering internal consistency reliability, several authors have suggested that a value of 0.90 is the minimum required for a clinical test (e.g., Nunnally & Bernstein, 1994). For research purposes, most authorities seem to view 0.70 as the minimum acceptable value for α (e.g., Cicchetti, 1994). Similar values have been proposed for inter-rater reliability estimates when assessed with Pearson correlations or intraclass correlations (Hunsley & Mash, 2018b). Kappa (κ) continues to be the most commonly used inter-rater reliability statistic, even though there are a number of statistics that are superior to κ (Xu & Lorber, 2014). When assessed with κ, acceptable reliability values are somewhat lower than these values for intraclass correlations (Cicchetti, 1994). Determining appropriate acceptable levels of test-retest reliability values can be very challenging, as not all constructs or measures are expected to show temporal stability (e.g., measures of state-like variables, life stress inventories). Hunsley and Mash (2018b) have provided guidance on how to interpret these values, with correlation values of 0.70 or greater interpreted as providing evidence of adequate reliability over a period of weeks for instruments designed to assess trait-like constructs.

To return to the point about the effect of measurement error on clinical assessment, it is critical that a clinician not assume that the client's score on an instrument represents the client's true and exact standing on the construct that is being assessed. Information about internal consistency can be used to establish confidence intervals around the client's score, with these intervals indicating the range of scores within which the true score is likely to lie. Although confidence intervals do not get around the problems associated with measurement error, they serve as an explicit reminder that clients' observed scores are unlikely to precisely reflect their true score on that construct. To construct confidence intervals, one uses the standard error of measurement (SEM), which is the standard deviation of a hypothetically infinite number of observed scores around the person's true score and is calculated as follows:

$$SEM = SD_T = \sqrt{(1 - r_{xx})}$$

where SD_T is the standard deviation of the total score for the sample on which the reliability was determined and r_{xx} is the reliability (typically coefficient α) of the instrument.

Although any confidence interval could be used, it is most common to see 90 percent (±1.65 SEM) or 95 percent (±1.96 SEM) intervals. Because of the importance of the SEM in interpreting a person's score, the *Standards for Educational and Psychological Testing* (AERA, APA, & NCME, 2014) require that the SEM must be reported for a psychological test. Confidence intervals can be extremely helpful in interpreting a person's scores on various measures. For example, Brooks and colleagues (2009) provided a good illustration of this using data from memory and intelligence tests. The reliability of the Verbal Comprehension Index (VCI; SEM = 2.88) scores on the Wechsler Adult Intelligence Scale-IV is higher than the reliability of the Visual Delayed Index (VDI; SEM = 6.18) scores on the Wechsler Memory Scale-III. This relative difference has important implications for making decisions on the basis of the scores on these indexes. For a patient who received a VCI score of 100, 95 times out of 100 the range of 94–106 includes the person's true score (i.e., the observed score minus/plus 1.96 times the SEM value). In contrast, because of having a larger SEM, if the same patient received a score of 100 on the VDI, 95 times out of 100 the range of 88–112 contains the person's true score. As this example illustrates, score reliability has a direct effect on the precision with which a clinician can interpret a person's test results.

Although not all reliability indices are relevant to all assessment methods and measures, reliability information is never irrelevant and information on reliability estimates is always germane to the scientific evaluation of scores from an assessment instrument. In short, some form of reliability is relevant for every instrument, regardless of whether they are nomothetic or idiographic in nature. For example, internal consistency estimates may not be relevant to measures that consist of items that, theoretically, should not demonstrate much inter-item correlation. Streiner (2003a) referred to instruments such as these as indexes, with stressful life events inventories being a prime example of instruments in which the endorsement or degree of endorsement of one item may be unrelated to responses to other items. The reliability of these indexes can be considered via test-retest reliability methods that use a retest interval brief enough to reduce the likelihood that recent events affect the responses to the index. As for idiographic assessment instruments, a number of strategies are available to assess intra-individual response consistency on behavioral, affective, or cognition checklists or self-monitoring diaries that are designed to be completed repeatedly within or across days (e.g., Moskowitz et al., 2009; Weisz et al., 2011). With these instruments the assessor must bear in mind that low reliability values may not necessarily be an indication of a poorly performing instrument; instead, they may indicate that certain target behaviors occur relatively infrequently, vary across short time periods, or are largely situationally determined.

Attending to Reliability

Inattention to reliability, or the use of an inappropriate statistic to estimate reliability, has the potential to undermine the validity of conclusions drawn about research studies or individual clients. Given the sample-specific nature of reliability, it is essential for researchers to calculate and report reliability coefficients from their own set of data, as failing to do so can lead to the interpretation of unreliable data (Henson, Kogan, & Vaccha-Haase, 2001). However, numerous reviews have found that up to three-quarters of research articles failed to provide information on the reliability estimates of the measures completed by participants in the studies (e.g., Barry et al., 2014; Vacha-Haase & Thompson, 2011). In such instances, authors appear to rely on findings of acceptable reliability estimates derived from either previous studies or the original test manual and, therefore, simply assume that their data are equally reliable. Before assuming the generalizability of reliability findings, those using a measure need to determine whether the reliability estimates previously reported are based on samples that have comparable composition and score variability to the group for which the measure will be used (Kieffer & Reese, 2002).

Because of the sample-specific nature of reliability, Vacha-Haase (1998) proposed a meta-analytic method known as reliability generalization in order to estimate the mean reliability score of a specific measure based on the obtained reliability coefficients of different studies. A growing number of studies have used a reliability generalization meta-analysis to examine the reliability estimates of instruments designed to assess a variety of psychological constructs (e.g., Henson et al., 2001; Therrien & Hunsley, 2013). As the mean reliability estimates and confidence intervals resulting from a meta-analysis are typically based on a large number of studies, these results provide valuable guidance for clinicians and researchers to consider when selecting an instrument for a specific assessment task. Reliability generalization meta-analysis can also provide an indication of how the reliability of the scores produced by the measure can vary due to sample and study characteristics.

VALIDITY

A standardized instrument with consistent evidence of score reliability does not necessarily yield valid data because, although purporting to measure a specific construct, it may actually be measuring a different construct, or the obtained scores may be misinterpreted. When we consider validity, we are evaluating both the degree to which there is evidence that the instrument truly measures what it purports to measure and the manner in which the test results are interpreted. Validity refers to whether the instrument (1) covers all aspects of the construct it is designed to assess (i.e., evidence of content validity), (2) provides data consistent with theoretical postulates associated with the construct being assessed (i.e., evidence of criterion validity [related to an outcome of interest such as a diagnosis or performance on a task], convergent validity [related to other measures of the same construct], and predictive validity [related to a future outcome of interest]), and (3) provides a relatively pure measure of the construct that is minimally contaminated by other psychological constructs (i.e., evidence of discriminant validity). In clinical contexts, it is also important to consider the extent to which data from an instrument add to our knowledge over and above the information gleaned from other data (i.e., evidence of incremental validity: Hunsley & Meyer, 2003; Sechrest, 1963). There can be considerable costs associated with the collection of assessment data in clinical settings (e.g., financial costs or opportunity costs such as reduced time available for treatment or rehabilitation services). Therefore, in clinical assessment settings, it is rarely a case of "the more data the better" (see Youngstrom et al., 2017).

Although it is common to describe an instrument as valid or invalid, validity, like reliability, is always conditional (Haynes et al., 2019). Many psychological tests consist of subscales designed to measure discrete aspects of a more global construct. In such situations, it is erroneous to consider the global validity of the test because it is the validity of each subscale that is crucial. Moreover, it is erroneous to refer to global validity of a test or subscale because validity can only be established within certain parameters, such that a test may be valid for specific purposes within specific groups of people (e.g., specific ages or gender). Finally, if a test is used for multiple purposes, its validity for each purpose must be empirically established. For example, knowing that a self-report symptom measure is a good indicator of diagnostic status does not automatically support its use for other clinical purposes.

Recent editions of the *Standards for Educational and Psychological Testing* (e.g., AERA et al., 2014) explicitly stated that validity is a unitary concept and that it was not appropriate to consider different types of validity. A major reason for this approach is the emphasis in the Standards on how the totality of validity evidence should inform the interpretation of a person's score on a measure. However, this overlooks the conditional nature of validity evidence, including the fact that evidence for the validity of scores on a measure is dependent on the purpose of the assessment being undertaken. For example, for a diagnostic instrument, evidence that scores on the instrument differentiate between those with and without the target diagnosis is critical, whereas, for an instrument that is intended to be used to monitor progress in treatment, evidence of sensitivity to change is essential. Research on validity continues to focus on concepts such as content validity, predictive validity, and incremental validity. Setting aside the wide range of conceptual and practical issues associated with the lack of consensus on the framing of validity (for a detailed discussion, see Newton & Shaw, 2013), it is clear that the vast majority of the literature on clinical assessment, both historically and currently, does not treat validity as a unitary concept (see Strauss & Smith, 2009).

In determining the extent and quality of validity evidence for an instrument, assessors should first consider the extent to which there is evidence of content validity. This is a basic, but frequently overlooked, step in developing and evaluating a psychological measure (Haynes, Richard, & Kubany, 1995). The extent to which items adequately represent the various aspects of the construct the instrument is designed to measure will directly affect the reliability and validity estimates for scores on the instrument (Smith, Fischer, & Fister, 2003). An instrument with poor evidence of content validity may fail to sufficiently capture the construct being assessed, which can result in clinical judgments being adversely affected and potentially inaccurate. For strong evidence of content validity, instrument developers must have clearly defined the construct being assessed and ensured that test items were representative of all aspects of the construct. Then, the instrument must have been evaluated and rated by judges (including domain experts and pilot research participants) to ensure clarity, relevance, and content coverage. Finally, these ratings should have led to modifications to the instrument prior to initial testing for the reliability and validity of scores on the instrument (Hunsley & Mash, 2018b).

Assuming that evidence of content validity has been established for an assessment purpose, assessors should then consider whether there is replicated evidence for a measure's criterion, convergent, discriminative, predictive, and, ideally, incremental validity. We have indicated already that validation is a context-sensitive concept – inattention to this fact can lead to inappropriate generalizations being made about the evidence for a measure's validity. There should be, therefore, replicated validity evidence, both for each assessment purpose and for each population/group for which the measure is intended to be used. This latter point is especially pertinent with clinical instruments for which it is very desirable to have evidence of validity generalization (i.e., evidence of adequate validity across a range of samples and settings: Messick, 1995; Schmidt & Hunter, 1977). Summaries of the validity evidence for many commonly used clinical instruments can be found in Hunsley and Mash (2018a) and in many chapters within this volume.

Of course, even when instruments with extensive validity evidence are used in an assessment, the person being assessed may respond in a biased and potentially invalid manner. This is of particular concern in forensic and neuropsychological assessments (Bush et al., 2005; Merten et al., 2013) and can occur with both self-report measures and performance tests. There are numerous possible forms of biased responding, including presenting oneself in an overly positive or overly negative manner, putting minimal effort into responding to performance tasks, and responding inconsistently to test items. Moreover, such responses can be either intentional or nonintentional. Fortunately there are a number of measures designed to detect likely biased responding. These include both standalone instruments (e.g., the Balanced Inventory of Desirable Responding [Paulhus, 1998] and the Test of Memory Malingering [Tombaugh, 1996]) and validity scales within commonly used self-report personality measures (e.g., the Defensiveness scale and the Variable Response Inconsistency scale in the Minnesota Multiphasic Personality Inventory-2 Restructured Form [Ben-Porath & Tellegen, 2008] and the Infrequency scale and the Negative Impression Management scale in the Personality Assessment Inventory [Morey, 1991]). Evaluating the validity and utility of such measures is a very important and active area of research (e.g., Fariña et al., 2017; McGrath et al., 2010; Rohling et al., 2011; Wiggins et al., 2012).

NORMS

For a psychological instrument to be potentially useful, it must be standardized and have replicated evidence of score reliability and validity. However, if the scores obtained on an instrument by an individual are to be meaningful, it is essential that the scores can be interpreted with norms, specific criterion-related cut scores, or both (AERA et al., 2014). A score only has meaning when such reference points are available. Knowing that, relative to the range of possible scores on a test, a person scored low or high on the test provides little interpretable information. Comparisons must be made (1) with criteria that have been set for a test (e.g., a minimum score that indicates the likely presence of a diagnosable disorder) or (2) with population norms. Norms and cut scores can also be used to determine a client's level of functioning pre- and posttreatment and to evaluate whether any change in functioning is clinically meaningful (Achenbach, 2001; Kendall et al., 1999). The development of appropriate cut scores is a complex undertaking that requires attention to sampling and measurement factors; we describe some aspects of this in the next section and more details on this can be found in Haynes and colleagues (2019) and Wood and colleagues (2006).

It is a challenging task to select the target population(s) for an instrument and then to develop norms. A number of options must be considered: Are the norms to be used for comparing a specific score with those that might be obtained within the general population or within specific subgroups of this population (e.g., gender-specific norms) or are the norms to be used for establishing the likelihood of membership in specific categories (e.g., nondistressed vs. psychologically disordered groups)? When establishing evidence of validity, it may be necessary to develop multiple norms for a test, based on the group being assessed and the purpose of the assessment. All too frequently this necessity is overlooked and data from a single normative sample are used to interpret scores on an instrument, regardless of the potential irrelevance of the norms to the person being evaluated. For example, in their review of anxiety measures commonly used with older adults, Therrien and Hunsley (2012) found that the majority of measures had neither age-relevant norms nor cut scores validated for use with older adults. Given that, compared to younger adults, older adults report more somatic symptoms overall (Fuentes & Cox, 1997), many anxiety measures, when used with older adults, may not provide an accurate assessment of anxiety symptoms.

Test norms are most commonly presented as developmental norms, percentile ranks, or standard scores (Hogan, 2014). Developmental norms are used when the psychological construct being assessed develops systematically over time: age equivalents (the age level in the normative sample at which the mean score is the same as the test score under consideration) and/or grade equivalents (the grade level in the normative sample at which the mean score is the same as the test score under consideration) are used to quantify achievement performance (e.g., the Woodcock-Johnson IV [McGrew, LaForte, & Schrank, 2014]). A percentile rank indicates the percentage of those in the normative group whose scores fell below a given test score (e.g., the Graduate Record Examination). Standard score norms are usually obtained in one of two ways, either (1) converting a score to a *T*-score with a distribution in which the mean score is 50 and the standard deviation is 10 (e.g., the Minnesota Multiphasic Personality Inventory-2-RF) or (2) converting a score to have a mean of 100 and a standard deviation of 15 (e.g., many intelligence and cognitive tests). Both types of standard scores are simply based on the use of *z*-scores to obtain means and standard deviation values are that easily remembered integers. Although percentile ranks and standard scores are very commonly used for clinical instruments, it is important to remember that they are based on the assumption that the distribution of scores approximates a normal distribution. To the extent that score distributions are skewed, these two types of norms will be inaccurate and could lead to errors in comparing scores (1) across test-takers and (2) across clinical measures within test-takers.

Regardless of the populations to which comparisons are to be made, a normative sample should be truly representative of the population with respect to demographics and other important characteristics (Achenbach, 2001; Wasserman & Bracken, 2013). This should involve, ideally, probability sampling in which data are obtained from the majority of contacted respondents. Unfortunately, such a sampling strategy is rarely used for the development of norms for clinical instruments and the frequent reliance on data collected from convenience samples (with unknown response rates) is likely to reduce the accuracy of the norms. Common convenience samples include undergraduate students, hospital inpatients, or clients from a single clinic. Norms based on samples such as these should be regarded with some skepticism, as little effort was made to ensure that the members of the normative group were comparable in age, gender, ethnicity, or educational level (for example) to those who are likely to complete the instrument as part of a clinical assessment.

CLASSIFICATION ACCURACY STATISTICS

Table 2.1 provides a way to think about the use of test scores to make clinical decisions and illustrates the nature of potential errors. When using assessment data, we are often making predictions about an "event," such as the ability of scores on a screening test to indicate the likelihood that a client has a specific disorder. There are four possible outcomes associated with our predictions: (1) a true positive, in that our prediction that the client has the disorder was true (the client does have the disorder), (2) a false positive, in that our prediction that the client has the disorder was false (the client does not have the disorder), (3) a true negative, in that our prediction that the client does not have the disorder was true (the client does not have the disorder), and (4) a false negative, in that our prediction that the client does not have the disorder was

Table 2.1 Accuracy and errors in clinical prediction

Prediction	True Event (Disorder)	True Non-Event (No Disorder)
Disorder	*True Positives (A)*	*False Positives (B)*
No Disorder	*False Negatives (C)*	*True Negatives (D)*

Hits: A and D
Misses: B and C
Sensitivity: A/(A + C)
Specificity: D/(D + B)
Positive Predictive Power = A/(A + B)
Negative Predictive Power = D/(D + C)

false (the client does have the disorder). True positive and true negative outcomes with our client would support the validity of our assessment-based decision about the presence or absence of the disorder because our prediction turned out to be accurate. Thus, both true positives and true negatives are decision-making "hits" and false positives and false negatives are decision-making "misses."

As described in the section on "Norms," the basis for a clinical decision/prediction often involves the determination of cut scores that divide scores on an instrument into two or more categories, with the implication being that there is something different about persons whose scores fall within the different categories. For example, a binary categorization might involve a decision such as client (1) passing or failing a test of cognitive performance or (2) having/not having a diagnosable disorder. The selection of a cut score involves balancing many competing considerations. This requires the clinician to consider the rate of hits and misses based on a cut score and the implications associated with the various forms of hits and misses. The consequences of errors are seldom equal for false positives and false negatives, as is abundantly clear when the assessment task is to determine whether a client is currently suicidal.

A common strategy for determining cut scores involves the use of the type of information contained in Table 2.1. For example, if the goal is to use scores from a self-report screening measure to classify individuals as meeting, or not meeting, diagnostic criteria for a disorder, two types of data from a group of research participants are needed: (1) information from a semi-structured diagnostic interview (that has replicated evidence supporting its use with this research sample) about which participants met diagnostic criteria for the disorder and (2) participants' score on the self-report screening measure. By using various cut scores on the screening measure and filling in the cells of the table, the researcher determines the best cut score. In large part, such a determination is based on the researcher's judgment of which of the four cells is most important.

The concepts of sensitivity and specificity are central for optimizing the predictive efficacy of cut scores. In our example, sensitivity describes the extent to which those who met diagnostic criteria based on the semi-structured interview were identified by the screening measure as having the disorder. As indicated in Table 2.1, sensitivity is calculated by dividing the number of true positives by the total number of people who met diagnostic criteria based on the interview. Accordingly, sensitivity is an indication of how well the measure performs in identifying those with the disorder. In contrast, specificity is an indication of how well the measure performs in identifying those who did not meet diagnostic criteria. As indicated in the table, specificity is calculated by dividing the number of true negatives by the total number of participants who did not meet diagnostic criteria. Moving the cut score affects sensitivity and specificity: as sensitivity increases, specificity decreases and vice versa. Setting a very low cut score maximizes the number of true positives and minimizes the number of false negatives, thus increasing sensitivity. A very low cut score also means, however, that the number of false positives will increase, thus reducing specificity.

Receiver operating characteristics (ROC) can be used to evaluate the predictive efficacy of scores on a measure across a range of cut scores. To construct the ROC curve, true positive rates associated with each cut score are plotted against the corresponding true negative rates (1-sensitivity). Values on the ROC curve can range from 0.5, indicating that the use of the cut score is accurate at chance levels, to 1.0, indicating that the use of the cut score results in perfect classification. An important feature of the ROC curve is that the area under the curve (AUC) yields an estimate of the predictive efficacy of the measure. AUCs can be used for many purposes, including comparing the predictive efficacy of (1) different measures of the same construct and (2) a measure when used with different populations.

Returning to Table 2.1, there is a second set of predicative efficacy statistics that can be calculated. Streiner (2003b) referred to sensitivity and specificity as "column-based" indicators of the predictive efficacy of cut scores because they use data from the columns of the table to determine the denominators used in calculating these statistics. The second set of statistics involves "row-based" indicators: positive predictive power (PPP; or sometimes called positive predictive value, PPV) and negative predictive power (NPP; or sometimes called negative predictive value, NPV). The shift from column- to row-based statistics is an important one. All of the calculations from the table assume that we have information about the true classification of individuals that is distinct from the measure that we are evaluating (e.g., the diagnostic interview data provided information for a "true" diagnosis of a disorder separate from the data obtained with the self-report screening instrument). Column-based statistics begin with information from the criterion (a diagnostic interview in our example) and evaluate how well scores on a separate measure classify people according to this criterion. In contrast, row-based statistics first consider those identified on the basis of the cut score as having (or not having) the disorder and then examine how many truly have (or do not have) the disorder based on the diagnostic interview. Therefore, in our example, PPP is the probability that a person identified by the screening measure has the disorder when the classification criterion indicates that the person has it. NPP is the probability that a person identified by the screening measure does not having the disorder when the classification criterion indicates that the person does not have it. In the typical clinical scenario, clinicians make determinations about the presence of a condition, disorder, trait, or other characteristic on the basis of whether a client's score on a measure is above or below a relevant cut score. PPP and NPP, not sensitivity and specificity, map directly onto this scenario. Unfortunately data on PPP and NPP values associated with a cut score on an instrument are rarely reported in the psychological literature.

Although the base rate (or prevalence) of a clinical criterion (such as a diagnosable disorder) has no impact on sensitivity and specificity, it does affect PPP and NPP. This is because accurate classification using assessment data (such as the self-report screening measure in our example) becomes more difficult as the base rate of the criterion decreases. In other words, the closer the base rate of the criterion is to 0.50, the more likely it is that assessment data can accurately predict the presence (or absence) of the criterion. Many of the decisions made by psychologists, psychiatrists, and other mental health professionals on the basis of assessment data have to do with relatively low base rate events such as mental disorders, suicide risk, and violence risk. Because the accurate detection of low base rate conditions is extremely difficult, assessment data may add little accurate information beyond the probability of the condition based simply on base rate information. However, assessment data may be extremely useful in "screening out" individuals unlikely to have a disorder, be suicidal, or be violent. Accordingly, Streiner (2003b) proposed that (1) when the base rate (or prevalence) is low, an assessment instrument is best used to rule out a condition, and (2) when the base rate (or prevalence) is high, an assessment instrument is best used to rule in a condition. One way to increase the value of assessment data is to change the base rate of the condition that is being predicted by using a sequential assessment strategy. This involves using a simple, inexpensive measure that has high sensitivity in order to minimize the number of false negatives. The sample that results from this initial assessment is likely to have a base rate for the condition that is much closer to 0.50 than was the case for the original sample. A second measure, with high specificity, can then be used to reduce the number of false positives as much as possible. Using a screening measure, followed by a semi-structured diagnostic interview, is a good example of this strategy for accurately identifying mental disorders.

UTILITY

Beyond the psychometric elements we have described thus far, it is also essential to know the utility of an instrument for a specific clinical purpose. The concept of utility has had a central role in the assessment literature in industrial, organizational, and personnel psychology for several decades, where the utility of assessment data is evaluated in terms of improvements in (1) decisions or services and (2) the financial implications of these improvements relative to the cost of collecting and using the data themselves (e.g., Anastasi & Urbina, 1997; Murphy & Davidshofer, 2005). Both of these elements – improvements in decisions/services and financial costs associated with these improvements – are key elements of the clinical utility of psychological assessment instruments. In sum, for present purposes, clinical utility considerations are concerned with evidence that use of the assessment data confers clinical benefits (e.g., better treatment outcomes, lower attrition rates, lower relapse rates) that are important to psychological service stakeholders (Youngstrom et al., 2017).

The application of the utility concept to the realm of clinical practice dates back to the mid-twentieth century (e.g., Cronbach & Meehl, 1955; Sechrest, 1963). Unfortunately, despite thousands of studies on the evidence for reliability and validity of scores on psychological instruments, scant attention has been paid to utility (see McGrath, 2001; Nelson-Gray, 2003). This has led to a situation in which there is very little replicated evidence that psychological assessment data have a direct impact on improved provision and outcome of clinical services. At present, therefore, for the majority of psychological instruments, clinical utility is assumed rather than demonstrated.

There are two exceptions to this general state of affairs for the clinical utility of assessment. The first exception is the use of functional assessments to guide interventions for children and adolescents with disruptive behavior problems. This behaviorally based assessment strategy focuses on identifying variables that influence the likelihood of occurrence of a target problem behavior. In their meta-analysis of nineteen within-subjects studies, Hurl and colleagues (2016) reported that, compared to interventions not based on functional assessments, those based on functional assessments showed greater reductions in the frequency of problem behaviors and greater increases in the frequency of appropriate behaviors. The second exception is the utility of using brief self-report symptom measures to monitor treatment progress on a session-by-session basis. In a meta-analysis conducted by Lambert and Shimokawa (2011), data were summarized from several large-scale randomized trials involving the tracking of treatment effects for thousands of adult clients, across a range of treatment approaches. The tracking of client progress had an impact on treatment successes and failures: Compared to the clients of therapists who did not receive treatment progress data, the clients of therapists who received these data had (1) 2.6 to 3.5 times higher odds of achieving reliable clinical change and (2) less than half the odds of experiencing deterioration during treatment. Although not as large as these effects, results of Tam and Rosen's (2017) meta-analysis of nine treatment studies indicated that the positive results associated with treatment monitoring measures are also evident in psychological treatments for children and adolescents. The use of such monitoring measures has also been found to improve medication-based treatments for psychological disorders (Fortney et al., 2017).

ITEM RESPONSE THEORY

CTT and IRT differ substantially. When psychometric tests are designed for the assessment of unidimensional constructs using CTT, the theoretical focus is at the level of the test, with the assumption that all test-takers will respond to a fixed set of items similarly. Each test item contributes an equal number of "units" of the measured construct to a summed outcome score, which describes the amount of the construct that has been observed. In CTT, there is also an assumption that a given test performs equally well in the detection of the underlying construct/trait across varying levels of that trait (i.e., the test will not become more or less accurate for those with differing levels of the trait). In contrast, IRT assumes that each item within a test has its own set of properties, called parameters. Item parameters can be mathematically modeled using curvilinear functions called item characteristic curves (ICCs), item characteristic functions (ICFs), or trace lines.

The Item Characteristic Curve

The ICC serves a purpose similar to the line of best fit in regression modeling in that it provides (1) a visual and mathematical representation of how participants with varying levels of a latent trait have responded to a particular item and (2) a basis for estimating the likelihood of participant responses (Lord, 1952). Examining item difficulty by plotting an ICC for each item allows us to rank items ordinally in terms of how each item is correlated with a specific outcome score or range of scores. For example, if we designed a test of mathematical ability, we would want to have questions that capture a range of ability levels. It would be practical to ensure that the test included questions that were adequate indicators spanning a continuum of low to high ability. To accomplish this, ICCs could be plotted for each test item and a range of items could be selected for inclusion on the test so that the test distribution of questions ranges from very easy to very difficult. Models with this structure (i.e., those examining only item difficulty) are referred to as Rasch models. Single-parameter models for items with binary response sets (response is correct/incorrect, true or false, yes or no) are referred to as dichotomous Rasch models (van der Linden, 2016a). Figure 2.1 is an illustration of what the ICC curves may look like for three test items of varying difficulty. The amount of the observed latent trait (e.g., mathematical ability) is measured using a logarithmic probability unit called a logit, which is conceptually similar to a z-score. Probability scores range from 0 to 1; 0 indicates the amount of the trait present at which the item is never answered correctly (0 percent of the time) and 1 indicates the amount of the trait that is present when

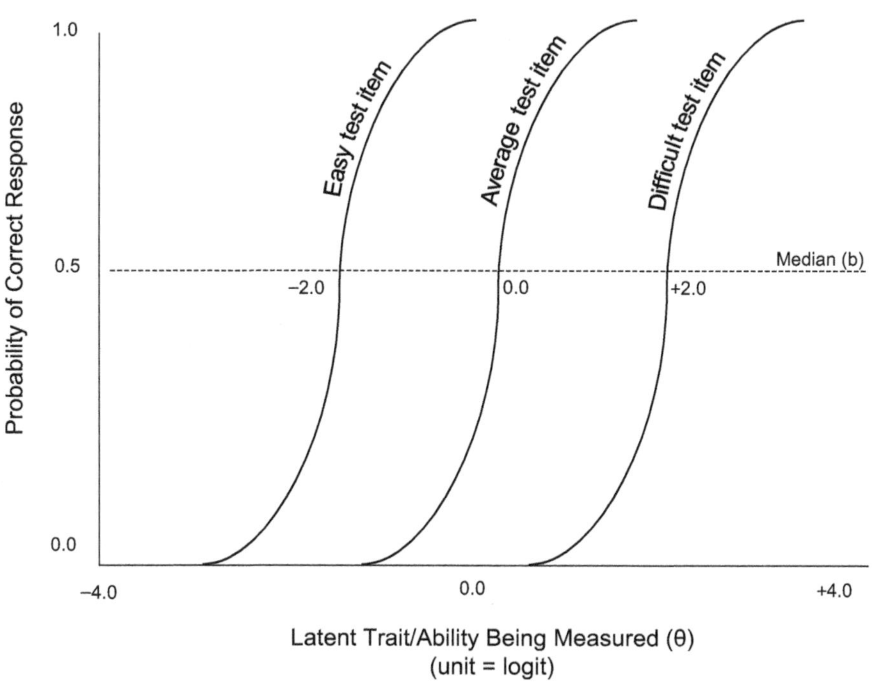

Figure 2.1 Item characteristic curves

the item is answered correctly always (100 percent of the time). The median probability (50 percent), and the logit value associated with this probability, is the value used to represent the item's level of difficulty. In many IRT equations, this median probability value in logit units is represented as *b* and the quantity of the observed latent trait is represented as theta, θ (van der Linden, 2016b).

Single-Parameter IRT Models

In addition to the relatively simple dichotomous Rasch model, numerous IRT models have been designed to fit both dichotomous and polytomous test response structures (true/false, multiple choice, Likert-type scales), testing item response distributions (e.g., normal, bimodal, multimodal), and overall patterns of responding (e.g., cumulative probabilities, likelihood of a given test outcome based on response patterns). One of the more common single-parameter IRT models is the partial credit model (PCM), which allows test developers to estimate item selection probabilities based on ability for polytomous (e.g., multiple choice) test items. PCM models are similar to dichotomous models in that the outcome of interest is the probability of each response at varying levels of θ; however, when there are more than two options it is not possible to calculate *b*. Instead, for each possible response option, a line may be used to illustrate the probability of selecting that response, given possible quantities of θ (Masters, 1982). Figure 2.2 depicts four possible hypothetical responses from a clinical instrument for symptoms of depression, the Patient Health Questionnaire-9 (PHQ-9; Kroenke, Spitzer, & Williams, 2001). For any given point along the x-axis (level of the latent trait of interest, θ), the total probability of all responses (choosing a, b, or c, in this example) will equal 100 percent. In Figure 2.2, θ is quantification of the client's experience of depression based on the frequency of experiencing a set of symptoms that are correlated with diagnoses of depression (as depression cannot be measured directly).

Two- and Three-Parameter IRT Models

Each of the models previously described focused on a single parameter, the probability of selecting a given response, given a quantity of a latent trait (θ). In IRT, it is also possible to model multiple item parameters. The IRT model used to investigate two items of interest (e.g., difficulty and discrimination) is referred to as a two-parameter logistic (2PL) model. A second parameter that is frequently of interest is discrimination, or how sensitive the item is for detecting a small increment of change or difference in θ, the latent trait being measured. Figure 2.3 depicts the two ICC curves where the item difficulty (*b*) is identical and the item slopes (*a*) differ, indicating that one item is more sensitive to changes in the measured latent trait (θ). Models that incorporate a third parameter (e.g., guessing) are substantially more complex mathematically and are referred to as three-parameter logistic (3PL) IRT models.

If we continue with the earlier example of designing a test to assess mathematical ability, we might hypothesize that very easy items would yield little information about an individual's skill level because the majority of participants would answer these correctly and that very difficult

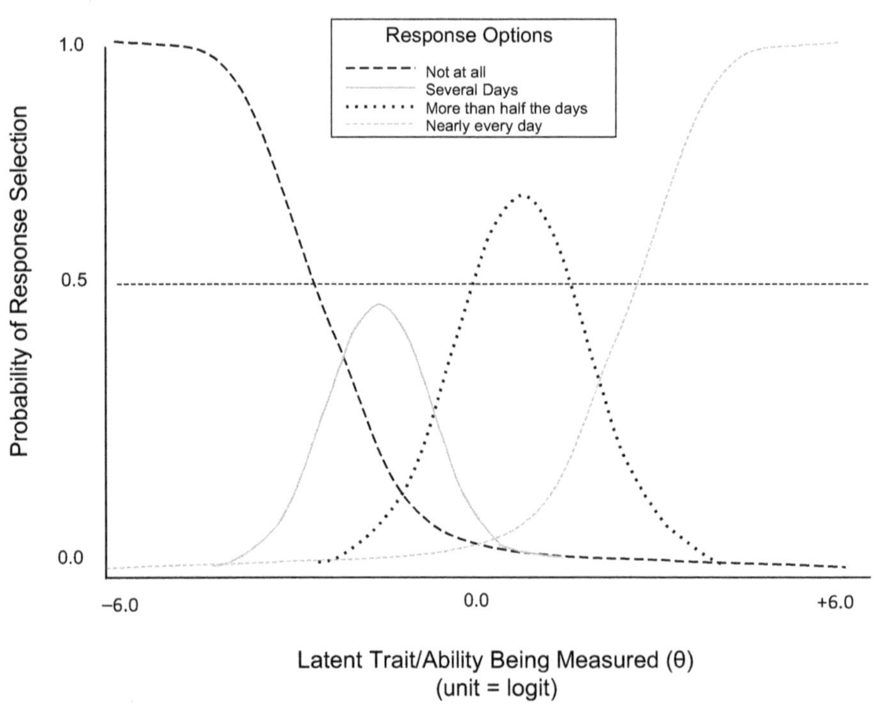

Figure 2.2 Partial credit model item characteristic curves

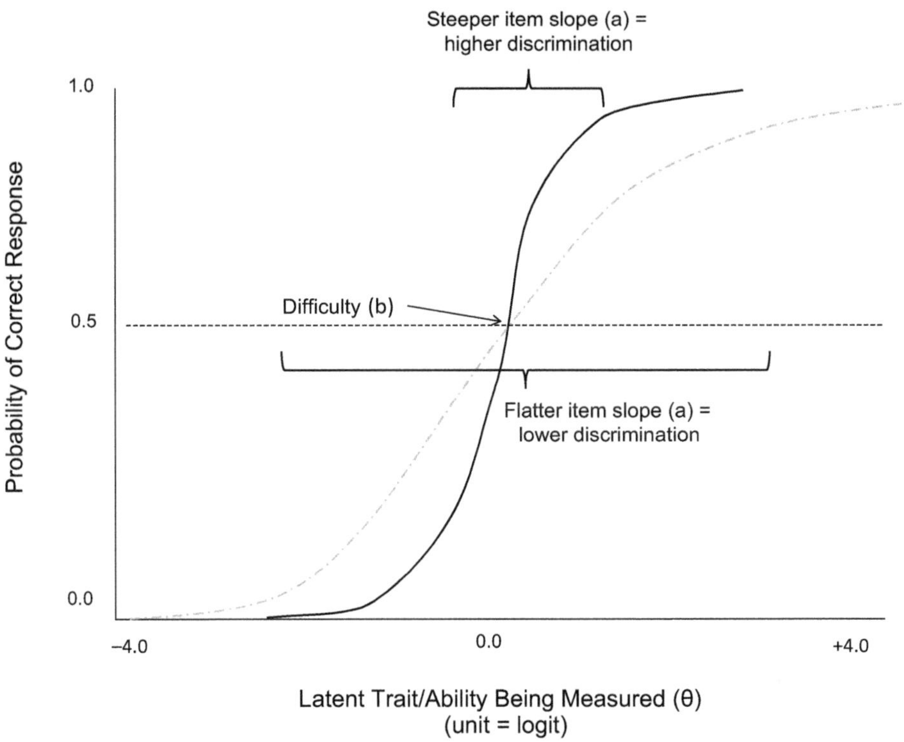

Figure 2.3 Two-parameter model item characteristic curves

items would also be minimally informative as the majority of participants would be likely to answer these incorrectly. Thus, in addition to assessing the relative difficulty of test items, it may also be useful to assess this second parameter, item discrimination (*a*). Discrimination/change sensitivity can be assessed by measuring the slope of the ICC for each item (Ferguson, 1942). A steeper slope indicates a smaller increase or decrease in logit units of the measured trait produces a response change and a flatter slope indicates that a larger logit unit increase or decrease in the amount of the measured trait must occur in order for the respondent's answer to change (van der Linden, 2016b). The mathematics to compute the discrimination parameter (*a*) become increasingly complex as the number of possible responses increases. These calculations also increase in complexity if there is a possibility that the respondent may be guessing (e.g., on knowledge and ability tests).

To summarize, IRT models may be examined in the context of cumulative probabilities using a single parameter but may also be comprised of response sets that can be used to model several items. One of these models is the Samejima graded response model (GRM) and, with it, a test developer may estimate the probability of a given response based on the discriminability parameter of the item in combination with a cumulative probability (threshold) based on the individual's pattern of responding to preceding test items (Samejima, 1969). A wide range of dichotomous and polytomous IRT models are available, including rating scale models for ordered response sets (RSM; Andrich, 1978), nominal response models (NRM; Bock, 1972), modified graded response models (MGRM; designed for Likert scale items, Muraki, 1990), and generalized partial credit models (a version of PCM that adds an item discrimination parameter to the model; Muraki, 1992). For readers interested in further information or computational formulae for the IRT models mentioned here, they can be found in sources such as Andrich (1978), Bock (1972), Masters (1982), Samejima (1969), and Muraki (1990, 1992). This is not a complete listing of all of currently available IRT procedures and there is ongoing, heated debate among statisticians regarding whether it is best to choose a single-parameter or two-parameter model (Andrich, 2004).

The Information Function at the Item Level and Test Level

After an ICC is derived, we can calculate an Information Function (IF), also commonly referred to at the item level as "information." Information is represented in IRT equations as *I*. Using the example above, the assessment of mathematical ability using a dichotomous model (correct/incorrect answer), the calculated value of information function is the product of the probability of producing a correct response multiplied by the probability of producing an incorrect response (Baker, 2001). Questions of varying difficulty (see Figure 2.1) are very likely to yield different quantities of *I*. Assume at a specific level of θ a test item that is an easy multiplication problem has the probability of producing a correct solution of 90 percent (0.9) and the probability of producing an incorrect solution of 10 percent (0.1). For this, $I_1 = 0.9 \times 0.1 = 0.09$. If a slightly more difficult question has a 70 percent probability of answering correctly and a 30 percent probability of answering incorrectly, at this same value for θ, $I_2 = 0.7 \times 0.3 = 0.21$. For a moderately difficult question, there may be a 50 percent probability of a correct response and a 50 percent probability of an incorrect response ($I_3 = 0.5 \times 0.5 = 0.25$). This value, where there is a 50/50 probability, is the median probability (*b*) (Figure 2.2). A difficult question may yield a 30 percent probability of a correct response and a 70 percent probability of an incorrect response for individuals at this same level of the latent trait ($I_4 = 0.3 \times 0.7 = 0.21$). The greatest relative value for *I* indicates which of the test items yields the most information for this level of θ. Conceptually, the moderately difficult question provides more information than the easy question because we would expect the easy question to be answered correctly by 90 percent of test-takers and we would not be distinguishing differing levels of the mathematical ability of the test-takers with much precision based on responses to this item.

Test information, in contrast to item information, is the sum of *I* across items at the given level of θ. In this example, our test had four items and, for this level of θ, test information would be calculated as $I_1 + I_2 + I_3 + I_4 = 0.76$. This test information value of 0.76 at a specific level of ability θ_A could be compared to the level of information yielded by this test at varying ability levels to determine the performance of this test across varying levels of ability. Tests that are so difficult that students at all ability levels produce few correct answers may yield as little information (i.e., lack precision to distinguish student ability) as tests where students of all ability levels score 90 percent. Comparatively, a test with a higher test information value indicates that, cumulatively, the test items are providing more information and can potentially be used to detect smaller changes in θ (Baker, 2001). Finally, the calculated values for item information and for test information are also used to calculate item reliability (standard error of θ) in IRT.

$$SE(\theta) = 1/\sqrt{Information(\theta)}$$

Referring back to Figure 2.2, the simulated response set indicates the greater level of θ (depressive symptoms) is associated with a greater probability of endorsing that a symptom is experienced either more than half the days or nearly every day. From this we would interpret that, although a key depressive symptom (such as low mood every day) is very likely to be endorsed by individuals with severe depression, a response of low mood more than half the days would provide more information about an individual with moderate depression because we would expect nearly all individuals with severe depression to endorse this item and fewer individuals with moderate depression to endorse it.

Advantages and Limitations of IRT

The global advantage of IRT over CTT is that more information is available on how test items relate to the measured construct, because characteristics are modeled for each item at all possible levels of the trait. This results in the following specific advantages for the IRT approach over the CTT approach: (1) evaluation of test item equivalence for the generation of test bank questions ordered by difficulty such that different sets of items may be used on differing assessment occasions and yield theoretically equivalent results; (2) differing items can be selected by clinicians based on the client's presumed level of a given construct or can be selected via algorithms to streamline the efficiency of the assessment process (i.e., computerized adaptive testing uses previous responses to select the questions that are the most likely to provide greater discriminability and greater accuracy in the estimation of the trait or ability being assessed); (3) differential item functioning across groups can be examined as a method of identifying item biases, which is important in assessing cultural fairness and equivalence of test items for use with diverse groups; and (4) measures of the same construct can be calibrated in order to generate integrated conclusions from large-scale studies that used similar methods but differing assessment instruments.

A limitation of IRT is that, like the majority of statistical procedures, certain parametric assumptions must be met: monotonicity, unidimensionality, local independence, and qualitative homogeneity. Logistic IRT models require that items responses occur in the form of monotonic functions. This means that the probability of endorsing an item (or providing the correct response to an ability test question) increases as θ increases. In our example, we hypothesize that the probability of answering a math question correctly increases with our observed latent trait "mathematical skill." The relation is not required to be precisely linear; however, latent traits that are best described using quartic, quadratic, or more complex trends would cause this assumption to be violated and the use of a logistic IRT model would not yield meaningful results. To satisfy the assumption of unidimensionality, item responses must be able to be characterized primarily by a unidimensional latent trait (θ) such that the amount of the trait present accounts for item covariance. Returning to our earlier example, unidimensionality would assume that the amount of the trait (e.g., mathematical skill) would explain individual differences in responding to questions of varying difficulty (e.g., easy vs. difficult multiplication problems). The assumption of local independence requires that item responses are uncorrelated after statistically controlling for the latent trait. If this assumption is violated by a correlation among several items, slope estimates may bias toward indicating that the scale yields greater-than-actual measurement precision. If this assumption is violated by a large correlation among only a few items, the scale may have insufficient construct validity. A final assumption that must be met for IRT analyses to be useful is the assumption that the population being assessed is qualitatively homogeneous, in that the same ICC would apply to all members of the population being studied. Differential Item Functioning (DIF) is a violation of this assumption. DIF occurs when all of the other assumptions have been met and individuals who are equivalent on the latent trait (θ) produce response differentials that exceed differences that would be expected due to measurement error.

Practical Applications of IRT

At present, IRT is a prevalent measurement model in both cognitive assessment and in computerized adaptive testing (CAT), as it is advantageous to be able to mathematically select the items most likely to provide the most relevant information based on the test-taker's initial responses. Recent applications of IRT also include explorations of item overlap among personality disorder diagnoses in the form of the CAT-PD Project (Wright & Simms, 2014) and the development of the Personality Inventory for DSM-5 (PID-5, Krueger et al., 2012). Although interest in both IRT and CAT for clinical testing is growing, it is likely due to the complexity of interpretation and the significantly larger sample sizes and resources required for useful and accurate IRT models that few clinical assessment instruments and clinical studies use IRT modeling methods.

PSYCHOMETRICS AND CULTURAL/DIVERSITY CONSIDERATIONS

In the preceding sections, we have emphasized the conditional nature of psychometric evidence. Nowhere is this more pertinent than when considering the culturally sensitive use of assessment instruments. Although the psychometric evidence supporting the use of a measure with one ethnic group may generalize to the use of the measure with other ethnic groups, there is no guarantee of this. The same is true not just for ethnicity but for other diversity dimensions as well (e.g., age, gender, sexual orientation). Moreover, the extent to which the measure's underlying construct is relevant to diverse groups should be empirically evaluated, not just assumed. To this end, a range of statistical procedures can be used to evaluate the applicability of a measure to groups other than those on which the measure was developed (e.g., Arbisi, Ben-Porath, & McNulty, 2002; Bingenheimer et al., 2005; Milfont & Fischer, 2010; van de Schoot, Lugtig, & Hox, 2012). These require data from multiple groups of interest and then (1) regression-based analyses to examine differential predictive validity across groups, (2) IRT-based DIF analyses to detect response differences across those with equivalent θ values, or (3) confirmatory factor analytic strategies to evaluate configural invariance (whether the same underlying measurement model fits across groups), metric invariance (whether scores on the measure have the same meaning across groups), and scalar invariance (whether the various group mean scores are similar).

So what is the clinician or researcher to do when deciding if it is appropriate to use an instrument with a client or research participant? In general, the clinician/researcher should determine whether there is relevant validity evidence based on research with members of the same ethnic group (or other diversity dimensions) as the client/participant, ideally based on the kinds of statistical procedures we just described. Fernandez, Boccaccini, and Noland (2007), for example, outlined a four-step process psychologists can use in identifying and selecting translated tests for Spanish-speaking clients (which is applicable to translated tests in other languages). First, the range of translated tests should be identified by reviewing the websites of test publishing companies and psychological test sites.[1] Next, research evidence for each relevant translated test, not just the original English-language versions, must be examined. Third, the nature of the Spanish-speaking samples used in the studies should be examined to determine if the results are likely to be relevant to the person who will be assessed (e.g., results of research conducted in Spain may not be generalizable to someone who recently emigrated from Honduras). Fourth, the overall strength of the validity evidence must be weighed in determining whether the test is likely to be appropriate and useful in assessing the person. As Haynes and colleagues (2019) have emphasized, no assessment instrument can demonstrate psychometric equivalence across all diversity dimensions. It is precisely for this reason that the clinician or researcher must remain cognizant of the conditional nature of psychometric evidence and, as much as possible, use multiple assessment methods and strategies when assessing an individual.

CONCLUSION

The use of psychometric evidence is critical for high-quality psychological assessment, whether the assessment is for research or clinical service purposes. Standardization, reliability, validity, norms, and utility are not just concepts that apply in a laboratory research context – they are critical in any context in which psychological assessments are conducted. Attention to psychometric evidence increases the likelihood that (1) the instruments we use to assess people are both appropriate and scientifically sound and (2) the conclusions we draw on the basis of scores on these instruments are as accurate and meaningful as possible.

[1] E.g., the American Psychological Association's PsycTESTS site: www.apa.org/pubs/databases/psyctests/index.aspx.

REFERENCES

Achenbach, T. M. (2001). What are norms and why do we need valid ones? *Clinical Psychology: Science and Practice, 8*, 446–450.

AERA (American Educational Research Association), APA (American Psychological Association), & NCME (National Council on Measurement in Education). (2014). *Standards for educational and psychological testing*. Washington, DC: AERA.

Anastasi, A., & Urbina, S. (1997). *Psychological testing* (7th ed.). Upper Saddle River, NJ: Prentice-Hall.

Andrich, D. (1978). A rating formulation for ordered response categories. *Psychometrika, 43*, 561–573.

Andrich, D. (2004). Controversy and the Rasch model. *Medical Care, 42*, 1–10.

Arbisi, P. A., Ben-Porath, Y. S., & McNulty, J. (2002). A comparison of MMPI-2 validity in African American and Caucasian psychiatric inpatients. *Psychological Assessment, 14*, 3–15.

Baker, F. (2001). *The basics of item response theory*. College Park, MD: ERIC Clearinghouse on Assessment and Evaluation.

Barry, A. E., Chaney, B. H., Piazza-Gardner, A. K., & Chavarria, E. A. (2014). Validity and reliability reporting in the field of health education and behavior: A review of seven journals. *Health Education and Behavior, 41*, 12–18.

Ben-Porath, Y. S., & Tellegen, A. (2008). *The Minnesota Multiphasic Personality Inventory – 2 Restructured Form: Manual for administration, scoring, and interpretation*. Minneapolis: University of Minnesota Press.

Bingenheimer, J. B., Raudenbush, S. W., Leventhal, T., & Brooks-Gunn, J. (2005). Measurement equivalence and differential item functioning in family psychology. *Journal of Family Psychology, 19*, 441–455.

Bock, R. D. (1972). Estimating item parameters and latent ability when responses are scored in two or more nominal categories. *Psychometrika, 37*, 29–51.

Brooks, B. L., Strauss, E., Sherman, E. M. S., Iverson, G. L., & Slick, D. J. (2009). Developments in neuropsychological assessment: Refining psychometric and clinical interpretive methods. *Canadian Psychology, 50*, 196–209.

Bush, S. S., Ruff, R. M., Tröster, A. I., Barth, J. T., Koffler, S. P., Pliskin, N. H., Reynolds, C. R., & Silver, C. H. (National Academy of Neuropsychology Policy & Planning Committee). (2005). Symptom validity assessment: Practice issues and medical necessity. *Archives of Clinical Neuropsychology, 20*, 419–426.

Chmielewski, M., Clark, L. A., Bagby, R. M., & Watson, D. (2015). Method matters: Understanding diagnostic reliability in DSM-IV and DSM-5. *Journal of Abnormal Psychology, 124*, 764–769.

Cicchetti, D. V. (1994). Guidelines, criteria, and rules of thumb for evaluating normed and standardized assessment instruments in psychology. *Psychological Assessment, 6*, 284–290.

Cronbach, L. J., Gleser, G. C., Nanda, H., & Rajaratnum, N. (1972). *The dependability of behavioral measures: Theory of generalizability for scores and profiles*. New York: John Wiley & Sons.

Cronbach, L. J., & Meehl, P. E. (1955). Construct validity in psychological tests. *Psychological Bulletin, 52*, 281–302.

Dunn, T. J., Baguley, T., & Brunsden, V. (2014). From alpha to omega: A practical solution to the pervasive problem of internal consistency estimation. *British Journal of Psychology, 105*, 399–412.

Fariña, F., Redondo, L., Seijo, D., Novo, M., & Arce, R. (2017). A meta-analytic review of the MMPI validity scales and indexes to detect defensiveness in custody evaluations. *International Journal of Clinical and Health Psychology, 17*, 128–138.

Ferguson, G. A. (1942). Item selection by the constant progress. *Psychometrika, 7*, 19–29.

Fernandez, K., Boccaccini, M. T., & Noland, R. M. (2007). Professionally responsible test selection for Spanish-speaking clients: A four-step approach for identifying and selecting translated tests. *Professional Psychology: Research and Practice, 38*, 363–374.

Fortney, J. C., Unützer, J., Wrenn, G., Pyne, J. M., Smith, G. R., Schoenbaum, M., & Harbin, H. T. (2017). A tipping point for measurement-based care. *Psychiatric Services, 68*, 179–188.

Fuentes, K., & Cox, B.J. (1997). Prevalence of anxiety disorders in elderly adults: A critical analysis. *Journal of Behavior Therapy and Experimental Psychiatry, 28*, 269–279.

Haynes, S. N., Richard, D. C. S., & Kubany, E. S. (1995). Content validity in psychological assessment: A functional approach to concepts and methods. *Psychological Assessment, 7*, 238–247.

Haynes, S. N., Smith, G., & Hunsley, J. (2019). *Scientific foundations of clinical assessment* (2nd ed.). New York: Taylor & Francis.

Henson, R., Kogan, L., & Vacha-Haase, T. (2001). A reliability generalization study of the Teacher Efficacy Scale and related instruments. *Educational and Psychological Measurement, 61*, 404–420.

Hogan, T. P. (2014). *Psychological testing: A practical introduction* (3rd ed.). Hoboken, NJ: John Wiley & Sons.

Hogan, T. P., Benjamin, A., & Brezinski, K. L. (2000). Reliability methods: A note on the frequency of use of various types. *Educational and Psychological Measurement, 60*, 523–531.

Hunsley, J., & Mash, E. J. (Eds.). (2018a). *A guide to assessments that work*. New York: Oxford University Press.

Hunsley, J., & Mash, E. J. (2018b). Developing criteria for evidence-based assessment: An introduction to assessments that work. In J. Hunsley & E. J. Mash (Eds.), *A guide to assessments that work* (pp. 3–14). New York: Oxford University Press.

Hunsley. J., & Meyer, G. J. (2003). The incremental validity of psychological testing and assessment: Conceptual, methodological, and statistical issues. *Psychological Assessment, 15*, 446–455.

Hurl, K., Wightman, J. K., Haynes, S. N., & Virués-Ortega, J. (2016). Does a pre-intervention functional assessment increase intervention effectiveness? A meta-analysis of within-subject interrupted time-series studies. *Clinical Psychology Review, 47*, 71–84.

Kendall, P. C., Marrs-Garcia, A., Nath, S. R., & Sheldrick, R. C. (1999). Normative comparisons for the evaluation of clinical significance. *Journal of Consulting and Clinical Psychology, 67*, 285–299.

Kieffer, K. M., & Reese, R. J. (2002). A reliability generalization study of the Geriatric Depression Scale (GDS). *Educational and Psychological Measurement, 62*, 969–994.

Kroenke, K., Spitzer, R. L., & Williams, J. B. W. (2001). The PHQ-9: The validity of a brief depression severity measure. *Journal of General Internal Medicine, 16*, 606–613.

Krueger, R. F., Derringer, J., Markon, K. E., Watson, D., & Skodol, A. E. (2012). Initial construction of a maladaptive personality trait model and inventory for DSM-5. *Psychological Medicine, 42*, 1879–1890.

Lambert, M. J., & Shimokawa, K. (2011). Collecting client feedback. *Psychotherapy*, *48*, 72–79.

Lord, F. (1952). *A theory of test scores*. Richmond, VA: Psychometric Corporation.

Masters, G. N. (1982). A Rasch model for partial credit scoring. *Psychometrika*, *47*, 149–174.

McGrath, R. E. (2001). Toward more clinically relevant assessment research. *Journal of Personality Assessment*, *77*, 307–332.

McGrath, R. E., Mitchell, M., Kim, B. H., & Hough, L. (2010). Evidence for response bias as a source of error variance in applied assessment. *Psychological Bulletin*, *136*, 450–470.

McGrew, K. S., LaForte, E. M., & Schrank, F. A. (2014). *Technical manual: Woodcock-Johnson IV*. Rolling Meadows, IL: Riverside

Merten, T., Dandachi-FitzGerald, B., Hall, V., Schmand, B. A., Santamaría, P., & González-Ordi, H. (2013). Symptom validity assessment in European countries: Development and state of the art. *Clínica y Salud*, *24*, 129–138.

Messick, S. (1995). Validity of psychological assessment: Validation of inferences from persons' responses and performances as scientific inquiry into score meaning. *American Psychologist*, *50*, 741–749.

Milfont, T. L., & Fischer, R. (2010). Testing measurement invariance across groups: Applications in cross-cultural research. *International Journal of Psychological Research*, *3*, 111–121.

Miller, C. S., Kimonis, E. R., Otto, R. K., Kline, S. M., & Wasserman, A. L. (2012). Reliability of risk assessment measures used in sexually violent predator proceedings. *Psychological Assessment*, *24*, 944–953.

Morash, V. S., & McKerracher, A. (2017). Low reliability of sighted-normed verbal assessment scores when administered to children with visual impairments. *Psychological Assessment*, *29*, 343–348.

Morey, L. C. (1991). *The Personality Assessment Inventory professional manual*. Odessa, FL: Psychological Assessment Resources.

Moskowitz, D. S., Russell, J. J., Sadikaj, G., & Sutton, R. (2009). Measuring people intensively. *Canadian Psychology*, *50*, 131–140.

Muraki, E. (1990). Fitting a polytomous item response model to Likert-type data. *Applied Psychological Measurement*, *14*, 59–71.

Muraki, E. (1992). A generalized partial credit model: application of an EM algorithm. *Applied Psychological Measurement*, *16*, 159–176.

Murphy, K. R., & Davidshofer, C. O. (2005). *Psychological testing: Principles and applications* (6th ed.). New York: Pearson.

Nelson-Gray, R. O. (2003). Treatment utility of psychological assessment. *Psychological Assessment*, *15*, 521–531.

Newton, P. E., & Shaw, S. D. (2013). Standards for talking and thinking about validity. *Psychological Methods*, *18*, 301–319.

Nunnally, J. C., & Bernstein, I. H. (1994). *Psychometric theory* (3rd ed.). New York: McGraw-Hill.

Paulhus, D. L. (1998). *Manual for the Paulhus Deception Scales: BIDR Version 7*. Toronto: Multi-Health Systems.

Reisse, S. P., & Revicki, D. A. (Eds.). (2015). *Handbook of item response theory modeling*. New York: Routledge.

Revelle, W., & Zinbarg, R.E. (2009). Coefficients alpha, beta, omega and the glb: Comments on Sijtsma. *Psychometrika*, *74*, 145–154.

Rodebaugh, T. L., Sculling, R. B., Langer, J. K., Dixon, D. J., Huppert, J. D., Bernstein, A., ... Lenze, E. J. (2016). Unreliability as a threat to understanding psychopathology: The cautionary tale of attentional bias. *Journal of Abnormal Psychology*, *125*, 840–851.

Rohling, M. L., Larrabee, G. J., Greiffenstein, M. F., Ben-Porath, Y. S., Lees-Haley, P., Green, P., & Greve, K. W. (2011). A misleading review of response bias: Response to McGrath, Mitchell, Kim, & Hough (2010). *Psychological Bulletin*, *137*, 708–712.

Rousse, S. V. (2007). Using reliability generalization methods to explore measurement error: An illustration using the MMPI-2 PSY-5 scales. *Journal of Personality Assessment*, *88*, 264–275.

Samejima, F. (1969). *Estimation of latent ability using a response pattern of graded scores* (Psychometric Monograph No. 17). Richmond, VA: Psychometric Society. www.psychometrika.org/journal/online/MN17.pdf

Schmidt, F. L., & Hunter, J. E. (1977). Development of a general solution to the problem of validity generalization. *Journal of Applied Psychology*, *62*, 529–540.

Sechrest, L. (1963). Incremental validity: A recommendation. *Educational and Psychological Measurement*, *23*, 153–158.

Smid, W. J., Kamphuis, J. H., Wever, E. C., & Van Beek, D. J. (2014). A comparison of the predictive properties of the nine sex offender risk assessment instruments. *Psychological Assessment*, *26*, 691–703.

Smith, G. T., Fischer, S., & Fister, S. M. (2003). Incremental validity principles in test construction. *Psychological Assessment*, *15*, 467–477.

Stanley, D. J., & Spence, J. R. (2014). Expectations for replications: Are yours realistic? *Perspectives on Psychological Science*, *9*, 305–318.

Strauss, M. E., & Smith, G. T. (2009). Construct validity: Advances in theory and methodology. *Annual Review of Clinical Psychology*, *5*, 89–113.

Streiner, D. L. (2003a). Starting at the beginning: An introduction to coefficient alpha and internal consistency. *Journal of Personality Assessment*, *80*, 99–103.

Streiner, D. L. (2003b). Diagnosing tests: Using and misusing diagnostic and screening tests. *Journal of Personality Assessment*, *81*, 209–219.

Tam, H. E., & Ronan, K. (2017). The application of a feedback-informed approach in psychological service with youth: Systematic review and meta-analysis. *Clinical Psychology Review*, *55*, 41–55.

Teglasi, H. (2010). *Essentials of TAT and other storytelling assessments* (2nd ed.). Hoboken, NJ: Wiley.

Therrien, Z., & Hunsley, J. (2012). Assessment of anxiety in older adults: A systematic review of commonly used measures. *Aging and Mental Health*, *16*, 1–16.

Therrien, Z., & Hunsley, J. (2013). Assessment of anxiety in older adults: A reliability generalization meta-analysis of commonly used measures. *Clinical Gerontologist*, *36*, 171–194.

Tombaugh, T. N. (1996). *The Test of Memory Malingering*. Toronto: Multi-Health Systems.

Vacha-Haase, T. (1998). Reliability generalization exploring variance in measurement error affecting score reliability across studies. *Educational and Psychological Measurement*, *58*, 6–20.

Vacha-Haase, T., Henson, R., & Caruso, J. (2002). Reliability generalization: Moving toward improved understanding and use of score reliability. *Educational and Psychological Measurement*, *62*, 562–569.

Vacha-Haase, T., & Thompson, B. (2011). Score reliability: A retrospective look back at 12 years of reliability generalization studies. *Measurement and Evaluation in Counseling and Development*, *44*, 159–168.

van de Schoot, R., Lugtig, P., & Hox, J. (2012). A checklist for testing measurement invariance. *European Journal of Developmental Psychology*, *9*, 486–492.

van der Linden, W. J. (Ed.). (2016a). *Handbook of item response theory*, Vol. *1*. Boca Raton, FL: CRC Press.

van der Linden, W. J. (Ed.). (2016b). *Handbook of item response theory*, Vol. *2*. Boca Raton, FL: CRC Press.

Wasserman, J. D., & Bracken, B. A. (2013). Fundamental psychometric considerations in assessment. In J. R. Graham & J. A. Naglieri (Eds.), *Handbook of psychology. Vol. 10: Assessment psychology* (2nd ed., pp. 50–81). Hoboken, NJ: John Wiley & Sons.

Weisz, J. R., Chorpita, B. F., Frye, A., Ng, M. Y., Lau, N., Bearman, S. K., & Hoagwood, K. E. (2011). Youth Top Problems: Using idiographic, consumer-guided assessment to identify treatment needs and to track change during psychotherapy. *Journal of Consulting and Clinical Psychology*, *79*, 369–380.

Wiggins, C. W., Wygant, D. B., Hoelzle, J. B., & Gervais, R. O. (2012). The more you say the less it means: Over-reporting and attenuated criterion validity in a forensic disability sample. *Psychological Injury and Law*, *5*, 162–173.

Wood, J. M., Garb, H. N., & Nezworski, M. T. (2006). Psychometrics: Better measurement makes better clinicians. In S. O. Lilienfeld & W. T. O'Donohue (Eds.), *The great ideas of clinical science: The 17 concepts that every mental health practitioner should understand* (pp. 77–92). New York: Brunner-Routledge.

Wright, A. G. C., & Simms, L. J. (2014). On the structure of personality disorder traits: Conjoint analyses of the CAT-PD, PID-5, and NEO-PI-3 Trait Models. *Personality Disorders: Theory, Research, and Treatment*, *5*, 43–54.

Xu, S., & Lorber, M. F. (2014). Interrater agreement statistics with skewed data: Evaluation of alternatives to Cohen's kappa. *Journal of Consulting and Clinical Psychology*, *82*, 1219–1227.

Youngstrom, E. A., Van Meter, A., Frazier, T. W., Hunsley, J., Prinstein, M. J., Ong, M.-L., & Youngstrom, J. K. (2017). Evidence-based assessment as an integrative model for applying psychological science to guide the voyage of treatment. *Clinical Psychology: Science and Practice*, *24*, 331–363.

3 Multicultural Issues in Clinical Psychological Assessment

FREDERICK T. L. LEONG, P. PRISCILLA LUI, AND ZORNITSA KALIBATSEVA

INTRODUCTION

There have been increasing theoretical developments and empirical research regarding multicultural issues in clinical psychological assessment and diagnosis over the past two decades. This is illustrated by a series of articles and chapters that have reviewed cross-cultural problems in assessment and clinical diagnosis with various ethnic and national groups (e.g., Adebimpe, 2004; Cheung, Leong, & Ben-Porath, 2003; Eap et al., 2010; Malgady, 1996). In this chapter, we add to this literature by addressing the multiple challenges in clinical psychological assessment and diagnosis from a multicultural perspective. We have undertaken this task by discussing the multicultural issues in relation to (1) clinical diagnosis and (2) psychological testing and assessment. In each of these two sections, we describe frameworks that represent best practices. For example, in terms of clinical diagnosis, the Cultural Formulations approach in the fifth edition of the *Diagnostic and Statistical Manual* (DSM-5; American Psychiatric Association, 2013a) represents the current major framework for conducting diagnosis with culturally diverse clients. In the third and final section, we discuss the remaining challenges and the future directions related to multicultural issues in clinical psychological assessment.

CLINICAL DIAGNOSIS

Regarding multicultural issues in clinical diagnosis, we will discuss the established system of the DSM-5 Outline for Cultural Formulation as an organizing framework that represents current best practice. This is followed by a summary of the model developed by Leong and Kalibatseva (2016) regarding Threats to Cultural Validity in Clinical Diagnosis and Assessment, which is another recommended best practice.

DSM-5 Outline for Cultural Formulation

One of the significant developments in multicultural diagnosis and assessment is the development of the Cultural Formulation approach in the fourth edition of the *Diagnostic and Statistical Manual* (DSM-IV; American Psychiatric Association, 1994). This edition of the DSM included cultural elements through its multiaxial system as steps toward greater cultural validity and this has been continued in the DSM-5. Therefore, any discussion of multicultural clinical diagnosis should begin with a review of the DSM-5 Outline for Cultural Formulation. The DSM-5 Outline for Cultural Formulation consists of the following five dimensions: (1) cultural identity of the individual; (2) cultural explanations of the individual's illness; (3) cultural factors related to the psychosocial environment and levels of functioning; (4) cultural elements of the relationship between the individual and the clinician; and (5) overall cultural assessment for diagnosis and care (DSM-5; American Psychiatric Association, 2013a). Familiarity with a cultural formulation approach like this one should serve as the foundation for multicultural diagnosis and assessment. It is the primary comprehensive approach to clinical diagnosis that accounts for cultural influences on mental disorders.

Cultural Identity

Regardless of culture, all individuals have multiple identities, including ethnic, gender, and vocational identity. Culture determines the specific content of these identities as well as which identities are more accessible or salient, and therefore will have the greatest impact on an individual's behavior (Heine, 2001; Markus & Kitayama, 1991). These fundamental cultural differences in identities have been linked to a wide range of cultural differences in affect, cognition, and behavior (for a recent review, see Cross, Hardin, & Gercek, 2011). Across various cultures, the same event can elicit different types of emotion; by the same token the same emotion can be elicited by different events. For example, research has shown that North Americans are more likely to score high on independent self-construals and tend to be motivated by self-enhancement presentations, whereas East Asians are more likely to score high on interdependent self-construals and may be motivated by self-criticism (for a review, see Heine, 2001). These tendencies are explained by East Asians' interdependent self-construal and their more accessible public and collective selves, which motivate behavior designed to avoid bringing shame to the group.

These cultural aspects of a client's cultural identity are likely to influence how they experience and manifest mental health problems. Language is a critical way people access their culture. Psycholinguistic studies have demonstrated that languages, which vary by culture, can influence how people think, feel, and behave. For example, the Chinese culture (and many other East Asian cultures) has a strong emphasis on group collectives and social relationships; it also has a larger vocabulary referencing relatives and kinship than cultures that have weaker emphases on the collective (e.g., Lui & Rollock, 2018). Of course, the degree of a client's cultural identity is moderated by the involvement and investment in their culture of origin. To understand how people adapt and psychologically function in their environments, it is critical to assess a client's level of acculturation to various contexts. In the US context, for example, clients who are highly acculturated to their mainstream host culture (i.e., Anglo American–oriented) are more likely to be similar to average White or Euro Americans than those who are lower on the acculturation continuum in terms of their behavioral practices, values and beliefs, and mental health statuses (Lui & Zamboanga, 2018a, 2018b).

According to the Cultural Formulations Interview in DSM-5, cultural identity is first assessed with a series of open-ended questions (see American Psychiatric Association, 2013b). For example, clients are asked: For you, what are the most important aspects of your background and identity? Based on these initial questions, further probes of cultural identity are conducted during the interview with a series of thirty-four questions (see American Psychiatric Association, 2013c). The responses to these questions are then integrated into the cultural formulation.

Cultural Explanation of an Illness

Anthropologists have long made a distinction between the disease and the illness behaviors. The former is a universal biological process such as metastatic breast cancer. The latter is often moderated by personality and culture and involves the behavioral responses to the disease. To the extent that the meaning and experience of a psychiatric disorder can be influenced by cultural factors, it is important for the clinician to assess and understand the client's culture-specific idioms of distress as well as the normative cultural explanatory models for the disease. These culturally moderated explanatory models are also likely to influence decisions regarding help-seeking and mental health service utilization. For example, clients who believe that their problems are due to spirit possession are likely to seek help from spiritualists. A respectful exploration of these explanatory models is likely to prove helpful in the diagnostic formulation. It also ensures that cultural factors do not mask underlying pathology and inadvertently result in underdiagnosis.

Cultural Context and Psychosocial Environment

Given the individualist focus of Western approaches to psychopathology and psychotherapy, clinicians tend to ignore the cultural context in the diagnosis of mental health problems. Just as the DSM had evolved to a multiaxial system to evaluate the psychosocial and environmental factors influencing the client in Axis IV, the Cultural Formulation approach also calls for the assessment of cultural factors in the psychosocial environment that may affect the functioning of the client. Although the DSM has moved away from the multiaxial system, we argue that clinical diagnosis and assessment need to continue to recognize the important role of contexts. From culture-specific social stressors (e.g., being an undocumented immigrant or a refugee, experiencing unfair treatment due to group identities) to extant social support within minority neighborhoods (e.g., Lau et al., 2013; Lui & Quezada, 2019; Rollock & Lui, 2016b), these contextual elements provide valuable information to guide the cultural formulation. In contrast to the decontextualized approach of traditional psychiatry, this is a more holistic approach to diagnosis and assessment that encourages clinicians and clients to consider supportive and risk factors in their cultural environments. Despite DSM-5 having removed the multiaxial system, few would argue against the important moderating effects of cultural context in diagnostic formulations.

Culture Dynamics in the Therapeutic Relationship

Cultural dynamics are important to consider in any therapeutic relationship because they can determine client–therapist alliance, and in turn increase the likelihood of better interventions and outcomes. Consideration of cultural factors influencing the client–therapist relationship can help ensure that the therapist understands the issues being presented by the client and uses the best interventions to facilitate the best outcomes. An important cultural factor to consider in this regard is individualism/collectivism (e.g., Hui & Triandis, 1986), which is closely related to the individual-level construct of self-construal (Markus & Kitayama, 1991).

Most common in Western societies, individualism emphasizes the individual's goals over the group's goals. As such, individualistic cultures tend to foster a more independent self-construal. Hence, in treatment-as-usual situations, the typical approaches to establishing and maintaining a therapeutic relationship when working with clients from individualistic cultures involve focusing on the individuals and understanding their unique experiences. Such approaches may not be culturally appropriate for clients from collectivistic cultures who tend to have more interdependent self-construals.

Collectivism, on the other hand, which is often associated many non-Western cultures, emphasizes group memberships such as extended family, workgroup, tribe, caste, or country. For collectivists, the self is usually considered part of the larger group. In the same way as a body part cannot function without being part of the whole body, collectivists cannot be understood apart from the group. In other words, members of individualistic cultures tend to have autonomous-selves, whereas those from collectivistic cultures tend to have relational-selves. For therapists working with collectivist individuals, this suggests a need to pay attention to the connection the person may have with their family and/or community. Special attention will need to be given to the roles and duties that would be determined by in-group membership. Treatment goals that are not congruent with the group's goals would not be considered acceptable by most collectivist clients.

Overall Cultural Assessment

As the final stage of the Cultural Formulations approach, the overall cultural assessment component integrates the elements from the previous sections into a coherent case conceptualization that pays due attention to all cultural factors that influence the clients and their approach to the therapists and the treatment. In arriving at this overall assessment, it would be useful for therapists to apply some of the current theories and models in cross-cultural psychotherapy (Sue & Sue, 2012). For example, the Integrative Multidimensional Model developed by Leong (1996) is based on an adaptation of the cross-cultural model to the therapeutic process and also recognizes and integrates clinical issues within the context of the following three dimensions: individual, group, and universal. Since this model is based on an eclectic style of therapy, it can be applied to almost any career model and/or theory and be adapted to work with most culturally diverse groups, thus providing practitioners with a complete and comprehensive model that allows for dynamic and in-depth insight into the career issues of the client (Leong & Hardin, 2002; Leong & Hartung, 2003).

Threats to Cultural Validity in Clinical Diagnosis

Clinical diagnosis and assessment are essential foundations for effective psychotherapy (Garfield, 1984). An accurate diagnosis serves as a fundamental prerequisite for the selection of the optimal intervention. Whereas the Cultural Formulations approach is a useful approach to clinical diagnosis, there are some underlying challenges that should be addressed in arriving at an accurate diagnosis with culturally diverse clients. Leong and Kalibatseva's (2016) review showed that there are threats to arriving at appropriate diagnosis and assessment for culturally diverse client populations. There are important clinical and research implications for the proper resolution of these threats to cultural validity in clinical diagnosis.

As pointed out by Leong and Kalibatseva (2016), there are several significant problems associated with the clinical diagnosis of psychopathology and the value of the diagnostic process has remained controversial (Garfield, 1984; Sadler, 2005). Leong and Kalibatseva (2016) have provided a detailed discussion of these threats to cultural validity in diagnosis and these threats are outlined immediately below. This model of threats to cultural validity helps us understand how cultural factors may negatively influence the accuracy and validity of clinical diagnoses.

Concept of cultural validity. According to Leong and Kalibatseva (2016), there has been a tendency in assessment and clinical diagnosis to neglect the role of cultural differences on psychopathology. They argued that cultural validity is an important corollary to psychometric properties (e.g., face, construct, predictive, and concurrent validity). The concept of cultural validity refers to the effectiveness of a measure or the accuracy of a clinical diagnosis to address the existence and importance of essential cultural factors. Such cultural factors may include values, beliefs, experiences, communication patterns, and epistemologies inherent to the client's cultural background (Solano-Flores & Nelson-Barber, 2001). The lack of cultural validity in clinical diagnosis could produce incorrect diagnoses and ineffective treatment for culturally diverse populations. Inappropriate overdiagnosis could unnecessarily lead to stigmatization and institutionalization of racial and ethnic minorities due to a lack of cultural validity in diagnoses.

Threats to cultural validity. As indicated in Leong and Kalibatseva's (2016) review, the interpretation of assessment data, the accuracy of clinical diagnosis, and the outcome of psychotherapy with culturally diverse populations can be influenced by many factors. In contrast, much of clinical diagnosis is often conducted from a universalist perspective, which assumes that all people, regardless of race, ethnicity, or culture, develop along uniform psychological dimensions (Canino & Alegría, 2008; Malgady, 1996). This assumption of uniformity has been applied to racial and ethnic minority clients in many treatment-as-usual situations. Leong and Kalibatseva (2016) have argued that this cultural uniformity assumption prevents clinicians from recognizing and attending to important cultural differences and may moderate the diagnostic process for culturally diverse clients.

Leong and Kalibatseva (2016) adopted Campbell and Stanley's (1966) concept of threats to validity in experiments to propose that the lack of cultural validity in clinical assessment and diagnosis can also be conceptualized in terms of multiple threats to validity. According to Leong and Kalibatseva (2016),

> these threats to cultural validity in clinical assessment are largely due to a failure to recognize, or a tendency to minimize, cultural factors in clinical assessment and diagnosis ... These factors include but are not limited to (1) pathoplasticity of psychological disorders; (2) cultural factors influencing symptom expression; (3) therapist bias in clinical judgment; (4) language capability of the client; and (5) inappropriate use of diagnostic and personality tests. (Leong & Kalibatseva, 2016, p. 59)

In our summary of Leong and Kalibatseva's (2016) model, we will only provide one or two studies to illustrate each threat due to space limitations.

Pathoplasticity of psychological disorders. Leong and Kalibatseva (2016) framed Westermeyer's (1985) concept of pathoplasticity of psychological disorders as the first threat to cultural validity. According to Westermeyer (1985), pathoplasticity refers to the variability in symptoms, course, outcome, and distribution of mental disorders among various cultural groups. Westermeyer (1985) delineated three different examples of pathoplasticity:

> First, features associated with schizophrenia may vary widely from one culture to another and even among ethnic groups in a single country. Such differences may include the content, severity, or relative frequency of symptoms. Second, the pathoplasticity of nonpsychotic disorders may be observed in the different rates of mood, anxiety, and somatoform disorders, which may differ from one culture to another. The third example of pathoplasticity is finding of better outcome of schizophrenia in developing countries than in developed countries, which has been attributed to sociocultural factors (e.g., more stable social networks, integration in the community). Fourth, it is possible that certain psychopathological states may be represented by different diagnoses in different cultures. (Summarized in Leong & Kalibatseva, 2016, p. 61)

For example, Kleinman (1982) found that 87 percent of Chinese outpatients diagnosed with neurasthenia met the criteria for major depressive disorder, suggesting that somatic symptoms may mask depression. To further illustrate pathoplasticity, the distribution of mental disorders may vary within ethnic subgroups. Jackson and colleagues (2011) examined the prevalence rates of a major depressive episode (MDE) among the various racial and ethnic groups in the Collaborative Psychiatric Epidemiological Surveys. The National Latino and Asian American Study included three specific Asian ethnic groups – Filipinos, Vietnamese, and Chinese – and Other Asian. The pan-Asian ethnic groups reported the lowest rates of lifetime MDE compared to all others (non-Latino Whites, Hispanics, Caribbean Blacks, and African Americans). Filipinos had the lowest MDE rate (7.2 percent). In addition, Jackson and colleagues compared the prevalence rates of MDE for US-born and non–US-born participants and consistently found that, among the Asian ethnic groups, non–US-born participants reported lower prevalence rates. Specifically, the MDE prevalence rate for US-born Chinese Americans was 21.5 percent as opposed to 7.7 percent for the non–US-born Chinese Americans. Thus, this study demonstrated the importance of examining the interactions of culture, race, ethnicity, and immigration in the assessment of individuals from diverse populations.

Therefore, the pathoplasticity of psychological disorders, as formulated by Westermeyer (1985), may serve as a major threat to cultural validity in clinical diagnosis. The failure to recognize the cultural plasticity often associated with various forms of psychopathology in clients from diverse cultures may undermine the diagnostic process. Several studies have demonstrated this pathoplasticity of psychological disorders among various racial and ethnic groups (Leong & Kalibatseva, 2016). Cultural misdiagnosis is likely to occur if clinicians are not aware of the pathoplasticity of psychological disorders and practice with an assumption of universal isomorphism of symptom expression.

Cultural factors influencing symptom expression. A second threat to cultural validity in clinical diagnosis noted by Leong and Kalibatseva (2016) concerns the influence of the client's cultural background on their symptom expression. In an older study, Malgady, Rogler, and Cortés (1996) demonstrated how low socioeconomic status, inner-city Puerto Ricans may use idioms of anger to express psychiatric symptoms. In particular, the authors found that idioms expressive of aggression, assertiveness, and vindictiveness were significantly associated with depressive and anxiety symptoms and predicted clinical status. Based on these findings, the authors argued for conceptualizing psychiatric symptoms from the cultural group's perspective (*emic*) instead of imposing a mainstream (*etic*) approach in assessment.

Similarly, Whaley and Hall (2009) proposed that mental health professionals need to recognize racial and ethnic differences owing to cultural factors in psychotic symptom expression among African Americans and European Americans. The authors performed a content analysis of the clinical interviews of 156 African American inpatients and identified race-related and religious themes in their psychotic symptoms. In particular, race-related themes emerged more frequently in persecutory delusions and religious themes were more common in other types of delusions. The authors suggested that clinicians need to elicit and understand the cultural themes associated with psychiatric symptoms to avoid misdiagnosis.

Finally, research showed that Canadian clients diagnosed with depression reported higher levels/more severe symptoms of depression than their Chinese counterparts (Ryder et al., 2008). Specifically, Chinese reported higher levels of somatic symptoms of depression than their Euro-Canadian counterparts. At the same time, Euro Canadian outpatients reported higher levels of psychological symptoms of depression than their Chinese counterparts. Ryder and colleagues explored depressive symptom expression and concluded that the assessment methods (i.e., spontaneous problem report, symptom self-report questionnaire, or structured clinical interview) influenced the type and frequency of the symptoms that the clients reported. In this study, Chinese clients were found to report more depressive somatic symptoms in spontaneous report and structured interviews than Euro Canadians, whereas Euro Canadian clients reported significantly more affective symptoms (e.g., depressed mood, anhedonia, worthlessness, guilt) in all three assessment methods than Chinese clients. Based on their findings, Ryder and colleagues suggested that discussing Chinese somatization of depression may not be warranted; instead, Westerners may overemphasize the affective or psychological aspects of depression compared to people from other cultures. In all cases, failure to recognize that a client's cultural background may mediate when and how symptoms are expressed may result in a threat to making an accurate diagnosis.

Therapist bias in clinical judgment. According to Leong and Kalibatseva (2016), therapist bias serves as the third source of threat to cultural validity in clinical diagnosis. Clinician bias may range from intentional prejudice to unintentional ignorance about the client's culture (Payne, 2012). Intentional biases may include the therapist's racial bias against clients' racial, ethnic, and cultural backgrounds (Constantine, 2007; Rosenberger & Hayes, 2002). Such biases could be conceptualized as culture-based countertransference where the skin color or accent of a client may elicit certain therapist reactions, which may then adversely affect the services provided. For instance, there may be racial bias in clinicians' perception of racial and ethnic minority psychiatric patients (Spector, 2001). To illustrate this, US psychiatrists routinely overestimated the violence potential of non-White male clients by rating them as more dangerous than White clients at intake, although the ratings were not based on their actual behavior (McNeil & Binder, 1995).

Another form of therapist bias may be due to ethnocentricism, that is, using one's cultural values and norms to evaluate members of another culture. For example, Li-Repac's (1980) study found that the degree of familiarity with the client's cultural background may influence the diagnostic process. Li-Repac had five White and five Chinese American therapists rate the same Chinese and White clients on a videotaped interview on several dimensions. The author found that the White therapists were more accurate in predicting self-descriptive responses of White clients than of Chinese clients. More importantly, Li-Repac found that the White therapists rated the Chinese clients higher on the "depression/inhibition" dimension and lower on the "social poise/interpersonal capacity" dimension than the Chinese American therapists. Moreover, the Chinese American therapists judged the White clients to be more severely disturbed than did the White therapists. These findings point to the subjective nature of assessment data interpretation and clinical diagnosis. Overall, it appears that cultural or ethnic differences may affect therapist clinical judgment and assessment such that a therapist may overpathologize a culturally different client (Whaley, 1997).

Language capability of the client. In Leong and Kalibatseva's (2016) model, the language capability of the client is the fourth source of threat to cultural validity in assessment and clinical diagnosis. As pointed out by Leong (1986), there are several ways in which language may serve as a barrier to effective therapeutic communication. Asian Americans who speak little or no English may be misunderstood by their therapists (D. Sue, 1981; S. Sue & Morishima, 1982). Additionally, Shuy's (1983) review of the literature revealed that the use of dialects or nonstandard English by clients may interfere with the effective exchange of information or even stimulate bias in the therapist performing the evaluation.

Leong and Kalibatseva (2016) also discussed the use of interpreters (and its effects on diagnostic evaluations) with racial and ethnic minority clients as another language problem in clinical diagnosis. Problems inherent in "interpreter-mediated interviews" are of particular relevance to immigrant/refugee clients, since many of them may not speak or understand English (Goh, Dunnigan, & Schuchman, 2004; Lee, 1980). Some studies have shown that the use of interpreters may result in distortions that could negatively influence the diagnostic evaluation process. In one study cited by Leong and Kalibatseva (2016), Sabin (1975) reviewed the clinical records of two suicide cases among Spanish-speaking clients who were evaluated by English-speaking psychiatrists using interpreters. It was found that the degree of clients' emotional suffering and despair may have been underestimated due to distortions by the interpretation process. The clinician-effect (i.e., error due to a particular clinician) was ruled out since both clinicians conducting the evaluations made the same errors. Sabin (1975) concluded that the diagnostic errors were due to the interpreter-effect and not the clinician-effect (Leong & Kalibatseva, 2016).

Inappropriate use of clinical and personality tests. The fifth source of threat to cultural validity proposed by Leong and Kalibatseva (2016) concerns the inappropriate use of clinical and personality tests. For example, studies of Asian Americans' clinical and personality test results (i.e., Minnesota Multiphasic Personality Inventory [MMPI-2], NEO Personality Inventory – Revised [NEO-PI-R], projective tests) have tended to show them as having more severe symptoms and profiles than Whites (Leong, 1986; Okazaki, Kallivayali, & Sue, 2002). Despite a convergence of data that Asian Americans have more neurotic and disturbed personality profiles on objective self-report measures, these results need to be interpreted with caution for several reasons. First, there is an absence of culture-specific test norms since most of these measures were developed and normed on White samples. Additionally, in terms of criterion-related validity, these tests were designed to be predictive for Whites and their predictive validity for other ethnic and cultural groups has seldom been directly investigated. Second, very few of the clinical diagnostic instruments have been translated into Asian languages and their validity remains undetermined for clients with English as a second language (Leong & Kalibatseva, 2016).

Relatedly, Leong and Kalibatseva (2016) pointed to Takeuchi and colleagues' (1989) challenge of the assumption that instruments standardized on Whites used to assess need for mental health services can be readily used on Asian Americans (Leong & Kalibatseva, 2016). In analyzing the data from the Symptom Checklist (SCL) for four ethnic groups in Hawaii (i.e., Whites, Filipinos, Japanese, and Native Hawaiians), they found that Whites had the highest number of items that fell into hypothesized factor dimensions (twenty-seven), although this number was still only half of the total number of items on the SCL (fifty-four). Interestingly, the number of items that loaded on the six factors was substantially lower for the ethnic minority groups.

Finally, Leong and Kalibatseva (2016) cited the main thesis from Leong, Leung, and Cheung's (2010) review of cross-cultural research, which pointed to the fundamental problem being the failure to examine the measurement equivalence of the tests and measures when applied to other cultural groups. Similarly, the measurement equivalence of personality and diagnostic tests is problematic in assessment and diagnosis. In particular, these tests may not be culturally appropriate if their linguistic, functional, conceptual, and metric equivalence have not specifically been established. Therefore, in using personality and diagnostic tests with racial and ethnic minority clients, there is a need to recognize that there may be important group differences in definitions of mental illness and mental health. Clinicians who use the existing diagnostic and personality tests to diagnose ethnic minority clients without being aware of these issues and limitations may formulate culturally invalid diagnoses (Leong & Kalibatseva, 2016).

Cultural variations in validity measures. In clinical practice, the validity of clinical diagnosis, symptom severity, and cognitive impairments is dependent on truthful and honest reports from clients. For a number of reasons, clients may provide inconsistent, exaggerated, or fake responses in clinical interviews, diagnostic tests, and on self-report personality/clinical measures. Feigning has been shown to be identified across various demographic categories, including cultural contexts, languages, and gender (Nijdam-Jones & Rosenfeld, 2017). For example, the MMPI-2 contains several validity scales to detect faking, nonresponsive, or acquiescent answers. Through content responsive faking, content nonresponsivity, variable response inconsistency, and true response inconsistency scales, research has shown that Korean nationals and Americans display different response patterns on the variable and true response inconsistency scales. These data indicate that many individuals from the Asian samples need to be excluded in cross-cultural comparisons (Ketterer et al., 2010). Research with Spanish-speaking Mexican Americans also suggests that the use of validity scales may be biased, given culturally variable response styles in some of these minority groups (Rogers et al., 1995). This body of literature is rather small, particularly with regard to clinical diagnoses, which has proven challenging to assess and summarize accuracies of existing symptom classifications across cultures (Nijdam-Jones & Rosenfeld, 2017). Nevertheless, clinicians should be vigilant in considering the cutoff scores for validity scales normed in one cultural group in other contexts.

Summary for Clinical Diagnosis

Clinical diagnosis is a complicated process and much more so when cultural factors are involved. In this section, we have provided two conceptual frameworks to guide the clinician. These are not meant to be protocols with specific steps to be taken in a particular sequence. Rather, they highlight how cultural factors may interfere with the diagnostic process and clinicians need to be aware of how they may be manifested. For example, the Cultural Formulations approach outlined in the DSM points to the critical importance of evaluation of the clients' cultural identity, which in turn would influence their response to the clinician's questions and approach during the clinical interview. Similarly, the Threats to Cultural Validity approach highlights the clinician's personal and training biases that may skew the interview process. This approach also argues that one needs to proceed cautiously with the "treatment-as-usual" approach used by clinicians in selecting, assigning, and interpreting clinical tests for diagnostic purposes.

PSYCHOLOGICAL TESTING AND ASSESSMENT

Cultural Validity from the Standpoint of Classical Test Score Theory

Multicultural issues in clinical assessments and diagnoses can manifest in both cross-cultural settings and ethnic minority settings. Whenever a measure is developed in one cultural context or validated and used predominantly with one group of people, cultural validity becomes a critical concern. Understanding of clinical phenomena rests on the availability and use of reliable and valid assessment tools. Threats to accurate clinical psychological assessment involve unreliable instruments and diagnoses over time or across informants and poorly validated measures. As illustrated in the classical test score theory, each individual's true score on any given psychological phenomenon would be obtained if measurement error does not exist. Inherent in psychology, however, the observed scores always deviate from the person's true scores because of measurement error. On the one hand, measurement error includes the inevitable natural variability in human behaviors, performance, and characteristics. For instance, assessment of depression in the past two weeks inherently contains people's stable traits associated with negative affectivity; thus, observed scale scores on state depression symptoms may include individual differences in trait depressivity. On the other hand, measurement error may be caused by the imprecision of assessment tools. This type of systematic measurement error hinders professionals' ability to capture an individual's true scores on a given characteristic. Whereas construct validation encompasses all aspects of psychometric properties of any given clinical measurement, there has been more attention given to internal consistency reliability, test-retest reliability, and inter-rater reliability, as well as convergent and discriminant validity and concurrent and predictive validity (see Chapter 2 for a detailed discussion). Comparatively, there has been less attention to cultural validity.

Cultural validity. Similar to our discussion regarding cultural validity in diagnosis, cultural validity is also relevant in determining an assessment tool's accuracy when applied to other cultural groups. Cultural validity is akin to external validity in some sense because it concerns the degree to which diagnoses and clinical assessment findings are generalizable to distinct cultural groups and multicultural contexts. The lack of cultural validity not only can yield inaccurate diagnoses and misinform plans for intervention but also risks stigmatizing or stereotyping certain groups. Cultural validity is also important to the internal validity of the measurement of a clinical phenomenon because it concerns whether or not it accurately reflects the construct equivalently across social groupings and cultural contexts. When measures lack cultural validity, the observed scores from a clinical measure would contain measurement error pertaining to cultural variations as well as some portion of the true scores. Therefore, the cultural validity of tests and assessments needs to be evaluated as to whether we can equivalently infer the true scores on a clinically relevant characteristic across cultural settings and populations. Examples of these group-related factors include cultural values and expectations, normative behavioral repertoires, communication styles, and specific lived experiences. In terms of assessing cultural validity, it is important to note that cultural variations can take place in terms of people's responses on various clinical measures, base rates of mental illness and maladaptive behaviors, nomological network of the psychological constructs, predictive relations among key concepts, and psychometric properties of the instruments.

Cultural bias in self-report responses. People across cultural contexts may differ in their response styles on self-reported psychological measures. For example, nationals and Americans of pan-Asian backgrounds have been found to use midpoint Likert scale options (as opposed to extreme values) more frequently than Euro Americans (e.g., Lui, Vidales, & Rollock, 2018; Rollock & Lui, 2016a; Shou, Sellbom, & Han, 2017). These cultural variations in responses can result in cultural bias in the observed scores and similarly render scoring comparisons of limited meaning. People also may respond to positively versus negatively worded items differently. For example, the Center for Epidemiologic Studies Depression Scale (CES-D), a frequently used screening tool for major depression symptoms, has been found to elicit cultural bias in self-report responses among Chinese Americans (Li & Hicks, 2010). Assessing depression symptoms, reverse coded items in the CES-D (e.g., "I felt that I was as good as other people" as opposed to a standard coded alternative such as "I felt worthless compared to other people") are less likely to be endorsed by Chinese Americans and therefore the observed depression scores may be inflated in the study sample. More notably, the existing cutoff score for depression has been shown to overpathologize Chinese Americans, because many individuals who score above this cutoff do not actually meet diagnostic criteria for a major depressive disorder.

Cultural bias in base rates of behaviors. Related to bias that stems from differential preferences for survey responses, psychological assessments also may contain measurement error pertaining to cultural variations in the opportunity for certain behaviors. For example, there is a great deal of cultural differences in children's social competence and parental involvement in supporting children's educational outcomes. Social competence and parental involvement both may require additional social and financial resources, resources that are often unavailable to underprivileged groups (e.g., Hornby & Lafaele, 2011). Relying on these indicators of social adjustment without critically considering meaningful contextual factors across cultural groups would likely introduce measurement bias.

Cultural variations in the nomological network of clinical phenomenon. Another example can be illustrated in the culturally distinct meaning of a clinical phenomenon that often is neglected in measures that have been constructed in another population. Given that personality has been found to predict psychopathology and a variety of other clinical outcomes, researchers and practitioners have been interested in personality traits across individuals and cultures. Despite the assumption about the universality of openness to experience, research in Chinese culture has suggested that many facets of this basic personality factor do not reflect what it means to be open among Chinese individuals (Cheung et al., 2008). Additionally, honesty-humility has been consistently found to be a distinct and robust factor in Japanese and other Asian samples that is independent of agreeableness in the prevailing five-factor model of personality (e.g., Wakabayashi, 2014). Although pessimism has been considered as a risk factor for many mental disorders such as depression, it may be related to realism and reflect a culture-specific sensibility that is adaptive in pan-Asian/Asian American populations (Chang, 1996; Lui et al., 2016).

Cultural variations in the predictability of psychological assessment. Even in cases where the measurement of a particular clinical phenomenon is equivalent across cultural groups, the extent to which this phenomenon robustly predicts another behavioral criterion may differ. For example, studies have shown that family's expressed emotions are not reliably predictive of greater relapse probability among people with schizophrenia (López et al., 2004). The impact of expressed emotions, whereas robustly observed among Euro Americans, either is negligible (criticism from families) or in fact positive (warmth from family members).

Measurement Invariance to Evaluate the Equivalence of Psychological Measures

Given the different scenarios that can threaten cultural validity of psychological measures, it would be important to systematically evaluate the degree to which these measures are in fact equivalent across the cultural groups of interest (Schmitt & Kuljanin, 2008). Multigroup structural equation analyses can be valuable methods to test the factorial invariance as a way of assessing group similarities or differences in the nomological network of a construct, base rates of the underlying behavior or phenomenon, or response styles. Separate regression analyses can be used to examine group similarities or differences in the predictability of clinical measures.

Factorial invariance. There are systematic, statistical ways by which factorial invariance of can be tested. Using multigroup factor analyses (e.g., confirmatory factor analysis, exploratory structural equation modeling), sources of cultural variations can be evaluated at the levels of configural, metric/weak, scalar/strong, and uniqueness/strict invariance (see descriptions in Meredith, 1993; Schmitt & Kuljanin, 2008). At the most rudimentary level, *configural invariance* is evident when cultural groups are similar in the number of latent factors and pattern of factor-item relations. In cases that the nomological networks vary across groups, the psychological measures therefore lack configural invariance and cannot be validly used for the comparative cultural group. The next step above configural invariance involves testing whether the scale items load onto the latent factors equivalently across groups. If so, *metric or weak invariance* is satisfied and the factor scores can be evaluated in their relative associations with external criteria across cultural groups. Furthermore, *scalar or strong invariance* is tested to determine whether the item means (or thresholds, if ordinal) are similarly estimated across groups, which is a necessary requirement for evaluating whether latent factor means are equivalent across groups, and, only if so, the latent factor scores can be compared and interpreted. Finally, *uniqueness or strict invariance* is evident when the residual variance of each scale item is equivalent across groups. Uniqueness invariance sometimes can account for the similarity of the reliability of the scale scores and reflect group similarities in response styles. Uniqueness or strict invariance permits direct comparisons of observed scale mean scores across cultural groups but is often difficult to achieve in reality. Although there are other more stringent tests of factorial invariance, these typically are not carried out in most research because of the small likelihood of being identified in most circumstances.[1]

Functional or predictive invariance. Separate from identifying the same underlying nomological network and meaning of the construct, clinical measures are as useful as their ability to predict an external criterion reliably and accurately across cultural groups. In order to determine whether some psychological measures are functionally related to a criterion behavior in similar ways across cultural groups, research using regression analyses should demonstrate similar predictability of the measures (Burlew et al., 2014). For example, on establishing measurement invariance of the Big Five personality measure, Lui and colleagues (2018) conducted a series of comparative regression models to examine the predictive relations between mental health problems (e.g., depression, anxiety), personality, and sociocultural factors across ethnic groups. Analyses revealed that, whereas personality traits were important determinants of mental health problems among pan-Asian nationals/Americans and Euro Americans, regression coefficients of sociocultural factors such as comfort with university campus environment and contact with Whites were relatively stronger among Asian individuals than their Euro American counterparts.

Etic and Emic Approaches to Psychological Assessment

Many of the sources of cultural bias in psychological assessment are related to the fact that measures for the same underlying psychological construct have been constructed and validated in one cultural group but applied to a different one. Cross-national and cross-cultural comparisons frequently rely on adopting the measures developed in one culture and translating them into another language to be administered in a different culture. Although best practices regarding test development and validation have emphasized the assurance of language equivalence through the process of translation-back translation in international research, this approach to psychological and clinical measurement relies on a universalist assumption. The universalist assumption is one that the construct has the same conceptual meaning, factor structure, and predictive function across cultural groups. The empirical approach that underlies the universalist assumption is one of the etic approach. To some extent, in order to make

[1] Readers interested in steps to apply measurement invariance analyses can consult Brown (2014, chap. 7), Kline (2011), and Meredith (1993).

cross-cultural comparisons, researchers and practitioners must be able to compare apples to apples. In order to ensure that one is indeed comparing apples across cultures, the previous methods for testing measurement invariance can be applied.

By contrast, there are group distinct experiences that should not be extrapolated from one culture to the other and therefore cannot be compared directly. Logically, comparing observed results from psychological measures developed in an emic approach would be analogous to comparing apples to oranges. For example, the assessment of historical trauma and colonialism among the indigenous people in North America must rely on emic approaches. Unlike etic approaches to measurement, emic approaches do not assume a universality in clinical phenomena. Rather, the focus of emic approaches is to uncover and understand culture-specific experiences.

Summary of Psychological Testing and Assessment

In this section, we propose that best practices require a more nuanced approach to testing and assessment. Instead of practicing with a client uniformity myth, clinicians need to recognize that cultural validity of our tests and measures cannot be assumed and instead needs to be directly evaluated. Research has shown that cultural factors can bias or influence a client's response to test items, which in turn would influence the validity of our test scores and even our psychological constructs. Hence, best practices require that we understand measurement invariance and directly evaluate the measurement equivalence of our measures before using with culturally diverse clients. Recent approaches have identified the use of Western, Educated, Industrialized, Rich, and Democratic (WEIRD) samples, which severely restricts the utility and generalizability of our tests and measures with respect to cultural validity. Caution should be the operating approach until more culturally relevant samples have been collected regarding the use of our common clinical and psychological tests and measures.

CHALLENGES AND FUTURE DIRECTIONS

One of the main challenges in clinical psychological assessment and diagnosis with culturally diverse clients remains the cultural specificity of the assessment instruments. In particular, the majority of clinical psychological assessment instruments were developed in WEIRD societies and the norms mainly pertain to Western populations (Henrich, Heine, & Norenzayan, 2010). Heinrich and colleagues reviewed research in a number of domains (e.g., cooperation, categorization, and inferential induction; reasoning styles; self-concepts and related motivations) and concluded that WEIRD societies "are among the least representative populations one could find for generalizing about humans" (p. 61). Despite the origin of the instruments and the frequent lack of empirical evidence for measurement equivalence, clinical tests and structured interviews are often used to inform clinical diagnosis and treatment with culturally diverse populations. To illustrate this, there was little or no information on psychometrics of translated tests for many of the tests available in Spanish (Fernandez, Boccaccini, & Noland, 2007). Out of thirty identified translated tests, the authors found only three that contained manual supplements with validity research and translation procedures. Yet some practitioners may mistakenly assume that translated tests can be used along with existing norms or still use the tests despite awareness of the lack of research since no other instruments are available. Thus, researchers and practitioners may encounter multiple challenges related to appropriate translation and validation of clinical assessment instruments as the majority of these instruments were developed and validated with WEIRD participants. Given this situation, it would be important for clinicians to go beyond test manuals and consult the latest empirical literature when using various tests with culturally diverse clients.

The movement of indigenous psychologies gained momentum in order to address some of the challenges associated with WEIRD psychology. The main goal of indigenous psychologies is to develop a scientific knowledge system that "reflects, describes, explains, and understands the psychological and behavioral activities in their native contexts" (Yang, 2000, pp. 245–246). The impetus to create local indigenous psychologies is a reaction to Euro-American dominance (Sinha, 1997). It stems from the realization that North American psychology is a type of indigenous psychology and not a universal human psychology (Triandis, 1997). In fact, Marsella (2013) discussed various culture-specific assumptions of Western psychology such as individuality, scientism, and quantification and asserted that "all psychologies are indigenous psychologies." Thus, clinical psychological assessment that was conceptualized and developed in a specific cultural context contains biases and assumptions related to that context. When such assessment measures are exported to other cultures using the cross-cultural approach, it is assumed the associated psychological theories are universal and applicable to other cultures, also known as "imposed etic" (Leong, Leung, & Cheung, 2010).

Indigenous psychologies can address this "imposed etic" issue by ensuring assessment instruments capture the unique facets of the native culture. However, one of the main challenges for the creation and use of indigenous measures remains the need for continued research and expansion of their scientific foundation. Furthermore, they may be conceptually biased toward the original culture where they were created (Leong et al., 2010). Therefore, it is important to consider how indigenous measures provide incremental validity to using universal measures of human behavior (Church,

2001). A good example of such a measure is the Chinese Personality Assessment Inventory (CPAI; Cheung et al., 1996). The CPAI is an indigenously derived multidimensional personality measure that was developed with mainstream scientific methodology. The researchers used a bottom-up approach, identifying universal and indigenous personality traits in Chinese culture through focus groups and review of contemporary literature and proverbs. Their findings point to four normal personality factors (Social Potency/Expansiveness, Dependability, Emotional Stability, and Interpersonal Relatedness) and two clinical factors (Emotional Problem and Behavioral Problem). The indigenous factor of Interpersonal Relatedness, which includes subscales on harmony and reciprocity in relationships, was distinct from other universal personality factors from universal personality measures. Yet the other factors were cross-culturally relevant, resulting in renaming the CPAI-2 to the Cross-Cultural Personality Assessment Inventory (Cheung, van de Vijver, & Leong, 2011).

In order to bridge the gap between WEIRD psychology and indigenous psychologies, a combined emic-etic approach in assessment may provide "the best of both worlds." This approach requires combining well-validated universal constructs with indigenously derived constructs in psychological assessment as demonstrated in the continuous research of the CPAI-2. To promote best practices in cross-cultural assessment, the International Test Commission (2017) developed and recently updated its guidelines for test translation and adaptation. The document contains eighteen guidelines focusing on preconditions, test development, confirmation, administration, scoring and interpretation, and documentation with suggestions for best practices. The American Psychological Association (2017) also recently updated its multicultural guidelines. The ten guidelines specifically address assessment-related issues by recommending the use of culturally and linguistically validated measures and appropriate norms.

Finally, as discussed in this chapter, there are specific challenges in multicultural clinical assessment and diagnosis of which both clinicians and researchers should be cognizant. At present, the DSM-5 Cultural Formulation approach is the dominant model in the field. And yet, there are additional factors to consider in this approach, including the various threats to cultural validity that can hamper or interfere with clinical diagnosis and assessment. Similarly, cultural validity is also a critical issue to be cognizant of with regard to our psychologist tests and assessment tools. This challenge of cultural validity can be evaluated by examining (rather than assuming) the measurement equivalence of tests and measures developed on majority cultural populations and applied to racial and ethnic minority clients. Finally, while the Cultural Formulation Interview provides some open-ended questions to guide the process, there are concerns regarding the reliability and validity of those responses. On the other hand, there are various measures of cultural identity and acculturation that clinicians can use (see Gamst, Liang, & Der-Karabetian, 2011) but it is important to note that their clinical validity and utility have yet to be evaluated.

REFERENCES

Adebimpe, V. R. (2004). A second opinion on the White norms in psychiatric diagnosis of Black patients. *Psychiatric Annals, 34*, 542–551.

American Psychiatric Association. (1994). *Diagnostic and statistical manual of mental disorders* (4th ed.). Washington, DC: American Psychiatric Association.

American Psychiatric Association. (2013a). *Diagnostic and statistical manual of mental disorders* (5th ed.). Washington, DC: American Psychiatric Association.

American Psychiatric Association. (2013b). Cultural Formulation Interview. www.multiculturalmentalhealth.ca/wp-content/uploads/2013/10/2013_DSM5_CFI.pdf

American Psychiatric Association. (2013c). Supplementary modules to the Core Cultural Formulation Interview (CFI). www.multiculturalmentalhealth.ca/wp-content/uploads/2013/10/CFI-Cultural-Identity.pdf

American Psychological Association. (2017). Multicultural guidelines: An ecological approach to context, identity, and intersectionality. www.apa.org/about/policy/multicultural-guidelines.pdf

Brown, T. A. (2014). *Confirmatory factor analysis for applied research* (2nd ed.). New York: Guilford Press.

Burlew, A. K., Feaster, D., Brecht, M., & Hubbard, R. (2014). Measurement and data analysis in research addressing health disparities in substance abuse. *Journal of Substance Abuse Treatment, 36*, 25–43. https://doi.org/10.1016/j.jsat.2008.04.003

Campbell, D. T., & Stanley, J. C. (1966). *Experimental and quasi-experimental designs for research*. Chicago: Rand McNally.

Canino, G., & Alegria, M. (2008). Psychiatric diagnosis: Is it universal or relative to culture? *Journal of Child Psychology and Psychiatry, 49*, 237–250.

Chang, E. C. (1996). Evidence for the cultural specificity of pessimism in Asians vs Caucasians: A test of a general negativity hypothesis. *Personality and Individual Differences, 21*, 819–822.

Cheung, F. M., Cheung, S. F., Zhang, J., Leung, K., Leong, F., & Yeh, K. H. (2008). Relevance of openness as a personality dimension in Chinese culture: Aspects of its cultural relevance. *Journal of Cross-Cultural Psychology, 39*, 81–108. https://doi.org/10.1177/0022022107311968

Cheung, F. M., Leong, F. T. L., & Ben-Porath, Y. S. (2003). Psychological assessment in Asia: Introduction to the special section. *Psychological Assessment, 15*, 243-247.

Cheung, F. M., Leung, K., Fan, R. M., Song, W.-Z., Zhang, J.-X., & Zhang, J.-P. (1996). Development of the Chinese Personality Assessment Inventory (CPAI). *Journal of Cross-Cultural Psychology, 27*, 181–199. https://doi.org/10.1177/0022022196272003

Cheung, F. M., van de Vijver, F. J. R., & Leong, F. T. L. (2011). Toward a new approach to the study of personality in culture. *American Psychologist, 66*, 593–603. https://doi.org/10.1037/a0022389

Church, A. T. (2001). Personality measurement in cross-cultural perspective. *Journal of Personality, 69*, 979–1006. https://doi.org/10.1111/1467-6494.696172

Constantine, M. G. (2007). Racial microaggressions against African American clients in cross-racial counseling relationships. *Journal of Counseling Psychology, 54*, 1–16.

Cross, S. E., Hardin, E. E., & Gercek, B. (2011). The what, how, why and where of self-construal. *Personality and Social Psychology, 15*, 142–179.

Eap, S., Gobin, R. L., Ng, J., & Nagayama Hall, G. C. (2010). Sociocultural issues in the diagnosis and assessment of psychological disorders. In J. E. Maddux & J. P. Tangney (Eds.), *Social psychological foundations of clinical psychology* (pp. 312–328). New York: Guilford Press.

Enright, J. B., & Jaeckle, W. R. (1963). Psychiatric symptoms and diagnosis in two subcultures. *International Journal of Social Psychiatry, 9*, 12–17.

Fernandez, K., Boccaccini, M. T., & Noland, R. M. (2007). Professionally responsible test selection for Spanish-speaking clients: A four-step approach for identifying and selecting translated tests. *Professional Psychology: Research and Practice, 38*, 363–374. https://doi.org/10.1037/0735-7028.38.4.363

Gamst, G. C., Liang, C. T. H., & Der-Karabetian, A. (2011) *Handbook of multicultural measures*. Thousand Oaks, CA: Sage Publications.

Garb, H. N. (1997). Race bias, social class bias, and gender bias in clinical judgment. *Clinical Psychology: Science and Practice, 4*, 99–120.

Garfield, S. (1984). Methodological problems in clinical diagnosis. In H. E. Adams & P. B. Sutker (Eds.), *Comprehensive handbook of psychopathology* (pp. 27–44). New York: Plenum.

Goh, M., Dunnigan, T., & Schuchman, K. M. (2004). Bias in counseling Hmong clients with limited English proficiency. In J. L. Chin (Ed.), *The psychology of prejudice and discrimination: Ethnicity and multiracial identity*, Vol. *2* (pp. 109–136). Westport, CT: Praeger and Greenwood Publishing.

Heine, S. J. (2001). Self as a cultural product. An examination of East Asian and North American selves. *Journal of Personality, 69*, 881–890.

Henrich, J., Heine, S. J., & Norenzayan, A. (2010). The weirdest people in the world? *Behavioral and Brain Sciences, 33*, 61–135. https://doi.org/10.1017/S0140525X0999152X

Hornby, G., & Lafaele, R. (2011). Barriers to parental involvement in education: An explanatory model. *Educational Review, 63*, 37–52. https://doi.org/10.1080/00131911.2010.488049

Hui, C. H., & Triandis, H. (1986). Individualism-collectivism: A study of cross-cultural researchers. *Journal of Cross-Cultural Psychology, 17*, 225–248.

International Test Commission. (2017). *The ITC guidelines for translating and adapting tests* (2nd ed.). www.intestcom.org/files/guideline_test_adaptation_2ed.pdf

Jackson, J. S., Abelson, J. M., Berglund, P. A., Mezuk, B., Torres, M., & Zhang, R. (2011). Ethnicity, immigration, and cultural influences on the nature and distribution of mental disorders: An examination of major depression. In D. Regier, W. Narrow, E. Kuhl, & D. Kupfer (Eds.), *Conceptual evolution of DSM-5* (pp. 267–285). Arlington, VA: American Psychiatric Publishing.

Ketterer, H. L., Han, K., Hur, J., & Moon, K. (2010). Development and validation of culture-specific Variable Response Inconsistency and True Response Inconsistency Scales for use with the Korean MMPI-2. *Psychological Assessment, 22*, 504–519. https://doi.org/10.1037/a0019511

Kleinman, A. (1982). Neurasthenia and depression: A study of somatization and culture in China. *Culture, Medicine, and Psychiatry, 6*, 117–190.

Kline, R. (2011). *Principles and practice of structural equation modeling*. New York: Guilford Publications.

Kluckhohn, F. R. (1953). *Personality in nature, society, and culture*. New York: Alfred A. Knopf.

Lau, A. S., Tsai, W., Shih, J., Liu, L. L., Hwang, W.-C., & Takeuchi, D. T. (2013). The Immigrant Paradox among Asian American Women: Are disparities in the burden of depression and anxiety paradoxical or explicable? *Journal of Consulting and Clinical Psychology, 81*(5), 901–911. http://doi.org/10.1037/a0032105

Lee, E. (1980). Mental health services for the Asian-Americans: Problems and alternatives. In L. Chin (Ed.), *U.S. Commission of Civil Rights, Civil rights issues of Asian and Pacific-Americans: Myths & realities* (pp. 676–680). Washington, DC: U.S. Government Printing Office.

Leong, F. T. L. (1996). Towards an integrative model for cross-cultural counseling and psychotherapy. *Applied and Preventive Psychology, 5*,189–209.

Leong, F. T. L. (1986). Counseling and psychotherapy with Asian Americans: Review of the literature. *Journal of Counseling Psychology, 33*, 196–206.

Leong, F. T. L., & Hardin, E. (2002). Career psychology of Asian Americans: Cultural validity and cultural specificity. In G. Hall and S. Okazaki (Eds.), *Asian American Psychology: Scientific Innovations for the 21st Century* (pp. 131–152). Washington, DC: American Psychological Association.

Leong, F. T. L., & Hartung, P. J. (2003). Cross-cultural career counseling. In G. Bernal, J. E. Trimble, A. K. Burlew, & F. T. L. Leong (Eds.), *Handbook of racial and ethnic minority psychology* (pp. 504–520). Thousand Oaks, CA: Sage Publications.

Leong, F. T. L., & Kalibatseva, Z. (2016). Threats to cultural validity in clinical diagnosis and assessment: Illustrated with the case of Asian Americans. In N. Zane, G. Bernal, & F. T. L. Leong (Eds.), *Culturally-informed evidence-based practice in psychology* (pp. 57–74). Washington, DC: American Psychological Association.

Leong, F. T. L., Leung, K., & Cheung, F. M. (2010). Integrating cross-cultural research methods into ethnic minority psychology. *Cultural Diversity and Ethnic Minority Psychology, 16*, 590–597. https://doi.org/10.1037/a0020127

Leong, F. T. L., Okazaki, S., & Tak, J. (2003). Assessment of depression and anxiety in East Asia. *Psychological Assessment, 15*, 290–305.

Li, Z., & Hicks, M. H.-R. (2010). The CES-D in Chinese American women: Construct validity, diagnostic validity for major depression, and cultural response bias. *Psychiatry Research, 175*, 227–232. https://doi.org/10.1016/j.psychres.2009.03.007

Li-Repac, D. (1980). Cultural influences on clinical perception: A comparison between Caucasian and Chinese-American therapists. *Journal of Cross-Cultural Psychology, 11*, 327–342.

López, S. R., Nelson Hipke, K., Polo, A. J., Jenkins, J. H., Karno, M., Vaughn, C., & Snyder, K. S. (2004). Ethnicity, expressed emotion, attributions, and course of schizophrenia: Family warmth matters. *Journal of Abnormal Psychology, 113*, 428–439. https://doi.org/10.1037/0021-843X.113.3.428

Lui, P. P., & Quezada, L. (2019). Associations between microaggression and adjustment outcomes: A meta-analytic and narrative review. *Psychological Bulletin, 145*, 45–78. https://doi.org/10.1037/bul0000172

Lui, P. P., & Rollock, D. (2018). Greater than the sum of its parts: Development of a measure of collectivism among Asians.

Cultural Diversity and Ethnic Minority Psychology, 24 (2),242–259. https://doi.org/10.1037/cdp0000163

Lui, P. P., Rollock, D., Chang, E. C., Leong, F. T. L., & Zamboanga, B. L. (2016). Big 5 personality and subjective well-being in Asian Americans: Testing optimism and pessimism as mediators. *Asian American Journal of Psychology, 7,* 274–286. https://doi.org/10.1037/aap0000054

Lui, P. P., Vidales, C. A., & Rollock, D. (2018). Personality and the social environment: Contributions to psychological adjustment among Asian and Euro American students. *Journal of Social and Clinical Psychology, 37,* 659–696. https://doi.org/10.1521/jscp.2018.37.9.659

Lui, P. P., & Zamboanga, B. L. (2018a). Acculturation and alcohol use among Asian Americans: A meta-analytic review. *Psychology of Addictive Behavior, 32,* 173–186. https://doi.org/10.1037/adb0000340

Lui, P. P., & Zamboanga, B. L. (2018b). A critical review and meta-analysis of the associations between acculturation and alcohol use outcomes among Hispanic Americans. *Alcoholism: Clinical and Experimental Research, 42,* 1841–1862. https://doi.org/10.1111/acer.13845

Malgady, R. G. (1996). The question of cultural bias in assessment and diagnosis of ethnic minority clients: Let's reject the null hypothesis. *Professional Psychology: Research and Practice, 27,* 73–77.

Malgady, R. G., Rogler, L. H., & Cortés, D. E. (1996). Cultural expression of psychiatric symptoms: Idioms of anger among Puerto Ricans. *Psychological Assessment, 8,* 265–268.

Markus, H. R., & Kitayama, S. (1991). Culture and self: Implications for cognition, emotion and motivation. *Psychological Review, 98,* 224–253.

Marsella, A. J. (2013). All psychologies are indigenous psychologies: Reflections on psychology in a global era. *Psychology International, 12.* www.apa.org/international/pi/2013/12/reflections.aspx

McNeil, D. E., & Binder, R. (1995). Correlates of accuracy in the assessment of psychiatric in-patient's risk of violence. *American Journal of Psychiatry, 152,* 901–906.

Meredith, W. (1993). Measurement invariance, factor analysis, and factorial invariance. *Psychometrika, 58,* 525–543. https://doi.org/10.1007/BF02294825

Nijdam-Jones, A., & Rosenfeld, B. (2017). Cross-cultural feigning assessment: A systematic review of feigning instruments used with linguistically, ethnically, and culturally diverse samples. *Psychological Assessment, 29,* 1321–1336. https://doi.org/10.1037/pas0000438

Okazaki, S., Kallivayalil, D., & Sue, S. (2002). Clinical personality assessment with Asian Americans. In J. N. Butcher (Ed.), *Oxford textbooks in clinical psychology, Vol. 2. Clinical personality assessment: Practical approaches* (pp. 135–153). New York: Oxford University Press.

Payne, J. S. (2012). Influence of race and symptom expression on clinicians' depressive disorder identification in African American men. *Journal of the Society for Social Work and Research, 3,* 162–177.

Rogers, R., Flores, J., Ustad, K., & Sewell, K. W. (1995). Initial validation of the Personality Assessment Inventory – Spanish version with clients from Mexican American communities. *Journal of Personality Assessment, 64,* 340–348. https://doi.org/10.1207/s15327752jpa6402_12

Rollock, D., & Lui, P. P. (2016a). Measurement invariance and the five-factor model of personality: Asian international and Euro American cultural groups. *Assessment, 23,* 571–587. https://doi.org/10.1177/1073191115590854

Rollock, D., & Lui, P. P. (2016b). Do spouses matter? Discrimination, social support, and psychological distress among Asian Americans. *Cultural Diversity and Ethnic Minority Psychology, 22,* 47–57. https://doi.org/10.1037/cdp0000045

Rosenberger, E., & Hayes, J. (2002). Therapist as subject: A review of the empirical countertransference literature. *Journal of Counseling and Development, 80,* 264–270.

Ryder, A. G., Yang, J., Zhu, X., Yao, S., Yi, J., Heine, S., et al. (2008). The cultural shaping of depression: Somatic symptoms in China, psychological symptoms in North America? *Journal of Abnormal Psychology, 117,* 300–313.

Sabin, J. E. (1975). Translating despair. *American Journal of Psychiatry, 132,* 197–199.

Sadler, J. Z. (2005). *Values and psychiatric diagnosis.* Oxford: Oxford University Press.

Schmitt, N., & Kuljanin, G. (2008). Measurement invariance: Review of practice and implications. *Human Resource Management Review, 18,* 210–222. https://doi.org/10.1016/j.hrmr.2008.03.003

Shou, Y., Sellbom, M., Xu, J., Chen, T., & Sui, A. (2017). Elaborating on the construct validity of Triarchic Psychopathy Measure in Chinese clinical and nonclinical samples. *Psychological Assessment, 29*(9), 1071–1081. http://dx.doi.org/10.1037/pas0000398

Shuy, R. W. (1983). Three types of interference to an effective exchange of information in the medical interview. In S. Fisher & A. D. Todd (Eds.), *The social organization of doctor-patient communication* (pp. 189–202). Washington, DC: Center for Applied Linguistics.

Sinha, D. (1997). Indigenizing psychology. In J. W. Berry, Y. H. Poortinga, & J. Pandey (Eds.), *Handbook of cross-cultural psychology,* Vol.*1* (2nd ed., pp. 129–169). Boston: Allyn & Bacon.

Solano-Flores, G., & Nelson-Barber, S. (2001). On the cultural validity of science assessments. *Journal of Research in Science Teaching, 38,* 553–573.

Spector, R. (2001). Is there racial bias in clinicians' perceptions of the dangerousness of psychiatric patients? A review of the literature. *Journal of Mental Health, 10,* 5–15.

Sue, D. W. (1981). *Counseling the culturally different: Theory and practice.* New York: John Wiley & Sons.

Sue, D. W., & Sue, D. (2012). *Counseling the culturally diverse: Theory and practice* (6th ed.). New York: John Wiley & Sons.

Sue, S., & Morishima, J. K. (1982). *The mental health of Asian Americans.* San Francisco: Jossey-Bass.

Takeuchi, D. T., Kuo, H., Kim, K., & Leaf, P. J. (1989). Psychiatric symptom dimensions among Asian Americans and Native Hawaiians: An analysis of the symptom checklist. *Journal of Community Psychology, 17,* 319–329.

Triandis, H. C. (1997). Cross-cultural perspectives on personality. In R. Hogan, J. Johnson, & S. Briggs (Eds.), *Handbook of personality psychology* (pp. 439–464). San Diego: Academic Press.

Wakabayashi, A. (2014). A sixth personality domain that is independent of the big five domains: The psychometric properties of the HEXACO personality inventory in a Japanese sample. *Japanese Psychological Research, 56,* 211–223. https://doi.org/10.1111/jpr.12045

Westermeyer, J. (1985). Psychiatric diagnosis across cultural boundaries. *American Journal of Psychiatry, 142,* 798–805.

Whaley, A. L. (1997). Ethnicity/race, paranoia, and psychiatric diagnoses: Clinical bias versus sociocultural differences. *Journal of Psychopathology and Behavioral Assessment*, *19*, 1–20.

Whaley, A. L., & Hall, B. N. (2009). Effects of cultural themes in psychotic symptoms on the diagnosis of schizophrenia in African Americans. *Mental Health, Religion and Culture*, *12*, 457–471.

Yakushko, O. (2010). Clinical work with limited English proficiency clients: A phenomenological study. *Professional Psychology: Research and Practice*, *41*, 449–455.

Yang, K.-S. (2000). Monocultural and cross-cultural indigenous approaches: The royal road to the development of a balanced global psychology. *Asian Journal of Social Psychology*, *3*, 241–263.

4 Ethical and Professional Issues in Assessment

LINDA K. KNAUSS

Ethical issues are important in all areas of psychology but especially in the area of assessment, where life and death issues can be decided, as in assessments related to death penalty cases (Atkins, 2002). This chapter covers both ethical and professional issues in assessment. Topics include informed consent, confidentiality, the involvement of third parties in assessment, external consequences, test construction, test revisions, obsolete tests and outdated test results, cultural competence, test data and test security, assessment in the digital age, report writing, and providing assessment feedback.

INFORMED CONSENT

Assessments should begin with an informed consent process. Informed consent is more than just an ethical obligation. It also reflects good clinical practice. The client's right to receive information and have the opportunity to make decisions about assessment encourages maximum participation in the assessment process (Knapp, VandeCreek & Fingerhut, 2017). While it is best to get written informed consent, oral informed consent can be obtained and documented in the client's record. There are three basic principles of informed consent: (1) the decision must be made knowledgeably, (2) it must be made voluntarily, and (3) it must be made by a person recognized as having the legal capacity to make the decision (Bersoff, Dematteo, & Foster, 2012). Thus, the person consenting must clearly understand to what they are consenting. The person seeking consent must make a good faith effort to disclose enough information so that consent is an informed choice. Although there are times when psychologists are in situations where they cannot provide the examinee with specific information on how test findings will be used or what the implications will be of the testing, and thus consent in these situations may not be truly informed, psychologists must still try to explain potential uses and implications of testing as early as possible (Knauss, 2009a). Voluntary means that consent is not coerced, induced, or given under duress. Children and cognitively impaired adults are at issue with regard to having the legal capacity to make a decision. Parents or legal guardians are authorized to consent for their minor children. Cognitively impaired adults can only be declared incompetent to consent by the court, which would then appoint a proxy decision-maker (Bersoff et al., 2012).

Standard 9.03 of the *Ethical Principles of Psychologists and Code of Conduct* (APA, 2017a) includes three exceptions to the requirement for informed consent: (1) testing is mandated by law or government regulations; (2) informed consent is implied because testing is conducted as a routine educational, institutional, or organizational activity (e.g., when participants voluntarily agree to assessment when applying for a job); or (3) one purpose of the testing is to evaluate decisional capacity. Thus, informed consent is not necessary when educational testing is done as part of regular school activities such as end-of-term reading or math achievement testing in elementary and high schools. The most complex aspect of informed consent in assessment is when the purpose of testing is to evaluate decisional capacity. This may be an issue in certain neuropsychological evaluations as well as when assessing clients for dementia or psychosis. The ability of the patient to understand the nature of the services being offered may not be ascertained until the evaluation is in process or perhaps completed (Knauss, 2009a).

When individuals are legally incapable of giving informed consent, it is still important to provide an appropriate explanation of the nature and purpose of the assessment and seek the individual's assent in order to gain active cooperation. If necessary, obtain permission from a legally authorized person, such as a parent or legal guardian. If there is no legally responsible person, consider the client's preferences and best interests and take reasonable steps to protect the person's rights and welfare (Fisher, 2017).

Assent is relevant in situations where assessment is requested by parents of minor children or family members of adults with suspected cognitive impairment. The Ethics Code (APA, 2017a) requires psychologists to provide assent information in a language and at a language level that is reasonably understandable to the person being assessed.

When working with children, practitioners are ethically obligated to explain the assessment process to the child in a manner that they understand even when the child does not have the choice to assent to or refuse services. Psychologists working with populations for whom English is not their primary language should be aware of their clients' language preferences and proficiencies (Fisher, 2017). To provide informed consent in a language that is understandable to a client, psychologists may use the services of an interpreter when they are not proficient in the language used by the client. An important consideration is the readability of consent forms. These documents are often complex, multiple pages, and written at a high school or college reading level. For this reason, it is important to take the time to talk with the examinee about the nature and purpose of the assessment (Knauss, 2009a).

The informed consent agreement form formalizes the informed consent process and informs clients of the rules of a practice. Although a great deal has been written about informed consent, very little has been written about how to construct an informed consent agreement form. There is a large amount of flexibility in the rules for any practice; the key to ethical practice is to inform clients in advance. There are several items that are frequently found in informed consent documents. The most common item is the limits of confidentiality. It is important for clients to know that not everything is confidential. Many practitioners begin their informed consent agreement forms with a paragraph about their treatment philosophy. They may also include an explanation of the therapy or assessment process. In addition, an assessment informed consent form may include a paragraph about the nature and purpose of psychological assessment, a checklist of various assessment measures, information about feedback, and whether a report will be generated.

Clients may be asked to take an active role in establishing treatment or assessment goals and be reminded that commitment to the therapeutic or assessment process is necessary for the most successful outcome. The practitioner may make a commitment to provide services that are helpful but may include the statement that they make no guarantee about the outcome of treatment or the findings of an assessment (Knauss. 2009b). A paragraph about emergency access or how to contact the psychologist is also a good idea but more important to a therapy practice than in an assessment setting.

Finally, the informed consent form should have a place for the client's signature and date indicating that he or she has read, understood, and agrees to the provisions of the informed consent agreement. There should also be a place for the signature of a parent or guardian in the event that the client is a minor.

CONFIDENTIALITY

There are several situations where confidentiality cannot be promised in an assessment. These circumstances must be part of the informed consent process. For example, there are special considerations for informed consent related to confidentiality when conducting forensic assessments. In addition to explaining to the person being tested the nature and purpose of the testing, it is also important for the examinee to know who has requested the testing and who will receive copies of the report (Fisher, 2017). There may also be circumstances where the examinee may not receive feedback or a copy of the testing report.

Another issue with regard to confidentiality has to do with background information. Often sensitive information such as medical or legal history is included about a variety of family members who may not know that testing is taking place, much less that they are being included in the report. For example, a report may include that a maternal grandparent was bipolar, or an uncle has a substance abuse problem, or a relative committed suicide. Once a report is completed, the psychologist has no control over where that report goes and, after the client has authorized the release of the report to a third party, there is even less certainty about who may have access to it. The report could be seen by an employer of a person mentioned or by the person included in the report. Thus, it is important to protect their confidentiality. This issue is seldom addressed in discussions of ethics or assessment (Knauss, 2012). Sometimes, a client will ask that sensitive information be removed from the background section. This is common when reports are being sent to a school. This raises questions for psychologists about when and why to comply with these requests. In general, it is reasonable to leave out sensitive information when it is not essential to the referral question or to the test findings. It is not necessary to indicate that a child's parent had an affair or to include the parent's legal history in an assessment to determine the presence of a learning disability. However, it would not be appropriate to omit the information that a child who usually takes medication for attention-deficit/hyperactivity disorder was not given his or her medication on the day of testing (Knauss, 2012).

THIRD PARTIES

The relevant American Psychological Association (APA) ethical standard is 3.07, Third Party Requests for Services (APA, 2017a). Psychologists are often asked by third parties to do evaluations. This is common in organizational, forensic, and neuropsychological contexts. In these situations, it is crucial for psychologists to clarify their roles before beginning the evaluation, including the probable use of the information from the evaluation and the fact that there may be limits to confidentiality.

The person being evaluated also has a right to know in advance whether he or she will have access to the report, test data, or feedback. Individuals who are assessed have the right to full informed consent regarding the planned evaluation before deciding whether to participate and psychologists need to provide enough information for this decision-making process.

It is a mistake to assume that people receiving services *automatically* give up their rights when services are requested by a third party. It is up to the client to accept the conditions of the third party, unless the services are court ordered. It is also important that clients understand the implications of not agreeing to arrangements requested by a third party. It may mean an inmate is not considered for parole, an employee is not eligible for promotion, or a physician cannot return to work.

Thus, the question of who is the client may not be the most useful way to conceptualize this dilemma. It may be more helpful to begin with the premise that the person receiving the services is always the client. This is because nothing other than a court order takes away a person's right to informed consent, confidentiality, and access to records. The fact that informed consent is a process that takes place with the person receiving the services, not with a third party, implies that the receiver of services is always a client.

However, the service provider may have additional obligations to a third party such as prison authorities and the human relations manager in an organization. It is through the informed consent process that the client who is to receive the assessment or therapeutic services learns of the obligations to the third party and agrees to whatever arrangements are necessary such as sending a test report directly to an organizational representative or giving up access to test data or records. It is best to have this agreement in writing either as part of the informed consent document or as a separate release of information form.

EXTERNAL CONSEQUENCES

Assessment can have a significant impact on an examinee's life. In addition, some assessments such as standardized testing can affect entire groups. Assessments with these types of consequences are considered high-stakes testing (Bersoff et al., 2012). Examples of high-stakes testing include assessments for organ transplantation or other types of surgery, screening for certain professions such as police officers or employees of nuclear power plants, and psychological testing to enter the seminary. Educational testing such as licensing examinations as well as forensic evaluations such as child custody and competency to be executed have serious consequences. It is essential that psychologists consider the ethical outcomes that may result from this type of testing.

In conducting high-stakes testing, there are two essential questions (Messick, 1980). One question is whether the test is a valid measure for the purpose for which it is used. The answer to this question depends on construct validity of the test. The second question is whether the test should be used for the proposed purpose in the proposed way. There is less clarity regarding the effectiveness of high-stakes tests with regard to accuracy of prediction.

When doing this type of testing, psychologists should be able to describe why they choose each test they used and why the test was appropriate for the referral question. Other considerations include whether the test is appropriate for the client with regard to reading level, language skills, or cultural background. The test also must be administered using standardized procedures. Any deviation from standardized procedures such as giving the test orally if the client does not have the necessary reading skills must be noted in the report.

TEST CONSTRUCTION

Test results are only as useful as the tests on which they are based. Therefore, test construction is the basis of ethical psychological assessment. Standard 9.05, Test Construction, of the Ethics Code states, "Psychologists who develop tests and other assessment techniques use appropriate psychometric procedures and current scientific or professional knowledge for test design, standardization, validation, reduction or elimination of bias, and recommendations for use" (APA, 2017a). At first, test development seems fairly straightforward. It is not physically invasive and no drugs are involved. However, psychologists who construct assessment techniques must be familiar with methods for establishing the validity and reliability of tests, develop standardized administration instructions, and select items that reduce or eliminate bias (Fisher, 2017). The *Standards for Educational and Psychological Testing* (AERA, APA, & NCME, 2014) is a good resource for this information. Chapter 2 of this volume covers many of the psychometric issues in detail.

TEST REVISIONS

A lot of attention is paid to issues related to test construction but issues related to test revision have not been as frequently addressed. There are many reasons that tests are revised. Although there are no specific guidelines to follow regarding when a test must be revised, if decisions that are based on the test will be inaccurate or harmful to a person's welfare, this is an indication that it is time to revise the test (Adams, 2000). The *Standards for Educational and Psychological Testing* (AERA et al., 2014) suggest revising a test when research data, changes in the field, or new interpretations make a test inappropriate for its intended use. However, old tests that continue to be useful do not need to be revised only because of the passage of time (Knauss, 2017). Revised tests often have advantages over prior versions such as better normative data and psychometric properties, ease of administration, and cultural fairness (Bush, 2010). Test stimuli also become outdated. Telephones, cars, and other objects change in appearance over time (Adams, 2000). The demographic characteristics of the population also change, requiring an updated standardization sample. According to the Flynn effect (Flynn, 1999), it is necessary to periodically update cognitive test norms based on society-wide changes in cognitive skill levels. The Flynn effect is the gradual population-wide improvement in intelligence test performance over time that causes IQ test norms to become obsolete with each generation. Personality tests may also need to incorporate changes in diagnoses as reflected in the most recent *Diagnostic and Statistical Manual of Mental Disorders* (5th ed.; American Psychiatric Association, 2013).

The ethical protection of patient welfare is the ultimate goal of test revision. Thus, tests are revised to reflect changes in cultural, educational, linguistic, and societal influences as well as changes in the demographic characteristics of the population (Fisher, 2017).

OBSOLETE TESTS AND OUTDATED TEST RESULTS

Many professionals begin using new versions of a test within one year of the publication date. However, the APA Ethics Code (APA, 2017a) and other guidelines are not this clear.

Standard 9.08(b) states: "Psychologists do not base such decisions or recommendations on tests and measures that are obsolete and not useful for current purposes" (APA, 2017a). Thus, the Ethics Code does not prescribe a specific time period in which psychologists should begin using a new version of a test. The decision about when to use a new version of a test is closely related to the reason tests are revised. Behnke (2005) indicated that this standard should not be interpreted to mean that anything older than a test's current edition is obsolete but that psychologists should determine what is most appropriate for a given purpose. The *Standards for Educational and Psychological Testing* (AERA et al., 2014, p. 152) state: "In the case of tests that have been revised, editions currently supported by the publisher usually should be selected. On occasion, use of an earlier edition of an instrument is appropriate (e.g., when longitudinal research is conducted, or when an earlier edition of an instrument contains relevant subtests not included in a later edition." In addition, the *Standards for Educational and Psychological Testing* (AERA et al., 2014) suggest using tests with the strongest validity for the purpose of the assessment and tests that are appropriate for the characteristics and the background of the test-taker. There was also a study by Leach and Oakland (2007) that reviewed thirty-one ethics codes in thirty-five countries and found that standards that discuss test construction and restrict the use of obsolete tests are rare. Thus, there does not seem to be any absolute standard or ethical guideline suggesting what version of a test to use (Knauss, 2017).

There are many considerations that go into the decision to adopt the revised version of a test. Improved normative data that correspond to the census of the country in which a test is used, increased inclusion of special populations in normative studies, the addition of new or additional relevant constructs, and significant cohort changes such as the Flynn effect provide support for the use of the revised version of a test as these elements could lead to improved clinical decision-making (Bush, 2010). However, there are many reasons for using earlier versions of revised tests, including comparing past and current test performance, such as before and after a head injury, and for longitudinal research purposes (Knauss, 2017). Also, an earlier version of a test may have more research associated with it or an older version of a test may be better suited to use with certain populations (Knapp et al., 2017; Knauss, 2014). It is also possible that only an older version of a test has been translated into the native language of an examinee. When using an older version of a test, it is important to document which version of the test was used, why that version was selected, and the test norms used to interpret the results (Fisher, 2017).

Previous test scores even from a current version of a test may be obsolete and misleading if the individual has changed over time, or due to certain circumstances such as maturational changes, educational advancement, job training or employment experience, changes in health, work, or family status, an accident or traumatic experience (Fisher, 2017). A student who meets the criteria for a learning disability one year may show a significant improvement in academic achievement, so that the diagnosis is no longer accurate the following year. Personality test results are also likely to change. A short term emotional crisis may cause an MMPI-2 (Butcher et al., 1989) profile to look pathological, while a short time later, when the crisis has passed, the test results could be within normal limits or a Beck Depression Inventory (BDI-II; Beck, Steer, & Brown, 1996) from yesterday could be inaccurate today. In contrast, Graduate Record Examination (GRE) test scores from years in the past may still be a valid predictor of performance in graduate school (Gregory, 2004). Thus, it is up to each practitioner to determine the need for reevaluation on an individual basis.

In some situations, it may be helpful to keep outdated test scores similarly to outdated test materials. They may be useful as a comparison with new test results to evaluate the effectiveness of an educational program or intervention, or they may be used to identify cognitive decline or the sudden change in emotional or adaptive functioning. They can also be useful to document a developmental disability. When outdated test results are used, psychologists should document the reason for their use and their limitations (Fisher, 2017).

CULTURAL COMPETENCE

Providing culturally competent psychological assessment is more than using the correct test or using an interpreter. The *APA Ethical Principles of Psychologists and Code of Conduct* (APA, 2017a) places an increased emphasis on cultural competency. The Ethics Code stresses increased sensitivity to the difficulties in providing psychological services when language fluency is not shared by the psychologist and client. Diversity considerations are also an important aspect of ethical decision-making in assessment (Brabender, 2018).

Cross-cultural sensitivity refers to understanding the client's unique worldview and ethnic, linguistic, racial, and cultural background. For example, individuals from diverse backgrounds differ with respect to responsiveness to speed pressures and willingness to elaborate on answers. Also, clients from certain backgrounds may value the relationship over the task or may experience disrespect if the procedure is not fully explained (APA, 2017b). The quality of the assessment may be improved if the psychologist takes some time in advance of the assessment to tell the client about the nature of the tests and the type of questions that will be asked, especially if there are questions on sensitive topics. Explaining the reason for the testing and how the results will be used is also important, especially for clients who are not generally familiar with the nature or purpose of psychological tests. Cultural competence means more than a list of stereotypes about particular cultures. It means being able to think in cultural terms and focus on both process and content (Knapp et al., 2017; Lopez, 1997).

To work effectively with individuals from different cultural backgrounds, psychologists must recognize the impact of their own cultural heritage on their values and assumptions (APA, 2017b). It is not likely that psychologists will become culturally competent with every ethnic group in the United States but they should be culturally competent with the ethnic groups with whom they expect to have frequent contact (Knapp et al., 2017). Accurate diagnosis requires culturally appropriate assessment instruments or the knowledge of how to adapt them. Appreciation of within-group differences prevents the assumptions that all persons of a particular race, ethnicity, or cultural background share the same worldview. Assimilation to American culture is another important variable, based in part but not entirely on the length of time the person or family has lived in the United States (Knauss, 2007).

Another area of consideration is how to assess clients who are from cultures in which no information is available on how to provide a culturally meaningful assessment. The APA (2017a) Ethics Code requires the use of appropriate caution in interpreting these test results. A major issue involves the idea of equivalence of the same measures used in different cultures. According to Knapp and colleagues (2013), "Historically, most psychological tests were normed with English-speaking, European Americans and may not have been appropriate for use with individuals who did not have English as a primary language or who were from other cultural backgrounds" (p. 157). More recently, many tests have incorporated members of diverse cultural and ethnic groups into their norms and research suggests that some tests are valid for members of many ethnic minority groups. When using psychological tests without established norms for the examinee or population being assessed, it is necessary to describe in the assessment report the limitations of the test results and interpretations. Also, if the administration of the test is modified to account for the cultural or linguistic background of the examinee, this should also be noted in the report.

Assessment methods should be appropriate to the individual's language preference and competence unless the use of an alternative language is relevant to the assessment issues. For example, there are times when proficiency in English or another language is essential to the goal of the assessment, such as when effective job performance or school placement requires the ability to communicate in that language. Psychologists may use tests in a language in which the examinee may not be proficient when the goal of the assessment requires the ability to communicate in that language. That is what is meant by "unless the use of an alternative language is relevant to the assessment issues" in the Ethics Code (APA, 2017a).

Inappropriate content or items is another problem when using a measure developed in one culture to assess individuals in another culture. It is not necessarily true that items have the same meaning for all people in all cultures. Chan, Shum, and Cheung (2003) suggest that, by developing assessment measures specifically for a particular cultural group, there is more freedom to take into account the specific needs and cultural realities of that population.

Psychology has traditionally been based on Western perspectives and has not always considered the influence and impact of racial and cultural factors. This has been detrimental to the needs of clients and to the public interest. The APA (2017a) Ethics Code stresses competence in all areas of diversity. This includes cultural sensitivity to the issues that arise when assessing individuals from a different cultural background and appropriately considering linguistic and cultural differences when interpreting assessment results. See Chapter 3 in this volume for more information on multicultural issues in assessment.

TEST DATA AND TEST SECURITY

Standard 9.04 of the Ethics Code (APA, 2017a), Release of Test Data, remains controversial more than sixteen years after it was written. Requests for test data are most likely to occur in forensic situations, although clients also sometimes request copies of their records. Standard of the 1992 Ethics Code (APA, 1992) stated that psychologists should not release raw test results or raw test data to people who are not qualified to use this information. This standard placed an affirmative duty on psychologists to take reasonable steps to ensure that "raw test results or raw data" were sent only to "qualified" persons (Knapp & VandeCreek, 2012). However, there were several problems with this standard. It did not define raw test results or raw test data, nor did it define who was a qualified person, and reasonable psychologists could disagree about who was qualified. Another problem was that the Health Insurance

Portability and Accountability Act (HIPAA) gives clients access to their assessment results. Under HIPAA, clients have the right to see and receive copies of medical records used to make decisions about them. Access must also be given to the client's personal representative. The 2002 Ethics Code (as amended in 2010 and 2017) has three major changes from the 1992 Ethics Code. Test data and test materials are defined, there is no longer a requirement to release only to qualified persons, and there is a trend toward more client autonomy consistent with HIPAA (Knapp & VandeCreek, 2012).

With a release from the client, psychologists provide test data to the client or other persons identified in the release. It is a good idea for psychologists to have a signed release or authorization from the client even if the information is being given directly to the client (Fisher, 2017). Test data refers to the client's actual responses to test items, raw and scaled scores, and psychologists' notes and recordings concerning clients' statements and behavior during an examination. Anything that includes client responses is considered test data. According to Campbell and colleagues (2010), "Once individualized information is entered onto a data sheet, the materials become test data because they contain information that is descriptive of the examinee" (p. 321). There is an affirmative duty to provide test data to clients in contrast to the previous Ethics Code (APA, 1992) in which there was a presumption that test data would be withheld. Test data can be released to anyone identified in a client release. This reflects greater respect for client autonomy. Psychologists may refrain from releasing such data in order to protect the client or others from substantial harm. According to HIPAA, this information must be released to clients unless it is reasonably likely to pose a threat to the life or physical safety of the client or another person, or likely to cause equally substantial harm (Fisher, 2017). Thus, before refusing to release test data, it is important to be sure there is a real threat of harm and it is important to recognize that such decisions may be regulated by law as stated in Standard 9.04 of the Ethics Code. Under HIPAA, if test data is withheld, clients have a right to have the denial reviewed by a licensed health care professional. Psychologists may also withhold test data to protect against misuse or misinterpretation of the data (violate test security). However, psychologists must document their rationale for assuming the data will be misused. If clients have the right to obtain their own test data that they can pass on to any individual of their choice, requiring psychologists to deny a request from a client to release information to other persons is ineffective and illogical. Thus, the standard went from *must* resist sending out test data to *may* resist. Without a release from the client, psychologists are to provide others with test data only as required by law or a court order (Knapp et al., 2017).

Concerns about the changes in the Ethics Code focus on protecting the security of copyrighted test materials because a protocol with test questions and answers provided by an examinee is considered test data and must be released if requested (although there are some exceptions as already noted). The usefulness of many psychological tests is based on test-takers having no knowledge of the test questions or the answers. Concerns include the possibility that attorneys may misinterpret or misuse information in court cases or may use test stimuli or manuals to coach future clients in other cases (anecdotal reports exist about attorneys who coach their clients on how to give favorable responses to the tests). One response to these concerns is that, if an attorney attempted to interpret the data, the opposing party would have experts available to correct any misinterpretation. Also, in spite of copyright protections, some test materials do enter the public domain especially through the Internet (Knapp et al., 2017).

The 2002 Ethics Code (and the 2010 and 2017 revisions) distinguishes between test materials and test data (Standard 9.11, Maintaining Test Security). *Test materials* are different from test data. *Test materials* are defined as manuals, instruments, blank protocols, and test questions or stimuli. In contrast to test data, psychologists are required to make reasonable efforts to maintain the integrity and security of test materials. However, Standard 9.11 only requires psychologists to make reasonable efforts to maintain the integrity and security of test materials, consistent with law and contractual obligations (Bersoff, DeMatteo, & Foster, 2012). It is important to note that those portions of test materials that include client responses are considered *test data*. Psychologists can withhold test data if they believe it violates test security. According to Fisher (2017), "When test data consisting of PHI [Protected Health Information] cannot be separated from test materials that are protected by copyright law, psychologists' decisions to withhold the release of test data would be consistent with HIPAA regulations and Standard 9.04a" (p. 385). However, as noted by Bersoff and colleagues (2012), "the boundary between the appropriate and inappropriate release of test materials and 'raw data' is best described as blurry" (p. 50). In an effort to protect test materials when releasing test data, psychologists should block out test questions or stimuli when releasing the examinee's responses or record responses on a form separate from the test items. It is also important that, in response to a court order, psychologists may release test materials (Knapp et al., 2017). Thus, there is no absolute restriction on the disclosure of test data or materials and there can be legal limits to protecting test security.

ASSESSMENT IN THE DIGITAL AGE

Psychological testing is becoming more and more computerized. Tests can now be administered on laptop computers and handheld devices either in a clinician's office or from a remote location. Testing can be done via the Internet or through email. However, advances in technology increase challenges in interpreting ethical codes and professional standards as they relate to computerized assessment (Knauss, 2013).

There are numerous advantages to computerized and online testing. It is less expensive than paper-and-pencil testing, provides faster results with greater accuracy, presents test stimuli more uniformly, permits faster revisions, and provides access to evaluations for individuals in rural areas (Naglieri et al., 2004). Computerized assessment also eliminates the need to purchase and transport test kits as well as eliminating the possibility of losing blocks, puzzle pieces, or other items (Knauss, 2013).

When testing individuals with disabilities, variable text and image size and digitalized voice may improve testing of individuals with visual impairments; and joysticks, the mouse, and touch-sensitive screens and pads can facilitate assessment of individuals with physical and communication disabilities (Jacob & Hartshorne, 2007). Digitalized voice or video clips providing instructions or asking questions in a person's native language or dialect may assist in assessment of individuals from linguistically and culturally diverse backgrounds (Black & Ponirakis, 2000). In addition, some examinees are more open and honest when answering sensitive questions via computer (e.g., drug use, suicidal thoughts) when compared to in-person interviews, resulting in more valid results (Black & Ponirakis, 2000).

In contrast to the benefits of computerized and online testing there are many challenges. One risk involves confidentiality. Standard 4.02c of the Ethics Code (APA, 2017a) specifically refers to psychological services or the transmission of records via electronic means. When using the Internet for psychological services, informed consent to assessment should provide a clear expectation of the extent and limits of confidentiality. According to Fisher and Fried (2003), "Psychologists providing services over the Internet must inform clients/patients about the procedures that are used to protect confidentiality and the threats to confidentiality unique to this form of electronic transmission of information" (p. 106). It is recommended that clinicians using computerized assessment tools use a secure server or encrypted communication to prevent interception by a third party. It is also important for clients to know, as part of the informed consent process, that absolute confidentiality cannot be assured by the clinician (Knauss, 2013).

Another challenge is client identification. When administering Web-based assessments, psychologists must ensure that the person who gave consent is the person completing the assessment (Fisher & Fried, 2003). For this reason, videoconferencing is preferred but the use of client passwords is also acceptable.

Competence is also a critical issue. Clinicians may rely on computerized administration, scoring of results, and interpretations to expand their competence into areas when they lack appropriate education, supervised training, experience, and credentialing. In these situations, the clinician is not qualified to evaluate the validity of the computer-generated results and interpretations for the clients tested. This places both the clients and the clinician at risk (Knauss, 2013).

In addition to the issues of client identification, confidentiality, and competence, when psychologists administer assessments using the Internet, they may not be able to observe behaviors or confirm relevant information typically available when using in-person testing procedures. For example, they may not be able to verify the client's ethnicity, competence in the language of the test, motor problems that might interfere with test-taking, or special conditions of the testing environment (Fisher & Fried, 2003). There has also been a proliferation of do-it-yourself "tests" on the Internet of uncertain validity or reliability without clearly identified responsible individuals (Koocher, 2007). There is no way to know what the potential damage members of the public have experienced by taking these "tests" to determine their IQ, level of happiness, or potential to develop dementia.

Internet services can also be provided across state lines, creating additional legal and ethical concerns for psychologists. It is important to know that, regardless of where the psychologist is practicing, services are provided wherever the client is located. Thus, if a psychologist is not licensed in the jurisdiction where the client is located, they are providing psychological services without a license in that jurisdiction (Knauss, 2011).

There are also varying opinions regarding the equivalence of traditional and computer-based or online versions of the same tests. In some cases, test developers adapt traditional tests for use on a computer. However, this may alter the test to the point that it may not be measuring the same construct as its traditional counterpart (Schulenberg & Yutrzenka, 2004), nor is it clear that the norms for standardized testing are the same for testing done via the Internet (Buchanan, 2002).

Computer-generated reports also have pros and cons. Test interpretation and report writing are the most difficult part of the assessment process for the clinician. Computerized psychological test reports save time and effort, making this task easier. However, "A major concern about computer generated reports is that they may not be as individualized as those generated in the conventional manner" (Bersoff & Hoffer, 2003, p. 301). Although some information such as demographic characteristics of the examinee can be entered into interpretation programs, no program can consider all the unique attributes of each individual. In most cases, the same programmed decision rules will be applied to all test scores (Bersoff & Hoffer, 2003). Computerized reports do not account for the context of the evaluations, demographic characteristics, or the employment and medical history of the client (Bersoff et al., 2012).

The *Standards for Educational and Psychological Testing* (AERA et al., 2014) and the APA Ethics Code (APA, 2017a) clearly indicate that test users are ultimately responsible for their test interpretations, no matter from what format the data are derived. This is found in the APA Ethics Code Standard 9.09(c) (Test Scoring and Interpretation Services): "Psychologists retain responsibility for the appropriate application, interpretation and use of assessment instruments, whether they score and interpret such tests themselves or use automated or other services" (APA, 2017a). When using computerized tests, interpretations, and reports, clinicians should have a coherent strategy for incorporating them in the assessment process and interpret them with caution. Automated scoring and interpretive services are only one component of an evaluation. Clinicians should carefully evaluate discrepant findings (Koocher & Keith-Spiegel, 2008)

Computerized testing and computer-generated reports can enhance the accuracy and sophistication of diagnostic decision-making. However, clinicians who use automated testing should accurately describe the purpose, norms, validity, and reliability of the measures they are using. The final decision in any assessment process should be made by a qualified practitioner who takes responsibility for both the testing process and the applicability of the interpretive report for the individual client. In spite of its limitations, the use of electronic technology to provide assessment services provides many benefits. These technological advances demand unique approaches to ethical decision-making. Psychologists must keep in mind the welfare of their clients. This is the most important guideline to help psychologists answer questions in emerging areas of practice.

REPORT WRITING

There is wide variability in psychological assessment report writing. There is variability in format, content, style, and purpose. In addition, there are several ethical considerations regarding assessment reports. As mentioned in the section on "Confidentiality," what to include in the background section of the report is one such issue.

Standard 9.01 of the APA *Ethical Principles of Psychologists and Code of Conduct* (APA, 2017a) states psychologists are urged to "base the opinions contained in their recommendations, reports, and diagnostic or evaluative statements ... on information and techniques sufficient to substantiate their findings." Thus, information in a psychological assessment report should be accurate and the conclusions based on data.

Psychologists should also indicate in assessment reports whether they deviated from standardized administration procedures. This would include noting whether an interpreter was used, whether the test was normed on a population different from the examinee, or whether there was a fire drill in the middle of testing. Any deviation or limitation within the testing situation should be noted in the report and taken into account when drawing conclusions from the data (Knauss, 2012).

The most important part of the assessment process is clearly communicating the test results and providing the recommendations. Unfortunately, it is often difficult to understand psychological reports because they are filled with jargon. Pelco and colleagues (2009) state the "literature is unequivocal in its conclusion that the use of technical terminology and phrases in written assessment reports hinders readers' comprehension of the report" (p. 20). In the more than four decades since these studies began, little seems to have changed. However, what has changed is client access to records.

Because clients have access to their records, it is recommended to write psychological reports for the client or at the very least with the expectation that they will be read by the client. Pelco and colleagues (2009) suggest that reports be written at an eighth-grade reading level without professional jargon. They compared reports written at different levels and found that no important information was lost from the report that was written at a lower reading level without jargon. Psychologists should also be sure that their reports answer the referral question. Too many reports use the administration of a standard test battery and a stereotyped report that does not provide answers to the questions being asked. This also makes psychologists responsible for only endeavoring to answer questions for which assessment is relevant. Some referral questions cannot be answered through the use of psychological assessment.

Recommendations need to be specific to the person being assessed, pragmatic, and relevant both to the referral question and to the context in which they will be delivered. Wolber and Carne (2002) suggest that, before a final psychological report is sent to the referral source or given to the client, it should be read by a colleague or supervisor. A final suggestion for making psychological assessment reports more useful has to do with timeliness. Turnaround time is a significant issue when decisions about an individual's future have to be made in a timely fashion. In a survey conducted by Berk (2005), respondents were unhappy with the amount of time that elapsed before they received the report. Thus, best practices in report writing include sensitivity to confidentiality of information in the background section of the report; basing conclusions on data; indicating any deviations from standardized procedures; keeping reading levels at or below the eighth grade; eliminating professional jargon; and making recommendations that are pragmatic and address the referral question. Keeping these issues in mind will improve the quality and usefulness of psychological assessment reports.

ASSESSMENT FEEDBACK

According to Kenneth Pope (1992), "Feedback may be the most neglected aspect of assessment" (p. 268). This leads to the question of why that may be the case when the *Ethical Principles of Psychologists and Code of Conduct* (APA, 2017a) clearly indicates in Standard 9.10 Explaining Assessment Results, that psychologists take reasonable steps to ensure that explanations of results are given to the individual or designated representative unless the nature of the relationship precludes providing an explanation of the results such as in certain forensic evaluations. When the examinee will not be given an explanation of the test results, this fact is to be clearly explained to the person being assessed in advance through the informed consent process.

Several hypotheses have been given for the reason that many psychological evaluations do not include test feedback as part of the assessment. Hypotheses include lack of training in test feedback techniques; feeling uncomfortable discussing the results of an assessment with a client; feeling uncertain as to how to present information to clients, especially negative results; and concern about the consequences of a client receiving potentially negative feedback (Butcher, 1992). It is also sometimes difficult to translate for the client the jargon that is used in many test reports. Finally, test results often leave many important questions unanswered, which can be frustrating to clients (Pope, 1992). It is also important to note that lack of time and reimbursement for assessment feedback contribute to the tendency to avoid or neglect providing feedback (Knauss, 2015).

Most people who are given psychological tests expect that the results will be discussed with them as part of the process. Sharing results with clients can build rapport between the client and the therapist, increase client cooperation with the assessment process, and leave the client with positive feelings. Assessment feedback itself can also be therapeutic for clients (Finn & Tonsager, 1992). Preparing for and giving feedback can also be beneficial for assessors. It requires the assessor to understand, integrate, and effectively organize the assessment findings and helps the psychologist to develop a clearer understanding of the assessment results and implications (Tharinger et al., 2008). Thus, providing effective feedback requires the skill of an effective therapist. The goal of most psychological assessments is to make recommendations that will affect the life of the examinee. In order for the assessment to be useful, the recommendations need to be followed. The effectiveness of the feedback session can determine whether or not the recommendations will be followed.

As noted, giving feedback is not always easy. However, there are some considerations that contribute to the success of a feedback session. First, clients should know what sort of feedback to expect and from whom it will come (Pope, 1992). The feedback session should enable the client to understand what the tests covered, what the scores mean, the accuracy of the scores, and how the information will be used (Knauss, 2015). It may be necessary to give feedback to several people such as a general practitioner and a therapist in addition to the client and their family members. In order to provide feedback to anyone other than the client (or the client's legal guardian if the client is a minor), it is necessary to get written permission from the client generally in the form of a signed release form or it could be part of the informed consent form (Wright, 2011).

There is no single model for providing feedback that has been widely adopted, although there are several options for organizing the session. The most common option is to give a copy of the written report to the client and then go through the report together, explaining everything that is written, answering any questions the client may have, and checking to make sure the person understands the information. Finn (2007) notes that research has shown that clients often continue to think about this information long after the feedback session. For some clients, receiving feedback may cause them to leave the assessment process with negative feelings (Wright, 2011) and is probably the most significant reason that psychologists do not give feedback.

Another consideration is whether psychologists assessing children and adolescents should provide feedback to the child as well as to their guardian. It is recommended to provide feedback to children and adolescents that is developmentally appropriate whenever possible and clinically appropriate (Fisher, 2017; Wright, 2011). It may be best to give feedback to parents (guardians) first and then to give feedback to the child with the parents in the room if you have tested a young child. This may occur in a separate session a few days or even a week later (Tharinger et al., 2008). As the client reaches adolescence, the opposite arrangement may be best so the client knows what information will be shared with their parents and the parents will not receive information without the adolescent present (Wright, 2011).

The final aspect of the feedback process is ensuring that the client understands as accurately as possible the information the psychologist was trying to communicate. A good feedback session includes providing an atmosphere where clients feel comfortable asking questions and this provides an opportunity to answer questions as they arise (Wright, 2011). It is also important to assess clients' reactions to the feedback process, especially when their reaction may be negative and result in terminating treatment or failure to follow recommendations. Understanding clients' reactions to feedback is as important as test administration, scoring, and interpretation (Pope, 1992).

It is important to note that there are times when the Ethics Code permits exceptions to the requirement of providing an explanation of assessment results. Assessment feedback is not usually given directly to the examinee when testing is court ordered or when assessments involve employment testing, eligibility for security clearances, or the ability to return to work. In those situations, reports are released to a third party and cannot be given to the examinees or anyone else without the consent of the third party. When feedback will not be given directly to clients or their guardians, psychologists are required to inform examinees of this prior to administering the assessment. If legally permissible, the psychologist should also provide the reason why feedback will not be given (Fisher, 2017).

Providing feedback is the final step in the assessment process. It is also required by the APA Ethics Code. The feedback process is valuable to both the assessor and the client. Effective feedback increases the probability that assessment recommendations will be followed and, in many cases, feedback has the potential to be an intervention in and of itself. Thus, it is important not to avoid or neglect giving assessment feedback but to consider it an essential part of the assessment process (Knauss, 2015).

CONCLUSION

This chapter has discussed the ethical issues of informed consent, collaborative assessment, confidentiality, the involvement of third parties in assessment, assessments with external consequences, test construction, test revisions, obsolete tests and outdated test results, cultural competence in assessment, test data and test security, assessments in the digital age, assessment report writing, assessment feedback, assessment supervision, and emerging areas in the field of assessment. Ethical issues do not necessarily result in ethical dilemmas. A good ethical decision-making framework as well as the APA *Ethical Principles of Psychologists and Code of Conduct* (APA, 2017a) and the *Standards for Educational and Psychological Testing* (AERA et al., 2014) provide guidance regarding ethical and professional issues in assessment. Good assessments begin with a thorough informed consent process, including information about third-party involvement and external consequences when relevant. Assessment reports should be written with the expectation that clients will read them and most assessors should provide feedback. New areas of assessment will continue to emerge, bringing new ethical challenges.

REFERENCES

Adams, K. A. (2000). Practical and ethical issues pertaining to test revisions *Psychological Assessment, 12*(3),281–286.

AERA (American Educational Research Association), APA (American Psychological Association), & NCME (National Council on Measurement in Education). (2014). *Standards for educational and psychological testing*. Washington, DC: AERA.

American Psychiatric Association. (2013). *Diagnostic and statistical manual of mental disorders* (5th ed.). Washington, DC: American Psychiatric Association.

APA (American Psychological Association). (1992). Ethical principles of psychologists and code of conduct. *American Psychologist, 47*, 1597–1611.

APA (American Psychological Association). (2017a). *Ethical principles of psychologists and code of conduct*. www.apa.org./ethics/code/ethics-code-2017.pdf

APA (American Psychological Association). (2017b). *Multicultural guidelines: An ecological approach to context, identity, and intersectionality*. www.apa.org/about/policy/multicultural-guidelines.pdf

Beck, A. T., Steer, R. A., & Brown, G. K. (1996). *Beck Depression Inventory – II*. San Antonio, TX: Pearson.

Behnke, S. (2005). Thinking ethically as psychologists: Reflections on Ethical Standards 2.01, 3.07, 9.08, and 10.04. *Monitor on Psychology, 36*(6). www.apa.org/monitor /jun05/ethics.html

Berk, S. N. (2005). Consumers speak. We need to listen. *The Pennsylvania Psychologist Quarterly, 68*(5), 2, 20.

Bersoff, D. N., & Hoffer, P. J. (2003). Legal issues in computerized psychological testing. In D. N. Bersoff (Ed.), *Ethical conflicts in psychology* (3rd ed., pp. 300–302). Washington, DC: American Psychological Association.

Bersoff, D. N., De Matteo, D., & Foster, E. E. (2012). Assessment and testing. In S. J. Knapp (Ed.), *APA handbook of ethics in psychology. Vol. 2: Practice, teaching, research* (pp. 45–74). Washington, DC: American Psychological Association.

Black, M. M., & Ponirakis, A. (2000). Computer-administered interviews with children about maltreatment. *Journal of Interpersonal Violence, 15*, 682–695.

Brabender, V. (2018). Ethics in diversity-sensitive assessment. In S. R. Smith & R. Krishnamurthy (Eds.), *Diversity-sensitive personality assessment* (pp. 333–348). New York: Routledge.

Buchanan, T. (2002). Online assessment: Desirable of dangerous? *Professional Psychology: Research and Practice, 33*, 148–154.

Bush, S. S. (2010). Determining whether or when to adopt new versions of psychological and neuropsychological tests: Ethical and professional considerations. *The Clinical Neuropsychologist, 24*, 7–16.

Butcher, J. N. (1992). Introduction to the special section: Providing psychological test feedback to clients. *Psychological Assessment, 4*(3), 267.

Butcher, J. N., Dahlstrom, W. G., Graham, J. R., Tellegen, A., & Kaemmer, B. (1989). *The Minnesota Multiphasic Personality Inventory-2 (MMPI-2): Manual for administration and scoring*. Minneapolis: University of Minnesota Press.

Campbell, L., Vasquez, M., Behnke, S., & Kinscherff, R. (2010). *APA ethics code commentary and case illustrations*. Washington, DC: American Psychological Association.

Chan, A. S., Shum, D., & Cheung, R. W. Y. (2003). Recent development of cognitive and neuropsychological assessment in Asian countries. *Psychological Assessment, 15*, 257–267.

Finn, S. E. (2007). *In our clients' shoes*. New York: Taylor and Francis.

Finn, S. E., & Tonsager, M. E. (1992). Therapeutic effects of providing MMPI-2 test feedback to college students awaiting therapy. *Psychological Assessment, 4*(3), 278–287.

Fisher, C. B. (2017). *Decoding the ethics code: A practical guide for psychologists* (4th ed.). Washington, DC: Sage.

Fisher, C. B., & Fried, A. L. (2003). Internet-mediated psychological services and the American Psychological Association Ethics Code. *Psychotherapy: Theory, Research, Practice, Training, 40*, 103–111.

Flynn, J. R. (1999). Searching for justice: The discovery of IQ gains over time. *American Psychologist, 54*, 5–20.

Gregory, R. J. (2004). *Psychological testing: History, principles, and applications* (4th ed.). Boston: Allyn and Bacon.

Jacob, S., & Hartshorne, T.S. (2007). *Ethics and law for school psychologists* (5th ed.). Hoboken, NJ: John Wiley & Sons.

Knapp, S. J., & Vandecreek, L. D. (2012). *Practical ethics for psychologists: A positive approach* (2nd ed.). Washington, DC: American Psychological Association.

Knapp, S. J., VandeCreek, L. D., & Fingerhut, R. (2017). *Practical ethics for psychologists: A positive approach* (3rd ed.). Washington, DC: American Psychological Association.

Knapp, S., Younggren, J. N., VandeCreek, L., Harris, E., & Martin, J. N. (2013). *Assessing and managing risk in psychological practice: An individualized approach* (2nd ed.). Rockville, MD: The Trust.

Knauss, L. K. (2007). Our ethical responsibility to provide culturally competent personality assessment. *SPA Exchange*, *19*(2), 4, 12–13.

Knauss, L. K. (2009a). Are you informed about informed consent? *SPA Exchange*, *21*(1), 4, 14, 15.

Knauss, L. K. (2009b). Informed consent, part II: Ideas for your informed consent agreement. *SPA Exchange*, *21*(2), 4, 14.

Knauss, L. K. (2011). Ethics, assessment, and the internet. *SPA Exchange*, *23*(1), 4, 12, 13.

Knauss, L. K. (2012). Ethical considerations in assessment report writing. *SPA Exchange*, *24*(1), 4, 13, 14.

Knauss, L. K. (2013). The pros and cons of computerized assessment. *SPA Exchange*, *25*(1), 4, 12, 13.

Knauss, L. K. (2014). Can I use this test? *SPA Exchange*, *26*(1), 7, 14.

Knauss, L. K. (2015). Ethical considerations in assessment feedback. *SPA Exchange*, *27*(2), 4, 16, 17.

Knauss, L. K. (2017). Response to article by Williams and Lally: What is the best test to use. *Professional Psychology Research and Practice*, *48*(4), 279–281.

Koocher, G. P. (2007). Twenty-first century ethical challenges for psychology. *American Psychologist*, *62*(5), 375–384.

Koocher, G. P., & Keith-Spiegel, P. (2008). *Ethics is psychology and the mental health profession: Standards and cases* (3rd ed.). New York: Oxford University Press.

Leach, M. M., & Oakland, T. (2007). Ethics standards impacting test development and use: A review of 31 ethics codes impacting practices in 35 countries. *International Journal of Testing*, *7*(1), 71–88.

Lopez, S. (1997). Cultural competence in psychotherapy: A guide for clinicians and their supervisors. In C. E. Watkins (Ed.), *Handbook of psychotherapy supervision* (pp. 570–588). New York: Wiley.

Messick, S. (1980). Test validity and the ethics of assessment. *American Psychologist*, *35*, 1012–1027.

Naglieri, J. A., Drasgow, F., Schmidt, M., Handler, L., Prifitera, A., Margolis, A., & Velasquez, R. (2004). Psychological testing on the Internet: New problems, old issues. *America Psychologist*, *59*, 150–162.

Pelco, L. E., Ward, S. B., Coleman, L., & Young, J. (2009). Teacher ratings of three psychological report styles. *Training and Education in Professional Psychology*, *3*(1), 19–27.

Pope, K. S. (1992). Responsibilities in providing psychological test feedback to clients. *Psychological Assessment*, *4*(3), 268–271.

Schulenberg, S. E., & Yutrzenka, B. A. (2004). Ethical issues in the use of computerized assessment. *Computers in Human Behavior*, *20*, 477–490.

Tharinger, D. J., Finn, S. E., Hersh, B., Wilkinson, A., Christopher, G. B., & Tran, A. (2008). Assessment feedback with parents and preadolescent children: A collaborative approach. *Professional Psychology: Research and Practice*, *39*(6), 600–609.

Wolber, G. J., & Carne, W. F. (2002). *Writing psychological reports: A guide for clinicians* (2nd ed.). Sarasota, FL: Professional Resource Press.

Wright, A. J. (2011). *Conducting psychological assessment: A guide for practitioners*. Hoboken, NJ: John Wiley & Sons.

5 Contemporary Psychopathology Diagnosis

CHRISTOPHER C. CONWAY, LEE ANNA CLARK, AND ROBERT F. KRUEGER

Classification systems for mental illness are intimately intertwined with clinical assessment. They define and codify mental disorder diagnoses, essentially our field's basic units. They reflect current expert opinion on the conditions that are public health, clinical, and research priorities and therefore effectively set the agenda for most mental health assessments. Accordingly, when classification systems are updated, popular assessment tools – including those used in specialized research settings and everyday clinical practice – are typically revised.

We describe four approaches to understanding and classifying mental illness. We begin with contemporary systems that have the broadest influence on clinical assessment today. In the United States, that overwhelmingly means the *Diagnostic and Statistical Manual of Mental Disorders* (DSM), which the US media often call the "bible" of psychiatry and allied disciplines. Outside the United States, the *International Classification of Diseases* (ICD) predominates. DSM and ICD have been the prevailing approaches for decades and they are revised periodically to be responsive to new research evidence.

Momentum is building, however, for systems that deviate in significant ways from traditional approaches. Just as other sciences intermittently revisit their basic assumptions (e.g., Is a virus alive? Is light a wave or a particle?), the mental health field is currently entertaining alternate views on the definition and basic structure of psychopathology. We present two emerging approaches that have divergent implications for clinical research and assessment: the Research Domain Criteria (RDoC; Cuthbert & Insel, 2013), a research framework for the biological correlates of mental illness; and the Hierarchical Taxonomy of Psychopathology (HiTOP; Kotov et al., 2017), an empirically derived model of the major phenotypic dimensions of psychopathology.

We begin with our view on the functions of nosology as it relates to clinical assessment to prepare readers to judge how well each classification system satisfies those functions. We then outline DSM and ICD and summarize limitations associated with these categorical approaches to diagnosis. Next, we explain how RDoC and HiTOP seek – in very different ways – to revamp classification and assessment to benefit various users (e.g., researchers, health professionals). We close by speculating about the future of mental health diagnosis and its implications for assessment.

CLINICAL FUNCTIONS OF A NOSOLOGY

Diagnostic systems shape the assessment process in various ways. Perhaps most obviously, they guide *diagnostic evaluations* – the end product of most clinical encounters in assessment settings. That is, nosologies delimit the clinical entities that diagnosticians assess. The most fundamental distinction is the threshold between health and illness. At what point does unusual or disruptive behavior become disordered? A useful classification system must also draw boundaries between separate conditions. This task has become more difficult as the list of syndromes compiled in DSM and ICD has proliferated. The validity of these boundaries is particularly relevant to differential diagnosis – choosing among various candidate diagnoses to find those that best explain a clinical presentation.

The role of clinical judgment in diagnosis differs across classification systems. Some nosologies (e.g., DSM) require adherence to a more or less detailed list of diagnostic criteria, whereas others (e.g., the ICD's *Clinical Descriptions and Diagnostic Guidelines*) provide clinicians with more flexible guidance. Other approaches to mental illness, such as RDoC, seek a more objective route (e.g., laboratory tests) to diagnosis, although this scenario is now highly speculative and would depend on significant progress in neuroscience-based research and theory.

Standardized diagnostic assessments generally leave little room for clinical judgment. Some structured interviews are almost a verbatim reformulation of DSM criteria. These instruments have the benefit of being very reliable and can be administered by lay interviewers and computers. Semi-structured interviews, which also correspond closely to diagnostic criteria, depend on clinicians to judge whether symptom and syndrome severity are sufficient to warrant a diagnosis (e.g., Structured Clinical Interview for DSM-5 [SCID]; First et al., 2015).

Unstructured interviews, which rarely cover all relevant diagnostic criteria systematically, rely most on clinical judgment and are the standard in routine practice.

Another function of diagnosis is to aid *treatment selection*. A basic assumption of clinical nosology – throughout the history of medicine and, later, mental health disciplines – is that diagnosis directs treatment type and intensity. Historically, diagnosis is presumed to capture the specific pathology or disrupted internal mechanisms underlying a health condition (Clark et al., 2017). Therefore, the optimal treatment addresses that pathological process (e.g., antibiotics are prescribed for a bacterial infection). Classification schemes for mental illness fall woefully short of that ideal scenario. Nevertheless, most psychological treatment manuals – and, to some extent, psychiatric medications – are marketed as interventions for a particular diagnostic entity (e.g., cognitive behavioral therapy for panic disorder). Finally, although diagnosis is intended to guide treatment selection, other clinical data (e.g., overall symptom severity or homicide risk) frequently play a major role in decisions about the style or intensity of indicated care (e.g., watchful waiting, outpatient, immediate psychiatric hospitalization).

Modern nosologies intend for diagnosis to connote *prognosis*, broadly speaking. That is, the results of a diagnostic evaluation are assumed to provide information about the temporal course of symptoms and impairment. Some syndromes are conceptualized as more enduring and chronically interfering (e.g., schizophrenia-spectrum disorders), whereas others are considered more episodic and milder on average (e.g., acute stress disorder). Prognosis informs not only expectations about naturalistic change over time but also treatment success. Personality disorders (PDs), for instance, were set apart from more acute disorders in DSM-III (American Psychiatric Association, 1980) to alert clinicians to their interfering effects on treatment for a focal clinical disorder (e.g., post-traumatic stress disorder, PTSD; panic disorder).

Periodically, through the history of mental illness classification, diagnosis has been framed around *etiology*. Prior to 1980, some DSM diagnoses (e.g., hysterical neurosis in DSM-II; American Psychiatric Association, 1968) were conceptualized from a psychodynamic perspective. This practice followed that of general medicine, where the ultimate goal of assessment is to identify observable symptoms' underlying pathophysiology. Since DSM-III, psychopathology diagnosis has been largely a descriptive enterprise, meaning that diagnoses are based on outward signs (e.g., motor tic) and patient-reported internal experiences (e.g., sadness). There are exceptions, though, in DSM-5, such as a traumatic event being considered an etiological requirement for PTSD. RDoC, however, proposes to go "back to the future" – paralleling DSM-I and DSM-II (American Psychiatric Association, 1952, 1968) in a conceptual sense – to discover and assess the causal factors involved in mental illness. Specifically, the RDoC philosophy seems to be that clarifying the neurobiological correlates of mental illness will lead to greater etiological understanding of psychopathology.

PREVAILING DIAGNOSTIC SYSTEMS

The DSM and ICD have governed most diagnosis and assessment worldwide for almost a century. For many US professionals, DSM is virtually *synonymous* with diagnosis. We describe the definition and organization of psychopathology within each of these systems, underlining how the content and structure of the nosologies relate to common assessment practices and decisions. Where relevant, we also highlight the ways in which these two classifications fulfill the main clinical functions of nosology.

Diagnostic and Statistical Manual of Mental Disorders

Diagnosis. The DSM-5 (American Psychiatric Association, 2013), like its three immediate predecessors (DSM-III, DSM-III-R, and DSM-IV; American Psychiatric Association, 1980, 1987, 1994), defines diagnoses according to specific sets of operational criteria. As alluded to earlier, these diagnostic criterion sets generally include outward signs and subjective symptoms, although very occasionally they also include objective tests (e.g., cognitive ability assessment for intellectual disability). Further, these criteria are generally considered "descriptive," in the sense that they invoke no specific theoretical orientation or etiological tradition that would explain the symptoms' origins, as was sometimes the case in the pre–DSM-III era. These precisely defined symptom sets enable the development of standardized questionnaire and interview measures that can increase diagnostic agreement across clinicians and assessment venues.

DSM-5 is oriented around diagnostic categories, implying (at least superficially) the existence of clear borders between normality and disorder and among disorder types. In fact, the DSM-5 acknowledges that evidence of discriminant validity for distinct diagnoses is limited for the vast majority of conditions, but the diagnoses have been reified over time so that many researchers, clinicians, and the lay public consider them to be valid, discrete disease entities (Clark et al., 2017). Therefore, diagnostic assessment results based on DSM-5 are often communicated to patients – and to research audiences – as a condition that someone "has," as opposed to as a useful summary of a complex symptom profile.

Patients need not satisfy all diagnostic criteria for a particular disorder to qualify for a diagnosis. DSM-5 has a polythetic approach to diagnosis, meaning that, for most disorders, only a subset of the listed symptoms is required to meet the diagnostic threshold. For example, only five of the nine diagnostic criteria for borderline PD are needed for a patient to be considered a "case." However, in some instances, cardinal symptoms are necessary but not sufficient for a diagnosis: For DSM-5 major depressive disorder, either depressed mood or anhedonia must be present for the diagnosis to apply in adults. As a result, for efficiency, some assessment routines – especially those concerned only with categorical diagnoses – forego the remainder of a symptom assessment if a patient does not endorse these necessary features.

In most cases, DSM-5 requires assessors to evaluate the *clinical significance* of a constellation of symptoms to determine whether a syndrome meets the cutoff of "caseness" or is a subthreshold symptom presentation. This typically entails a determination of whether a patient experiences significant distress as a result of symptoms *or* whether the symptoms produce clinical levels of impairment in social and/or occupational roles (e.g., romantic relationships, leisure activity, employment). Many categories in DSM-5 also involve subtypes or specifiers that reflect an overall severity rating (e.g., mild vs. moderate substance use disorder).

Organization. The primary targets of assessment in DSM-5 are the mental disorders in the manual's Section II, "Diagnostic Criteria and Codes." This section is subdivided into clusters of similar conditions, such as Anxiety Disorders or Dissociative Disorders, which often shape the format of assessment tools. For example, a diagnostic interview at a panic disorder treatment center might only cover conditions in DSM-5's Anxiety Disorders subsection. This focused approach to assessment – often a byproduct of time constraints – usually leads to an incomplete view of the clinical picture (i.e., underdiagnosis; Wilk et al., 2006) and it can reify historical divisions between conditions that in fact share significant pathology and may be functionally related (e.g., panic disorder often co-occurs with major depression).

In earlier DSM versions, these clusters were based on symptom similarity or the subjective experience of psychological symptoms (i.e., phenomenology). For example, DSM-IV mood disorders were grouped due to marked affective disturbance, regardless of whether it manifested in depressive or manic episodes. In the most recent revision, there is progress toward a more evidence-based organization that reflects disorders' patterns of empirical relations with eleven "validators," such as cognitive deficits or neural abnormalities (Andrews et al., 2009). As a result, DSM-5 designated separate sections for unipolar versus bipolar mood disorders, broke off obsessive-compulsive and related disorders, as well as trauma- and stressor-related disorders (e.g., PTSD) from anxiety disorders, and cross-listed schizotypal PD with schizophrenia-spectrum and other psychotic disorders, to name a few examples.

In DSM-III through DSM-IV, a comprehensive evaluation of psychopathology and related problems in living entailed a "multiaxial" assessment to draw attention to not only clinical disorders but also PDs and mental retardation (now called intellectual disability), general medical conditions, psychosocial problems, and a global assessment of functioning (Axes I through V, respectively). By organizing assessments around these domains, it was thought that diagnosticians would be reminded to document other areas in need of clinical attention (e.g., Type II diabetes, marital discord) that might otherwise be overlooked.

Although the multiaxial system was eliminated in DSM-5, to bring it in line with standard practice in general medicine, other assessment procedures appear in DSM-5 Section III ("Emerging Measures and Models") to help gather clinical information that can supplement[1] the (Section II) diagnostic formulation. This set of inventories – an optional part of DSM-5 diagnosis – includes a number of cross-cutting symptom domains (e.g., sleep problems, anger) that might benefit from clinical attention (Narrow et al., 2013). Section III also presents a Cultural Formulation Interview, which aids clinicians in understanding how patients' cultural backgrounds (broadly construed; e.g., ethnicity, socioeconomic status) might play a role in the origins, manifestation, and effective treatment for mental illness.

Finally, perhaps the most controversial entry in Section III is the Alternative DSM-5 Model of Personality Disorders (AMPD). The AMPD was supported by the DSM-5 Personality and Personality Disorders Workgroup and by the DSM-5 Task Force as a viable new model for PD diagnosis (in Section II) but was rejected by the American Psychiatric Association Board of Trustees at the eleventh hour of the DSM revision process and assigned to Section III. Briefly, the AMPD involves first a determination of whether personality dysfunction – disrupted self and interpersonal functioning – is present. Next, patients' scores on five pathological trait domains – and, time permitting, twenty-five constituent trait facets – are recorded (negative affectivity, detachment, antagonism, disinhibition, psychoticism) (Krueger et al., 2012). The combination of personality dysfunction and aberrant trait standing is sufficient for either one of six "familiar" diagnoses (antisocial, avoidant, borderline, narcissistic, obsessive-compulsive, schizotypal) *or* personality disorder trait-specified, which captures the maladaptive trait profile without requiring it to match a traditional PD category. The AMPD thus represents a hybrid of categorical and dimensional perspectives that can provide a more detailed and idiographic account of personality dysfunction and maladaptive traits.

International Classification of Diseases

Comparison with DSM. The ICD is published by the World Health Organization (WHO) as a resource for clinicians around the world for identifying and recording health conditions. The mental, behavioral, and neurodevelopmental disorders constitute one chapter in this sweeping document. The ICD serves a broad audience of practitioners in a diversity of health care settings across the full range of cultural backgrounds. Because the ICD must be interpretable by all types of health

[1] Or replace in the case of PD.

professionals around the globe, *clinical utility* is an overriding consideration in *ICD* development (Clark et al., 2017). Thus, the ICD above all else aims to be a user-friendly assessment tool, leading to some structural differences with DSM.

The latest iteration of this manual, ICD-11, was released in summer 2018. There have been efforts over the evolution of ICD to harmonize it with DSM (and vice versa) and these two classification systems have a great deal of overlap. The principal similarity for our purposes is that they both assert a largely categorical model of psychopathology diagnosis. In this section, though, we focus on the main deviation from DSM. Specifically, the WHO produces three *different versions* of ICD to suit the needs of particular assessment settings.

Multiple versions. The ICD-11 version that bears that closest resemblance to DSM-5 is the Diagnostic Criteria for Research (DCR). Like DSM, its categories are defined by lists of operationally defined symptoms. The relatively precise wording and decision rules in the DCR promote standardized, reliable assessment. As the name implies, this precision is a priority especially in research settings, where investigators aim to establish homogeneous patient groups for clinical trials and other experimental and observational studies.

The WHO recognizes that this format is not optimal for all assessment contexts. The ICD also includes a *Clinical Descriptions and Diagnostic Guidelines* (CDDG) version, which offers more prototypic conceptualizations by describing the main clinical and associated features of each diagnosis without requiring strict adherence to them. The CDDG is in fact the predominant method of clinical assessment worldwide, other than for research purposes. It is widely used because it is flexible and user-friendly and allows for more clinical judgment, taking into account how mental illness presents in particular local contexts. For instance, symptoms of social phobia take on different presentations across various regions of the world and cultural subgroups (Clark et al., 2017).

The CDDG is thus especially attuned to diversity issues. It acknowledges that most (perhaps all) mental illnesses are not "natural kinds" that exist independent of sociocultural context. DSM-5 or DCR criterion lists represent one index of diagnostic constructs but they are not isomorphic with "true" latent constructs. Indeed, the simple fact that diagnostic criterion lists are revised across editions of DSM and ICD signals that categories are fluid approximations. This more flexible conceptualization of mental illness suggests that slightly different symptom presentations can be reasonably judged to reflect the same health phenomenon. To make a culinary metaphor, in Indonesia, a Balinese meringue is a dessert made with palm sugar, which imbues an umami taste. In the West, in contrast, this dish is known for its sweetness, related to the use of cane sugar. Despite these significant cross-cultural differences, both desserts are sensibly identified as meringue. The same logic applies to varying presentations of, say, social phobia across gender and cultural groups. More flexible versus more rigid systems each have both strengths and weaknesses. The more flexible CDDG reduces the use of "not elsewhere classified"/"not otherwise specified" diagnoses that are rampant in the DSM but accordingly increases both prevalence and diagnostic heterogeneity. Whether this means the CDDG tends to overdiagnose or the *DSM* tends to underdiagnose is unknown, absent an infallible "gold standard." The effect on reliability appears to be more a function of whether a single assessment or test-retest method is used, with the former yielding higher estimates than the latter (e.g., Regier et al., 2013).

The ICD also provides a version of the mental, behavioral, or neurodevelopmental disorders chapter for primary care settings. In the United States and around the world, many patients are first diagnosed in primary care, where assessment time may be most limited and health care professionals have the least specialized knowledge and training. The ICD is responsive to those constraints by having a catalog of diagnoses that demands less fine-grain assessment. That is, the primary care version includes broad diagnostic classes that are expected to be easier to detect than more specific, operationally defined conditions. It is unclear, though, whether a less precise diagnostic routine might promote overdiagnosis (i.e., Type I error). This organization is analogous to the DSM-5 configuration of diagnostic "spectra," such as autism spectrum disorder, which encompasses several related conditions that were classified separately in DSM-IV (e.g., Asperger's disorder, autistic disorder, Rett syndrome); indeed, DSM-5 does not provide subspectrum diagnostic codes.

Personality disorder. Structural changes to the PD section have brought about a radically different PD assessment process in ICD-11 (Tyrer et al., 2015). This new model is similar to the AMPD in DSM-5 but differs in some important ways. The first step to PD diagnosis in ICD-11 is evaluating personality dysfunction in self and interpersonal arenas. If this essential impairment is detected, then the clinician determines the severity of dysfunction – mild, moderate, or severe PD. A subthreshold designation called "personality difficulty" allows identification of significant, but subclinical, levels of pathology. A recommended but optional next step is to specify which of five maladaptive traits best describe the PD style. These five dimensions are conceptually equivalent to those of the AMPD trait model, except that ICD-11 includes Anankastia – compulsive and controlling attitudes and behaviors – and does not include psychoticism (because, among other reasons, schizotypal PD is listed in the schizophrenia or other primary psychotic disorders section). This redesign of the ICD PD model substantially simplifies PD assessment but might require adjustment by professionals used to the old system.

Standard Assessment Tools

Various measures guide assessment of categorical disorders in clinical practice. In the United States, the SCID, mentioned previously (see the section "Clinical Functions of a Nosology"), is often used. It features separate versions for assessing acute clinical disorders versus PDs and there are corresponding self-report screening instruments to identify salient symptoms that are then evaluated more thoroughly in the SCID proper. For dedicated assessment of PD, the SCID and International Personality Disorder Examination (IPDE; Loranger, 1999) are prevalent tools. The IPDE is the only current interview measure that includes an assessment of criteria for both DSM-IV and ICD-10 models, making it an attractive option for international audiences.

Although reliability for categorical diagnosis has improved markedly since the transition to more precise operational criteria in DSM-III, inter-rater agreement and temporal stability for the SCID and related tools remain limited. This observation is critically important not only because reliability is essential for clinical utility of diagnostic constructs (e.g., judging treatment effectiveness) but also because reliability is a prerequisite for disorder validity. A widely publicized instance of poor test-retest reliability using standard assessments occurred in the DSM-5 field trials, during which many common diagnoses – including alcohol use disorder and major depressive disorder – fell in an unacceptable or questionable range of inter-rater reliability (Regier et al., 2013).

LIMITATIONS OF A CATEGORICAL DIAGNOSTIC SYSTEM

DSM and ICD are based on an essentially categorical approach to psychopathology diagnosis, arranging signs and symptoms of mental illness as indicators of nominally discrete disorder categories. Although the categorical model is widely popular and arguably the best available approach for applied assessment on a broad scale, many experts believe that the field must seek a more scientifically tenable system. Here, we review the primary limitations of categorical diagnosis before presenting emerging research programs into alternative dimensional nosologies.

Comorbidity

After the transition to more precisely defined disorder categories in DSM-III, data from large, nationally representative samples showed that people with any diagnosis were as likely as not to receive *two or more* diagnoses (Kessler et al., 1994). In clinical groups, this co-occurrence, or comorbidity, was even more pronounced (Brown et al., 2001). Comorbidity complicates the clinical functions of nosology that we raised at the outset. For example, treatment selection is thorny when a patient carries multiple diagnoses. Practitioners must decide, with little evidence base as guidance, whether to treat these conditions simultaneously or sequentially. If sequentially, there are scant data regarding the optimal order of interventions and it may not be feasible to obtain sufficient training in multiple disorder-specific treatments.

Heterogeneity

Most diagnostic categories in DSM and ICD reflect a diverse constellation of symptoms. In the "Prevailing Diagnostic Systems" section, we alluded to the fact that only five of nine diagnostic criteria are needed to assign a borderline PD diagnosis in DSM-5 Section II. Not only does this mean that there are 256 ways to qualify for the diagnosis but two patients can receive the diagnosis and yet have only one criterion in common. Such heterogeneity in modern diagnostic categories is problematic for treatment researchers because interventions may have differential effectiveness for the various components of the syndrome. For example, it is easy to imagine a cognitive psychotherapy addressing cognitive symptoms of panic disorder (e.g., fear of dying or going crazy) but having little immediate impact on physiological symptoms (e.g., tachycardia, dizziness, and other aspects of the fight-or-flight response).

Reliability

It has proven difficult to assess many categorical diagnoses – or even the presence versus absence of *any* mental illness – in contemporary classification systems reliably. Inter-rater disagreement can arise from the inherent difficulty in discerning the health–illness boundary, as well as varying approaches to differential diagnosis (i.e., selecting a primary diagnosis).

Disorder categories also can be temporally unstable, appearing to remit and recur even over short intervals, such that a patient diagnosed with generalized anxiety disorder one week ago might be disorder-free when assessed again today. Longitudinal studies that have systematically examined the continuity of mental illness have shown convincingly that categorical measures of psychopathology are more variable over time than dimensional ones (Morey et al., 2012).

RECENT DEVELOPMENTS IN NOSOLOGY

Today, most practitioners tend to use categorical models but they are not the only option. Motivated by the many problems with categorical diagnosis – such as excessive comorbidity, heterogeneity, and unreliability – nosologists currently are pushing for new ways to understand and diagnose psychopathology. Next, we review two emerging systems, RDoC and HiTOP, that seek to supplement – and perhaps eventually to supplant – prevailing diagnostic models.

Research Domain Criteria

Motivation. The US National Institute of Mental Health (NIMH) launched the RDoC initiative in 2009, signaling a divergence with the American Psychiatric Association's (DSM's publisher) approach to assessing and understanding mental illness. Fundamentally, NIMH was concerned that mental disorder categories, at least as currently constituted, were inhibiting discovery of psychopathology's causal mechanisms. It advocated for research toward an approach that would eventually define psychopathology according to etiology, as opposed to observable features (Cuthbert & Insel, 2013).

It is important to note, however, that RDoC is unusual in this chapter because *it is not actually a diagnostic system*. Although its eventual goal is to revolutionize our understanding of psychopathology, RDoC is currently strictly a framework for research. Its focus is explicating the pathogenesis of mental illness, centered on the level of neural circuitry. NIMH hopes that improved understanding of the etiologies of psychopathology will lead eventually to more informative, accurate clinical assessment and, in turn, treatments targeted on pathophysiological mechanisms underlying clinical problems.

The NIMH perspective is that research must pivot away from existing diagnostic categories to facilitate new breakthroughs in understanding the etiology of mental illness. A common refrain in the recent history of biological psychiatry is that there are no known laboratory tests for any DSM diagnosis. With the possible exception of narcolepsy, there is no biological "signature" unique to any diagnosis, no pathognomonic marker. The NIMH views this misalignment of the insights into biological functioning possible with new technologies (e.g., neuroimaging, genomics) and mental disorder diagnoses as a failure of the current diagnostic system. It aims to boost the observed signal of neurobiological risk factors – and the technologies used to measure them – by decomposing traditional categories into more homogeneous processes that are theoretically more proximal to fundamental biological systems.

Structure. NIMH's initial set of new constructs is cataloged in the RDoC "matrix," which, as mentioned, is a research framework, not a diagnostic system. Its constructs are conceptualized as the building blocks of psychological problems. The development process took place in expert workgroups, in which consensus emerged on the pathological mechanisms most important to various types of mental illness and the assessment procedures that best capture them.

As of the time of writing, there are five functional domains that form the rows of the RDoC matrix:[2] Negative Valence, Positive Valence, Cognitive Systems, Social Processes, and Arousal and Regulatory Systems. Each domain is subdivided into narrower functional dimensions that represent the basic units (and assessment targets) of this system. To illustrate, Table 5.1 presents an abridged version of the Negative Valence subconstructs and their associated phenotypes to illustrate the RDoC matrix.

The five functional domains are crossed with seven "units of analysis," which are essentially assessment modalities: genes, molecules, cells, circuits, physiology, behavior, and self-reports.[3] They cover the full range from molecular to molar perspectives on mental illness, although genetic and neurobiological aspects are emphasized. The NIMH developers assert that articulating these units of analysis is intended to ensure that research takes a multilevel, pluralistic approach to evaluating each construct. They envision systematic research into the pathways from molecular constructs (e.g., genetic polymorphisms) up through neural circuits (e.g., amygdala-prefrontal cortex connectivity) and ending in manifest behavior (e.g., response inhibition). In fact, an inclusion criterion for RDoC constructs was evidence that the proposed construct had empirical links to both neural *and* behavioral systems. At the same time, NIMH has indicated that neural circuits are the central hub of the RDoC matrix, consistent with other statements from RDoC architects that mental health problems are "disorders of neural circuits" (e.g., Insel & Cuthbert, 2015).

More recent NIMH presentations of the RDoC project have underscored that the functional domains must be understood within neurodevelopmental and environmental contexts. It is clear that normative developmental processes shape the expression of RDoC constructs (i.e., brain and behavior) and environmental forces – capturing everything from lead exposure to traumatic stressors to poverty to cultural factors – influence and are influenced by biological systems in a dynamic cycle. Thus, the matrix is considered to be embedded in these contextual factors and NIMH urges investigators explicitly to consider their role whenever possible.

What does psychopathology assessment look like in the RDoC framework? As an example, we describe a potential study of the Negative Valence system. Suppose researchers are interested in the role of threat reactivity (a construct in the Acute Threat subdomain) in the development of emotion dysregulation (e.g., severe anxious and/or depressed mood). They recruit a series of patients from a primary care center who are flagged as reporting elevated anxiety *or* depressive symptoms during a routine medical visit. Notably, the researchers do not seek out participants on the basis of a DSM or ICD diagnosis; as mentioned, RDoC is agnostic regarding traditional diagnostic constructs. Instead, they invite patients who express more general

[2] See www.nimh.nih.gov/research-priorities/rdoc/constructs/rdoc-matrix.shtml

[3] An eighth unit of analysis, Paradigms, lists specific research procedures; for example, the Trier Social Stress Test (Kirschbaum, Pirke, & Hellhammer, 1993) is listed under Acute Threat.

Table 5.1 Example Negative Valence system phenotypes in the Research Domain Criteria (RDoC) matrix

Construct/ Subconstruct	Genes[a]	Molecules	Cells	Circuits	Physiology	Behavior	Self-Report	Paradigms
Acute Threat ("Fear")		Dopamine	Glia	Insular cortex	Context startle	Analgesia	Fear Survey Schedule	Trier Social Stress Test
Potential Threat ("Anxiety")		Cortisol	Pituitary cells	Bed nucleus of stria terminals	Potentiated startle	–	Anxiety Sensitivity Index	No-shock, predictable shock, unpredictable shock (NPU) Threat Task
Sustained Threat		Adrenocorticotropic hormone	Hippocampal	Attention network	Error-related negativity	Anhedonia	Risky Families Questionnaire	–
Loss		Androgens	–	Amygdala	Autonomic nervous system	Crying	Life Events and Difficulties Schedule	Sadness-eliciting film clips
Frustrative Nonreward		Vasopressin	–	Amygdala	–	Physical aggression	Questionnaire of Daily Frustrations	"Locked Box" Task

Note. For clarity, we list only one entry per cell. The full matrix, including all elements per cell, for Negative Valence Systems and all other RDoC domains are available at www.nimh.nih.gov/research-priorities/rdoc/constructs/rdoc-matrix.shtml.

[a] Starting in May 2017, this column is left blank on the RDoC website due to concerns regarding reproducibility of individual molecular genetic (i.e., measured genes, such as single nucleotide polymorphisms) on psychopathology outcomes.

vulnerability to internalizing distress and are thus vulnerable to a full gamut of emotional disorder diagnoses.

In the lab, patients and their significant others complete a battery of questionnaires regarding the severity of patients' internalizing problems. Patients then respond to a series of computer-based tasks to evaluate information-processing and memory biases for threatening material (e.g., angry and fearful faces). The lab session ends with a fear-conditioning paradigm, in which patients' startle eyeblink is recorded (via electromyography) as they are presented with stimuli that were either previously paired with a noxious unconditional stimulus (e.g., shock) or not. The researchers hypothesize that both cognitive biases and fear-potentiated startle will be correlated with the severity of self- and informant-reported internalizing problems.

Provisional status. At best, RDoC can be considered a research approach that is "under construction." It is explicitly not intended for *clinical* assessment purposes at present. Instead, the RDoC matrix currently is designed to guide psychopathology research, which may eventually yield insights that will transform existing nosologies. Thus, RDoC paves the way for basic research – possibly for decades – that ideally will have long-term applied payoff for assessment practice.

Innovation. RDoC departs from traditional diagnosis by adopting a *dimensional* approach. The project aims to understand biological and behavioral processes relevant to mental health along the complete spectrum of normality through pathology. For instance, in the hypothetical study on threat reactivity, researchers would be concerned with examining the entire range of responsiveness to potential danger, including hyper-reactivity (e.g., exaggerated startle eyeblink to a fear-inducing stimulus), healthy reactions (i.e., adaptive defensive responding that undoubtedly has been conserved through the course of human evolution), and *hypo*-reactivity to threat that characterizes imperturbable groups of people ranging from emergency-room doctors to psychopaths.

Another potential, albeit very speculative, advancement inherent in RDoC is minimizing the potential for *noncredible responding*. Traditional assessment measures are open to bias from inconsistent, careless, or misleading reports of symptom information. Because many DSM and ICD diagnostic criteria reflect internal processes, assessment routinely relies on patients' introspection. However, patients arguably are not always the best source of information. Sometimes as a feature of their psychopathology, they deliberately or unwittingly offer inaccurate responses. Malingering, whereby patients intentionally mislead the assessor for secondary gain, is a prominent instance of such misreporting. These problems could be addressed by securing collateral reports from an informant and relying on validity scales to assist in interpreting assessment responses (e.g., those that detect response inconsistency, nay-saying, and excessively socially desirable responses). RDoC takes a different approach to noncredible responding by emphasizing objective tests (e.g., genomic analysis, hormone assays), which generally run a lower risk of falsification, relative to self-report. Although the psychometric properties of many of these tests have yet to be firmly established, they could in the near-term usefully complement traditional assessment practices. It remains to be seen, though, how assessors would manage a situation in which self-reports and lab test results conflict or point to different diagnosis or treatment decisions.

Practical assessment implications. It remains unclear how or when (or if) the RDoC approach will make its way into routine practice. Clinical application is not among the priorities of the RDoC initiative at present. We speculate that the assessment process would rely largely on genetic, neurobiological, and peripheral psychophysiological data in connection with self-reported subjective states. Also, any subjective phenomena or outward symptoms that are queried will probably be those that are empirically related to presumed biological mechanisms of disorder etiology, as opposed to the rationally derived syndromes that populate DSM/ICD.

It seems safe to say that, under the RDoC framework, any assessment process would be dominated by putatively objective biological and behavioral measurements. RDoC emphasizes these types of observations because they are supposedly proximal to the neural circuitry that forms the crux of the RDoC matrix. This observation raises the question of how accessible and familiar these assessment procedures will be to frontline practitioners. Most clinical assessors receive little training in the methodologies (e.g., neuroimaging) that have been the bread and butter of RDoC studies thus far.

We reiterate that RDoC is not ready for clinical implementation; and it is unlikely that RDoC-based assessment would appreciably improve prediction of clinical outcomes (e.g., treatment success, suicide risk), because the effect sizes associated with many biobehavioral phenotypes emphasized in RDoC are comparatively very small. Therefore, for the foreseeable future, we believe that diagnosis and clinical decisions will be most guided effectively by traditional assessment of observable signs and subjective symptoms of mental illness.

Hierarchical Taxonomy of Psychopathology

Motivation. Like RDoC, HiTOP is a reaction to inherent limitations of categorical diagnostic rubrics. Its guiding principle is that categories are not the optimal way to represent and organize mental illness, judging by diagnostic heterogeneity, comorbidity, unreliability, and other known problems with DSM and ICD. Instead, HiTOP advocates a nosology based on empirical patterns of covariation among the signs and symptoms of psychopathology. These observed associations are thought to reflect the true structure of mental illness more accurately and to allow researchers to "carve nature at its joints."

The drive toward a quantitative-empirical classification system follows from the desire not only to represent the natural structure of mental illness more accurately but also to build an optimally evidence-based nosology. In the early stages of DSM and ICD development, the lines between different conditions and those separating health from illness were drawn mostly on the basis of clinical heuristics. A *New Yorker* magazine profile of Robert Spitzer, the psychiatrist who shepherded DSM-III development, described how Spitzer formulated some DSM criterion sets in an office alone with his typewriter (Spiegel, 2005). Of course, in more recent revisions to DSM, research evidence played a much larger role but expert opinion was often unavoidably the largest reason for change (or inaction). Moreover, the bar for change was set much higher than that for the original inclusion of criteria or diagnoses, making it very difficult to expunge even highly problematic diagnoses. HiTOP proponents argue that using quantitative data as the deciding factor will lead to a more accurate, scientific nosology and, in turn, more effective assessment.

An international team of researchers has come together to develop HiTOP. In the past few years, the consortium has published multiple papers that describe the current HiTOP structure and potential utility (e.g., Kotov et al., 2017; Krueger et al., 2018). Its ultimate goal is to translate existing (and future) research on the architecture of mental illness into a quantitative nosology that can optimize research, assessment, and treatment activities.

Structure. The origins of the HiTOP model can be traced back decades to early factor analyses of youth psychopathology symptoms. This seminal research showed that diverse anxiety, depressive, and somatic features clustered together empirically to form a coherent "internalizing" dimension, whereas disruptive and delinquent behaviors coalesced into an "externalizing" dimension (e.g., Achenbach, 1966). These psychometric results were hugely influential on the subsequent course of developmental psychopathology research and they formed the basis for popular youth assessment tools.

Following this example, a series of studies beginning in the late 1990s recovered the same two dimensions in factor analyses of psychological disorders in nationally representative samples of adults (Krueger, 1999; Krueger et al., 1998). These findings galvanized a new era of research into the patterning of mental illness comorbidity and the internalizing and externalizing factors were replicated consistently in diverse international datasets spanning countries, developmental stages, and assessment instruments (Rodriguez-Seijas et al., 2015). Internalizing and externalizing dimensions thus formed the anchors of the HiTOP system but more recent research has articulated the psychopathology "factor space" in more detail, establishing constructs that explain – at various levels of resolution – a progressively wider array of psychopathology symptoms.

A key property of these factor-analytic findings is the hierarchical organization of the resulting structural model of psychopathology. The HiTOP hierarchy currently has five levels. It combines symptoms, signs, and maladaptive behaviors into tight-knit *symptom-sign components* (e.g., aggression) and maladaptive traits (e.g., dishonesty). These, in turn, are combined with closely related components/traits into dimensional *syndromes*, such as conduct problems. Similar syndromes are combined into *subfactors*, such as antisocial behavior that includes inattention, hyperactivity, oppositionality, antisocial personality, and conduct problems. Larger constellations of syndromes form broad *spectra*, such as a disinhibited externalizing dimension that consists of antisocial behavior and substance abuse. Finally, spectra may be aggregated into a general factor of psychopathology that reflects characteristics shared by all mental disorders.

Dimensions. The term taxonomy (the *T* in HiTOP) is actually a misnomer because the HiTOP model at present *features no taxa*. Instead, quantitative analyses of the latent structure of virtually all mental health problems examined to date indicate that psychopathology is best understood dimensionally. Taxometric research has produced little to no evidence of discrete natural kinds and there is weak evidence for the discriminant validity of DSM and ICD conditions (Markon, Chmielewski, & Miller, 2011). As a data-driven system, however, HiTOP would be expected to incorporate categories if evidence consistently pointed to the existence of latent psychopathology classes.

Dimensional constructs confer many nosological advantages. First, psychopathology variables are assessed much more reliably continuously than discretely (Markon et al., 2011). Relatedly, categorizing a continuous construct discards information, whereas dimensions permit discrimination at all levels of their underlying distributions. Further, when cut points along a distribution must be imposed for categorical decision-making purposes (e.g., to treat, hospitalize, or follow up), they can be established on the basis of empirical evidence versus arbitrary conventions. Both general medicine and psychology have long categorized dimensions, creating accepted thresholds for blood pressure, body mass index, and IQ selected using population norms.

Hierarchy. Compared to the other classifications reviewed here, HiTOP is much more explicitly hierarchical. Kotov and colleagues (2017, fig. 1) illustrate that the model includes narrow, homogeneous constructs near the bottom and broad, heterogeneous constructs near the top. This structure is analogous to the architecture of personality and intelligence domains, which were also explicated over decades of factor-analytic research. For instance, personality is considered a multilevel system with overarching dimensions at the apex and fine-grained nuances at the base. Although it is most often examined at the five-factor model level, these well-known traits (Neuroticism,

Extraversion, Conscientiousness, Agreeableness, Openness to experience) represent a more differentiated version of the Big Three, which in turn reflect higher order factors originally termed simply alpha and beta (Digman, 1990) but more recently conceptualized as stability and plasticity dimensions (DeYoung, Peterson, & Higgins, 2002).

In a hierarchical structure, psychopathology can be flexibly conceptualized at varying levels of resolution, responsive to the assessment context. When an in-depth profile is needed for treatment planning, assessment might target symptom-sign components and maladaptive traits. On the other hand, if the objective is an expedient risk assessment for the development or progression of mental illness more generally, the spectrum level is a more likely target. When time is limited, computerized adaptive testing may also help to establish which broad spectra are most problematic and direct the assessment efficiently toward the salient subfactors, syndromes, and symptom/sign components within those areas.

Utility. HiTOP promises to make assessment and treatment more effective and functional. Emerging data suggest that psychiatrists base medication prescriptions more on dimensional constructs (e.g., performance anxiety) than categorical diagnoses (e.g., social phobia; Waszczuk et al., 2017). This study showed that two people with the same diagnosis are often prescribed different medication because of divergent lower order symptoms. For instance, those with major depression marked by agitation were more likely to be prescribed neuroleptics, whereas those with prominent insomnia were prescribed hypnotics. Other research in a nationally representative sample indicates that patients themselves select into treatment largely on the basis of internalizing and externalizing spectrum levels, rather than the specific syndromes that compose them (Rodriguez-Seijas et al., 2017).

New psychological treatments *designed* to act on transdiagnostic processes are gaining momentum (Hopwood, 2018). These interventions are based on the observation that syndromes that are normally targeted individually in routine practice (e.g., depression, social phobia) have significant overlap in terms of pathology, as reflected in higher order dimensions (e.g., internalizing). The rationale behind transdiagnostic treatment strategies is that addressing mental illness at the level of higher order dimensions can remediate multiple syndrome–level constructs simultaneously. This theory implies a much more efficient treatment dissemination process; instead of training practitioners in many individual treatment approaches tailored to specific syndromes, training on the transdiagnostic treatment would suffice for addressing many different presenting problems.

Currently the most widely used of these transdiagnostic treatments is the Unified Protocol for Transdiagnostic Treatment of Emotional Disorders (Barlow et al., 2014). Based on the extensive comorbidity among anxiety, depressive, and related disorders, the Unified Protocol intervenes on the internalizing spectrum, targeting cognitive and behavioral processes thought to underlie all subfactors and syndromes in this domain (e.g., behavioral avoidance, risk misperception). The most recent randomized control trial compared the Unified Protocol to established cognitive behavioral therapy manuals *tailored to the primary diagnosis* (e.g., generalized anxiety disorder, dysthymia) of patients presenting to an anxiety disorder treatment center (Barlow et al., 2017). Results suggested that the Unified Protocol worked just as well as disorder-specific treatments at reducing anxiety and depressive symptoms over a six-month follow-up. This finding indicates that considering HiTOP dimensions in treatment planning could lead to more efficient and easily disseminated intervention approaches.

Prognosis is another key function of diagnosis and there is evidence that the HiTOP approach has added value, relative to categorical disorders, for forecasting important clinical outcomes. First, the temporal stability of HiTOP spectra appears to explain the continuity of DSM diagnoses over time (Kessler, Petukhova, & Zaslavsky, 2011). In other words, the majority of variation in new onsets and recurrences of categorical entities is attributable to more stable individual differences on spectra like internalizing and disinhibited externalizing. Second, other research suggests that higher order HiTOP constructs can enhance detection of suicide potential. Specifically, HiTOP's distress subfactor of internalizing explained ~34 percent of the variation in suicide attempt history in an epidemiological study, whereas diagnoses accounted for at most 1 percent (Eaton et al., 2013). Third, dimensional constructs are superior predictors of psychosocial impairment (e.g., occupational trouble, romantic problems), which simultaneously represents a major cost of mental illness and a barrier to recovery (e.g., Markon, 2010). In a ten-year longitudinal study of personality pathology, a dimensional assessment of maladaptive personality (Clark, 2014) at baseline surpassed DSM PD categories in predicting multiple long-term outcomes, including various types of functioning, Axis I psychopathology, and medication use (Morey et al., 2012).

Practical assessment implications. In contrast to RDoC, HiTOP is poised, if not yet fully prepared, for clinical implementation. Various assessment instruments allow practitioners to measure HiTOP model dimensions (Kotov et al., 2017). For example, the Externalizing Spectrum Inventory and Inventory of Depression and Anxiety Symptoms are two broad-bandwidth dimensional measures of the clinical problems comprising most common anxiety, depressive, somatic symptom, conduct, antisocial, and substance use disorders in DSM (Krueger et al., 2007; Watson et al., 2012). These measures were factor analytically derived to include various lower order dimensions of mental illness that account for the heterogeneity of categorical mental illnesses and they also include broader dimensions (e.g., dysphoria, disinhibition) that capture the overarching features of collections of disorders. They improve on traditional self-report and interview-based instruments for these clinical disorders by explicitly parsing the lower order components of diagnoses that contribute to diagnostic heterogeneity and the higher order components that account for comorbidity across diagnoses.

Some HiTOP spectra, such as Antagonistic Externalizing and Detachment, are closely connected with PD constructs from traditional nosologies. There are several assessment measures of the PD domain that also tap the maladaptive traits that constitute higher order HiTOP dimensions. The Personality Inventory for DSM-5 (PID-5; Krueger et al., 2012) has twenty-five facets (e.g., callousness, withdrawal) that coalesce around five broader trait domains (i.e., negative affectivity, detachment, antagonism, disinhibition, and psychoticism). The PID-5 has generated a great deal of research into novel dimensional models of PD and psychopathology writ large. Short and informant versions of the PID-5 are also available.

The Schedule for Nonadaptive and Adaptive Personality – Second Edition (SNAP-2; Clark et al., 2014) is another measure of PD space with outstanding psychometric properties. The SNAP is composed of twelve specific traits (e.g., mistrust, exhibitionism) and three higher order temperament dimensions (i.e., negative temperament, positive temperament, disinhibition) that form the scaffolding for personality pathology. SNAP scales demonstrate excellent internal consistency, appropriate discriminant validity, reasonable temporal stability, and good predictive power for important clinical outcomes (e.g., treatment effectiveness, suicide; Morey et al., 2012; Vittengl et al., 2013).

We await normative data for some of these HiTOP-informed assessment instruments and efforts to collect such normative samples would surely accelerate the uptake of these measures in routine practice. There are published norms for the SNAP (Clark et al., 2014) and IDAS-II (Nelson, O'Hara, & Watson, 2018). Meanwhile, comparison data from large samples of university students and prisoners exist for the ESI brief version (Patrick et al., 2013) and descriptive data have been reported across diverse samples for the PID-5 (Krueger et al., 2012), although norms per se have not yet been established.

Perhaps the greatest obstacle holding HiTOP back from everyday use, though, is the absence of a comprehensive assessment instrument for the full model. That is a current priority of the HiTOP consortium and a self-report scale development process is now underway. Eventually, interview and clinician rating measures also will need to be developed to accommodate the needs of various assessment settings.

Case illustration. Here we present a hypothetical patient who might have been recruited to the RDoC project on mood dysregulation described in the "Recent Developments in Nosology" section. Our patient is a thirty-five-year-old woman who presents to outpatient care complaining of feeling panicky in social situations, worrying constantly regarding her health and that of her three-year-old son, and a pervasive sense of fatigue that has caused her to withdraw from most social activity. Traditionally, based on these intake data, her clinician probably would consider a range of diagnoses across DSM-5 anxiety, depressive, and somatic symptom and related disorders sections. In this case, the clinician uses the SCID to assign diagnoses of panic disorder, recurrent major depressive disorder, and illness anxiety disorder.

HiTOP-guided assessment would follow a different course. The clinician first would screen for clinical problems across all six spectra. Elevations would signal the clinician to delve deeper into that area of the hierarchy to identify problems with more precision. In our case, we would expect spikes, relative to norms, on the somatoform, internalizing, and detachment spectra. Time permitting, the clinician would next assess lower order HiTOP constructs with interviews or self-report measures. The Interview for Mood and Anxiety Symptoms (IMAS) might be administered to examine the symptom components underpinning the internalizing spectrum (Kotov et al., 2015). Other measures might evaluate the lower levels of somatoform and detachment problems. Here, the clinician might compare IMAS results to relevant clinical norms and discover elevations on dysphoria, anhedonia, lassitude, physical panic, interactive social anxiety, and irritability dimensions.

This profile of internalizing problems could be used to communicate to the patient the nature of her problems and prognosis and guide treatment selection. Dimensional measures can be administered periodically over the course of treatment to judge progress and watch for other symptom domains that might affect treatment effectiveness or psychosocial functioning. The HiTOP consortium maintains a website that provides an evolving list of factor analytically derived measures, such as the IMAS, for various domains of psychopathology.[4] Also, a more detailed presentation of the clinical application of HiTOP in assessment and treatment settings can be found in Ruggero et al. (2018).

Provisional status. HiTOP is a work in progress. It builds on decades of factor analyses of disorder signs and symptoms and there is a solid evidence base for many model components, such as the internalizing spectrum. However, there are uncertainties about other aspects, including the validity of the *p*-factor and the optimal location of several lower order components (e.g., mania). Also, a comparatively small – but growing – research literature has examined the validity and utility of lower order dimensions. We previously mentioned the need for a comprehensive measurement instrument.

[4] HiTOP measures can be found at the following website: https://psychology.unt.edu/hitop

This unified assessment system ideally will also address noncredible responding. This issue has not been a central consideration to date in model development, although investigators recognize that biased response patterns will likely distort the observed clustering of psychopathology signs and symptoms. For instance, an alternative, albeit unlikely, explanation for the *p*-factor is high rates of yea-saying, or inappropriately endorsing all (or many) clinical problems (Lahey et al., 2017). Currently, HiTOP-informed assessment can catch many types of noncredible responding via validity indices in component measures of the HiTOP system, such as the Schedule for Nonadaptive and Adaptive Personality (Clark, 2014) and the Personality Inventory for DSM-5 (Krueger et al., 2012; for sample validity indices, see Keeley et al., 2016; Sellbom, Dhillon, & Bagby, 2018).

SUMMARY AND CONCLUSIONS

In this chapter, we reviewed four systems for understanding and classifying psychopathology. Two are prevailing approaches familiar to health professionals around the world, whereas two are evolving models now gaining purchase in research and clinical settings. No two systems have exactly the same objectives or serve the same audiences (Clark et al., 2017) and they all have different implications for clinical assessment.

Today the DSM and ICD represent the status quo. They are a part of graduate training for almost all mental health professionals and they set the agenda for most diagnostic evaluations. Their widespread use will make them difficult to unseat. Nevertheless, momentum is building for new approaches that overcome critical limitations of categorical diagnostic systems. In particular, diagnostic heterogeneity, comorbidity, and unreliability constrain the utility of DSM and ICD. More evidence pours in every month for the scientific superiority of a dimensional perspective.

Two new contenders – RDoC and HiTOP – both seek a nosology oriented around dimensions of mental illness. RDoC is fundamentally an experimental research program intended to discover the key biological and behavioral mechanisms at the root of psychopathology. But it does not claim to have any applied benefit for clinical assessment per se *right now*. HiTOP, on the other hand, synthesizes decades of research on the structure of clinical problems to create a multilevel model that can guide ongoing research, assessment, and treatment.

In the coming years, we will see whether either of these systems is ready for clinical use. Each has a claim to superior validity over DSM and ICD but the priority in most clinical settings is *utility*, including familiarity, feasibility, and ease of use. Categories have been the dominant paradigm in health settings for more than a century and clinical stakeholders – and the professional organizations that represent them – will need to perceive significant benefits in new nosologies before they are widely adopted. We look forward to future nosological research that paves the way toward diagnostic systems that optimally meet patients' mental health needs.

REFERENCES

Achenbach, T. M. (1966). The classification of children's psychiatric symptoms: A factor-analytic study. *Psychological Monographs: General and Applied*, *80*, 1–37.

American Psychiatric Association. (1952). *Diagnostic and statistical manual of mental disorders*. Washington, DC: Author.

American Psychiatric Association. (1968). *Diagnostic and statistical manual of mental disorders* (2nd ed.). Washington, DC: Author.

American Psychiatric Association. (1980). *Diagnostic and statistical manual of mental disorders* (3rd ed.). Washington, DC: Author.

American Psychiatric Association. (1987). *Diagnostic and statistical manual of mental disorders* (rev. 3rd ed.). Washington, DC: Author.

American Psychiatric Association. (1994). *Diagnostic and statistical manual of mental disorders* (4th ed.). Washington, DC: Author.

American Psychiatric Association. (2000). *Diagnostic and statistical manual of mental disorders* (rev. 4th ed.). Washington, DC: Author.

American Psychiatric Association. (2013). *Diagnostic and statistical manual of mental disorders* (5th ed.). Washington, DC: Author.

Andrews, G., Goldberg, D. P., Krueger, R. F., Carpenter, W. T., Hyman, S. E., Sachdev, P., & Pine, D. S. (2009). Exploring the feasibility of a meta-structure for DSM-V and ICD-11: Could it improve utility and validity? *Psychological Medicine*, *39*, 1993–2000.

Barlow, D. H., Farchione, T. J., Bullis, J. R., Gallagher, M. W., ... & Cassiello-Robbins, C. (2017). The Unified Protocol for Transdiagnostic Treatment of Emotional Disorders compared with diagnosis-specific protocols for anxiety disorders: A randomized clinical trial. *JAMA Psychiatry*, *74*, 875–884.

Barlow, D. H., Sauer-Zavala, S., Carl, J. R., Bullis, J. R., & Ellard, K. K. (2014). The nature, diagnosis, and treatment of neuroticism: Back to the future. *Clinical Psychological Science*, *2*, 344–365.

Brown, T. A., Campbell, L. A., Lehman, C. L., Grisham, J. R., & Mancill, R. B. (2001). Current and lifetime comorbidity of the DSM-IV anxiety and mood disorders in a large clinical sample. *Journal of Abnormal Psychology*, *110*, 585–599.

Clark, L. A. (2014). *Schedule for Nonadaptive and Adaptive Personality, Second Edition (SNAP-2)*. Notre Dame, IN: University of Notre Dame.

Clark, L. A., Cuthbert, B., Lewis-Fernández, R., Narrow, W. E., & Reed, G. M. (2017). Three approaches to understanding and classifying mental disorder: ICD-11, DSM-5, and the National Institute of Mental Health's Research Domain Criteria (RDoC). *Psychological Science in the Public Interest*, *18*, 72–145.

Clark, L. A., Simms, L. J., Wu, K. D., & Casillas, A. (2014). *Schedule for Nonadaptive and Adaptive Personality – Second Edition*. Notre Dame, IN: University of Notre Dame.

Cuthbert, B. N., & Insel, T. R. (2013). Toward the future of psychiatric diagnosis: The seven pillars of RDoC. *BMC Medicine*, *11*, 126–134.

DeYoung, C. G., Peterson, J. B., & Higgins, D. M. (2002). Higher-order factors of the big five predict conformity: Are there neuroses of health? *Personality and Individual Differences*, *33*(4), 533–552.

Digman, J. M. (1990). Personality structure: Emergence of the five-factor model. *Annual Review of Psychology*, *41*, 417–440.

Eaton, N. R., Krueger, R. F., Markon, K. E., Keyes, K. M., Skodol, A. E., Wall, M., ... & Grant, B. F. (2013). The structure and predictive validity of the internalizing disorders. *Journal of Abnormal Psychology, 122,* 86–92.

First, M. B., Williams, J. B. W., Karg, R. S., & Spitzer, R. L. (2015). *Structured clinical interview for DSM-5 – Clinician version (SCID-5-CV).* Arlington, VA: American Psychiatric Association.

Hopwood, C. J. (2018). A framework for treating DSM-5 alternative model for personality disorder features. *Personality and Mental Health, 12,* 107–125.

Insel, T. R., & Cuthbert, B. N. (2015). Brain disorders? Precisely. *Science, 348,* 499–500.

Keeley, J. W., Webb, C., Peterson, D., Roussin, L., & Flanagan, E. H. (2016). Development of a response inconsistency scale for the personality inventory for DSM–5. *Journal of Personality Assessment, 98,* 351–359.

Kessler, R. C., McGonagle, K. A., Zhao, S., Nelson, C. B., Hughes, M., Eshleman, S., ... & Kendler, K. S. (1994). Lifetime and 12-month prevalence of DSM-III-R psychiatric disorders in the United States: Results from the national comorbidity study. *Archives of General Psychiatry, 51,* 8–19.

Kessler, R. C., Petukhova, M., & Zaslavsky, A. M. (2011). The role of latent internalizing and externalizing predispositions in accounting for the development of comorbidity among common mental disorders. *Current Opinion in Psychiatry, 24,* 307–312.

Kirschbaum, C., Pirke, K., & Hellhammer, D. H. (1993). The "trier social stress test": A tool for investigating psychobiological stress responses in a laboratory setting. *Neuropsychobiology, 28*(1–2), 76–81.

Kotov, R., Krueger, R. F., Watson, D., Achenbach, T. M., Althoff, R. R., Bagby, R. M., ... & Zimmerman, M. (2017). The Hierarchical Taxonomy of Psychopathology (HiTOP): A dimensional alternative to traditional nosologies. *Journal of Abnormal Psychology, 126,* 454–477.

Kotov, R., Perlman, G., Gámez, W., & Watson, D. (2015). The structure and short-term stability of the emotional disorders: A dimensional approach. *Psychological Medicine, 45*(8), 1687–1698.

Krueger, R. F. (1999). The structure of common mental disorders. *Archives of General Psychiatry, 56,* 921–926.

Krueger, R. F., Caspi, A., Moffitt, T. E., & Silva, P. A. (1998). The structure and stability of common mental disorders (DSM-III-R): A longitudinal-epidemiological study. *Journal of Abnormal Psychology, 107,* 216–227.

Krueger, R. F., Derringer, J., Markon, K. E., Watson, D., & Skodol, A. E. (2012). Initial construction of a maladaptive personality trait model and inventory for DSM-5. *Psychological Medicine, 42,* 1879–1890.

Krueger, R. F., Kotov, R., Watson, D., Forbes, M. K., Eaton, N. R., Ruggero, C. J., et al. (2018). Progress in achieving quantitative classification of psychopathology. *World Psychiatry, 17,* 282–293.

Krueger, R. F., Markon, K. E., Patrick, C. J., Benning, S. D., & Kramer, M. D. (2007). Linking antisocial behavior, substance use, and personality: An integrative quantitative model of the adult externalizing spectrum. *Journal of Abnormal Psychology, 116,* 645–666.

Lahey, B. B., Krueger, R. F., Rathouz, P. J., Waldman, I. D., & Zald, D. H. (2017). A hierarchical causal taxonomy of psychopathology across the life span. *Psychological Bulletin, 143,* 142–186.

Loranger, A. W. (1999). *IPDE: International Personality Disorder Examination: DSM-IV and ICD-10 interviews.* Odessa, FL: Psychological Assessment Resources.

Markon, K. E. (2010). Modeling psychopathology structure: A symptom-level analysis of Axis I and II disorders. *Psychological Medicine, 40,* 273–288.

Markon, K. E., Chmielewski, M., & Miller, C. J. (2011). The reliability and validity of discrete and continuous measures of psychopathology: a quantitative review. *Psychological Bulletin, 137,* 856–877.

Morey, L. C., Hopwood, C. J., Markowitz, J. C., Gunderson, J. G., Grilo, C. M., McGlashan, T. H., ... & Skodol, A. E. (2012). Comparison of alternative models for personality disorders, II: 6-, 8- and 10-year follow-up. *Psychological Medicine, 42,* 1705–1713.

Narrow, W. E., Clarke, D. E., Kuramoto, S. J., Kraemer, H. C., Kupfer, D. J., Greiner, L., & Regier, D. A. (2013). DSM-5 field trials in the United States and Canada, Part III: Development and reliability testing of a cross-cutting symptom assessment for DSM-5. *American Journal of Psychiatry, 170,* 71–82.

Nelson, G. H., O'Hara, M. W., & Watson, D. (2018). National norms for the Expanded Version of the Inventory of Depression and Anxiety Symptoms (IDAS-II). *Journal of Clinical Psychology, 74,* 953–968.

Patrick, C. J., Kramer, M. D., Krueger, R. F., & Markon, K. E. (2013). Optimizing efficiency of psychopathology assessment through quantitative modeling: Development of a brief form of the Externalizing Spectrum Inventory. *Psychological Assessment, 25,* 1332–1348.

Regier, D. A., Narrow, W. E., Clarke, D. E., Kraemer, H. C., Kuramoto, S. J., Kuhl, E. A., & Kupfer, D. J. (2013). DSM-5 field trials in the United States and Canada, Part II: Test-retest reliability of selected categorical diagnoses. *American Journal of Psychiatry, 170,* 59–70.

Rodriguez-Seijas, C., Eaton, N. R., Stohl, M., Mauro, P. M., & Hasin, D. S. (2017). Mental disorder comorbidity and treatment utilization. *Comprehensive Psychiatry, 79,* 89–97.

Rodriguez-Seijas, C., Stohl, M., Hasin, D. S., & Eaton, N. R. (2015). Transdiagnostic factors and mediation of the relationship between perceived racial discrimination and mental disorders. *Journal of the American Medical Association Psychiatry, 72,* 706–713.

Ruggero, C. (2018). Integrating a dimensional, hierarchical taxonomy of psychopathology into clinical practice, PsyArXiv Preprints, August 18. psyarxiv.com/r2jt6

Sellbom, M., Dhillon, S., & Bagby, R. M. (2018). Development and validation of an overreporting scale for the personality inventory for DSM–5 (PID-5). *Psychological Assessment, 30*(5), 582–593.

Spiegel, A. (2005). The dictionary of disorder. *New Yorker, 80,* 56–63.

Tyrer, P., Reed, G. M., & Crawford, M. J. (2015). Classification, assessment, prevalence and effect of personality disorder. *Lancet, 385,* 717–726.

Waszczuk, M. A., Zimmerman, M., Ruggero, C., Li, K., MacNamara, A., Weinberg, A., ... & Kotov, R. (2017). What do clinicians treat: Diagnoses or symptoms? The incremental validity of a symptom-based, dimensional characterization of emotional disorders in predicting medication prescription patterns. *Comprehensive Psychiatry, 79,* 80–88.

Watson, D., O'Hara, M. W., Naragon-Gainey, K., Koffel, E., Chmielewski, M., Kotov, R., ... Ruggero, C. J. (2012). Development and validation of new anxiety and bipolar symptom scales for an expanded version of the IDAS (the IDAS-II). *Assessment*, *19*, 399–420.

Vittengl, J. R., Clark, L. A., Thase, M. E., & Jarrett, R. B. (2013). Nomothetic and idiographic symptom change trajectories in acute-phase cognitive therapy for recurrent depression. *Journal of Consulting and Clinical Psychology*, *81*, 615–626.

Wilk, J. E., West, J. C., Narrow, W. E., Marcus, S., Rubio-Stipec, M., Rae, D. D., ... & Regier, D. A. (2006). Comorbidity patterns in routine psychiatric practice: Is there evidence of under-detection and under-diagnosis? *Comprehensive Psychiatry*, *47*, 258–264.

6 Assessment of Noncredible Reporting and Responding

DUSTIN B. WYGANT, DANIELLE BURCHETT, AND JORDAN P. HARP

Mental health assessment is a complex endeavor that involves consideration of emotional/psychological, neurocognitive, and physical functioning. Each of these domains involves specific assessment techniques and approaches. For example, as internal experiences, psychological and emotional symptoms are often manifest through an individual's self-report or inferred from behavioral observations. Neurocognitive functioning, on the other hand, is often established through performance on various neuropsychological tests. Somatic and physical symptoms are often assessed via self-report and various medical examination procedures. Consequently, the assessment of response bias must incorporate various techniques and approaches to assess these different domains. In this chapter, we will review the assessment of noncredible reporting and responding across psychological, neurocognitive, and somatic/physical domains, emphasizing evidence-based approaches that integrate psychological testing and assessment data.

The importance of considering response bias in mental health assessment cannot be overstated. Given the frequency with which self-report methods (tests/surveys and clinical interviews) serve as the primary means of gathering clinical data, it is important for clinicians to understand the reasons and manner by which that data can be distorted. Indeed, research has shown that distorted responding can impact the validity of neurocognitive test scores (e.g., Green et al., 2001) and attenuate the psychometric properties of self-report measures (Burchett & Ben-Porath, 2010; Wiggins et al., 2012).

In this chapter, we will review the ways in which evaluations of psychopathology, neurocognitive symptoms, and medical/somatic presentations can be compromised due to noncredible responding and invalidating test-taking approaches. We will cover a variety of strategies and measures that have been developed to assess invalid responding. Further, we will discuss evaluation contexts in which invalid responding is most likely to occur. We will also conclude with some remarks regarding cultural considerations as well as how technology can be incorporated into the assessment of response bias.

Although noncredible reporting can occur in any evaluation for a variety of reasons that may be intentional or unintentional (e.g., carelessness, confusion, indecisiveness, distractibility, disengagement, tendency toward socially desirable or negativistic responding, desire to be taken seriously enough to receive psychological help; Graham, 2012; Jackson & Messick, 1958), it is especially likely in forensic settings, where evaluees (either criminal defendants or civil litigants) have an inherent motivation to misrepresent their functioning (e.g., evasion of criminal responsibility or awarding of disability). Symptom exaggeration is relatively common in pretrial evaluations of competency to stand trial and sanity at the time of an offense (Boccaccini, Murrie, & Duncan, 2006; Vitacco et al., 2007), worker's compensation (Bianchini, Curtis, & Greve, 2006), and determination of veterans' PTSD-related service connection disability (Frueh et al., 2000). In surveying a group of neuropsychologists, Mittenberg and colleagues (2002) estimated that symptom exaggeration or probable malingering occurs in 27–31 percent of civil cases and 11–21 percent of criminal cases. Intentional symptom exaggeration or fabrication may also occur when a client is seeking access to academic accommodations or stimulant or opioid medications (Alfano & Boone, 2007; Chang, Szczyglinski, & King, 2000). On the opposite side of response bias, symptom minimization may be likely in preemployment screening evaluations (Corey & Ben-Porath, 2018) and child custody evaluations (Ackerman & Ackerman, 1997; Arce et al., 2015; Bathurst, Gottfried, & Gottfried, 1997). Outside of forensic settings, clinicians must nevertheless be concerned about overly negativistic and distorted self-impressions, a point made by Morey (2007) and others (Hopwood et al., 2007) with respect to the Personality Assessment Inventory (PAI). This style of responding also has the potential to distort findings and limit their utility in treatment planning.

INVALIDATING TEST-TAKING APPROACHES

In addition to clinical interviews, psychological testing plays a significant role in the assessment process. Clinicians rely on psychological test results for a variety of reasons, such as clarifying diagnostic impressions and treatment needs, assessing suicidality and violence risk, informing the hiring process, and making recommendations in criminal and civil court proceedings, among others. In each of these contexts, evaluators integrate reliable and valid test instruments with interview information, behavioral observations, and collateral records in an effort to formulate accurate impressions regarding an examinee's psychopathology and neuropsychological functioning (Burchett & Bagby, 2014). In addition to selecting nomothetically sound measures, clinicians are tasked with the challenge of ascertaining whether evaluation data for individual examinees accurately reflects genuine functioning or, alternatively, whether the accuracy of assessment results has been unintentionally or intentionally compromised.

Ben-Porath (2013) discussed several threats to the validity of self-report instrument protocols, such as those often used to assess for psychopathology and personality dysfunction. *Noncontent-based invalid responding* occurs when an examinee does not engage with the meaning of items as they complete a measure. This responding could occur in the form of *nonresponding* (e.g., skipping items), *acquiescent responding* (i.e., responding in the affirmative to several items regardless of whether the statements accurately reflect their functioning), *counter-acquiescent responding* (i.e., responding in the negative to items even if the statements would accurately reflect their functioning), or *random responding*. Noncontent-based invalid responding has been linked to intellectual disability (Lewis & Morrissey, 2010), uncooperativeness (Gervais et al., 2018), language and reading comprehension problems (Himsl et al., 2017), cognitive effort, and sustained attention (Friedhoff et al., 2014) and can significantly distort scales designed to measure genuine psychopathology (Bagby & Sellbom, 2018; Dragon, Ben-Porath, & Handel, 2012; Handel et al., 2010; Keeley et al., 2016; Neo, Sellbom, & Wygant, in press), overreporting, and underreporting (Burchett et al., 2016).

Content-based invalid responding encompasses both *overreporting* and *underreporting* of symptoms. Overreporting, sometimes referred to as feigning, exaggerating, faking bad, or negative impression management, occurs when an individual fabricates or exaggerates psychological difficulties (Rogers, 2018a). Examinees may overreport symptoms of psychopathology, somatic complaints, and/or physical pain in combination or selectively (i.e., only cognitive problems) (Hoelzle, Nelson, & Arbisi, 2012; Rogers, 2018a). Underreporting, sometimes referred to as minimizing, faking good, defensiveness, or positive impression management, occurs when an individual denies or minimizes psychological symptoms they genuinely experience or exaggerate virtuous qualities. Overreporting and underreporting may significantly impact substantive scale interpretations and predictive utility (Anderson et al., 2013; Burchett & Ben-Porath, 2010; Crighton et al., 2017; Dhillon et al., 2017; Wiggins, et al., 2012).

As noted in the previous section, individuals may engage in intentional invalid responding (sometimes called feigning) or unintentional invalid responding (e.g., due to distractibility, reading problems, or low insight into their actual symptoms) – and, in most cases, indicators that detect invalid responding do not inform the evaluator about intentionality. Thus, extra-test, contextual information regarding motivational factors, discrepancies between reported and observed symptoms, and discrepancies with medical records is often needed to determine intentionality (Burchett & Bagby, 2014). A determination of intent is important to consider in the context of assessing the diagnostic classification of malingering since "the essential feature of malingering is the intentional production of false or grossly exaggerated physical or psychological symptoms, motivated by external incentives" (American Psychiatric Association, 2013, p. 726). Regardless of intentionality, indicators of response bias should be considered because of the significant impact that invalid responding has on test protocol accuracy and interpretation.

CULTURAL CONSIDERATIONS IN THE ASSESSMENT OF RESPONSE BIAS

Consistent with the broader field of psychological assessment, it is important for clinicians to consider the influence of cultural differences in response styles. This consideration should go beyond just examining potential group differences with respect to scores on response bias measures to examine whether these measures exhibit differential prediction of response bias criteria across individuals from different cultural groups.

Previous research indicates that differences exist across cultural groups related to extremity of responding, tendency to overreport or underreport physical health or psychological difficulties, and acquiescence level (Johnson et al., 2005; Jürges, 2007). Correa (2018) noted that there were several important issues that must be taken into consideration with respect to cultural issues in the assessment of response bias. These include language issues and the availability of properly translated measures, acculturation and culturally specific response styles (e.g., *machismo*), and diversity within a measure's norms.

DETECTING NONCREDIBLE RESPONDING ON PSYCHOPATHOLOGY MEASURES

The assessment of psychopathology relies heavily on an examinee's self-report of their internal experiences. Data from medical records, family members, and unstructured and structured interviews can provide important nuanced information about the scope and duration of symptoms. However, psychological tests are particularly effective for reliable and efficient measurement of the severity of a wide variety of symptoms in a manner that allows for comparisons of an examinee to normative and clinical samples. Further, some standardized psychopathology inventories offer streamlined methods for the evaluation of noncredible responding, as do stand-alone measures of invalid responding. Clinicians utilizing these measures should be familiar with how they were designed, as the methods used to develop them may impact their effectiveness. Moreover, clinicians should be aware of the various research methodologies used to evaluate the effectiveness of response bias indicators (see Rogers, 2018a).

With omnibus psychopathology measures, it is ideal to screen for nonresponding, random responding, and fixed responding before interpreting indicators of overreporting or underreporting, given the impact that noncontent-based responding can have on content-based validity scale scores (Burchett et al., 2016). Because nonresponding can deflate test scores on measures that do not involve imputed scores, such as the Minnesota Multiphasic Personality Inventory-2 (MMPI-2; Butcher et al., 2001) and PAI (Morey, 1991/2007), raw counts of unscorable items can alert examiners about potentially suppressed test protocols (Dragon et al., 2012). Creative strategies utilizing item pairs have been used to detect fixed inconsistent (e.g., endorsement of two conceptually opposite items in the same direction) and random (e.g., endorsement of two conceptually consistent items in the opposite direction) responding (Ben-Porath & Tellegen, 2008).

Rogers (2018a) described several detection strategies that have been used to develop indicators of overreported psychopathology in measures embedded in omnibus instruments as well as on stand-alone overreporting measures. Most of these detection strategies are premised on the notion that feigning individuals typically lack nuanced knowledge about psychopathology. Some scales are developed by selecting items with *quasi-rare* (infrequently endorsed in normative samples) or *rare* (infrequently endorsed in patient samples) frequencies. Some include *improbable symptoms* items – those that are so implausible that a genuine respondent would be unlikely to report experiencing them. The *symptom combinations* method involves two symptoms that are individually common but that rarely occur together. *Symptom severity* methods allow responders to record the severity of symptoms with the idea that individuals who endorse a high number as severe may be overreporting. The *indiscriminant symptom endorsement* method assumes that malingerers are likely to endorse a larger quantity of symptoms across many domains of psychopathology, compared to genuine patients. Other scales consist of items that clearly distinguish between valid and invalid criterion groups. The *obvious symptoms* approach involves face-valid symptom items and is premised on the notion that feigning individuals are more likely to endorse obvious symptoms but miss endorsing subtle symptoms. The *erroneous stereotypes* method utilizes items that many people might assume are characteristic of genuine psychopathology but that are not actually common symptoms. *Composite indexes*, which utilize tallies of profile characteristics rather than raw scores, have also been developed to distinguish valid and invalid groups (Burchett & Bagby, 2014; Rogers, 2018a).

Rogers (2018a) also described methods that have been used to capture underreporting. For instance, the *denial of psychopathology or patient characteristics* method includes items that distinguish between normative samples and known patients who score within normal limits (i.e., those believed to be underreporting their symptoms). The *spurious patterns of simulated adjustment* method utilizes configurations of scales that are common in defensive patients but less common in clinical or nonclinical samples. The *denial of minor flaws or personal faults* strategy involves items about minor foibles most people would admit are true for them, such that someone who admits to very few may be presenting themselves in an especially favorable light (Graham, 2012). Similarly, the *social desirability* method focuses on items related to the presentation of a highly favorable image. Some scales utilize a *blended affirmation of virtuous behavior and denial of personal faults* strategy that includes both types of items on the same measure (Rogers, 2018a).

Embedded measures. Several multiscale self-report personality and psychopathology measures included embedded validity indicators – some of which are broadly designed to detect symptom exaggeration and others that more specifically focus on a particular domain, such as exaggeration of psychopathology, somatic complaints, or cognitive difficulties (see Table 6.1). Some of the most common include the Minnesota Multiphasic Personality Inventory-2 (MMPI-2; Butcher et al., 2001), MMPI-2 Restructured Form (MMPI-2-RF; Ben-Porath & Tellegen, 2008), PAI (Morey, 1991/2007), and Millon Clinical Multiaxial Personality Inventory-IV (MCMI-IV; Millon, Grossman, & Millon, 2015) (Bow, Flens, & Gould, 2010; Camara, Nathan, & Puente, 2000; Stedman, McGeary, & Essery, 2017). Most brief symptom measures (e.g., Beck Depression Inventory-II; Beck, 1996) do not include measures of invalid responding. One exception is the Trauma Symptom Inventory-II (TSI-2; Briere, 2010), which includes the Atypical Responses scale. However, there is not much empirical support for the TSI-2 in detecting invalid responding at this time.

MMPI-2/MMPI-2-RF. Both the 567-item MMPI-2 (Butcher et al., 2001) and the 338-item Restructured Form (MMPI-2-RF; Ben-Porath & Tellegen, 2008/2011) include a comprehensive set of validity scales. Most of the MMPI-2-RF Validity Scales are revised versions of their MMPI-2 counterparts (for a review of the revision process, see Ben-Porath, 2012). Both assess noncontent-based invalid responding with Cannot Say (CNS), a raw count of skipped or double-marked items. Variable and fixed responding are measured with Variable Response Inconsistency (VRIN/VRIN-r) and True Response Inconsistency (TRIN/TRIN-r), respectively. Overreporting is measured in both measures with several scales. The MMPI-2 includes the Infrequency (F) and Back Infrequency (F_B) scales, while the MMPI-2-RF includes Infrequent Responses (F-r),

Table 6.1 Common indicators of noncredible responding based on self-report

	Noncontent-Based Invalid Responding			Overreporting			Underreporting	
	Nonresponding	Random Responding	Fixed Responding	Psychopathology	Cognitive Complaints	Somatic Complaints	Denial of Psychopathology	Exaggeration of Virtues
Minnesota Multiphasic Personality Inventory-2 (MMPI-2)								
Cannot Say (CNS)	X							
Variable Response Inconsistency (VRIN)		X						
True Response Inconsistency (TRIN)			X					
Infrequency (F)				X				
Back Infrequency (F_B)				X				
Infrequency Psychopathology (F_P)				X				
Symptom Validity (FBS)					X	X		
Lie (L)								X
Correction (K)							X	
Superlative Self-Presentation (S)							X	X
MMPI-2 Restructured Form (MMPI-2-RF)								
Cannot Say (CNS)	X							
Variable Response Inconsistency (VRIN-r)		X						
True Response Inconsistency (TRIN-r)			X					
Infrequent Responses (F-r)				X				
Infrequent Psychopathology Responses (Fp-r)				X				
Infrequent Somatic Responses (Fs)						X		
Symptom Validity (FBS-r)					X	X		
Response Bias (RBS)					X			
Uncommon Virtues (L-r)								X
Adjustment Validity (K-r)							X	
Personality Assessment Inventory (PAI)								
Missing items	X							
Inconsistency (ICN)		X						
Infrequency (INF)		X						
Negative Impression Management (NIM)				X				
Malingering Index (MAL)				X				
Rogers Discriminant Function (RDF)				X				
Malingered Pain-Related Disability-Discriminant Function (MPRDF)						X		
Positive Impression Management (PIM)								X
Defensiveness Index (DEF)							X	X
Cashel Discriminant Function (CDF)							X	X

Continued

Millon Clinical Multiaxial Inventory-IV (MCMI-IV)					
Invalidity (V)	X				
Inconsistency (W)	X				
Disclosure (X)		X		X (low scores)	X (low scores)
Desirability (Y)				X	X
Debasement (Z)		X			
Structured Interview of Reported Symptoms (SIRS-2)					
Rare Symptoms (RS)		X			
Symptom Combinations (SC)		X			
Improbable or Absurd Symptoms (IA)		X			
Blatant Symptoms (BL)		X			
Subtle Symptoms (SU)		X			
Selectivity of Symptoms (SEL)		X			
Severity of Symptoms (SEV)		X			
Reported versus Observed Symptoms (RO)		X			
Direct Appraisal of Honesty (DA)		X			
Defensive Symptoms (DS)					X
Overly Specified Symptoms (OS)		X			
Improbable Failure (IF)			X		
Inconsistency of Symptoms (INC)	X				
Rare Symptom (RS) Total		X			
Modified Total (MT) Index		X			
Supplementary Scale (SS) Index		X			
Structured Inventory of Malingered Symptomatology (SIMS)					
Psychosis (P)		X			
Neurological Impairment (N)			X		
Amnestic Disorders (Am)			X		
Low Intelligence (LI)			X		
Affective Disorders (Af)		X			
Miller Forensic Assessment of Symptoms Test (M-FAST)					
Reported versus Observed (RO)		X			
Extreme Symptomatology (ES)		X			
Rare Combinations (RC)		X			
Unusual Hallucinations (UH)		X			
Unusual Symptom Course (USC)		X			
Negative Image (NI)		X			
Suggestibility (S)		X			
Total Score		X			

which consist of items rarely endorsed in the MMPI-2/RF normative sample. Because these items are not always rare in psychiatric patients reporting genuine problems, Infrequency Psychopathology (F_P; Arbisi & Ben-Porath, 1995) was introduced (and slightly revised with the MMPI-2-RF Infrequent Psychopathology Responses [Fp-r]), using items rarely endorsed in inpatient settings, to more specifically measure exaggeration of psychopathology symptoms. Symptom Validity (FBS; Lees-Haley, English, & Glenn, 1991), developed using a rational item selection approach, is sensitive to somatic as well as cognitive symptom overreporting (see Ben-Porath, Graham, & Tellegen, 2009). A slightly revised version, FBS-r, was released for the MMPI-2-RF. New to the MMPI-2-RF are Infrequent Somatic Responses (Fs; Wygant, Ben-Porath, & Arbisi, 2004) and Response Bias Scale (RBS; Gervais et al., 2007). Fs consists of somatic items that are rarely endorsed in normative and medical samples whereas RBS consists of items that were found to distinguish between disability claimants who passed versus failed performance validity tests.

Both measures include underreporting scales that include Lie (MMPI-2 L) and Uncommon Virtues (MMPI-2-RF L-r), which was designed to identify individuals who deny minor flaws and report rare desirable qualities. Correction (MMPI-2 K) and Adjustment Validity (MMPI-2-RF K-r) are sensitive to underreporting of psychological symptoms. Finally, the MMPI-2 includes the Superlative Self-Presentation (S; Butcher & Han, 1995) scale that consists of items that distinguished between individuals in the normative sample and airline pilot applicants.

Graham (2012) and Wygant and colleagues (2018) provide thorough reviews of the rich literature for the MMPI-2 and MMPI-2-RF that has demonstrated the utility of these indicators in general clinical as well as forensic practice. Research has examined the utility of the MMPI-2-RF Validity Scales to screen for noncontent-based invalid responding (Burchett et al., 2016; Dragon et al., 2012; Handel et al., 2010) and to detect underreporting (Crighton et al., 2017; Sellbom & Bagby, 2008b). Despite positive findings, these are less well-studied than are the MMPI-2-RF's overreporting indices. Two recent meta-analyses have supported the utility of the MMPI-2-RF overreporting scales, with Fp-r demonstrating particular relative strengths across thirty studies. One limitation is that some scales (i.e., F-r, FBS-r, RBS) may be notably elevated in the presence of genuine depression or somatoform disorder. Further, FBS-r appears to behave as a general feigning indicator rather than one that is specific to cognitive symptom overreporting (see Ingram & Ternes, 2016; Sharf et al., 2017). A notable strength of the MMPI-2-RF is its inclusion of indices that screen for symptom exaggeration across psychopathology, cognitive, and somatic domains. In light of existing research, we find the MMPI-2-RF Validity Scales are particularly effective at screening for protocol invalidity and may be followed up with more thorough measures of symptom distortion, as needed.

With respect to cross-cultural research on the MMPI-2-RF Validity Scales, Glassmire, Jhawar, Burchett, and Tarescavage (2016) examined item frequencies of the Fp-r scale in a sample of forensic inpatients. They found that one of the twenty-one Fp-r items had an endorsement rate above 20 percent for African American and Hispanic/Latino patients, underscoring the need to consider cultural differences in interpreting Validity Scale results. Sanchez and colleagues (2017) utilized a sample of Spanish-speaking individuals who completed the MMPI-2 (from which the MMPI-2-RF Validity Scales were scored) and found that all five overreporting scales could discriminate between individuals drawn from the general population who completed the test under standard instructions from those instructed to feign psychopathology. F-r and Fp-r were effective at discriminating between the feigning group and a sample of psychiatric patients.

It should be noted that development of the MMPI-3 is currently underway. This updated version of the MMPI will include a new normative sample. The basic structure of the MMPI-3, including the Validity Scales will closely resemble the MMPI-2-RF.

PAI. The 344-item PAI (Morey, 1991/2007) includes eight validity indicators. Inconsistency (ICN) is designed to detect variable responding utilizing a paired-item approach whereas Infrequency (INF) is intended to detect careless responding with nonsymptom items that are too bizarre to be frequently endorsed by most people. Negative Impression Management (NIM) includes items capturing symptoms related to a variety of disorders or personal problems that are unrealistically severe. The Malingering Index (MAL) incorporates scores from eight PAI profile characteristics that are more likely to occur with overreporting versus honest responders. The Rogers Discriminant Function (RDF; Rogers et al., 1996) includes a weighted combination of twenty PAI scores that were found to distinguish between honest and feigning responders in simulation study. Positive Impression Management (PIM) includes favorable items that are infrequently endorsed by nonclinical and clinical samples. Similar to RDF, the Cashel Discriminant Function (CDF; Cashel et al., 1995) involves a weighted combination of indicators that were found to distinguish between honest and underreporting responders in a simulation study. The Defensiveness Index (DEF) is scored based on eight PAI profile characteristics that are more likely to occur with underreporters than with honest responders. The Negative Distortion Scale (NDS; Mogge et al., 2010) includes rarely endorsed symptoms and the Malingered Pain-Related Disability-Discriminant Function (MPRDF; Hopwood, Orlando, & Clark, 2010) was designed to distinguish between pain patients and coached pain-related disability overreporters.

Research demonstrates the utility of the PAI indicators of random or careless responding when using computer-generated data, although additional research is needed to examine the impact of response styles that involve endorsing more extreme versus more middle-road answers. The utility of PAI symptom overreporting indicators has also been well-studied, with most indices evidencing strong specificity with relatively weaker sensitivity; NIM and MAL exhibit the largest effects across studies. Studies of PAI underreporting indices suggest that PIM and DEF exhibit consistently large effects (Boccaccini & Hart, 2018). Hawes and Boccaccini (2009) conducted a meta-analysis of PAI overreporting indices, concluding the measures are more effective in classifying exaggeration of severe psychological impairment as compared to less severe impairment (e.g., mood or anxiety symptoms). In light of supportive research, the PAI Validity Scales should be considered effective for screening for protocol invalidity and may be followed up with more thorough measures of symptom distortion, as needed. Moreover, Fernandez and colleagues (2008) found similar performance for the PAI Validity Scales across the English and Spanish versions of the test.

MCMI-IV. The MCMI-IV (Millon, Grossman, & Millon, 2015) is a measure of psychopathology and personality dysfunction normed on a clinical sample. It includes five validity indicators. The Validity (V) index is designed to detect non-content-based invalid responding using very improbable symptoms. Inconsistency (W) is intended to detect variable responding. Disclosure (X) is intended to detect whether a patient responded in an open or secretive manner whereas Desirability (Y) is designed to measure underreporting (including both virtuousness and emotional stability) and Debasement (Z) is designed to detect overreporting and self-deprecation. Sellbom and Bagby (2008a) reviewed literature on the MCMI-III Validity Scales, citing concerns regarding low sensitivity and concluded "Under no circumstances should practitioners use this instrument in forensic evaluations to determine response styles" (p. 205). Boccaccini and Hart (2018) reviewed MCMI validity scale studies published after Sellbom and Bagby's (2008) chapter. None of the three articles they reviewed examined the MCMI-IV validity scales. Consequently, Boccaccini and Hart (2018) shared Sellbom and Bagby's (2008a) concerns about use of the MCMI validity scales in forensic evaluations. We agree and also recommend that these scales not be utilized in any significant fashion in gauging response bias until more research has demonstrated their utility.

Stand-alone measures. A variety of stand-alone measures are available to assess overreporting of psychopathology, although the three most popular include the Structured Interview of Reported Symptoms-2 (SIRS-2; Rogers, Sewell, & Gillard, 2010), Structured Inventory of Malingered Symptomatology (SIMS; Widows & Smith, 2005), and Miller Forensic Assessment of Symptoms Test (M-FAST; Miller, 2001).

SIRS-2. Utilizing the 172-item set from the SIRS (Rogers, Bagby, & Dickens, 1992) and a revised scoring strategy, the structured interview-based SIRS-2 (Rogers, Sewell, & Gillard, 2010) includes a variety of methods to detect overreporting with varied strategies. The Primary Scales include Rare Symptoms (RS), Symptom Combinations (SC), Improbable or Absurd Symptoms (IA), Blatant Symptoms (BL), Subtle Symptoms (SU), Selectivity of Symptoms (SEL), Severity of Symptoms (SEV), and Reported versus Observed Symptoms (RO). Supplementary Scales, include Direct Appraisal of Honesty (DA). Additionally, Defensive Symptoms (DS), Overly Specified Symptoms (OS), Improbable Failure (IF), and Inconsistency of Symptoms (INC) provide further information about overreporting as well as about inconsistent responding, cognitive symptom overreporting, and exaggeration of virtues. Three indexes include the Rare Symptoms (RS) Total, Modified Total (MT) Index, and Supplementary Scale (SS) Index (Rogers et al., 2010). Much of the robust SIRS literature is applicable to the SIRS-2, as the item content and Primary Scales are identical across measures. Often referred to as a "gold standard" for identifying overreported psychopathology, the SIRS/SIRS-2 exhibits strong inter-rater reliability, internal consistency (in English, Spanish, and Chinese translations), and small standard errors of measurement. Further, a well-established literature documents it has strong discriminant validity (Rogers, 2018b). We would not recommend that the SIRS-2 be used as a measure of cognitive response bias until research is available to showcase its utility in this domain of functioning.

The Spanish SIRS-2 showed fairly equivalent psychometric properties with the English version of the test (Correa & Rogers, 2010). The Chinese (Mandarin) version of the SIRS-2 was examined in a simulation sample of Chinese undergraduate students and a known groups sample (utilizing the Chinese version of the MMPI-2) of psychiatric outpatients compared to a group of suspected malingerers (Liu et al., 2013). While the study showed promising results with respect to discriminant validity, additional work is needed to fully examine the Chinese translation of the SIRS-2.

SIMS. The 75-item SIMS (Widows & Smith, 2005) includes five indices designed to screen for overreporting of both psychopathology and neurological symptoms. Psychosis (P) items involve symptoms rarely reported in psychiatric patients. Neurological Impairment (N) items involve illogical or atypical neurological symptoms. Amnestic Disorders (Am) items involve memory problems not common in brain-injured patients. Low Intelligence (LI) items assess for general simple knowledge. Finally, Affective Disorders (Af) involve atypical depression and anxiety items. A Total Score is used to provide an overall measure of overreporting (Smith, 2008). Cut scores were derived from honest and simulation samples of predominantly female European-American undergraduates. The SIMS demonstrated acceptable internal consistency and moderate associations with M-FAST scores in an inmate sample, although the two measures demonstrated low feigning classification concordance (Nadolny & O'Dell, 2010; Smith, 2018). Of note, the SIMS is not recommended for screening feigned intellectual disability (Smith, 2018).

Although the body of literature on the SIMS is somewhat limited, strong sensitivity and negative predictive power coupled with low specificity and positive predictive power suggest the SIMS may be a useful screener, with more extensive research needed in real-world settings before conclusions regarding overreporting are made (Lewis, Simcox, & Berry, 2002). Van Impelen and colleagues (2014) completed a systematic review and meta-analysis of the SIMS, noting that the measure is largely successful in differentiating feigners and simulators in analogue studies but, owing to limited specificity, may overestimate feigning among those with schizophrenia, intellectual disability, and seizure disorders. These authors recommended using a higher cut score than is recommended in the test manual (Total Score > 14) and combining the measure with other symptom validity indicators. A Dutch version of the SIMS showed similar findings with the original English version of the test (Merckelbach & Smith, 2003).

M-FAST. The 25-item M-FAST (Miller, 2001) is a brief structured interview that allows for screening of overreported psychopathology within forensic settings. The M-FAST has primarily been utilized as a screener for longer and more comprehensive feigning instruments, such as the SIRS/SIRS-2. Each of the seven indices – including Reported versus Observed (RO), Extreme Symptomatology (ES), Rare Combinations (RC), Unusual Hallucinations (UH), Negative Image (NI), Suggestibility (S), and a Total Score – is designed to screen for overreported psychopathology.

The M-FAST has been examined with MMPI-2/RF, PAI, and SIRS scores (Clark, 2006; Gaines, 2009; Glassmire, Tarescavage, & Gottfried, 2016; Guy & Miller, 2004; Miller, 2004; Veazey et al., 2005). This literature supports the use of the M-FAST as a screener for overreported psychopathology, with scores ≥ 6 suggesting the need to follow up with a more comprehensive evaluation of overreporting and scores ≥ 16 indicating stronger confidence in conclusions of feigning (Glassmire, Tarescavage, & Gottfried, 2016). Research does not support the M-FAST as a screener for cognitive symptom exaggeration and future research is needed to examine its utility in the detection of feigned mood and anxiety symptoms (Smith, 2018). Only one study has examined a Spanish translation of the M-FAST. Montes and Guyton (2014) translated the M-FAST into Spanish and administered it to a sample of 102 bilingual (English/Spanish-speaking) incarcerated males. Their results suggest similar psychometric performance between the two versions of the instrument.

In sum, a rich literature exists to examine the utility of embedded and stand-alone measures of noncredible responding of psychopathology symptoms. As noted in this section, each tool is distinct in regard to the depth of research examining its accuracy in various evaluation settings. They are also varied in their administration time, minimum reading comprehension levels, breadth of scales to cover various domains of invalid responding (e.g., noncontent- and content-based; overreporting subdomains; scales designed with varied detection strategies), and susceptibility to be influenced by genuine psychopathology. Evaluators should consider each of these factors when deciding on measures to administer to examinees. It is recommended that examiners avoid relying on any one indicator of response bias – especially a screening tool. Further evaluation with more comprehensive measures is recommended and interpretation of test results in the context of other data (e.g., additional test results, medical and/or legal records, interview, collateral contacts) is imperative. Additionally, determinations of malingering should be reserved for cases when both intentionality and secondary gain can be documented (see Burchett & Bagby, 2014).

ASSESSMENT OF NEUROCOGNITIVE RESPONSE BIAS

Response bias is a major concern in the assessment of cognitive functions (such as memory, attention/concentration, and processing speed, among others), especially in the context of diagnostic evaluation for neurocognitive disorder secondary to traumatic brain injury (TBI), attention deficit/hyperactivity disorder (ADHD), learning disabilities, and other medical and psychiatric conditions. In these contexts, assessment relies to a great extent on the use of performance-based measures in addition to self-report, collateral records, and clinical observation. Performance-based measures (or performance validity tests; PVTs) are well-suited to the assessment of response bias and several detection approaches have been developed in this modality. Clinical researchers have used these approaches to create several, well-validated "stand-alone" PVTs for inclusion in cognitive assessment batteries. A growing research literature has also identified and validated numerous "embedded" PVTs, which can be computed from standard administrations of traditional neuropsychological assessment instruments. This section will describe the most common performance-based detection approaches, briefly review stand-alone and embedded PVTs that employ those approaches, and introduce the malingered neurocognitive dysfunction (MND) criteria proposed by Slick, Sherman, and Iverson (1999) to provide a framework for methodical use of such measures within a comprehensive clinical or forensic assessment. The following review of detection approaches provides a somewhat simplified, narrative discussion of the subject to promote conceptual clarity. For more in-depth discussions of the below approaches, please see Berry and Schipper (2008); Sweet, Condit, and Nelson (2008); Slick and colleagues (1999); and Heilbronner and colleagues (2009).

Performance-Based Detection Approaches

Below-chance performance. One strong indicator of response bias is performance significantly below what would be expected by chance. Consider a forced-choice paradigm (Pankratz, 1979) in which the test-taker must choose between two response options for each item, one correct and one incorrect. If one were to choose responses entirely at random, the expected test score would be 50 percent correct. That is, if a test-taker were to provide responses without any test-relevant knowledge or ability, the test-taker's score would be expected to fall close to 50 percent. Scores significantly below 50 percent (using a chosen statistical cutoff for "significance") are very unlikely, even in the case of zero ability, and are strong grounds for inferring a content-responsive and deliberate suppression of performance. In the two-option forced-choice example above, one may use the binomial probability distribution to determine the cutoff below which content-responsive performance suppression is likely.

Criterion cutoffs. In a clinical or forensic evaluation, though, random responding or total absence of knowledge or ability is often far below expectation even among individuals with true impairments, meaning that the below-chance approach would result in a high false negative rate. Only test-takers with the most profoundly aberrant response style would be detected and more moderate cases of response bias would go undetected. A more sensitive approach, the use of "criterion cutoffs," relies on empirically established expected levels of performance within impaired populations. For example, a measure such as the two-item forced-choice task above would be administered to a known clinical population (e.g., severe TBI patients), cutoff scores would be either rationally identified – that is, statistically significantly below the average in that impaired population – or empirically identified, using estimates of sensitivity and specificity classifying individuals with known impairment versus individuals either asked to feign impairment or otherwise identified as exhibiting response bias. Thompson (2003) and Tombaugh (2002) followed such an approach in developing well-known performance validity measures discussed in more detail later in this section. The criterion cutoff makes use of empirical knowledge to improve sensitivity over the below-chance approach but it requires more extensive and careful validation under a variety of research designs to adequately address internal and external validity concerns and support inference of response bias in less egregious cases.

Performance curve analysis. The "performance curve" detection strategy makes use of the objective difficulty level of test items. The general expectation under an ideal response style is that an individual will perform better on easier items and more poorly on more difficult items. To the extent that an individual's responses depart from this expectation, one may surmise the presence of response bias. Moreover, the extent to which an individual's pattern of failures matches the apparent difficulty rather than the objective difficulty is a potential indicator of response bias.

Floor item analysis. Related somewhat to performance curve analysis, the examination of "floor" item failure involves evaluating rare or atypical responses on very low difficulty items that even very neurologically compromised patients tend to answer correctly. A typical example is the patient forgetting their own name. To add some nuance to the "floor" item approach, comparison of performances within or across cognitive domains may allow the examiner to establish, ipsatively, a reasonable performance floor (Frederick, 2000). For example, relatively intact memory performance may identify severely impaired performance on attention tasks as a "floor" violation. Other examples include intact recall with impaired recognition.

Performance Validity Tests

Though most PVTs were initially developed or validated in the context of brain injury evaluation, nearly all have shown evidence of validity for detecting cognitive response bias in other clinical contexts as well. It is important to remember that all PVTs are not validated for all assessment contexts. Specificity and sensitivity per se do not exist as test properties and it is critical for clinicians to think in terms of "sensitivity to X condition" and "specificity to X condition versus Y condition." Development and validation of PVTs remains an active field of research and clinicians are highly encouraged to review recent literature particular to the assessment context when selecting and interpreting PVTs (e.g., Bender & Frederick, 2018).

Stand-alone PVTs. The Rey 15-Item Test (FIT; Lezak, 1983; Rey, 1964) relies on a forced-choice recognition memory paradigm and the Dot Counting Test (Boone, Lu, & Herzberg, 2002; Lezak, Howieson, & Loring, 2004; Rey, 1941) relies on failure of the floor-level, overlearned task of counting grouped dots versus ungrouped dots. These are among the earliest stand-alone tasks for detecting response bias. Research has shown these tasks to have problematic predictive powers, at least partially because they can be confounded by genuine impairment (Millis & Kler, 1995). Vickery and colleagues (2001) performed a meta-analytic review of the literature, which confirmed the weakness of the DCT and the 15-Item Test relative to other stand-alone PVTs in use at the time. The best performers in that review were the Digit Memory Test (DMT; Hiscock & Hiscock, 1989), which showed very good specificity and sensitivity to cognitive feigning versus mixed neurologic samples and known TBI (generally moderate to severe) samples, the Portland Digit Recognition Test (PDRT; Binder, 1993), which showed very good specificity and good sensitivity to cognitive feigning versus primarily known TBI (generally moderate to severe) samples as well as mixed neurologic samples, and the 21-Item Test (Iverson, 1998), which showed very good specificity and modest sensitivity to cognitive feigning versus mixed neurologic samples and one known memory disorder sample. The DMT and PDRT are both forced-choice number recognition tasks that use various features in increased perceived task or item difficulty and both have been revised to computerized formats that measure response latency as well (the Victoria Symptom Validity Test, VSVT, is a revision of the DMT; the PDRT is now the PDRT-C). The 21-Item Test is a forced-choice word recognition task following verbal presentation of a word list and it relies on criterion cutoffs for scoring.

Sollman and Berry (2011) performed a more recent meta-analysis of stand-alone PVTs not included in the Vickery and colleagues (2001) review. After they reviewed the empirical research on sixteen additional stand-alone PVTs, only five instruments were found to have sufficient studies available for meta-analysis. These included the Test of Memory Malingering (TOMM; Tombaugh, 1996; a forced-choice, visual recognition memory task), the Word Memory Test (WMT; Green, 2003; a set of verbal learning, recall, and recognition memory tasks), the Letter Memory Test (LMT; Inman et al., 1998; a forced-choice task of recognition memory for strings of letters, with features designed to vary perceived item difficulty), the Medical Symptom Validity Test (MSVT; Green, 2004; a screening task for verbal memory dysfunction with forced-choice components and a consistency index), and the VSVT (Slick et al., 1997). The TOMM, WMT, and LMT had the most robust support in the literature and all showed good sensitivity to malingered cognitive impairment. The TOMM showed excellent specificity versus head injury (often moderate to severe but also non–compensation-seeking mild TBI as well), mixed neurologic disorders, and mild intellectual and developmental disability (IDD), inpatient and outpatient psychiatric disorders, and ADHD. The LMT showed excellent specificity versus head injury (often moderate to severe but also non–compensation-seeking mild TBI as well), mixed neurologic disorders, mild intellectual disability, and ADHD. The WMT showed significantly lower but acceptable specificity in general – stronger versus pain disorders, learning disability, and inpatient psychiatric disorders; and weaker versus head injury and mild IDD. The MSVT showed excellent specificity as well but somewhat lower sensitivity to cognitive feigning versus head injury and inpatient dementia. Likewise, few eligible studies of the VSVT were available but both specificity and sensitivity to cognitive feigning were very high versus head injury and mixed neurologic disorders. Examining the issue of specificity of PVTs with respect to brain injury, McBride and colleagues (2013) examined ninety-two suspected head injury litigants who underwent neuroimaging with MRI and CT. The presence (and location if present) of brain injury showed no statistical association to scores on the TOMM, VSVT, or LMT.

Additional stand-alone PVTs include the Computerized Assessment of Response Bias (CARB; Conder, Allen, & Cox, 1992), another forced-choice digit recognition task with some support for use in head injury and non–head injury disability evaluation contexts (Gervais et al., 2004; Green & Iverson, 2001); the b Test (Boone et al., 2000), a timed test of the overlearned skill of identifying the letter "b" from among distracters, which has some support for use in a variety of clinical populations (Roberson et al., 2013) and in Spanish-speaking populations (Robles et al., 2015); and the Validity Indicator Profile (VIP; Frederick, 2003a), a forced-choice test with word definition and nonverbal abstraction items that relies on performance curve analysis to classify profiles as "compliant" (high effort to respond correctly), "irrelevant" (low effort to respond incorrectly), "careless" (low effort to respond correctly), or "malingering" (high effort to respond incorrectly). The limited literature addressing the VIP suggests some support for use in head injury evaluation (Frederick, 2003b) and possible concerns regarding specificity to cognitive feigning versus active psychosis (Hunt, Root, & Bascetta, 2013).

Embedded PVTs. Identification and validation of embedded PVTs is a very active area of research due to potential time savings and retrospective assessment of response bias in prior evaluations (Berry & Schipper, 2008). The sheer number of embedded indices under study precludes an exhaustive list. More recognizable indices include the forced-choice tasks included within the California Verbal Learning Test (CVLT-II and CVLT-III; Delis et al., 2000, 2017) and the Rey Auditory Verbal Learning Test (RAVLT; Schmidt, 1996). The Reliable Digit Span index of the WAIS-III and WAIS-IV Digit Span subtest (Greiffenstein, Baker, & Gola, 1994) shows evidence of validity for the detection of cognitive response bias in the context of a mild head injury evaluation (Jasinski, Berry et al., 2011), though its use may be limited outside of that context (Jasinski, Harp et al., 2011) and in veteran populations (Spencer et al., 2013). Promising embedded indices have been identified in many other instruments, including several nonmemory/attention tasks (Trail Making Test A and B, Speech Sounds Perception Test, Conners' Continuous Performance Test), the Finger Tapping Test, Benton Visual Form Discrimination and Judgment of Line Orientation, Rey-Osterrieth Complex Figure, Wisconsin Card Sorting Test, and the FAS verbal fluency test). We highly recommend Schutte and Axelrod (2013) for a recent, well-organized review of these and other embedded indices. That chapter also details and presents the evidence supporting several discriminant functions and multiple regression models developed to aid in the combination of embedded PVTs without inflating the false positive rate.

Malingered Neurocognitive Dysfunction

Slick and colleagues (1999) proposed diagnostic criteria for MND to encourage consensus and reliability in the identification of malingering involving cognitive response bias, especially in medicolegal contexts. MND is defined as "the volitional exaggeration or fabrication of cognitive dysfunction for the purposes of obtaining substantial material gain, or avoiding or escaping formal duty or responsibility" (p. 552) and diagnosis is stratified into definite, probable, and possible MND. All levels of MND require the presence of a substantial and clearly identifiable external incentive to exaggerate or fabricate symptoms. Likewise, a diagnosis of MND at any level requires that the behaviors used as evidence of volitional exaggeration or fabrication are not fully accounted for by psychiatric, neurological, or developmental factors. A diagnosis of definite MND requires evidence of definite negative response bias, meaning significantly below-chance performance on one or more forced-choice measures of cognitive response bias.

A classification of probable MND requires either (1) two or more types of evidence from neuropsychological evaluation – including probable response bias using well-validated PVTs; discrepancy between test data and known patterns of brain function; discrepancy between test data and observed behavior, between test data and reliable collateral reports, or between test data and documented background history – or (2) one such type of evidence from neuropsychological testing, plus one or more type of evidence from self-report – including discrepancies between self-reported and documented history; self-reported symptoms and known patterns of brain functioning; self-reported symptoms and behavioral observations or collateral informants; or evidence of fabricated or exaggerated psychological dysfunction. Possible MND requires only (1) one or more types of evidence from self-report or (2) all criteria met for either definite or probably MND except that psychiatric, neurological, or developmental etiologies cannot be ruled out.

The proposed criteria for MND have gained wide acceptance in the fields of clinical and forensic neuropsychology and, though not a part of an official diagnostic system or manual, have provided a common language and framework for professionals working with cognitive response bias. The framework both supports clinicians in responsible use of PVTs and holds them to account for overgeneralizing the meaning of a positive results on a PVT. The proposed criteria provide important reminders that evidence in malingering assessment (1) can be staged by overall strength of the evidence, (2) must come from other sources in addition to PVTs, (3) when it does come from PVTs, must come from PVTs well-validated for the specific disorder and population, and (4) should take into account the whole context of the performance, including other explanations that may account for aberrant performance. Though assessment of MND involves significant application of clinical judgment, such judgment should be well supported by the responsible use of measures of cognitive response bias. Finally, clinicians should remain aware that failure to meet criteria for MND by no means suggests that symptom and performance validity data should be ignored; rather, variable or suboptimal response validity must be considered when interpreting other test scores in a given case.

ASSESSING FEIGNED SOMATIC AND MEDICAL PRESENTATIONS

Assessing feigned somatic and medical presentations is particularly challenging for psychologists. Whereas the assessment response bias in psychopathology and cognitive impairment has exploded over the last twenty years, the assessment of somatic and physical feigning has received much less attention, even though it occurs with some frequency. Indeed, Greve and colleagues (2009) estimated a malingering prevalence range of 20–50 percent in chronic pain patients with financial incentive. This domain of assessment is particularly challenging for psychologists because examination of medical symptoms and physical ailment is generally outside of our scope of competency. Thus, assessment of feigned somatic and medical presentations must be undertaken in conjunction with medical colleagues. Further complicating matters, the assessment of feigned somatic and medical symptoms lacks any "gold standard." Consequently, mental health practitioners must often focus on self-reported descriptions of medical symptoms. Two brief self-report measures of pain (Pain Disability Index; Pollard, 1984) and perception of somatic symptoms (Modified Somatic Perception Questionnaire; Main, 1983) have shown utility in differentiating those with bona fide pain disability and malingered pain disability (Bianchini et al., 2014; Crighton et al., 2014; Larrabee, 2003a). As noted earlier, the MMPI-2-RF Infrequent Somatic Responses (Fs) scale has shown some utility in detecting feigned somatic symptoms (Sellbom, Wygant, & Bagby, 2012; Wygant et al., 2017). It is also worth noting that individuals presenting with pain and other somatic symptoms often report a high number of psychological symptoms and cognitive complaints. Consequently, much of what we have already covered in the chapter will be useful in this context.

Several medical techniques have been identified as potentially associated with feigned medical issues and pain, such as the effort indicators on isometric strength measures (Bianchini et al., 2005) and "signs" of nonorganic back pain (Waddell et al., 1980). Utilizing the Waddell signs as a symptom feigning measure has not been without controversy. Fishbain and colleagues (2004) found that Waddell signs were not consistently correlated with disability status and improved with treatment. Moreover, they found no association between MMPI/MMPI-2 validity scales and scores on the Waddell signs. It is not surprising, however, since the studies they reviewed only examined the L, F, and K scales, which conceptually are not related to somatic overreporting. In a more recent study, Wygant and colleagues (2017) examined the Waddell signs in a sample of 230 outpatient chronic pain patients and found a large effect size between the signs and scores on MMPI-2-RF validity scales, most prominently Fs (d = 1.31), comparing patients with elevated signs (> 2) to those who received score of 0.

Finally, assessing feigned somatic and medical presentations is complicated by several diagnoses in the DSM-5 that are characterized by somatic symptoms (i.e., somatic symptom disorder, conversion disorder, and factitious disorder). Clinicians must carefully examine the role that potential exaggeration plays in both the clinical presentation and secondary gain motivations that are external (e.g., disability status) versus internal (e.g., emotional support from others). One recent study addressed this particular challenge with the MMPI-2-RF and found that scales utilizing the rare symptoms approach (Fp-r, Fs) were more successful in differentiating somatic malingering from bona fide somatoform and genuine medical symptoms than scales that utilize other approaches (FBS-r, RBS) (Sellbom, Bagby, & Wygant, 2012).

Similar to the assessment of malingered neurocognitive impairment (Slick et al., 1999), Bianchini and colleagues (2005) developed a similarly organized set of criteria aimed at characterizing malingered pain-related disability (MPRD). While the MPRD criteria are explicitly focused on pain as a somatic symptom, the criteria include consideration of broad somatic functioning, as well as indicators designed to capture both feigned cognitive presentations (e.g., PVTs) and amplified somatic issues (e.g., Waddell signs). The MPRD criteria added a set of criteria that incorporated evidence from physical evaluation that was consistent with symptom feigning. Aside from this addition, the remaining structure for the MPRD criteria is consistent with MND. The criteria incorporate neuropsychological testing, clinical interview data/observations, self-report measures, and physical examinations. While the construct validity of the criteria themselves has not been directly empirically investigated, several studies using the criteria have shown expected results on external validity measures, including the MMPI-2-RF Validity Scales (Bianchini et al., 2018; Wygant et al., 2011), and the MSPQ and PDI (Bianchini et al., 2014; Crighton et al., 2014). These studies have shown that individuals scoring in the probable/definite range of MPRD exhibit higher scores on these validity indicators than those with genuine pain, which indirectly supports the construct validity of the MPRD criteria.

TECHNOLOGY AND THE ASSESSMENT OF RESPONSE BIAS

Technology has largely not been a big focus in the area of malingering and response bias assessment. Many of the techniques described in this chapter involve paper and pencil measures (e.g., PAI) and structured clinical interviews (e.g., SIRS-2). Perhaps the one exception is in the area of neuropsychological assessment, which has increasingly utilized computer and tablet-based assessment approaches in recent years. With respect to the assessment of response bias, several measures utilize computer-based administration, such as the Word Memory Test (WMT; Green, 2003) and Victoria Symptom Validity Test (VSVT, Slick, Hopp, & Strauss, 1997).

Nevertheless, technology may offer interesting insights in the detection of response bias. One area where that has been explored is utilizing computer-based administrations to capture latency in responding to response bias measures. Reviewing the research on response latency in response bias research, Burchett & Ben-Porath (in press) noted that intentional response distortion has been found to be associated with differences in response times. Some of this research has focused on the congruence model (Holden et al., 1992), which posits that response latency for any particular item is influenced by the congruence between the generated response and the response set (i.e., whether the individual is attempting to feign or response honestly). As noted by Burchett and Ben-Porath (in press), recent findings from Holden and Lambert (2015) found that subjects instructed to feign responded quicker to items that were congruent with their response set than to items that are noncongruent with their response set. Nevertheless, there have been inconsistencies across studies, which necessitates additional research in the area of response latency and response bias detection. As computer-based administration of psychological assessment measures becomes increasingly available, research can incorporate response latency into the assessment process.

CONCLUDING REMARKS AND FUTURE DIRECTIONS

We close this chapter by again emphasizing the importance of routine assessment of response bias in mental health assessment. Clinical and diagnostic assessment has far-reaching implications for those evaluated by mental health professionals, with records of diagnosis and treatment following the individual for years. Thus, it is critical we routinely consider the effects and impact of noncredible responding in our assessments. As we have noted, in some areas of assessment (i.e., forensic assessment), the issue of noncredible responding is particularly crucial in that clinicians must often defend clinical and diagnostic impressions as they are deliberated during the adversarial context of the legal system.

In line with the recent push for evidence-based psychological assessment (Bornstein, 2017) and empirically supported forensic assessment (Archer, Wheeler, & Vauter, 2016), we recommend a multimethod approach to the assessment of response bias and noncredible responding, particularly in assessment situations that involve various domains of functioning (e.g., neuropsychological assessment of mild TBI). Fortunately, as we discussed throughout the chapter, there are numerous screening instruments and clinical instruments (e.g., MMPI-2-RF, PAI) available that have embedded measures of response bias.

Researching methods of assessing noncredible responding and response bias continues to be an important topic. There are several topics in this area that need additional exploration. As noted throughout this chapter, one such topic involves cross-cultural considerations in assessing response bias. Few studies investigate the important demographic and cultural variables' impact on the accuracy of response bias indicators. Additionally, we need to continue collecting data that differentiate feigning and genuine psychopathology and impairment. This will inevitably involve collecting data from various clinical groups to reduce possible false positive indications of response bias.

REFERENCES

Ackerman, M. J., & Ackerman, M. C. (1997). Custody evaluation practices: A survey of experienced professionals (revisited). *Professional Psychology: Research and Practice*, *28*(2), 137–145.

Alfano, K., & Boone, K. B. (2007). The use of effort tests in the context of actual versus feigned attention-deficit/hyperactivity disorder and learning disability. In K. B. Boone (Ed.), *Assessment of feigned cognitive impairment: A neuropsychological perspective* (pp. 366–383). New York: Guilford.

American Psychiatric Association. (2013). *Diagnostic and statistical manual of mental disorders* (5th ed.). Washington, DC: Author.

Anderson, J. L., Sellbom, M., Wygant, D. B., Edens, J. F. (2013). Examining the necessity for and utility of the Psychopathic Personality Inventory – Revised (PPI-R) validity scales. *Law and Human Behavior*, *37*, 312–320.

Arbisi, P. A., & Ben-Porath, Y. S. (1995). An MMPI-2 infrequent response scale for use with psychopathological populations: The Infrequency-Psychopathology Scale, F(p). *Psychological Assessment*, *7*, 424–431.

Arce, R., Fariña, F., Seijo, D., & Novo, M. (2015). Assessing impression management with the MMPI-2 in child custody litigation. *Assessment*, *22*(6), 769–777.

Archer, R.P., Wheeler, E.M.A., & Vauter, R.A. (2016). Empirically supported forensic assessment. *Clinical Psychology: Science and Practice*, *23*, 348–364.

Baer, R. A., & Miller, J. (2002). Underreporting of psychopathology on the MMPI-2: A meta-analytic review. *Psychological Assessment*, *14*, 84–94.

Bagby, R. M., Nicholson, R. A., Bacchiochi, J. R., Ryder, A. G., & Bury, A. S. (2002). The predictive capacity of the MMPI-2 and PAI Validity Scales and Indexes to detect coached and uncoached feigning. *Journal of Personality Assessment*, *78*(1), 69–86.

Bagby, R.M., & Sellbom, M. (2018). The Validity and Clinical Utility of the Personality Inventory for DSM-5 (PID-5) Response Inconsistency Scale. *Journal of Personality Assessment*, *100*, 398–405.

Bathurst, K., Gottfried, A. W., & Gottfried, A. E. (1997). Normative data for the MMPI-2 in child custody litigation. *Psychological Assessment*, *9*(3), 205–211.

Beck, A. T., Steer, R. A., & Brown, G. K. (1996). *Beck Depression Inventory-II*. San Antonio: Psychological Corporation.

Bender, S. D., & Frederick, R. (2018). Neuropsychological models of feigned cognitive deficits. In R. Rogers & S. D. Bender (Eds.), *Clinical assessment of malingering and deception* (4th ed., pp. 42–60). New York: Guilford.

Bender, S. D., & Rogers, R. (2004). Detection of neurocognitive feigning: Development of a multi-strategy assessment. *Archives of Clinical Neuropsychology*, *19*, 49–60.

Ben-Porath, Y. S. (2012). *Interpreting the MMPI-2-RF*. Minneapolis: University of Minnesota Press.

Ben-Porath, Y. S. (2013). Self-report inventories: Assessing personality and psychopathology. In A. M. Goldstein (Ed.), *Handbook of psychology, Vol. 10: Assessment psychology* (pp. 622–644). Hoboken, NJ: Wiley.

Ben-Porath, Y. S., Graham, J. R., & Tellegen A. (2009). *The MMPI-2 Symptom Validity (FBS) scale development, research findings, and interpretive recommendations*. Minneapolis: University of Minnesota Press.

Ben-Porath, Y. S., & Tellegen, A. (2008). *MMPI-2-RF manual for administration, scoring, and interpretation*. Minneapolis: University of Minnesota Press.

Berry, D. T. R., & Schipper, L. J. (2008). Assessment of feigned cognitive impairment using standard neuropsychological tests. In R. Rogers (Ed.), *Clinical assessment of malingering and deception* (3rd. ed., pp. 237–253). New York: Guilford.

Bianchini, K. J., Aguerrevere, L. E., Curtis, K. L., Roebuck-Spencer, T. M., Greve, K. W., & Calamia, M. (2018). Classification accuracy of the Minnesota Multiphasic Personality Inventory-2 (MMPI-2)-Restructured form validity scales in detecting malingered pain-related disability. *Psychological Assessment*, *30*, 857–869.

Bianchini, K. J., Aguerrevere, L. E., Guise, B. J., Ord, J. S., Etherton, J. L., Meyers, J. E., Soignier, R. D., Greve, K. W., Curtis, K. L., & Bui, J. (2014). Accuracy of the Modified Somatic Perception Questionnaire and Pain Disability Index in the detection of malingered pain-related disability in chronic pain. *The Clinical Neuropsychologist*, *28*, 1376–1394.

Bianchini, K. J., Curtis, K. L., & Greve, K. W. (2006). Compensation and malingering in traumatic brain injury: A dose-response relationship? *Clinical Neuropsychology*, *20*(4), 831–847.

Bianchini, K. J., Greve, K. W., & Glynn, G. (2005). Review article: On the diagnosis of malingered pain-related disability: Lessons from cognitive malingering research. *The Spine Journal*, *5*, 404–417.

Binder, L. M. (1993). Assessment of malingering after mild head trauma with the Portland Digit Recognition Test. *Journal of Clinical and Experimental Neuropsychology*, *15*, 170–182.

Boccaccini, M. T., & Hart, J. R. (2018). Response style on the Personality Assessment Inventory and other multiscale inventories. In R. Rogers & S. D. Bender (Eds.), *Clinical assessment of malingering and deception* (4th ed., pp. 208–300). New York: The Guilford Press.

Boccaccini, M. T., Murrie, D. C., & Duncan, S. A. (2006). Screening for malingering in a criminal-forensic sample with the Personality Assessment Inventory. *Psychological Assessment*, *18*(4), 415–423.

Boone, K., Lu, P., & Herzberg, D. (2002). *The Dot Counting Test*. Los Angeles: Western Psychological Services.

Boone, K. B., Lu, P., Sherman, D., Palmer, B., Back, C., Shamieh, E., et al. (2000). Validation of a new technique to detect malingering of cognitive symptoms: The b Test. *Archives of Clinical Neuropsychology*, *15*, 227–241.

Boone, K. B., Salazar, X., Lu, P., Warner-Chacon, K., & Razani, J. (2002). The Rey 15-item recognition trial: A technique to enhance sensitivity of the Rey 15-item memorization test. *Journal of Clinical and Experimental Neuropsychology*, *24*(5), 561–573.

Bornstein, R. F. (2017). Evidence-based psychological assessment. *Journal of Personality Assessment*, *99*, 435–445.

Bow, J. N., Flens, J. R., & Gould, J. W. (2010). MMPI-2 and MCMI-III in forensic evaluations: A survey of psychologists. *Journal of Forensic Psychology Practice*, *10*, 37–52.

Briere, J. (2010). *Trauma Symptom Inventory (TSI-2) professional manual* (2nd ed.). Odessa, FL: Psychological Assessment Resources.

Burchett, D., & Bagby, R. M. (2014). Multimethod assessment of response distortion: Integrating data from interviews, collateral records, and standardized assessment tools. In C. Hopwood & R. Bornstein (Eds.), *Multimethod clinical assessment* (pp. 345–378). New York: Guilford.

Burchett, D. L., & Ben-Porath, Y. S. (2010). The impact of over-reporting on MMPI-2-RF substantive scale score validity. *Assessment*, *17*, 497–516.

Burchett, D. L., & Ben-Porath, Y. S. (in press). Methodological considerations for developing and evaluating response bias indicators. *Psychological Assessment*.

Burchett, D., Dragon. W. E., Smith Holbert, A. M., Tarescavage, A. M., Mattson, C. A., Handel, R. W., & Ben-Porath, Y. S. (2016). "False feigners": Examining the impact of non-content-based invalid responding on the Minnesota Multiphasic Personality Inventory-2 Restructured Form content-based invalid responding indicators. *Psychological Assessment*, *28* (5), 458–470.

Bury, A. S., & Bagby, R. M. (2002). The detection of feigned uncoached and coached posttraumatic stress disorder with the MMPI-2 in a sample of workplace accident victims. *Psychological Assessment*, *14*(4), 472–484.

Bush, S. S. (2012). *Mild traumatic brain injury: Symptom validity assessment and malingering*. New York: Springer.

Butcher, J. N., Graham, J. R., Ben-Porath, Y. S., Tellegen, A., Dahlstrom, W. G., & Kaemmer, B. (2001). *MMPI-2 manual for administration, scoring, and interpretation* (rev. ed.). Minneapolis: University of Minnesota Press.

Butcher, J. N., & Han, K. (1995). Development of an MMPI-2 scale to assess the presentation of self in a superlative manner: The S scale. In J. N. Butcher & C. D. Spielberger (Eds.), *Advances in personality assessment*, Vol. *10* (pp. 25–50). Hillsdale, NJ: Lawrence Erlbaum Associates.

Camara, W. J., Nathan, J. S., & Puente, A. E. (2000). Psychological test usage: Implications in professional psychology. *Professional Psychology: Research and Practice*, *31*, 141–154.

Cashel, M. L., Rogers, R., Sewell, K., & Martin-Cannici, C. (1995). The Personality Assessment Inventory and the detection of defensiveness. *Assessment*, *2*, 333–342.

Chang, J. T., Szczyglinski, J. A., & King, S. A. (2000). A case of malingering: Feigning a painful disorder in the presence of true medical illness. *Pain Medicine*, *1*(3), 280–282.

Clark, J. A. (2006). Validation of the Miller Forensic Assessment of Symptoms Test (M-FAST) in a civil forensic population. Master's thesis, University of Kentucky. (Retrieved from University of Kentucky, Paper No. 399.)

Conder, R., Allen, L., & Cox, D. (1992). *Computerized assessment of response bias test manual*. Durham, NC: CogniSyst.

Corey, D., & Ben-Porath, Y. S. (2018). *Assessing police and other public safety personnel using the MMPI-2-RF: A practical guide*. Minneapolis: University of Minnesota Press.

Correa, A. A. (2018). Beyond borders: Cultural and translational perspectives of feigning and other response styles. In R. Rogers & S. D. Bender (Eds.), *Clinical assessment of malingering and deception* (4th ed., pp. 61–80). New York: Guilford.

Correa A. A., & Rogers, R. (2010). Validation of the Spanish SIRS with monolingual Hispanic outpatients. *Journal of Personality Assessment*, *92*, 458–464.

Crighton, A. H., Marek, R. J., Dragon, W. R., & Ben-Porath, Y. S. (2017). Utility of the MMPI-2-RF Validity Scales in detection of simulated underreporting: Implications of incorporating a manipulation check. *Assessment*, *24*(7), 853–864.

Crighton, A. H., Wygant, D. B., Applegate, K. C., Umlauf, R. L., & Granacher, R. P. (2014). Can brief measures effectively screen for pain and somatic malingering? Examination of the Modified Somatic Perception Questionnaire and Pain Disability Index. *The Spine Journal*, *14*, 2042–2050.

DeClue, G. (2011). Harry Potter and the structured interview of reported symptoms. *Open Access Journal of Forensic Psychology*, *3*, 1–18.

Delis, D. C., Kramer, J. H., Kaplan, E., & Ober, B. A. (2000). *CVLT-II: California verbal learning test: Adult version*. . San Antonio, TX: Psychological Corporation.

Delis, D. C., Kramer, J. H., Kaplan, E., & Ober, B. A. (2017). *CVLT-3: California verbal learning test* (3rd ed.). Bloomington, MN: Psychological Corporation.

Dhillon, S., Bagby, R. M., Kushner, S. C., & Burchett, D. (2017). The impact of underreporting and overreporting on the validity of the Personality Inventory for DSM–5 (PID-5): A simulation analog design investigation. *Psychological Assessment*, *29*, 473–478.

Dragon, W. R., Ben-Porath, Y. S., & Handel, R. W. (2012). Examining the impact of unscorable responses on the validity and interpretability of MMPI-2/MMPI-2-RF Restructured Clinical (RC) Scale scores. *Assessment*, *19*(1), 101–113.

Fernandez, K., Boccaccini, M. T., & Noland, R. M. (2008). Detecting over- and underreporting of psychopathology with the Spanish-language Personality Assessment Inventory: Findings from a simulation study with bilingual speakers. *Psychological Assessment*, *20*, 189–194.

Fishbain, D. A., Cole, B., Cutler, R.B., Lewis, J., Rosomoff, H. L., & Rosomoff, R. S. (2003). A structured evidenced-based review on the meaning of nonorganic physical signs: Waddell signs. *Pain Medicine*, *4*, 141–181.

Fishbain, D. A., Cutler, R. B., Rosomoff, H. L., & Rosomoff, R. S. (2004). Is there a relationship between nonorganic physical findings (Waddell Signs) and secondary gain/malingering? *Clinical Journal of Pain*, *20*, 399–408.

Frederick, R. I. (2000). A personal floor effect strategy to evaluate the validity of performance on memory tests. *Journal of Clinical and Experimental Neuropsychology*, *22*, 720–730.

Frederick, R. I. (2003a). *Validity Indicator Profile (enhancement and profile report)*. Minnetonka, MN: Pearson Assessments.

Frederick, R. I. (2003b). Review of the validity indicator profile. *Journal of Forensic Neuropsychology*, *2*(3–4), 125–145.

Friedhoff, L. A., Burchett, D., Alosco, M., Rapier, J. L., Benitez, A., Gunstad, J., & Ben-Porath, Y. S. (2014). MMPI-2-RF VRIN-r and TRIN-r associations with neuropsychological measures in a university-based neuropsychological evaluation setting. Paper presented at the Annual Symposium on Recent MMPI-2, MMPI-2-RF, & MMPI-A Research, Scottsdale, AZ, April 25–26.

Frueh, B. C., Hamner, M. B., Cahill, S. P., Gold, P. B., & Hamlin, K. (2000). Apparent symptom overreporting among combat veterans evaluated for PTSD. *Clinical Psychology Review*, *20*(7), 853–885.

Gaines, M. V. (2009). An examination of the combined use of the PAI and the M-FAST in detecting malingering among inmates. Unpublished doctoral dissertation, Texas Tech University.

Gervais, R. O., Ben-Porath, Y. S., Wygant, D. B., & Green, P. (2007). Development and validation of a Response Bias Scale (RBS) for the MMPI-2. *Assessment*, *14*, 196–208.

Gervais, R. O., Rohling, M. L., Green, P., & Ford, W. (2004). A comparison of WMT, CARB, and TOMM failure rates in non-head injury disability claimants. *Archives of Clinical Neuropsychology*, *19*, 475–87.

Gervais, R. O., Tarescavage, A. M., Greiffenstein, M. F., Wygant, D. B., Deslauriers, C., & Arends, P. (2018). Inconsistent responding on the MMPI-2-RF and uncooperative attitude: Evidence from cognitive performance validity measures. *Psychological Assessment, 30*, 410–415.

Glassmire, D. M., Jhawar, A., Burchett, D., & Tarescavage, A. M. (2016). Evaluating item endorsement rates for the MMPI-2-RF F-r and Fp-r scales across ethnic, gender, and diagnostic groups with a forensic inpatient unit. *Psychological Assessment, 29*, 500–508.

Glassmire, D. M., Tarescavage, A. M., & Gottfried, E. D. (2016). Likelihood of obtaining Structured Interview of Reported Symptoms (SIRS) and SIRS-2 elevations among forensic psychiatric inpatients with screening elevations on the Miller Forensic Assessment of Symptoms Test. *Psychological Assessment, 28*(12), 1586–1596.

Graham, J. R. (2012). *MMPI-2: Assessing Personality and Psychopathology* (5th ed.). New York: Oxford University Press.

Green, P. (2003). *Green's word memory test*. Edmonton: Green's Publishing.

Green, P. (2004). *Medical Symptom Validity Test (MSVT) for Microsoft Windows: User's manual*. Edmonton: Green's Publishing.

Green, P., & Iverson, G. L. (2001). Validation of the Computerized Assessment of Response Bias in litigating patients with head injuries. *The Clinical Neuropsychologist, 15*, 492–497.

Green, P., Rohling, M. L., Lees-Haley, P. R., & Allen, L. (2001). Effort has a greater effect on test scores than severe brain injury in compensation claimants. *Brain Injury, 15*, 1045–1060.

Greiffenstein, M. F., Baker, W. J., & Gola, T. (1994). Validation of malingered amnesia measures with a large clinical sample. *Psychological Assessment, 6*, 218–224.

Greve, K. W., Ord, J. S., Bianchini, K. J., & Curtis, M. S. (2009). Prevalence of malingering in patients with chronic pain referred for psychologic evaluation in a medico-legal context. *Archives of Physical Medicine and Rehabilitation, 90*, 1117–1126.

Guy, L. S., & Miller, H. A. (2004). Screening for malingered psychopathology in a correctional setting: Utility of the Miller-Forensic Assessment of Symptoms Test (M-FAST). *Criminal Justice and Behavior, 31*, 695–716.

Handel, R. W., Ben-Porath, Y. S., Tellegen, A., & Archer, R. P. (2010). Psychometric functioning of the MMPI-2-RF VRIN-r and TRIN-r scales with varying degrees of randomness, acquiescence, and counter-acquiescence. *Psychological Assessment, 22*, 87–95.

Hawes, S. W. & Boccaccini, M. T. (2009). Detection of overreporting of psychopathology on the Personality Assessment Inventory: A meta-analytic review. *Psychological Assessment, 21*, 112–124.

Heilbronner, R. L., Sweet, J. J., Morgan, J. E., Larrabee, G. J., Millis, S. R., & Conference Participants. (2009). American Academy of Clinical Neuropsychology Consensus Conference Statement on the neuropsychological assessment of effort, response bias, and malingering. *The Clinical Neuropsychologist, 23*(7), 1093–1129.

Himsl, K., Burchett, D., Tarescavage, A., & Glassmire, D. M. (2017). Assessing reading ability for psychological testing in forensic assessments: An investigation with the WRAT-4 and MMPI-2-RF. *International Journal of Forensic Mental Health, 16* (3), 239–248.

Hiscock, M., & Hiscock, C. K. (1989). Refining the forced-choice method for the detection of malingering. *Journal of Clinical and Experimental Neuropsychology, 11*(6), 967–974.

Hoelzle, J. B., Nelson, N. W., & Arbisi, P. A. (2012). MMPI-2 and MMPI-2-Restructured Form validity scales: Complimentary approaches to evaluate response validity. *Psychological Injury and Law, 5*, 174–191.

Holden, R. R., Kroner, D. G., Fekken, G. C., & Popham, S. M. (1992). A model of personality test item response dissimulation. *Journal of Personality and Social Psychology, 63*, 272–279.

Holden, R. R., & Lambert, C. E. (2015). Response latencies are alive and well for identifying fakers on a self-report personality inventory: A reconsideration of van Hooft and Born (2012). *Behavioral Research, 47*, 1436–1442.

Hopwood, C. J., Morey, L. C., Rogers, R., & Sewell, K. (2007). Malingering on the Personality Assessment Inventory: Identification of specific feigned disorders. *Journal of Personality Assessment, 88*, 43–48.

Hopwood, C. J., Orlando, M., & Clark, T. C. (2010). The detection of malingered pain-related disability with the Personality Assessment Inventory. *Rehabilitation Psychology, 55*, 307–310.

Hopwood, C. J., Talbert, C. A., Morey, L. C., & Rogers, R. (2008). Testing the incremental utility of the Negative Impression-Positive Impression differential in detecting simulated Personality Assessment Inventory profiles. *Journal of Clinical Psychology, 64*(3), 338–343.

Hunt, S., Root, J. C., & Bascetta, B. L. (2013). Effort testing in schizophrenia and schizoaffective disorder: Validity indicator profile and test of memory malingering performance characteristics. *Archives of Clinical Neuropsychology, 29*, 164–172.

Ingram, P. B., & Ternes, M. S. (2016). The detection of content-based invalid responding: A meta-analysis of the MMPI-2 Restructured Form's (MMPI-2-RF) over-reporting Validity Scales. *The Clinical Neuropsychologist, 30*(4), 473–496.

Inman, T. H., Vickery, C. D., Berry, D. T., Lamb, D. G., Edwards, C. L., & Smith, G. T. (1998). Development and initial validation of a new procedure for evaluating adequacy of effort given during neuropsychological testing: The letter memory test. *Psychological Assessment, 10*(2), 128.

Iverson, G. L. (1998). *21-Item Test research manual*. Vancouver: University of British Columbia.

Jackson, D. N., & Messick, S. (1958). Content and style in personality assessment. *Psychological Bulletin, 55*(4), 243–252.

Jasinski, L. J., Berry, D. T., Shandera, A. L., & Clark, J. A. (2011). Use of the Wechsler Adult Intelligence Scale Digit Span subtest for malingering detection: A meta-analytic review. *Journal of Clinical and Experimental Neuropsychology, 33*(3), 300–314.

Jasinski, L. J., Harp, J. P., Berry, D. T., Shandera-Ochsner, A. L., Mason, L. H., & Ranseen, J. D. (2011). Using symptom validity tests to detect malingered ADHD in college students. *The Clinical Neuropsychologist, 25*(8), 1415–1428.

Johnson, T., Kulesa, P., Cho, Y. I., & Shavitt, S. (2005). The relation between culture and response styles: Evidence from 19 countries. *Journal of Cross-Cultural Psychology, 36*, 264–277.

Jürges, H. (2007). True health vs response styles: Exploring cross-cultural differences in self-reported health. *Health Economics, 16*, 163–178.

Keeley, J. W., Webb, C., Peterson, D., Roussin, L., & Flanagan, E. H. (2016). Development of a Response Inconsistency Scale for the Personality Inventory for DSM-5. *Journal of Personality Assessment, 98*(4), 351–359.

Larrabee, G. J. (2003a). Exaggerated MMPI-2 symptom report in personal injury litigants with malingered neurocognitive deficit. *Archives of Clinical Neuropsychology, 18*, 673–686.

Larrabee, G. J. (2003b). Detection of malingering using atypical performance patterns on standard neuropsychological tests. *The Clinical Neuropsychologist*, *17*, 410–425.

Lees-Haley, P. R., English, L. T., & Glenn, W. J. (1991). A fake bad scale on the MMPI-2 for personal-injury claimants. *Psychological Reports*, *68*, 203–201.

Lewis, C., & Morrissey, C. (2010). The association between self-report and informant reports of emotional problems in a high secure intellectual disability sample. *Advances in Mental Health and Intellectual Disabilities*, *4*(2), 44–49.

Lewis, J. L., Simcox, A. M., & Berry, D. T. R. (2002). Screening for feigned psychiatric symptoms in a forensic sample by using the MMPI-2 and the Structured Inventory of Malingered Symptomatology. *Psychological Assessment*, *14*, 170–176.

Lezak, M. (1983). *Neuropsychological Assessment* (2nd ed.). New York: Oxford University Press.

Lezak, M., Howieson, D.B., & Loring, D.W. (2004). *Neuropsychological Assessment* (4th ed.). New York: Oxford University Press.

Liu, C., Liu, Z., Chiu, H. F. K., Carl, T. W., Zhang, H., Wang, P., et al. (2013). Detection of malingering: Psychometric evaluation of the Chinese version of the structured interview of reported symptoms-2. *BMC Psychiatry*, *13*, https://doi.org/10.1186/1471-244X-13-254

Main, C.J. (1983). The Modified Somatic Perception Questionnaire (MSPQ). *Journal of Psychosomatic Research*, *27*, 503–514.

McBride, W. F., Crighton, A. H., Wygant, D. B., & Granacher, R .P. (2013). It's not all in your head (or at least your brain): Association of traumatic brain lesion presence and location with performance on measures of response bias and forensic evaluation. *Behavioral Sciences and the Law*, *31*, 774–778.

Merckelbach, H., & Smith, G. P. (2003). Diagnostic accuracy of the Structured Inventory of Malingered Symptomatology (SIMS) in detecting instructed malingering. *Archives of Clinical Neuropsychology*, *18*, 145–152.

Miller, H. A. (2001). *Miller-Forensic Assessment of Symptoms Test (M-FAST): Professional manual*. Odessa, FL: Psychological Assessment Resources.

Miller, H. A. (2004). Examining the use of the M-FAST with criminal defendants incompetent to stand trial. *International Journal of Offender and Comparative Criminology*, *48*, 268–280.

Millis, S. R., & Kler, S. (1995). Limitations of the Rey Fifteen-Item Test in the detection of malingering. *The Clinical Neuropsychologist*, *9*(3), 241–244.

Millon, T., Millon, C., & Grossman, S. (2015). *Millon Clinical Multiaxial Inventory – IV manual* (4th ed.). Bloomington: NCS Pearson.

Mittenberg, W., Patton, C., Canyock, E. M., & Condit, D. C. (2002). Base rates of malingering and symptom exaggeration. *Journal of Clinical and Experimental Neuropsychology*, *24*, 1094–1102.

Mogge, N. L., Lepage, J. S., Bell, T., & Ragatz, L. (2010). The negative distortion scale: A new PAI validity scale. *Journal of Forensic Psychiatry and Psychology*, *21*, 77–90.

Montes, O., & Guyton, M. R. (2014). Performance of Hispanic inmates on the Spanish Miller Forensic Assessment of Symptoms Test (M-FAST). *Law and Human Behavior*, *38*, 428–438.

Morey, L. C. (1991/2007). *Personality Assessment Inventory professional manual* (2nd ed.). Odessa, FL: Psychological Assessment Resources.

Musso, M. W., Hill, B. D., Barker, A. A., Pella, R. D., & Gouvier, W. D. (2016). Utility of the Personality Assessment Inventory for detecting malingered ADHD in college students. *Journal of Attention Disorders*, *20*(9), 763–774.

Nadolny, E., & O'Dell, R. T. (2010). Measures of central tendency and intercorrelations within and between the SIMS and the M-FAST among medium security prison inmates. *American Journal of Forensic Psychology*, *28*, 51–67.

Neo, B., Sellbom, M., & Wygant, D. B. (in press). Evaluating the Psychometric Effects and Assessment of Inconsistent Responding on the Psychopathic Personality Inventory-Revised in a Correctional Sample. *Journal of Personality Disorders*.

Pankratz, L. (1979). Symptom validity testing and symptom retraining: Procedures for the assessment and treatment of functional sensory deficits. *Journal of Consulting and Clinical Psychology*, *47*, 409–410.

Pollard, C. A. (1984). Preliminary validity study of the Pain Disability Index. *Perceptual Motor Skills*, *59*, 974.

Rey, A. (1941). L'examen psychologique dans les cas d'encephalopathie traumatique. *Archives de Psychologie*, *28*, 286–340.

Rey, A. (1964). *L'examen clinique en psychologie*. Paris: Presses universitaires de France.

Roberson, C. J., Boone, K. B., Goldberg, H., Miora, D., Cottingham, M., Victor, T. et al. (2013). Cross validation of the b Test in a large known groups sample. *The Clinical Neuropsychologist*, *27*, 495–508.

Robles, L., Salazar, L. E., Boone, K. B., & Glaser, D. F. (2015). Specificity data for the b Test, Dot Counting Test, Rey-15 Item Plus Recognition, and Rey Word Recognition Test in monolingual Spanish-speakers. *Journal of Clinical and Experimental Neuropsychology*, *37*, 614–621.

Rogers, R. (2018a). Detection strategies for malingering and defensiveness. In R. Rogers & S. D. Bender (Eds.), *Clinical assessment of malingering and deception* (4th ed., pp. 18–41). New York: Guilford.

Rogers, R. (2018b). Structured interviews and dissimulation. In R. Rogers & S.D. Bender (Eds.), *Clinical assessment of malingering and deception* (4th ed., pp. 423–448). New York: Guilford.

Rogers, R., Bagby, R. M., & Dickens, S. E. (1992). *Structured Interview of Reported Symptoms (SIRS) and professional manual*. Odessa, FL: Psychological Assessment Resources.

Rogers, R., Ornduff, S. R., & Sewell, K. W. (1993). Feigning specific disorders: A study of the Personality Assessment Inventory (PAI). *Journal of Personality Assessment*, *60*, 554–560.

Rogers, R., Sewell, K. W., & Gillard, N. D. (2010). *Structured Interview of Reported Symptoms* (2nd ed.). Odessa, FL: Psychological Assessment Resources.

Rogers, R., Sewell, K. W., Morey, L. C., & Ustad, K. L. (1996). Detection of feigned mental disorders on the Personality Assessment Inventory: A discriminant analysis. *Journal of Personality Assessment*, *67*, 629–640.

Rubenzer, S. (2010). Review of the Structured Interview of Reported Symptoms-2 (SIRS-2). *Open Access Journal of Forensic Psychology*, *2*, 273–286.

Sanchez, G., Ampudia, A. Jimenez, F., & Amado, B. G. (2017). Contrasting the efficacy of the MMPI-2-RF overreporting scales in the detection of malingering. *The European Journal of Psychology Applied in the Legal Context*, *9*, 51–56.

Schmidt, M. (1996). Rey auditory verbal learning test: A handbook. Los Angeles: Western Psychological Services.

Schutte, C., & Axelrod, B. N. (2013). Use of embedded cognitive symptom validity measures in mild traumatic brain injury cases. In S. S. Bush (Ed.), *Mild traumatic brain injury: Symptom validity assessment and malingering* (pp. 159–181). New York: Springer.

Sellbom, M., & Bagby, R. M. (2008a). Response styles on multiscale inventories. In R. Rogers (Ed.), *Clinical assessment of malingering and deception* (3rd ed., pp. 182–206). New York: Guilford.

Sellbom, M., & Bagby, R. M. (2008b). Validity of the MMPI-2-RF (Restructured Form) L-r and K-r scales in detecting underreporting in clinical and nonclinical samples. *Psychological Assessment, 20*, 370–376.

Sellbom, M., Wygant, D. B., & Bagby, R. M. (2012). Utility of the MMPI-2-RF in detecting non-credible somatic complaints. *Psychiatry Research, 197*, 295–301.

Sharf, A. J., Rogers, R., Williams, M. M., & Henry, S. A. (2017). The effectiveness of the MMPI-2-RF in detecting feigned mental disorders and cognitive deficits: A meta-analysis. *Journal of Psychopathology and Behavioral Assessment, 39*, 441–455. https://doi.org/10.1007/s10862-017-9590-1

Slick, D., Hopp, G., Strauss, E., & Thompson, G. (1997). *The Victoria Symptom Validity Test*. Odessa, FL: Psychological Assessment Resources.

Slick, D. J., Sherman, E. M., & Iverson, G. L. (1999). Diagnostic criteria for malingered neurocognitive dysfunction: Proposed standards for clinical practice and research. *The Clinical Neuropsychologist, 13*, 545–561.

Smith, G. P. (2008). Brief screening measures for the detection of feigned psychopathology. In R. Rogers (Ed.), *Clinical assessment of malingering and deception* (3rd ed., pp. 323–339). New York: Guilford.

Smith, G. (2018). Brief measures for the detection of feigning and impression management. In R. Rogers & S. D. Bender (Eds.), *Clinical assessment of malingering and deception* (4th ed., pp. 449–472). New York: Guilford.

Sollman, M. J., & Berry, D. T. (2011). Detection of inadequate effort on neuropsychological testing: A meta-analytic update and extension. *Archives of Clinical Neuropsychology, 26*(8), 774–789.

Spencer, R. J., Axelrod, B. N., Drag, L. L., Waldron-Perrine, B., Pangilinan, P. H., & Bieliauskas, L. A. (2013). WAIS-IV reliable digit span is no more accurate than age corrected scaled score as an indicator of invalid performance in a veteran sample undergoing evaluation for mTBI. *The Clinical Neuropsychologist, 27*(8), 1362–1372.

Stedman, J. M., McGeary, C. A., & Essery, J. (2017). Current patterns of training in personality assessment during internship. *Journal of Clinical Psychology*. Advance online publication. https://doi.org/10.1002/jclp.22496

Sullivan, K., & King, J. (2010). Detecting faked psychopathology: A comparison of two tests to detect malingered psychopathology using a simulation design. *Psychiatry Research, 176*, 75–81.

Sweet, J. J., Condit, D. C., & Nelson, N. W. (2008). Feigned amnesia and memory loss. In R. Rogers (Ed.), *Clinical assessment of malingering and deception* (3rd ed., pp. 218–236). New York: Guilford.

Tarescavage, A. M., & Glassmire, D. M. (2016). Differences between structured interview of reported symptoms (SIRS) and SIRS-2 sensitivity estimates among forensic inpatients: A criterion groups comparison. *Law and Human Behavior, 40*, 488–502.

Thompson, G. B. (2003). The Victoria Symptom Validity Test: An enhanced test of symptom validity. *Journal of Forensic Neuropsychology, 2*, 43–67.

Tombaugh, T. N. (1996). Test of *Memory Malingering*: TOMM. New York: MHS Assessments.

Tombaugh, T. N. (2002). The Test of Memory Malingering (TOMM) in forensic psychology. *Journal of Forensic Neuropsychology, 2*, 69–96.

Tylicki, J. L. Wygant, D. B., Tarescavage, A. M., Frederick, R. I., Tyner, E. A., Granacher, R. P., & Sellbom, M. (2018). Comparability of Structured Interview of Reported Symptoms (SIRS) and Structured Interview of Reported Symptoms – 2nd Edition (SIRS-2) classifications with external response bias criteria. *Psychological Assessment, 30*, 1144–1159.

Van Impelen, A., Merckelbach, H., Jelicic, M., & Merten. T. (2014). The Structured Inventory of Malingered Symptomatology (SIMS): A systematic review and meta-analysis. *The Clinical Neuropsychologist, 28*, 1336–1365.

Veazey, C. H., Hays, J. R., Wagner, A. L., & Miller, H. A. (2005). Validity of the Miller Forensic Assessment of Symptoms Test in psychiatric inpatients. *Psychological Reports, 96*, 771–774.

Vickery, C. D., Berry, D. T., Inman, T. H., Harris, M. J., & Orey, S. A. (2001). Detection of inadequate effort on neuropsychological testing: A meta-analytic review of selected procedures. *Archives of Clinical Neuropsychology, 16*(1), 45–73.

Vitacco, M. J., Rogers, R., Gabel, J., & Munizza, J. (2007). An evaluation of malingering screens with competency to stand trial patients: a known-groups comparison. *Law and Human Behavior, 31*, 249–260.

Waddell, G., McCulloch, J.A., Kummel, E., & Venner, R. M. (1980). Nonorganic physical signs in low-back pain. *Spine, 5*, 117–125.

Weiss, R. A., Rosenfeld, B., & Farkas, M. R. (2011). The utility of the Structured Interview of Reported Symptoms in a sample of individuals with intellectual disabilities. *Assessment, 18*(3), 284–290.

Widows, M., & Smith, G. P. (2005). *Structured Inventory of Malingered Symptomatology (SIMS): Professional manual*. Odessa, FL: Psychological Assessment Resources.

Wiggins, C. W., Wygant, D. B., Hoelzle, J. B., & Gervais, R. O. (2012). The more you say the less it means: Overreporting and attenuated criterion validity in a forensic disability sample. *Psychological Injury and Law, 5*, 162–173.

Wygant, D. B., Anderson, J. L., Sellbom, M., Rapier, J. L., Allgeier, L. M., & Granacher, R. P. (2011). Association of the MMPI-2 Restructured Form (MMPI-2-RF) Validity Scales with structured malingering criteria. *Psychological Injury and Law, 4*, 13–23.

Wygant, D. B., Arbisi, P. A., Bianchini, K. J., & Umlauf, R. L. (2017). Waddell nonorganic signs: New evidence suggests somatic amplification among outpatient chronic pain patients. *The Spine Journal, 17*, 505–510.

Wygant, D. B., Ben-Porath, Y. S., & Arbisi, P. A. (2004). Development and initial validation of a scale to detect infrequent somatic complaints. Poster presented at the 39th Annual Symposium on Recent Developments of the MMPI-2/MMPI-A, Minneapolis, MN, May.

Wygant, D. B., Walls, B. D., Brothers, S. L., & Berry, D. T. R. (2018). Assessment of malingering and defensiveness on the MMPI-2 and MMPI-2-RF. In R. Rogers & S. D. Bender (Eds.), *Clinical assessment of malingering and deception* (4th ed., pp. 267–279). New York: Guilford Press.

7 Technological Advances in Clinical Assessment

Ambulatory Assessment

TIMOTHY J. TRULL, SARAH A. GRIFFIN, AND ASHLEY C. HELLE

Traditionally, clinical assessment is conducted in a psychologist's consulting room or, less frequently, in a dedicated laboratory. The results of the questionnaires, interviews, or tasks are viewed as an "assay" of an individual's characteristics or tendencies that reflect or influence real-world behavior. That is, scores from these measures form the basis of judgments regarding individuals' relative standing on dimensions/constructs relevant to psychopathology, as compared to that of peers or comparison groups. The important point here is that clinicians make inferences or predictions from these results concerning real-world mood, cognitions, and behavior of clients or patients. To be sure, this perspective developed due to the difficulty of assessing a person's mood, cognitions, behavior, and physiology as these unfold in daily life. However, because clinical assessment is most useful when it can accurately reflect real-world experiences of individuals, whether they be depressed, anxious, impulsive, or engaged in maladaptive behavior, a new assessment approach was needed.

Advances in technology have profoundly influenced the possibilities for clinical assessment. Perhaps the biggest beneficiary is a method of assessment that targets the moods, cognitions, behaviors, physiological states, and experiences of individuals as they are living their daily life. *Ambulatory assessment* (AA), which is also sometimes referred to as *ecological momentary assessment* (EMA; Stone & Shiffman, 1994), differs from traditional forms of assessment (e.g., self-report questionnaires, laboratory tasks, clinical and diagnostic interviews) in several important ways (Trull & Ebner-Priemer, 2013). First, because AA involves multiple assessments over time, it is uniquely suited to focus on *within-individual processes*. For example, depression is a dynamic process that ebbs and flows over time, often as a result of contextual or environmental factors. Yet traditional, cross-sectional assessment requires individuals to somehow characterize depression by aggregating in some unspecified way over, perhaps, extended periods of time (e.g., two weeks). Furthermore, traditional clinical assessment often requires some degree of retrospection (in extreme cases, over one's lifetime). In contrast, AA can be used to target momentary experiences (e.g., "within the last fifteen minutes"; "right now"), *minimizing retrospective biases and memory heuristics* (e.g., the peak-end rule; Fredrickson & Kahneman, 1993). AA captures slices of these processes in real or near real time, allowing an evaluation of not only the mood process (e.g., how much one's depression changes within and across days) but also potential internal and external influences on these processes. Thus, AA adds a needed *time dimension* to the assessment of psychological constructs. Finally, owing to the collection of data during the daily lives of individuals, the implicit *ecological validity and external validity* of these assessments matches, if not exceeds, that of more traditional measures that are completed in the artificial environment of the clinic, laboratory, or hospital. This chapter will review the clinical applications of AA, but we do not believe that AA methods are at a place yet of standing alone as a clinical assessment approach. However, when used appropriately and mindful of current limitations, AA and EMA can be useful in a variety of clinical contexts.

Although AA and EMA may seem new to most, these methods have roots that date back to antiquity in the form of written records or diaries that catalogued events, private experiences, and observations (Wilhelm, Perrez, & Pawlik, 2012). By the late nineteenth and early twentieth centuries, these methods were used as part of early scientific investigations into affective states and behavior in daily life (Stone et al., 2007; Wilhelm et al., 2012). Even at this stage, investigators were skeptical of the reliability and validity of *retrospective* reports and used these new methods to capture momentary experiences that were less vulnerable to retrospective bias as well as more ecologically valid. The nascent fields of health psychology and behavior therapy took great advantage of these "self-observation" procedures to inform both theories of and interventions for problematic behavior as it occurred in daily life.

Early daily life research used paper-and-pencil diaries to record thoughts, feelings, and experiences (typically referred to as the *experience sampling method*; ESM).

Often participants were given packets of paper diaries and instructed when to complete the individual surveys or were prompted by pagers or timers to complete the surveys. These surveys were then returned to the researchers at designated intervals or at the end of the study. However, several seminal studies demonstrated that individuals were prone to "hoard" responses until close to the deadline for submission and to subsequently "back-fill" responses from previous days (e.g., Stone et al., 2002). Fortunately, advances in technology such as digital diaries allowed for a more accurate assessment of compliance, the time-stamping of responses, an array of sampling options, the digitization of responses, and flexible software options that could be tailored for individual projects or studies (Wilhelm et al., 2012).

The widespread availability and use of smartphones has been a game-changer for AA. Approximately 77 percent of adults in the United States own smartphones (Pew Research Center, 2018) and there are more than 2 billion smartphone users worldwide. The smartphone not only can serve as an electronic diary but also can collect data using many of its own built-in sensors and functions. Furthermore, using Bluetooth connections, the smartphone can serve as a wireless hub that collects and transmits data from both internal and external sensors. Thus, the smartphone can serve as a nexus hub for a range of AA devices and sensors.

The introduction of smartphones (and, originally, electronic diaries) in daily life research for recording experiences represented a major advancement for several reasons: (1) all entries are time-stamped; (2) there is no need to transcribe or score responses by hand; and (3) these devices are more convenient for participants and can store large amounts of data. Many refer to this method of collecting self-reported data as *ecological momentary assessment* (EMA) since self-reports on states, experiences, and behaviors are obtained in real or near real time in participants' natural environments. Perhaps less familiar, there are "passive" data collection methods available to the AA clinician or researcher as well, wherein behaviors or states can be "observed" by electronic devices. For example, devices can record the opening of medication bottles (including digital time stamps) and smartphones can record or be programmed to record audio or video. In addition, as mentioned in this section and discussed further later, a number of wireless sensor products currently on the market can record physical activity, cardiac activity, respiration, and electrodermal activity, for example. These sensors, in turn, can transmit data to the smartphone via Bluetooth.

CURRENT TECHNOLOGIES

Current AA methods incorporate tools, techniques, and technologies from a variety of fields, including medicine. Existing reviews cover the array of AA technology and systematically examine the nuances of the topic (e.g., Carpenter, Wycoff, & Trull, 2016; Perna et al., 2018); therefore, for space conservation, every technology relevant to AA will not be detailed here. Instead, we highlight three primary categories of information currently being captured using available AA technologies: self-report, environment- or context-specific, and psychophysiology.

Self-report. Self-report information is typically gathered via mobile phone or electronic diary, either through texting prompts, Internet-based survey platforms (e.g., SurveyMonkey, Qualtrics), or native applications installed on the device itself. Pragmatism must be employed in implementing sampling designs, giving consideration to issues including timing and frequency of prompts, conditions under which reports are collected, and length of survey, among others (for in-depth discussions, see Carpenter et al., 2016; Fisher & To, 2012; Intille, 2007). Importantly, self-report information collected through AA is "active" data collection, in that individuals are actively providing the information, contrasting other passive methods. Unfortunately, relatively few self-report measures have been validated across AA studies and samples; instead, typically, researchers select items from a larger cross-sectional measure and adapt the instructions to fit the desired time frame (e.g., over the last fifteen minutes). For purposes of reliability and validity within the AA framework, it is recommended that complex constructs be assessed with at least three items, while discrete phenomena or behavior may be assessed with a single item (Shrout & Lane, 2011). It is worth noting that self-report AA ratings may still rely on retrospective recall, depending on the instructions given. For example, responding to a prompt to rate one's mood since the last prompt or receiving a prompt but completing the survey hours later may involve some degree of retrospective recall. Therefore it is important to monitor both signal and response time (using time stamps) and to be clear about rating instructions, as these are directly relevant to analysis and interpretation.

Despite the temptation of ease and convenience, we cannot assume that cross-sectional measures will retain original, or even similar, psychometric properties when administered repeatedly in short intervals. Currently, there is a lack of psychometric evaluation of AA questionnaires, which may be due to unfamiliarity with methods to assess psychometric properties of repeated longitudinal data; several authors have fortunately outlined options for responding to this issue (e.g., Fisher & To, 2012). It is also of note that current publication standards are inconsistent for AA and traditional, cross-sectional measures. Although details on the psychometric qualities of traditional self-report measures are required for publication, typically the reliability and validity of AA measures are assumed but not evaluated or reported. As such, it is difficult to judge the psychometric properties of AA surveys because the metrics are not reported routinely beyond the reporting of the cross-sectional reliabilities of the instruments modified for AA studies. That being said, investigators are now starting to report psychometric properties of AA measures used in their studies (Dubad et al., 2018), and many self-report scales administered via AA show reasonable to excellent convergent relationships with related criteria, likely owing to the implicit increased external validity of administering scales within a person's daily life and the scale's proximity to the dependent variables of interest.

As mentioned, cross-sectional questionnaires whose manuals provide norm-based cutoffs or ranges should not be applied naively with different instructions within an AA framework. Any norms would need to be recalculated based on information gathered over the intended AA time frame and future administrations of that measure would need to adhere to a similar time frame and sampling schedule to accurately employ those norms. For example, response level ratings increase as the time frames for rating increase (Walentynowicz, Schneider, & Stone, 2018). Given that self-report is the most commonly used method in AA, significant work remains to evaluate the psychometric properties of momentary self-report measures already in use in AA, particularly those assessing complex constructs captured in multi-item scales as well as those scales with norm-referenced cutoffs.

Context-specific. The second cluster of data collected through AA is environmental and context-specific information. There are several ways in which data like these can be collected, depending primarily on the targets of interest. To understand more about a person within a given situation or context while having them actively provide information, some AA designs require individuals to opt in to surveys or reports when they are in specific scenarios or situations. Context or environmental data can also be collected passively, without an individual actively interacting with the data collection platform. For example, an early technology to capture environmental data without user initiation was the *Electronically Activated Recorder* (EAR; Mehl et al., 2001), a small audio recorder programmed to capture sound bites throughout the day that then are coded for variables of interest. Smartphones now also have this capability. In addition, it is possible to track GPS location using smartphones with participant consent and activation of this feature. GPS can be used to track physical location, to better understand activity or movement by combining these data with self-reported experience, or to prompt participants to complete location-specific tasks or reports (e.g., report on alcohol use when in a bar). Passive data collection methods, like GPS monitoring, have the benefit of placing relatively little burden on the individual. Combining self-report and context data provides real-time insight into human phenomena, which is particularly useful for improving our understanding of infrequent or maladaptive behaviors or events.

Psychophysiology. Lastly, AA can incorporate psychophysiological measurement from external devices to identify physiological processes associated with subjective experience in real time. It should be noted that ambulatory monitoring devices (e.g., Holter monitors, home blood pressure monitoring) have been used successfully (reliably and validly) in physical medicine for decades; however, recent advances provide increased comfort and discretion in the user experience, facilitating extended periods of use and expanded device utility beyond medical necessity. Devices such as wrist monitors, biometric shirts (e.g., Hexoskin; Villar, Beltrame, & Hughson, 2015), and even smartphone sensors can be used to record physiological indicators in real time. Physiological indices of interest monitored via AA include heart rate (HR), heart rate variability (HRV), electrodermal activity (EDA), respiration, movement, and sleep, among others. Latest technologies also allow for momentary assessment of complex indicators like blood alcohol level and gait via smartphone applications and sensors. Despite the proliferation and promise of these sensors, it cannot be assumed that there is no measurement error involved. For example, wearable devices vary in their hardware precision, sampling rates, and dependency on close contact with the body. Wrist sensors that can assess HR and EDA are appealing because they are relatively unobtrusive but, if they are not worn properly, the data collected will be unreliable. In addition, these devices may drain the battery on smartphones when using Bluetooth connections, sometimes requiring recharging within a day. One approach may be to simply collect the physiological data for later download but the investigator may find out much too late that the data are unreliable or even missing due to technical malfunctions.

It is also important to collect enough information from the individual to place the physiological data within context, as it may be difficult to interpret or extrapolate psychological meaning with physiological data alone. For example, intense physical activity will greatly influence cardiac and respiratory activity indices. Therefore, it is important to assess the content of activity (through self-report) as well as the physiological correlates of activity. In combination with the methods discussed in this section, these technologies enable a better understanding of the link between physiology and behavior, mood, life events, and symptoms.

As AA technologies and capabilities continue to evolve and expand, so too do the possible applications of these methods. To illustrate the potential utility of AA, we highlight the utility and functions of AA within both research and clinical realms in turn.

APPLICATION: RESEARCH

Using AA in Research

AA can improve understanding of clinical symptoms and experiential phenomena through the use of a rich contextual framework set within individuals' daily lives. In this section, we begin by describing the application of AA in psychological research by discussing several methodological benefits, including limiting retrospective recall and adapting sampling frequency to the construct of interest. Next, we provide illustrations of these applications as related to specific disorders, such as major depressive disorder (MDD) and social anxiety disorder (SAD). Finally, we highlight the unique advantages of AA data, through discussion of contextual and temporal features not well captured by other data collection methods. This section is not an exhaustive review of the application of AA research methodology, nor the outcomes of clinical research using AA. Rather, examples are highlighted to illustrate the utility of this methodology.

By nature of the AA method, gathering information in the moment and iteratively, we can glean insight into individuals' daily lives that may be otherwise lost or distorted in the bias of retrospective recall. To illustrate, comparing retrospective with momentary reports, individuals with depression on an inpatient unit tended to retrospectively overreport severity of symptoms, including anhedonia, sadness, and suicidality, in comparison to momentary reports of those same symptoms (Ben-Zeev & Young, 2010). Interestingly, nondepressed controls were also inaccurate in their recall. In fact, both groups were equally biased in their overreporting of tension, concentration difficulty, guilt, and fear. However, controls tended to underreport helplessness, detachment, and self-control (Ben-Zeev & Young, 2010). Therefore, people, regardless of clinical diagnosis or mental health status tend to show bias in their retrospective recall of behaviors, attitudes, cognitions, and emotions and the nature of those biases may depend on diagnostic status or clinical impairment. This type of systematic bias highlights the utility of AA methods regardless of the population being studied.

Additionally, by sampling small snapshots of individuals' lives intensively (e.g., frequent monitoring for forty-eight hours), one can assess distinctions between and within constructs germane to many areas of importance in the field of human behavior and psychophysiology. The ability to adjust sampling frequency in a very precise manner is a strength of AA methodology and increases the accuracy and precision of assessing human phenomena in the real world. For example, it is more appropriate to capture affective instability in borderline personality disorder (BPD) with frequent assessments within one day, whereas affect fluctuations of manic and major depressive episodes within bipolar disorder might best be captured by daily assessments over multiple weeks or months (Ebner-Priemer & Trull, 2009; Ebner-Priemer & Sawitzki, 2007).

Examples of AA in clinical research. AA is used in psychopathology research targeting a range of clinical problems, including mood, anxiety, substance, and personality disorders. For example, multiple AA studies have found that spikes in anticipatory anxiety *did not precede* panic attacks; rather, anticipatory anxiety spiked *after* panic attacks related to possible future panic attacks (Walz, Nauta, & aan het Rot, 2014). This finding challenges conventional clinical wisdom and suggests that large increases in anticipatory anxiety do not actually predict or cause panic attacks. AA research has also revealed differential symptom expression, such that patients with PTSD showed greater instability of self-reported physiological anxiety indicators and shorter symptom lapses than patients who experience panic attacks (Pfaltz et al., 2010).

Work in the field of psychotic disorders highlights the importance of AA to our conceptualization and assessment of clinical phenomena. Anhedonia, or the blunted capacity to experience pleasure, has long been considered a negative symptom of schizophrenia spectrum disorders. This has been supported by cross-sectional findings that individuals with schizophrenia self-report lower levels of pleasure on trait measures (Horan et al., 2006; Oorschot et al., 2009). Recent research, including select AA investigations, has challenged this, demonstrating that individuals who experience psychosis may actually show similar capacity for positive emotion when elicited in the lab or captured in real life (e.g., Gard et al., 2007, & Myin-Germeys, Delespaul, & DeVries, 2000; for a thorough review of emotion and schizophrenia, see Kring & Moran, 2008). These findings, compiled by Kring and Moran (2008), are cited within the online text of the fifth edition of the *Diagnostic and Statistical Manual of Mental Disorders* (DSM-5; American Psychiatric Association, 2013) as evidence for expanding the diagnostic definition of anhedonic experiences within criteria for schizophrenia spectrum disorders to include "degradation in the recollection of pleasure previously experienced." Since this update in DSM-5, additional AA studies have been conducted to field-test laboratory-based hypotheses about emotional experience in psychosis. Several studies to date have showed that individuals who experience psychosis show an intact capability of experiencing enjoyment and pleasure in the moment; however, individuals with psychosis also tend to report fewer pleasant events in their daily lives than do emotional controls (e.g., Oorschot et al., 2013).

As evidenced by this research, AA can capture dynamic processes as they unfold in daily life. Thus, AA can aid in the detection and clarification of unique and common features of syndromes, allowing for further clarification on the true processes and mechanisms and impairment, as well as providing more targeted directions for intervention. Ebner-Priemer and Trull (2009) provide an overview of EMA for assessing dynamic processes within mood disorders, highlighting the importance of utilizing appropriate analytic and sampling strategies to capture the essence of the appropriate constructs, as previously described. For instance, AA has played a critical role in understanding affective dynamics, the ebb and flow of emotional experience in daily life (Trull et al., 2015). AA methods allow for the assessment of mood fluctuation as a dynamic process – as opposed to retrospective report and aggregate data, which fail to capture the fluid and oscillating nature of emotion. In fact, multiple dynamic features of affect have been identified from AA techniques, including affective instability, emotional inertia, and emotion differentiation (Trull et al., 2015). These features of mood dynamics expand our ability to understand, assess, and discuss emotional experiences while also elucidating meaningful differences in experience across disorders. For instance, individuals with BPD and MDD have similar *average levels* of negative affect; however, when examining AA data, those with BPD had a higher frequency of affective *instability*, with more extreme variability, compared to those with MDD (Trull et al., 2008). Conversely, *emotional inertia*, or the maintenance of similar levels of affect despite changes in the environment, has been highlighted as a warning sign of transition into major depressive episodes (van de Leemput et al., 2014) and is highly relevant to the maintenance of negative emotion in those with MDD (Trull et al., 2015). Emotional inertia has even been shown to predict future onset of MDD in adolescents, above and beyond other risk factors (Kuppens et al., 2012). *Emotional differentiation*, a third dynamic feature of mood, refers to the empirical differentiation between emotional states (e.g., sadness from fear from anger; Barrett et al., 2001). This feature may manifest itself differently across diagnoses, including MDD, BPD, generalized anxiety, and schizophrenia, and has shown predictive relationships with several important clinical outcomes, such as nonsuicidal self-injury, impulsivity, and alcohol use (see Trull et al., 2015). Because AA methods can collect tens or even hundreds of responses over time within each person, we can start to distinguish disorders from one another based on intricacies of symptom profiles and dynamics in daily life. These important distinctions are likely to be missed with retrospective reporting and can be captured using AA assessments to aid in differential diagnoses of complex cases in the future.

Examining temporal and contextual associations with AA. AA data can reveal temporal precedence and dynamic patterns because they uncover both internal and environmental antecedents of clinically relevant events and behaviors. However, it is important to note that AA and other longitudinal data cannot "prove" causality; given that random assignment to life circumstances or daily events is impossible, all data are inherently correlational (Conner & Lehman, 2012). As such, here we discuss antecedents of human experience and phenomena rather than "causes."

It is well-established that there is a temporal association between substance craving and use or relapse (e.g., Schneekloth et al., 2012). AA studies have further elucidated the intricacies of this process. For example, a recent study identified that, among individuals currently addicted to alcohol, tobacco, cannabis, or heroin, person-specific cues and associations, not substance-specific cues, preceded increases in substance craving, which, in turn, preceded increased substance use (Fatseas et al., 2015). Additional work has highlighted the temporal association between craving and alcohol use, demonstrating that increased craving predicted alcohol relapse within the following twelve hours (Moore et al., 2014) and alcohol craving within the first two drinks of a drinking episode predicted higher alcohol consumption during that episode (Ray et al., 2010). Repeated and temporally sensitive measurement of craving and substance use allowed for these insights into what individuals might retrospectively report as a muddied and unclear process, clarifying the temporal relationships between risk factors.

AA methodologies can clarify and test competing theories of processes of interactions between symptoms or behaviors and contextual factors. For example, to further assess timing and motive for cannabis use among patients with social anxiety, Buckner and colleagues (2012) utilized AA and found that cannabis users with social anxiety were more likely to use cannabis when they were in social situations where others were using and they reported high anxiety in these situations rather than before or after social events (Buckner et al., 2012). Another study examined symptom exacerbation through reactions to stressors in daily life between three groups: individuals with psychosis, with BPD, and controls. Those with BPD demonstrated a significantly larger change in negative affect (increased) and positive affect (decreased) following a stressful daily event than did those in the other groups (Glaser et al., 2007). Similar work has been conducted across disorders (e.g., depression, bipolar disorder, psychosis), with the goal of examining changes in mood associated with various contextual factors including daily stressors, time of day, and social interactions (Delespaul & DeVries, 1987; Myin-Germeys et al., 2003; Stiglmayr et al., 2008).

APPLICATION: INTERVENTION

Using Ambulatory Assessment in Treatment

AA allows for gathering data on relevant clinical constructs (e.g., symptoms, mood) in the patients' real world and in real time (Myin-Germeys et al., 2018). This can inform and improve treatment and AA can be utilized as a platform for intervention itself. Several review papers have discussed important considerations when integrating AA into intervention (e.g., Heron & Smyth, 2010; Kaplan & Stone, 2013; Shiffman, Stone & Hufford, 2008). This integration aligns with the current paradigm shift toward personalized medicine, personally tailored interventions, and the delivery of specialized, targeted care to increase efficiency and efficacy in patient care (Perna et al., 2018). Tailored interventions can assist in providing evidence-based predictions based on large amounts of information (e.g., electronic medical records and AA data). For instance, noninvasive wearable devices can provide a great amount of detail about daily activity and biomarkers associated with psychiatric illness, thereby supporting the identification of treatment targets (Hsin et al., 2018).

Treatment planning and diagnosis. Initial assessment of presenting concerns is generally the first step in treatment planning. Utilizing AA at this stage can provide rich data to aid in this process. Collecting information from patients can establish a baseline level of symptoms and also capture their day-to-day experiences, level of functioning, and impairment. Furthermore, AA reporting of these experiences provides a level of detail and granularity at the outset of treatment that is not as biased by retrospective recall as traditional clinical methods; these data capture current levels of distress and symptomatology better. It can be helpful to think of AA as supplemental to data gathered from the client in the session, which are typically collected via self-report measures and clinical interviews. When used in conjunction with other types of supplemental information (e.g., family report), active or passively collected AA data can contribute to a rich, full clinical picture and inform treatment planning. AA can also help refine diagnostic impressions given modest agreement between retrospective and momentary recall, concerns well-documented in recall bias research. For example, studies show that the agreement between recalled mood instability and mood instability assessed with EMA is poor (e.g., Solhan et al., 2009). More recently, diagnostic systems using EMA technology have been proposed (van Os et al., 2013) and the trend of integrating traditional and AA data to inform diagnosis and treatment is likely to continue.

Active treatment. Monitoring symptoms throughout treatment is a hallmark of numerous evidence-based treatment (EBT) approaches (e.g., cognitive behavioral therapy for anxiety, dialectical behavior therapy, exposure and response prevention for obsessive-compulsive disorder) and is not a new concept. For example, DBT patients track mood and behaviors daily, often on a paper diary card. AA can provide more detailed and precise information compared to weekly or biweekly reports of symptoms, bypassing reliance on retrospective recall while also providing valuable incremental information (i.e., real-time, real-world experience). Some patients may actually prefer to enter and track this information on a smartphone, which is more readily accessible, compared to a paper log. The end result is more reliable and compliant data entry.

Monitoring experiences of daily life in treatment can provide a number of benefits for patients and providers. In addition to increasing accuracy of information, the ease of usage for patients may be the chief benefit. Many EMA/EMI applications have been deemed acceptable by participants (Heron & Smyth, 2010). Furthermore, as a direct benefit, research has shown symptom-tracking itself can increase self-awareness and, in some cases, a reduction in symptoms (for a review, see Dubad et al., 2018).

In the spirit of collaborative treatment, feedback and discussion with the patient, from the initial assessment phase, to establishing treatment goals, and monitoring treatment progress, are a central part of psychological treatment. Utilizing AA methods can assist in each step of this process, supplementing weekly or biweekly rating scales if desired. AA of symptoms throughout treatment may also provide the client with a structured platform to monitor their symptoms in collaboration with the provider (e.g., communicated through a secured shared server or discussed in weekly session), similar to many medical models in which patients can share electronic medical record (EMR) messaging systems with physicians. For example, Shiffman and colleagues (2008) refer to the microanalysis of process, in which the clinician and patient then systematically analyze behavior, including context and mood – an intervention that may be more effective and efficient when incorporating the contextual data from the patient's AA reports. Thus, incorporating AA of symptoms into treatment may increase agency and investment with treatment process, can provide rich contextual information, and is consistent with patient-focused care.

In addition to patient-oriented benefits, monitoring symptoms can provide substantive information to providers regarding responses (e.g., behavioral, physiological) to interventions. This information, in turn, can be used to inform decisions regarding continuing or modifying treatment in a timely manner. This may be particularly germane in research assessing new interventions and/or to monitor and respond to side effects or adverse events as they occur, rather than at extended follow-up periods.

Treatment on the Go: Ecological Momentary Intervention

EMI and just-in-time intervention (JIT) are interventions delivered with an emphasis on ecological validity, the utilization of smartphone applications, delivered in the context of patients' real life and in real time (Heron & Smyth, 2010). At the present stage of development and utilization, EMIs appear to be most commonly used adjunctively to in-person therapies. EMIs have the capability to be tailored to individuals, allowing them to fit well within the paradigm shift toward personalized patient care (e.g., Perna et al., 2018).

EMI can be implemented in a variety of ways. EMIs typically are prompted based on active or passive data collected from the participant (e.g., self-reported depression, GPS location). For example, if there is a reported increase in a distress, an urge to use drugs, or an increase in heart rate, the programmed EMI may send a message encouraging the person to practice a skill or showing a short video offering guidance on a skill. A major benefit of these interventions over traditional treatment is the ability to target behavioral change in these salient moments (i.e., "just in time") to influence the outcome (e.g., effective skill use rather than engaging in problematic behavior). When used in the context of traditional psychological treatment, the clinician can review the momentary intervention with the patient in session and discuss its effectiveness.

Research outcomes. Although the use of AA in interventions, and EMI research more specifically, is in early stages of testing and refinement, research indicates mixed results. On the one hand, participants and patients have largely rated EMIs as acceptable and easy to use. For example, Wright and colleagues (2018) conducted a randomized control trial (RCT) of EMI for risky alcohol consumption in young adults, and individuals who received the EMI rated acceptability as high. A review of twenty-seven EMIs spanning a variety of health behaviors (e.g., alcohol use, smoking cessation, healthy eating) concluded that the EMIs were well-received (Heron & Smyth, 2010). On the other hand, however, evidence on the effectiveness of EMIs remains equivocal. Some EMIs have not shown significant treatment effects (e.g., Wright et al., 2018), while others show more promise. EMIs were found efficacious for targeting behavior change when used in conjunction with individual or group therapy (Heron & Smyth, 2010). An EMI for smoking cessation delivered automated, tailored messages targeting risk factors (e.g., being around a smoker, availability of cigarettes, urge to smoke, motivation to quit, and stress) as reported in the moment by participants and these messages were associated with reduction in risk factors (Hebert et al., 2018). Nevertheless, before they can be considered stand-alone EBTs, more research into the efficacy of EMIs is needed (using RCTs; see Byambasuren et al., 2018), particularly research that is sensitive to different presenting problems and symptom manifestation.

CHALLENGES AND RECOMMENDATIONS

Utilizing AA in treatment settings and research as well as the use of EMIs as stand-alone interventions are all exciting areas of growth in the psychological and medical research sectors. Although these are burgeoning areas, as previously mentioned, there is currently limited support for the efficacy of a wide range of EMIs. The field of EMIs is in its infancy and rigorous RCTs are a necessary first step (Byambasuren et al., 2018; Perna et al., 2018). However, several recent "proof of concept" papers do suggest promise. Even in these early stages of establishing empirical support for EMIs, AA can be used to aid in the development and refinement of EMI or more traditional interventions. For instance, AA methods can enhance our understanding about motivations for drinking (Crooke et al., 2013) and provide evidence for the "functions" of behaviors directly related to targets of change in therapy (e.g., substance use, risky sexual behavior).

Data security and privacy considerations are central issues in utilizing technology, AA, and EMI in psychological interventions; this adds a layer of complexity above and beyond traditional clinical work and requires special attention. Psychologists, for instance, should review principles and codes in their Ethical Principles of Psychologists and Code of Conduct, HIPAA (Health Insurance Portability and Accountability Act of 1996), and HITECH (Health Information Technology for Economic and Clinical Health Act) requirements, as well as other more intervention/research-specific recommendations (e.g., secure encryption for diary data, requiring passcode for device entry). A review of privacy and security considerations and practical recommendations can be found in other sources (e.g., Carpenter et al., 2016; Luxton et al., 2011; Piasecki et al., 2007; Prentice & Dobson, 2014). Further investigation into such concerns is recommended for those considering using AA within clinical work, given that anticipating risk and risk mitigation planning are a necessary component of utilizing AA methods in clinical settings.

There are numerous recommendations consistent with continued advancements of using AA in intervention. First is a continued focus on scientific rigor, both by conducting scientifically sound studies and by utilizing AA and EMI protocols in the way they have been validated. This includes assessment of the feasibility, acceptability, and reliability of the technology, as well as the efficacy of the intervention itself. The manner in which EBT components of traditional psychotherapies function cannot be assumed to automatically transfer to EMI. Additionally, response styles of AA reports should be investigated to determine the rates, patterns, and impact of noncredible responding. As with more traditional self-report methods, individuals may overreport, underreport, or provide invalid (random) responding. The reasons and times in which people may engage in these response styles may differ with AA or as a function of factors unique to AA. Exploring these patterns within an AA framework is important to understanding and addressing these concerns. Also, accurate packaging and marketing within the large technological world of applications ("apps") and smart devices are essential. For instance, there are a number of "treatment-based" apps targeting alcohol use; however, analysis of the apps indicated that most tracked consumption and few implemented evidenced-based components of treatment, despite advertising themselves as an "intervention" (Cohn et al., 2011). Using existing systems (e.g., *Purple*; Schueller et al., 2014) and guides (e.g., Nahum-Shani, Hekler, & Spruijt-Metz, 2015) can assist researchers and treatment developers to develop EMI platforms and provide support around key issues such as functionality and data privacy.

Another crucial issue concerning the implementation and application of EMI platforms, and AA in general, is the reach and accessibility of these technologies to diverse groups of people. Research examining multicultural issues for AA, from the perspective of collecting AA data in a sensitive way, to administering evidence-based treatments for these populations, and tailoring treatment outcome targets, is vital to the further development of this methodology. Before AA is fully implemented in clinical practice, these issues must be studied and appropriate modifications made to data collection methods, to momentary interventions, and to appropriate clinical symptom targets. In this way, the validity and utility of AA methodology across the many domains of identity including race, ethnicity, socioeconomic status, sexual orientation, and geographic location can be established.

Finally, a more global recommendation is the need to invite and populate researchers and clinicians into the same intellectual space of AA and EMIs. As has been noted by others (e.g., Heron & Smyth, 2010; Perna et al., 2018), AA research and implementation of these applications within treatment have been largely parallel, yet separate, efforts on the part of researchers and clinicians, which could only be improved by increased collaboration within the field.

CONCLUSIONS

Traditional clinical assessment is limited in what it can tell us about the daily life experiences of our clients and patients because it is cross-sectional and cannot adequately account for or predict dynamic real-world influences on mood, cognitions, and behavior. AA promises to address these limitations through the use of multiple, momentary assessments in the real world that do a better job of describing daily life problems, uncover important situational and contextual influences, and point to targets for intervention. Technological advances have made AA more feasible and acceptable to clients and patients, such that these assessments can be completed without too much disruption in one's daily life. As individuals, clinicians, and clinical researchers become more familiar with AA methods and the insights that can be gained, AA holds promise to revolutionize the field of clinical assessment and intervention. Before this occurs, however, much more work needs to be done in terms of demonstrating AA's acceptability and utility, convincing more clinicians and clinical researchers to use AA, documenting the reliability and validity of AA assessments, and developing and refining EMIs that are efficacious. At this point in time, we believe AA can be a beneficial, complementary assessment tool used in clinical settings. As more research explores the reliability, validity, and utility of AA, we are optimistic that AA will become an important, perhaps even preferred, method of clinical assessment that provides rich, granular, and ecologically valid information on clinical phenomena that will inform treatment approaches for years to come.

REFERENCES

American Psychiatric Association. (2013). *Diagnostic and statistical manual of mental disorders* (5th ed.). Washington, DC: American Psychiatric Association. https://dsm.psychiatryonline.org/doi/full/10.1176/appi.books.9780890425596.dsm02

Barrett, L. F., Gross, J., Christensen, T. C., & Benvenuto, M. (2001). Knowing what you are feeling and knowing what to do about it: Mapping the relation between emotion differentiation and emotion regulation. *Cognition and Emotion, 15*, 713–724.

Ben-Zeev, D., & Young, M. A. (2010). Accuracy of hospitalized depressed patients' and healthy controls' retrospective symptom reports: An experience sampling study. *The Journal of Nervous and Mental Disease, 198*(4), 280–285.

Buckner, J. D., Crosby, R. D., Wonderlich, S. A., & Schmidt, N. B. (2012). Social anxiety and cannabis use: An analysis from ecological momentary assessment. *Journal of Anxiety Disorders, 26*, 297–304.

Byambasuren, O., Sanders, S., Beller, E., & Glasziou, P. (2018). Prescribable mHealth apps identified from an overview of systematic reviews. *npj Digital Medicine, 1*(1), 12.

Carpenter, R. W., Wycoff, A. M., & Trull, T. J. (2016). Ambulatory assessment: New adventures in characterizing dynamic processes. *Assessment, 23*, 414–424.

Cohn, A. M., Hunter-Reel, D., Hagman, B. T., & Mitchell, J. (2011). Promoting behavior change from alcohol use through mobile technology: The future of ecological momentary assessment. *Alcoholism: Clinical and Experimental Research, 35*(12), 2209–2215.

Conner, T. S., & Lehman, B. J. (2012). Getting started: Launching a study in daily life. In M. R. Mehl & T. S. Connor (Eds.), *Handbook of research methods for studying daily life* (pp. 89–107). New York: Guilford Press.

Crooke, A. H., Reid, S. C., Kauer, S. D., McKenzie, D. P., Hearps, S. J., Khor, A. S., & Forbes, A. B. (2013). Temporal mood changes associated with different levels of adolescent drinking: Using mobile phones and experience sampling methods to explore motivations for adolescent alcohol use. *Drug and Alcohol Review, 32*, 262–268.

Delespaul, P. A., & DeVries, M. W. (1987). The daily life of ambulatory chronic mental patients. *The Journal of Nervous and Mental Disease, 175*, 537–544.

Dubad, M., Winsper, C., Meyer, C., Livanoud, M., & Marwaha, S. (2018). A systematic review of the psychometric properties, usability and clinical impacts of mobile mood-monitoring applications in young people. *Psychological Medicine, 48*, 208–228.

Ebner-Priemer, U. W., & Sawitzki, G. (2007). Ambulatory assessment of affective instability in borderline personality disorder: The effect of sampling frequency. *European Journal of Psychological Assessment, 23*, 238–247.

Ebner-Priemer, U. W., & Trull, T. J. (2009). Ecological momentary assessment of mood disorders and mood dysregulation. *Psychological Assessment, 21*, 463–475.

Fatseas, M., Serre, F., Alexandre, J. M., Debrabant, R., Auriacombe, M., & Swendsen, J. (2015). Craving and substance use among patients with alcohol, tobacco, cannabis or heroin addiction: A comparison of substance-and person-specific cues. *Addiction, 110*(6), 1035–1042.

Fisher, C. D., & To, M. L. (2012). Using experience sampling methodology in organizational behavior. *Journal of Organizational Behavior, 33*(7), 865–877.

Fredrickson, B. L., & Kahneman, D. (1993). Duration neglect in retrospective evaluations of affective episodes. *Journal of Personality and Social Psychology, 65*, 45–55.

Gard, D. E., Kring, A. M., Gard, M. G., Horan, W. P., & Green, M. F. (2007). Anhedonia in schizophrenia: Distinctions between anticipatory and consummatory pleasure. *Schizophrenia Research, 93*(1–3), 253–260.

Glaser, J. P., van Os, J., Mengelers, R., Myin-Germeys, I. (2007). A momentary assessment study of the reputed emotional phenotype associated with borderline personality disorder. *Psychological Medicine, 38*, 1–9.

Hebert, E. T., Stevens, E. M., Frank, S. G., Kendzor, D. E., Wetter, D. W., Zvolensky, M. J. et al. (2018). An ecological momentary intervention for smoking cessation: The associations of just-in-time, tailored messages with lapse risk factors. *Addictive Behaviors, 78*, 30–35.

Heron, K. E., & Smyth, J. M. (2010). Ecological momentary interventions: Incorporating mobile technology into psychosocial and health behaviour treatments. *The British Journal of Health Psychology, 15*, 1–39.

Horan, W. P., Green, M. F., Kring, A. M., & Nuechterlein, K. H. (2006). Does anhedonia in schizophrenia reflect faulty memory for subjectively experienced emotions? *Journal of Abnormal Psychology, 115*(3), 496.

Hsin, H., Fromer, M., Peterson, B., Walter, C., Fleck, M., Campbell, A. et al. (2018). Transforming psychiatry into data-driven medicine with digital measurement tools. *npj Digital Medicine, 1*(1), 37.

Intille, S. S. (2007). Technological innovations enabling automatic, context-sensitive ecological momentary assessment. In A. A. Stone & S. Shiffman (Eds.), *The science of real-time data capture: Self-reports in health research* (pp. 308–337). Oxford: Oxford University Press.

Kaplan, R. M., & Stone, A. A. (2013). Bringing the laboratory and clinic to the community: Mobile technologies for health promotion and disease prevention. *Annual Review of Psychology, 64*, 471–498.

Kring, A. M., & Moran, E. K. (2008). Emotional response deficits in schizophrenia: Insights from affective science. *Schizophrenia Bulletin, 34*(5), 819–834.

Kuppens, P., Sheeber, L. B., Yap, M. B., Whittle, S., Simmons, J. G., & Allen, N. B. (2012). Emotional inertia prospectively predicts the onset of depressive disorder in adolescence. *Emotion, 12*, 283–289.

Luxton, D. D., McCann, R. A., Bush, N. E., Mishkind, M. C., & Reger, G. M. (2011). mHealth for mental health: Integrating smartphone technology in behavioral healthcare. *Professional Psychology: Research and Practice, 42*, 505–512.

Mehl, M. R., Pennebaker, J. W., Crow, D. M., Dabbs, J., & Price, J. H. (2001). The Electronically Activated Recorder (EAR): A device for sampling naturalistic daily activities and conversations. *Behavior Research Methods, Instruments, and Computers, 33*(4), 517–523.

Moore, T. M., Seavey, A., Ritter, K., McNulty, J. K., Gordon, K. C., & Stuart, G. L. (2014). Ecological momentary assessment of the effects of craving and affect on risk for relapse during substance abuse treatment. *Psychology of Addictive Behaviors, 28*(2), 619–624.

Myin-Germeys, I., Delespaul, P. A., & DeVries, M. W. (2000). Schizophrenia patients are more emotionally active than is assumed based on their behavior. *Schizophrenia Bulletin, 26* (4), 847–854.

Myin-Germeys, I., Peeters, F., Havermans, R., Nicolson, N. A., DeVries, M. W., Delespaul, P. et al. (2018). Experience sampling methodology in mental health research: New insights and technical developments. *World Psychiatry, 17*, 123–132.

Myin-Germeys, I., Peeters, F. P. M. L., Havermans, R., Nicolson, N. A., DeVries, M. W., Delespaul, P. A. E. G., & Van Os, J. (2003). Emotional reactivity to daily life stress in psychosis and affective disorder: An experience sampling study. *Acta Psychiatrica Scandinavica, 107*(2), 124–131.

Nahum-Shani, I., Hekler, E. B., & Spruijt-Metz, D. (2015). Building health behavior models to guide the development of just-in-time interventions: A pragmatic framework. *Health Psychology, 34*, 1209–1219.

Oorschot, M., Kwapil, T.R., Delespaul, P., & Myin-Germeys, I. (2009). Momentary assessment research in psychosis. *Psychological Assessment, 21*, 498–505.

Oorschot, M., Lataster, T., Thewissen, V., Lardinois, M., Wichers, M., van Os, J. et al. (2013). Emotional experience in negative symptoms of schizophrenia: No evidence for a generalized hedonic deficit. *Schizophrenia Bulletin, 39*(1), 217–225.

Perna, G., Grassi, M., Caldi, D., & Nemeroff, C. B. (2018). The revolution of personality psychiatry: Will technology make it happen sooner? *Psychological Medicine, 48*, 705–713.

Pew Research Center. (2018). Mobile fact sheet. February 5. www.pewinternet.org/fact-sheet/mobile/

Pfaltz, M. C., Michael, T., Grossman, P., Margraf, J., & Wilhelm, F. H. (2010). Instability of physical anxiety symptoms in daily life of patients with panic disorder and patients with posttraumatic stress disorder. *Journal of Anxiety Disorders, 24*(7), 792–798.

Piasecki, T. M., Hufford, M. R., Solhan, M., & Trull, T. J. (2007). Assessing clients in their natural environments with electronic diaries: Rationale, benefits, limitations, and barriers. *Psychological Assessment, 19*, 25–43.

Prentice, J. L., & Dobson, K. S. (2014). A review of the risk and benefits associated with mobile phone applications and psychological interventions. *Canadian Psychology, 55*, 282–290.

Ray, L. A., Miranda R., Jr., Tidey, J. W., McGeary, J. E., MacKillop, J., Gwaltney, C. J. et al. (2010). Polymorphisms of the μ-opioid receptor and dopamine D_4 receptor genes and subjective responses to alcohol in the natural environment. *Journal of Abnormal Psychology, 119*(1), 115–125.

Schneekloth, T. D., Biernacka, J. M., Hall-Flavin, D. K., Karpyak, V. M., Frye, M. A., Loukianova, L. L. et al. (2012). Alcohol craving as a predictor of relapse. *The American Journal on Addictions, 21*, S20–S26.

Schueller, S. M., Begale, M., Penedo, F. J., & Mohr, D. C. (2014). Purple: A modular system for developing and deploying behavioral intervention technologies. *Journal of Medical Internet Research, 16*, e181.

Shiffman, S., Stone, A. A., & Hufford, M. R. (2008). Ecological momentary assessment. *Annual Review of Clinical Psychology, 4*, 1–32.

Shrout, P. E., & Lane, S. P. (2011). Psychometrics. In M. R. Mehl & T. S. Conner (Eds.), *Handbook of research methods for studying daily life* (pp. 302–320). New York: Guilford Press.

Solhan, M. B., Trull, T. J., Jahng, S., & Wood, P. K. (2009). Clinical assessment of affective instability: Comparing EMA indices, questionnaire reports, and retrospective recall. *Psychological Assessment, 21*, 425–436.

Stiglmayr, C. E., Ebner-Priemer, U. W., Bretz, J., Behm, R., Mohse, M., Lammers, C. H. et al. (2008). Dissociative symptoms are positively related to stress in borderline personality disorder. *Acta Psychiatrica Scandinavica*, *117*, 139–147.

Stone, A. A., & Shiffman, S. (1994). Ecological momentary assessment (EMA) in behavioral medicine. *Annals of Behavioral Medicine*, *16*(3), 199–202.

Stone, A. A., Shiffman, S., Atienza, A. A., & Nebeling, L. (2007). Historical roots and rationale of ecological momentary assessment (EMA). In A. A. Stone & S. Shiffman (Eds.), *The science of real-time data capture: Self-reports in health research* (pp. 3–10). Oxford: Oxford University Press.

Stone, A. A., Shiffman, S., Schwartz, J. E., Broderick, J. E., & Hufford, M. R. (2002). Patient non-compliance with paper diaries. *BMJ*, *324*(7347), 1193–1194.

Trull, T. J., & Ebner-Priemer, U. (2013). Ambulatory assessment. *Annual Review of Clinical Psychology*, *9*, 151–176.

Trull, T. J., Lane, S. P., Koval, P., & Ebner-Priemer, U. W. (2015). Affective dynamics in psychopathology. *Emotion Review*, *7*(4), 355–361.

Trull, T. J., Solhan, M. B., Traggesser, S. L., Jahng, S., Wood, P. K., Piasecki, T. M., & Watson, D. (2008). Affective instability: Measuring a core feature of borderline personality disorder with ecological momentary assessment. *Journal of Abnormal Psychology*, *117*, 647–661.

Van de Leemput, I. A., Wichers, M., Cramer, A. O., Borsboom, D., Tuerlinckx, F., Kuppens, P., et al. (2014). Critical slowing down as early warning for the onset and termination of depression. *Proceedings of the National Academy of Sciences*, *111*, 87–92.

Van Os, J., Delespaul, P., Wigman, J., Myin-Germeys, I., & Wichers, M. (2013). Beyond DSM and ICD: Introducing "precision diagnosis" for psychiatry using momentary assessment technology. *World Psychiatry*, *12*, 113–117.

Villar, R., Beltrame, T., & Hughson, R. L. (2015). Validation of the Hexoskin wearable vest during lying, sitting, standing, and walking activities. *Applied Physiology, Nutrition, and Metabolism*, *40*(10), 1019–1024.

Walentynowicz, M., Schneider, S., & Stone, A. A. (2018). The effects of time frames on self-report. *PloS ONE*, *13*(8), e0201655.

Walz, L. C., Nauta, M. H., & aan het Rot, M. (2014). Experience sampling and ecological momentary assessment for studying the daily lives of patients with anxiety disorders: A systematic review. *Journal of Anxiety Disorders*, *28*(8), 925–937.

Wilhelm, P., Perrez, M., & Pawlik, K. (2012). Conducting research in daily life: A historical review. In M. R. Mehl & T. A. Connor (Eds.), *Handbook of research methods for studying daily life* (pp. 62–86). New York: Guilford Press.

Wright, C., Dietze, P. M., Agius, P. A., Kuntzche, E., Livingston, M., Black, O. C. et al. (2018). Mobile phone-based ecological momentary intervention to reduce young adults' alcohol use in the event: A three-armed randomized controlled trial. *Journal of Medical Internet Research mHealth and uHealth*, *6*(7), e149.

8 Psychological Assessment as Treatment

Collaborative/Therapeutic Assessment

E. HALE MARTIN

Psychological assessment today is often used as an adjunct to psychotherapy or to psychiatric interventions. By uncovering the dynamics and their roots underlying clients' issues, assessment can inform psychological and/or pharmacological interventions to be appropriately targeted and thus increase their efficiency and effectiveness. In both instances, psychological assessment can save time and resources in the provision of mental health services. Thus, the goal of assessment traditionally has been to understand esoteric dynamics in the service of guiding treatment providers. Psychotherapists at times use assessment measures to guide their work but, generally, full psychological assessment batteries are not conducted by a client's therapist but rather by a consultant who specializes in assessment. This is especially the case with master's-level psychotherapists who are generally not trained in psychological assessment. Collaboration with the patient has not been a central focus of psychological assessment other than to facilitate gathering accurate information. With the development of collaborative assessment, there is mounting evidence that the role of therapist and assessor can be profitably merged (Poston & Hanson, 2010). This chapter will explore the emergence of assessment designed to be therapeutic and the evidence supporting it.

In recent years, we have learned that psychological effects arise from altering clients' narratives that explain and guide their lives (Adler, 2012; Epston & White, 1995; Wilson, 2011). Furthermore, these effects do not arise as much from esoteric discussions as from experiences and understandings that connect closely to a person's unique lived experience (Epston & White, 1995; Schore, 2009). While psychology certainly has a wealth of esoteric knowledge that informs its practitioners, we are learning that this knowledge is most useful when clients can effectively apply it to their own lives (Fischer, 1985/1994). Constance Fischer (1985/1994) understood that assessment techniques used collaboratively can provide an avenue to increase clients' self-understanding, change their stories about themselves and the world, and ultimately better manage their problems in living.

There is growing acknowledgment of the value of collaborative techniques in psychological assessment (Finn, 2007; Fisher 1985/1994). Fischer's efforts to make assessment helpful to clients has fueled a full-fledged movement. She used tests to help clients understand why they struggled and what they realistically could do about their difficulties. Fischer's approach enlisted the client as a collaborator, hence earning the moniker Collaborative Assessment (CA).

Fisher's work dovetailed nicely with Stephen Finn's ideas about the potential of psychological assessment. In fact, Finn tells the story of staying up all night with tears in his eyes as he read the just-published Fisher (1985/1994) book *Individualizing Assessment* (Finn, personal communication). Subsequently, he and Mary Tonsager (1992) conducted a study that demonstrated that clients can indeed benefit therapeutically from a collaborative approach to assessment. They collected a sample of students on the wait list for psychological services at a university counseling center who were willing to participate in a psychological study while they waited for services. The sample was randomly divided into two groups. The experimental group (thirty-two students) participated in a brief assessment conducted by a graduate student, which involved a thirty-minute interview focused on developing questions they had about their struggles, completing an MMPI-2, and participating in a feedback session two weeks later, which was conducted in accordance with a collaborative model developed by Finn, which he called Therapeutic Assessment (TA). The control group (twenty-eight students) received an equal amount of attention, meeting twice with a graduate student to discuss their struggles and completing the same outcome measures as the experimental group. Outcome measures included the Self-Esteem Questionnaire (Cheek & Buss, 1981), the Symptom Checklist-90-Revised (SCL-90-R) (Derogatis, 1983), the Self-Consciousness Inventory (Fenigstein, Scheier, & Buss, 1975), and the Assessment Questionnaire (AQ), which was developed for their study to assess the relationship with the graduate student with whom students met. The dependent variables were collected at three times: Time 1 at the beginning of the first session,

Time 2 immediately after the feedback session, and Time 3 approximately two weeks after the feedback session.

The results showed no significant differences between the groups on the dependent variables at Time 1 but significant differences between groups on key variables at Time 2 and Time 3, including differences on the Global Symptom Index of the SCL-90-R [Time 2: $t(56) = 0.57$, ns; Time 3: Cohen's $d = 0.36$, $t(57) = 2.98$, $p < 0.01$); with no significant decrease in the control group across time] and the Self-Esteem Questionnaire (Time 2: Cohen's $d = 0.38$, $t(58) = -3.16$, $p < 0.01$; Time 3: Cohen's $d = 0.46$, $t(57) = -3.93$, $p < 0.001$). Another scale that assessed hope was added at Time 2 and Time 3 but no data were available from the beginning, so no overall conclusions can be drawn about hope. However, the hope variable showed significant differences between the experimental group and control group at Time 2 ($p < 0.05$) and Time 3 ($p < 0.01$). On the other hand, the AQ scale assessing the relationship with the examiner did not show significant differences between groups at any of the three times dependent variables were measured. Thus, the observed effects supported the value of a simple TA intervention in reducing symptoms and increasing self-esteem that were not merely due to a positive relationship with the graduate student. Newman and Greenway (1997) replicated these results, altering the design somewhat by having both experimental and control groups take the Minnesota Multiphasic Personality Inventory-2 (MMPI-2) to control for possible effects from simply taking the MMPI-2 but with the control group receiving feedback only after completion of the study. More recent studies have continued to provide evidence that CA and TA produce positive effects in a variety of clients who have diverse problems in living (De Saeger et al., 2014; Hilsenroth, Peters, & Ackerman, 2004; Smith, Handler, & Nash, 2010).

This initial empirical evidence ignited the quest for an optimal approach for TA, which Finn has spearheaded. Since 1992, Finn and colleagues have thoughtfully honed a semi-structured approach to collaborative psychological assessment focused on increasing the likelihood of therapeutic effects and maximizing those effects. Finn has carefully mined other areas of psychology (e.g., self-psychology, attachment theory, social psychology) to incorporate the best understandings of the day into the approach and he and others have researched, tested, and honed the approach. The result offers added advantages to psychological assessment, namely opportunities to increase the therapeutic effects assessment can have. Today Finn leads the nonprofit Therapeutic Assessment Institute centered in Austin, Texas, with a European Center for Therapeutic Assessment in Milan, Italy, and an Asian Center for Therapeutic Assessment in Tokyo, Japan.

THERAPEUTIC ASSESSMENT

A brief overview of the semi-structured TA is in order. TA typically includes several sequential components: an initial session in which the nature of the assessment is determined; testing sessions in which standardized tests are used to gather both nomothetic and idiographic data; an Assessment Intervention Session in which efforts are made to help clients experience the results of the assessment for themselves; a Summary/Discussion session, in which findings are discussed and contextualized in the client's world; a personal letter that conveys in writing what has been understood through the experience; and a follow-up session, which addresses any lingering concerns or additional questions that arise. The TA process has been more thoroughly described by Finn and Martin (2013) but will be addressed briefly in the seven succeeding sections. Readers should keep in mind that the TA process is flexible and tailored to the particular client. As Jan Kamphuis, a trainer and researcher of TA noted recently, TA is designed to help clients "bake their own cake" (Kamphuis, personal communication).

Like many assessments, TA often begins with referral from a mental health provider who is uncertain or confused by a client. Therapeutic progress may feel stuck or a client may be difficult and auxiliary help and understanding are sought. In TA, we work to collaborate with the therapist as well as the client for several reasons. Therapists can offer important information and insights that aid the assessment. The therapist can also be witness to important findings, allowing the assessor to introduce difficult information that the therapist can then titrate over the course of future therapy. For example, they might offer at an opportune moment in subsequent therapy, "I wonder if this is what Dr. Martin meant when he said . . ." Furthermore, having two professionals work together can magnify the client's sense of being seen and understood. Finally, involving the therapist can further model the spirit of collaboration. TA can also be an intervention in itself for people who are not in therapy but are seeking answers to problems in their lives. Either in concert with a therapist or at the request of a person not in therapy, it usually begins with one to two phone conversations to set up an initial meeting.

INITIAL SESSION

The essential core values of TA are collaboration, compassion, curiosity, humility, openness, and respect, which are expressed throughout the assessment process (Finn, 2015a). TA begins with strong efforts to establish collaboration with the referral source and especially with the client. In TA, clients are not passive participants in the assessment process merely following directions or receiving results; rather, they are actively engaged throughout the process. From the initial contact, clients are encouraged to consider what they need to know in order to better manage their problems in living. These personal contemplations are transformed into specific questions the client poses in the initial session and these will guide the assessment. Questions that come from the client in their own words reflect areas in which the client is seeking answers and they give the assessor a clear idea of how a client currently understands their life. Understanding the client's world is essential for the assessor because, as Fisher (1985/1994) points out, "For an optional route to be personally viable, it must be a variation of present approaches; it must branch off from where the client is now, and it must accommodate familiar action" (p. 100). The client's questions signal the next step in their personal growth, about which assessment techniques can provide powerful insights. Developing a good working relationship is important in the initial session; in fact, the relationship between assessor and client is of paramount importance in TA. Aschieri, Fantini, and Smith (2016) have expounded on this importance by mining attachment theory.

Important aspects of attachment theory are incorporated in the TA process. Finn (2009; Finn et al., 2012) argues that to activate the client's exploratory system, the client's attachment strivings must be calmed through a satisfactory relationship with the assessor. Optimal conditions for this arise when the assessor–client relationship resembles a secure attachment. (Note that assessors are not attachment figures but can act like them.) Hence, Finn incorporates essential components of secure attachment, including emotional attunement, collaborative communication, and repair of disruptions (Tronick, 2007). To the extent the assessor can create a secure attachment environment, the client will be increasingly receptive to exploring new ways of being in the world. Secure attachment occurs in an intersubjective field in which communication involves not only words but also "right brain to right brain" resonance (Schore, 2009). Finn describes effective emotional attunement as arising from spontaneous, empathic responsiveness from the assessor. Collaborative communication involves reciprocal patterns of interaction that emerge from the attunement that evolves as the relationship deepens. Noticing the disruptions that inevitably occur in the evolving relationship and addressing these (directly or indirectly) is also part of secure attachment relationships as they foster increasing trust and openness. Thus, in the initial session, strong efforts are made to create an environment that will facilitate the client's growth, including embodying the core essential values of TA mentioned at the beginning of this section – collaboration, compassion, curiosity, humility, openness, and respect (Finn, 2015a).

Testing Sessions

Following the initial session, and with the scope of the testing to be done established, testing sessions largely focus on gathering accurate nomothetic data, which will provide the backbone of the answers to the client's questions. Standardized administration procedures are followed in order to get reliable and valid data. Like any responsible assessment, TA is firmly committed to using multiple methods to gather data, in order to reduce error and to deepen understanding (Bornstein, 2017). The testing process begins with a test clearly focused on the client's questions in order to demonstrate to the client that the assessor honors the client's personal interests. For example, if the client is concerned about cognitive abilities, the first test might be a well-validated intelligence test. Furthermore, the assessor makes an effort to introduce all tests by explaining how they are related to the client's questions. This increases the client's motivation, knowing they are working together to address his or her personal concerns.

Extended Inquiry

While nomothetic data are essential, they are not enough to effectively understand the client. In TA, we make a practice of asking clients to help us understand responses or processes that are pregnant with unknown meaning – unknown to us or to the client. Discussing responses with clients often clarifies understanding in ways that the nomothetic data alone cannot. In TA, these discussions occur in a loosely structured Extended Inquiry (EI), which employs a half-step technique, which involves staying just slightly ahead of a client in the discussion in slowly leading them to insights. This technique allows the client to discover their own answers and also helps the assessor stay in contact with what is possible for the client. It is important to note that EI occurs *after* the standard administration has been completed in a reliable manner. EIs are done by first asking the client to explain their experience of the just-completed test and then deepened by asking leading questions to facilitate ideographic understanding. For example, the assessor notices that the client who has asked about attention-deficit/hyperactivity disorder (ADHD) loses points on timed subtests of an intelligence test because they repeatedly check their work and sometimes change correct answers to incorrect ones. A discussion afterwards reveals the client's fear of making a mistake leads to overthinking and interferes with their cognitive performance. EIs not only provide a rich source of information useful in enhancing the assessor's understanding but they also further enhance collaboration and motivation and, importantly, help the client move toward answering their questions themselves; that is, baking their own cake. The self-discovery process is a highly valued element in facilitating meaningful change.

Assessment Intervention Session

The next step in the TA process is intended to further enhance the process of self-discovery. The Assessment Intervention session (AIS) is perhaps the most intriguing component of TA. It might also be the most therapeutic, though that speculation is based only on clinical experience voiced by a number of assessors and not yet on empirical research. The AIS comes after all nomothetic testing has been completed. With what we have come to understand through testing about potential answers to the client's questions, we do our best to select an activity that will provoke in the testing room a characteristic, problematic response from the client that is related to one (or more) of their assessment questions. Thus, we try to get the potentially problematic behavior active in the room. An example of an AIS would be selecting cards from the Thematic Apperception Test (Murray, 1943) that pull for conflict or anger and potentially demonstrate a client's avoidance of anger in that the client might not include anger or conflict in their stories. By being curious about that omission, the assessor can help the client explore why that might be. Then, by having the client tell a story full of anger, they both can explore the emotions that emerge or, if the client is unable to tell an angry story, the client and assessor together can explore what is blocking the simple task. Again, using the half-step technique allows the assessor to lead the client to useful insights. The ultimate goal of the AIS is to make findings a client is likely to reject accessible to that client, again in ways connected to their own life. The AIS is similar to EI but it is carefully planned rather than spontaneous and it is often more involved than an EI.

The AIS also provides opportunities to try on new solutions that could be more adaptive for the client. Fischer focused on helping clients create new ways of addressing old problems. She asserts, "Trying out alternatives during the assessment is intended to serve three related functions: to explore what is personally viable, to help the client recognize when they are headed toward trouble (landmarks) and develop pivot points where the client could shift to an optional route, and to practice the optional route so it feels familiar and reliable" (Fischer, 1985/1994, p. 99). It is by collaboratively selecting a viable target behavior, anticipating and troubleshooting difficulties that might arise, and formulating possible ways to manage those difficulties that prepares the client to go out into their world and try new ways of being. In this way, meaningful change can begin. Fischer adds, "It is in these practicings [sic] of alternative approaches that self-deceptions, incompatible goals, and other previously non-focal concerns – in short, unconscious motivations – become concretely available for collaborative explorations" (Fischer, 1985/1994, p. 99).

Summary Discussion Session

The Summary Discussion session (SDS) is not like traditional feedback sessions. The name change is meant to capture the important difference that the SDS emphasizes a two-way interaction between assessor and client more than most traditional feedback sessions. The goal of the SDS is to answer the assessment questions collaboratively, incorporating the insights the data have provided and the understandings that have emerged in the collaboration with the client. The assessor and client work to see how the findings fit the client and their unique problems in living. It is an opportunity to reconsider, tweak, develop memorable metaphors, and confirm meaningful and usable answers to the assessment questions. The SDS is also an opportunity to complete a successful relationship with another person, which is an experience some clients have rarely experienced. Having worked together throughout the assessment process, the client and the assessor have developed a healthy bond revolving around the client feeling accurately seen and respected.

The SDS is informed by self-schema theories of change (Martin & Young, 2010) and, more directly, by self-verification theory as detailed by social psychologist William Swan (1997). Swan asserts that people search for information that verifies how they see themselves and the world and postulates that the predictability is reassuring even if it confirms undesirable things (e.g., "I am unlovable"). It is a source of comfort that the world is as one thinks it is. A person is more likely to assimilate information that is congruent with their self-schema and reject information that is incongruent with that self-schema (Martin & Young, 2010). Furthermore, working carefully between what a person does and does not see in themselves helps the assessor avoid triggering a disintegration experience (Kohut, 1984). In this effort, Finn (2007) teaches TA assessors to organize the information presented to the client into three levels:

Level 1. Information the client will recognize and agree with, that is self-verifying information (again, this may not be a positive, encouraging finding).

Level 2. Information that is slightly at odds with the way the client sees themselves and the world. The majority of the SDS is spent at this level, with the goal of helping the client see new possibilities, which may be accessible now due to the preceding work (e.g., AIS) providing glimpses into new possibilities.

Level 3. Information that the client is likely to claim is not accurate. We include this level because we are often surprised at what the client now can accommodate and because it plants seeds for future consideration.

If a client has a therapist, the therapist is encouraged to join the SDS as a witness and perhaps as a voice for the client as needed. This expanded collaboration with the therapist offers a broader model of collaboration for the client as well as a magnified sense of feeling understood and held by others. The session is organized keeping in mind the anticipated feelings the client brings into the room. Processing those feelings, expressly setting the structure of the session, and offering opportunities to end the session when the client is ready to stop can all help the client manage their anxiety. The secure attachment strategies mentioned in the "Initial Session" section also help the client feel psychologically safe and thus more open to new understandings. Hopefully, the client leaves the SDS feeling deeply understood, cared about, and hopeful and with a more coherent, accurate, useful, and compassionate narrative about their problems in living as well as what next steps could be useful.

Written Results

The written communication to the client is also different from traditional assessment. Rather than the highly structured and often esoteric understandings presented in traditional psychological reports, which may not be directly related to the client's concerns, the TA written feedback is directly focused on answering the client's questions, pulling from all that has transpired during the assessment. The language is tailored to the individual, images and metaphors that the client offered during the assessment are employed to make the letter personally meaningful, and findings are couched in the context of the work that has been done together, often referencing the client's contribution (e.g., "The testing suggested ... but you helped me understand this only occurs when you ...").

Written feedback is also provided to children in the child TA adaptation. It takes the form of an age-appropriate fable or story that captures the essence of the assessment in an engaging narrative. Children are often encouraged to illustrate the story as the session unfolds. These stories can convey significant meaning for the child. Diane Engelman and Janet Allyn (2012) have been exploring therapeutic stories for adults. As the field of psychology is learning (Adler, 2012; Epston & White, 1995; Wilson, 2011), stories people have about their lives seem to be compelling guides that regulate their beliefs, attitudes, and behaviors. If they can be shifted even a little to be more accurate and self-compassionate, a powerful therapeutic effect is possible.

Follow-up Sessions

Follow-up sessions are the latest addition to the TA structure. They were initially provided at the request of clients but later it became clear that they could be an important part of smoothing the client's transition into new ways of being. They typically occur a couple of months after the SDS with the goal of checking in with the client to remind them of findings, review the feedback letter, answer lingering questions, troubleshoot remaining obstacles, and reinforce positive developments. The client's therapist is included in the follow-up session unless the client or therapist prefers otherwise. There are instances in which periodic "follow-up sessions" (e.g., an annual meeting) provide a client who is not in therapy with sufficient support to continue their growth (Finn, 2007).

Adaptations of TA to Children and Families, Adolescents, and Couples

TA for adults has been adapted to various clinical populations, including children, adolescents, and couples, which represent the four areas in which certification in TA is offered through the Therapeutic Assessment Institute.[1] In child TA, family system issues are usually central. Thus, the goal is to help the parents gain understanding and empathy for their child's struggles. The AIS with children usually involves the family doing something together, such as each family member drawing a picture of the family doing something together and then presenting it to others in the family for reactions. The assessor can expand this intervention to ask questions about family life (for a thorough discussion of child TA, see Tharinger et al., 2008). Adolescent TA is designed to fit the age-appropriate strivings for autonomy and to help the family adjust to developing teen issues and needs. Tharinger, Gentry, and Finn (2013) present details of adolescent TA. A unique application of TA is using it with couples. TA with couples typically involves individual TAs with each partner sandwiched between an initial meeting with the couple to formulate couple's questions and a couple's AIS, which often asks the couple to do a task that requires them to negotiate in order to jointly decide on answers. It is helpful to videotape their interaction to play back for them to see. They then process what they observe and are hopefully guided to more adaptive responses to each other, which they can then practice in the room (for more information, see Finn, 2015b).

EMPIRICAL EVIDENCE

Empirical evidence that Collaborative/Therapeutic Assessment (C/TA) is an effective intervention has been mounting since the seminal study by Finn and Tonsager (1992). Studies demonstrate the effectiveness of C/TA with a range of clinical issues, including chronic pain (Miller, Cano, & Wurm, 2013), oppositional defiant disorder (Smith et al., 2010), borderline personality disorder (Morey, Lowmaster, & Hopwood, 2010), complex PTSD (Smith & George, 2012; Tarocchi et al., 2013), and families with children with emotional problems (Tharinger et al., 2009). There is also evidence that C/TA facilitates therapeutic alliance in subsequent treatment (Hilsenroth et al., 2004; Hilsenroth & Cromer, 2007), improves clients' relationships with staff and other inpatients in residential treatment (Blonigen et al., 2015); increases follow-through with recommendations for therapy (Ackerman et al., 2000); increases motivation to attend follow-up sessions for self-harming adolescents after treatment in an emergency room (Ougrin, Ng & Low, 2008); and enhances engagement with therapy in work with children and families in a child inpatient setting (Pagano, Blattner, & Kaplan-Levy, 2018). These results suggest that TA not only reduces symptoms but also increases participation in future therapeutic interactions.

In 2010, Poston and Hanson undertook a meta-analysis to understand what benefits psychological assessment that

[1] For additional information about the TA certification process as well as a bibliography of readings, upcoming trainings, a list of certified TA assessors, and membership in the Therapeutic Assessment Institute, see www.therapeuticassessment.com

uses personalized, collaborative feedback offers to clients (Poston & Hanson, 2010). They identified seventeen studies published between 1954 and 2007 involving 1,496 participants that met the criteria of offering feedback with the intention of being therapeutic. They admittedly included studies that offered only the "bare bones of assessment as an intervention" (p. 205). Dependent variables included any variable "designed to demonstrate potential client improvement or enhanced therapy process" (p. 205). They calculated fifty-two nonindependent Cohen's *d* effect sizes with a resulting overall effect size of 0.423, which falls in the small range. Considering control groups included in the constituent studies, they also found evidence that traditional evidence-gathering assessment offered no significant therapeutic effects, which led them to speculate that those who practice traditional assessment may not observe any therapeutic effects and thus be resistant to suggestions that assessment can have a therapeutic impact. It is noteworthy that some studies included in the meta-analysis involved only two sessions in the assessment process (e.g., Finn & Tonsager, 1992), a very brief intervention to have such impressive results.

From these results, the authors recommend that

> clinicians should familiarize themselves with therapeutic models of assessment ... Clinicians should also seek out continuing-education training related to these models. Those who engage in *assessment and testing as usual* may miss out, it seems, on a golden opportunity to effect client change and enhance clinically important treatment processes. Similarly, applied training programs in clinical, counseling, and school psychology should incorporate therapeutic models of assessment into their curricula, foundational didactic classes, and practica. (p. 210)

They continue, "Furthermore, managed care policy makers should take these results into account, especially as they make future policy and reimbursement decisions regarding assessment and testing practices" (p. 210).

Ilaria Durosini and Filippo Aschieri (2018) are currently finishing a new meta-analysis exploring the effectiveness of TA. The new meta-analysis partials therapeutic effects into three areas: (1) the effect of TA on treatment processes (i.e., alliance with mental health professionals, motivation to change, trust in treatment, and time in subsequent treatment); (2) symptom reduction (i.e., self-reported symptoms including demoralization); and (3) client enhancement (i.e., self-understanding, self-confidence, and self-esteem). It includes some studies common to the Poston and Hansen study but inclusion is limited to studies that employed at least one standardized test, involved collaborative feedback, was conducted with willing participants, and involved at least one additional element of TA from the following: client assessment questions; EI; AIS; feedback arranged according to Level 1, 2, and 3 information; written feedback in the form of a personal letter; or interaction with the client's parents or therapist.

Results addressing the effect of TA on *treatment processes* are based on eight studies and twenty-five dependent variables. The random effect multilevel analysis showed a statistically significant medium effect size (Cohen's $d = 0.58$; (95% CI [0.36; 0.81]; $p < 0.001$), suggesting that TA enhances the treatment processes. Results derived from variables reflecting *symptom reduction* included seven studies and sixteen nonindependent effect sizes revealed that TA has a medium effect size (Cohen's $d = 0.49$; 95% CI [0.12; 0.86]; $p < 0.05$) on clients' psychological problems. Finally, results based on six studies and ten dependent variables grounded in *client enhancement* demonstrated that TA has a medium mean effect size (Cohen's $d = 0.56$; 95% CI [0.23; 0.90], $p < 0.01$), suggesting significant effects on clients' psychological resources. Thus, the results of this meta-analysis suggest significant positive results on all three dimensions of outcomes considered therapeutic and thus support and augment the findings of Poston and Hansen (2010).

Both of these meta-analyses provide evidence that the evolving C/TA model is grounded in evidence of its effectiveness. Moreover, it is important to note that, as compelling as these meta-analyses are, the results may significantly underestimate potential effects of C/TA when infused with all the techniques now incorporated in the TA model, including enhanced techniques fostering collaboration (e.g., focusing on the client's questions) and leveraging knowledge of attachment, self-psychology, effective feedback practices, and experiential techniques designed to enhance therapeutic effects (e.g., EIs and AISs).

A final noteworthy aspect of the evidence supporting C/TA is that, unlike most interventions, there is evidence that the therapeutic effects of C/TA continue to grow after the intervention (Aldea et al., 2010; Finn & Tonsager, 1992; Newman & Greenway, 1997; Smith et al., 2010). As an example, the Finn and Tonsager (1992) study presented in the opening section of this chapter showed symptomatology decreases after the final session (from not significant at Time 2 to $p < 0.01$ at Time 3) and self-esteem increases after the final session (from significant change at $p < 0.01$ at Time 2 to $p < 0.001$ at Time 3). Additional studies that investigate longer follow-up periods are needed.

BROADER VALUE OF TA

Before I introduce TA to groups of students or professionals, I ask them to offer what they think is wrong with assessment. I get a lengthy list! Many criticisms are related to poor training but many voice other concerns: traditional assessment lacks connection with the real person; emphasizes the power differential between client and assessor; lacks empathy; pathologizes; produces results that are unrelated to the real problems; overvalues data with no checks and balances; relies on static understanding of dynamic problems; lacks sensitivity to cultural issues; produces results that are not used; expresses conclusions that are vague or in language the client does not understand; does not provide effective feedback; disempowers the client; and is often unnecessary.

I believe TA offers an antidote to many shortcomings of assessment as usual. To begin, TA is collaborative. It develops and maintains a strong connection to the client's life and concerns and thus is connected to the real person. Additionally, TA deemphasizes the power differential between assessor and client. By acknowledging that clients are the expert on themselves while the assessor is the expert on testing, both parties have important information to bring to the table. This dynamic elevates the need for collaboration (and is important to cross-cultural assessment to be discussed later in this section). Furthermore, the fact that TA is focused on the relationship, specifically striving to create a secure attachment environment, emphasizes empathy as a central element of TA, as well as collaborative communication and repair of ruptures.

Because TA is connected to clients' real-life problems, it relates intimately to the client's concerns and focuses the work on addressing those concerns. This focus deemphasizes pathology and, in fact, strives to go deeper than pathology by uncovering the roots of the client's problems. For example, rather than diagnosing narcissistic personality disorder, TA might focus on the lack of attention and effective mirroring a client experienced growing up and highlight reported experiences as evidence of inaccurate mirroring. By explaining the importance of mirroring and the adaptive strategies the client employed as a child, the client develops more compassion for themselves. This is likely more useful and therapeutic for the client than a pathologizing label. It may also be useful to a referring therapist not versed in developmental deficits (Kohut, 1984).

Because TA is intimately related to the client's world, it is contextualized. The person and their unique circumstances are not lost. While TA values data, it also values the context in which the data developed and now exist. This balance between nomothetic and idiographic data is an important check against overvaluing nomothetic data. It also prevents static understandings that do not capture dynamic problems.

One of the most promising aspects of TA is that it seems to be a tailor-made approach to diversity issues (Martin, 2018). By using the client as the expert on their own life, the assessor listens carefully to the client's life experience, learns from the client about the influences on their life, and integrates the unique influences on them into any derived understandings. Thus, TA acknowledges and integrates cultural and diversity factors into understanding our clients' unique experiences by focusing intently on the person in front of us, not on categories or vague stereotypes. Understanding the unique influences that have shaped clients' lives – including cultural and systemic factors, how clients have been affected by those influences, and how they have integrated them into their way of being, thinking, and feeling is the precise insight that an assessor seeks in order to be most accurate and helpful for their client. Thus, TA is exceptionally sensitive to cultural issues. Further research can explore this promising value of TA with diverse clients.

The criticism that assessment results are not used is contradicted in that TA is experiential and that a hallmark of TA is carefully crafted feedback. The EI and AIS provide experiences the client feels and which hopefully have an enduring impact. The SDS is focused on co-creating a meaningful understanding of the client's problems in living. Furthermore, the letter written to clients answering their questions is a document to which clients can refer back through their lives. Thus, there are a number of important ways that TA results are used.

The SDS offers further rebuttal to criticisms of assessment. Its goals are the exact opposite of vague conclusions that the client does not understand. By using the client's words and images when possible (i.e., from a client's questions, the SDS, and the feedback letter), the results are exquisitely tailored to the client. Most important, TA is therapeutic, as the evidence indicates. Thus, rather than disempowering and unnecessary, TA is empowering and integral to clients' personal growth.

A final value of TA is that it has the potential to reduce noncredible and defensive responding. Because the entire process is geared to address clients' own concerns, clients are likely motivated to do their job as expert on themselves in order to be acknowledged and well-represented in the assessment outcome. Because it is focused on clients' real-life problems and uses tests and techniques that provide helpful insights, and because the focus is not on pathologizing but rather on understanding their life experience, clients are likely motivated to reveal themselves in the drive to be understood.

RECENT DEVELOPMENTS

While there is evidence that TA is an effective intervention, recent work by Kamphuis and Finn (2018) explores further *why* it is an effective intervention. The exciting insights they offer stem in part from a large study of the efficacy of TA with personality disorders at the Viersprong Institute for Studies on Personality Disorders, Halsteren, the Netherlands (De Saeger, Kamphuis et al., 2014; De Saeger, Bartak et al., 2016). Briefly, this study compared an experimental group that received a four-session TA to a control group that received four sessions of the well-validated, structured, goal-focused pretreatment intervention used at the institute. Results showed that the TA was superior to the control treatment in producing significantly higher expectations for therapy success (Cohen's d = 0.65), increased sense of progress in therapy (Cohen's d = 0.56), and increased satisfaction with treatment (Cohen's d = 0.68). Results did not show differences between the two interventions in changes in symptomatology (which might partly be explained by the fact that personality disordered clients are notoriously resistant to change). However, the positive effects of TA demonstrated in this study are consistent with research that shows C/TA has effects beyond symptom reduction in paving the way for better alliance with mental health professionals, greater motivation to engage in treatment, and better outcomes in subsequent treatment.

Kamphuis and Finn (2018) mine the research of Fonagy, Luyten, and Alison (2015) and Sperber and colleagues (2010) to conclude that TA is an effective approach to epistemic hypervigilance/epistemic petrification. The distinction is made between epistemic trust (ET), which is the ability to learn from others in order to enhance survival; epistemic vigilance (EV), which is discerning who to trust to deliver useful information; and epistemic hypervigilance (EH) or epistemic petrification (EP), which is pervasive distrust of information others offer and difficulty assimilating it. They contend that the extent to which a person is guarded about taking in new information depends on their experiences with trust in life. EH can be adaptive when a child is subjected to abuse, but it may become a feature of their personality and attachment status. Thus, EH may be an underlying feature of personality disorders, reflecting the inability to incorporate and effectively use important information that comes from others. Attachment status may also reflect issues with EH by limiting the value of information offered by others. Clearly, the inability to use well-meant and useful information that comes from others is a hindrance to effective functioning and successful relationships and certainly a barrier to effective therapy.

Kamphuis and Finn (2018) explore how TA helps rehabilitate damaged ET. They state,

> we believe that in principle and procedures, TA is optimally geared to promote an individual's willingness to (re-) consider communication conveying new knowledge from someone else as trustworthy, generalizable and relevant to the self; that is, to lower EH and promote ET. Further, we have come to believe that this process of restoring ET and lowering EH may be the general meta-theoretical ingredient that may help account for the remarkable efficacy of TA across setting and disorder. (p. 5)

Their rationale for this conclusion begins with the core values of TA: collaboration, compassion, curiosity, humility, openness, and respect (Finn, 2015a). These attributes in an assessment set the stage for a different kind of experience for clients with low ET. The focus of assessment on a client's problems also signals a personal relevance that catches the attention of those with low ET. Further, the effort to engage the client as an expert on themselves working in concert with an expert in testing reduces the power imbalance people with low ET have generally suffered. Kamphuis and Finn believe the following TA steps all help clients move beyond their current inability to trust helpful information and to ultimately change: promotion of mentalization; efforts to create a secure attachment environment; the process of self-verification in confirming clients' working models before attempting to change them; using experiential techniques (EI, AIS), which allow for a bottom-up strategy of learning that emerges from within clients rather than from an external source; using tests allowing top-down learning from an impersonal authoritative source; sensitively anticipating and modulating shame that, if activated, would shut down exploration of important areas; and conducting an AIS, which provides the opportunity to scaffold clients in their zone of proximal development and which requires empathy, attunement, and collaborative communication. In the case of personality disorders, change is exceedingly difficult but studies suggest that TA may affect EH (Durosini & Aschieri, 2018; Hilsenroth et al., 2004; Hilsenroth & Cromer, 2007; Pagano et al., 2018). Further studies are needed to determine if modification of EH is indeed the underlying mechanism of such effects on treatment processes.

THE FUTURE

While there is significant evidence establishing the efficacy of psychological assessment as an intervention (Durosini & Aschieri, 2018; Poston & Hanson, 2010), more research is needed to empirically ground TA and to explore its limits. Additional research can answer important questions:

- While there are theoretical reasons to believe that TA's attention to establishing the assessor–client alliance before testing begins and focusing on the client's questions reduce noncredible and general defensiveness in reporting, does it actually do so? A comparison of rates of noncredible/defensive reporting when using traditional assessment to those rates when using TA would provide important insight into this expectation, given that increasing honesty improves the value of assessment. Furthermore, research could be useful in guiding the application of TA to settings particularly susceptible to noncredible/defensive reporting.
- Which of the specific steps and elements of TA are important in producing therapeutic change? Understanding the contributions to change that result from developing client questions, the AIS or the EI would be helpful. There is some evidence that different clients respond to different TA steps (Smith et al., 2010). Studies comparing the effects of TA with and without client questions or AIS or EI would be useful in refining the TA approach. The results of such studies would also inform efforts to shorten TA.
- Would TA prior to beginning therapy increase the effectiveness or duration of that subsequent therapy? There have been studies showing that TA leads to increased treatment compliance and improved alliance with subsequent treatment (Ackerman et al., 2000; Hilsenroth et al., 2004), but no research has yet investigated the possibility that TA before therapy enhances the following therapy. There is one study that shows that TA mid-therapy leads to better outcomes (Smith et al., 2014). If TA prior to therapy can improve results and/or shorten therapy, it would lead to cost savings.

- Is TA an effective approach to assessment of clients with substantial cultural differences from the assessor? While there are case studies that show TA's value in assessments conducted in challenging cultural situations (Finn, 2016; Martin & Jacklin, 2012), the value of TA in assessing clients from diverse cultures has not been empirically established. Further empirical work could guide implementation of TA in multicultural contexts.
- Does the overall TA process alter clients' stories about themselves and the world? If so, what aspects of TA are potent in changing clients' life narratives? Adler (2012) tracked client narratives during psychotherapy and showed that shifts in narratives preceded symptomatic improvement. The technology he employed could also be used to study narrative change in TA.
- With the increasing focus on the central role that life narratives play in guiding a person's life (Adler, 2012; Epston & White, 1995; Wilson, 2011), how effective are therapeutic stories written for children or for adults in enhancing the effects of TA (Engelman & Allyn, 2012)? While stories are highly individualized, research might even identify potent aspects of stories that maximize the impact of stories.
- Can TA be an effective approach working with personality disorders? Kamphuis and Finn (2018) point to research that supports the conclusion that TA effectively addresses EH and could be useful in work with clients with personality disorders. Further research documenting this usefulness is needed, including identifying the active ingredients of TA's effectiveness in restoring ET.
- How enduring are the effects of TA? While there is evidence that the therapeutic effects of TA continue for up to eight weeks (Smith et al., 2010), longer longitudinal studies are important in determining the long-term effects of TA.

Research is also needed to explore the limits of TA:

- What are contraindications for TA? Are there circumstances in which TA or any form of CA is inadvisable? A preliminary qualitative study suggests there are areas in forensic assessment in which CTA is not recommended (Tekeste, 2013). Are these suggestions corroborated and are there other circumstances when TA should not be used?
- Can TA be shortened at least in some situations? With affordability an increasingly salient factor in mental health services, shortening TA to its essential components is important in increasing its utility. Finn and Kamphuis (2006) described TA using only one self-report personality inventory and Finn, De Saeger, and Kamphuis (2017) more recently presented an ultra-brief model of TA. The intensity that maximizes the utility of a TA will likely vary depending on the client and the issues presented. For instance, when EH is a factor, an assessor might expect that a longer intervention will be required than with clients without personality disorder issues. Research to determine optimal intensity of TA would be helpful in reining in health care costs and making TA viable in more situations than it is currently practiced.
- Technology has demonstrated enormous power to change the world. How might technology be applied to TA? This is a complicated question in that TA seems to rest heavily on interpersonal connection. Its reliance on attunement, empathy, and attachment make it doubtful that technology could replace an assessor any time soon. However, research investigating the use of virtual reality (VR) in treating mental health issues has been extensive in recent years. For example, a recent meta-analysis of treatments for social anxiety showed equal effects derived from traditional in vivo and imaginal therapy compared to VR techniques (Chesham, Malouff, & Schutte, 2018). These findings and the possibility of customizing VR experiences suggest that VR could play a role in TA. For instance, VR might create the basis for a powerful AIS by getting a problem behavior in the room. Rather than using picture story cards, an assessor might use VR to activate a problematic response. An assessor could then explore that response with the client and perhaps even arrange for the client to experience a VR alternative experience. Such possibilities are increasing as VR technology advances, and TA might profit from research applying technological advances. Another technological question involves the online delivery of TA. Could TA be effectively conducted online? Attunement and empathy could still play a role, though not as immediately and intimately as face-to-face sessions provide. Research to establish the efficacy of TA delivered remotely could be useful in spreading the use of this effective intervention.

These are exciting times for psychological assessment. C/TA offers new direction and life to psychological assessment. Using psychological assessment as a therapeutic intervention itself is a reality, one that is enormously promising. According to Poston and Hansen (2010), "Those who engage in *assessment and testing as usual* may miss out, it seems, on a golden opportunity to effect client change and enhance clinically important treatment processes" (p. 210).

REFERENCES

Ackerman, S. J., Hilsenroth, M. J., Baity, M. R., & Blagys, M. D. (2000). Interaction of therapeutic process and alliance during psychological assessment. *Journal of Personality Assessment*, *75*, 82–109.

Adler, J. M. (2012). Living into the story: Agency and coherence in a longitudinal study of narrative identity development and mental health over the course of psychotherapy. *Journal of Personality and Social Psychology*, *102*(2), 367–389.

Aldea, M. A., Rice, K. G., Gormley, B., & Rojas, A. (2010). Testing perfectionists about their perfectionism: Effects of providing feedback on emotional reactivity and psychological symptoms. *Behavior Research and Therapy*, *48*, 1194–1203.

Aschieri, F., Fantini, F., & Smith, J. D. (2016). Collaborative/therapeutic assessment: Procedures to enhance client outcomes. In S. Maltzman (Ed.), *The Oxford handbook of treatment processes and outcomes in psychology: A multidisciplinary, biopsychosocial approach* (pp. 241–269). Oxford: Oxford University Press.

Blonigen, D. M., Timko, C., Jacob, T., & Moos, R. H. (2015). Patient-centered feedback on the results of personality testing increases early engagement in residential substance use disorder treatment: A pilot randomized control trial. *Addiction Science and Clinical Practice*, *10*(9). https://doi.org/10.1186/s13722-015-0030-9

Bornstein, R. F. (2017). Evidence-based psychological assessment. *Journal of Personality Assessment*, *99*(4), 435–445.

Cheek, J. M., & Buss, A. H. (1981). Shyness and sociability. *Journal of Personality and Social Psychology*, *41*, 330–339.

Chesham, R. K., Malouff, J. M., & Schutte, N. S. (2018). Meta-analysis of the efficacy of virtual reality exposure therapy for social anxiety. *Behaviour Change*, *25*, 152–166. https://doi.org/10.1017/bec2018.15

Derogatis, L. R. (1983). *SCL-90-R Administration, scoring, and procedures manual – II for the R(evised) version*. Towson, MD: Clinical Psychometric Research.

De Saeger, H., Bartak, A., Eder, E. E., & Kamphuis, J. H. (2016). Memorable experiences in Therapeutic Assessment: Inviting the patient's perspective following a pretreatment randomized controlled trial. *Journal of Personality Assessment*, *98*(5), 472–479. doi.org/10.1080/00223891.2015.1136314

De Saeger, H., Kamphuis, J. H., Finn, S. E., Verheul, R., Smith, J. D., van Busschbach, J. J. V., Feenstra, D., & Horn, E. (2014). Therapeutic Assessment promotes treatment readiness but does not affect symptom change in patients with personality disorders: Findings from a randomized clinical trial. *Psychological Assessment*, *26*(2), 474–483.

Durosini, I., & Aschieri, F. (2018). Therapeutic Assessment effectiveness: A meta-analytic study. Paper presented at Performance Based Assessment Around the World session, Society for Personality Assessment, Annual Convention, Washington, DC, March 17.

Engelman, D. H., & Allyn, J. B. (2012). Collaboration in neuropsychological assessment: Metaphor as intervention with a suicidal adult. In S. E. Finn, C. T. Fischer, & L. Handler (Eds.), *Collaborative/Therapeutic Assessment: A casebook and guide*. New York: Wiley.

Epston, D., & White, M. (1995). Consulting your consultants: A means to the co-construction of alternative knowledges. In S. Friedman (Ed.), *The reflecting team in action: Collaborative practice in family therapy* (pp. 277–313). New York: Guilford Press.

Fenigstein, A., Scheier, M. F., & Buss, A. H. (1975). Public and private self-consciousness: Assessment and theory. *Journal of Consulting and Clinical Psychology*, *43*, 522–527.

Finn, S. E. (2007). *In our clients' shoes: Theory and techniques of Therapeutic Assessment*. Mahwah, NJ: Lawrence Erlbaum Associates.

Finn, S. E. (2009). The many faces of empathy in experiential, person-centered, collaborative assessment. *Journal of Personality Assessment*, *91*, 20–23.

Finn, S. E. (2015a). Core values in Therapeutic Assessment. Therapeutic Assessment Institute (website). www.therapeuticassessment.com

Finn, S. E. (2015b). Therapeutic Assessment with couples. *Pratiques Psychologues*, *21*, 345–373.

Finn, S. E. (2016). Using therapeutic assessment in psychological assessment required for sex reassignment surgery. In V. Brabender & J. L. Mihura (Eds.), *Handbook of gender and sexuality in psychological assessment* (pp. 511–533). New York: Routledge.

Finn, S. E., De Saeger, H., & Kamphuis, J. H. (2017). An ultra-brief model of Therapeutic Assessment. Workshop presented at the annual meeting of the Society for Personality Assessment, San Francisco, March.

Finn, S. E., Frackowiak, M., Schaber, P., Tharinger, D. J., & Smith, J. D. (2012). Building a strong alliance in the initial session of adult and adolescent assessments. Workshop presented at the annual meeting of the Society for Personality Assessment, Chicago, March.

Finn, S. E., & Kamphuis, J. H. (2006). Therapeutic Assessment with the MMPI-2. In J. N. Butcher (Ed.), *MMPI-2: A practitioners guide* (pp. 165–191). Washington, DC: APA Books.

Finn, S. E., & Martin, E. H. (2013). Therapeutic Assessment: Using psychological testing as brief therapy. In K. F. Geisinger (Ed.), *APA handbook of testing and assessment in psychology*, Vol. *2* (pp. 453–465). Washington, DC: American Psychological Association.

Finn, S. E., & Tonsager, M. E. (1992). The therapeutic effects of providing MMPI-2 test feedback to college students awaiting psychotherapy. *Psychological Assessment*, *4*, 278–287.

Fischer, C. T. (1985/1994). *Individualizing psychological assessment*. Mahwah, NJ: Lawrence Erlbaum Associates.

Fonagy, P., Luyten, P., & Allison, E. (2015). Epistemic petrification and the restoration of epistemic trust: A new conceptualization of borderline personality disorder and its psychosocial treatment. *Journal of Personality Disorders*, *29*, 575–609.

Hilsenroth, M. J., & Cromer, T. D. (2007). Clinician interventions related to alliance during the initial interview and psychological assessment. *Psychotherapy: Theory, Research, and Practice*, *44* (2), 205–218.

Hilsenroth, M. J., Peters, E. J., & Ackerman, S. J. (2004). The development of therapeutic alliance during psychological assessment: Patient and therapist perspectives across treatment. *Journal of Personality Assessment*, *83*, 332–344.

Kamphuis, J. H., & Finn, S.E. (2018). Therapeutic Assessment in personality disorders: Toward the restoration of epistemic trust. *Journal of Personality Assessment*, doi.org.du.idm.oclc.org/10.1080/00223891.2018.1476360

Kohut, H. (1984). *How does analysis cure?* Chicago: University of Chicago Press.

Martin, H. (2018). Collaborative Therapeutic Assessment and diversity: The complexity of being human. In R. Krishnamurthy & S. Smith (Eds.), *Diversity sensitive psychological assessment book*. Cambridge University Press.

Martin, E. H., & Jacklin, E. (2012). Therapeutic Assessment involving multiple life issues: Coming to terms with problems of health, culture, and learning. In S. E. Finn, C. T. Fischer, & L. Handler (Eds.), *Collaborative/Therapeutic Assessment: A casebook and guide* (pp. 157–177). Hoboken, NJ: Wiley.

Martin, R., & Young, J. (2010). Schema therapy. In K.S. Dobson (Ed.), *Handbook of cognitive-behavioral therapies* (3rd ed.). New York: Guilford Press.

Miller, L. R., Cano, A., & Wurm, L. H. (2013). A motivational therapeutic assessment improves pain, mood, and relationship satisfaction in couples with chronic pain. *The Journal of Pain, 14*(5), 525–537.

Morey, L. C., Lowmaster, S. E., & Hopwood, C. J. (2010). A pilot study of Manual Assisted Cognitive Therapy with a Therapeutic Assessment augmentation for Borderline Personality Disorder. *Psychiatry Research, 178*, 531–535.

Murray, H. A. (1943). *Thematic Apperception Test manual*. Cambridge, MA: Harvard University Press.

Newman, M. L., & Greenway, P. (1997). Therapeutic effects of providing MMPI-2 test feedback to clients in a university counseling service: A collaborative approach. *Psychological Assessment, 9*, 122–131.

Ougrin, D., Ng, A. V., & Low, J. (2008). Therapeutic assessment based on cognitive-analytic therapy for young people presenting with self-harm: Pilot study. *Psychiatric Bulletin, 32*, 423–426.

Pagano, C. J., Blattner, M. C. C., & Kaplan-Levy, S. (2018). Therapeutic Assessment with child inpatients. *Journal of Personality Assessment*. https://doi.org/10.1080/00223891.2018.1447945

Poston, J. M., & Hanson, W. M. (2010). Meta-analysis of psychological assessment as a therapeutic intervention. *Psychological Assessment, 22*, 203–212.

Schore, A. (2009). Right brain affect regulation: An essential mechanism of development, trauma, dissociation, and psychotherapy. In D. Fosha, M. Solomon, & D. Siegel (Eds.), *The healing power of emotions: Integrating relationships, body, and mine. A dialogue among scientists and clinicians* (pp. 112–144). New York: Norton.

Smith, J. D., Eichler, W. C., Norman, K. R., & Smith, S. R. (2014). The effectiveness of Collaborative/Therapeutic Assessment for psychotherapy consultation: A pragmatic replicated single case study. *Journal of Personality Assessment, 97*(3), 261–270.

Smith, J. D., & George, C. (2012). Therapeutic Assessment case study: Treatment of a woman diagnosed with metastatic breast cancer and attachment trauma. *Journal of Personality Assessment, 94*(4), 331–344.

Smith, J. D., Handler, L., & Nash, M. R. (2010). Family Therapeutic Assessment for preadolescent boys with oppositional defiant disorder: A replicated single-case time-series design. *Psychological Assessment, 22*, 593–602.

Sperber, D., Clément, F., Heitz, C., Mascaro, O., Mercier, H., Origgi, G., & Wilson, D. (2010). Epistemic vigilance. *Mind and Language, 25*(4), 359–393.

Swann, W. B., Jr. (1997). The trouble with change: Self-verification and allegiance to the self. *Psychological Science, 8*, 177–180.

Tarocchi, A., Aschieri, F., Fantini, F., & Smith, J. D. (2013). Therapeutic Assessment of complex trauma: A single-case time-series study. *Clinical Case Studies, 12*(3), 228–245.

Tekeste, M. (2013). Therapeutic assessment with forensic populations. Dissertation, University of Denver.

Tharinger, D. J., Finn, S. E., Austin, C., Gentry, L, Bailey, E., Parton, V., & Fisher, M. (2008). Family sessions in psychological assessment with children: Goals, techniques, and clinical utility. *Journal of Personality Assessment, 90*, 547–558.

Tharinger, D. J., Finn, S. E., Gentry, L., Hamilton, A., Fowler, J., Matson, M., Krumholz, L., & Walkowiak, J. (2009). Therapeutic Assessment with children: A pilot study of treatment acceptability and outcome. *Journal of Personality Assessment, 91*, 238–244.

Tharinger, D. J., Gentry, L., & Finn, S. E. (2013). Therapeutic Assessment with adolescents and their parents: A comprehensive model. In D. Saklofske, C. R. Reynolds, & V. L. Schwean (Eds.), *Oxford handbook of psychological assessment of children and adolescents* (pp. 385–422). New York: Oxford University Press.

Tronick, E. Z. (2007). *The neurobehavioral and social-emotional development of infants and children*. New York: W.W. Norton & Co.

Wilson, T. D. (2011). *Redirect: The surprising new science of psychological change*. New York: Little, Brown and Company.

9 Writing a Psychological Report Using Evidence-Based Psychological Assessment Methods

R. MICHAEL BAGBY AND SHAUNA SOLOMON-KRAKUS

Psychological assessment and report writing are arguably two of the more important tasks of clinical psychologists. The administration, scoring, and interpretation of evidence-based tests that comprise evidence-based psychological assessments (EBPA) are skills that distinguish clinical psychologists from other mental health professionals (Meyer et al., 2001). Irving Weiner, president of Division 5 (Evaluation, Measurement, and Statistics) of the American Psychological Association (APA) and past president of Division 12 (Society of Clinical Psychology) stated, "testing was the seed from which modern-day psychology grew" (Novotney, 2010, p. 26) and the demand for psychological assessments is only continuing to grow today (Novotney, 2017). Considering that psychological report writing is an integral component of psychological assessment, the overall purpose of this chapter is to provide some recommendations and guidelines on how to write a psychological report using EBPA methods. Our definition of EBPA methods assumes that psychological assessment is an objective performance-based measure that adheres to the Standards for Educational and Psychological Testing (AERA, APA, & NCME, 2014). Bornstein's (2017) recommendations on how to operationalize EBPA also informed this chapter.

ASSESSMENT PRACTICES OF PSYCHOLOGISTS

A recent survey found about one-quarter of professional psychologists' direct clinical hours were spent conducting psychological assessments (Wright et al., 2017). The referral questions for these psychological assessments typically centered around assisting in psychodiagnosis, making treatment, academic, or vocational recommendations, and screening for cognitive or neuropsychological deficits. The writing of psychological reports was an integral and time-consuming component of the psychological assessments; among psychologists who conducted assessments regularly, more time was spent scoring and writing the psychological report (6.6 hours per week on average) compared to the assessment itself (6.1 hours per week on average).

THE EVOLUTION OF PSYCHOLOGICAL REPORT WRITING: FROM PSYCHODYNAMIC INFERENCE TO INTERPRETATION OF OBJECTIVE NORMATIVE-BASED DATA

The evolution of psychological report writing is noteworthy with what we see as the de-emphasis on psychodynamic terminology and inference to the transition from test-by-test reporting to assessment (e.g., meaningful associations between the client and objective data) (see, e.g., Neukrug & Fawcett, 2010; Tallent, 1993). Given the wide array of techniques used by clinical psychologists, there is no clear consensus regarding the contents of a psychological report. Readers of this chapter should be aware that this guide and the recommendations on how to write a psychological report are only one example and that the nature and content of a psychological report depend ultimately on the referral source and question(s). In this chapter, we do, however, adhere to the general shift from psychodynamic theory to the substantive interpretation of normative-based test results, which reflect more mainstream and contemporary approaches to psychological assessment.

In general, evidence-based practice in psychology has been defined as the "integration of the best available research with clinical expertise in the context of patient characteristics, culture, and preferences" (APA, 2006, p. 273). Although the focus to date has been on evidence-based psychological treatments, clinical psychologists are beginning to emphasize the importance of EBPA (Bornstein, 2017). Bornstein (2017) outlines nine steps to operationalize and implement EBPA that include but are not limited to (1) using empirically validated psychological tests that have demonstrated strong psychometric properties and clinical utility in the literature, (2) understanding the limitations of these psychological tests (i.e., generalizability to individuals with varying cultures, ages, ethnicities), and (3) using multiple psychological tests to measure a construct when possible. Indeed, these steps outline that EBPA consist of the administration, scoring, and interpretation of multiple evidence-based psychological tests. This chapter adds to the growing literature that emphasizes the importance of EBPA by guiding readers on how to write a psychological report using results from the psychological tests that comprise EBPA.

PRINCIPLES OF REPORT WRITING USING EVIDENCE-BASED PSYCHOLOGICAL ASSESSMENT METHODS

Nearly twenty years ago, Heilbrun (2001) articulated twenty-nine general principles for forensic psychological assessments – a context in which evidence-based report writing is of a high premium (see also Heilbrun, DeMatteo, and Marczyk, 2004; Heilbrun et al., 2009). Since then, Young (2016) identified that twenty-two of these twenty-nine principles can be applied to forensic psychological report writing. We use these principles (hereafter to referred to as the Principles) as a framework and an organizing tool on how to write all varieties of a psychological report using EBPA methods. Given that Young (2016) and Heilbrun and colleagues (2001) focused on forensic contexts, we included some unique principles that adhere to our opinions and comply with psychological report writing outside of forensic contexts (see Table 9.1). To exemplify how we believe these principles should inform the content and wording of any psychological report, examples from the first author's "closed" case file reports (i.e., older than seven years) are excerpted. These excerpts have been partially fictionalized and anonymized to mask the identity of those assessed.

THE PSYCHOLOGICAL REPORT: A TEMPLATE

Section 1: Biographical Sketch. A short yet thorough description of the evaluator's qualifications, degrees, and competencies should be listed at the beginning of the psychological report (Principle #4; Young, 2016).[1] If relevant, affiliations with academic institutions and peer-reviewed journals should be noted. The registration number(s) of the evaluator's professional regulatory bodies must be included. We also recommend the inclusion of how long the evaluator has been conducting psychological assessments, any specializations (e.g., forensic assessments), and whether or not they have experience testifying in court if applicable. The APA's Ethical Principles of Psychologists and Code of Conduct (EPPCC) (APA, 2017a) Section 2 outlines that all licensed psychologists must have the proper training, qualifications, and supervised experience to provide their services and that these qualifications are accurately and clearly described to the client.

In summary, the following points should be covered in a biographical sketch:

- Occupation(s) and respective registration number(s)
- An exhaustive list of declared competencies
- Number of previous assessments relevant to the psychological report
- A list of relevant education and training, including where and when degrees were obtained. Note that clinical psychologists should list where and when their postdoctoral training was completed
- Positions at any academic institutions, including membership(s) to specific departments
- Involvement in peer-reviewed academic journals
- Number of peer-reviewed publications that speak to the author's expertise and competency to write this psychological report
- Private practice experience if applicable and relevant
- Experience at testifying in court if applicable

Section 2: Identifying Information and Referral Question. A description of the client is needed, including basic demographic information (e.g., client's full name and date of birth). The date of the assessment and the date of the final report must also be reported. As per Principle #2 (Young, 2016), the referral question (e.g., *Why* is the assessment needed?) and referral source (e.g., *Who* requested the assessment?) must be clearly identified at the very beginning:

Mr. W is a 33-year-old married male referred for a comprehensive psychological evaluation by his family physician [name of family physician], in order to inform the client's medical team about whether psychological symptoms are impacting Mr. W's social and occupational functioning.

Some referral sources (e.g., insurance companies) may have specific questions (e.g., *"Based on established DSM-5 diagnostic criteria what is your diagnosis? Please provide diagnostic coding, including specifiers."*) We believe it is important that these questions are copied into the report verbatim. Evidence-based responses to referral questions are included in a subsequent section of the report.

This section also provides a broad overview of what transpired in the assessment. For example, what time did the assessment commence and terminate? What was the duration of the assessment? Who assisted with the assessment? Were any breaks needed (e.g., lunch breaks) and why were breaks needed (e.g., was the client upset by questioning?)? The context (e.g., quiet room with few distractions), as per Principle #5 (Young, 2016), should also be described here.

The final portion of Section 2 (i.e., Identifying Information and Referral Question) describes the assessment in more detail. Any aids that could have influenced the assessment and/or interpretation of the test results should be outlined here. For example, was an interpreter needed?[2] Was there any indication that a question was

[1] It is our general practice to always include qualifications into a report, although this is more characteristic of forensic rather than non-forensic reports.

[2] The use of an interpreter should be noted in the report. It is best practice that interpreters consent to not reveal any information obtained during the assessment. Ethical principles surrounding confidentiality should also be explained to the interpreter. The informed consent process with the interpreter should be noted in the report.

Table 9.1 Principles of psychological report writing

Principle #	Principle Name
1	Avoid scientific jargon and provide definitions as needed.
2	The referral source, referral/legal question, and relevant legal information (if applicable) should be listed at the beginning of the report.
3	The informed consent process must be described in detail and near the beginning of the report.
4	A biographical sketch that outlines the report writer's competence and areas of expertise (e.g., degrees, years of experience) is needed.
5	A detailed description of the assessment should be provided including the context of the assessment (e.g., private room with few distractions).
6	Clients, third parties, and collaterals must be aware of the purpose of the assessment and who will have access to the final psychological report.
7	Limits of confidentiality must be explained to the client and described in the psychological report.
8	The language and tone of a psychological report must be objective and impartial.
9	Objective empirical evidence must inform all aspects of the psychological report including the data collection method(s) and the interpretations of the results.[a]
10	Multiple sources of information (e.g., self-report measures, structured and/or semi-structured clinical interviews, file reviews) will improve the objectivity of the report.
11	When using evidence-based psychological assessment methods, only psychological tests with evidence of reliability and validity in the empirical literature should be administered and interpreted in the psychological reports.[a]
12	If applicable, the functioning of the client before and after the incident in question (e.g., forensic cases) should be clearly described.
13	Results from evidence-based psychological assessments should be compared to other sources of information including the structured or semi-structured interview. Discrepancies between any sources of information should be outlined.
14	If applicable, assess legally relevant behavior with the data gathered from the multiple sources including evidence-based assessments (e.g., functionality, clinical characteristics).
15	Response style (e.g., inconsistent responding, malingering) should be assessed objectively with validity scales.[a]
16	If the results from the validity scales indicate that the results are not interpretable, this should be described in the report and the results should not be interpreted in any way.[a]
17	Idiographic and nomothetic evidence should be used in a psychological report. Idiographic evidence (e.g., client's current clinical condition, affect, demeanor, and functional abilities) should not be used alone.[a]
18	Using evidence-based psychological assessment methods, nomothetic evidence (e.g., substantive interpretations from evidence-based assessments) is preferred relative to idiographic evidence.[a]
19	Interpretations in the report must correspond to list of assessments found in the "Sources of Information" section.
20	Causal links between clinical conditions (or the legal event in question) and functional abilities/impairments should be provided with caution and supported with objective and empirical evidence. Limitations as to why causal connections cannot be made should be noted in the report.
21	Only the referral questions should be addressed however; in legal cases, the ultimate legal question should never be answered.
22	Report writers should anticipate that their reports will be thoroughly examined. Any indication of bias must be removed.

[a] These revised and unique principles were included to adhere to the opinions of the authors. This table was informed by principles of forensic psychological report writing outlined by Young (2016), which adhere to the principles of forensic assessment published in Heilbrun (2001), Heilbrun, DeMatteo, and Marczyk (2004), and Heilbrun et al. (2009).

unclear to the client due to cultural differences?[3] Should the results be interpreted with caution given the lack of empirical evidence supporting the reliability and/or validity of a particular assessment among the client's cultural group? A review of the empirical literature is needed to decipher whether the psychometric properties of the EBPA are generalizable to the client and any limitations to interpretation due to cultural differences should be noted in the psychological report in either this section or Section 10: Case Formulation described below.

Section 3: Sources of Information. All interpreted data must correspond to an exhaustive list of sources of information (Principle #19; Young, 2016). To ensure the

[3] We adhere to the definition of culture articulated by the APA (2017b).

psychological report is based on EBPA methods, the "Sources of Information" list will include psychological tests that comprise EBPA exclusively. Sources of information must also include a review of collateral information (e.g., any previous evaluations of the client, medical records, and/or court records that informed the psychological report). Any previous psychological assessment of the client should also be compared with the current assessment and discrepancies in the results should be noted (Principle #13; Young, 2016). As per Principle #10 (Young, 2016), multiple and diverse sources of information improve the objectivity of the report.

Section 4: Informed Consent. It is imperative that the informed consent process is clearly outlined in the psychological report (Principles #3, 6, and 7; Young, 2016). According to the EPPCC, informed consent (Standard 3.10) is completed when assessors explain (1) the purpose of the assessment, (2) limitations to confidentiality, including who will have access to the final psychological report, and (3) involvement of third parties if applicable. Informed consent also requires that clients are provided with sufficient time and opportunity to ask questions (APA, 2017a). Documentation of the informed consent process is essential in the psychological report:

Prior to beginning the assessment, Mrs. B was informed that a psychological assessment had been requested by [referral source] to assist in her psychiatric evaluation. It was explained that the results of the psychological assessment would be summarized in a report that would be provided to [referral source]. She appeared to comprehend the purpose of the assessment and its use. She consented to the assessment verbally and also signed an informed consent document.

Assessors and psychological report writers are encouraged to review their respective code of ethics and privacy laws (e.g., the Health Insurance Portability and Accountability Act; HIPAA) to ensure humane and ethical informed consent processes are followed.[4]

Section 5: Presenting Problem(s) and Symptoms(s) and/or Background Situation. This section describes the client's presenting problem (e.g., symptoms of depression, anxiety), the severity of the problem (e.g., level of impairment), and how the presenting problem(s) has impacted the client's level of functioning if applicable (e.g., social, occupational; Principle #12). It is important to consider onset, duration, and course, as well as any historical manifestations of the reported problem. Other factors that directly relate to the presenting problems (e.g., going through a divorce; lost a job) can be included here. This section may also require a brief background of the situation behind why a client may have been referred for an assessment (e.g., forensic reports). In forensic reports, a defendant's account of the offense or a summary of a plaintiff's complaints can be useful.

[4] The Canadian privacy laws are outlined in the Personal Information Protection and Electronic Documents Act (PIPEDA)

Section 6: Psychosocial Background. The Psychosocial Background section is an integral component of the report; the client's personal history creates the context for which all objective test results should be interpreted (Lichtenberger et al., 2004). Several pieces of information should be gathered for this section, including but not limited to personal history, including the client's current living situation and occupational status; immigration process if relevant; employment history; developmental history, including whether the client experienced any developmental delays (e.g., walking, talking) and/or experienced any learning difficulties at school; current relationship status and relationship history if relevant; educational history; legal history if applicable; medical history, including prior psychiatric diagnoses; and family psychiatric history. This section can be informed by collateral information (e.g., file review) and can be complemented by the unstructured interview in the assessment for which the report is being written. Overall, the Psychosocial Background section is intended to (1) build the foundation for the assessment, (2) place the objective test results within the client's context, and (3) help inform the Case Formulation and Recommendations sections. The Psychosocial Background section should be pertinent to the current assessment; personal information that does not fulfill the above-mentioned purposes of the Psychosocial Background section should be omitted. Some psychological reports have included this section (Section 6: Psychosocial Background) before Section 5: Presenting Problem(s) and Symptoms(s) and/or Background Situation. The order of sections will depend on the case and is ultimately at the discretion of the report writer.

Section 7: Mental Status and Behavioral Observations. Assessors may consider reporting the client's punctuality, attire (e. g., appropriately dressed for a formal assessment or not), eye contact, rapport, demeanor (e.g., friendly, unapproachable), speech including the rate, rhythm, volume, and tangentiality, attributional style (e.g., was the client arrogant or self-effacing?), and affect (e.g., was the client tearful/smiling throughout the assessment?). It should also be noted whether prominent symptoms are immediately apparent (e.g., mania, thought disorder) and should be highlighted for the reader of the report.

Ms. V presented on time for her appointment. She was casually attired and appropriately groomed appearing somewhat older than her stated age. She easily established adequate rapport and was cooperative and pleasant. She made appropriate eye contact. Her speech was of normal rate, rhythm, and volume and she elaborated spontaneously and appropriately when asked questions. She was fully oriented and showed no signs of tangentiality, thought disorder, responding to internal stimuli, racing thoughts or pressured speech. She did not evidence psychomotor retardation or agitation. Her affect was appropriate to the content of her speech. She cried frequently, especially when discussing her symptoms of depression. She evidenced an attributional style that was internalizing and self-blaming (e.g., she blamed herself for "putting her family in this position"). She did not refuse to answer any interview questions posed. She completed all the psychological tests in a timely manner and denied significant difficulty reading the test materials.

Section 8: Evidence-Based Psychological Tests. It is our position that EBPA consists of the administration, scoring, and interpretation of multiple psychological tests that have empirical support for their psychometric properties and clinical utility. Interpretations from evidence-based psychological tests provide substantial nomothetic evidence that, in the authors' opinion, is preferred when conducting assessments and writing psychological reports (Principle #18).

Before examples of substantive interpretations are provided, we believe it is essential for five types of invalid response style to be assessed in EBPA (Sellbom & Bagby, 2008). Three forms of noncontent-based response styles include nonresponding (i.e., scores cannot be computed because a response is missing, or multiple responses are given for the same item), random responding (i.e., participants unintentionally answer items in an unsystematic manner, perhaps due to issues of comprehension), and fixed responding (i.e., participants are responding either in an acquiescent [yea-saying] or counter-acquiescent [nay-saying] manner). Two forms of content-based responding should also be examined: underreporting (e.g., intentional minimization of psychological difficulties) and overreporting (e.g., intentional exaggeration of psychological difficulties). Objective tests of response style should be used in all EBPA and results from the tests should be described in the psychological report (Principle #9). Examples of such objective tests include validity scales from the Minnesota Multiphasic Personality Inventory-2-Restructured Form (MMPI-2-RF; Ben-Porath & Tellegen, 2008/2011) and the Personality Assessment Inventory (PAI; Morey, 1991) (see descriptions of these scales below). The feigning of memory complaints can also be assessed using performance validity tests (e.g., Test of Memory Malingering, TOMM; Tombaugh, 1996). The exaggeration of psychiatric symptoms can be assessed with the Miller Forensic Assessment of Symptoms Test (M-FAST; Miller, 2001) or the Structured Interview of Reported Symptoms 2nd Edition (SIRS-2; Kocsis, 2011), to mention a few. For more on this issue, see Chapter 6 in this volume.

It is our position that the substantive interpretations from the psychological tests comprise the most important content of an evidence-based psychological report. The following psychological tests are frequently used in the first author's practice due to the extensive empirical evidence that supports their reliability and validity (Principle #11).[5]

The Minnesota Multiphasic Personality Inventory-2-Restructured Form (MMPI-2-RF). Chapter 16 in this volume provides extensive coverage of the MMPI-2-RF (Ben-Porath & Tellegen, 2008/2011). In brief, the MMPI-2-RF is a revised and psychometrically improved version of the MMPI-2.[6] It is a measure of personality and psychopathology that provides information regarding the possible presence of a mental disorder as well as information relevant to the assessment of dysfunctional personality patterns or personality disorders as measured by a number of "substantive" clinical scales. In addition, it contains a number of "validity scales"; these scales assess consistency of responding (i.e., if the client responded to the content of the item, as opposed to random endorsement of items or a simple pattern of repeatedly responding to the questions with either "true" or "false") and the degree to which clients may have engaged in excessive or "noncredible" levels of underreporting or overreporting response style bias. If either of the consistency or response style validity scales are elevated to any significant degree (as specified by the MMPI-2-RF test manual), then the clinical scales of the instrument cannot be interpreted as the test protocol is considered "invalid" (Principle #15; Young, 2016). Clear reasons as to why the test is not interpreted should be outlined in the psychological report (Principle #16).

Mr. S's MMPI-2-RF profile did not indicate inconsistent responding or overt attempts at gross misrepresentation.

Mr. S's "higher-order" clinical scale profile, a set of scales capturing overarching or higher-order dimensions of psychopathology including symptoms of internalizing mental disorders (e.g., depression, anxiety), externalizing disorder (e.g., problematic substance use and antisocial behaviors), and thought dysfunctions (e.g., psychosis), indicated no significant psychopathology.

On the remaining "lower-order" clinical and specific problem scales, Mr. S's profile indicated minor and clinically insignificant elevations on scales measuring somatic health complaints, low positive emotion (e.g., depressive states/anhedonia), and ideas of persecution. These minor elevations, again, do not indicate clinical levels of pathology. The only significant clinical subscale elevation evident in his profile was an elevation on the suicide subscale. This elevation reflects Mr. S's positive endorsement of a single item, "My thoughts these days turn more and more to death and the life hereafter," which was only endorsed by 13.5% of the MMPI-2-RF normative sample and thus is typically flagged for further inquiry, as a precautionary measure. Given that Mr. S's elevation on this scale is based upon his endorsement of only one item, it cannot by itself be concluded to provide firm support for imminent suicide risk. Mr. S did not endorse imminent suicidal ideation in his responses to more direct queries about suicide (e.g., on the PAI) and in the clinical interview.

In sum, Mr. S's MMPI-2-RF clinical profile, overall, does not support a picture of significant psychopathology or of clinically significant personality dysfunction. It is, essentially, indicative of overall "normal" range functioning.

[5] Given the first author's expertise, there is an emphasis on personality inventories. Thorough descriptions of intelligence and other neuropsychological test measures can be found elsewhere (Lezak et al., 2012), including in Chapters 12 and 15 in this volume.

[6] According to a recent survey of practicing psychologist in the United States (Wright et al., 2017), the MMPI (any version) was the second most frequently administered psychological test after symptom specific measures such as the Beck Depression Inventory (BDI).

The Personality Assessment Inventory (PAI). Chapter 17 provides extensive coverage of the PAI (Morey, 1991). In brief, the PAI, like the MMPI-2-RF, is a measure of personality and psychopathology and provides information regarding the possible presence of a major mental disorder and dysfunctional personality patterns or personality disorders.[7] The PAI also provides an array of scales and indices that are designed to identify factors that could influence the results of testing. Such factors include idiosyncratic responding due to carelessness, confusion, reading difficulties, or other sources of random responding, and a variety of willful or self-deceptive manipulations and distortions such as exaggerations, malingering, and defensiveness.

Mr. S's PAI profile did not indicate inconsistent responding or deliberate attempts at self-misrepresentation. An elevation on the alcohol scale suggested occasional problems caused by alcohol consumption, but this elevation was below the range considered clinically significant. Other clinical scales on the PAI reflected no significant psychopathology.

In terms of clinical subscales, Mr. S's profile showed minor elevations on subscales reflecting antisocial behavior and verbal aggression. These were likewise below the range considered clinically significant.

The Treatment Resistance Index of the PAI reflected a somewhat lower than average motivation to receive psychological treatment, indicating that Mr. S may not feel he requires further psychological intervention.

The NEO Personality Inventory-3. The NEO-PI-3 (McCrae, Costa, & Martin, 2005) is a multidimensional test of normative personality factors following the well-supported five-factor model of personality. The five broad (higher-order) factors (or domains; neuroticism, extraversion, openness, agreeableness, and conscientiousness) are further subdivided into multiple "lower-order" facets (e.g., achievement seeking, depression). Evidence for convergent and discriminant validity as well as internal reliability have been consistently reported (McCrae et al., 2005). It should be noted that the NEO-PI-3 does not include validity scales like the MMPI-2-RF and the PAI.

In terms of individual facets within the five domains, Mr. S did not exhibit any facet scores within the very low or very high range, a pattern that does not support any major personality pathology.

Mr. S's overall profile is inconsistent with a clinical picture of personality disorder. It is consistent, however, with an individual with average ranged emotional stability, self-esteem, need for achievement and ability to cope with stress.

These evidence-based psychological tests can provide valuable information for almost all referral questions; however, additional testing may be required depending on the presenting problem(s) and referral question(s). The first author has used other evidence-based tests including the Beck Depression Inventory (BDI-II; Beck, Steer, & Brown, 1996) and the second edition of the Trauma Symptom Inventory (TSI-2; Briere, 2011). Although the BDI and the TSI-2 are evidence-based, it should be noted that, unlike the PAI and MMPI-2-RF, they do not include a formal set of validity scales that assess response style, which is important to acknowledge in psychological reports that use EBPA methods.

Reporting Interpretations from Psychological Tests in EBPA. Competency and the ability to provide an informed interpretation are integral to this section of the report. In some cases, referral questions may be outside the scope of the report writer's competencies. Should this be the case, it is important to contextualize an interpretation in light of limitations to competency:

Q: Within the scope of your medical discipline, what are the Plan Member's current symptoms? Based on your examination, are the symptoms supported by clinical pathology?

A: Depressed mood, anhedonia, poor concentration, sleep problems and poor appetite. Limited physical mobility. All the psychiatric symptoms are linked to depression and the physical limitation to her surgery, although I am not a medical doctor.

In part, yes.

Competency is also important when complementing computer-based test interpretations (CBTI). CBTI are available for several psychological tests, including the MMPI-2-RF and PAI. It has been considered as an ethical violation, however, to copy CBTI verbatim into the psychological report as a stand-alone (see Michaels, 2006 for a review). CBTI should rather be paraphrased and complemented with clinical judgment, the client's context, and competency. The report writer must carefully review each CBTI, interpret each statement within the context of the assessment, compare the statement with the objective data, and determine whether it is applicable to each individual client and the client's culture. The recommendation to avoid using CBTI is a good example of why the integration of idiographic and nomothetic evidence is preferred when writing a psychological report using EBPA methods (Principles #17 & 18). The following case exemplifies the importance of complementing CBTI with clinical judgment and the client's history (e.g., previous psychological assessments):

When I rescored the raw test data using a computerized scoring system, I obtained interpretative statements that are inconsistent with the absence of personality disorder. For example, the interpretive report states, "notable may be (i.e., the test respondent's) tendencies to intimidate and exploit others, and to expect special recognition and consideration without assuming reciprocal responsibilities." In addition, "he may display a rash willingness to risk harm and he may be notably fearless in the face of threats and punitive action. In fact, punishment may only reinforce his rebellious and hostile feelings." Further, "carrying a chip on the shoulder attitude he may exhibit a readiness to attack those he distrusts. If he is unsuccessful in channeling these omnipresent aggressive impulses, his resentment may mount into periods of manic excitement or into acts of brutal hostility." This interpretation seems to be consistent with the presence of an antisocial personality disorder, and is similar to

[7] Both the MMPI-2-RF and the PAI are administered to provide corroborative information or "back-up" information should one of the tests prove to be invalid.

the results obtained from the MMPI-2-RF. While one cannot rely solely on the interpretive statements provided by the test publisher, it is important to note that these descriptions are consistent with the [previous assessors'] clinical opinion that Mr. K in fact did meet the diagnostic criteria for antisocial personality disorder. It is my opinion, that antisocial personality disorder is the prominent feature of Mr. K's clinical profile.

When providing interpretations, report writers may also consider citing empirical sources to validate their own interpretations. Indeed, interpretative statements from the MMPI-2-RF are accompanied by empirical references.[8] Should interpretative statements be used verbatim in the report, we recommend that they should be identified with quotations and seamlessly integrated into the report.

It is imperative that, when reporting interpretations from psychological tests, the language is clear, simple, and accessible to an audience beyond mental health professionals who are familiar with these tests (Principle #1). Language must also be objective and impartial (Principle #8), as interpretations should never simply advocate for the referral source. The following example demonstrates how this common pitfall of psychological report writing can be avoided:

It is not possible to conclude definitively or otherwise disentangle with a reasonable level of certainty whether Ms. Q's current psychopathology stems primarily from her alleged misdiagnosis and her accompanying sense of mistrust of medical doctors and medical procedures, or from the disability that resulted directly from her diagnosis independent of alleged delayed diagnosis. Further complicating any inference of a reliable causal assignment or connection to her misdiagnosis with her current psychiatric symptoms is the fact that her choice to file a law suit against the hospital and various physicians is also a likely source of her current anxiety and depression.

This example illustrates how to use objective language (e.g., "It is not possible to conclude **definitively** or otherwise disentangle with a **reasonable level of certainty** whether ... "), how to incorporate multiple sources of data when providing an interpretation (Principle #14; Young, 2016), and how the ultimate question (in this case, legal question) should never be answered with absolute certainty (Principles #20 & 21; Young, 2016).

It is also our position to omit raw data or test scores in the psychological report. Though other qualified mental health professionals may argue that they can provide their own unique interpretations, not all readers of the psychological report possess these skills and qualifications. Single data points can be easily misinterpreted without other information (e.g., behavioral observations, the client's culture and other demographic factors, the clinical interview, tests of malingering, among other limitations of the assessments; Groth-Marnat & Horvath, 2006).

Section 9: Clinical Interview Results. There are many different structured clinical interviews (e.g., the Clinician-Administered PTSD Scale for DSM-5 [CAPS-5; Weathers et al., 2013] and the Mini-International Neuropsychiatric Interview [MINI; Sheehan et al., 1998]; see, e.g., Chapter 10 in this volume). We apply the Structured Clinical Interview for DSM-5 (SCID-5; First et al., 2015) in our practice to comprehensively assess and diagnose the client's past and current mental disorders as contained within the fifth edition of the American Psychiatric Association's *Diagnostic and Statistical Manual of Mental Disorders* (DSM-5; American Psychiatric Association, 2013). We emphasize the importance of administering structured interviews to facilitate greater diagnostic accuracy and inter-rater reliability (Miller et al., 2001). It is our opinion that using clinical impressions based on unstructured interviews as stand-alones when making psychiatric diagnoses may be subjected to a number of unintentional biases that lead to potentially nonveridical clinical inference. Though structured interviews help inform psychiatric diagnoses, the SCID does not collect information regarding the client's psychosocial background, which, as previously mentioned, builds the context for which all objective data (including data from the SCID) should be interpreted. An unstructured interview should precede the SCID in order to gather sufficient information for the Psychosocial Background and the Case Formulation sections.

Depending on the referral question and the client's presenting problem(s), the assessor would decide which module should be administered (e.g., may only administer modules A [Mood Episodes] and F [Anxiety Disorders]). The DSM-5 Self-Rated Level 1 Cross-Cutting Symptoms Measure (Narrow, Clarke, & Kuramoto, 2013) can help inform which modules are selected. The First and colleagues (2015) citation and the Cross-Cutting Symptoms Measure are both used in the first author's practice. A detailed description of the results from the SCID-5 should be listed in this section. In this example, only the results from module A (Mood Episodes) are listed:

With regard to mood symptoms, Ms. N reported feelings of low mood nearly every day, with no significant periods of remission. She stated that she has experienced loss of interest and motivation to perform many activities she enjoyed prior to [date], such as swimming, going for runs, and trying new restaurants. She reported frequent waking on a nightly basis since [date], resulting in her getting 5 ½ hours of sleep on a typical night and feeling tired throughout the day. She noted that occasionally she is awakened by "night terrors." She also endorsed occasional psychomotor agitation with accompanying periods of elevated anxiety but denied that this occurred on most days. She endorsed daily anergia and the feeling that tasks require more effort than they did prior to [date]. She reported feelings of worthlessness, which she attributed to her failure to adapt to a life of relative dependency and her perception of low job

[8] An example of an interpretative report of Mr. I, a middle-aged man presenting with psychotic thinking and assaultive behavior can be found online at: http://images.pearsonclinical.com/images/Assets/MMPI-2-RF/MMPI-2-RF_Interp_PsyInpatient.pdf. Interpretative statements from Mr. I's clinical profile along with citations that support these statements can be found on this website.

performance, whereas she emphasized that prior to [date] she felt highly independent and successful. She further reported difficulty concentrating, retrieving/retaining information and comprehending written material. She denied any suicidal ideation or intent, current or past. She stated that these symptoms have had an impact on her functioning; for example, straining her marriage and her relationship with her children due to heightened irritability, making daily tasks, such as cleaning difficult, and leading to some neglect of these tasks.

Similar to when writing interpretations from the evidence-based psychological tests, language used to describe results from structured and unstructured clinical interview must be clear, simple, and accessible to a lay audience (Principle #1; Young, 2016). Furthermore, considering a psychiatric diagnosis could influence a reader's interpretation of the report; it is also essential that a diagnosis be supported with substantial empirical evidence (e.g., results from the SCID in addition to results from the evidence-based psychological tests). Pejoratives (Resnick & Soliman, 2012) and language that reifies an illness (e.g., "a schizophrenic individual") should never be used. Rather, "an individual *with* schizophrenia" would be a more appropriate description. It should be noted that structured diagnostic interviews including the SCID do not include formal validity scales. Notwithstanding, there is empirical evidence indicating that elevated validity scales on the MMPI-2-RF, which are associated with inflated (i.e., overreporting) or deflated (i.e., underreporting) scores on the substantive scales on the MMPI-2-RF are also accompanied by alterations in test scale scores on instruments administered alongside the MMPI-2-RF (Forbey & Lee, 2011).

Section 10: Case Formulation. Report writers have the challenging task of synthesizing a vast amount of information from the EBPA into a meaningful narrative that is the case formulation, which, in clinical settings, is critical to guide intervention goals and recommendations. The first part of the case formulation is a summary of the presenting problem, informed by subjective interpretations from the client, clinical judgment, and from objective data collected in the assessment. According to Persons and Tompkins (2007), the summary of the presenting problem can be broken down into three levels: (1) the symptom (e.g., negative mood), (2) the disorder (e.g., major depressive disorder) or the problem (e.g., impairment to functioning), and (3) the case (understanding the presenting problem in the context of the client, including their culture and environment, among other important variables that are listed in the Psychosocial Background section). Report writers may also be required to hypothesize causes of the presenting problem (for a review, see Persons & Tompkins, 2007), including potential origins (e.g., biomarkers), mechanisms (e.g., coping strategies such as avoidance), and precipitants (e.g., environmental triggers such as a major role transition), all of which can be described in this section of the psychological report.

Depending on the referral question, psychological report writers should consider all presenting problems, how the problems affect or are related to one another, and the repercussions on all domains of life (e.g., psychological, interpersonal, occupational, educational functioning; Persons & Tompkins, 2007). Cultural factors that may speak to the origin or precipitant of the problem(s) should also be noted:

Although Mr. K denied any currently ongoing or residual symptoms of posttraumatic stress disorder (PTSD) or any other psychopathology, it is possible that he is experiencing symptoms but simply not admitting their presence. This is not an unusual phenomenon in "front line" public safety or military personnel in which a culture of invincibility diminishes the probability of any individual disclosure of mental health problems.

Arguably, the most important aspect of a case formulation is whether the recommendations, including treatment recommendations that are derived from the formulation, are suitable and relevant for the individual client and their context.

Section 11: Recommendations. Recent empirical evidence suggests that results from EBPA can inform treatment planning (e.g., the five-factor model of personality assessed by the NEO-PI-3; Bagby et al., 2016). It should be remembered, however, that official diagnoses and treatment recommendations can only be provided if this is within the report writer's realm of competency:

Given the presence of Mr. D's depression and generalized anxiety disorder (GAD)-related symptoms, and the level of impairment and interpersonal distress he perceives and reports these symptoms have caused, it is recommended that he pursue more structured and frequent psychotherapy (e.g., 20-week, once weekly trial of Cognitive Behavior Therapy – [CBT]), than he is currently receiving. I also recommend that he receive a psychiatric consultation to determine whether a trial of medication is indicated for his depression and anxiety; such a consultation might also include some psychoeducation about the short- and long-term effects of such medication(s).

All psychological report writers must consider that their final document will be reviewed and may impact the client's life in a significant way. Any indication of biases, particularly when describing the results from the clinical interview and interpreting the results from the EBPA, must be removed before the finalized version is submitted (Principle #22).

Section 12: Summary and Conclusions. This section summarizes the case at hand, who the client is, and whether the results indicate any clinical psychopathology. Codes from the DSM-5 and The International Classification of Disease – Eleventh Revision (ICD-11; World Health Organization, 2018) should be listed here to accompany any diagnosis provided in the report. The final portion of this section will reiterate answers to referral question(s) or explain limitations as to why referral question(s) could not be answered.

Table 9.2 Headings and subheadings of a psychological report using evidence-based psychological assessment methods

Suggested Order of (sub)headings	Title of (sub)headings
Section 1	Biographical Sketch
Section 2	Identifying Information and Referral Question
Section 3	Sources of Information
Section 4	Informed Consent
Section 5	Presenting Problem(s) and Symptoms(s) and/or Background Situation
Section 6	Psychosocial Background
Section 7	Mental Status and Behavioral Observations
Section 8	Evidence-Based Psychological Tests
Section 9	Clinical Interview Results
Section 10	Case Formulation
Section 11	Recommendations
Section 12	Summary and Conclusions

CONCLUSIONS

Our approach was to provide a template for how one might write a psychological report using EBPA methods. Table 9.2 summarizes our suggested headings and subheadings for this psychological report template. Revised principles from Young (2016) were used as an organizing tool and framework for this template and partially fictionalized and anonymized excerpts from the first author's practice were used to illustrate these principles. We would like to reiterate that some clinical psychologists might use other psychological assessment methods in their reports, including a reliance on performance-based/projective-based measures. Here we focus on one type of EBPA (e.g., objective performance-based measures) and follow the Standards for Educational and Psychological Testing (AERA, APA, & NCME, 2014). Report writers who share similar approaches to EBPA may find this outline helpful when formatting their psychological reports.

REFERENCES

AERA (American Educational Research Association), APA (American Psychological Association), & NCME (National Council on Measurement in Education). (2014). *Standards for educational and psychological testing*. Washington, DC: AERA.

American Psychiatric Association. (2013). *Diagnostic and statistical manual of mental disorders* (5th ed.). Washington, DC: American Psychiatric Association.

APA (American Psychological Association). (2006). Evidence-based practice in psychology. *American Psychologist*, *61*, 271–285.

APA (American Psychological Association). (2017a). *Ethical Principles of Psychologists and Code of Conduct*. www.apa.org/ethics/code/index.aspx

APA (American Psychological Association). (2017b). *APA Guidelines on Multicultural Education, Training, Research, Practice and Organizational Change for Psychologists*. www.apa.org/pi/oema/resources/policy/multicultural-guidelines.aspx

Bagby, R. M., Gralnick, T. M., Al-Dajani, N., & Uliaszek, A. A. (2016). The role of the Five Factor Model in personality assessment and treatment planning. *Clinical Psychology: Science and Practice*, *23*, 365–381. http://doi.org/10.1111/cpsp.12175

Beck, A. T., Steer, R. A., & Brown, G. K. (1996). *Manual for the Beck Depression Inventory-II*. San Antonio, TX: Psychological Corporation.

Ben-Porath, Y. S., & Tellegen, A. (2008/2011). *MMPI–2–RF (Minnesota Multiphasic Personality Inventory–2 Restructured Form) manual for administration, scoring, and interpretation*. Minneapolis: University of Minnesota Press.

Bornstein, R. F. (2017). Evidence-based psychological assessment. *Journal of Personality Assessment*, *99*, 435–445. https://doi.org/10.1080/00223891.2016.1236343.

Briere, J. (2011). *Trauma Symptom Inventory–2 (TSI–2)*. Odessa, FL: Psychological Assessment Resources.

First, M. B., Williams, J. B. W., Karg, R. S., Spitzer, R. L. (2015). *Structured Clinical Interview for DSM-5 Disorders, clinician version (SCID-5-CV)*. Arlington, VA: American Psychiatric Association.

Forbey, J. D., & Lee, T. T. C. (2011). An exploration of the impact of invalid MMPI-2 protocols on collateral self-report measure scores. *Journal of Personality Assessment*, *93*, 556–565.

Groth-Marnat, G., & Horvath, L. S. (2006). The psychological report: A review of current controversies. *Journal of Clinical Psychology*, *62*, 73–81. http://doi.org/10.1002/jclp.20201

Heilbrun, K. (2001). *Principles of forensic mental health assessment*. New York: Kluwer Academic/Plenum.

Heilbrun, K., DeMatteo, D., & Marczyk, G. (2004). Pragmatic psychology, forensic mental health assessment, and the case of Thomas Johnson: Applying principles to promote quality. *Psychology, Public Policy, and Law*, *10*, 31–70. http://doi.org/10.1037/1076–8971.10.1–2.31

Heilbrun, K., Grisso, T., & Goldstein, A. M. (2009). *Foundations of forensic mental health assessment*. New York: Oxford University Press.

Kocsis, R. N. (2011). The structured interview of reported symptoms 2nd edition (SIRS-2): The new benchmark towards the assessment of malingering. *Journal of Forensic Psychology Practice*, *11*, 73–81. https://doi.org/10.1080/15228932.2011.521726.

Lezak, M. D., Howieson, D. B., Bigler, E. D., & Tranel, D. (2012). *Neuropsychological Assessment* (5th ed.). New York: Oxford University Press.

Lichtenberger, E. O., Mather, N., Kaufman, N. L., & Kaufman, A. S. (2004). *Essentials of assessment report writing*. Hoboken, NJ: John Wiley & Sons.

McCrae, R. R., Costa, P. T. T., Jr., & Martin, T. A. (2005). The NEO–PI–3: A more readable revised NEO personality inventory. *Journal of Personality Assessment*, *84*(3), 261–270. http://doi.org/10.1207/s15327752jpa8403_05

Meyer, G. J., Finn, S. E., Eyde, L. D., Kay, G. G., Moreland, K. L., Dies, R. R. et al. (2001). Psychological testing and psychological assessment. A review of evidence and issues. *American Psychologist*, *56*, 128–165. http://dx.doi.org/10.1037/0003-066X.56.2.128

Michaels, M. H. (2006). Ethical considerations in writing psychological assessment reports. *Journal of Clinical Psychology*, *62*, 47–58. http://doi.org/10.1002/jclp.20199.

Miller, H. A. (2001). *Miller-Forensic Assessment of Symptoms Test (M-FAST): Professional manual*. Odessa, FL: Psychological Assessment Resources.

Miller, P. R., Dasher, R., Collins, R., Griffiths, P., & Brown, F. (2001). Inpatient diagnostic assessments: 1. Accuracy of structured vs. unstructured interviews. *Psychiatry Research*, *105*(3), 255–264.

Morey, L. C. (1991). *Personality Assessment Inventory: Professional manual*. Odessa, FL: Psychological Assessment Resources. http://doi.org/10.1002/9781118625392.wbecp284

Narrow, W., Clarke, D., & Kuramoto, J. (2013). DSM-5 field trials in the United States and Canada, part III: Development and reliability testing of a cross-cutting symptom assessment for DSM-5. *American Journal of Psychiatry*, *170*, 71–82. http://doi.org/10.1176/appi.ajp.2012.12071000

Neukrug, S. E., & Fawcett, C. R. (2010). The assessment report process: Interviewing the client and writing the report. In E. S. Neukrug & R. C. Fawcett (Eds.), *Essentials of testing and assessment: A practical guide for counselors, social workers, and psychologists* (3rd ed., pp. 59–80). Belmont, CA: Brooks/Cole.

Novotney, A. (2010). Postgrad growth area: Assessment psychology. *American Psychological Association's gradPSYCH magazine*. www.apa.org/gradpsych/2010/03/postgrad.aspx

Novotney, A. (2017). Helping courts and juries make educated decisions. *American Psychological Association's Monitor on Psychology*, *48*(8). www.apa.org/monitor/2017/09/courts-decisions.aspx

Persons, J. B., & Tompkins, M. A. (2007). Cognitive-behavioral case formulation. In T. D. Eells (Ed.), *Handbook of psychotherapy case formulation* (pp. 290–316). New York: Guilford Press.

Resnick, P. J., & Soliman, S. (2012). Planning, writing, and editing forensic psychiatric reports. *International Journal of Law and Psychiatry*, *35*(5–6), 412–417. http://doi.org/10.1016/j.ijlp.2012.09.019

Sellbom, M., & Bagby, R. M. (2008). Response styles on multiscale inventories. In R. Rogers (Ed.), *Clinical assessment of malingering and deception* (3rd ed., pp. 182–206). New York: Guilford Press.

Sheehan, D. V., Lecrubier, Y., Sheehan, K. H., Amorim, P., Janavs, J., Weiller, E. et al. (1998). The Mini-International Neuropsychiatric Interview (MINI): the development and validation of a structured diagnostic psychiatric interview for DSM-IV and ICD-10. *Journal of Clinical Psychiatry*, *59*, 22–33.

Tallent, N. (1993). *Psychological report writing* (4th ed.). Englewood Cliffs, NJ: Prentice Hall.

Tombaugh, T. N. (1996). *Test of Memory Malingering (TOMM)*. Toronto: Multi-Health Systems.

Weathers, F. W., Blake, D. D., Schnurr, P. P., Kaloupek, D. G., Marx, B. P., & Keane, T. M. (2013). *The Clinician-Administered PTSD Scale for DSM-5 (CAPS-5)*. National Center for PTSD (Full interview). www.ptsd.va.gov/professional/assessment/adult-int/caps.asp

World Health Organization. (2018). International statistical classification of diseases and related health problems (11th revision). https://icd.who.int/browse11/l-m/en

Wright, C. V., Beattie, S. G., Galper, D. I., Church, A. S., Bufka, L. F., Brabender, V. M., & Smith, B. L. (2017). Assessment practices of professional psychologists: Results of a national survey. *Professional Psychology: Research and Practice*, *48*(2), 73–78. http://dx.doi.org/10.1037/pro0000086

Young, G. (2016). Psychiatric/psychological forensic report writing. *International Journal of Law and Psychiatry*, *49*, 214–220. http://doi.org/10.1016/j.ijlp.2016.10.008

PART II

SPECIFIC CLINICAL ASSESSMENT METHODS

10 Clinical Interviewing

JOHN SOMMERS-FLANAGAN, VERONICA I. JOHNSON, AND MAEGAN RIDES AT THE DOOR

The clinical interview is a fundamental assessment and intervention procedure that mental and behavioral health professionals learn and apply throughout their careers. Psychotherapists across all theoretical orientations, professional disciplines, and treatment settings employ different interviewing skills, including, but not limited to, nondirective listening, questioning, confrontation, interpretation, immediacy, and psychoeducation. As a process, the clinical interview functions as an assessment (e.g., neuropsychological or forensic examinations) or signals the initiation of counseling or psychotherapy. Either way, clinical interviewing involves formal or informal assessment.

Clinical interviewing is dynamic and flexible; every interview is a unique interpersonal interaction, with interviewers integrating cultural awareness, knowledge, and skills, as needed. It is difficult to imagine how clinicians could begin treatment without an initial clinical interview. In fact, clinicians who do not have competence in using clinical interviewing as a means to initiate and inform treatment would likely be considered unethical (Welfel, 2016).

Clinical interviewing has been defined as

> a complex and multidimensional interpersonal process that occurs between a professional service provider and client [or patient]. The primary goals are (1) assessment and (2) helping. To achieve these goals, individual clinicians may emphasize structured diagnostic questioning, spontaneous and collaborative talking and listening, or both. Clinicians use information obtained in an initial clinical interview to develop a [therapeutic relationship], case formulation, and treatment plan. (Sommers-Flanagan & Sommers-Flanagan, 2017, p. 6)

Given their breadth and multidisciplinary nature, clinical interviews have one or more of the following goals and objectives:

1. initiate and develop a therapeutic relationship
2. provide a role induction or orientation to therapy
3. acquire assessment and diagnostic information
4. formulate a case conceptualization and treatment plan
5. implement a psychological or educational intervention (adapted from Sommers-Flanagan, 2016).

Tackling and managing all or some of these goals and objectives during a limited time frame is no small feat, even for experienced clinicians. In cases when clinical interviewing is used solely for assessment purposes, there is still an art to balancing information gathering with efforts to develop rapport and solicit client cooperation.

In this chapter, we describe and explore clinical interviewing as foundational to mental health assessment and intervention. To start, we review the origins and development of clinical interviewing, including how interviews can vary with respect to theoretical orientation, setting, client problem, and purpose. Subsequently, we present a generic, atheoretical interviewing model, along with several variations for clinicians who are required or inspired to use the clinical interview as a specific assessment procedure. We close the chapter with a discussion of limitations, cultural issues, technological advances, and the future of clinical interviewing.

THE CLINICAL INTERVIEW: ORIGINS, DIALECTICS, AND INFLUENTIAL FORCES

In the 1920s, Swiss psychologist Jean Piaget first used the term "semi-clinical interview" to describe an assessment process (Elkind, 1964). Piaget's efforts to understand how children acquire and understand concepts related to religion and God led him to blend psychiatric interviewing with standardized mental testing questions. Piaget's approach was foundational to how contemporary mental health professionals later came to think about and practice clinical interviewing. Although the ideas and applications of clinical interviewing have moved beyond Piaget's original strategies, many of the core attitudes required to conduct successful clinical interviews remain the same (e.g., "a liking for [clients], a respect for their individuality, and patience"; Elkind, 1964, p. 41).

Piaget's purpose was primarily assessment (i.e., information gathering). More recently, postmodern theorists and psychotherapists have emphasized that initial interviews are therapeutic. Specifically, during interviews, clinicians are viewed as not just "taking [a] history" but also "making history" (Hoyt, 2000, p. 3). Hoyt's description speaks to the therapeutic component of clinical interviewing.

An Interviewing Dialectic

Clinical interviewing's flexibility includes a dialectic in purpose and process. On the one hand, many researchers view clinical interviews primarily as a means for gathering objective, quantifiable data. In contrast, practitioners value clinical interviews as a relational process that facilitates client and clinician collaboration. Despite polarization regarding the true purpose and process of clinical interviews, interviews can and should integrate *both* scientific *and* relational components (Sommers-Flanagan & Sommers-Flanagan, 2017). Overall, clinical interviewing exists within a large tent; it encompasses the richness of witnessing and empathically resonating with human experiences; it also involves collecting reliable and valid assessment data.

Factors That Influence and Drive Clinical Interviews

Clinical interviews look and feel quite different depending on many factors.

Interview setting and purpose. Interview purpose and clinical setting are intimately intertwined. For example, a clinician working at an adoption agency might interview prospective parents with the singular goal of assessing their suitability as adoptive parents. In other settings, clinicians focus on mental status examinations (MSEs), violence potential, collecting forensic assessment data, or psychotherapy preparation. Interviews conducted in private practice settings look very different from interviews in inpatient settings or those conducted in outpatient mental health agency settings. Some settings (e.g., employee assistance programs) emphasize interventions from first contact.

Client factors. Clinicians should be sensitive to unique client characteristics (Sue & Sue, 2016). Clients who present in crisis will likely benefit from brief and structured clinical interviews, whereas clients struggling with divorce might appreciate less structure and more opportunity to talk freely. Common client factors that influence clinical interviewing process and content include, but are not limited to, (1) presenting problems or goals, (2) preferences about therapy, (3) religious or spiritual identity, (4) coping style, (5) expectations, (6) culture, and (7) client resources (Norcross & Lambert, 2011). Identifying and addressing these characteristics can determine whether or not clients return to psychotherapy following an initial session (Sue & Sue, 2016).

Clinician factors. Several clinician factors drive the interview. At minimum, these include professional discipline, theoretical orientation, and clinician skills.

Clinicians from psychiatry, psychology, social work, and professional counseling use interviews for overlapping purposes. However, each discipline also has a primary emphasis. Specifically, psychiatrists and psychologists tend to use interviews for assessment, including psychiatric diagnosis, MSE, psychological or psychiatric evaluations, and treatment planning. Social workers typically focus more on psychosocial history, family history, and systemic or cultural issues. In contrast, professional counselors orient toward relationship development, collaborative engagement, and client wellness or strengths.

Clinician theoretical orientation and skills also influence how professionals conduct interviews. An Adlerian therapist is likely to conduct a family constellation interview during a first session. Family systems therapists might engage clients in a similar process but call it a genogram assessment. Clinicians with a behavioral orientation conduct in-session or in vivo functional behavioral assessments; their focus would be on defining specific problem behaviors and identifying behavioral antecedents and consequences. These theory-based interview approaches contribute to case formulation and treatment planning.

Structured, semi-structured, and unstructured interviews. Clinical interviews also vary based on time and structure. The most prescriptive clinical interview is the structured interview. Structured interviews follow a predetermined question list. Nearly all structured interviews are psychodiagnostic interviews; clinicians gather symptom-related information with diagnostic formulation or behavioral prediction as their ultimate goal. In contrast, unstructured interviews allow clients to talk freely while clinicians respond with reflections, summaries, and open questions. Semi-structured interviews, a middle ground of sorts, provide clinicians with structure and focus while retaining flexibility to explore content areas that emerge organically.

A GENERIC CLINICAL INTERVIEWING MODEL

All clinical interviews follow a common process or outline. Shea (1998) offered a generic or atheoretical model, including five stages: (1) introduction, (2) opening, (3) body, (4) closing, and (5) termination. Each stage includes specific relational and technical tasks.

Introduction

The introduction stage begins at first contact. An introduction can occur via telephone, online, or when prospective clients read information about their therapist (e.g., online descriptions, informed consents). Client expectations, role induction, first impressions, and initial rapport-building are central issues and activities.

First impressions, whether developed through informed consent paperwork or initial greetings, can exert powerful influences on interview process and clinical outcomes. Mental health professionals who engage clients in ways that are respectful and culturally sensitive are likely to facilitate trust and collaboration, consequently resulting in more reliable and valid assessment data (Ganzini et al., 2013). Technical strategies include authentic opening statements that invite collaboration. For example, the clinician might say something like, "I'm looking forward to getting to know you better" and "I hope you'll feel comfortable asking me whatever questions you like as we talk together today." Using friendliness and small talk can be especially important to connecting with diverse clients (Hays, 2016; Sue & Sue, 2016). The introduction stage also includes discussions of (1) confidentiality, (2) therapist theoretical orientation, and (3) role induction (e.g., "Today I'll be doing a diagnostic interview with you. That means I'll be asking lots of questions. My goal is to better understand what's been troubling you."). The introduction ends when clinicians shift from paperwork and small talk to a focused inquiry into the client's problems or goals.

Opening

The opening provides an initial focus. Most mental health practitioners begin clinical assessments by asking something like, "What concerns bring you to counseling today?" This question guides clients toward describing their presenting problem (i.e., psychiatrists refer to this as the "chief complaint"). Clinicians should be aware that opening with questions that are more social (e.g., "How are you today?" or "How was your week?") prompt clients in ways that can unintentionally facilitate a less focused and more rambling opening stage. Similarly, beginning with direct questioning before establishing rapport and trust can elicit defensiveness and dissembling (Shea, 1998).

Many contemporary therapists prefer opening statements or questions with positive wording. For example, rather than asking about problems, therapists might ask, "What are your goals for our meeting today?" For clients with a diverse or minority identity, cultural adaptations may be needed to increase client comfort and make certain that opening questions are culturally appropriate and relevant. When focusing on diagnostic assessment and using a structured or semi-structured interview protocol, the formal opening statement may be scripted or geared toward obtaining an overview of potential psychiatric symptoms (e.g., "Does anyone in your family have a history of mental health problems?"; Tolin et al., 2018, p. 3).

Body

The interview purpose governs what happens during the body stage. If the purpose is to collect information pertaining to psychiatric diagnosis, the body includes diagnostic-focused questions. In contrast, if the purpose is to initiate psychotherapy, the focus could quickly turn toward the history of the problem and what specific behaviors, people, and experiences (including previous therapy) clients have found more or less helpful.

When the interview purpose is assessment, the body stage focuses on information gathering. Clinicians actively question clients about distressing symptoms, including their frequency, duration, intensity, and quality. During structured interviews, specific question protocols are followed. These protocols are designed to help clinicians stay focused and systematically collect reliable and valid assessment data.

Closing

As the interview progresses, it is the clinician's responsibility to organize and close the session in ways that assure there is adequate time to accomplish the primary interview goals. Tasks and activities linked to the closing include (1) providing support and reassurance for clients, (2) returning to role induction and client expectations, (3) summarizing crucial themes and issues, (4) providing an early case formulation or mental disorder diagnosis, (5) instilling hope, and, as needed, (6) focusing on future homework, future sessions, and scheduling (Sommers-Flanagan & Sommers-Flanagan, 2017).

Termination

Termination involves ending the session and parting ways. The termination stage requires excellent time management skills; it also requires intentional sensitivity and responsiveness to how clients might react to endings in general or leaving the therapy office in particular. Dealing with termination can be challenging. Often, at the end of an initial session, clinicians will not have enough information to establish a diagnosis. When diagnostic uncertainty exists, clinicians may need to continue gathering information about client symptoms during a second or third session. Including collateral informants to triangulate diagnostic information may be useful or necessary. See Chapter 11 of this volume for more details on collateral reports.

CLINICAL INTERVIEWING AS ASSESSMENT

The clinical interview often involves more assessment and less intervention. Interviewing assessment protocols or procedures may not be limited to initial interviews; they can be woven into longer term assessment or therapy encounters. Allen Frances (2013), chair of the DSM-IV task force, recommended that clinicians "be patient," because accurate psychiatric diagnosis may take "five minutes," "five hours," "five months, or even five years" (p. 10).

Four common assessment interviewing procedures are discussed next: (1) the intake interview, (2) the psychodiagnostic interview, (4) MSEs, and (4) suicide assessment interviewing.

The Intake Interview

The intake interview is perhaps the most ubiquitous clinical interview; it may be referred to as the initial interview, the first interview, or the psychiatric interview. What follows is an atheoretical intake interview model, along with examples of how theoretical models emphasize or ignore specific interview content.

Broadly speaking, intake interviews focus on three assessment areas: (1) presenting problem, (2) psychosocial history, and (3) current situation and functioning. The manner in which clinicians pursue these goals varies greatly. Exploring the client's presenting problem could involve a structured diagnostic interview, generation and analysis of a problem list, or clients free associating to their presenting problem. Similarly, the psychosocial history can be a cursory glimpse at past relationships and medical history or a rich and extended examination of the client's childhood. Gathering information about the client's current situation and functioning can range from an informal query about the client's typical day to a formal MSE (Yalom, 2002).

Psychodiagnostic Interviewing

The psychodiagnostic interview is a variant of the intake interview. For mental health professionals who embrace the medical model, initial interviews are often diagnostic interviews. The purpose of a psychodiagnostic interview is to establish a psychiatric diagnosis. In turn, the purpose of psychiatric diagnosis is to describe the client's current condition, prognosis, and guide treatment.

Psychodiagnostic interviewing is controversial. Some clinicians view it as essential to treatment planning and positive treatment outcomes (Frances, 2013). Others view it in ways similar to Carl Rogers (1957), who famously wrote, "I am forced to the conclusion that … diagnostic knowledge is not essential to psychotherapy. It may even be … a colossal waste of time" (pp. 102–103). As with many polarized issues, it can be useful to take a moderate position, recognizing the potential benefits and liabilities of diagnostic interviewing. Benefits include standardization, a clear diagnostic focus, and identification of psychiatric conditions to facilitate clinical research and treatment (Lilienfeld, Smith, & Watts, 2013). Liabilities include extensive training required, substantial time for administration, excess structure and rigidity that restrain experienced clinicians, and questionable reliability and validity, especially in real-world clinical settings (Sommers-Flanagan & Sommers-Flanagan, 2017).

Clinicians who are pursuing diagnostic information may integrate structured or semi-structured diagnostic interviews into an intake process. The research literature is replete with structured and semi-structured diagnostic interviews. Clinicians can choose from broad and comprehensive protocols (e.g., the *Structured Clinical Interview for DSM-5 Disorders – Clinician Version*; First et al., 2016) to questionnaires focusing on a single diagnosis (e.g., *Autism Diagnostic Interview – Revised*; Zander et al., 2017). Additionally, some diagnostic interviewing protocols are designed for research purposes, while others help clinicians attain greater diagnostic reliability and validity. Later in this chapter we focus on psychodiagnostic interviewing reliability and validity.

The Mental Status Examination

The MSE is a semi-structured interview protocol. MSEs are used to organize, assess, and communicate information about clients' current mental state (Sommers-Flanagan, 2016; Strub & Black, 1977). To achieve this goal, some clinicians administer a highly structured Mini-Mental State Evaluation (MMSE; Folstein, Folstein, & McHugh, 1975), while others conduct a relatively unstructured assessment interview but then organize their observations into a short mental status report. There are also clinicians who, perhaps in the spirit of Piaget's semi-clinical interviews, combine the best of both worlds by integrating a few structured MSE questions into a less structured interview process (Sommers-Flanagan & Sommers-Flanagan, 2017).

Although the MSE involves collecting data on diagnostic symptoms, it is not a psychodiagnostic interview. Instead, clinicians collect symptom-related data to communicate information to colleagues about client mental status. Sometimes MSEs are conducted daily or hourly. MSEs are commonly used within medical settings. Knowledge of diagnostic terminology and symptoms is a prerequisite to conducting and reporting on mental status.

Introducing the MSE. When administering an MSE, an explanation or role induction is needed. A clinician might state, "In a few minutes, I'll start a more formal method of getting … to know you. This process involves me asking you a variety of interesting questions so that I can understand a little more about how your brain works" (Sommers-Flanagan & Sommers-Flanagan, 2017, pp. 580–581).

Common MSE domains. Depending on setting and clinician factors, the MSE may focus on neurological responses or psychiatric symptoms. Nine common domains included in a psychiatric-symptom oriented MSE are

1. Appearance
2. Behavior/psychomotor activity
3. Attitude toward examiner (interviewer)
4. Affect and mood
5. Speech and thought
6. Perceptual disturbances
7. Orientation and consciousness
8. Memory and intelligence
9. Reliability, judgment, and insight.

Given that all assessment processes include error and bias, mental status examiners should base their reports on direct observations and minimize interpretive statements. Special care to cross-check conclusive statements is necessary, especially when writing about clients who are members of traditionally oppressed minority groups (Sommers-Flanagan & Sommers-Flanagan, 2017). Additionally, using multiple assessment data sources (aka triangulation; see "Using multiple (collateral) data sources") is essential in situations where patients may have memory problems (e.g., confabulation) or be motivated to over- or underreport symptoms (Suhr, 2015).

MSE reports. MSE reports are typically limited to one paragraph or one page. The content of an MSE report focuses specifically on the previously listed nine domains. Each domain is addressed directly with at least one statement.

Suicide Assessment Interviewing

The clinical interview is the gold standard for suicide assessment and intervention (Sommers-Flanagan, 2018). This statement is true, despite the fact that suicide assessment interviewing is not a particularly reliable or valid method for predicting death by suicide (Large & Ryan, 2014). The problem is that, although standardized written assessments exist, they are not a stand-alone means for predicting or intervening with clients who present with suicide ideation. In every case, when clients endorse suicide ideation on a standardized questionnaire or scale, a clinical interview follow-up is essential. Although other assessment approaches exist, they are only supplementary to the clinical interview. Key principles for conducting suicide assessment interviews are summarized below.

Contemporary suicide assessment principles. Historically, suicide assessment interviewing involved a mental health professional conducting a systematic suicide risk assessment. Over the past two decades, this process has changed considerably. Now, rather than taking an authoritative stance, mental health professionals seek to establish an empathic and collaborative relationship with clients who are suicidal (Jobes, 2016). Also, rather than assuming that suicide ideation indicates psychopathology or suicide risk, clinicians frame suicide ideation as a communication of client distress. Finally, instead of focusing on risk factors and suicide prediction, mental health professionals gather information pertaining to eight superordinate suicide dimensions or drivers and then work with suicidal clients to address these dimensions through a collaborative and therapeutic safety planning process (Jobes, 2016). The eight superordinate suicide dimensions include:

- *Unbearable emotional or psychological distress*: Unbearable distress can involve one or many trauma, loss, or emotionally disturbing experiences.
- *Problem-solving impairments*: Suicide theory and empirical evidence both point to ways in which depressive states can reduce client problem-solving abilities.
- *Interpersonal disconnection, isolation, or feelings of being a social burden*: Joiner (2005) has posited that thwarted belongingness and perceiving oneself as a burden contributes to suicidal conditions.
- *Arousal or agitation*: Many different physiological states can increase arousal/agitation and push clients toward using suicide as a solution to their unbearable distress.
- *Hopelessness*: Hopelessness is a cognitive variable linked to suicide risk. It can also contribute to problem-solving impairments.
- *Suicide intent and plan*: Although suicide ideation is a poor predictor of suicide, when ideation is accompanied by an active suicide plan and suicide intent, the potential of death by suicide is magnified.
- *Desensitization to physical pain and thoughts of death*: Fear of death and aversion to physical pain are natural suicide deterrents; when clients lose their fear of death or become desensitized to pain, suicide behaviors can increase.
- *Access to firearms*: Availability of a lethal means, in general, and access to firearms, in particular, substantially increase suicide risk.

(For additional information on suicide assessment interviewing and the eight suicide dimensions, see Sommers-Flanagan, 2018; and Chapter 23 in this volume.)

LIMITATIONS, CULTURAL ISSUES, AND INNOVATIONS

Although clinical interviews are a flexible assessment and therapy tool, they also have limitations. These limitations vary depending on the particular approach being implemented.

Diagnostic Reliability and Validity

The publication of the third edition of the *Diagnostic and Statistical Manual of Mental Disorders* (DSM-III; American Psychiatric Association, 1980) was greeted with high praise from the psychiatric-medical community. Previous versions of the DSM adhered to a psychoanalytic model and had vague symptom criteria sets. Advocates for psychiatric diagnosis emphasized that DSM-III's improved specificity and atheoretical model approach had solved previous problems with diagnostic reliability. Later, with the publication of the DSM-III-R (American Psychiatric Association, 1994), structured diagnostic interviewing protocols like the *Structured Clinical Interview for DSM-III-R* (then the SCID-III-R, now the SCID-5; First et al., 2016) were praised as greatly improving clinician inter-rater reliability. Currently, most diagnostic interview protocols or schedules are based on diagnostic criteria from the DSM-5 (American Psychiatric Association, 2013).

Despite apparent improvements, inter-rater reliability for specific diagnostic conditions remains questionable (Lobbestael, Leurgans, & Arntz, 2011; Salamon et al., 2018). In 1997, Kutchins and Kirk wrote, "Twenty years after the reliability problem became the central scientific focus of DSM, there is still not a single major study showing that DSM (any version) is routinely used with high reliability by regular mental health clinicians ... The DSM revolution in reliability has been a revolution in rhetoric, not in reality" (Kutchins & Kirk, 1997, p. 53).

Over the past twenty years, researchers and reviewers have described structured diagnostic interviews as demonstrating "adequate" or "moderate" or "excellent" inter-rater reliability (Lilienfeld et al., 2013; Lobbestael et al., 2011; Tolin et al., 2018). Although these claims provide surface support for diagnostic reliability, a deeper examination raises questions and doubts. Specifically, studies focusing on inter-rater reliability utilize highly trained diagnostic raters. These raters are not clinicians in everyday practice; consequently, results based on their inter-rater reliability are unlikely to generalize to real-world clinical practice. Additionally, the language used to describe and label the acceptability of kappa coefficients (a reliability measure) is derived from DSM field trial recommendations. For example, following the DSM-5 field trial recommendations, one study described the kappa coefficient for an attention-deficit/hyperactivity disorder (ADHD) diagnosis as "very good." The label *very good* was used despite researchers reporting a confidence interval for the ADHD-related kappa reliability index as in the range "0.33–0.87" (Tolin et al., 2018). In this case, using the DSM convention for labeling kappa coefficients made a coefficient with an R^2 (coefficient of determination) ranging as low as $R^2 = 0.10$ sound "very good" (which is clearly misleading). Further, even highly trained diagnostic interviewers have only modest agreement regarding specific diagnoses; they perform more acceptably when using the simple categorical criterion of determining the presence or absence of a mental disorder (Widiger & Edmundson, 2011).

Beyond reliability issues, many practicing clinicians avoid using structured diagnostic interviews because they take too much time and are not helpful for establishing therapy relationships. Nevertheless (and this makes both sides of the argument more complex), if the purpose of a clinical interview is psychiatric diagnosis, using a structured diagnostic interviewing protocol based on the DSM system has significant scientific support, especially if clinicians are trained to use these protocols. In fact, diagnostic reliabilities for major mental disorders (e.g., depression, anxiety) typically have alpha or kappa coefficients similar to what physicians obtain when diagnosing medical disorders (Lilienfeld et al., 2013).

Diagnostic validity is a more difficult issue. There are no genetic markers or gold standard for determining whether a specific diagnosis is true or valid. To support diagnostic validity, researchers often rely on longitudinal studies focusing on predictive validity. Unfortunately, results from diagnostic predictive validity studies tend to be mixed (Edens et al., 2015).

Noncredible or Invalid Client (Self-) Report

Diagnostic clinical interviews rely on clients disclosing truthful or accurate information via self-report. Unfortunately, client self-report is notoriously suspect (Rogers, 2008; Sommers-Flanagan & Sommers-Flanagan, 1998; Suhr, 2015). It is not unusual for clients to over- or underreport their symptoms, particularly in some contexts where individuals have a substantial incentive (e.g., a forensic assessment).

Contemporary researchers and practitioners refer to inaccurate client responses as noncredible responding (Suhr & Berry, 2017). As Suhr (2015) summarized, noncredible responding is a substantial problem for clinical interviewers; under certain circumstances, "the base rate for noncredible responding in individuals reporting psychological, physical, and/or cognitive symptoms and concerns is higher than the base rate of most actual disorders!" (p. 61).

Overreporting symptoms. Clients who exaggerate symptoms to obtain external gain are often referred to as malingering or feigning (Green & Rosenfeld, 2011; Rogers, 2008). Several assessment tools have been designed to detect malingering. An interview-based example is the *Structured Interview of Reported Symptoms-2* (SIRS-2; Rogers, Sewell, & Gillard, 2010). The SIRS-2 includes 172 interview items (with thirty-two items repeated to evaluate for consistency) and takes one to two hours to administer. The original SIRS was often regarded as the gold standard for measuring malingering. However, more recently, researchers have critiqued the SIRS as being susceptible to misclassifying patients as feigning (Green & Rosenfeld, 2011) and the SIRS-2 has been questioned as possibly having less sensitivity and utility than the original SIRS (Green, Rosenfeld, & Belfi, 2013).

Underreporting symptoms. Research on symptom underreporting is generally within the substance use arena (Bahorik et al., 2014; Hormes, Gerhardstein, & Griffin, 2012). To avoid being viewed as ill, clients with addiction problems are inclined to underestimate or deny substance use. Underreporting is also common in settings where full symptom disclosure could have significant negative consequences or in situations where having mental disorder symptoms are in violation of social norms (e.g., athletic or military settings; Kroshus et al., 2015; Vannoy et al., 2017).

There are no published interview protocols designed to identify underreporting. Often, clinicians feel an urge to confront clients who appear to be minimizing their problems. Alternatives to using confrontation are integrated into the next section.

Strategies for Addressing Noncredible Responding in a Clinical Interview

Clinical interviewing strategies for dealing with noncredible client responses include (1) developing clinician awareness, (2) managing countertransference, (3) using specific questioning or interpersonal strategies, and (4) using additional or supplementary data sources.

Clinician awareness. Clinician awareness of the potential for noncredible responding is the foundation for dealing with this common client response style. Specifically, clinicians should be aware that, due to motivational, contextual, and other factors, clients may systematically overreport, underreport, or misreport their presenting symptoms, personal history, social-cultural-sexual orientation, and/or current functioning (i.e., impairment). As Suhr (2015) wrote, "It might help for the assessor to remember that inaccuracy of self-report is normal and often adaptive behavior, even outside of the clinical context" (p. 100).

To avoid decision-making biases, it is recommended that clinicians adopt a "scientific mindedness" frame during assessment interviews (S. Sue, 1998). Scientific mindedness was originally described as a means to help clinicians avoid making premature cultural assumptions. However, adopting a mentality of intentionally forming and testing hypotheses about the accuracy of client self-reports can also help mitigate clinician bias (Shea, 1998).

Managing countertransference. Clinicians can have countertransference reactions to clients before, during, or after clients engage in noncredible responding. Countertransference reactions may, in turn, adversely affect rapport and relationship development. When this happens, clinicians may prompt clients to provide noncredible responses. For example, countertransference or lack of skills might lead clinicians to stray from an accepting stance and ask a question that includes a judgmental tone: "You aren't using substances to help you sleep are you?" This sort of question can easily stimulate a noncredible, underreporting response of denial, "No. I wouldn't do that."

Several strategies can be used to manage countertransference. Most commonly, personal therapy or additional skills-based training is helpful. For example, motivational interviewing was designed, in part, to help clinicians move away from judgmental-confrontational approaches with substance-using clients. The central philosophy of motivational interviewing is person-centered, with a strong emphasis on the "profound acceptance of what the client brings" (Miller & Rollnick, 2013, p. 16). If countertransference reactions occur, rather than engaging in confrontation, clinical interviewers can refocus on adopting an attitude of profound acceptance. Otherwise, relational ruptures and under- or overreporting of symptoms may occur (Sommers-Flanagan & Sommers-Flanagan, 2017).

Using specific questioning or interpersonal strategies. Specific clinical skills or strategies can be used to address underreporting. These skills and strategies include (1) modeling openness, (2) using normalizing statements, and (3) phrasing questions to make it easier for clients to disclose symptoms.

Clinicians who begin sessions with an open and transparent informed consent process and role induction may be able to mitigate underreporting. Transparency can also include statements that invite collaboration. Examples include "I'd like to be helpful, but you know yourself best, and so I'll need to rely on what you tell me" and "Please ask me any questions at any time and I'll do my best to answer them."

Normalizing statements are recommended for interviewing potentially suicidal clients. Specifically, it can be useful to precede direct questions about suicide ideation with a statement like, "It's not unusual for people who are feeling stressed to have thoughts of suicide." Similar normalizing statements can be used with other symptoms (e.g., "Lots of college students have difficulty sleeping, I wonder if that's the case for you?").

When interviewing clients with high potential for substance use, Shea (1998) recommended using a questioning strategy called gentle assumption. To use gentle assumption, interviewers presume that specific embarrassing or illegal behaviors are a regular occurrence in the client's life. For example, instead of asking, "Do you drink alcohol?," an interviewer might ask, "When was your most recent drink?"

Using multiple (collateral) data sources. Stand-alone clinical interviews are especially vulnerable to over- or underreporting of symptoms. This is particularly true when situational factors offer external rewards and/or the avoidance of negative consequences for symptom exaggeration or minimizing. For example, personal injury cases, learning disability or ADHD evaluations, athletic or military settings, and assessments conducted for forensic purposes can motivate clients to present as having more or fewer symptoms (Sellbom & Hopwood, 2016; Suhr, Cook, & Morgan, 2017; Sullivan, May, & Galbally, 2007; Vannoy et al., 2017).

Collateral information is data or information obtained via a third party. For example, when conducting child assessments, clinicians commonly conduct collateral interviews with, or gather information via questionnaire from, parents or teachers. Collateral interviews can provide illuminating alternative perspectives. Unfortunately, parents, teachers, and other collateral informants also may have motivational and memory issues that cause them to provide inaccurate information. Finding significant discrepancies between parents, teachers, and child reports is a common occurrence (see Chapter 11 in this volume; Sommers-Flanagan & Sommers-Flanagan, 2017).

Medical, educational, and psychological/psychiatric records constitute additional sources of collateral assessment information. Unfortunately, clients' previous records also are not free from bias or inaccuracy. Consequently, although gathering collateral information is recommended for clinicians who are using a clinical interview for assessment purposes, collateral information is also susceptible to error. In the end, the best approach typically involves gathering information from at least three sources and then triangulating data in an effort to present a reasonably accurate assessment report (see Chapter 11, this volume).

Cultural Considerations: Cultural Validity and Cultural Humility

Cultural validity refers to how well assessment procedures address and are sensitive to client-specific cultural perspectives (Basterra, Trumbull, & Solano-Flores, 2011). Client cultural perspectives can include, but are not limited to, "the sets of values, beliefs, experiences, communication patterns, teaching and learning styles, and epistemologies inherent in the [clients'] cultural backgrounds, and the socioeconomic conditions prevailing in their cultural groups" (Solano-Flores & Nelson-Barber, 2001, p. 55). If cultural validity is not considered, conclusions may be inaccurate and cause client harm.

Clinicians are encouraged to make cultural adaptations to address cultural validity. These adaptations may involve administering assessments in the client's native language, consulting with cultural experts, and using multidimensional assessment models (Hays, 2016). Using cultural validity checks and balances is especially important when implementing diagnostic assessment and mental status protocols (Sommers-Flanagan & Sommers-Flanagan, 2017).

Cultural humility is also linked to successful clinical interviewing. Clinicians who demonstrate cultural humility go beyond the core multicultural competencies of clinician self-awareness, culture-specific knowledge, and culturally specific skills. Culturally humble clinicians are defined as (1) other-oriented, (2) seeing clients as experts of their cultural experience, and (3) approaching relationships from a position of respect and curiosity (Hook et al., 2013). Clients' perceptions of their clinician's cultural humility are associated with the development of a working alliance and positive therapy outcomes.

Cultural humility applies to all clinician–client relationships. Clinical interviews inherently place clinicians in an expert position and can leave clients feeling leery of clinician judgments. To collect valid and reliable information, clinicians must create environments where clients feel welcomed, accepted, and valued no matter what information is shared. Adopting a culturally humble stance can help clinicians communicate respect to clients.

Information gathered in the clinical interview can drive psychotherapy and should therefore be gathered in a collaborative and culturally sensitive manner. The tricky business of clinical interviewing is to integrate relevant questions with the core conditions of congruence, unconditional positive regard, and empathic understanding (Rogers, 1957; Suhr, 2015). These core conditions, particularly empathic understanding, transcend theory, setting, and client presenting problems.

Technological Advances in Psychotherapy and Clinical Interviewing

Clinical interviewing procedures shift and change with time. Clinical interviewing has flexed and changed in the past; it will continue to flex along with various new social and cultural dynamics, including the rise of technology in the delivery of mental health services.

Technological advancements have affected mental and behavioral health assessment and treatment in many ways. Some mental health professionals believe that technology can improve their ability to acquire information, support treatment plans, and track client outcomes. Others believe technology detracts from therapeutic relationship development. Controversies around technology have been incorporated into professional ethical guidelines; clinicians should consult their respective ethical codes when using technology (e.g., American Counseling Association, 2014; APA, 2010).

Computer-based assessments sometimes outperform clinician-based assessments (Richman et al., 1999). This is particularly true when clients are expected to reveal sensitive personal information (e.g., sexual behavior, suicide ideation). Regardless of computer-based assessment efficiency, therapeutic follow-up requires face-to-face or virtual human contact. Integrating technology for data gathering and note-taking appears to have no adverse effects on assessment process or the development of therapeutic relationships (Wiarda et al., 2014).

Online assessment and psychotherapy is growing as a method of mental health service delivery. Proponents include research scientists and medical practitioners who deliver services from a distance, as well as entrepreneurial independent practitioners seeking to expand their practice domain. Technological methods for delivering assessment and therapy services include (1) text-only synchronous or asynchronous communication, (2) voice-only synchronous or asynchronous communication, and (3) video-link synchronous communication. Overall, researchers have reported that telephonic and online assessments are equal to face-to-face assessment interviewing (Sommers-Flanagan & Sommers-Flanagan, 2017). Similarly, non–face-to-face therapy outcomes are similar to face-to-face outcomes, at least for clients who choose non–face-to-face therapeutic modalities (Hanley & Reynolds, 2009).

FUTURE DEVELOPMENTS

The clinical interview is a time-honored and flexible procedure that encompasses mental health assessment and intervention. Given its traditional status and flexibility of application, it is doubtful that the future of clinical interviewing process or content will drastically change. However, for the past several decades, clinical and psychodiagnostic interviewing has consistently, albeit slowly, evolved and expanded its reach. Specifically, practitioners who adhere to postmodern psychotherapy models have used language to transform the form and function of traditional clinical interviews. These transformations can be captured, in part, with the relabeling of the initial clinical interview as an initial therapeutic conversation. Additionally, but in the opposite direction, substantial time and energy has been devoted to structuring clinical interviews as a diagnostic procedure; this has involved operationalizing and standardizing clinical interviewing data collection and interpretation, as well as research focusing on methods for discerning when clients are over-reporting, underreporting, and/or providing inaccurate assessment information. Finally, clinical interviews have simultaneously evolved in a third direction – toward greater cultural sensitivity, relevance, and validity. No doubt, these past developments will continue forward but the course and trajectory of clinical interviewing appears predictable: learning and applying clinical interviews for assessment and treatment purposes will remain central to the role and function of all mental health professionals.

REFERENCES

American Counseling Association. (2014). *The American Counseling Association code of ethics*. Alexandria, VA: Author.

American Psychiatric Association. (1980). *Diagnostic and statistical manual of mental disorders* (3rd ed.). Washington, DC: Author.

American Psychiatric Association. (1994). *Diagnostic and statistical manual of mental disorders* (3rd ed., rev.). Washington, DC: Author.

American Psychiatric Association. (2013). *Diagnostic and statistical manual of mental disorders* (5th ed.). Washington, DC: Author.

APA (American Psychological Association). (2010). *Ethical principles for psychologists and code of conduct*. Washington, DC: Author.

Bahorik, A. L., Newhill, C. E., Queen, C. C., & Eack, S. M. (2014). Under-reporting of drug use among individuals with schizophrenia: Prevalence and predictors. *Psychological Medicine, 44* (1), 61–69.

Basterra, M. D., Trumbull, E., & Solano-Flores, G. (2011). *Cultural validity in assessment: Addressing linguistic and cultural diversity*. New York: Routledge.

Edens, J. F., Kelley, S. E., Lilienfeld, S. O., Skeem, J. L., & Douglas, K. S. (2015). DSM-5 antisocial personality disorder: Predictive validity in a prison sample. *Law and Human Behavior, 39*(2), 123–129.

Elkind, D. (1964). Piaget's semi-clinical interview and the study of spontaneous religion. *Journal for the Scientific Study of Religion, 4*, 40–47.

First, M. B., Williams, J. B. W., Karg, R. S., & Spitzer, R. L. (2016). *Structured Clinical Interview for DSM-5 Disorders, clinician version (SCID-5-CV)*. Arlington, VA: American Psychiatric Association.

Folstein, M. F., Folstein, S. E., & McHugh, P. R. (1975). Mini-mental state: A practical method for grading the cognitive state of patients for the clinician. *Journal of Psychiatric Research, 12* (3), 189–198.

Frances, A. (2013). *Essentials of psychiatric diagnosis: Responding to the challenge of DSM-5* (rev ed.). New York: Guilford Press.

Ganzini, L., Denneson, L. M., Press, N., Bair, M. J., Helmer, D. A., Poat, J., & Dobscha, S. K. (2013). Trust is the basis for effective suicide risk screening and assessment in veterans. *Journal of General Internal Medicine, 28*(9), 1215–1221.

Green, D., & Rosenfeld, B. (2011). Evaluating the gold standard: A review and meta-analysis of the structured interview of reported symptoms. *Psychological Assessment, 23*(1), 95–107.

Green, D., Rosenfeld, B., & Belfi, B. (2013). New and improved? A comparison of the original and revised versions of the structured interview of reported symptoms. *Assessment, 20*(2), 210–218.

Hanley, T., & Reynolds, D. J. (2009). Counselling psychology and the internet: A review of the quantitative research into online outcomes and alliances within text-based therapy. *Counselling Psychology Review, 24*(2), 4–13.

Hays, P. A. (2016). *Addressing cultural complexities in practice: Assessment, diagnosis, and therapy* (3rd ed.). Washington, DC: American Psychological Association.

Hook, J. N., Davis, D. E., Owen, J., Worthington, E. L., & Utsey, S. O. (2013). Cultural humility: Measuring openness to culturally diverse clients. *Journal of Counseling Psychology, 60*(3), 353–366.

Hormes, J. M., Gerhardstein, K. R., & Griffin, P. T. (2012). Under-reporting of alcohol and substance use versus other psychiatric symptoms in individuals living with HIV. *AIDS Care, 24*(4), 420–423.

Hoyt, M. F. (2000). *Some stories are better than others: Doing what works in brief therapy and managed care*. Philadelphia: Brunner/Mazel.

Jobes, D. A. (2016). *Managing suicidal risk: A collaborative approach* (2nd ed.). New York: Guilford Press.

Joiner, T. (2005). *Why people die by suicide*. Cambridge, MA: Harvard University Press.

Kroshus, E., Kubzansky, L. D., Goldman, R. E., & Austin, S. B. (2015). Norms, athletic identity, and concussion symptom under-reporting among male collegiate ice hockey players: A prospective cohort study. *Annals of Behavioral Medicine, 49*(1), 95–103.

Kutchins, H., & Kirk, S. A. (1997). *Making us crazy*. New York: Free Press.

Large, M. M., & Ryan, C. J. (2014). Suicide risk categorisation of psychiatric inpatients: What it might mean and why it is of no use. *Australasian Psychiatry, 22*(4), 390–392.

Lilienfeld, S. O., Smith, S. F., & Watts, A. L. (2013). Issues in diagnosis: Conceptual issues and controversies. In W. E. Craighead & D. J. Miklowitz (Eds.), *Psychopathology: History, diagnosis, and empirical foundations* (2nd ed., pp. 1–35). Hoboken, NJ: Wiley.

Lobbestael, J., Leurgans, M., & Arntz, A. (2011). Inter-rater reliability of the structured clinical interview for DSM-IV axis I disorders (SCID I) and axis II disorders (SCID II). *Clinical Psychology and Psychotherapy, 18*(1), 75–79.

Miller, W. R., & Rollnick, S. (2013). *Motivational interviewing: Preparing people for change* (3rd ed.). New York: Guilford Press.

Norcross, J. C., & Lambert, M. J. (2011). Psychotherapy relationships that work II. *Psychotherapy: Theory, Research, and Practice, 48*, 4–8.

Richman, W. L., Weisband, S., Kiesler, S., & Drasgow, F. (1999). A meta-analytic study of social desirability distortion in computer-administered questionnaires, traditional questionnaires, and interviews. *Journal of Applied Psychology, 84*(5), 754–775.

Rogers, C. R. (1957). The necessary and sufficient conditions of therapeutic personality change. *Journal of Consulting Psychology, 21*, 95–103.

Rogers, R. (2008). *Clinical assessment of malingering and deception* (3rd ed.). New York: Guilford Press.

Rogers, R., Sewell, K. W., & Gillard, N. D. (2010). *SIRS-2: Structured Interview of Reported Symptoms: Professional manual*. Odessa, FL: Psychological Assessment Resources.

Salamon, S., Santelmann, H., Franklin, J., & Baethge, C. (2018). Test-retest reliability of the diagnosis of schizoaffective disorder in childhood and adolescence: A systematic review and meta-analysis. *Journal of Affective Disorders*, *230*, 28–33.

Sellbom, M., & Hopwood, C. J. (2016). Evidence-based assessment in the 21st century: Comments on the special series papers. *Clinical Psychology: Science and Practice*, *23*(4), 403–409.

Shea, S. C. (1998). *Psychiatric interviewing: The art of understanding* (2nd ed.). Philadelphia: Saunders.

Solano-Flores, G., & Nelson-Barber, S. (2001). On the cultural validity of science assessments. *Journal of Research in Science Teaching*, *38*, 553–573. https://doi.org/10.1002/tea.1018

Sommers-Flanagan, J. (2016). Clinical interview. In J. C. Norcross, G. R. VandenBos, & D. K. Freedheim (Eds.), *APA handbook of clinical psychology* (pp. 3–16). Washington, DC: American Psychological Association.

Sommers-Flanagan, J. (2018). Conversations about suicide: Strategies for detecting and assessing suicide risk. *Journal of Health Service Psychology*, *44*, 33–45.

Sommers-Flanagan, J., & Sommers-Flanagan, R. (1998). Assessment and diagnosis of conduct disorder. *Journal of Counseling and Development*, *76*, 189–197.

Sommers-Flanagan, J., & Sommers-Flanagan, R. (2017). *Clinical interviewing* (6th ed.). Hoboken, NJ: Wiley.

Strub, R. L., & Black, F. W. (1977). *The mental status exam in neurology*. Philadelphia: Davis.

Sue, D. W., & Sue, D. (2016). *Counseling the culturally diverse* (7th ed.). Hoboken, NJ: Wiley.

Sue, S. (1998). In search of cultural competence in psychotherapy and counseling. *American Psychologist*, *53*(4), 440–448.

Suhr, J. A. (2015). *Psychological assessment: A problem-solving approach*. New York: Guilford Press.

Suhr, J. A., & Berry, D. T. R. (2017). The importance of assessing for validity of symptom report and performance in attention deficit/hyperactivity disorder (ADHD): Introduction to the special section on noncredible presentation in ADHD. *Psychological Assessment*, *29*(12), 1427–1428.

Suhr, J. A., Cook, C., & Morgan, B. (2017). Assessing functional impairment in ADHD: Concerns for validity of self-report. *Psychological Injury and Law*, *10*(2), 151–160.

Sullivan, B. K., May, K., & Galbally, L. (2007). Symptom exaggeration by college adults in attention-deficit hyperactivity disorder and learning disorder assessments. *Applied Neuropsychology*, *14* (3), 189–207.

Tolin, D. F., Gilli Tolin, D. F., Gilliam, C., Wootton, B. M., Bowe, W., Bragdon, L. B. et al. (2018). Psychometric properties of a structured diagnostic interview for DSM-5 anxiety, mood, and obsessive-compulsive and related disorders. *Assessment*, *25* (1), 3–13.

Vannoy, S. D., Andrews, B. K., Atkins, D. C., Dondanville, K. A., Young-McCaughan, S., & Peterson, A. L. (2017). Under reporting of suicide ideation in US Army population screening: An ongoing challenge. *Suicide and Life-Threatening Behavior*, *47* (6), 723–728.

Welfel, E. R. (2016). *Ethics in counseling and psychotherapy: Standards, research, and emerging issues* (6th ed.). Boston: Cengage.

Wiarda, N. R., McMinn, M. R., Peterson, M. A., & Gregor, J. A. (2014). Use of technology for note taking and therapeutic alliance. *Psychotherapy*, *51*(3), 443–446.

Widiger, T. A., & Edmundson, M. (2011). Diagnoses, dimensions, and DSM-5. In D. H. Barlow (Ed.), *The Oxford handbook of clinical psychology* (pp. 254–278). New York: Oxford University Press.

Yalom, I. D. (2002). *The gift of therapy*. New York: HarperCollins.

Zander, E., Willfors, C., Berggren, S., Coco, C., Holm, A., Jifält, I. et al. (2017). The interrater reliability of the autism diagnostic interview-revised (ADI-R) in clinical settings. *Psychopathology*, *50*(3), 219–227.

11 Multi-Informant Assessment of Psychopathology from Preschool through Old Age

THOMAS M. ACHENBACH, MASHA Y. IVANOVA, AND LESLIE A. RESCORLA

This chapter addresses use of mental health assessment data from various informants, including the people who are assessed. The methods for obtaining and using data from different informants vary with the developmental levels of the people assessed, the kinds of problems that are assessed, the relevant informants, the purposes of assessment, and statistical considerations. We first review findings from research on levels of agreement between informants. We then present findings on the predictive power of data from various sources. Thereafter, we present practical tools for obtaining, comparing, and using data from multiple informants.

In mental health services for children (we use "children" to include adolescents), parents are usually the help-seekers as well as the key sources of assessment data, although referrals may be prompted by school personnel, health care providers, or social service agencies. In services for adults, the people who seek help from providers are usually the main sources of assessment data regarding the problems for which help is sought. For older adults, referrals are often instigated by health care providers or family members who also contribute assessment data.

CORRELATIONS BETWEEN RATINGS BY DIFFERENT INFORMANTS

Providers who work with children have long recognized the need to obtain assessment data from informants other than the children for whom help is sought. Providers of child services customarily ask parents about the problems for which help is sought. When problems involve school, providers may request information from teachers, as well. Providers may then consider information from parents and teachers when they form clinical judgments on the basis of their own interactions with the child in the clinical setting.

To evaluate levels of agreement between different informants regarding children's problems, meta-analyses have been performed on published correlations between ratings of children's problems by mothers, fathers, teachers, clinicians, observers, and children themselves (Achenbach, McConaughy, & Howell, 1987). The ratings were obtained with various assessment instruments, including interviews, rating forms, and questionnaires. Between informants who played similar roles with respect to the children and who saw the children in similar contexts (pairs of parents, teachers, clinicians, or observers), the mean cross-informant Pearson correlation (r) was 0.60. Between informants who played different roles and saw the children in different contexts (e.g., parents vs. teachers; teachers vs. clinicians), the mean r was 0.28. Between adult informants' ratings versus children's self-ratings, the mean r was 0.22.

Since the meta-analyses were published in 1987, the modest levels of cross-informant agreement regarding child psychopathology have received a great deal of attention, with the 1987 meta-analyses being cited in some 6,000 publications (Google Scholar, January 31, 2019). Subsequent meta-analyses have supported the 1987 meta-analytic findings (e.g., De Los Reyes et al., 2015), which are among "the most robust findings in clinical child research" (De Los Reyes & Kazdin, 2005, p. 483).

Mental health providers obtain assessment data from multiple informants far less often for adult clients than for child clients. Accordingly, far less attention has been paid to cross-informant agreement for adult psychopathology than for child psychopathology. However, meta-analyses of correlations between self-ratings and informant-ratings on parallel instruments for assessing adult psychopathology have yielded a mean cross-informant $r = 0.43$ for internalizing problems (anxiety, depression, social withdrawal, somatic complaints without apparent medical cause) and $r = 0.44$ for externalizing problems (aggressive and rule-breaking behaviors) (Achenbach et al., 2005). (Findings for internalizing and externalizing problems have been reported in >75,000 publications; Achenbach et al., 2016.) When self- and informant-ratings of adult psychopathology were obtained on nonparallel instruments, the mean cross-informant r across all kinds of problems was only 0.30.

In addition to the modest meta-analytic correlations between self- and informant-ratings for adult psychopathology, Meyer and colleagues (2001) found a mean kappa coefficient of only 0.12 between psychiatric diagnoses based on interviews with adult clients versus diagnoses based on data from informants. Meyer and colleagues concluded that, "after correcting for agreements due to chance, about 70 percent of the interview-based diagnoses were in error" when compared with diagnoses derived from multimethod evaluations (p. 151).

The abundant evidence for differences between self-reports and reports by various informants makes it clear that no one source of data is apt to provide a comprehensive picture of a person's functioning.

Multicultural Cross-Informant Correlations for Child Psychopathology

Much of the research and theory regarding psychopathology has originated in a few rather similar societies. (We use "societies" to include countries, plus geopolitically demarcated populations that are not countries, such as Hong Kong and Puerto Rico.) To test the generalizability of assessment procedures and of findings, it is essential to extend research beyond those few societies. To test the multicultural generalizability of cross-informant correlations, Rescorla and colleagues (2012, 2013, 2014) analyzed cross-informant correlations between parent and teacher ratings and between parent and self-ratings for population samples of children in dozens of societies from around the world. In the participating societies, indigenous researchers asked parents to complete the Child Behavior Checklist for Ages 6–18 (CBCL/6–18), asked teachers to complete the Teacher's Report Form (TRF), and asked eleven-to-eighteen-year-olds to complete the Youth Self-Report (YSR) in a language appropriate for the informants. Each form can be completed on paper or online in about fifteen to twenty minutes. For respondents who may be unable to complete forms independently, interviewers with no specialized training can read the items aloud and enter the responses.

On each form, informants rate more than 100 items that describe a broad spectrum of problems, such as *Acts too young for age*; *Can't concentrate*; *Can't get mind off certain thoughts*; *Cruelty, bullying, or meanness to others*; *Fears going to school*; *Gets in many fights*; and *Unhappy, sad, or depressed* (Achenbach & Rescorla, 2001). The items are worded appropriately for each type of informant (parent, teacher, self). Some items do not have counterparts on all three forms (e.g., *Nightmares* is on the CBCL/6–18 and YSR but not on the TRF). Each item is rated on a Likert scale as *0 = not true*, *1 = somewhat or sometimes true*, or *2 = very true or often true*. The items are scored on eight factor-analytically derived syndromes, plus six DSM-oriented scales comprising items corresponding to diagnostic categories of the American Psychiatric Association's (2013) *Diagnostic and Statistical Manual* (DSM). The items are also scored on broad-spectrum Internalizing, Externalizing, and Total Problems scales.

Rescorla and colleagues (2014) computed correlations between corresponding scales scored from parent and teacher ratings of problem items that had counterparts on the CBCL/6–18 and TRF. Averaged across problem scales scored from CBCL/6–18 and TRF forms completed for 27,962 children in twenty-one societies, the mean *r* was 0.26, which approximates the mean *r* of 0.27 found between parent and teacher ratings in the Achenbach and colleagues (1987) meta-analyses of correlations between parent and teacher ratings reported in studies that were mostly from the United States. Moreover, for 7,380 preschool children in thirteen societies, Rescorla and colleagues (2012) found a mean cross-informant *r* of 0.27 between problem scales scored from ratings by parents on the CBCL/1½–5 and from ratings by preschool teachers or daycare providers on the parallel Caregiver-Teacher Report Form (C-TRF).

Averaged across problem scales scored from CBCL/6–18 and YSR forms completed for 27,861 eleven-to-eighteen-year-olds in twenty-five societies, Rescorla and colleagues (2013) found a mean *r* of 0.41, which was substantially higher than the mean *r* of 0.25 between parent and child ratings in the Achenbach and colleagues (1987) meta-analyses. The smaller mean *r* found in the meta-analyses may reflect the inclusion of ratings by younger children in the meta-analyzed studies than in the Rescorla and colleagues (2013) YSR samples, which spanned ages eleven to eighteen. Rescorla and colleagues (2013) also reported that mean item ratings by parents were highly correlated with mean item ratings by adolescents within each society (mean = 0.85), indicating that parents and adolescents in all twenty-five societies agreed strongly, on average, regarding which items were rated as low, medium, or high. However, within-dyad item agreement was much lower on average (mean = 0.33), with large variations among parent–adolescent dyads on item ratings in every society. When agreement was measured dichotomously using an 84th percentile cut point for deviance, most parents agreed when the YSR yielded a nondeviant score and most adolescents agreed when the CBCL yielded a nondeviant score (mean agreement = 87%). However, <50% of dyads agreed when either the CBCL or the YSR was in the deviant range.

For 6,762 eleven-to-eighteen-year-olds referred to mental health services in seven societies, Rescorla and colleagues (2017) found a mean *r* of 0.47 between parents' CBCL/6–18 ratings and YSR ratings by their eleven-to-eighteen-year-old offspring. Although the mean *r* of 0.41 for population samples and the mean *r* of 0.47 for clinical samples are substantially higher than the mean meta-analytic *r* of 0.25 that included younger children, all the mean correlations indicate that parents and their children, as well as parents and teachers, often provide different information. Rescorla and colleagues (2017) found large correlations between parents and clinically referred adolescents across the seven societies for mean item ratings (mean = 0.87), consistent with the mean $r = 0.85$ for the twenty-five population samples. Like the Rescorla and colleagues (2013) findings for population samples, mean dyadic correlations were smaller than mean item correlations and varied widely in the clinical samples from all seven societies, indicating that some parent–adolescent pairs agree much better than others.

Multicultural Cross-Informant Correlations for Adult Psychopathology

Rescorla and colleagues (2016) analyzed cross-informant correlations between problem scales scored from Adult Self-Reports (ASRs) and Adult Behavior Checklists (ABCLs) completed by 8,302 eighteen-to-fifty-nine-year-olds and their collaterals in fourteen societies. Like the YSR and the CBCL/6–18, the ASR and ABCL have more than 100 items that describe a broad spectrum of problems rated *0 = not true*, *1 = somewhat or sometimes true*, or *2 = very true or often true* (Achenbach & Rescorla, 2003). Some of the items have counterparts on forms for younger ages (e.g., *Unhappy, sad, or depressed*) whereas others do not (e.g., *Has trouble managing money or credit cards*). The problem items are scored on eight factor-analytically derived syndromes and six DSM-oriented scales, plus Internalizing, Externalizing, and Total Problems scales. Averaged across all problem scales, Rescorla and colleagues found a mean cross-informant r of 0.47, which approximates the mean r of 0.45 found for self-ratings versus collateral ratings on parallel forms of many different assessment instruments in meta-analyses of samples that were mainly from the United States (Achenbach et al., 2005). Rescorla and colleagues (2016) also reported very large correlations (mean = 0.92 across fourteen societies) between adult participants and their collateral informants regarding which problem items received low, medium, or high ratings. On the other hand, within-society mean dyadic correlations averaged only 0.39, indicating that dyads varied quite widely in agreement on ASR–ABCL item ratings.

For older adults, a mean r of 0.60 was found between self-ratings of problems on the Older Adult Self-Report (OASR) and collateral ratings on the Older Adult Behavior Checklist (OABCL) in population samples from eleven societies (Achenbach & Rescorla, 2019).

Conclusions Regarding Cross-Informant Correlations

Meta-analyses have yielded cross-informant correlations averaging 0.60 for ratings of child psychopathology by pairs of informants who play similar roles and see children in similar contexts, including pairs of parents, teachers, clinicians, and observers (Achenbach et al., 1987). However, the mean cross-informant correlations between ratings by pairs of informants who play different roles and see children in different contexts are considerably lower. Subsequent research has yielded similarly modest cross-informant correlations for ratings of children in many societies around the world. Moreover, meta-analytic and multicultural studies have yielded mean cross-informant rs in the 0.40s between self-ratings and collateral ratings for adult psychopathology assessed with various parallel forms, although a mean r of 0.60 was found between self-ratings and collateral ratings on the parallel OASR and OABCL for older adults in multicultural samples.

Findings from very diverse samples thus show that informants often provide different information than is provided by the people who are assessed. Moreover, reports by informants who play different roles and see the assessed people in different contexts also differ from each other.

THE VALUE OF DATA FROM DIFFERENT INFORMANTS

Discrepancies between reports by different informants may reflect differences in what they see, which, in turn, may be affected by the contexts in which the informants see the assessed person and also by the nature of the informants' relationships and interactions with the assessed person. For example, a teacher may observe that a child does not attend to schoolwork while in a classroom of thirty children. The child's parent, on the other hand, may observe that the child attends closely to computer games at home. Discrepancies between the teacher's and parent's ratings of attention problems would therefore reflect real differences between what is seen at school versus home, in addition to the possible effects of differences between the teacher's and parent's mindsets and their sensitivity to the child's attention problems.

Discrepancies between informants' ratings may also be affected by the informants' behavior toward the assessed person. For example, if one parent is much more punitive than the other parent toward their child, the more punitive parent is apt to elicit different behavior than the less punitive parent. Equally important, informants may differ in how they perceive and remember behavior. For example, one informant may interpret and remember an assessed person's signs of unhappiness as anger, whereas the assessed person reports unhappiness. Because there is no objective gold standard for psychopathology, assessment always involves human judgments. In our example of discrepancies between teacher versus parent ratings of attention problems, discrepancies may reflect true differences between the child's behavior at school versus home but may also reflect differences between the teacher's perceptions and memory of the disruptive effect of the child's inattention in the classroom versus the parent's perception and memory of the child's behavior in the family context. And discrepancies between ratings of a child by a mother versus father or by a collateral and an assessed adult may reflect various characteristics of the informants as well as of the assessed child or adult. Factors that may increase discrepancies between self-ratings and collateral ratings include the informants' personal traits (e.g., narcissistic, antisocial), as well as cognitive characteristics.

Informant discrepancies can provide clinically valuable data about the informants and their views of the assessed person, as well as providing data about the assessed person. Consequently, when informants' data are discrepant, it is wrong to ask "Who should I believe?" Instead, it is better to examine the discrepancies and to explore possible reasons for the discrepancies. In subsequent sections on comparing data from multiple informants, we will present ways to clinically use both discrepancies and consistencies between informants' data. However, it is helpful to first consider research evidence regarding the value of data from different informants.

Predictions from Different Kinds of Informants

It seems clear that comprehensive clinical assessment should include data from multiple informants whenever possible. In addition to the value of multi-informant data for comprehensive assessment, data from various informants can improve the accuracy of predicting clinically important variables. As an example, Ferdinand and colleagues (2003) tested prediction of three-year outcomes for Dutch six-to-twelve-year-old psychiatry outpatients from parents' CBCL ratings, teachers' TRF ratings, and clinicians' ratings on scales of the Semistructured Clinical Interview for Children and Adolescents (SCICA; McConaughy & Achenbach, 2001). It was found that the TRF Aggressive Behavior syndrome was the only significant predictor of school problems three years later, while the TRF Social Problems syndrome was the only significant predictor of police/judicial contacts. The CBCL Social Problems syndrome and the SCICA Attention Problems syndrome both predicted psychiatric hospitalizations, while the SCICA Aggressive Behavior syndrome predicted parents' desire for additional professional help three years later. Teacher, parent, and clinician ratings thus contributed to prediction of different aspects of outcomes following child psychiatric services.

For adult psychopathology, Klein (2003) compared self-reports versus informants' reports of depressed outpatients' personality disorders and other characteristics as predictors of outcomes assessed seven and a half years later. Each patient and each informant was interviewed separately at the initial clinical evaluation. The patients were interviewed again seven and a half years later. The initial interviews included scales for rating depression and global functioning, plus the Personality Disorder Examination (Loranger, 1988). Klein found that initial personality disorder diagnoses and dimensional scores based on self-reports and on informants' reports independently predicted depressive symptoms and global functioning. However, only the informants' reports made significant additional contributions to prediction of global functioning and social adjustment. Klein concluded that "Informants' reports appeared to be particularly useful in predicting social adjustment, despite the fact that the outcomes were assessed using patients' reports" (p. 221). Meta-analyses have also shown that informants' ratings of personality traits predict aspects of functioning such as academic and job performance more accurately than self-ratings do (Connelly & Ones, 2010).

For older adults, research has demonstrated the value of informants' reports for predicting Alzheimer's disease. In a Canadian study, nondemented older adults underwent baseline diagnostic assessments that included the Mini-Mental State Examination (MSSE; Folstein, Folstein, & McHugh, 1975), which is a widely used test of memory impairment (Tierney et al., 2003). The baseline assessments also included self-ratings and informants' ratings of cognitive difficulties. When reassessed two years later, 20 percent of the older adults were found to meet criteria for Alzheimer's disease. Informants' baseline ratings contributed significantly to prediction of Alzheimer's disease over and above prediction by the MMSE and self-ratings. In a US study, informants' OABCL ratings significantly augmented MMSE scores in discriminating between patients with Alzheimer's disease versus mood disorders (Brigidi et al., 2010). The informants' ratings also discriminated significantly between patients with either Alzheimer's disease or mood disorders versus nonclinical samples of older adults.

Questions of Validity

Studies summarized in the section on "Predictions from Different Kinds of Informants" support the validity of data from different kinds of informants for predicting different aspects of outcomes. Another important aspect of validity is the validity of a single individual's report. Some self-report assessment instruments include validity scales that are intended to detect overreporting, defensiveness, and inconsistent responding. Scores on such scales are primarily used to flag protocols deemed to be invalid but sometimes also to adjust scores on content scales, though the utility of this latter practice has been questioned (e.g., Barthlow et al., 2002).

Validity scales scored from the Minnesota Multiphasic Personality Inventory (MMPI) have generated more research than perhaps any other scales for evaluating the validity of self-reports of psychopathology. Various validity scales were developed for the first edition of the MMPI (Hathaway & McKinley, 1943) and for the second edition (MMPI-2; Butcher et al., 1989). The most advanced scales are those developed for the MMPI-2-Restructured Form (MMPI-2-RF; Ben-Porath & Tellegen, 2008/2011), which employs the MMPI-2's normative data but provides different ways of scoring the MMPI-2's 338 True/False items. (See Chapter 16 in this volume for full coverage of the MMPI-2 –RF and its validity scales.)

Meta-analyses of mainly forensic and neuropsychological assessment studies have yielded significant effects for the ability of the MMPI-2-RF Infrequent Pathology (Fp-r), Infrequent Responses (F-r), Infrequent Somatic (Fs), Response Bias (RBS), and Symptom Validity (FBS-r) scales to discriminate significantly between respondents who were instructed to simulate certain response patterns versus those who were instructed to respond honestly and also between criterion groups of real clients (Ingram & Ternes, 2016; Sharf et al., 2017). The findings on deliberately simulated response patterns suggest that self-report validity scales may detect overreporting response styles by forensic and neuropsychological assessment clients.

Research on detection of malingering and overreporting of symptoms in mainly forensic and neuropsychological assessment of adults thus shows that users of self-report instruments must be sensitive to clients' motives to distort their reports. Research also shows that experimental manipulation of the percentage of random, acquiescent, and counter-acquiescent item responses can affect scores on content-based validity scales (Burchett et al., 2016). Informant-report scales typically do not include validity scales. Because many items of instruments like the MMPI-2-RF assess clients' reports of their subjective experiences, it is difficult to populate informant-report instruments with parallel items that assess the same subjective content as the self-report items. While validity scales on self-report instruments such as the MMPI-2-RF can alert users to possibly invalid scale scores, the need for data from other sources argues for also obtaining informant reports whenever possible. Because informant reports are especially valuable when they can be compared with self-reports, more research is needed on the validity of parallel informant reports and self-reports and on the validity of various algorithms for combining them.

For assessment of individuals, it is clearly helpful to obtain and compare data from multiple informants. Data from different informants can reveal similarities and differences in how the assessed person functions in different contexts and also in how the assessed person is perceived by people who may be relevant to helping that person. The following sections present methods for obtaining data from multiple informants and for documenting both similarities and discrepancies between data from different informants. When important discrepancies are detected, providers can tailor their explorations of reasons for the discrepancies to the specifics of the case. To facilitate such explorations, the methods presented in the following sections provide explicit comparisons and correlations between data from different informants, including printouts that can be shown to informants for discussion, if deemed appropriate by providers.

HOW TO OBTAIN DATA FROM MULTIPLE INFORMANTS

When parents apply for mental health services for their children, they typically expect to fill out forms to provide information about the children. Assessment forms can be mailed to parents, made available online, filled out in waiting rooms, or read aloud by interviewers who enter the parents' responses as part of the application process. For youths, self-report forms can likewise be mailed, made available online, filled out in waiting rooms, or administered by interviewers. Most youths are willing to complete self-report forms, as indicated by the 97 percent rate found for youths' completion of the YSR after their parents had completed the CBCL/6–18 in a US national household survey (Achenbach & Rescorla, 2001). For children who attend school, parents can be asked to sign a consent form to permit providers to ask teachers to complete assessment forms, which can also be done on paper or online. If the application process routinely includes completion of forms for assessing the child by parents and – when appropriate – by teachers and by the assessed child (if old enough), providers can view the completed forms and scales scored from the forms prior to meeting with the parents and child.

When meeting with parents, the provider can ask if they have any questions about the forms they completed. Parents often express reactions to certain items and provide additional details. The data on the forms and the parents' reactions give providers opportunities for follow-up questions and discussion. If a child has completed a self-report form, the provider can also use it as a takeoff point for interviewing the child by inviting questions and following up on what was entered on the form. Self-report forms often provide entrée to issues that children may be more willing to acknowledge on a form than to verbalize in response to oral questions. For example, self-ratings may affirm problems such as *I think about killing myself*, *I feel that others are out to get me*, or *I feel that no one loves me*, which the provider can then ask about.

For adult clients, providers can request that self-report forms be completed on paper or online prior to the initial meeting. At the first or second meeting, the provider can discuss the value of obtaining the perspective of somebody who knows the client well and can give examples of collaterals who complete assessment forms, such as spouses, partners, parents, grown children, other family members, roommates, and friends. The provider can show the client an ABCL form, give assurance of confidentiality, and encourage the client to think of one or more people who could complete the ABCL. If the client nominates one or more people, the provider can ask the client to sign consents for each nominated informant to complete an ABCL. The provider can then send each informant a cover letter, the signed consent, and an ABCL to complete on paper or online.

Although it might be objected that adult clients would not agree to having informants complete the ABCL, completed ABCLs were obtained for 81.0 percent of eighteen-to-fifty-nine-year-olds who completed the ASR in a US national household survey (Achenbach & Rescorla,

2003). This means that most adults who completed the ASR nominated an informant and gave written consent for the informant to be contacted, the informant was successfully contacted, and the informant completed the ABCL.

For many older clients, potential informants accompany the clients or are otherwise involved in help-seeking. After a client has completed the OASR on paper or online, the provider can ask if the client would consent to have one or more informants complete the OABCL. As evidence that most older adults are inclined to permit informants to complete the OABCL, completed OABCLs were obtained for 80.4 percent of sixty-to-ninety-eight-year-olds who completed the OASR in a US national household survey (Achenbach et al., 2004). If an older adult is unable to complete the OASR, one or more informants can nevertheless be asked to complete the OABCL.

HOW TO COMPARE DATA FROM MULTIPLE INFORMANTS

It is easy to compare data from multiple informants if they complete parallel forms that assess the same aspects of functioning in the same formats and are scored in the same way. However, a few items may not be assessable by all informants. For example, problems such as nightmares are not assessable by teachers, whereas problems such as disrupting class discipline are not assessable by parents.

Even when scale scores are based only on items that have clear counterparts on parallel forms, differences between mean scale scores obtained from different kinds of informants' ratings have been found that are consistent across population samples from many societies, as follows: For both preschool and school-age children, mean problem scale scores from parents' ratings are higher than from teachers' ratings; mean problem scale scores from eleven-to-eighteen-year-olds' self-ratings are higher than from parents' or teachers' ratings; mean problem scale scores from eighteen-to-fifty-nine-year-olds' self-ratings are higher than from informants' ratings (Rescorla et al., 2013, 2014, 2016). However, between adults over age fifty-nine and informants, the differences in mean problem scale scores are smaller and inconsistent (Achenbach & Rescorla, 2019).

In addition to differences between scores obtained from different kinds of informants, scores may differ in relation to the gender and age of the people assessed, as well as in relation to their society of origin and, for immigrants, their society of residence. To take account of gender, age, and informant differences, different sets of norms have been constructed for people of each gender within particular age ranges assessed with collateral- versus self-rated forms. To take account of differences associated with particular societies, different sets of multicultural norms have been constructed for each form. One set of multicultural norms is based on data from societies where problem scores are relatively low on a particular form. A second set of multicultural norms is based on data from societies where problem scores are intermediate on that form. A third set of multicultural norms is based on data from societies where problem scores are relatively high on that form.

The research that obtained normative data from population samples in dozens of societies revealed that problem scale scores from ratings by different kinds of informants in a society did not necessarily qualify for the same multicultural norm group. For example, problem scale scores from ratings by parents and teachers in Japan and Mainland China qualified for the CBCL/6–18 and TRF low norm group but problem scale scores from self-ratings by Japanese and Mainland Chinese eleven-to-eighteen-year-olds qualified for the YSR intermediate norm group. To take account of societal differences in tendencies for each kind of informant to rate problems relatively low, intermediate, or high, software computes normalized *T* scores that are standardized for the multicultural norm group appropriate for a particular kind of informant from a particular society.

As an example, norms for scales scored from CBCL/6–18 and TRF forms completed by Japanese and Mainland Chinese parents and teachers are based on data from low-scoring societies, whereas norms for scales scored from YSRs completed by Japanese and Mainland Chinese eleven-to-eighteen-year-olds are based on data from intermediate-scoring societies. Consequently, scores for Japanese and Mainland Chinese eleven-to-eighteen-year-olds rated by parents, teachers, and youths are all displayed in terms of *T* scores based on user-selected multicultural norm groups, types of informants (parent, teacher, youth), age groups, and gender. Note, however, that norms for Chinese people in Hong Kong, Singapore, and Taiwan do not necessarily correspond to those that are derived from Mainland Chinese population samples.

Bar Graph Comparisons

To help providers evaluate similarities and differences between levels of scale scores obtained from ratings by different informants, the software displays bar graphs in which the *T* score for each scale is standardized for the appropriate multicultural norm group (low, intermediate, high), the type of informant (e.g., parent, teacher, self), the age of the assessed person, and the gender of the assessed person. As an illustration, Figure 11.1 displays bar graphs of syndrome scale *T* scores for fourteen-year-old Cathy. (Names and personal details are fictitious.)

In Figure 11.1, scores below the bottom broken line (<93rd percentile; $<T$ 65) are in the normal range. Scores between the two broken lines (93rd–97th percentile; *T* 65–69) are in the borderline clinical range while scores above the top broken line (>97th percentile; $T > 69$) are in the clinical range. By looking at the bars in the upper left-hand box in Figure 11.1, you can see that Cathy obtained an Anxious/

Cross-Informant Comparison - Syndrome Scale T Scores CBCL/TRF/YSR

ID: Name: Cathy W Gender: Female Birth Date: 09/09/1992 Comparison date: 12/11/2006

Form	Eval ID	Age	Informant Name	Relationship	Date	Form	Eval ID	Age	Informant Name	Relationship	Date
CBC1	001	14	Not displayed	Unknown	10/10/2006						
TRF2	002	14	Not displayed	Unknown	11/11/2006						
YSR3	003	14	Not displayed	Self	11/12/2006						

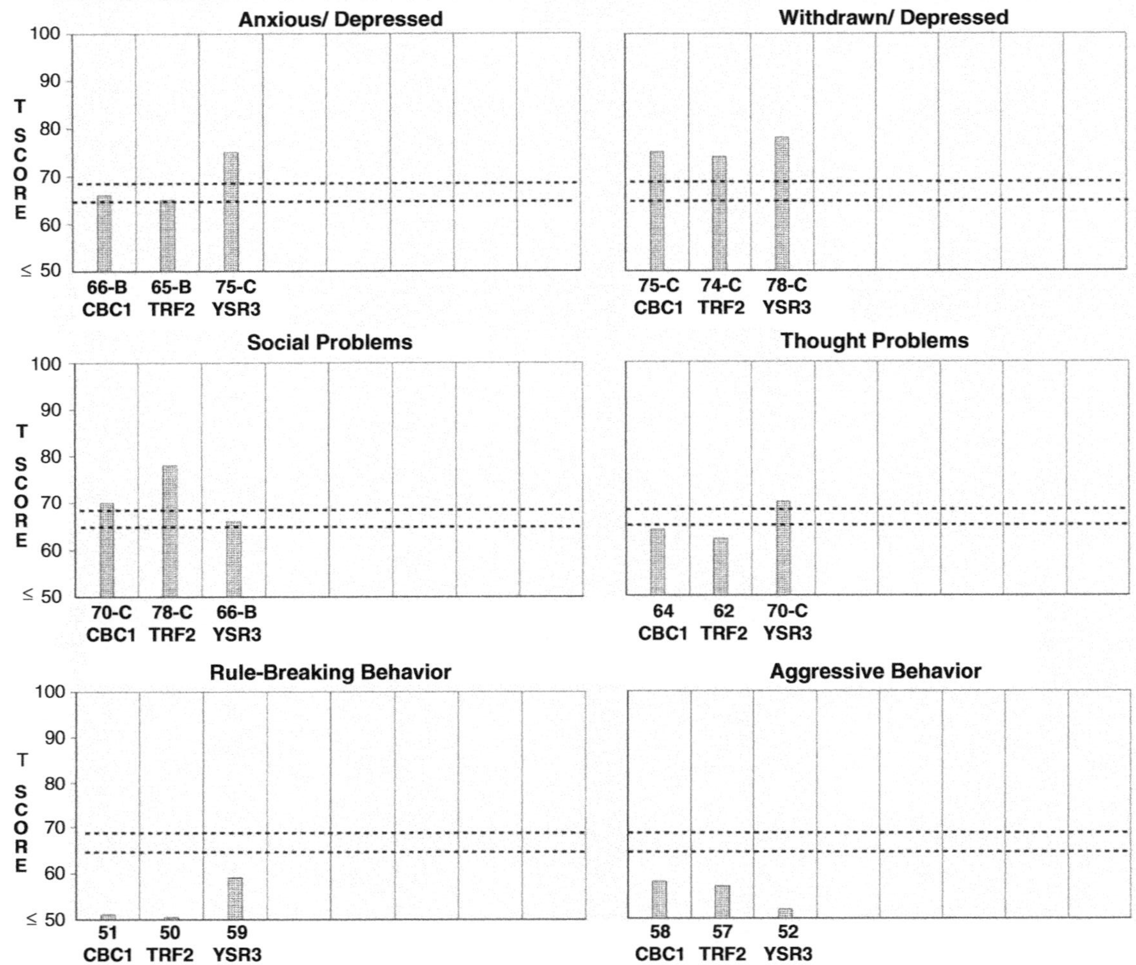

Multicultural Society Information

Form	Society Name	Society Code
CBC1	Society M	000M
TRF2	Society M	000M
YSR3	Society M	000M

Broken lines = Borderline clinical range *B = Borderline clinical range; C = Clinical range* *nc = not calculated due to insufficient data*

(From Achenbach & Rescorla, 2007). Copyright © 2007 by authors; reproduced by permission from authors.

Figure 11.1 Cross-informant comparisons of Cathy's scores on syndrome scales in relation to Society M norms

Depressed syndrome score in the clinical range on the YSR and in the borderline clinical range on the CBCL/6–18 and TRF. Cathy also obtained scores in the borderline or clinical range on the Withdrawn/Depressed, Somatic Complaints, and Social Problems syndromes, but in the normal range on the Rule-Breaking and Aggressive Behavior syndromes. However, on the Thought Problems syndrome, Cathy's YSR score was in the clinical range, while her CBCL/6–18 and TRF scores were in the high normal range. On the Attention Problems syndrome, Cathy's CBCL/6–18 and TRF scores were in the borderline clinical range, while her YSR score was in the normal range.

Based on ratings by Cathy, her mother, and her teacher, it is clear that Cathy does not need help with rule-breaking or aggressive behavior. However, scores in the clinical range for the Withdrawn/Depressed syndrome in ratings on all three forms argue for giving problems comprising this syndrome especially high priority in efforts to help Cathy. Borderline or clinical range scores for the Anxious/Depressed, Somatic Complaints, and Social Problems syndromes on all three forms also argue for prioritizing help in these areas. On the Attention Problems syndrome, borderline clinical scores on the CBCL/6–18 and TRF but not on the YSR suggest that Cathy may be unaware of moderate attention problems that her mother and teacher notice. Conversely, on the Thought Problems syndrome, scores in the clinical range on the YSR but in the high normal range on the CBCL/6–18 and TRF suggest that thought problems experienced by Cathy are not fully evident to her mother and teacher.

Assessing Parents

To help children who are referred for mental health services, providers need a clear picture of parental characteristics that may affect the children, as well as affecting efforts to improve the children's functioning. For example, Vidair and colleagues (2011) found that parents' psychopathology was significantly associated with diagnoses and CBCL/6–18 scores of their clinically referred children. To document parent problems as part of the intake process, parents can be asked to fill out the ASR to describe themselves and the ABCL to describe their partner. The *Multicultural Family Assessment Module* (MFAM) can then display parents' scale scores on bar graphs that also display their child's scale scores (Achenbach, Rescorla, & Ivanova, 2015). As an example, Figure 11.2 displays syndrome scale scores for CBCL/6–18, ASR, and ABCL forms filled out by ten-year-old Clark's parents, plus the TRF filled out by Clark's teacher. The bar graphs show scores in the clinical range on several syndromes for Clark's parents, as well as for Clark. The elevated scores for Clark's parents suggest that they, as well as Clark, may need help. If the provider deems it appropriate, the MFAM bar graphs can be shown to Clark's parents in order to teach them about informant differences in how Clark and they are viewed and also to show them areas in which they may need help.

Side-by-Side Displays of Item Ratings

In addition to displaying bar graph comparisons of scale scores like those shown in Figure 11.2, the software helps providers compare data from multiple informants by displaying side-by-side comparisons of 0–1–2 ratings of each problem item from each form on which the item was rated (item ratings are not shown in Figure 11.2). The problem items are grouped by scale. This enables providers to look down the list of a scale's items in order to see which items were endorsed by all informants, which items were endorsed by some informants, and which items were endorsed by no informants. In Clark's case, the lower left box of Figure 11.2 shows that Clark obtained Aggressive Behavior syndrome scores in the clinical range from CBCL/6–18 ratings by both parents and TRF ratings by his teacher. However, the CBCL/6–18 completed by Clark's mother (designated as CBC2 in Figure 11.2) yielded an Aggressive Behavior *T* score of 89, whereas the CBCL/6–18 completed by Clark's father (designated as CBC1) and the TRF completed by Clark's teacher (designated as TRF3) yielded Aggressive Behavior *T* scores of 72 and 80, respectively. The provider can look at the side-by-side display of item ratings to identify problem items that were rated 1 or 2 only by Clark's mother. The discrepancies between item ratings by Clark's mother, father, and teacher can then provide guidance for interviewing Clark and his parents to determine why his mother reported more aggressive behavior than his father or teacher.

Q Correlations between Informants' Item Ratings

The bar graphs and side-by-side displays of item ratings show providers the specific consistencies and discrepancies between scale scores and between item ratings obtained from different informants. To help providers evaluate the overall level of cross-informant agreement, the software computes and displays *Q* correlations between problem item ratings from each pair of informants. (A *Q* correlation is computed by applying the formula for *r* to two sets of items, such as the CBCL/6–18 problem items rated by a child's parent and the corresponding TRF items rated by the child's teacher.) A *Q* correlation of 1.00 means that the two patterns of 0–1–2 ratings agree perfectly, whereas a *Q* correlation of 0.00 means that there is no consistency between the two sets of ratings.

To help providers interpret *Q* correlations between particular kinds of informants (e.g., two parents or a parent and teacher), the software also displays the 25th percentile, mean, and 75th percentile *Q* correlations found in large reference samples of those kinds of informants. The software generates text that describes *Q* correlations <25th percentile as *below average*; *Q* correlations from the 25th to 75th percentiles as *average*; and *Q* correlations >75th percentile as *above average*. If a *Q* correlation is below average for a particular pair of informants, the provider can explore possible reasons, such as a lack of contact with

Cross-Informant Comparison - Syndrome Scale T Scores

Form	Eval ID	Assessed Person	Age	Informant	Relation	Society	Date
CBC1	1	V, Clark	10	V, Paul	Father	ASEBA Standard	2015-02-06
CBC2	2	V, Clark	10	V, Melissa	Mother	ASEBA Standard	2015-02-04
TRF3	3	V, Clark	10	R, Sarah	Teacher	ASEBA Standard	2015-02-06
ABC4	4	V, Melissa	35	P, Olivia	Friend	ASEBA Standard	2015-02-06
ASR5	5	V, Melissa	35	V, Melissa	Self	ASEBA Standard	2015-02-06
ABC6	6	V, Paul	35	W, Abby	Girlfriend	ASEBA Standard	2015-02-06
ASR7	7	V, Paul	35	V, Paul	Self	ASEBA Standard	2015-02-06

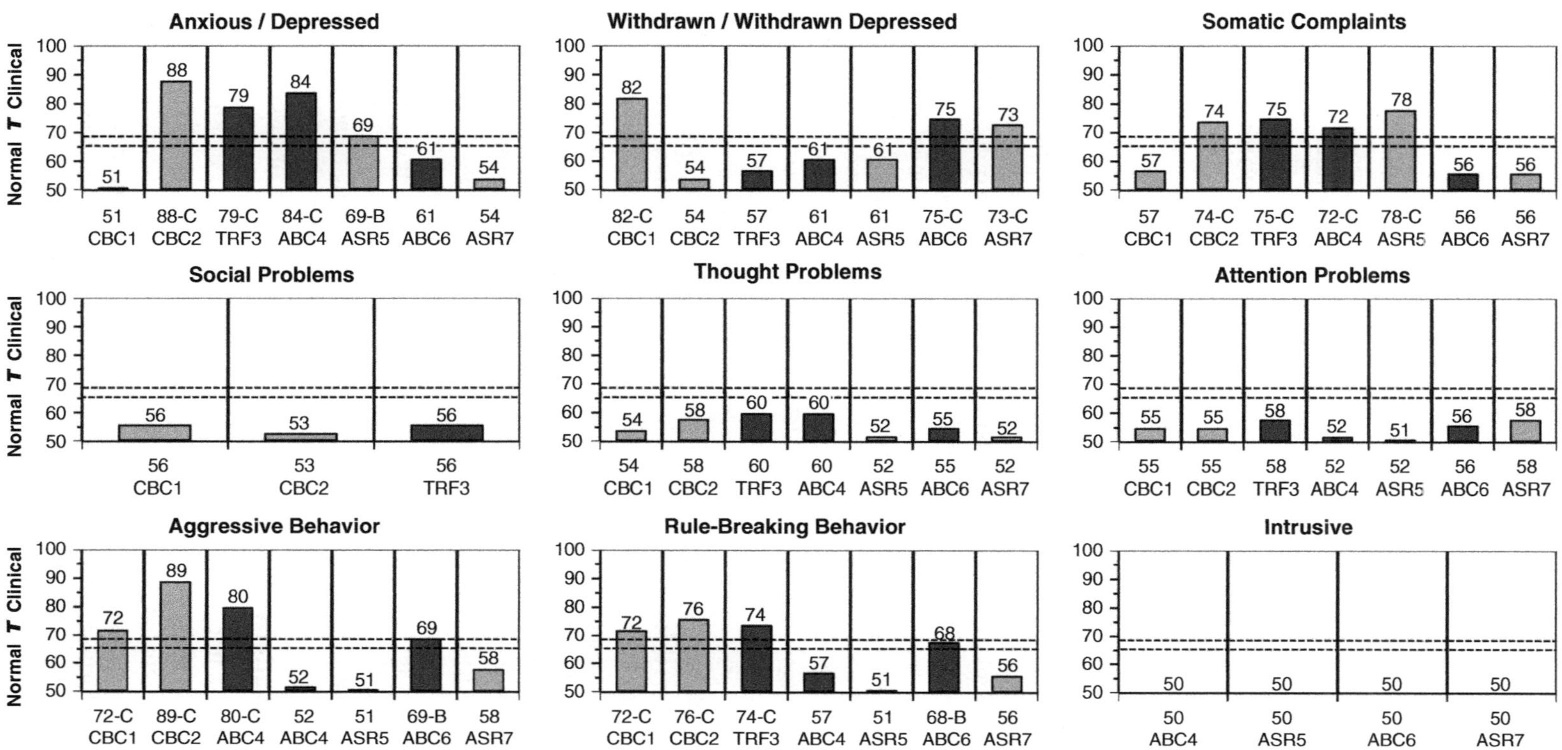

B = Borderline clinical range; C = Clinical range; Broken Lines = Borderline clinical range

** nc = The scores are not computed due to missing data.*

Printed by: ASEBA\Admin

(From Achenbach, Rescorla, & Ivanova, 2015). Copyright © 2015 by authors; reproduced by permission from authors.

Figure 11.2 MFAM bar graphs scored for ten-year-old Clark, Melissa (Clark's mother), and Paul (Clark's father)

the child, or an especially easy or difficult relationship with the child, or tendencies to underreport or overreport problems.

HOW TO USE MULTI-INFORMANT DATA

The foregoing sections described tools for helping providers compare data from informants who fill out parallel assessment forms. Providers in diverse contexts can use the tools for designing interventions and for helping their clients in other ways. In this section, we describe an additional tool for helping providers integrate assessment data from multiple informants in evaluating six-to-eighteen-year-olds for services and in evaluating progress and outcomes. The tool is the Integration, Progress, and Outcomes App for Ages 6–18 (IPO App/6–18; Achenbach, 2020). The app focuses on ages six to eighteen because providers often obtain data from more informants (e.g., two parents, teachers, self-reports) for these ages than for preschoolers or adults. However, similar principles can be applied to assessment of these other age groups.

When CBCL/6–18, TRF, and/or YSR data are obtained for a child, the app identifies scale scores that are in the borderline or clinical range. It then lists scales for which scores are in the borderline or clinical range. If any scale scores are in the borderline or clinical range on more than one form, the app generates text stating that help *is probably needed* for the problems assessed by the scale(s) with scores in the borderline or clinical range on more than one form. If any scale scores are in the borderline or clinical range on only one form, the app generates text stating that help *may be needed* for the problems assessed by the scale(s) with scores in the borderline or clinical range on only one form.

In addition to alerting providers to deviant scale scores, the app also displays critical items that were rated *1* or *2* by any informant. Expert clinicians have identified the critical items that warrant particular concern. For ages six to eighteen, the critical items include: *Deliberately harms self or attempts suicide*; *Hears sounds or voices that aren't there*; *Physically attacks people*; *Runs away from home*; *Sees things that aren't there*; *Sets fires*; *Talks about killing self*; *Uses drugs for nonmedical purposes (not including alcohol or tobacco)*. The app generates text stating that help is probably needed for the problems described by critical items that were rated *1* or *2* on any form.

Progress and Outcome Evaluations

If services are implemented, it is important to assess clients' progress in order to decide whether services should be continued, changed, or terminated. Informants who completed forms for the initial assessment (Date 1) can be asked to complete the same forms again at one or more subsequent points (Date 2, Date 3, etc.) to assess progress. The IPO App/6–18 can display bar graphs that compare scale scores from Date 1 to scale scores obtained at each subsequent assessment. The app also generates text stating whether changes from the Date 1 assessment to each subsequent assessment exceed chance expectations. The app uses statistical computations to determine whether changes exceed chance expectations. However, providers do not need any statistical knowledge to use the app.

When termination of a service is being considered or after termination occurs, providers can evaluate outcomes by asking informants to fill out the assessment forms again. The app can evaluate changes in scale scores from Date 1, Date 2, and so on to the outcome assessment in the same way as it evaluates changes from an initial assessment to one or more progress assessments. If providers wish to do subsequent outcome evaluations (e.g., six months after termination), they can repeat the process.

FUTURE DIRECTIONS

Providers who work with children or with older adults have long recognized the need to routinely obtain assessment data from people who know the assessed person, in addition to data from the assessed person. Evidence reviewed in this chapter argues for routinely obtaining collateral reports for eighteen-to-fifty-nine-year-olds, as well as for children and older adults.

Existing research and evidence-based assessment instruments provide foundations for using multi-informant assessment to advance mental health services along multiple paths. One possible path forward involves using multi-informant data to detect specific disorders. Martel, Markon, and Smith (2017), for example, have proposed research on "Developmental models of cross-informant integration for individual disorders based on theory and tests of incremental validity" (p. 116). These authors mention "longitudinal trajectories and outcomes, treatment response, and behavior genetic etiology" (p. 116) as external validity criteria for multi-informant assessment research. They also stress the need for "disorder-specific theories for understanding the presence and nature of informant discrepancies" (p. 125).

The research path outlined by Martel and colleagues is apt to be very long, in view of the years needed for evidence-based construction of "developmental models of cross-informant integration for individual disorders" and validation against "longitudinal trajectories and outcomes, treatment responses, and behavior genetic etiology." This path also assumes that theories, assessment, and amelioration of psychopathology should be organized according to constructs for many specific disorders, analogous to DSM diagnostic categories. However, the Introduction to the DSM-5 states that "The historical aspiration of achieving diagnostic homogeneity by progressively subtyping within disorder categories no longer is sensible; like most common human ills, mental disorders are heterogeneous at many levels, ranging from genetic risk factors to symptoms" (American Psychiatric Association, 2013, p. 12). Moreover, "dimensional approaches to diagnosis ... will likely supplement or supersede current categorical approaches" (p. 13). DSM-5 thus implies that efforts to model psychopathology in terms of many specific disorders may be obsolete.

A shorter path forward involves helping today's trainees and providers systematically use data from multiple informants to document diverse aspects of each client's functioning. Advances along this path need not wait for "disorder-specific theories" nor validation against "longitudinal trajectories and outcomes, treatment response, and behavior genetic etiology." Although such aspirations are commendable for long-term research, applications of existing knowledge, instruments, and procedures outlined in this chapter can advance mental health services in the near term, while also preparing providers to apply the future fruits of long-term research.

SUMMARY AND CONCLUSIONS

For ages one and a half to ninety plus, findings from many societies reveal important differences between reports of psychopathology by people who are being assessed versus collaterals who know them. These findings argue for routinely obtaining multi-informant data whenever possible. Parallel forms completed by different informants provide standardized item and scale score comparisons that highlight similarities and differences between perceptions of clients' functioning in different contexts. Standardized multi-informant data provide evidence on which to base interventions, as well as evaluations of progress and outcomes.

To advance mental health services, today's trainees and providers can routinely use existing tools to obtain and compare data from multiple informants. To strengthen therapeutic alliances, they can also display the results of multi-informant assessment for discussion with clients at intake, progress, and outcome evaluations. Over the longer term, research can build on the foundations laid by existing instruments and on findings that more precisely personalize use of multi-informant data to address clients' specific problems, strengths, and amenability to various intervention options.

REFERENCES

Achenbach, T. M. (2020). *Integration, progress, and outcomes app for ages 6–18*. Burlington, VT: University of Vermont, Research Center for Children, Youth, & Families.

Achenbach, T. M., Ivanova, M. Y., Rescorla, L. A., Turner, L. V., & Althoff, R. R. (2016). Internalizing/externalizing problems: Review and recommendations for clinical and research applications. *Journal of the American Academy of Child and Adolescent Psychiatry*, *55*, 647–656.

Achenbach, T. M., Krukowski, R. A., Dumenci, L., & Ivanova, M. Y. (2005). Assessment of adult psychopathology: Meta-analyses and implications of cross-informant correlations. *Psychological Bulletin*, *131*, 361–382. https://doi.org/10.1037/0033-2909.131.3.361

Achenbach, T. M., McConaughy, S. H., & Howell, C. T. (1987). Child/adolescent behavioral and emotional problems: Implications of cross-informant correlations for situational specificity. *Psychological Bulletin*, *101*, 213–232. https://doi.org/10.1037/0033-2909.101.2.213

Achenbach, T. M., Newhouse, P. A ., & Rescorla, L. A. (2004). *Manual for the ASEBA older adult forms & profiles*. Burlington, VT: University of Vermont Research Center for Children, Youth, and Families.

Achenbach, T. M., & Rescorla, L. A. (2001). *Manual for the ASEBA school-age forms & profiles*. Burlington, VT: University of Vermont Research Center for Children, Youth, and Families.

Achenbach, T. M., & Rescorla, L. A. (2003). *Manual for the ASEBA adult forms & profiles*. Burlington, VT: University of Vermont Research Center for Children, Youth, and Families.

Achenbach, T. M., & Rescorla, L. A. (2007). *Multicultural supplement to the Manual for the ASEBA School-Age Forms & Profiles*. Burlington, VT: University of Vermont Research Center for Children, Youth, and Families.

Achenbach, T. M., & Rescorla, L. A. (2019). *Multicultural supplement to the Manual for the ASEBA Older Adult Forms & Profiles*. Burlington, VT: University of Vermont Research Center for Children, Youth, and Families.

Achenbach, T. M., Rescorla, L. A., & Ivanova, M. Y. (2015). *Guide to family assessment using the ASEBA*. Burlington, VT: University of Vermont Research Center for Children, Youth, and Families.

American Psychiatric Association. (2013). *Diagnostic and statistical manual of mental disorders* (5th ed.). Washington, DC: Author.

Barthlow, D. L., Graham, J. R., Ben-Porath, Y. S., Tellegen, A., & Mcnulty, J. L. (2002). The appropriateness of the MMPI-2 K correction. *Assessment*, *9*, 219–229.

Ben-Porath, Y., & Tellegen, A. (2008/2011). *Minnesota Multiphasic Personality Inventory-Restructured Form: Manual for administration, scoring, and interpretation*. Minneapolis: University of Minnesota Press.

Brigidi, B. D., Achenbach, T .M., Dumenci, L., & Newhouse. P. A. (2010). Broad spectrum assessment of psychopathology and adaptive functioning with the Older Adult Behavior Checklist: A validation and diagnostic discrimination study. *International Journal of Geriatric Psychiatry*, *25*, 1177–1185.

Burchett, D., Dragon, W. R., Smith Holbert, A. M., Tarescavage, A. M., Mattson, C. A., Handel, R. W., & Ben-Porath, Y. S. (2016). "False Feigners": Examining the impact of non-content-based invalid responding on the Minnesota Multiphasic Personality Inventory-2 Restructured Form content-based invalid responding indicators. *Psychological Assessment*, *28*, 458–470. http://dx.doi.org/10.1037/pas0000205

Butcher, J. N., Dahlstrom, W. G., Graham, J.R ., Tellegen, A., & Kaemmer, B. (1989). *Minnesota Multiphasic Personality Inventory (MMPI-2). Manual for administration and scoring*. Minneapolis: University of Minnesota Press.

Connelly, B. S., & Ones, D. S. (2010). An other perspective on personality: Meta-analytic integration of observers' accuracy and predictive validity. *Psychological Bulletin*, *136*, 1092–1122.

De Los Reyes, A., Augenstein, T. M., Wang, M., Thomas, S. A., Drabick, D. A. G., Burgess, D. E., & Rabinowitz, J. (2015). The validity of the multi-informant approach to assessing child and adolescent mental health. *Psychological Bulletin*, *141*, 858–900. https://doi.org/10.1037/a0038498

De Los Reyes, A., & Kazdin, A. E. (2005). Informant discrepancies in the assessment of childhood psychopathology: A critical review, theoretical framework, and recommendations for further study. *Psychological Bulletin, 131*, 483–509. https://doi.org/10.1037/0033-2909.131.4.483

Ferdinand, R. F., Hoogerheide, K. N., van der Ende, J., Heijmens Visser, J. H., Koot, H. M., Kasius, M. C., & Verhulst, F. C. (2003). The role of the clinician: Three-year predictive value of parents', teachers', and clinicians' judgment of childhood psychopathology. *Journal of Child Psychology and Psychiatry, 44*, 867–876.

Folstein, M. F., Folstein, S. E., & McHugh, P. R. (1975). "Mini-mental state." A practical method for grading the cognitive state of patients for the clinician. *Journal of Psychiatry Research, 12*, 189–198.

Hathaway, S. R., & McKinley, J. C. (1943). *The Minnesota Multiphasic Personality Schedule*. Minneapolis: University of Minnesota Press.

Ingram, P. B., & Ternes, M. S. (2016). The detection of content-based invalid responding: a meta-analysis of the MMPI-2-Restructured Form's (MMPI-2-RF) over-reporting validity scales. *The Clinical Neuropsychologist, 30*, 473–496. http://dx.doi.org/10.1080/13854046.2016.1187769

Klein, D. N. (2003). Patients' versus informants' reports of personality disorders in predicting 7½ year outcome in outpatients with depressive disorders. *Psychological Assessment, 15*, 216–222.

Loranger, A. W. (1988). *Personality Disorder Examination (PDE) Manual*. Yonkers, NY: DV Communications.

Martel, M. M., Markon, K., & Smith, G. T. (2017). Research review: Multi-informant integration in child and adolescent psychopathology diagnosis. *Journal of Child Psychology and Psychiatry, 58*, 116–128.

McConaughy, S. H., & Achenbach, T. M. (2001). *Manual for the Semistructured Clinical Interview for Children and Adolescents* (2nd ed.). Burlington, VT: University of Vermont Research Center for Children, Youth, and Families.

Meyer, G. J., Finn, S. E., Eyde, L. D., Kay, G. G., Moreland, K. L., Dies, R. R. et al. (2001). Psychological testing and psychological assessment: A review of evidence and issues. *American Psychologist, 56*, 128–165.

Rescorla, L. A., Achenbach, T. M., Ivanova, M. Y., Bilenberg, N., Bjarnadottir, G., Denner, S., et al. (2012). Behavioral/emotional problems of preschoolers: Caregiver/teacher reports from 15 societies. *Journal of Emotional and Behavioral Disorders, 20*, 68–81. https://doi.org/10.1177/1063426611434158

Rescorla, L. A., Achenbach, T. M., Ivanova, M. Y., Turner, L. V., Árnadóttir, H. A., Au, A. et al. (2016). Collateral reports of problems and cross-informant agreement about adult psychopathology in 14 societies. *Journal of Psychopathology and Behavioral Assessment, 38*, 381–397.

Rescorla, L. A., Bochicchio, L., Achenbach, T. M., Ivanova, M. Y., Almqvist, F., Begovac, I. et al. (2014). Parent-teacher agreement on children's problems in 21 societies. *Journal of Clinical Child and Adolescent Psychology, 43*, 627–642. https://doi.org/10.1080/15374416.2014.900719

Rescorla, L. A., Ewing, G., Ivanova, M. Y., Aebi, M., Bilenberg, N., Dieleman, G. C. et al. (2017). Parent-adolescent cross-informant agreement in clinically referred samples: Findings from seven societies. *Journal of Clinical Child and Adolescent Psychology, 46*, 74–87.

Rescorla, L., Ginzburg, S., Achenbach, T. M., Ivanova, M. Y., Almqvist, F., Begovac, I. et al. (2013). Cross-informant agreement between parent-reported and adolescent self-reported problems in 25 societies. *Journal of Clinical Child and Adolescent Psychology, 42*, 262–273.

Sharf, A. J., Rogers, R., Williams, M. M., & Henry, S. A. (2017). The effectiveness of the MMPI-2-RF in detecting feigned mental disorders and cognitive deficits: A meta-analysis. *Journal of Psychopathology and Behavioral Assessment, 39*, 441–455. http://dx.doi.org.10.1007/s10862-017-9590-1

Tierney, M., Herrmann, N., Geslani, D. M., & Szalai, J. P. (2003). Contribution of informant and patient ratings to the accuracy of the Mini-Mental State Examination in predicting probable Alzheimer's disease. *Journal of the American Geriatrics Society, 51*, 813–818.

Vidair, H. B., Reyes, J. A., Shen, S., Parrilla-Escobar, M. A., Heleniak, C. M., Hollin, I. L. et al. (2011). Screening parents during child evaluations: Exploring parent and child psychopathology in the same clinic. *Journal of the American Academy of Child and Adolescent Psychiatry, 50*, 441–450. https://doi.org/10.1016/j.jaac.2011.02.002

12 Intellectual Assessment

LISA WHIPPLE DROZDICK AND JENNIFER PUIG

Practitioners have long sought methods of classifying individuals by various physiological and cognitive factors. Intellectual assessment has a unique role in psychological assessment, as it has been front and center in public debate and policy. Popular ideas of what intelligence means may not be related to constructs included in measures of intelligence. Moreover, the definition of intelligence varies across cultures, such that what is considered intelligent in one culture may or may not be considered intelligent in another culture (Ang, VanDyne, & Tan, 2011). Multiple surveys of and books by experts in intelligence have resulted in multiple definitions of intelligence, making the operationalization and measurement of intelligence difficult (e.g., Sternberg & Detterman, 1986). Thus, tests of intelligence are often described as measures of general cognitive ability.

Results from intelligence tests describe an individual's cognitive abilities at the time of testing and are highly correlated with outcome variables, such as academic achievement, occupational success, health, and mortality (Deary, Weiss, & Batty, 2010; Gottfredson & Deary, 2004; Hunter & Schmidt, 1996; Kaufman & Lichtenberger, 2006; Kendler et al., 2016; Schmidt & Hunter, 2004). Although intelligence is relatively stable over time, it is influenced by environmental and biological factors (Deary, 2014; Deary et al., 2012; Larsen, Hartmann, & Nyborg, 2008; Sameroff et al., 1993). Thus, an individual's IQ score may vary across instruments or time. However, the extensive information on a person's global cognitive ability, cognitive strengths and weaknesses, and underlying cognitive processes is essential for researchers and clinicians. This chapter briefly describes the major theories of intelligence, the instruments currently used to assess intelligence, and issues surrounding the use and interpretation of intelligence measures.

CURRENT THEORIES OF INTELLIGENCE

While multiple theories of intelligence have been proposed, the measurement of intelligence relies heavily on two distinct approaches: psychometric and information processing. Both approaches endorse the presence of overall intellectual ability, first defined as *g* (for general factor) by Spearman in 1927. However, the composition of *g* and the breakdown of the components of intelligence vary between these approaches. The psychometric approach describes *g* as comprised of discrete, measurable cognitive abilities. The information processing approach describes the process of cognition and defines the subcomponents of *g* as those abilities required to utilize higher skills. While other theories of intelligence have been proposed, such as biological, contextual, or integrative theories, they have not resulted in widely adopted instruments and are not included in this chapter.

Psychometric Theories

In the psychometric approach to assessing intelligence, factor analysis is typically utilized to group test results into different subgroups or factors based on how closely results are related. In addition to *g*, Spearman (1927) described specific factors related to cognitive performance on specific tasks. Spearman emphasized the importance of *g* in understanding intelligence and downplayed the specific factors. The earliest intellectual assessments endorsed a global score measuring general intelligence (e.g., Full Scale Intelligence Quotient in Wechsler Adult Intelligence Scale [WAIS; Wechsler, 1955] and Stanford-Binet Intelligence Scale [Terman, 1916]).

Cattell (1941, 1943) built on Spearman's work but increased the emphasis on the specific factors, proposing two specific factors: fluid intelligence and crystalized intelligence. Fluid intelligence reflects the ability to reason and solve problems and crystallized intelligence reflects the ability to acquire and use knowledge from experience. Continuous research led to additional factors being identified, although the weight of the various factors in relation to *g* was debated (Carroll, 1993; Horn, 1965, 1968, 1972; Horn & Cattell, 1966). Carroll (1993) introduced a model placing general and specific abilities into a hierarchical system, incorporating *g*, and multiple broad and narrow cognitive abilities comprising intelligence.

The Cattell-Horn-Carroll (CHC) theory of intelligence has become the dominant taxonomy for understanding intelligence from a psychometric perspective (Flanagan & McGrew, 1998; Flanagan, McGrew, & Ortiz, 2000; McGrew, 1997; Schneider & McGrew, 2012) and is widely used to describe cognitive abilities measured in intelligence tests. CHC theory is the basis of many psychometrically based intelligence assessments, guiding test development and interpretation. In addition, it is frequently used to classify results for interpretation, even within tests not developed explicitly from the CHC model. It is continuously being revised and expanded to reflect the most contemporary research (Flanagan & Dixon, 2014), which creates difficulty in test interpretation, as the theory may change after a test's publication. Clinicians utilizing CHC for test interpretation need to stay abreast of changes in the model (see Table 12.1 for a brief description of the CHC broad and narrow abilities). For a comprehensive review of the evolution of the CHC theory over time, see Flanagan and Alfonso (2017), Flanagan, Ortiz, and Alfonso (2013), and Schneider and McGrew (2018).

Information Processing Theories

The information processing approaches to the evaluation of intelligence examine how specific neuropsychological processes responsible for sensory, perceptual, motor, social-emotional, and cognitive functioning (Luria 1973, 1980) facilitate the learning and acquisition of skills and understanding of and adjustment to one's environment (Dehn, 2013; Miller, 2013; Reynolds & Fletcher-Janzen, 2007). Research has identified multiple cognitive processes related to intellectual functioning, including attention, sensory processing, executive functioning, fluid reasoning, memory, language, phonological processing, processing speed, visual-spatial processing, social cognition, and working memory (Dehn, 2013; Lezak et al., 2012). Some of these constructs are measured directly in assessments of intelligence, while others are evaluated as processes influencing performance on higher-level functions.

Luria (1973, 1980) organized brain functions into four neurocognitive abilities within three interrelated functional units: Attention, Simultaneous and Successive

Table 12.1 CHC broad and narrow abilities

Global Ability	Broad CHC Ability (code)	Narrow CHC Ability (code) ***Major abilities are in bold; minor abilities are in regular font***
G	**Fluid reasoning (*Gf*)**	**Induction (I)** **Quantitative reasoning (RQ)** General sequential reasoning (RG)
	Short-term working memory (*Gwm*)	**Auditory short-term storage (Wa)** **Visual-spatial short-term storage (Wv)** **Attentional control (AC)** **Working memory capacity (WM)**
	Learning efficiency (*Gl*)	**Associative memory (MA)** **Meaningful memory (MM)**
	Visual-spatial processing (*Gv*)	**Visualization (Vz)** **Speeded rotation (SR)** **Imagery (IM)** Closure speed (CS) Flexibility of closure (CF) Visual memory (MV) Spatial scanning (SS) Serial perceptual Integration (PI) Length estimation (LE) Perceptual illusions (IL) Perceptual alternations (PN) Perceptual speed (P)
	Auditory processing (*Ga*)	**Phonetic coding (PC)** **Maintaining and judging rhythm (U8)** Speech sound discrimination (US) Resistance to auditory stimulus distortion (UR) Memory for sound patterns (UM) Musical discrimination and judgment (U1 U9) Absolute pitch (UP) Sound localization (UL)

Continued

Table 12.1 (cont.)

Global Ability	Broad CHC Ability (code)	Narrow CHC Ability (code) ***Major abilities are in bold; minor abilities are in regular font***
	Comprehension-knowledge (*Gc*)	**Language development (LD)** **Lexical knowledge (VL)** **General verbal information (K0)** Listening ability (LS) Communication ability (CM) Grammatical sensitivity (MY)
	Domain-specific knowledge (*Gkn*)	**General science information (K1)** **Knowledge of culture (K2)** Mechanical knowledge (MK) Foreign language proficiency (KL) Knowledge of signing (KF) Skill in lip reading (LP)
	Reading and writing (*Grw*)	**Reading comprehension (RC)** **Reading decoding (RD)** **Writing ability (WA)** **Reading speed (RS)** Spelling ability (SG) Writing speed (WS) English usage (EU)
	Quantitative knowledge (*Gq*)	**Mathematical knowledge (KM)** **Mathematical achievement (A3)**
	Retrieval fluency (*Gr*)	**Ideational fluency (FI)** **Expressional fluency (FE)** **Speed of lexical access (LA)** **Naming facility (NA)** **Word fluency (FW)** Associational fluency (FA) Sensitivity to problems/alternative solution fluency (SP) Originality/creativity (FO) Figural fluency (FF) Figural flexibility (FX)
	Processing speed (*Gs*)	**Perceptual speed (P)** **Perceptual speed-search (Ps)** **Perceptual speed-compare (Pc)** Number facility (N) Reading speed (fluency) (RS)
	Reaction and decision speed (*Gt*)	Simple reaction time (R1) Choice reaction time (R2) Inspection time (IT) Semantic processing speed (R4) Mental comparison speed (R7)
	Psychomotor speed (*Gps*)	Speed of limb movement (R3) Writing speed (fluency) (WS) Speed of articulation (PT) Movement time (MT)

abilities, and Planning. While Luria described three functional units, he did not believe that the units functioned independently. Owing to the interactivity of the functional units, impairments in one area influence performance within the other areas. Das, Naglieri, and Kirby (1994) developed the Planning, Attention, Simultaneous, and Successive (PASS) model based on Luria's work along with research in the fields of neuropsychology and cognitive psychology. The four factors of the PASS model are arranged in the same manner as Luria's model but Simultaneous and Successive processing are separated for measurement purposes, although they both are used in the perception, encoding, and processing of information. The PASS model does not delineate further factors but groups mental processes into these four areas. Similar to the Lurian theory, the PASS model supports the interplay of the four functional areas both in functionality of the processes involved and in the interactions within the related brain structures involved.

Intelligence tests are not generally designed to serve as neuropsychological measures; however, many instruments have incorporated process scores of procedures to allow examination of cognitive processes within the context of intellectual assessment (e.g., Wechsler Intelligence Scale for Children – Fifth Edition Integrated [WISC-V; Wechsler & Kaplan, 2015] and Advanced Clinical Solutions for Wechsler Adult Intelligence Scale – Fourth Edition and Wechsler Memory Scale – Fourth Edition [ACS, WAIS-IV, WMS-IV; Pearson, 2009b]). Neuropsychological approaches examine the relation between neuropsychological or cognitive processes and performance.

MEASURES OF INTELLIGENCE

This section focuses on the most widely used measures in psychological assessment. In general, the instruments fall into the psychometric and information processing approaches to assessment. This is not intended to exclude other approaches to defining and assessing intelligence but to describe those instruments with the greatest acceptance and use within the field (Rabin, Barr, & Burton, 2005; Rabin, Paolillo, & Barr, 2016). In addition, while some group-administered intelligence tests are available (e.g., Naglieri Nonverbal Ability Test – Third Edition [NNAT-3; Naglieri, 2015]; Beta-4 [Kellogg & Morton, 2016]), this review focuses on individually administered assessments.

When selecting an instrument to use for a particular client, there are many features that need to be considered, including construct coverage, psychometric soundness, normative sample characteristics, relations to other measures, and logistical issues such as administration time, material requirements, and usability. It is important to understand how these issues relate to test selection.

Intellectual instruments are used within a variety of evaluations that require the assessment of a multitude of cognitive functions. Multiple instruments are often needed in order to measure all the constructs required to answer a particular referral question. For example, an assessment for a specific learning disability may require measures within the intelligence test that address various cognitive constructs associated with learning (e.g., verbal comprehension, working memory, visual-spatial ability), as well as additional measures of constructs not commonly included in intelligence measures (e.g., reading fluency, reading comprehension, mathematics ability). Evaluating multiple constructs allows for an evaluation of an individual's cognitive strengths and weaknesses that aid in diagnosis and treatment planning. Since each instrument measures different constructs, it is important to be familiar with the constructs required before selecting an instrument.

Published measures of intelligence are required to provide information on the psychometric properties of the instrument (see *The Standards for Educational and Psychological Testing* [*The Standards*; AERA, APA, & NCMA, 2014]). Measures of reliability and validity should support the use of the instrument in the populations of interest and provide sufficient support for the validity of the scores provided. The comprehensive measures described in this chapter have sufficient evidence of reliability and validity to be considered valid measures of cognitive and intellectual ability, at least at the global and index scale levels. Some subtests have less psychometric support; therefore, familiarity with each measure is key to appropriately using the instruments.

In addition to psychometric support, it is important to understand the standardization sample utilized in the creation of norms in order to interpret results appropriately. Samples should be sufficiently large to allow variability across ages, representative of the population in terms of demographic variables known to impact test performance (e.g., age, grade, socioeconomic status, gender) and cover the range of ability within the population. Mitrushina and colleagues (2005) indicate that normative samples containing at least fifty participants per normative band are sufficient to establish reliability and validity information, while Sattler (2008) suggests normative bands of 100 provide greater stability. Norfolk and colleagues (2014) examined the impact of the standardization sample size in seventeen intelligence tests and found that 47 percent did not meet the minimum requirement of thirty per norm group provided. While most published measures of intelligence meet these criteria, one major difference across measures is the inclusion of special cases in the normative sample.

Normative samples collected only in typically developing and aging samples provide a comparison of an individual to a nonimpaired group of individuals. Thus, scores can be interpreted in light of a cognitively intact group. Pena, Spaulding, and Plante (2006) describe the diagnostic strength this type of sample provides for assessments of clinical populations. However, McFadden (1996) raises concerns that norms gathered in only typically developing individuals may lead to the identification of typically developing children as impaired. Some normative samples include clinical populations at the extremes of the population, ensuring the full range of abilities are sampled and incorporated in the norms. Holdnack and colleagues (2004) indicate that this may provide a better estimate of the actual distribution of the population, as both individuals with intellectual giftedness and those with intellectual disability (ID) are included in the sample. Other normative samples include special populations across the entire distribution, including gifted and talented, ID, and clinical disorders, such as specific learning disability (SLD) and attention-deficit/hyperactivity disorder (ADHD), to provide a representative sample of the whole population. Thus, scores can be discussed in relation to the population as a whole. In cases where special groups are distributed across the sample, they are typically included in proportion to the percentages found in the population. It is important to understand the normative sample to which you are comparing your individual examinee in order to make appropriate interpretations. See Strauss, Sherman, and Spreen (2006) for detailed information on the impact of various approaches to sampling stratification on the interpretation of results.

In addition to capturing a representative sample of current populations, the age of normative data needs to be considered when selecting an instrument. Older norms produce inflated scores on intelligence measures, a phenomenon known as the Flynn effect. On intelligence tests, research describes an increase of approximately three IQ points per decade or roughly a third of a point per year (Flynn, 1984, 1987, 1999; Kaufman & Weiss, 2010) on global intelligence scores. Test norms are static and provide a snapshot of a population's intelligence abilities at the time of standardization; however, population characteristics are dynamic and change over time. From the moment a test is published, a gap between the norms and the true intellectual level of the population appears and continues to widen until new norms are developed (Gregoire et al., 2016). Thus, cognitive tests with older norms may yield higher IQs and other global index scores, with scores becoming more inflated as the norms age. Caution is warranted when interpreting scores from tests with older norms to ensure accurate and appropriate score interpretations.

Measures of intelligence are rarely used in isolation. They are frequently administered along with measures of achievement, memory, personality, mood, and other cognitive and psychological constructs. In evaluating performances across instruments, it is important to understand how the instruments are related and how they interact. Achievement and memory tests are frequently administered along with measures of intelligence (see Chapters 13 and 15). Many intelligence measures are co-normed or linked with other measures. Co-normed measures share normative samples while linking or correlational studies describe the relation between instruments normed in separate samples. Co-norming provides greater support for comparisons of scores across instruments as sample variance does not contribute to observed differences. Russell, Russell, and Hill (2005) suggest that comparison of scores across instruments that are not co-normed is not supported psychometrically. However, other studies provide support for the use of cross-battery comparisons by describing the relation among instruments in both typically developing and clinical populations without co-norming. Rohling and colleagues (2015) found only small differences when comparing the methods and concluded that co-norming is not required to utilize instruments together. Therefore, while it is important to be aware of normative sample differences when comparing scores across batteries, such comparisons are valid when similar normative samples are used and the relation between instruments is known.

Logistical issues also need to be considered when administering intelligence measures. Client-specific needs, such as administration time, location constraints, and client care needs, may influence the selection of an instrument. For example, a medically frail child may need to be assessed bedside in multiple sessions, requiring an instrument that allows for multiple sessions with relatively independent subtests. While the ability to modify an instrument to accommodate the needs of a particular client can allow a valid assessment of ability in individuals with sensory, motor, language, or health differences, it is always important to note these modifications from standardization in reports and to consider the modifications when interpreting results. Portability of materials, response requirements, and language requirements may also be considered in the selection of an instrument. For example, selecting appropriate instruments is key to obtaining valid results among clients who are bilingual or who have limited English proficiency. It is important not to assume language preferences when testing individuals but to use the client's preferred or primary language.

The selection of an appropriate assessment for measuring intelligence is complex and requires consideration. Research demonstrates that examiner preferences, often acquired during training or early career experiences, and situational factors (e.g., availability of an instrument within a school or hospital system) often drive choices in the selection of instruments, even more than the needs of a specific client or referral question (Cottrell & Barrett, 2017). It is important to note that the selection of an instrument influences the results available for diagnostic and interpretive information. Evaluating each instrument in the context of a specific client will require knowledge of test structure, psychometric soundness, normative sample characteristics, relation to other measures, and client-specific issues.

COMPREHENSIVE MEASURES OF INTELLIGENCE

Wechsler Scales of Intelligence

Three instruments were developed by David Wechsler to measure intelligence across the life span and have been revised multiple times: the WAIS for ages sixteen to ninety years; the WISC for ages six to sixteen years; and the Wechsler Preschool and Primary Scale of Intelligence (WPPSI) for ages two years six months to seven years and seven months. Wechsler viewed intelligence as a global entity comprised of different, although related, cognitive elements. Although the test structure of all three instruments follows the psychometric approach, the Wechsler scales are not tied to a particular theory of intelligence. The scales incorporate research from multiple fields to provide a comprehensive measure that reflects the current research on cognitive ability.

The scales are developmentally appropriate and address the referral questions frequently encountered in the specific age group of each instrument. Although some subtests are valid measures across the life span and appear in all three scales, other subtests are included in a single scale to assess developmental aspects of a cognitive domain. For example, WISC-V contains measures related to reading acquisition and WPPSI-IV utilizes measures assessing the early development of working memory. Subtests are either core, used to derive index scores, or supplemental, used for substitution or to provide additional information on specific cognitive abilities.

Each Wechsler scale provides an overall global intelligence score, the Full Scale Intelligence Quotient (FSIQ), and multiple cognitive domain index scores that describe the individual's ability within a cognitive domain. There are three types of index scores. Primary index scores are the main factor-derived composite scores for the scale and provide a comprehensive evaluation of intellectual abilities. Ancillary index scores measure important cognitive skills related to intelligence. Complementary index scores provide information on cognitive domains that may have clinical importance in specific evaluations.

The Wechsler scales are the most widely used measures of intelligence (Archer et al., 2006; Camara, Nathan, & Puente, 2000; Rabin et al., 2016) and have significant research support for their psychometric strength and clinical utility. The Wechsler scales have been translated and adapted into numerous languages, including Spanish, Norwegian, German, Japanese, Italian, and Chinese. All three scales are available in paper and digital format.

Wechsler Adult Intelligence Scale – Fourth Edition

WAIS-IV is the most widely used psychological assessment with adults. Table 12.2 provides an overview of the properties of the WAIS-IV. It contains subtests measuring specific cognitive abilities in four cognitive domains: Verbal Comprehension, Working Memory, Perceptual Reasoning, and Processing Speed. It provides the Full Scale IQ (FSIQ) and four domain-specific index scores. An additional ancillary index is available, the General Ability Index (GAI), comprised of the scores from the Verbal Comprehension and Perceptual Reasoning subtests. For individuals with neurodevelopmental disorders that impact working memory and processing speed, the GAI allows comparisons with other cognitive functions, such as memory and achievement, when the FSIQ is low due to impairments in working memory and cognitive speed. It is important to note that the GAI is not intended to replace the FSIQ in describing global ability, as working memory and processing speed are important aspects of intellectual ability (Blalock & McCabe, 2011; Bunting, 2006; Kaufman, Raiford, & Coalson, 2016; Rowe, Kingsley, & Thompson, 2010; Weiss et al., 2006).

Standardization. The WAIS-IV was normed on 2,200 individuals ages sixteen to ninety stratified on age, gender, education level, race/ethnicity, and geographic region. It was co-normed with the Wechsler Memory Scale – Fourth Edition (WMS-IV; Wechsler, 2009) and linked to the Wechsler Individual Achievement Test – Second Edition (WIAT-II; Harcourt Assessment, 2005). A subsequent publication, the Advanced Clinical Solutions for WAIS-IV and WMS-IV (ACS) provided additional measures and psychometric data (for a detailed description of the ACS, see Holdnack et al., 2013). With the publication of the WIAT-III (Pearson, 2009a), the Ability-Achievement discrepancy analysis was updated.

Reliability. WAIS-IV reliabilities are high for all index and core subtest scores (Wechsler, 2008). Reliabilities in the clinical groups are consistent with those observed in the normative sample. The test-retest stability coefficients are also high. Finally, interscorer agreement is also quite high.

Validity. All subtest and index scores intercorrelate to some degree; however, within each domain, the subtests correlate most highly with the index to which they contribute and less to other domains (Wechsler, 2008). The confirmatory factor analysis reported supports the four-factor model in both the sixteen-to-sixty-nine-year old and seventy-to-ninety-year old samples. In the initial publication, correlations are reported with other measures of cognitive ability, achievement, and related constructs. Each study supported the constructs described in the manual and the WMS-IV and WIAT-II samples were used to create ability-memory analysis and ability-achievement analysis data, respectively. Clinical data were also collected for individuals with special conditions (see Table 12.2).

Independent factor-analytic studies verify the factor structure (Bowden, Saklofske, & Weiss, 2011a, 2011b; Ward, Bergman, & Hebert, 2012) and also indicate that the basic factor structure of the WAIS-IV holds for individuals with clinical syndromes such as schizophrenia and traumatic brain injury (TBI; Goldstein & Saklofske, 2010). Similarly, factor analyses in samples of individuals with

Table 12.2 Intelligence measures overview: construct coverage, administration time, standardization normative group, age of norms, psychometric soundness, and links to related measures

Measure	Constructs Covered	Admin Time	Normative Sample	Year of Norms	Links to Other Measures	Other Measures	Clinical Groups
WAIS-IV	Verbal Comprehension Perceptual Reasoning Working Memory Processing Speed	60–90 minutes for core	Ages 16–90 *N* = 2,200 Special groups at ends of distributions	2008	Co-norm: WMS-IV; Links: WIAT-II WIAT-III	WISC-IV, CMS, Brown ADD Scales, KAIT, SB5, D-KEFS, CVLT-II, RBANS	GT, ID-Mild, ID-moderate, Borderline IQ, SLD-R, SLD-M, ADHD, TBI, ASD, Asperger's, depression, MCI, Alzheimer's
WISC-V	Verbal Comprehension Visual Spatial Fluid Reasoning Working Memory Processing Speed *Quantitative Reasoning* *Auditory Working Memory* *Nonverbal* *General Ability* *Cognitive Proficiency* *Naming Speed* *Symbol Translation* *Storage and Retrieval*	60 minutes for core	Ages 6–16 *N* = 2,200 Special groups at ends of distributions	2014	Co-norm: WISC-V Integrated Links: WIAT-III KTEA-3 Also WISC-V Spanish	WPPSI-IV, WAIS-IV, K-ABC-II, KTEA-3, Vineland-II, BASC-2	GT, ID-Mild, ID-moderate, Borderline IQ, SLD-R, SLD-RW, SLD-M, ADHD, disruptive behavior, TBI, ELL, ASD-L, ASD-NL
WPPSI-IV	Verbal Comprehension Visual Spatial Fluid Reasoning Working Memory Processing Speed *Vocabulary Acquisition* *Nonverbal* *General Ability* *Cognitive Proficiency*	30–45 for core ages 2:6–3:11; 45–60 minutes for core ages 4:0–7:7	Ages 2:6–7:3 *N* = 1,700 Special groups at ends of distributions	2012	Links: WIAT-III	Bayley-III, DAS-II, NNAT, NEPSY-II, BASC-2 PRS	GT, ID-Mild, ID-moderate, DD-cognitive, DD-risk, preliteracy concerns, ADHD, disruptive behavior, ELD, MERL, ASD, Asperger's
KABC-II	Sequential/*Gsm* Simultaneous/*Gv* Learning/*Glr* Planning/*Gf* Knowledge/*Gc* *Delayed Recall*	25–55 minutes for Luria Core battery; 35–70 minutes for core CHC battery	Ages 3–18 *N* = 3,025 Special groups throughout distribution *N* =700 for NU	2004 2018 (NU)	Co-norm: KTEA-II; Links: WIAT-III KABC-II NU Links: KTEA-3, WIAT-III	For K-ABC-II: WISC-III, WPPSI-III, KAIT, WJ-III COG and ACH, KTEA-II, WIAT-II	SLD-R, SLD-M, SLD-W, ID-Mild, ASD, ADHD, emotional disturbance, GT, Hearing loss

Continued

Table 12.2 (cont.)

Measure	Constructs Covered	Admin Time	Normative Sample	Year of Norms	Links to Other Measures	Other Measures	Clinical Groups
DAS-II	Verbal Ability Nonverbal Ability Spatial Ability Special Nonverbal *School Readiness* *Working Memory* *Processing Speed*	45–60 minutes KABC-II for Core battery; 30 minutes for diagnostic subtests	Ages 2:6–17:11 *N* = 3,480 Special groups throughout distribution	2007	Links: WIAT-II KTEA-II WJ-III ACH DAS-II Early Years Spanish	WPPSI-III, WISC-IV, Bayley III, WIAT-II, KTEA-II, WJ-III ACH, Bracken-R	GT, ID, SLD-R, SLD-RW, SLD-M, ADHD, ADHD with SLD, ELD, MERL, LEP, deaf/hard of hearing
CAS-2	Attention Simultaneous Sequential Planning *Executive Function without Working Memory* *Executive Function with Working Memory* *Working Memory* *Verbal Content* *Nonverbal Content*	40–60 minutes	Ages 2:6–17:11 *N* = 1,342 Special groups throughout distribution	2014		WISC-IV, CTONI-2, PTNI, WJ-III ACH, TSCRF-II, GORT-5, CMAT, WRAT-4	GT, SLI, SLD, ADHD, emotional/behavioral disorder, anxiety disorder, ASD
WJ-IV	Comprehension/Knowledge Fluid Reasoning Short-Term Working Memory Processing Speed Auditory Processing Long-Term Retrieval Visual Processing Perceptual Speed Quantitative Reasoning Number Facility	60 minutes for standard battery	Ages 2:0–90+ *N* = 7,416	2014	Co-norm: WJ-III ACH; WJ-III OL Integrated Links: WIAT-III KTEA-3	WISC-IV, WAIS, IV, WPPSI-III, KABC-II, DAS-II	SLD-R, SLD-M, SLD-W, TBI, Language delay, ASD, ADHD, GT, ID
SB5	Verbal IQ Nonverbal IQ Fluid Reasoning Knowledge Quantitative Reasoning Visual-Spatial Processing Working Memory	45–75 minutes for the full battery	Ages 2–85+ *N* = 4,800 Special groups throughout distribution	2014		WPPSI-R, WISC-III, WAIS-III, UNIT, WJ-III COG and ACH, WIAT-II	GT, ID, DD, ASD, ELL, SLI, SLD, serious emotional disorder, ADHD, motor delay

Note. GT = gifted and talented; ID-Mild = Intellectual disability – mild; ID-moderate = intellectual disability – moderate; Borderline IQ = borderline intellectual functioning; SLD-R = specific learning disability – reading; SLD-M = specific learning disability – mathematics; ADHD = attention-deficit/hyperactivity disorder; TBI = traumatic brain injury; ASD = autism spectrum disorder; MCI = mild cognitive disorder; SLD-RW = specific learning disability – reading and writing; ELL = English language disorder; ASD-L = autism spectrum disorder with language difficulty; ASD-NL = autism spectrum disorder without language difficulty; DD-cognitive = developmental delay – cognitive; DD-risk = developmental delay risk factors; ELD = expressive language disorder; MERL = mixed expressive/receptive language disorder; ASD = autism spectrum disorder; SLD-W = specific learning disability – writing; LEP = limited English proficiency; SLI = speech/language impairment. *Note*. WISC = Wechsler Intelligence Scale for Children; WMS= Wechsler Memory Scale; CMS = Children's Memory Scale (Cohen, 1997), WIAT = Wechsler Individual Achievement Test; Brown ADD Scales = Brown Attention Deficit Disorder Scales (Brown, 1996); D-KEFS = Delis-Kaplan Executive Function System (Delis, Kaplan, & Kramer, 2001), CVLT = California Verbal Learning Test (Delis et al., 2000), RBANS = Repeatable Battery for the Assessment in Neuropsychological Status (Randolph, 1998). K-ABC = Kaufman Assessment Battery for Children (Kaufman & Kaufman, 1983), WPPSI = Wechsler Preschool and Primary Scale of Intelligence; KAIT = Kaufman Adult Intelligence Test; WJ-III COG = Woodcock-Johnson III Tests of Cognitive Abilities (Woodcock, McGrew, & Mather, 2001a; PIAT-R = Peabody Individual Achievement Test-Revised (Markwardt, 1989, 1997); KTEA = Kaufman Test of Educational Achievement (Kaufman & Kaufman, 2004b); WJ-III-ACH = Woodcock-Johnson III Tests of Achievement (Woodcock, McGrew, & Mather, 2001b); Bracken = Bracken Basic Concept Scale – Revised (Bracken, 1998); CAS = Cognitive Assessment System (Naglieri & Das, 1997; Naglieri, Das, & Goldstein, 2014b); CAS-2 R = Cognitive Assessment System – Second Edition: Rating Scale (Naglieri, Das, & Goldstein, 2014c); CTONI = Comprehensive Test of Nonverbal Intelligence – Second Edition (Hammill, Pearson, & Wiederholt, 2009), Primary Test of Nonverbal Intelligence (Ehrler & McGhee, 2008); WJ-III-SCR = Woodcock-Johnson Tests of Achievement – Third Edition, Test of Silent Contextual Reading Fluency – Second Edition (Hammill, Weiderholt, & Allen, 2014); Gray = Gray Oral Reading Tests – Fifth Edition (Weiderholt & Bryant, 2012); CMAT = Comprehensive Mathematical Abilities Test (Hresko et al., 2003); WRAT = Wide Range Achievement Test – Fourth Edition (Wilkinson & Robertson, 2006); SB4 = Stanford-Binet – Fourth Edition (SB-IV; Thorndike, Hagen, & Sattler, 1986); UNIT = Universal Nonverbal Intelligence Test (Bracken & McCallum, 1998).

autism spectrum disorder (ASD) have revealed factors of verbal comprehension, perceptual reasoning, and freedom from distractibility, as well as a social cognition factor (Goldstein et al., 2008; Goldstein & Saklofske, 2010). Additional factor analysis with WMS-IV confirms the construct validity of the instruments (Drozdick et al., 2013; Miller et al., 2013). Since the publication of the WAIS-IV, investigators have identified an alternative five-factor structure of the WAIS-IV (Benson, Hulac, & Kranzler, 2010; Weiss et al., 2013a, 2013b). In the five-factor model, the perceptual reasoning domain is split into visual-spatial and fluid reasoning factors, similar to the five-factor structure of the WISC-V and consistent with CHC theory (Weiss et al., 2013a, 2013b). Both the four- and five-factor models have shown support across different groups and geographies (Abad et al., 2016; Bowden et al., 2011a, 2011b; Niileksela, Reynolds, & Kaufman, 2013; Staffaroni et al., 2018).

In addition, the WAIS-IV and its predecessors correlate highly with other measures of intelligence. WAIS scores correlate highly with the Kaufman Adolescent and Adult Intelligence Test (KAIT; Kaufman & Kaufman, 1993) and the Stanford-Binet Intelligence Scale – Fifth Edition (SB5; Roid, 2003). Finally, the WAIS-IV correlates highly with composites from the WIAT-III, the D-KEFS, the CVLT-II, and the RBANS. High correlations are found between similar constructs, such as the WAIS-IV Perceptual Reasoning Index and the RBANS Visuospatial/Constructional scale, and lower correlations between dissimilar constructs, such as WAIS-IV indexes and delayed memory scores on the CVLT-II and RBANS (Wechsler, 2008).

Wechsler Intelligence Scale for Children – Fifth Edition

The WISC-V measures the cognitive abilities of children and adolescents ages six to sixteen. Table 12.2 provides an overview of the properties of the WISC-V. It provides a global score, the FSIQ, and five primary index scores comprising subtests across five domains: Verbal Comprehension, Visual Spatial, Fluid Reasoning, Working Memory, and Processing Speed. In addition to the primary indexes, five secondary index scores and three complementary index scores are provided. It comprises ten primary subtests, six secondary subtests, and five complementary subtests. The complementary subtests are used to derive the complementary index scores and were designed to provide information on abilities related to the evaluation of specific learning disabilities and are not considered measures of intellectual ability.

Standardization. The WISC-V was normed on 2,200 children and adolescents ages six to sixteen stratified on age, gender, parent education level, race/ethnicity, and geographic region. It was linked to the WIAT-III and Kaufman Test of Educational Achievement – Third Edition (KTEA-3; Kaufman & Kaufman, 2014). A subsequent publication, the WISC-V Integrated, allows for assessment of the processes involved in completing the WISC-V. Supplemental subtests and measures provide greater depth of examination of specific cognitive processes contributing to performance on the WISC-V. See Raiford (2017) for a detailed overview of the WISC-V Integrated. The WISC-V Spanish (Wechsler, 2017) allows for the assessment of children whose primary language is Spanish and who are acculturating to the United States. This battery is composed of eleven of the WISC-IV Spanish (Wechsler, 2004) subtests and three new subtests adapted for the WISC-V. The WISC-V Spanish does not include the complementary subtests of the WISC-V.

Reliability. WISC-V reliabilities are high for all index and subtests scores (Wechsler, 2014). Reliabilities in the clinical groups are consistent with those observed in the normative sample. The test-retest stability coefficients are also high for the indexes and subtests. Finally, interscorer agreement is also quite high.

Validity. All subtest and index scores intercorrelate to some degree; however, within each domain, the subtests correlate most highly with the index to which they contribute and less to other domains (Wechsler, 2014). The confirmatory factor analysis supports the five-factor model. Interestingly, Fluid Reasoning correlated perfectly with the higher-order FSIQ. This is a consistent finding across instruments and studies (Kaufman & Kaufman, 2004a; Keith et al., 2006; Wechsler, 2008, 2012; Weiss et al., 2013a, 2013b). The factor structure of WISC-V has been supported across genders and geographies (Chen et al., 2015).

In the initial publication, correlations are reported with other measures of cognitive ability, achievement, and related constructs. Each study supported the constructs described in the manual. Clinical data were also collected for individuals with special conditions (see Table 12.2). Several analyses completed following publication of the WISC-V question the separation of the fluid reasoning and visual-spatial factors. Sattler (2016) demonstrated that while Verbal Comprehension, Working Memory, and Processing Speed are relatively clean factors, Fluid Reasoning and Visual-Spatial subtests tend to cross factors and, therefore, these factors are less well-defined. Two independent factor analyses support an alternate four-factor structure for the WISC-V (Canivez, Watkins, & Dombrowski, 2016, 2017).

Wechsler Preschool and Primary Scale of Intelligence – Fourth Edition

The WPPSI-IV measures the cognitive abilities of children ages two years six months to seven years seven months. Table 12.2 provides an overview of the properties of the WPPSI-IV. It includes two batteries, one for ages two years six months to three years eleven months and one for ages four years zero months to seven years seven months. Both batteries provide the FSIQ but differ in the included subtest and index scores. The 2:6–3:11 battery provides three primary index scores (Verbal Comprehension, Visual Spatial, Working Memory) and three ancillary index scores (Vocabulary Acquisition, Nonverbal, General Ability). The 4:0–7:7 battery provides five primary index scores (Verbal Comprehension, Visual Spatial, Fluid Reasoning, Working Memory, Processing Speed) and four ancillary index scores (Vocabulary Acquisition, Nonverbal, General Ability, Cognitive Proficiency).

The WPPSI-IV subtests measure specific cognitive abilities and are designed to be developmentally appropriate for preschool and early school–age children. The six or ten core subtests in each battery are required to derive the FSIQ and available primary index scores. The secondary subtests allow for substitution of an invalid primary subtest for the FSIQ, to provide additional support for the assessment of a domain, or to derive the ancillary index scores.

Standardization. The WPPSI-IV was normed on 1,700 children ages two years six months through seven years seven months stratified on age, gender, parent education level, race/ethnicity, and geographic region. It was linked to the WIAT-III.

Reliability. WPPSI-IV reliabilities are high for all index and subtest scores (Wechsler, 2012). Reliabilities in the clinical groups are consistent with those observed in the normative sample. In addition, the test-retest stability coefficients are high for the indexes and the subtests. Finally, interscorer agreement is also quite high.

Validity. All subtest and index scores intercorrelate to some degree; however, within each domain, the subtests correlate most highly with the index to which they contribute and less to other domains, with the core subtests generally producing the highest correlations (Wechsler, 2012). The correlations across domains are higher than observed in WISC-V and WAIS-IV, likely due to the developmental expression of specific cognitive abilities (Bjorklund, 2012; Vig & Sanders, 2007). The confirmatory factor analysis reported supports a three-factor model in the younger children and a five-factor model in older children. In the initial publication, correlations are reported with other measures of cognitive ability, achievement, and related constructs. Each study supported the constructs described in the manual. Clinical data were also collected for individuals with special conditions (see Table 12.2).

At younger ages, fewer factors are differentiated in intellectual measures than in older children, with greater focus placed on global ability (Bjorklund, 2012; Vig & Sanders, 2007). In an examination of the WPPSI-IV batteries, Watkins and Beaujean (2014) found that general intelligence accounted for the greatest amount of variance in performance, more than all the domain scores combined. This suggests a greater emphasis on global ability may be warranted in measures assessing younger children.

Kaufman Assessment Battery for Children – Second Edition

The Kaufman Assessment Battery for Children – Second Edition (KABC-II; Kaufman & Kaufman, 2004a) measures the processing and cognitive abilities of children and adolescents ages three to eighteen years. Table 12.2 provides an overview of the properties of the KABC-II. Since its publication in 2004, the KABC-II has been one of the most widely used assessments in evaluations with preschool and school-age children (Ford, Kozey, & Negreiros, 2012; Oakland, Douglas, & Kane, 2016; Sotelo-Dynega & Dixon, 2014; Visser et al., 2012). In addition, it has been adapted and translated into multiple languages, including French, German, Italian, Korean, and Japanese (e.g., Kaufman & Kaufman, 2008; Kaufman et al., 2014; Kaufman, Kaufman, & Publication Committee of Japanese Version of KABC-II, 2013). Numerous books, chapters, and articles have described the research support for the KABC-II (e.g., Drozdick et al., 2018; Kaufman et al., 2005; Mays, Kamphaus, & Reynolds, 2009) in various clinical and demographic populations. The Kaufman Assessment Battery for Children – Second Edition, Normative Update (KABC-II NU; Kaufman & Kaufman, 2018) provides updated normative information for the KABC-II collected on a sample of children and adolescents in 2017.

The KABC-II is grounded in two theoretical models, namely the CHC psychometric theory of cognitive abilities and Luria's neuropsychological theory of processing (Kaufman, 2009; McGrew, 1997; McGrew & Evans, 2004; Sotelo-Dynega & Dixon, 2014; Taub & McGrew, 2004). This dual-theoretical foundation allows the examiner to select an interpretive model based on the child's background and reason for referral. The CHC model is the recommended interpretation model and utilizes the Fluid-Crystallized Index (FCI) as the global index. The Mental Processing Index (MPI), which is based on the information processing approach, is for situations in which excluding measures of acquired knowledge/crystallized ability may provide a fairer assessment of a child's or adolescent's cognitive ability. Individuals with receptive or expressive language difficulties, who are bilingual, or who have had limited experiences with mainstream American culture may be more fairly assessed with the MPI. A third global score, the Nonverbal Index (NVI), is provided for instances in which the child's ability to communicate adequately in English is limited. Spanish translations of teaching text and scoring keys for verbal subtests are provided to assist in bilingual assessment. Differential predictive validity studies assessing typically developing Caucasian, African American, and Hispanic students found all three KABC-II global indexes to be unbiased, with the FCI producing the lowest differences in predicting academic achievement (Scheiber & Kaufman, 2015). In addition to the three global scores, the KABC-II provides five core scale scores and one supplementary scale score. The KABC-II contains eighteen subtests across the age range, with different core and supplementary subtests across ages. It is important to note that, although the FCI, MPI, and NVI are available for all ages, the content of the scales differ across ages. Three-year-olds are given seven core subtests and three supplementary subtests to derive the three global scores but no scales are available for this age. For ages four to six, eleven core subtests and eight supplementary subtests are available to derive the three global scores and four scale scores. For ages seven to eighteen, eleven core subtests and seven supplementary subtests are available to derive the three global scores and five scale scores.

Standardization. The KABC-II was normed on 3,025 children and adolescents ages three to eighteen stratified on age, gender, education level, race/ethnicity, and region. In addition, a representative portion of individuals with various special education classifications were included in the sample, comprising roughly 13 percent of the total sample. KABC-II was co-normed with the KTEA-II and linked to the WIAT-III (Pearson, 2009a). A link to the KTEA-3 was established with the publication of KTEA-3 (Kaufman & Kaufman, 2014).

The KABC-II NU was normed on 700 children and adolescents ages three to eighteen stratified on age, gender, education level, race/ethnicity, and region. Representative proportions of children from various special education classifications were included in the normative sample to reflect the US population as a whole and provide variance of cognitive ability. As with the KABC-II, the KABC-II NU was linked to the KTEA-3 and the WIAT-III (Kaufman & Kaufman, 2018).

Reliability. KABC-II reliabilities are high for all scale scores and moderate to high for the core subtests (Kaufman & Kaufman, 2004a). Test-retest stability coefficients were moderate to high for the scales and for the core subtests. Finally, interscorer agreement is also quite high.

Reliabilities of the KABC-II NU global scale indexes are quite high, averaging in the mid-to-upper 0.90s for the FCI and MPI and in the low-to-mid 0.90s for the NVI. In general, the reliabilities are as high as or higher than the original KABC-II reliabilities; this finding supports the consistency of the instrument over time. Overall, the subtests show very good internal consistency across ages. The median reliability (averaged across ages) for core subtests is 0.89 for ages three to six and 0.91 for ages seven to eighteen; supplementary subtests have slightly lower reliabilities on average.

Validity. Correlational studies conducted with the original KABC-II compared the test with several intelligence and achievement measures (see Table 12.2). Results showed consistently high correlations between the KABC-II FCI and the MPI and the global intelligence scores on other instruments, although correlations with the MPI were generally slightly lower. Moreover, similar constructs across instruments correlated moderately. Clinical data were also collected for individuals with special conditions (see Table 12.2). The KABC-II NU was examined in relation to the KABC-II, the WISC-V, and the KTEA-3. Results showed consistently high correlations between the KABC-II and the KABC-II NU supporting the application of research on the KABC-II to the KABC-II NU (Kaufman et al., 2018). Correlations with the WISC-V demonstrated high correlations between the FCI and FSIQ and higher correlations between similar construct scales/indexes than between dissimilar scales. Overall, results supported the constructs measured in the KABC-II NU.

Numerous published studies (see Drozdick et al., 2018; Kaufman et al., 2005; Mays et al., 2009) continue to support the construct validity of the KABC-II. The CFA completed for the original publication supported four factors for ages four to six and five factors for ages seven to eighteen, with the factor structure supporting the scale structure for these broad age groups. In addition, the factor structure has been supported in a reanalysis of standardization data for all age groups (Reynolds et al., 2007) and in preschool children ages four to five years (Hunt, 2008; Morgan et al., 2009). The four-factor structure was supported in preschool children; however, the data also fit into a five-factor model, similar to the broad ability factors laid out for the older children (Potvin et al., 2015). The factor structure of the KABC-II has been supported in high- and low-ability groups (Reynolds et al., 2007), across gender (Reynolds, Ridley, & Patel, 2008), across ethnicity (Fletcher-Janzen, 2003; Scheiber, 2016a, 2016b), and across cultures (Fujita et al., 2011; Kaufman et al., 2013, 2014; Malda et al., 2010).

Differential Ability Scales – Second Edition

The DAS-II measures the cognitive abilities of children and adolescents ages two years six months to seventeen years. Table 12.2 provides an overview of the properties of the DAS-II. It was adapted from the British Ability Scales, which was developed to assess the cognitive abilities of preschool and school-age children. The DAS-II is closely tied to the CHC psychometric theory of cognitive abilities but also incorporates research from multiple fields to ensure construct coverage, clinical utility, and examiner usability; however, it can be interpreted from multiple theoretical perspectives.

The DAS-II provides one global score, the General Conceptual Ability (GCA), which measures reasoning and conceptual abilities. It important to note that DAS-II does not use the term intelligence due to the ambiguity of the term intelligence and the use and misuse of the term intelligence in the general public. The DAS-II provides two batteries, the Early Years battery for ages two years six months to six years eleven months and the School-Age battery for children ages seven to seventeen years. The Early Years battery is divided into two levels: the Lower

Level for two years six months to three years eleven months and the Upper Level for ages four to six years. In addition to the GCA, domain-specific cluster scores are provided. The cluster scores available differ across ages following the developmental trend of increased cognitive differentiation with age.

The DAS-II contains twenty subtests across the age range, with different core and diagnostic subtests across ages. Core subtests are used to derive the core global and cluster scores, diagnostic subtests provide assessment of important, nonconceptual abilities related to performance on the DAS-II or in school, and allow for diagnostic clarity. The Early Years battery includes four core subtests and three diagnostic subtests in the lower level and six core subtests and five diagnostic subtests in the upper level. The School Age battery contains ten core subtests and eight diagnostic subtests. Many of the subtests were collected on children outside of the age range, allowing for out-of-level testing. The use of item response theory (IRT) to derive item sets for most subtests allows assessment time to be focused on the ability level of the child, rather than being tied to the chronological age of the child.

Standardization. The DAS-II was normed on 3,480 children and adolescents ages 2:6–17:11 stratified on age, gender, parent education level, race/ethnicity, and geographic region. It was linked to the KTEA-II, WIAT-II, and WJ-III ACH. A subsequent publication, the DAS-II Spanish Early Years (Elliott, 2012), provided adaptations and translations for all core and diagnostic subtests in the Early Years battery as well as new normative data collected in Spanish-speaking children.

Reliability. DAS-II reliabilities are high for all cluster scores and moderate to high for the subtests in both typically developing and clinical populations (Elliott, 2007). In addition, test-retest stability coefficients are moderate to high for the cluster scores and the core subtests. Finally, interscorer agreement was very high.

Validity. Correlational studies conducted for the DAS-II publication compared the test with several other cognitive and achievement measures (see Table 12.2). Results showed consistently high correlations between the GCA and the global intelligence scores on the other instruments. GCA tended to correlate more highly with the domain scores reflecting fluid reasoning or conceptualization abilities, and similar constructs across instruments correlated moderately. Subsequent factor analyses support the factor structure and measurement invariance of the DAS-II across the age range (Keith et al., 2010). Correlational studies with the measures of achievement produced moderate to high correlations between the GCA and the global measures of achievement and supported the constructs measured in the DAS-II. Clinical data were also collected within the DAS-II standardization (see Table 12.2). Spanish and American Sign Language translations of the nonverbal tasks were provided in the administration manual of the DAS-II.

Cognitive Assessment System – Second Edition

The Cognitive Assessment System – Second Edition (CAS-2; Naglieri, Das, & Goldstein, 2014a) measures the neurocognitive abilities of children and adolescents ages five to eighteen years. Table 12.2 provides an overview of the properties of the CAS-2. It is the only intelligence assessment tied exclusively to the PASS theory, integrating neuropsychological and information processing theory. The CAS-2 measures the four neuropsychological abilities observed across the three functional units described by Luria (1973), namely attention, memory/learning and information processing, and planning. The CAS-2 measures the three functional units through the abilities expressed in the cognitive abilities of attention, sequential processing, simultaneous processing, and planning. The abilities are not expected to be independent but to interrelate; thus, overall ability is also assessed.

The CAS-2 provides one global score, the Full Scale score that summarizes the child's overall cognitive ability. Like the DAS-II, the CAS-2 does not use the term intelligence in its global score, instead focusing on overall neurocognitive ability. The CAS-2 provides two batteries, the Core battery and the Extended battery. In addition to the Full Scale score, four core process-specific scale scores and five supplemental scale scores are provided. Core scale scores and the global score are the primary focus of interpretation and are given equal weight in interpretation. The core scale scores differ in composition across batteries with an additional subtest included in each scale score in the Extended battery. The CAS-2 contains thirteen subtests that each fall into one of the four cognitive abilities of the PASS theory. Core subtests are used to derive the core global and cluster scores; supplemental subtests provide additional assessment for the Extended battery and feed into the core and supplemental scales.

Standardization. The CAS2 was normed on 1,342 children and adolescents ages five to eighteen stratified on age, gender, parental education, race/ethnicity, and geographic region. In addition, a representative portion of individuals with exceptionality were included in the sample, comprising roughly 13 percent of the total sample. Exceptionalities included gifted and talented, ID, deaf and hard of hearing, ADHD, articulation disorder, TBI, developmental delay (DD), emotional disturbance, behavioral disorder, learning disability, physical or health impairment, language impairment, and ASD.

Reliability: CAS2 reliabilities are high for all scale scores and for the subtests in the normative sample and in most demographic and clinical subgroups (Naglieri et al., 2014a). Reliability is in the 0.70s for some subgroups, likely due to small sample sizes in the calculation of reliability. In addition, test-retest stability coefficients are moderate to high for the scales and the core subtests. Finally, interscorer agreement was very high.

Validity: Confirmatory Factor Analysis of the CAS-2 scores yielded support for the four factors described in the CAS-2 manual. Correlational studies conducted for the CAS-2 publication compared the test with several other cognitive measures and within several key clinical groups (see Table 12.2). Results showed consistently high correlations between the Full Scale and the global intelligence scores on the other instruments; however, they also demonstrated that the CAS-2 measures some unique aspects of intelligence, particularly in the area of planning. In addition, CAS-2 scores correlated moderately with measures of reading and mathematics achievement. Overall, clinical group results supported the clinical utility of the constructs measured in the CAS-2. A study of children with ADHD who took both the CAS-2 and WISC-IV demonstrated lower Full Scale IQ scores on CAS-2 than on the WISC-IV, primarily attributable to low scores on the Planning scale, a scale measuring abilities not directly measured in the WISC-IV (Naglieri et al., 2014a).

Woodcock-Johnson Tests of Cognitive Abilities – Fourth Edition

The Woodcock-Johnson Tests of Cognitive Abilities – Fourth Edition (WJ-IV COG; Schrank, McGrew, & Mather, 2014) was co-normed with the Woodcock-Johnson Tests of Achievement – Fourth Edition (WJ-IV ACH; Schrank, Mather, & McGrew, 2014a) and the Woodcock-Johnson Tests of Oral Language – Fourth Edition (WJ-IV OL; Schrank, Mather, & McGrew, 2014b). Table 12.2 provides an overview of the properties of the WJ-IV. The development of the initial Woodcock-Johnson battery (Woodcock & Johnson, 1977) was atheoretical and relied on the scientific-empirical method of test development, which used factor and cluster analyses to characterize the areas of cognitive functioning assessed. Subsequent revisions of the Woodcock-Johnson Tests have been heavily influenced by CHC theory. Ten core subtests compose the Standard battery and yield an overall cognitive ability measure called the General Intellectual Ability (GIA). Three subtests may be used as a brief assessment of cognitive functioning and yield a Brief Intellectual Ability (BIA) estimate. Eight additional supplemental subtests are designed to help with interpretation of results obtained on the ten core subtests.

Standardization. The WJ-IV COG was co-normed with the WJ-IV ACH and the WJ-IV OL on 7,416 individuals. This sample was stratified by geographic region, sex, country of birth, race, ethnicity, community type, parent education, type of school, type of college, educational attainment, employment status, and occupational level. Due to the length of the test batteries, a Multiple Matrix Sampling design was used in which different parts of a test battery were administered to random subsamples to total the complete norming sample. A core set of tests were administered to all participants and the remaining subtests were matrix sampled.

Reliability. Split-half reliabilities were moderate to high for the summary and subtest scores. For speeded tests or subtests with multi-point items, test-retest reliabilities were also quite high.

Validity. Validity was established through a combination of exploratory and confirmatory factor analyses that took place in three stages. Results supported a broad CHC factor top-down model that included nine broad CHC factors (i.e., *Gc, Grw, Gf, Gs, Gq, Gv, Glr, Gwm,* and *Ga*) as well as *g*. Subsequent factor-analytic research indicated that a four-factor model including Verbal, Working Memory, Processing Speed, and Perceptual Reasoning was a better fit for individuals ages nine to nineteen (Dombrowski, McGill, & Canivez, 2016, 2018). Correlations between the GIA, BIA, and *Gc-Gf* composite were highly correlated with main composite indices from several other tests of intellectual functioning (see Table 12.2). The clinical validity of the WJ-IV COG was also examined. It should be noted that, in order to avoid examinee fatigue, a diagnostic group-targeted approach was used in which a selection of subtests hypothesized to be clinically important for each diagnosis was administered as opposed to the full battery of all three WJ-IV tests. Patterns of results across clinical groups, age bands, and different demographic groups provide support for the primary WJ-IV clusters.

Stanford-Binet Intelligence Scales – Fifth Edition

The Stanford-Binet Intelligence Scales – Fifth Edition is the descendant of the original Stanford-Binet developed by Terman in 1916. It is a battery of ten ability subtests for ages two to eighty-five plus, which yields a FSIQ score. Separate verbal and nonverbal IQ scores can also be derived from these subtests. There are two forms: the standard form for ages two to eighty-five plus and an early childhood assessment for ages two to seven, which is derived from the standard version. The SB5 measures five cognitive abilities in both verbal and nonverbal domains and the composition and test structure are based on the CHC model.

Administration begins with routing subtests that are used to determine the ability-based starting point for the following subtests. The scores on these subtests can be combined to obtain an abbreviated battery IQ that provides an estimate of the individual's functional level. Based on the results of the routing subtests, the examinee is administered the nonverbal subtests of the SB5 and then the verbal subtests of the SB5. The nonverbal and verbal subtests are comprised of several testlets organized according to six different levels of difficulty; these were designed to be analogous to the age levels used on the original Stanford-Binet (Terman, 1916).

Standardization. The SB5 was normed on 4,800 individuals ages two to ninety-six stratified on age, sex, ethnicity, socioeconomic level, and geographic region. The standardization sample included individuals who were enrolled in special education services for less than 50 percent of their day (approximately 5 percent of the school-age sample). Otherwise, individuals who were members of special groups were excluded from the normative sample but included in the validity sample. The sample was stratified across thirty age groups.

Reliability. SB5 reliabilities were high for all index scores and moderate for the subtest scores. Test-retest stability coefficients were also moderate to high for the factor indexes, the IQ scores, and for the individual subtests. The stability coefficients are higher than observed in other measures, suggesting higher consistency of scores across testing. Interscorer agreement is also quite high.

Validity. Correlational studies were conducted with several other assessments of cognitive abilities and achievement. The FSIQ score from the SB5 was generally highly correlated with the overall cognitive estimates from these measures and the SB5 Verbal IQ was generally highly correlated with measures of reading and math achievement. Clinical data were also collected (see Table 12.2). Subsequent factor-analytic studies indicated that the two-factor structure (i.e., verbal and nonverbal abilities) was supported for preschool and school-age children but a single factor solution was the best fit for individuals over the age of ten (DiStefano & Dombrowski, 2006). Overall, results supported the clinical utility of the constructs measured in the SB5.

Shorter Batteries Assessing Intelligence

Multiple shorter batteries have also been developed to assess intelligence. Shorter batteries offer some of the same benefits as the comprehensive batteries, including global ability scores and evidence of reliability and validity but do not provide the same level of information provided in the comprehensive measures. There are many situations in which a shorter battery provides the information required from an intelligence measure. Some examples include evaluations in which intelligence is not a key element, group evaluations, screening for determining needs for further evaluation, evaluations requiring a large number of domains to be assessed, or research. It is important to ensure that the battery selected meets the needs of the evaluation. Shorter batteries are not recommended when diagnoses reliant on IQ are required, in evaluations of cognitive strengths and weaknesses, or for placement decisions. Comprehensive batteries provide greater depth of construct coverage.

Some short forms were developed from items or subtests of a comprehensive battery (e.g., short forms of the WAIS-IV developed by Denney, Ringe, and Lacritz [2015] or Meyers et al. [2013]). Kaufman and Lichtenberger (2006) recommend that practitioners utilize batteries developed as shorter batteries over the use of short forms derived from longer assessments to reduce the impact of order effects and statistical impacts on the norms derived for short forms. Some of the most common brief batteries used are the Reynolds Intellectual Assessment Scales – Second Edition (Reynolds & Kamphaus, 2015), Raven's Progressive Matrices – Second Edition (Raven, 2018), the NNAT, the Kaufman Brief Intelligence Test – Second Edition (Kaufman & Kaufman, 2004c), the Peabody Picture Vocabulary Test – Fourth Edition (Dunn & Dunn, 2007), and the Wechsler Ability Scale of Intelligence – Second Edition (Wechsler, 2011).

Technological Advances in Intelligence Testing

In its initial release, the Q-interactive digital platform served as a digital administration, recording, and scoring tool while maintaining paper stimuli, manipulatives, and response booklets used directly by examinees. More recently, paper response booklets were replaced with fully digitally interactive equated subtests. The transition from paper to digital required research supporting the acceptability of the user interface and the equivalency or equating of measures across formats. Equivalency studies ensure that differences in administration procedures between digital and paper do not significantly alter client performance in a way that makes standardization data collected on the paper format invalid for the digital format.

The subtests of the WAIS-IV, WISC-IV, and WISC-V were among the first to be examined for equivalence using a nonrandom equivalent groups method. For the WAIS-IV, an overrepresentation of older individuals and individuals with low educational status were recruited as these groups were anticipated to be most impacted by the new digital format of the tests (Daniel, 2012). In instances where the effect size exceeded 0.20, the standard set for equivalence, further investigation was completed to determine potential sources of differences. If differences were attributable to more accurate administration and scoring procedures in Q-interactive, corrections were not made to the digital platform. However, if differences were attributable to an effect of the digital platform (e.g., changes in client response requirements) modifications were made to the digital platform and then retested. After identifying and correcting errors with the digital interface, the majority of WAIS-IV subtests were found to be equivalent according to predefined effect size thresholds (Daniel, Wahlstrom, & Zhang, 2014).

Initial equivalency studies maintained paper response booklets for examinees. Hence, further testing was required when fully digital Coding and Symbol Search subtests were developed for the WISC-V (Raiford, Drozdick, & Zhang, 2016). Owing to the differences in response format, it was assumed that the paper and digital Coding and Symbol Search subtests were not equivalent and would require equating procedures. Changes to the digital build following two pilot studies yielded results that facilitated the development of equating procedures. A third pilot study found that children with clinical conditions did not demonstrate any adverse reactions to the new digital format of the Coding and Symbol Search subtests. An equivalence study conducted on the equated digital and paper scores demonstrated that the differences between the paper and digital subtests were not sufficient to result in a substantial difference between scores (Raiford et al., 2016).

Equivalency studies were also conducted for the WPPSI-IV (Drozdick et al., 2016). Early usability studies of WPPSI-IV subtests among very young children found that visible touch-state changes (i.e., highlighting a selected answer) were positively reinforcing in this age group and prompted additional touching not observed in older children and adults. As a result of this finding, visible touch-state responses were removed from the digital form of the WPPSI-IV. A sample of subtests representative of the different ways in which the examiner and examinee interact with the tablet was selected for this equivalency study. All subtests examined were determined to be equivalent.

Clinical Groups Equivalency Studies

Clinical equivalency studies with the WISC-V were conducted among children with intellectual giftedness, ID (mild), ASD with language impairment (ASD-L), ADHD, Specific Learning Disorder-Reading (SLD-R), and Specific Learning Disorder-Math (SLD-M) (Raiford et al., 2014; Raiford, Drozdick, & Zhang, 2015, 2016). Performance on the digital administration was compared to a demographically matched sample from the WISC-V paper standardization sample (variations in demographics occurred across groups and are described in the original research). Results from the digital version of the WISC-V demonstrated the expected performances for each group and were consistent with results from other comparison studies for the intellectually gifted, ID (mild), SLD-R, SLD-M, and ASD-L groups. Results were less consistent in the comparison studies for the ADHD group but were generally in the same direction as the comparison studies for the paper WISC-V. In general, results from the digital version of the WISC-V were consistent with previous research and with the literature describing these disorders, indicating that both versions assess the same target constructs (Raiford et al., 2014; Raiford et al., 2015, 2016).

A limitation of this initial clinical study was the lack of data from the digital processing speed tests, as these were under development at the time the research was conducted. During development of the digital versions of the WISC-V Coding and Symbol Search subtests, several groups were collected to evaluate clinical validity (Raiford et al., 2016). The clinical groups in this study included intellectually gifted, ID (mild), SLD-R, SLD-M, ADHD, ASD-L, and motor impairment. The demographics of these samples were matched with individuals from the normative sample of the WISC-V paper version, which served as the control group. In general, results were consistent with previous research and the clinical performances generally observed in these clinical populations. Among the group of individuals with motor impairments, scores on the Coding subtest remained lower than scores on the Symbol Search subtest, despite the reduction in motor requirements in the digital version. This discrepancy, observed in paper as well, may be due to task complexity and associative learning in the digital version and not to graphomotor speed (Raiford, Zhang et al., 2016).

TOWARD CULTURALLY COMPETENT INTELLIGENCE TESTING

Intelligence tests are uniquely controversial in the educational and psychological sciences, as well as public discourse. The abuses of results from intelligence testing are well documented. For example, the argument that general intelligence is unitary and predominately hereditable has been used to bolster an entire scientific literature on racial differences in results from intelligence testing (for recent examples, see Jensen, 2000; Rushton & Rushton, 2003). Fortunately, the study and practice of psychology are moving away from reductionist arguments of nature versus nurture toward examining the manifestations of genetics through environmental influences. For example, behavioral genetics research suggests that the heritability of IQ scores is moderated by socioeconomic status (SES; Turkheimer et al., 2003), such that low SES has a greater impact on IQ scores for children than middle or high SES. It is important to understand that intelligence tests, and their results, are the product of a specific culture and results may be less valid when applied to individuals who are not of the culture in which a measure was standardized (Sternberg, 1999). Although test developers utilize developmental approaches and psychometric methods to create culturally fair assessments, it is incumbent on the practitioner to develop habits that facilitate the unbiased interpretation of results.

Multiple Forms of Test Bias

It is important to understand different sources of bias, both statistical and nonstatistical, and the impact these biases can have on test results, interpretation, and on the individual being tested. Statistical bias focuses on properties inherent to the actual test, which is influenced by the content in the measure or the methodological approach to standardization, while nonstatistical bias focuses on the use of the test in clinical practice. This can include the knowledge, experience, and training of the practitioner, the physical environment of the testing session, and the interactions between the client and practitioner.

Aspects of a test's validity can present sources of bias, including differential content validity, statistical differences, and differential predictive validity (Ford, 2004). However, these types of bias are often heavily scrutinized during test development and are less likely to be a source of bias when using a well-developed and standardized instrument like the described measures. Expert reviews, statistical analyses of bias, and review of performance across demographic and clinical subgroups can help minimize test bias due to statistical sources of error.

Nonstatistical sources of error focus on predictive validity (how the use of test results leads to different outcomes for different groups). Potential sources of bias that may affect outcomes for different groups include the environment in which the testing takes place, the characteristics of the examiner administering the test, and the reaction of the examinee to these characteristics. For example, social psychology research indicates that the interaction between the examiner and the examinee can have a profound impact on standardized testing results, particularly when individuals from marginalized groups are taking the test and a "stereotyped threat" is activated (Steele & Aronson, 1995). Although this research has not demonstrated group differences in test results, it suggests that the behavior of the examiner may affect the examinee's test performance in unintended ways.

Approaches to Culturally Competent Cognitive Assessment

It is important to view intelligence testing through the lens of underserved communities in order to understand the controversy surrounding these tests. It is well documented that the average lower scores of traditionally underserved populations (i.e., African Americans, Hispanic Americans, and Native Americans) have a disproportionately negative impact on educational attainment and experiences, as members of these groups are frequently underrepresented in Gifted and Talented programs and overrepresented in Special Education programs (Council of State Directors for the Gifted and National Association of Gifted and Talented, 2015; Ford, 2004). Given this context, individuals from minority groups may be leery of intelligence testing. In order to develop unbiased interpretations of results from cognitive testing, it is important to identify the ways in which extraneous factors can impact assessment results. These include culture, ethnicity, and language (Howieson, Loring, & Hannay, 2004; Wong et al., 2000).

The influence of ethnicity on cognitive testing is reflected in the normative samples of published assessments as nearly all are stratified according to various subgroups of the population. The stratification variables are selected due to the expected impact of the demographic variables on performance and are collected in proportions representative of the overall comparison population (e.g., Wechsler, 2008). When interpreting results from cognitive testing, it is important to consider whether the sample drawn from the broader population is representative of the specific subpopulation (Ford, 2004). Subpopulation norms may offer additional information on how the examinee's performance ranks in relation to more demographically similar peers.

Demographic adjustments to normative data may be helpful when used appropriately. Differences in scores across subgroups on well-stratified normed measures are frequently small and have similar predictive and clinical value; thus the normative scores are valid for use across groups. However, in some cases, not making appropriate demographic adjustments may decrease the specificity of cognitive tests (Heaton et al., 1999; Heaton, Taylor, & Manly, 2003; Norman et al., 2000); particularly in cases where comparisons to a person's demographically similar peers help address the referral question. However, consideration for the ways in which demographic adjustments may have a differential impact on outcomes for examinees must also be considered. Manly and Echemendia (2007) observed that using subgroup normative data may lead to minority examinees not being placed in needed services, as their use can increase their scores above established cutoffs. In addition, the use of race/ethnicity in normative data ignores the underlying cultural, health, and educational factors that influence test performance disparities (Manly, 2005; Manly & Echemendia, 2007). Ultimately, the use of demographic adjustments should be made to answer the referral question. Practitioners must fully understand how demographic adjustments affect test scores, understand how to interpret these norms, understand the appropriate use of such norms, and apply these norms ethically (Brickman, Cabo, & Manly, 2006). For a comprehensive review on the topic of demographic adjustments, see Heaton, Taylor, and Manly (2003).

Language is an important factor in cognitive assessment, not only because it is a vehicle for building rapport but because it is an essential characteristic on which the examinee is evaluated. Although some difficulties can be overcome with the help of a translator, specialized training is required in order to not influence testing results by unintentionally helping the client or reporting inaccurate or incomplete answers to the clinician. Even with training, the implications of various translations of instructions and test questions are unknown and may influence the client in unintended ways (Wong et al., 2000).

Given the controversial uses and misuses of intelligence testing throughout history, it is important to highlight approaches specific to the culturally competent interpretation of these tests. It is first and foremost essential to recognize when the characteristics of an individual differ in ways that may impact their performance on an assessment. This requires a broad knowledge of different assessments of cognitive abilities as well as the types of samples on which these tests were normed. For example, the DAS-II includes directions for individuals who communicate with American Sign Language, and the WISC-V and DAS-II have been translated and normed for Spanish-speaking populations in the United States (Elliott, 2007, 2012; Wechsler, 2017). It is also important to maintain up-to-date knowledge of best practices in the culturally competent practice of psychology. The American Psychological Association (APA) recently updated its guidelines for the multicultural practice of psychology (APA, 2017). For more specific information regarding the culturally competent practice of psychological assessment, the interested reader is referred to *The Handbook of Cross-Cultural Neuropsychology* (Fletcher-Janzen, Strickland, & Reynolds, 2000).

The ultimate product of any psychological assessment is not the scores but the diagnosis, interventions, accommodations, and services justified by the interpretation of these scores. It is the clinical judgment of the examiner, gained through training and experience, applied to psychological test scores within context that serves to connect clients to services. Hence, cultural competence is an essential component of ensuring equal access to these scarce resources.

PERFORMANCE VALIDITY AND COGNITIVE TESTING

The ability to determine whether an examinee is putting forth their best effort within the context of a psychological assessment is important but often fraught with difficulties. The inherent nature of psychological assessment, inferring dysfunction based on behavioral observations in the absence of conclusive medical procedures or tests, leaves open to interpretation the question of whether a person's performance is a symptom of their neurological condition or fabricated in order to obtain a secondary gain. Several general indicators of low performance validity (i.e., determining whether or not an examinee's performance on a series of tests is consistent with the nature of their injury or condition; Pearson, 2009b) can be observed across an assessment. First and foremost are inconsistencies in test performance, which can include test results that are inconsistent with the referral information, scoring below chance on forced choice tests, and unlikely improvements in performance across multiple testing sessions. Other examples include relatively poor performance on sensory and motor tasks in the presence of good performance on tests of higher cognitive functioning. Complaints of memory problems including poor performance on simple digit span tasks, in the absence of a speech or language disorder, and/or good performance on other tests of verbal memory can also indicate low performance validity (Howieson et al., 2004). The presence of severe symptoms disproportionate to the injury sustained may also be a sign of low performance validity (Mittenburg et al., 2002). Because it is difficult to attribute willful manipulation of test results to a client, the term malingering is infrequently used. Rather, the discrepancy between the test results and the nature of the presenting conditions is emphasized in reports (Pearson, 2009b). Additionally, a thorough understanding of the client's history and current status is essential in determining their insight regarding the nature of their difficulties.

In addition to general indicators, there are also measures of performance validity. These fall into two categories: independent measures of performance validity, such as the Test of Memory and Malingering (TOMM; Tombaugh, 1997), and embedded measures of performance validity, such as Reliable Digit Span (RDS; Greiffenstein, Baker, & Gola, 1994, Pearson 2009b). Independent measures are designed to assess performance validity directly and often provide comparison data across multiple groups with different expected levels of performance. Embedded measures are included within larger batteries and may not be designed specifically for the assessment of performance validity. For example, RDS utilizes data from the Digit Span Forward and Digit Span Backward conditions of the Digit Span subtest on WAIS and WISC. Greiffenstein and colleagues (1994) defined RDS as the sum of the longest sequence of digits accurately repeated over two trials for both Digit Span Forward and Digit Span Backward. The ACS for WAIS-IV and WMS-IV also provides measures to assess effort using external and embedded measures, providing base rates for ten clinical groups (Pearson, 2009b).

Although performance validity is typically conducted in adult assessments, it is increasingly being done in psychological evaluations with children (e.g., Kirkwood, 2015). RDS has been studied as a potential measure of performance validity in the assessment of children and adolescents with the WISC-IV. Kirkwood, Hargrave, and Kirk (2011) examined the utility of RDS among a sample of children who were referred for an evaluation due to concussion. Within a broader neuropsychological evaluation, participants were administered the Medical Symptom Validity Test (MSVT; Green, 2004), the TOMM, and the WISC-IV Digit Span subtest. Children who failed both the MSVT and the TOMM were considered to have suboptimal performance validity. The scaled score of ≤5 on the Digit Span subtest had a sensitivity of 51 percent and a specificity of 95 percent in classifying children with suboptimal performance. An RDS of ≤6 was found to have a sensitivity of 51 percent and a specificity of 92 percent in identifying children with suboptimal performance (Kirkwood et al., 2011). Kirkwood and colleagues (2011) make an important developmental distinction when evaluating children for suboptimal performance. They noted that the majority of children in their sample were not eligible for a tangible secondary gain (e.g., financial compensation or disability services) and suggest that the motivations of children to perform poorly may be more varied than observed in adults.

INTERPRETING COGNITIVE ABILITY TESTS

The proper interpretation of cognitive assessment results begins with an acknowledgment of cognitive errors and biases that lead to invalid interpretations. Several of these errors include, but are not limited to, the overgeneralization of test findings in which a set of findings is used to support conclusions beyond what the data support, confirmation bias or the tendency to focus on data that supports one's preexisting theory and to ignore data that contradicts it, and the over- or underinterpretation of data (Hannay & Lezak, 2004). Many of these phenomena can be combated by utilizing base rates, the likelihood that an individual in a population will achieve a specific score or pattern of scores on a test (Meehl & Rosen, 1955), when drawing inferences from psychological assessments.

Although most intelligence tests provide a singular, omnibus, estimate of overall cognitive ability, best practices discourage drawing diagnostic conclusions based on this estimate (Lezak, Howieson, & Loring, 2004; Lichtenberger & Kaufman, 2009; Sattler & Ryan, 2009). Overall scores such as the FSIQ from the Wechsler scales or the FCI or MPI from the KABC-II do not reflect the individual's pattern of strengths and weaknesses that often provides clues into the nature of a person's deficit and informs treatment recommendations (Sattler & Ryan, 2009). Several approaches to the interpretation of the Wechsler scales have been developed that are equally applicable to other tests of cognitive abilities and that provide habits of thought that prevent the clinician from overinterpreting singular IQ scores. Sattler and Ryan (2009) utilize profile or scatter analysis as a means of interpreting the Wechsler scales. This procedure allows for the comparison of the examinee's individual subtest and index scores in order to identify that person's unique set of strengths and weaknesses. Differences between scaled or standard scores are sufficient to draw meaningful hypotheses when there is a statistically significant difference between scores or when a score discrepancy is infrequently found in the standardization sample (i.e., the base rate; Sattler & Ryan [2009]). Although this approach utilizes multiple data points in order to generate hypotheses regarding an individual's functioning, results from a profile analysis alone are not sufficient in drawing diagnostic conclusions (Sattler & Ryan, 2009).

In addition to understanding the mechanics of interpreting cognitive tests, it is important to cultivate a holistic approach to test interpretation that looks beyond the numbers to the person and the context within which the scores are generated. Lichtenberger and Kaufman (2009) describe an approach to test interpretation that places the scores within the context of the client's lived experience, the testing environment, the theoretical framework from which the test was created, and data from additional tests, which the authors refer to as the *Intelligent Testing Philosophy*. This approach emphasizes the potential of the examinee and the limitations of the assessment measures, as the results from a test should be interpreted as a snapshot of the examinee's abilities and the behaviors assessed by any given measure are not exhaustive. The artifice of the testing environment is also noted, as standardized test administration procedures create an environment that limits the generalizability of the test's findings (Lichtenberger & Kaufman, 2009). During the course of an evaluation, it is important to generate and test hypotheses and results with the guidance of a theoretical model. Although it is sometimes helpful to apply the theoretical model on which the test was created, test results can be interpreted through the lens of other theoretical models as well (Lichtenberger & Kaufman, 2009). Finally, it is important to support or disconfirm one's hypotheses using multiple levels of analysis (e.g., standardized tests, questionnaires, and behavioral observations) from multiple sources of information (e.g., parents, caregivers, teachers; Lichtenberger & Kaufman, 2009).

Regardless of one's approach to and philosophy of intelligence test interpretation, it is essential to never focus on the scores to the exclusion of the person completing the tests. It is equally important to never view the results from any single measure of cognitive functioning, even an intelligence test, as the sum total of a person's skills and abilities. Results from intelligence tests should only serve as a launching point for testing hypotheses regarding the individual's overall cognitive functioning and results should be supported by additional evidence gathered at multiple levels of analysis and from multiple sources. The history of psychological testing is rife with examples of clinicians engaging in unintelligent interpretations of assessment data that cast a shadow over standardized testing to this day.

In 1912, the psychologist Henry Goddard published *The Kallikak Family: A Study in the Heredity of Feeble-Mindedness*. The book's premise was to establish the heritability of "feeble-mindedness" or low intellectual functioning through a full genealogy of Deborah Kallikak, a patient of Dr. Goddard's. Interpretations of intelligence test scores and genealogy provide excellent examples of overgeneralization and overinterpretation of insufficient data. Results from repeated administration of the Binet Scales, indicated a mental level above nine years of age resulting in a diagnosis of "high grade feeble-minded person" or "moron." Inherent in this diagnosis is the assumption that the Binet Scales captured a full sample of intelligent behavior. In order to support his conclusions about hereditability through a genealogy of the Kallikak family, no consideration was given to the social, economic, and cultural contexts in which the branches of the family developed.

Within the context of the time it was written, this book serves as a useful warning of how far biases in judgment and errors of thought can lead one astray. Dr. Goddard used his theory of the hereditability of intelligence to justify the forced sterilization of "feeble-minded" individuals with the ultimate goal of establishing colonies in which those who were deemed "feeble-minded" were to be segregated from the "normal" population. This book supported public policy initiatives across the United States of sterilization programs that were ongoing until a few years ago. The last known program sterilized 148 female prisoners, without their consent, in California between 2006 and 2010 (Schwartz, 2014). Although it is highly unlikely that the interpretation of any single psychological assessment will lead to dire outcomes such as this, poor test interpretation practices can have an enormously negative impact on examinees including, but not limited to, denial or loss of services, misdiagnosis, and perpetuating stereotypes.

REFERENCES

Abad, F. J., Sorrel, M. A., Roman, F. J., & Colom, R. (2016). The relationships between WAIS-IV factor index scores and educational level: A bifactor model approach. *Psychological Assessment, 28*, 987–1000.

AERA (American Educational Research Association), APA (American Psychological Association), & NCME (National Council on Measurement in Education). (2014). *The standards for educational and psychological testing*. Washington, DC: Author.

Ang, S., VanDyne, L., & Tan, M. I. (2011). Cultural intelligence. In R. J. Sternberg & S. B. Kaufman (Eds.) *Cambridge handbook of intelligence* (pp. 582–602). Cambridge: Cambridge University Press.

APA (American Psychological Association). (2017). *Multicultural guidelines: An ecological approach to context, identity, and intersectionality*. www.apa.org/about/policy/multicultural-guidelines.pdf

Archer, R. P., Buffington-Vollum, J. K., Stredny, R., & Handel, R. W. (2006). A survey of psychological test use patterns among forensic psychologists. *Journal of Personality Assessment, 87*, 84–94. https://doi.org/10.1207/s15327752jpa8701_07

Bayley, N. (2006). *Bayley scales of infant and toddler development* (3rd ed.). San Antonio, TX: Harcourt Assessment.

Benson, N., Hulac, D. M., & Kranzler, J. H. (2010). Independent examination of the Wechsler Adult Intelligence Scale-Fourth Edition (WAIS-IV): What does the WAIS-IV measure? *Psychological Assessment, 22*(1), 121–130. https://doi.org/10.1037/a0017767

Bjorklund, D. F. (2012). *Children's thinking: Cognitive development and individual differences* (5th ed.). Belmont, CA: Wadsworth/Cengage Learning.

Blalock, L. D., & McCabe, D. P. (2011). Proactive interference and practice effects in visuospatial working memory span task performance. *Memory, 19*(1), 83–91. https://doi.org/10.1080/09658211.2010.537035

Bowden, S. C., Saklofske, D. H., & Weiss, L. G. (2011a). Augmenting the core battery with supplementary subtests: Wechsler Adult Intelligence Scale-IV measurement invariance across the United States and Canada. *Assessment, 18*, 133–140.

Bowden, S. C., Saklofske, D. H., & Weiss, L. G. (2011b). Invariance of the measurement model underlying the Wechsler Adult Intelligence Scale-IV in the United States and Canada. *Educational and Psychological Measurement, 71*, 186–189.

Bracken, B. A. (1998). *Bracken basic concept scale – Revised*. San Antonio, TX: Psychological Corporation.

Bracken, B.A., & McCallum, R.S. (1998). *Universal nonverbal intelligence test*. Riverside Publishing.

Brickman, A. M., Cabo, R., & Manly, J. J. (2006). Ethical issues in cross-cultural neuropsychology. *Applied Neuropsychology, 13*, 91–100.

Brown, T. E. (1996). *Brown attention deficit disorder scales for adolescents and adults*. Bloomington, MN: Pearson.

Bunting, M. (2006). Proactive interference and item similarity in working memory. *Journal of Experimental Psychology: Learning, Memory, and Cognition, 32*(2), 183–196. https://doi.org/10.1037/0278-7393.32.2.183

Camara, W. J., Nathan, J. S., & Puente, A. E. (2000). Psychological test usage: Implications in professional psychology. *Professional Psychology: Research and Practice, 31*(2), 141–154.

Canivez, G. L., Watkins, M. W., & Dombrowski, S. C. (2016). Factor structure of the Wechsler Intelligence Scale for Children-Fifth Edition: Exploratory factor analyses with the 16 primary and secondary subtests. *Psychological Assessment, 28*(8), 975–986.

Canivez, G. L., Watkins, M. W., & Dombrowski, S. C. (2017). Structural validity of the Wechsler Intelligence Scale for Children-Fifth Edition: Confirmatory factor analyses with the 16 primary and secondary subtests. *Psychological Assessment, 29*(4), 458–472.

Carroll, J. B. (1993). *Human cognitive abilities: A survey of factor-analytic studies*. Cambridge: Cambridge University Press.

Cattell, R. B. (1941). Some theoretical issues in adult intelligence testing. *Psychological Bulletin, 38*, 592.

Cattell, R. B. (1943). The measurement of adult intelligence. *Psychological Bulletin, 40*, 153–193.

Chen, H., Zhang, O., Raiford, S. E., Zhu, J., & Weiss, L. G. (2015). Factor invariance between genders on the Wechsler Intelligence Scale for Children-Fifth Edition. *Personality and Individual Differences, 86*, 1–5.

Cohen, M. J. (1997). *Children's memory scale*. San Antonio, TX: Psychological Corporation.

Cottrell, J. M., & Barrett, C. A. (2017). Examining school psychologists' perspectives about specific learning disabilities: Implications for practice. *Psychology in the Schools, 54* (3), 294–308. doi:10.1002/pits.21997

Council of State Directors for the Gifted and National Association of Gifted and Talented. (2015). *State of the States in Gifted Education: Policy and Practice Data*. www.nagc.org/sites/default/files/key%20reports/2014-2015%20State%20of%20the%20States%20%28final%29.pdf

Daniel, M. H. (2012). *Q-interactive technical report 1: Equivalence of Q-interactive administered cognitive tasks: WAIS-IV*. Bloomington, MN: Pearson. www.helloq.com/research.html

Daniel, M. H., Wahlstrom, D., & Zhang, O. (2014). *Q-interactive technical report 8: Equivalence of Q-interactive and paper administrations cognitive tasks: WISC-V*. Bloomington, MN: Pearson. www.helloq.com/research.html

Das, J. P., Naglieri, J. A., & Kirby, J. R. (1994). Assessment of cognitive processes: The PASS theory of intelligence. Needham Heights, MA: Allyn & Bacon.

Deary, I. J. (2014). The stability of intelligence from childhood to old age. *Current Directions in Psychological Science, 23*, 239–245.

Deary, I. J., Weiss, A., & Batty, G. D. (2010). Intelligence and personality as predictors of illness and death: How researchers in differential psychology and chronic disease epidemiology are collaborating to understand and address health inequalities. *Psychological Science in the Public Interest, 11*(2), 53–79.

Deary, I. J., Yang, J., Davies, G., Harris, S. E., Tenesa, A., Liewald, D. et al. (2012). Genetic contributions to stability and change in intelligence from childhood to old age. *Nature, 482*, 212–215.

Dehn, M. J. (2013). Enhancing SLD diagnoses through the identification of psychological processing deficits. *The Educational and Developmental Psychologist, 30*(2), 119–139. https://doi.org/10.1017/edp.2013.19

Delis, D. C., Kaplan, E., & Kramer, J. H. (2001). *Delis-Kaplan executive function system*. San Antonio, TX: Psychological Corporation.

Delis, D. C., Kramer, J. H., Kaplan, E., & Ober, B. A. (2000). *California verbal learning test* (2nd ed.). San Antonio, TX: Psychological Corporation.

Denney, D. A., Ringe, W. K., & Lacritz, L. H. (2015). Dyadic short forms of the Wechsler Adult Intelligence Scale-IV. *Archives of Clinical Neuropsychology, 30*(5), 404–412. https://doi.org/10.1093/arclin/acv035

DiStefano, C., & Dombrowski, S. C. (2006). Investigating the theoretical structure of the Stanford–Binet-Fifth Edition. *Journal of Psychoeducational Assessment, 24*(2), 123–126. https://doi.org/10.1177/0734282905285244

Dombrowski, S. C., McGill, R. J., & Canivez, G. L. (2016). Exploratory and hierarchical factor analysis of the WJ-IV Cognitive at school age. *Psychological Assessment. 29*(4), 394–407. https://doi.org/dx.doi.org/10.1037/pas0000350

Dombrowski, S. C., McGill, R. J., & Canivez, G. L. (2018). An alternative conceptualization of the theoretical structure of the Woodcock-Johnson IV Tests of Cognitive Abilities at school age: A confirmatory factor analytic investigation. *Archives of Scientific Psychology, 6*, 1–13. http://dx.doi.org/10.1037/arc0000039

Drozdick, L. W., Getz, K., Raiford, S. E., & Zhang, O. (2016). *Q-interactive technical report 14: WPPSI-IV: Equivalence of Q-interactive and paper formats*. Bloomington, MN: Pearson. www.helloq.com/research.html

Drozdick, L. W., Holdnack, J. A., Weiss, L. G., & Zhou, X. (2013). Overview of the WAIS-IV/WMS-IV/ACS. In J. A. Holdnack, L W. Drozdick, L. G. Weiss, & G. L. Iverson (Eds.), *WAIS-IV, WMS-IV, and ACS: Advanced clinical interpretation* (pp. 1–73). San Diego, CA: Academic Press.

Drozdick, L. W., Singer, J. K., Lichtenberger, E. O., Kaufman, J. C., Kaufman, A. S., & Kaufman, N. L. (2018). The Kaufman Assessment Battery for Children-second edition and the KABC-II Normative Update. In D. Flanagan & P. Harrison (Eds.), *Contemporary intellectual assessment: Theories, tests, and issues* (4th ed.). New York: Guilford Press.

Dunn, L. M., & Dunn, D. M. (2007). *Peabody picture vocabulary test* (4th ed.). San Antonio, TX: Pearson.

Ehrler, D. J., & McGhee, R. L. (2008). *Primary test of nonverbal intelligence*. Austin, TX: PRO-ED.

Elliott, C. D. (2007). *Differential ability scales* (2nd ed.). San Antonio, TX: Harcourt Assessment.

Elliott, C. D. (2012). *Differential ability scales: Early Years Spanish supplement* (2nd ed.). Bloomington, MN: Pearson.

Flanagan, D. P., & Alfonso, V. C. (2017). *Essentials of WISC-V assessment*. Hoboken, NJ: John Wiley & Sons.

Flanagan, D. P., & Dixon, S. G. (2014). The Cattell-Horn-Carroll theory of cognitive abilities. In *Encyclopedia of Special Education*. Hoboken, NJ: John Wiley & Sons. https://doi.org/10.1002/9781118660584.ese0431

Flanagan, D. P., & McGrew, K. S. (1998). Interpreting intelligence tests from contemporary Gf-Gc theory: Joint confirmatory factor analysis of the WJ-R and KAIT in a non-white sample. *Journal of School Psychology, 36*(2), 151–182. https://doi.org/10.1016/s0022-4405(98)00003-x

Flanagan, D. P., McGrew, K. S., & Ortiz, S. O. (2000). *The Wechsler intelligence scales and Gf-Gc theory: A contemporary approach to interpretation*. Boston, MA: Allyn & Bacon.

Flanagan, D. P., Ortiz, S. O., & Alfonso, V. C. (2013). *Essentials of cross-battery assessment* (3rd ed.). Hoboken, NJ: John Wiley & Sons.

Fletcher-Janzen, E. (2003). *A validity study of the KABC-II and the Taos Pueblo children of New Mexico*. Circle Pines, MN: American Guidance Service.

Fletcher-Janzen, E., Strickland, T. L., & Reynolds, C. (2000). *Handbook of cross-cultural neuropsychology*. New York: Springer Publishing.

Flynn, J. R. (1984). The mean IQ of Americans: Massive gains 1932 to 1978. *Psychological Bulletin, 95*(1), 29–51. https://doi.org/10.1037//0033-2909.95.1.29

Flynn, J. R. (1987). Massive IQ gains in 14 nations: What IQ tests really measure. *Psychological Bulletin, 101*(2), 171–197. https://doi.org/10.1037/0033-2909.101.2.171

Flynn, J. R. (1999). Searching for justice: The discovery of IQ gains over time. *American Psychologist, 54*(1), 5–20. https://doi.org/10.1037//0003-066x.54.1.5

Ford, D. Y. (2004). *The National Research Center for the Gifted and Talented Senior Scholar Series: Intelligence testing and cultural diversity: Concerns, cautions, and considerations*. Nashville, TN: Vanderbilt University.

Ford, L., Kozey, M. L., & Negreiros, J. (2012). Cognitive assessment in early childhood: Theoretical and practical perspectives. In D. P. Flanagan & P. L. Harrison (Eds.), *Contemporary intellectual assessment: Theories, tests, and issues* (3rd ed., pp. 585–622). New York: Guilford Press.

Fujita, K., Ishikuma, T., Aoyama, S., Hattori, T., Kumagai, K., & Ono, J. (2011). Theoretical foundation and structure of the Japanese version of KABC-II. *Japanese Journal of K-ABC Assessment, 13*, 89–99. [In Japanese.]

Goddard, H. H. (1912). *The Kallikak family: A study in the heredity of feeble-mindedness*. New York: The Macmillan Company.

Goldstein, G. A., Allen, D. N., Minshew, N. J., Williams, D. L., Volkmar, F., Klin, A., & Schultz, R. T. (2008). The structure of intelligence in children and adults with high functioning autism. *Neuropsychology, 22*(3), 301–312.

Goldstein, G., & Saklofske, D. H. (2010). The Wechsler Intelligence Scales in the assessment of psychopathology. In L. G. Wess, D. H. Saklofske, D. Coalson, & S. E. Raiford (Eds.), *WAIS-IV clinical use and interpretation: Scientist-practitioner perspectives* (pp. 189–216). London: Academic Press.

Gottfredson, L. S., & Deary, I. J. (2004). Intelligence predict health and longevity, but why? *Current Directions in Psychological Science, 13*, 1–4.

Gregoire, J., Daniel, M., Llorente, A. M., & Weiss, L. G. (2016). The Flynn effect and its clinical implications. In L. G. Weiss, D. H. Saklofske, J. A. Holdnack, & A. Prifitera (Eds.), *WISC-V assessment and interpretation: Scientist-practitioner perspectives* (pp. 187–212). San Diego, CA: Academic Press. https://doi.org/10.1016/B978-0-12-404697-9.00006-6

Green, P. (2004). *Medical symptom validity test*. Kelowana, BC: Paul Green Publishing.

Greiffenstein, M. F., Baker, W. J., & Gola, T. (1994). Validation of malingered amnesia measures with a large clinical sample. *Psychological Assessment*, *6*, 218–224.

Hammill, D. D., Pearson, N. A., & Wiederholt, J. L. (2009). *Comprehensive test of nonverbal intelligence* (2nd ed.). Austin, TX: PRO-ED.

Hammill, D. D., Weiderholt, J. L., & Allen, E. A. (2014). *Test of silent contextual reading fluency* (2nd ed.). Austin, TX: PRO-ED.

Hannay, H. J., & Lezak, M. D. (2004). The neuropsychological examination: Interpretation. In M. D. Lezak, D. B. Howieson, & D. W. Loring (Eds.), *Neuropsychological Assessment* (4th ed.). New York: Oxford.

Harcourt Assessment. (2005). *Wechsler individual achievement test* (2nd ed.). San Antonio, TX: Author.

Heaton, R. K., Avitable, N., Grant, I., & Matthews, C. G. (1999). Further cross validation of regression based neuropsychological norms with an update for the Boston Naming Test. *Journal of Clinical and Experimental Neuropsychology*, *21*, 572–582.

Heaton, R. K., Taylor, M. J., & Manly, J. (2003). Demographic effects and the use of demographically corrected norms with the WAIS–III and WMS–III. In D. S. Tulsky, D. H. Saklofske, G. J. Chelune, R. K. Heaton, R. J. Ivnik, R. Bornstein, et al. (Eds.), *Clinical interpretation of the WAIS–III and WMS–III* (pp. 181–210) San Diego: Academic Press.

Holdnack, J. A., Drozdick, L. W., Weiss, L. A., & Iverson, G. L. (2013) *WAIS-IV, WMS-IV, and ACS: Advanced Clinical Interpretation*. San Diego, CA: Academic Press.

Holdnack, J. A., Lissner, D., Bowden, S. C., & McCarthy, K. A. L. (2004). Utilising the WAIS-III/WMS-III in clinical practice: Update of research and issues relevant to Australian normative research. *Australian Psychologist*, *39*, 220–227.

Horn, J. L. (1965). Fluid and crystallized intelligence: A factor analytic study of the structure among primary mental abilities. Unpublished doctoral dissertation, University of Illinois, Champaign.

Horn, J. L. (1968). Organization of abilities and the development of intelligence. *Psychological Review*, *75*, 242–259.

Horn, J. L. (1972). State, trait and change dimensions of intelligence: A critical experiment. *British Journal of Educational Psychology*, *42*, 159–185.

Horn, J. L., & Cattell, R. B. (1966). Refinement and test of the theory of fluid and crystallized intelligence. *Journal of Educational Psychology*, *57*, 253–270.

Howieson, D. B., Loring, D. W., & Hannay, H. J. (2004). Neurobehavioral variables and diagnostic issues. In M. D. Lezak, D. B. Howieson, & D. W. Loring, *Neuropsychological assessment* (4th ed.). New York: Oxford University Press.

Hresko, W., Schlieve, P., Herron, S., Swain, C., & Sherbenou, R. (2003). *Comprehensive mathematical abilities test*. Austin, TX: PRO-ED.

Hunt, M. S. (2008). A joint confirmatory factor analysis of the Kaufman Assessment Battery for Children, second edition, and the Woodcock-Johnson tests of cognitive abilities, third edition, with preschool children. *Dissertation Abstracts International Section A: Humanities and Social Sciences*, *68*(11-A), 4605.

Hunter, J. E., & Schmidt, F. L. (1996). Intelligence and job performance: Economic and social implications. *Psychology, Public Policy, and Law*, *6*, 447–472.

Jensen, A. R. (2000). TESTING: The dilemma of group differences. *Psychology, Public Policy, and Law*, *6*, 121–127. https://doi.org/10.1037/1076-8971.6.1.121

Kaufman, A. S. (2009). *IQ testing 101*. New York: Springer Publishing.

Kaufman, A. S., & Kaufman, N. L. (1983). *Kaufman assessment battery for children*. Circle Pines, MN: American Guidance Service.

Kaufman, A. S., & Kaufman, N. L. (1993). *Kaufman adolescent and adult intelligence test*. Circle Pines, MN: American Guidance Service.

Kaufman, A. S., & Kaufman, N. L. (2004a). *Kaufman assessment battery for children, second edition (KABC-II) manual*. Circle Pines, MN: American Guidance Service.

Kaufman, A. S., & Kaufman, N. L. (2004b). *Kaufman test of educational achievement, second edition (KTEA-II) comprehensive form manual*. Circle Pines, MN: American Guidance Service.

Kaufman, A. S., & Kaufman, N. L. (2004c). *Kaufman brief intelligence test* (2nd ed.). Bloomington, MN:Pearson.

Kaufman, A. S., & Kaufman, N. L. (2008). *KABC-II batterie pour l'examen psychologique de l'enfant-deuxième édition*. Montreuil: Éditions du Centre de Psychologie Appliquée.

Kaufman, A. S., & Kaufman, N. L. (2014). *Kaufman test of educational achievement* (3rd ed.). Bloomington, MN: NCS Pearson.

Kaufman, A. S., & Kaufman, N. L. (2018). *Kaufman assessment battery for children, second edition, normative update*. Bloomington, MN: NCS Pearson.

Kaufman, A. S., & Kaufman, N. L., Drozdick, L. W., & Morrison, J. (2018) *Kaufman assessment battery for children, second edition, normative update manual supplement*. Bloomington, MN: NCS Pearson.

Kaufman, A. S., Kaufman, N. L., Melchers, P., & Melchers, M. (2014). *German-language adaptation of the Kaufman assessment battery for children* (2nd ed.). Frankfurt: Pearson.

Kaufman, A. S., Kaufman, N. L., & Publication Committee of Japanese Version of the KABC-II. (2013). *Japanese version of Kaufman assessment battery for children* (2nd ed.). Tokyo: Maruzen.

Kaufman, A. S., & Lichtenberger, E. O. (2006). *Assessing adolescent and adult intelligence* (3rd ed.). Hoboken, NJ: John Wiley & Sons.

Kaufman, A. S., Lichtenberger, E. O., Fletcher-Janzen, E., & Kaufman, N. L. (2005). *Essentials of KABC-II assessment*. Hoboken, NJ: John Wiley & Sons.

Kaufman, A. S., Raiford, S. E., & Coalson, D. L. (2016). *Intelligent testing with the WISC-V*. Hoboken, NJ: John Wiley & Sons.

Kaufman, A. S., & Weiss, L. G. (2010). Guest editors' introduction to the special issue of JPA on the Flynn effect. *Journal of Psychoeducational Assessment*, *28*(5), 379–381. https://doi.org/10.1177/0734282910373344

Keith, T. Z., Fine, J. G., Taub, G. E., Reynolds, M. R., & Kranzler, J. H. (2006). Higher order, multisample, confirmatory factor analysis of the Wechsler Intelligence Scale for Children – Fourth Edition: What does it measure? *School Psychology Review*, *35*, 108–127.

Keith, T. Z., Low, J. A., Reynolds, M. R., Patel, P. G., & Ridley, K. P. (2010). Higher-order factor structure of the Differential Ability Scales-II: Consistency across ages 4 to 17. *Psychology in the Schools*, *47*, 676–697.

Kellogg, C. E., & Morton, N. W. (2016). *Beta* (4th ed.). San Antonio, TX: Pearson.

Kendler, K. S., Ohlsson, H., Mezuk, B., Sundquist, J. O., & Sundquist, K. (2016). Observed cognitive performance and deviation from familial cognitive aptitude at age 16 years and ages 18 to 20 years and risk for schizophrenia and bipolar illness in a Swedish national sample. *JAMA Psychiatry; 73*, 465–471. https://doi.org/10.1001/jamapsychiatry.2016.0053

Kirkwood, M. W. (2015). *Validity testing in child and adolescent assessment: Evaluating exaggerating, feigning and noncredible effort*. New York: Guilford Press.

Kirkwood, M. W., Hargrave, D. D., & Kirk, J. W. (2011). The value of the WISC-IV digit span subtest in noncredible performance during pediatric neuropsychological examinations. *Archives of Clinical Neuropsychology, 26(5)*, 377–385. https://doi.org/10.1093/arclin/acr040.

Larsen, L., Hartmann, P., & Nyborg, H. (2008). The stability of general intelligence from early adulthood to middle-age. *Intelligence, 36*, 29–34.

Lezak, M. D., Howieson, D. B., Bigler, E. D., & Tranel, D. (2012). *Neuropsychological assessment* (5th ed.). New York: Oxford University Press.

Lezak, M. D., Howieson, D. B., & Loring, D. W. (2004). *Neuropsychological assessment* (4th ed.). New York: Oxford University Press.

Lichtenberger, E. O., & Kaufman, A. S. (2009). *Essentials of WAIS-IV assessment*, Vol. *50*. John Wiley & Sons.

Luria, A. R. (1973). *The working brain: An introduction to neuropsychology* (trans. B. Haigh). London: Penguin Books.

Luria, A. R. (1980). *Higher cortical functions in man* (trans. B. Haigh, 2nd ed.). New York: Basic Books.

Malda, M., van de Vijver, F. J. R., Srinivasan, K., & Sukumar, P. (2010). Traveling with cognitive tests: Testing the validity of a KABC-II adaptation in India. *Assessment, 17*, 107–115.

Manly, J. J. (2005). Advantages and disadvantages of separate norms for African Americans. *The Clinical Neuropsychologist, 19*, 270–275. https://doi.org/10.1080/13854040590945346

Manly, J. J., & Echemendia, R. J. (2007). Race-specific norms: Using the model of hypertension to understand issues of race, culture, and education in neuropsychology. *Archives of Clinical Neuropsychology, 22*, 319–325.

Markwardt, F. C. (1989). *Peabody individual achievement test-revised*. Circle Pines, MN: American Guidance Service.

Markwardt, F. C. (1997). *Peabody individual achievement test-revised/normative update*. Circle Pines, MN: American Guidance Service.

Mays, K. L., Kamphaus, R. W., & Reynolds, C. R. (2009) Applications of the Kaufman assessment battery for children, 2nd edition in neuropsychological assessment. In C. R. Reynolds & E. Fletcher-Janzen (Eds.), *Handbook of clinical child neuropsychology* (3rd ed., pp. 281–296). Boston, MA: Springer.

McFadden, T. U. (1996). Creating language impairments in typically achieving children: The pitfalls of "normal" normative sampling. *Language, Speech, and Hearing Services in Schools, 27*, 3–9.

McGrew, K. S. (1997). Analysis of the major intelligence batteries according to a proposed comprehensive Gf-Gc framework. In D. P. Flanagan, J. L. Genshaft, & P. L. Harrison (Eds.), *Contemporary intellectual assessment: Theories, tests, and issues* (pp. 151–179). New York: Guilford.

McGrew, K. S., & Evans, J. J. (2004). *Internal and external factorial extensions to the Cattell-Horn-Carroll (CHC) theory of cognitive abilities: A review of factor analytic research since Carroll's seminal 1993 treatise*. St. Joseph, MN: Institute for Applied Psychometrics.

Meehl, P. E., & Rosen, A. (1955). Antecedent probability and the efficiency of psychometric signs, patterns, or cutting scores. *Psychological Bulletin, 52*(3), 194–216. https://doi.org/10.1037/h0048070.

Meyers, J. E., Zellinger, M. M., Kockler, T., Wagner, M., & Miller, R. M. (2013). A validated seven-subtest short form for the WAIS-IV. *Applied Neuropsychology: Adult, 20*, 249–256.

Miller, D. C. (2013). *Essentials of school neuropsychological assessment* (2nd ed.). Hoboken, NJ: John Wiley & Sons.

Miller, D. I., Davidson, P. S. R., Schindler, D., & Meisser, C. (2013). Confirmatory factor analysis of the WAIS-IV and WMS-IV in older adults. *Journal of Psychoeducational Assessment, 31*, 375–390.

Mitrushina, M., Boone, K. B., Razani, J., & D'Elia, L. F. (2005). *Handbook of normative data for neuropsychological assessment* (2nd ed.). New York: Oxford University Press.

Mittenburg, W., Patton, C., Canyock, E. M., & Condit, D. C. (2002). Base rates of malingering and symptom exaggeration. *Journal of Clinical and Experimental Neuropsychology, 24*, 1094–1102.

Morgan, K. E., Rothlisberg, B. A., McIntosh, D. E., & Hunt, M. S. (2009). Confirmatory factor analysis of the KABC-II in preschool children. *Psychology in the Schools, 46*(6), 515–525. https://doi.org/10.1002/pits.20394

Naglieri, J. A. (2015). *Naglieri nonverbal ability test* (3rd ed.). Bloomington, MN: Pearson.

Naglieri, J. A., & Das, J. P. (1997). *Cognitive assessment system*. Itasca, IL: Riverside.

Naglieri, J. A., Das, J. P., & Goldstein, S. (2014a). *Cognitive assessment system* (2nd ed.). Itasca, IL: Riverside.

Naglieri, J. A., Das, J. P., & Goldstein, S. (2014b). *Cognitive assessment system – second edition: Brief*. Itasca, IL: Riverside.

Naglieri, J. A., Das, J. P., & Goldstein, S. (2014c). *Cognitive assessment system – second edition: Rating scale*. Itasca, IL: Riverside.

Niileksela, C. R., Reynolds, M. R., & Kaufman, A. S. (2013). An alternative Cattell-Horn-Carroll (CHC) factor structure of the WAIS-IV: Age invariance of an alternative model for ages 70–90. *Psychological Assessment, 25*, 391–404.

Norfolk, P. A., Farner, R. L., Floyd, R. G., Woods, I. L., Hawkins, H. K., & Irby, S. M. (2014). Norm block sample sizes: A review of 17 individually administered intelligence tests. *Journal of Psychoeducational Assessment, 33*, 544–554.

Norman, M. A., Evans, J. D., Miller, S. W., & Heaton, R. K. (2000). Demographically corrected norms for the California Verbal Learning Test. *Journal of Clinical and Experimental Neuropsychology, 22*, 80–94.

Oakland, T., Douglas, S., & Kane, H. (2016). Top ten standardized tests used internationally with children and youth by school psychologists in 64 countries: A 24-year follow-up study. *Journal of Psychoeducational Assessment, 34*(2), 166–176. https://doi.org/10.1177/0734282915595303

Pearson. (2009a). *Wechsler individual achievement test* (3rd ed.). San Antonio, TX: Author.

Pearson. (2009b). *Advanced clinical solutions for WAIS-IV and WMS-IV*. San Antonio, TX: Author.

Pena, E. D., Spaulding, T. J., & Plante, E. (2006). The composition of normative groups and diagnostic decision making: Shooting ourselves in the foot. *American Journal of Speech-Language Pathology, 15*, 247–254.

Potvin, D. C. H., Keith, T. Z., Caemmerer, J. M., & Trundt, K. M. (2015). Confirmatory factor structure of the Kaufman Assessment Battery for Children-Second Edition With

Preschool children: Too young for differentiation? *Journal of Psychoeducational Assessment*, *33*(6), 522–533. https://doi.org/10.1177/0734282914568538

Rabin, L. A., Barr, W. B., & Burton, L. A. (2005). Assessment practices of clinical neuropsychologists in the United States and Canada: A survey of INS, NAN, and APA Division 40 members. *Archives of Clinical Neuropsychology*, *20*(1), 33–65. https://doi.org/10.1016/j.acn.2004.02.005

Rabin, L. A., Paolillo, E., & Barr, W. B. (2016). Stability in test-usage practices of clinical neuropsychologists in the United States and Canada over a 10-year period: A follow-up survey of INS and NAN members. *Archives of Clinical Neuropsychology*, *31*, 206–230. https://doi.org/10.1093/arclin/acw007

Raiford, S. E. (2017). *Essentials of WISC-V integrated assessment*. Hoboken, NJ: John Wiley & Sons.

Raiford, S. E., Drozdick, L. W., & Zhang, O. (2015). *Q-interactive technical report 11: Q-Interactive special group studies: The WISC-V and children with autism spectrum disorder and accompanying language impairment or attention-deficit/hyperactivity disorder*. Bloomington, MN: Pearson. www.helloq.com/research.html

Raiford, S. E., Drozdick, L. W., & Zhang, O. (2016). *Q-interactive technical report 13: Q-interactive Special group studies: The WISC-V and children with specific learning disorders in reading and mathematics*. Bloomington, MN: Pearson. www.helloq.com/research.html

Raiford, S. E., Holdnack, J., Drozdick, L. W., & Zhang, O. (2014). *Q-interactive technical report 9: Q-interactive Special Group Studies: The WISC-V and children with intellectual giftedness and intellectual disabilities*. Bloomington, MN: Pearson. www.helloq.com/research.html

Raiford, S. E., Zhang, O., Drozdick, L. W., Getz, K., Wahlstorm, D., Gabel, A., Holdnack, J., & Daniel, M. H. (2016). *Q-Interactive technical report 12: WISC-V coding and symbol search in digital format: Reliability, validity, special group studies, and interpretation*. Bloomington, MN: Pearson. www.helloq.com/research.html

Randolph, C. (1998). *Repeated battery for the assessment of neuropsychological status*. San Antonio, TX: Pearson.

Raven, J. C. (2018). *Ravens 2 progressive matrices: Clinical edition*. Bloomington, MN: Pearson.

Reynolds, C. R., & Fletcher-Janzen, E. (Eds.). (2007). *Encyclopedia of special education: A reference for the education of children, adolescents, and adults with disabilities and other exceptional individuals*, Vol. *3* (3rd ed.). Hoboken, NJ: John Wiley & Sons.

Reynolds, C. R., & Kamphaus, R. W. (2015). *Reynolds intellectual assessment scales* (2nd ed.). Lutz, FL: Psychological Assessment Resources.

Reynolds, M. R., Keith, T. Z., Fine, J. G., Fisher, M. E., & Low, J. A. (2007). Confirmatory factor structure of the Kaufman Assessment Battery for Children—Second Edition: Consistency with Cattell–Horn–Carroll theory. *School Psychology Quarterly*, *22*(4), 511–539. https://doi.org/10.1037/1045-3830.22.4.511

Reynolds, M. R., Ridley, K. P., & Patel, P. G. (2008). Sex differences in latent general and broad cognitive abilities for children and youth: Evidence from higher-order MG-MACS and MIMIC Models. *Intelligence*, *26*, 236–260.

Rohling, M. L., Miller, R. M., Axelrod, B. N., Wall, J. R., Lee, A. J. H., & Kinikini, D. T. (2015). Is co-norming required? *Archives of Clinical Neuropsychology*, *30*, 611–633.

Roid, G. H. (2003). *Stanford-Binet intelligence scales – fifth edition: Technical manual*. Itasca, IL: Riverside.

Rowe, E. W., Kingsley, J. M., & Thompson, D. F. (2010). Predictive ability of the general ability index (GAI) versus the full scale IQ among gifted referrals. *School Psychology Quarterly*, *25*(2), 119–128. https://doi.org/10.1037/a0020148

Rushton, J. P., & Rushton, E. W. (2003). Brain size, IQ, and racial group differences: Evidence from musculoskeletal traits. *Intelligence*, *31*, 139–155. https://doi.org/10.1016/S0160-2896(02)00137-X.

Russell, E. W., Russell, S. L., & Hill, B. D. (2005). The fundamental psychometric status of neuropsychological batteries. *Archives of Clinical Neuropsychology*, *20*(6), 785–794. https://doi.org/10.1016/j.acn.2005.05.001.

Sameroff, A. J., Seifer, R., Baldwin, A., & Baldwin, C. (1993). Stability of intelligence from preschool to adolescence: The influence of social and family risk factors. *Child Development*, *64*, 80–97.

Sattler, J. M. (2008). *Assessment of children: Cognitive foundations* (5th ed.). La Mesa, CA: Author.

Sattler, J. M. (2016). *Assessment of children: WISC-V and WPPSI-IV*. La Mesa, CA: Author.

Sattler, J. M., & Ryan, J. J. (2009). *Assessment with the WAIS-IV*. La Mesa, CA: Author.

Scheiber, C. (2016a). Do the Kaufman tests of cognitive ability and academic achievement display construct bias across a representative sample of Black, Hispanic, and Caucasian school-age children in grades 1 through 12? *Psychological Assessment*, *28*(8), 942–952. https://doi.org/10.1037/pas0000236

Scheiber, C. (2016b). Is the Cattell-Horn-Carroll-based factor structure of the Wechsler Intelligence Scale for Children-fifth edition (WISC-V) construct invariant for a representative sample of African-American, Hispanic, and Caucasian male and female students ages 6 to 16 years? *Journal of Pediatric Neuropsychology*, *2*(3–4), 79–88. https://doi.org/10.1007/s40817-016-0019-7

Scheiber, C. & Kaufman, A. S. (2015). Which of the three KABC-II global scores is the least biased? *Journal of Pediatric Neuropsychology*, *1*, 21–35.

Schmidt, F. L., & Hunter, J. E. (2004). General mental ability in the work place. *Journal of Personality and Social Psychology*, *86*, 162–173.

Schneider, W. J., & McGrew, K. S. (2012). The Cattell-Horn-Carroll model of intelligence. In D. P. Flanagan & P. L. Harrison (Eds.), *Contemporary intellectual assessment: Theories, tests, and issues* (3rd ed., pp. 99–114). New York: Guilford Press.

Schneider, W. J., & McGrew, K. S. (2018). The Cattell-Horn-Carroll theory of cognitive abilities. In D. P. Flanagan & E. M. McDonough (Eds.), *Contemporary intellectual assessment: Theories, tests and issues* (4th ed., pp. 73–163). New York: Guilford Press.

Schrank, F. A., Mather, N., & McGrew, K. S. (2014a). *Woodcock-Johnson-IV tests of achievement*. Rolling Meadows, IL: Riverside.

Schrank, F. A., Mather, N., & McGrew, K. S. (2014b). *Woodcock-Johnson-IV tests of oral language*. Rolling Meadows, IL: Riverside.

Schrank, F. A., McGrew, K. S., & Mather, N. (2014). *Woodcock-Johnson–IV tests of cognitive abilities*. Rolling Meadows, IL: Riverside.

Schwartz, H. (2014). Following reports of forced sterilization of female inmates, California passes ban. *Washington Post*, 26 September. www.washingtonpost.com/blogs/govbeat/wp/2014/09/26/following-reports-of-forced-sterilization-of-female-prison-inmates-california-passes-ban/?utm_term=.0085bcae1945

Sotelo-Dynega, M., & Dixon, S. G. (2014). Cognitive assessment practices: A survey of school psychologists. *Psychology in the Schools*, *51*(10), 1031–1045.

Spearman, C. (1927). *The abilities of man, their nature, and measurement*. New York: Macmillan.

Staffaroni, A. M., Eng, M. E., Moses, J. A., Jr., Zeiner, H. K., & Wickham, R. E. (2018). Four- and five-factor models of the WAIS-IV in a clinical sample: Variations in indicator configuration and factor correlational structure. *Psychological Assessment*, *30*, 693–706.

Steele, C. M., & Aronson, J. (1995). Stereotype threat and the intellectual test performance of African Americans. *Journal of personality and social psychology*, *69*(5), 797–811.

Sternberg, R. J. (1999). A triarchic approach to the understanding and assessment of intelligence in multicultural populations. *Journal of School Psychology*, *37*(2), 145–159. https://doi.org/10.1016/S0022-4405(98)00029-6.

Sternberg, R. J., & Detterman, D. K. (Eds.). (1986). *What is intelligence?* Norwood, NJ: Ablex.

Strauss, E., Sherman, E. M. S., & Spreen, O. (2006). *A compendium of neuropsychological tests: Administration, norms, and commentary* (3rd ed.). New York: Oxford University Press.

Taub, G. E., & McGrew, K. S. (2004). A confirmatory factor analysis of Cattell-Horn-Carroll theory and cross-age invariance of the Woodcock-Johnson Tests of Cognitive Abilities III. *School Psychology Quarterly*, *19*(1), 72–87.

Terman, L. M. (1916). *The measurement of intelligence: An explanation of and a complete guide for the use of the Stanford revision and extension of the Binet-Simon Intelligence Scale*. Oxford: Houghton Mifflin.

Thorndike, R. L., Hagen, E. P., & Sattler, J. M. (1986). *Stanford-Binet intelligence scale* (4th ed.). Chicago: Riverside.

Tombaugh, T. N. (1997). The Test of Memory Malingering (TOMM): Normative data from cognitively intact and cognitively impaired individuals. *Psychological Assessment*, *9*, 260–268.

Turkheimer, E., Haley, A., Waldron, M., D'Onofrio, B., & Gottesman, I. I. (2003). Socioeconomic status modifies heritability of IQ in young children. *Psychological Science*, *14(6)*, 623–628. https://doi.org/10.1046/j.0956-7976.2003.psci_1475.x

Vig, S., & Sanders, M. (2007). Cognitive assessment. In M. R. Brassard, & A. E. Boehm (Eds.), *Preschool assessment: Principles and practices* (pp. 383–419). New York: Guilford Press.

Visser, L., Ruiter, S. A., van der Meulen, B. F., Ruijssenaars, W. A., & Timmerman, M. E. (2012). A review of standardized developmental assessment instruments for young children and their applicability for children with special needs. *Journal of Cognitive Education and Psychology*, *11*(2), 102–127.

Ward, L. C., Bergman, M. A., & Hebert, K. R. (2012). WAIS-IV subtest covariance structure: Conceptual and statistical considerations. *Psychological Assessment*, *24*(2), 328–340. https://doi.org/10.1037/a0025614

Watkins, M. W., & Beaujean, A. A. (2014). Bifactor structure of the Wechsler Preschool and Primary Scale of Intelligence – Fourth Edition. *School Psychology Quarterly*, *29*, 52–63.

Wechsler, D. (1955). *Wechsler adult intelligence scale*. New York: Psychological Corporation.

Wechsler, D. (2004). *Wechsler intelligence scale for children: Spanish* (4th ed.). Bloomington, MN: NCS Pearson.

Wechsler, D. (2008). *Wechsler adult intelligence scale* (4th ed.). Bloomington, MN: NCS Pearson.

Wechsler, D. (2009). *Wechsler memory scale* (4th ed.). Bloomington, MN: NCS Pearson, Inc.

Wechsler, D. (2011). *Wechsler abbreviated scale of intelligence* (2nd ed.). Bloomington, MN: NCS Pearson.

Wechsler, D. (2012). *Wechsler preschool and primary scale of intelligence* (4th ed.). Bloomington, MN: NCS Pearson.

Wechsler, D. (2014). *Wechsler intelligence scale for children* (5th ed.). Bloomington, MN: NCS Pearson.

Wechsler, D. (2017). *Wechsler intelligence scale for children: Spanish* (5th ed.). Bloomington, MN: NCS Pearson.

Wechsler, D., & Kaplan, E. (2015). *Wechsler intelligence scale for children: Integrated* (5th ed.). Bloomington, MN: NCS Pearson.

Weiderholt, J. L., & Bryant, B. R. (2012). *Gray oral reading tests* (5th ed.). Austin, TX: PRO-ED.

Weiss, L. G., Keith, T. Z., Zhu, J., & Chen, H. (2013a). WAIS-IV clinical validation of the four- and five factor interpretive approaches [special edition]. *Journal of Psychoeducational Assessment*, *31*(2), 94–113. https://doi.org/10.1177/0734282913478030

Weiss, L. G., Keith, T. Z., Zhu, J., & Chen, H. (2013b). WISC-IV and clinical validation of the four- and five-factor interpretive approaches [special edition]. *Journal of Psychoeducational Assessment*, *31*(2), 114–131. https://doi.org/10.1177/0734282913478032

Weiss, L. G., Saklofske, D. H., Prifitera, A., & Holdnack, J. A. (2006). WISC-IV: Advanced clinical interpretation. Burlington, MA: Academic Press.

Wilkinson, G. S., & Robertson, G. J. (2006). *WRAT4 wide range achievement test* (4th ed.). Lutz, FL: Psychological Assessment Resources.

Wong T. M., Strickland, T. L., Fletcher-Janzen, E., Ardilla, A., & Reynolds, C. R. (2000). Theoretical and practical issues in the neuropsychological treatment and assessment of culturally dissimilar patients. In Fletcher-Janzen, E., Strickland, T.L., & Reynolds, C.R. (Eds.) *Handbook of cross-cultural neuropsychology* (pp. 3–18). New York: Springer Science & Business Media.

Woodcock, R. W., & Johnson, M. B. (1977). *Woodcock-Johnson psycho-educational battery*. Rolling Meadows, IL: Riverside.

Woodcock, R. W., McGrew, K. S., & Mather, N. (2001a). *Woodcock-Johnson III: Tests of cognitive abilities*. Chicago: Riverside Publishing.

Woodcock, R. W., McGrew, K. S., & Mather, N. (2001b). *Woodcock-Johnson III: Tests of achievement instrument*. Itasca, IL: Riverside Publishing.

13 Achievement Assessment

JENNIFER WHITE, NANCY MATHER, DEBORAH ANNE SCHNEIDER, AND JENNIFER BRADEN KIRKPATRICK

Achievement tests are instruments designed to measure performance in a single academic domain or across multiple academic domains. They may be administered to groups or individuals. The information derived from achievement tests may be used for a variety of purposes in education, including formative evaluation, summative evaluation, course or program placement, and/or special education placement. The results may also be used to help identify specific learning disabilities, document an individual's strengths and weaknesses, design instructional programs, monitor progress, and conduct research. The most common types of these tests are comprehensive achievement batteries that measure many aspects of achievement; single subject area tests, such as reading, writing, or mathematics; curriculum-based measurements (CBMs), designed to provide ongoing evaluation of a student's progress toward curriculum-based achievement goals; and informal tests of achievement, such as teacher-made tests.

Comprehensive achievement batteries measure an individual's performance across major academic areas (reading, written language, and mathematics), whereas standardized single-subject tests measure performance in only one achievement area, though typically in much greater detail and depth. Both of these types of assessments are norm-referenced and produce scores that provide an estimate of an individual's group standing or rank relative to peers. CBMs are typically brief, time-efficient probes of achievement that are closely aligned to curricular and learning objectives. They may be standardized or nonstandardized and are designed to provide information that can be used to inform teaching on an ongoing basis (Hosp, Hosp, & Howell, 2016; Hosp & Suchey, 2014). As an example, a CBM probe of reading may constitute a one-minute timed test of reading fluency at grade level or at the student's instructional level, whereas a CBM probe of mathematics may include a one-minute timed test of subtraction problems, also at grade level or at the student's instructional level. Finally, informal measures of achievement include various types of teacher-developed assessments, such as oral and written exams. The results of these assessments may be used formatively, to monitor student progress and develop and revise instructional goals, or summatively, to assess student achievement at the end of a unit or course.

In this chapter, we provide a more thorough description of comprehensive achievement tests, single-subject achievement tests, and curriculum-based measurements. We also discuss advances in technology, issues related to achievement testing, matters of culture and diversity, and misuses and misinterpretations of achievement testing. Finally, we include several interpretive and practical recommendations for achievement testing.

COMMONLY USED COMPREHENSIVE ACHIEVEMENT TESTS

Three examples of widely used norm-referenced achievement tests are the Woodcock-Johnson Tests of Achievement – Fourth Edition (WJ ACH IV; Schrank, Mather, & McGrew, 2014a), the Wechsler Individual Achievement Test – Third Edition (WIAT-III; Wechsler, 2009), and the Kaufman Test of Educational Achievement – Third Edition (KTEA-3; Kaufman & Kaufman, 2014). See Table 13.1 for an overview of the major norm-referenced achievement tests.

Woodcock-Johnson Tests of Achievement – Fourth Edition

The WJ IV ACH (Schrank et al., 2014a) is a companion instrument to the Woodcock-Johnson IV Tests of Cognitive Abilities (WJ IV COG: Schrank, McGrew, & Mather, 2014b) and Tests of Oral Language (WJ IV OL: Schrank, Mather, & McGrew, 2014b). These three instruments form the Woodcock-Johnson IV (WJ IV: Schrank, McGrew, & Mather, 2014a), a comprehensive system of individually administered tests that is designed based on Cattell-Horn Carroll (CHC) theory to measure important broad and narrow factors. Overall measures include general intellectual ability, specific CHC abilities, oral language abilities, and achievement. Depending on the purpose of the assessment, the WJ IV batteries may be used independently,

Table 13.1 Major norm-referenced achievement tests

Achievement Battery	Standard Domain/Cluster Scores	Subtests	Normative Sample	Psychometrics	Scoring	Alternate Forms	Time
Woodcock-Johnson Tests of Achievement IV **Age range:** 2 years to 90+ years	Broad Reading Basic Reading Skills Reading Fluency Reading Comprehension Reading Rate Phoneme-Grapheme Knowledge Broad Mathematics Math Calculation Skills Math Problem Solving Broad Written Language Written Expression Basic Writing Skills Academic Skills Academic Fluency Academic Applications Academic Knowledge Brief Achievement Broad Achievement	20 subtests in standard and extended battery covering: Reading, Mathematics, Writing, Academic Knowledge (Science, Social Studies, Humanities), Oral Language subtests in separate battery	7,416 individuals ages 2 to 95 years; representing 46 states and District of Columbia (matching demographics of US population)	Cluster reliability over 0.90 ages 5 to adult Test reliability over 0.80 Content Validity – Compared to WIAT III (grades 1 to 8) and K-TEA II (ages 8 to 12) correlations: 0.50 to 0.90	Online only	3 alternate for the Standard battery only	-Core battery (subtests 1 to 6) 40 minutes; 5 to 10 minutes per subtest; Test 6 – Writing Samples – 15 to 20 minutes
Wechsler Individual Achievement Test III **Age range:** 4 years to 50 years 11 months	Oral Language Total Reading Basic Reading Reading comprehension Oral Reading Fluency Written Expression Mathematics Math Fluency Total Achievement	16 subtests covering Reading, Mathematics, Written Expression, and Oral Language	2775 students pre-K to grade 12; Stratified by grade, age, sex, race/ethnicity, parent education, geographic region to represent US demographics. Adult norms also available	Internal consistency reliability: .80 for all subtests but Listening Comp (.75) Validity – stronger correlations between math composites with intercorrelations ranging from 0.46 to 0.93 among 8 composite scores	Online using scoring software (Q-Global) or by hand	None	Average student K to 12th grades: 1 to 15 minutes per subtest 13 to 30 minutes for each composite
Kaufman Test of Educational Achievement 3	Reading Math Written Language	19 subtests covering Reading, Mathematics,	3,000 individuals ages 4 to 25 (age norms)	Internal consistency reliability range 0.72 to 0.98	Online using scoring software (Q-	2 alternate forms	Pre-K to 12th grades: 3 to 18 minutes per subtest

Continued

Table 13.1 (cont.)

Achievement Battery	Standard Domain/Cluster Scores	Subtests	Normative Sample	Psychometrics	Scoring	Alternate Forms	Time
Age range: 4 years to 25 years	Academic Skills Battery Composite Sound-Symbol Decoding Reading Fluency Reading Understanding Oral Language Oral Fluency Comprehension Expression Orthographic Processing Academic Fluency	Written Language, and Oral Language	2,600 individuals pre-K to grade 12. Based on two samples: Fall/Spring to Norming sample is representative of the US population related to race, ethnicity geographic region, special education status, gifted & talented status	Academic skills battery composite 0.98 a across grades and forms	Global) or by hand		7 to 35 minutes per composite 16 to 81 minutes Academic Skills Battery

in conjunction with each other, or with other assessment instruments. All of the tests are contained in two easel test books called the Standard Battery and the Extended Battery. A compact disk (CD) is provided with the technical manual and an audio recording is provided for the Spelling of Sounds test for standardized administration. The Extended Battery can be used with any of the three forms of the Standard Battery and includes tests that provide greater breadth of coverage in each academic area.

Normative data and psychometric properties. The WJ IV ACH was normed for use with individuals ranging from the preschool to geriatric ages. Grade norms are reported for each tenth of a year from grades K.0 through 17.9. The age norms are reported for each month from ages two through eighteen and then by one-year intervals from nineteen through ninety-five plus years of age. Complete technical information is available in the *Woodcock-Johnson IV: Technical Manual* (McGrew, LaForte, & Schrank, 2014).

Unique features. Two unique features of the WJ IV ACH are the variation and comparison procedures. For the intra-achievement variation procedure, the results from six core tests (two reading tests, two written language tests, and two mathematics tests) can be compared to determine relative strengths and weaknesses among the measures of achievement. An individual's obtained standard score for each test is compared to a predicted standard score that is based on the average of the other five core tests. For example, the standard score on Test 1: Letter-Word Identification would be compared to a predicted score that is derived from the average standard score obtained from the other five core tests. Additional tests and clusters can also be included in this comparison procedure.

For the ability-achievement comparison procedure, the Academic Knowledge cluster, which consists of the orally administered Science, Social Studies, and Humanities tests, can be compared to all other areas of achievement (reading, written language, and mathematics). This comparison helps evaluators determine if an individual's levels of reading, written language, and mathematics achievement are commensurate with their overall level of acquired academic knowledge and whether or not a more comprehensive evaluation should be considered. For example, the comparison can reveal that a student has significantly higher academic knowledge than basic reading skills, which can suggest the existence of a reading disability and should be explored more extensively.

Wechsler Individual Achievement Test – Third Edition

The WIAT-III (Wechsler, 2009) is another standardized, comprehensive assessment used in schools, private practice, and clinical settings. The WIAT-III provides information about the achievement of individuals, prekindergarten (pre-K) to fifty years, in reading, writing, math, listening, and speaking. Similar to the WJ IV ACH, this assessment can be used to assess specific skill areas or a broad range of academic achievement, based on the subtests administered. The WIAT-III is often used in conjunction with the Wechsler Intelligence Scale for Children – Fifth Edition (WISC-V; Wechsler, 2014) to provide a comprehensive evaluation of academic skills and intellectual abilities, as well as patterns of strengths and weaknesses between and within cognitive and achievement profiles.

To guide evaluators, the test kit includes two administration manuals: (1) the Examiner's manual, which includes guidelines for administration, scoring, and interpretation of results; and (2) a CD containing the Technical manual, which describes the development, standardization, reliability, and validity of the assessment. Administration materials correspond to specific subtests and include the Stimulus book for subtests including visual stimuli, the Oral Reading Fluency booklet for reading passages, the Word Card and Pseudo Word Card for reading isolated words and non-words, and an audio CD for listening comprehension.

Normative data and psychometric properties. The WIAT-III was most recently standardized in 2008 on 2,775 students in pre-K through grade 12. Adult norms are also available, based on a normative sample that was collected a year after the initial release of the WIAT-III. The WIAT-III technical manual (Breaux, 2009) provides detailed information concerning the instrument's psychometric properties and norming data.

Unique features. For the WIAT-III, the subtests that contribute to each composite score vary, depending on the grade of the individual being tested. For example, thirteen of the sixteen subtests contribute to the Total Achievement composite score but the Early Reading Skills subtest and Alphabet Writing Fluency subtest only contribute to the Total Achievement composite for grades Pre-K–1; the Oral Reading subtest score is available only for grades 2–12; and the Spelling subtest only contributes to the Total Achievement composite score in grades 2–12. This type of grade-dependent clustering is also present in the composite scores of Total Reading, Math Fluency, and Written Expression.

Another feature of the WIAT-III is that, depending on the purpose of the assessment, practitioners have the ability to interpret scores both broadly, through analysis of standard scores, and narrowly, through item-level skill analysis. The item-level skills analysis is available for seven subtests and identifies the skills involved in each item. For example, if an individual scores poorly on the Word Reading subtest, an item-level analysis can be completed through Q-Global. This breaks down each item into the specific features of the words read (i.e., morphology, vowel types, consonant types, etc.) for missed items, allowing evaluators to determine which skills the participant is having difficulty with and which specific skills area to target for intervention. The patterns of strengths and weakness analysis are available if the WIAT-III has been paired with the WISC-V, the Wechsler Preschool and Primary Scale of Intelligence – Fourth Edition (WPPSI–IV), the Wechsler Adult Intelligence Scale – Fourth Edition (WAIS-IV), the Differential Ability Scales – Second Edition (DAS-II), or the Kaufman Assessment Battery for Children – Second Edition (KABC-II) and will provide information comparing cognitive strengths and weaknesses to achievement strengths and weaknesses.

Intervention goal statements that provide examples of annual goals with short-term objectives are also available through the Q-Global program. These goals are based on the specific subtest skills on which the individual made one or more errors and include recommended intervention tasks to assist the practitioner with developing goals for individualized education plans and selecting academic interventions. As with all scoring software, an evaluator would also consider additional factors such as the student's background, educational history, classroom performance, and available resources when interpreting results and developing program goals.

Kaufman Test of Educational Achievement – Third Edition

A third comprehensive, standardized assessment is the KTEA-3 (Kaufman & Kaufman, 2014). Similar to the WJ IV and WIAT-III, this assessment is an individually administered battery with measures of reading, math, written language, and oral language. As with other standardized achievement tests, the KTEA-3 is designed for use in initial evaluations and reevaluations to gain information about specific academic skills and/or broad academic abilities, as well as to measure progress or response to intervention.

The KTEA-3 includes the following materials: an administration manual, scoring manual, stimulus books, written expression booklets, record forms, response booklets, and a stopwatch. The KTEA-3 includes a flash drive that contains the Technical and Interpretive Manual (Kaufman, Kaufman, & Breaux, 2014) and the audio files for administering the Listening Comprehension subtest. It also includes demonstrations of administration for several of the subtests, forms and normative data for hand scoring, qualitative observation forms, and letter checklists.

Normative data and psychometric properties. Normative data were collected for the KTEA-3 over two years (2011–2013). Half were tested in the fall and half were tested in the spring to create fall and spring norms. Approximately half of the norm group received Form A and half received Form B, to establish parallel forms. The KTEA-3 Technical manual (Kaufman, Kaufman, & Breaux, 2014) provides detailed information concerning the instrument's psychometric properties and norming data.

Unique features. The KTEA-3 content has been mapped to Common Core Standards and provides measures of the eight specific learning disability areas specified by the Individuals with Disabilities Education Improvement Act (IDEA; 2004), as well as areas of impairment listed in the fifth edition of the *Diagnostic and Statistical Manual of Mental Disorders* (DSM-5) (American Psychiatric Association, 2013). Additionally, the Administration Manual provides guidance for practitioners using a CHC approach to assessment as well as to those using an Information Processing Approach (Kaufman Kaufman, 2014).

Online scoring software Q-global is available for the KTEA-3. Optional error analysis with norm tables is also available. In this analysis, the number of errors made by an individual is compared to the number of errors made by grade-level peers who attempted the same items. Two types of error coding are included: item-level and within item-level analysis. In the case of item-level analysis, some subtests provide error categories that correspond to each missed item. For example, on the written expression subtest, practitioners can determine whether an individual missed an item due to errors in categories such as capitalization, punctuation, structure, word form, or task. Qualitative analyses of errors explain why an item was missed rather than just assigning an error category. For instance, on subtests such as Spelling, Nonsense Word Decoding, and Letter and Word Recognition, an examiner has the option to determine if errors were made for reasons such as using an incorrect vowel or consonant sound, confusing single and double consonants, or making errors on consonant blends and digraphs. By understanding the nature of individual errors, an evaluator can gain a much greater understanding of an individual's specific instructional needs. A special issue of *Journal of Psychoeducational Assessment*, devoted to research investigations on the kinds of errors students make on the KTEA-3 subtests, provides useful data for interpreting achievement errors – within the contexts of cognitive profiles and educational interventions – for both normal and clinical samples (Breaux et al., 2017).

Summary. Comprehensive batteries such as the WJ IV ACH, WIAT-III, and KTEA-3 are useful in evaluating student achievement across multiple content areas; however, there are situations in which using a comprehensive assessment of multiple domains is not the most appropriate choice. Single-subject achievement tests that focus on a specific academic area provide a more in-depth understanding of that particular skill and can also be more time- and cost-efficient than administering a comprehensive achievement battery.

SINGLE-SUBJECT ACHIEVEMENT TESTS

A variety of content-specific achievement tests are available for a more in-depth assessment in specific academic domains, such as reading, writing, and mathematics. Three examples of norm referenced, content-specific achievement tests are the Woodcock Reading Mastery Test – Third Edition (WRMT-III; Woodcock, 2011), the Test of Written Language – Fourth Edition (TOWL-4; Hammill & Larsen, 2009), and the Key Math – Third Edition (Key Math-3) Diagnostic Assessment (Connolly, 2007).

The WRMT-III provides an evaluation of a wide variety of reading readiness and achievement skills within nine subtests, including phonemic awareness, oral reading fluency, word identification, listening comprehension, passage comprehension, and rapid automatized naming. This comprehensive reading test is designed for individuals aged four years and six months to seventy-nine years and eleven months, as well as those in grades K–12.

The TOWL-4 is a diagnostic test of written expression that measures conventional linguistic and conceptual aspects of student writing such as vocabulary, spelling, punctuation, sentence building, and story composition. This assessment was intended for use with individuals between the ages of nine years and seventeen years and eleven months.

Finally, the Key Math-3 provides specific measurement of a range of essential math skills from rote counting to factoring polynomials. All subtests are categorized into three broad math abilities: basic concepts, operations, and applications to provide information about overall math achievement, as well as an individual's performance on particular math skills.

These types of single-subject assessments are valuable for identifying specific strengths and weaknesses in a particular subject area, developing detailed instructional goals, documenting growth and monitoring progress, and supporting decisions regarding additional educational services and supports.

CURRICULUM-BASED MEASUREMENTS

CBMs are brief, curriculum-aligned assessments of student's achievement, most often in the foundational skills of reading and math. These instruments have been shown to provide valid and reliable insights into students' progress and provide data that can be used to assess response to or effectiveness of instruction and inform instructional planning (Fuchs, 2016; Fuchs & Fuchs, 2002). Curriculum-based measurements – which may be norm-referenced, criterion-referenced, or both – are generally used to measure fluency in basic skills in a particular area over time. CBMs are considered general outcome measures and do not provide an extensive or thorough understanding of students' achievement in a broad domain. They can, however, provide practitioners with an overall indicator of student progress in a particular skill area. In schools, they often serve as critical data for making decisions in a Multi-Tiered System of Supports (MTSS) or a Response to Intervention (RTI) model for addressing students' specific academic needs. Within these models, the information obtained from CBMs is often used as part of a process of assessing individual student skills, growth, and response to instruction through frequent progress monitoring (Jones, Southern, & Brigham, 1998).

CBMs have a variety of uses in education and administration frequency may vary, depending on the assessment purpose. Typically, CBMs are administered based on student need – three times a year for universal screening and at regular intervals, often one to two times per week, for students in need of intensive intervention. In most cases, teachers count the number of correct responses and errors and then chart each student's score on a graph. When students also participate in the recording and tracking of their CBM data, they make more progress and have a greater understanding of and involvement in their own learning processes (Davis & Fuchs, 1995).

Extensive research supports the use of CBMs in the areas of reading, math, and writing, most commonly on timed tasks (Fuchs, 2016; Fuchs et al., 2001). CBMs used in these domains may include measurement of reading fluency on specific levels of text, solving math fact problems, and spelling words. The speed and accuracy with which tasks are performed have been linked to academic success, especially with respect to oral reading fluency (ORF). ORF is frequently evaluated using CBMs and provides a strong proxy measurement of overall reading proficiency, including comprehension (Fuchs et al., 2001; Shinn et al., 1992; Van Norman, Nelson, & Parker, 2018). Many CBMs use a measure of words read correctly per minute (WCPM), which is used to assess the rate and accuracy of ORF. Assessments that also include measurements of prosody and passage comprehension, in addition to rate and accuracy, provide a more precise measurement of ORF and comprehension ability (Valencia et al., 2010). To date, Hasbrouck and Tindal (2017) have published the most comprehensive set of ORF norms that provide benchmark guidelines for students in grades 1–6. Several popular, evidence-based CBM tools have been adopted by schools and districts for educators to use in their classrooms. Table 13.2 provides web addresses for several popular commercially available CBM tools.

Strengths of Curriculum-Based Measurements

The greatest benefits of CBM measures are that they are quick, easy to administer and score, sensitive to growth, and provide immediate feedback regarding student performance. This information allows educators to frequently gauge the success of an intervention as well as the student's response to instruction, so that instruction can be adjusted and altered accordingly, if needed. The information produced by CBMs can also be used as a piece of data in determining special education placement and services. CBM data in isolation, however, are not adequate to determine that a student has a disability. The main utility is to assist educators in finding interventions that work for students, as well as determining whether a student exhibits a need for specialized instruction.

Table 13.2 Websites that provide information on curriculum-based measurements (CBMs)

AIMSweb	www.aimsweb.com
CBM Warehouse	www.interventioncentral.org/cbm_warehouse
DIBELS	http://dibels.uoregon.edu
Edcheckup	www.edcheckup.com
FAST	www.fastbridge.org
McGraw-Hill	www.mhdigitallearning.com
National Center on Student Progress Monitoring	www.studentprogress.org

Specific training is required to ensure the fidelity of CBM administration and scoring procedures. Reliability checks should be in place to monitor fidelity. The process, however, does not require specialized knowledge and teachers, paraprofessionals, and even peer tutors can learn to administer CBMs correctly (VanDerHeyden, Witt & Gilberson, 2007).

CBMs are also cost-effective, as teachers can create materials or only need to print or copy the required materials. The flexibility in materials allows for adaptation to each student's learning goals. A further benefit of CBMs is the easy production of a number of alternate forms, allowing for repeated testing. Frequent administration and measurement help to track a student's progress over time, as opposed to measurement from one assessment at one point in time.

Weaknesses of Curriculum-Based Measurements

Despite their usefulness in measuring student growth and informing instructional planning, CBMs have several important limitations. Because CBMs are general outcome indicators, they only provide a general overview of a student's fluency in a given area. While CBMs produce a snapshot of a student's progress relative to specific curricular goals, they are not intended to provide an in-depth picture of student achievement across a domain. While they may be used as part of a multimethod, multisource, multisetting approach to assessment typically used in the schools (NASP, 2016), they are not meant to be used in isolation to make diagnostic inferences. Furthermore, the focus of many CBMs is on the measurement of the acquisition of fluency in basic skills, making them more appropriate for use in elementary settings than in secondary schools, where the subject matter becomes more complex and difficult to assess.

CBMs are fluency measures and thus timed tasks in which the speed of production is key. This may render them ineffective for students with significant weaknesses in processing speed and may produce anxiety in struggling students (Deeney & Shim, 2016). Moreover, CBMs may not adequately capture the progress of students who tend to work slowly and carefully. The validity and reliability of inferences produced by CBMs also vary greatly due to the lack of standardization among certain CBM materials, especially those that are teacher-designed. While commercially produced CBMs are often standardized, problems may occur when these assessments are not administered with fidelity. A final consideration is that potential differences exist for identifying students for additional intervention when using different instruments and cut scores to make screening decisions (Ford et al., 2017). For example, students have been shown to read fewer words using DIBELS Next than with Formative Reading Assessment System for Teachers (FAST) or AIMSWeb (Ford et al., 2017). Such differences in results could affect the type, frequency, and intensity of interventions prescribed. Thus, while there are a great number of advantages, these weaknesses need to be considered when using CBMs for assessment and progress monitoring.

TECHNOLOGICAL ADVANCES

Information and computer technology–based (ICT-based) assessments of achievement use digital technologies to generate, deliver, score, and/or interpret tests (Singleton, 2001). In this section, we provide a brief overview of the history of ICT-based assessments of achievement and a description of their current uses, as well as a discussion of the advantages and disadvantages of ICT-based achievement assessment.

Overview

Though rudimentary ICT-based assessment has been attested to as early as the 1960s (Rome et al., 1962), early computers lacked the processing power and storage capacity sufficient to facilitate ICT-based testing in the classroom environment. Consequently, their use in assessment remained limited through the mid-twentieth century. The use of computers to perform simple assessments of declarative knowledge began to develop in earnest in the United States in the 1970s; however, computer-based assessments of achievement generally remained constrained to the evaluation of content knowledge through the mid-1990s (Shute & Rahimi, 2017). By the late 1990s, computing capacity had grown to the point where it became possible to assess not only declarative knowledge but also problem-solving ability and other more complex academic skills using digital technologies (Shute & Rahimi, 2017). Today's ICT-based assessments have become even more sophisticated. While some continue to assess simple content knowledge much in the same way as paper-and-pencil tests, others immerse students in virtual worlds or simulations designed to stealthily evaluate critical thinking and practical application of learned skills. Many ICT assessments adapt to students' instructional level, streamlining the assessment process and improving the accuracy of evaluation (Shute et al., 2016).

Contemporary ICT-based assessments of achievement may be used for diagnostic, formative, or summative purposes. When used for diagnostic purposes, ICT-based assessments of achievement allow the evaluator to identify and target strengths and weaknesses in student achievement, often at key points during the instructional cycle, such as the beginning and end of a term. Diagnostic assessments may be used at the individual level to identify areas in need of remediation or they may be used at the cohort level to detect common gaps in students' learning. Similarly, formative ICT-based assessments provide feedback on students' learning, so teachers can adjust instruction at the individual or group level. Summative ICT-based assessments, by contrast, are used to evaluate student learning relative to expected achievement targets or learning goals, often at the end of a unit or course.

Whether it is for formative, summative, or diagnostic purposes, the use of ICT-based assessment of achievement has grown exponentially since its inception. An article in *Education Week* indicated that ICT-based assessments are rapidly displacing print assessments and their use is expected to increase by 30 percent in only three years (Molnar, 2017). Because the stakes of these assessments are often high, both in terms of monetary cost and in terms of educational decisions affected by student outcomes (e.g., placement, tracking, teacher evaluation, and school funding), it is important to understand both the advantages and the potential disadvantages of ICT-based assessments of achievement.

Advantages

ICT-based assessments of achievement have several potential advantages over traditional paper-and-pencil assessments. One important potential advantage is the availability of computer-adaptive testing. ICT-based assessments may be designed such that item difficulty and/or content are adaptive in response to student performance on previous items, streamlining the assessment and ensuring that the item difficulty remains consistent with the student's actual level of proficiency. This increased efficiency leads to reduced fatigue, boredom, and frustration for students. On a computer-adaptive assessment, when a student answers an item or items correctly, the next item may increase in difficulty, whereas when a student answers an item or items incorrectly, the next item may decrease in difficulty. It is therefore possible to quickly establish, with fewer items, a student's present level of proficiency. Furthermore, the potential for administration of out-of-grade–level items improves both measurement accuracy and test efficiency for students who perform significantly above or below their grade-level peers (Wei & Lin, 2015). By contrast, most paper-and-pencil tests require all students to answer the same questions, without respect to the proficiency level of the individual student. As a result, such tests may provide little information about individual students whose proficiency levels differ substantially from the level for which the test was designed.

As ICT-based tests of achievement have become more sophisticated, item pools have grown larger, potentially improving content validity by providing broader construct coverage (Huff & Sireci, 2001). Furthermore, innovative item types have become increasingly available, improving construct validity by permitting the measurement and evaluation of higher-order skills. For example, the use of audio, video, and simulated performance tasks in item design has allowed for the measurement of facets of achievement that might be far more difficult to evaluate using more conventional means of assessment (Huff & Sireci, 2001). Furthermore, such items may provide content in multiple modalities, potentially improving accessibility among diverse learners. More sophisticated ICT-based assessments may also permit for the evaluation of complex problem-solving skills in a manner less easily achieved using paper-and-pencil–based assessments (Greiff et al., 2013).

On a practical level, most ICT-based standardized tests of achievement allow numerous students to be tested at the same time with less intrusion on instructional time than comparable paper-and-pencil tests. Data produced by these tests are often immediately available and can frequently be aggregated across classes, schools, and/or school districts. Furthermore, in the case of most standardized ICT-based assessments, large item pools are used and it is impossible to preview item content, making it much more difficult to teach to the test. This is particularly the case with computer adaptive tests, whose content is individualized in response to student responses.

Disadvantages

While ICT-based tests of achievement offer many potential advantages, they have some potential disadvantages as well. Perhaps the most obvious of these is that schools may lack the ability to meet technical requirements. For example, some schools may not have enough computers capable of hosting the tests and others, particularly those in rural areas, might lack the bandwidth necessary to support online delivery.

Concerns also exist in regard to validity, in particular construct and content validity, that is, the degree to which the assessments measure what they purport to measure and the degree to which they provide adequate coverage of the constructs measured. Ironically, this is particularly true of computer-adaptive assessments of achievement and those with innovative item times, such as simulated performance tasks (Huff & Sireci, 2001). As to computer-adaptive tests, poor item-selection algorithms may contribute to inadequate coverage of a construct and, with performance task and other innovative item types, the probability that the items measure content outside of the construct may increase (Huff & Sireci, 2001). In addition, student characteristics can influence the validity of online assessment results. For example, some students experience heightened test anxiety when using ICT-based assessments and others may struggle to maintain attention given the potentially distracting aspects of the medium. Still others may lack the computer literacy or keyboarding skills required to be successful.

Another potential disadvantage of ICT-based testing is the reduced opportunity for practitioners to make qualitative observations regarding the student's testing behaviors. When testing in-person, an evaluator can observe when a student is struggling with a particular task or topic and garner insights into the nature of the difficulty. Observations of behaviors such as hesitating, guessing, fidgeting, losing focus, and failing to use strategies are often key factors in accurate test interpretation. More than eight decades ago, Monroe (1932) observed: "Two children, reading the same paragraph, may make the same number of errors, and yet their mistakes may be wholly different in nature. Their reading performances may be quantitatively the same but qualitatively unlike" (p. 34).

As with paper-and-pencil assessments, ICT-based assessments also have some security threats. Someone may provide a student with inappropriate assistance during test administration or the student may be able to access outside resources, such as consulting their smartphones for information. Furthermore, without careful monitoring, an individual may take an exam for another person. Finally, ICT-based assessments, like paper-and-pencil–based assessments, may be poorly designed or inadequately validated. When selecting such assessments, it is therefore essential to review the instrument's technical specifications to ensure that the psychometric properties are sound.

Examples of Online Assessments

Many ICT-based assessments of achievement have been developed to measure and evaluate reading skills. Brief descriptions of several instruments follow to illustrate examples of the types of assessments that are available.

One example of an online reading assessment is the FAST, which is a suite of progress-monitoring tools designed for students in kindergarten to grade 5.[1] These assessment tools measure different various reading skills and are individualized for each student. The FAST provides a CBM-Reading assessment, which monitors a student's progress and provides a measure of oral reading fluency; an Early Primary Reading assessment (kindergarten to grade 3), which includes print concepts, phonological awareness (blending and segmenting), letter sounds and names, decoding sight words, and sentence reading; and an Adaptive Reading tool that is similar to the testing format of many statewide assessments. These adaptive tests are all individualized, making them an efficient and effective way to monitor student reading progress.

Renaissance STAR Reading is another example of a computerized, adaptive, standardized (norm-referenced) reading achievement test for students in grades 1–12.[2] The assessment may be administered in either English or Spanish. The assessment identifies the skills that students have mastered and suggests future content. The test is adaptive, so item content and difficulty are adjusted in response to student responses. Furthermore, it can be used repeatedly to measure progress without repetition of content. A variety of district, school, and individual student reports are available.[3]

The MindPlay Universal Screener is an online diagnostic reading assessment that assesses an individual's reading skills within five to thirty minutes.[4] It can be used with a single student, a classroom, or an entire school district. One unique feature of this screener is that, after the assessment, the program creates an individualized prescriptive plan for each student. A student can then receive targeted instruction through the MindPlay Virtual Reading Coach. This online instructional and practice program addresses the student's specific areas of need and is designed to be used for thirty minutes, four to five days a week. The instruction is delivered by speech language pathologists and reading specialists.

A few online assessments address one specific area of reading. For example, MOBY.READ (ami) provides a measure of reading accuracy and rate. This program is an iPad app where the student reads passages aloud. The app records the reading and then calculates the words read correctly per minute, the accuracy, and the expressiveness. The app can identify students in need of intervention, as well as track student progress. A teacher may print out reports and compare readings across time.

Another example of an online assessment is the Partnership for Assessment of Readiness for College and Careers (PARCC).[5] The PARCC is a set of assessments designed to measure student performance in English-language arts and mathematics. It is designed to determine if a student is on a successful pathway to college. It includes a paper-based version, as well as an ICT-based version.

ALEKS is a comprehensive program for mathematics that includes both assessment and instructional components.[6] It was developed from research at New York University and the University of California, Irvine, by software engineers, mathematicians, and cognitive scientists. ALEKS is an artificial intelligence engine that assesses each student's knowledge individually and continuously so that instruction is only provided in topics that

[1] See FAST progress monitoring tools at: www.fastbridge.org

[2] See Renaissance Star Reading at: www.renaissance.com/products/assessment/star-360/star-reading-skills

[3] Ibid.

[4] See Mindplay Universal Screener the Virtual Reading Coach at: www.mindplay.com

[5] See PARCC at: https://parcc-assessment.org

[6] See ALEKS at: www.aleks.com

the student is ready to learn. The ALEKS Assessment asks the student about twenty to thirty questions to determine the current level of math knowledge. The questions are determined on the basis of the student's answers to all the previous questions. Thus, each student receives an individualized set of assessment questions. Once the assessment is completed, the student enters the Learning Mode where a choice of appropriate topics to learn is presented.

Technological advances, including the examples provided in this section, have expanded assessment options for administrators and can be a viable option for formative, summative, and diagnostic assessment. Whether it be a technology-based assessment or a traditional paper-and-pencil test, factors can impact the reporting of results and interpretation of scores. The following sections of this chapter will focus on situations of noncredible reporting and factors to consider when interpreting results.

FACTORS IMPACTING VALIDITY

A number of factors can impact validity of achievement tests, including lack of motivation or effort on the part of the examinee (Adelman et al., 1989), noncredible performance by the examinee, and administrator error (e.g., inappropriate test administration, scoring errors, or misinterpretation of results by the examiner). As with all standardized assessments, achievement assessment is built on the foundation of examiner competence in administration, scoring, and interpretation. Similar to this, when interpreting achievement test results, examiners assume a reasonable, valid effort on the part of the examinee. This speaks to the importance of the examiner establishing rapport with the examinee prior to administering the test and having an awareness of what the student is able to do both in and out of the classroom (Adelman et al., 1989).

Another concern with all types of testing is the possibility of intentional falsification of results or noncredible performance by the examinee. Research has indicated that rates of noncredible performance in college populations for students being evaluated for learning disabilities may be as high as 15 percent (Harrison & Edwards, 2010; Sullivan, May, & Galbally, 2007). Related to this, examinees who feign performance on psychoeducational tests often do so in a way that is not detectable by the examiner (Harrison & Edwards, 2010; Harrison, Edwards, & Parker, 2008). As a result, researchers recommend including measures of performance validity (PVT) to psychoeducational batteries, especially when there is a perceived benefit from being labeled as having a learning disability (e.g., access to additional resources or accommodations) (DeRight & Carone, 2015; Harrison & Edwards, 2010; Harrison et al., 2010; Harrison et al., 2008). PVTs are typically measures that are easily passed, even by those with a diagnosed impairment; thus, poor performance is indicative of feigned poor performance (DeRight & Carone, 2015; Harrison et al., 2010, Harrison et al., 2008). Whereas the majority of the research in this area has been with college or adult populations, some data suggest that feigned impairment also occurs in children as young as eight or nine years old (Kirkwood et al., 2010; Lu & Boone, 2002). To minimize this factor when evaluating children, DeRight and Carone (2015) advised: "In both research and clinical practice, a combination of multitest and multimethod approaches is the current gold standard in the evaluation of test-taking effort with children" (p. 19).

In our practice, we have seen one example of such a case. A twenty-one-year-old woman claimed that she had dyslexia and that she needed extended time on all examinations. Apparently, she had read or been told that a major characteristic of dyslexia was poor spelling and reversed and transposed letters. On the WJ III Writing Samples test, she misspelled simple words (e.g., spelling the word "to" as "ot," the word "the" as "hte," the word "sun" as "snu" and "fresh air" as "frehs iar"). Three of her written responses are presented in Figure 13.1.

When she completed the WJ III Spelling test, however, she obtained a standard score of 105 and was able to spell numerous words correctly, with no reversals or transpositions. Examples of words that she spelled correctly are provided in Figure 13.2.

After closer examination, we determined that this young woman suffered from anxiety regarding test-taking and that she clearly did not have dyslexia. Certainly, if she could not spell the word *the* correctly, she would not have been able to spell the word *congenial* correctly!

As with examinees, intentional misrepresentation is rare among examiners; it is extremely unusual for an examiner to falsify test results. Nonvalid scores more often occur if an examiner has failed to administer tests appropriately addressing the referral question(s) or has made an error in test administration and/or scoring. An example of a scoring error from a recent report on the core tests of the WJ IV ACH is in Figure 13.3.

In this report, the examiner failed to notice the discrepancies between the standard scores and percentile ranks on the Spelling and Passage Comprehension tests. An average standard score would convert to an average percentile rank (25th to 75th percentile). A standard score of 105 would result in a percentile rank of 63, not 25. In this case, the evaluator's discussion focused on the percentile ranks, so the interpretation of the tests' results was inaccurate and misleading. This type of error can occur if an evaluator fails to review the obtained scores critically or does not verify that the tables created for a report are accurate. Another error that occurs is a miscalculation when totaling scores.

Examiners need to be alert to potential threat to the validity of assessment results. A careful review of scoring and administration procedures, as well as the interpretation of performance, can mitigate examiner error. Sound assessment practices using multiple data sources, including, when called for, the use of Symptom Validity Testing, can alert examiners that an examinee may not be putting forth the required level of effort whether due to noncredible performance or a simple lack of motivation.

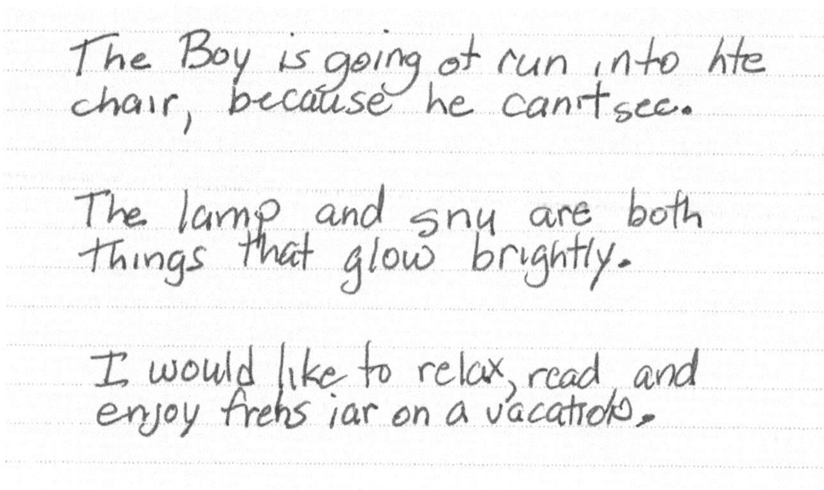

Figure 13.1 WJ III Writing Samples test: three example responses

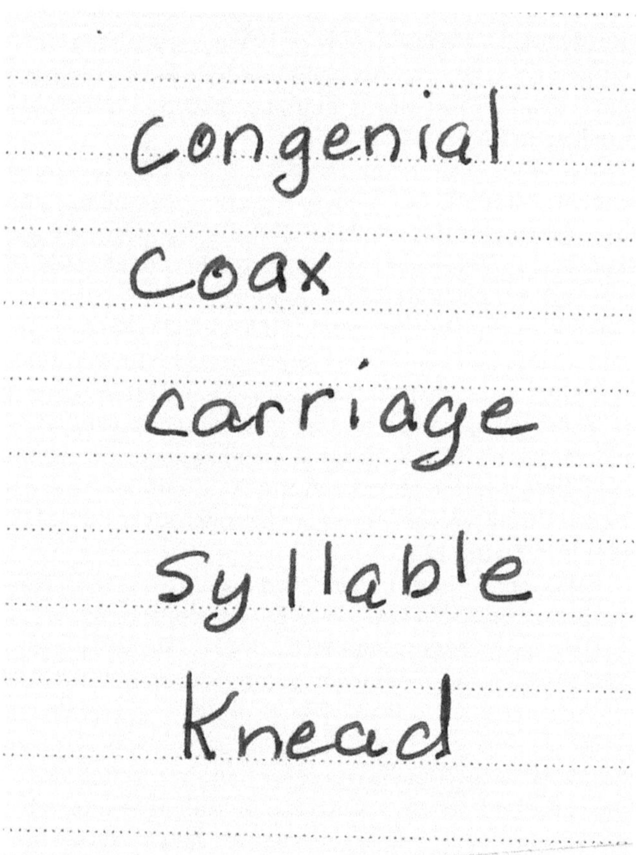

Figure 13.2 WJ III Spelling test: spelling samples

Six Core Tests	Standard Score (68% band)	RPI	Percentile Rank
Letter-Word Identification	127 (122–131)	100/90	98
Applied Problems	120 (115–125)	99/90	84
Spelling	105 (101–109)	95/90	25
Passage Comprehension	105 (99–110)	94/90	24
Calculation	111 (106–116)	97/90	53
Writing Samples	104 (99–109)	93/90	30

Figure 13.3 WJ IV ACH test: scoring error example

MISUSES AND MISUNDERSTANDINGS

As noted, one common error in the reporting of achievement test results is misreporting or misinterpretation of the obtained scores. Substantial misunderstanding often exists among educators regarding the meaning of test scores (Gardner, 1989). The types of scores that can be particularly confusing to untrained educators are (1) grade and age equivalents, (2) percentile ranks, and (3) standard scores. Although much of this discussion will seem rather obvious to seasoned evaluators, teachers and parents may be confused or lack understanding of this information.

Grade and Age Equivalents

Grade-equivalent scores are expressed as a whole number and decimal representing the grade and month of the school year. For example, 3.7 would represent grade 3, month 7. These scores are derived from the median raw score attained by sample participants at a particular grade level. Age-equivalent scores are much the same; however, they are reported using a whole number and hyphen representing the year and month at which the median sample participant attained a particular raw score. For example, 8-4 would represent eight years and four months.

Grade and age equivalent scores are somewhat problematic in that, despite a common misconception, they do not represent a standard to be attained or the grade at which a student should be receiving instruction (Gardner, 1989). If a student obtains a fifth-grade score on a computation test, it does not necessarily follow that the student can perform fifth-grade–level computations; rather, the score indicates that the student performed computations as well as the median fifth-grade student. A fifth-grade–equivalent score also should not be taken to indicate that fifth-grade instructional materials are appropriate for a student, as instructional materials are not typically aligned to grade-equivalent scores and a great deal of variability in difficulty exists among instructional materials produced by different publishers.

Although grade- and age-equivalent scores may provide some useful information concerning the relative achievement of students, they are not equal-interval scores and thus provide a very imprecise measure of growth. Additionally, a standard score in the average range may be represented by a grade- or age-equivalent score one grade above or below the student's current level if the student scores at either the top or the bottom of the average range. Owing to the high likelihood of misuses of these types of scores, age- and grade-equivalent scores must be interpreted with caution.

Percentile Rank

A percentile rank shows the percentage of obtained scores in a particular sample that is equal to or less than the specified obtained score. Percentile ranks are typically expressed using a range from 1 to 99, ranking the individual's obtained score within a distribution of 100, or from 0.1 to 99.9, ranking the individual's obtained score within a distribution of 1,000. For example, a rank at the 25th percentile would indicate that 25 percent of the participants taking a test had a score equal to or less than that of a specified individual. A percentile rank of 99.9 would indicate that the individual's score equaled or exceeded those of 999 out of 1,000 sample participants.

People who are unfamiliar with test interpretation may confuse percentile rank with percent correct. A rank at the 50th percentile does not indicate that an individual answered 50 percent of items correctly but rather that the individual's obtained score was equal to or exceeded that of 50 percent of the norm group sample. To minimize the possibility of confusion, it is best not to abbreviate a percentile rank with the percent sign (e.g., 25th %ile). As with age- and grade-equivalent scores, percentile ranks are norm-referenced and do not provide interval-level data for establishing improvement in achievement. Thus, they also provide an imprecise measure of growth. Although test developers assign different qualitative descriptors to score ranges and by association percentile ranks, typically the "average range" is considered to be from the 25th to the 75th percentile.

Standard Scores

Like percentile ranks, standard scores are norm-referenced and indicate an individual's relative group standing: They compare the individual to others of the same age or grade who took the same test. Unlike percentile ranks, standard scores are expressed in standard deviation units, that is, the number of standard deviations from the mean of the sample at which a particular obtained score falls. Achievement tests frequently have a mean of 100 and a standard deviation of 15 for their composite scores; however, there is some variation, particularly with respect to subtests, which sometimes use scaled scores that have a mean of 10 and a standard deviation of 3.

Both parents and teachers can be confused about how to interpret statements about standard scores and percentile ranks. Consider this example from Schneider and colleagues (2018) regarding the clarity and interpretation of these two statements:

> 1. Josie's score on the Woodcock-Johnson IV Spelling test was 95, which corresponds to a percentile rank of 37.
> 2. Josie can spell about as well as most children her age.
>
> The first statement is quite precise but not particularly clear – at least not to an audience of nonexperts. One can imagine the thoughts of an intelligent but psychometrically naive parent: What is this test, the Woodcock-Johnson Eye-Vee Spelling test? Does it tell us all we need to know about a person's ability to spell? Is 95 a good score? What is a percentile rank? Does that mean Josie came in 37th place? ... 'cause there aren't that many kids in her class. Or does it mean she got 37 percent correct? That does not sound like a good performance – we called that an *F* when I was in school. That's the thing about spelling tests, if you don't study in advance, you can really bomb 'em. I know a few times I sure did. Did Josie have the opportunity to study the spelling words in advance? If not, I don't see how the test is fair.
>
> The second statement avoids these possible sources of confusion. Although it is in some ways less precise than the first statement, it has the virtue of being easy to understand correctly, keeping the focus squarely on what the reader actually needs to know (i.e., that spelling is not a problem for Josie). (p. 4)

Both teachers and parents may also become confused when examining standard scores to understand how much progress a student has made. For example, in grade 3, Rebecca obtained a standard score of 80 on the WIAT-III Math Fluency subtest. In grade 5, Rebecca had a standard score of 80 on the same test. At the school meeting, her father remarked that she had made absolutely no progress as her score had stayed exactly the same. The truth, however, is that Rebecca did make progress as she kept her place in the group standing across the two years (e.g., a fifth-grade student would need to answer more items correctly than a third-grade student to obtain a standard score of 80).

Additional Factors

Several other factors can also affect test interpretation or cause confusion. One arises from placing too much emphasis on a single score or measure. A second stems from the various verbal labels assigned to test scores by the test authors or publishers. A third involves the misinterpretation of composite scores. A fourth revolves around the misuse of age or grade norms. A fifth and final factor centers on content validity, particularly among reading comprehension tests.

Drawing conclusions from one score or one test. Reliance on a single score, or even the results of a single composite test, is inadvisable for educational decision-making. Numerous factors contribute to an individual's achievement at any point in time and all measurement is subject to bias and error. Reflecting on the weaknesses inherent in testing, Linn (2000) cautioned: "Don't put all of the weight on a single test. Instead, seek multiple indicators" (p. 15). Brooks, Holdnack, and Iverson (2011) in their work with adults with traumatic brain injuries, also cautioned against the use of single subtest scores when measuring impairments in individuals. They emphasized that a low score on a subtest given in isolation may appear meaningful but a single low score from a composite or battery of tests is fairly common in the general population. This supports that use of multiple methods and sources of data, including factors such as client demographic characteristics, as well as having examiners with a sound background in psychometrics who are able to take into account factors such as the intercorrelations between subtests and the impact of interpreting a single score versus a battery of tests concurrently.

Furthermore, the evaluator also needs to consider contextual factors. In order to understand an individual's test performance, scores must be interpreted within the full context of gathered information, which would often include background information (e.g., prior services and interventions); classroom work samples; behavioral observations; interviews; and parent, teacher, and examinee self-reports. Gardner (1989) explains that a test score is just a numeric description of a sample of performance at a given point in time but the score does not tell us anything about why the individual performed a particular way or what caused the performance described by the score.

Qualitative classification of achievement. An additional factor that may create misunderstanding regarding test scores is the different qualitative descriptors used by the test authors and publishers to classify achievement scores. Different publishers describe the same norm-referenced score using different labels. What one test publisher describes as "low average," another test publisher describes as "below average." As Dr. John Willis (2015) noted in a presentation: "My score is 110! I am adequate, average, high average, or above average. I'm glad that much is clear!" He went on to say: "It is essential that [we] know (and be reminded) precisely what classification scheme(s) we are using with the scores," as failure to do so increases the probability of inaccurate interpretation and use of testing data. Additionally, examiners should be well versed in the psychometric properties of tests, as well as various theoretical models related to disability identification when making clinical decisions and recommendations.

Interpretation of composite scores. Achievement tests routinely have individual subtest scores that are combined into composite scores. On most tests, the composite scores are not means or averages of the obtained scores across subtests; rather, they are a weighted composite that shows how the individual performed compared to those in the norm group across measures. Thus, if a composite consists of three subtests, the overall score reflects how the individual performed across all three measures, when compared to peers. Consequently, there is often not a readily apparent equivalence among subtest scores and composite scores. An individual who had a standard score of 70 on each of the four subtests comprising a composite may have a composite standard score lower than 70 (unless the particular test determines the cluster score as the mean of the four subtests) because of the decreased likelihood that an individual would perform uniformly low on each of the four subtests comprising the composite.

Another consideration regarding composite scores is that sometimes they mask the underlying concern or an individual's specific areas of strengths and weaknesses. For example, a reading battery may be composed of three different subtests: basic reading skills, reading fluency or rate, and reading comprehension. A composite score may obscure a weakness in one of these areas if individual subtest scores are not also considered. As an illustration, Manuel, a sixth-grade student, was referred for a reading evaluation. Although his overall reading composite score fell in the Average range, his individual subtest scores showed that he had a specific weakness in reading fluency; his reading fluency score was significantly lower than those of the other subtests. Without examining specific subtest scores, the evaluator may draw erroneous conclusions and fail to provide appropriate recommendations for intervention or accommodations.

Use of age or grade norms. Many achievement tests provide both age and grade norms, so an evaluator can decide whether to compare the student to individuals of the same chronological age or to those of the same grade placement. If the results of an achievement test are going to be compared to the results of an intelligence test (which is sometimes done in evaluations for specific learning disabilities), then the achievement test should be scored with age norms, as most intelligence tests only provide age norms.

The selection of age or grade norms becomes most problematic in cases of retention. Should the student be compared to age peers who are in a higher grade or to grade peers? Some would argue grade peers, as the student has not yet been exposed to the next grade level of material. Others would argue age peers, as it provides a more accurate indication of how far behind the student really is. The best advice is to report both, adding an explanation to assist with interpretation.

Reading comprehension tests and what they purport to measure. A variety of tests are available for evaluating reading comprehension. Two major concerns, however, have been raised about these measures. One is that the comprehension questions can often be answered correctly without reading the passage. Another is that the results from various tests are often widely discrepant, owing to the different cognitive and linguistic abilities on which they place demands.

Several studies have shown that many commonly used reading comprehension measures have problems with passage independence, that is, students may be able to answer the items correctly without having read the associated passages. Consequently, these instruments may end up measuring acquired knowledge rather than reading comprehension. Keenan and Betjemann (2006) examined the content validity of the Gray Oral Reading Test – Fourth Edition (GORT-4; Wiederholt & Bryant, 2001) by assessing whether or not students could answer the questions correctly without reading the passages. Undergraduate students (n = 77) were able to answer 86 percent of the questions correctly without reading the associated passages and a small group of students ages seven to fifteen (n = 10) were able to answer the questions with 47 percent accuracy, also without having read the associated passages.

Based on these findings, Keenan and Betjemann (2006) concluded that these items were unlikely to be sensitive measures for measuring reading comprehension or identifying reading disability. Additionally, they found that performance on these items correlated closely with performance on other comprehension tests and noted that the field of comprehension assessment needs to be more concerned about the passage independence of items. On the most recent version of the GORT-5 (Wiederholt & Bryant, 2012), the publishers noted that the comprehension questions had been completely revised and studies were conducted to demonstrate and ensure that the questions were passage-dependent.

Authors of another study (Coleman et al., 2010) investigated the content validity of the comprehension section of the Nelson-Denny Reading Test (Brown, Fishco, & Hanna, 1993) and obtained similar results. The authors asked university students with and without learning disorders to answer the multiple-choice comprehension questions without reading the associated passages. They found that the students' accuracy rates were well above chance for both forms of the test, as well as for both groups of students.

Kendeou, Papadopoulos, and Spanoudis (2012) examined the cognitive processes underlying performance on three different reading comprehension tests administered to students in grades 1 and 2: WJ III Passage Comprehension test (WJPC), a cloze-based format that requires students to read a passage and fill in a missing word in a sentence (Woodcock, McGrew, & Mather, 2001); the CBM-Maze,[7] a curriculum-based measurement timed test that requires students to read a passage with every sixth word omitted and choose the missing word from three options; and a test of reading recall that requires students to read a text and then recall it orally from memory. All three tests placed processing demands on decoding, whereas the CBM-Maze test also placed demands on fluency and vocabulary and the WJPC placed additional demands on working memory. The authors noted that cognitive processes underlying performance on tests of reading comprehension are dependent on a number of factors, including test format; test length; and the availability of the text, that is, whether the person can continue to view the text while answering the questions. The authors concluded that, owing to the different cognitive processes on which performance on tests of comprehension may depend, an individual's performance on one measure would not necessarily correlate well to performance on another. For this reason, as well as the others previously discussed, it is important to use multiple measures of reading comprehension, as opposed to only one measure.

In another study, Keenan, Betjemann, and Olson (2008) examined the content validity of some of the most popular reading comprehension measures, including the GORT, WJPC, the Reading Comprehension test from the Peabody Individual Achievement Test (PIAT; Markwardt, 1997), and the retellings and comprehension questions from the Qualitative Reading Inventory (QRI; Leslie & Caldwell, 2001). They found that the tests only had modest intercorrelations and that decoding skill accounted for most of the variance on both the WJPC and the PIAT.

More recently, Keenan and Meenan (2014) reaffirmed that reading comprehension tests are not interchangeable and that they do not necessarily provide equivalent measures of the construct. Nine-hundred and ninety-five children were assessed with the GORT-3, the WJPC, the PIAT, and the QRI-3. Results were more consistent for younger students, for whom weaknesses were most often caused by poor decoding skills, than for older students, for whom weaknesses had more variable causes. When examining the bottom 10 percent of performers, Keenan and Meenan (2014) found that the average overlap between the tests in diagnosing reading disabilities was only 43 percent and inconsistencies in scores were just as apparent in the top performers. Furthermore, the authors found that working memory was more important for tests with short texts (WJPC and PIAT) rather than for tests with longer texts (GORT-3 and QRI-3). Thus, format differences among the tests created differences in the types of skills that they assessed, reducing the correlations among scores. The

[7] See CBM-Maze at: interventioncentral.org

authors reiterated the suggestion that evaluators use more than one test to assess reading comprehension. They also noted that it is important to evaluate component skills such as listening comprehension, vocabulary, and working memory to identify the source of deficits.

DIVERSITY AND CULTURAL ISSUES

Because the results of achievement tests play a central role in educational decision-making and may be associated with high stakes for examinees and schools alike, the validity of the inferences derived from these tests is of utmost importance. This is of particular concern with respect to culturally and ethnically diverse learners, as well as those who are non-native speakers of the language of instruction. While issues of cultural and ethnic bias in assessment have been better studied in relation to cognitive testing than to achievement testing, modest evidence suggests that such bias, as well as other related factors, including linguistic barriers to item comprehension, teacher expectancy effects, and stereotype threat, may negatively affect achievement test performance among members of cultural, ethnic, and linguistic minorities.

Ethnic or Cultural Bias

Ethnic or cultural bias in achievement testing may occur when characteristics of a test item unrelated to the achievement construct being assessed differentially affect the responses of members of different ethnic and cultural groups (Banks, 2006). For example, a test designed to evaluate examinees' English-language arts achievement might contain items whose distractors employ constructs common in a regional or ethnic dialect, potentially causing speakers of that dialect to respond inaccurately, irrespective of their mastery of the English-language arts construct assessed. To illustrate this concept, one culturally sensitive item derived from a widely used standardized assessment of English-language arts achievement asked examinees to identify the grammatically correct phrase among options; however, it contained a distractor that employed a construction commonly used in African American English (AAE) – a construction that would be perfectly grammatical to speakers of that sociolect (Banks, 2006). Not surprisingly, this item functioned differently for African American students than for matched Hispanic or white students, demonstrating an increased probability of an incorrect response among members of that population (Banks, 2006).

Other types of culturally sensitive item content may also promote differential functioning. In a 2006 study of ethnic and cultural bias in assessment, Banks performed simultaneous item bias test (SIBTEST) analyses on a large set of fifth-grade reading cluster data derived from the Terra Nova Test (CTB/McGraw-Hill, 1999). The results of these analyses revealed that, while matched Black, Hispanic, and white examinees did not differ significantly in their overall cluster scores, Black examinees were disproportionately likely to respond incorrectly to items whose distractors contained culturally sensitive information. In a follow-up study using the same dataset, Banks (2012) found evidence to indicate that inferential reading items were more susceptible to cultural bias than were literal items, suggesting that such items are more likely to draw on culturally bound knowledge, potentially disadvantaging students whose cultural experiences are not well-aligned with those reflected in the test items.

Linguistic Impediments

Linguistic impediments to valid assessment of achievement are another important concern, especially when evaluating English-language learners (Martiniello, 2009). Abedi and colleagues (Abedi, 2002; Abedi et al., 2001; Abedi & Leon, 1999; Abedi, Leon, & Mirocha, 2003) have performed numerous studies of extant testing data derived from major standardized tests of achievement and have consistently found that English-language proficiency is positively correlated to standardized test performance across academic domains, inclusive of mathematics and science. Furthermore, the relationship between test performance and linguistic competence does not appear to be a simple function of differential access to content knowledge based on language mastery. In their research, Abedi and colleagues found that the greater the linguistic complexity of the test item, even among items for which language was presumed to be irrelevant to the achievement construct, the greater the difference in performance tended to be between examinees classified as English-language learners and those who were not. In fact, in one study of extant achievement testing data from several locations in the United States, Abedi (2002) revealed that English-language learners and non–English-language learners had measurable differences in overall math performance, whereas performance on the computation subtest was nearly identical between the groups. These findings suggest that English-language proficiency was an important moderator of achievement test performance independent of construct mastery, even in mathematics, a subject for which linguistic competence should be of minimal importance.

Testing Accommodations

Testing accommodations are often discussed as a means by which to improve the access of English-language learners to assessment content and, by consequence, promote test performance more reflective of their knowledge of the relevant achievement construct. Unfortunately, research has not generally borne out the efficacy of the most commonly used accommodations in effecting improvements in achievement test performance among English-language learners. In a meta-analysis of the extant literature, Kieffer and colleagues (2009) found that only one (providing dictionaries or glossaries) of the seven commonly used testing accommodations studied[8] had a statistically significant positive effect on achievement test performance among English-language learners; their apparent lack of efficacy notwithstanding, none of the common accommodations were found to threaten the validity of the inferences produced by the assessments.

Teacher Expectancy Effects and Stereotype Threats

Factors independent of the tests themselves, including teacher expectancy effects and stereotype threat, may also affect the performance of ethnically and culturally diverse examinees on standardized evaluations of achievement and these factors merit consideration when examining the results of achievement tests in academic decision-making. Expectancy effects can be characterized as the results of a self-fulfilling prophecy: Biased perceptions lead to biased behavior and the effects of the biased behavior further reinforce the initial biased perceptions (Babad, Inbar, & Rosenthal, 1982). In the case of teacher–student relationships, expectancy effects may result from biases on the part of teachers, which may then color those teachers' interactions with their students, ultimately moderating student achievement outcomes (Hinnant, O'Brien, & Ghazarian, 2009). Teachers' biases may also be the result of implicit or explicit prejudice, leading to subtle behavioral changes that may negatively affect students' achievement. As an example, a multilevel analysis of the effects of prejudices on students' achievement in more than forty classrooms revealed that teachers' implicit prejudices explained part of the ethnic achievement gap among classrooms via teacher expectancy effects (Van den Bergh et al., 2010).

Stereotype threat is another form of self-fulfilling prophecy relevant to achievement assessment. Stereotype threat may occur when individuals of a negatively stereotyped group risk confirming stereotype, not because of any inherent or acquired trait or quality but because of the effects of negative expectancies or anxiety produced by the stereotype itself (Steele & Aronson, 1995). As an example, Spencer, Steele, and Quinn (1999) found that women participants significantly underperformed equally qualified men participants on a difficult test of mathematics achievement when primed with a suggestion that the test produced gender differences favoring men; however, when women participants were given a difficult test of mathematics achievement and primed with the suggestion that the test did not produce gender differences, their achievement was not significantly different than that of equally qualified men participants. Stereotype threat is relevant to the interpretation of the results of standardized assessments of achievement because it has been shown to disadvantage members of minority groups on high-stakes tests (Kellow & Jones, 2008). A meta-analysis of more than 100 experimental studies examining the effects of stereotype threat on the achievement and cognitive test performance of both women and members of racial and ethnic minorities revealed that stereotype cues had substantial negative impacts on the achievement and cognitive test performance of members of these groups, serving as an important moderator of outcomes (Nguyen & Ryan, 2008).

[8] Accommodations included extra time, dual-language booklets, dual-language questions, Spanish-language tests, simplified English tests, bilingual dictionaries or glossaries, and English dictionaries or glossaries.

Limitations of Standardized Assessments of Achievement

Whereas the authors and publishers of standardized assessments of achievement strive to minimize bias and maximize the validity of their instruments, some bias in assessment is nevertheless unavoidable – and sometimes factors independent of the assessments themselves produce performance that is unreflective of a student's mastery of an achievement construct. Therefore, educators and clinical practitioners alike should bear the limitations of standardized tests of achievement in mind when making decisions concerning a student's education or placement. Consistent with the American Psychological Association's *Code for Fair Testing Practices in Education* (APA, 2004), educators and clinical practitioners should avoid basing any educationally meaningful decision on a single test or source of information. They should also consider the limitations of the tests used, including any potential sources of bias or threats to validity. Use of multiple sources of data provides the best overall picture of an examinee and helps reduce problems caused by threats to validity such as examiner error and examinee effort or feigning. Examiners should evaluate the totality of the information required for making appropriate educational inferences while considering the rationale, procedures, and evidence for performance standards or cut scores. Finally, they should use appropriate testing practices for the student, particularly in the case of students with limited linguistic proficiency or those with identified disabilities; however, any deviation from standardization should be described and considered with respect to the validity of the inferences made based on the assessment.

INTERPRETIVE OR PRACTICAL RECOMMENDATIONS

As has been discussed in this chapter, the purposes of achievement testing are varied. In some cases, testing is done to determine which students are struggling, so interventions can be provided in a timely fashion; in other cases, evaluation is more in-depth and focused on determining why a particular student is struggling and informing solutions that will address and help resolve the specific referral question(s). This type of clinical evaluation requires specific training expertise and achievement testing in this context is often performed with concurrent assessment of cognitive abilities. Although it is relatively easy to administer and score a test properly, it is far more difficult to interpret the data produced by the test and draw meaningful conclusions.

In order to interpret the results of achievement tests with validity, an evaluator must have an understanding of the deep and reciprocal relationships between language abilities and achievement. Language abilities, including both oral and written, underlie achievement in all other areas, as instruction is typically delivered via written and oral modalities. Furthermore, achievement assessment tends to draw on oral and written languages abilities, even in areas, such as mathematics, where linguistic abilities are less relevant to the achievement construct.

Across domains, achievement tests draw on skills and cognitive factors that may not appear immediately relevant to the achievement construct. For example, passage reading tasks place demands on a variety of skills and abilities, including phonological awareness, orthographic awareness, syntactic knowledge, memory, breadth and depth of vocabulary knowledge, and background knowledge. Even a timed test of math facts knowledge assesses more than simple arithmetic knowledge, as demands are placed on processing speed and the rapid interpretation of symbols. Therefore, when interpreting the results of achievement testing, an evaluator should consider a variety of underlying cognitive factors.

As part of the assessment process, an evaluator must also decide which tests to administer based on the referral question and the goals of the assessment. A poorly defined referral question can make this task far more complex and difficult than it needs to be (Kaufman, Raiford, & Coalson, 2016). Therefore, evaluators should endeavor to clarify an ambiguous referral question so that review of existing data and subsequent data collection clarifies the nature of the student's difficulties and appropriately informs the goals of the assessment process. In some instances, achievement testing may be sufficient to answer a referral question. In many others, an achievement test or tests would be only a part of a more comprehensive evaluation, which might also include various cognitive, oral language, and/or behavioral measures.

Once appropriate assessments have been selected, the evaluator should refer to the examiner's manual of the assessment they are using to decide if standard accommodations and/or modifications are appropriate for a student during the assessment process (e.g., large print for students with a visual impairment). While educators should use appropriate accommodations for students with disabilities in classroom assessments, accommodations and modifications on standardized individual assessments are often not appropriate. While legal definitions and usage of assessment vary from state to state, appropriate assessment accommodations and modifications are an integral part of a protocol for appropriately assessing those whose disabilities affect their ability to take a test. Thurlow, Lazarus, and Christensen (2013) described assessment accommodations as "an essential part of the validity argument for assessments; to obtain valid results for students with disabilities, it is necessary to provide accommodations that help them show what they know and can do without interference from the barriers that their disabilities pose, as long as the accommodations do not change what the assessment is intended to measure" (p. 103).

The challenge for practitioners is determining whether accommodations are appropriate for an individual on a particular assessment. For example, for classroom achievement testing, a student with attention-deficit/hyperactivity disorder may benefit from taking the test individually, away from distractions, and with frequent breaks. These accommodations do not alter the content of the assessment but provide the student with an optimal testing environment. Another example of an appropriate accommodation would be the use of large print on a CBM reading probe for a student with a visual impairment. This accommodation would allow the student to access the testing material without changing the nature of the assessment. On the other hand, an accommodation of extended time on a standardized fluency assessment would likely not be appropriate for any student, regardless of disability, because it would invalidate the assessment by failing to provide an accurate measure of fluency or the student's reading accuracy and speed. Practitioners must thoroughly understand the assessment protocols they use, the purposes of the assessment, and the needs of the student in order to determine which accommodations and modifications may be appropriate and when to use them in an evaluation. Use of accommodations not specified in examiners' manuals will limit the validity of normative comparisons and should only be used after tests are administered in a standardized way to "test the limits." Testing the limits allows the evaluator to test the conditions under which the student's more optimal performance is achieved (Sattler, 2008). Sattler emphasizes that testing of limits may be used after scores have been obtained from a complete standardized administration of an assessment, so as to not provide any cues that may assist a student on any items. Further, he recommends that testing the limits may include "providing additional cues or aids," "changing the stimulus modality" (e.g., question format), or "eliminating time limits" (pp. 206–207). Sattler provides additional suggested procedures for testing the limits.

Within the evaluation process, the results of achievement testing often play a key role in helping to determine whether or not a student may be eligible for special services or which accommodations a student may need in an academic setting. In school settings, these types of determinations are made by a multidisciplinary team of professionals who consider data from a variety of sources. If a student qualifies for special education, they are provided with an Individual Education Plan (IEP) that describes individualized goals based on identified student needs. As part of the IEP, the team would also consider whether the student is in need of specific accommodations, such as extended time on certain types of tests or the use of some kind of assistive technology when completing an assessment.

Although achievement test results play a central role in the diagnosis of a disability, as with any type of clinical assessment, the evaluator should use the results to inform practical recommendations and accommodations that can be implemented with fidelity in the current setting. Cruickshank (1977) advised that "Diagnosis must take second place to instruction, and must be made a tool of instruction, not an end in itself" (p. 194). A careful analysis of the test results can help an evaluator develop a plan that includes a description of the implementation and monitoring of targeted interventions that are designed to increase student achievement. In order to write targeted recommendations, an evaluator needs to have extensive knowledge of effective academic interventions. Cruickshank further explained that "A variety of programs must be available for children who have a variety of needs" (p. 194). Fortunately, numerous effective interventions exist and the National Association of School Psychologists includes in their domains of practice knowledge of data-based decision-making as well as appropriateuse of evidence-based interventions (NASP, n.d.). Thus, school psychology programs today are requiring students to take courses related to linking academic assessment data to evidence-based interventions (Joseph, Wargelin, & Ayoub, 2016).

In addition, the evaluator must communicate with others regarding the nature of instructional interventions, as well as how, where, and when those interventions should occur. For one student, systematic instruction could be provided every day after school in a math lab; for another student, instruction should be delivered daily for forty-five minutes in a resource setting by a special education teacher; for still another, the parents may decide to provide tutoring for their son or daughter at home.

This chapter provided an introduction to commonly used comprehensive achievement tests, single-subject achievement tests, CBMs, technological advances, threats to validity of results including noncredible reporting, and interpretive and practical recommendations. Achievement testing is an integral component of assessment. When used and interpreted appropriately, the results can help document a student's current academic performance levels and can provide key information for improving student outcomes by informing the need for specific academic interventions, instructional or testing accommodations and/or modifications, and appropriate educational services.

REFERENCES

Abedi, J. (2002). Standardized achievement tests and English language learners: Psychometrics issues. *Educational Assessment, 8*, 231–257.

Abedi, J., Hofstetter, C, Baker, E., & Lord, C. (2001). *NAEP math performance test accommodations: Interactions with student language background* (CSE Technical Report 536). Los Angeles: National Center for Research on Evaluation, Standards, and Student Testing.

Abedi, J., & Leon, S. (1999). *Impact of students' language background on content-based performance: Analyses of extant data*. Los Angeles: University of California, National Center for Research on Evaluation, Standards, and Student Testing.

Abedi, J., Leon, S., & Mirocha, J. (2003). *Impact of student language background on content-based performance: Analyses of extant data* (CSE Technical Report 603). Los Angeles: National Center for Research on Evaluation, Standards, and Student Testing.

Adelman, H. S., Lauber, B. A., Nelson, P., & Smith, D. C. (1989). Toward a procedure for minimizing and detecting false positive diagnoses of learning disability. *Journal of Learning Disabilities, 22*, 234–244.

American Psychiatric Association. (2013). *Desk reference to the diagnostic criteria from DSM-5*. Washington, DC: American Psychiatric Publishing.

APA (American Psychological Association). (2004). *Code of fair testing practices in education*. Washington, DC: Joint Committee on Testing Practices.

Babad, E. Y., Inbar, J., & Rosenthal, R. (1982). Pygmalion, Galatea, and the Golem: Investigations of biased and unbiased teachers. *Journal of Educational Psychology, 74*, 459–474.

Banks, K. (2006). A comprehensive framework for evaluating hypotheses about cultural bias in educational testing. *Applied Measurement in Education, 19*, 115–132.

Banks, K. (2012). Are inferential reading items more susceptible to cultural bias than literal reading items? *Applied Measurement in Education, 25*, 220–245.

Breaux, K. C. (2009). *Wechsler individual achievement test: Technical manual* (3rd ed.). San Antonio, TX: Pearson.

Breaux, K. C., Bray, M. A., Root, M. M., & Kaufman, A. S. (Eds.) (2017). Special issue on studies of students' errors in reading, writing, math, and oral language. *Journal of Psychoeducational Assessment, 35*. https://doi.org/10.1177/0734282916669656

Brooks, B. L., Holdnack, J. A., & Iverson, G. L. (2011). Advanced clinical interpretation of the WAIS-IV and WMS-IV: Prevalence of low scores varies by level of intelligence and years of education. *Assessment, 18*, 156–167.

Brown, J. I., Fishco, V. V., & Hanna, G. (1993). *Nelson-Denny reading test (forms G and H)*. Austin, TX: PRO-ED.

Coleman, C., Lindstrom, J., Nelson, J., Lindstrom, W., & Gregg, K. N. (2010). Passageless comprehension on the Nelson Denny Reading Test: Well above chance for university students. *Journal of Learning Disabilities, 43*, 244–249.

Connolly, A. (2007). *Key Math-3 Diagnostic Assessment*. Austin, TX: Pearson.

Cruickshank, W. M. (1977). Least-restrictive placement: Administrative wishful thinking. *Journal of Learning Disabilities, 10*, 193–194.

CTB/McGraw-Hill. (1999). *Teacher's guide to Terra Nova: CTBS battery, survey, and plus editions, multiple assessments*. Monterey, CA: Author.

Davis, L. B., & Fuchs, L. S. (1995). "Will CBM help me learn?": Students' perception of the benefits of curriculum-based measurement. *Education and Treatment of Children, 18*(1), 19–32.

Deeney, T. A., & Shim, M. K. (2016). Teachers' and students' views of reading fluency: Issues of consequential validity in adopting one-minute reading fluency assessments. *Assessment for Effective Instruction, 41*(2), 109–126.

DeRight, J., & Carone, D. A. (2015). Assessment of effort in children: A systematic review. *Child Neuropsychology, 21*, 1–24.

Ford, J. W., Missall, K. N., Hosp, J. L., & Kuhle, J. L. (2017). Examining oral passage reading rate across three curriculum-based measurement tools for predicting grade-level proficiency. *School Psychology Review, 46*, 363–378.

Fuchs, L. S. (2016). Curriculum based measurement as the emerging alternative: Three decades later. *Learning Disabilities Research and Practice, 32*, 5–7.

Fuchs, L. S., & Fuchs, D. (2002). Curriculum-based measurement: Describing competence, enhancing outcomes, evaluating treatment effects, and identifying treatment nonresponders. *Peabody Journal of Education, 77*(2), 64–84.

Fuchs, L. S., Fuchs, D., Hosp, M., & Jenkins, J. R. (2001). Oral reading fluency as an indicator of reading competence: A theoretical, empirical, and historical analysis. *Scientific Studies of Reading, 5*, 239–256.

Gardner, E. (1989). *Five common misuses of tests*. ERIC Digest No. 108. Washington, DC: ERIC Clearinghouse on Tests Measurement and Evaluation.

Greiff, S., Wüstenberg, S., Holt, D. V., Goldhammer, F., & Funke, J. (2013). Computer-based assessment of complex problem solving: Concept, implementation, and application. *Educational Technology Research and Development, 61*, 407–421.

Hammill, D. D., & Larsen, S. C. (2009). *Test of written language* (4th ed.). Austin, TX: PRO-ED.

Harrison, A. G., & Edwards, M. J. (2010). Symptom exaggeration in post-secondary students: Preliminary base rates in a Canadian sample. *Applied Neuropsychology, 17*, 135–143.

Harrison, A. G., Edwards, M. J., Armstrong, I., & Parker, K. C. H. (2010). An investigation of methods to detect feigned reading disabilities. *Archives of Clinical Neuropsychology, 25*, 89–98.

Harrison, A. G., Edwards, M. J., & Parker, K. C. H. (2008). Identifying students feigning dyslexia: Preliminary findings and strategies for detection. *Dyslexia, 14*, 228–246.

Hasbrouck, J., & Tindal, G. (2017). An update to compiled ORF norms (Technical Report No. 1702). Eugene, OR: Behavioral Research and Teaching, University of Oregon.

Hinnant, J. B., O'Brien, M., & Ghazarian, S. R. (2009). The longitudinal relations of teacher expectations to achievement in the early school years. *Journal of Educational Psychology, 101*, 662–670.

Hosp, M. K., Hosp, J. L., & Howell, K. W. (2016). *The ABCs of CBM: A practical guide to curriculum-based measurement* (2nd ed.). New York: Guilford Press.

Hosp, J. L., & Suchey, N. (2014). Reading assessment: Reading fluency, reading fluently, and comprehension – Commentary on the special topic. *School Psychology Review, 43*, 59–68.

Huff, K. L., & Sireci, S. G. (2001). Validity issues in computer-based testing. *Educational Measurement: Issues and Practice, 20*, 16–25.

Jones, E. D., Southern, W. T., & Brigham, F. J. (1998). Curriculum-based assessment: Testing what is taught and teaching what is tested. *Intervention in School and Clinic, 33*, 239–249.

Joseph, L. M., Wargelin, L., & Ayoub, S. (2016). Preparing school psychologists to effectively provide services to students with dyslexia. *Perspectives on Language and Literacy, 42*(4), 15–23.

Kaufman, A. S., & Kaufman, N. L. (2014). *Kaufman test of educational achievement* (3rd ed.). San Antonio, TX: Pearson.

Kaufman, A. S., Kaufman, N. L., & Breaux, K. C. (2014). *Technical and interpretive manual. Kaufman Test of Educational Achievement – Third Edition (KTEA-3) Comprehensive Form*. Bloomington, MN: NCS Pearson.

Kaufman, A. S., Raiford, S. E., & Coalson, D. L. (2016). *Intelligent testing with the WISC-V*. Hoboken, NJ: John Wiley & Sons.

Keenan, J. M., & Betjemann, R. S. (2006). Comprehending the Gray Oral Reading Test without reading it: Why comprehension tests should not include passage-independent items. *Scientific Studies of Reading, 10*, 363–380.

Keenan, J. M., Betjemann, R. S., & Olson, R. K. (2008). Reading comprehension tests vary in the skills that they assess: Differential dependence on decoding and oral comprehension. *Scientific Studies of Reading, 12*, 281–300.

Keenan, J. M., & Meenan, C. E. (2014). Test differences in diagnosing reading comprehension deficits. *Journal of Learning Disabilities, 47*, 125–135.

Kellow, J. T., & Jones, B. D. (2008). The effects of stereotypes on the achievement gap: Reexamining the academic performance of African American high school students. *Journal of Black Psychology, 34*(1), 94–120.

Kendeou, P., Papadopoulos, T. C., & Spanoudis, G. (2012). Processing demands of reading comprehension tests in young readers. *Learning and Instruction, 22*, 354–367.

Kieffer, M. J., Lesaux, N. K., Rivera, M., & Francis, D. J. (2009). Accommodations for English language learners taking large-scale assessments: A meta-analysis on effectiveness and validity. *Review of Educational Research, 79*, 1168–1201.

Kirkwood, M. W., Kirk, J. W., Blaha, R. Z., Wilson, P. (2010). Noncredible effort during pediatric neuropsychological exam: A case series and literature review. *Child Neuropsychology, 16*, 604–618.

Leslie, L., & Caldwell, J. (2001). *Qualitative reading inventory–3*. New York: Addison Wesley Longman.

Linn, R. L. (2000). Assessments and accountability. *Educational Researcher, 29*, 4–16.

Lu, P. H., & Boone, K. B. (2002). Suspect cognitive symptoms in a 9-year old child: Malingering by proxy? *The Clinical Neuropsychologist, 16*, 90–96.

Markwardt, F. C. (1997). *Peabody individual achievement test – revised* (normative update). Bloomington, MN: Pearson Assessments.

Martiniello, M. (2009). Linguistic complexity, schematic representations, and differential item functioning for English language learners in math tests. *Educational Assessment, 14*, 160–179.

McGrew, K. S., LaForte, E. M., & Schrank, F. A. (2014). *Woodcock-Johnson IV: Technical manual* [CD]. Itasca, IL: Houghton Mifflin Harcourt.

Molnar, M. (2017). Market is booming for digital formative assessments. *Education Week*, May 24. http://edweek.org/ew/articles/2017/05/24/market-is-booming-for-digital-formative-assessments.html

Monroe, M. (1932). *Children who cannot read*. Chicago. IL: University of Chicago Press.

NASP (National Association of School Psychologists). (n.d.). NASP practice model: 10 domains. www.nasponline.org/standards-and-certification/nasp-practice-model/nasp-practice-model-implementation-guide/section-i-nasp-practice-model-overview/nasp-practice-model-10-domains

NASP (National Association of School Psychologists). (2016). *School psychologists' involvement in assessment*. Bethesda, MD: Author.

Nguyen, H. H. D., & Ryan, A. M. (2008). Does stereotype threat affect test performance of minorities and women? A meta-analysis of experimental evidence. *Journal of Applied Psychology, 93*, 1314–1334.

Rome, H. P., Swenson, W. M., Mataya, P., McCarthy, C. E., Pearson, J. S., Keating, F. R., & Hathaway, S. R. (1962). Symposium on automation techniques in personality assessment. *Proceedings of the Staff Meetings of the Mayo Clinic*, *37*, 61–82.

Sattler, J. M. (2008). *Assessment of children: Cognitive foundations*. CA: Author.

Schneider, J. W., Lichtenberger, E. O., Mather, N., & Kaufman, N. L. (2018). *Essentials of assessment report writing*. Hoboken, NJ: John Wiley & Sons.

Schrank, F. A., Mather, N., & McGrew, K. S. (2014a). *Woodcock-Johnson IV tests of achievement*. Itasca, IL: Houghton Mifflin Harcourt.

Schrank, F. A., Mather, N., & McGrew, K. S. (2014b). *Woodcock-Johnson IV tests of oral language*. Itasca, IL: Houghton Mifflin Harcourt.

Schrank, F. A., McGrew, K. S., & Mather, N. (2014a). *Woodcock-Johnson IV*. Itasca, IL: Houghton Mifflin Harcourt.

Schrank, F. A., McGrew, K. S., & Mather, N. (2014b). *Woodcock-Johnson IV tests of cognitive abilities*. Itasca, IL: Houghton Mifflin Harcourt.

Shinn, M. R., Good, R. H., Knutson, N., & Tilly, D. W. (1992). Curriculum-based measurement of oral reading fluency: A confirmatory analysis of its relation to reading. *School Psychology Review*, *21*, 5, 459–479.

Shute, V. J., Leighton, J. P., Jang, E. E., & Chu, M. W. (2016). Advances in the science of assessment. *Educational Assessment*, *21*(1), 34–59.

Shute, V. J., & Rahimi, S. (2017). Review of computer-based assessment for learning in elementary and secondary education. *Journal of Computer Assisted Learning*, *33*(1), 1–19.

Singleton C. H. (2001). Computer-based assessment in education. *Educational and Child Psychology*, *18*(3), 58–74.

Spencer, S. J., Steele, C. M., & Quinn, D. M. (1999). Stereotype threat and women's math performance. *Journal of Experimental Social Psychology*, *35*, 4–28.

Steele, C. M., & Aronson, J. (1995). Stereotype threat and the intellectual test performance of African Americans. *Journal of Personality and Social Psychology*, *69*, 797–811.

Sullivan, B. K., May, K., & Galbally, L. (2007). Symptom exaggeration by college adults in Attention-Deficit Hyperactivity Disorder and Learning Disorder assessments. *Applied Neuropsychology*, *14*, 189–207.

Thurlow, M., Lazarus, S., & Christensen, L. (2013). Accommodations for assessment. In J. Lloyd, T. Landrum, B. Cook, & M. Tankersley (Eds.)., *Research-based approaches for assessment* (pp. 94–110). Upper Saddle River, NJ: Pearson.

Valencia, S. W., Smith, A. T., Reece, A. M., Li, M., Wixson, K. K., & Newman, H. (2010). Oral reading fluency assessment: Issues of construct, criterion, and consequential validity. *Reading Research Quarterly*, *45*, 270–291.

Van den Bergh, L., Denessen, E., Hornstra, L., Voeten, M., & Holland, R. W. (2010). The implicit prejudiced attitudes of teachers: Relations to teacher expectations and the ethnic achievement gap. *American Educational Research Journal*, *47*, 497–527.

VanDerHeyden, A. M., Witt, J. C., & Gilbertson, D. (2007). A multi-year evaluation of the effects of a response to intervention (RTI) model on identification of children for special education. *Journal of School Psychology*, *45*, 225–256. https://doi.org/10.1016/j.jsp.2006.11.004

Van Norman, E. R., Nelson, P. M., & Parker, D. C. (2018). A comparison of nonsense-word fluency and curriculum-based measurement of reading to measure response to phonics instruction. *School Psychology Quarterly*, *33*, 573–581. https://doi.org/10.1037/spq0000237

Wechsler, D. (2009). *Wechsler individual achievement test* (3rd ed.). San Antonio, TX: Psychological Corporation.

Wechsler, D. (2014). *Wechsler intelligence scale for children* (5th ed.). San Antonio, TX: Psychological Corporation.

Wei, H., & Lin, J. (2015). Using out-of-level items in computerized adaptive testing. *International Journal of Testing*, *15*, 50–70.

Wiederholt, J. L., & Bryant, B. R. (2001). *Gray oral reading test* (4th ed.). Austin, TX: PRO-ED.

Wiederholt, J. L., & Bryant, B. R. (2012). *Gray oral reading test* (5th ed.). Austin, TX: PRO-ED.

Willis, J. (2015). The historical role and best practice in identifying Specific Learning Disabilities. Paper presented at the New York Association of School Psychologists annual conference. Verona, NY, October.

Woodcock, R. W. (2011). *Woodcock reading mastery test* (3rd ed.). San Antonio, TX: Pearson.

Woodcock, R. W., McGrew, K. S., & Mather, N. (2001). *Woodcock–Johnson III tests of achievement*. Itasca, IL: Riverside.

14 Using Vocational Assessment Tests

JANE L. SWANSON

Assessment has long held a central role in professional psychology, although its purpose and implementation differ among specialty areas, due in part to the disparate historical roots of specialties early in the twentieth century. Vocational psychology (along with the broader specialty within which it is typically located, counseling psychology) emerged from the vocational guidance movement, developed in the environment of educational institutions, and has a continued emphasis on assessment of career and developmental concerns in well-functioning individuals. This chapter focuses on the unique nature of vocational assessment, as well as the points of commonality with other psychological assessment.

Vocational psychology as a defined specialty encompasses the study of vocational behavior across the life span, from initial career exploration and choice by adolescents to occupational entry and work adjustment by adults. The history of vocational psychology is traced to the social reform movement in the early part of the twentieth century and is tied to the publication of Frank Parsons's (1909/1989) book *Choosing a Vocation*. Parsons described an oft-cited triumvirate: "in the wise choice of a vocation there are three broad factors: (1) a clear understanding of yourself, ... (2) knowledge of the requirements ... in different lines of work, [and] (3) true reasoning on the relations of these two groups of facts" (p. 5). Parsons's approach, later labeled as "trait-and-factor" approaches to assessment (measuring traits of individuals and matching them to measured factors of occupations), formed the basis of the majority of work conducted in vocational psychology since his time. The rise of vocational psychology was intertwined with the development of psychometrics as a set of practical quantitative tools for developing, evaluating, and improving psychological assessment, with an emphasis on *individual differences* and how to quantify these differences (Dawis, 1992).

Owing to these different historical influences, assessment within the context of vocational decisions is grounded in a somewhat different view of assessment than in other arenas in which assessment is used. The following section describes some broad models of assessment, as well as ways in which vocational assessment differs from "traditional" assessment.

MODELS OF ASSESSMENT

Although vocational psychology is historically connected to the development of the professional field of counseling psychology (Dawis, 1992), other professionals also use vocational assessment, such as school counselors, industrial/organizational (I/O) psychologists, rehabilitation professionals, as well as others. Because *counseling psychology* as a broader field encompasses at least a portion of the practice of vocational assessment, it is useful to briefly consider various models of assessment within counseling psychology that also are relevant to other specialties that conduct diagnostic or clinical assessment.

The current practice of assessment in counseling psychology varies widely, from the traditional use of testing as an integrated part of career counseling, where clients frequently expect to participate in testing, to full-scale evaluation in medical or forensic settings, with specific referral questions that are addressed in written reports to relevant parties (Swanson, 2012). The unique aspects of counseling psychology's approach to the use of testing were outlined nearly thirty years ago by Duckworth (1990): In contrast to other applied specialties, counseling psychologists tend to use testing to enhance short-term therapy, focus on developmental issues, facilitate problem-solving, assist with decision-making, and provide psychoeducational opportunities for clients. Duckworth (1990) further described the "counseling psychological approach" to testing, in which (1) testing is done for the benefit of client *and* therapist, (2) testing is done to generate information for both client *and* counselor, (3) the client needs to be an active participant, (4) the client is assumed to be able to profit from the testing process, (5) testing should focus on both strengths and weaknesses, (6) the test-taker is more likely to be "normal," (7) clients are capable of change, (8) vocational tests are an important part of assessment, and (9) the goal of testing is empowerment of the test-taker.

The practice of professional psychology has evolved substantially since Duckworth (1990) proposed this approach, so that there really are two different models of assessment within counseling psychology: one that focuses on the use of tests in counseling with career and/or "normal" developmental adjustment as its primary focus (a "traditional" model) and one that focuses on what might be considered a clinical psychology application of assessment (a "diagnostic" model) (Swanson, 2012).

Another heuristic framework that illuminates how vocational assessment may differ from other types of psychological assessment was proposed by Haverkamp (2013). She defined two dimensions underlying the use of assessment, representing epistemological and axiological bases. The first dimension describes the *purpose* of assessment, specifically addressing whose needs are being met by assessment, with "expert" (clinical or organizational needs) anchoring one end of the dimension and "collaborative" (client needs) anchoring the other end. The second dimension describes the *type of information* that is provided by assessment or the basis on which inferences are made, with one end being a traditional, data-driven, nomothetic stance and the other end being a contextual, intuitive, and idiographic stance. Combining these two dimensions creates four quadrants, each describing different types of assessment or different ways in which assessment is used. Vocational assessment clearly corresponds to the "client needs" or "collaborative" end of the dimension related to the purpose of assessment, encompassing two of the four quadrants. The first quadrant includes traditional forms of assessment, which provide the client with objective and standardized results based on their responses to a set of items, using well-developed norm groups. More broadly, this quadrant characterizes assessment typically considered "diagnostic," to answer neuropsychological, school, and career questions. Examples of this type of vocational assessment include the Strong Interest Inventory and the Minnesota Importance Questionnaire (discussed in the "Vocational Interests" and "Work Values" sections of this chapter). The second relevant quadrant is referred to as "collaborative assessment" (Haverkamp, 2013) and includes idiographic methods of assessment. For example, card sorts and other qualitative methods have been developed to use in session for exploration of interests, skills, and values (Chope, 2015; McMahon, Watson, & Lee, 2019).

The remaining two quadrants embody either data-driven information or idiographic information that is gathered to meet the needs of an organization or clinician. Examples of the former include personnel selection or college admissions, whereas the latter includes selection interviews or evaluations conducted for forensic or custody purposes. Vocational assessment rarely is used to address questions in either of these quadrants. Haverkamp's (2013) model offers a comprehensive basis to discuss the fundamental reasons for using vocational assessment, as well as the specific tools and their uses, which constitutes the remainder of the present chapter.

THE NATURE AND SCOPE OF VOCATIONAL ASSESSMENT TOOLS

Vocational assessment may be defined as any test or assessment designed to measure work-related characteristics, such as interests, values, personality, skills, abilities, and self-efficacy. The primary goals of the majority of vocational assessment are both proximal and distal in nature: to increase individuals' present self-exploration and self-understanding, so as to improve later outcomes such as career choice fit or job satisfaction. Vocational assessment includes formal standardized tests with well-established psychometric properties but may also include less formal, qualitative methods of gathering information, such as card sorts or other activities designed to enhance self-understanding.

Vocational assessment is almost always shared directly with the client when it occurs as part of career counseling (Duckworth, 1990), given that the goal is self-understanding. Moreover, vocational assessment instruments are specifically designed to be directly communicated to the client; in fact, the client is expected to be an integral part of the process of interpreting assessment results (Duckworth, 1990; Haverkamp, 2013) and test interpretation often serves as an in-session intervention.

Traditionally, a large portion of vocational assessment occurs in the context of individual career counseling, in which a single counselor meets face-to-face with a single client. Further, the client is frequently engaged in the process of deciding whether to use assessment, what types of assessment might be useful, and in the interpretation of results and integration into ongoing counseling. However, there are other settings in which vocational assessment is used. In fact, because work often plays a central role in individuals' lives, vocational assessment could be implemented in nearly any setting (Juntunen, 2006; Swanson & Fouad, in press), such as personnel selection, admissions decisions, rehabilitation, and career management.

Viewed from another perspective, some vocational interventions and assessment focus on career exploration, helping clients gain an awareness of their interests, values, and skills and explore various occupations that might be a good fit. Other vocational interventions (and assessment) focus on helping individuals prepare for various transitions involving work, such as preparing for a job, finding a job, or managing career transitions.

Types of Tests

Vocational assessment has traditionally focused on the measurement of four broad constructs viewed as central to career decisions and vocational behavior: interests, values, ability/achievement, and personality. Theoretically, these are separate and distinct constructs and initial development of assessment tools treated them as such. However, the assessment of many of these constructs now is offered in a comprehensive or integrated manner, which is particularly true in online platforms such as the Kuder Career Planning System.

A distinction is often made between career choice *content* and career choice *process*. Career choice content refers to the actual choice, or the *what* or product of career decision-making; career choice process refers to *how* the decision is made. This distinction is useful in considering the purpose of assessment. Vocational assessment that focuses on content includes measures of interests, values, abilities, skills, and personality. All of these instruments are used *for* the client; in other words, the information gleaned from the assessment is shared directly with the client and becomes interwoven with what occurs in career counseling or educational interventions. This type of assessment is most amenable to the recommendations of Duckworth (1990) related to the client's involvement in all aspects of assessment, from initial selection of measures through interpretation of scores. Moreover, assessment of career choice content is frequently viewed as an intervention in and of itself within career counseling. Thus, a client may enter career counseling with the express purpose of taking a test to "tell me what to do" or the counselor may propose an assessment as an initial data-gathering intervention.

In contrast, the assessment of career choice *process* often serves a screening function, to determine whether the client is ready to move forward with career decisions and to identify factors that may impede decision-making. Assessment of career choice process also is frequently used as a criterion by which to judge the efficacy of interventions. Thus, measures of process may be more oriented toward use primarily by counselors than are measures of content, although some recent test developers have made materials more directly accessible to clients. A core set of process constructs include vocational maturity or adaptability, identity, decision-making, and adjustment.

Vocational Interests

The measurement of vocational interests forms the bedrock of vocational assessment and counseling. The earlier version of current interest measures were published in the 1920s by E. K. Strong and Fritz Kuder and evolved into the current Strong Interest Inventory (Harmon et al., 2005) and the Kuder Career Interests Assessment (now incorporated into an online platform). Interest inventories continue to be the most commonly used assessment tool in assisting clients with work-related decisions (Hansen, 2005, 2013).

Nearly all available interest inventories are designed to measure, at least in part, constructs from Holland's (1959, 1997) theory of vocational personality types. Holland posited that career choice is an expression of vocational personality and that individuals in an occupation have similar personalities. He categorized vocational personalities into six vocational types: realistic, investigative, artistic, social, enterprising, and conventional (RIASEC). Although Holland's theory has been primarily used as a framework for vocational interests, each type also includes characteristic aspects of skills, abilities, personality, and values. Environments may also be categorized into the same six RIASEC types. If a person's type(s) matches the environment's type(s) (or are *congruent*), the individual is predicted to be satisfied in that occupation. Thus, this theory predicts that person–environment fit leads to positive vocational outcomes such as job satisfaction and life satisfaction.

Holland (1997) hypothesized that the six types are ordered around a hexagon in the R-I-A-S-E-C configuration and the distances between the themes are hypothesized to be equal around the hexagon. Those that are adjacent are presumed to be more related and those that are directly opposite (A-C, R-S, and I-E) on the hexagon are predicted to be least related to one another. This hexagonal structure is evident in the presentation of individuals' results on interest inventories. Holland's theory has received considerable support for the existence and ordering of the RIASEC types (Nauta, 2010).

Interest inventories may provide a straightforward and focused assessment of Holland's themes, such as the Self-Directed Search, ACT's UNIACT, or the Interest Profiler. In addition to Holland's themes, interest measures may also provide scales on clusters of interests and comparison of an individual's interests to incumbents in a variety of occupations. The Strong Interest Inventory, the Campbell Interest and Skills Survey, and the Kuder Career Search are examples of the latter.

Three interest inventories are discussed in the next section to illustrate the types of inventories available to measure interests: the Strong Interest Inventory (SII), the Self-Directed Search, and the Interest Profiler. The SII is commercially available from Consulting Psychologists Press and must be computer scored (either paper-and-pencil or taken online). The Self-Directed Search was developed by Holland to be a counselor-free intervention and is available from Psychological Assessment Resources (paper-and-pencil or online). The Interest Profiler is part of the O*NET suite of materials published by the US Department of Labor and is free and readily available to the public. Psychometric information for each inventory is summarized in Table 14.1.

Strong Interest Inventory (SII). The SII (Harmon et al., 2005) consists of 291 items assessing an individual's preferences for various activities, using a five-point scale to rate liking of occupational titles, activities, school subjects, and various types of people and whether various characteristics are descriptive of the test-taker. Scores are reported on four types of scales, normed on same-sex and combined-sex groups. The six General Occupational Themes (GOT) are broad, theoretically driven scales measuring Holland's six vocational personality themes (RIASEC). The thirty Basic Interest Scales (BIS) provide more information on clusters of preferences for specific activities (e.g., Sales, Performing Arts, Office Management). Five personal style scales constitute the third set and include Work Style, Learning Environment Scale, Leadership Style, Risk Taking and Team Orientation. The fourth set, with the longest history,

Table 14.1 Representative psychometric information for vocational assessment tests

Measure	Reliability	Validity	Diversity
Interests			
Strong Interest Inventory			
General Occupational Themes	Alpha: 0.90–0.95 [a] Test-retest (8–23 mos): 0.80–0.92 [a]	Differentiation of occupational groups Correlations with other RIASEC scales [b]	Similarity of hexagonal structure across sex and R/E groups [c]
Basic Interest Scales	Alpha: 0.80–0.92 [c] Test-retest (1–6 mos): mean = 0.84 [c]	Differentiation of occupational groups [a]	Sex differences as predicted; minimal differences across five R/E groups [m]
Occupational Scales	Test-retest (2–23 mos): 0.71–0.93 [a]	Prediction of concurrent education or eventual occupation [d]	Similar prediction of education or occupation across sex and R/E groups [c]
Personal Style Scales	Alpha 0.82–0.87 [a] Test-retest (2–23 mos): 0.74–0.91 [a]	Correlations with like-named scales; group differences [a]	No information available
Self-Directed Search	KR-20: 0.90–0.94 [e] Test-retest (1–3 mos): 0.76–0.89 [e]	Correlations with other RIASEC scales [b e]	Sex differences as predicted; R/E representation in samples [e]
Interest Profiler	Alpha: 0.93–0.96 [f] Test-retest (1 mo): 0.82–0.92 [f]	Correlations with other RIASEC scales [f] Confirmed RIASEC structure [f]	Sex differences as predicted; R/E representation in samples [f]
Self-Efficacy			
Skills Confidence Inventory	Alpha: 0.84–0.94 [g] Test-retest (3 wks): 0.83–0.87 [g]	Correlations with like-named *Strong* scales [g] Differentiation of occupational groups [h]	Sex differences as predicted, similar correlational patterns with *Strong* scales; R/E representation in samples [g]
Values			
Minnesota Importance Questionnaire	Hoyt coefficients: 0.77–0.81 [i] Test-retest (6 wks): 0.65–0.83 [i]	Correlations with like-named scales [j]	Minimal sex differences; R/E representation in samples [j]
Work Importance Profiler	Alpha: 0.50–0.86 [k] Test-retest (1–2 mos): needs, 0.53–0.76; values 0.59–0.66 [k]	Correlations with MIQ: needs, 0.55–0.84; values, 0.67–0.84 [k] Confirmed six-factor structure [k]	Minimal sex and R/E differences and similar structure across groups [k]
Career Maturity/Adaptability			
Career Adapt-Abilities Scale	Alpha: US, 0.80–0.90, total score 0.94; international 0.74–0.85, total score 0.92 [l] Test-retest: n/a	Correlations with identity status; confirmed factor structure [l]	Developed with samples from 13 countries [l]

Abbreviations. "mos" = months, "wks" = weeks, "R/E" = racial/ethnic
Notes.[a] Donnay et al. (2005); [b] Savickas, Taber, and Spokane (2002); [c] Hansen (2013); [d] Hansen and Dik (2005), Hansen and Swanson (1983); [e] Holland, Fritzsche, and Powell (1997); [f] Rounds, Mazzeo et al. (1999); [g] Betz et al. (2003); [h] Donnay and Borgen (1999); [i] Gay et al. (1971), Rounds et al. (1981); [j] Leuty and Hansen (2011); [k] McCloy et al. (1999); [l] Porfeli and Savickas (2012), Savickas and Porfeli (2012); [m] Fouad and Mohler (2004).

is the Occupational Scales, which are empirically derived via the use of contrast groups to select items characteristic of occupational incumbents; currently, there are 122 occupations on the SII, representing benchmark occupations (e.g., Actuary, Graphic Designer, Social Worker). Administrative indices also are reported on the SII profile, including a typicality index that flags potentially inconsistent or random responses by examining pairs of highly correlated items.

Another feature of the SII is a companion measure, the *Skills Confidence Inventory* (Betz, Borgen, & Harmon, 2005), designed to assess the level of confidence an individual has in completing tasks associated with the six Holland themes. Results are presented in tandem with the SII and test-takers' results are prioritized according to the comparison of interests and skills confidence, such as High Priority if both interests and skills confidence are high, versus high interest but low confidence, or high confidence but low interest.

Psychometric properties of the SII have been well documented since its introduction in 1927 and substantial evidence exists for content, concurrent, predictive, and construct validity of the various SII scales (Hansen, 2013). Concurrent and predictive validity evidence also has been demonstrated for the SCI, although at a lesser volume due to its more recent development (Jenkins, 2013). See Table 14.1 for more information.

Self-Directed Search. Holland (Holland, 1985; Holland & Messer, 2013) developed the SDS to be a self-help measure of the six RIASEC themes and it continues to be available to individuals in such a fashion, either via paper-and-pencil administration or online. The SDS consists of items related to aspirations, activities, self-rated competencies and abilities, and interest in specific occupations, resulting in a three-letter summary code corresponding to an individual's three highest RIASEC raw scores. Test-takers are then directed to a listing of occupations that are classified according to the RIASEC codes, either through printed workbooks or online via the O*NET.

There is substantial psychometric information for the SDS, in part because it has been used extensively in vocational psychology research for nearly forty years and includes strong test-retest and internal consistency reliability as well as concurrent and predictive validity. In addition, content validity was addressed through development and subsequent revisions to ensure that the six RIASEC summary codes are adequately measuring the interest domains.

Interest Profiler. The Interest Profiler Short Form (Rounds et al., 2010) is a sixty-item measure of Holland's six RIASEC themes. The original 180-item Interest Profiler (Lewis & Rivkin, 1999) was designed to be an accessible, self-administered, and culture-fair instrument and to include activities from highly complex to less skilled occupations.

The Interest Profiler Short Form takes ten minutes to complete and is available online. Individuals indicate level of interest on a five-point scale and scores are summed for each the six scales. Individuals are then directed to occupations in their highest interest area from more than 1,000 occupations in the O*NET database. The Interest Profiler was developed with particular attention to reducing gender and racial/ethnic bias, as well as to ensuring strong and comprehensive reliability and validity evidence (Rounds et al., 2010).

Work Values

The assessment of work values is used to predict job satisfaction as well as vocational choice, and values assume a central role in some theories of vocational choice and adjustment (Pope, Flores, & Rottinghaus, 2014). Work values may be assessed to clarify individuals' motivations for working or what they expect to gain from specific jobs or occupations (Rounds & Jin, 2013).

The constructs of values and needs are central in the Theory of Work Adjustment (TWA; Dawis & Lofquist, 1984; Swanson & Schneider, in press), which postulates that job satisfaction is highest when an individual's needs are matched by reinforcers within their employing organization. In TWA terms, if an individual's needs correspond to the reinforcers provided by the environment, they will be satisfied. When they do not match, such as, for example, dissatisfaction with level of pay, the individual engages in adjustment behavior. The individual will either actively seek changes in the environment (e.g., ask for more pay) or reactively make changes in their level of need (e.g., reduce expenses).

Work values may be assessed with the Minnesota Importance Questionnaire (MIQ; Rounds, Henley, Dawis, Lofquist, & Weiss, 1981) or the Work Importance Profiler (WIP; McCloy et al., 1999). Other extant measures that may be used in vocational interventions measure general values rather than work-related values.

Minnesota Importance Questionnaire. The MIQ measures twenty-one work-related needs, grouped into six underlying values. Two forms are available: The paired comparison format presents each need statement compared to every other need statement (total of 420 pairs) and the rank format presents need statements in groups of five, which are rank-ordered by test-takers. The MIQ also provides an index of the degree of match between an individual's needs and those of ninety occupations, which is a strength of the MIQ. An index of Logically Consistent Triads, the LCT, provides information about nonrandomness in responding. The MIQ has been extensively researched, providing evidence for its construct and structural validity (Rounds & Jin, 2013), undergirding the development of the Work Importance Profiler.

Work Importance Profiler. The Work Importance Profiler (WIP; McCloy et al., 1999) is part of the O*NET career exploration tools available at no cost to the general public. The WIP was designed to be similar to the MIQ and MIQ developers were senior consultants to the US Department of Labor during the development of the WIP. Individuals are presented with groups of five need statements to rank order, followed by absolute ratings of the importance of each statement in an ideal job. The WIP profile summarizes the relative importance of six values: Achievement, Independence, Recognition, Relationships, Support, and Working Conditions. Results are linked to the extensive occupational database in the O*NET, providing individuals with occupations that may be a good fit with their work values.

Ability, Achievement, and Aptitude

Assessment of ability and achievement was an integral part of early career interventions, particularly those that focused on the "trait" aspect of trait-and-factor counseling. Ability was viewed, justifiably so, as an important component of an individual's characteristics vis-à-vis vocational choice. One of the earliest measures built on strong psychometric principles was the General Aptitude Test Battery (GATB), developed by the US Employment Service in the 1940s; this test was the precursor of today's Armed Services Vocational Aptitude Battery (ASVAB), used to select and place military personnel. For more information on assessment of aptitude and achievement, see Chapter 12 ("Intellectual Assessment") and Chapter 13 ("Achievement Assessment") in this volume.

However, the formal assessment of ability per se is unlikely to occur in the context of contemporary vocational interventions; rather, proxy indicators are used, such as measures of achievement (ACT and similar measures administered for educational admission), grade point average and other indicators of academic performance, or even self-estimates (Metz & Jones, 2013). Further, in organizational settings, work-based performance indicators take on greater importance (particularly as related to TWA).

Measures of aptitude may also be used in personnel selection, although not strictly for traditional "vocational" purposes (i.e., assisting an individual in determining career direction) but rather as a screening measure for organizational purposes. For example, the Wonderlic Basic Skills Test is often used as a brief screening measure of cognitive ability.

A contemporary interpretation of measuring ability/achievement/aptitude is the measurement of *self-efficacy*. Starting with Taylor and Betz (1983), researchers applied Bandura's (1977) concept of self-efficacy to vocational choice in two ways: self-efficacy about interest-related areas (such as Holland's RIASEC) and self-efficacy about the decision-making process itself. The former is represented by the Skills Confidence Inventory (SCI; Betz et al., 2005), which is available as an add-on to the Strong Interest Inventory, as noted in the "Strong Interest Inventory" section. Self-efficacy about career decision-making is more accurately classified as a process variable (see discussion of process vs. content in vocational assessment in the "Types of Tests" section) and is measured via instruments such as the Career Decision Self-Efficacy Scale (CDSE; Betz & Taylor, 2012), which has been widely used in vocational research.

Personality

The measurement of personality occupies an interesting role within vocational assessment. Personality variables are of obvious importance in the selection and implementation of career choice (influencing the *content* of career interventions) but are also relevant to the *process* of career intervention itself (Brown & Hirschi, 2013; Rossier, 2015); yet stand-alone measurement of personality is not often included as part of vocational assessment. On the other hand, as noted in the "Vocational Interests" section, Holland's (1997) theory purports to encompass "vocational personalities," as evidenced by the inclusion of personality traits in descriptions of the six RIASEC types, and so interpretation of interest inventories with RIASEC types frequently incorporates discussion of personality. When personality instruments are used as part of vocational assessment, they may either be measures developed for use in other settings or developed specifically to augment measures of other constructs for educational/vocational uses.

An important feature of personality inventories in the context of vocational assessment is a focus on "normal" personality (versus psychopathology). So, measures most commonly used as part of vocational assessment include the California Psychological Inventory (CPI), the NEO Personality Inventory (NEO-PI), the Sixteen Personality Factor Questionnaire (16PF), and the Eysenck Personality Questionnaire. Readers are referred to reviews of personality and vocational behavior, such as Brown and Hirschi (2013) and Rossier (2015).

A unique approach to using extant personality inventories entails test publishers tailoring profile reports for vocational or personnel uses, such as the NEO-PI-3 Four-Factor Version (NEO-PI-3:4FV), which eliminates Neuroticism from the Big Five domain scales to make results more relevant to work settings. Inventories such as the 16PF produce the same numeric results regardless of the purpose of assessment but offer interpretive information geared toward career exploration. Another approach is personality inventories that were added to measures originally designed for another purpose, such as the Personal Characteristics Inventory, built to accompany the Wonderlic, and ACT's WorkKeys Assessments, which incorporate measures of aptitude, interests, values, and personality.

It is crucial to recall the purpose of measuring personality variables in the context of vocational assessment, in comparison to other settings. That is, results of personality assessment are aimed at increasing individuals' self-awareness and then integrating that awareness with other information to enhance career-related decisions. The test-taker is an active participant in the selection and interpretation of test results (Duckworth, 1990). In contrast, personality assessment in other settings (such as forensic or custody evaluations, presurgical screenings) may be more susceptible to clients' desires to "fake good" or "fake bad," depending on the purpose and outcome of the assessment (Goldfinger, 2019).

Career maturity and adaptability. The concept of "career development" emerged from the work of Donald E. Super (1953), in recognition of the ongoing nature of vocational decisions across a person's life span rather than as a single decision point. Super's theory led to efforts to measure relevant constructs, including *vocational maturity* (Super, 1955), *career maturity* (Crites, 1973), and, more recently, *career adaptability* (Savickas, 1997; Super & Knausel, 1981). Savickas (2013, 2018) identified four components of career adaptability: *concern* refers to the degree to which individuals think about their future and begin to increase personal *control* over, *curiosity* about exploring, and *confidence* in pursuing that future. Measuring constructs related to career maturity and adaptability has proved difficult, however, in part due to the inherently transitory nature of constructs expected to change with time (Swanson, 2013). On the other hand, one might argue that the construct of adaptability has increased in relevance given the changes in the world of work (Blustein, 2013; DeBell, 2006) and more recent theoretical formulations emphasize the utility of adaptability (Glavin, 2015).

Several measures have been developed to assess readiness to make career decisions, including the Career Development Inventory (CDI; Super, 1990) and the Career Maturity Inventory (CMI; Crites, 1973). The Career Adapt-Abilities Scale (CAAS; Porfeli & Savickas, 2012; Savickas & Porfeli, 2012) is the most recent evolution of the CMI and was developed by an international collaboration of researchers across thirteen countries. The CAAS provides a general measure of adaptability regardless of age, with an overall score obtained for Career Adaptability and subscale scores on Career Concern, Career Control, Career Curiosity, and Career Confidence.

A Comment about Psychometric Characteristics

The instruments discussed in this chapter were chosen based on their psychometric rigor, longevity, and utility, as summarized in Table 14.1, as well as the attention paid to issues of cultural diversity in their development and interpretation. Given that many vocational instruments are used with adolescents and young adults, it is important to consider the nature of the trait being measured and to disentangle stability of the trait from reliability and validity of the measure. For example, measures of vocational interests tend to be increasingly stable with age and thus validity or reliability evaluated in children's or adolescent's test scores must be interpreted in the context of a construct that is developmental in nature.

In addition to the traditional tripartite view of validity (content, criterion-related, and construct validity), several other conceptualizations of validity have been proposed as specifically relevant to vocational assessment. *Exploration validity* (Randahl, Hansen, & Haverkamp, 1993) refers to the degree to which an assessment tool stimulates the test-taker to explore additional career options based on test results. Similarly, *interpretive validity* (Walsh & Betz, 2001) refers to the degree to which test results and interpretations are presented in a useful and valid manner. These newer conceptualizations of validity are focused on test results and how they are interpreted to the test-taker. While this is a useful conceptualization, it has not received the same empirical attention as more traditional views of validity.

Further, the desired outcomes of vocational assessment may vary widely based on the reasons individuals enter counseling or other interventions. For example, the Strong Interest Inventory may be used to expand a client's view of possible occupations early in the process of career exploration or to narrow or focus a client's view prior to choosing a specific occupational path. Such disparate outcomes complicate determination of a "good" outcome of an intervention.

DIVERSITY/CULTURAL ISSUES

Issues related to diversity are particularly important in vocational assessment because these inventories offer access to the opportunity structure of society. That is, if a goal of using vocational assessment is to encourage career exploration or to facilitate decision-making, then the instruments themselves must be as free from bias as possible and not reflect historical limits to occupational access. Attention to gender and racial-ethnic diversity must begin during test development by constructing items that are free from bias and by ensuring that normative samples are representative of the population. Moreover, the results and interpretation of instruments must be presented in a manner that does not foreclose options. Attention to cultural diversity in career assessment is a natural outgrowth of counseling psychology being rooted in the individual differences paradigm and has been folded into models that systematically address broader issues in career counseling, such as Bingham and Ward's (1994) model of culturally appropriate career counseling or Fouad and Kantamneni's (2008) three-dimensional model of contextual factors in vocational psychology. In addition, guidelines regarding multicultural assessment have been developed by professional organizations relevant to career practitioners, such as *Standards for Multicultural Assessment* by the Association for Assessment in Counseling (AAC, 2003) and *Minimum Standards for Multicultural Career Counseling* by the National Career Development Association (NCDA, 2009).

Empirical evidence supports the use of vocational assessment with diverse cultural groups, including sex and racial-ethnic groups (see Table 14.1). It is important to distinguish between valid group differences on the constructs that instruments are designed to measure versus the ability of the instruments to predict important outcomes for a variety of groups. For example, sex differences in vocational interests are "quite stable and robust" in studies spanning a fifty-year period (Hansen, 2013, p. 410); yet the important question regarding validity is whether a measure of interests predicts with the same level of accuracy for men and women. In other words, finding sex or racial-ethnic differences in interests or values does not necessarily suggest a lack of support for these measures; rather, it is important to examine the validity of the interpretations resulting from these measures. Measures of vocational constructs developed in recent years frequently build on evidence from earlier measures and one approach to validating the newer measure is to compare it to the previous measure. However, evidence specifically pertaining to diversity requires additional updating.

Inclusivity regarding gender and race/ethnicity has long been a focus in career assessment, whereas attention has only recently turned to LGBTQ representation and access in assessment (Prince & Potoczniak, 2012; Schaubhut & Thompson, 2016). Further research is also needed to examine the effect of intersecting identities on the development and use of vocational assessment.

TECHNOLOGICAL ADVANCES IN VOCATIONAL ASSESSMENT

Some of the technological advances in vocational assessment parallel those in any type of psychological testing, particularly in regard to computer-assisted or online administration and interpretation, with concomitant issues related to test security and integrity of scores. In addition, there are several technological advances unique to vocational assessment, primarily in connecting one set of test scores to another and to occupational information.

Integrated Assessment

As noted in the "Vocational Interests" section, many of the stand-alone measures of single constructs (e.g., interests or values) have been connected to or merged with measures of other constructs, producing an integrated profile of results. For example, the Strong Interest Inventory may be linked to the Skills Confidence Inventory with the goal of comparing an individual's interests and self-efficacy for sets of activities. Similarly, the Kuder Career Planning System includes measures of interests, values, and skills confidence. These results may either be fully integrated (such as the Strong and Skills Confidence Inventory, in which interest scores are compared to like-named confidence scales to create high-high, high-low, low-high, and low-low categories) or simply be presented as contiguous results that require integration by the counselor and client (such as the Interest Profiler and the Work Importance Profiler, both available on the O*NET, in which results are presented separately).

Creating comprehensive and integrated assessment platforms was a natural development. If a publisher owns copyrights and scoring services for related instruments, the packaging of results could be accomplished with relative ease. Moreover, a test publisher with a well-established instrument in one domain may choose to expand by developing or acquiring another instrument. Further, advances in internet-based technology also made integration feasible. For example, the ACT, initially developed for use in college admissions decisions, was extended downward into the middle-school range and an interest test was incorporated into results. Labeled EXPLORE (for grades 8–9) and PLAN (for grade 10), these results offer achievement/aptitude scores along with interest scores based on Holland's theory. Because of the preeminence of achievement data in educational institutions, however, the interpretation and use of the interest portion are often overlooked.

The Kuder Career Planning System is another example of a set of "traditional" assessments that have been revised and reformatted into an online platform that is accessible, for a fee, by anyone from elementary school through middle adulthood. This system includes a version of the original Kuder Preference Record, an interest test developed in the 1930s, the Work Values Inventory developed by Donald Super in the 1960s, as well as a skills and abilities self-assessment.

Connection of Assessment Results to Occupational Information

An important component of vocational assessment in the context of career- and work-related decisions is the provision of occupational information; in Parsons's (1909) original treatise, he defined world-of-work information as "knowledge of the requirements and conditions of success, advantages and disadvantages, compensation, opportunities and prospects in different lines of work" (p. 5). Many of the integrated systems include such a component, by linking an individual's assessment results with occupational information. For example, the O*NET system includes the largest available database of empirically based occupational information and test-takers may access the database using their assessment results. Unfortunately, the O*NET does not yet provide users with an intersection of their results: A user can take the Work Importance Profiler and the Interest Profiler, and use each independently to explore the database, but not examine the ways in which interests and values intersect and connect to the occupations.

Online Assessment and Interpretation

Assessment administered online has grown exponentially in the past decade. Although there are unique problems involved in using online assessment, there are also technological solutions. In the context of vocational assessment, however, concerns about test security or integrity are less prevalent than for aptitude tests or tests administered for personnel selection (Sampson et al., 2013).

It is important to make a distinction between online administration and online interpretation. Some publishers offer the option of administering a test online through a secure portal, with the test results delivered electronically to the counselor. The Kuder Career Planning System, with its measures of interests, skills confidence, and values, may be purchased for individual use by nonprofessionals; in fact, some age levels of the system are marketed to parents rather than to an educational institution. Whether or not these test results are properly interpreted requires further investigation.

Because a major focus of vocational assessment is on *self-exploration*, it would seem particularly well-suited for self-guided assessments, which, in turn, are particularly well-suited for online delivery. The Self-Directed Search (SDS) was initially developed by John Holland to foster self-assessment, even arguing that career counselors should become obsolete. One consequence of the availability of online assessment, however, is the proliferation of unsubstantiated "quizzes" with little or no psychometric foundation or theoretical grounding (for an illustration, type "career assessment" into a search engine).

Other Innovations

Little has been done in terms of adaptive testing in vocational assessment. For example, when measuring an individual's relative standing on the six Holland RIASEC types, it would be useful to drill down into areas of interest rather than wasting items in areas of little interest.

A logical extension of the development of online assessment is scaling down to mobile platforms and delivering brief assessments via smartphones. For example, C'reer was developed to assess high-school students' interests and match them with relevant educational programs, as was a short, mobile-based version of the O*NET Interest Profiler (Rounds et al., 2016). More of these apps are surely around the corner; it will be important for professional psychological organizations to weigh in on the psychometric integrity of new options.

While not a technological advance per se, the changing nature of work will continue to have an immense impact on how career assessment is implemented. Scales that measure a test-taker's similarity to occupational incumbents may be less relevant given the rise in precarious work and a decline in lifelong occupations (Blustein, 2013, 2019).

INTERPRETIVE AND/OR PRACTICAL RECOMMENDATIONS

Traditionally, discussion of how to integrate assessment results into counseling occurs primarily within the realm of vocational (vs. nonvocational) counseling, because nowhere else is it as central to the role and purpose of counseling. A word of warning, though, comes from Hartung (2005), who cautions against a "career-counseling-as-testing" mindset, in which testing is viewed as *the* equivalent of counseling. In fact, earlier applications of trait-and-factor vocational counseling were characterized as "test 'em and tell 'em" or "three interviews and a cloud of dust." In contrast, contemporary models of vocational counseling are a far cry from these earlier approaches. As noted throughout the present chapter, the practice of vocational assessment typically entails a client who is active in decisions about whether to use assessment, about the specific types of assessment, and, not surprisingly, in the interpretation of results.

Zytowski (2015), noting that test manuals vary widely in terms of guidance for interpretation, suggested five general principles for interpreting interest inventories, which would apply to other types of vocational assessment results: (1) prepare for the discussion of results, (2) involve clients in communication of results, (3) use simple, emphatic communication, (4) ask clients to recapitulate their results in their own words, and (5) stimulate continuing development, such as further exploration of possible occupations.

Whether in traditional career counseling or as part of another intervention, practitioners using vocational assessment tests are encouraged to keep in mind the client-focused nature of these tests. They provide valuable information for work-related decisions, particularly given the collaborative manner in which they were intended to be used.

In summary, vocational assessment is a valuable tool for career practitioners and other professionals, whether administered and interpreted in traditional one-on-one counseling settings or delivered online or via mobile apps. The increasing diversity of the workforce, as well as the changing nature of work itself, requires continued attention from test developers and researchers.

REFERENCES

Association for Assessment in Counseling. (2003). *Standards for multicultural assessment*. http://aac.ncat.edu/Resources/documents/STANDARDS%20FOR%20MULTICULTURAL%20ASSESSMENT%20FINAL.pdf

Bandura, A. (1977). Self-efficacy: Toward a unifying theory of behavioral change. *Psychological Review*, *84*, 191–215.

Betz, N. E., Borgen, F. H., & Harmon, L. (2005). *Skills confidence inventory manual* (revised ed.). Palo Alto, CA: Consulting Psychologists Press.

Betz, N. E., Borgen, F. H., Rottinghaus, P., Paulsen, A., Halper, C. R., & Harmon, L. W. (2003). The expanded Skills Confidence Inventory: Measuring basic dimensions of vocational activity. *Journal of Vocational Behavior*, *62*, 76–100.

Betz, N. E., & Taylor, K. M. (2012). *Manual for the career decision self-efficacy Scale and CDSE-short form*. Menlo Park, CA: Mindgarden.

Bingham, R. P., & Ward, C. M. (1994). Career counseling with ethnic minority women. In W. B. Walsh & S. Osipow (Eds.), *Career counseling with women* (pp. 165–195). Hillsdale, NJ: Lawrence Erlbaum.

Blustein, D. L. (Ed.). (2013). *The Oxford handbook of the psychology of working*. New York: Oxford University Press.

Blustein, D. L. (2019). *The importance of work in an age of uncertainty: The eroding work experience in America*. New York: Oxford University Press.

Brown, S. D., & Hirschi, A. (2013). Personality, career development, and occupational attainment. In S. D. Brown & R. W. Lent (Eds.), *Career development and counseling: Putting theory and research to work* (2nd ed., pp. 299–328). New York: Wiley.

Chope, R. C. (2015). Card sorts, sentence completions, and other qualitative assessments. In P. J. Hartung, M. L. Savickas, & W. B. Walsh (Eds.), *APA handbook of career intervention, Vol. 2: Applications* (pp. 71–84). Washington, DC: American Psychological Association. doi:10.1037/14439-006

Crites, J. O. (1973). *The career maturity inventory*. Monterey, CA: CTB/McGraw-Hill.

Dawis, R. V. (1992). The individual differences tradition in counseling psychology. *Journal of Counseling Psychology*, *39*, 7–19.

Dawis, R. V., & Lofquist, L. H. (1984). *A psychological theory of work adjustment*. Minneapolis: University of Minnesota Press.

DeBell, C. (2006). What all applied psychologists need to know about the world of work. *Professional Psychology: Research and Practice*, *37*, 325–333.

Donnay, D. A. C., & Borgen, F. H. (1999). The incremental validity of vocational self-efficacy: an examination of interest, self-efficacy, and occupation. *Journal of Counseling Psychology*, *46*(4), 432–447.

Donnay, D. A. C, Morris, M., Schaubhut, N., & Thompson, R. (2005). *Strong Interest Inventory manual: Research, development, and strategies for interpretation*. Palo Alto, CA: Consulting Psychologists Press.

Duckworth, J. (1990). The counseling approach to the use of testing. *The Counseling Psychologist*, *18*, 198–204.

Flores, L. Y., Berkel, L. A., Nilsson, J. E., Ojeda, L., Jordan, S. E., Lynn, G. L., & Leal, V. M. (2006). Racial/ethnic minority vocational research: A content and trend analysis across 36 years. *The Career Development Quarterly*, *55*, 2–21.

Fouad, N. A., & Kantamneni, N. (2008). Contextual factors in vocational psychology: Intersections of individual, group, and societal dimensions. In S. D. Brown & R. W. Lent (Eds.), *Handbook of counseling psychology* (4th ed., pp. 408–425). Hoboken, NJ: John Wiley.

Fouad, N. A., & Mohler, C. E. (2004). Cultural validity of Holland's theory and the Strong Interest Inventory for five racial/ethnic groups. *Journal of Career Assessment*, *12*(4), 432–439. doi:10.1177/1069072704267736

Gay, E. G., Weiss, D. J., Hendel, D. D., Dawis, R. V., & Lofquist, L. H. (1971). *Manual for the Minnesota Importance Questionnaire*. http://vpr.psych.umn.edu/instruments/miq-minnesota-importance-questionnaire

Glavin, K. (2015). Measuring and assessing career maturity and adaptability. In P. J. Hartung, M. L. Savickas, & W. B. Walsh (Eds.), *APA handbook of career intervention, Vol. 2: Applications* (pp. 183–192). Washington, DC: American Psychological Association.

Goldfinger, K. B. (2019). *Psychological testing in everyday life: History, science, and practice*. Thousand Oaks, CA: SAGE.

Hansen, J. C. (2005). Assessment of interests. In S. D. Brown & R. W. Lent (Eds.), *Career development and counseling: Putting theory and research to work* (pp. 281–304). New York: Wiley.

Hansen, J. C. (2013). Nature, importance, and assessment of interests. In S. D. Brown & R. W. Lent (Eds.), *Career development and counseling: Putting theory and research to work* (2nd ed., pp. 387–416). New York: Wiley.

Hansen, J. C., & Dik, B. J. (2005). Evidence of 12-year predictive and concurrent validity for SII Occupational Scale scores. *Journal of Vocational Behavior*, *67*, 365–378.

Hansen, J. C., & Swanson, J. L. (1983). The effect of stability of interests on the predictive and concurrent validity of the SCII for college majors. *Journal of Counseling Psychology*, *30*, 194–201.

Harmon, L. W., Hansen, J. C., Borgen, F. H., & Hammer, A. C. (2005). *Strong interest inventory: Applications and technical guide*. Palo Alto, CA: Consulting Psychologists Press.

Hartung, P. J. (2005). Integrated career assessment and counseling: Mindsets, models, and methods. In W. B. Walsh and M. L. Savickas (Eds.), *Handbook of vocational psychology* (3rd ed., pp. 371–395). Mahwah, NJ: Lawrence Erlbaum.

Haverkamp, B. E. (2013). Education and training in assessment for professional psychology: Engaging the "reluctant student." In K. F. Geisinger (Ed.), *APA handbook of testing and assessment in psychology, Vol. 2: Testing and assessment in clinical and counseling psychology* (pp. 63–82). Washington, DC: American Psychological Association.

Holland, J. L. (1959). A theory of vocational choice. *Journal of Counseling Psychology*, *6*, 35–45.

Holland, J. L. (1985). *The self-directed search professional manual*. Odessa, FL: Psychological Assessment Resources.

Holland, J. L. (1997). *Making vocational choices: A theory of vocational personalities and work environments* (3rd ed.). Odessa, FL: Psychological Assessment Resources.

Holland, J. L., Fritzsche, B. A., & Powell, A. B. (1997). *The self-directed search technical manual*. Odessa, FL: Psychological Assessment Resources.

Holland, J. L., & Messer, M. A. (2013). *The self-directed search professional manual*. Odessa, FL: Psychological Assessment Resources

Jenkins, J. A. (2013). Strong Interest Inventory and Skills Confidence Inventory. In C. Wood & D. G. Hayes (Eds.), *A counselor's guide to career assessment instruments* (6th ed., pp. 280–284). Broken Arrow, OK: National Career Development Association.

Juntunen, C. L. (2006). The psychology of working: The clinical context. *Professional Psychology: Research and Practice*, *37*(4), 342–350.

Leuty, M. E., & Hansen, J. C. (2011). Evidence of construct validity for work values. *Journal of Vocational Behavior*, *79*, 379–390.

Lewis, P., & Rivkin, D. (1999). *Development of the O*NET interest profiler*. www.onetcenter.org/dl_files/IP.pdf

McCloy, R., Waugh, G., Medsker, G., Wall, J., Rivkin, D., & Lewis, P. (1999). *Development of the O*NET computerized Work Importance Profiler*. www.onetcenter.org/dl_files/DevCWIP.pdf

McMahon, M., Watson, M., & Lee, M. C. Y. (2019). Qualitative career assessment: A review and reconsideration. *Journal of Vocational Behavior*, *110*, 420-432doi.org/10.1016/j.jvb.2018.03.009

Metz, A. J., & Jones, J. E. (2013). Ability and aptitude assessment in career counseling. In S. D. Brown & R. W. Lent (Eds.), *Career development and counseling: Putting theory and research to work* (2nd ed., pp. 449–476). New York: Wiley.

Nauta, M. (2010). The development, evolution, and status of Holland's theory of vocational personalities: Reflections and future directions for counseling psychologists. *Journal of Counseling Psychology, 57*(1), 11–22.

NCDA (National Career Development Association). (2009). *Multicultural career counseling minimum competencies*. www.ncda.org/aws/NCDA/pt/sp/guidelines

Parsons, F. (1989). *Choosing a vocation*. Garrett Park, MD: Garrett Park Press. (Original work published 1909.)

Pope, M., Flores, L. Y., & Rottinghaus, P. J. (Eds.). (2014). *The role of values in careers*. Charlotte, NC: Information Age Publishing.

Porfeli, E. J., & Savickas, M. L. (2012). Career Adapt-Abilities Scale-USA form: Psychometric properties and relation to vocational identity. *Journal of Vocational Behavior, 80*, 748–753.

Prince, J. P., & Potoczniak, M. J. (2012). Using psychological assessment tools with lesbian, gay, bisexual, and transgender clients. In S. H. Dworkin & M. Pope (Eds.), *Casebook for counseling lesbian, gay, bisexual, and transgender persons and their families*. Alexandria, VA: American Counseling Association.

Randahl, G. J., Hansen, J. C., & Haverkamp, B. E. (1993). Instrumental behaviors following test administration and interpretation: Exploration validity of the Strong Interest Inventory. *Journal of Counseling and Development, 71* (4), 435–439.

Rossier, J. (2015). Personality assessment and career interventions. In P. J. Hartung, M. L. Savickas, & W. B. Walsh (Eds.), *APA handbook of career intervention, Vol. 1: Foundations* (pp. 327–350). Washington, DC: American Psychological Association.

Rounds, J. B., Henley, G. A., Dawis, R. V., Lofquist, L. H., & Weiss, D. J. (1981). *Manual for the Minnesota importance questionnaire*. Minneapolis: University of Minnesota.

Rounds, J. B., & Jin, J. (2013). Nature, importance and assessment of needs and values. In S. D. Brown & R. W. Lent (Eds.), *Career development and counseling: Putting theory and research to work* (2nd ed., pp. 417–448). New York: Wiley.

Rounds, J. B., Mazzeo, S. E., Smith, T. J., Hubert, L., Lewis, P., & Rivkin, D. (1999). *O*NET Computerized Interest Profiler: Reliability, validity, and comparability*. www.onetcenter.org/dl_files/CIP_RVC.pdf

Rounds, J. B., Ming, C. W. J., Cao, M., Song, C., & Lewis, P. (2016). *Development of an O*NET® Mini Interest Profiler (Mini-IP) for mobile devices: Psychometric characteristics*. www.onetcenter.org/reports/Mini-IP.html

Rounds, J. B., Su, R., Lewis, P. & Rivkin, D. (2010). *O*NET interest profiler short form psychometric characteristics: Summary*. www.onetcenter.org/dl_files/IPSF_Psychometric.pdf

Sampson, J. P., Jr., McClain, M., Dozier, C., Carr, D. L., Lumsden, J. A., & Osborn, D. S. (2013). Computer-assisted career assessment. In C. Wood & D. G. Hayes (Eds.), *A counselor's guide to career assessment instruments* (6th ed., pp. 33–47). Broken Arrow, OK: National Career Development Association.

Savickas, M. L. (1997). Career adaptability: An integrative construct for life-span, life-space theory. *Career Development Quarterly, 45*, 247–259.

Savickas, M. L. (2013). Career construction theory and practice. In R. W. Lent & S. D. Brown (Eds.), *Career development and counseling: Putting theory and research to work* (2nd ed., pp. 147–186). Hoboken, NJ: Wiley.

Savickas, M. L. (2018). *Career counseling* (2nd ed.). Washington, DC: American Psychological Association.

Savickas, M. L., & Porfeli, E. J. (2012). Career Adapt-Abilities Scale: Construction, reliability, and measurement equivalence across 13 countries. *Journal of Vocational Behavior, 80*, 661–673.

Savickas, M. L., Taber, B. J., & Spokane, A. R. (2002). Convergent and discriminant validity of five interest inventories. *Journal of Vocational Behavior, 61*, 139–184.

Schaubhut, N. A., & Thompson, R. C. (2016). *Technical brief for the Strong Interest Inventory assessment: Using the Strong with LGBT populations*. Palo Alto, CA: Consulting Psychologists Press.

Super, D. E. (1953). A theory of vocational development. *American Psychologist, 8*, 185–190.

Super, D. E. (1955). The dimensions and measurement of vocational maturity. *Teachers College Record, 57*, 157–163.

Super, D. E. (1990). A life-span, life-space approach to career development. In D. Brown & L. Brooks (Eds.), *Career choice and development: Applying contemporary theories to practice* (pp. 197–261). San Francisco, CA: Jossey-Bass.

Super, D. E., & Knausel, E. G. (1981). Career development and adulthood: Some theoretical problems and a possible solution. *British Journal of Guidance and Counselling, 9*, 194–201.

Swanson, J. L. (2012). Measurement and assessment. In E. M. Altmaier & J. C. Hansen (Eds.). *The Oxford handbook of counseling psychology* (pp. 208–236). New York: Oxford University Press.

Swanson, J. L. (2013). Assessment of career development and maturity. In K. F. Geisinger (Ed.), *APA handbook of testing and assessment in psychology, Vol. 2: Testing and assessment in clinical and counseling psychology* (pp. 349–362). Washington, DC: American Psychological Association.

Swanson, J. L., & Fouad, N. A. (in press). *Career theory and practice: Learning through case studies* (4th ed.). Thousand Oaks, CA: Sage.

Swanson, J. L., & Schneider, M. (in press). Theory of Work Adjustment. In S. D. Brown & R. W. Lent (Eds.), *Career development and counseling: Putting theory and research to work* (3rd ed.). New York: Wiley.

Taylor, K. M., & Betz, N. E. (1983). Application of self-efficacy theory to the understanding and treatment of career indecision. *Journal of Vocational Behavior, 22*, 63–81.

Walsh, W. B., & Betz, N. E. (2001). *Tests and assessment*. Upper Saddle River, NJ: Prentice Hall.

Zytowski, D. G. (2015). Test interpretation: Talking with people about their test results. In P. J. Hartung, M. L. Savickas, & W. B. Walsh (Eds.), *APA handbook of career intervention, Vol. 2: Applications* (pp. 3–9). Washington, DC: American Psychological Association.

15 Neuropsychological Testing and Assessment

JULIE A. SUHR AND KALEY ANGERS

Neuropsychology, as defined by the Society for Clinical Neuropsychology, is "the study of brain-behavior relationships and the clinical application of that knowledge to human problems" (SCN, 2015). The terms neuropsychology and neuropsychologist emphasize two core components. The first, "neuro," refers to the need for advanced knowledge of neuroscience and biological bases of behavior. The second, "psychology," refers to the need for advanced knowledge of behavioral and emotional components of disorders, as well as of normal psychological development. Simply put, a neuropsychologist must be well trained in both clinical psychology and neuroscience, as the role of the neuropsychologist is to integrate biological, cognitive, psychological, and social assessment information in order to evaluate patients' presenting problems. Further, the neuropsychologist needs advanced skills in application of that knowledge (i.e., understanding of psychometric issues that arise when assessing neuropsychological constructs). These components are necessary for evidence-based clinical neuropsychology practice (Chelune, 2010). As such, although many health care psychologists and other health care providers administer neuropsychological screenings, and neuropsychological tests are often used in research, the clinical practice of neuropsychological assessment requires specialty training.

Clinical neuropsychology is a specialization recognized by both the American Psychological Association and the Canadian Psychological Association. Since its inception as a specialty area in 1996, neuropsychology has defined aspirational training standards. As outlined at the Houston Conference in 1997, clinical neuropsychology requires advanced training at the predoctoral, internship, and postdoctoral level (Hannay et al., 1998). At a minimum, to practice as a neuropsychologist, one should hold a doctoral degree in psychology (most often in clinical psychology or clinical neuropsychology) from an accredited program, the predoctoral internship (required for a doctoral degree in clinical psychology) should provide at least some training in clinical neuropsychology, and a two-year postdoctoral residency in clinical neuropsychology must be completed (Hannay et al., 1998). From there, a neuropsychologist is recommended, though not required, to complete a two-year board certification process. Details about training consistent with this model can be found in Chapter 34 in this volume.

Neuropsychological assessment can help to determine cognitive, psychological, and behavioral strengths/weaknesses that assist in establishing diagnosis, indicating prognosis, or predicting treatment outcome. It can also serve as a way to document outcome following treatment or other interventions. Results of a neuropsychological assessment may indicate early signs of a neurodegenerative disease process, which may lead to better preventive care. There is some evidence that neuropsychological tests serve as endophenotypes by showing more clear and proximal relationships to genetic variability associated with neuropsychiatric disorders than the behavioral/clinical symptoms (Jagaroo & Santangelo, 2016). Neuropsychological assessment is also common in forensic settings (although this specialty is beyond the scope of the chapter).

The purpose of the present chapter is to describe neuropsychological tests and assessment processes in both clinical and research settings. As neuropsychologists commonly use broad-band personality instruments, self-report instruments that assess individual constructs, and intelligence and achievement tests as part of their neuropsychological battery, readers should refer to other chapters within this volume for coverage of assessment issues for these measures (Chapters 11–13; Chapters 16–19). In the present chapter, we will focus on more unique issues beyond those that present in traditional psychological or intellectual assessment. We will first provide a description of approaches to neuropsychological assessment and discuss commonly assessed constructs (with exemplar tests). Then we will provide coverage of issues relevant for empirically informed clinical decision-making in neuropsychological assessment, including issues that arise when selecting tests, interpreting their scores, and integrating them with other data. We will also briefly discuss relatively unique ethical and professional issues that arise in the context of neuropsychological assessment.

APPROACHES TO NEUROPSYCHOLOGICAL ASSESSMENT

In the clinical setting, a neuropsychological evaluation typically includes collecting relevant medical, psychological, developmental, and sociocultural history, administering and interpreting neuropsychological tests, and integrating those components into a comprehensive report that addresses a referral question. Medical history is often collected through medical records and patient interview. Educational records can provide relevant information for neurodevelopmental presentations or to establish an estimation of premorbid functioning following an acquired neurological condition. Collateral information from family members may be collected to provide additional information regarding history and current symptomatology and functioning (see Chapter 11 in this volume for discussion of collateral reports).

The majority of a typical neuropsychological examination consists of formal tests of cognitive functioning involving oral and written responses, as well as manipulations of presented stimuli (for example, solving puzzles, building structures) (American Academy of Clinical Neuropsychology, 2017). Increasingly, computerized tests are also used in neuropsychological evaluation, which can allow for better control of both stimulus delivery and behavioral response recording (especially in regards to reaction time). Together, these tests serve to assess different cognitive domains, including verbal and nonverbal memory, visuospatial skills, executive function, language, motor function, and perception, to name a few. The neuropsychological examination also typically assesses psychological function through patient interview, as well as self-report questionnaires addressing affect, mood, motivation, personality, and substance use.

Table 15.1 outlines the most commonly assessed neuropsychological domains and tests used to measure them. In most cases, exemplar tests were selected based on results of a survey of clinical neuropsychologists in the United States and Canada, who reported on the tests they used most often to measure each construct (Rabin, Paolillo, & Barr, 2016). Exemplars for measures of validity of test data were drawn from surveys of neuropsychologists in multiple countries (Dandachi-FitzGerald, Ponds, & Merten, 2013; Martin, Schroeder, & Odland, 2015).

In neuropsychological evaluation, the tests administered are a critical component and thus should be chosen carefully. First, the tests should aid in addressing the presenting problem or referral question. For example, if a patient presents with memory concerns, tests that reflect learning and memory ability should be administered as part of the neuropsychological examination. However, given that an individual needs adequate "input" of information in order to learn and later recall it, other relevant cognitive constructs must also be assessed, such as basic attention and receptive language skills (if material is presented orally, for example). Second, tests should be selected based on known or suspected neurological, neuromedical, neurodevelopmental, or neuropsychiatric history of the patient.

There are additional critical test selection factors to consider, including age, education, primary language, reading level, and race/ethnicity/culture of the patient (Smith, Ivnik, & Lucas, 2008). Selected tests should have appropriate normative data relevant for the patient being assessed, with regard to gender, age, education, and race/ethnicity. Further, tests should be able to be comprehended and completed by the patient and thus should be appropriate for their reading level and in their primary language (Smith et al., 2008).

A collection of neuropsychological tests is called a test battery. In neuropsychological assessment, the two most common approaches are fixed and flexible batteries. In the fixed battery approach, the same test battery is used with each patient assessed. The most widely used fixed battery is the Halstead-Reitan Neuropsychological Battery (HRNB; Reitan & Wolfson, 1985), which is comprised of ten tests assessing several cognitive domains, including executive function, attention, working memory, psychomotor ability, language, and sensory and perception (see Table 15.1). A recent variation on the fixed battery approach that is used in the research setting is the common metric assessment battery (Casaletto & Heaton, 2017). These are population-specific research-based batteries developed as a standard method for neuropsychological assessment within specific populations in order to allow for combining data across multiple research sites, providing greater statistical power for epidemiological and clinical trial studies. One example is the Measurement and Treatment Research to Improve Cognition in Schizophrenia (MATRICS; Nuechterlein et al., 2008)

A major advantage of a fixed battery is that it provides a common metric for which performance across tests can be measured, in that they were all normed on the same sample of individuals (Meyers, 2017). However, there are also limitations to using a fixed battery approach. The first is that this approach does not necessarily assess all patients' concerns. As such, fixed batteries must often be augmented to include neuropsychological measures that assess domains not assessed in the fixed battery (Suhr, 2015). Moreover, using a fixed battery does not allow for the incorporation of new/updated tests or new technology (e.g., computerized assessments).

A flexible battery approach is often preferred in neuropsychological evaluation. Two types of flexible battery approaches are commonly used: a "fixed" flexible approach in which a group of tests is routinely administered for the assessment of particular referral questions, such as dementia or learning disorder evaluations, but with the flexibility to add or remove tests as warranted by the specific patient's presentation; and a fully flexible approach in which test selection is made on a completely individual basis and not routinized in any way across

Table 15.1 Popular constructs assessed in neuropsychological evaluation

Construct/Domain	Description	Exemplar Tests[a] (Flexible Approach)	Fixed Battery Equivalents (HRNB)
Orientation	Awareness of time, place, personal information	Mini-Mental State Exam	N/A
Attention and Concentration	Selecting of, filtering of, and focusing on information	Digit Span (from the Wechsler Adult Intelligence Scale-IV)	Seashore Rhythm Test; Speech-sounds Perception Test
Perception	Awareness and perception of tactile, auditory, and visual perception	Often informally screened	Sensory Perceptual Examination
Motor Function	Motor strength, fine and gross motor movements	Grooved Pegboard	Tactual Performance Test; Finger Tapping; Strength of Grip; Lateral Dominance Examination
Visuospatial and Visuoconstructional Skills	Visuospatial orientation, mental rotation, drawing tasks, ability to construct 2-D and 3-D stimuli	Rey-Osterrieth Complex Figure Test	Reitan-Indiana Aphasia Screening Test (item drawing)
Language Skills	Receptive language (comprehension), expressive language (speaking and writing skills), fluency	Boston Naming Test-2	Reitan-Indiana Aphasia Screening Test
Learning and Memory	Learning efficiency, immediate memory, delayed memory (verbal and nonverbal), potentially retrograde or nondeclarative memory	Wechsler Memory Scale-IV, California Verbal Learning Test	N/A
Executive Function Skills	Abstract reasoning, cognitive flexibility, decision-making, inhibition, working memory	Wisconsin Card Sort Test (WCST)/ WCST-64; Trail Making Test; Delis-Kaplan Executive Functioning Scale; Stroop Test; Category Test	Category Test; Trail Making Test
Psychological Functioning	Affect, mood, motivation, personality, social behavior, substance use	Minnesota Multiphasic Personality Inventory-2-Restructured Form (MMPI-2-RF)	Minnesota Multiphasic Personality Inventory (original)
Measures of Noncredible Presentation	Validity and reliability of self-reported functioning, and behavior	Amsterdam Short-Term Memory Test; Rey 15 Item Test, Test of Memory Malingering, Word Memory Test, MMPI-2-RF validity scales for self-report[b]	None

Note. [a] Survey of clinical neuropsychologists in the United States and Canada (Rabin et al., 2016). [b] Survey of neuropsychologists in six European countries (Dandachi-FitzGerald et al., 2013) and survey of North American neuropsychologists (Martin et al., 2015).

patients. In a survey of neuropsychologists in the United States, only 3 percent of neuropsychologists reported using a fixed battery, while 14 percent used a flexible approach; the vast majority of neuropsychologists (82 percent) reported using a fixed flexible battery approach (Sweet et al., 2015).

One key advantage to using a flexible battery approach is that it is patient-centered; tests are selected specifically for a patient to address their problems rather than taking a "one-size-fits-all" approach as in the fixed battery (Meyers, 2017). Using a flexible battery also allows for the incorporation of new instruments and technology as the field of neuropsychology advances. Flexible batteries can be (but are not always) shorter than fixed batteries. There are, however, some limitations to this approach. First, the flexible battery requires the neuropsychologist to engage in a decision-making process to guide test selection, which may be prone to biases (for example, choosing only tests that confirm what the neuropsychologist already knows or suspects about the patient). Another disadvantage is that the tests administered do not typically have a common metric by which to determine impairment because they were not co-normed. As noted in this section, many neuropsychologists take a combination approach by administering a small relatively fixed battery to all of their referrals and then supplementing with additional measures based on various hypotheses that arise during the course of the evaluation, which can mitigate concerns.

PSYCHOMETRIC AND OTHER ISSUES RELEVANT FOR EMPIRICALLY INFORMED CLINICAL DECISION-MAKING IN NEUROPSYCHOLOGICAL ASSESSMENT

As Robin Hilsabeck (2017) recently indicated, psychometrics and statistics are "pillars" of empirically informed neuropsychological assessment. While Chapter 2 in this text presents information on psychometrics, in this section, we will discuss psychometric issues that arise in the selection of which neuropsychological tests to administer. We will also discuss decision-making issues related to psychometrics and statistics, such as how to determine whether someone is showing neuropsychological impairment or determine whether there has been significant change in neuropsychological status over time.

Reliability

To decide on the use of specific neuropsychological tests for either research or clinical purposes, their reliability must be examined. However, there is no set "value" for any particular form of reliability that is crucial for deciding whether a test is appropriate to use for either clinical or research purposes. Lower reliabilities may occur for some neuropsychological tests, even though the test accurately reflects the underlying construct being assessed. For example, the measures of the construct of effort/noncredible presentation are likely to be inconsistent, as effort on tests may wax and wane as a function of the difficulty level of the items or tests or as a function of the communication style of the examinee (i.e., consciously performing more poorly on items that seem on the surface to assess skills in which the individual would like to be seen as having impairment). Reaction time and processing speed are also domains in which scores may be unreliable as a function of time of day, amount of sleep, amount of stimulant (caffeine, nicotine) in the examinee's system, or other individual characteristics (for example, for individuals with disorders known to cause high response variability, such as attention-deficit/hyperactivity disorder). In some instances, lower reliability may accurately reflect the construct of interest; however, higher standard error of measurement (SEM) and larger confidence intervals may result, which can affect interpretation of test results.

Construct Validity

A further consideration in neuropsychological test selection is the construct validity of the test. As with reliability, construct validity cannot be reflected in only one number and requires a good understanding of the construct at hand, followed by careful consideration of all the evidence that supports any given test as a measure of that construct. It is important to note that, while many neuropsychological instruments are purposed to measure narrower constructs than, for example, tests of intelligence, most still require multiple cognitive abilities to perform successfully. Thus, impaired scores on even relatively specific neuropsychological tests can reflect many different cognitive processes or implicate many brain regions.

While the most common components of construct validity are concurrent validity (correlation with other measures of the same construct) and criterion validity (correlation with criterion such as diagnosis or some other "real-world" variable), there are other important components of construct validity that should be considered when determining whether any given neuropsychological test is an accurate measure of the construct of interest. These include neurodevelopmental evidence and neuroimaging evidence. For example, if a particular neuropsychological construct shows changes across different stages of brain development, then a valid test of that construct should also reflect those developmental changes. If a particular neuropsychological construct is related to function/dysfunction of particular brain regions, then structural findings (so-called lesion studies) should be related to performance on tests designed to measure that construct. Similarly, in functional neuroimaging studies (in both clinical and nonclinical populations), further evidence for the construct validity of the test can be seen when test scores correlate with activation of brain regions associated with the construct the test is supposed to assess. Further, if a particular intervention affects a brain region associated with a neuropsychological construct, then a valid test of that construct should show consistent postintervention changes. Ideally, data from all of these aspects of construct validity should be available from diverse populations.

Two psychometric issues of special importance in the applied use of neuropsychological tests are diagnostic validity and ecological validity. Both relate to criterion validity: the degree to which variation in performance on a test is related to variation in a specific criterion (diagnosis or real-world functioning), which helps determine whether you can draw conclusions from the test score. With respect to diagnostic validity, neuropsychological measures are often used to aid in establishing an etiology or diagnosis for presenting problems. Thus, the accuracy of neuropsychological assessment tools is essential to establish and requires understanding the sensitivity, specificity, positive predictive power, and negative predictive power of neuropsychological measures (for a good overview of these accuracy statistics in neuropsychological assessment, see Lange & Lippa, 2017). It is important for assessors to recognize that accuracy statistics are affected by the base rates of the disorder in question; for example, data reflecting the accuracy of a neuropsychological measure in an outpatient setting may not apply in an inpatient setting. For use in diverse groups, data should be available with regard to these accuracy parameters across a wide range of populations.

Even when an etiology or diagnosis is known, knowledge of neuropsychological strengths/weaknesses should provide implications for an individual's functioning in the real world, which is known as ecological validity. In the clinical setting, this is essential for patient management, including whether a patient is able to live independently, could benefit from treatment or rehabilitation, can safely drive a car, and so on. Thus, data on the relationship of scores on neuropsychological tests to real-world outcomes are essential to the use of these tests in clinical practice. These data can be difficult to obtain, as one needs valid measures of "real-world" functioning as the criteria. For example, in driving, criterion measures might include vehicular accident records, driving in a driving simulator, collateral report of driving errors, and so on. Further, to ensure that the tests show ecological validity in diverse groups, there should be data indicating that the relationship between test scores and real-world outcome is similar across different groups. It is important to provide a cautionary note with regard to the recent trend of assuming that self-reported functioning is an accurate measure of real-world impairment. This trend is especially seen in the assessment of executive functioning (Dekker et al., 2017). However, in a typical self-report measure of executive functioning, there is no control for validity of self-report.

One critical issue that arises when considering whether neuropsychological test scores predict real-world outcomes is the use of raw scores versus demographically corrected scores. In order to determine whether someone is scoring out of an expected range for peers, which would suggest impairment, demographically corrected scores are useful. However, to predict functioning in an important task that everyone must perform to a certain level of competency (such as driving), it does not make sense to use demographically corrected scores, as raw scores may be more predictive of impairment (Barrash et al., 2010; Silverberg & Millis, 2009).

Validity at the $N = 1$ Level

When using neuropsychological tests in either the clinical or the research setting, it is important to consider the existing research data on the reliability and validity of that test for individuals similar to whom you plan to assess. However, this still does not guarantee that any single patient or research participant has produced reliable and valid data at the time they are evaluated. Thus, assessment for the validity of neuropsychological test performance is crucial to interpreting findings from any individual's neuropsychological battery. Neuropsychologists have been front and center in the development of performance validity tests (PVTs) to assess for the validity of an individual's performance on cognitive measures and neuropsychologists have been champions for the use of and further development of measures of invalid symptom reporting (symptom validity tests, or SVTs), as well. Chapter 6 in this volume provides a more detailed discussion of issues related to the assessment of self-report and performance validity and Chapter 35 provides further discussion of assessing for validity within neuropsychological assessment settings. In Table 15.1, we included survey results for the most commonly administered PVTs and SVTs within neuropsychological assessment.

Standard Scores and Norms

As noted in the previous section, a neuropsychologist must know an individual's relative standing on a neuropsychological test to understand its implications for diagnosis. For many neuropsychological tests, there are multiple populations of comparison available in the research literature and differences in those populations can impact the relative standing of an individual being assessed. For example, compilations of normative data for neuropsychological tests are provided in several texts (Lezak et al., 2012; Mitrushina et al., 2005; Strauss, Sherman, & Spreen, 2006). As previously indicated, this is a potential limitation of flexible neuropsychological batteries, as individuals are not compared to the same relative population standard across tests in the battery.

Another issue for some neuropsychological tests is that their scores are not normally distributed; some are highly skewed, some have truncated distributions, and so on. For example, confrontational naming tests typically involve the naming of common objects and are highly negatively skewed, with most people performing at/near the mean, which falls near the very top of the score distribution. While such distributions might reflect the construct of interest accurately, this can have a major impact on the relative standing of an individual with regard to standard scores and/or percentiles. Thus, assessors interpreting scores from such neuropsychological tests should always review the general distribution of scores for those tests and consider the raw score obtained by the individual when interpreting the results. This can be especially important when trying to determine if a score is out of the range of normal (high average or superior, which may not be measurable by neuropsychological tests with negative skew; or for determining impairment). For example, if a confrontational naming task were made more difficult so that scores could reflect high average or superior performance, it would likely no longer measure a person's ability to retrieve common words but instead reflect a person's vocabulary level.

PSYCHOMETRIC OVERVIEW OF EXEMPLAR NEUROPSYCHOLOGICAL TESTS

In this section, we provide a brief psychometric overview of commonly administered neuropsychological tests. Tests were selected from those illustrated in Table 15.1. We provide a brief summary of reliability, validity, and available normative data. More detailed discussion of these tests (as well as many other neuropsychological tests) can be found in reference volumes (Lezak et al., 2012; Mitrushina et al., 2005; Strauss et al., 2006).

Orientation Tests

Orientation refers to the awareness of oneself in the context of one's surroundings, including time and space (Lezak et al., 2012). Tests of orientation allow the examiner to assess whether the patient is alert, attentive, and oriented enough to participate in a cognitive evaluation. The Mental State Examination (MSE)/Mini-Mental State Examination (MMSE; Folstein, Folstein, & McHugh, 1975) is generally used to screen global cognitive functioning, including orientation (temporal and spatial), but also registration of information, attention and calculation, immediate recall, visuoconstructional skills, and language. The MMSE requires five to ten minutes for administration and asks patients/participants to complete simple tasks such as stating the date, the location of the evaluation, naming objects, obeying simple commands, counting backward by 7's, and so on. It is recommended that individuals completing the MMSE speak English fluently and have a minimum of an eighth-grade education (Tombaugh & McIntyre, 1992).

Normative data for the MMSE is available for both children and adults through age eighty-five; some norms provide data divided by age and education level (for norms, see Strauss et al., 2006). Internal consistency is variable, ranging from 0.31 in a sample of community participants to 0.96 in a sample of mixed medical patients (see Strauss et al., 2006). It should be noted, however, that, because the MMSE measures a broad range of cognitive skills, low reliability estimates might be expected (Tombaugh & McIntrye, 1992). Test-retest reliability estimates over a two-month interval (or less) fall between 0.80 and 0.95 (Folstein et al., 1975; Tombaugh & McIntrye, 1992) in both healthy controls and those with dementia. With respect to validity, scores on the MMSE correlate modestly to highly with other cognitive screening instruments (for a detailed review of construct validity, see Strauss et al., 2006).

Attention, Concentration, and Working Memory Tests

Tests of attention and concentration involve measuring an individual's ability to focus and are required for focused behavior. Working memory is the ability to hold and manipulate information during a short period of time. Because working memory requires both attention and concentration, and poor performance on tests of working memory may reflect attentional distraction, working memory is often grouped with the cognitive domain of attention and concentration but is also often considered a component of executive functioning (see "Executive Functioning Tests" section). Span tests are commonly used to measure attentional capacity (Lezak et al., 2012), with simple span (immediate repetition of digits or a spatial pattern) reflecting attention/short-term memory and more complex span tasks requiring manipulation of digits or spatial patterns reflecting working memory. The most commonly administered test of attention, concentration, and working memory is the Digit Span subtest of the Wechsler Adult Intelligence Scale – Fourth Edition (WAIS-IV; Wechsler, 2008), which has norms for ages seventeen to eighty-nine across a sample of adults representative of the demographics of the US population. Digit Span requires the examinee to listen as the examiner reads a span of digits ranging in length from two to nine digits. The examinee is then asked to recall the digits either forward, backward, or sequenced in ascending order.

The Digit Span subtest has excellent internal consistency, ranging from 0.89 to 0.94 depending on the age group, with an overall average internal consistency of 0.93 for ages sixteen to ninety (Wechsler, 2008). Reliability coefficients are also available for specific clinical groups (see WAIS-IV manual). Test-retest reliability over a span ranging from eight to eight-two days across all ages is good ($r = 0.83$; Wechsler, 2008). Confirmatory factor-analytic studies demonstrate that the Digit Span (and Arithmetic) subtest best fits the Working Memory factor (as opposed to other factors: Verbal Comprehension, Perceptual Reasoning, Processing Speed).

Motor Tests

Tests of motor agility and dexterity have long been included in neuropsychological evaluations. Initially, it was believed that poor performance on motor tasks might be an indication of lesion lateralization (Lezak et al., 2012). While that is not necessarily the case for all motor tasks, motor tests help neuropsychologists discern the extent to which one's dexterity, coordination, and motor agility are intact or impaired.

One commonly administered test of fine-motor dexterity is the Grooved Pegboard (Kløve, 1963). The test includes a pegboard consisting of twenty-five holes (5 × 5) with slots that are angled in different directions and pegs with ridges, which are to be placed into the pegboard by aligning the ridge with the angled, slotted hole. The examinee is asked to place the pegs into the holes in the pegboard as quickly as they can, one peg at a time and in order, row by row. The examinee performs the task with their dominant and non-dominant hands, respectively. The examinee is scored on their completion time and "drops" are also recorded (i.e., when the examinee cannot hold onto the peg while attempting to place it).

Of note, there is an age effect for this test such that completion time increases as age increases, as can be seen in the normative references (Lezak et al., 2012; Mitrushina et al., 2005; Strauss et al., 2006). Several normative datasets exist for the Grooved Pegboard test, some of which provide norms specifically organized by age, education, and racial/ethnic group (African American) (Strauss et al., 2006). Mitrushina and colleagues (2005) developed meta-norms by incorporating data from six studies. Test-retest reliabilities have demonstrated acceptable results, with some evidence for practice effects (see Lezak et al., 2012; Strauss et al., 2006).

There is limited support for a relationship between Grooved Pegboard performance and performance on other, more simple tests of motor ability. One study in healthy older adults (ages fifty-five to seventy-four) suggested that performance on the Grooved Pegboard test is instead related to other tests of cognitive ability (including tests of memory, processing speed, perceptual reasoning, and executive function), reflecting the cognitive complexity of the Grooved Pegboard (Ashendorf, Vandslice-Barr, & McCaffrey, 2009). However, dramatic differences in left-handed and right-handed performance are related to evidence of contralateral brain damage/dysfunction (Bohnen et al., 2007; Haaland & Delaney, 1981).

Visuospatial and Visuoconstructional Tests

Successful performance on tests of visuospatial and visuocontructional ability reflects intact integration of perception, motor, and spatial skills. Impaired performance is generally associated with right hemisphere dysfunction (Lezak et al., 2012) and may indicate impairment in perception, or spatial or motor ability, with implications for everyday life skills that involve such abilities (e.g., driving).

One commonly administered test of visuospatial and visuoconstructional ability, as noted in Table 15.1, is the Rey-Osterrieth Complex Figure Test (ROCFT; Osterrieth, 1944; Meyers & Meyers, 1995). In this test, the examinee is asked to copy a complex figure. Some examiners may only complete the copy trial, while others use the immediate and delayed recall trials, which require the examinee to draw the figure from memory three minutes and thirty minutes (respectively) following the copy trial, allowing for assessment of visual memory. There is also a recognition trial that requires the examinee to select parts of the original figure from among targets and foils. The constructed figure is scored on the accuracy and placement of various elements of the figure. Examiners who choose to administer only the copy trial may be interested in the examinee's approach to drawing the figure; to do so, the examiner may ask the examinee to switch the color of ink they are using to draw the figure every thirty seconds, every six to eight marks drawn, or during each third (or fourth) of the drawing (Lezak et al., 2012).

The ROCFT can be administered to examinees ranging in age from six to eighty-nine years. Parallel forms of the ROCFT exist to address readministration needs. Normative adult data is available for ages eighteen to ninety in the ROCFT manual. Mistrushina and colleagues (2005) developed meta-norms using a sample of nine studies, resulting in 1,340 participants. Internal consistency estimates for the ROCFT have been reported as sufficient (above 0.60 for the copy trial and greater than 0.80 for recall trials; Strauss et al., 2006). Performance on the ROCFT is related to performance of other tasks of constructional ability and to memory (Meyers & Meyers, 1995). Moreover, lesion studies have demonstrated that area of brain lesion is associated with performance on the ROCFT. For example, in one seminal study examining thirty-two patients with lesions of the frontal lobe, 75 percent of those who made a defective copy made mistakes related to the disorganization of their copy, such as copying a portion of the figure that had already been copied (Messerli, Seron, & Tissot, 1979). Further, a study of constructional abilities following unilateral brain damage found that individuals with left hemisphere damage took a piecemeal approach to constructing the complex figure, breaking individual units up into smaller pieces more often than did normal controls, while those with right hemisphere damage showed greater distortions in their complex figure copies and excluded details from the figure more often than did normal controls and those with left hemisphere damage (Binder, 1982).

Language Tests

A comprehensive assessment of language skills is useful when a patient presents with either expressive or receptive language problems following brain injury or illness or due to a neurodegenerative condition. There are full batteries of language tasks meant to assess acquired language disorders; the most common are the Multilingual Aphasia Exam (Benton, Hamsher, & Sivan, 1994) and the Boston Diagnostic Aphasia Examination – Third Edition (Goodglass, Kaplan, & Barresi, 2001), which is available in English, Spanish, Portuguese, French, Hindi, Finnish, and Greek. However, speech/language pathologists also administer a wide variety of speech and language batteries to patients, and neuropsychologists often encounter patients for whom an aphasia diagnosis has already been established or are simply screening for language ability in the patients they are referred. Informally, major difficulties with either expressive or receptive communication can be identified in the conversational speech of a patient during clinical interview and their ability to comprehend test instructions and respond appropriately during completion of other neuropsychological tests. However, the examiner must consider the effects of age and education on both expressive and receptive language skills, which often indicates a need for formal assessment.

A commonly administered language measure is the Boston Naming Test – Second Edition (BNT-2; Kaplan, Goodglass, & Weintraub, 2001), which assesses confrontational naming ability. The test requires an individual to name an object depicted in a black-and-white drawing within twenty seconds. If the individual does not respond correctly, a stimulus cue is given and another twenty seconds is allowed for a response; if the individual still does not respond correctly, a phonemic cue is offered. The first items are words that have a high frequency of use; over time, items with decreasing use frequency are presented. The full measure has sixty items but short forms have also been developed. There are adaptations for Chinese, Italian, Jamaican, Dutch, Korean, French-Canadian, and Spanish-speaking people in the United States (Lezak et al., 2012), although there has been much less examination of the psychometric properties of these translations.

The BNT-2 can be administered to individuals from five to thirteen years of age and to adults age eighteen and older and there are a variety of normative samples available for English speakers, with Heaton and colleagues (2004) providing a compilation of US norms divided by age, gender, education, and race/ethnicity (White and Black/African American). Ivnik and colleagues (1996) also provided norms from the Mayo Older Americans Normative Studies (MOANS) that correct for both age and education; and Lucas and colleagues (2005) provided norms from the Mayo Older African American Normative Studies (MOAANS) sample. Child norms are much less substantive and are summarized in Strauss and colleagues (2006).

Normative data show that scores on the test are highly negatively skewed, with most individuals obtaining high scores on the test; thus, the test is most useful for identifying impairment in confrontational naming. Internal consistency of the Boston Naming Test is high (0.78–0.96; Lezak et al., 2012). Short-term test-retest reliability is also high (above 0.90). Scores on the test correlate highly with other measures of naming ability and moderately high with other measures of verbal fluency. However, scores on the test are also related moderately with both verbal and nonverbal IQ, suggesting scores should not be interpreted in isolation of performance on intelligence measures (Lezak et al., 2012). Furthermore, level of acculturation and language background have a significant relationship to performance and at least one study has suggested a "cohort effect" for some of the items in that their frequency of use in the English language may have changed over time (Storms, Saerens, & DeDeyn, 2004).

Clinical data also generally support the construct validity of the measure. Individuals with diagnoses of neurological conditions that lead to anomia show deficits on the test (Strauss et al., 2006). Structural neuroimaging studies show that performance is most associated with dysfunction in left anterior to posterior middle temporal gyrus and its underlying white matter (Baldo et al., 2013). At least one study has shown that the test is sensitive to language change following epilepsy surgery (Sawrie et al., 1996).

Learning and Memory Tests

To assess learning and memory, a neuropsychologist must provide the individual with new and novel information to be encoded, stored, and then later retrieved (episodic memory). Tests of episodic memory can include verbal or nonverbal material and may include semantically unrelated material (such as a list of unrelated words) or involve semantic cues (such as a list of words that are semantically related) or other forms of organizational structure (learning and recall of a short story). Tests of episodic memory usually include both free retrieval of the material and recognition of the material in order to assess storage of the learned material versus retrieval of the learned material. Finally, tests of episodic memory often include both immediate and delayed recall and recognition trials.

A commonly administered battery of memory tests is the Wechsler Memory Scale – Fourth Edition (WMS-IV; Wechsler, 2008). The WMS-IV is a measure of encoding and retrieval of novel verbal and nonverbal material, which takes about sixty minutes to complete. Verbal memory is assessed with short stories and word pairs as stimuli and nonverbal memory are assessed with abstract visual designs that require the individual to remember the content of, and spatial location of, the designs, as well as a test requiring the individual to draw abstract visual designs from memory. All four of the subtests tests have immediate and delayed recall trials and a delayed recognition trial. The WMS-IV also includes two subtests of nonverbal working memory.

WMS-IV norms are based on a national sample representative of 2005 US Census data (ages sixteen to ninety) and were stratified for age, sex, race/ethnicity, educational level, and four geographic regions. The test was co-normed with the WAIS-IV, which allows for discrepancy scores between the two tests to be calculated. The psychometric properties of the WMS-IV are summarized in detail in the technical manual (Wechsler, 2008). Generally, the test shows strong internal consistency and test-retest reliability. There are practice effects on repeated administration, which vary by subtest but must be taken into account when testing a patient a second time with the test. Unfortunately, there are no alternative forms of the test. Scores on the WMS-IV correlate strongly with other neuropsychological measures of learning and memory. There have been many studies of clinical groups with known memory impairments, which provide further construct validity for the test; these are summarized in the technical manual.

The WMS-IV does not include a list-learning and retrieval test. The most commonly administered list-learning and retrieval task is the California Verbal Learning Test – Third Edition (Delis, Kramer, Kaplan, & Ober, 2017). This is a sixteen-item word list-learning task in which the words are members of four different semantic categories. The list is presented to individuals over five trials to assess learning of the words. An interference list is then presented, followed by a free recall of the word list and then a cued recall in which individuals are given the four semantic categories to help guide retrieval. After a twenty-minute delay, the free recall and cued recall trials are readministered, followed by a yes/no recognition trial. To address practice effects when there is a need for retesting, there is an alternative form available.

Norms exist for individuals age sixteen to ninety and were generated from a representative sampling of the US population with regard to sociodemographic variables, including education, age, region, and ethnicity (Delis et al., 2017). The construct validity is primarily based on the preceding versions of the test but supports the test as a reliable and valid measure of verbal learning and memory (Lezak et al., 2012; Strauss et al., 2006).

Executive Functioning Tests

Executive functioning (EF) is a complex construct and many definitions of the construct overlap with definitions of intelligence, including the capacity to direct behavior purposefully toward goals and the ability to adapt routine cognitive skills to novel or complex situations that require one to monitor success toward obtaining a goal. Given the complexity of EF, and the fact that EF requires that other underlying cognitive skills are intact to carry it out correctly, measures of EF often assess many other cognitive skills. Thus, a neuropsychologist needs to determine what specific EF process they desire to measure and then examine the psychometric properties of specific tests with regard to their ability to assess that specific EF process. Further, EF performance can only be interpreted in the context of performance on measures of component basic cognitive skills. At the very least, assessment of general intelligence is necessary to the interpretation of EF tests (Lezak et al., 2012). Finally, EF is best assessed with multiple measures within the same battery, not with just one test.

Based on results of factor analyses of many tests of EF, Miyake and colleagues (2000) proposed three major aspects of EF – updating, inhibition, and shifting – which we will use to organize discussion of commonly administered EF tests, using exemplars from Table 15.1. Updating is the continuous monitoring and quick addition or deletion of contents within one's working memory. Working memory was discussed in the "Attention, Concentration, and Working Memory Tests" section.

Inhibition is one's capacity to supersede responses that are prepotent in a given situation. A classic inhibition test is the Stroop task, which assesses an individual's ability to suppress a habitual and automatic response (reading a word) in favor of a less familiar one (stating the color of ink a word is printed in). There are many normed versions available but the Golden (Golden & Freshwater, 2002) version is used here to describe general psychometrics. As in many Stroop tasks, scores can be obtained for word reading speed, color naming speed, and the interference task. An examiner must consider the scores in the context of one another, as general slowing on all tasks reflects processing speed and not EF.

The Golden version has normative data for individuals ranging from age fifteen to ninety. Ivnik and colleagues (1996) also provide MOANS norms for the Golden version and Lucas and colleagues (2005) provided normative data from the MOAANS. Performance is overall slower in bilingual individuals and there have been some racial/ethnic differences noted, even when accounting for education (Moering et al., 2004). Test-retest reliability is high over short intervals but with huge practice effects, and reliability for the interference subtest tends to be lower (Strauss et al., 2006). Strauss and colleagues (2006) provide a nice summary of construct validity data for the test. With regard to the EF construct, the interference score correlates well with other measures of attention and response inhibition; performance on the interference subtest is also associated with working memory ability and with speed of processing. Construct ability is also supported by clinical findings, in that poor Stroop interference has been seen in a variety of patient groups that are known to have EF deficits, including head injury, dementia, schizophrenia, and individuals with frontal lesions. Functional neuroimaging studies show that the frontal lobes are activated in individuals when performing the interference component of the Stroop task (for a brief summary of imaging findings, see Lezak et al., 2012). Both age and intelligence are strongly associated with Stroop performance and thus performance should be interpreted in the context of both age (reflected in norms) and general intelligence (Strauss et al., 2006).

Shifting is the cognitive flexibility to alternate between different tasks or mental states. The Wisconsin Card Sorting Test (WCST), the Trail Making Test (TMT), and the Category Test are commonly used to assess this component of EF.

The WCST (Heaton et al., 1993) and its short form (Kongs et al., 2000) assess an individual's ability to abstract and to use feedback and shift cognitive set. Four stimulus cards are placed in front of the individual, along with a deck of cards. The individual must determine how the cards match the stimulus cards and is given feedback each time as to whether the match was correct or incorrect. Without warning, the category that applies to a successful match changes and the individual must ascertain this switch and try different categorization rules based on error feedback. There are also computerized versions available.

The original standardization sample for the WCST included individuals age six years, five months to age eighty-nine but did not provide data on race/ethnicity. The sample was slightly more educated than the US population of the time. Rhodes (2004) conducted a meta-analysis of thirty-four studies that included about 3,000 adult participants and provided supplemental norms to the manual; other supplemental adult norms are provided by Mitrushina and colleagues (2005) and supplemental child norms are provided by Strauss and colleagues (2006). Supplemental norms are also available for Spanish-speaking and Italian adults; for details, see Strauss and colleagues (2006).

The WCST shows poor test-retest reliability and significant practice effects, which reflects the lack of novelty of the problem-solving and set-shifting components after a first administration. Performance on the WCST correlates with performance on other EF measures reasonably well and factor analyses show that the WCST tends to load with EF measures but also with memory and working memory measures (Miyake et al., 2000; Strauss et al., 2006). Although initial neuroanatomical studies suggested a strong relationship of poor WCST performance to frontal lobe lesions, accumulating evidence suggests the relationship is not so clear as to allow WCST performance to have diagnostic classifiability. Nevertheless the WCST appears to be sensitive to dysfunction in individuals with disorders known to be associated with impaired EF (Strauss et al., 2006). Further, WCST performance has been shown to be useful in predicting competency and impairment in everyday life (Strauss et al., 2006). As with other EF measures, education and IQ are related to performance (Lezak et al., 2012; Strauss et al., 2006) and overall performance should not be interpreted outside of the context of measures of more general cognitive functioning.

The TMT (Reitan, 1955) requires individuals to connect numbers in order in part A and then numbers in letters in alternating order in part B. TMT thus assesses visual scanning speed, psychomotor speed, and, in part B, cognitive flexibility. Alternative forms have been developed to account for practice effects (Lezak et al., 2012).

Many normative samples are available for the TMT and the quality of the normative samples varies. Because the TMT is part of the Halstead-Reitan Battery, Heaton and colleagues (2004) provide a relatively large set of norms. In addition, other normative data was compiled by Mitrushina and colleagues (2005). Lucas and colleagues (2005) also provide MOANNS data on the TMT. Most TMT norms provide adjustment for age and education. Steinberg and colleagues (2005) also provide IQ-adjusted TMT norms for individuals over fifty-five (from the MOANS data).

Test-retest reliability is generally low and lower for part A than part B (Strauss et al., 2006). There are practice effects over short intervals (Strauss et al., 2006) but there are alternative forms available that show high correlation with the original version. Performance on the TMT correlates well with other measures of speeded processing as well as other EF measures (Lezak et al., 2012; Strauss et al., 2006). While many studies have shown that the TMT is sensitive to cognitive dysfunction in a variety of neuropsychiatric, neurodevelopmental, neuromedical, and neurological disorders, it is not specific to any particular disorder or to dysfunction in any particular brain region (Lezak et al., 2012; Strauss et al., 2006). However, several studies have demonstrated its strong relationship to real-world functioning for adults of all ages; thus, its value may be as a measure of prognosis rather than diagnosis (Strauss et al., 2006).

The mostly commonly administered version of the Category Test is the Booklet Category Test – Second Edition (BCT; DeFillipps & McCampbell, 1997). The BCT was developed to assess concept formation and ability to think flexibly in the fact of changing and complex problem-solving. The test provides items that are organized on the basis of different principles that represent the numbers one to four in some way. The participant must deduce the classification principle based on feedback from the examiner. Interestingly, although on the surface the task seems similar to the WCST, they do not share much variance (Lezak et al., 2012).

The adult version has good normative data for ages twenty to eighty-five. There are some norms available for adolescents and there are other versions available for children (see Lezak et al., 2012). While the normative datasets vary in quality, there are meta-norms available broken down by age, education, gender, and race (White, Black/African American) (Lezak et al., 2012; Mitrushina et al., 2005). There is some evidence that performance is affected by level of acculturation for minority groups (Manly et al. 1998).

The BCT shows high internal consistency for the total score but test-retest reliabilities have been quite variable, likely reflecting the loss of novelty of the task after a first admission (Lezak et al., 2012). There are very strong practice effects, which should be taken into account when comparing scores across two time points (Lezak et al., 2012). Factor analyses show that the task loads with other reasoning tasks, especially for clinical samples (Strauss et al., 2006). While the BCT has been shown to be sensitive to brain damage and dysfunction generally, impairment on the BCT is not associated with any specific location of brain damage (Strauss et al., 2006). There is a high correlation between level of intelligence and performance on the task, which must be considered when interpreting test scores. There are varying data on the contribution of education to performance (Lezak et al., 2012).

A commonly administered EF battery is the Delis-Kaplan Executive Function System (DKEFS; Delis, Kaplan, & Kramer, 2001). The DKEFS includes nine subtests that assess both verbal and nonverbal EF. Subtests include Word Context (a test of deductive reasoning), Sorting Test (a test of concept formation and conceptual reasoning skills), Twenty Questions Test (a test of concept formation and abstract thinking), Tower Test (a test of spatial planning, rule learning, impulsivity, inhibition, and maintaining set), Color-Word Interference Test (a Stroop task that includes an extra component assessing cognitive flexibility), Verbal Fluency Test (a test of word generation and set shifting), Design Fluency Test (a test of design generation and cognitive shifting), Trail Making Test (similar to the TMT previously described but also including a fourth subtest involving more cognitive shifting, plus assessment of component processes to help isolate the EF component from the other abilities), and the Proverb Test (a test of verbal abstraction). To address the issue of EF measures assessing several cognitive abilities in concert, the subtests have different indices within them to control for underlying cognitive abilities in interpretation of scores. Alternative forms are available for three of the subtests that are most susceptible to practice effects.

The normative sample in the manual was matched to the US population at the time and ranged in age from eight to eighty-nine. The sample was sociodemographically representative of the 2000 US Census data with regard to race and ethnicity, gender, and education. The subtests and scores vary in their internal consistency, test-retest, and alternate form reliability but are generally adequate (see test manual for details). A limitation of the battery is that so many different scores are generated and they do not show high intercorrelations even though they purport to assess similar constructs (Lezak et al., 2012). While various subtests correlate with other independent measures of EF, they also correlate as strongly with neuropsychological measures of other constructs (such as memory), suggesting weak discriminant validity (Lezak et al., 2012; Strauss et al., 2006).

WHAT IS IMPAIRMENT?

An important decision-making task for neuropsychologists is to determine whether test scores suggest impairment. Given that a typical neuropsychological evaluation includes multiple measures of various constructs, each of which may not assess the construct of interest perfectly and may have different normative comparison groups, this task is a complex one. The task is made even more complex by the fact that, with an increase in the number of tests administered and test scores being interpreted for any individual, the chance that at least one of those tests will falsely indicate impairment is increased (Binder, Iverson, & Brooks, 2009; Huizenga et al., 2016). This problem is not unique to neuropsychology but should also be considered when interpreting intelligence and achievement tests (see Chapters 12 and 13). The probabilities of a false positive indication of impairment are further increased if the assessor is using liberal cutoffs for impairment; for example, using a cutoff of only 1 SD below the mean to indicate impairment on one isolated test would identify 16 percent of the normative population (Binder et al., 2009). Lower reliabilities (and thus higher standard error of measurement, or SEM) for some neuropsychological tests may also increase the probability of error in judgments about impairment (Binder et al., 2009). Some researchers have provided helpful tables to calculate the likelihood of having one or more test scores that fall into the "impaired" range within the entirety of outcome scores that are obtained within common test batteries. For examples, see Brooks, Holdnack, and Iverson (2011) for the WAIS-IV/WMS-IV and Crawford and colleagues (2012) for the Repeatable Battery for the Assessment of Neuropsychological Status (RBANS).

The probabilities of an "impaired" score on a neuropsychological test are also influenced by the baseline general cognitive functioning level of the individual being assessed. For example, Binder and Binder (2011) demonstrated the differential base rates of obtaining impaired range scores on any subtest of the WAIS-IV based on highest obtained subtest score. Such data are important to consider because it is common for neuropsychologists to determine impairment by comparing current test scores to "expected" levels of cognitive functioning, which might be based on scores on neuropsychological or intelligence tests expected to reflect premorbid functioning. However, individuals with extremely high/low levels of premorbid functioning are more likely to show high variability of test scores within a neuropsychological battery and are thus more likely to show significant test discrepancies (Brooks et al., 2008; Brooks et al., 2011; Donell, Belanger, & Vanderploeg, 2011).

DETECTING CHANGE OVER TIME

Detecting whether an individual has improved or declined over time is another important clinical decision in neuropsychological assessment and is often an important research question as well. Thus, it is useful for neuropsychological tests to have parallel forms that can be administered when tracking change over time, to minimize practice effects, although it should be noted that there is still potential for test familiarity and sophistication to affect test results on a second administration. For example, individuals administered memory tasks for the first time are not aware that they will be asked to recall those items after a delay but, when they are administered those same tasks on reevaluation, they may be aware of the impending recall at the point of the learning trials, which may affect their behavior during the learning portion of the memory task. Individuals at higher levels of premorbid functioning are also more likely to show practice effects (Heilbronner et al., 2010). In addition, psychometric properties of the neuropsychological tests may affect the ability of the test to show any reliable change (i.e., skewed tests with floor or ceiling effects). Regression to the mean will also affect the ability to determine whether there is reliable change over time and tests with lower reliability (and thus larger SEM) are more likely to show regression toward the mean (Heilbronner et al., 2010). At the very least, reliable change scores should be calculated in order to determine whether two test scores show change over time, even though such methods tend to assume the same level of practice effect for all individuals over that time period (Heilbronner et al., 2010).

ETHICAL AND PROFESSIONAL ISSUES IN THE CONTEXT OF NEUROPSYCHOLOGICAL ASSESSMENT

There are several salient ethical and professional issues that arise in the context of neuropsychological assessment. We will briefly touch on several of these, including assessment of diverse patients, informed consent, third-party observers, use of raw test data, use of technicians, and computerized assessment.

Assessment of Diverse Patients

It is important for neuropsychologists to consider diversity factors in all facets of an evaluation, from test selection to test administration and test interpretation. In the process of test selection, a neuropsychologist should consider whether tests have reliability and validity data from groups that represent relevant diversity characteristics that apply to the patient that is being assessed. Further, during the process of test selection, a neuropsychologist should consider whether the normative sample includes individuals who are similar to the client being tested. However, even these decisions are complicated by the fact that it is not always clear what the relevant diversity characteristics are. For example, it is clear that administering a test developed for children ages four to twelve is likely not to have reliability, validity, nor normative data that would make this test appropriate to administer to a thirty-year-old. However, data suggest that race/ethnicity may actually be a proxy for other more relevant variables that are directly related to variation in cognitive performance, such as educational level, literacy, language fluency, and socioeconomic status (Romero et al., 2009). Thus, it can be hard to determine whether the psychometric data that are available do in fact "apply" to any given individual being assessed. In the review of exemplar tests, attention to diversity issues in regard to normative data was presented. Studies examining whether tests show any racial/ethnic bias in terms of their ability to detect brain dysfunction or real-world impairment are sparse and more studies are needed.

Further, it can be difficult to determine whether any group-specific or demographically adjusted norms should be used to make assessment-related decisions for a particular client. It is not always clear that such adjustments improve accuracy and, in fact, they may make it worse. For example, Lucas and colleagues (2005) found that adjusting norms for older African Americans based on reading level made the data less accurate for diagnostic classification. Overall, there remain many challenges in the assessment of diverse groups (Elbulok-Chacape et al., 2014; Romero et al., 2009) and more studies need to be conducted. In the meanwhile, neuropsychologists should be conscious of diversity issues throughout a neuropsychological evaluation. Additional discussion of diversity considerations within the context of neuropsychological assessment can be found in Chapter 35.

Informed Consent in the Context of Neuropsychological Impairment

The American Psychological Association (APA) Ethics Code requires informed consent for patients, provided in a way that allows adequate comprehension by the patient (Ethical Standard 9.03, APA, 2010). Comprehension of consent procedures can be more difficult when the patient has neurocognitive impairments that preclude their ability to comprehend, which may require that a neuropsychologist provide extra attention to the consent process. Further, there may be an exception to the requirement of informed consent when concerns are raised about the decisional capacity of the patient, a not uncommon scenario in neuropsychological referrals. In such circumstances, assent is considered appropriate for the purposes of the evaluation (National Academy of Neuropsychology, 2003). In instances where assent is sufficient and consent is not required, neuropsychologists are still required to provide an explanation of assessment procedures, consider the examinee's preferences and best interests, and obtain permission by a legally authorized person if permitted or required by law, in addition to seeking the examinee's assent (Ethical Standard 3.01, APA, 2010). The Ethics Code also requires that the obtained consent be documented. While written consent is the preferred means of obtaining consent, in some cases, clients may not be able to provide written consent (e.g., psychosis, acute illness, hospitalization); in such cases, oral consent is appropriate (National Academy of Neuropsychology, 2003). Because of the more complex issues regarding obtaining informed consent with individuals who have cognitive impairments associated with brain dysfunction, the National Academy of Neuropsychology's (2003) consensus statement for informed consent in clinical neuropsychology practice provides a flow chart for informed consent and sample informed consent document.

Third-Party Observers

A third-party observer can be defined as any observer who is present for the neuropsychological evaluation who is not the examiner or examinee, or the use of any device intended to record the evaluation for the purposes of later review (Sweet & Breting, 2012). As outlined by the American Academy of Clinical Neuropsychology's position paper on third-party observation during neuropsychological evaluation, there are two ethical issues concerning third-party observers: validity of test results and test security (Sweet & Breting, 2012).

Neuropsychological assessment requires a distraction-free environment that allows the patient to feel comfortable with testing procedures and with the neuropsychologist administering these tests. In the presence of third-party observers, patients may become distracted or uncomfortable by the physical presence of another person or recording device in the testing room, compromising the validity of the test results obtained during the evaluation (Sweet & Breting, 2012). Indeed, research literature suggests that presence of a third-party observer may impede neuropsychological test performance (Constantinou, Ashendorf, & McCaffrey, 2005; Horwitz & McCaffrey, 2008; Yantz & McCaffrey, 2005), calling into question the validity of obtained test results and any diagnostic impressions or summaries made during the evaluation.

The presence of a third-party observer also warrants special attention to the maintenance of test security. A third-party observer is exposed to secure test stimuli, which may invalidate the use of those tests in future evaluations of the observer or of any person to whom the observer discloses information about those tests. Individuals who observe neuropsychological evaluations are not held to the same ethical standards as clinicians and may disclose information related to test content (stimuli, specific test questions, instructions) without repercussion (Otto & Krauss, 2009). Furthermore, recording neuropsychological evaluations where test questions, stimuli, and instructions are disclosed may violate the copyright agreements of test publishers (Sweet & Breting, 2012).

Protecting Neuropsychological Test Data

When evaluations are completed in a forensic context, patients and/or lawyers will often ask for the release of raw test data. As defined by the APA Ethics Code, data includes raw and scaled scores, as well the client's responses to test questions, and behavioral observation notes taken during the assessment (Ethical Standard 9.04a, APA, 2010). Principle 9.04 requires psychologists to provide test data to the client/patient or other persons identified in an authorization to release but also emphasizes that psychologists can decline to release test data (if allowed by law) if it is believed that release could cause harm to a client/patient or others or result in misuse/misrepresentation of the data or the test.

While releasing test data when requested by a patient might appear to be consistent with the aspirational principle of respect for people's rights and dignity, a misinterpretation or misuse of test results may harm the patient, which stands in contrast to the aspirational principle of beneficence and nonmaleficence, or avoiding harm (Bush & Lees-Haley, 2005). For example, it is not uncommon for individuals to misunderstand percentiles, interpreting a score at the 50th percentile (which is normal) as not normal because they think it is the same as 50 percent correct, or believe they should be above normal in all domains (Bowman, 2002). Consequently, the patient could mistakenly think they have cognitive impairment, while their test score suggests their performance on the task fell within normal limits as compared to peers of their same age.

Another complication to the release of test data is that, as previously discussed, psychologists should maintain the integrity and security of test materials, where materials are defined as test questions, stimuli, instruments, protocols, and manuals (Ethical Standard 9.11, APA, 2010). It may not be difficult to release a patient's exact responses to a self-report questionnaire while deleting the actual item content but it is much more difficult to release an exact response to a memory test item, for example, without also revealing the actual test content. In releasing neuropsychological test data then, the integrity and security of tests can become compromised.

In accordance with the American Academy of Clinical Neuropsychology's consensus statement regarding the protection of raw test data (Kaufman, 2009), the following recommendations are suggested in an effort to protect raw data and neuropsychological tests from wrongful disclosure. First, neuropsychologists should become familiar with laws regarding release of raw test data and test materials in their state of practice. Second, dependent on the legislature of the practicing state, neuropsychologists should adhere to (if required) or utilize existing psychologist nondisclosure privilege, which allows the psychologist the right to refuse the release of raw test data and test materials during litigation in an effort to protect the validity of neuropsychological tests and maintain test security (Kaufman, 2009). If it is necessary or mandated by law to release test data or materials, neuropsychologists should ensure that the person the data are going to be released to understands the data or that the data are released to a psychologist or other qualified user.

Technological Advances in Neuropsychological Assessment

Clinical neuropsychology has been affected by the widespread use of technology. In a survey of doctorate-level psychologists (n = 495), 19.6 percent endorsed utilizing computerized test batteries sometimes, 18.2 percent endorsed using them often, and 2.6 percent endorsed using them always (Rabin et al., 2014). Recently, there have been large governmental initiatives toward developing and standardizing computerized neuropsychological batteries. For example, the National Institutes of Health developed a set of computerized neuropsychological tests (NIH EXAMINER, Kramer et al., 2014; NIH Toolbox, Gershon et al., 2013) and the Department of Defense developed the Automatic Neuropsychological Assessment Metrics (Reeves et al., 2007) to use in pre- and postdeployment assessment. Emerging computerized tests that take advantage of online data collection, use of tablets and smartphones, virtual reality, or other wearable devices have also been developed (Parsons, 2015). Many of these advancements allow for repeated serial assessments that can occur outside of the laboratory or clinic, allowing for ambulatory data that appear to have good psychometric properties, although more data are needed. There have also been initiatives to use computerized technology to conduct cognitive screening, automatic scoring and analysis, visualization of the data, and educational materials to other health care providers, allowing for better dissemination of neuropsychological information outside of the specialist setting (Casaletto & Heaton, 2017).

There are significant advantages associated with the use of computerized assessment. For example, there is less variability in and consequently more control over test administration and scoring (Parsey & Schmitter-Edgecombe, 2013). Other advantages include increased accuracy in the timing of stimulus presentation and response latency (Bilder, 2011) and the ease of both administering tests in different languages and exporting participant responses for the purposes of data analysis (Bauer et al., 2012). Moreover, administration of computerized neuropsychological tests may save time and increase the accessibility of neuropsychological services (Bauer et al., 2012). However, computerized assessment is also associated with disadvantages. First, problems with software or hardware may lead to incomplete or unusable test data. Reaction time is especially problematic to assess, given differences in computers across settings, and especially if an examiner is trying to collect data using a web-based format, in which there is no knowledge of the computer system being utilized on the patient's end of data collection. Second, given the constant changes in computer technology, there are constant alterations and adaptations of measures that may affect their psychometric properties, creating a need for expensive retesting and renorming prior to use. Third, the use of computerized assessments does not capture behavioral observations that are important in informing diagnostic impressions. Fourth, in computerized assessment, determining effort/noncredible performance may prove more difficult (Bauer et al., 2012) and computerized tests do not allow the examiner to provide encouragement or assess motivation during the testing session. Accordingly, when deciding whether to use computerized tests or develop such tests, several risks and benefits must be weighed. A joint position paper of the American Academy of Clinical Neuropsychology and National Academy of Neuropsychology outlines expectations of computerized test developers and users (Bauer et al., 2012) and more thorough discussion of computerized testing in neuropsychological assessment settings can be found in Chapter 35. However, it is worth highlighting that the neuropsychologist still retains the responsibility of interpreting computerized test scores and integrating their results into all other data available for a patient. Thus, the assessor should still be trained and have expertise in neuropsychological assessment to use computerized tests appropriately, in either the clinical or the research setting. Ultimately, regardless of how the data are gathered, it is the neuropsychologist who must integrate test data together with medical, developmental, psychological, educational, and other history to answer a neuropsychological referral question.

REFERENCES

American Academy of Clinical Neuropsychology. (2017). *Adult neuropsychology*. https://theaacn.org/adult-neuropsychology

APA (American Psychological Association). (2010). *Ethical principles of psychologists and code of conduct*.

Ashendorf, L., Vanderslice-Barr, J. L., & McCaffrey, R. J. (2009). Motor tests and cognition in healthy older adults. *Applied Neuropsychology, 16*, 171–179.

Baldo, J. V., Arevalo, A., Patterson J. P., & Dronkers, N. F. (2013). Gray and white matter correlates of picture naming: Evidence from a voxel-based lesion analysis of the Boston Naming Test. *Cortex, 49*, 658–667.

Barrash, J., Stillman, A., Anderson, S. W., Uc, E. Y., Dawson, J. D., & Rizzo, M. (2010). Prediction of driving ability with neuropsychological testing: Demographic adjustments diminish accuracy. *Journal of the International Neuropsychological Society, 16*, 679–686.

Bauer, R. M., Iverson, G. L., Cernich, A. N., Binder, L. M., Ruff, R. M., & Nagle, R. I. (2012). Computerized neuropsychological assessment devices: Joint position paper of the American Academy of Clinical Neuropsychology and the National Academy of Neuropsychology. *Archives of Clinical Neuropsychology, 27*, 362–373.

Benton, A. L., Hamsher, K. deS., & Sivan, A. B. (1994). *Multilingual aphasia examination* (3rd ed.). San Antonio, TX: Psychological Corporation.

Bilder, R. (2011). Neuropsychology 3.0: Evidence-based science and practice. *Journal of the International Neuropsychological Society, 17*, 7–13.

Binder, L. M. (1982). Constructional strategies on Complex Figure drawings after unilateral brain damage. *Journal of Clinical Neuropsychology, 4*, 51–58.

Binder, L. M., & Binder, A. L. (2011). Relative subtest scatter in the WAIS-IV standardization sample. *The Clinical Neuropsychologist, 25*, 62–71.

Binder, L. M., Iverson, G. L., & Brooks, B. L. (2009). To err is human: "Abnormal" neuropsychological scores and variability are common in healthy adults. *Archives of Clinical Neuropsychology, 24*, 31–46.

Bohnen, N. I., Kuwabara, H., Constantine, G. M., Mathis, C. A., & Moore, R. Y. (2007). Grooved Pegboard as a test of biomarker nigrostriatal denervation in Parkinson's disease. *Neuroscience Letters, 424*, 185–189.

Bowman, M. L. (2002). The perfidy of percentiles. *Archives of Clinical Neuropsychology, 17*, 295–303.

Brooks, B. L., Holdnack, J. A., & Iverson, G. L. (2011). Advanced clinical interpretation of the WAIS-IV and the WMS-IV: Prevalence of low scores varies by level of intelligence and years of education. *Assessment, 18*, 156–167.

Brooks, B. L., Iverson, G. L., Holdnack, J. A., & Feldman, H. H. (2008). Potential for misclassification of mild cognitive impairment: A study of memory scores on the Wechsler Memory Scale-III in healthy older adults. *Journal of the International Neuropsychological Society*, *14*, 463–478.

Bush, S., & Lees-Haley, P. R. (2005). Threats to the validity of forensic neuropsychology data: Ethical considerations. *Journal of Forensic Psychology*, *4*, 45–66.

Casaletto, K. B., & Heaton, R. K. (2017). Neuropsychological assessment: Past and future. *Journal of the International Neuropsychological Society*, *23*, 9–10.

Chelune, G. J. (2010). Evidence-based research and practice in clinical neuropsychology. *The Clinical Neuropsychologist*, *24*, 454–467.

Constantinou, M., Ashendorf, L., & McCaffrey, R. J. (2005). Effects of a third party observer during neuropsychological assessment: When the observer is a video camera. *Journal of Forensic Neuropsychology*, *4*, 39–47.

Crawfold, J. R., Garthwaite, P. H., Morrice, N., & Duff, K. (2012). Some supplementary methods for the analysis of the RBANS. *Psychological Assessment*, *24*, 365–374.

Dandachi-FitzGerald, B., Ponds, R. W. H. M., & Merten, T. (2013). Symptom validity and neuropsychological assessment: A survey of practices and beliefs of neuropsychologists in six European countries. *Archives of Clinical Neuropsychology*, *28*, 771–783.

DeFillips, N.A., & McCampbell, E. (1997). *Booklet category test* (2nd ed.). Odessa, FL: Psychological Assessment Resources.

Dekker, M. C., Ziermans, T. B., Spruijt, A. M., & Swaab, H. (2017). Cognitive, parent, and teacher rating measures of executive functioning: Shared and unique influences on school achievement. *Frontiers in Psychology*, *8*. doi:103389/fpsyg.2017.00048

Delis, D. C., Kaplan, E., & Kramer, J. L. (2001). *The Delis-Kaplan executive function system examiner's manual*. San Antonio, TX: Psychological Corporation.

Delis, D. C, Kramer, J. H., Kaplan, E., & Ober, B. A. (2017) *California verbal learning test* (3rd ed.). San Antonio, TX: Psychological Corporation.

Donnell, A., Belanger, H., & Vanderploeg, R. (2011). Implications of psychometric measurement for neuropsychological interpretation. *The Clinical Neuropsychologist*, *25*, 1097–1118.

Elbulok-Chacape, M. M., Rabin, L. A., Spadaccini, A. T., & Barr, W. B. (2014). Trends in the neuropsychological assessment of ethnic/racial minorities: A survey of clinical neuropsychologists in the US and Canada. *Cultural Diversity and Ethnic Minority Psychology*, *20*, 353–361.

Folstein, M. F., Folstein, S. E., & McHugh, P. R. (1975). "Mini-mental state": A practical method for grading the cognitive state of patients for the clinician. *Journal of Psychiatric Research*, *12*, 189–198.

Gershon, R.C., Wagster, M.V., Hendrie, H.G., Fox, N.A., Cook, K. A., & Nowinski, C.J. (2013). NIH Toolbox for assessment of neurological and behavioral function. *Neurology*, *80*, S2–S6.

Golden, C. J., & Freshwater, S. M. (2002). *Stroop Color and Word Test: Revised examiner's manual*. Wood Dale, IL: Stoelting Co.

Goodglass, H., Kaplan, E., & Barresi, B. (2001). *Boston Diagnostic Aphasia Examination* (3rd ed.). Philadelphia, PA: Lippincott Williams & Wilkins.

Haaland, K. Y., & Delaney, H. D. (1981). Motor deficits after left or right hemisphere damage due to stroke or tumor. *Neuropscyhologia*, *19*, 17–27.

Hannay, H. J., Bieliaukas, L., Crosson, B. A., Hammeke, T. A., Hamsher K. deS., & Koffler, S. (1998). Proceedings of the Houston Conference on specialty education and training in clinical neuropsychology. *Archives of Clinical Neuropsychology*, *13*, 157–250.

Heaton, R. K., Chelune, G. J., Talley, J. L., Kay, G. G., & Curtis, G. (1993). *Wisconsin Card Sorting Test (WCST) manual, revised and expanded*. Odessa, FL: Psychological Assessment Resources.

Heaton, R. K., Miller, S. W., Taylor, M. J., & Grant, I. (2004). *Revised comprehensive norms for an expanded Halstead-Reitan battery: Demographically adjusted neuropsychological norms for African-American and Caucasian adults*. Lutz, FL: Psychological Assessment Resources.

Heilbronner, R.L., Sweet, J.J., Attix, D.K., Krull, K.R., Henry, G. K., & Hart, R.P. (2010). Official position of the American Academy of Clinical Neuropsychology on serial neuropsychological assessments: The utility and challenges of repeat test administrations in clinical and forensic contexts. *The Clinical Neuropsychologist*, *24*, 1267–1278.

Hilsabeck, R. C. (2017). Psychometrics and statistics: Two pillars of neuropsychological practice. *The Clinical Neuropsychologist*, *31*, 995–999.

Horwitz, J. E., & McCaffrey, R. J. (2008). Effects of a third party observer and anxiety on tests of executive function. *Archives of Clinical Neuropsychology 23*, 409–417.

Huizenga, H.M., ven Rentergem, J.A., Agelink, G., Raoul, P.P.P, Muslimovic, D., & Schmand, B. (2016). Normative comparisons for large neuropsychological test batteries: User-friendly and sensitive solutions to minimize familywise false positives. *Journal of Clinical and Experimental Neuropsychology*, *38*, 611–629.

Ivnik, R. J., Malec, J. F., Smith, G. E., Tangalos, E. G., & Peterson, R. C. (1996). Neuropsychological test norms above age 55: COWAT, BNT, MAE Token, WRAT-R Reading, AMNART, Stroop, TMT, and JLO. *The Clinical Neuropsychologist*, *10*, 262–278.

Jagaroo, V., & Santangelo, S. L. (Eds.). (2016). *Neurophenotypes: Advancing psychiatry and neuropsychology in the "OMICS" era*. New York: Springer.

Kaplan, E., Goodglass, H., & Weintraub, S. (2001). *The Boston naming test-II*. Philadelphia: Lea & Febinger.

Kaufman, P. M. (2009). Protecting raw data and psychological tests from wrongful disclosure: A primer on the law and other persuasive strategies. *The Clinical Neuropsychologist*, *23*, 1130–1159.

Kløve, H. (1963). Clinical neuropsychology. In F. M. Forster (Ed.), *The medical clinics of North America*. New York: Saunders.

Kongs, S. K., Thompson, L. L., Iverson, G. L., & Heaton, R. K. (2000). *Wisconsin Card Sorting Test-64 Card Version*. Lutz, FL: Psychological Assessment Resources.

Kramer, J.H., Mungas, D., Possin, K.L., Rankin, K.P., Boxer, A. L., ... Widmeyer, M. (2014). NIH EXAMINER: conceptualization and developmental of an executive function battery. *Journal of the International Neuropsychological Society*, *20*, 11–19.

Lange, R. T., & Lippa, S. M. (2017). Sensitivity and specificity should never be interpreted in isolation without consideration of other clinical utility metrics. *The Clinical Neuropsychologist*, *31*, 1015–1028.

Lezak, M. D., Howieson, D.B., Bigler, E.D., & Tranel, D. (2012). *Neuropsychological assessment* (5th ed.). New York: Oxford University Press.

Lucas, J. A., Ivnik, R. J., Smith, G. E., Ferman, T. J., Willis, F. B., Peterson, R. C., & Graff-Radford, N. R. (2005). Mayo's Older

African Americans Normative Studies: Norms for Boston Naming Test, Controlled Oral Word Association, Category Fluency, Animal Naming, Token Test, WRAT-3 Reading, Trail Making Test, Stroop Test, and Judgment of Line Orientation. *The Clinical Neuropsychologist*, *19*, 243–269.

Lucas, J. A., Ivnik, R. J., Willis, F. B., Ferman, T. J., Smith, G. E., Parfit et al. (2005). Mayo's older African Americans normative studies: Normative data for commonly used neuropsychological tests. *The Clinical Neuropsychologist*, *19*, 162–183.

Manly, J. J., Jacobs, D. M., Sano, M., Bell, K., Merchant, C. A., Small, S. A., & Stern, Y. (1998). Cognitive test performance among nondemented elderly African Americans and Whites. *Neurology*, *50*, 1238–1245.

Martin, P. K., Schroeder, R.W., & Odland, A. P. (2015). Neuropsychologists' validity testing beliefs and practices: A survey of North American professionals. *The Clinical Neuropsychologist*, *29*, 741–776.

Messerli, P., Seron, X., & Tissot, R. (1979). Quelques aspects des troubles de la programmation dans le syndrome frontal. *Archives Suisse de Neurologie, Neurchirugie et Psychiatrie*, *125*, 23–35.

Meyers, J. E. (2017). Fixed battery. In J. Kreutzer, J. DeLuca, & B. Caplan (Eds.), *Encyclopedia of clinical neuropsychology* (pp. 1–2). New York: Springer.

Meyers, J. E., & Meyers, K. (1995). *The Meyers scoring system for the Rey complex figure and the recognition trial: Professional manual*. Odessa, FL: Psychological Assessment Resources.

Mitrushina, M. N., Boone, K. B., Razani, J., & d'Elia, L. F. (2005). *Handbook of normative data for neuropsychological assessment* (2nd ed.). New York: Oxford University Press.

Miyake, A., Friedman, N.P., Emerson, M.J., Witzki, A.H., & Howerter, A. (2000). The unity and diversity of executive functions and their contributions to complex 'frontal lobe' tasks: A latent variable analysis. *Cognitive Psychology*, *41*, 49–100.

Moering, R.G., Schinka, J.A., Mortimer, J.A., & Graves, A.B. (2004). Normative data for elderly African Americans for the Stroop Color and Word Test. *Archives of Clinical Neuropsychology*, *9*, 61–71.

National Academy of Neuropsychology. (2003). *Test security: An update. Official statement of the National Academy of Neuropsychology*. Author. https://www.nanonline.org/docs/PAIC/PDFs/NANTestSecurity Update.pdf

Nuechterlein, K. H., Green, M. F., Kern, R. S., Baade, L. E., Barch, D. M., Cohen, T. D. et al. (2008). The MATRICS Consensus Cognitive Battery, part 1: Test selection, reliability, and validity. *American Journal of Psychiatry*, *165*, 203–213.

Osterrieth, P. A. (1944). Le test de copie d'une figure complexe. *Archives de Psychologie*, *30*, 206–356 [trans. J. Corwin and F. W. Bylsma (1993), *The Clinical Neuropsychologist*, *7*, 9–15].

Otto, R. K., & Krauss, D. A. (2009). Contemplating the presence of third party observers and facilitators in psychological evaluations. *Assessment*, *16*, 362–372.

Parsey, C. M., & Schmitter-Edgecombe, M. (2013). Applications of technology in neuropsychological assessment. *The Clinical Neuropsychologist*, *27*, 1328–1361.

Parsons, T. D. (2015). Virtual reality for enhanced ecological validity and experimental control in the clinical, affective, and social neurosciences. *Frontiers in Human Neuroscience*, *9*, 660.

Rabin, L. A., Paolillo, E., & Barr, W. B. (2016). Stability in test-usage practices of clinical neuropsychologists in the United States and Canada over a 1 10-year period: A follow-up survey of INS and NAN. *Archives of Clinical Neuropsychology*, *31*, 206–230.

Rabin, L. A., Spadaccini, A. T., Brodale, D. L., Grant, K. S., Elbulok-Charcape, M. M., & Barr, W. B. (2014). Utilization rates of computerized tests and test batteries among clinical neuropsychologists in the United States and Canada. *Professional Psychology: Research and Practice*, *45*, 368–377.

Reeves, D.L., Winter, K.P., Bleiberg, J., & Kane, R.L. (2007). ANAM Genogram: Historical perspectives, description, and current endeavors. *Archives of Clinical Neuropsychology*, *22*, S15–S37.

Reitan, R. M. (1955). The relation of the Trail Making Test to organic brain damage. *Journal of Consulting Psychology*, *19*, 393–394.

Reitan, R. M., & Wolfson, D. (1985). *The Halstead-Reitan neuropsychological test battery: Theory and clinical interpretation*. Tucson, AZ: Neuropsychology Press.

Reitan, R. M., & Wolfson, D. (1993). *The Halstead-Reitan Neuropsychological Test Battery: Theory and clinical interpretation* (2nd ed.). Tucson, AZ: Neuropsychology Press.

Rhodes, M. G. (2004). Age-related differences in performance on the Wisconsin Card Sorting Test: A meta-analytic review. *Psychology and Aging*, *19*, 482–494.

Romero, H. R., Lageman, S. K., Kamath, V., Irani, F., Sim, A., Suarez, P. et al. (2009). Challenges in the neuropsychological assessment of ethnic minorities: Summit proceedings. *The Clinical Neuropsychologist*, *23*, 761–779.

Sawrie, S. M., Chelune, G. J., Naugle, R. I., & Luders, H. O. (1996). Empirical methods for assessing meaningful change following epilepsy surgery. *Journal of the International Neuropsychological Society*, *2*, 556–564.

SCN (Society for Clinical Neuropsychology Division 40 of the American Psychological Association). (2015). *About the Society for Clinical Neuropsychology*. www.scn40.org/about-scn.html

Silverberg, N. D., & Millis, S. R. (2009). Impairment versus deficiency in neuropsychological assessment: Implications for ecological validity. *Journal of the International Neuropsychological Society*, *15*, 94–102.

Smith, G. E., Ivnik, R. J., & Lucas, J. (2008). Assessment techniques: Tests, test batteries, norms, and methodological approaches. In J. E. Morgan & J. H. Ricker (Eds.), *Textbook of Clinical Neuropsychology* (pp. 38–57). New York: Taylor & Francis.

Steinberg, B. A., Bieliauskas, L. A., Smith, G. E., & Ivnik, R. J. (2005). Mayo Older Americans Normative Studies: Age- and IQ-adjusted norms for the Trail-Making Test, the Stroop Tees, and MAE Controlled Oral Word Association Test. *The Clinical Neuropsychologist*, *19*, 329–377.

Storms, G., Saerens, J., & DeDeyn, P. P. (2004). Normative data for the Boston Naming Test in native Dutch-speaking Belgian children and the relation with intelligence. *Brain and Language*, *91*, 274–281.

Strauss, E., Sherman, E. M. S., & Spreen, O. (2006). *A compendium of neuropsychological tests* (3rd ed.). New York: Oxford University Press.

Suhr, J. A. (2015). *Empirically based assessment: A problem-solving approach*. New York: Guilford Press.

Sweet, J. J., & Breting, L. G. (2012). *Affidavit regarding opposition to the presence of third party observers and recording of neuropsychological and psychological assessments performed in the state of Illinois*. https://theaacn.org/wp- content/uploads/2015/

10/third-party-observer-affidavit-completed-2013-all-abcn-illinois-practicing-psychologists.pdf

Sweet, J. J., Benson, L. M., Nelson, N. W., & Moberg, P. J. (2015). The American Academy of Clinical Neuropsychology, National Academy of Neuropsychology, and Society for Clinical Neuropsychology (APA, Division 40) 2014 TCN professional practice and 'salary survey': Professional practices, beliefs, and incomes of U.S. neuropsychologists. *The Clinical Neuropsychologist*, *29*, 1069–1162.

Tombaugh, T. N., & McIntyre, N. J. (1992). The Mini-Mental State Examination: A comprehensive review. *Journal of American Geriatric Society*, *40*, 922–935.

Wechsler, D. (2008). *Wechsler Memory Scale – Fourth Edition (WMS-IV): Technical and interpretive manual*. San Antonio, TX: Pearson.

Yantz, C. L., & McCaffrey, R. J. (2005). Effects of a supervisor's observation on memory test performance of the examinee: Third party observer effect confirmed. *Journal of Forensic Neuropsychology*, *4*, 27–38.

16 Minnesota Multiphasic Personality Inventory-2-Restructured Form (MMPI-2-RF)

YOSSEF S. BEN-PORATH, MARTIN SELLBOM, AND JULIE A. SUHR

The Minnesota Multiphasic Personality Inventory (MMPI) has been a mainstay of psychological assessment for nearly eight decades, a testament to the richness and clinical utility of the test. We begin this chapter by tracing the history and evolution of the MMPI instruments, including the rationale for and development of the MMPI-2-RF. In the following section, we provide an overview of the test scales and the documents available to guide its administration, scoring, and interpretation. The next section provides an overview of the psychometric features of the MMPI-2-RF scales and a review of the literature on its use in a broad range of applied settings. Next, we review the literature on multicultural considerations when using the MMPI-2-RF. A brief description of the adolescent version of the inventory, the MMPI-Adolescent-Restructured Form (MMPI-A-RF) is then followed by a concluding section that illustrates MMPI-2-RF interpretation with a case study.

HISTORY AND EVOLUTION OF THE MMPI INSTRUMENTS

The item pool, assembled by Hathaway and McKinley (1940) to "create a large reservoir of items from which various scales might be constructed in the hope of *evolving* a greater variety of valid personality descriptions than are available at the present time" (p. 249, emphasis added) and augmented by Butcher and colleagues (1989) for the MMPI-2, has proven to be remarkably fruitful. It is noteworthy that, as early as 1940, Hathaway and McKinley viewed their initial efforts at scale development as a starting point for what they hoped would be an evolving instrument. This statement proved to be prescient, as evolution wound up being one of the defining characteristics of the test, undoubtedly contributing to its longevity. In this section, we review the history and evolution of the MMPI instruments to date.

Rationale for and Development of the MMPI

The MMPI was developed by Hathaway and McKinley (1943) to assist in the process of differential diagnosis of patients admitted to the University of Minnesota Hospital. Ben-Porath (2012) noted that it is incorrect to view the original MMPI (as some have done) as atheoretical and strictly the product of "blind" empiricism. Rather, he noted that the theoretical foundations of the MMPI included

1. initial development of items and designation of scales based on the then contemporary Kraepelinian descriptive nosology
2. treatment of test items as stimuli for behavioral responses, the aggregates of which may have certain empirical correlates, including diagnostic group membership
3. rejection of content-based test interpretation as overly susceptible to the influences of overt (intentional) and covert (unconscious) distortion
4. recognition that, point 3 notwithstanding, test-takers do attend to item content and may intentionally or unintentionally respond in a misleading manner

Hathaway and McKinley described the development of several of the original Clinical Scales in a series of articles (Hathaway & McKinley, 1940, 1942). For each of the Clinical Scales, they selected items that statistically differentiated a designated patient group from "normals." The nonclinical sample consisted primarily of visitors to the University of Minnesota Hospital, mostly rural Minnesotans with an average of eight years of education and employed primarily as skilled and semiskilled laborers and farmers. This sample was also used to develop norms for the MMPI.

Hathaway and McKinley did not realize their goal of constructing a test to be used as a direct differential diagnostic indicator. Attempts to replicate the validity of the Clinical Scales as predictors of diagnostic group membership were only marginally successful for some scales and largely unsuccessful for others (Hathaway, 1960). Instead, led by Paul Meehl, Hathaway's students and colleagues reinvented the MMPI by directing its use away from the narrow task of differential diagnosis to a considerably broader application and, within a decade, the prevailing use of the MMPI had changed dramatically. MMPI users observed that certain patterns of scores tended to recur and test-takers who produced these combinations shared certain clinical and personality characteristics. The Kraepelinian nosological model was dropped in favor of a considerably broader and more ambitious goal of assessing normal and abnormal personality characteristics. Code types, representing the patterns just mentioned rather than individual scales, were viewed as the primary source of information provided by the test. To facilitate the MMPI's transformation from a single-scale differential diagnostic tool to an omnibus measure of personality and psychopathology, Meehl (1956) called for developing MMPI "cookbooks." Researchers were implored to identify a new, clinically useful set of MMPI-based classes and establish their empirical correlates. Investigators responded with a number of comprehensive efforts to develop such systems (e.g., Gilberstadt & Duker, 1965; Marks & Seeman, 1963).

Hathaway and McKinley, for the most part, ignored item content when selecting items for the Clinical Scales, whereas Wiggins (1966) set the standard for rigorous construction of Content Scales for the MMPI. Wiggins offered cogent arguments favoring development of content-based scales for the test, citing research that had demonstrated equivalence, if not superiority, of content-based measures over empirically keyed ones and the desirability of developing psychometrically sound dimensional means of gauging the information conveyed by the test-taker. The development of Validity Scales for the MMPI, intended to measure how a test-taker approached the instrument, also reflected early recognition that item content could not be ignored.

Hathaway's appraisal of the MMPI might best be characterized as ambivalent. In a paper titled "Where Have We Gone Wrong? The Mystery of the Missing Progress," Hathaway (1972) lamented the lack of further development of the Clinical Scales, indicating that, to a large extent, this could be attributed to the absence of an improved (or, for that matter, equally useful) alternative to the Kraepelinian diagnostic system. Nevertheless, he anticipated that "Even if it has little more to offer us in research, I fear that the aged MMPI will be tolerated for some time by those concerned with practical problems in psychological evaluation" (Hathaway, 1972, p. 23).

Hathaway's (1972) paper was one of several presented at a conference convened in his honor in 1970 (the Fifth Annual Symposium on Recent Developments in the Use of the MMPI), devoted to consideration of whether the time had come for a revision of the MMPI and, if so, what form it should take. The conference produced an edited volume (Butcher, 1972) that included most of the presentations and a detailed discussion of the topic by Meehl (1972), who conceded that the unwavering empirical rationale outlined in his early defense of the MMPI (Meehl, 1945) was overstated. In particular, he agreed that sound psychometric practice should include consideration of item content at the various stages of scale development. He also now advocated reliance on statistical analyses, including possibly factor analyses, to control for competing (with the targeted construct) sources of variance at the stage of scale development. Relatedly, he now viewed internal consistency of scales as desirable and heterogeneity as undesirable.

Rationale for and Development of the MMPI-2

The 1989 publication of a revised version of the MMPI, the MMPI-2 (Butcher et al., 1989), represented the culmination of nearly a decade of research. Among the main objectives for revising the test was an update of the test norms, a task that was not the focus of the 1970 conference just discussed. While the MMPI normative sample represented well the initial target population for the test, patients receiving services at the University Hospital, it was no longer adequate as the MMPI became more widely used in a variety of settings throughout the United States.

Problematic MMPI items were a second focus of the revision. The item pool of the inventory had come under considerable criticism over the years. Foremost among these concerns was the inclusion of item content that was no longer clear, relevant, or appropriate for assessing personality and psychopathology. In addition, a relatively large set of MMPI items was not scored on any of the Clinical, Validity, or widely used Supplementary Scales. These "nonworking" items were candidates for deletion and replacement. A final item-level issue was the absence of content dealing with matters relevant to contemporary clinical personality assessment (e.g., suicidal ideation, Type A behavior, use of drugs such as marijuana, work-related difficulties, and treatment readiness). A trade-off between nonworking and new items was viewed as the appropriate strategy for confronting both problems.

In the 1989 MMPI-2 manual and the writings of the three original Restandardization Committee members (Butcher, Dahlstrom, and Graham), there is little or no discussion of the proposals for addressing fundamental problems with the MMPI Clinical Scales summarized in the edited volume by Butcher (1972). Early on, these committee members made a strategic decision to keep the Clinical Scales essentially intact to allow for continued and unchanged reliance on the reported empirical correlates of code types formed by these scales, which, as discussed, had become the primary focus of MMPI interpretation. The Restandardization Committee thus assigned itself two goals: to improve the test, while maintaining as much continuity as possible with the original MMPI. Improvement was to be attained by updating the normative base and correcting the item-level deficiencies just noted. Continuity was to be accomplished by minimizing changes to the Clinical Scales, making it possible for test interpreters to continue to rely on decades of accumulated research and clinical experience with these measures.

The MMPI-2 normative sample was collected throughout the United States. The final normative sample was made up of 2,600 individuals, 1,138 men and 1,462 women. A number of additional clinical and nonclinical datasets were compiled and used in various scale development and validation studies. Altogether, more than 10,000 individuals were tested as part of the Restandardization Project.

As discussed, the Restandardization Project had two potentially conflicting goals: to improve the instrument, while maintaining continuity with its empirical and experiential foundations. Continuity was achieved by leaving the thirteen basic Validity and Clinical Scales of the MMPI largely intact. Improvement at the scale level was accomplished primarily through the introduction of twenty-one new measures, including three new Validity Scales, the MMPI-2 Content Scales (Butcher et al., 1990), and three Supplementary Scales, two designed to measure gender roles and a post-traumatic stress disorder (PTSD) indicator.

Judged by the frequency with which the MMPI-2 came to be used in practice and research, the revision was clearly successful. This is particularly true in light of the skeptical reaction of some original MMPI researchers, who opined that the test had changed too much and mistakenly predicted that, as a result, the MMPI-2 would fail to replace its "classic" predecessor (Adler, 1990). The strategic decision to leave the Clinical Scales essentially unchanged did, however, have negative consequences. Up until the 1960s, the MMPI played a significant role in basic research in personality and psychopathology and in studies of important applied questions in personality assessment. As concerns about the psychometric soundness of the Clinical Scales mounted, basic researchers lost interest in the MMPI, as did many investigators seeking to foster improvements in applied personality assessment. This schism disadvantaged MMPI users, who could no longer rely on direct links to these lines of investigation, and it was also detrimental to investigators in these areas, who lost access to the wealth of clinically rich data available on the hundreds of thousands of individuals tested yearly with the inventory.

Successful efforts to link the MMPI-2 to more modern approaches to the measurement and study of psychopathology and personality were nevertheless carried out. The Personality Psychopathology Five (PSY-5) Scales, developed by Harkness, McNulty, and Ben-Porath (1995) to assess what was then an innovative dimensional model of personality disorder–related psychopathology (Harkness & McNulty, 1994), could be linked, for example, with the widely studied five-factor model of personality. Nevertheless, the continuity achieved for the MMPI-2 with the Clinical Scales ensured that the host of problems detailed in the volume by Butcher and colleagues (1972) continued to challenge its users.

Rationale for and Development of the MMPI-2-RF

Ben-Porath (2012) noted that the authors' goal for developing the MMPI-2-RF was to represent the clinically significant substance of the MMPI-2 item pool with a comprehensive set of psychometrically adequate measures. This goal reflected recognition of the MMPI item pool's long-standing record of providing relevant information about the psychological functioning of individuals who completed the inventory. Nevertheless, the primary sources of information on the original MMPI and MMPI-2, the Clinical Scales, had some long-recognized limitations. Auke Tellegen, the only member of the MMPI Restandardization Committee who had advocated for updating the Clinical Scales for the MMPI-2, embarked on a project to address these challenges directly.

A primary shortcoming of the Clinical Scales involved their limited discriminant validity, which resulted from excessive correlations between them, magnified by considerable item overlap. Discriminant validities of Clinical Scale scores were particularly problematic with respect to differentiation between emotional dysfunction and other types of psychopathology. This shortcoming was in part a product of how the empirical keying technique was applied when items were assigned to the Clinical Scales, based primarily on their ability to discriminate between different patient groups and a common "normal" comparison sample. Because of this approach, each of the eight original Clinical Scales wound up including some items that characterized the designated patient group, in addition to others that reflected common (across disorders) differences between being a patient and not being one. A second critical limitation of the Clinical Scales was their heterogeneous makeup, including items unrelated to the targeted constructs both statistically and conceptually, which diminished their convergent validity. Finally, a near-total absence of theory to help guide their interpretation restricted the ability of MMPI users to rely on construct validity in Clinical Scale interpretation.

Tellegen's goal was to restructure the Clinical Scales in a manner that would directly address the limitations just noted and make available scales with improved discriminant and (in some cases) convergent validities, which can be linked to contemporary theories and models of personality and psychopathology. Scale construction proceeded in four steps. The first involved developing a marker of the MMPI common factor, which, as just noted, was overrepresented in the Clinical Scales as a result of how they were assembled. Tellegen labeled this factor *Demoralization* and conceptualized it within the framework of his (Tellegen, 1985) two-factor model of affect as the MMPI-2 equivalent of pleasant versus unpleasant or happy versus unhappy mood. Ben-Porath (2012) provides a detailed discussion of this construct as it applies to the MMPI-2-RF. The second step was designed to identify the major distinctive core component of each Clinical Scale with the aid of factor analyses. In Step 3, these core markers were refined further to yield a maximally distinct set of *Seed* scales. Step 4 involved correlational analyses with the entire MMPI-2 item pool. An item was added to a Seed scale and included on the final Restructured Scale derived from it if (1) that item correlated more highly with that Seed scale than it did with the others; (2) the correlation exceeded a certain specified value; and (3) it did not correlate beyond a specified level with any other Seed scale. The specific criteria varied across scales as specified by Tellegen and colleagues (2003).

The result of this four-step process was a set of nine nonoverlapping scales representing Demoralization and a major distinctive core component of each of the eight original Clinical Scales. Restructured Scales were not developed for Clinical Scales 5 (Masculinity–Femininity) or 0 (Social Introversion) because the focus of the Restructured Clinical (RC) Scales was on assessment of psychopathology. The final set of nine RC Scales consisted of 192 MMPI-2 items. Research reported initially by Tellegen and colleagues (2003), and later in the peer-reviewed literature, demonstrated that the RC Scales had successfully met their developer's goals, showing substantial improvement in discriminant and convergent (and therefore also construct) validity (for a review, see, e.g., Tellegen, Ben-Porath, & Sellbom, 2009).

The nine RC Scales, designed to assess major distinctive core components of the original MMPI Clinical Scales, were carried over to the MMPI-2-RF in identical composition and augmented by thirty-three substantive measures and nine validity indicators intended to canvass the full range of constructs that can be reliably and validly assessed with the MMPI-2 item pool. Tellegen and Ben-Porath (2008/2011) and Ben-Porath (2012) provide detailed descriptions of the development processes for these scales. Briefly, a set of Specific Problems and Interest Scales was developed using methods similar to how the RC Scales were constructed, with the aim of representing constructs more narrowly focused than the RC Scales or ones not assessed by the Clinical or RC Scales. Higher-Order Scales were developed to represent three broad psychopathology domains identified in factor analyses of the RC Scales. The Personality Psychopathology Five (PSY-5) scales were developed to provide revised measures of the five dimensions of personality disorder–related psychopathology represented by the MMPI-2 PSY-5 Scales (Harkness et al., 2012). A central aspect of the development of the MMPI-2-RF was to link the test to contemporary concepts and models of personality and psychopathology. Ben-Porath (2012) provides a detailed description of the constructs assessed by the forty-two MMPI-2-RF substantive scales and the literature supporting their construct validity. The MMPI-2-RF Validity Scales include seven revised versions of MMPI-2 validity indicators and two new measures.

OVERVIEW OF THE MMPI-2-RF

The MMPI-2-RF consists of 338 items scored on fifty-one scales. Two test manuals are available to guide use of the inventory. The *MMPI-2-RF Manual for Administration Scoring and Interpretation* (Ben-Porath & Tellegen, 2008/2011) includes information about intended uses of the inventory, the normative sample, methods used to develop standard scores for the scales, and guidelines for standard administration, scoring, and interpretation of test results. Unlike the MMPI-2 manual, this document includes detailed interpretive guidelines that establish a common standard for interpreting test findings.

The MMPI-2-RF normative sample is essentially the same one used in standardizing the MMPI-2, with the exception that nongendered norms are used with the MMPI-2-RF. The practice of reporting and interpreting gendered norms for MMPI scales began with the original test and was maintained with the MMPI-2. However, the use of tests in certain areas, particularly in personnel screening, is governed by laws that prohibit reliance on some group-specific norms. The federal Civil Rights Act of 1991 explicitly prohibits consideration of race, color, religion, sex, or national origin in employment practices and has been interpreted to prohibit using gendered norms in personnel screening. To address the resulting need for gender-neutral norms, a set of nongendered norms for all MMPI-2 scales included in the test manual (Butcher et al., 2001) was developed by Ben-Porath and Forbey (2003), who reported finding little to no interpretable differences between gender-normed and nongendered MMPI-2 scale scores. Consequently, the MMPI-2-RF standard scores were developed based on a combined-gender sample made up of 2,276 (1,138 men and 1,138 women) of the 2,600 individuals that made up the MMPI-2 normative sample.

The *MMPI-2-RF Technical Manual* (Tellegen & Ben-Porath, 2008/2011) includes a description of the test development procedures and detailed information about the psychometric properties (reliability and validity) of scores on the fifty-one scales of the inventory. Correlations between scores on the MMPI-2-RF substantive scales and collateral information collected with large samples representing settings in which the test is used are reported in Appendix A of the Technical Manual (Tellegen & Ben-Porath, 2008/2011). The thousands of external correlates (53,970) reported in Appendix A are based on data provided by 4,336 men and 2,337 women using 605 different criteria. These validity findings served as the primary source for identifying the empirical correlates of substantive scale scores listed in the interpretive guidelines provided in the MMPI-2-RF Manual for Administration, Scoring, and Interpretation (Ben-Porath & Tellegen, 2008/2011). Correlates were included on these lists if they replicated across setting, gender, and criterion source. Appendix D of the Technical Manual includes descriptive data (means and standard deviations) on the fifty-one MMPI-2-RF scales for samples of more than 65,000 individuals tested in a broad range of settings where the test is used.

MMPI-2-RF Scales

Listed and described briefly in Table 16.1, the MMPI-2-RF scales are divided into six sets. The *Validity Scales* consist of nine MMPI-2-RF measures designed to alert the

Table 16.1 MMPI-2-RF scale: labels, abbreviations, number of items, and brief description

Scale	Abbreviation	Items	Description
Validity Scales			
Variable Response Inconsistency	VRIN-r	53 pairs	Random responding
True Response Inconsistency	TRIN-r	26 pairs	Fixed responding
Infrequent Responses	F-r	32	Responses infrequent in community populations
Infrequent Psychopathology Responses	F_P-r	21	Responses infrequent in both community and patient populations
Infrequent Somatic Responses	F_S	16	Physical health complaints infrequent in medical patient populations
Symptom Validity	FBS-r	30	Noncredible physical and cognitive complaints
Response Bias Scale	RBS	28	Exaggerated memory complaints
Unlikely Virtues	L-r	14	Rarely claimed virtuous attributes or behaviors
Adjustment Validity	K-r	14	Avowals of psychological adjustment
Higher-Order (H-O) Scales			
Emotional/Internalizing Dysfunction	EID	41	Substantial problems associated with mood and affect
Thought Dysfunction	THD	26	Substantial problems associated with disordered thinking
Behavioral/Externalizing Dysfunction	BXD	23	Substantial problems associated with disinhibited behavior
Restructured Clinical (RC) Scales			
Demoralization	RCd	24	Nonspecific emotional distress; general unhappiness and dissatisfaction
Somatic Complaints	RC1	27	Preoccupation with a diverse set of health complaints
Low Positive Emotions	RC2	17	Lack of positive emotional experiences; anhedonia
Cynicism	RC3	15	Non–self-referential beliefs expressing distrust and a generally low opinion of others
Antisocial Behavior	RC4	22	Social deviance, rule-breaking, impulsivity, and irresponsible behavior
Ideas of Persecution	RC6	17	Self-referential beliefs that others pose a threat; paranoid delusions
Dysfunctional Negative Emotions	RC7	24	Maladaptive anxiety, anger, irritability
Aberrant Experiences	RC8	18	Unusual perceptions or thoughts
Hypomanic Activation	RC9	28	Hyperactivation, aggression, impulsivity, and grandiosity
Specific Problem (SP) Scales			
Somatic/Cognitive Scales			
Malaise	MLS	8	Overall sense of physical debilitation, poor health
Gastrointestinal Complaints	GIC	5	Complaints about nausea, recurring upset stomach, and poor appetite
Head Pain Complaints	HPC	6	Complaints about head and neck pains
Neurological Complaints	NUC	10	Complaints about dizziness, weakness, paralysis, loss of balance, etc.
Cognitive Complaints	COG	10	Memory problems, difficulties concentrating
Internalizing Scales			
Suicidal/Death Ideation	SUI	5	Direct reports of suicidal ideation and suicide attempts
Helplessness/Hopelessness	HLP	5	Belief that goals cannot be reached or problems solved
Self-Doubt	SFD	4	Lack of confidence, feelings of uselessness
Inefficacy	NFC	9	Belief that one is inefficacious; indecisiveness
Stress/Worry	STW	7	Stress reactivity; preoccupation with disappointments; difficulty with time pressure
Anxiety	AXY	5	Pervasive anxiety; frights; frequent nightmares
Anger Proneness	ANP	7	Becoming easily angered; impatient with others
Behavior-Restricting Fears	BRF	9	Fears that significantly inhibit normal activities

Continued

Table 16.1 (cont.)

Scale	Abbreviation	Items	Description
Multiple Specific Fears	MSF	9	Fears of a diverse set of stimuli, such as blood, fire, thunder, etc.
Externalizing Scales			
Juvenile Conduct Problems	JCP	6	Difficulties at school and at home; stealing as a youngster
Substance Abuse	SUB	7	Current and past misuse of alcohol and drugs
Aggression	AGG	9	Verbally and physically aggressive; violent behavior
Activation	ACT	8	Heightened excitation and energy level; euphoria; racing thoughts
Interpersonal Scales			
Family Problems	FML	10	Conflictual family relationships
Interpersonal Passivity	IPP	10	Being unassertive and submissive with others
Social Avoidance	SAV	10	Avoiding or not enjoying social events
Shyness	SHY	7	Bashful; prone to feel inhibited and anxious around others
Disaffiliativeness	DSF	6	Disliking people and being around them
Interest Scales			
Aesthetic-Literary Interests	AES	7	Interests in literature, music, the theater
Mechanical-Physical Interests	MEC	9	Interested in fixing and building things, the outdoors, sports
Personality Psychopathology Five (PSY-5) Scales			
Aggressiveness-revised	AGGR-r	18	Instrumental, goal-directed aggression; dominance and assertiveness; grandiosity
Psychoticism-revised	PSYC-r	26	Disconnection from reality
Disconstraint-revised	DISC-r	20	Undercontrolled behavior; impulsivity; sensation seeking
Negative Emotionality/ Neuroticism-revised	NEGE-r	20	Dispositional proclivity to experience anxiety, insecurity, worry, anger, and fear
Introversion/Low Positive Emotionality-revised	INTR-r	20	Dispositional proclivity for social disengagement and anhedonia

interpreter to various threats to the validity of an individual test protocol. They include measures of inconsistent responding, overreporting, and underreporting. The MMPI-2-RF Validity Scales include seven revised versions of MMPI-2 validity indicators and two new measures. Revisions were intended primarily to eliminate item overlap, which reduced the distinctiveness of the MMPI-2-Validity Scales. The two new indicators were developed by identifying items with somatic content answered uncommonly in the keyed direction by medical patients (*Infrequent Somatic Responses*) and items correlated with scoring below established cutoffs on performance validity indicators in neuropsychological assessments (*Response Bias Scale*).

The remaining forty-two substantive scales include three *Higher-Order Scales*, which indicate whether and to what extent a test-taker is likely experiencing problems in the domains of mood and affect, thought processes, and/or behavior; the nine *Restructured Clinical Scales* just discussed, which provide an indication of the individual's standing on the nine psychological constructs identified by Tellegen and colleagues (2003) as major distinctive core components of the original MMPI Clinical Scales; twenty-three *Specific Problems Scales*, the most narrowly focused MMPI-2-RF measures, which are subdivided into indicators of somatic and cognitive complaints, internalizing difficulties, externalizing behaviors, and interpersonal functioning; two *Interest Scales*, derived from the original MMPI Scale 5; and five *Personality Psychopathology Five (PSY-5) Scales*, which are revised versions of similarly labeled MMPI-2 scales, designed to provide a dimensional perspective on features of personality disorder–related psychopathology.

MMPI-2-RF Administration, Scoring, and Interpretation

The primary source of guidance for MMPI-2-RF administration, scoring, and interpretation is the test manual (Ben-Porath & Tellegen, 2008/2011). Another resource available for MMPI-2-RF users is the book *Interpreting the MMPI-2-RF* (Ben-Porath, 2012), which provides a detailed review of the evolution of the MMPI instruments, a description of the construction of the instrument, a framework for interpreting Validity Scale scores, and, as mentioned, a detailed discussion of the constructs assessed by the forty-two substantive scales of the inventory. The recommended process for MMPI-2-RF interpretation is only briefly reviewed here and is illustrated with a case study presented at the end of this chapter.

The first step in interpreting the MMPI-2-RF is considering scores on the Validity Scales. Specifically, test interpreters need to determine (in order) the presence of unscorable responding (Cannot Say-Revised and proportion of scorable responses for each scale), random/inconsistent and indiscriminant fixed responding (VRIN-r and TRIN-r; see Table 16.1), overreporting (F-r, Fp-r, Fs, FBS-r, and RBS; see Table 16.1), and underreporting (L-r and K-r; see Table 16.1). If a protocol is deemed valid for clinical interpretation, the substantive scales are considered next. This interpretation begins with the Higher-Order scales and, specifically, the most elevated scale, which indicates to the clinician which domain of functioning (i.e., emotional, thought, behavioral) is considered first. All RC, Specific Problems (SP), and PSY-5 scales within the indicated domain are interpreted before moving on to the next domain as indicated by the next highest elevated Higher-Order scale. Once no Higher-Order scale remains to be interpreted, any uninterpreted RC Scales at that stage are considered, and scales within the domain to which that RC scale belongs are interpreted as well. Finally, any remaining elevated scales are interpreted. Ben-Porath and Tellegen (2008/2011) recommended that Somatic/Cognitive scales (RC1 and corresponding SP scales; see Table 16.1) be interpreted immediately after scales from the emotional dysfunction domain are covered. This interpretative strategy is demonstrated in the case illustration provided at the end of this chapter.

PSYCHOMETRICS

Reliability

One-week test-retest reliability for the MMPI-2-RF was calculated from MMPI-2 data, using a subset of the normative sample (collapsed over genders) who completed developmental versions of the MMPI-2 on two occasions. Test-retest reliability values for the Validity scales are generally above 0.70, with the exception of Fs (0.51), VRIN-r (0.52), and TRIN-r (0.40), which would not be expected to be temporally stable. Test-retest values for most substantive subscales exceed 0.70, with many at 0.80 or higher. Generally speaking, the Higher-Order Scales, RC Scales, and PSY-5 Scales show higher test-retest reliability (Tellegen & Ben-Porath, 2008/2011). Internal consistency of the MMPI-2-RF scales is based on the normative sample, as well as three patient samples (community mental health outpatients, psychiatric inpatients, and male Veterans Administration (VA) psychiatric inpatients). As with test-retest reliability, internal consistency values tend to be stronger for the longer Higher-Order Scales, RC Scales, and PSY-5 Scales, with most values falling at 0.80 or higher (Tellegen & Ben-Porath, 2008/2011). SP scales are substantially shorter, and therefore penalized by Cronbach's alpha, but were otherwise by and large adequate with respect to internal consistency, particularly in clinical samples. Overall, both test-retest and internal consistency values are stronger for the MMPI-2-RF than the MMPI-2, resulting in smaller standard errors of measurement (SEM) for most scales. For scales with higher SEM values, higher *T*-scores are used before those scales are clinically interpreted (Tellegen & Ben-Porath, 2008/2011).

Construct Validity

The research on the MMPI-2-RF and its scales has been voluminous over the past decade and half, beginning with the introduction of the RC Scales on the MMPI-2 in 2003. Sellbom (2019) provides a detailed review of the construct validity and applied utility of MMPI-2-RF scale scores. In this section, we summarize several lines of important findings.

Tellegen and Ben-Porath (2008/2011) provided validity evidence for all fifty-one MMPI-2-RF scales across a range of samples, including from various outpatient and inpatient facilities, criminal forensic, civil forensic, and nonclinical populations. This evidence allowed the test authors to generate a set of descriptive correlates to guide scale interpretation.

Validity Scales. The MMPI-2-RF Validity Scales have been the subject of a large number of research studies. Handel and colleagues (2010) have established the impact of random and indiscriminant fixed responding on MMPI-2-RF substantive scale scores as well as determining the optimal cut scores to detecting such responding on the VRIN-r and TRIN-r scales, respectively, in a large psychiatric sample. They found support for 80T for both scales as indicative of invalid responding and that 30–40 percent of such responding had deleterious effects on both scale elevations and psychometric validity.

In terms of overreporting, there have been two recent meta-analyses published, which provide good support for the various scales and clearly indicate that the best scales depend on context and population (Ingram & Ternes, 2016; Sharf et al., 2017). Ingram and Ternes (2016) reviewed twenty-five studies of the MMPI-2-RF overreporting scales, covering a wide range of populations and research designs; they reported that, overall, effect size estimates (Hedge's *g*) ranged from 1.08 (FBS-r) to 1.43 (Fp-r). Most recently, Sharf and colleagues (2017) examined thirty studies that met their stringent criteria for clinical applicability. Similar to Ingram and Ternes (2016), they reported that the effect size estimates (Cohen's *d*) ranged from 0.75 (FBS-r) to 1.35 (Fp-r) for studies for which genuine patients were used as the comparison group. Furthermore, these researchers also reported good classification accuracies for the overreporting scales in detecting both feigned mental disorders (FMD), feigned cognitive impairment (FCI), and feigned medical complaints (FMC). F-r was associated with the best sensitivity for FMD, including at the manual's recommended cut score, whereas (as expected) Fp-r was associated with the best specificity (98 percent at $T \geq 100$). RBS was associated with the best balance of sensitivity and specificity for detecting FCI, whereas Fs exhibited the best such balance for FMC. Overall, overreporting scales are more specific (often > 95 percent at optimal cut scores) than sensitive, which serves to reduce false positive classification errors.

The underreporting scales (L-r and K-r) have received far less research attention relative to their overreporting counterparts but research has been supported their utility. Simulation studies across various university, community, and patient populations have indicated that the effect sizes range from 0.65 to 1.50, with a mean of 1.09 for L-r and 1.02–1.65, with a mean of 1.33, for K-r (Brown & Sellbom, in press; Crighton et al., 2017; Sellbom & Bagby, 2008). Moreover, Detrick and Chibnall (2014) used a differential prevalence design in which they compared MMPI-2-RF scores of a preemployment sample (who were motivated to be hired as police officers) with scores generated by the same individuals after they had successfully completed their training, with no stake in the results of the second assessment (and thus with less motivation to underreport). The authors observed L-r and K-r differences between the two administrations with large effect sizes, which was consistent with conceptual expectations. Finally, research that has examined classification accuracy (Brown & Sellbom, in press; Crighton et al., 2017) have shown very good specificity rates for recommended cut scores (> 95 percent) but lower sensitives at recommended screening cut scores (54–63 percent) for these scales.

Substantive Scales. There are too many published studies on these scales across contexts and settings to efficiently summarize here. One of the goals of the restructuring effort was to better align the instrument's scales with contemporary models of personality and psychopathology. To this end, research has clearly demonstrated impressive convergent and discriminant validity for various MMPI-2-RF scales in their relation to well-established personality models, such as the five-factor model of personality (Sellbom, Ben-Porath, & Bagby, 2008a), Tellegen's Multidimensional Personality Questionnaire (Avdeyeva, Tellegen, & Ben-Porath, 2011; Sellbom & Ben-Porath, 2005; Tellegen & Ben-Porath, 2008), and the interpersonal circumplex (Ayearst et al., 2013).

Furthermore, the MMPI-2-RF scales have also shown good alignment with emerging dimensional models of personality disorders, particularly the personality trait model embedded within the alternative DSM-5 model of personality disorders (AMPD; American Psychiatric Association, 2013). In a series of studies, Anderson and colleagues (2013) and Anderson, Sellbom, Ayearst and colleagues (2015) examined undergraduate students and psychiatric patients, respectively, who had been administered the MMPI-2-RF and the Personality Inventory for DSM-5 (PID-5) – the most common operationalization of the AMPD trait model. Across both studies, the MMPI-2-RF PSY-5 and PID-5 domain scales converged as conceptually expected (e.g., Negative Affectivity with NEGE-r; Detachment with INTR-r). Other studies (Anderson, Sellbom, Ayearst et al., 2015; Sellbom et al., 2013) have also demonstrated substantial overlap between the MMPI-2-RF scales and PID-5 trait facet scales in a manner that was consistent with conceptual expectations in both psychiatric inpatient and university student samples. Sellbom and colleagues (2013) observed that conceptually relevant MMPI-2-RF scales could explain a substantial proportion of variance (47–60 percent) in trait aggregate scores representing Antisocial, Avoidant, Borderline, and Schizotypal personality disorders, with smaller (albeit still large) amounts in Narcissistic and Obsessive-Compulsive personality disorders.

More recently, emergence of the Hierarchical Taxonomy of Psychopathology (HiTOP; Kotov et al., 2017), which represents an effort at organizing psychopathology and maladaptive personality symptoms and traits in a manner that is consistent with psychiatric and psychological science, has led to demonstrations that the MMPI-2-RF scales and associated hierarchical structure align well with the HiTOP framework (Lee, Sellbom, & Hopwood, 2017; Sellbom, 2019). Although a detailed examination is beyond the scope of this chapter, Sellbom (2019) recently demonstrated through a review of the MMPI-2-RF literature, particularly studies that examined the internal structure of various sets of MMPI-2-RF scales (e.g., Hoelzle & Meyer, 2008; McNulty & Overstreet, 2014; Sellbom, 2016, 2017a; Sellbom, Ben-Porath, & Bagby, 2008a; Van der Heijden et al., 2013), that the scales align closely with various levels of the HiTOP structure, as conceptually expected.

Applied Assessment. The MMPI instruments are the most frequently used inventories of personality and psychopathology in clinical practice as well as the most frequently emphasized in clinical psychology training (e.g., Camara et al., 2000; Mihura, Roy, & Graceffo, 2017; Neal & Grisso, 2014). It is therefore not surprising that many scholars who conduct research on the instrument have been especially interested in addressing questions that pertain to its applied utility, with such research occurring in mental health, substance abuse treatment, correctional, criminal forensic, civil forensic, medical, and nonclinical settings, as well as presurgery candidate and public safety personnel evaluations (for a review, see Sellbom, 2019). Some highlights of this extensive literature are reviewed here.

In terms of mental health evaluations, the MMPI-2-RF scales have demonstrated good utility in differential diagnosis and specifically aligning with various symptoms of mental health disorders in conceptually expected ways. This literature includes personality disorders (e.g., Anderson, Sellbom, & Pymont et al., 2015; Sellbom, Smid et al., 2014; Sellbom & Smith, 2017; Zahn et al., 2017), PTSD (Arbisi et al., 2011; Choi, 2017; Koffel et al., 2016; Sellbom, Lee et al., 2012; Wolf et al., 2008) as well as the explicit differentiation between depressive, bipolar, and schizophrenic disorders (Sellbom, Bagby et al., 2012;

Lee et al., 2018; Watson et al., 2011). Furthermore, several studies have also reported that MMPI-2-RF scales can predict premature termination in psychotherapy in both university counseling centers (Anestis, Finn et al., 2015; Anestis, Gottfried, & Joiner, 2015) and community outpatient clinics (Tarescavage, Finn et al., 2015).

The MMPI-2-RF has also demonstrated good utility in forensic settings, including characterizing those undergoing evaluations to address different psycho-legal questions, such as competence to stand trial, criminal responsibility (Sellbom, 2017b), sex offender risk (Tarescavage, Cappo, & Ben-Porath, 2018), child custody, and parental capacity (Archer et al., 2012; Kauffman, Stolberg, & Madero, 2015; Pinsoneault & Ezzo, 2012; Resendes & Lecci, 2012). Several studies have also begun to emerge that support the utility of the externalizing MMPI-2-RF scales and thought dysfunction scales as potent predictors of general and violent offense risk (Grossi et al., 2015; Sellbom, Ben-Porath, Baum et al., 2008; Tarescavage, Glassmire, & Burchett, 2016; Tarescavage, Luna-Jones, & Ben-Porath, 2014).

The MMPI-2-RF has also been demonstrated to be useful in medical settings. Various medical populations, such as patients with epilepsy (e.g., Locke et al., 2010, 2011; Myers et al., 2012, 2013), with chronic pain (Tarescavage, Scheman, & Ben-Porath, 2015, 2018), and those undergoing smoking cessation treatment (Martinez et al., 2017; Martinez et al., 2018) to mention a few have been studied. The majority of scholarly work in medical settings has occurred in the context of presurgery evaluations. This body of literature has demonstrated that the MMPI-2-RF can be quite useful in predicting concurrent and future risk in bariatric surgery (e.g., Marek et al., 2014, 2015, 2017), spine surgery, and spinal cord stimulator (e.g., Block, Ben-Porath, Marek, 2013; Block et al., 2014; Marek et al., 2015a, 2017b) candidates. For instance, Marek and colleagues have examined the prospective validity of MMPI-2-RF scale scores in predicting both poor treatment adherence and adverse outcomes postsurgery, including one to three months (Marek et al., 2014), up to one year (Marek et al., 2015b), and up to five years (Marek et al., 2017a). One particularly notable finding in this prospective research is that MMPI-2-RF scores become stronger outcome predictors as the time span from presurgery to follow-up increases.

A final applied area in which the MMPI-2-RF is frequently recommended and used is preemployment evaluations of candidates for public safety positions, such as law enforcement (Corey & Ben-Porath, 2018). This literature has shown that MMPI-2-RF scale scores are associated with a wide range of problematic outcomes in the police academy and later on the job using a variety of different forms of criterion modalities (e.g., clinician ratings, supervisor ratings, employment records) (Corey, Sellbom, & Ben-Porath, 2018; Sellbom, Fischler, & Ben-Porath, 2007; Tarescavage, Brewster et al., 2015; Tarescavage, Corey, & Ben-Porath, 2015, Tarescavage et al., 2016; Tarescavage, Corey, Gupton et al., 2015c; Tarescavage, Fischler et al., 2015).

The literature just reviewed represents merely a snapshot of the extensive body of publications available to guide the applied use of the MMPI-2-RF. Interested readers are encouraged to examine the literature in greater depth. What is clear is that the MMPI-2-RF has demonstrated utility in the measurement of a number of important factors in various contexts (e.g., treatment implications in mental health settings; adverse surgical outcomes in medical settings; future risk for violence in forensic assessments; and future disciplinary and behavioral problems among public safety officers) but, of course, individual scale interpretations in these settings should always be consistent with specific findings.

MULTICULTURAL CONSIDERATIONS FOR THE USE OF THE MMPI-2-RF

The MMPI-2-RF is appropriate to use in adults across a wide range of ages (from eighteen to eighty). The reading level is about grade 4.5–5, allowing for use in individuals with low literacy; in addition, the test can be administered orally using standard audio recordings for those who cannot read the items (Ben-Porath & Tellegen, 2008/2011). The MMPI-2-RF has been translated into many other languages, including Croatian, Dutch, French, French-Canadian, German, Hebrew, Italian, Korean, Norwegian, Spanish for Mexican/Central Americans, Spanish for South Americans, Spanish for the United States, and Swedish.

One weakness of the MMPI-2-RF with regard to diversity is the normative database. The norms were based on the 1990 US Census and there was a slight underrepresentation of African Americans and Hispanic/Latinx individuals in the normative sample relative to the Census numbers at the time. However, males and females were equally represented (Tellegen & Ben-Porath, 2008/2011). This shortcoming will be addressed in the new normative sample collected for the MMPI-3 (Ben-Porath & Tellegen, under development), which will match the population demographics projected for the 2020 Census.

The most important empirical data with regard to use of any instrument in diverse groups is evidence for differential validity/construct invariance. There have been only a few MMPI-2-RF studies to date that have addressed this issue; however, the studies suggest the MMPI-2-RF is appropriate to use in diverse groups. With regard to factorial invariance, Kim and colleagues (2015) conducted an exploratory factor analysis of the RC scales using data from the Korean translation of the MMPI-2-RF in a large sample of North Korean female refugees. They found that a three-factor model similar to that identified in the technical manual showed the best fit to the data.

Two studies to date have examined predictive bias in the MMPI-2-RF. Marek, Ben-Porath, and colleagues (2015) examined empirical correlates of MMPI-2-RF scores across gender, race/ethnicity (African American, Hispanic/Latinx, and Caucasian groups), and age in bariatric surgery candidates. Of the gender analyses, twelve of forty were statistically significant (all suggesting intercept bias) and all suggested overprediction for males relative to females; however, effect sizes were negligible to small. Of the racial/ethnicity analyses, ten out of forty were statistically significant (nine of which suggested slope bias). All showed underprediction for African Americans; however, effect sizes were small. Overall, results did not suggest concerns with bias for interpretation of the MMPI-2-RF in this population. Whitman and colleagues (2019) examined gender and race/ethnicity bias (Caucasian, African American, and Hispanic/Latinx groups) in the prediction of future suicidal and/or violent behavior within a forensic psychiatric inpatient sample. Of a total of 320 analyses, only eighteen were statistically significant, consistent with chance. Of the eighteen, two showed intercept bias and sixteen showed slope bias. Of note, the effect sizes for the statistically significant results were negligible to small. With regard to prediction of suicidal behavior, there were no consistent patterns among the statistically significant results with regard to prediction of suicidal behavior between genders or across racial/ethnic groups. With regard to bias in the prediction of violent behavior, several predictors were more strongly associated with the criterion for men than women but of small effect size. For six of the scales, the correlation between scale scores and future violent behavior were stronger for African Americans than Caucasians and for two other scales the correlations were stronger for African Americans than Hispanic/Latinx. However, all of the findings were of small effect size. Overall, results do not suggest gender or racial/ethnic bias in the interpretation of MMPI-2-RF scores in forensic psychiatric inpatients.

Another study did not conduct formal bias analyses but provided evidence that the F-r and Fp-r scales can be used successfully in a diverse sample of criminally committed inpatients who ware adjudicated as not guilty by reason of insanity (Glassmire et al., 2016). They found that the endorsement rate of items was generally similar across genders and racial/ethnic groups. Only one Fp-r item showed differential endorsement rates, with Hispanic/Latinx and African Americans endorsing the item at higher rates than Caucasians and females endorsing the item at a higher rate than males. Overall, their findings suggest that these two validity scales are acceptable to use across diverse groups in this particular setting.

Two international studies did not compare diverse groups to one another but examined the empirical correlates of MMPI-2-RF scales to determine whether interpretation guidelines from the standard manual could apply in their respective countries. Moultrie and Engel (2017) conducted a chart review of psychiatric inpatients at a German university hospital and determined that the MMPI-2-RF manual empirical correlates were generally similar in their sample, suggesting the standard interpretation guidelines from the manual could be applied in their setting. Similarly, Laurinaityte and colleagues (2017) found that the correlations between MMPI-2-RF scales and external criteria in a large male Lithuanian correctional sample were similar to those identified by the interpretative manual.

The available literature raises no concerns about the use of MMPI-2-RF in diverse samples, although additional research is needed.

TECHNOLOGICAL ADVANCES IN MMPI-2-RF ASSESSMENT

In some ways, MMPI "technology" is remarkably similar to what has been used for the past seven decades. The test is still administered by asking individuals to respond to a fixed set of items, these responses are scored using standard keys that count, for a set of predefined scales, the number of items answered in the designated direction (true or false), and the resulting raw scores are converted to standard *T*-scores derived from responses provided by a common normative sample. Some technological advances have, nonetheless, occurred during this time frame and their pace has accelerated with the MMPI-2-RF. Indeed, development of the MMPI-2-RF provided opportunities to build on the advances just described while avoiding the pitfalls just mentioned. Efforts to do so produced the following features:

Administration

MMPI-2-RF administration can be accomplished with Pearson's desktop and web-based systems. The former requires use of computers or laptops running Microsoft Windows software; the latter can be used with any hardware device, including Apple products, running any operating system, and with tablets. The primary benefit offered by digital administration is time. Most test-takers can complete a paper-and-pencil administration of the test in 35–50 minutes. Digital administration takes an average of 25–35 minutes. In addition, the Pearson software used to administer the test is the same as that used to score it. Thus, test results can be produced as soon as the examinee responds to the final item of the test, saving the time/cost needed to input their responses into the system, which requires either expensive scanning technology or manual response input, which takes additional time and is subject to error.

Scoring

The MMPI-2-RF Score Report (Ben-Porath & Tellegen, 2011) includes several previously unavailable features. Foremost among them are options for report customization. These include the availability of standard comparison groups, made of samples of individuals tested in specified settings (e.g., psychiatric inpatients) or evaluations (e.g., preemployment). These data complement the test's general population norms by indicating how the examinee's scores compare with those obtained by comparison group members. The output includes for each of the 51 MMPI-2-RF scales the percent of comparison group members scoring at or below the test-taker. In addition to providing a menu of more than two dozen standard comparison groups, the scoring software allows users to create their own custom comparison groups made up of individuals they have assessed.

A second customizable feature allows users the option of obtaining extended item-level information. The test authors designated seven MMPI-2-RF scales as having critical item content that might require immediate attention and follow-up: Suicidal/Death Ideation (SUI), Helplessness/Hopelessness (HLP), Anxiety (AXY), Ideas of Persecution (RC6), Aberrant Experiences (RC8), Substance Abuse (SUB), and Aggression (AGG). Items answered by the individual in the keyed direction on a critical scale are listed if the test-taker's *T*-score on that scale is clinically elevated (sixty-five or higher). The percentage of the MMPI-2-RF normative sample who answered each item listed in the keyed direction is provided as is the percentage of members of any comparison group selected. The software also provides an option for the user to designate additional scales and/or alternative cutoff levels for generating item-level information. Users can select any MMPI-2-RF scale for inclusion in this part of the report. The ability to customize cutoffs can be particularly helpful in settings in which interpretable deviations from reference group means occur at lower levels.

Interpretation

Two features of the *MMPI-2-RF Interpretive Report for Clinical Settings* (Ben-Porath & Tellegen, 2011) set it apart from its predecessors. First, the statements in the report are based entirely on the interpretive guidelines provided in the test manual. In essence, the report applies the interpretive recommendations presented in the MMPI-2-RF Manual for Administration, Scoring, and Interpretation to a specific set of scores. Examining the interpretive report is tantamount to looking up the interpretive recommendations for the test-taker's scores and saves the time needed to do so. A second unique aspect of the interpretive report is its transparency. The annotated version of the report, which is provided unless the test user opts to suppress it, identifies the source (i.e., scale scores) for each statement and indicates whether it is based on test responses (i.e., reflects the content of the test-taker's responses to the test items), empirical correlates, or is an inference of the report authors. For statements identified as being based on empirical correlates, the report provides references to the literature where the correlational data supporting these statements can be found. These references include hyperlinks that, when viewed on an Internet-connected device, can be used to navigate to the cited publications.

In addition to the Computer-Based Test Interpretation (CBTI) system for clinical settings just mentioned, interpretive reports are available for use with police recruits and individuals undergoing presurgical evaluations for spine surgery or spinal cord stimulators. The *MMPI-2-RF Police Candidate Interpretive Report* (PCIR; Corey & Ben-Porath, 2014) incorporates all of the elements of the clinical report just described, augmented by sections focused specifically on police candidate comparison group findings and job-relevant correlates. The MMPI-2-RF Spine Surgery and Spinal Cord Stimulator Candidate Interpretive Reports (Block & Ben-Porath, 2018) also include all of the elements of the clinical report as well as specialized sections on comparison group findings, presurgical risk factors, postsurgical outcomes, and treatment recommendations. Both the police candidate and the spine reports incorporate findings from an extensive setting-specific empirical literature.

Future Directions

The MMPI-2-RF technological advances just described involve scoring and interpretation. Unlike the areas of ability and aptitude testing, and with the exception of digitally administering the test in standard order in its entirety, very limited progress has been made to date in capitalizing on computer technology in MMPI administration. In a recent effort, Tarescavage and Ben-Porath (2017) describe and examine the feasibility of *Flexible and Conditional Administration* (FCA) of the MMPI-2-RF. In this approach, elevated scores on higher-level substantive scales are used to trigger administration of lower-level scales within the same assessment domain to minimize administration time. The authors conducted a real-data simulation to derive rules for and evaluate this administration strategy using the MMPI-2-RF normative sample and a community mental health center comparison group. The flexible and conditional administration strategy resulted in minimal loss of information in separate subsamples used to evaluate the method. However, item savings were more pronounced in the normative sample, in which administration time was decreased by 40–80 percent depending on the number of substantive domains assessed. Tarescavage and Ben-Porath (2017) concluded that FCA holds particular promise to make testing more efficient in settings with time constraints and relatively low base rates of psychopathology, such as medical patient and neuropsychological evaluations as well as assessments of candidates for public safety positions.

ASSESSMENT OF ADOLESCENT PSYCHOPATHOLOGY: THE MMPI-A-RF

Shortly after its formal publication, the MMPI was being used with adolescents. Even at the time of its release, Capwell (1945) published a study on MMPI characteristics of juvenile delinquents. Hathaway and Monachesi (1951) administered the MMPI as part of a large-scale longitudinal study that included 15,000 adolescents. Eventually, Marks and Seeman (1963) provided normative data for 1,800 adolescents, which were published in Dahlstrom, Welsh, and Dahlstrom (1972). By the mid-1980s, the MMPI was one of the most frequently used personality inventories for adolescents (Archer et al., 1991) but there were growing concerns about the length, norms, and language of items for adolescents, with recognition that a more developmentally sensitive version of the MMPI was necessary. As a result, the 478-item MMPI-A was published in 1992 (Butcher et al., 1992), with adolescent-specific norms and several constructs better suited for the assessment of adolescent psychopathology and personality. However, recognizing the many similar psychometric problems with the MMPI-2, which were articulated in the section describing the rationale for developing the MMPI-2-RF, Archer, Handel, Ben-Porath, and Tellegen began work on a restructured form of the MMPI-A, which was eventually published in 2016 (Archer et al., 2016).

There are many similarities between the MMPI-2-RF and MMPI-A-RF, including underlying conceptual models, scale development, administration, scoring, and interpretative framework. Therefore, in this section, we will help the reader with understanding some of the main differences across the MMPI-2-RF and MMPI-A-RF.

The most significant difference across the two version is length, with the MMPI-A-RF consisting of 241 true/false items. The MMPI-A-RF normative sample is based on the MMPI-A normative sample with, similar to the MMPI-2-RF, one major modification: nongendered norms. As such, the normative sample has been slightly reduced from 1,620 to 1,610 to facilitate an equal number of boys and girls. The normative sample covers the age ranges of fourteen to eighteen, though the MMPI-A-RF manual outlines circumstances during which administration to twelve- and thirteen-year-olds might be possible. Such decision-making should among other things be based on reading ability and psychological maturity of the adolescent. Furthermore, unlike the MMPI-2-RF, the MMPI-A-RF also relies on a slightly lower threshold for determining a clinical elevation on a substantive scale: $T \geq 60$ as opposed to $T \geq 65$. Finally, while both instruments make use of a list of "Critical Responses," the MMPI-A-RF also uses a revised version of Forbey and Ben-Porath's (1998) critical items list used for the MMPI-A.

The structure and general composition of scales of the MMPI-A-RF are very similar to those of its adult counterpart, with an identical hierarchy of scales that inform interpretation in the same manner. There are some differences, however, in individual scales included, which are briefly articulated here. In terms of the validity scales, there are two major differences. First, the MMPI-A-RF has included a Combined Response Inconsistency (CRIN) scale to complement the VRIN-r and TRIN-r scales in the assessment of inconsistent and fixed indiscriminant responding, with Archer and colleagues (2016) determining that the two scales were insufficient in capturing the full range of such responding (as response styles can sometimes alternate). Second, the MMPI-A-RF only makes use of one overreporting scale, Infrequent Responses-Revised (F-r) as opposed to five scales for the MMPI-2-RF. The F-r scale is a hybrid of the F-r and Fp-r scales on the MMPI-2-RF, in that items that were infrequently endorsed in a combined sample from a range of settings (e.g., normative, community, correctional) were selected.

There are also differences in the substantive scale composition, which occur exclusively at the SP scale level. Among the internalizing scales, the MMPI-A-RF does not have a full scale for SDI (such items do appear in the revised critical item list) but instead has an Obsessions/Compulsions (OCS) scale that measures obsessional thinking, rumination, and compulsive behaviors. Moreover, the externalizing SP scales provide for a more nuanced assessment of such psychopathology vis-à-vis the MMPI-2-RF. Both inventories share the SUB and AGG scales, but the MMPI-A-RF also assesses the constructs of Negative School Attitudes (NSA), Antisocial Attitudes (ASA), Conduct Problems (CNP), and Negative Peer Influence (NPI), which are developmentally appropriate constructs that in many respects are less applicable to adult functioning. Finally, unlike the MMPI-2-RF, the MMPI-A-RF does not include a set of Interest Scales.

In summary, the MMPI-A-RF has very much been modeled after its adult counterpart, with an almost identical set of scales and an identical interpretative framework. A good underlying understanding of how to use the MMPI-2-RF will provide for a smooth transition for using the MMPI-A-RF, much like transitioning between the Wechsler Adult Intelligence Scale – Fourth Edition (WAIS-IV) and the Wechsler Intelligence Scale for Children – Fifth Edition (WISC-V) for intelligence assessment.

CASE ILLUSTRATION

The following case study is designed to illustrate the use of the MMPI-2-RF in a psychological evaluation. Although the profile is from an actual case, the background information represents a combination of multiple clients with highly similar presenting problems and circumstances.

Background

A.B. is a twenty-three-year-old man who came to a university psychology clinic to seek treatment for longstanding concerns about social anxiety, had a lengthy history of isolation, and described himself as "a loner" who will never find a meaningful romantic relationship. He explained that he had friends while growing up but lost them in high school. He had no friends at all in university. In terms of previous mental health history, A.B. said that his father had died from cancer when A.B. was aged five, which was very traumatic for the family, and he attended grief counseling. A.B. further reported that he was so upset by his loss of friends in high school that he once threatened suicide to his mother so he would get counseling to cope with his distress. He was prescribed antidepressant medication but did not find psychotherapy helpful. He denied current suicidal ideation.

A.B. performed well academically in high school but was placed on probation and eventually expelled from his first university due to poor grades. He explained that, in an effort to make friends, he began drinking alcohol heavily and using drugs (cannabis, cocaine, and psilocybin mushrooms) and his academic work suffered as a result. He also stopped attending class because he was too overwhelmed by anxiety. He reported that his effort to make friends was unsuccessful. A.B. reenrolled at his current university after a couple of years in the workforce that had also been difficult for him, as he had been fired from two jobs due to absenteeism owing to social anxiety.

MMPI-2-RF Interpretation

As part of A.B.'s intake and assessment process, he completed the MMPI-2-RF, which was used to assist the student therapist with a psychological formulation and develop a treatment plan. Figure 16.1 shows the Validity Scales. A.B. left one item unanswered, which means the various "Response %" underneath each scale should be consulted to determine the impact of unscorable responding; scales with less than 90 percent of scorable responses should not be interpreted. In the Validity Scale profile, K-r is affected by the nonresponse but remains interpretable at 93 percent scorable responding. The VRIN-r and TRIN-r scales are consulted next; neither scale reached a level that would indicate an invalid profile (80T or higher) nor any concern at all with random or fixed indiscriminant responding. Moreover, all of the overreporting scales (F-r, Fp-r, Fs, FBS-r, and RBS) were within normal limits with respect to profile invalidity, indicating that his reported symptoms on the MMPI-2-RF are unlikely to be the product of exaggeration or fabrication. Finally, the two underreporting scales, L-r and K-r, indicate that A.B. was unlikely to appear overly virtuous or well-adjusted in his responding. Overall, his profile was deemed valid for clinical interpretation.

Next, we turn to the scores of A.B.'s substance scales. The H-O, RC, SP, and PSY-5 scales appear in Figures 16.2–16.5. We use the formal interpretative MMPI-2-RF framework (Ben-Porath, 2012; Ben-Porath & Tellegen, 2008/2011), which indicates that we should start with the most elevated H-O scale that dictates which domain of functioning is covered first. In A.B.'s profile, EID was the only elevated scale and therefore guides us to the emotional dysfunction domain. EID in itself indicates the likelihood of pervasive emotional distress, unhappiness, and anxiety but further scales within this domain require consultation for a clearer picture. The RC Scale profile (see Figure 16.2) indicates that RC7 is the only elevated scale within the emotional dysfunction domain. Per this elevation, A.B. is likely to be experiencing a range of negative emotions, including anxiety, fear, guilt, and anger, though the internalizing SP scales (see Figure 16.3) can further disentangle his emotional dysfunction. These scales reveal elevations on STW and AXY, which indicate significant anxious apprehension, stress reactivity, obsessive thinking, and rumination (STW), with likely intense and intrusive anxious ideation and possibly traumatic stress (AXY), though the latter was generally ruled out from his history. The PSY-5 scales (see Figure 16.5), which include elevation on NEGE-r and INTR-r, suggest long-standing difficulties with emotional regulation, proneness to experience negative affect across context, as well as reduced capacity for positive emotions and social disengagement. Next, Ben-Porath (2012) recommends interpreting the somatic/cognitive domain after the emotional domain has been covered, if warranted. HPC was the only such elevated scale (see Figure 16.3), indicating a preoccupation with head pain complaints with a likely psychological underpinning; indeed, no medical history could rule this out. Next, because no further RC scales were elevated (see Figure 16.2), we examine any remaining SP scales that have not yet been interpreted, which includes the interpersonal SP scales (see Figure 16.4). Three such scales, IPP, SAV, and SHY, are elevated, indicating that A.B. is likely to be unassertive and submissive in his relations with others, be socially withdrawn and prefer solitude over the company of others, and be socially inhibited, bashful, and anxious; he likely fears negative evaluation from others. A.B. also has a low score on the AGGR-r PSY-5 scale (see Figure 16.5), which is similarly associated with a passive-submissive and dependent interpersonal style.

Considering the totality of A.B.'s MMPI-2-RF scores, two non–mutually exclusive major diagnostic possibilities seem most likely: Generalized Anxiety Disorder and Social Anxiety/Avoidant Personality Disorder. The elevations on RC7, STW, and AXY indicate the possibility of a more generalized pattern to his anxiety; however, research has indicated that these scales are also elevated in the context of Avoidant Personality Disorder (Anderson, Sellbom, Pymont et al., 2015; Sellbom & Smith, 2017; Zahn et al., 2017) in addition to the interpersonal scales (especially SAV and SHY) and the PSY-5 scales (INTR-r, NEGE-r), which reflect enduring dispositional tendencies, with NEGE-r, INTR-r, and sometimes low AGGR-r, being an oft-replicated pattern (e.g., Sellbom, Smid et al., 2014). A.B.'s unassertiveness (IPP; low AGGR-r) is likely a function of his social anxiety and associated impairment.

Conclusion

The clinical interview and MMPI-2-RF testing results converged on a clear pattern of long-standing, recurrent, and pervasive social anxiety with high levels of noncoping and significant interpersonal difficulties. It was recommended that A.B. receive cognitive behavioral psychotherapy to work on reducing maladaptive cognitions that perpetuate

MMPI-2-RF® Score Report
08/03/2019, Page 2

ID: 986

MMPI-2-RF Validity Scales

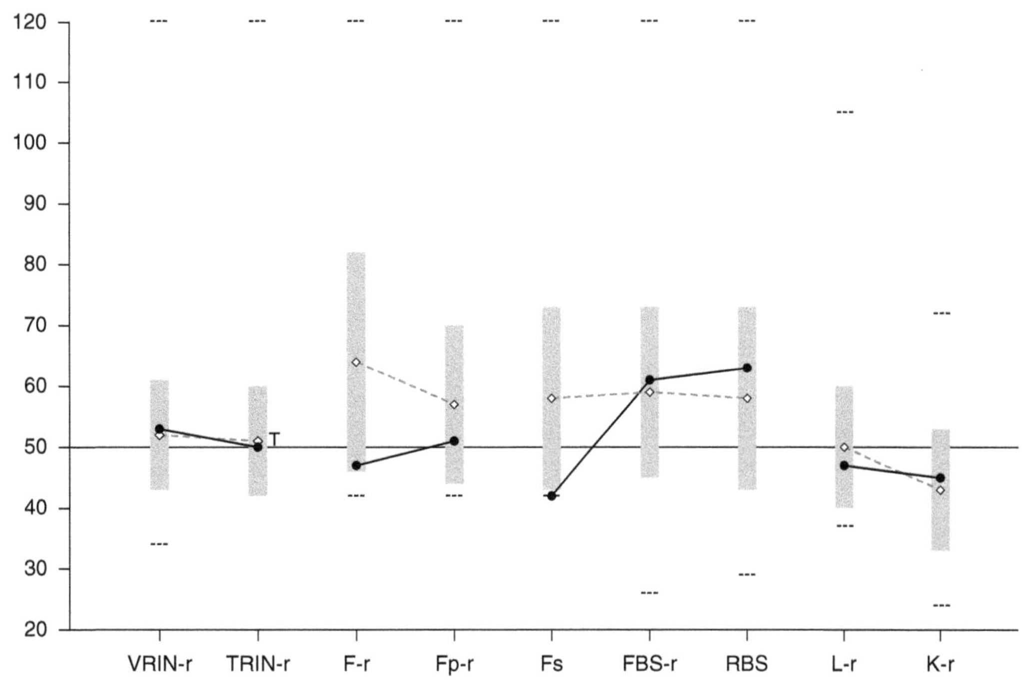

	VRIN-r	TRIN-r	F-r	Fp-r	Fs	FBS-r	RBS	L-r	K-r
Raw Score:	4	11	1	1	0	11	8	2	6
T Score:	53	50	47	51	42	61	63	47	45
Response %:	100	100	100	100	100	100	100	100	93

Cannot Say (Raw): 1   Percent True (of items answered): 39%

Comparison Group Data: College Counseling Clinic (Men), N = 367

	VRIN-r	TRIN-r	F-r	Fp-r	Fs	FBS-r	RBS	L-r	K-r
Mean Score (◇--◇):	52	51 T	64	57	58	59	58	50	43
Standard Dev (±1 SD):	9	9	18	13	15	14	15	10	10
Percent scoring at or below test taker:	66	35	24	52	25	65	73	57	66

The highest and lowest T scores possible on each scale are indicated by a "---"; MMPI-2-RF T scores are non-gendered.

VRIN-r	Variable Response Inconsistency	Fs	Infrequent Somatic Responses	L-r	Uncommon Virtues
TRIN-r	True Response Inconsistency	FBS-r	Symptom Validity	K-r	Adjustment Validity
F-r	Infrequent Responses	RBS	Response Bias Scale		
Fp-r	Infrequent Psychopathology Responses				

Excerpted from the MMPI-2-RF Score Report. Copyright © 2008, 2011, 2012 by the Regents of the University of Minnesota. All rights reserved. Portions excerpted from the MMPI-2-RF® Manual for Administration, Scoring, and Interpretation, copyright © 2008, 2011 by the Regents of the University of Minnesota. Reproduced by permission of the University of Minnesota Press. All rights reserved. "Minnesota Multiphasic Personality Inventory-2-RF®" and "MMPI-2-RF®" are trademarks owned by the Regents of the University of Minnesota.

Figure 16.1 MMPI-2-RF Validity Scales

MMPI-2-RF® Score Report
08/03/2019, Page 3

ID: 986

MMPI-2-RF Higher-Order (H-O) and Restructured Clinical (RC) Scales

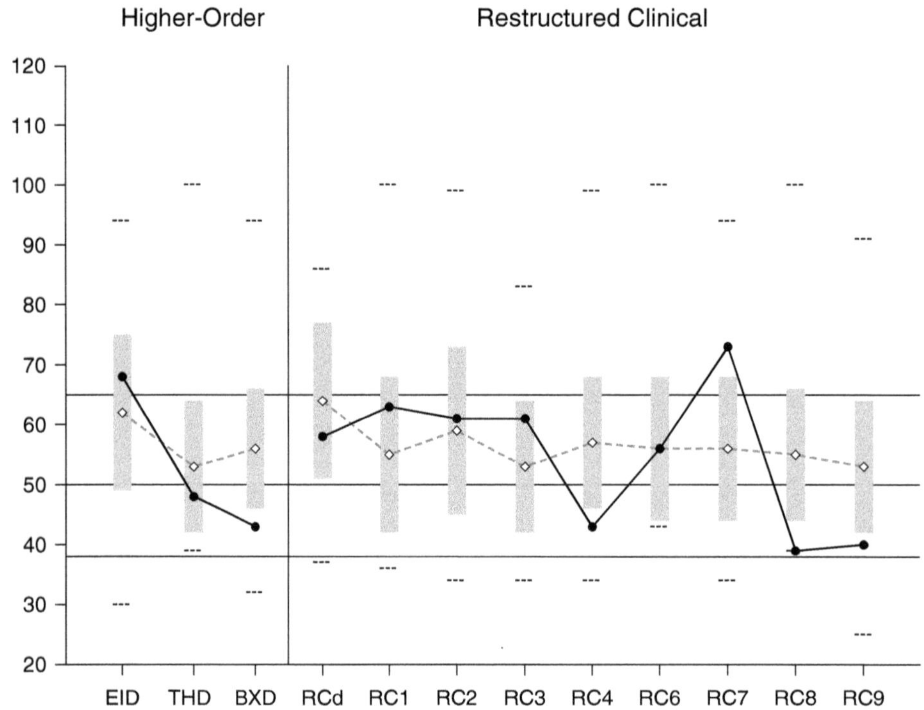

	EID	THD	BXD	RCd	RC1	RC2	RC3	RC4	RC6	RC7	RC8	RC9
Raw Score:	23	1	3	9	8	7	10	2	1	16	0	6
T Score:	68	48	43	58	63	61	61	43	56	73	39	40
Response %:	100	100	100	100	100	100	93	100	100	100	100	100

Comparison Group Data: College Counseling Clinic (Men), N = 367

	EID	THD	BXD	RCd	RC1	RC2	RC3	RC4	RC6	RC7	RC8	RC9
Mean Score (◇--◇):	62	53	56	64	55	59	53	57	56	56	55	53
Standard Dev (±1 SD):	13	11	10	13	13	14	11	11	12	12	11	11
Percent scoring at or below test taker:	66	44	7	37	78	66	82	9	59	93	19	9

The highest and lowest T scores possible on each scale are indicated by a "---"; MMPI-2-RF T scores are non-gendered.

EID Emotional/Internalizing Dysfunction
THD Thought Dysfunction
BXD Behavioral/Externalizing Dysfunction

RCd Demoralization
RC1 Somatic Complaints
RC2 Low Positive Emotions
RC3 Cynicism
RC4 Antisocial Behavior

RC6 Ideas of Persecution
RC7 Dysfunctional Negative Emotions
RC8 Aberrant Experiences
RC9 Hypomanic Activation

Excerpted from the MMPI-2-RF Score Report. Copyright © 2008, 2011, 2012 by the Regents of the University of Minnesota. All rights reserved. Portions excerpted from the MMPI-2-RF® Manual for Administration, Scoring, and Interpretation, copyright © 2008, 2011 by the Regents of the University of Minnesota. Reproduced by permission of the University of Minnesota Press. All rights reserved. "Minnesota Multiphasic Personality Inventory-2-RF®" and "MMPI-2-RF®" are trademarks owned by the Regents of the University of Minnesota

Figure 16.2 MMPI-2-RF Higher-Order and Restructured Clinical Scales

MMPI-2-RF® Score Report
08/03/2019, Page 4

ID: 986

MMPI-2-RF Somatic/Cognitive and Internalizing Scales

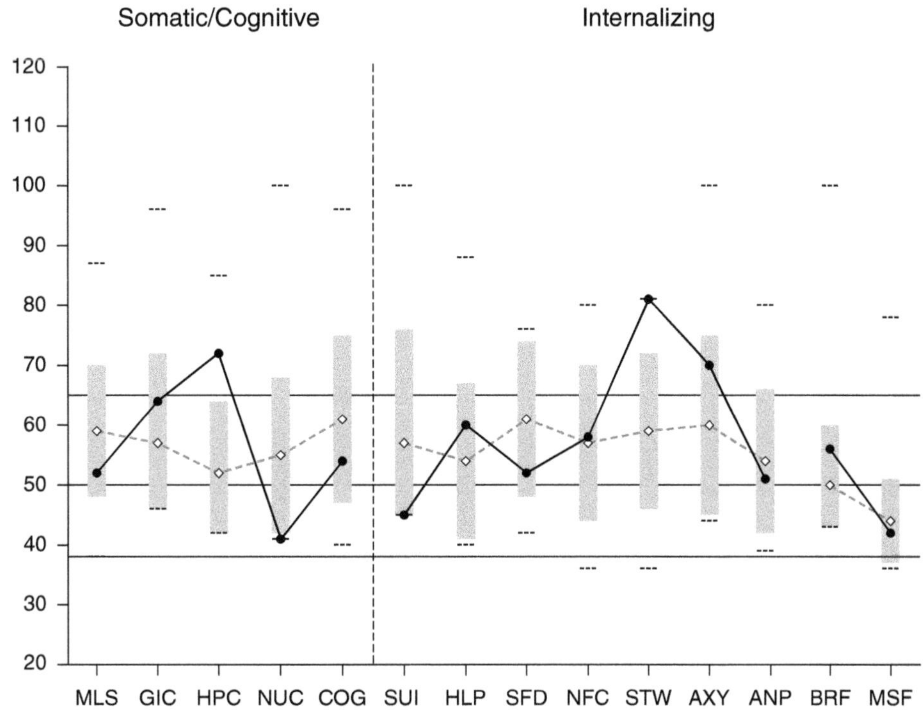

	MLS	GIC	HPC	NUC	COG	SUI	HLP	SFD	NFC	STW	AXY	ANP	BRF	MSF
Raw Score:	2	1	4	0	2	0	2	1	5	7	2	2	1	1
T Score:	52	64	72	41	54	45	60	52	58	81	70	51	56	42
Response %:	100	100	100	100	100	100	100	100	100	100	100	100	100	100

Comparison Group Data: College Counseling Clinic (Men), N = 367

	MLS	GIC	HPC	NUC	COG	SUI	HLP	SFD	NFC	STW	AXY	ANP	BRF	MSF
Mean Score (◇--◇):	59	57	52	55	61	57	54	61	57	59	60	54	50	44
Standard Dev (±1 SD):	11	15	12	13	14	19	13	13	13	13	15	12	10	7
Percent scoring at or below test taker:	40	75	94	32	42	66	79	35	65	100	83	51	84	52

The highest and lowest T scores possible on each scale are indicated by a "---"; MMPI-2-RF T scores are non-gendered.

MLS	Malaise	SUI	Suicidal/Death Ideation	AXY	Anxiety
GIC	Gastrointestinal Complaints	HLP	Helplessness/Hopelessness	ANP	Anger Proneness
HPC	Head Pain Complaints	SFD	Self-Doubt	BRF	Behavior-Restricting Fears
NUC	Neurological Complaints	NFC	Inefficacy	MSF	Multiple Specific Fears
COG	Cognitive Complaints	STW	Stress/Worry		

Excerpted from the MMPI-2-RF Score Report. Copyright © 2008, 2011, 2012 by the Regents of the University of Minnesota. All rights reserved. Portions excerpted from the MMPI-2-RF® Manual for Administration, Scoring, and Interpretation, copyright © 2008, 2011 by the Regents of the University of Minnesota. Reproduced by permission of the University of Minnesota Press. All rights reserved. "Minnesota Multiphasic Personality Inventory-2-RF®" and "MMPI-2-RF®" are trademarks owned by the Regents of the University of Minnesota.

Figure 16.3 MMPI-2-RF Somatic/Cognitive and Internalizing Specific Problems Scales

MMPI-2-RF® Score Report
08/03/2019, Page 5

ID: 986

MMPI-2-RF Externalizing, Interpersonal, and Interest Scales

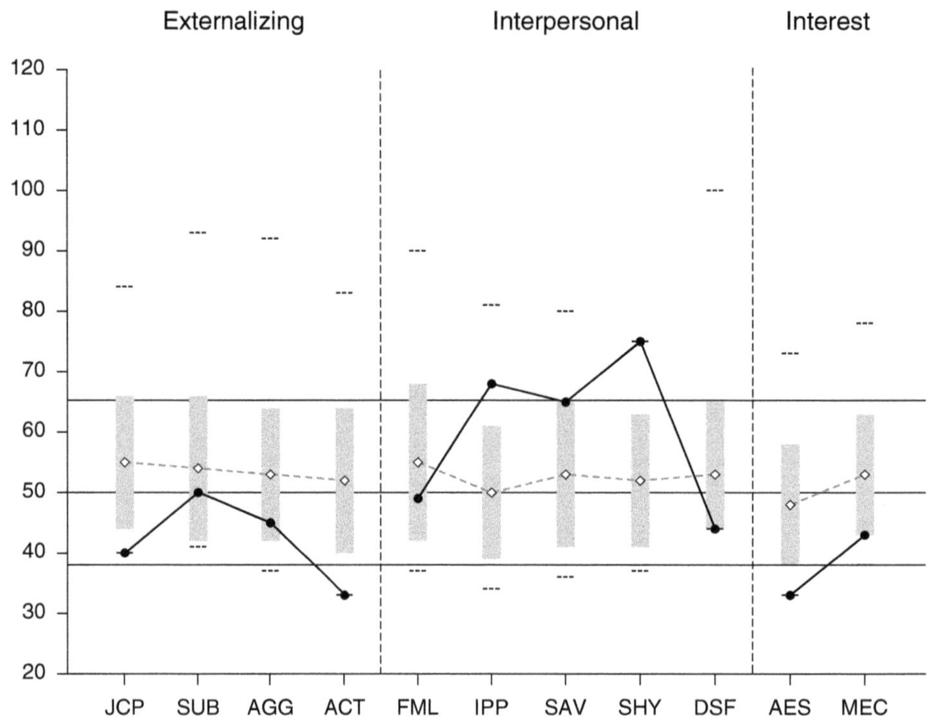

	JCP	SUB	AGG	ACT	FML	IPP	SAV	SHY	DSF	AES	MEC
Raw Score:	0	1	1	0	2	8	7	7	0	0	1
T Score:	40	50	45	33	49	68	65	75	44	33	43
Response %:	100	100	100	100	100	100	100	100	100	100	100

Comparison Group Data: College Counseling Clinic (Men), N = 367

Mean Score (◇--◇):	55	54	53	52	55	50	53	52	53	48	53
Standard Dev (±1 SD):	11	12	11	12	13	11	12	11	12	10	10
Percent scoring at or below test taker:	24	48	35	5	42	94	83	100	57	12	25

The highest and lowest T scores possible on each scale are indicated by a "---"; MMPI-2-RF T scores are non-gendered.

JCP Juvenile Conduct Problems
SUB Substance Abuse
AGG Aggression
ACT Activation

FML Family Problems
IPP Interpersonal Passivity
SAV Social Avoidance
SHY Shyness
DSF Disaffiliativeness

AES Aesthetic-Literary Interests
MEC Mechanical-Physical Interests

Excerpted from the MMPI-2-RF Score Report. Copyright © 2008, 2011, 2012 by the Regents of the University of Minnesota. All rights reserved. Portions excerpted from the MMPI-2-RF® Manual for Administration, Scoring, and Interpretation, copyright © 2008, 2011 by the Regents of the University of Minnesota. Reproduced by permission of the University of Minnesota Press. All rights reserved. "Minnesota Multiphasic Personality Inventory-2-RF®" and "MMPI-2-RF®" are trademarks owned by the Regents of the University of Minnesota.

Figure 16.4 MMPI-2-RF Externalizing, Interpersonal, and Interest Scales

MMPI-2-RF® Score Report
08/03/2019, Page 6

ID: 986

MMPI-2-RF PSY-5 Scales

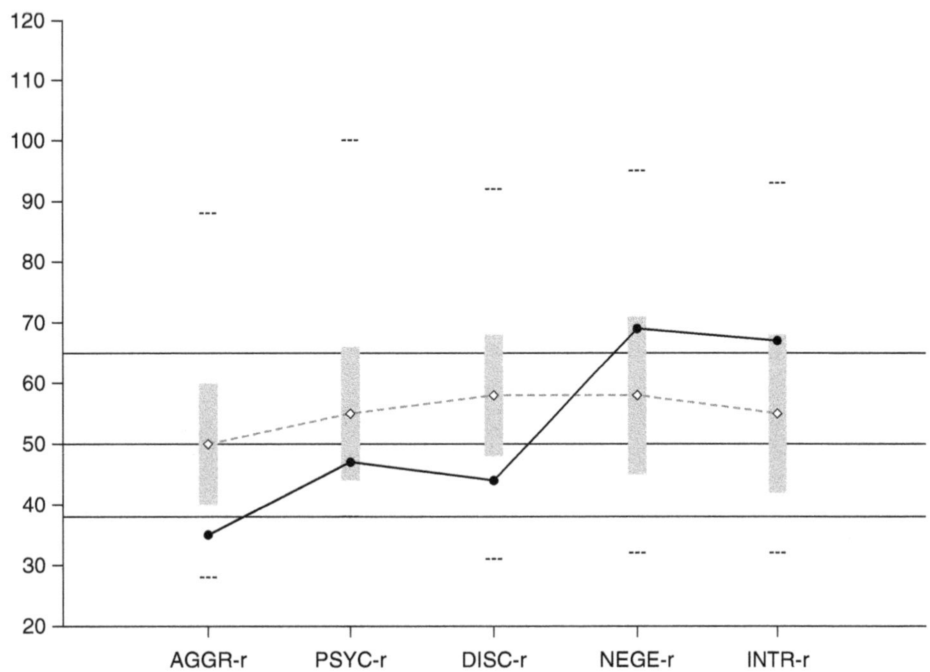

	AGGR-r	PSYC-r	DISC-r	NEGE-r	INTR-r
Raw Score:	2	1	4	13	12
T Score:	35	47	44	69	67
Response %:	100	100	100	100	100

Comparison Group Data: College Counseling Clinic (Men), N = 367

Mean Score (◇--◇):	50	55	58	58	55
Standard Dev (±1 SD):	10	11	10	13	13
Percent scoring at or below test taker:	4	35	10	78	84

The highest and lowest T scores possible on each scale are indicated by a "---"; MMPI-2-RF T scores are non-gendered.

AGGR-r Aggressiveness-Revised
PSYC-r Psychoticism-Revised
DISC-r Disconstraint-Revised
NEGE-r Negative Emotionality/Neuroticism-Revised
INTR-r Introversion/Low Positive Emotionality-Revised

Excerpted from the MMPI-2-RF Score Report. Copyright © 2008, 2011, 2012 by the Regents of the University of Minnesota. All rights reserved. Portions excerpted from the MMPI-2-RF® Manual for Administration, Scoring, and Interpretation, copyright © 2008, 2011 by the Regents of the University of Minnesota. Reproduced by permission of the University of Minnesota Press. All rights reserved. "Minnesota Multiphasic Personality Inventory-2-RF®" and "MMPI-2-RF®" are trademarks owned by the Regents of the University of Minnesota.

Figure 16.5 MMPI-2-RF Personality Psychopathology Five (PSY-5) Scales

his social anxiety, relaxation to combat anxious arousal and stress-induced headaches (as evidenced per follow-up), and social skills training to improve on the quality of his interactions with others.

THE FUTURE: MMPI-3

At the time of this writing, the MMPI-3 is under development (Ben-Porath & Tellegen, under development) and it will likely be published shortly after this handbook. This publication will not make this chapter moot, however, as the MMPI-3 is being heavily modeled after the MMPI-2-RF. Indeed, the same set of Validity Scales, Higher-Order Scales, RC, and PSY-5 scales will be available with some modifications to improve on and (in some cases) shorten them. Although the Interest Scales will be removed, virtually all of the SP scales will be retained with minor modifications. A few new constructs will be covered as well, including eating concerns, compulsivity, impulsivity, and excessive self-regard/grandiosity. In addition, a new normative sample has been collected with demographics importantly mapping onto the projected 2020 US Census data. Moreover, the MMPI-3 will employ the same interpretative strategy as the MMPI-2-RF and many of the features described for the MMPI-2-RF will be available for the MMPI-3 as well. Finally, because the scale sets will remain so similar, most of the research base on the MMPI-2-RF will apply to the MMPI-3 as well.

REFERENCES

Adler, T. (1990). Does the "new" MMPI beat the "classic"? *APA Monitor*, April, pp. 18–19.

American Psychiatric Association. (2013). *Diagnostic and statistical manual of mental disorders* (5th ed.). Washington, DC: American Psychiatric Association.

Anderson, J. L., Sellbom, M., Ayearst, L., Quilty, L. C., Chmielewski, M., Bagby, R. M. (2015). Associations between DSM-5 Section III personality traits and the Minnesota Multiphasic Personality Inventory 2-Restructured Form (MMPI-2-RF) scales in a psychiatric patient sample. *Psychological Assessment*, *27*, 811–815.

Anderson, J. L., Sellbom, M., Bagby, R. M., Quilty, L. C., Veltri, C. O. C., Markon, K. E., & Krueger, R. F. (2013). On the convergence between PSY-5 domains and PID-5 domains and facets: Implications for assessment of DSM-5 personality traits. *Assessment*, *20*, 286–294.

Anderson, J. L., Sellbom, M., Pymont, C., Smid, W., De Saeger, H., & Kamphuis, J. H. (2015). Measurement of DSM-5 Section II personality disorder constructs using the MMPI-2-RF in clinical and forensic samples. *Psychological Assessment*, *27*, 786–800.

Anestis, J. C., Finn, J. A., Gottfried, E. D., Arbisi, P. A., & Joiner, T. E. (2015). Reading the road signs: The utility of the MMPI-2 Restructured Form Validity Scales in prediction of premature termination. *Assessment*, *22*, 279–288.

Anestis, J. C., Gottfried, E. D., & Joiner, T. E. (2015). The utility of MMPI-2-RF substantive scales in prediction of negative treatment outcomes in a community mental health center. *Assessment*, *22*, 23–35.

Arbisi, P. A., Polusny, M. A., Erbes, C. R., Thuras, P., & Reddy, M. K. (2011). The Minnesota Multiphasic Personality Inventory 2 Restructured Form in National Guard soldiers screening positive for Posttraumatic Stress Disorder and mild traumatic brain injury. *Psychological Assessment*, *23*, 203–214.

Archer, R. P., Maruish, M., Imhof, E. A., & Piotrowski, C. (1991). Psychological test usages with adolescent clients: 1990 survey findings. *Professional Psychology Research and Practice*, *22*, 247–252.

Archer, E. M., Hagan, L. D., Mason, J., Handel, R. W., & Archer, R. P. (2012). MMPI-2-RF characteristics of custody evaluation litigants. *Assessment*, *19*, 14–20.

Archer, R. P., Handel, R. W., Ben-Porath, Y. S., & Tellegen, A. (2016). *Minnesota Multiphasic Personality Inventory – Adolescent Restructured Form (MMPI-A-RF): Administration, scoring, interpretation, and technical manual.*Minneapolis: University of Minnesota Press.

Avdeyeva, T. V., Tellegen, A., & Ben-Porath, Y. S. (2011). Empirical correlates of low scores on MMPI-2/MMPI-2-RF Restructured Clinical Scales in a sample of university students. *Assessment*, *19*, 388–393.

Ayearst, L. E., Sellbom, M., Trobst, K. K., & Bagby, R. M. (2013). Evaluating the interpersonal content of the MMPI-2-RF Interpersonal Scales. *Journal of Personality Assessment*, *95*, 187–196.

Ben-Porath, Y. S. (2012). *Interpreting the MMPI-2-RF*. Minneapolis: University of Minnesota Press.

Ben-Porath, Y. S., & Forbey, J. D. (2003). *Non-gendered norms for the MMPI-2*. Minneapolis: University of Minnesota Press.

Ben-Porath, Y. S., & Tellegen, A. (2008/2011). *Minnesota Multiphasic Personality Inventory-2- Restructured Form (MMPI-2-RF): Manual for administration, scoring, and interpretation*. Minneapolis: University of Minnesota Press.

Block, A. R., & Ben-Porath, Y. S. (2018). *MMPI-2-RF (Minnesota Multiphasic Personality Inventory-2 Restructured Form): User's guide for the Spine Surgery Candidate and Spinal Cord Stimulator Candidate Interpretive Reports*. Minneapolis: University of Minnesota Press.

Block, A. R., Ben-Porath, Y. S., & Marek, R. J. (2013). Psychological risk factors for poor outcome of spine surgery and spinal cord stimulator implant: A review of the literature and their assessment with the MMPI-2-RF. *The Clinical Neuropsychologist*, *27*, 81–107.

Block, A. R., Marek, R. J., Ben-Porath, Y. S., & Ohnmeiss, D. D. (2014). Associations between MMPI-2-RF scores, workers' compensation status, and spine surgery outcome. *Journal of Applied Biobehavioral Research*, *19*, 248–267.

Brown, T. A., & Sellbom, M. (in press). The utility of the MMPI-2-RF validity scales in detecting underreporting. *Journal of Personality Assessment*.

Butcher, J. N. (1972). *Objective personality assessment: Changing perspectives*. New York: Academic Press.

Butcher, J. N., Dahlstrom, W. G., Graham, J. R., Tellegen, A., & Kaemmer, B. (1989). *Minnesota Multiphasic Personality Inventory-2 (MMPI-2): Manual for administration and scoring*. Minneapolis: University of Minnesota Press.

Butcher, J. N., Graham, J. R., Ben-Porath, Y. S., Tellegen, A., Dahlstrom, W. G., & Kaemmer, B. (2001). MMPI-2: *Manual for administration and scoring* (rev. ed.). Minneapolis: University of Minnesota Press.

Butcher, J. N., Graham, J. R., Williams, C. L., & Ben-Porath, Y. S. (1990). *Development and use of the MMPI-2 Content Scales*. Minneapolis: University of Minnesota Press.

Butcher, J. N., Williams, C. L., Graham, J. R., Archer, R. P., Tellegen, A., Ben-Porath, Y. S., & Kaemmer, B. (1992). *Minnesota Multiphasic Personality Inventory (MMPI-A): Manual for administration, scoring and interpretation*. Minneapolis: University of Minnesota Press.

Camara, W. J., Nathan, J. S., & Puente, A. E. (2000). Psychological test usage: Implications in professional psychology. *Professional Psychology: Research and Practice, 31*, 141–154.

Capwell, D. F. (1945). Personality patterns of adolescent girls. II. Delinquents and non-delinquents. *Journal of Applied Psychology, 29*, 284–297.

Choi, J. Y. (2017). Posttraumatic stress symptoms and dissociation between childhood trauma and two different types of psychosis-like experience. *Child Abuse and Neglect, 72*, 404–410.

Corey, D. M., & Ben-Porath, Y. S. (2014). *MMPI-2-RF (Minnesota Multiphasic Personality Inventory-2-Restructured Form): User's guide for the Police Candidate Interpretive Report*. Minneapolis, MN: University of Minnesota Press.

Corey, D. M., & Ben-Porath, Y. S. (2018). *Assessing police and other public safety personnel using the MMPI-2-RF*. Minneapolis, MN: University of Minnesota Press.

Corey, D. M., Sellbom, M., & Ben-Porath, Y. S. (2018). Risks Associated with Overcontrolled Behavior in Police Officer Recruits. *Psychological Assessment, 30*, 1691–1702.

Crighton, A. H., Tarescavage, A. M. Gervais, R. O., & Ben-Porath, Y. S. (2017). The generalizability of over-reporting across a battery of self-report measures: An investigation with the Minnesota Multiphasic Personality Invemtory-2 Restructured Form (MMPI-2-RF) and the Personality Assessment Inventory (PAI) in a civil disability sample. *Assessment, 24*, 555–574.

Dahlstrom, W. G., Welsh, G. S., & Dahlstrom, L. E. (1972). *An MMPI handbook, Vol. 1: Clinical interpretation* (rev. ed.). Minneapolis: University of Minnesota Press.

Detrick, P., & Chibnall, J. T. (2014). Underreporting on the MMPI-2-RF in a high demand police officer selection content: An illustration. *Psychological Assessment, 26*, 1044–1049.

Forbey, J.D., & Ben-Porath, Y.S. (1998). *A critical Item set for the MMPI-A*. Minneapolis: University of Minnesota Press.

Gilberstadt, H., & Duker, J. (1965). *A handbook for clinical and actuarial MMPI interpretation*. Philadelphia: Saunders.

Glassmire, D. M., Jhawar, A., Burchett, D., & Tarescavage, A. M. (2016). Evaluating item endorsement rates for the MMPI-2-RF F-r and Fp-r scales across ethnic, gender, and diagnostic groups with a forensic inpatient unit. *Psychological Assessment, 29*, 500–508.

Grossi, L. M., Green, D., Belfi, B., McGrath, R.E., Griswald, H., & Schreiber, J. (2015). Identifying aggression in forensic inpatients using the MMPI-2-RF: An examination of MMPI-2-RF scale scores and estimated psychopathy indices. *International Journal of Forensic Mental Health, 14*, 231–244.

Handel, R. W., Ben-Porath, Y. S., Tellegen, A., & Archer, R. P. (2010). Psychometric Functioning of the MMPI-2-RF VRIN-r and TRIN-r scales with varying degrees of randomness, acquiescence, and counter-acquiescence. *Psychological Assessment, 22*, 87–95.

Harkness, A. R., Finn, J. A., McNulty, J. L., & Shields, S. M. (2012). The Personality Psychopathology Five (PSY-5): Recent constructive replication and assessment literature review. *Psychological Assessment, 24*, 432–443.

Harkness, A. R., & McNulty, J. L. (1994). The Personality Psychopathology Five (PSY-5): Issues from the pages of a diagnostic manual instead of a dictionary. In S. Strack & M. Lorr (Eds.), *Differentiating normal and abnormal personality* (pp. 291–315). New York: Springer.

Harkness, A. R., McNulty, J. L., & Ben-Porath, Y. S. (1995). The Personality Psychopathology Five (PSY-5): Constructs and MMPI-2 scales. *Psychological Assessment, 7*, 104–114.

Hathaway, S. R. (1960). Foreword. In W. G. Dahlstrom & G. S. Welsh (Eds.), *An MMPI handbook: A guide to use in clinical practice and research* (pp. vii–xi). Minneapolis: University of Minnesota Press.

Hathaway, S. R. (1972). Where have we gone wrong? The mystery of the missing progress. In J. N. Butcher (Ed.), *Objective personality assessment: Changing perspectives* (pp. 21–43). Oxford: Academic Press.

Hathaway, S. R., & McKinley, J. C. (1940). A multiphasic personality schedule (Minnesota): I. Construction of the schedule. *Journal of Psychology, 10*, 249–254.

Hathaway, S. R., & McKinley, J. C. (1942). A multiphasic personality schedule (Minnesota): III. The measurement of symptomatic depression. *Journal of Psychology, 14*, 73–84.

Hathaway, S. R., & McKinley, J. C. (1943). *The Minnesota Multiphasic Personality Inventory*. Minneapolis: University of Minnesota Press.

Hathaway, S. R., & Monachesi, E. D. (1951). The prediction of juvenile delinquency using the Minnesota Multiphasic Personality Inventory. *American Journal of Psychiatry, 108*, 469–473.

Hoelzle, J. B., & Meyer, G. J. (2008). The factor structure of the MMPI-2 Restructured Clinical (RC) Scales. *Journal of Personality Assessment, 90*, 443–455.

Ingram, P. B., & Ternes. M. S. (2016). The detection of content-based invalid responding: a meta-analysis of the MMPI-2--Restructured Form's (MMPI-2-RF) over-reporting validity scales. *The Clinical Neuropsychologist, 30*, 473–496.

Kauffman, C. M., Stolberg, R., & Madero, J. (2015). An examination of the MMPI-2-RF (Restructured From) with the MMPI-2 and MCMI-III in child custody litigants. *Journal of Child Custody, 12*, 129–151.

Kim, S., Goodman, G. M., Toruno, J. A., Sherry, A. R., & Kim, H. K. (2015). The cross-cultural validity of the MMPI-2-RF Higher-Order scales in a sample of North Korean female refugees. *Assessment, 22*, 640–649.

Koffel, E., Kramer, M. D., Arbisi, P. A., Erbes, C. R., Kaler, M., & Polusny, M. A. (2016). Personality traits and combat exposure as predictors of psychopathology over time. *Psychological Medicine, 46*, 209–220.

Kotov R., Krueger, R. F, Watson. D., Achenbach, T. M., Althoff, R. R., Bagby, R. M., et al. (2017). The Hierarchical Taxonomy of Psychopathology (HiTOP): A dimensional alternative to traditional nosologies. *Journal of Abnormal Psychology, 126*, 454–477.

Laurinaityte, I., Laurinavicius, A., Ustinaviciute, L., Wygant, D.B., & Sellbom, M. (2017). Utility of the MMPI-w Restructured Form (MMPI-2-RF) in a sample of Lithuanian male offenders. *Law and Human Behavior, 41*, 494–505.

Lee, T. T. C., Graham, J. R., & Arbisi, P. A. (2018). The utility of MMPI-2-RF scale scores in differential diagnosis of Schizophrenia and Major Depressive Disorder. *Journal of Personality Assessment, 100*, 305–312.

Lee, T. T. C., Sellbom, M., & Hopwood, C.J. (2017). Contemporary psychopathology assessment: Mapping major personality inventories onto empirical models of psychopathology. In S. C. Bowden (Ed.), *Neuropsychological assessment in the age of evidence-based practice: Diagnostic and treatment evaluations* (pp. 64–94). New York: Oxford University Press.

Locke, D. E. C., Kirlin, K. A., Thomas, M. L., Osborne, D., Hurst, D. F., Drazkowsi, J. F., et al. (2010). The Minnesota Multiphasic Personality Inventory–Restructured Form in the epilepsy monitoring unit. *Epilepsy and Behavior*, *17*, 252–258.

Locke, D. E. C., Kirlin, K. A., Wershaba, R., Osborne, D., Drazkowski, J. F., Sirven, J. I., & Noe, K. H. (2011). Randomized comparison of the Personality Assessment Inventory and the Minnesota Multiphasic Personality Inventory-2, in the epilepsy monitoring unit. *Epilepsy and Behavior*, *21*, 397–401.

Marek, R. J., Ben-Porath, Y. S., Epker, J. T., Kreymar, J. K., & Block, A. R. (2018). Reliability and Validity of the Minnesota Multiphasic Personality Inventory-2-Restructured Form (MMPI-2-RF) in Spine Surgery and Spinal Cord Stimulator Samples. *Journal of Personality Assessment.*

Marek, R. J., Ben-Porath, Y. S., Merrell, J., Ashton, K., & Heinberg, L. J. (2014). Predicting one and three month post-operative somatic concerns, psychological distress, and maladaptive eating behavior in bariatric surgery candidates with the Minnesota Multiphasic Personality Iniventory-2 Restructured Form (MMPI-2-RF). *Obesity Surgery*, *24*, 631–639.

Marek, R. J., Ben-Porath, Y. S., Sellbom, M., McNulty, J. L., & Heinberg, L. J. (2015). Validity of Minnesota Multiphasic Personality Inventory-2-Restructured Form (MMPI-2-RF) scores as a function of gender, ethnicity, and age of bariatric surgery candidates. *Surgery for Obesity and Related Diseases*, *11*, 627–636.

Marek, R. J., Ben-Porath, Y. S., Van Dulmen, M., Ashton, K., & Heinberg, L. J. (2017). Using the pre-surgical psychological evaluation to predict 5-year weight-loss outcomes in bariatric surgery patients. *Surgery for Obesity and Related Diseases*, *13*, 514–521.

Marek, R. J., Ben-Porath, Y. S., Windover, A. K., Tarescavage, A. M., Merrell, J., Ashton, K., Lavery, M., & Heinberg, L. J. (2013). Assessing psychosocial functioning of bariatric surgery candidates with the Minnesota Multiphasic Personality Inventory-2-Restructured Form. *Obesity Surgery*, *23*, 1864–1873.

Marek, R. J., Block, A. R., & Ben-Porath, Y. S. (2015). The Minnesota Multiphasic Personality Inventory-2-Restructured Form (MMPI-2-RF): Incremental validity in predicting early post-operative outcomes in spine surgery candidates. *Psychological Assessment*, *27*, 114–124.

Marek, R. J., Tarescavage, A. M., Ben-Porath, Y. S., Ashton, K., Heinberg, L. J., & Rish, J.M. (2017). Associations between psychological test results and failure to proceed with bariatric surgery. *Surgery for Obesity and Related Diseases*, *13*, 507–513.

Marek, R. J., Tarescavage, A. M., Ben-Porath, Y. S., Ashton, K., Rish, J. M., & Heinberg, L. J. (2015). Using presurgical psychological testing to predict 1-year appointment adherence and weight loss in bariatric surgery candidates: Predictive validity and methodological considerations. *Surgery for Obesity and Related Diseases*. *11*, 1171–1181.

Marks, P. A., & Seeman, W. (1963). *The actuarial description of abnormal personality: An atlas for use with the MMPI*. Baltimore, MD: Williams & Wilkins.

Martinez, U., Fernandez del Rio, E., Lopez-Duran, A., & Becona, E. (2017). The utility of the MMPI-2-RF to predict the outcome of a smoking cessation treatment. *Personality and Individual Differences*, *106*, 172–177.

Martinez, U., Fernandez del Rio, E., Lopez-Duran, A, Martinez-Vispo, C., & Becona, E. (2018). Types of smokers who seek smoking cessation treatment according to psychopathology. *Journal of Dual Diagnosis*, *14*, 50–59.

McNulty, J. L., & Overstreet, S. R. (2014). Viewing the MMPI-2-RF structure through the Personality Psychopathology Five (PSY-5) lens. *Journal of Personality Assessment*. *96*, 151–157.

Meehl, P. E. (1945). The dynamics of "structured" personality tests. *Journal of Clinical Psychology*, *1*, 296–303.

Meehl, P. E. (1956). Wanted – a good cook-book. *American Psychologist*, *11*(6), 263–272.

Meehl, P. E. (1972). Reactions, reflections, projections. In J. N. Butcher (Ed.), *Objective personality assessment: Changing perspectives* (pp. 131–189). Oxford: Academic Press.

Meyers, J. E., Miller, R. M., & Tuita, A. R. R. (2014). Using pattern analysis matching todifferentiate TBI and PTSD in a military sample. *Applied Neuropsychology: Adult*, *21*, 60–68.

Mihura, J. L., Roy, M., & Graceffo, R. A. (2017). Psychological assessment training in clinical psychology doctoral programs. *Journal of Personality Assessment*, *99*, 153–164.

Moultrie, J. K., & Engel, R. R. (2017). Empirical correlates for the Minnesota Multiphasic Personality Inventory-2-Restructured From in a German inpatient sample. *Psychological Assessment*, *29*, 1273–1289.

Myers, L., Lancman, M., Laban-Grant, O., Matzner, B., & Lancman, M. (2012). Psychogenic non-epileptic seizures: Predisposing factors to diminished quality of life. *Epilepsy and Behavior*, *25*, 358–362.

Myers, L., Matzner, B., Lancman, M., Perrine, K., & Lancman, M. (2013). Prevalence of alexithymia in patients with psychogenic non-epileptic seizures and epileptic seizures and predictors in psychogenic non-epileptic seizures. *Epilepsy and Behavior*, *26*, 153–157.

Neal, T. M., & Grisso, T. (2014). Assessment practices and expert judgment methods in forensic psychology and psychiatry: An international snapshot. *Criminal Justice and Behavior*, *41*, 1406–1421.

Pinsoneault, T. B., & Ezzo, F. R. (2012). A comparison of MMPI-2-RF profiles between child maltreatment and non-maltreatment custody cases. *Journal of Forensic Psychology Practice*, *12*, 227–237.

Resendes, J., & Lecci, L. (2012). Comparing the MMPI-2 scale scores of parents involved in parental competency and child custody assessments. *Psychological Assessment*, *24*, 1054–1059.

Sellbom, M. (2016). Elucidating the validity of the externalizing spectrum of psychopathology in correctional, forensic, and community samples. *Journal of Abnormal Psychology*, *125*, 1027–1038.

Sellbom, M. (2017a). Mapping the MMPI-2-RF Specific Problems scales onto Extant Psychopathology Structures. *Journal of Personality Assessment*, *99*, 341–350.

Sellbom, M. (2017b). Using the MMPI-2-RF to Characterize Defendants Evaluated for Competency to Stand Trial and Criminal Responsibility. *International Journal of Forensic Mental Health*, *16*, 304–312.

Sellbom, M. (2019). The MMPI-2-Restructured Form (MMPI-2-RF): Assessment of personality and psychopathology in the twenty-first century. *Annual Review of Clinical Psychology*, *15*, 149–177.

Sellbom, M., Anderson, J. L., & Bagby, R. M. (2013). Assessing DSM-5 Section III personality traits and disorders with the MMPI-2-RF. *Assessment*, *20*, 709–722.

Sellbom, M., & Bagby, R. M. (2008). Validity of the MMPI-2-RF (Restructured Form) L-r and K-r scales in detecting underreporting in clinical and nonclinical samples. *Psychological Assessment*, *20*, 370–376.

Sellbom, M., Bagby, R. M., Kushner, S., Quilty, L. C., & Ayearst, L. E. (2012). Diagnostic construct validity of MMPI-2 Restructured Form (MMPI-2-RF) scale scores. *Assessment*, *19*(2), 176–186.

Sellbom, M., & Ben-Porath, Y. S. (2005). Mapping the MMPI-2 Restructured Clinical Scales onto normal personality traits: Evidence of construct validity. *Journal of Personality Assessment*, *85*, 179–187.

Sellbom, M., Ben-Porath, Y. S., & Bagby, R. M. (2008a). On the hierarchical structure of mood and anxiety disorders: Confirmatory evidence and elaboration of a model of temperament markers. *Journal of Abnormal Psychology*, *117*, 576–590.

Sellbom, M., Ben-Porath, Y. S., & Bagby, R. M. (2008b). Personality and psychopathology: Mapping the MMPI-2 Restructured Clinical (RC) Scales onto the Five Factor Model of personality. *Journal of Personality Disorders*, *22*, 291–312.

Sellbom, M., Ben-Porath, Y. S., Baum, L. J., Erez, E., & Gregory, C. (2008). Predictive validity of the MMPI-2 Restructured Clinical (RC) Scales in a batterers' intervention program. *Journal of Personality Assessment*, *90*, 129–135.

Sellbom, M., Fischler, G. L., & Ben-Porath, Y. S. (2007). Identifying MMPI-2 predictors of police officer integrity and misconduct. *Criminal Justice and Behavior*, *34*, 985–1004.

Sellbom, M., Lee, T. T. C., Ben-Porath, Y. S., Arbisi, P. A., & Gervais, R. O. (2012). Differentiating PTSD symptomatology with the MMPI-2-RF (Restructured Form) in a forensic disability sample. *Psychiatry Research*, *197*, 172–179.

Sellbom, M., Smid, W., De Saeger, H., Smit, N., & Kamphuis, J. H. (2014). Mapping the Personality Psychopathology Five domains onto DSM-IV personality disorders in Dutch clinical and forensic samples: Implications for the DSM-5. *Journal of Personality Assessment*, *96*, 185–191.

Sellbom, M., & Smith, A. (2017). Assessment of DSM-5 Section II personality disorders with the MMPI-2-RF in a nonclinical sample. *Journal of Personality Assessment*, *99*, 384–397.

Sharf, A. J., Rogers, R., Williams, M. M., & Henry, S. A. (2017). The effectiveness of the MMPI-2-RF in detecting feigned mental disorders and cognitive deficits: A meta-analysis. *Journal of Psychopathology and Behavioral Assessment*, *39*, 441–455.

Tarescavage, A. M., & Ben-Porath, Y. S. (2017). Examination of the feasibility and utility of Flexible and Conditional Administration (FCA) of the Minnesota Multiphasic Personality Inventory-2-Restructured Form (MMPI-2-RF). *Psychological Assessment*, *29*, 1337–1348.

Tarescavage, A. M., Brewster, J., Corey, D. M., & Ben-Porath, Y. S. (2015). Use of pre-hire MMPI-2-RF police candidate scores to predict supervisor ratings of post-hire performance. *Assessment*, *22*, 411–428.

Tarescavage, A. M., Cappo, B. M., & Ben-Porath, Y. S. (2018). Assessment of sex offenders with the Minnesota Multiphasic Personality Inventory-2-Restructured Form (MMPI-2-RF). *Sexual Abuse: A Journal of Research and Treatment*, *30*, 413–437.

Tarescavage, A. M, Corey, D. M., & Ben-Porath, Y. S. (2015). Minnesota Multiphasic Personality Inventory Restructured form (MMPI-2-RF) predictors if police officer problem behavior. *Assessment*, *22*, 116–132.

Tarescavage, A. M., Corey, D. M., & Ben-Porath, Y. S. (2016). A prorating method for estimating MMPI-2-RF Scores from MMPI responses: Examination of score fidelity and illustration of empirical utility in the PERSEREC Police Integrity Study sample. *Assessment*, *23*, 173–190.

Tarescavage, A. M., Corey, D. M., Gupton, H. M., & Ben-Porath, Y. S. (2015). Criterion validity and clinical utility of the Minnesota Multiphasic Personality Inventory-2-Restructured Form (MMPI-2-RF) in assessments of police officer candidates. *Journal of Personality Assessment*, *97*, 382–394.

Tarescavage, A. M., Finn, J. A., Marek, R. J., Ben-Porath, Y. S., & van Dulmen, M. H. M (2015). Premature termination from psychotherapy and internalizing psychopathology: The role of demoralization. *Journal of Affective Disorders*, *174*, 549–555.

Tarescavage, A. M., Fischler, G. L., Cappo, B., Hill, D. O., Corey, D. M., & Ben-Porath, Y. S. (2015). Minnesota Multiphasic Personality Inventory-2-Restructured Form (MMPI-2-RF) predictors of police officer problem behavior and collateral self-report test scores. *Psychological Assessment*, *27*, 125–137.

Tarescavage, A. M., Glassmire, D. M., & Burchett, D. (2016). Introduction of a conceptual model for integrating the MMPI-2-RF into HCR-20V3 violence risk assessments and associations between the MMPI-2-RF and institutional violence. *Law and Human Behavior*, *40*, 626–637.

Tarescavage, A. M., Luna-Jones, L., & Ben-Porath, Y. S. (2014). Minnesota Multiphasic Personality Inventory-2-Restructured Form (MMPI-2-RF) predictors of violating probation after felonious crimes. *Psychological Assessment*, *26*, 1375–1380.

Tarescavage, A. M., Scheman, J., & Ben-Porath, Y. S. (2015). Reliability and validity of the Minneapolis Multiphasic Personality Inventory-2-Restructured Form (MMPI-2-RF) in evaluations of chronic low back pain patients. *Psychological Assessment*, *27*, 433–446.

Tarescavage, A. M., Scheman, J., & Ben-Porath, Y. S. (2018). Prospective comparison of the Minnesota Multiphasic Personality Inventory-2 (MMPI-2) and MMPI-2 Restructured From (MMPI-2-RF) in predicting treatment outcomes among patients with chronic low back pain. *Journal of Clinical Psychology in Medical Settings*, *25*, 66–79.

Tellegen, A. (1985). Structures of mood and personality and their relevance to assessing anxiety, with an emphasis on self-report. In A. H. Tuna & J. D. Maser (Eds.), *Anxiety and the anxiety disorders* (pp. 681–706). Hillsdale, NJ: Lawrence Erlbaum Associates.

Tellegen, A., & Ben-Porath, Y. S. (2008/2011). *MMPI-2-RF (Minnesota Multiphasic Personality Inventory-2-Restructured Form): Technical manual*. Minneapolis: University of Minnesota Press.

Tellegen, A., Ben-Porath, Y. S., McNulty, J. L., Arbisi, P. A., Graham, J. R., & Kaemmer, B. (2003). *MMPI-2 Restructured Clinical (RC) Scales: Development, validation, and interpretation*. Minneapolis: University of Minnesota Press.

Tellegen, A., Ben-Porath, Y. S., & Sellbom, M. (2009). Construct validity of the MMPI-2 Restructured Clinical (RC) Scales: Reply to Rouse, Greene, Butcher, Nichols, & Williams. *Journal of Personality Assessment*, *91*, 211–221.

Van der Heijden, P. T., Rossi, G. M., Van der Veld, M. M., Derksen, J. J. L., & Egger, J. I. M. (2013). Personality and psychopathology: Higher order relations between the Five Factor Model of personality and the MMPI-2 Restructured Form. *Journal of Research in Personality*, *47*, 572–579.

Watson, C., Quilty, L. C., & Bagby, R. M. (2011). Differentiating bipolar disorder from major depressive disorder using the MMPI-2-RF: A receiver operating characteristics (ROC) analysis. *Journal of Psychopathology and Behavioral Assessment, 33*, 368–374.

Whitman, M. R., Tarescavage, A. M., Glassmire, D. M., Burchett, D., & Sellbom, M. (2019). Examination of differential validity of MMPI-2-RF scores by gender and ethnicity in predicting future suicidal and violent behaviors on a forensic sample. *Psychological Assessment, 31*, 404–409.

Wiggins, J. S. (1966). Substantive dimensions of self-report in the MMPI item pool. *Psychological Monographs, 80*.

Wolf, E. J., Miller, M. W., Orazem, R. J., Weierich, M. R., Castillo, D. T., Milford, J., et al. (2008). The MMPI-2 Restructured Clinical Scales in the assessment of Posttraumatic Stress Disorder and comorbid disorders. *Psychological Assessment, 20*, 327–340.

Zahn, N., Sellbom, M., Pymont, C., & Schenk, P. W. (2017). Associations between MMPI-2-RF scale scores and self-reported personality disorder criteria in a private practice sample. *Journal of Psychopathology and Behavioral Assessment, 39*, 723–741.

17 Personality Assessment Inventory

LESLIE C. MOREY AND MORGAN N. MCCREDIE

The *Personality Assessment Inventory* (PAI; Morey, 1991) is a multiscale, self-administered questionnaire designed to provide a comprehensive picture of client personality and psychopathology. The measure has been widely used in clinical, research, and training settings (Archer et al., 2006; Stedman, McGeary, & Essery, 2018), with practical applications across a number of assessment specialties, including forensics, health, and personnel selection. The inventory consists of a total of 344 items with a four-alternative scale, including *False, Not at all True (F)*, *Slightly True (ST)*, *Mainly True (MT)*, and *Very True (VT)*. These items comprise twenty-two non-overlapping scales of four different types: four validity scales, eleven clinical scales, five treatment scales, and two interpersonal scales. Ten of the full scales are further broken down into subscales to provide breadth of coverage within diagnostic constructs, and several additional indicators have been developed since the test was first introduced to allow for more extensive interpretation. See Table 17.1 for more details. This chapter provides an overview of the theory and development of the PAI, summarizes the relevant psychometric literature, and highlights noteworthy research and practical applications of the PAI across a variety of assessment contexts. Primary resources should be consulted for a more detailed discussion beyond the scope of this chapter (Blais, Baity, & Hopwood, 2010; Morey, 1996, 2003, 2007a; Morey & Hopwood, 2007).

THEORY AND DEVELOPMENT

The PAI was developed within a construct validation framework that simultaneously balanced a theoretically informed approach to item development and selection with the empirical assessment of the psychometric properties of those items. Included constructs were selected on the basis of both demonstrated historical import in research literature and relevance to practicing clinicians, with the conceptual and empirical literature of each construct providing the guiding framework for the phenomena to be sampled for each scale. Following a sequential construct validation strategy similar to that described by Loevinger (1957) and Jackson (1970), an original pool of 2,200 items was subjected to four iterations of testing, using a variety of item selection criteria that included convergent and discriminant validity, differential item functioning, bias panel review, feigning simulations, and variability of thresholds for item characteristic curves.

Particular emphasis throughout the item selection process was placed on the simultaneous use of a variety of quantitative parameters, as overreliance on a single parameter for item selection often results in an instrument that fares well on one desirable psychometric property but is lacking in other important areas. Throughout the development of the PAI, attention was paid to both the *breadth* and the *depth* of content coverage, as to provide a balanced sampling of the core aspects of each psychological construct measured. Content *breadth* refers to the coverage of the diversity of symptoms and features encompassed by a construct. For example, if one were to measure the construct of anxiety, it would be important to assess both the physiological expression (e.g., autonomic nervous system reactivity) and the cognitive and affective manifestations (e.g., rumination, apprehensiveness). Failing to consider the full range of characteristics associated with a construct would result in a measure with limited breadth of coverage and thus compromised content validity. Thus, the PAI subscales are useful for capturing the diverse range of symptoms and elements that may be present within a given construct.

The *depth* of content coverage refers to the ability to assess a construct across a spectrum of severity. PAI scales were designed to include items representing a variety of symptoms and features from the mildest to most severe. Item characteristic curves were used to select items that provide information across the full range of construct severity, with the nature of the severity continuum varying across the constructs. For example, affective elements of anxiety may vary from mild apprehension to full-blown panic; degree of suicidal ideation may vary from vague and ill-articulated thoughts about suicide to immediate plans for self-harm. The PAI's inclusion of items that represent

Table 17.1 PAI scales and subscales

	Scale	Interpretation of High Scores
Validity Scales		
ICN	*Inconsistency*	Poor concentration or inattention
INF	*Infrequency*	Idiosyncratic or random response set
NIM	*Negative Impression Management*	Negative response set due to pessimistic worldview and/or intentional dissimulation
PIM	*Positive Impression Management*	Positive response set due to naivety or intentional dissimulation
Clinical Scales		
SOM	*Somatic Complaints*	Focus on physical health-related issues
SOM-C	*Conversion*	Rare sensorimotor symptoms associated with conversion disorders or certain medical conditions
SOM-S	*Somatization*	The occurrence of common physical symptoms or vague complaints of ill health or fatigue
SOM-H	*Health Concerns*	Preoccupation with physical functioning and symptoms
ANX	*Anxiety*	Experience of generalized anxiety across different response modalities
ANX-C	*Cognitive*	Ruminative worry and impaired concentration and attention
ANX-A	*Affective*	Experience of tension, difficulty relaxing, nervousness, and fatigue
ANX-P	*Physiological*	Overt signs of anxiety, including sweating, trembling, shortness of breath, and irregular heartbeat
ARD	*Anxiety-Related Disorders*	Symptoms and behaviors related to specific anxiety disorders
ARD-O	*Obsessive-Compulsive*	Intrusive thoughts, compulsive behaviors, rigidity, indecision, perfectionism, and affective constriction
ARD-P	*Phobias*	Common fears, including social situation, heights, and public or enclosed places; low scores suggest fearlessness
ARD-T	*Traumatic Stress*	Experience of trauma that continues to cause distress
DEP	*Depression*	Experience of depression across different response modalities
DEP-C	*Cognitive*	Worthlessness, hopelessness, indecisiveness, and difficulty concentrating; low scores indicate personal confidence
DEP-A	*Affective*	Feelings of sadness, diminished interest, and anhedonia
DEP-P	*Physiological*	Diminished level of physical functioning and activity; dysfunctional sleep and diet patterns
MAN	*Mania*	Experience of behavioral, affective, and cognitive symptoms of mania and hypomania
MAN-A	*Activity Level*	Disorganized overinvolvement in activities; accelerated thought processes and behavior
MAN-G	*Grandiosity*	Inflated self-esteem and expansiveness; low scores indicate low self-esteem
MAN-I	*Irritability*	Frustration intolerance, impatience, and resulting strained relationships
PAR	*Paranoia*	Experience of paranoid symptoms and traits
PAR-H	*Hypervigilance*	Suspiciousness and tendency to closely monitor environment; low scores suggest interpersonal trust
PAR-P	*Persecution*	Belief that others have intentionally constructed obstacles to one's achievement
PAR-R	*Resentment*	Bitterness and cynicism in relationships, tendency to hold grudges, and externalization of blame
SCZ	*Schizophrenia*	Symptoms relevant to the broad spectrum of schizophrenic disorders
SCZ-P	*Psychotic Experiences*	Unusual perceptions and sensations, magical thinking, and unusual ideas
SCZ-S	*Social Detachment*	Social isolation, discomfort, and awkwardness
SCZ-T	*Thought Disorder*	Confusion, concentration difficulties, and disorganization

Continued

Table 17.1 (cont.)

	Scale	Interpretation of High Scores
BOR	*Borderline Features*	Attributes indicative of borderline levels of personality functioning
BOR-A	*Affective Instability*	Emotional responsiveness, rapid mood change, poor modulation
BOR-I	*Identity Problems*	Uncertainty about major life issues and feelings of emptiness or lack of fulfillment or purpose
BOR-N	*Negative Relationships*	History of intense, ambivalent relationships and feelings of exploitation or betrayal
BOR-S	*Self-Harm*	Impulsivity in areas likely to be dangerous
ANT	*Antisocial Features*	Focuses on behavioral and personological features of antisocial personality
ANT-A	*Antisocial Behaviors*	History of antisocial and illegal behavior
ANT-E	*Egocentricity*	Lack of empathy or remorse, exploitive approach to relationships
ANT-S	*Stimulus-Seeking*	Cravings for excitement, low boredom tolerance, recklessness
ALC	*Alcohol Problems*	Use of and problems with alcohol
DRG	*Drug Problems*	Use of and problems with drugs
Treatment Consideration Scales		
AGG	*Aggression*	Characteristics and attitudes related to anger, assertiveness, and hostility
AGG-A	*Aggressive Attitude*	Hostility, poor control over anger, and belief in instrumental utility of violence
AGG-V	*Verbal Aggression*	Assertiveness, abusiveness, and readiness to express anger to others
AGG-P	*Physical Aggression*	Tendency to be involved in physical aggression
SUI	*Suicidal Ideation*	Frequency and intensity of thoughts of self-harm or fantasies about suicide
STR	*Stress*	Perception of an uncertain or difficult environment
NON	*Nonsupport*	Perception that others are not available or willing to provide support
RXR	*Treatment Rejection*	Low motivation for treatment; lack of openness to change in the self and acceptance of help from others
Interpersonal Scales		
DOM	*Dominance*	Desire and tendency for control in relationships; low scores suggest meekness and submissiveness
WRM	*Warmth*	Interest and comfort with close relationships; low scores suggest hostility, anger, and mistrust

varying severity is important to capture the full range of possible presentations.

PAI SCALES

Brief descriptions of the PAI scales, subscales, and select supplemental indices are presented in Tables 17.1 and 17.2. The PAI contains scales of four types: validity scales, clinical scales, treatment consideration scales, and interpersonal scales. The four validity scales were intended to identify response patterns that deviate from accurate and honest responding, including random, careless, or manipulated response sets. There are two scales for the assessment of random response tendencies (Inconsistency, ICN; Infrequency, INF), as well as one scale each for the assessment of systematic negative (Negative Impression Management, NIM) or positive (Positive Impression Management, PIM) responding. Several supplemental validity indicators have also been developed and added to the standard scoring protocol, including the Defensiveness Index (DEF; Morey, 1996), Malingering Index (MAL; Morey, 1996), Rogers Discriminant Function (RDF; Rogers et al., 1996), and Cashel Discriminant Function (CDF; Cashel et al., 1995).

The eleven clinical scales of the PAI were intended to assess a range of historically stable and clinically relevant phenomena. There are four neurotic spectrum scales, including Somatic Problems (SOM), Anxiety (ANX), Anxiety-Related Disorders (ARD), and Depression (DEP), and three psychotic spectrum scales, including Paranoia (PAR), Schizophrenia (SCZ), and Mania (MAN). There are additionally two scales assessing personality pathology, Borderline Features (BOR) and Antisocial Features (ANT), and two scales assessing substance use and associated consequences, Alcohol Problems (ALC) and Drug Problems (DRG).

The five treatment consideration scales were intended to provide clinically relevant information for individual treatment planning beyond psychiatric diagnosis. Two scales offer information about whether an individual may pose a threat of harm to themselves or others: the Suicidal Ideation (SUI) scale and the Aggression (AGG) scale. Two additional scales, the Stress (STR) scale and Nonsupport (NON) scale, provide an evaluation of environmental factors that may be contributing to psychological difficulties. The Treatment Rejection (RXR) scale additionally serves as a predictor of the course of treatment. Several supplemental indices, including the Suicide Potential Index (SPI), Violence Potential Index (VPI), and the Treatment Process Index (TPI), have also been developed as supplemental indicators to assess other treatment-related risk factors. Finally, the PAI contains two interpersonal scales, Dominance (DOM) and Warmth (WRM), which correspond to the orthogonal axes of two dimensions of interpersonal style: (1) dominant control vs. meek submission and (2) warm affiliation vs. cold rejection.

PSYCHOMETRICS

Reliability

The reliability of the PAI scales and subscales has been examined in numerous studies in terms of internal consistency (Alterman et al., 1995; Boyle & Lennon, 1994; Karlin et al., 2005; Morey, 1991; Rogers et al., 1995), test-retest reliability (Boyle & Lennon, 1994; Morey, 1991; Rogers et al., 1995), and configural stability (Morey, 1991). Median internal consistency alphas of the standardization sample were 0.85 and 0.74 for the scales and subscales, respectively (Morey, 1991), with similar results obtained across different age, gender, and race/ethnicity groups. Similar internal consistencies have been reported across a variety of unique setting contexts, including with psychiatric inpatients (Siefert et al., 2009), women with eating disorders (Tasca et al., 2002), chronic pain patients (Karlin et al., 2005), bariatric surgery candidates (Corsica et al., 2010), and deployed combat troops (Morey et al., 2011). The PAI has also demonstrated psychometric equivalence across diverse samples, including with African American and Latino respondents (Alterman et al., 1995; Hopwood et al., 2009).

The median test-retest reliability of the eleven clinical scales over a four-week interval was 0.86 for the full scales and 0.78 for the subscales in the standardization sample (Morey, 1991). Overall standard error of measurement estimates for the scales were three to four *T*-score points, with 95 percent confidence intervals of +/– six to eight *T*-score points. Absolute *T*-score change values over time were approximately two to three *T*-score points for most of the full scales, demonstrating very little change over the test-retest interval (Morey, 1991). In a nonclinical sample, Boyle and Lennon (1994) reported a similar median test-retest reliability of 0.73 over an interval of twenty-eight days.

Another important reliability consideration on multiscale inventories is the stability of the configurations of scales (i.e., the elevations of scales in relation to each other within the same profile). This analysis is often conducted by determining the inverse (or Q-type) correlation between each subject's profile at Time 1 and Time 2. These correlations were calculated for each of the 155 subjects in the full retest standardization sample, and a distribution of the within-subject profile correlations was obtained. Results indicated that the median correlation of the clinical scale configuration was 0.83, demonstrating considerable stability in profile configurations over time (Morey, 1991).

Validity

As reported in the test manual (Morey, 1991, 2007a), a number of initial validation studies were conducted to examine the relationships between PAI scales and subscales and other well-validated measurements of their corresponding constructs. Convergent and discriminant validity were assessed by concurrently administering the PAI and a variety of external clinical indicators to various samples. Further evaluation was conducted regarding diagnostic and clinical judgments to determine if PAI correlates were consistent with hypothesized relations. Lastly, the PAI was administered under various simulation protocols in order to assess the measure's efficacy at identifying various types of response sets. A large number of these correlations are presented in the PAI manual (Morey, 1991, 2007a), and hundreds of subsequent independent studies have also provided further evidence of validity in relation to a broad range of criteria and across various racially and ethnically diverse groups (e.g., Alterman et al., 1995; Hovey & Magaña, 2002; Patry & Magaletta, 2015). Although a comprehensive discussion of the PAI validity literature is beyond the scope of this chapter, the following section presents some of the more noteworthy validity findings.

Validity scales. One possible concern for profile validity is response sets that are non-systematically distorted, reflecting potentially random or careless responding. Various studies have used computer-generated random data to test the capacity of ICN and INF at differentiating random and genuine response sets (Morey, 1991). In general, when the entire PAI protocol is answered randomly, ICN and INF detect random responding at very high sensitivity rates. However, in cases where the protocol has only been partially answered randomly, ICN and INF are less sensitive to distortion (Clark, Gironda, & Young, 2003). For these cases, Morey and Hopwood (2004) developed an indicator of back random responding (BRR) utilizing short-form/full-scale score discrepancies ≥ 5*T* on the Alcohol (ALC) and Suicide (SUI) scales, which demonstrated satisfactory positive and negative predictive power across levels and base rates of back random responding – results replicated in an independent inpatient sample (Siefert et al., 2006).

Response sets may also be systematically biased in the positive or negative direction, or both, as a result of either intentional (i.e., faking) or implicit (e.g., defensiveness, negative exaggeration) distortion. Identifying such profiles is particularly crucial in contexts where the PAI is being used to make major decisions, such as in treatment planning, forensic evaluations, and personnel selection, among others. Several PAI indicators have been developed to detect underreporting of symptomatology, potentially as a result of naivety, defensiveness, or purposeful concealment. Validation studies consistently demonstrate that those scoring above 57*T* on PIM are much more likely to be in a positive dissimulation sample than a community sample (Cashel et al., 1995; Fals-Stewart, 1996; Morey, 1991; Morey & Lanier, 1998; Peebles & Moore, 1998). However, these rates do vary and tend to be higher in testing contexts where individuals are motivated to present themselves as favorably as possible (e.g., personnel selection, child custody evaluation). PIM has additionally been shown to moderate the predictive validity of other PAI scales in settings where such motivation is common (e.g., Edens & Ruiz, 2006; Lowmaster & Morey, 2012).

DEF is a supplemental indicator of positive response distortion that was designed to augment PIM. DEF is a composite of eight configural features that represent combinations of one or more scale scores that are unlikely to occur naturally (e.g., elevated grandiosity [MAN-G] without irritability [MAN-I]). Simulation studies of "fake good" profiles have demonstrated hit rates ranging in the high 0.70s to mid-0.80s (Baer & Wetter, 1997; Peebles & Moore, 1998), although there is some evidence that coaching respondents to escape detection may decrease DEF's sensitivity (Baer & Wetter, 1997). Along similar lines, the CDF is an empirically derived function designed to maximize differences between honest responders and individuals who have been instructed to "fake good" in both college student and forensic populations. Follow-up studies (Morey, 1996; Morey & Lanier, 1998) indicated that the CDF demonstrated substantial cross-validation when applied to new, independent samples. A key feature of the CDF is that, unlike PIM, the CDF is largely independent of psychopathological factors that may minimize problems (e.g., naivety, lack of insight), an inference supported by its relatively modest association with the PAI validity scales (Morey & Lanier, 1998) and clinical scales (Morey, 1996).

Additionally, several PAI indicators have also been developed to detect overreporting of symptomatology. Converse to the PIM scale, elevated scores on NIM may indicate an exaggerated presentation of symptoms, possibly as a cry for help or a result of purposeful malingering. Morey (1991) demonstrated that individuals instructed to feign mental illness produced markedly elevated NIM scores relative to actual clinical clients. This finding has been replicated by numerous subsequent studies (e.g., Blanchard et al., 2003; Rogers, Ornduff, & Sewell, 1993; Wang et al., 1997), which have generally found that the scale distinguishes simulators from actual protocols across a variety of response set conditions that can potentially moderate the effectiveness of NIM, such as population (e.g., clinical, forensic, college student), coaching, and sophistication of respondents (e.g., graduate student, undergraduate). In general, hit rates range from 0.50 to 0.80 but there is evidence to suggest that NIM's sensitivity is negatively affected by coaching and positively related to the severity of feigned disorders (Rogers et al., 1993).

The Malingering Index (MAL; Morey, 1996) was developed as a supplement to NIM in order to more directly identify purposeful feigning of mental illness as opposed to amplification due to genuine psychopathology (e.g., exaggeration associated with depression). Similar to DEF, MAL is a composite of eight configural features that represent combinations of one or more scale scores that are unlikely to occur naturally among clinical clients (e.g., elevated egocentricity [ANT-E] without specific antisocial behavior [ANT-A]). The RDF is an empirically derived function that was developed as a supplement to MAL. Like the CDF, the RDF is unrelated to psychopathology and thus serves as a potentially important distinguisher between intentional malingering and exaggeration related to genuine clinical issues (Morey, 1996). Both indices have generally been quite successful at differentiating "faking" protocols from standard protocols across a number of simulation studies (Bagby et al., 2002; Blanchard et al., 2003; Edens, Poythress, & Watkins-Clay, 2007; Morey & Lanier, 1998; Rogers et al., 2012). The most recently introduced indicator of malingering is the Negative Distortion Scale (NDS; Mogge et al., 2010), which is comprised of the fifteen most infrequently endorsed items across two inpatient samples. The NDS demonstrated remarkable sensitivity and specificity in the initial validation study (Mogge et al., 2010), and some follow-up studies have indicated that the NDS may outperform the other three PAI feigning indicators in the detection of malingering (Rogers et al., 2013; Thomas et al., 2012).

Clinical scales. An abundance of research has been conducted regarding the neurotic spectrum scales and their relationships with neurotic-level diagnoses and related clinical issues. SOM tends to be the highest clinical elevation in medical samples (Clark, Oslund, & Hopwood, 2010; Karlin et al., 2005; Keeley, Smith, & Miller, 2000; Osborne, 1994). One important area of research pertaining to SOM and its subscales has been in the detection of malingered physical health conditions. For example, Whiteside and colleagues (2010) found that extremely elevated SOM scores (> 87*T*) were associated with a 91 percent classification rate of suboptimal cognitive effort in a neuropsychological population, per the Test of Memory Malingering (TOMM; Tombaugh, 1996). Hopwood, Orlando, and Clark (2010) reported that coached (80.8*T*, *SD* = 18.0) and naive feigners (89.3*T*, SD = 17.1) of chronic pain demonstrated markedly higher SOM scores than genuine chronic pain patients (76.5*T*, *SD* = 10.6), although the effect was strongest for naive malingerers (Cohen's *d* = 1.08). Elevations on SOM have also been demonstrated in several studies examining PAI profiles of compensation-seeking individuals, including those presenting with mild traumatic brain injury (Whiteside et al., 2012) and chronic back pain (Ambroz, 2005).

Research findings related to DEP reflect the broad range of clinical phenomena associated with depression. Elevated DEP scores have been associated with nonsuicidal self-injury in college women (Kerr & Muehlenkamp, 2010), sleep difficulties (Tkachenko et al., 2014), substance use (Shorey et al., 2015), and poor performance on memory tasks (Keiski, Shore, & Hamilton, 2003), among a multitude of other clinical issues. Keeley and colleagues (2000) demonstrated that DEP can also be used as a clinical outcome measure, as adults in a family medical center experienced an average decline of 8.6*T* over the course of a fourteen-week antidepressant treatment.

Like depression, anxiety is a broad psychological construct, as reflected by the range of research pertaining to the ANX scale. For example, ANX has demonstrated significant associations with indices of anxiety sensitivity (Killgore et al., 2016), sleep difficulties (Tkachenko et al., 2014), acculturative stress (Hovey & Magaña, 2002), dissociation (Briere, Weathers, & Runtz, 2005), sexual dysfunction (Bartoi, Kinder, & Tomianovic, 2000), and problem gambling (Hodgins et al., 2012). Woods, Wetterneck, and Flessner (2006) reported that individuals with trichotillomania treated with ten sessions of Acceptance and Commitment Therapy demonstrated an 8 percent decrease in ANX scores (from 63.8*T* to 58.3*T*) that persisted at three-month follow-up (57.2*T*) while ANX scores increased on average for a wait-list control group, suggesting that ANX may have utility as an outcome measure.

Much of the current research to date regarding the ARD scale has focused on the Traumatic Stress (ARD-T) subscale. As expected, ARD tends to elevate among individuals diagnosed with post-traumatic stress disorder (PTSD) as well as those attempting to malinger PTSD (Liliquest, Kinder, & Schinka, 1998; McDevitt-Murphy et al., 2005; Thomas et al., 2012; Wooley & Rogers, 2015). McDevitt-Murphy and colleagues (2005) reported significant correlations between ARD-T and measures of PTSD, while also demonstrating that ARD-T scores significantly differentiated women with PTSD (74.9*T*, SD = 11.3) from women without PTSD (57.0*T*, SD = 10.8) in a community sample. Thomas and colleagues (2012) reported higher ARD-T scores in both naive feigners (88.6*T*, SD = 15.5) and coached feigners (84*T*, SD = 16.8) as compared to individuals diagnosed with PTSD reporting honestly (73.8*T*, SD = 12.6). These findings highlight the importance of evaluating the validity indicators when interpreting ARD-T elevations.

Several studies have examined the utility of the PAI in relation to the assessment of psychotic spectrum disorders and symptoms. Douglas, Hart, and Kropp (2001) found that a model including the social detachment (SCZ-S) and grandiosity (MAN-G) subscales differentiated psychotic inmates from nonpsychotic inmates in a male forensic psychiatric sample. Paranoia (PAR) scale scores have also been linked to a variety of psychotic behaviors. For example, Gay and Combs (2005) demonstrated that individuals with persecutory delusions scored significantly higher on the Persecutory Ideation subscale (PAR-P; *M* = 75*T*) than did individuals without such delusions (5*T*). In another study, Combs and Penn (2004) found that, even at subclinical levels, individuals with relatively high PAR scores (*M* = 62*T*) performed poorly on an emotion-perception task, sat further away from the examiner, and took longer to read the research consent forms than individuals with low PAR scores (44*T*). The Schizophrenia (SCZ) subscale demonstrated a significant association with the Rorschach schizophrenia index (*r* = 0.42), while also outperforming the Rorschach in the differentiation of schizophrenic individuals (SCZ = 77*T*) from individuals with other psychiatric disorders (59*T*; Klonsky, 2004).

Both Borderline Features (BOR) and Antisocial Features (ANT) have demonstrated significant relationships to both the diagnosis of their corresponding personality disorders and related clinical issues and behavioral outcomes. Stein, Pinsker-Aspen, and Hilsenroth (2007) reported that clients diagnosed with borderline personality disorder scored significantly higher on the PAI BOR scale (67*T*, SD = 10) than clients with other psychiatric disorders (60*T*, SD = 11; Cohen's *d* = .70), including other personality disorders, with an overall correct classification rate of 73 percent. DeShong and Kurtz (2013) reported significant associations between PAI BOR and the NEO-PI-3 (McCrae, Costa, & Martin, 2005) facets of urgency (*r* = 0.56), perseverance (*r* = −0.44), and premeditation (*r* = −0.36), reflecting the relationship between borderline features and impulsivity. Abundant support has also been found for the convergent validity of ANT with other similar measures of psychopathology. Edens and colleagues (2000) reported moderately strong correlations between the ANT scale and the Psychopathy Checklist: Screening Version (PCL: SV; Hart, Cox, & Hare, 1995; *r* = 0.54) and the PCL-R (Hare, 1991; *r* = 0.40). Reidy, Sorenson, and Davidson (2016) found that, among a large sample of inmates, those who committed a disciplinary infraction scored significantly higher on ANT (63*T*) than those who did not (58*T*), with the most prominent difference being on the Antisocial Behavior (ANT-A) subscale.

Ruiz, Dickinson, and Pincus (2002) found that the Alcohol Problems (ALC) scale correlated significantly with quantity and frequency of drinking (*r* = 0.63), frequency of binge drinking (*r* = 0.60), and maladaptive coping (*r* = 0.66) among college students. Correct classification rates of 74 percent and 84 percent were found for alcohol abuse and dependence, respectively. Among a clinical population, Parker, Daleiden, and Simpson (1999) reported that ALC correlated significantly (*r* = 0.49) with the Alcohol Composite score of the Alcohol Severity Index (ASI; McLellan et al., 1992), while demonstrating discriminant validity with the ASI Drug Composite (*r* = 0.10). Likewise, the Drug Problems (DRG) scale correlated significantly with the ASI Drug Composite (r = 0.39) but not the ASI Alcohol Composite (r = −0.20), again demonstrating good convergent and discriminant validity. Both the PAI ALC and the DRG scales were also significantly related to the likelihood of their corresponding diagnoses, r = 0.47 in both cases.

Treatment consideration scales. Correlations between the treatment consideration scales and a variety of other well-validated measures provide support for their construct validity (Costa & McCrae, 1992; Morey, 1991), and a number of validation studies of these scales for treatment-related issues are described in the "Applications" section of this chapter.

Interpersonal scales. The orthogonal axes of interpersonal behavior assessed by the interpersonal scales serve as useful clinical tools in the conceptualization and guidance of therapeutic process (Kiesler, 1996; Tracey, 1993), while also providing information about normal variations in personality and within the context of mental disorders (Kiesler, 1996; Pincus, 2005). These scales have been shown to correlate well with other measures of the circumplex model of interpersonal behavior (Ansell et al., 2011), and inconsistent responding on the items of these scales appears to be related to conflicts regarding interpersonal attachment (Hopwood & Morey, 2007).

ADMINISTRATION AND SCORING

The PAI was developed and standardized as a clinical assessment instrument for use with adults eighteen years of age and older; a parallel version, the PAI-Adolescent (PAI-A: Morey, 2007b), is available with norms covering ages twelve to eighteen. The PAI scale and subscale raw scores are linearly transformed to T-scores (mean of 50, standard deviation of 10) to provide interpretation relative to a standardization sample of 1,000 community-dwelling adults that was chosen to match US Census projections on the basis of gender, race, and age. The PAI does not calculate T-scores differently for men and women; rather, combined norms are used for both genders. Several procedures were used throughout the PAI item selection process to ensure that any items that risked being biased by demographic features would be eliminated in the course of selecting final items for the test. With relatively few exceptions, differences across item responses as a function of demographic characteristics were minimal in the community sample. The most noteworthy effects pertained to the tendency for younger adults to score higher on the BOR and ANT scales, as well as the tendency for men to obtain higher scores on ANT and ALC relative to women. Such differences are unlikely to be the result of systematic bias, as these findings are consistent with observed epidemiological differences in these disorders.

To facilitate comparisons with scale elevations typical in clinical settings, the PAI profile form indicates T-scores that correspond to marked elevations when referenced against a representative clinical sample. These T-scores form a "skyline" on the profile that indicates the score for each scale and subscale that represents the raw score that is two standard deviations above the mean for a clinical sample of 1,246 clients selected from a variety of professional settings. The configuration of this skyline serves as a guide to base rate expectations of elevations when the setting shifts from a community to a clinical frame of reference, which becomes useful when crafting diagnostic hypotheses. Thus, PAI profiles can be interpreted in comparison to both community and clinical samples as appropriate.

Computerization

There are different computer software packages designed to enhance the use of the PAI in clinical, correctional (i.e., inmate assessment), and public safety personnel selection contexts. The PAI Software Portfolio (Morey, 2000) can be used for online administration of the test and provides scoring of PAI scales and several additional indices that are difficult to compute by hand, such as RDF, CDF, MAL, and DEF. This portfolio also provides a narrative report of results, diagnostic hypotheses, and critical items relevant for clinical assessment.

The PAI Law Enforcement, Corrections, and Public Safety Selection Report Module (Roberts, Thompson, & Johnson, 2000) provides scoring of PAI scales and T-transformation based on data from a normative sample of approximately 18,000 public safety applicants. The software package also compares the applicant's scores to a sample of individuals who have successfully completed a post-hiring probation period to further facilitate assessment predictions, and it provides a probability estimate of the likelihood that a given applicant would be judged acceptable based on the observed PAI scores.

Finally, the PAI Correctional Software (Edens & Ruiz, 2005) transforms raw PAI scores based on normative data gathered from multiple correctional settings. In addition to providing a narrative report, the software also provides several indices relevant to correctional populations, including front and back infrequency scales, an inconsistency scale that focuses on criminal behavior, and an addictive characteristics scale designed to assist the clinician in the assessment of substance use denial (see Table 17.2 for descriptions of these supplemental scales).

APPLICATIONS

Clinical Uses

Diagnostic decision-making. Diagnostic decision-making is a complex process that involves formulating an array of clinical judgments from a variety of data sources. Two important diagnostic decisions specifically pertaining to the PAI profile are (1) an estimation of the degree of distortion in an individual's presentation as well as the nature of the distortion and (2) derivation of psychiatric

Table 17.2 Supplementary PAI indices

	Index	Development	Interpretation of High Scores
Validity Indices			
MAL	*Malingering Index*	Eight configural features observed with relatively high frequency in malingering samples	Negative response set; malingering
RDF	*Rogers Discriminant Function*	Function found to discriminate patients from naïve and coached malingerers	Malingering
DEF	*Defensiveness Index*	Eight configural features observed with relatively high frequency in positive dissimulation samples	Self and/or other deception in the positive direction
CDF	*Cashel Discriminant Function*	Function found to discriminate real from fake good inmates and college students	Intentional concealment of specific problems
ALCe	*ALC Estimated Score*	ALC estimated by other elements of the profile	ALCe > ALC suggests deception regarding alcohol use
DRGe	*DRG Estimated Score*	DRG estimated by other elements of the profile	DRGe > DRG suggests deception regarding drug use
ACS*	*Addictive Characteristics Scale*	Algorithm used to predict addictive potential	Deception regarding substance use (with low ALC, DRG)
BRR	*Back Random Responding*	Differences > 5*T* on front and back halves of ALC and SUI scales	Random responding on back half of PAI
INF-F*	*Infrequency-Front*	First four INF items	Random responding on first half of PAI
INF-B*	*Infrequency-Back*	Last four INF items	Random responding on second half of PAI
ICN-C*	*Inconsistency-Corrections*	Inconsistent responses to two similar items regarding illegal behavior	Inattention
NDS	*Negative Distortion scale*	Scale developed to distinguish true and feigned patients	Malingering
MPRD	*Malingered Pain-Related Disability*	Function developed to identify overreported disability from chronic pain	Overreporting of pain-related disability
Predictive Indices			
TPI	*Treatment Process Index*	Twelve configural features of the PAI associated with treatment amenability	Difficult treatment process, high probability of reversals
VPI	*Violence Potential Index*	Twenty configural features of the PAI associated with dangerousness to others	Increased likelihood of violence to others
SPI	*Suicide Potential Index*	Twenty configural features of the PAI associated with suicide	Increased likelihood of suicide

diagnoses. These two facets of diagnostic decision-making will be discussed in relation to their corresponding indicators.

Profile validity. A crucial first step in profile interpretation is the evaluation of the setting context, demand characteristics, and other potential factors that may have contributed to profile distortion. Although it is necessary to attend to the assessment milieu before interpreting validity scale scores, as cut scores may vary by setting and context, research findings have pointed to cut-score suggestions that have demonstrated diagnostic utility in a variety of clinical assessments. In detecting nonsystematic or random response distortion, elevations on ICN and/or on INF can indicate probable distortion that may have resulted from factors such as confusion, inattention, or reading difficulties, suggesting that the rest of the profile should be interpreted cautiously. Elevations at or above 73*T* for ICN and/or 75*T* for INF, which fall two standard deviations above the mean of the PAI clinical standardization sample, suggest problematic responding that is likely to hinder interpretation of the rest of the profile.

Also of concern are systematic distortions that might result in a protocol appearing healthier or more pathological than is merited. With respect to identifying positive distortion, moderate elevations at or above 57*T* on PIM indicate a profile in which an individual is presenting themselves generally favorably and denying common faults, potentially as a result of defensiveness or naivety (Cashel et al., 1995; Morey & Lanier, 1998; Peebles & Moore, 1998). Significant elevations exceeding 68*T* indicate marked positive distortion that may invalidate the profile. Research suggests appropriate cut scores on DEF of 5 (64*T*; Morey, & Lanier, 1998) and of CDF at 148 (57*T*; Morey & Lanier, 1998) in most samples. Interpreting these three positive response distortion scales in relation to each other offers the examiner insight as to the relative effects of clinical issues and intentional faking when interpreting test data (Morey, 1996, 2003; Morey & Hopwood, 2007). For example, a profile in which PIM is elevated, DEF is moderate, and CDF is within normal limits suggests a defensive or naive respondent who may be self-deceptive. Conversely, a profile in which all three are elevated suggests intentional deceptiveness or denial of psychological issues.

For detecting negatively distorted profiles, scores above 92*T* on NIM fall two standard deviations above the mean of the clinical standardization sample and indicate marked distortion; a meta-analysis by Hawes and Boccaccini (2009) suggests that 81*T* represents a useful cutting score for identifying feigned psychopathology. Scores at or above 3 (84*T*) on MAL suggest interpretive caution, as do RDF scores at or above 0.57 (65*T*; Morey & Lanier, 1998). As with indicators of positive dissimulation, examining the combination of these three negative dissimulation scales in relation to each other allows for a more critical analysis of the nature of the distortion. For example, a profile in which NIM is elevated, MAL is moderate, and RDF is within normal limits suggests significant negative distortion that is likely to be a result of genuine psychological issues rather than purposeful feigning. Conversely, a profile with elevations across all three indicators is more likely to indicate purposeful malingering. Recently developed supplemental negative distortion indications, such as the NDS (Mogge et al., 2010) or the Malingered Pain-Related Disability discriminant function (Hopwood et al., 2010) also show promise for identifying negative profile distortion.

While these validity indicators are useful for identifying systematic profile distortion, it is also important to assess the effects of such distortion in order to glean useful information from a distorted profile. There are two strategies that can assist in this process. In the first, a regression-based approach is used to predict PAI scale scores on the basis of the observed NIM or PIM score, thus evaluating the expected contribution of the response style to the observed profile. For example, in an exaggerated profile (e.g., NIM elevated, RDF within normal limits), an observed score on DEP that is no higher than the predicted score based on the NIM elevation would suggest that elevations in DEP are likely a reflection of negative distortion across the profile rather than a specific clinical issue with depression. Conversely, if the observed DEP score was significantly higher than the NIM-predicted DEP score, one could presume that depression is a prominent clinical issue for this client despite potential exaggeration across a number of problem areas. For cases where malingering is suspected (e.g., elevated on both NIM and RDF), Hopwood, Morey, Rogers, and Sewell (2007) suggested that NIM-predicted discrepancies can also be used to identify the specific disorder the respondent is attempting to malinger.

A second strategy involves the comparison of an observed profile to a sample of individuals from the standardization studies with similar PIM or NIM elevations. For example, examiners can use PIM-specific profiles to highlight elevations on an individual's profile relative to similar defensive/naive respondents, allowing for the identification of significant clinical problems despite general suppression of psychological issues. Such differences are often referred to as "leaks" in the profile, referring to the test-taker's inability to conceal genuine psychological issues to the same extent as other problem areas. As an example, Kurtz and colleagues (2015) demonstrated that larger than expected discrepancies from PIM-predicted results were useful in identifying elevations in the actual protocols of individuals subsequently instructed to respond in a defensive manner.

Specific indicators of positive dissimulation have also been developed for the substance abuse scales (Fals-Stewart, 1996; Morey, 1996). Items on the ALC and DRG scales are primarily explicit in nature, meaning that one can fairly easily misrepresent themselves on these scales by outwardly denying substance use behaviors and the corresponding consequences. To assess possible substance use denial, ALC and DRG estimated scores make regression-based predictions of the substance use scales based on the other PAI scales that are commonly associated with substance abuse behaviors. These scores can then be compared to observed scores as a means of estimating the degree of dissimulation regarding substance use.

Psychiatric diagnosis. Although diagnostic decisions should be based on multiple sources of information, the PAI can serve as a useful tool in the diagnosis process. One noteworthy feature of the PAI is that most of the clinical scales correspond to specific diagnoses or symptomatic constructs, so a marked elevation on a particular scale generally represents the most likely diagnosis or symptom. However, given the complexity of diagnosis, there are several other methods that incorporate data from multiple aspects of the profile in order to suggest, confirm, or disconfirm a diagnostic hypothesis. Two such diagnostic methods are facilitated through the PAI scoring software.

In the first method, the profile is compared to an assortment of mean profiles from a variety of diagnostic groups, and coefficients of fit of the observed profile (represented as Q-correlations) to the various other mean profiles are provided in rank order. This system allows clinicians to assess the similarity of a client's overall profile to others with known psychiatric diagnoses or clinical issues, thus potentially offering further evidence in the confirmation or disconfirmation of a hypothesized diagnosis. The second approach involves a logistic function-based method that calculates the probability of an observed profile fitting a particular diagnosis on the basis of scores of individuals with that diagnosis in the standardization sample. The PAI software then uses this function to provide diagnostic hypotheses in the automated report.

Another method for generating diagnostic hypotheses involves a "structural summary" approach to PAI profile interpretation (Morey & Hopwood, 2007). In this strategy, relative elevations and suppressions on the PAI profile that correspond to particular psychiatric diagnoses are evaluated. For example, Major Depressive Disorder is indicated by relative elevations on all three Depression (DEP-C, depressive cognitions; DEP-A, subjective sadness; and DEP-P, physical symptoms) subscales, the thought disorder (SCZ-T; concentration difficulties) and social withdrawal (SCZ-S; lack of interest, anhedonia) subscales, and the Suicidal Ideation (SUI) scale, in conjunction with relative suppressions on grandiosity (MAN-G; worthlessness) and activity (MAN-A; lethargy). Configural algorithms such as this have been provided for most common psychiatric diagnoses (Morey, 1996).

Treatment planning and progress. In addition to diagnosis, the PAI was designed to also provide clinical information relevant to treatment. For example, one of the most important considerations during psychiatric evaluations is whether a client poses a risk to self or others, but such judgments are often only loosely tied to psychiatric diagnosis. Thus, the SUI scale offers an assessment of the degree to which a client is thinking about suicide, while other risk factors are included on the SPI. Such risk factors include features such as affective lability (BOR-A) and lack of social support (NON). Individuals who have needed suicide precaution measures or who have made a suicide or self-harm attempt tend to score above a raw score of nine on the SPI, whereas individuals in the community standardization sample generally do not score above a six (Morey, 1996; Sinclair et al., 2012). Sinclair and colleagues (2012) reported significant correlations between SPI scores and history of suicidal ideation, suicide attempts, and inpatient psychiatric hospitalization among psychiatric outpatients, and Patry and Magaletta (2015) provide support for the SUI scale and the SPI in a large, racially and ethnically diverse sample of federal inmates.

With respect to potential harm to others, there is an abundance of research pertaining to the relationships between PAI indicators and violence and misconduct (see Gardner et al., 2015 for a meta-analytic review). Most notably, the AGG scale assesses aggressive tendencies, while the VPI aggregates twenty PAI criteria that have been empirically and theoretically linked to an elevated risk of dangerousness toward others, including features such as impulsivity (BOR-S) and substance abuse (ALC, DRG). Individuals with violent histories tend to score above a six on the VPI, while individuals from the community standardization sample rarely score above a four (Morey, 1996). Sinclair and colleagues (2012) demonstrated significant relationships between the VPI and behavioral indicators of violent tendencies among psychiatric inpatients, including history of violence/assault and arrests. Reidy and colleagues (2016) reported a similar relationship among a large sample of inmates, demonstrating significant correlations between ANT, AGG, and VPI and disciplinary violations, including serious and assaultive inmate infractions (Cohen's d = 0.34–0.44).

Two PAI indicators in particular have demonstrated utility as predictors of treatment process and outcome. The first, the RXR scale, consists of eight items that rely on a client's self-report of motivation for treatment, with higher scores indicating elevations in treatment rejection and thus implying lower treatment motivation. Given that T-scores are based on a community standardization sample, the standardization average score of 50T on RXR is indicative of a client who is generally satisfied with their current life circumstances and not driven to seek treatment. T-scores of forty or below suggest that a client is more likely to recognize problem areas, acknowledge responsibility for those problems, and accept help in making appropriate changes. Conversely, individuals with elevated T-scores are openly expressing resistance to change and thus are particularly likely to be difficult to engage in treatment. In the prediction of therapeutic amenability and outcome, Caperton, Edens, and Johnson (2004) found that, among incarcerated men in a mandated sex offender treatment program, elevated scores on the RXR scale modestly but significantly predicted treatment noncompliance. In an outpatient university training clinic, Charnas and colleagues (2010) found that those who withdrew from treatment had significantly higher RXR scores than those who continued (d = 0.56), offering some evidence that treatment rejection may be predictive of premature termination.

The TPI is a cumulative index of twelve features that are theoretically and empirically identified as potential impediments to effective treatment, such as hostility or defensiveness (Constantino, Castonguay, & Schut, 2002; Clarkin & Levy, 2004; Morey, 1996). Each feature is represented by one or more scale elevations on the PAI profile. Low scores on the TPI indicate a number of positive attributes that may assist the treatment process, whereas high scores (7+) indicate a number of problematic characteristics that may act as obstacles to the treatment process. The TPI has demonstrated utility in predicting premature treatment termination (Hopwood, Ambwani, & Morey, 2007; Hopwood et al., 2008; Percosky et al., 2013). Furthermore, treatment amenability (as measured by TPI) and treatment motivation (as measured by RXR) have been found to interact in predicting such termination (e.g., Hopwood et al., 2008), which should be expected as motivation for treatment must be evaluated in the context of the need for treatment.

Finally, the PAI has also proved to be useful in evaluating change over the course of treatment. Given test-retest reliability coefficients offered in the manual, *T*-score differences of 7–8 points or greater generally indicate reliable change that is in excess of two standard errors of measurement for most PAI scales. The PAI has been used to document outcome in a number of different studies; for example, Harley and colleagues (2007) demonstrated that Dialectical Behavior Therapy led to reductions in BOR scores, while Moadel and colleagues (2015) found that ANX scores were reduced in right (but not left) temporal lobe epilepsy patients following anterior temporal lobectomy.

Assessing strengths. Although clinical measures such as the PAI are generally associated with the assessment of psychological difficulties, it is equally important that such instruments can also identify respondents' strengths. In general, a lack of distress or dysfunction in a nondefensive profile suggests overall psychological health and adaptive coping. However, specific strengths can often also be identified by particular scale configurations. In the PAI Structural Summary (Morey & Hopwood, 2007), these configurations are organized around three specific psychological constructs: self-concept (focusing on the MAN-G, DEP-C, and BOR-I subscales), interpersonal style (focusing on DOM and WRM), and perception of potential resources in one's environment (focusing on NON and STR).

Other PAI scales that measure pathology may also offer information about specific strengths. For example, balanced scores on the validity indicators suggest an individual has a realistic perception of their environment. Mild to moderate scores on the obsessive-compulsive scale (ARD-O) may be indicative of an individual's conscientiousness and organizational capacity, and can be a positive predictor of performance in work settings such as police work (DeCoster-Martin et al., 2004). Additionally, where scores in one direction may indicate pathology, scores in the other may indicate positive attributes. For instance, low scores on ANT-E suggest capacity for empathy, low scores on ANT-S indicate boredom tolerance, and low scores on MAN-I may relate to above-average frustration tolerance. Likewise, low BOR scale scores suggest overall ego strength, and low scores on the self-harm and affective instability subscales (BOR-S, BOR-A) suggest impulse-control and emotional regulation skills, respectively.

Other Uses

Use of the PAI has extended beyond standard clinical assessment to a large variety of other assessment contexts. The PAI has demonstrated particular utility in correctional settings, including predicting criminal reoffending (Boccaccini et al., 2010; Ruiz et al., 2014) and inmate disciplinary infractions (Reidy et al., 2016). Further, the PAI meets expert legal standards for court admissibility for a variety of purposes, including violence risk assessment, competency to stand trial evaluation, and malingering assessment (Lally, 2003; Morey, Warner, & Hopwood, 2006). Some of the demonstrated psycho-legal applications of the PAI include parenting capacity evaluations (Loving & Lee, 2006), assessment of motor vehicle accident claimants (Cheng, Frank, & Hopwood, 2010), and evaluation of legal incompetence related to cognitive impairment (Matlasz et al., 2017). The PAI has also been used widely in personnel selection, particularly in the mental health screening of individuals applying for sensitive occupations, such as law enforcement officials (Lowmaster & Morey, 2012; Weiss, 2010) or the military (Calhoun et al., 2010; Morey et al., 2011), as well as in third-party reproduction screenings (Sims et al., 2013).

The PAI is also often used in health settings (Clark et al., 2010). For example, the PAI has shown to be useful in predicting completion of an outpatient chronic pain treatment program (Hopwood et al., 2008), and substantial research has been conducted regarding use of the PAI with individuals with traumatic brain injury and epilepsy. Keiski and colleagues (2003) demonstrated that the DEP scale of individuals with brain injuries affected scores on a memory task after controlling for global cognitive impairment, while several studies (e.g., Locke et al., 2011; Wagner et al., 2005) have found that SOM and the conversion subscale (SOM-C) are capable of distinguishing epileptic from non-epileptic (conversion) seizures, with evidence to suggest that PIM may augment the positive predictive power of these scales (Purdom et al., 2012).

Cross-Cultural Considerations

As noted in the "Psychometrics" section of this chapter, research regarding the utility of the PAI with diverse racial and ethnic groups has generally been supportive. For use with non-English speakers, the PAI has been translated into several languages, and similar psychometric properties have been demonstrated across translations, including the Spanish (Fernandez, Boccaccini, & Noland, 2008), German (Groves & Engel, 2007), and Greek (Lyrakos, 2011) versions.

Among diverse groups of English speakers, several studies have examined differences in responding related to cultural influences. Although there were numerous efforts to minimize test bias in the developmental stages of the PAI, the influence of ethnic identity and cultural factors should be taken into careful consideration when interpreting test results. Worldviews and cultural values may influence the way in which diverse groups experience, interpret, and respond to item content and thus it is important that these factors be considered before psychopathology (or lack thereof) is assumed. Studies generally suggest that differences in PAI scores attributable to cultural factors are generally less than or equal to the standard error of measurement for a given scale but notable findings regarding multicultural differences in responding are presented in the following two paragraphs. It is important to note that such differences do not necessarily constitute test bias but more likely reflect the different experiences of individuals with diverse backgrounds. Nonetheless, it is important for evaluators to understand how these diverse worldviews may influence test scores.

As presented in the original manual (Morey, 1991), the most prominent difference between African American and European American mean scale scores is found on PAR, with a tendency for African Americans to score approximately 7*T* higher than European Americans. When examined critically in the context of cultural experience, it is conceivable that enduring prejudice and social injustices may contribute to group-wide feelings of resentment and isolation as represented by modest elevations on PAR. A similar study was conducted by Chang and Smith (2015) comparing nonclinical Asian Americans to European Americans. In addition to also scoring higher on PAR, Asian American respondents also tended to score significantly higher on the ANX, ARD, and NIM scales, while scoring significantly lower on WRM. As discussed by the researchers, these group differences are in line with the traditional Asian values of formality, humility, and internalization of affect and thus should be interpreted in light of their cultural context.

In another example, Estrada and Smith (2017) conducted a comparison of PAI scores between nonclinical Latinos and European Americans. Latinos scored significantly higher than European Americans on PAR as well as several additional scales, including INF, ARD, SCZ, NON, and STR. Elevations on ARD, NON, and STR were partially attributed to the potential for isolation, injustice, and trauma accompanying the cultural experience of being a minority group in the United States, particularly in light of recent anti-Latino immigrant sentiments. Additionally, the researchers suggested that elevations on INF and SCZ may be explained by the greater tendency for many Latinos to endorse spiritual or fate-based explanations for experiences, which may appear as bizarre or unusual thinking without context. There is also some suggestion that Latinos may score higher than Anglo participants on some positive distortion indicators, such as DEF and CDF (Hopwood et al., 2009), without necessarily demonstrating any differences in elevations on PAI clinical scales. In general, current evidence suggests that, although modest scale score differences have been observed, scores do not vary in their relationships with external criteria as a function of race or ethnicity and thus such differences do not appear to be indicative of test bias.

CASE EXAMPLE

Julie is a forty-nine-year-old divorced white woman who was tested shortly following admission to a psychiatric inpatient unit (her third psychiatric hospitalization). Julie was referred to the unit after presenting to the emergency room with severe depression, panic attacks, and recurrent suicidal ideation. She also reports a number of physical ailments, including nausea, vomiting, diarrhea, and abdominal pain as a result of an eight-year history of pancreatitis. Despite numerous operations, she reports no notable improvement in her physical condition. Julie states that she assuages her physical discomfort by overusing medications prescribed to her by a variety of different doctors, as well as heavy use of marijuana. Her mother's death came shortly following the onset of her somatic symptoms and Julie has a history of psychotic symptoms – auditory and visual hallucinations and delusions – that began shortly thereafter. Julie reports that the panic attacks are a recent phenomenon and are preceded by disorientation and feelings of lost time.

Julie reports a long history of abuse both in childhood and in adulthood. At age six, her parents reportedly dropped her off at a relative's house with the promise of being right back but did not return for several months. Julie remembers this incident as causing her to feel abandoned, unwanted, and unloved. Julie was physically and emotionally abused by both parents, including the constant reminder that she was "an accident." At age nine, she was raped by her brother at knifepoint. Julie's first reported history of depression dates back sixteen years to her divorce from her first husband, who was physically abusive and adulterous. Her mother's death was sudden, causing feelings of rage that she was unable to properly say goodbye. Following her mother's death, Julie began to experience hallucinations and delusions, which were exacerbated by her father's attempt to sexually molest her. She currently reports poor relationships with her daughters, who appear to suffer from substance abuse problems themselves and may also be abusive.

Julie's physical symptoms have progressed over time and are now the central focus of her existence. She has had four suicide attempts in the last five years. The examiner described Julie as being visually depressed and often self-deprecating, although she was cooperative with all testing procedures. The remainder of this vignette will address profile validity, suggest how her PAI data (presented in Figures 17.1 and 17.2; Table 17.3) might be interpreted to better understand Julie's recent feelings and behaviors and infer treatment recommendations based on this data.

Profile Validity

The validity scales (ICN, INF) suggest that Julie attended to item content and responded in a coherent manner. NIM is moderately elevated, raising some concern of negative distortion. However, MAL and RDF were within normal

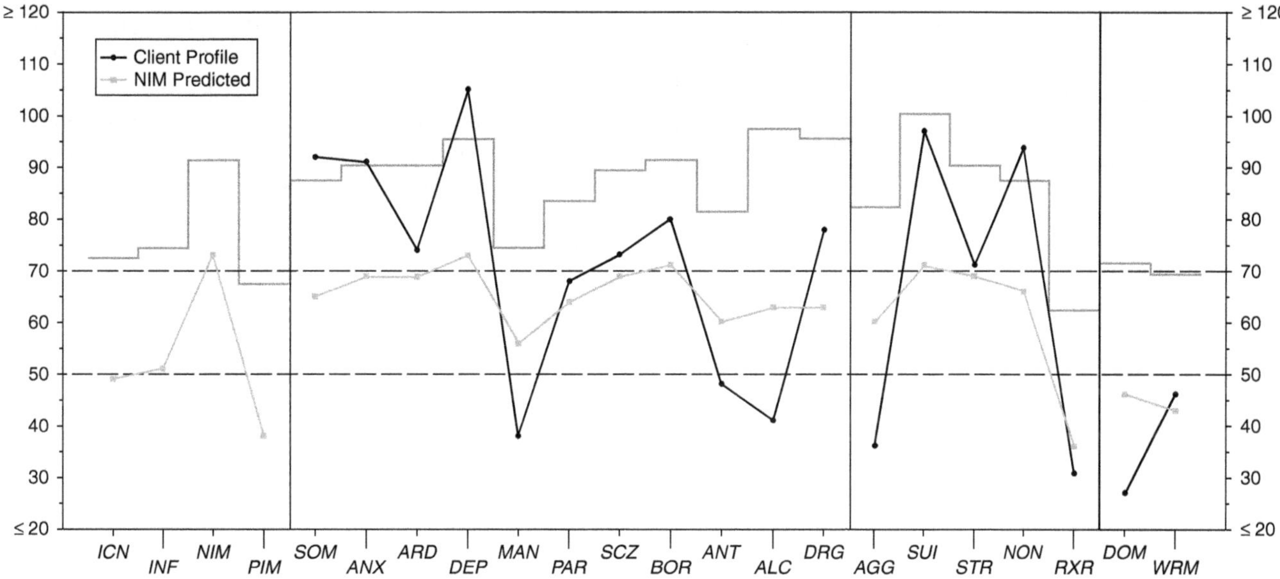

Figure 17.1 Julie's scores on the PAI validity, clinical, treatment consideration, and interpersonal scales

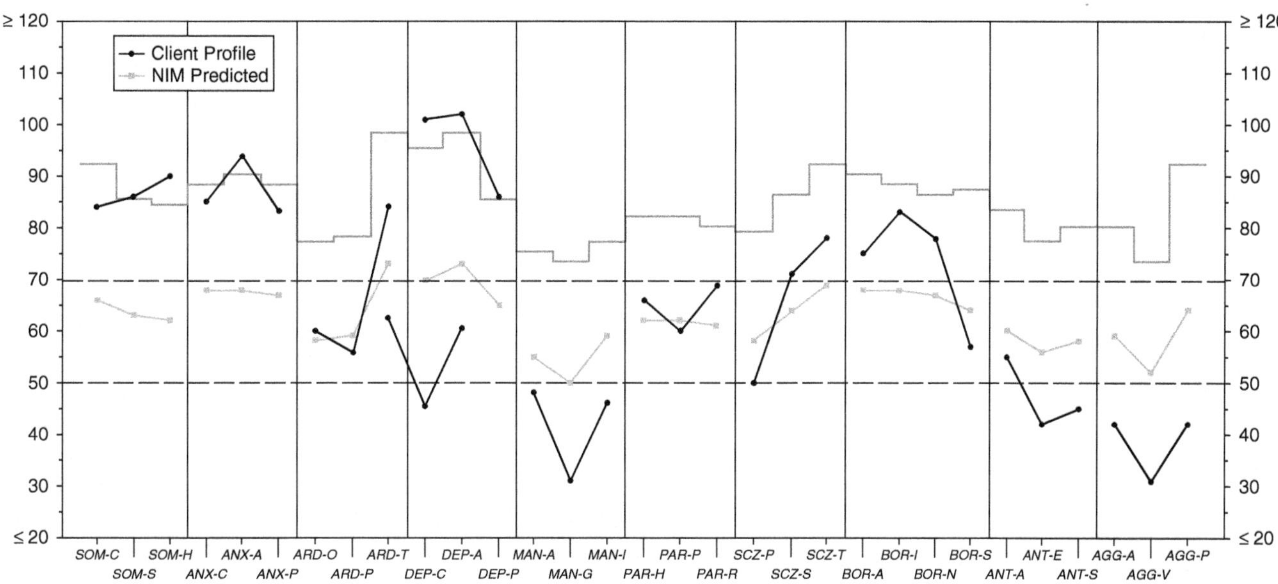

Figure 17.2 Julie's scores on the PAI subscales

limits, suggesting that Julie's exaggerated presentation of her symptoms is likely a result of genuine psychopathology rather than intentional feigning. As previously discussed, the NIM Predicted Method (obtained through the PAI Interpretive Software or the Structural Summary Form) may offer greater clarity in distinguishing salient clinical issues from elevations due to general distress. On Julie's profile, several prominent concerns stand out beyond what might be expected from her NIM score, including health concerns (SOM), depression (DEP), anxiety (ANX), suicidal ideation (SUI), trauma history (ARD-T), identity instability (BOR-I), self-esteem issues (MAN-G), problematic relationships (BOR-N), perceived lack of social support (NON), drug use (DRG), and submission (DOM). Conversely, several moderate elevations may be more attributable to Julie's negative perceptual style, including psychotic spectrum issues (PAR, SCZ) and current stress (STR). Activity level (MAN-A), frustration tolerance (MAN-I), antisocial attitudes or behaviors (ANT), and anger control issues (AGG) do not appear to be significant clinical issues on this profile.

Clinical Presentation

Julie is currently experiencing markedly severe depression (DEP), coupled with active suicidal ideation (SUI, SPI).

Table 17.3 PAI supplemental indices and coefficients of profile fit for Julie

Supplemental Indices		
	Raw	*T*
Defensiveness Index (DEF)	0	32
Cashel Discriminant Function (CDF)	146.82	56
Malingering Index (MAL)	2	71
Rogers Discriminant Function (RDF)	−0.84	51
Suicide Potential Index (SPI)	16	90
Violence Potential Index (VPI)	7	75
Treatment Process Index (TPI)	6	76
ALC Estimated Score		53
DRG Estimated Score		51
Mean Clinical Elevation		72
Coefficients of Profile Fit		
Antipsychotic medications	0.878	
Cluster 7	0.875	
Major Depressive Disorder	0.874	
Current suicide	0.869	

She feels helpless, hopeless (DEP-C), and severely distressed (DEP-A) to the extent that life no longer seems worth living. As represented by her recent panic attacks, she is also experiencing significant levels of anxiety (ANX), including heightened tensions (ANX-A) and rumination (ANX-C), as well as physiological manifestations, such as racing heartbeat, sweaty palms, and dizziness (ANX-P). Julie's health concerns are a central aspect of her distress (SOM) and she feels pessimistic and powerless regarding the possibility of finding a remedy (DEP-C), likely exacerbating her other psychological issues (DEP, ANX, SUI). She has a tendency to use maladaptive coping strategies to address her distress, including abusing drugs (DRG). Although Julie's health issues do not seem to be an issue of conversion (SOM-C), it is still quite likely that her physical and psychological health problems are mutually reinforcing.

Despite a reported history of psychotic symptoms, Julie does not report active hallucinations or delusions (SCZ-P) at this time. Nevertheless, she displays evidence of thinking inefficiencies (SCZ-T), likely related to her severe depression. Julie's sense of self appears to be very poorly established. She is unsure of who she really is (BOR-I) and she is lacking in both self-esteem (MAN-G) and self-efficacy (DEP-C). Julie's long history of abuse, mistreatment, and abandonment continues to affect the way she views herself and the world (ARD-T). Her interpersonal relationships have left her feeling exploited and disappointed (BOR-N) and she is thus mistrustful (PAR-H), resentful, and bitter (PAR-R) toward others. She does not believe that she is receiving the help and support from others that she needs (NON); however, her highly passive (AGG) and submissive (DOM) interpersonal style makes her unable to appropriately assert herself. Thus, Julie's needs for care and support continue to be unmet and her view of others as unhelpful and manipulative is reinforced. Nevertheless, Julie has greater capacity for empathy and attachment (ANT-E, WRM) than might be expected given her history of abuse. With a supportive therapeutic environment and assertiveness skill-building, Julie should be able to gain the trust and confidence necessary to forge meaningful interpersonal relationships.

Treatment Considerations and Recommendations

Julie's active suicidal ideation (SUI) and vulnerability to making a suicidal gesture (SPI) require immediate attention. She does not have aggressive tendencies (AGG) and is unlikely to pose a serious risk of danger to others (VPI). Julie is quite motivated to seek treatment (RXR) and is likely to be ready and willing to engage in therapy. She understands that she has problems that need to be addressed, acknowledges some responsibility in those problems, and actively seeks change. Nevertheless, it is important to acknowledge that she will likely present a difficult therapy case (TPI) and would be best placed with a skilled and experienced therapist. She has a complex and severe range of pathology, as well as a tendency to be wary and mistrustful toward others. Establishing trust will be a crucial first step in creating a therapeutic environment where Julie feels safe enough to explore the difficult and upsetting aspects of both her past and her current circumstances. Julie's preoccupation with her health and physical symptoms seems to be fueling her depression and anxiety, and skills that can help her to better live with physical discomfort (e.g., mindfulness, breathing exercises) will likely also help decrease the severity of her psychological symptoms. These skills will also be beneficial in building Julie's self-efficacy, in addition to practicing assertiveness in her interpersonal relationships with others. Learning to trust those who deserve trust and building healthy relationships will be important additional treatment targets.

REFERENCES

Alterman, A. I., Zaballero, A. R., Lin, M. M., Siddiqui, N., Brown, L. S., Rutherford, M. J., & McDermott, P. A. (1995). Personality Assessment Inventory (PAI) scores of lower-socioeconomic African American and Latino methadone maintenance patients. *Assessment*, *2*, 91–100.

Ambroz, A. (2005). Psychiatric disorders in disabled chronic low back pain workers' compensation claimants. Utility of the Personality Assessment Inventory. *Pain Medicine*, *6*, 190.

Ansell, E. B., Kurtz, J. E., DeMoor, R. M., & Markey, P. M. (2011). Validity of the PAI interpersonal scales for measuring the dimensions of the interpersonal circumplex. *Journal of Personality Assessment*, *93*, 33–39.

Archer, R. P., Buffington-Vollum, J. K., Stredny, R. V., & Handel, R. W. (2006). A survey of psychological test use patterns among forensic psychologists. *Journal of Personality Assessment*, *87*, 84–94.

Baer, R. A., & Wetter, M. W. (1997). Effects of information about validity scales on underreporting of symptoms on the Personality Assessment Inventory. *Journal of Personality Assessment*, *68*, 402–413.

Bagby, R. M., Nicholson, R. A., Bacchiochi, J. R., Ryder, A. G., & Bury, A. S. (2002). The predictive capacity of the MMPI-2 and PAI validity scales and indexes to detect coached and uncoached feigning. *Journal of Personality Assessment*, *78*, 69–86.

Bartoi, M. G., Kinder, B. N., & Tomianovic, D. (2000). Interaction effects of emotional status and sexual abuse on adult sexuality. *Journal of Sex and Marital Therapy*, *26*, 1–23.

Blais, M. A., Baity, M. R., & Hopwood, C. J. (Eds.). (2010). *Clinical applications of the Personality Assessment Inventory*. New York: Routledge.

Blanchard, D. D., McGrath, R. E., Pogge, D. L., & Khadivi, A. (2003). A comparison of the PAI and MMPI-2 as predictors of faking bad in college students. *Journal of Personality Assessment*, *80*, 197–205.

Boccaccini, M. T., Murrie, D. C., Hawes, S. W., Simpler, A., & Johnson, J. (2010). Predicting recidivism with the Personality Assessment Inventory in a sample of sex offenders screened for civil commitment as sexually violent predators. *Psychological Assessment*, *22*, 142–148.

Boyle, G. J. & Lennon, T. (1994). Examination of the reliability and validity of the Personality Assessment Inventory. *Journal of Psychopathology and Behavioral Assessment*, *16*, 173–187.

Briere, J., Weathers, F. W., & Runtz, M. (2005). Is dissociation a multidimensional construct? Data from the Multiscale Dissociation Inventory. *Journal of Traumatic Stress*, *18*, 221–231.

Calhoun, P. S., Collie, C. F., Clancy, C. P., Braxton, L. E., & Beckham, J. C. (2010). Use of the PAI in assessment of post-traumatic stress disorder among help-seeking veterans. In M. A, Blais, M. R. Baity, & C. J. Hopwood (Eds.), *Clinical applications of the Personality Assessment Inventory* (pp. 93–112). New York: Routledge.

Caperton, J. D., Edens, J. F., & Johnson, J. K. (2004). Predicting sex offender institutional adjustment and treatment compliance using the Personality Assessment Inventory. *Psychological Assessment*, *16*, 187–191.

Cashel, M. L., Rogers, R., Sewell, K., & Martin-Cannici, C. (1995). The Personality Assessment Inventory and the detection of defensiveness. *Assessment*, *2*, 333–342.

Chang, J., & Smith, S. R. (2015). An exploration of how Asian Americans respond on the Personality Assessment Inventory. *Asian American Journal of Psychology*, *6*, 25–30.

Charnas, J. W., Hilsenroth, M. J., Zodan, J., & Blais, M. A. (2010). Should I stay or should I go? Personality Assessment Inventory and Rorschach indices of early withdrawal from psychotherapy. *Psychotherapy: Theory, Research, Practice, Training*, *47*, 484–499.

Cheng, M. K., Frank, J. B., & Hopwood, C. J. (2010). Assessment of motor vehicle accident claimants with the PAI. In M. A, Blais, M. R. Baity, & C. J. Hopwood (Eds.), *Clinical applications of the Personality Assessment Inventory* (pp. 177–194). New York: Routledge.

Clark, M. E., Gironda, R. J., & Young, R. W. (2003). Detection of back random responding: Effectiveness of MMPI-2 and Personality Assessment Inventory validity indices. *Psychological Assessment*, *15*, 223–234.

Clark, T. S., Oslund, S. R., & Hopwood, C. J. (2010). PAI assessment in medical settings. In M. A, Blais, M. R. Baity, & C. J. Hopwood (Eds.), *Clinical applications of the Personality Assessment Inventory* (pp. 149–162). New York: Routledge.

Clarkin, J. F., & Levy, K. N. (2004). The influence of client variables on psychotherapy. In M. J. Lambert (Ed.), *Handbook of psychotherapy and behaviour change* (5th ed., pp. 194–226). New York: John Wiley & Sons.

Combs, D. R., & Penn, D. L. (2004). The role of subclinical paranoia on social perception and behavior. *Schizophrenia Research*, *69*, 93–104.

Constantino, M. J., Castonguay, L. G., & Schut, A. J. (2002). The working alliance: A flagship for the "scientist-practitioner" model in psychotherapy. In G. S. Tyron (Ed.), *Counseling based on process research: Applying what we know* (pp. 81–131). Boston, MA: Allyn & Bacon.

Corsica, J. A., Azarbad, L., McGill, K., Wool, L., & Hood, M. (2010). The Personality Assessment Inventory: Clinical utility, psychometric properties, and normative data for bariatric surgery candidates. *Obesity Surgery*, *20*, 722–731.

Costa, P. T., & McCrae, R. R. (1992). Normal personality assessment in clinical practice: The NEO Personality Inventory. *Psychological Assessment*, *4*, 5–13.

DeCoster-Martin, E., Weiss, W. U., Davis, R. D., & Rostow, C. D. (2004). Compulsive traits and police officer performance. *Journal of Police and Criminal Psychology*, *19*, 64–71.

DeShong, H. L., & Kurtz, J. E. (2013). Four factors of impulsivity differentiate antisocial and borderline personality disorders. *Journal of Personality Disorders*, *27*, 144–56.

Douglas, K. S., Hart, S. D., & Kropp, P. R. (2001). Validity of the Personality Assessment Inventory for forensic assessments. *International Journal of Offender Therapy and Comparative Criminology*, *45*, 183–197.

Edens, J. F., Hart, S. D., Johnson, D. W., Johnson, J. K., & Olver, M. E. (2000). Use of the Personality Assessment Inventory to assess psychopathy in offender populations. *Psychological Assessment*, *12*, 132–139.

Edens, J. F., Poythress, N. G., & Watkins-Clay, M. M. (2007). Detection of malingering in psychiatric unit and general population prison inmates: A comparison of the PAI, SIMS, and SIRS. *Journal of Personality Assessment*, *88*, 33–42.

Edens, J. F., & Ruiz, M. A. (2005). *PAI interpretive report for correctional settings (PAI-CS)*. Odessa, FL: Psychological Assessment Resources.

Edens, J. F., & Ruiz, M. A. (2006). On the validity of validity scales: The importance of defensive responding in the prediction of institutional misconduct. *Psychological Assessment*, *18*, 220–224.

Estrada, A. R., & Smith, S. R. (2017). An exploration of Latina/o respondent scores on the Personality Assessment Inventory. *Current Psychology*, *38*, 782-791.

Fals-Stewart, W. (1996). The ability of individuals with psychoactive substance use disorders to escape detection by the Personality Assessment Inventory. *Psychological Assessment*, *8*, 60–68.

Fernandez, K., Boccaccini, M. T., & Noland, R. M. (2008). Detecting over-and underreporting of psychopathology with the Spanish-language Personality Assessment Inventory: Findings from a simulation study with bilingual speakers. *Psychological Assessment*, *20*, 189–194.

Gardner, B. O., Boccaccini, M. T., Bitting, B. S., & Edens, J. F. (2015). Personality Assessment Inventory scores as predictors of misconduct, recidivism, and violence: A meta-analytic review. *Psychological Assessment*, *27*, 534–544.

Gay, N. W., & Combs, D. R. (2005). Social behaviors in persons with and without persecutory delusions. *Schizophrenia Research*, *80*, 361–362.

Groves, J. A., & Engel, R. R. (2007). The German adaptation and standardization of the Personality Assessment Inventory (PAI). *Journal of Personality Assessment*, *88*, 49–56.

Hare, R. D. (1991). *The Hare Psychopathy Checklist– revised*. Toronto, ON: Multi-Health Systems.

Harley, R. M., Baity, M. R., Blais, M. A., & Jacobo, M. C. (2007). Use of dialectical behavior therapy skills training for borderline personality disorder in a naturalistic setting. *Psychotherapy Research*, *17*, 351–358.

Hart, S. D., Cox, D. N., & Hare, R. D. (1995). Manual for the Psychopathy Checklist – Screening Version (PCL: SV). Unpublished manuscript, University of British Columbia.

Hawes, S. W., & Boccaccini, M. T. (2009). Detection of overreporting of psychopathology on the Personality Assessment Inventory: A meta-analytic review. *Psychological Assessment*, *21*, 112–124.

Hodgins, D. C., Schopflocher, D. P., Martin, C. R., el-Guebaly, N., Casey, D. M., Currie, S. R. ... & Williams, R. J. (2012). Disordered gambling among higher-frequency gamblers: Who is at risk? *Psychological Medicine*, *42*, 2433–44.

Hopwood, C. J., Ambwani, S., & Morey, L. C. (2007). Predicting non-mutual therapy termination with the Personality Assessment Inventory. *Psychotherapy Research*, *17*, 706–712.

Hopwood, C. J., Creech, S., Clark, T. S., Meagher, M. W., & Morey, L. C. (2008). Predicting the completion of an integrative and intensive outpatient chronic pain treatment. *Journal of Personality Assessment*, *90*, 76–80.

Hopwood, C. J., Flato, C. G., Ambwani, S., Garland, B. H., & Morey, L. C. (2009). A comparison of Latino and Anglo socially desirable responding. *Journal of Clinical Psychology*, *65*, 769–780.

Hopwood, C. J., & Morey, L. C. (2007). Psychological conflict in borderline personality as represented by inconsistent self–report item responding. *Journal of Social and Clinical Psychology*, *26*, 1065–1075.

Hopwood, C. J., Morey, L. C., Rogers, R., & Sewell, K. W. (2007). Malingering on the PAI: The detection of feigned disorders. *Journal of Personality Assessment*, *88*, 43–48.

Hopwood, C. J., Orlando, M. J., & Clark, T. S. (2010). The detection of malingered pain-related disability with the Personality Assessment Inventory. *Rehabilitation Psychology*, *55*, 307–310.

Hovey, J. D., & Magaña, C. G. (2002). Psychosocial predictors of anxiety among immigrant Mexican Migrant Farmworkers: Implications for prevention and treatment. *Cultural Diversity and Ethnic Minority Psychology*, *8*, 274–289.

Jackson, D. N. (1970). A sequential system for personality scale development. In C. D. Spielberger (Ed.). *Current topics in clinical and community psychology*, vol. 2 (pp. 62–97). New York: Academic Press.

Karlin, B. E., Creech, S. K., Grimes, J. S., Clark, T. S., Meagher, M. W., & Morey, L. C. (2005). The Personality Assessment Inventory with chronic pain patients: Psychometric properties and clinical utility. *Journal of Clinical Psychology*, *61*, 1571–1585.

Keeley, R., Smith, M., & Miller, J. (2000). Somatoform symptoms and treatment nonadherence in depressed family medicine outpatients. *Archives of Family Medicine*, *9*, 46–54.

Keiski, M. A., Shore, D. L., & Hamilton, J. M. (2003). CVLT-II performance in depressed versus nondepressed TBI subjects. *The Clinical Neuropsychologist*, *17*, 107.

Kerr, P. L., & Muehlenkamp, J. J. (2010). Features of psychopathology in self-injuring female college students. *Journal of Mental Health Counseling*, *32*, 290–308.

Kiesler, D. (1996). *Contemporary interpersonal theory and research: Personality, psychopathology, and psychotherapy*. New York: Wiley.

Killgore, W. D., Sonis, L. A., Rosso, I. M., & Rauch, S. L. (2016). Emotional intelligence partially mediates the association between anxiety sensitivity and anxiety symptoms. *Psychological Reports*, *118*, 23–40.

Klonsky, E. D. (2004). Performance of Personality Assessment Inventory and Rorschach indices of schizophrenia in a public psychiatric hospital. *Psychological Services*, *1*, 107–110.

Kurtz, J. E., Henk, C. M., Bupp, L. L., & Dresler, C. M. (2015). The validity of a regression-based procedure for detecting concealed psychopathology in structured personality assessment. *Psychological Assessment*, *27*, 392–402.

Lally, S. J. (2003). What tests are acceptable for use in forensic evaluations? A survey of experts. *Professional Psychology: Research and Practice*, *34*, 491–498.

Liljequist, L., Kinder, B. N., & Schinka, J. A. (1998). An investigation of malingering posttraumatic stress disorder on the Personality Assessment Inventory. *Journal of Personality Assessment*, *71*, 322–336.

Locke, D. E. C., Kirlin, K. A., Wershba, R., Osborne, D., Drazkowski, J. F., Sirven, J. I., & Noe, K. H. (2011). Randomized comparison of the Personality Assessment Inventory and the Minnesota Multiphasic Personality Inventory-2 in the epilepsy monitoring unit. *Epilepsy and Behavior*, *21*, 397–401.

Loevinger, J. (1957). Objective tests as instruments of psychological theory. *Psychological Reports*, *3*, 635–694.

Loving, J. L., & Lee, A. J. (2006). Use of the Personality Assessment Inventory in parenting capacity evaluations. Paper presented at the Society of Personality Assessment Annual Conference, San Diego, CA, March 22–26.

Lowmaster, S. E., & Morey, L. C. (2012). Predicting law enforcement officer job performance with the Personality Assessment Inventory. *Journal of Personality Assessment*, *94*, 254–261.

Lyrakos, D. G. (2011). The development of the Greek Personality Assessment Inventory. *Psychology*, *2*, 797–803.

Matlasz, T. M., Brylski, J. L., Leidenfrost, C. M., Scalco, M., Sinclair, S. J., Schoelerman, R. M., ... & Antonius, D. (2017). Cognitive status and profile validity on the Personality Assessment Inventory (PAI) in offenders with serious mental illness. *International Journal of Law and Psychiatry*, *50*, 38–44.

McCrae, R. R., Costa, P. T., & Martin, T. A. (2005). The NEO–PI–3: A more readable revised NEO personality inventory. *Journal of Personality Assessment*, *84*, 261–270.

McLellan, A. T., Kushner, H., Metzger, D., Peters, R., Smith, I., Grissom, G., ... & Argeriou, M. (1992). The fifth edition of the Addiction Severity Index. *Journal of Substance Abuse Treatment*, *9*, 199–213.

McDevitt-Murphy, M., Weathers, F. W., Adkins, J. W., & Daniels, J. B. (2005). Use of the Personality Assessment

Inventory in assessment of posttraumatic stress disorder in women. *Journal of Psychopathology and Behavioral Assessment*, *27*, 57–65.

Moadel, D., Doucet, G. E., Pustina, D., Rider, R., Taylor, N., Barnett, P., . . . Tracy, J. L. (2015). Emotional/psychiatric symptom change and amygdala volume after anterior temporal lobectomy. *JHN Journal*, *10*, 12–14.

Mogge, N. L., LePage, J. S., Bella T., & Ragatzc, L. (2010). The Negative Distortion Scale: A new PAI validity scale. *The Journal of Forensic Psychiatry and Psychology*, *21*, 77–90.

Morey, L. C. (1991). *Personality Assessment Inventory professional manual*. Odessa, FL: Psychological Assessment Resources.

Morey, L. C. (1996). *An interpretive guide to the Personality Assessment Inventory*. Odessa, FL: Psychological Assessment Resources.

Morey, L. C. (2000). *PAI software portfolio manual*. Odessa, FL: Psychological Assessment Resources.

Morey, L. C. (2003). *Essentials of PAI assessment*. New York: John Wiley.

Morey, L. C. (2007a). *Personality Assessment Inventory professional manual* (2nd ed.). Lutz, FL: Psychological Assessment Resources.

Morey, L. C. (2007b). *Personality Assessment Inventory – Adolescent (PAI-A)*. Lutz, FL: Psychological Assessment Resources.

Morey, L. C., & Hopwood, C. J. (2004). Efficiency of a strategy for detecting back random responding on the Personality Assessment Inventory. *Psychological Assessment*, *16*, 197–200.

Morey, L. C., & Hopwood, C. J. (2007). *Casebook for the Personality Assessment Inventory: A structural summary approach*. Lutz, FL: Psychological Assessment Resources.

Morey, L. C., & Lanier, V. W. (1998). Operating characteristics for six response distortion indicators for the Personality Assessment Inventory. *Assessment*, *5*, 203–214.

Morey, L. C., Lowmaster, S. E., Coldren, R. L., Kelly, M. P., Parish, R. V., & Russell, M. L. (2011). Personality Assessment Inventory profiles of deployed combat troops: An empirical investigation of normative performance. *Psychological Assessment*, *23*, 456–462.

Morey, L. C., Warner, M. B., & Hopwood, C. J. (2006). The Personality Assessment Inventory: Issues in legal and forensic settings. In A. Goldstein (Ed.) *Forensic Psychology: Advanced Topics for Forensic Mental Experts and Attorneys* (pp. 97–126). Hoboken, NJ: John Wiley & Sons.

Osborne, D. (1994). Use of the Personality Assessment Inventory with a medical population. Paper presented at the meetings of the Rocky Mountain Psychological Association, Denver, CO.

Parker, J. D., Daleiden, E. L., & Simpson, C. A. (1999). Personality Assessment Inventory substance-use scales: Convergent and discriminant relations with the Addiction Severity Index in a residential chemical dependence treatment setting. *Psychological Assessment*, *11*, 507–513.

Patry, M. W., & Magaletta, P. R. (2015). Measuring suicidality using the Personality Assessment Inventory: A convergent validity study with federal inmates. *Assessment*, *22*, 36–45.

Peebles, J., & Moore, R. J. (1998). Detecting socially desirable responding with the Personality Assessment Inventory: The Positive Impression Management Scale and the Defensiveness Index. *Journal of Clinical Psychology*, *54*, 621–628.

Percosky, A. B., Boccaccini, M. T., Bitting, B. S., & Hamilton, P. M. (2013). Personality Assessment Inventory scores as predictors of treatment compliance and misconduct among sex offenders participating in community-based treatment. *Journal of Forensic Psychology Practice*, *13*, 192–203.

Pincus, A. L. (2005). A contemporary integrative theory of personality disorders. In M. F. Lenzenweger & J. F. Clarkin (Eds.), *Major theories of personality disorder* (pp. 282–331). New York: Guilford Press.

Purdom, C. L., Kirlin, K. A., Hoerth, M. T., Noe, K. H., Drazkowski, J. F., Sirven, J. I., & Locke, D. E. (2012). The influence of impression management scales on the Personality Assessment Inventory in the epilepsy monitoring unit. *Epilepsy and Behavior*, *25*, 534–538.

Reidy, T. J., Sorensen, J. R., & Davidson, M. (2016). Testing the predictive validity of the Personality Assessment Inventory (PAI) in relation to inmate misconduct and violence. *Psychological Assessment*, *28*, 871–884.

Roberts, M. D., Thompson, J. A., & Johnson, M. (2000). *PAI law enforcement, corrections, and public safety selection report module*. Odessa, FL: Psychological Assessment Resources.

Rogers, R., Flores, J., Ustad, K., & Sewell, K. W. (1995). Initial validation of the Personality Assessment Inventory-Spanish Version with clients from Mexican American communities. *Journal of Personality Assessment*, *64*, 340–348.

Rogers, R., Gillard, N. D., Wooley, C. N., & Kelsey, K. R. (2013). Cross-validation of the PAI Negative Distortion Scale for feigned mental disorders: A research report. *Assessment*, *20*, 36–42.

Rogers, R., Gillard, N. D., Wooley, C. N., & Ross, C. A. (2012). The detection of feigned disabilities: The effectiveness of the Personality Assessment Inventory in a traumatized inpatient sample. *Assessment*, *19*, 77–88.

Rogers, R., Ornduff, S. R., & Sewell, K. (1993). Feigning specific disorders: A study of the Personality Assessment Inventory (PAI). *Journal of Personality Assessment*, *60*, 554–560.

Rogers, R., Sewell, K. W., Morey, L. C., & Ustad, K. L. (1996). Detection of feigned mental disorders on the Personality Assessment Inventory: A discriminant analysis. *Journal of Personality Assessment*, *67*, 629–640.

Ruiz, M. A., Cox, J., Magyar, M. S., & Edens, J. F. (2014). Predictive validity of the Personality Assessment Inventory (PAI) for identifying criminal reoffending following completion of an in-jail addiction treatment program. *Psychological Assessment*, *26*, 673–678.

Ruiz, M. A., Dickinson, K. A., & Pincus, A. L. (2002). Concurrent validity of the Personality Assessment Inventory Alcohol Problems (ALC) Scale in a college student sample. *Assessment*, *9*, 261–270.

Shorey, R. C., Gawrysiak, M. J., Anderson, S., & Stuart, G. L. (2015). Dispositional mindfulness, spirituality, and substance use in predicting depressive symptoms in a treatment-seeking sample. *Journal of Clinical Psychology*, *71*, 334–345.

Siefert, C. J., Kehl-Fie, K., Blais, M. A., & Chriki, L. (2007). Detecting back irrelevant responding on the Personality Assessment Inventory in a psychiatric inpatient setting. *Psychological Assessment*, *19*, 469–473.

Siefert, C. J., Sinclair, S. J., Kehl-Fie, K. A., & Blais, M. A. (2009). An item-level psychometric analysis of the Personality Assessment Inventory: Clinical scales in a psychiatric inpatient unit. *Assessment*, *16*, 373–383.

Sims, J. A., Thomas, K. M., Hopwood, C. J., Chen, S. H., & Pascale, C. (2013). Psychometric properties and norms for the Personality Assessment Inventory in egg donors and gestational carriers. *Journal of Personality Assessment*, *95*, 495–499.

Sinclair, S. J., Bello, I., Nyer, M., Slavin-Mulford, J., Stein, M. B., Renna, M., ... & Blais, M. A. (2012). The Suicide (SPI) and Violence Potential Indices (VPI) from the Personality Assessment Inventory: A preliminary exploration of validity in an outpatient psychiatric sample. *Journal of Psychopathology and Behavioral Assessment*, *34*, 423–431.

Stedman, J. M., McGeary, C. A., & Essery, J. (2018). Current patterns of training in personality assessment during internship. *Journal of Clinical Psychology*, *74*, 398–406.

Stein, M. B., Pinsker-Aspen, J., & Hilsenroth, M. J. (2007). Borderline pathology and the Personality Assessment Inventory (PAI): An evaluation of criterion and concurrent validity. *Journal of Personality Assessment*, *88*, 81–89.

Tasca, G. A., Wood, J., Demidenko, N., & Bissada, H. (2002). Using the PAI with an eating disordered population: Scale characteristics, factor structure and differences among diagnostic groups. *Journal of Personality Assessment*, *79*, 337–356.

Thomas, K. M., Hopwood, C. J., Orlando, M. J., Weathers, F. W., & McDevitt-Murphy, M. E. (2012). Detecting feigned PTSD using the Personality Assessment Inventory. *Psychological Injury and the Law*, *5*, 192–201.

Tkachenko, O., Olson, E. A., Weber, M., Preer, L. A., Gogel, H., & Killgore, W. D. S. (2014). Sleep difficulties are associated with increased symptoms of psychopathology. *Experimental Brain Research*, *232*, 1567–1574.

Tombaugh, T. N. (1996). *Test of memory malingering: TOMM*. North Tonawanda, NY: Multi-Health Systems.

Tracey, T. J. (1993). An interpersonal stage model of therapeutic process. *Journal of Counseling Psychology*, *40*, 396–409.

Wagner, M. T., Wymer, J. H., Topping, K. B., & Pritchard, P. B. (2005). Use of the Personality Assessment Inventory as an efficacious and cost-effective diagnostic tool for nonepileptic seizures. *Epilepsy and Behavior*, *7*, 301–304.

Wang, E. W., Rogers, R., Giles, C. L., Diamond, P. M., Herrington-Wang, L. E., & Taylor, E. R. (1997). A pilot study of the Personality Assessment Inventory (PAI) in corrections: Assessment of malingering, suicide risk, and aggression in male inmates. *Behavioral Sciences and the Law*, *15*, 469–482.

Weiss, P. A. (2010). Use of the PAI in personnel selection. In M. A. Blais, M. R. Baity, &, C. J. Hopwood (Eds.), *Clinical applications of the Personality Assessment Inventory* (pp. 163–176). New York: Routledge.

Whiteside, D., Clinton, C., Diamonti, C., Stroemel, J., White, C., Zimberoff, A., & Waters, D. (2010). Relationship between suboptimal cognitive effort and the clinical scales of the Personality Assessment Inventory. *The Clinical Neuropsychologist*, *24*, 315–325.

Whiteside, D. M., Galbreath, J., Brown, M., & Turnbull, J. (2012). Differential response patterns on the Personality Assessment Inventory (PAI) in compensation-seeking and non-compensation-seeking mild traumatic brain injury patients. *Journal of Clinical and Experimental Neuropsychology*, *34*, 172–182.

Woods, D. W., Wetterneck, C. T., & Flessner, C. A. (2006). A controlled evaluation of acceptance and commitment therapy plus habit reversal for trichotillomania. *Behaviour Research and Therapy*, *44*, 639–656.

Wooley, C. N., & Rogers, R. (2015). The effectiveness of the Personality Assessment Inventory with feigned PTSD: An initial investigation of Resnick's model of malingering. *Assessment*, *22*, 449–458.

18 The Millon Clinical Multiaxial Inventory-IV (MCMI-IV)

SETH GROSSMAN

Users of the Millon Clinical Multiaxial Inventory – Fourth Edition (MCMI-IV; Millon, Grossman, & Millon, 2015), as well as the legacy MCMI instruments, frequently laud and appreciate the close concordance of its constructs with established diagnostic criteria of the DSM-5 (American Psychiatric Association, 2013) and its predecessors. The rather straightforward relationship between MCMI-IV scales and DSM categories is the oft-cited motivation for its inclusion in a given battery, as it readily lends incremental validity to the diagnostic enterprise. Many clinicians will argue that this is the instrument's raison d'être, and this may be its most common usage but it is also its most basic. The narrative of this chapter will guide the reader "beyond the basics" in order to deepen skills in interpreting the personality constructs of the instrument; this begins with a firm foundation in the history, development, scope, and intent of the MCMI from its initial development to the current edition. It will then continue with a practical review of Millon's evolutionary theory (Millon, 1990, 2011; Millon & Davis, 1996) and its clinical application as the theoretical backbone of the MCMI-IV. The chapter continues by describing an interpretive sequence that lends itself to integrative assessment. It will then conclude with feedback and therapeutic direction derived from MCMI-IV personality data and its theoretical correlates.

The MCMI-IV is a 195-item adult self-report clinical personality inventory that identifies and delineates complex personality patterns in concert with clinical symptomology, also contextualizing noteworthy concerns and test-taking approach and attitude. Beyond simple diagnostic support, the instrument's intent is to provide information that cogently maximizes therapeutic plans that are integrative and germane to the individual assessed. Broken down into several sections of information, the instrument maintains the "multiaxial" perspective of prior DSMs in that it places personality and clinical symptomology in separate prominent positions such that they may be effectively examined for their relative influence on one another, rather than collapsed into discrete clinical entities within the same class with no meaningful relationship to one another. The profile page also includes a section comprised of validity measures and modifying indices that measure various aspects of an examinee's approach to the instrument, as well as a "High-Point Code" indicating a personality code combination. Table 18.1 lists all primary MCMI-IV scales; of particular note, and consistent with the most current theoretical augmentations (Millon, 2011), each of the fifteen familiar personality scales of the instrument are presented here and on the instrument as "spectra," or continua of severity from relatively adaptive to more severely maladaptive. The fourth edition of the instrument emphasizes these gradations in greater detail than in the legacy instruments. Additionally, a new scale abbreviation system allows for a printout of the profile page without emphasis on the full diagnostic label, facilitating feedback by granting the clinician more descriptive power over scale combinations that do not conform cleanly to a categorical label. A second profile page breaks down the *Grossman Facet Scales*, the more finite measures of the three most integral domains of each personality scale.

The MCMI-IV is a clinically oriented instrument and was primarily standardized using a sample population presenting for clinical services at a variety of inpatient and outpatient settings in North America. Its use should be limited to circumstances wherein a clinical referral question exists. However, this is a wider bandwidth than is generally presumed, as there is a common misconception that the instrument presumes the examinee to have marked personality pathology (Grossman & Amendolace, 2017), and the MCMI-IV makes this wider bandwidth more explicit in its demarcation of three ranges of personologic functioning (Normal Style, Abnormal Type, and Clinical Disorder, consistent with Millon's [2011] theory revision) and two ranges of clinical symptomology (Present and Prominent). These are recorded at specific base rate (BR) score elevations, as explicated in the "MCMI-IV Development" section of this chapter.

DEVELOPMENT OF LEGACY MCMI INSTRUMENTS

The origins of the MCMI-IV may be traced to Millon's (1969) initial biosocial learning theory and his quest to

Table 18.1 MCMI-IV primary profile page scales

Scale no.	Scale Abbreviation	Scale Name	No. of Items	Spectra (Style > Type > Disorder)
Personality Pattern Scales				
1	AASchd	Schizoid	15	Apathetic > Asocial > Schizoid
2A	SRAvoid	Avoidant	18	Shy > Reticent > Avoidant
2B	DFMelan	Melancholic	19	Dejected > Forlorn > Melancholic
3	DADepn	Dependent	14	Deferential > Attached > Dependent
4A	SPHistr	Histrionic	17	Sociable > Pleasuring > Histrionic
4B	EETurbu	Turbulent	17	Ebullient > Exuberant > Turbulent
5	CENarc	Narcissistic	16	Confident > Egotistical > Narcissistic
6A	ADAntis	Antisocial	14	Aggrandizing > Devious > Antisocial
6B	ADSadis	Sadistic	13	Assertive > Denigrating > Sadistic
7	RCComp	Compulsive	18	Reliable > Constricted > Compulsive
8A	DRNegat	Negativistic	18	Discontented > Resentful > Negativistic
8B	AAMasoc	Masochistic	18	Abused > Aggrieved > Masochistic
Severe Personality Pattern Scales				
S	ESSchizoph	Schizotypal	21	Eccentric > Schizotypal > Schizophrenic
C	UBCycloph	Borderline	20	Unstable > Borderline > Cyclophrenic
P	MPParaph	Paranoid	16	Mistrustful > Paranoid > Paraphrenic
Clinical Syndrome Scales				
A	GENanx	Generalized Anxiety	13	Anxiety, tension, generalized agitation
H	SOMsym	Somatic Symptom	10	Preoccupation with physical symptoms
N	BIPspe	Bipolar Spectrum	13	Range of cyclothymic > bipolar symptoms
D	PERdep	Persistent Depression	21	Chronic dysphoria, apathy, ineffectiveness
B	ALCuse	Alcohol Use	8	Recurrent or recent alcohol use difficulty
T	DRGuse	Drug Use	11	Recurrent or recent drug use difficulty
R	P-Tstr	Post-Traumatic Stress	14	Range of PTSD reactions and symptoms
Severe Clinical Syndromes				
SS	SCHspe	Schizophrenic Spectrum	21	Incongruous, disorganized, regressive behavior and affect
CC	MAJdep	Major Depression	17	Acute and disruptive dysphoric symptoms
PP	DELdis	Delusional	14	Irrational, suspicious, grandiose thought patterns
Validity				
V		Invalidity	3	Highly unlikely response endorsement
W		Inconsistency	50	Matched-endorsement item pairs
Modifying Indices				
X		Disclosure	121	Tendency to overreport
Y		Desirability	24	Tendency to portray oneself favorably
Z		Debasement	30	Tendency to portray oneself disfavorably

organize the theory's original set of personality prototypes into comparable, measurable entities (Millon, 2002). Millon felt that this could, at once, describe the core motivations of individuals, while also providing a system of personality taxonomy. The driving force of this exercise was to make the case that personality, rather than syndromal phenomena such as anxiety and depression, should be the central concern for clinical psychology, owing to its influence on, and ability to modulate, clinical symptomology. The fruits of this labor then set the stage not only for the original Millon Clinical Multiaxial Inventory (MCMI; Millon, 1977) but for the designation of personality on its own separate axis in the multiaxial systems of DSM-III (American Psychiatric Association, 1980) through to DSM-IV (American Psychiatric Association, 1994).

Beginning with the first MCMI, and through the current, fourth edition, the instrument has held a unique position among its peers owing to its deductive method of test development. Conceived specifically as a theoretically derived, empirically supported instrument, Millon worked to ensure a consistency of intent and an explanatory framework for *how* the personality prototypes related to one another yet remained unique entities.

The resulting MCMI featured eight primary personality scales corresponding to Millon's eight personality styles, as well as three "severe" personality scales (Schizotypal, Cycloid [Borderline], and Paranoid) measuring personality prototypes conceived as more structurally compromised variants of the basic personality patterns. Additionally, nine clinical syndrome scales measured classic psychopathology (e.g., depression, anxiety, alcohol abuse) and one validity scale was developed to detect random response patterns.

As the theory further developed into the "evolutionary model" and supported an expanded group of personality prototypes and updated MCMI iterations, Millon became an influential member of subsequent DSM Personality Disorder workgroup committees (Piotrowski & Keller, 1989; Piotrowski & Lubin, 1989, 1990). Personality patterns measured by the instrument overlapped considerably with, but were not identical to, the personality disorders of the diagnostic system, encompassing all critical criteria identified in the DSMs but going beyond the DSM's "atheoretical intent" to integrate aspects of theoretical constructs. In this way, the instrument offered clinicians a system in which they could further contextualize official diagnostic criteria via the explanatory principles embedded in Millon's theory (Choca & Grossman, 2015). Subsequent MCMIs remained inclusive of subsequent DSM iterations but remained more comprehensive both in theoretical inclusion and in included disorders (i.e., DSM patterns Depressive, Negativistic [Passive-Aggressive], Sadistic, and Masochistic were all eventually relegated to the Appendix of their respective DSMs, while they remained fully validated in the MCMIs).

Throughout the history of the MCMI, there were also several non-DSM innovations. The first was the decision to utilize an alternative standardized score to the commonly used *T*-score. Reflective of actuarial prevalence rates of a given disorder, the BR system rejected a core *T*-score assumption of the existence of a common, normal distribution shared by the various disorders (personality or clinical syndrome) being measured. In other words, prevalence rates for psychiatric measures, as opposed to other classes of measurement such as cognitive attributes, may be vastly different between two different personality patterns, or between a personality pattern and a psychiatric syndrome. Using a BR score system, then, provides greater idiographic accuracy by setting a core "cutting" point at a specified percentile rank reflective of estimates of how those diagnosed with a given disorder would score and using an iterative process to reflect further predictions of the prevalence of traits to establish a series of BR score conversions unique to each pattern (Wetzler, 1990). Further innovations appeared in the MCMI-II, including a differential item weighting system, emphasizing those items that were written specifically for a given scale (the scale's *prototypal* items) and deemphasizing those that supplement a given scale (prototypal items from other scales), as well as the advent of the classic three *modifying indices*, *Disclosure*, *Desirability*, and *Debasement*. MCMI-III, then, was the first to reflect Dr. Millon's most major theory advance, moving his constructs from the original biosocial-learning platform to the more expansive evolutionary model. Through several editions of the MCMI-III, other innovations were incorporated, including a simplified item weighting system, the addition of the Grossman Facet Scales, an *Inconsistency* scale, and the incorporation of combined-gender norms.

MCMI-IV DEVELOPMENT

Theodore Millon's last theory revision (Millon, 2011) set the stage for the development of the current instrument, the MCMI-IV. While this theory revision was a modest expansion of the evolutionary theory, it contained some crucial enhancements and clarifications, two of which are most relevant to specific points of clarity on the MCMI-IV. First, a new personality prototype – the *Turbulent* spectrum – was developed, inspired by early psychoanalytic descriptions (e.g., Kraepelin, 1921) as well as more current reference in popular culture (e.g., Jamison, 2005). Second, the theory more fully articulated a wider bandwidth from adaptive to maladaptive levels of personality functioning. While the evolutionary theory always specified a continuum, the revision sought to highlight characteristics at mild, moderate, and severe personologic pathology levels, designated as "Style," "Type," and "Disorder," respectively. These ultimately equated with critical cutting points at the levels of BR 60, BR 75, and BR 85 on the scale's personality measures.

As with the legacy MCMI instruments, as well as all of the Millon Inventories, the revision followed the three-stage deductive strategy described briefly here (the reader is encouraged to review the manual for a fuller explication of this test development sequence).

Theoretical-Substantive Stage

Following the revised theory's publication, Millon and his colleagues began composing new items for use in the MCMI-IV. The new item content was derived from the revised theory, as well as from the newly published DSM-5 criteria (American Psychiatric Association, 2013). This stage of development also saw a focus on contemporary social problems as well as concern for increased clinical focus on cognitive areas not generally associated with MCMI assessment, leading to several new noteworthy response categories and content (e.g., "Vengefully Prone," "Adult ADHD"). One unusual step during this first phase was a pilot study of all 245 new items administered to both clinical and nonclinical subjects in an effort to examine not only the general quality and clarity of the items but the extent to which the bandwidth of the traditionally clinically oriented measure might be expanded. While this effort ultimately did not result in a decision to move forward with an MCMI-IV encompassing a range from full adaptiveness to maladaptiveness, these data aided in shaping the instrument's larger clinical bandwidth. A second developmental study at the "item tryout" stage used the surviving new items added to the MCMI-III, administered along with two collateral measures, the Minnesota Multiphasic Personality Inventory-2-Restructured Form (MMPI-2-RF; Ben-Porath and Tellegen, 2008) and the Brief Symptom Inventory (BSI; Derogatis, 1993) to 235 individuals who were part of a general clinical US population. The new items retained after this stage were then also translated into Spanish, as well as back-translated, to evaluate their usefulness and appropriateness for US Spanish-speaking populations. Both an English and a Spanish final Research Form composed of the MCMI-III and the new items were then assembled for administration in the standardization (internal-structural) stage.

Internal-Structural Stage

The standardization form was administered and assessed through the Pearson Q-global platform to patients of then current MCMI-III users to determine final item selection from MCMI-III and new item content, as well as final scale composition. A primary selection factor, in keeping with Millon's vision for the instrument, was a concordance between empirical and theoretical considerations, with a specific focus on clinical utility of the constructs. This included, but was not limited to, an item's correlation with the targeted scale, representativeness of the clinical construct under consideration, and endorsement frequency. Items retained in this first round of analysis were then assigned as prototypal items for the target MCMI-IV scale.

External-Criterion Stage

Items surviving this stage as prototypal were then subjected to both external measure comparisons (i.e., collateral measures collected at earlier stages) and Confirmatory Factor Analysis, or CFA. This statistical method was chosen for its ability to incorporate theoretical considerations in guiding scale composition, without allowing the theory to *predetermine* this (Hoyle, 1991). Items were then assessed for use as *non-prototypal* or *supportive* content on other primary personality or syndrome scales. It is important to note, in this system of scale construction, that any given item may be used on several scales as a non-prototypal item but may only be used as a prototypal item on the single scale for which it was deliberately written. Final Cronbach's alpha measures were calculated for each scale, which finalized the 195-item content of the MCMI-IV. Alphas and test-retest correlations were employed for final reliability ratings, as were sensitivity/specificity measures for discriminant validity; the reader is referred to the test manual (Millon, Grossman, & Millon, 2015) for a review of these measures.

Table 18.2 details the standardization sample characteristics of the MCMI-IV, inclusive of all pilot groups and the general normative sample. Of the 1,884 total cases collected, 1,547 passed general exclusion criteria (see Millon, Grossman, & Millon, 2015, for specifics) and were included in the normative group. Employing the MCMI-III user-base in data collection allowed for a largely representative normative sample reflective of individuals seeking clinical psychotherapeutic services. While largely successful in achieving this reflection, typical challenges arose with respect, particularly, to age and race/ethnicity, as individuals from diverse groups and of older age tend to seek services less frequently than do younger adults and majority-race persons. This data collection, notably, also took place at what might be observed

Table 18.2 MCMI-IV standardization sample characteristics

Category/Range Overall N: 1,547	Percentage
AGE	
18–25	22.4
26 49	56.0
50–85	21.7
EDUCATION	
0–12 years, no high school diploma	8.1
High school/GED	24.6
Some college, associate degree, technical certificate beyond high school	29.9
Bachelor's degree and above	37.3
RACE/ETHNICITY	
African American	8.0
Asian	3.2
Caucasian	72.4
Hispanic	11.1
Other	5.4
GENDER	
Female	54.7
Male	45.3
REGION	
Midwest	19.7
Northeast	15.0
South	38.5
West	26.8
SETTING/STATUS	
Inpatient	9.9
Outpatient	90.1
MARITAL STATUS	
Never married	34.5
First marriage	29.3
Remarried	10.5
Separated	5.0
Divorced	13.8
Widowed	2.4
Cohabitating	3.1
Other	1.5

as the "young" phase of our field's understanding and mainstreaming of nonbinary gender definitions, and, for this reason, there is no discernable data for individuals who identify as gender nonbinary. It is the hope and intent of the authors to encourage post-publication research to address challenges inherent in the administration and interpretation of the MCMI-IV with diverse populations.

Final Test Development Considerations

Final test development tasks included redevelopment of the Grossman Facet Scales, a group of subscales representing dimensional trait measures drawn from each of the fifteen primary personality scales in accordance with the theory, as well as normative inclusion considerations, assignment of BR score transformations, creation of *Modifying Indices* scales, redevelopment of interpretive report material, and finalization of *Noteworthy Response* items and categories.

For the Facet Scales, consistent with the MCMI-III Faces Scales, the goal was to identify the three best represented of eight theoretically defined functional and structural personologic domains (see subsequent "Theory" section) from each primary personality scale and to assign approximately seven scale and supplemental items to each construct to compose each facet scale. CFA was then used to refine the resultant facet scales.

As the normative sample for the instrument is designed as a broad reflection of therapeutic service seekers in the US population, this is the most appropriate comparison group; the instrument may evidence distorted results if utilized for general counseling purposes or if a given patient may be a member of a more unusual subgroup that influences their experience much more profoundly than the overall dominant culture. As the vast majority of therapy-seeking adults in the United States are young adult to middle-age, college-educated, and white, the normative group emphasizes this mainstream population, despite concerted efforts to collect data from more diverse sources. That said, it is important to note that it *is* appropriate to utilize the MCMI-IV with individuals who do *not* show obvious signs of personality pathology, as long as they are seeking treatment for mental health concerns ranging from adjustment disorders to more profound psychiatric or personality pathology. It is also appropriate to use the instrument for all populations included in the normative group (adult age range, wide educational/marital status, major ethnic groups) that are considered part of the overall makeup of US and Western culture. An American-Spanish translation, developed with assistance from the publisher's bilingual language specialists for translation and back-translation, was utilized with American Spanish-speaking participants within the standardization sample and has been available since the test publication; the European Spanish version was released in late 2018.

BR score transformations for all MCMI-IV scales anchor a score to the prevalence rate of a given characteristic in question. For each attribute, the cutoff scores of BR 75 and 85 (as well as 60 with all personality and facet scales) gain significance in terms of the degree of a characteristic or personality pattern being measured. The most significant score point for all measures is at BR 75, which can be thought of as an "anchor point" at which the attribute or characteristic being measured gains pathological significance. The shape of the score distribution, however, may differ from one measure to another, although the key points (85, and, with personality measures, 60) may be interpreted similarly. This is consistent with the reality that measures of personality and psychopathology do not conform to a normal distribution and are idiographic in nature.

Psychometrically, the MCMI-IV evidences internal consistency by the inclusion of Cronbach's α calculated on both the English form cases in the normative sample and a subset of the Spanish form cases, and by a test-retest stability estimate. For the α estimates, overall results were found to fall in the "good" range (i.e., > 0.80), with a median score in the English cases of 0.84 for personality patterns, 0.83 for the clinical syndromes, and 0.80 for the facet scales. For the Spanish cases, these values also fell in the "good" range, with values at 0.86, 0.83, and 0.80, respectively. Some outliers were found; of particular note were seven of the forty-five facet scale values falling below 0.70. These were retained, however, owing to the understanding of a weaker statistical precision inherent in a smaller item pool size and the integral nature of the constructs being measured. In the Spanish cases, there was generally a wider range for the α values, partially due to the smaller sample size. However, there were differences between the Spanish and English scores on some measures that could not be attributed to sample size. These included the Drug Use and Antisocial scales, two constructs seen as infrequently disclosed by Hispanic/Latinx individuals to strangers (Freeman, Lewis, & Colon, 2002; Suarez-Morales & Beitra, 2013). Test-retest correlations also indicate adequate to good stability across administrations, with most corrected stability coefficients 0.80 or larger.

Validity for the MCMI-IV was established using scale intercorrelations, as well as correlations with collateral measures (BSI, Derogatis, 1993; MMPI-2 RF, Ben-Porath & Tellegen, 2008; MCMI-III, Millon et al., 2009; MCMI-IV Clinician's Rating Form). Overall, scales expected to negatively correlate with others performed as expected (e.g., Histrionic and Turbulent with most other personality scales, Antisocial with Compulsive), and those with known comorbidity tended to correlate positively (e.g., the clinical syndromes Generalized Anxiety, Persistent Depression and Somatic Symptom all moderately correlating). Correlations with the collateral measures were found to be in the good range for related scales and constructs. The reader is referred to the MCMI-IV manual for a detailed iteration of these reliability and validity measures developed in the instrument's external-validation stage.

Little independent validity research been conducted, to date, with the MCMI-IV and none has yet been published. However, the instrument is now in its fourth major iteration and there are only two notable construct modifications out of its twenty-five primary clinical measures (i.e., the addition of personality scale 4B: EETurbu, and a reformulation of scale SS – Schizophrenic Spectrum – from the MCMI-III "Thought Disorder" scale). With these exceptions, all other constructs are well-established in legacy. For this reason, validity studies conducted on the MCMI legacy instruments (in particular, the MCMI-III) may be cautiously applied to the newer instrument for its related constructs, with the understanding that some more nuanced changes have yet to be thoroughly assessed.

As established criteria reflections of DSM-based constructs, the syndrome scales rely largely on clinician rating forms and collateral measures collected during the development and standardization processes. The personality scales have, over time, been more thoroughly studied. As a general trend, validity has improved in these scales through iterations I–III (Rossi et al., 2003). Rossi and colleagues (2003) noted that the MCMI-III personality scales have shown promising concurrent validity with other measures, most notably the Somwaru and Ben-Porath (1995) MMPI-2 personality scales. An exception, however, found in this and other reviews (e.g., Choca, 2004; Craig, 1999), lies with the Compulsive scale. As this is a consistent finding, it may evidence a more integral difference in conceptualization between Millon's Compulsive construct and that of other test developers. Finally, there is no published peer-reviewed research examining MCMI-IV scale performance across cultural contexts, which is a weakness that needs to be remediated as research on the instrument continues to accumulate.

THEORY

A clear understanding of the *workings* of the theory adds immeasurably to the potential for meaningful and integrated interpretation and feedback as described in the latter parts of the chapter. This is an area of Millon Inventories assessment that often seems daunting to many clinicians. What follows is a breakdown of the major sections of the theory and a cross-section of the theory's dynamics, rather than an expansive catalogue of its assertions. This is meant more as a primer than an interpretive guide; the reader is directed to some of the more recent, comprehensive resources (e.g., Grossman & Amendolace, 2017; Millon, 2011; Millon, Grossman, & Millon, 2015) for content guidance for specific clinical presentations.

Millon focused his theory on the centrality of personologic functioning and designed his instruments to be "personality-centric" (Millon, 1990, 2011; Millon & Davis, 1996). To aim treatment at the personality level, Millon professed, was to strengthen the person's psychological immune system (Millon, 1999; Millon & Grossman, 2007a, 2007b, 2007c). It is with this perspective in mind that the core focus of the Millon Inventories is on personality functioning, with an ultimate intent of facilitating intervention by helping the person better adapt and traverse the environment, thereby alleviating psychiatric symptomology.

The most recent theoretical revision (Millon, 2011) details fifteen personality prototypes that are represented on the MCMI-IV as the primary and severe personality patterns. The twelve primary patterns are derived from varying emphases and simple conflicts or discordances along this limited set of overarching principles (see "Motivating Aims," below), while three (Schizotypal, Borderline, and Paranoid) trend toward greater maladaptation, as seen in a form of structural compromise in the personality.

Motivating Aims

The evolutionary theory posits three basic motivational strategies, termed *Motivating Aims*, that are each set up as *polarity* continua and are each related directly to evolutionary imperatives (see Figure 18.1). When taken together, different patterns of emphasis, conflict, or other dynamics along these three strategies derive each personality prototype. Simpler organisms of the living world, Millon posited, could also be described using this schema but they would generally be described via stable points on each of these continua. Humans and their personalities, conversely, would tend to show some movement and flexibility along these lines, as different situations and internal states would call for reasonable changes to adaptive strategies. A higher

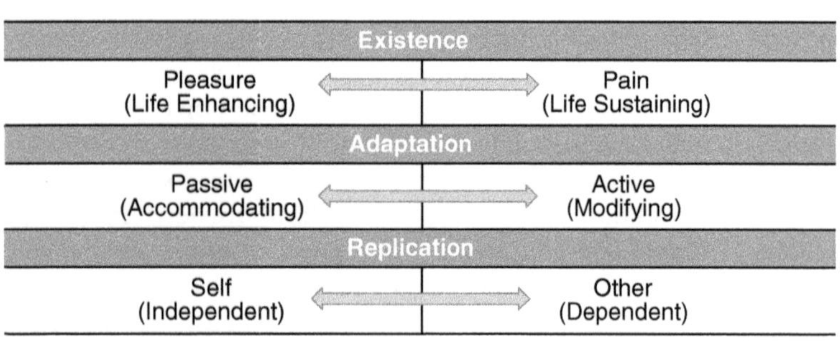

Figure 18.1 Motivating aims

level of personality dysfunction, however, would evidence less adaptivity and flexibility in navigating life demands.

The fifteen prototypes representing the fifteen MCMI-IV personality scales are each derived by their profile of favored strategies across the three polarities as follows:

Survival strategy. An organism must first exist as a living entity. These strategies range from actions that decrease threat (*pain* avoidance) to actions aimed at enhancing life (*pleasure*-seeking).

Adaptation strategy. Following survival, the organism must interact with its environment. Strategies range from influencing the environment to conform to its needs (*active-modification*) to modifying itself to fit in (*passive-accommodation*).

Replication strategy. Recognizing its finite lifespan, an organism must regenerate. These strategies are *self-propagating* or *other-nurturing* in nature.

In general, adaptive, healthy personalities will evidence well-defined favored strategies with a modicum of flexibility. For example, an independent individual may tend to rely mostly on themselves, may show only moderate concern for risks, and may take solace in being and acting alone. These characteristics, when moderated, are neither adaptive nor maladaptive by definition. This same pattern, at a more maladaptive level, however, will evidence pervasive fixedness, enacting strong active-self motivations of the antisocial prototype and displaying poor impulse control and insatiable self-needs

Several problematic patterns can hinder adaptiveness, manifesting within a single prototype and/or in admixtures of prototypes:

Disbalance. This is the simplest and most prevalent of these problematic patterns, wherein a given personality strongly favors one side of the polarity structure over the other.

Conflict. This process emanates from the subjugation of unwanted favoring of one motivating aim producing an even less desired effect. These conflicts may manifest across one polarity, or several, with greater personality structural compromise occurring with more discord.

Reversal. In this process, a motivating aim is reversed into its opposite, thereby creating an inverse of expected motivations and the experience of a phenomenon as its apparent opposite.

Wavering. This process represents a disintegration of usual motivating aims to the point where motivations become ill-defined and chaotic.

Unalterable. This process manifests immovability across all polarities. In this structural compromise, extant motivations become concretized, showing severe resistance to flexibility.

Structural and Functional Domains

At a more molecular level of the theory, Millon outlines a trait-domain system that dimensionalizes prototypes in a manner in which they can be directly comparable to one another. Each prototype has eight dimensional domains classified within a general psychological framework (behavioral, phenomenological, intrapsychic, or biophysical) as well as being either functional or structural in nature. The eight functional/structural domains are listed in Table 18.3.

It is actually highly unusual for a person to fit cleanly into one category alone (Millon et al., 2004). Rather, a given person may match *primarily* with one prototype but evidence traits more typical of others. Because the domains of personality are comparable across prototypes, it is possible, and even likely, to see this manifest in highly individualized profiles.

In the MCMI-IV, this system of domain delineation is partially represented by the Grossman Facet Scales

Table 18.3 Functional and structural domains

Domain	General Definition	Structural/ Functional	Class
Expressive Emotion	Individual behavior inferring emotion	Functional	Behavioral
Interpersonal Conduct	Behavioral interactions with others	Functional	Behavioral
Self-Image	Sense of self-as-object, unique from others	Structural	Phenomenological
Cognitive Style	Allocation of attention and focus; mental set	Functional	Phenomenological
Intrapsychic Content	Template of expectation of others drawn from early experience	Structural	Intrapsychic
Intrapsychic Dynamics	Defense mechanisms	Functional	Intrapsychic
Intrapsychic Architecture	Internal organization of psychic principles and content	Structural	Intrapsychic
Mood/Temperament	Physical substrates influencing psychic processes	Structural	Biophysical

Table 18.4 Personality levels across evolutionary spectra

Spectrum Acronym	Normal Style	Abnormal Type	Clinical Disorder
AASchd	Apathetic	Asocial	Schizoid
SRAvoid	Shy	Reticent	Avoidant
DFMelan	Dejected	Forlorn	Melancholic
DADepn	Deferential	Attached	Dependent
SPHistr	Sociable	Pleasuring	Histrionic
EETurbu	Ebullient	Exuberant	Turbulent
CENarc	Confident	Egotistical	Narcissistic
ADAntis	Aggrandizing	Devious	Antisocial
ADSadis	Assertive	Denigrating	Sadistic
RCComp	Reliable	Constricted	Compulsive
DRNegat	Discontented	Resentful	Negativistic
AAMasoc	Abused	Aggrieved	Masochistic
ESSchizoph	Eccentric	Schizotypal	Schizophrenic
UBCycloph	Unstable	Borderline	Cyclophrenic
MPParaph	Mistrustful	Paranoid	Paraphrenic

(Grossman, 2004; Millon, Grossman, & Millon, 2015). Facet scales were constructed primarily from primary scale item pools and supplemented from statistically correlated and clinically related items from other scales in the inventory. A set of three of the eight domains per scale (differing from scale to scale) was developed to be clinical hypothesis-builders and finer-grade measures of more prominent trait personology, as measured by theory (Millon, 2011).

Levels of Adaptiveness

A long-standing question regarding the Millon clinical instruments has been centered on most appropriate target usage. The theory focuses primarily on personality pathology, and the MCMI-IV is normed on a clinical population. The instrument, then, is best suited for those individuals who are *presenting for clinical services.* This does not presume personality pathology but it does not automatically exclude other specialized populations (e.g., adults involved in family law matters). The most recent update to the theory specifies three different adaptiveness levels, ranging from mostly adaptive to disordered, and reflected on the MCMI-IV by anchoring to specified BR scores. *Normal style* (BR 60–74), the first of these three levels, reflects generally adaptive personality functioning. These individuals may, at times, evidence less adaptive traits when under duress but generally are able to cope adequately. The moderate level comprises the *abnormal type* (BR 75–84). At this level, the individual may predictably show vulnerability to repetitive stressors or impairments owing to deficits in flexibility and adaptivity. While there may be patternistic personality difficulties that impair the individual's functioning, this range is not usually reflective of diagnosable personality disorders, or, if it is, it reflects the so-called high functioning level of disordered personality. *Clinical disorders*, then, fall at the most maladaptive end (BR 85+) and reflect individuals who chronically evidence functional personologic impairment, self-perpetuated vicious cycles of social and internal distress, and overall limited ability to satisfactorily function in a community. This range is generally most reflective of the DSM-5 level of maladaptiveness required to consider a diagnosis.

Table 18.4 presents each pattern of the spectrum in relation to these levels of severity and reiterates an acronym system initiated in Millon (2011). This acronym set is utilized in the alternative MCMI-IV profile report, which is designed to provide an additional tool for clinicians seeking to more directly share results from the instrument and to reduce vulnerability to "false positives" as an unanticipated result of the diagnostic labels appearing on the standard profile page.

From Theory to MCMI-IV Personality Assessment

The aforementioned theoretical elements serve as "building blocks" to the central feature of the MCMI-IV – that is, its primary personality and facet scales. Each of the primary personality scales is conceptualized as a prototypal personality construct, reflective of the motivating aims inherent in each prototype. Scale composition is derived from items that are written as operational statements reflective of the various functional and structural domains in each prototype.

The usefulness of the theory in assessment and, ultimately, in intervention, then, is manifold. First, a single personality scale, when elevated, offers prototypal information beyond a diagnostic category or construct. Each single elevation details aspects of the individual's basic motivation. Multiple-scale elevations, as MCMI-IV protocols usually present, then consider how these isolated elevations may blend to form further disbalance, conflicts, and so on between prototypal scales. Next, as domains are identified as salient via the Grossman Facet Scales and examination with the theory, specific trait expressions may offer insights into treatment approaches. Finally, with personologic insights gained from the personality scales, insights are possible in terms of how a given individual may express and experience a given syndromal complication.

INTERPRETIVE PRINCIPLES AND STRATEGIES

The process of interpreting the many data points of an MCMI-IV profile involves a recommended progressive sequence, an ability to contextualize diverse but related information, and a sensitivity to, but not an obsession with, specific score quantities. The instrument's design sets the stage for integrating response-set biases (Modifying Indices and Validity measures), immediate concerns and differentials (Noteworthy Responses), and more fully articulated psychiatric concerns (Clinical/ Severe Symptoms) through the lens of the person being assessed (Clinical and Severe Personality Patterns). The following sequence was first outlined by Retzlaff (1995) and later updated and further delineated by Grossman and Amendolace (2017):

Examine Response Bias Measures (Scales V–Z). These five scales, subdivided into "Validity measures" (scales V and W) and "Modifying Indices" (Scales X, Y, and Z), work together to compose a picture of the assessee's overall attitude and approach to completing the MCMI-IV. The first of these, scale V (Invalidity), is composed of three highly unlikely and almost nonsensical items designed to identify random or nonserious response bias depending on their endorsement (one deeming the protocol questionable, and two rendering it invalid). Scale W was developed for the fourth edition of the MCMI-III (Millon et al., 2009), in recognizing the limitations of the scale V methodology. This scale is composed of 25 extant MCMI-IV item pairs identified as statistically and semantically related, and expected to be endorsed with predictable consistency owing to their close relationship. A moderate level of unusual endorsement will render a protocol questionable, while a high level of unusual endorsement designates the protocol invalid.

Scales X (Disclosure), Y (Desirability), and Z (Debasement) are together known as the classic "Modifying Indices" of the Millon instruments. Overall, these three scales are used to shape the overall interpretation. Scale X represents a continuum of response style from secretiveness through to frankness to overdisclosure. Scales Y and Z represent attempts to appear virtuous, highly well-adjusted, and socially attractive, or self-deprecating, mentally unstable, and unappealing, respectively. These three scales may be interpreted both independently and configuratively.

Noteworthy Responses. The MCMI-IV now has thirteen noteworthy response categories wherein select individual items are grouped, but not scaled, according to vulnerability/safety concerns or clinical distinctions. Some more finite distinctions are now included (e.g., there is a differentiation between self-injurious behaviors intended to relieve discomfort and intentional suicidal behaviors, though both may be life-threatening) and there are now two overall intentions embedded in the Noteworthy Response categories (risk amelioration and differential diagnoses). While primary focus remains on risk and safety concerns, some of the newer categories also offer an alert to clinicians that a clinical issue that falls outside of the main purview of the MCMI-IV (e.g., ADHD, ASD) may be present.

Personality scales: An overview. In considering the fifteen MCMI-IV personality scales, it may be useful to compare them to a color wheel. Red, yellow, and blue are but three perceivable colors, yet their various combinations can produce thousands of color variants. To take a simple example from this metaphor: Green is neither yellow nor blue but these two colors, in approximately equal amounts of their primary form, blend to create green. What is created is unique and distinct from its components. It maintains the core material of the original two colors but the blending is transformational.

Millon's theory posits a similar process with human personality. The theory, and hence the MCMI-IV personality scales, takes the approach of utilizing fifteen "primary colors" (i.e., the primary personality scales), inclusive of their motivating aims, structure, and facets as identified by the functional and structural personologic domains, and attempts to reflect an examinee using this data. For example, a person who produces a profile with elevated scores on 2A (Avoidant) and 2B (Melancholic) may exhibit some characteristics of each prototype but will likely be qualitatively and quantitatively different from either. Further, the personality structure will be transformed. Both prototypes appear strong on the "pain" end of the survival polarity but are opposites on the adaptation polarity. This conflict may create ambivalence, seeking psychological protection on the one hand (as would a prototypal avoidant) while giving in and accepting vulnerability to psychic pain on the other (as would a prototypal melancholic). This presentation, then, evidences unique problems in living from either prototype.

Assess severe personality pathology. In order to integrate possible structural compromise of an individual's personality into the clinical interpretation, the three severe personality patterns – Schizotypal, Borderline, and Paranoid – should be examined before assessing the basic personality patterns (Scales 1–8B). With the severe personality patterns, in general, the theory lays emphasis on the structural integrity of each construct, with each showing frailty and/or lack of coherence in the personality system due to polarity wavering (Schizotypal), polarity conflict (Borderline), or unalterable polarities (Paranoid). The guidelines for examining these scales are as follows:

1. *If one or more of the scales S, C, or P are among the highest 2–3 elevations across all personality scales*, those high-elevated scales should be considered for possible diagnostic implications and interpreted as a primary elevation. This means, for example, that, if Scale C (Borderline) is the first or second highest elevation along with Scale 4A (Histrionic), the Borderline scale should be co-interpreted directly with scale 4A, given similar weight, and may be considered supportive of, but not determinative of, a diagnosis of borderline personality disorder (assuming an elevation above BR 75).
2. *If one or more of the scales S, C, or P are elevated above BR 60, but* not *among the highest 2–3 elevations across all scales*, the elevated scale(s) (S, C, P) should be assessed for contribution as a modifier of other more highly elevated scales. While the S, C, or P scale in this scenario will not likely be considered for a given diagnosis, its effects, as specified in the theory, should be considered in terms of any potential personality structural compromise. Example: A given profile evidences a very high 4B/5 (Turbulent/Narcissistic) elevation, with both scores above 85. If the profile also includes an elevated S, C, or P, the interpretation is modified as follows:
   a. *Scale S*: The *wavering/disintegrating* effect on the motivating aims across all polarity dimensions may create a more chaotic presentation, with this otherwise narcissistically guarded, energetic, and ambitious person evidencing lack of focus and an alienation from and misattunement to others.
   b. *Scale C*: Owing to pervasive conflicts across all polarities, this elevation may indicate fragility of personality cohesion, and any unusual stressors may create intense and unpredictable lability.
   c. *Scale P*: In this scenario, the immutability across polarities is likely to present in an unrealistically determined, unalterable "agenda" in which any outside doubt is met with projection and guardedness.
3. *No elevations over BR 60 on Scales S, C, P*: These scales may be disregarded for the current profile and the clinician should move on to a more straightforward interpretation of Clinical Personality Patterns, Scales 1–8B.

Assess clinical personality patterns (Scales 1–8B). Keeping in mind any elevations on Scales S, C, or P, interpretation moves to the Clinical Personality Pattern scales. In this section, each high score elevation is examined separately, with primary focus on the highest 2–3 scale scores. When examining these scales, as with the Severe Personality Pathology, it is as important to consider the structure of the construct as defined by the theory's Motivating Aims (polarities, as discussed in the "Theory" section in this chapter) as it is to look at the DSM-5, where applicable. Polarity disbalance, conflict, and discord in each prototype offers key information regarding different evolutionary motivations.

Most profiles feature multiple scale elevations. As with the color wheel metaphor of how prototypal personality patterns ("primary colors") coalesce into subtypes ("secondary colors"), the next part of the interpretive process involves an understanding of each prototype as well as a dynamic view as to how two or more prototypal patterns may coalesce. This is an area of MCMI-IV interpretation that involves clinical practice and skill-building to become fluent in assessing these combinations and relating results to the examinee's presentation and other sources of information. The following are some basic guidelines for interpretation:

1. *Matching/aligning polarities*: Examination of several prototypes represented by elevated scale scores may yield more than one "matching" polarity description. For example, if scales 3 (Dependent) and 4A (Histrionic) are elevated, both prototypes feature a strong emphasis on the "Other" end of the Replication polarity. It is likely, especially if there are no other major elevations in opposition to this, that this examinee places an even more distinct emphasis on using relationship with others for self-definition.
2. *Opposing polarities*: In some combinations, two elevated scales will represent prototypes wherein a polarity continuum will highlight opposing ends of the continuum. In these instances, the clinician must examine the meaning of this difference. This often relates to current level of functioning. When not distressed, a simple difference such as this may indicate an ability to modulate between motivational strategies but, under distress, this may highlight a conflict. In the same example with a co-elevation of the Dependent and Histrionic scales, while the Replication strategy matches (both emphasizing "Other"), the Adaptation strategy is opposed (Dependent being a "Passive" strategy and Histrionic being an "Active" one). It is possible, when this person is not experiencing unusual pressure,

that the two differing emphases may balance one another and the person may be able to switch between adjusting to expectations and acting on the environment as outside cues arise. However, in more distress, the same personality structure may create a conflict in which the person feels ambivalence as to whether to draw attention (act on the environment) or to become much more of a compliant, obedient entity (passively fit in).

3. *Combinations where one or more prototypes feature a single conflict or discordance*: These situations often highlight the need to assess whether the prototypal amalgam exacerbates or subdues the prototypal conflict or discord. For example, Scale 2A (Avoidant) and Scale 6B (Sadistic) are structured similarly, with each oriented toward an "Active–Pain" motivating strategy. Of course, their outward expression is very different but their core motivations may be similar. The key difference is the reversal on "Pain" for the Sadistic, wherein this person reorients the focus on pain to deflect psychic pain outward onto others. Wherein a single Sadistic elevation may be reflective of a person less aware of their own psychic pain experience, the combination likely reflects an individual well aware of their own struggle with social acceptance, possibly being more conscious of their strategy to hurt others as a means of deflection.
4. *Combinations involving Scales S, C, or P*: A determination will need to be made as to whether an elevation on one of these three scales represents a probable co-elevation with other scales contending for a diagnostic assignment or whether a more moderate elevation (above BR 60; more significantly separated from other higher elevations) serves mainly to "colorize" the more elevated scales. See the preceding subsection, "Assess severe personality pathology" for a more detailed review of this process.

While there may be many scales elevated beyond a BR of 60, key interpretive information should be focused on the highest of these scales. An elevated scale not among the highest scores may contribute some meaningful colorization to the overall profile but primary consideration should still be focused on the highest elevations. For example, a profile may feature a cluster of high scores, perhaps BRs in the 80s, for Scale 1 (Schizoid), 2A (Avoidant), and 3 (Dependent), with a secondary score of Scale 6B (Sadistic) at a BR of 67. In this example, most of the motivation and key personologic information will be found in the solitude, fear of rejection, and self-uncertainty in the first three scales. However, Scale 6B adds an important colorization in that it may speak to this person's chosen defense of presenting a kind of "meanness" in their interactions. Exploration of this scale with the examinee may lead to an understanding that, owing to their fears, they are more comforted by leading people to believe in their unfriendliness.

Integrate the facet scales. After formulating the overall personality framework, focus shifts to more finite specifications detailed by the Grossman Facet Scales. To review, these scales are derived from the three out of eight most prominent structural and functional domains in each prototypal scale and largely match with those predicted to be most prominent within the theory. Although the specific three out of eight domains may differ between prototypal scales, the eight domains are consistent across all prototypes and scales.

Facet scales are best seen as clinical hypothesis-builders, useful in helping determine specific problem areas and linking these challenges to treatment approaches. Assessment of facet scales is a relatively straightforward process. First, priority is given to facet scales, as a general rule, in order of the primary scale elevations. The highest three primary scale scores are shown in descending order graphically on page 2 of the profile report, with the full listing of all facet scales below that graph. In some instances, the same domain may be elevated on two different primary scales, with two different descriptions. The clinician will need to determine, based on primary scale elevation, facet scale elevation, and clinical presentation, which of the two descriptions (or whether a combination of both descriptions) is most appropriate.

Assess severe clinical symptomology. Following the same logic from the personality scales, wherein severe personality patterns were appraised before examining the basic personality patterns, this sequence suggests using the severe clinical syndrome scales – Scales SS (Schizophrenic Spectrum), CC (Major Depression) and PP (Delusional) – as "colorizers" for the basic clinical syndrome scales. In protocols wherein there is no major elevation in these three scales, individual and configural interpretation of the basic clinical syndrome scales (described next) is relatively straightforward. However, elevations in any of these three scales may prompt the following considerations:

1. *If any of the Severe Clinical Syndrome Scales is the highest among all Clinical Syndrome Scales*, this should warrant consideration for the construct in question to be among the primary diagnoses.
2. *If any of the Severe Clinical Syndrome Scales are elevated significantly, but less than scales in the basic Clinical Syndrome group*, consider how the more severe construct affects the more basic clinical syndrome. For example, if scale CC (Major Depression) is elevated at BR 76 and scale D (Persistent Depression) from the basic syndrome group is elevated at BR 89, you may consider a clinical classification of "Double Depression," wherein a pronounced persistent pattern of dysphoria and negative perspective are setting the stage for a moderate onset of a major depressive episode and there is a common occurrence of treatment

delay owing to the individual accepting worsening symptoms as inevitable and natural (Klein et al., 2000).

Assess the clinical syndrome scales (Scales A, H, N, D, B, T, R). After considering the influence of the Severe Clinical Syndrome scales (if any), the last section to be assessed as a unit is the clinical syndrome scales. These are reflective of the most common diagnostic categories across adult psychiatric symptomology and are constructed, as are the severe syndrome scales, to correspond closely to DSM-5 syndromal constructs. They are not explicitly designed to be interpreted configurally among one another, though some configural interpretation is possible (e.g., the common co-occurrence of *Anxiety* and *Persistent Depression*). As a general rule, when a clinical syndrome scale and a severe clinical syndrome scale are similarly elevated, consideration should be given first to the more severe syndrome, owing to greater vulnerability.

Integrate the overall profile. In formulating an overall clinical impression with the MCMI-IV, the foregoing sequence is explicitly designed to help organize these related but substantively different sections of clinical inquiry. Each step builds on the next. By initiating with a clear sense of the profile's validity and any unusual response pattern, the clinician may develop an overall framework for interpretation. The next section focusing on noteworthy responses rules out the need for tertiary intervention, provides some perspective for distress responding, and alerts the clinician to the potential need for a differential diagnosis using other measures. The third section, looking at both severe and basic clinical personality patterns, gives the central context of the overall protocol, which emphasizes understanding the person and their personality (in this light, as the psychological immune system), and *who the person is* that is experiencing clinical symptomology is assessed in the fourth, clinical syndrome, section of the instrument.

FEEDBACK AND THERAPEUTIC APPLICATIONS

By the end of the twentieth century, Millon had become more focused on the application of assessment to intervention (Millon, 1999, 2002; Millon & Grossman, 2007a, 2007b, 2007c). Consistent with his (2011) text shift emphasizing the larger bandwidth of personality severity and adaptiveness across all fifteen personality prototypes, the MCMI-IV vision was to focus on useful clinical information beyond the label/diagnosis and its applicability to intervention. A major initiative in developing the new instrument was to make the information it produced as useful to the examinee as it may be to a treating clinician receiving the profile pages and interpretive material. A decision was made to offer an alternative profile that could be printed in addition to, or in lieu of, the standard profile page. The "Abbreviated Scale Names" option produces identical information to the standard profile page but uses Millon's most recent abbreviations representative of the personality spectra, in lieu of the classic labels (e.g., "EETurbu" in place of "Turbulent"; refer to "Spectra Acronym" column of Table 18.3 for the full listing). This is aligned with the American Psychological Association (APA) trends and directives toward greater openness in assessment, as well as with some modalities' encouragement of more direct and collaborative feedback in psychological testing while avoiding misguidance of diagnostic labeling (e.g., Therapeutic Assessment). This innovation, according to the authors, is designed to support a more thorough and candid review of assessment findings with the examinee and to facilitate the examinee's self-understanding via enhanced use of the descriptive language inherent in these theoretical assertions that then are translated to therapeutic alliance building (Ackerman et al., 2000; Grossman & Amendolace, 2017; Millon, Grossman, & Millon, 2015).

Using the Theory's Assertions to Evolve a Therapeutic Language

Effective feedback relies strongly on the clinician's ability to translate the theoretical language of the MCMI-IV into more personalized, descriptive ideas that engage the examinee, but an instrument that directly suggests diagnostic categories often encourages a less than sensitive, immediate description of labels. A rather matter-of-fact and less sensitive clinician, for example, may describe a single elevation on Scale 3 (Dependent) as, "These elevations reflect how you may be similar to, [or 'responded similarly to', in more collaborative terms] dependent individuals." Using a translated form of the theory's Motivating Aims, however, opens the possibility of a more helpful, disarming, and therapeutic dialogue. Using theoretical language to construct a more descriptive feedback, this client would likely benefit from this information delivered along the lines of, "You tend to take, [or more collaboratively, 'You responded similarly to people who take . . . '], a more passive role in relationships, often relying on others to provide direction and a sense of safety." By focusing on the dynamic within this personality structure that pulls strongly on the passive and other evolutionary polarities, the clinician is able to communicate the manifestation of the dependent personality without overemphasizing the categorical label.

After considering information gleaned from the highest scale elevations and examining their theoretical (polarity) structure, a next step will be to describe several personality scales in context with one another. It may be useful, once again, to consider the color wheel analogy. By combining prototypal personality patterns ("primary colors"), you may then derive a much wider spectrum of secondary colors and further admixtures (multiple scale elevations creating "subtypes"). This begins, however, with considering the relative contribution of each prototypal pattern.

When describing the personality expression of one specific scale, it may be helpful to preface or explain certain findings by using language such as, "If this said everything about you . . . but it, of course, doesn't." Examiners should be mindful of occurrences when evolutionary polarities may align, complement, or conflict with each other. During those instances, it may be helpful to inform the examinee that, "at times, these tendencies may balance each other out, but other times, you may find yourself feeling stuck or caught up in an attempt to find what way of being works best for you in a given moment." Assuming the results are valid and that there is at least a modicum of openness about this person's interpersonal concerns, the examinee is then invited to respond, explore, and reconsider means of dealing with environmental challenges.

This building-block process of understanding and subsequently relating MCMI-IV information to the examinee in a manner that builds a therapeutic alliance continues with integration of the Grossman Facet Scales. The facet score data provide descriptions from the eight functional and structural domains of the fifteen primary personality scales. Remember, too, that the facet scales correspond to the three most salient personologic domains for each prototypal patterns and that different facet configurations across elevated scales will yield valuable information related to focused areas of personologic concern.

Another way to further link facet score findings to more practical utility for an examinee is to help them understand which approaches to psychotherapy may best suit their unique personality pattern composition and to explain some basic tenets of the approaches that emerge. The major therapeutic schools of thought (e.g., cognitive, behavioral, interpersonal, intrapsychic) logically correspond to the functional/structural domains of personality and, therefore, information gleaned from the facet scales. This information lends a degree of comfort to the examinee in that the data points not only relate to the explanation of personal characteristics but are further linked to means of mental health improvement.

SUMMARY

The fourth edition of the Millon Clinical Multiaxial Inventory continues a tradition of examining personality from an integration of theory and empirical methodologies rarely still seen in a rapidly changing personality assessment field that is now largely favoring dimensional constructs over the problematic categories of neo-Kraepelin psychiatry. However, as may be evident from the foregoing, its constructs, while adhering to the still-active DSM-5 categorical model, also feature rich dimensional elements. Future research, integral to the continued viability of the instrument in terms of changing assessment paradigms as well as diversity concerns, may reveal considerable overlap with some proposed alternative models, while retaining what Millon believed to be an integral perspective: that of cross-assessing long-standing personality variables to contextualize current symptomology of mental health service seekers.

REFERENCES

Ackerman, S. J., Hilsenroth, M. J., Bairy, M. R., & Blagys, M. D. (2000). Interaction of therapeutic process and alliance during psychological assessment. *Journal of Personality Assessment, 75* (1), 82–109.

American Psychiatric Association. (1980). *Diagnostic and statistical manual of mental disorders* (3rd ed.). Washington, DC: Author.

American Psychiatric Association. (1994). *Diagnostic and statistical manual of mental disorders* (4th ed.). Washington, DC: Author.

American Psychiatric Association. (2013). *Diagnostic and Statistical Manual of Mental Disorders* (5th ed.). Washington, DC: Author.

Ben-Porath, Y., & Tellegen, A. (2008). *MMPI-2-RF manual for administration, scoring and interpretation*. Minneapolis: University of Minnesota Press.

Choca, J. P. (2004). *Interpretive guide to the Millon Clinical Multiaxial Inventory* (3rd ed.). Washington, DC: American Psychological Association.

Choca, J. P., & Grossman, S. (2015). Evolution of the Millon Clinical Multiaxial Inventory. *Journal of Personality Assessment, 97*, 541–549.

Craig, R. J. (1999). Overview and status of the Millon Clinical Multiaxial Inventory. *Journal of Personality Assessment, 72*, 390–406.

Derogatis, L. (1993). *Brief Symptom Inventory (BSI) manual*. Minneapolis, MN: National Computer Systems.

Freeman, R. C., Lewis, Y. P., & Colon, H. M. (2002). Instrumentation, data collection, and analysis issues. In R. C. Freeman, Y.P. Lewis, & H. M. Colon (Eds.). *Handbook for conducting drug abuse research with Hispanic populations* (pp. 167–188). Westport, CT: Praeger.

Grossman, S. D. (2004). Facets of personality: A proposal for the development of MCMI-III content scales (Doctoral Dissertation, Carlos Albizu University, 2004). *Dissertation Abstracts International, 65*, 5401.

Grossman, S. D. (2015). Millon's evolutionary model of personality assessment: A case for categorical/dimensional prototypes. *Journal of Personality Assessment, 97*, 436–445.

Grossman, S., & Amendolace, B. (2017). *Essentials of MCMI-IV Assessment*. Hoboken, NJ: Wiley.

Hoyle, R. H. (1991). Evaluating measurement models in clinical research: Covariance structure analysis of latent variable models of self-conception. *Journal of Consulting and Clinical Psychology, 59*, 67–76.

Jamison, K. A. (2005). *Exuberance (The passion for life)*. New York: Knopf.

Klein, D. N., Schwartz, J. E., Rose, S., & Leader, J. B. (2000). Five-year course and outcome of dysthymic disorder: A prospective, naturalistic follow-up study. *American Journal of Psychiatry, 157*, 931–939.

Kraepelin, E. (1921). *Manic-depressive insanity and paranoia*. Edinburgh: Livingstone.

Millon, T. (1969). *Modern Psychopathology*. Philadelphia, PA: Saunders.

Millon, T. (1977). *Millon Clinical Multiaxial Inventory*. Minneapolis, MN: National Computer Systems.

Millon, T. (1990). *Toward a new personology: An evolutionary model*. New York: Wiley.

Millon, T. (1999). *Personality-guided therapy*. New York: Wiley.

Millon, T. (2002). A blessed and charmed personal odyssey. *Journal of Personality Assessment*, *79*, 171–194.

Millon, T. (2011). *Disorders of personality: Introducing a DSM-ICD spectrum from normal to abnormal*. Hoboken, NJ: Wiley.

Millon, T., & Davis, R. D. (1996). *Disorders of personality: DSM-IV and beyond*. New York: Wiley.

Millon, T., Davis, R., Millon, C., & Grossman, S. (2009). *Millon Clinical Multiaxial Inventory-III manual* (4th ed.). Minneapolis, MN: NCS Pearson Assessments.

Millon, T., & Grossman, S. D. (2007a). *Resolving difficult clinical syndromes: A personalized psychotherapy approach*. Hoboken, NJ: Wiley.

Millon, T., & Grossman, S. D. (2007b). Overcoming resistant personality disorders: *A personalized psychotherapy approach*. Hoboken, NJ: Wiley.

Millon, T., & Grossman, S. D. (2007c). Moderating severe personality disorders: *A personalized psychotherapy approach*. Hoboken, NJ: Wiley.

Millon, T., Grossman, S., & Millon, C. (2015). *Millon Clinical Multiaxial Inventory-IV manual*. Minneapolis, MN: Pearson Assessments.

Millon, T., Grossman, S., Millon, C., Meagher, S., & Ramnath, R. (2004). *Personality disorders in modern life*. Hoboken, NJ: Wiley.

Piotrowski, C., & Keller, J. W. (1989). Psychological testing in outpatient mental health facilities: A national study. *Professional Psychology: Research and Practice*, *20*, 423–425.

Piotrowski, C., & Lubin, B. (1989). Assessment practices of Division 38 practitioners. *Health Psychologist*, *11*, 1.

Piotrowski, C., & Lubin, B. (1990). Assessment practices of health psychologists: Survey of APA Division 38 clinicians. *Professional Psychology: Research and Practice*, *21*, 99–106.

Retzlaff, P. D. (1995). Clinical Application of the MCMI-III. In P. D. Retzlaff (Ed.), *Tactical psychotherapy of the personality disorders: An MCMI-III approach* (pp. 1–23). Needham, MA: Allyn & Bacon.

Rossi, G., Van den Brande, L, Tobac, A., Sloore, H., & Hauben, C. (2003). Convergent validity of the MCMI-III personality disorder scales and the MMPI-2 scales. *Journal of Personality Disorders*, *17*, 330–340.

Somwaru, D. P., & Ben-Porath, Y. S. (1995). *Development and reliability of MMPI-2 based personality disorder scales*. Paper presented at the 30th Annual Workshop and Symposium on Recent Developments in Use of the MMPI-2 &MMPI-A, St. Petersburg Beach, FL.

Suarez-Morales, L., & Beitra, D. (2013). Assessing substance-related disorders in Hispanic clients. In L. T. Benuto (Ed.), *Guide to psychological assessment with Hispanics* (pp. 163–181). New York: Springer.

Wetzler, S. (1990). The Millon Clinical Multiaxial Inventory (MCMI): A review. *Journal of Personality Assessment*, *55*, 445–464.

19 Self-Report Scales for Common Mental Disorders

An Overview of Current and Emerging Methods

MATTHEW SUNDERLAND, PHILIP BATTERHAM, ALISON CALEAR, AND NATACHA CARRAGHER

Self-report scales that measure the severity of common mental disorders (e.g., unipolar depression and anxiety disorders) based on subjective signs and symptoms have formed the cornerstone of assessment in clinical psychology and psychiatry for many years. The large degree of heterogeneity and subjective nature of symptoms associated with mental disorders necessitates high-quality self-report measures to validly capture these experiences and inform diagnosis, assist with treatment decisions, and facilitate patient monitoring and assessment of outcomes. Indeed, studies have identified poor to moderate correlations between self-report and informant-report measures of psychopathology, which may reflect different but clinically important and meaningful information about how one views their own behaviors and experiences versus how others perceive them (Achenbach et al., 2005). These findings have been expanded to self-report and clinician-rated scales, with the results suggesting that both self-report and clinician-rated versions of the same instrument provide unique information toward the prediction of depression treatment outcomes (Uher et al., 2012; Zimmerman et al., 2018). Accordingly, the importance of self-report instruments has been increasingly recognized in clinical research and practice, with ongoing efforts seeking to combine unique self-report information with complementary clinician or informant-rated scales, and cognitive and neurobiological measures to create a broader picture of psychopathology (Venables et al., 2018; Yancey, Venables, & Patrick, 2016).

Self-report instruments for mental disorders represent the most cost-effective and time-efficient method for obtaining large amounts of data when compared to other forms of assessment, such as clinician-rated or observational data. This is particularly pertinent when considering self-administered forms of self-report data, which are highly amendable to automated data collection and online administration. A recent systematic review of studies examining the online administration of existing scales for mental disorders found mounting evidence for adequate psychometric properties relative to pen-and-paper administration, with studies testing the Center for Epidemiologic Studies – Depression Scale (CES-D), the Montgomery-Asberg Depression Rating Scale Self Report (MADRS-S), and the Hospital Anxiety and Depression Scale (HADS) (van Ballegooijen et al., 2016). These findings suggest that social media, online research panels, and crowdsourcing internet marketplaces (e.g., Amazon's Mechanical Turk) can be used to validly and efficiently obtain data on common mental disorders, which allows researchers to better target low prevalence disorders or hard-to-reach populations and provides increased power to detect significant interactions and comorbid relationships (Batterham, 2014; Cunningham, Godinho, & Kushnir, 2017; Kosinski et al., 2015; Thornton et al., 2016). Similarly, online/electronic integration of self-report instruments and automated treatment decisions form the core components of emerging computer-based person-centered tailored treatments and assessment-based care, which have demonstrated better patient outcomes in comparison to standard care (T. Guo et al., 2015; Scott & Lewis, 2015).

Despite the above advantages and increased utility of self-report scales, threats to validity and specific response patterns have long been discussed in the literature, with researchers consistently questioning the veracity of self-report data. Threats to validity and nonoptimal response strategies are particularly pertinent in settings where external incentives exist to misrepresent oneself, such as clinical, public health, or hospital settings where a diagnosis is often required to receive treatment or for health insurance coverage. However, it should be noted that these potential biases are not limited to self-report scales and can influence other clinical assessments, given that symptoms of mental disorders are rarely observable and rely on subjective reports regardless of the assessment modality. Some key examples of nonoptimal response patterns include socially desirable responding (both "faking good" to appear in a normal positive light and "faking bad" to appear in a negative light as a mechanism for receiving enhanced or expedited treatment or avoiding such treatment) (Paulhus, 2002); acquiescent responding (the tendency to automatically agree with statements without regard to content); extreme responding (the tendency to generate floor or ceiling effects) (Paulhus & Vazire, 2007); inaccurate or invalid data due to limitations in self-knowledge or a lack of insight; limited levels of mental health literacy (Streiner & Norman, 2008); poor cognitive capacity (particularly for children, individuals with comorbid severe mental illness, or older adults with cognitive impairment); problems with recall (particularly for lifetime-based self-report scales) (Takayanagi et al., 2014); and cultural differences in self-report resulting in biased responses (Hamamura, Heine, & Paulhus, 2008).

A plethora of studies have demonstrated that different types of response styles can have large effects on both individual scores and the psychometric validity of self-report scales in mental health. For example, Conijn, van der Ark, and Spinhoven (2017) recently examined nonoptimal response strategies to self-report questionnaires using data from the Netherlands Study of Depression and Anxiety. Their results indicated that respondents with anxiety or comorbid anxiety and depression were more likely to use nonoptimal response strategies, according to satisficing indicators on the NEO Five-Factor Inventory, in comparison to healthy respondents. Conijn, van der Ark, and Spinhoven (2017) concluded that, in their sample, nonoptimal response strategies were common and therefore the quality of the data in mental health care requires further attention. However, quantifying the impact of response bias on a specific population can be difficult, with studies showing that the effects of response styles can vary dramatically according to the specific nature of the self-report scale (and what the scale purports to measures) as well as the match between the individual patient characteristics/personality, scale content, and context of use (Chan, 2009; Plieninger, 2017). Furthermore, many widely used scales to measure self-reported symptoms of depression and anxiety (particularly those discussed in the current chapter) do not include built-in mechanisms, such as validity scales commonly used in personality tests, to measure the possibility of nonoptimal response styles and therefore adjust individual results accordingly. In any case, it is clear from the existing literature that additional research on the issue of nonoptimal response styles and the influence of bias on data obtained from self-report scales of mental disorders is warranted.

In addition to nonoptimal response styles, the issue of cross-cultural bias inherent in self-report scales for mental disorders has received increasing attention. Most widely used scales that measure mental disorders have been developed and primarily validated in high-income Western populations (e.g., North America, Europe, Australia) and therefore assume a Western understanding of mental disorders and symptoms, as exemplified in the American Psychiatric Association's *Diagnostic and Statistical Manual of Mental Disorders* (DSM) or the International Classification of Diseases (ICD) by the World Health Organization (WHO). The practice of utilizing Western-developed scales across diverse cultural and ethnic populations is widespread. For example, a review of 183 published studies on the mental health status of refugees indicated that 78 percent of the findings were based on instruments that were not developed or tested specifically in refugee populations (Hollifield et al., 2002). To investigate the potential extent of this bias, Haroz and colleagues (2017) reviewed 138 qualitative studies of depression reflecting seventy-seven different nationalities and ethnicities. Of the fifteen most frequently mentioned features of depression across non-Western populations, only seven reflect DSM criteria for major depression, whereas other features, including social isolation, general pain, and headaches, are typically missing in existing scales. The findings of Haroz and colleagues (2017) suggest that scales developed using a DSM model of mental disorders may not accurately capture the varied cross-cultural perceptions of depression or may measure an alternate construct of depression not widely accepted by all cultures. Any comparisons drawn between cultures may be inaccurate or inappropriate. In short, there is a pressing need for culturally specific scales developed using a bottom-up and open-ended approach or at the very least a greater degree of local adaptation and testing of existing scales across different cultures and ethnicities.

Notwithstanding the above limitations, self-report scales investigating psychopathology continue to be widely used in research and clinical settings. As such, the current chapter aims to provide a broad overview of existing, widely used, self-report scales for assessing the presence and frequency of symptoms of depression and anxiety. This overview will focus on some of the more widely used scales in research and clinical settings with specific reference to their psychometric properties and cross-cultural applicability. This overview is followed by a discussion of emerging methods that apply modern psychometric techniques to develop the next generation of self-report scales, with the aim of improving the reliability, validity, and comparability of self-report data, while minimizing respondent burden and increasing efficiency via electronic administration.

OVERVIEW OF EXISTING SELF-REPORT SCALES FOR DEPRESSION AND ANXIETY

Numerous self-report scales exist that measure common mental disorders such as depression and anxiety, too many to provide a comprehensive overview for each mental disorder in the space of this chapter. As such, a brief overview of some of the most widely used scales for depression and anxiety and their psychometric properties will be provided (brief details of each scale are provided in Table 19.1), as well as a discussion of self-report scales that measure the presence and frequency of symptoms of mental disorders outlined in the most recent fifth edition of the American Psychiatric Association's *Diagnostic and Statistical Manual of Mental Disorders* (DSM-5; American Psychiatric Association, 2013). References to recent

Table 19.1 Summary of included self-report scales to measure depression and anxiety

Scale	Abbreviation	Total Number of Items	Key Published Psychometric Study/ies	Brief Description	Reliability
Depression					
Center for Epidemiologic Studies – Depression Scale	CES-D	20	(Carleton et al., 2013; Radloff, 1977)	A short scale created for measuring symptoms of depression in the general population. The scale asks respondents to endorse one of four options indicating how often they have experienced certain feelings and behaviors in the past week. Possible scores range from 0 to 60, with higher scores indicating more severe symptomology. Original analysis identified a four-factor structure comprising Depressed affect, Positive affect, Somatic and retarded activity, and Interpersonal factors, while more recent research supports a three-factor (Negative affect, Anhedonia, Somatic symptoms), fourteen-item model.	Internal consistency for several clinical and community samples ranges from $\alpha = 0.85$ to 0.94 (Carleton et al., 2013; Radloff, 1977) Test-retest reliability ranges from $r = 0.45$ to 0.70 (Radloff, 1977)
Beck Depression Inventory-II	BDI-II	21	(Dozois, Dobson, & Ahnberg, 1998; Wang et al., 2013)	The most recent version of the BDI, the BDI-II is a short scale for measuring depression severity, for ages 13–80. The scale asks respondents to endorse one of four statements indicating increasing severity of key depression symptoms experienced in the past two weeks. The inventory can be used for assessing those with existing diagnoses as well as for detecting depression in the general population. Possible scores range from 0 to 63, with higher scores indicating increased severity. A two-factor structure of the scale has been identified, comprising Cognitive-affective and Somatic-vegetative factors.	Internal consistency ranges from $\alpha = 0.83$ to 0.96 (Wang et al., 2013) Test-retest reliability ranges from $r = 0.73$ to 0.96 (Wang et al., 2013)
Patient Health Questionnaire-9	PHQ-9	10 (9 +1)	(Chilcot et al., 2013; El-Den, Chen, Gan, Wong, & O'Reilly, 2018; Granillo, 2012; B. Guo et al., 2017; Kroenke et al., 2001; E. J. Richardson & Richards, 2008)	A brief scale assessing depressive symptoms experienced in the past two weeks. The scale is administered in primary care settings and can be used for both detecting depression and assessing severity. The scale asks respondents to endorse one of four options indicating how frequently they are troubled by nine depression-related problems. Possible scores range from 0 to 27, with higher scores indicating increased severity. A tenth question (applicable to those who indicated experiencing any depression-related problems) asks about the impact of those problems on daily life and contributes when using the scale to detect depression. While a one-factor structure has been identified, more recent studies support a two-factor model composed of Affective and Somatic factors.	Internal consistency ranges from $\alpha = 0.67$ to 0.91 in primary health care settings (El-Den et al., 2018). Test-retest reliability in primary health care settings ranges from $r = 0.84$ to 0.94 (El-Den et al., 2018).
Anxiety					
Generalized Anxiety Disorder-7	GAD-7	8 (7 + 1)	(Löwe et al., 2008; Spitzer et al., 2006)	A brief clinical scale used for screening and severity assessment of Generalized Anxiety Disorder. The scale asks respondents to endorse one of four options indicating the frequency of seven anxiety-related problems experienced in the past two weeks. Possible scores range from 0 to 21, with higher scores indicating increased severity. An eighth item (applicable to those who indicated experiencing any anxiety-related problems) asks respondents to select the level of interpersonal difficulty they have experienced. Research supports a unidimensional structure for the scale.	Internal consistency has been reported as $\alpha = 0.89$ and 0.92 (Löwe et al., 2008; Spitzer et al., 2006). Test-retest reliability has been reported as $r = 0.83$ (Spitzer et al., 2006).

Continued

Table 19.1 (cont.)

Beck Anxiety Inventory	BAI	21	(Beck et al., 1988; Creamer, Foran, & Bell, 1995; Fydrich, Dowdall, & Chambless, 1992; Osman, Kopper, Barrios, Osman, & Wade, 1997)	A scale for measuring clinical anxiety, designed to minimize confounding with depression. Respondents are asked to endorse one of four options indicating the severity of twenty-one anxiety-related symptoms experienced in the past month. Possible scores range from 0 to 63, with higher scores indicating increased severity. The original development paper describes two factors (Somatic and Subjective anxiety and panic), while other research supports a four-factor model (Subjective, Neurophysiological, Autonomic, and Panic).	Internal consistency ranges from $\alpha = 0.90$ to 0.94 (Beck et al., 1988; Creamer et al., 1995; Fydrich et al., 1992; Osman et al., 1997). Test-retest reliability ranges from $r = 0.62$ to 0.75 (Beck et al., 1988; Creamer et al., 1995; Fydrich et al., 1992).
State-Trait Anxiety Inventory	STAI	40	(Barnes, Harp, & Jung, 2002; Vigneau & Cormier, 2008)	A scale for measuring state (twenty items) and trait (twenty items) anxiety. Its most current version is known as Form Y. The scale asks respondents to endorse one of four options indicating the extent to which they currently (state items) or generally (trait items) experience a list of anxiety-related feelings. Possible scores range from 20 to 80, with higher scores indicating increased severity. Both a four-factor (State anxiety present, State anxiety absent, Trait anxiety present, State anxiety absent) and a two-construct, two-method model have been identified for the scale in its current form.	Internal consistency ranges from $\alpha = 0.65$ to 0.96 (state subscale) and $\alpha = 0.72$ to 0.96 (trait subscale) (Barnes et al., 2002). Test-retest reliability for the state subscale ranges from $r = 0.34$ to 0.96, and for the trait subscale ranges from $r = 0.82$ to 0.94 (Barnes et al., 2002).
Penn State Worry Questionnaire	PSWQ	16	(Brown, 2003; Fresco, Heimberg, Mennin, & Turk, 2002; Hazlett-Stevens, Ullman, & Craske, 2004; Meyer, Miller, Metzger, & Borkovec, 1990)	A scale for measuring the worry trait. The scale asks respondents to endorse one of five options indicating how typical of themselves they find certain anxiety-related statements. Possible scores range from 16 to 80, with higher scores indicating increased severity. Results are conflicting as to whether the scale is best represented by a unidimensional or two-factor structure.	Internal consistency was reported in the scale's development paper as $\alpha =$ 0.91–0.95 (Meyer et al., 1990). For various time intervals, test-retest reliability was reported in the scale's development paper as $r =$ 0.74 –0.93 (Meyer et al., 1990).
Worry Behaviors Inventory	WBI	10	(Mahoney et al., 2016; Mahoney, Hobbs, Newby, Williams, & Andrews, 2018)	A scale used to assess avoidant behaviors associated with GAD. Respondents are asked to endorse one of five options indicating how often they engage in a list of worry-related behaviors. Possible scores range from 0 to 40, with higher scores indicating increased severity. Factor analyses support a two-factor structure (Safety behaviors and Avoidance).	Internal consistency ranges from $\alpha = 0.83$ to 0.86 (Mahoney et al., 2016, 2018). Test-retest reliability has been reported as $r = 0.89$ (Mahoney et al., 2018).

reviews of scales for specific anxiety disorders will also be provided, so interested readers might use this section as a starting point when investigating suitable self-report scales for their own research or clinical work.

With respect to depression, the CES-D (Radloff, 1977) is one of the most widely used and validated scales to measure symptom frequency across different settings, age groups, gender, and those with poor distress and physical ill health (Eaton et al., 2004). Despite the widespread use, the CES-D has several potential shortcomings. A review of the literature identified inconsistent support for more than twenty alternative factor solutions since the scale was first published (Carleton et al., 2013). Moreover, researchers have questioned the appropriateness of the CES-D when informing diagnostic decisions or screening for depression, with revisions and short form versions aiming to reduce the overall length and improve the diagnostic and case-finding properties of the original CES-D (Björgvinsson et al., 2013; Santor & Coyne, 1997). Despite the CES-D having been translated into multiple languages, there is mixed support for cross-cultural invariance of the factor structure across Latino and Anglo-American populations (Crockett et al., 2005; Posner et al., 2001). Similarly, Asian and Armenian populations exhibit a different factor structure, yield higher depressive symptom scores, and exhibit a tendency to over-endorse positive affect items in comparison to Anglo-Americans (Demirchyan, Petrosyan, & Thompson, 2011; Iwata & Buka, 2002). These observed cross-cultural differences have the potential to significantly influence the diagnostic accuracy of the CES-D for some cultures, as demonstrated in a study comparing Korean and Anglo-American older adults (Lee et al., 2011).

The second edition of the Beck Depression Inventory (BDI-II), like the CES-D, is one of the most widely used scales to detect and assess the severity of depression. In contrast to the CES-D, revisions were made to the twenty-one items of the original BDI to better align them with the DSM-IV diagnostic criteria for major depression (Beck et al., 1996). A comprehensive review of the psychometric literature of the BDI-II has indicated good reliability, evidence to support concurrent and discriminant validity, a strong general factor according to bifactor models, and sufficient diagnostic properties as a first-stage screening tool (McElroy et al., 2018; Wang et al., 2013). Among clinical inpatients, the BDI-II has good psychometric properties and a consistent factor structure but exhibits poor diagnostic properties when screening for depression, suggesting that in clinical populations the use of the BDI-II may be limited to assessing symptom severity and monitoring changes to depressive symptomatology (Subica et al., 2014). The BDI-II has been translated into multiple languages, with studies demonstrating acceptable and comparable psychometric properties as the original English version (Ghassemzadeh et al., 2005; Kojima et al., 2002; Wiebe & Penley, 2005). Despite good psychometric properties, some limitations restrict the use of the BDI-II in everyday clinical settings, including: copyright restrictions, cost per use, and its length (at twenty-one items). There is also mixed support for the measurement equivalence of the BDI-II across cultures. Byrne and colleagues (2007) provided sound evidence of measurement equivalence of the BDI-II factorial structures across Hong Kong and American adolescents. Similarly, Dere and colleagues (2015) found evidence of strong measurement equivalence across Chinese-heritage and European-heritage students on the BDI-II. In contrast, Nuevo and colleagues (2009) could not find evidence to support measurement equivalence across five European countries, with the greatest bias associated with the Spanish sample and only eight items exhibiting nonsignificant bias. Likewise, a large degree of bias was found in twelve of the BDI-II items across Turkish and US college student samples (Canel-Çınarbaş, Cui, & Lauridsen, 2011). These findings suggest that it may be inappropriate to assume that the BDI-II mean scores can be compared across different cultures without first examining the extent and potential impact of bias.

The Patient Health Qustionnaire-9 (PHQ-9) is a widely used alternative to the BDI-II given it is a brief, easy to administer, free to use scale that directly maps onto the DSM-IV and DSM-5 symptom criteria for major depressive disorder (Kroenke, Spitzer, & Williams, 2001). The PHQ-9 has acceptable diagnostic screening properties across various clinical settings, age groups, and cultures/ethnicities (Huang et al., 2006; Manea, Gilbody, & McMillan, 2012; Moriarty et al., 2015; L. P. Richardson et al., 2010). A recent meta-analysis of the sensitivity and specificity of case-finding instruments for a clinical diagnosis of DSM major depression indicated the PHQ-9 with a cutoff of ten demonstrated on average the highest sensitivity and specificity relative to the BDI-II, CES-D, and the HADS (Pettersson et al., 2015). Another systematic review of screening tools for depression across low- and middle-income countries found that the PHQ-9 performed well in student samples but performed poorly in several clinical samples with lower than average education, suggesting that caution is required when using the PHQ-9 as a screening tool in middle to low income countries with low levels of literacy (Ali, Ryan, & De Silva, 2016).

The close alignment between the PHQ-9 and the DSM has resulted in criticisms that can be applied to both, including the possibility that the nine symptoms of depression measure a different, more constrained construct of depression, relative to longer scales, or that the PHQ-9 neglects to measure important symptoms and features of depression experienced by non-Western cultures (Haroz et al., 2017; McGlinchey et al., 2006). As such, scales with more constrained symptom sets, like the PHQ-9, have the potential to differ significantly in their distribution of patients categorized as "severe" relative to other lengthier scales or across different cultures and ethnicities (Zimmerman et al., 2012). Furthermore, new findings from a burgeoning line of self-report symptom-based research have led some researchers to conclude that the use of single sum-scores and clinical cutoffs to estimate a proxy diagnosis of major depression may obfuscate crucial clinical insights and scientific progress in depression research (Fried, 2017; Fried & Nesse, 2015). Moving forward, Fried and Nesse (2015) have recommended the use of multiple depression scales to generate robust and generalizable conclusions; utilize scales that include important non-DSM symptoms (e.g., the Symptoms of Depression Questionnaire; Pedrelli et al., 2014); distinguish between sub-symptoms, such as insomnia and hypersomnia, rather than assessing broad sleep problems; and increase the precision and reliability of symptom measurement.

With respect to anxiety (or broad/generalized anxiety), the seven-item Generalized Anxiety Disorder (GAD-7) scale has demonstrated substantial promise as a severity measure for DSM-defined GAD, given strong psychometric properties and the brief and easy to use nature of the scale (Spitzer et al., 2006). The GAD-7 and a modified version of the GAD-7 covering symptoms experienced in the past twenty-four hours have also demonstrated good internal consistency, convergent validity, and sensitivity to change in a sample of patients receiving treatment for anxiety disorders (Beard & Björgvinsson, 2014). The modified twenty-four-hour version shows promise for use in studies that collect intensive longitudinal data to model dynamic relationships across symptoms. However, the GAD-7 performed quite poorly as a diagnostic screener for anxiety disorders, particularly within the subgroup of patients with social anxiety disorder (Beard & Björgvinsson, 2014). The GAD-7 has been successfully translated into multiple languages and local dialects but relatively few studies have examined the GAD-7 specifically for cross-cultural bias. One study identified a consistent factor structure across White/Caucasian, Hispanic, and Black/African American undergraduates; however, differential item functioning analysis revealed that Black/African American participants tended to score lower on the GAD-7 in comparison to other participants despite being matched in terms of mean latent GAD severity. This bias was most evident among items examining nervousness, restlessness, and irritability (Parkerson et al., 2015).

Like the PHQ-9, the close alignment of the GAD-7 with the DSM criteria may limit coverage of the targeted construct relative to other, more comprehensive scales, such as the Beck Anxiety Inventory (BAI) or the State-Trait Anxiety Inventory (STAI) (Beck et al., 1988; Spielberger, Gorsuch, & Lushene, 1970). Both scales have solid psychometric properties established by numerous studies although both have copyright restrictions and costs for administration that may restrict implementation (Bardhoshi, Duncan, & Erford, 2016). The BAI and STAI have been shown to target broader definitions of anxiety that also include somatic and panic-like symptoms as well as trait-like anxious-distress or negative affectivity. The STAI, in particular, has been criticized as targeting multiple factors, including depression and well-being, due to item overlap (Caci et al., 2003). Moreover, the general and broad nature of these anxiety scales, much like the GAD-7, can result in a lack of specificity to assess anxiety symptom severity or screen for a diagnosis of other anxiety disorders, such as social anxiety disorder (Kabacoff et al., 1997; Muntingh et al., 2011). In terms of assessing GAD, the BAI focuses more on somatic symptoms (heart racing, dizziness) of anxiety as a means of reducing the overlap with depression, but this focus has been shown to increase the propensity of overlap with other physical aspects of medical conditions and neglects to include key symptoms of worry and ruminative aspects of anxiety (Morin et al., 1999).

The Penn State Worry Questionnaire (PSWQ) is a widely used scale to measure the trait-like tendency toward excessive worry that has been shown to adequately differentiate between GAD and other anxiety disorders (D. M. Fresco et al., 2003). More recently, attention has been directed toward the measurement of additional behavioral features associated with GAD, such as subtle and varied forms of situational avoidance and safety behaviors, to complement cognitive and somatic symptoms (Beesdo-Baum, Jenjahn, et al., 2012). The Worry Behavior Inventory has been developed for this purpose, with preliminary analyses demonstrating good psychometric properties in research and clinical settings (Mahoney et al., 2016). Yet, like all scales of GAD or broad anxiety, there is an ongoing need for research examining cross-cultural differences associated with symptom presentation or alternative/additional symptoms of anxiety. With respect to the measurement of specific anxiety disorders, multiple scales are freely available and widely used but, given space constraints, interested readers are referred to literature reviews that address self-report scales for panic disorder/agoraphobia (Bouchard et al., 1997), social anxiety disorder (Wong, Gregory, & McLellan, 2016), post-traumatic stress disorder (PTSD) (Sijbrandij et al., 2013), obsessive-compulsive disorder (Overduin & Furnham, 2012), and suicidal thoughts and behaviors (Batterham, Ftanou, et al., 2015).

In recent years, the American Psychiatric Association has gradually moved toward dimensional approaches to measurement in comparison to the long-standing categorical structure of the DSM. In response to this shift, they have encouraged the use of several self-report severity scales for mental disorders. These include cross-cutting symptom measures for broad depression and anxiety but also existing and newly developed scales for specific disorders, such as separation anxiety disorder, specific phobia, social anxiety disorder, panic disorder, agoraphobia, GAD, PTSD, acute stress symptoms, and dissociative symptoms.[1] Despite a few notable exceptions (Beesdo-

[1] All freely available from the American Psychiatric Association website: www.psychiatry.org

Baum, Klotsche, et al., 2012; Knappe et al., 2014; LeBeau, Mesri, & Craske, 2016; Möller & Bögels, 2016), the psychometric properties of these scales have yet to be extensively tested and replicated, particularly with respect to tracking and monitoring severity over time in clinical settings. Yet the widespread use of these scales may further encourage the migration from a strictly categorical-diagnostic approach to a more dimensional-symptom–driven approach to the measurement of psychopathology, which has seen increasing attention in the recent literature (Kotov et al., 2017).

EMERGING METHODS IN SELF-REPORT SCALE DEVELOPMENT AND ADMINISTRATION

The widely used instruments outlined in the previous section reflect a standard pen-and-paper approach with simple sum-scoring (based on classical test theory) to quantify the degree of disorder severity. Pen-and-paper instruments have been converted to electronic administration while maintaining the simple sum-scoring approach, with some success (van Ballegooijen et al., 2016). However, advances in psychometric models, computational statistics, and computer testing have heralded a significant array of novel developments associated with the administration and scoring of self-report scales. These developments rely heavily on the application of modern psychometric methods, including item response theory (IRT), to improve the validity, accuracy, comparability, and efficiency of mental health scales (Caspi et al., 2014). These new methods have also shown substantial promise in the advanced analysis of cross-cultural differences through IRT-based differential item functioning as well as the use of item anchoring or equating to adjust for any significant bias (Dere et al., 2015; Gibbons & Skevington, 2018; Vaughn-Coaxum, Mair, & Weisz, 2016). Similarly, new IRT models have emerged that can estimate and correct for extreme response styles more effectively than classical methods and quantify the tendency of extreme responding on a particular scale (Dowling et al., 2016; Jin & Wang, 2014). In the following sections, we focus on three applications of modern test theory to the self-report assessment of mental disorders: *item banking*, *adaptive testing and data-driven short scales*, and *scale equating*. We outline the strengths and some current criticisms of these techniques and highlight future directions for research.

Item Banking

An item bank is a large collection of questions or symptoms that represent the manifestation of a latent construct, disorder, or trait. The key difference between item banks and classical symptom scales is the application of IRT models to generate information about the statistical relationship between a person's underlying disorder severity score (or latent trait score) and the probability of endorsing a particular response option on each of the symptom indicators (i.e., the item parameters) (Embretson & Reise, 2000). Determining the values for these parameters and the associated severity scores is known as *calibration*. The unique properties of IRT make it possible to generate severity scores that are comparable across different respondents using any combination of items from the total bank, even when using two sets of completely different items (Cella et al., 2007). This advantage increases the flexibility of assessment by enabling the use of multiple short forms to better suit a variety of purposes or populations without compromising on precision or relevance, and providing a foundation for highly efficient, dynamic computerized adaptive tests (Lai et al., 2011). Moreover, item banks can facilitate the standardization of measurement by calibrating multiple scales onto a new joint metric (referred to as concurrent calibration; Wahl et al., 2014) or via equating scores from existing scales to that of a newly developed item bank metric (referred to as fixed calibration; Choi et al., 2014).

Item banks seek to substantially improve the relevance and content validity of traditional self-report symptom scales developed using classical test theory. Content validity is maximized by collating items and developing the bank using a systematic process that seeks to cover all aspects of the construct as well as address a wide range of severity. DeWalt and colleagues (2007), as part of their work on the Patient Reported Outcomes Measurement and Information System (PROMIS), outlined the steps required to develop an effective item bank that begins with first establishing comprehensive item pools and subjecting those items to extensive qualitative testing. These steps have since been utilized and extended by Batterham and colleagues (2015) to develop multiple items banks for common mental disorders. Data is obtained on the item pools and used to test the various assumptions of IRT models, including unidimensionality, local independence, and invariance across key sociodemographic characteristics (Batterham et al., 2016). Items that do not meet these requirements are removed from the final item banks, which are calibrated using an appropriate IRT model, commonly the graded response model (Samejima, 1997) or generalized partial credit response model (Muraki, 1992), to provide interpretable scores that are representative of the calibration sample.

Making use of this approach, researchers have developed a range of item banks that measure various mental disorders with more precision across the full spectrum of disorder severity relative to existing, widely used, scales. This includes item banks for major depressive disorder (Fliege et al., 2005; Forkmann et al., 2009; Gibbons et al., 2012; Pilkonis et al., 2011; Wahl et al., 2014), generalized anxiety disorder (Gibbons, Weiss, et al., 2014; Pilkonis et al., 2011; Walter et al., 2007), anger (Pilkonis et al., 2011), social anxiety disorder (Batterham et al., 2016), panic disorder (Batterham et al., 2016), obsessive-compulsive disorder (Batterham et al., 2016), PTSD (Batterham et al., 2016;

Del Vecchio et al., 2011), adult attention-deficit/hyperactivity disorder (Batterham et al., 2016), suicidal thoughts and behaviors (Batterham et al., 2016; R. Gibbons et al., 2017), psychosis (Batterham et al., 2016), self-harm (Latimer, Meade, & Tennant, 2014), and multiple facets of the externalizing spectrum (Krueger et al., 2007).

Despite the relative validity of item banks, controversies exist regarding the appropriate use of IRT models to calibrate item banks when measuring mental disorders, particularly regarding the use of unidimensional models. Croudace and Böhnke (2014) argued that the IRT unidimensional assumption may artificially restrict the item content representing heterogeneous mental disorders. They conclude that additional item banking studies would benefit from the application of multidimensional IRT models to better capture the true nature of mental health constructs. Indeed, Gibbons and colleagues (2012; Gibbons, Weiss et al., 2014) applied a specific multidimensional model, the bifactor model, to develop item banks for depression and anxiety. The bifactor model assumes that all items concurrently load on a single dimension accounting for common variance as well as at least one other subdimension accounting for specific variance across groups of related items (Gibbons et al., 2007). Gibbons and colleagues demonstrated that these models better represent the multidimensional nature of depression and anxiety in comparison to unidimensional models, with the added benefit of facilitating the use of very large item banks to better capture the full spectrum and multiple subdomains of mental disorders (Gibbons et al., 2016). While multidimensional models dramatically increase complexity, mental health assessment and clinical practice may ultimately benefit from integrating methods that better account for the nature and structure of mental disorders when examining the validity of new item banks (Batterham et al., 2016; Eisen et al., 2016). In particular, the development of item banks that incorporate new multidimensional and hierarchical frameworks of psychopathology informed by empirical evidence rather than the existing psychiatric classification systems may be of benefit (Kotov et al., 2017).

Computerized Adaptive Tests and Data-Driven Short Scales

As previously mentioned, a key advantage of IRT-based item banking is the ability to generate comparable scores using any subset of items contained within the item bank. This feature is critical to the operation of computerized adaptive tests (CAT) and fixed short scales, which seek to efficiently administer the item bank while maximizing precision and accuracy. CATs utilize the responses provided by the respondent to items at the beginning of the test to tailor the administration of subsequent items that better target the respondent's probable severity level. Only items relevant to the respondent's severity level are administered and more precise estimates are obtained without needlessly administering the full item bank (Embretson & Reise, 2000). For clinical applications, efficiency in assessment is paramount given the tight time pressures faced by clinicians. Lengthy assessment batteries are often seen as a major roadblock to the administration of evidenced-based assessments to inform diagnostic and treatment decisions (Gibbons et al., 2008). For research applications, the ability to assess multiple disorders in one efficient assessment battery can potentially reduce the probability of missing data and poor retention rates while facilitating data collection for intensive longitudinal analyses, such as ecological momentary assessments or ambulatory monitoring (Devine et al., 2016; Rose et al., 2012).

The efficiency of adaptive tests to assess mental disorders has been demonstrated extensively in simulation studies. Gibbons and colleagues (2012, 2014) demonstrated correlations of 0.95 and 0.94 between depression and anxiety scores across two twelve-item mean length CATs and the full item banks consisting of 389 items and 431 items, respectively. The administration time of the depression and anxiety CATs averaged 2.3 and 2.5 minutes, respectively. Similarly, Fliege and colleagues (2005) demonstrated that scores from a full bank of sixty-four items assessing depression could be replicated with a high degree of precision (standard error < 0.32) and high correlation ($r = 0.95$) using on average six items. Likewise, scores from a fifty-item measure of anxiety could be replicated with a high degree of precision ($SE < 0.32$) and accuracy ($r = 0.97$) using approximately six to eight items (Walter et al., 2007). Similar reductions in the mean number of items administered have been observed without significant decreases in reliability and precision associated with CAT administration of existing scales, such as the CES-D, the Mood and Anxiety Symptom Questionnaire, the Beck Scale for Suicide Ideation, and multiple facets of the Externalizing Spectrum Inventory (De Beurs et al., 2014; Flens et al., 2016; Smits, Cuijpers, & van Straten, 2011; Sunderland, Slade, et al., 2017).

Despite the substantial promise associated with CATs to improve the efficiency of mental health assessment, several criticisms have emerged regarding the use and implementation of CATs. Predominately, CATs involve an increased level of complexity associated with calibrating, recalibrating, and scoring the tests; they are restricted to electronic administration; and they involve additional costs associated with developing and ongoing maintenance of the item banks. Importantly, researchers have queried whether the gains offered by adaptive testing in terms of efficiency and precision outweigh the increased level of complexity, particularly when comparing scores from CATs to short static tests developed by selecting a small fixed subset of items with optimal IRT parameters.

Choi and colleagues (2010) compared the performance of adaptive and static short tests of similar length when assessing depression severity and concluded that the measurement precision of a static short test was almost as good as a CAT for respondents who fall within the middle to upper regions of the severity distribution. In contrast, the CAT provided considerably higher precision for respondent scores at the extreme ranges of severity in comparison to the short test. Interestingly, Choi and colleagues (2010) further demonstrated that a simpler two-stage semi-adaptive strategy could be applied to develop a short test that came very close to replicating the results of the CAT across the full severity distribution. The added benefit of using the simpler semi-adaptive test includes the ability to implement pen-and-paper administration in settings that are limited in the use of electronic tests. Similar results were found in a study by Sunderland, Batterham, and colleagues (2017), who developed and compared adaptive and static short tests that assess the severity of social anxiety disorder, obsessive-compulsive disorder, and panic disorder. Across the three disorders, the CATs generated marginally higher or similar correlations with scores from the full item banks and marginally higher precision across the severity continuum in comparison to static short tests of similar length (Sunderland, Batterham, et al., 2017). As such, the question of whether the incremental gains in precision and accuracy obtained by adaptive tests outweigh the increases in complexity relative to short static or semi-adaptive tests, particularly for clinical applications, requires further empirical investigation.

Self-Report Scale Equating

One major limitation in the field of mental health assessment is the lack of any standardized test that can objectively detect and monitor levels of psychopathology. A corollary of this lack of standardization has been the proliferation of multiple self-report scales that purportedly measure the same construct or disorder but differ in terms of their content, context, and psychometric rigor. This heterogeneity in measurement and a lack of a common metric have made it difficult to directly compare severity scores across multiple scales. One approach for improving the comparability of scores across self-report scales involves the use of various statistical techniques to equate scores on a common or unified metric, which adjusts for differences in relative severity across multiple scales (Dorans, 2007).

Item banking and IRT is again central to this endeavor. The approach requires a representative dataset and a single item bank that jointly calibrates items from two or more scales either concurrently (generating a new common metric informed by every item in the bank) or by fixing the metric to that of a single anchor scale (overlaying the scores of other scales onto the anchor scale). The item parameters that are estimated from either approach to joint calibration can be used to generate scores on the equated IRT metric using response data from any subset of items in the bank, including each subset of items that form the separate scales (Curran et al., 2008). Any existing or newly collected datasets that obtain responses from any of the previously equated scales can be re-scored on the equated IRT metric, forming a bridge between scales and allowing researchers to more accurately combine individual results with other re-scored datasets (Gibbons, Perraillon, & Kim, 2014).

Several noteworthy studies have equated self-report scales that measure specific mental disorders. Wahl and colleagues (2014) used a variant of concurrent calibration to equate fourteen scales from eleven separate measures of depression across multiple clinical and general population samples. Independent validation testing indicated that it was possible to accurately estimate latent depression scores on the common metric using PHQ-9 response data (Liegl et al., 2016). However, as mentioned previously, the use of a unidimensional IRT approach resulted in the exclusion of many items from the initial item bank, drawing into question the interpretability of the "common metric" and scores generated by this item bank (Croudace & Böhnke, 2014). Other approaches to item banking based on multidimensional IRT models may produce different, perhaps more valid results (Gibbons, Perraillon, et al., 2014).

Choi and colleagues (2014) used the alternative equating approach, fixed-parameter calibration, to equate three scales of depression, the CES-D, BDI-II, and PHQ-9, using the PROMIS depression item bank as the anchor scale to set the metric. Scores for this metric can be interpreted based on a normative sample representative of the US general population with a mean of fifty and standard deviation of ten. They found high correlations ($r > 0.83$) and low mean differences (0.21 to 0.36) between PROMIS depression scores estimated using the actual PROMIS item bank versus scores estimated using the equated CES-D, PHQ-9, and BDI-II items. Additionally, Gibbons and colleagues (2011) demonstrated the utility of equating existing legacy scales like the PHQ-9 on the PROMIS depression common metric to facilitate migration from fixed-form measures to CATs based on the PROMIS item banks described in the previous section. Finally, Schalet and colleagues (2014) equated three measures of anxiety, the Mood and Anxiety Symptom Questionnaire (MASQ), the Positive and Negative Affect Schedule (PANAS), and GAD-7, to the PROMIS anxiety item bank that generates a common metric for general anxious-distress. They again found high correlations ($r > 0.83$) and small mean differences (−0.07 to 0.16) when comparing actual PROMIS anxiety scores with equated anxiety scores using the MASQ, PANAS, and GAD-7.

CONCLUSIONS

There are a sizable number of self-report scales currently available that can be used to assess the diagnostic status and severity of common mental disorders, with some scales demonstrating better psychometric properties for more specific purposes or populations. Given the high degree of heterogeneity and the use of self-report scales across multiple applications, it is difficult to recommend one specific set of self-report scales over others. Clinicians and researchers need to ultimately weigh up the strengths and weaknesses of each scale with specific consideration to their research or clinical purpose and targeted population. Nevertheless, the application of modern psychometric methods, namely IRT and item banking, offers substantial improvements in the flexibility and utility of self-report scales, including the potential for greater integration of evidence-based frameworks of psychopathology and increased efficiency and standardization to overcome several barriers to implementation in clinical care. Self-report scales continue to provide unique information regarding the experience of mental disorders and the associated signs and symptoms. Moving forward, additional work is required to investigate the impact and adjust for cross-cultural differences and bias, as well as combining multiple self-report symptom scales with additional informant data and corresponding biological or cognitive-based measures to provide a more valid, comprehensive, and nuanced picture of psychopathology.

REFERENCES

Achenbach, T. M., Krukowski, R. A., Dumenci, L., & Ivanova, M. Y. (2005). Assessment of adult psychopathology: Meta-analyses and implications of cross-informant correlations. *Psychological Bulletin*, *131*(3), 361–382.

Ali, G.-C., Ryan, G., & De Silva, M. J. (2016). Validated screening tools for common mental disorders in low and middle income countries: A systematic review. *PLoS ONE*, *11*(6), e0156939. https://doi.org/10.1371/journal.pone.0156939

American Psychiatric Association. (2013). *Diagnostic and statistical manual of mental disorders* (5th ed.). Arlington, VA: American Psychiatric Publishing.

Bardhoshi, G., Duncan, K., & Erford, B. T. (2016). Psychometric meta-analysis of the English version of the Beck Anxiety Inventory. *Journal of Counseling and Development*, *94*(3), 356–373. https://doi.org/10.1002/jcad.12090

Barnes, L. L. B., Harp, D., & Jung, W. S. (2002). Reliability generalization of scores on the Spielberger State-Trait Anxiety Inventory. *Educational and Psychological Measurement*, *62*(4), 603–618. https://doi.org/10.1177/0013164402062004005

Batterham, P. J. (2014). Recruitment of mental health survey participants using Internet advertising: Content, characteristics and cost effectiveness. *International Journal of Methods in Psychiatric Research*, *23*(2), 184–191. https://doi.org/10.1002/mpr.1421

Batterham, P. J., Brewer, J. L., Tjhin, A., Sunderland, M., Carragher, N., & Calear, A. L. (2015). Systematic item selection process applied to developing item pools for assessing multiple mental health problems. *Journal of Clinical Epidemiology*, *68* (8), 913–919. https://doi.org/10.1016/j.jclinepi.2015.03.022

Batterham, P. J., Ftanou, M., Pirkis, J., Brewer, J. L., Mackinnon, A. J., Beautrais, A., ... Christensen, H. (2015). A systematic review and evaluation of measures for suicidal ideation and behaviors in population-based research. *Psychological Assessment*, *27*(2), 501–512. https://doi.org/10.1037/pas0000053

Batterham, P. J., Sunderland, M., Carragher, N., & Calear, A. L. (2016). Development and community-based validation of eight item banks to assess mental health. *Psychiatry Research*, *243*, 452–463. https://doi.org/10.1016/j.psychres.2016.07.011

Beard, C., & Björgvinsson, T. (2014). Beyond generalized anxiety disorder: Psychometric properties of the GAD-7 in a heterogeneous psychiatric sample. *Journal of Anxiety Disorders*, *28*(6), 547–552. https://doi.org/10.1016/J.JANXDIS.2014.06.002

Beck, A. T., Epstein, N., Brown, G., & Steer, R. A. (1988). An inventory for measuring clinical anxiety: Psychometric properties. *Journal of Consulting and Clinical Psychology*, *56*, 893–897.

Beck, A. T., Steer, R. A., Ball, R., & Ranieri, W. F. (1996). Comparison of Beck depression inventories -IA and -II in psychiatric outpatients. *Journal of Personality Assessment*, *67*(3), 588–597. https://doi.org/10.1207/s15327752jpa6703_13

Beesdo-Baum, K., Jenjahn, E., Höfler, M., Lueken, U., Becker, E. S., & Hoyer, J. (2012). Avoidance, safety behavior, and reassurance seeking in generalized anxiety disorder. *Depression and Anxiety*, *29*(11), 948–957. https://doi.org/10.1002/da.21955

Beesdo-Baum, K., Klotsche, J., Knappe, S., Craske, M. G., Lebeau, R. T., Hoyer, J., ... Wittchen, H. U. (2012). Psychometric properties of the dimensional anxiety scales for DSM-V in an unselected sample of German treatment seeking patients. *Depression and Anxiety*, *29*(12), 1014–1024. https://doi.org/10.1002/da.21994

Björgvinsson, T., Kertz, S. J., Bigda-Peyton, J. S., McCoy, K. L., & Aderka, I. M. (2013). Psychometric properties of the CES-D-10 in a psychiatric sample. *Assessment*, *20*(4), 429–436. https://doi.org/10.1177/1073191113481998

Bouchard, S., Pelletier, M.-H., Gauthier, J. G., Côté, G., & Laberge, B. (1997). The assessment of panic using self-report: A comprehensive survey of validated instruments. *Journal of Anxiety Disorders*, *11*(1), 89–111. https://doi.org/10.1016/S0887-6185(96)00037-0

Brown, T. A. (2003). Confirmatory factor analysis of the Penn State Worry Questionnaire: Multiple factors or method effects? *Behaviour Research and Therapy*, *41*, 1411–1426. https://doi.org/10.1016/S0005-7967(03)00059-7

Byrne, B. M., Stewart, S. M., Kennard, B. D., & Lee, P. W. H. (2007). The Beck Depression Inventory-II: Testing for measurement equivalence and factor mean differences across Hong Kong and American adolescents. *International Journal of Testing*, *7*(3), 293–309. https://doi.org/10.1080/15305050701438058

Caci, H., Baylé, F. J., Dossios, C., Robert, P., & Boyer, P. (2003). The Spielberger trait anxiety inventory measures more than anxiety. *European Psychiatry*, *18*(8), 394–400. https://doi.org/10.1016/J.EURPSY.2003.05.003

Canel-Çınarbaş, D., Cui, Y., & Lauridsen, E. (2011). Cross-cultural validation of the Beck Depression Inventory–II across U.S. and Turkish samples. *Measurement and Evaluation in Counseling and Development*, *44*(2), 77–91. https://doi.org/10.1177/0748175611400289

Carleton, R. N., Thibodeau, M. A., Teale, M. J. N., Welch, P. G., Abrams, M. P., Robinson, T., & Asmundson, G. J. G. (2013). The Center for Epidemiologic Studies Depression Scale: A review with a theoretical and empirical examination of item content and factor structure. *PLoS ONE*, *8*(3), e58067. https://doi.org/10.1371/journal.pone.0058067

Caspi, A., Houts, R. M., Belsky, D. W., Goldman-Mellor, S. J., Harrington, H., Israel, S., ... Moffitt, T. E. (2014). The p factor: One general psychopathology factor in the structure of psychiatric disorders? *Clinical Psychological Science: A Journal of the Association for Psychological Science*, *2*(2), 119–137. https://doi.org/10.1177/2167702613497473

Cella, D., Gershon, R., Lai, J.-S., & Choi, S. (2007). The future of outcomes measurement: Item banking, tailored short-forms, and computerized adaptive assessment. *Quality of Life Research*, *16*(S1), 133–141. https://doi.org/10.1007/s11136-007-9204-6

Chan, D. (2009). So why ask me? Are self-report data really that bad? In C. E. Lance & R. J. Vandenberg (Eds.), *Statistical and methodological myths and urban legends: Doctrine, verity and fable in organizational and social sciences* (pp. 309–336). New York: Routledge.

Chilcot, J., Rayner, L., Lee, W., Price, A., Goodwin, L., Monroe, B., ... Hotopf, M. (2013). The factor structure of the PHQ-9 in palliative care. *Journal of Psychosomatic Research*, *75* (1), 60–64. https://doi.org/10.1016/j.jpsychores.2012.12.012

Choi, S. W., Reise, S. P., Pilkonis, P. A., Hays, R. D., & Cella, D. (2010). Efficiency of static and computer adaptive short forms compared to full-length measures of depressive symptoms. *Quality of Life Research*, *19*(1), 125–136. https://doi.org/10.1007/s11136-009-9560-5

Choi, S. W., Schalet, B., Cook, K. F., & Cella, D. (2014). Establishing a common metric for depressive symptoms: Linking the BDI-II, CES-D, and PHQ-9 to PROMIS Depression. *Psychological Assessment*, *26*(2), 513–527. https://doi.org/10.1037/a0035768

Conijn, J. M., van der Ark, L. A., & Spinhoven, P. (2017). Satisficing in mental health care patients: The effect of cognitive symptoms on self-report data quality. *Assessment*. https://doi.org/10.1177/1073191117714557

Creamer, M., Foran, J., & Bell, R. (1995). The Beck Anxiety Inventory in a non-clinical sample. *Behaviour Research and Therapy*, *33*(4), 477–85.

Crockett, L. J., Randall, B. A., Shen, Y.-L., Russell, S. T., & Driscoll, A. K. (2005). Measurement equivalence of the Center for Epidemiological Studies Depression Scale for Latino and Anglo adolescents: A national study. *Journal of Consulting and Clinical Psychology*, *73*(1), 47–58. https://doi.org/10.1037/0022-006X.73.1.47

Croudace, T. J., & Böhnke, J. R. (2014). Item bank measurement of depression: Will one dimension work? *Journal of Clinical Epidemiology*, *67*, 4–6 https://doi.org/10.1016/j.jclinepi.2013.08.002

Cunningham, J. A., Godinho, A., & Kushnir, V. (2017). Can Amazon's Mechanical Turk be used to recruit participants for internet intervention trials? A pilot study involving a randomized controlled trial of a brief online intervention for hazardous alcohol use. *Internet Interventions*, *10*, 12–16. https://doi.org/10.1016/j.invent.2017.08.005

Curran, P. J., Hussong, A. M., Cai, L., Huang, W., Chassin, L., Sher, K. J., & Zucker, R. A. (2008). Pooling data from multiple longitudinal studies: The role of item response theory in integrative data analysis. *Developmental Psychology*, *44*(2), 365–80. https://doi.org/10.1037/0012-1649.44.2.365

De Beurs, D. P., de Vries, A. L., de Groot, M. H., de Keijser, J., & Kerkhof, A. J. (2014). Applying computer adaptive testing to optimize online assessment of suicidal behavior: A simulation study. *Journal of Medical Internet Research*, *16*(9), e207. https://doi.org/10.2196/jmir.3511

Del Vecchio, N., Elwy, A. R., Smith, E., Bottonari, K. A., & Eisen, S. V. (2011). Enhancing self-report assessment of PTSD: Development of an item bank. *Journal of Traumatic Stress*, *24*(2), 191–199. https://doi.org/10.1002/jts.20611

Demirchyan, A., Petrosyan, V., & Thompson, M. E. (2011). Psychometric value of the Center for Epidemiologic Studies Depression (CES-D) scale for screening of depressive symptoms in Armenian population. *Journal of Affective Disorders*, *133*(3), 489–498. https://doi.org/10.1016/J.JAD.2011.04.042

Dere, J., Watters, C. A., Yu, S. C.-M., Bagby, R. M., Ryder, A. G., & Harkness, K. L. (2015). Cross-cultural examination of measurement invariance of the Beck Depression Inventory–II. *Psychological Assessment*, *27*(1), 68–81. https://doi.org/10.1037/pas0000026

Devine, J., Fliege, H., Kocalevent, R., Mierke, A., Klapp, B. F., & Rose, M. (2016). Evaluation of Computerized Adaptive Tests (CATs) for longitudinal monitoring of depression, anxiety, and stress reactions. *Journal of Affective Disorders*, *190*, 846–853. https://doi.org/10.1016/j.jad.2014.10.063

DeWalt, D. A., Rothrock, N., Yount, S., Stone, A. A., & PROMIS Cooperative Group. (2007). Evaluation of item candidates: the PROMIS qualitative item review. *Medical Care*, *45*(5 Suppl. 1), S12–S21. https://doi.org/10.1097/01.mlr.0000254567.79743.e2

Dorans, N. J. (2007). Linking scores from multiple health outcome instruments. *Quality of Life Research*, *16*(S1), 85–94. https://doi.org/10.1007/s11136-006-9155-3

Dowling, N. M., Bolt, D. M., Deng, S., & Li, C. (2016). Measurement and control of bias in patient reported outcomes using multidimensional item response theory. *BMC Medical Research Methodology*, *16*(1), 63. https://doi.org/10.1186/s12874-016-0161-z

Dozois, D. J. A., Dobson, K. S., & Ahnberg, J. L. (1998). A psychometric evaluation of the Beck Depression Inventory-II. *Psychological Assessment*, *10*(2), 83–89. https://doi.org/10.1037/1040-3590.10.2.83

Eaton, W. W., Smith, C., Ybarra, M., Muntaner, C., & Tien, A. (2004). Center for Epidemiologic Studies Depression Scale: Review and revision (CESD and CESD-R). In M. E. Maruish (Ed.), *The use of psychological testing for treatment planning and outcomes assessment: Instruments for adults* (pp. 363–377). Mahwah, NJ: Lawrence Erlbaum Associates.

Eisen, S. V., Schultz, M. R., Ni, P., Haley, S. M., Smith, E. G., Spiro, A., ... Jette, A. M. (2016). Development and validation of a computerized-adaptive test for PTSD (P-CAT). *Psychiatric Services*, *67*(10), 1116–1123. https://doi.org/10.1176/appi.ps.201500382

El-Den, S., Chen, T. F., Gan, Y.-L., Wong, E., & O'Reilly, C. L. (2018). The psychometric properties of depression screening tools in primary healthcare settings: A systematic review. *Journal of Affective Disorders*, *225*, 503–522. https://doi.org/10.1016/j.jad.2017.08.060

Embretson, S. E., & Reise, S. P. (2000). *Item response theory for psychologists*. Mahwah, NJ: Lawrence Erlbaum Associates.

Flens, G., Smits, N., Carlier, I., van Hemert, A. M., & de Beurs, E. (2016). Simulating computer adaptive testing with the Mood and Anxiety Symptom Questionnaire. *Psychological Assessment*, *28*(8), 953–62. https://doi.org/10.1037/pas0000240

Fliege, H., Becker, J., Walter, O. B., Bjorner, J. B., Klapp, B. F., & Rose, M. (2005). Development of a computer-adaptive test for depression (D-CAT). *Quality of Life Research*, *14*(10), 2277–2291. https://doi.org/10.1007/s11136-005-6651-9

Forkmann, T., Boecker, M., Norra, C., Eberle, N., Kircher, T., Schauerte, P., ... Wirtz, M. (2009). Development of an item bank for the assessment of depression in persons with mental illnesses and physical diseases using Rasch analysis.

Rehabilitation Psychology, *54*(2), 186–197. https://doi.org/10.1037/a0015612

Fresco, D. M., Heimberg, R. G., Mennin, D. S., & Turk, C. L. (2002). Confirmatory factor analysis of the Penn State Worry Questionnaire. *Behaviour Research and Therapy*, *40*, 313–323.

Fresco, D. M., Mennin, D. S., Heimberg, R. G., & Turk, C. L. (2003). Using the Penn State Worry Questionnaire to identify individuals with generalized anxiety disorder: a receiver operating characteristic analysis. *Journal of Behavior Therapy and Experimental Psychiatry*, *34*(3–4), 283–291. https://doi.org/10.1016/J.JBTEP.2003.09.001

Fried, E. I. (2017). The 52 symptoms of major depression: Lack of content overlap among seven common depression scales. *Journal of Affective Disorders*, *208*, 191–197. https://doi.org/10.1016/J.JAD.2016.10.019

Fried, E. I., & Nesse, R. M. (2015). Depression sum-scores don't add up: Why analyzing specific depression symptoms is essential. *BMC Medicine*, *13*(1), 72. https://doi.org/10.1186/s12916-015–0325–4

Fydrich, T., Dowdall, D., & Chambless, D. L. (1992). Reliability and validity of the Beck Anxiety Inventory. *Journal of Anxiety Disorders*, *6*(1), 55–61. https://doi.org/10.1016/0887–6185(92)90026–4

Ghassemzadeh, H., Mojtabai, R., Karamghadiri, N., & Ebrahimkhani, N. (2005). Psychometric properties of a Persian-language version of the Beck Depression Inventory – second edition: BDI-II-PERSIAN. *Depression and Anxiety*, *21*(4), 185–192. https://doi.org/10.1002/da.20070

Gibbons, C., & Skevington, S. M. (2018). Adjusting for cross-cultural differences in computer-adaptive tests of quality of life. *Quality of Life Research*,*27*, 1027–1039. https://doi.org/10.1007/s11136-017–1738–7

Gibbons, L. E., Feldman, B. J., Crane, H. M., Mugavero, M., Willig, J. H., Patrick, D., . . . Crane, P. K. (2011). Migrating from a legacy fixed-format measure to CAT administration: Calibrating the PHQ-9 to the PROMIS depression measures. *Quality of Life Research*, *20*(9), 1349–1357. https://doi.org/10.1007/s11136-011–9882–y

Gibbons, R., Bock, R. D., Hedeker, D., Weiss, D. J., Segawa, E., Bhaumik, D. K., . . . Stover, A. (2007). Full-information item bifactor analysis of graded response data. *Applied Psychological Measurement*, *31*(1), 4–19. https://doi.org/10.1177/0146621606289485

Gibbons, R., Kupfer, D., Frank, E., Moore, T., Beiser, D. G., & Boudreaux, E. D. (2017). Development of a Computerized Adaptive Test Suicide Scale: The CAT-SS. *The Journal of Clinical Psychiatry*, *78*, 1376–1382. https://doi.org/10.4088/JCP.16m10922

Gibbons, R., Perraillon, M. C., & Kim, J. B. (2014). Item response theory approaches to harmonization and research synthesis. *Health Services and Outcomes Research Methodology*, *14*(4), 213–231. https://doi.org/10.1007/s10742-014–0125–x

Gibbons, R., Weiss, D. J., Frank, E., & Kupfer, D. (2016). Computerized adaptive diagnosis and testing of mental health disorders. *Annual Review of Clinical Psychology*, *12*(1), 83–104. https://doi.org/10.1146/annurev-clinpsy–021815–093634

Gibbons, R., Weiss, D. J., Kupfer, D. J., Frank, E., Fagiolini, A., Grochocinski, V. J., . . . Immekus, J. C. (2008). Using computerized adaptive testing to reduce the burden of mental health assessment. *Psychiatric Services*, *59*(4), 361–8. https://doi.org/10.1176/appi.ps.59.4.361

Gibbons, R., Weiss, D. J., Pilkonis, P. A., Frank, E., Moore, T., Kim, J. B., & Kupfer, D. J. (2012). The CAT-DI: Development of a computerized adaptive test for depression. *Archives of General Psychiatry*, *69*(11), 1104–12. https://doi.org/10.1001/archgenpsychiatry.2012.14

Gibbons, R., Weiss, D., Pilkonis, P., Frank, E., Moore, T., Kim, J., & Kupfer, D. (2014). Development of the CAT-ANX: A computerized adaptive test for anxiety. *American Journal of Psychiatry*, *171*(2), 187–194. https://doi.org/10.1038/nature13314.A

Granillo, M. T. (2012). Structure and function of the Patient Health Questionnaire-9 among Latina and non-Latina white female college students. *Journal of the Society for Social Work and Research*, *3*(2), 80–93. https://doi.org/10.5243/jsswr.2012.6

Guo, B., Kaylor-Hughes, C., Garland, A., Nixon, N., Sweeney, T., Simpson, S., . . . Morriss, R. (2017). Factor structure and longitudinal measurement invariance of PHQ-9 for specialist mental health care patients with persistent major depressive disorder: Exploratory Structural Equation Modelling. *Journal of Affective Disorders*, *219*, 1–8. https://doi.org/10.1016/j.jad.2017.05.020

Guo, T., Xiang, Y.-T., Xiao, L., Hu, C.-Q., Chiu, H. F. K., Ungvari, G. S., . . . Wang, G. (2015). Measurement-based care versus standard care for major depression: A randomized controlled trial with blind raters. *American Journal of Psychiatry*, *172*(10), 1004–1013. https://doi.org/10.1176/appi.ajp.2015.14050652

Hamamura, T., Heine, S. J., & Paulhus, D. L. (2008). Cultural differences in response styles: The role of dialectical thinking. *Personality and Individual Differences*, *44*(4), 932–942. https://doi.org/10.1016/j.paid.2007.10.034

Haroz, E. E., Ritchey, M., Bass, J. K., Kohrt, B. A., Augustinavicius, J., Michalopoulos, L., . . . Bolton, P. (2017). How is depression experienced around the world? A systematic review of qualitative literature. *Social Science and Medicine*, *183*, 151–162. https://doi.org/10.1016/j.socscimed.2016.12.030

Hazlett-Stevens, H., Ullman, J. B., & Craske, M. G. (2004). Factor Structure of the Penn State Worry Questionnaire. *Assessment*, *11*(4), 361–370. https://doi.org/10.1177/1073191104269872

Hollifield, M., Warner, T. D., Lian, N., Krakow, B., Jenkins, J. H., Kesler, J., . . . Westermeyer, J. (2002). Measuring trauma and health status in refugees. *JAMA*, *288*(5), 611. https://doi.org/10.1001/jama.288.5.611

Huang, F. Y., Chung, H., Kroenke, K., Delucchi, K. L., & Spitzer, R. L. (2006). Using the patient health questionnaire-9 to measure depression among racially and ethnically diverse primary care patients. *Journal of General Internal Medicine*, *21*(6), 547–552. https://doi.org/10.1111/j.1525–1497.2006.00409.x

Iwata, N., & Buka, S. (2002). Race/ethnicity and depressive symptoms: A cross-cultural/ethnic comparison among university students in East Asia, North and South America. *Social Science & Medicine*, *55*(12), 2243–2252. https://doi.org/10.1016/S0277–9536(02)00003–5

Jin, K.-Y., & Wang, W.-C. (2014). Generalized IRT models for extreme response style. *Educational and Psychological Measurement*, *74*(1), 116–138. https://doi.org/10.1177/0013164413498876

Kabacoff, R. I., Segal, D. L., Hersen, M., & Van Hasselt, V. B. (1997). Psychometric properties and diagnostic utility of the Beck Anxiety Inventory and the state-trait anxiety inventory with older adult psychiatric outpatients. *Journal of Anxiety*

Disorders, *11*(1), 33–47. https://doi.org/10.1016/S0887-6185(96)00033-3

Knappe, S., Klotsche, J., Heyde, F., Hiob, S., Siegert, J., Hoyer, J., ... Beesdo-Baum, K. (2014). Test–retest reliability and sensitivity to change of the dimensional anxiety scales for DSM-5. *CNS Spectrums*, *19*(3), 256–267. https://doi.org/10.1017/S1092852913000710

Kojima, M., Furukawa, T. A., Takahashi, H., Kawai, M., Nagaya, T., & Tokudome, S. (2002). Cross-cultural validation of the Beck Depression Inventory-II in Japan. *Psychiatry Research*, *110*(3), 291–299. https://doi.org/10.1016/S0165-1781(02)00106-3

Kosinski, M., Matz, S. C., Gosling, S. D., Popov, V., & Stillwell, D. (2015). Facebook as a research tool for the social sciences: Opportunities, challenges, ethical considerations, and practical guidelines. *American Psychologist*, *70*(6), 543–556. https://doi.org/10.1037/a0039210

Kotov, R., Krueger, R. F., Watson, D., Achenbach, T. M., Althoff, R. R., Bagby, R. M., ... Zimmerman, M. (2017). The Hierarchical Taxonomy of Psychopathology (HiTOP): A dimensional alternative to traditional nosologies. *Journal of Abnormal Psychology*, *126*(4), 454–477. https://doi.org/10.1037/abn0000258

Kroenke, K., Spitzer, R. L., & Williams, J. B. W. (2001). The PHQ-9: Validity of a brief depression severity measure. *Journal of General Internal Medicine*, *16*(9), 606–613.

Krueger, R. F., Markon, K. E., Patrick, C. J., Benning, S. D., & Kramer, M. D. (2007). Linking antisocial behaviour, substance use, and personality: An integrative quantitative model of the adult externalizing spectrum. *Journal of Abnormal Psychology*, *116*(4), 645–666. https://doi.org/10.1037/0021-843X.116.4.645

Lai, J.-S., Cella, D., Choi, S., Junghaenel, D. U., Christodoulou, C., Gershon, R., & Stone, A. (2011). How item banks and their application can influence measurement practice in rehabilitation medicine: A PROMIS fatigue item bank example. *Archives of Physical Medicine and Rehabilitation*, *92*(10), S20–S27. https://doi.org/10.1016/j.apmr.2010.08.033

Latimer, S., Meade, T., & Tennant, A. (2014). Development of item bank to measure deliberate self-harm behaviours: Facilitating tailored scales and computer adaptive testing for specific research and clinical purposes. *Psychiatry Research*, *217*(3), 240–247. https://doi.org/10.1016/j.psychres.2014.03.015

LeBeau, R. T., Mesri, B., & Craske, M. G. (2016). The DSM-5 social anxiety disorder severity scale: Evidence of validity and reliability in a clinical sample. *Psychiatry Research*, *244*, 94–96. https://doi.org/10.1016/j.psychres.2016.07.024

Lee, J. J., Kim, K. W., Kim, T. H., Park, J. H., Lee, S. B., Park, J. W., ... Steffens, D. C. (2011). Cross-cultural considerations in administering the Center for Epidemiologic Studies Depression Scale. *Gerontology*, *57*(5), 455–61. https://doi.org/10.1159/000318030

Liegl, G., Wahl, I., Berghofer, A., Nolte, S., Pieh, C., Rose, M., & Fischer, F. (2016). Using Patient Health Questionnaire-9 item parameters of a common metric resulted in similar depression scores compared to independent item response theory model reestimation. *Journal of Clinical Epidemiology*, *71*, 25–34. https://doi.org/10.1016/j.jclinepi.2015.10.006

Löwe, B., Decker, O., Müller, S., Brähler, E., Schellberg, D., Herzog, W., & Herzberg, P. Y. (2008). Validation and standardization of the Generalized Anxiety Disorder Screener (GAD-7) in the general population. *Medical Care*, *46*(3), 266–274. https://doi.org/10.1097/MLR.0b013e318160d093

Mahoney, A., Hobbs, M. J., Newby, J. M., Williams, A. D., & Andrews, G. (2018). Psychometric properties of the Worry Behaviors Inventory: Replication and extension in a large clinical and community sample. *Behavioural and Cognitive Psychotherapy*, *46*(1), 84–100. https://doi.org/10.1017/S1352465817000455

Mahoney, A., Hobbs, M. J., Newby, J. M., Williams, A. D., Sunderland, M., & Andrews, G. (2016). The Worry Behaviors Inventory: Assessing the behavioral avoidance associated with generalized anxiety disorder. *Journal of Affective Disorders*, *203*, 256–264. https://doi.org/10.1016/j.jad.2016.06.020

Manea, L., Gilbody, S., & McMillan, D. (2012). Optimal cut-off score for diagnosing depression with the Patient Health Questionnaire (PHQ-9): A meta-analysis. *CMAJ*, *184*(3), E191-6. https://doi.org/10.1503/cmaj.110829

McElroy, E., Casey, P., Adamson, G., Filippopoulos, P., & Shevlin, M. (2018). A comprehensive analysis of the factor structure of the Beck Depression Inventory-II in a sample of outpatients with adjustment disorder and depressive episode. *Irish Journal of Psychological Medicine*, *35*, 53–61. https://doi.org/10.1017/ipm.2017.52

McGlinchey, J. B., Zimmerman, M., Young, D., & Chelminski, I. (2006). Diagnosing major depressive disorder VIII: Are some symptoms better than others? *The Journal of Nervous and Mental Disease*, *194*(10), 785–790. https://doi.org/10.1097/01.nmd.0000240222.75201.aa

Meyer, T. J., Miller, M. L., Metzger, R. L., & Borkovec, T. D. (1990). Development and validation of the Penn State Worry Questionnaire. *Behaviour Research and Therapy*, *28*, 487–495.

Möller, E. L., & Bögels, S. M. (2016). The DSM-5 Dimensional Anxiety Scales in a Dutch non-clinical sample: Psychometric properties including the adult separation anxiety disorder scale. *International Journal of Methods in Psychiatric Research*, *25*(3), 232–239. https://doi.org/10.1002/mpr.1515

Moriarty, A. S., Gilbody, S., McMillan, D., & Manea, L. (2015). Screening and case finding for major depressive disorder using the Patient Health Questionnaire (PHQ-9): A meta-analysis. *General Hospital Psychiatry*, *37*(6), 567–576. https://doi.org/10.1016/j.genhosppsych.2015.06.012

Morin, C. M., Landreville, P., Colecchi, C., McDonald, K., Stone, J., & Ling, W. (1999). The Beck Anxiety Inventory: Psychometric properties with older adults. *Journal of Clinical Geropsychology*, *5*(1), 19–29. https://doi.org/10.1023/A:1022986728576

Muntingh, A. D. T., van der Feltz-Cornelis, C. M., van Marwijk, H. W. J., Spinhoven, P., Penninx, B. W. J. H., & van Balkom, A. J. L. M. (2011). Is the Beck Anxiety Inventory a good tool to assess the severity of anxiety? A primary care study in the Netherlands Study of Depression and Anxiety (NESDA). *BMC Family Practice*, *12*, 66. https://doi.org/10.1186/1471-2296-12-66

Muraki, E. (1992). A generalized partial credit model: Application of an EM algorithm. *Applied Psychological Measurement*, *16*(2), 159–176.

Nuevo, R., Dunn, G., Dowrick, C., Vázquez-Barquero, J. L., Casey, P., Dalgard, O. S., ... Ayuso-Mateos, J. L. (2009). Cross-cultural equivalence of the Beck Depression Inventory: A five-country analysis from the ODIN study. *Journal of Affective Disorders*, *114*(1–3), 156–162. https://doi.org/10.1016/J.JAD.2008.06.021

Osman, A., Kopper, B. A., Barrios, F. X., Osman, J. R., & Wade, T. (1997). The Beck Anxiety Inventory: Reexamination of factor structure and psychometric properties. *Journal of Clinical Psychology*, *53*(1), 7–14.

Overduin, M. K., & Furnham, A. (2012). Assessing obsessive-compulsive disorder (OCD): A review of self-report measures. *Journal of Obsessive-Compulsive and Related Disorders*, *1*(4), 312–324. https://doi.org/10.1016/j.jocrd.2012.08.001

Parkerson, H. A., Thibodeau, M. A., Brandt, C. P., Zvolensky, M. J., & Asmundson, G. J. G. (2015). Cultural-based biases of the GAD-7. *Journal of Anxiety Disorders*, *31*, 38–42. https://doi.org/10.1016/J.JANXDIS.2015.01.005

Paulhus, D. L. (2002). Socially desirable responding: the evolution of a construct. In H. I. Braun, D. N. Jackson, & D. E. Wiley (Eds.), *The role of constructs in psychological and education measurement* (pp. 49–69). Mahwah, NJ: Lawrence Erlbaum Associates.

Paulhus, D. L., & Vazire, S. (2007). The self-report method. In R. W. Robins, C. Fraley, & R. F. Krueger (Eds.), *Handbook of research methods in personality psychology* (pp. 224–239). New York: Guilford Press.

Pedrelli, P., Blais, M. A., Alpert, J. E., Shelton, R. C., Walker, R. S. W., & Fava, M. (2014). Reliability and validity of the Symptoms of Depression Questionnaire (SDQ). *CNS Spectrums*, *19*(6), 535–46. https://doi.org/10.1017/S1092852914000406

Pettersson, A., Boström, K. B., Gustavsson, P., & Ekselius, L. (2015). Which instruments to support diagnosis of depression have sufficient accuracy? A systematic review. *Nordic Journal of Psychiatry*, *69*(7), 497–508. https://doi.org/10.3109/08039488.2015.1008568

Pilkonis, P. A., Choi, S. W., Reise, S. P., Stover, A. M., Riley, W. T., Cella, D., & Group, P. C. (2011). Item banks for measuring emotional distress from the Patient-Reported Outcomes Measurement Information System (PROMIS®): Depression, anxiety, and anger. *Assessment*, *18*(3), 263–283. https://doi.org/10.1177/1073191111411667

Plieninger, H. (2017). Mountain or molehill? A simulation study on the impact of response styles. *Educational and Psychological Measurement*, *77*(1), 32–53. https://doi.org/10.1177/0013164416636655

Posner, S. F., Stewart, A. L., Marín, G., & J. Pérez-Stable, E. (2001). Factor variability of the Center for Epidemiological Studies Depression Scale (CES-D) among urban Latinos. *Ethnicity and Health*, *6*(2), 137–144. https://doi.org/10.1080/13557850120068469

Radloff, L. S. (1977). The CES-D Scale: A self-report depression scale for research in the general population. *Applied Psychological Measurement*, *1*, 385–401.

Richardson, E. J., & Richards, J. S. (2008). Factor structure of the PHQ-9 screen for depression across time since injury among persons with spinal cord injury. *Rehabilitation Psychology*, *53*(2), 243–249. https://doi.org/10.1037/0090–5550.53.2.243

Richardson, L. P., McCauley, E., Grossman, D. C., McCarty, C. A., Richards, J., Russo, J. E., . . . Katon, W. (2010). Evaluation of the Patient Health Questionnaire-9 item for detecting major depression among adolescents. *Pediatrics*, *126*(6), 1117–23. https://doi.org/10.1542/peds.2010–0852

Rose, M., Bjorner, J. B., Fischer, F., Anatchkova, M., Gandek, B., Klapp, B. F., & Ware, J. E. (2012). Computerized adaptive testing: Ready for ambulatory monitoring? *Psychosomatic Medicine*, *74*(4), 338–348. https://doi.org/10.1097/PSY.0b013e3182547392

Samejima, F. (1997). Graded response model. In *Handbook of modern item response theory* (pp. 85–100). New York: Springer. https://doi.org/10.1007/978–1-4757–2691-6_5

Santor, D. A., & Coyne, J. C. (1997). Shortening the CES-D to improve its ability to detect cases of depression. *Psychological Assessment*, *9*(3), 233–243. https://doi.org/10.1037/1040–3590.9.3.233

Schalet, B. D., Cook, K. F., Choi, S. W., & Cella, D. (2014). Establishing a common metric for self-reported anxiety: Linking the MASQ, PANAS, and GAD-7 to PROMIS Anxiety. *Journal of Anxiety Disorders*, *28*(1), 88–96. https://doi.org/10.1016/j.janxdis.2013.11.006

Scott, K., & Lewis, C. C. (2015). Using measurement-based care to enhance any treatment. *Cognitive and Behavioral Practice*, *22*(1), 49–59. https://doi.org/10.1016/j.cbpra.2014.01.010

Sijbrandij, M., Reitsma, J. B., Roberts, N. P., Engelhard, I. M., Olff, M., Sonneveld, L. P., & Bisson, J. I. (2013). Self-report screening instruments for post-traumatic stress disorder (PTSD) in survivors of traumatic experiences. In M. Sijbrandij (Ed.), *Cochrane database of systematic reviews*. Chichester: John Wiley & Sons. https://doi.org/10.1002/14651858.CD010575

Smits, N., Cuijpers, P., & van Straten, A. (2011). Applying computerized adaptive testing to the CES-D scale: A simulation study. *Psychiatry Research*, *188*(1), 147–155. https://doi.org/10.1016/j.psychres.2010.12.001

Spielberger, C. D., Gorsuch, R. L., & Lushene, R. E. (1970). *Manual for the State-Trait Anxiety Inventory*. Palo Alto, CA: Consulting Psychologists Press.

Spitzer, R. L., Kroenke, K., Williams, J. B. W., & Lowe, B. (2006). A brief measure for assessing generalized anxiety disorder: The GAD-7. *Archives of Internal Medicine*, *166*, 1092–1097.

Streiner, D. L., & Norman, G. R. (2008). Biases in responding. In D. L. Streiner & G. R. Norman (Eds.), *Health Measurement Scales: A practical guide to their development and use*. Oxford: Oxford University Press.

Subica, A. M., Fowler, J. C., Elhai, J. D., Frueh, B. C., Sharp, C., Kelly, E. L., & Allen, J. G. (2014). Factor structure and diagnostic validity of the Beck Depression Inventory–II with adult clinical inpatients: Comparison to a gold-standard diagnostic interview. *Psychological Assessment*, *26*(4), 1106–1115. https://doi.org/10.1037/a0036998

Sunderland, M., Batterham, P. J., Calear, A. L., & Carragher, N. (2017). The development and validation of static and adaptive screeners to measure the severity of panic disorder, social anxiety disorder, and obsessive compulsive disorder. *International Journal of Methods in Psychiatric Research*, *26*(4), e1561. https://doi.org/10.1002/mpr.1561

Sunderland, M., Slade, T., Krueger, R. F., Markon, K. E., Patrick, C. J., & Kramer, M. D. (2017). Efficiently measuring dimensions of the externalizing spectrum model: Development of the Externalizing Spectrum Inventory-Computerized Adaptive Test (ESI-CAT). *Psychological Assessment*, *29*(7), 868–880. https://doi.org/10.1037/pas0000384

Takayanagi, Y., Spira, A. P., Roth, K. B., Gallo, J. J., Eaton, W. W., & Mojtabai, R. (2014). Accuracy of reports of lifetime mental and physical disorders: Results from the Baltimore Epidemiological Catchment Area study. *JAMA Psychiatry*, *71*(3), 273–80. https://doi.org/10.1001/jamapsychiatry.2013.3579

Thornton, L., Batterham, P. J., Fassnacht, D. B., Kay-Lambkin, F., Calear, A. L., & Hunt, S. (2016). Recruiting for health, medical or psychosocial research using Facebook: Systematic review. *Internet Interventions*, *4*(1), 72–81. https://doi.org/10.1016/j.invent.2016.02.001

Uher, R., Perlis, R. H., Placentino, A., Dernovšek, M. Z., Henigsberg, N., Mors, O., ... Farmer, A. (2012). Self-report and clinician-rated measures of depression severity: Can one replace the other? *Depression and Anxiety*, *29*(12), 1043–9. https://doi.org/10.1002/da.21993

van Ballegooijen, W., Riper, H., Cuijpers, P., van Oppen, P., & Smit, J. H. (2016). Validation of online psychometric instruments for common mental health disorders: A systematic review. *BMC Psychiatry*, *16*(1), 45. https://doi.org/10.1186/s12888-016–0735–7

Vaughn-Coaxum, R. A., Mair, P., & Weisz, J. R. (2016). Racial/ethnic differences in youth depression indicators. *Clinical Psychological Science*, *4*(2), 239–253. https://doi.org/10.1177/2167702615591768

Venables, N. C., Yancey, J. R., Kramer, M. D., Hicks, B. M., Krueger, R. F., Iacono, W. G., ... Patrick, C. J. (2018). Psychoneurometric assessment of dispositional liabilities for suicidal behavior: Phenotypic and etiological associations. *Psychological Medicine*, *48*(3), 463–472. https://doi.org/10.1017/S0033291717001830

Vigneau, F., & Cormier, S. (2008). The factor structure of the State-Trait Anxiety Inventory: An alternative view. *Journal of Personality Assessment*, *90*(3), 280–285. https://doi.org/10.1080/00223890701885027

Wahl, I., Lowe, B., Bjorner, J. B., Fischer, F., Langs, G., Voderholzer, U., ... Rose, M. (2014). Standardization of depression measurement: A common metric was developed for 11 self-report depression measures. *Journal of Clinical Epidemiology*, *67*(1), 73–86. https://doi.org/10.1016/j.jclinepi.2013.04.019

Walter, O. B., Becker, J., Bjorner, J. B., Fliege, H., Klapp, B. F., & Rose, M. (2007). Development and evaluation of a computer adaptive test for "Anxiety" (Anxiety-CAT). *Quality of Life Research*, *16*, 143–155. https://doi.org/10.1007/s11136-007–9191–7

Wang, Y.-P., Gorenstein, C., Wang, Y.-P., & Gorenstein, C. (2013). Psychometric properties of the Beck Depression Inventory-II: A comprehensive review. *Revista Brasileira de Psiquiatria*, *35*(4), 416–431. https://doi.org/10.1590/1516–4446–2012–1048

Wiebe, J. S., & Penley, J. A. (2005). A psychometric comparison of the Beck Depression Inventory-II in English and Spanish. *Psychological Assessment*, *17*(4), 481–485. https://doi.org/10.1037/1040–3590.17.4.481

Wong, Q. J. J., Gregory, B., & McLellan, L. F. (2016). A review of scales to measure social anxiety disorder in clinical and epidemiological studies. *Current Psychiatry Reports*, *18*(4), 38. https://doi.org/10.1007/s11920-016–0677–2

Yancey, J. R., Venables, N. C., & Patrick, C. J. (2016). Psychoneurometric operationalization of threat sensitivity: Relations with clinical symptom and physiological response criteria. *Psychophysiology*, *53*(3), 393–405. https://doi.org/10.1111/psyp.12512

Zimmerman, M., Martinez, J. H., Friedman, M., Boerescu, D. A., Attiullah, N., & Toba, C. (2012). How can we use depression severity to guide treatment selection when measures of depression categorize patients differently? *The Journal of Clinical Psychiatry*, *73*(10), 1287–1291. https://doi.org/10.4088/JCP.12m07775

Zimmerman, M., Walsh, E., Friedman, M., Boerescu, D. A., & Attiullah, N. (2018). Are self-report scales as effective as clinician rating scales in measuring treatment response in routine clinical practice? *Journal of Affective Disorders*, *225*, 449–452. https://doi.org/10.1016/j.jad.2017.08.024

20 Performance-Based Techniques

GREGORY J. MEYER AND JONI L. MIHURA

This chapter focuses on methods used to know people based on their spontaneous productions in response to semi-structured task demands. These methods are in contrast to other avenues for knowing a person, bringing with them some inherent strengths and some other inherent limitations.

WAYS OF KNOWING AND THE SCOPE OF THIS CHAPTER

Two primary ways to know information about another person exist: asking questions to obtain information or observing the person in particular contexts as a way to see for oneself what they are like. Psychological assessment measures mine these distinct strategies by employing standardized structures for implementing these methods of knowing. At a minimum, psychological assessment instruments provide standardized stimuli and administration guidelines, and often standardized scoring, norms, and interpretive routines as well. This formal structure makes assessment measures distinct from the kind of questioning and observation that accompanies interviews or psychotherapy.

With respect to question-based methods of knowing, two main types exist: questions asked of the target provide *self-reported* information and questions asked of someone who knows the target provide *informant-reported* information. Standardized assessment measures that rely on in vivo observation also are of two main types, *maximum* and *typical* performance measures. Maximum performance tasks provide a context where there is a correct and desirable way of responding, such as stating the correct definition of a word. They provide clear guidance about what constitutes success and how to achieve it, a limited number of response options, and testing conditions that foster success and motivated performance. Typical performance tasks – the focus of this chapter – provide a context with general guidelines for completing the task but without clear standards for correct or desirable performance. They generally provide wide latitude for responding and conditions that foster individualized solutions rather than a predetermined goal. Consequently, maximum performance tasks indicate what a person *can do* when motivated to perform optimally, while typical performance tasks indicate what a person *will do* when left to their own preferences (Cronbach, 1990).

Within typical performance measures, we focus on tasks that have been used by clinical psychologists to understand personality and psychopathology, in contrast to those used in other domains of psychology. Thus, our scope is limited to inkblot, picture-story, sentence completion, and prompted drawing tasks. We focus most attention on the Rorschach inkblot task, as its base of research is directly relevant to how it is used in practice. Other methods and measures often have a substantial research foundation, though those scales generally are not used in clinical practice, which has contributed to the substantial criticism directed at these measures (e.g., Lilienfeld, Wood, & Garb, 2000).

THE BROAD NATURE OF RESPONSES TO INKBLOTS, PICTURES, SENTENCE STEMS, AND DRAWING PROMPTS

Table 20.1 summarizes the key dimensions across which the four typical performance method families differ. Their stimuli vary in the extent to which they are visual, conceptual, or verbal. Similarly, the response generated by the respondent varies in the extent to which it is orally communicated, written, or drawn. Each method family has alternative versions that further narrow and shape the task demands. Nonetheless, each of the methods shares some common features, which includes whether personal embellishments are encouraged, whether administration involves interaction with an examiner, and the extent to which each method family is culturally embedded versus transportable across cultures.

Finally, the method families can be further subdivided into more specific sub-methods, which are the discrete sources of information that can inform an assessment. As indicated in the first four sets of entries in this section, to some extent each method family draws on thematic content, the logical coherence of the completed task,

Table 20.1 Similarities and differences on key dimensions among the four typical performance method families reviewed in this chapter

Dimension	Inkblot Task	Picture-Story	Sentence Stems	Prompted Drawings
Stimuli	Visual (Inkblots)	Visual (Pictures, Drawings)	Written phrases	Conceptual-Verbal or Visual
Response Mode	Visual-Verbal	Visual-Verbal	Written language	Drawn
Alternate Versions	Rorschach, Zulliger, Holtzman	TAT, PSE, AAP, Roberts, TEMAS	Loevinger, Rotter, Forer	DAP, HTP, KFD, CWS
Task	Provide an attribution; say what it looks like	Provide an attribution and a narrative; explain what is happening, what led up to it, what happens next, and what the characters are thinking and feeling	Provide a conclusion or completion	Provide a figural representation; possibly a verbal elaboration
Embellishment Encouraged	No	Yes	Yes	Varies
Interactive with Examiner	Almost always	Generally	Typically not	Minimal during, possibly after
Cultural Embeddedness	Low	High	Moderate	Low
Sub-methods	Thematic content perceived Logic and coherence of communication Relational representations Interactions with stimuli or examiner Fit of object to features Conventionality of perception Movement embellishments Determinants of perception Structure of perception Locus of attention	Thematic content attributed Logic and coherence of communication Relational representations Interactions with stimuli or examiner Narrative coherence Spontaneous inclusion of narrative elements Communal and agentic motives and attitudes Affective attributions Quantity of verbalization Level of detail	Thematic content stated Logic and coherence of completion Relational references Interactions with stems or replies Amount written Sophistication of language & writing	Thematic content represented Logic and coherence of representation For KFD, relational representations Interactions with productions Line quality Figure size Figure placement Emphasis or omission of elements Level of effort and detail

Note. TAT = Thematic Apperception Test; PSE = Picture Story Exercise; AAP = Adult Attachment Projective; TEMAS = Tell Me a Story Test; DAP = Draw a Person; HTP = House-Tree-Person; KFD = Kinetic Family Drawing; CWS = Crisi Wartegg Test.

potential information about relational representations, and the respondents' interactive behavior with the test stimuli, their own productions, or the examiner. However, the method families are not equally infused by each of these sources. The gray font in Table 20.1 indicates sources of information that generally contribute less. Ultimately, however, each method family draws on unique sources of information that are shaped by its particular stimuli and task demands.

HOW FREQUENTLY METHODS AND MEASURES ARE USED IN PRACTICE AND TAUGHT

The most recent survey data on test use among psychologists in practice (Wright et al., 2017) indicate that narrowly focused self-report symptom-specific scales are used most frequently, followed by multiscale self-report inventories and maximum performance tasks of cognitive functioning, with overall frequencies ranging from 54 to 78 percent of clinicians. These measures are followed by typical performance measures, including the Rorschach (54 percent) and an undifferentiated category of other typical performance measures (49 percent) that includes picture-story, sentence completion, and drawing tasks. The most recent survey of accredited clinical psychology doctoral programs (Mihura, Roy, & Graceffo, 2017) shows that training in multiscale tests of maximum performance (the Wechsler scales and Woodcock-Johnson Achievement battery) and self-reported symptomatology (MMPI-2 or RF, PAI, MCMI) is required in 59–98 percent of programs. This is followed by required training in typical performance measures, including the Thematic Apperception Test (45 percent), Rorschach (43 percent), a sentence completion task (35 percent), and figure drawing tasks (28 percent). Thus, the measures covered in this chapter are used and taught regularly, though not uniformly across all programs or settings.

INKBLOT TASKS

Over the years, several sets of inkblots have been developed for potential use in assessment. However, none are used or researched as often as Rorschach's inkblots, which are the focus in this chapter.

The Rorschach Inkblot Task

Searls (2017) provides a fascinating scholarly account of both Rorschach the person and the controversial test he introduced almost 100 years ago. Rorschach's task includes a standard series of ten inkblots that he carefully created, pilot tested, and artistically refined over time. Five inkblots are variegated black and gray, two are variegated black and gray with prominent sections of bold red, and three are fully chromatic with elements ranging from pastel to brightly saturated color. Each inkblot was created on a white background, which Rorschach (1942) deliberately used as part of the inkblot pattern on many cards. During administration, the cards are sequentially handed to respondents in a fixed order and respondents are asked to answer the question "What might this be?" The examiner then records the verbatim responses to that question across all ten cards. Following this, the examiner proceeds to a clarification phase, going back to each response to gain information from the respondent about where in the card response objects reside and what inkblot features contributed to the perception.

Each inkblot provides many response possibilities that vary across multiple stimulus dimensions. Solving the problem posed in the query thus invokes a series of perceptual problem-solving operations related to scanning the stimuli, selecting locations for emphasis, comparing potential inkblot images to mental representations of objects, filtering out responses judged less optimal, and articulating those selected for emphasis to the examiner (Exner, 2003). Each response or solution to the task is coded across a number of dimensions and the codes are then aggregated across all responses and summarized into scores. The summary scores thus quantify what occurred in the process of repeatedly attributing meaning to the visual stimuli and then explaining to another person how one looks at things in the context of multiple competing possibilities. A sample of behavior collected under standardized conditions like this provides the foundation for the Rorschach's empirically demonstrated validity.

The Development and Nature of the Rorschach Inkblots

Rorschach died shortly after the book describing his inkblot "experiment" was published in 1921. Consequently, many details remain unknown about how the inkblots were created and why Rorschach constructed them the way he did. It is clear, however, that Rorschach used his artistic skills to iteratively refine and embellish the inkblots over time. He did not describe the specific end he had in mind, though his apparent goal was twofold. First, he embedded a reasonably recognizable structure into each of the inkblots – the commonly reported conventional response objects. Second, he simultaneously embedded a textured array of suggestive "critical bits" (Exner, 1996) that lend themselves to incomplete or imperfect perceptual likenesses and form competing visual images as potential responses to the task. The latter are based on the form, color, shading, or symmetrical features of the inkblots. They provide wide latitude for people to generate an almost unlimited number of unique and idiographic responses.

These two elements combine to create what is known as a Zipf or power-law distribution of objects perceived (Meyer et al., 2011). Such a distribution is distinctly nonnormal. If one plots frequency on the vertical axis and rank order on the horizontal axis, the result is a near vertical "arm" on the left for the relatively few objects that occur with a high frequency and a near horizontal "tail" on the right for the numerous uncommonly reported objects. Indeed, even in very large samples, about 70 percent of the distinct objects identified on the Rorschach are seen by just one person. Thus, the nature of the task has both clearly embedded structure and wide latitude for idiographically unique perceptions.

The task provides an in vivo sample of perceptual problem-solving behavior obtained under standardized conditions. Responses include a visual attribution of what the stimulus looks like, a set of verbal and nonverbal communications, and a range of behaviors as the respondent interacts with the cards and the examiner. These behaviors can be coded along many dimensions (e.g., perceptual fit, logical coherence, organizational efforts, thematic content). The popularity of the Rorschach in clinical settings despite recurrent psychometric challenges (e.g., Lilienfeld et al., 2000) is likely because it provides a method of gathering information about an individual that cannot be obtained using other popular assessment methods.

Rorschach Systems for Applied Use

Given Rorschach's untimely death, different systems developed for its use in clinical practice. In the United States, the primary approaches were first developed by Samuel Beck and Bruno Klopfer. Subsequently, three other systems were developed by Marguerite R. Hertz, Zygmunt Piotrowski, and David Rapaport, Merton Gill, and Roy Schafer. Because these systems used Rorschach's original inkblots, all five have been referred to as "the Rorschach." However, they were distinctive in many respects.

In 1974, John Exner compiled what he believed were the best and most empirically defensible elements of the five previous systems. His Comprehensive System became the most popular approach to using the Rorschach in the United States and many other countries (e.g., Meyer et al., 2013; Shaffer, Erdberg, & Meyer, 2007), largely due to its empirical foundation. From 1974 to 2005, Exner published three volumes (a general text, an interpretative text, and a youth text) and a workbook, each with multiple editions, attesting to its popularity and continual refinement.

In 1997, Exner created what he called the Rorschach Research Council, consisting of seven members who met biannually for several days in order to advance research on his system. Exner (1997) planned to have the Research Council develop the system after he retired or passed away. However, he died unexpectedly in 2006 and left no formal guidelines for how this could occur. Consequently, four Research Council members and another co-author developed what they call the Rorschach Performance Assessment System (R-PAS; Meyer et al., 2011), applying solutions to problems they had been working on from 1997 to 2006, as well as extending work initiated within the Research Council.

The solutions included fixing problems with the Comprehensive System norms (Meyer, Erdberg, & Shaffer, 2007) and the excessive variability in the number of responses given to the task, both of which were long-standing concerns actively addressed by the Research Council (e.g., Dean et al., 2007; Meyer et al., 2004). Other innovations initiated within the Research Council included updated tables to classify the conventionality of perceptions, more fully specified administration guidelines, enhanced guidelines to increase inter-coder agreement, emphasizing variables with systematically gathered evidence for validity, dropping variables that lacked validity or were redundant with other variables, adding new variables based on contemporary reviews of the literature, and refining interpretation by emphasizing transparent links between observed testing behaviors and inferred behavior in everyday life.

Use in Practice

After administering the task, the examiner classifies the responses along multiple dimensions, summarizes the codes across all responses to generate summary scores, compares the summary scores to normative expectations, and interprets the results based on formal interpretive guidelines. The main types of coded variables include test-taking behaviors; the location(s) selected for a response; the type of content seen; the way that objects were perceived independently or in relation to each other; the conventionality and fit of the object(s) in relation to the contours of the inkblot location used; the features of the inkblots contributing to a perception; the logical coherence of communication; and the type of themes present in the response, including the ways in which people and relationships were construed.

Within R-PAS, the primary variables considered for interpretation are displayed on two pages of norm-based profiles. The test manual provides a review of reliability and validity data and a regularly updated library of research is available at the R-PAS website.[1] R-PAS also provides extensive free teaching and training resources (e.g., checklists and videos to learn administration, cases for practice coding, teaching PowerPoints). Both hand-scoring and online computerized scoring are available, with the latter recommended to minimize mistakes and take full advantage of normative adjustments for protocol complexity or youth age.

Psychometrics

Controversy has surrounded the Rorschach throughout its history (Searls, 2017). During the two decades from 1995 to 2015, it received heated criticisms in the literature (e.g., Lilienfeld et al., 2000). The main critiques focused on Exner's Comprehensive System, though they also encompassed the Rorschach more generally. These critiques led to debates focused on normative data, reliability, validity, utility in practice, and incremental validity (for a sequential, structured debate addressing these issues, see Meyer, 2001; Meyer & Archer, 2001).

Normative data. An important goal for R-PAS was to have improved estimates of expected performance among nonclinical individuals. Over time, evidence accumulated that the standard reference samples for the Comprehensive System looked notably healthier than other nonpatient samples from the United States and other countries on many variables (e.g., Viglione & Hilsenroth, 2001; Wood et al., 2001). A ten-year effort to understand this culminated in the publication of a Special Supplement to the *Journal of Personality Assessment* (*JPA*) devoted to internationally collected reference samples for the Comprehensive System (Shaffer et al., 2007). This effort brought together a multicultural set of twenty-one samples of adult data from sixteen countries encompassing North and South America, Europe, Asia, and Oceania, as well as thirty-one samples of youth data from five

[1] See www.r-pas.org

countries encompassing North America, Europe, and Asia. The adult samples looked very similar to each other – but also distinct from the standard Comprehensive System norms (Meyer et al., 2007; Meyer, Shaffer et al., 2015). The homogeneity among adult samples justified forming composite international reference values that could be applied globally to correct the problematic Comprehensive System norms. For youth, the picture was more complicated because the norms at similar ages were not as homogeneous as for adults.

As of 2018, the R-PAS norms for adults draw on the same samples used in the *JPA* Supplement, taking as its base up to 100 randomly selected protocols from fifteen donated samples of data from Argentina, Belgium, Brazil, Denmark, Finland, France, Greece, Israel, Italy, Portugal, Romania, Spain, and the United States (Meyer et al., 2011). These protocols formed two sets of norms: 1,396 protocols to use with Comprehensive System administration procedures and 640 protocols to use if examiners follow the R-PAS recommendations for modified administration to control excess variability in the number of responses. Research has confirmed the two forms of administration lead to identical norms except for the intended targets of reduced variability in responding and slightly more responses overall (Hosseininasab et al., 2017).

Meyer, Viglione, and Mihura (2017) compared demographics for the R-PAS adult norms to several benchmark standards. Relative to the US Census, the norms are similar in gender, level of education, and White vs. Other ethnicities, though they are younger (*M* age = 37 vs. 48). Relative to the United Nations' classification of fifty-eight Developed countries, the norms have a similar proportion of men, are lower in average age (37 vs. 50), have about two more years of education, and show substantially more ethnic diversity using approximate country-based ethnic classifications. Relative to a global standard of all living adults, the R-PAS norms have somewhat fewer men, are younger by about six years, are much more educated (*M* years 13.3 vs. 7.9), and are ethnically imbalanced, with many more people of White European ancestry and many fewer people of Asian ancestry than is the case for the world population. However, research has documented that R-PAS scores do not vary as a function of gender, ethnicity, or adult age; they do vary by adult levels of education and youth age (Meyer, Giromini et al., 2015). Thus, the R-PAS adult norms, with an average of 13.3 years of education, are more applicable to people in the United States and from other Developed countries than to people from countries with much lower standards for education.

As of 2018, the R-PAS norms for children and adolescents rely on transitional norms collected in Brazil and the United States using R-PAS guidelines, supplemented by a small number of protocols from Italy (Meyer et al., 2017). The norms rely on 346 youth protocols ranging in age from six to seventeen, with adult age expectations anchored by the sample of 640 adult protocols. Continuous inferential norming accompanied by age-specific bootstrap resampling to estimate equally plausible alternative norm samples was used to fit polynomial regression curves to the developmental data. This approach allowed protocols across all ages to identify the most accurate and generalizable normative expectations. After correcting problematic skew, regression equations were fit to predict key raw score percentiles from age, which were then converted to standard score equivalents, resulting in raw score to standard score conversions for each variable at each age from six to seventeen. These norms ultimately will be replaced by larger age-based samples from multiple countries. In the interim, they provide reasonable, developmentally sensitive expectations for what youth see, say, and do when completing the task at various ages. Importantly, they correct for the overpathologizing nature of the previous Comprehensive System youth norms and the irregularities seen in the *JPA* Supplement for youth (Meyer & Erdberg, 2018).

Reliability. Meta-analytic research has found good to excellent scoring reliability for most variables used in clinical practice or research (e.g., Meyer et al., 2017). Similar results were observed for the twenty-eight normative samples from sixteen countries in the *JPA* Supplement (Shaffer et al., 2007) and for studies specifically examining R-PAS in the United States and Italy (e.g., Pignolo et al., 2017; Viglione et al., 2012). Thus, coding for trained examiners is fairly straightforward with good agreement across coders. However, interrater reliability is dependent on the training, skill, and conscientiousness of the examiner, so practice and calibration are essential.

Meta-analytic research has found good temporal consistency, though most of the literature is older. Using twenty-six samples from the United States and Europe, Grønnerød (2003) found average stability of $r = 0.65$ over an average retest interval of thirty-eight months. Only one comprehensive stability study has been published since. In a sample of seventy-five French nonpatients, the median three-month stability across eighty-seven scores was $r = 0.55$ (Sultan et al., 2006), showing that generally healthy research volunteers can provide noticeably different protocols when tested by two different reasonably trained examiners three months apart. Meyer and colleagues (2011) noted how the stability of Rorschach scores may be more like the stability of memory or job performance scores, which have a one-to-two-month average stability of about 0.50 to 0.70, rather than the relatively high stability of intelligence scores or introspectively assessed self-reported characteristics.

Meyer, Mihura, and Smith (2005) examined interpretive reliability for Rorschach results using fifty-five patient protocols and judgments from twenty clinicians residing in multiple countries. Substantial reliability was observed across four datasets and the findings compared favorably to meta-analytic summaries of inter-rater agreement for other types of applied judgments in psychology, psychiatry, and medicine. Thus, when presented with the same Rorschach data, experienced clinicians drew similar conclusions about patients.

Validity. In 2001, Meyer and Archer summarized the available meta-analytic evidence on the global validity of Rorschach scores, all of which compared the validity of the Rorschach to the validity of the Minnesota Multiphasic Personality Inventory (MMPI; Hathaway & McKinley, 1942). They found the Rorschach and MMPI had equivalent validity; each with an average $r = 0.32$ for individual hypothesized effects (523 effects for the Rorschach and 533 for the MMPI) or $r = 0.29$ for cross-method validity coefficients aggregated within samples (seventy-three samples for the Rorschach and eighty-five for the MMPI). These data clearly supported the general validity of the Rorschach (and the MMPI).

These data indicated Rorschach scores were *generally* valid, and generally *as valid as MMPI scores*, but not which *specific scores* were valid and which were not. The absence of systematic meta-analytic data for individual variables led Garb (1999) to call for a moratorium on the use of the Rorschach in clinical and forensic settings until that kind of data was available. Although no multiscale assessment instrument used in practice would meet Garb's standard for use, Mihura and colleagues (2013) responded to that challenge by completing a systematic review of the published literature on the sixty-five variables central to interpretation in the Comprehensive System (Exner, 1974, 2003), drawing on studies completed in twenty countries across North and South America, Europe, Asia, and Oceania. The authors reliably identified all instances of validity coefficients in the published literature that had been hypothesized by any author (3,106 findings) and then reliably classified these with respect to their construct relevance to systematically identify 1,156 core findings that directly targeted their construct validity. As expected, Rorschach scores in general were more strongly associated with externally assessed criteria ($r = 0.27$) than with conceptually related self-reported characteristics ($r = 0.08$). Relative to externally assessed criteria, thirteen of the variables had excellent support, seventeen had good support, ten had modest support, thirteen had no support, and twelve variables had no construct-relevant validity studies in the peer-reviewed literature.

Interestingly, the classification of the sixty-five variables studied by Mihura and colleagues (2013) as having no, modest, good, or excellent validity were strongly correlated (0.51) with the average ratings of validity from a separately conducted study of 246 clinicians working in twenty-six countries who were blind to the meta-analytic results (Meyer et al., 2013). However, both the aggregated clinical judgments and the meta-analytic research findings diverged from the existing authoritative review of validity for these variables, which was Exner's (2003) text that essentially endorsed the validity of all variables. Thus, while diverging from Exner, both sources converged on the same two conclusions: Some variables lacked validity and probably should not be used in practice and other variables were valid and should be emphasized in practice. These results strongly influenced the variables included in R-PAS (Meyer et al., 2011).

In response to the Mihura and colleagues' (2013) meta-analyses, the self-described "Rorschach critics" published a follow-up Comment (Wood et al., 2015; see also Mihura et al., 2015). They made two noteworthy statements, given the years of debate associated with the Rorschach. First, they said that Mihura and colleagues' results "provided an unbiased and trustworthy summary of the published literature" (p. 243). Second, they rescinded the global moratorium Garb (1999) had called for on use of the Rorschach in clinical and forensic settings.

Other systematic reviews and meta-analyses provide validity support for individual Rorschach variables in R-PAS that were not in the Comprehensive System, including Oral Dependency (e.g., Bornstein, 1999), the Ego Impairment Index (Deiner et al., 2011), the Mutuality of Autonomy Scale (e.g., Graceffo, Mihura, & Meyer, 2014), and Space Reversal and Space Integration (Mihura et al., 2018). Somewhat paradoxically, because of the ongoing controversies concerning the Rorschach, the variables included in R-PAS now have more meta-analyses documenting their construct validity than the variables included in any other multiscale assessment measure, such as the MMPI or the Wechsler scales.

Summary

Interview-based measures and self-report inventories require clients to introspectively describe what they are like; the Rorschach requires them to provide an in vivo behavioral illustration of what they are like via their responses to each card. Thus, the Rorschach task allows an examiner to observe what people do, as opposed to learning about how they think of themselves. R-PAS does not contain formal response validity scales like many self-report inventories but it does provide two measures (overall protocol complexity and a summary score of dramatic contents) that are sensitive to defensive inhibition or exaggerated overpathologizing (Meyer, 1997; Meyer et al., 2000; Meyer et al., 2011). However, like any psychological measure, the task is vulnerable to noncredible responding, either from embellishments to appear pathological or from inhibition of response content to appear healthy (e.g., Sewell & Helle, 2018).

Not surprisingly, given their very different natures as sources of information, Rorschach assessed variables of all types are essentially independent of self-reports of seemingly similar constructs (e.g., Meyer, 1997; Meyer et al., 2000; Mihura et al., 2013). As such, the Rorschach can provide psychological information that may reside outside of the client's immediate or conscious awareness, much like the maximum performance assessment of memory, impulsivity, and executive functioning provides information that people are unable to volunteer reliably or validly in self-report (e.g., Beaudoin & Desrichard, 2011). The average correlation of these cognitive abilities with self-report (*r*s from 0.00 to 0.15) is about the same as that found with Rorschach-assessed characteristics and self-reported characteristics ($r = 0.08$). Accessing information obtained from observing a client's personality in action, as is the case with the Rorschach, can be an important resource for clinicians engaged in the idiographic challenge of trying to understand a person in their full complexity because valid Rorschach scores will incrementally add information that cannot be obtained from other sources of information.

PICTURE-STORY TASKS

In applied practice, having clients tell stories to pictorial stimuli has been almost as popular as using the Rorschach, although without as much directly supportive research. In large part, this is because the most commonly researched storytelling scales are not regularly scored in practice. In clinical psychology training (Mihura et al., 2017), the original Thematic Apperception Test (TAT) is the most popular, followed by the Roberts Apperception Test: 2 (Roberts-2). Several other less popular storytelling tests exist, such as the Children's Apperception Test, Tell-Me-A-Story Test (TEMAS), and Picture Story Exercise. The latter is used often in research on motives, though not in clinical practice. Although the TAT can be used with adults or children, the Roberts-2 and TEMAS were specifically designed for use with children and both have parallel sets of cards for use with different ethnic groups. Our review focuses on the TAT and a more recently developed measure that is increasingly used and researched, the Adult Attachment Projective Picture System (AAP). For additional stimuli and scoring approaches, see Jenkins (2008).

For all picture-story tasks, respondents are presented with figural stimuli, which may encompass fairly ambiguous scenes or clearly depicted scenarios with one or more people, and asked to create a story. Typical instructions indicate the story should describe what is happening in the picture, what led up to it, what will happen next, and what each of the characters are thinking and feeling. The examiner records what the respondent says, including any examiner prompts for missing elements. The cards vary in their characteristics, with each pulling for particular kinds of themes. The respondent's stories are then interpreted for any recurring themes and for ways in which the respondent's story matches or deviates from the typical pull for that particular card. These interpretations are used to understand a person's typical way of constructing or applying narrative meaning to situations. As such, storytelling tasks address a person's mental schema, or style of conceptualizing situations, and can provide examples of how they tend to interpret somewhat ambiguous interpersonal situations. For example, the characters in a person's TAT story might frequently be cast as heroes rescuing helpless people. In everyday life, the respondent may tend to be dependent on others or, vice versa, identify with the helping characters and play this role in their lives (e.g., nurse, therapist, or waiter).

The TAT (Murray, 1943) consists of thirty pictures and one blank card: fourteen cards depict a single person, fourteen have two or more people, and two depict outdoor scenes. The images are all achromatic and generally have a gloomy tone. The task was designed to elicit stories that would exemplify important psychological characteristics, including motivations, needs, drives, and personal or interpersonal conflicts. Most practitioners select between eight to ten cards, which typically include cards they use with most clients and others based on the referral questions and the card's pull for typical stories (e.g., Weiner & Greene, 2017). Clinicians generally use an intuitive approach to identify recurring themes or salient departures from what is typical and their implications. Inferences typically encompass attending to the form or structure of the stories (e.g., organization, injection of content not depicted, typicality), themes (e.g., endings, emotional tone, nature of interactions), and interactive behaviors around the task (e.g., reactions to the task demands or the examiner). Several recent resources provide useful illustrations of drawing clinical inferences with the TAT (e.g., Teglasi, 2010; Weiner & Greene, 2017).

Common and generally supportive research with the TAT encompasses implicit motives, including achievement, power, and affiliation or intimacy (e.g., McClelland, Koestner, & Weinberger, 1989; Winter et al., 1998), and three developmentally ordered defense mechanisms, denial, projection, and identification (see Cramer, 2015). Another is the Social Cognition and Object Relations Scale: Global Rating Method (SCORS-G; Stein & Slavin-Mulford, 2018) with eight scales assessing Complexity of Representation of People, Affective Quality of Representations, Emotional Investment in Relationships, Emotional Investment in Values and Moral Standards, Understanding of Social Causality, Experience and Management of Aggressive Impulses, Self-Esteem, and Identity and Coherence of Self. Across studies, samples have been diverse in gender and ethnicity.

Because the TAT does not have a uniform set of cards or standardized scoring and norms for practice, it is more accurately considered an assessment method or task rather than a psychological test. Published case studies show that the TAT can be helpful when used by psychologists to explore personal and idiographic meanings with their patients, especially when used in a collaborative or therapeutic assessment (e.g., Smith et al., 2015). Yet psychologists should use caution with their interpretive hypotheses and ensure that the interpretation is experienced as valid with their client or that other evidence independently supports their interpretations. Also, very little research is available on motivated efforts to bias stories in a pathological or healthy direction, with almost all of it being older and generating mixed results (Sewell & Helle, 2018). The only study published in the last decade found children instructed to fake good in their thematic stories did not differ from controls on clinical variables (Fantini et al., 2017).

The AAP (George & West, 2012) is a recently developed storytelling test for use with adults that has generated fairly substantial empirical support across ethnically diverse samples. It is focused exclusively on assessing attachment and consists of eight line drawings designed to sequentially increase activation of attachment representations, specifically focused on potential threats of separation, loss, and aloneness. Although the coding system is complicated to learn, it has shown decent inter-rater agreement and reasonable test-retest reliability (George & West, 2012). The scores are criterion-referenced as opposed to norm-referenced, with the full set of narratives classified as Unresolved, Secure, Dismissing, or Preoccupied Attachment. The AAP has shown validity in relation to maternal caregiving and child adjustment, attachment difficulties following trauma, and developmental adversities (e.g., George & West, 2012), as well as neurophysiological correlates across multiple multinational studies (e.g., Buchheim et al., 2016; Müller et al., 2018).

SENTENCE COMPLETION TASKS

Sentence completion methods require the examinee to create a sentence that builds on a stimulus word or phrase. These measures hold appeal because they are time-efficient and provide a nonthreatening task that can promote rapport, especially with children. Many sentence completion measures have been developed (Sherry, Dahlen, & Holaday, 2004); the Rotter Incomplete Sentences Blank (RISB) is the most popular in clinical practice and the Washington University Sentence Completion Test (WUSCT) is the most frequently studied in research. Both use written, not oral, responses to sentence stems. Neither measure has been evaluated for non-credible or biased responding, though sentence completion measures are not immune to such efforts (e.g., Picano et al., 2002; Sewell & Helle, 2018).

The RISB-2 (Rotter, Lah, & Rafferty, 1992) is available in three parallel forms for adults, college students, and high school students. Most of the sentence stems (twenty-nine of forty) have just one or two words (e.g., "People ..., " "I like ... "), with the remaining items having just three to five words. The test authors provide a quantitative scoring system that yields an overall adjustment score, derived from weighted ratings of each response. The manual reports an optimal cutting score to differentiate adjustment from maladjustment using college students, with the caveat that it needs to be adjusted for other populations. However, interpretation typically involves a qualitative analysis of response content to ascertain thoughts, feelings, self-attitudes, interpersonal relationships, and problem areas. Weiner and Greene (2017) provide a guide for interpretation, as well as a more detailed review of the available research on its reliability, validity, and norms when formally scored.

Loevinger (e.g., 1998) developed the thirty-six-item WUSCT as a research instrument specifically to assess the construct of ego development, which is understood as a key dimension of psycho-emotional maturity, distinct from age or general intelligence. Items include stems such as "When I am criticized ... " or "Being with other people ... " Each item is classified into one of eight levels of ego development (Impulsive, Self-Protective, Conformist, Self-Aware, Conscientious, Individualistic, Autonomous, and Integrated) that is converted to a final score. Scoring criteria for each item are rigorously defined, leading to high levels of inter-rater reliability among trained individuals (Westenberg, Hauser, & Cohn, 2004). Extensive research supports the validity of the WUSCT as a measure of ego development and psychological maturity, with more than 300 empirical studies completed by the early 1990s (Westenberg et al., 2004), including longitudinal predictive validity for various indices of adaptability and effective functioning. A meta-analysis showed just modest associations with intelligence and incremental validity over and above intelligence (Cohn & Westenberg, 2004).

PROMPTED PICTURE DRAWING TASKS

Picture drawing techniques prompt clients to create an illustration. Like sentence completion tasks, they are often used as an initial nonthreatening task to promote rapport and as an adjunct to other assessment measures. They are considered particularly useful for assessing young children because they do not require verbal expression and are congruent with children's age-appropriate activities. Many scoring approaches have been introduced over the years, with the most common being a global summary approach that counts either expected or atypical features. Within that approach, there are two primary uses of drawings: one to estimate intellectual maturity and the other to identify maladjustment or psychopathology. The validity literature for each is substantially different.

Assessing Intellectual Maturity

Harris (1964) completed the first large standardization of drawings as a nonverbal index of intellectual maturity in children, norming the task on 2,975 youth aged five to fifteen years. Harris selected scoring characteristics (e.g., trunk longer than breadth, arms attached to trunk) using four classes of evidence: progressive age change, item-total associations, correlations with intelligence, and presence in drawings from intellectually impaired students. Naglieri (1988) revised his measure, using sixty-four criteria that were normed in the 1980s on a large (N = 2,622) and nationally representative sample of youth. Most recently,

Reynolds and Hickman (2004) created a simplified system using just one figure of the self that is coded for twenty-three characteristics, and extended the age range to encompass adults, with norms from four to ninety years.

In general, because these measures count the presence of certain characteristics, they tend to have excellent inter-rater reliability ($r > 0.90$) and good stability ($r = 0.60$ to 0.80 for intervals up to four months; e.g., Scott, 1981). However, their validity has been much more hotly contested. The major critical reviews (e.g., Imuta et al., 2013; Scott, 1981) do not dispute the magnitude of the validity coefficients, which typically are in the range 0.30–0.65 with maximum performance measures of general intelligence. Rather, the argument is that the correlations are not sufficiently high to be interchangeable with the maximum performance measures or suitable for use in high-stakes decisions, such as qualifications for intellectual disability. Although we agree with the latter, the validity coefficients for these drawing tasks are regularly larger than the typical heteromethod validity coefficients found when comparing maximum performance measures with alternative methods for assessing conceptually parallel constructs (e.g., see table 3 in Meyer et al., 2001).

Ironically, findings from the largest and most representative datasets are never mentioned in reviews of the literature, even though they are available to interested researchers. Their robust findings contradict arguments suggesting that figure drawing measures of intelligence in youth are invalid. Two large datasets jointly examined about 14,000 youth who were nationally representative of the US population aged six to seventeen, and were collected in the 1960s for the National Health Examination Survey (Series 11).[2] The drawings showed expected monotonic increases with age, correlated well with two Wechsler subtests, and had an expected pattern of correlates with family background variables, conditions at birth, developmental milestones, medical problems, and school experiences that was similar to the Wechsler scales (e.g., Roberts & Engel, 1974). Two ongoing British projects collectively continue to follow more than 34,000 people, collecting multisource information on many health, development, economic, and interpersonal factors.[3] Each study used figure drawings and three or four other ability measures to assess intellect in childhood. Most research has created a general factor of intelligence, with the figure drawing task showing strong *g* loadings (e.g., Kanazawa, 2012; Parsons, 2014). This factor has been linked to various criteria, including how intelligence impacts subsequent health, drug use, voting behaviors, social class, and educational attainment years later (e.g., Batty et al., 2007; White & Batty, 2012).

Maladjustment or Psychopathology

The other main use of figure drawings is to make inferences about psychological functioning and maladjustment based on drawn features. As noted by Weiner and Greene (2017), this tradition began in the 1940s and most commonly encompasses interpreting drawings of human figures; the combination of a house, tree, and person; or family members engaged in an activity. Naglieri, McNeish, and Bardos (1991) revised a list first developed by Koppitz of features atypically seen in children's drawings (e.g., gross asymmetries, teeth, genitals, no eyes), clarified coding criteria, and normed the measure on 2,260 nationally representative youth aged six to seventeen. Although the norms may now be somewhat dated, the manual reported good reliability and promising validity, with subsequent research showing moderately supportive validity for differentiating clinical from nonclinical samples.

In practice, most clinicians do not formally score figure drawings but rather interpret them impressionistically. Although impressionistic interpretation is challenging to study, Tharinger and Stark (1990) developed an approach to doing so that can be applied to both individual figures and family drawings. Initial reliability and validity results were promising, but the system appears not to have been researched since that time. Thomas (1966) published a potential resource for research, providing the male and female drawings from 870 participants in an ongoing seventy plus–year longitudinal study of medical students that could be used to evaluate validity in relation to a wealth of follow-up data obtained over time.

A very different type of drawing task is the Wartegg Drawing Completion Test, which consists of a two-by-four grid of squares, with each square containing a unique symbol (e.g., three dots) that respondents incorporate into a drawing. The Wartegg has been used regularly with adults in countries such as Finland, Italy, Brazil, and Germany; its familiarity is growing in the United States, with a new English-language monograph to guide its use (Crisi, 2018). A meta-analysis supported the general reliability and global validity of the Wartegg (Grønnerød & Grønnerød, 2012); however, it did not indicate what constructs the test was better or worse at assessing and did not summarize evidence for specific scales or variables.

Tharinger and Roberts (2014) and Weiner and Greene (2017) provide guidelines for drawing conservative inferences from different types of figure drawings. However, although drawings are easy to use, clinicians should be cautious relying on them to assess personality or psychopathology.

Strengths and Limitations Associated with Methods of Knowing

The measures reviewed in this chapter have strengths and limitations relative to other standardized ways of knowing based on self-report, informant rating, or maximum

[2] Studies using these data are available at: www.cdc.gov/nchs/products/series/series11.htm

[3] Details and individual studies can be obtained at: https://cls.ucl.ac.uk/

performance. We briefly review these qualities to better contextualize typical performance measures for informing a multimethod assessment.

The reported methods (i.e., self and informant) always require linguistic mediation of stimuli via statements, questions, or possibly short vignettes. In response, the reporter, when optimally engaged with the task, reflects on experiences, retrospectively recalls exemplars consistent with and inconsistent with the verbal stimulus, and then decides how to reply. The linguistically mediated results of this introspective reflection are provided in the form of an endorsed response to an anchored rating scale. Strengths of reported methods are the almost limitless range of potential constructs they can assess and the highly flexible time scope they can encompass including the past, present, and future.

In contrast, the performed methods (maximum and typical) rely on various types of visual, auditory, tactile, and verbal stimuli, often presented together as a package. The respondent's task is to engage spontaneously with the stimuli and provide a behavioral response that can include words, actions, narratives, imagery, drawings, or other productions, which recruit processes beyond the verbal-linguistic process that dominate the reported methods. The specific requirements of the task define the constructs assessed by these methods and, because the tasks entail behavior in the moment, these constructs are dependent on the respondent's current functioning and behavior. Responses thus have high occasion sensitivity, which cannot indicate what the respondent might have done on a different occasion. Thus, the extent to which task behavior generalizes to everyday life depends on the actions completed at the time of measurement being meaningfully characteristic of the person.

Considering more specifically typical performance tasks, their instructions carry an expectation for the respondent to generate some kind of response, though the respondent decides what kind of response is sufficient or desirable. Because the face validity of most typical performance methods is low, the social desirability demands are typically minimal, though impression management generally operates on the extent to which the respondent spontaneously engages with the task authentically, including their propensity to censure certain types of response content. In general, typical performance measures are optimal for observing and classifying a person's natural predilections, which may not be present fully or clearly in their verbal self-concept. However, these measures generally are poor for assessing specific beliefs, symptoms, experiences, or historical events. With these tasks, it is not possible to determine what a client consciously feels, believes, or has experienced, or whether they meet criteria for a specific diagnosis.

Consequently, it is optimal to use typical performance measures in a multimethod collaborative assessment anchored by self-report (Finn, Fischer, & Handler, 2012). Literature reviews examining the validity of assessment methods have found the midrange of cross-method validity effect sizes was $r = 0.21$ to 0.33 (Meyer et al., 2001), though lower when comparing self-report with either maximum performance tests of attention ($r = 0.06$) or memory ($r = 0.13$) or typical performance measures of parallel constructs from the Rorschach ($r = 0.04$) or TAT ($r = 0.09$). This low degree of construct convergence across different methods means any single method provides only a partial representation of the assessed domain, which is the evidence-based rationale for employing multimethod assessment so psychologists can more fully understand their clients.

Working in a multimethod context also forces psychologists to contend with disagreements across sources. Doing so effectively requires recognition of how methods differ from each other and how those distinct sources of information shape the construct assessed. What may seem like a single construct, such as hostile aggression, actually varies substantially depending on whether the source for that information is self-report on a questionnaire, informant-report on a rating scale, imagery in response to Rorschach inkblots, or narrative stories in response to the TAT. Recognizing these distinctions, psychologists also need to avoid thinking of *either-or* decisions that pick which source of information is most correct in favor of using *both-and* decisions to empathically understand what it means to be a person for whom all sources of information are true.

Finally, a collaborative assessment ensures both the psychologist and the client have a common understanding of the test findings. Each typical performance method reviewed here has exemplar scales that can be coded reliably and show reasonable or good evidence of validity. However, with the exception of the Rorschach, other typical performance measures are used impressionistically by clinicians rather than scored using the scales with documented validity support. Psychologists engaged in idiographic theorizing about the meaning of specific test behaviors can develop inferences that are biased or have little basis in the reality of a client's life. However, coming to a collaboratively constructed understanding of these behaviors with the client can be an immediate and effective antidote to potentially inaccurate inferences. Collaborative assessment thus allows psychologists to use the idiographically rich and personally relevant responses from the assessment tools covered in this chapter in an ethical and optimally helpful manner.

REFERENCES

Batty, G. D., Deary, I. J., Schoon, I., & Gale, C. R. (2007). Mental ability across childhood in relation to risk factors for premature mortality in adult life: The 1970 British Cohort Study. *Journal of Epidemiology and Community Health*, *61*, 997–1003. doi:10.1136/jech.2006.054494

Beaudoin, M., & Desrichard, O. (2011). Are memory self-efficacy and memory performance related? A meta-analysis. *Psychological Bulletin, 137*, 211–241. doi:10.1037/a0022106

Bornstein, R. F. (1999). Criterion validity of objective and projective dependency tests: A meta-analytic assessment of behavioral prediction. *Psychological Assessment, 11*, 48–57. doi:10.1037/1040-3590.11.1.48

Buchheim, A., Erk, S., George, C., Kächele, H., Martius, P., Pokorny, D., ... Walter, H. (2016). Neural response during the activation of the attachment system in patients with borderline personality disorder: An fMRI study. *Frontiers in Human Neuroscience, 10*, 389.

Cohn, L. D., & Westenberg, P. M. (2004). Intelligence and maturity: Meta-analytic evidence for the incremental and discriminant validity of Loevinger's measure of ego development. *Journal of Personality and Social Psychology, 86*, 760–772. doi:10.1037/0022-3514.86.5.760

Cramer, P. (2015). Defense mechanisms: 40 years of empirical research. *Journal of Personality Assessment, 97*, 114–123. doi:10.1080/00223891.2014.947997

Crisi, A. (2018). *The Crisi Wartegg System (CWS): Manual for administration, scoring, and interpretation*. New York: Routledge.

Cronbach, L. J. (1990). *Essentials of psychological testing* (5th ed.). New York: Harper Collins.

Dean, K. L., Viglione, D. J., Perry, W., & Meyer, G. J. (2007). A method to optimize the response range while maintaining Rorschach Comprehensive System validity. *Journal of Personality Assessment, 89*, 149–161. doi:10.1080/00223890701468543.

Diener, M. J., Hilsenroth, M. J., Shaffer, S. A., & Sexton, J. E. (2011). A meta-analysis of the relationship between the Rorschach Ego Impairment Index (EII) and psychiatric severity. *Clinical Psychology and Psychotherapy, 18*, 464–485. doi:10.1002/cpp.725

Exner, J. E. (1974). *The Rorschach: A Comprehensive System, Vol. 1: Basic foundations*. New York: Wiley.

Exner, J. E. (1996). Critical bits and the Rorschach response process. *Journal of Personality Assessment, 67*, 464–477.

Exner, J. E. (1997). Rorschach workshops and the future. 1997 Alumni Newsletter. Rorschach Workshops, Asheville, NC, July 7.

Exner, J. E. (2003). *The Rorschach: A comprehensive system, Vol. 1: Basic foundations* (4th ed.). Hoboken, NJ: Wiley.

Fantini, F., Banis, A., Dell'Acqua, E., Durosini, I., & Aschieri, F. (2017) Exploring children's induced defensiveness to the Tell Me a Story Test (TEMAS). *Journal of Personality Assessment, 99*, 275–285, doi:10.1080/00223891.2016.1261359

Finn, S. E., Fischer, C. T., & Handler, L. (Eds.). (2012). *Collaborative/therapeutic assessment: A casebook and guide*. Hoboken, NJ: John Wiley.

Garb, H. N. (1999). Call for a moratorium on the use of the Rorschach Inkblot Test in clinical and forensic settings. *Assessment, 6*, 313–317. doi:10.1177/107319119900600402

George, C., & West, M. (2012). *The Adult Attachment Projective Picture System*. New York: Guilford Press.

Graceffo, R. A., Mihura, J. L., & Meyer, G. J. (2014). A meta-analysis of an implicit measure of personality functioning: The Mutuality of Autonomy Scale. *Journal of Personality Assessment, 96*, 581–595. doi:10.1080/00223891.2014.919299

Grønnerød, C. (2003). Temporal stability in the Rorschach method: A meta-analytic review. *Journal of Personality Assessment, 80*, 272–293. doi:10.1207/S15327752JPA8003_06

Grønnerød, J. S., & Grønnerød, C. (2012). The Wartegg Zeichen Test: A literature overview and a meta-analysis of reliability and validity. *Psychological Assessment, 24*, 476–489. doi:10.1037/a0026100

Harris, D. B. (1964). *Children's drawings as measures of intellectual maturity: A revision and extension of the Goodenough Draw-A-Man test*. Oxford: Harcourt, Brace & World.

Hathaway, S. R., & McKinley J. C. (1942). *Manual for the Minnesota Multiphasic Personality Inventory*. Minneapolis: University of Minnesota Press.

Hosseininasab, A., Meyer, G. J., Viglione, D. J., Mihura, J. L., Berant, E., Resende, A. C., Reese, J., & Mohammadi, M. R. (2017). The effect of CS administration or an R-Optimized alternative on R-PAS Variables: A meta-analysis of findings from six studies. *Journal of Personality Assessment, 101*(2), 199–212. doi:10.1080/00223891.2017.1393430

Imuta, K., Scarf, D., Pharo, H., & Hayne, H. (2013). Drawing a close to the use of human figure drawings as a projective measure of intelligence. *PLoS ONE, 8*, e58991. doi:10.1371/journal.pone.0058991

Jenkins, S. R. (Ed.). (2008). *A handbook of clinical scoring systems for thematic apperceptive techniques*. Mahwah, NJ: Lawrence Erlbaum Associates.

Kanazawa, S. (2012). Intelligence, birth order, and family size. *Personality and Social Psychology Bulletin, 38*, 1157–1164. doi:10.1177/0146167212445911

Lilienfeld, S. O., Wood, J. M., & Garb, H. N. (2000). The scientific status of projective techniques. *Psychological Science in the Public Interest, 1*, 27–66. doi:10.1111/1529-1006.002

Loevinger, J. (1998). *Technical foundations for measuring ego development: The Washington University sentence completion test*. Mahwah, NJ: Lawrence Erlbaum Associates.

McClelland, D. C., Koestner, R., & Weinberger, J. (1989). How do self-attributed and implicit motives differ? *Psychological Review, 96*, 690–702. doi:10.1037/0033-295X.96.4.690

Meyer, G. J. (1997). On the integration of personality assessment methods: The Rorschach and MMPI. *Journal of Personality Assessment, 68*, 297–330. doi:10.1207/s15327752jpa6802_5.

Meyer, G. J. (Ed.). (2001). Special Section II: The utility of the Rorschach for clinical assessment [Special Section]. *Psychological Assessment, 13*, 419–502.

Meyer, G. J., & Archer, R. P. (2001). The hard science of Rorschach research: What do we know and where do we go? *Psychological Assessment, 13*, 486–502. doi:10.1037/1040-3590.13.4.486

Meyer, G. J., & Erdberg, P. (2018). Using the Rorschach Performance Assessment System (R-PAS) norms with an emphasis on child and adolescent protocols. In J. L. Mihura & G. J. Meyer (Eds.). *Using the Rorschach Performance Assessment System (R-PAS)* (pp. 46–61). New York: Guilford Press.

Meyer, G. J., Erdberg, P., & Shaffer, T. W. (2007). Towards international normative reference data for the Comprehensive System. *Journal of Personality Assessment, 89*, S201–S216. doi:10.1080/00223890701629342

Meyer, G. J., Finn, S. E., Eyde, L., Kay, G. G., Moreland, K. L., Dies, R. R. et al. (2001). Psychological testing and psychological assessment: A review of evidence and issues. *American Psychologist, 56*, 128–165. doi:10.1037/0003-066X.56.2.128

Meyer, G. J., Giromini, L., Viglione, D. J., Reese, J. B., & Mihura, J. L. (2015). The association of gender, ethnicity, age, and education with Rorschach scores. *Assessment, 22*, 46–64. doi:10.1177/1073191114544358

Meyer, G. J., Hsiao, W., Viglione, D. J., Mihura, J. L., & Abraham, L. M. (2013). Rorschach scores in applied clinical practice: A survey of perceived validity by experienced clinicians. *Journal of Personality Assessment, 95*, 351–365. doi:10.1080/00223891.2013.770399

Meyer, G. J., Mihura, J. L., & Smith, B. L. (2005). The interclinician reliability of Rorschach interpretation in four data sets. *Journal of Personality Assessment, 84*, 296–314. doi:10.1207/s15327752jpa8403_09

Meyer, G. J., Riethmiller, R. J., Brooks, R. D., Benoit, W. A., & Handler, L. (2000). A replication of Rorschach and MMPI-2 convergent validity. *Journal of Personality Assessment, 74*, 175–215. doi:10.1207/S15327752JPA7402_3

Meyer, G. J., Shaffer, T. W., Erdberg, P., & Horn, S. L. (2015). Addressing issues in the development and use of the Composite International Reference Values as Rorschach norms for adults. *Journal of Personality Assessment, 97*, 330–347. doi:10.1080/00223891.2014.961603

Meyer, G. J., Viglione, D. J., Erdberg, P., Exner, J. E., Jr., & Shaffer, T. (2004). CS scoring differences in the Rorschach Workshop and Fresno nonpatient samples. Paper presented at the annual meeting of the Society for Personality Assessment, Miami, FL, March 11.

Meyer, G. J., Viglione, D. J., & Mihura, J. L. (2017). Psychometric foundations of the Rorschach Performance Assessment System (R-PAS). In R. Erard & B. Evans (Eds.), *The Rorschach in multimethod forensic practice* (pp. 23–91). New York: Routledge.

Meyer, G. J., Viglione, D. J., Mihura, J. L., Erard, R. E., & Erdberg, P. (2011). *Rorschach Performance Assessment System: Administration, coding, interpretation, and technical Manual*. Toledo, OH: Rorschach Performance Assessment System.

Mihura, J. L., Dumitrascu, N., Roy, M., & Meyer, G. J. (2018). The centrality of the response process in construct validity: An illustration via the Rorschach Space response. *Journal of Personality Assessment, 100*, 233–249. doi:10.1080/00223891.2017.1306781

Mihura, J. L., Meyer, G. J., Bombel, G., & Dumitrascu, N. (2015). Standards, accuracy, and questions of bias in Rorschach meta-analyses: Reply to Wood, Garb, Nezworski, Lilienfeld, and Duke (2015). *Psychological Bulletin, 141*, 250–260. doi:10.1037/a0038445

Mihura, J. L., Meyer, G. J., Dumitrascu, N., & Bombel, G. (2013). The validity of individual Rorschach variables: Systematic reviews and meta-analyses of the comprehensive system. *Psychological Bulletin, 139*, 548–605. doi:10.1037/a0029406

Mihura, J. L., Roy, M., & Graceffo, R. A. (2017). Psychological assessment training in clinical psychology doctoral programs. *Journal of Personality Assessment, 99*, 153–164. doi:10.1080/00223891.2016.1201978

Müller, L. E., Bertsch, K., Bülau, K., Herpertz, S. C., & Buchheim, A. (2018). Emotional neglect in childhood shapes social dysfunctioning in adults by influencing the oxytocin and the attachment system: Results from a population-based study. *International Journal of Psychophysiology*. doi:10.1016/j.ijpsycho.2018.05.011

Murray, H. A. (1943). *Thematic Apperception Test manual*. Cambridge, MA: Harvard University Press.

Naglieri, J. A. (1988). *Draw a Person: A quantitative scoring system*. San Antonio, TX: Psychological Corporation.

Naglieri, J. A., McNeish, T., & Bardos, A. (1991). *Draw a person: Screening procedure for emotional disturbance*. Austin, TX: Pro-Ed.

Parsons, S. (2014). *Childhood cognition in the 1970 British Cohort Study*. London: Centre for Longitudinal Studies, Institute of Education, University of London.

Picano, J. J., Roland, R. R., Rollins, K. D., & Williams, T. J. (2002). Development and validation of a sentence completion test measure of defensive responding in military personnel assessed for nonroutine missions. *Military Psychology, 14*(4), 279–298. doi:10.1207/S15327876MP1404_4

Pignolo, C., Giromini, L., Ando', A., Ghirardello, D., Di Girolamo, M., Ales, F., & Zennaro, A. (2017). An interrater reliability study of Rorschach Performance Assessment System (R–PAS) raw and complexity-adjusted scores. *Journal of Personality Assessment, 99*, 619–625. doi:10.1080/00223891.2017.1296844

Reynolds, C. R., & Hickman, J. A. (2004). *Draw-A-Person Intellectual Ability Test for children, adolescents, and adults: Examiner's manual (DAP:IQ)*. Austin, TX: Pro-Ed.

Roberts, J., & Engel, A. (1974). Family background, early development, and intelligence of children 6–11 years: United States. Vital and Health Statistics Series 11(142). www.cdc.gov/nchs/products/series/series11.htm

Rorschach, H. (1942). *Psychodiagnostics: A diagnostic test based on perception*. Bern: Verlag Hans Huber.

Rotter, J. B., Lah, M. I., & Rafferty, J. E. (1992). *Rotter Incomplete Sentences Blank manual* (2nd ed.). Orlando, FL: Psychological Corporation.

Scott, L. H. (1981). Measuring intelligence with the Goodenough-Harris Drawing Test. *Psychological Bulletin, 89*, 483–505. doi:10.1037/0033-2909.89.3.483

Searls, D. (2017). *The inkblots: Hermann Rorschach, his iconic test, and the power of seeing*. New York: Crown Publishers.

Sewell, K. W., & Helle, A. C. (2018). Dissimulation on projective measures: An updated appraisal of a very old question. In R. Rogers & S. D. Bender (Eds.), *Clinical assessment of malingering and deception* (pp. 301–313). New York: Guilford Press.

Shaffer, T. W., Erdberg, P., & Meyer, G. J. (Eds.). (2007). International reference samples for the Rorschach Comprehensive System [Special issue]. *Journal of Personality Assessment, 89*(Suppl. 1).

Sherry, A., Dahlen, E., & Holaday, M. (2004). The use of sentence completion tests with adults. In M. J. Hilsenroth & D. L. Segal (Eds.), *Comprehensive handbook of psychological assessment, Vol. 2: Personality assessment* (pp. 372–386). Hoboken, NJ: John Wiley & Sons.

Smith, J. D., Eichler, W. C., Norman, K. R., & Smith, S. R. (2015). The effectiveness of collaborative/therapeutic assessment for psychotherapy consultation: A pragmatic replicated single-case study. *Journal of Personality Assessment, 97*, 261–270. doi:10.1080/00223891.2014.955917

Stein, M. B., & Slavin-Mulford, J. (2018). *The Social Cognition and Object Relations Scale-Global Rating Method (SCORS-G): A comprehensive guide for clinicians and researchers*. New York: Guilford Press.

Sultan, S., Andronikof, A., Réveillère, C., & Lemmel, G. (2006). A Rorschach stability study in a nonpatient adult sample. *Journal of Personality Assessment, 87*, 330–348. doi:10.1207/s15327752jpa8703_13

Teglasi, H. (2010). *Essentials of TAT and other storytelling assessments* (2nd ed.). Hoboken, NJ: John Wiley.

Tharinger, D. J., & Roberts, G. (2014). Human figure drawings in therapeutic assessment with children: Process, product, context, and systemic impact. In L. Handler & A. D. Thomas (Eds.), *Drawings in assessment and psychotherapy: Research and application* (pp. 17–41). New York: Routledge.

Tharinger, D. J., & Stark, K. D. (1990). A qualitative versus quantitative approach to evaluating the Draw-A-Person and Kinetic Family Drawing: A study of mood- and anxiety-disorder children. *Psychological Assessment, 2*, 365–375. doi:10.1037/1040-3590.2.4.365

Thomas, C. B. (1966). *An atlas of figure drawings: Studies on the psychological characteristics of medical students – III*. Baltimore, MD: Johns Hopkins Press.

Viglione,D. J., Blume-Marcovici. A. C., Miller, H. L., Giromini, L., & Meyer, G. J. (2012). An initial inter-rater reliability study for the Rorschach Performance Assessment System. *Journal of Personality Assessment, 94*, 607–612. doi:10.1080/00223891.2012.684118

Viglione, D. J., & Hilsenroth, M. J. (2001). The Rorschach: Facts, fiction, and future. *Psychological Assessment, 13*, 452–471. doi:10.1037/1040-3590.13.4.452

Weiner, I. B., & Greene, R. L. (2017). *Handbook of personality assessment* (2nd ed.). Hoboken, NJ: John Wiley & Sons.

Westenberg, P. M., Hauser, S. T., & Cohn, L. D. (2004). Sentence completion measurement of psychosocial maturity. In M. J. Hilsenroth & D. L. Segal (Eds.), *Comprehensive handbook of psychological assessment, Vol. 2: Personality assessment* (pp. 595–616). Hoboken, NJ: John Wiley & Sons.

White, J., & Batty, G. D. (2012). Intelligence across childhood in relation to illegal drug use in adulthood: 1970 British Cohort Study. *Journal of Epidemiology and Community Health, 66*, 767–774. doi:10.1136/jech-2011-200252

Winter, D. G., John, O. P., Stewart, A. J., Klohnen, E. C., & Duncan, L. E. (1998). Traits and motives: Toward an integration of two traditions in personality research. *Psychological Review, 105*, 230–250. doi:10.1037/0033-295X.105.2.230

Wood, J. M., Garb, H. N., Nezworski, M. T., Lilienfeld, S. O., & Duke, M. C. (2015). A second look at the validity of widely used Rorschach indices: Comment on Mihura, Meyer, Dumitrascu, and Bombel (2013). *Psychological Bulletin, 141*, 236–249. doi:10.1037/a0036005

Wood, J. M., Nezworski, M. T., Garb, H. N., & Lilienfeld, S. O. (2001). The misperception of psychopathology: Problems with norms of the Comprehensive System for the Rorschach. *Clinical Psychology: Science and Practice, 8*, 350–373. doi:10.1093/clipsy/8.3.350

Wright, C. V., Beattie, S. G., Galper, D. I., Church, A. S., Bufka, L. F., Brabender, V. M., & Smith, B. L. (2017). Assessment practices of professional psychologists: Results of a national survey. *Professional Psychology: Research and Practice, 48*, 73–78. doi:10.1037/pro0000086

PART III

ASSESSMENT AND DIAGNOSIS OF SPECIFIC MENTAL DISORDERS

21 Assessment of Childhood Neurodevelopmental Disorders

LINDSEY WILLIAMS, RACHEL SANDERCOCK, AND LAURA GROFER KLINGER

DIFFERENTIAL DIAGNOSIS FOR NEURODEVELOPMENTAL DISORDERS

Many neurodevelopmental disorders have shared risk factors and one neurodevelopmental disorder often confers an increased likelihood of additional neurodevelopmental problems. For example, abnormalities of the MECP2 gene are associated with greater risk of autism spectrum disorder (ASD), intellectual disability, and Rett syndrome; individuals with Rett syndrome have an increased likelihood of being diagnosed with ASD compared to the general population (see Woodbury-Smith & Scherer, 2018, for a review). Differential diagnosis for neurodevelopmental disorders will almost always include assessing for symptoms of ASD, both because it is one of the most common neurodevelopmental disorders (Baio et al., 2018) and because of the frequent overlap in symptoms between ASD and other disorders.

While being alert that multiple neurodevelopmental disorders may exist concurrently, the clinician should be mindful not to overdiagnose concurrent disorders based on overlapping symptomatology. While it may be the case, for example, that comorbid ASD is more common in children with Trisomy 21 than in the general population, there may also be considerable overlap in symptom presentation in children who do not have both disorders. Young children with Trisomy 21 may have notable differences in communication (e.g., poor eye contact), play (e.g., preoccupation with parts of objects, restricted interests), and stereotyped behaviors (e.g., body rocking, hand flapping) that are similar to children with ASD but lack the core deficits in social relatedness (Channell et al., 2015; Hepburn et al., 2008). Individuals with Prader-Willi syndrome frequently show restricted and repetitive behaviors and may show social deficits similar to ASD (Dimitropoulos & Schultz, 2007; Greaves et al., 2006). Given similarities in some aspects of behavioral presentation, it is common for children with other neurodevelopmental disorders to score high on measures of ASD symptoms, which may lead to overdiagnosis of ASD. Further complicating differential diagnosis, comorbid psychiatric problems are common in individuals with neurodevelopmental disorders and should also be evaluated.

Owing to these issues of diagnostic complexity, a thorough developmental and medical history is crucial for guiding assessment. History should include a review of genetics, sensory perceptual functioning, sleep, and nutrition. For example, moderate vision and hearing problems may go undiagnosed in individuals with intellectual disability but have a significant impact on learning, daily living skills, and quality of life (Evenhuis et al., 2009). Hearing impairments can be associated with decreased language as well as peer and emotional difficulties (Fellinger et al., 2009). Clinicians should inquire about the child's most recent hearing and vision screening and any related concerns. It is also important to ask about the child's sleep and dietary habits, episodes of "spacing out" or other behaviors that could indicate possible seizure activity, and any other potential medical concerns, and make referrals as appropriate (for more information about seizures, pain, feeding disorders, and other medical concerns in the context of intellectual disability, see Matson & Matson, 2015). An intake interview should also include questions about past trauma, as individuals with neurodevelopmental disorders are disproportionately victims of abuse (US Department of Health and Human Services, 2012), which may affect behavior and psychological well-being.

After developmental and medical history, the clinician's evaluation may include symptom-specific assessment, cognitive functioning, adaptive functioning, and concurrent psychological/behavioral concerns. Depending on the presenting concerns, achievement testing may be needed (e.g., if there is concern about a specific learning disorder). Results of a comprehensive assessment will guide the clinician in making an accurate diagnosis and appropriate recommendations.

SYMPTOM-SPECIFIC ASSESSMENT FOR AUTISM SPECTRUM DISORDER

As previously mentioned, the frequency of ASD in the general population, comorbidity with other neurodevelopmental disorders, and overlap of ASD symptoms with other neurodevelopmental issues make it prudent to assess for ASD symptoms in many cases. The diagnostic symptoms and other areas of importance in ASD assessment are outlined in the sections titled "Diagnostic Symptoms" and "Research Domain Criteria Symptoms," followed by information on ASD-specific measures. Assessment for ASD will yield pertinent information for assessing other neurodevelopmental areas, as well as inform treatment recommendations regardless of whether a diagnosis of ASD is given.

In the ASD field, it is common to hear, "Once you've met one person with ASD . . . you've met one person with ASD." This phrase emphasizes the heterogeneity in symptom presentation and severity encompassed in the ASD diagnosis. Heterogeneity is likely due to several factors, including association with a known genetic disorder, developmental level, and symptom severity. This variability in clinical presentation has important implications for the diagnostic process.

DSM-5 Diagnostic Symptoms

The DSM-5 (American Psychiatric Association, 2013) conceptualizes ASD as defined by behavioral symptoms in two core domains: social communication and the presence of restricted/repetitive behaviors. To address heterogeneity, symptom severity in each domain is rated on a three-point scale based on the level of support required (some, substantial, or very substantial support). An ASD diagnosis should also specify if there is accompanying intellectual or language impairment; association with a known medical or genetic condition or environmental factor; association with another neurodevelopmental, mental, or behavioral disorder; or comorbid catatonia.

Persistent deficits in social communication and social interaction. Social communication deficits in ASD impact multiple areas of social behavior, including social-emotional reciprocity (e.g., appropriately sharing interests with others, initiating and responding to interactions), nonverbal communication (e.g., understanding and use of gestures, facial expressions, and eye contact), and understanding (e.g., peer interactions, adapting behavior to different social contexts). Symptom expression varies based on several factors, including the individual's developmental level. For example, difficulties understanding and maintaining relationships may look like difficulty engaging in pretend play with peers in a preschooler, while an older child may have difficulty engaging in reciprocal conversation with classmates. Symptom severity also affects presentation. An individual with severe deficits in social reciprocity may fail entirely to respond to others, while an individual with less severe symptoms may desire social relationships but monologue about a topic to disinterested peers.

Restricted, repetitive behaviors, interests, or activities (RRBIs). Atypical RRBIs include a variety of symptoms: stereotyped and repetitive motor movements (e.g., hand flapping), use of objects (e.g., lining up toys instead of playing with them) or speech (e.g., echolalia, "scripting"), preoccupations with unusual objects (e.g., manhole covers) or topics (e.g., train schedules), rigid adherence to routines (e.g., insisting on taking the same route to school or eating dinner at precisely 5:00 p.m.), and unusual interest in or response to sensory input (e.g., fascination with lights; under-responsivity to pain). It is important to note, however, that while repetitive behaviors are more common in individuals with ASD, they can be observed in typically developing children (e.g., Watt et al., 2008) and in the context of other developmental and psychiatric disorders (see Leekam, Prior, & Uljarevic, 2011, for a review).

Research Domain Criteria Symptoms

The recently proposed Research Domain Criteria (RDoC) suggest that a dimensional rather than categorical approach is needed to understand psychopathology. An RDoC approach cuts across diagnostic categories and incorporates many areas commonly identified as problematic in individuals with neurodevelopmental disorders, including social processes, cognitive systems (e.g., attention, perception, working memory), positive valence/reward systems, negative valance systems (e.g., defeat, depression, loss), systems of arousal regulation (sleep, activity, circadian rhythms), and motor systems (Garvey & Cuthbert, 2017; Insel, 2017). Although researchers have only recently begun incorporating an RDoC approach in understanding neurodevelopmental disorders, this approach offers a strong foundation for ensuring adequate assessment of areas likely to be affected in neurodevelopmental disorders.

Measures of Core ASD Symptoms

Unlike neurodevelopmental disorders diagnosed based on genetic or chromosomal abnormalities, there is no medical test to diagnose ASD. While recent research has highlighted the potential for future diagnosis of ASD through imaging (e.g., Hazlett et al., 2017), current best practices rely on behavioral observations and caregiver reports.

Autism Diagnostic Observation Schedule – Second Edition (ADOS-2). The semi-structured, standardized Autism Diagnostic Observation Schedule – Second Edition (ADOS-2; Lord et al., 2012) is a play-based observational assessment designed to probe for symptoms of ASD. It takes approximately forty-five minutes to administer and assesses communication, social interaction, play, and restricted/repetitive behaviors in individuals of different ages with different levels of expressive language. Five different modules exist providing appropriate assessment probes for individuals across the lifespan and across verbal ability.

Owing to the relatively recent update, the ADOS-2 has not been as thoroughly researched as the original ADOS. The ADOS has been widely studied, however, with researchers concluding that it is a reliable and valid measure of ASD symptoms (e.g., Bastiaansen et al., 2011; Gray, Tong & Sweeny, 2008). Kanne, Randolph, and Farmer (2008) endorsed the ADOS as one of the "gold standard" measures for assessing ASD and, in a review of ASD measures, Falkmer and colleagues (2013) included the ADOS as one of only three measures with strong evidence for diagnostic accuracy (see Falkmer at al., 2013 for further review of the ADOS). The extended validation sample for the ADOS-2 included 1,351 cases with clinical diagnoses of ASD (83 percent of the sample) and 279 with non-spectrum conditions (17 percent), such as intellectual disability, language disorders, oppositional defiant disorder, and attention-deficit /hyperactivity disorder (ADHD); ethnicity across module and diagnostic groups ranged from 71 percent to 91 percent Caucasian. Within this sample, the authors reported sensitivity ranging from 50 percent (Module 1: Few to No Words, nonverbal mental age ≤ 15 months) to 94 percent (Module 1: Few to No Words, nonverbal mental age > 15 months) across modules and age categories, with an average sensitivity of 0.84. Reported specificity ranged from 0.91 (Module 3) to 0.98 (Module 2), with an average specificity of 0.96 (Lord et al., 2012). The ADOS-2 has been successfully translated into several languages and assessed for usability in countries around the world (e.g., Rudra et al., 2014; Smith, Malcolm-Smith, & de Vries, 2017).[1] However, racial and socioeconomic disparities in ASD diagnosis persist (Mandell et al., 2009) and more research on the use of the ADOS-2 in diverse populations is needed.

Autism Diagnostic Interview-Revised (ADI-R). The ADI-R (Rutter, Le Couteur, & Lord, 2003) is a standardized, semi-structured interview for parents or caregivers. It includes ninety-three items in three domains of functioning: language/communication; reciprocal social interactions; and restricted, repetitive, and stereotyped behaviors and interests. Like the ADOS-2, the ADI-R is available in several languages,[2] though there is limited research available about its use with diverse populations. The ADI-R is less expensive than the ADOS-2; however, administration takes approximately two hours. The authors reported that sensitivity and specificity on the ADI-R were both above 0.90 for identifying ASD versus non-ASD conditions, such as intellectual disability and language impairments; however, the initial validation sample was small (fifty individuals) and relatively homogeneous (82 percent Caucasian; Lord, Rutter, & LeCouteur, 1994). Additional research has supported the ADI-R's utility in discriminating between ASD and developmental delay (Cox et al., 1999) and language impairment (Mildenberger et al., 2001). Additionally, Falkmer and colleagues (2013) found that the ADOS and ADI-R together have correct classification rates for ASD of 88 percent in children under age three and 84 percent for individuals over age three.

Research in toddler and preschool samples found that the standard ADI-R diagnostic algorithm was not appropriate for children with a nonverbal mental age below two years (Lord et al., 1993; Ventola et al., 2006; Wiggins & Robins, 2008). As a result, a new algorithm was created specifically for use with toddlers and young preschoolers (Kim & Lord, 2012). Research on the revised algorithm conducted by the authors and in a multi-site follow-up study found acceptable sensitivity and specificity (> 0.80) for identifying ASD versus non-spectrum concerns (e.g., language and behavioral disorders, developmental delays; Kim et al., 2013).

Even well-validated measures such as the ADI-R and ADOS-2 should not be used in isolation but should be used in combination with thorough developmental history, caregiver report, other standardized testing, and observation in order to make an accurate diagnosis. For example, Grzadzinski and colleagues (2016) found that 21 percent of children with ADHD met ASD cutoffs on the original ADOS and 30 percent met ASD cutoffs on all domains of the ADI-R. Thus, even in the most highly researched, validated, and "gold standard" measures of ASD symptoms, it is important to consider other diagnoses that may create symptom overlap.

Childhood Autism Rating Scale – Second Edition (CARS-2). The CARS-2 (Schopler et al., 2010) is a fifteen-item observational screening tool that the clinician completes after a review of developmental history/caregiver interview and direct observation of the individual's behavior. The CARS-2 comes in two forms: one for use with young children or with older children/adults who have IQ below 80 (CARS-2-ST) and a "high functioning" version (CARS-2-HF) for use with individuals over the age of six years with an IQ of eighty or above. The CARS-2-ST is identical to the original CARS and has strong psychometric properties, though estimates vary depending on the age of the child, severity of ASD, and which DSM version was being used at the time (the DSM-III was still in use at the time of original development). The authors report a sensitivity value of 0.88 and a specificity value of 0.86 for identifying ASD versus non-ASD developmental or intellectual disabilities using the CARS-2-ST. Subsequent research has supported the CARS-2-ST's strength in discriminating between children with ASD and non-ASD diagnoses (Perry et al., 2005). Ventola and colleagues (2006) also found good agreement between the CARS-2-ST and the ADOS (Lord et al., 2003) and found that the original CARS had very good sensitivity and specificity compared to clinical judgment. On the

[1] As of this writing, the ADOS-2 is available in twenty-one languages, including English. For a list of available translations, see www.wpspublish.com/app/OtherServices/PublishedTranslations.aspx

[2] As of this writing, the ADI-R is available in twenty languages, including English. For a list of available translations, see www.wpspublish.com/app/OtherServices/PublishedTranslations.aspx

CARS-2-HF, the authors report a sensitivity of 0.81 and specificity of 0.87 in the development sample (Schopler et al., 2010). Individuals included in this sample had a variety of DSM-IV-TR clinical diagnoses, including autistic disorder, Asperger's disorder, pervasive development disorder – not otherwise specified (PDD-NOS), ADHD, learning disorders, and other internalizing and externalizing disorders; a small group of general education and students without ASD in a special education sample were also included to verify an absence of symptoms rated on the CARS-2-HF in those groups. See Ibañez, Stone, and Coonrod (2014) for further review.

Social Communication Questionnaire (SCQ). The SCQ (Rutter, Bailey, & Lord, 2003) is a forty-item caregiver rating scale to assess for ASD symptoms in persons at least four years old with a mental age of two plus years. The items are based on the *ADI-R,* but the *SCQ* only takes about ten minutes to complete and five minutes to score, making the measure useful as a screener to decide whether a full ASD assessment is needed. The Lifetime form is more useful for diagnostic purposes and inquires about the entire developmental history, while the Current Behavior form assesses the past three months and is more useful for treatment planning and tracking change over time. The authors report that, using ROC analysis for the total *SCQ* score, a cutoff score of fifteen had a sensitivity of 0.96 and specificity of 0.80 for Autism (using DSM-IV-TR criteria) versus other diagnoses (e.g., fragile X syndrome) excluding intellectual disability; analyses indicated a sensitivity of 0.96 and specificity of 0.67 for autism versus intellectual disability.

Johnson and colleagues (2011) used the SCQ to screen for ASD in young children who were born extremely preterm. These researchers reported 0.82 sensitivity and 0.88 specificity for identifying ASD versus typical development and other neurodevelopmental impairments, behavioral concerns, and socio-communicative impairments. The authors concluded that the presence of other neurodevelopmental disorders, particularly those with motor disorders, complicates the use and interpretation of the SCQ; given the overlap in symptoms between ASD and other neurodevelopmental disorders, this is true for many caregiver report rating scales.

Social Responsiveness Scale – Second Edition (SRS-2). The SRS-2 (Constantino & Gruber, 2012) is a screening tool designed to assess behaviors associated with developmentally expected social responsiveness across the lifespan beginning at two years, and also includes a scale related to restricted behaviors/interests. The SRS-2 is a sixty-five-item Likert-type rating scale that can be given to caregivers, teachers, or other close observers (e.g., spouses or friends); an adult self-report form is also available. The SRS-2 takes fifteen to twenty minutes to complete and yields subscales for Social Awareness, Social Cognition, Social Communication, Social Motivation, and Restricted Interests/Repetitive Behaviors in addition to a total overall score. The SRS-2 manual reports internal consistency for total scores ranging from 0.94 to 0.96 for the total sample. Inter-rater reliability coefficients ranged from 0.61 to 0.92 across the various forms of the scale. The authors report moderate to high correlations with other rating scales of social communication and social behavior. Lower correlations were found with diagnostic instruments based on observation or interview (i.e., the ADI-R and ADOS).

Various studies have found large effect sizes when comparing individuals with and without ASD (e.g., Constantino, 2011; Turner-Brown et al., 2013). For the School-Age form, the authors of the SRS-2 used ROC analysis to obtain sensitivity and specificity estimates of 0.92 and 0.92, respectively, for identifying ASD among a large sample containing typically developing individuals, individuals with varying levels of related symptomatology (e.g., previous Asperger's or PDD-NOS diagnoses), and individuals with other diagnostic concerns. However, Moody and colleagues (2017) reported that specificity for the SRS-2 decreased with lower maternal education, lower family income, lower developmental functioning, and higher rates of behavior problems. Mandell and colleagues (2012) found lower predictive validity for the adult form, with specificity of 0.60 and sensitivity of 0.86 compared to other psychiatric diagnoses in an inpatient setting, suggesting this form may not discriminate as well as the School-Age form. For further review of the SRS-2, see Bruni (2014).

ASSESSMENT OF COGNITIVE FUNCTIONING

In addition to these core behavioral features of ASD, cognitive processing impairments have consistently been identified (for a review, see Klinger et al., 2014). For example, Brunsdon and colleagues (2014) reported that a majority of children (72 percent) with ASD had multiple cognitive atypicalities in attention, executive function, and perspective taking, with only 18 percent having no apparent cognitive deficits. Sixty-eight percent of children with ASD were found to have problems with executive functioning. Children with multiple learning differences also had more severe ASD symptoms than those without cognitive atypicalities, suggesting a need to consider ASD as a disorder with an inherent underlay of differences in multiple cognitive functions. Impairments in these areas are not specific to ASD and are important targets for determining recommendations/treatment plans in ASD, specifically, as well as in many other neurodevelopmental disabilities, and can be important components of differential diagnosis. The most commonly evaluated assessment areas and appropriate measures are described in the following sections "Intelligence," "Language," "Attention and Executive Functioning," "Adaptive Behavior," and "Psychiatric Comorbidities"; further review, including psychometrics and validation samples, can be found in Chapters 11 and 12 in this volume.

Intelligence

Intellectual disability is common in the context of neurodevelopmental disabilities and assessment will generally include broad developmental or intelligence tests. The Council on Children with Disabilities (Johnson & Meyers, 2007) recommends cognitive testing as a part of any interdisciplinary diagnostic evaluation for developmental disorders, as cognitive testing provides a framework for interpreting an individual's social and communication delays as well as behaviors that may be affected by deficits in these areas. For example, if testing suggests a four-year-old is functioning on a two-year-old level, then social and communication deficits should be interpreted accordingly. Social and communication deficits in ASD must be significantly below expected for *developmental* age, not chronological age.

Intellectual testing highlights any changes in cognitive functioning across development. Young children with or suspected to be at risk for neurodevelopmental disabilities (e.g., extremely low birth weight infants) may show significant change in scores on developmental/cognitive tests over time (Hack et al., 2005). Testing also provides information about neurocognitive strengths and weaknesses. The cognitive profile of individuals with ASD can vary widely, both within and between individuals. Many show wide scatter across domains on tests of cognitive ability, often rendering the interpretation of a full-scale IQ score meaningless (see Klinger, Mussey, & O'Kelley, 2018 for review). It is a common stereotype that individuals with ASD have higher nonverbal than verbal IQ, and some research has supported this idea. However, other researchers have not found this, or have found that this pattern often presents in younger children but gradually disappears during school-age years. It may be that, for many children, verbal processing is initially more impaired but may improve over time (see Klinger et al., 2018).

Developmental assessments. Children with neurodevelopmental disorders often exhibit early signs of motor and/or language delay and are referred for testing prior to our ability to measure stable intellectual functioning. For these young children, developmental assessments cover cognitive, receptive and expressive language, and motor skills. The Mullen Scales of Early Learning (Mullen, 1995) and Bayley Scales of Infant Development – Third Edition (Bayley-III; Bayley, 2006) are commonly used to evaluate young children who, due to developmental delays, would not meet basal requirements on other standardized tests. The *Mullen* can be used up to five and a half years of age, and the Bayley-III through three and a half years (though the lowest possible *T*-score on the Bayley-III is fifty, so extremely delayed children may not score high enough to get a standard score, in which case age-equivalence scores can be used). When assessing an older individual unlikely to meet the basal score on intelligence tests appropriate for their age, developmental tests are sometimes used to provide age equivalencies in lieu of standard scores. The Differential Ability Scales – Second Edition (DAS-II; Elliott, 2007) is a brief developmental battery designed for ages 2:6 through 17:11 years. There are various batteries for different age groups, yielding Verbal, Nonverbal, and General Conceptual Ability scores at all levels and an additional Spatial Ability score for older children. The examiner can administer the lower level battery for children ages 5:0–8:11 if significant intellectual disability is suspected and still compute a standard score.

Verbally based intelligence tests. Commonly used intelligence tests including the Wechsler tests and the Stanford-Binet – Fifth Edition (SB5; Roid, 2003) will not be discussed extensively here. However, certain considerations are worth mentioning. In general, tests that allow computation of a General Abilities Index (GAI) in addition to an overall Full-Scale IQ (e.g., Wechsler tests) have utility in assessing individuals with motor or attention problems. The GAI is computed without indices most likely to be impacted by motor or attentional difficulties (e.g., working memory, processing speed).

The SB5 has the advantage of covering a wide age range (two to eighty-five plus years), which is useful when testing an older child who may be cognitively functioning on a preschool level. Studies comparing Wechsler and SB5 scores in individuals with ASD or intellectual disability have shown interesting differences: Baum and colleagues (2015) found that on average, children with ASD scored substantially better on the SB5 overall, though scores on verbal indices were higher on the Wechsler Intelligence Scale for Children – Fourth Edition. In a study of adults with intellectual disability, Silverman and colleagues (2010) found the opposite pattern, with every individual scoring higher on the Wechsler Adult Intelligence Scale – Fourth Edition than on the SB5. See Chapter 12 in this volume for a general review of these instruments.

Assessing nonverbal or minimally verbal children. One disadvantage of using the nonverbal indices on the SB5 or the Wechsler tests to obtain estimates of nonverbal ability is that subtest administration still requires some verbal comprehension. Measures are sometimes referred to as nonverbal tests if they do not require the *examinee* to speak, but instructions may be given verbally, thus making these measures more accurately described as language-reduced. There are a few truly nonverbal assessments that make no receptive or expressive verbal language demands for examiner or examinee. These assessments may be useful for individuals with speech or hearing difficulties, who are not fluent in English, or who have verbal processing difficulties.

The Leiter International Performance Scale – Third Edition (Leiter-3; Roid et al., 2013) is a commonly used test for individuals with limited verbal ability. The Leiter-3 is also untimed, which is helpful for individuals with motor/coordination difficulties. Designed for ages three to seventy-five years, the Leiter-3 includes instructions for standardized nonverbal instructions (gestures, facial expressions). The Test of Nonverbal Intelligence – Fourth Edition (TONI-4; Brown, Sherbenou, & Johnson, 2010), is a language-free and motor-free assessment. Goldberg Edelson, Edelson, and Jung (1998) noted that, because it does not require real-world knowledge, the TONI may be a more culturally fair measure of intelligence than nonverbal measures that use analogies (e.g., the Universal Nonverbal Intelligence Test; Bracken & McCallum, 2016). The DAS-II includes a nonverbal reasoning cluster and comes with a CD or DVD of signed administration directions in ASL.

Language

A diagnostic evaluation for suspected neurodevelopmental disorders should include broad assessment of both expressive and receptive language. It may be challenging to obtain an inventory of words and speech sounds in individuals with neurodevelopmental disorders. Many of the assessment tasks for expressive abilities involve instructions that can be difficult for some to follow; assessment can be particularly difficult for individuals who have poor imitation skills or are anxious in new settings. The clinician can solicit parent report of words/vocalizations and nonverbal behaviors (Kasari et al., 2013) or ask the parent to record and bring in samples of their child's communication during a routine ten-to-fifteen-minute caregiving interaction. Caregiver-completed measures of adaptive behaviors (e.g., Vineland – Third Edition [Sparrow, Cicchetti, & Saulnier, 2016] and Adaptive Behavior Checklist – Third Edition [Harrison & Oakland, 2015]) often include assessment of language abilities via caregiver report.

At times, more specific assessment by a trained professional (e.g., speech pathologist) may be warranted, particularly when discrepancies exist across communication domains, which is not uncommon in neurodevelopmental disorders. For example, individuals with ASD may have significantly greater deficits in receptive language when compared to individuals with other language problems (Paul et al., 2007), whereas many with Trisomy 21 show greater deficits in expressive than in receptive communication (Chapman, 1997; Chapman et al., 1998). A significant discrepancy between cognitive skills/academic functioning and pragmatic or higher-level language deficits presents a need for adequate assessment of pragmatic language through clinical observation or standardized testing.

A comprehensive review of language and communication assessments is beyond the scope of this chapter. A diagnosis of specific speech/language problems likely necessitates collaboration with or referral to a speech-language pathologist. The interested reader may refer to Paul and Wilson (2009) for more information about assessing prelinguistic, pragmatic, and nonverbal communication, including discussion of measures; the reader may also refer to Shipley and McAfee (2015) for additional information on this topic.

Attention and Executive Functioning

The ultimate goal of cognitive assessment is a thorough understanding of patterns of strengths and weaknesses; given the high variability in different cognitive skills across ASD and other neurodevelopmental disabilities, this may mean assessing specific cognitive features including attention and executive function. Measures of attention and executive function, while not necessary to make a diagnosis of a neurodevelopmental disorder, are useful in identifying areas of particular difficulty, determining whether a comorbid diagnosis is appropriate, and making treatment recommendations. Overall, children with ASD have been shown to have difficulties with shifting attention, while those with ADHD have been found to have difficulties with inhibition (Happé et al., 2006); however, the overlap between these disorders makes it difficult to use these constructs for diagnostic purposes.

As attention and executive function measures are presented in other chapters (see Chapter 15, this volume, in particular), they will only be discussed briefly here. Parent and teacher report measures are perhaps the most widely utilized for their ease of administration and ability to get input from multiple sources across environments; the Behavior Rating Inventory of Executive Functioning (BRIEF; Gioia et al., 2000) is one such scale. Another commonly used report measure is the Conners-3 (Conners, 2008), which focuses on cognitive, behavioral, and emotional problems, with a focus on ADHD and commonly co-occurring mood/behavior disorders. Three performance-based measures that have traditionally been used to measure executive functioning in neurodevelopmental disorders include the Wisconsin Card Sorting Test (WCST; Grant & Berg, 1948; Heaton et al., 1993), which tests the ability to think flexibly; the Tower of Hanoi (Borys, Spitz, & Dorans, 1982), which assesses working memory and planning; and the Stroop Color-Word Test (Stroop, 1935), which measures behavioral inhibition. It is important to note that self-report and collateral-report measures of executive function cannot control for validity and have not been found to correlate well with behavioral measures (Vriezen & Pigott, 2010); this may be due to reporters failing to observe executive function difficulties that are assessed by behavioral measures, or perhaps existing behavioral measures do not adequately reflect everyday difficulties captured by reporter-based questionnaires. A review examining cognitive flexibility in ASD found a large gap between the inflexible everyday behaviors that occur in this population and the cognitive flexibility deficits that existing clinical and experimental measures aim to capture (Geurts, Corbett, & Solomon, 2009). These issues point to the potential limitations of existing behavioral, self-report, and collateral-report measures, and highlight the importance of assessing factors that may lead to discrepancies between behavioral and collateral-report measures (Cook, Bolinger, & Suhr, 2016). An additional caution in interpreting caregiver rating scales in the context of neurodevelopmental disabilities is that clinical elevations may occur due to overall developmental delay and results for a child who has intellectual disability should be considered in the context of developmental age. Additionally, caregivers may overestimate a child's understanding. For example, in instances when a child has a very uneven skill profile (e.g., they are very good at tasks involving visual/spatial abilities or when instructions are printed but have very poor verbal/auditory processing), or have learned to do something in one context but have not generalized this skill to other settings, difficulties with comprehension may be mistaken for inattention.

ASSESSMENT OF ADAPTIVE FUNCTIONING

Any neurodevelopmental assessment should include a measure of adaptive functioning. Adaptive behavior refers to personal independence and social responsibility necessary to take care of oneself and get along with others (Burger-Caplan, Saulnier, & Sparrow, 2018). Broad measures of adaptive functioning covering multiple domains (e.g., self-help skills, communication, leisure skills) are an efficient way to gather information about areas of concern as well as relative strengths that can assist with both diagnosis and recommendations. Documentation of impaired adaptive functioning is also a critical component to diagnosing intellectual disability. Documentation of impairment in various domains is necessary for qualification for services for individuals with neurodevelopmental disabilities, especially in adulthood (e.g., to qualify for services from Vocational Rehabilitation, or community supports). Assessing adaptive behaviors is particularly essential in a comprehensive assessment of ASD, as research suggests that children and adolescents with ASD have fewer daily living skills than both typically developing children and children with other developmental disorders. Furthermore, daily living skills are often below expectations compared to IQ and may decline with age for individuals with ASD because they are not acquiring skills at the same rate as typical peers (Klin et al., 2007; Meyer et al., 2018). The developmental trajectory has been characterized by a pattern of initial increase in adaptive behavior skills in early childhood followed by a plateau during adolescence and a decline in adulthood across all levels of functioning (Meyer et al., 2018; L. E. Smith, Maenner, & Seltzer, 2012). Commonly used measures of adaptive functioning include the Vineland-3: Vineland Adaptive Behavior Scales (Sparrow et al., 2016) and the Adaptive Behavior Assessment System – Third Edition (ABAS-3; Harrison & Oakland, 2015).

The Vineland-3 covers communication, daily living skills, and socialization and also includes an optional motor skills domain. There are three available administration forms: the Interview Form, the Parent/Caregiver Form, and the Teacher Form. The original iteration of the Vineland Adaptive Behavior Scales (Sparrow, Balla, & Cicchetti, 1984) and its subsequent second edition (Sparrow, Cicchetti, & Balla, 2005) are the most studied adaptive behavior measures for ASD (Klin et al., 2007). While there has been less research on the Vineland-3 due to its more recent publication, it continues to be a reliable and well-validated measure of adaptive behavior in this population. The Vineland-3 has been standardized for individuals from birth through age ninety; each form is also available in a brief Domain-Level version that can be used for individuals aged three to twenty-one years. Because the Vineland-3 covers a wide age range and has significant normative data tracking typical growth, it is particularly useful for developmental assessments and monitoring change or progress over time (Burger-Caplan et al., 2018). The standardization sample was stratified on the basis of the 2014 US Census data on sex, race/ethnicity, parents' or individual's education level, and geographic region. Data were also collected specifically for a sample of individuals with ASD and for other populations that fall under IDEA classification. Additionally, all items have undergone bias review to improve cultural sensitivity. The Parent/Caregiver Form is available in Spanish and previous versions of the Vineland have been translated into several other languages. Reported inter-rater and inter-interviewer reliability estimates range from 0.70 to 0.81 for the Comprehensive Interview Form and 0.69 to 0.84 for the Domain-Level Interview Form (Sparrow et al., 2016).

The Adaptive Behavior Assessment System – Third Edition (ABAS-3; Harrison and Oakland 2015) provides an assessment of adaptive behavior and skills from birth through to age eighty-nine. Five forms are available: Parent/Primary Caregiver Form (ages 0–5 years), Teacher/Day-Care Provider Form (2–5 years), Parent Form (5–21 years), Teacher Form (5–21 years), and Adult Form (16–89 years). The ABAS-3 assesses ten skill areas to provide scaled scores, which fall under three broad domains: conceptual (communication, functional academics, and self-direction), social (social skills and leisure), and practical (self-care, home or school living, community use, health and safety, and work for adults). Motor skill is also an optional skill area that can be assessed for children. The ABAS-3 standardization samples are representative of 2010 US Census data with respect to gender, race/ethnicity, and socioeconomic status (SES) and included individuals with typical abilities as well as those with disabilities, including ASD and other neurodevelopmental disorders. Internal consistency is high, with manual-reported reliability coefficients of 0.85–0.99 for the General Adaptive Composite and three domains and somewhat lower coefficients for the briefer adaptive skill areas. Test-retest and inter-rater reliability coefficients on the ABAS-3 are reported to fall in the 0.70s and 0.80s for the General Adaptive Composite, three domains, and skill areas. The ABAS-3 demonstrates strong concurrent validity with the Vineland Adaptive Behavior Scales – Second Edition (Sparrow et al., 2005). ABAS-3 validity is also supported by evidence that its scores distinguish between individuals with typical functioning and those in clinical groups, such as individuals with ASD, intellectual disabilities, and attention disorders (Harrison & Oakland, 2015).

Both measures have pros and cons to clinical use. Both have caregiver report forms that can be filled out by the parent independently and both have been translated into Spanish and other languages. Choice of which measure to administer may depend on the type of information sought. For example, the Vineland-3 provides a communication score that is not provided by the ABAS-3. However, the ABAS-3 provides a broad assessment of conceptual knowledge that is not provided by the Vineland-3. The ABAS-3 is shorter with less complex sentence structure and includes only one domain per page, making it easier for parents to fill out correctly. The formatting of the Vineland-3 includes a lengthy page of instructions and multiple domains may appear on each page. Thus, caregivers may be confused about where to start (i.e., they start with the child's chronological age regardless of developmental level) and which sections to complete. Therefore, the Vineland-3 caregiver report may be best administered in the clinic with time for the clinician to review and make sure it is filled out correctly, whereas the ABAS-3 may be sent home with parents for later return. On the other hand, the ABAS-3 is not ideal for severely impaired adults or older children, who may fail to get a *T*-score beyond 1 on multiple domains. If there is concern a basal score may not be reached, the Vineland-3 may be a better choice, and the age equivalencies (not provided on the ABAS-3) can be particularly meaningful for severely impaired individuals.

PSYCHIATRIC COMORBIDITIES

Concurrent psychiatric problems are common within the context of neurodevelopmental disorders. For example, in a population-derived sample of ten-to-fourteen-year-old children with ASD, Simonoff and colleagues (2008) found that 70 percent had at least one comorbid psychiatric disorder and 41 percent had two or more. Intellectual disability and learning disabilities are both significant risk factors for psychiatric concerns, including mood and anxiety problems (Mammarella et al., 2016).

A thorough review of measures used to assess for comorbid psychiatric disorders in neurodevelopmental assessment is beyond the scope of this chapter. Many of the more commonly used measures (discussed in Chapters 19 and 22–28) may be used to screen for psychiatric problems, though validation and standardization in the context of neurodevelopmental disabilities is, in many cases, lacking. Accordingly, the clinician should bear in mind the possibility of overinflated scores if neurodevelopmental symptoms mimic those of psychological problems, the possibility that symptoms may be underreported for individuals who lack the capacity or insight to verbally express their mood/worries, and the possibility that measures appropriate for an individual's chronological age may nonetheless be developmentally inappropriate. The clinician should always be mindful of the risk of diagnostic overshadowing, taking into consideration the increased frequency of genuine psychological problems in the context of neurodevelopmental disabilities. In particular, self-injurious behavior may be viewed as a stereotypy and treated as due entirely to a neurodevelopmental disorder, when in some cases treatment of underlying mood disorders can sharply reduce or eliminate the behavior (e.g., Wachtel, Jaffe, & Kellner, 2011).

Though some researchers have developed measures specifically to assess for psychiatric problems in individuals with neurodevelopmental disorders, evidence for many measures is limited and, in many cases, the existing research has been conducted only by instrument author(s). For a review of measurement tools for mental health in individuals with severe or profound intellectual disability, see Flynn and colleagues (2017). For assessing mental health in the context of ASD, see Matson (2016), Pearl and Mayes (2016), and Pandolfi and Magyar (2016).

ADDITIONAL CONSIDERATIONS IN ASSESSMENT

Because ASD is diagnosed based on behavioral features rather than a medical test, there are potential cultural and gender biases that impact accurate diagnoses and access to treatment.

Cultural Concerns

Most studies have struggled to disentangle the complex influence of race, education, and income with regard to diagnosis of neurodevelopmental disorders, particularly an ASD diagnosis. The most recent Centers for Disease Control (CDC) report indicates that Caucasian children are 1.1 times more likely than African American children and 1.2 times more likely than Hispanic children to be identified as having an ASD (Baoi et al., 2018). In addition, children from minority backgrounds were more likely to receive ASD diagnoses at later ages compared to Caucasian children (Baio et al., 2018; Christensen et al., 2016). Race and ethnicity also play a role in the accuracy of diagnosis. For example, Black children who ultimately received an ASD diagnosis were three times more likely than White children to first receive a diagnosis of conduct or adjustment disorder (Mandell et al., 2007). It is likely that SES is also highly influential in the ability to attain a diagnosis of ASD. Discrepancies in availability and access to health care resources across the board and, specifically, to diagnostic services for families from lower SES backgrounds may disproportionately affect minority populations. Children of mothers who have some college education were also more likely to have a documented ASD diagnosis. In these cases, higher maternal education may imply greater knowledge of expected developmental milestones or more awareness of the access to services a documented diagnosis can provide. Like SES, the intersection of education and race/ethnicity is difficult to disentangle, as White mothers were most likely and Hispanic mothers least likely to have some college education (Mandell et al., 2009). Residence has been also reported to be associated with ASD, in that living in an urban compared to a rural area is associated with a higher prevalence – though this, too, may be an artifact of greater access to diagnostic services (Lauritsen, Pedersen, & Mortensen, 2005).

While differences in referral and diagnostic rates of ASD have been well-studied, research is needed to examine potential test bias due to racial/ethnic and socioeconomic diversity for individual assessment measures. Moreover, our knowledge of existing assessment tools may be incomplete due to the concentration of research in high-income settings and with disproportionately more White participants (Durkin et al., 2015). Future assessment measures for ASD should be developed with more careful consideration of issues related to culture and diversity, including considerations of accessibility. As Durkin and colleagues (2015) note, one factor that perpetuates the imbalance of knowledge and access to diagnostic services is that current "gold standard" assessment measures, such as the ADI-R (Rutter, Le Couteur, & Lord, 2003) and the ADOS-2 (Lord et al., 2012), are expensive, require extensive training, and are lengthy to administer; barriers due to cost and feasibility limit access to low-resource communities.

Sex Differences

The prevalence of ASD in males versus females is consistently reported at an average ratio of approximately 4:1, both in the United States and internationally (Baio et al., 2018). Studies have also found that girls are significantly older when they receive an ASD diagnosis (Begeer et al., 2012) and are less likely to receive an autism diagnosis even with equivalent levels of ASD symptoms compared to male peers (Dworzynski et al., 2012). Because of the increased prevalence rates in males, standardization samples for diagnostic instruments are often predominantly male (Koenig & Tsatsanis, 2005). Consequently, diagnostic criteria may be biased to reflect the presentation of symptoms typically seen in males (Rivet & Matson, 2011). Previous research examining gender differences in ASD has suggested that males and females tend to differ in several areas, including restricted and repetitive behaviors, IQ, and cognitive profile. For example, researchers have found that females with ASD tend to demonstrate fewer repetitive behaviors than males (Zwaigenbaum et al., 2012), though the quality of these repetitive behaviors may be different: While a male with ASD may be more likely to engage in visible repetitive body movements, a female with ASD may be more likely to engage in repetitive thoughts or have restricted interests in less eccentric areas, such as books or dolls (Halladay et al., 2015). It has also been suggested that males show more behaviors that trigger evaluation broadly, such as hyperactivity or aggression, which may result in more frequent identification of ASD (Rivet & Matson, 2011). More recent research with a large sample across the lifespan found small or nonexistent differences between males and females with regard to age at diagnosis, IQ scores, cognitive profile, and symptom severity. While subtle differences were noted supporting the idea that females with higher communication skills may show less social impairment or may be able to more easily "camouflage" their symptoms, these findings indicate overall that males and females with ASD may be more similar than previously believed (Mussey, Ginn, & Klinger, 2017). Because of the limited number of females included in normative samples, however, current assessment tools are not able to reflect existing differences, or to take into account the amount/type of previous intervention, such as therapies with a focus on improving eye contact and other social skills that are often specifically assessed. The clinician should consider these factors throughout the diagnostic process.

Multi-informant and Self-Report Approaches

An important consideration in the assessment of neurodevelopmental disorders is including information from multiple sources and contexts, as symptom presentation may be impacted by environmental factors (Ozonoff, Goodlin-Jones, & Solomon, 2005). While a child or adolescent with ASD may be perceived as "precocious" or "quirky" when interacting with adults, the same child may show significantly more impairment when interacting with peers. Conversely, a toddler who has no experience in a structured setting or a child with more impairing behavioral difficulties may look much more symptomatic during an evaluation in an unfamiliar environment with significant demands. Consequently, parent and teacher report measures, naturalistic observation, cognitive and behavioral assessments, and clinical judgment may all be essential to a comprehensive assessment. See Chapter 11 in this volume on collateral reports for additional discussion of this issue.

Unlike assessments with children, adult assessments for the purposes of diagnosis and treatment planning often involve self-report. Particularly for intellectually capable adults, clinicians often need to rely on self-report as they do with other adult populations. However, several issues arise in the effort to accurately assess adults with ASD, including the unique symptom profile of adults and potential biases in caregiver-report due to difficulty remembering early milestones. Additionally, the hallmark symptoms of ASD are poor insight into social and communicative difficulties, which may hinder adults' ability to accurately report their own symptoms, even in those with average intelligence (Berthoz & Hill, 2005; Bishop & Seltzer, 2012). Research on self-report in other areas, such as ADHD, indicates that overreporting or exaggerating of symptoms may undermine the validity of such measures but that noncredible reporting may be difficult to detect (Cook et al., 2016; Suhr, Sullivan, & Rodriguez, 2011). A limitation of existing self-report and informant-report measures used in ASD is that they do not assess for the validity of reporting, emphasizing the need for evidence of symptoms and impairment from sources outside of questionnaires.

Despite the growing demand for self-report measures in this population, there has been little research examining the convergence of self-report and informant-report or the validity of self-report for individuals with ASD. Recent research by Sandercock, Klinger, and colleagues (Sandercock, 2018) found that, for adults with ASD with average to above-average IQs, there were no significant discrepancies between caregiver and self-report ratings of symptom severity. However, there were significant differences between reporters on ratings of daily living skills and quality of life, with caregivers reporting more challenges. Despite discrepancies, caregiver and self-report scores were significantly positively correlated on all measures. Additionally, combining caregiver-report and self-report measures provided significantly higher predictive value of objective employment and independent living outcomes than did measures from a single reporter. These results indicate that self-report is likely valid for this population but emphasize the importance of a multi-informant approach in assessment of the severity of daily live challenges and in making appropriate treatment recommendations.

Age-Related Concerns in Assessment

Differentiating neurodevelopmental disorders from one another can be particularly challenging in young children. For example, parents of children with ASD and parents of children with intellectual disability or other developmental disorders have reported similar numbers of symptoms on measures of social, communication, and repetitive behaviors until approximately thirteen to twenty-four months of age, at which point socialization differences (e.g., lack of joint attention, use and comprehension of gestures, lack of shared enjoyment) become more apparent for those with ASD (Ozonoff et al., 2008; Zwaigenbaum et al., 2007). Deficits in symbolic play, functional toy use, repetitive behavior and object play, and differences in motor activity are frequently seen in the context of cognitive delay and are unreliable indicators of ASD or other specific developmental disorders in very young children (Saint-Georges et al., 2010; Wetherby et al., 2004).

It is also important to address issues in the assessment of adults with ASD. As ASD has often been thought of as a disorder of childhood, the majority of currently available measures were developed to target the symptoms of ASD in children. However, ASD is a lifelong developmental disability and changes in presentation with age should also be considered. Clinical presentation is often more complex in adulthood, developmental history may be unavailable (Bastiaansen et al., 2011), and assessment measures must be able to reliably capture the aspects of ASD that change over the lifespan and the differential presentation of the disorder in adults. Research on this population suggests that the positive symptoms of ASD – such as repetitive behaviors or emotional outbursts – tend to decline with age, and social and communicative deficits instead become more pronounced (Taylor & Seltzer, 2010).

Addressing Behavior Concerns

Choosing developmentally appropriate tests will decrease the likelihood of behavior problems related to frustration; in choosing tests, the clinician must be mindful that many individuals with suspected neurodevelopmental disability have widely varying ability levels across domains. With appropriate test selection, many individuals will be able to complete standardized evaluations, particularly with some strategies to improve understanding of expectations. For example, checking off a list of subtests may reduce anxiety about when testing will be finished; checking off a certain number of items or sections before a play break or reward may increase motivation and attention. For individuals with significant social skill difficulties, establishing social routines may be helpful in minimizing the social component of testing and making the unfamiliar examiner seem more predictable. For example, as Klinger and colleagues (2018) suggest, the examiner may establish a routine by saying "Time to work. Look," before presenting a test item, waiting for a response, and then responding with a phrase such as "Good working" that praises appropriate behavior without indicating whether the examinee responded correctly. At times, additional accommodations may be necessary, including taking breaks or allowing the child to stand or to sit on the floor. Even so, behavioral concerns may preclude the likelihood of obtaining valid results on lengthy evaluations. The clinician is encouraged to consider the most succinct measures that will provide the necessary information.

Selecting the Appropriate Cognitive Tests

The information learned in an evaluation is directly influenced by which measures are chosen as part of the assessment battery and how suitable they are in answering referral questions. The choice of both domains assessed and assessment instruments has a significant impact on the reliability and validity of obtained information and subsequent decision-making. Language ability, delayed processing, attention, developmental level in comparison to chronological age, and problems with motor planning/coordination should be considered in choosing appropriate instruments.

Keeping in mind the purpose(s) of the test will also guide test selection. Does the purpose demand a full evaluation of diagnostic symptoms or cognitive domains, or will a symptom screener or abbreviated assessment of cognitive ability suffice? This may depend on whether and by whom the evaluation report may be used to make decisions about service eligibility. Some agencies and school systems require comprehensive measures and full-scale IQ scores to meet eligibility requirements; some managed care plans have been known to require the assessments to be chosen from a short list of options to meet reimbursement requirements. If the evaluation will be used as a baseline to track development over time, the clinician may use measures that cover a wider age range. For individuals with significant delays, perhaps there are no age-appropriate measures that are suitable for the developmental level of the individual; in such cases, the clinician may consider using a measure that provides age equivalents rather than standard scores.

In selecting cognitive assessments for individuals suspected of having an uneven profile of strengths and weaknesses, the clinician should again keep in mind the purposes of the test. In the case of highly discrepant verbal and nonverbal abilities, the individual may score in the higher range on a nonverbal test of cognitive abilities, highlighting areas of strength. However, if the evaluation results will be used to inform intervention planning by identifying strengths and weaknesses that impact performance in the typical classroom or workplace setting, or to qualify for service provision, then an instrument that assesses areas of weakness will be important. In such cases, it may be appropriate to administer both a traditional cognitive test and a nonverbal test to provide a more comprehensive picture of the individual's capabilities.

CONCLUSION

The assessment of individuals with neurodevelopmental disorders requires an understanding of both typical and atypical development across domains. Assessment with an intellectual test is an important component of evaluation for those with neurodevelopmental disorders but is rarely sufficient. For example, if the referral question asks whether an individual has an ASD diagnosis, an ASD-specific measure (e.g., ADOS-2) is needed to evaluate the DSM-5–defined social communication and repetitive behavior symptoms of this disorder. If a referral question asks about supports needed for independent living, an adaptive behavior assessment is essential. Because individuals with neurodevelopmental disorders often have a scattered profile of strengths and weaknesses, it is important to choose assessment measures that identify this profile. In addition to intellectual delays, individuals with neurodevelopmental disorders often have comorbid developmental and/or psychiatric conditions. Thus, a comprehensive evaluation should include a thorough developmental and medical history as well as assessments across multiple domains, including diagnostic symptoms (social skills, communication skills, repetitive behaviors), cognitive skills (intellectual, language, attention, executive functioning), adaptive behavior, and psychiatric comorbidities. However, given the challenges of assessing individuals with neurodevelopmental disorders – particularly young children – it is unlikely that all developmental areas can be assessed through formal testing. Thus, the examiner often relies on caregiver report in addition to standardized assessments. Issues of culture and gender are important with regard to conducting an appropriate caregiver interview. The examiner must carefully consider which developmental areas to assess and which assessment measures to administer to answer the referral question and provide accurate diagnoses and treatment recommendations.

REFERENCES

American Psychiatric Association. (2013). *Diagnostic and statistical manual of mental disorders* (5th ed.). Arlington, VA: American Psychiatric Publishing.

Baio, J. B., Wiggins, L., Christensen, D. L., Maenner, M. J., Daniels, J., Warren, Z., Kurzuis-Spencer, M. ... Dowling, N.F. (2018). Prevalence of autism spectrum disorder among children aged 8 years: Autism and Developmental Disabilities Monitoring Network, 11 Sites, United States, 2014. *Morbidity and Mortality Weekly Report Surveillance Summaries*, *67*(6), 1–23.

Bastiaansen, J. A., Meffert, H., Hein, S., Huizinga, P., Ketelaars, C., Pijnenborg, M., ... & de Bildt, A. (2011). Diagnosing autism spectrum disorders in adults: The use of Autism Diagnostic Observation Schedule (ADOS) module 4. *Journal of Autism and Developmental Disorders*, *41*(9), 1256–1266.

Baum, K. T., Shear, P. K., Howe, S. R., & Bishop, S. L. (2015). A comparison of WISC-IV and SB-5 intelligence scores in adolescents with autism spectrum disorder. *Autism*, *19*(6), 736–745.

Bayley, N. (2006). *Bayley scales of infant and toddler development, third edition: Technical manual*. San Antonio, TX: Harcourt.

Begeer, S., Mandell, D., Wijnker-Holmes, B., Venderbosch, S., Rem, D., Stekelenburg, F., & Koot, H. M. (2012). Sex differences in the timing of identification among children and adults with autism spectrum disorders. *Journal of Autism and Developmental Disorders*, *43*(5), 1151–1156. http://doi.org/10.1007/s10803-012-1656-z

Berthoz, S., & Hill, E. L. (2005). The validity of using self-reports to assess emotion regulation abilities in adults with autism spectrum disorder. *European Psychiatry*, *20*(3), 291–298. http://doi.org/10.1016/j.eurpsy.2004.06.013

Bishop, S. L., & Seltzer, M. M. (2012). Self-reported autism symptoms in adults with autism spectrum disorders. *Journal of Autism and Developmental Disorders*, *42*(11), 2354–2363. http://doi.org/10.1007/s10803-012-1483-2

Borys, S. V., Spitz, H. H., & Dorans, B. A. (1982). Tower of Hanoi performance of retarded young adults and nonretarded children as a function of solution length and goal state. *Journal of Experimental Child Psychology*, *33*(1), 87–110.

Bracken, B. A., & McCallum, R. S. (2016). *Universal Nonverbal Intelligence Test*. Austin, TX: PRO-ED.

Brown, L., Sherbenou, R. J., & Johnsen, S. K. (2010). *Test of Nonverbal Intelligence: TONI-4*. Austin, TX: PRO-ED.

Bruni, T. P. (2014). Test review: Social responsiveness scale–Second edition (SRS-2). *Journal of Psychoeducational Assessment*, *32*(4), 365–369.

Brunsdon, V. E., Colvert, E., Ames, C., Garnett, T., Gillan, N., Hallett, V., ... & Happé, F. (2015). Exploring the cognitive features in children with autism spectrum disorder, their co-twins, and typically developing children within a population-based sample. *Journal of Child Psychology and Psychiatry*, *56*(8), 893–902.

Burger-Caplan, R., Saulnier, C. A., & Sparrow, S. S. (2018). Vineland adaptive behavior scales. In J. Kreutzer, J. DeLuca, & B. Caplan (Eds.), *Encyclopedia of clinical neuropsychology*. Cham: Springer.

Channell, M. M., Phillips, B. A., Loveall, S. J., Conners, F. A., Bussanich, P. M., & Klinger, L. G. (2015). Patterns of autism spectrum symptomatology in individuals with Down syndrome without comorbid autism spectrum disorder. *Journal of Neurodevelopmental Disorders*, *7*(5), 1–9. https://doi.org/10.1186/1866-1955-7-5

Chapman, R. S. (1997). Language development in children and adolescents with Down syndrome. *Developmental Disabilities Research Reviews*, *3*(4), 307–312.

Chapman, R. S., Seung, H. K., Schwartz, S. E., & Bird, E. K. R. (1998). Language skills of children and adolescents with Down syndrome: II. Production deficits. *Journal of Speech, Language, and Hearing Research*, *41*(4), 861–873.

Christensen, D. L., Baio, J., Braun, K. V. N., Bilder, D., Charles, J., Constantino, J. N., ... & Yeargin-Allsopp, M. (2016). Prevalence and characteristics of autism spectrum disorder among children aged 8 years: Autism and Developmental Disabilities Monitoring Network, 11 Sites, United States, 2012. *Morbidity and Mortality Weekly Report. Surveillance Summaries*, *65*(3), 1–23. http://doi.org/10.15585/mmwr.ss6503a1

Conners, C. K. (2008). *Conners-3*. Toronto, ON: Multi-Health Systems.

Cook, C. M., Bolinger, E., & Suhr, J. (2016). Further validation of the Conners' adult attention deficit/hyperactivity rating scale infrequency index (CII) for detection of non-credible report of attention deficit/hyperactivity disorder symptoms. *Archives of Clinical Neuropsychology*, *31*(4), 358–364. http://doi.org/10.1093/arclin/acw015

Constantino J. N. (2011). The quantitative nature of autistic social impairment. *Pediatric Research*, *69*, 55–62.

Constantino, J. N., & Gruber, C. P. (2012). *Social Responsiveness Scale – Second Edition (SRS-2)*. Torrance, CA: Western Psychological Services.

Cox, A., Klein, K., Charman, T., Baird, G., Baron-Cohen, S., Swettenham, J., ... & Wheelwright, S. (1999). Autism spectrum disorders at 20 and 42 months of age: Stability of clinical and ADI-R diagnosis. *The Journal of Child Psychology and Psychiatry and Allied Disciplines*, *40*(5), 719–732.

Dimitropoulos, A., & Schultz, R. T. (2007). Autistic-like symptomatology in Prader-Willi syndrome: A review of recent findings. *Current Psychiatry Reports*, *9*(2), 159–164.

Durkin, M. S., Elsabbagh, M., Barbaro, J., Gladstone, M., Happe, F., Hoekstra, R. A., ... & Shih, A. (2015). Autism screening and diagnosis in low resource settings: Challenges and opportunities to enhance research and services worldwide. *Autism Research*, *8*(5), 473–476. http://doi.org/10.1002/aur.1575

Dworzynski, K., Ronald, A., Bolton, P., & Happé, F. (2012). How different are girls and boys above and below the diagnostic threshold for autism spectrum disorders? *Journal of the American Academy of Child and Adolescent Psychiatry*, *51*(8), 788–797. http://doi.org/10.1016/j.jaac.2012.05.018

Elliott, C. D. (2007). *Differential Ability Scales* (2nd ed.). San Antonio, TX: Harcourt Assessment.

Evenhuis, H. M., Sjoukes, L., Koot, H. M., & Kooijman, A. C. (2009). Does visual impairment lead to additional disability in adults with intellectual disabilities? *Journal of Intellectual Disability Research*, *53*(1), 19–28.

Falkmer, T., Anderson, K., Falkmer, M., & Horlin, C. (2013). Diagnostic procedures in autism spectrum disorders: A systematic literature review. *European Child and Adolescent Psychiatry*, *22*(6), 329–340.

Fellinger, J., Holzinger, D., Beitel, C., Laucht, M., & Goldberg, D. P. (2009). The impact of language skills on mental health in teenagers with hearing impairments. *Acta Psychiatrica Scandinavica*, *120*(2), 153–159.

Flynn, S., Vereenooghe, L., Hastings, R.P., Adams, D., Cooper, S., Gore, N., ... & Waite, J. (2017). Measurement tools for mental health problem and mental well-being with severe or profound intellectual disabilities: A systematic review. *Clinical Psychology Review*, *57*, 32–44.

Garvey, M. A., & Cuthbert, B. N. (2017). Developing a motor systems domain for the NIMH RDoC Program. *Schizophrenia Bulletin*, *43*(5), 935–936.

Geurts, H. M., Corbett, B., & Solomon, M. (2009). The paradox of cognitive flexibility in autism. *Trends in Cognitive Sciences*, *13* (2), 74–82. http://doi.org/10.1016/j.tics.2008.11.006

Gioia, G. A., Isquith, P. K., Guy, S. C., & Kenworthy, L. (2000). *Behavior rating inventory of executive function: BRIEF*. Odessa, FL: Psychological Assessment Resources.

Goldberg Edelson, M., Edelson, S. M., & Jung, S. S. (1998). Assessing the intelligence of individuals with autism: A cross-cultural replication of the usefulness of the TONI. *Focus on Autism and Other Developmental Disabilities*, *13*(4), 221–227.

Grant, D. A., & Berg, E. (1948). A behavioral analysis of degree of reinforcement and ease of shifting to new responses in a Weigl-type card-sorting problem. *Journal of Experimental Psychology*, *38*(4), 404.

Gray, K. M., Tonge, B. J., & Sweeney, D. J. (2008). Using the Autism Diagnostic Interview-Revised and the Autism Diagnostic Observation Schedule with young children with developmental delay: Evaluating diagnostic validity. *Journal of Autism and Developmental Disorders*, *38*(4), 657–667.

Greaves, N., Prince, E., Evans, D. W., & Charman, T. (2006). Repetitive and ritualistic behaviour in children with Prader–Willi syndrome and children with autism. *Journal of Intellectual Disability Research*, *50*(2), 92–100.

Grzadzinski, R., Dick, C., Lord, C., & Bishop, S. (2016). Parent-reported and clinician-observed autism spectrum disorder (ASD) symptoms in children with attention deficit/hyperactivity disorder (ADHD): Implications for practice under DSM-5. *Molecular Autism*, *7*(1), 7.

Hack, M., Taylor, H. G., Drotar, D., Schluchter, M., Cartar, L., Wilson-Costello, D., ... & Morrow, M. (2005). Poor predictive validity of the Bayley Scales of Infant Development for cognitive function of extremely low birth weight children at school age. *Pediatrics*, *116*(2), 333–341.

Halladay, A. K., Bishop, S., Constantino, J. N., Daniels, A. M., Koenig, K., Palmer, K., ... & Szatmari, P. (2015). Sex and gender differences in autism spectrum disorder: Summarizing evidence gaps and identifying emerging areas of priority. *Molecular Autism*, *6*(1), 1–5. http://doi.org/10.1186/s13229-015–0019-y

Happé, F., Booth, R., Charlton, R., & Hughes, C. (2006). Executive function deficits in autism spectrum disorders and attention-deficit/hyperactivity disorder: Examining profiles across domains and ages. *Brain and Cognition*, *61*, 25–39. http://doi.org/10.1016/j.bandc.2006.03.004

Harrison, P., & Oakland, T. (2015). Adaptive behavior assessment system – third edition (ABAS-3). Torrance, CA: WPS Publishing.

Hazlett, H. C., Hongbin, G., Munsell, B. C., Kim, S. H., Styner, M., Wolff, J. J. ... & the IBIS Network. (2017). Early brain development in infants at high risk for autism spectrum disorder. *Nature*, *542*, 348–351. https://doi.org/10.1038/nature21369

Heaton, R. K., Chelune, G. J., Talley, J. L., Kay, G. G., & Curtiss, G. (1993). Wisconsin card *Sorting Test* manual revised and expanded. Lutz, FL: Psychological Assessment Resources.

Hepburn, S., Philofsky, A., Fidler, D. J., & Rogers, S. (2008). Autism symptoms in toddlers with Down syndrome: A descriptive study. *Journal of Applied Research in Intellectual Disabilities*, *21*(1), 48–57.

Ibañez, L. V., Stone, W. L., & Coonrod, E. E. (2014). Screening for autism in young children. In F. Volkmar, S. Rogers, R. Paul, & K. Pelphrey (Eds.), *Handbook of autism and pervasive developmental disorders* (4th ed., pp. 585–608). Hoboken, NJ: John Wiley & Sons.

Insel, T. R. (2017). Digital phenotyping: Technology for a new science of behavior. *JAMA*, *318*(13), 1215–1216.

Johnson, C. P., & Myers, S. M. (2007). Identification and evaluation of children with autism spectrum disorders. *Pediatrics*, *120* (5), 1183–1215.

Johnson, S., Hollis, C., Hennessy, E., Kochhar, P., Wolke, D., & Marlow, N. (2011). Screening for autism in preterm children: Diagnostic utility of the Social Communication Questionnaire. *Archives of Disease in Childhood*, *96*(1), 73–77.

Kanne, S. M., Randolph, J. K., & Farmer, J. E. (2008). Diagnostic and assessment findings: A bridge to academic planning for children with autism spectrum disorders. *Neuropsychology Review*, *18*(4), 367–384.

Kasari, C., Brady, N., Lord, C., & Tager-Flusberg, H. (2013). Assessing the minimally verbal school-aged child with autism spectrum disorder. *Autism Research*, *6*(6), 479–493.

Kim, S. H., & Lord, C. (2012). New autism diagnostic interview-revised algorithms for toddlers and young preschoolers from 12 to 47 months of age. *Journal of Autism and Developmental Disorders*, *42*(1), 82–93. http://doi.org/10.1007/s10803-011–1213-1

Kim, S. H., Thurm, A., Shumway, S., & Lord, C. (2013). Multisite study of new Autism Diagnostic Interview-Revised (ADI-R) algorithms for toddlers and young preschoolers, *Journal of Autism and Developmental Disorders* *43*(7), 1527–1538. https://doi.org/10.1007/s10803-012–1696–4

Klin, A., Saulnier, C. A., Sparrow, S. S., Cicchetti, D. V, Volkmar, F. R., & Lord, C. (2007). Social and communication abilities and disabilities in higher functioning individuals with autism spectrum disorders: The Vineland and the ADOS. *Journal of Autism and Developmental Disorders*, *37*(4), 748–59. http://doi.org/10.1007/s10803-006–0229-4

Klinger, L. G., Dawson, G., Barnes, K., & Crisler, M. (2014). Autism spectrum disorder. In E. J. Mash & R. A. Barkley (Eds.), *Child psychopathology* (3rd ed., pp. 531–572). New York: Guilford Press.

Klinger, L. G., Mussey, J. L., & O'Kelley, S. (2018). Assessment of intellectual functioning in autism spectrum disorder. In S. Goldstein & S. Ozonoff (Eds.). Assessment of *autism spectrum disorder* (2nd ed., pp. 215–262). New York: Guilford Press.

Koenig, K., & Tsatsanis, K. D. (2005). Pervasive developmental disorders in girls. In D. J. Bell, S. L. Foster, & E. J. Mash (Eds.), *Handbook of behavioral and emotional problems in girls* (pp. 211–237). New York: Kluwer Academic/Plenum Publishers.

Lauritsen, M. B., Pedersen, C. B., & Mortensen, P. B. (2005). Effects of familial risk factors and place of birth on the risk of autism: A nationwide register-based study. *Journal of Child Psychology and Psychiatry and Allied Disciplines*, *46*(9), 963–971. http://doi.org/10.1111/j.1469–7610.2004.00391.x

Leekam, S. R., Prior, M. R., & Uljarevic, M. (2011). Restricted and repetitive behaviors in autism spectrum disorders: A review of research in the last decade. *Psychological Bulletin*, *137*(4), 562.

Lord, C., Rutter, M., Dilavore, P., & Risi, S. (2003). *Autism diagnostic observation schedule*. Los Angeles, CA: Western Psychological Services.

Lord, C., Rutter, M., DiLavore, P., Risi, S., Gotham, K., & Bishop, S. (2012). *Autism diagnostic observation schedule* (2nd ed.). Torrance, CA: Western Psychological Services.

Lord, C., Rutter, M., & LeCouteur, A. (1994). Autism diagnostic interview: A revised version of a diagnostic interview for caregivers of individuals with possible pervasive developmental disorders. *Journal of Autism and Developmental Disorders*, *24* (5), 659–685.

Lord, C., Storoschuk, S., Rutter, M., & Pickles, A. (1993). Using the ADI-R to diagnose autism in preschool children. *Infant Mental Health Journal*, *14*(3), 234–252.

Mammarella, I. C., Ghisi, M., Bomba, M., Bottesi, G., Caviola, S., Broggi, F., & Nacinovich, R. (2016). Anxiety and depression in children with nonverbal learning disabilities, reading disabilities, or typical development. *Journal of Learning Disabilities*, *49* (2), 130–139.

Mandell D. S., Lawer L. J., Branch K., Brodkin E. S., Healey K., Witalec R., ... & Gur R. E. (2012). Prevalence and correlates of autism in a state psychiatric hospital. *Autism*, *16*, 557–567.

Mandell, D. S., Ittenbach, R. F., Levy, S. E., & Pinto-Martin, J. A. (2007). Disparities in diagnoses received prior to a diagnosis of autism spectrum disorder. *Journal of Autism and Developmental Disorders*, *37*(9), 1795–1802. http://doi.org/10.1007/s10803-006–0314-8

Mandell, D. S., Wiggins, L. D., Carpenter, L. A., Daniels, J., DiGuiseppi, C., Durkin, M. S., ... & Kirby, R. S. (2009). Racial/ethnic disparities in the identification of children with autism spectrum disorders. *American Journal of Public Health*, *99*(3), 493–498. http://doi.org/10.2105/AJPH.2007.131243

Matson, J. L. (Ed.). (2016). *Handbook of assessment and diagnosis of autism spectrum disorder*. New York: Springer International.

Matson, J. L., & Matson, M. L. (Eds.). (2015). *Comorbid conditions in individuals with intellectual disabilities*. New York: Springer International.

Meyer, A. T., Powell, P. S., Buttera, N., Klinger, M. R., & Klinger, L. G. (2018). Brief Report: Developmental trajectories of adaptive behavior in children and adolescents with ASD diagnosed between 1968–2000. *Journal of Autism and Developmental Disorders*, *48*(8), 2870–2878.

Mildenberger, K., Sitter, S., Noterdaeme, M., & Amorosa, H. (2001). The use of the ADI-R as a diagnostic tool in the differential diagnosis of children with infantile autism and children with a receptive language disorder. *European Child and Adolescent Psychiatry*, *10*(4), 248–255.

Moody, E. J., Reyes, N., Ledbetter, C., Wiggins, L., DiGuiseppi, C., Alexander, A., . . . & Rosenberg, S. A. (2017). Screening for autism with the SRS and SCQ: Variations across demographic, developmental and behavioral factors in preschool children. *Journal of Autism and Developmental Disorders*, *47*(11), 3550–3561.

Mullen, E. (1995). *Mullen Scales of Early Learning*. Circle Pines, MN: American Guidance Service.

Mussey, J. L., Ginn, N. C., & Klinger, L. G. (2017). Are males and females with autism spectrum disorder more similar than we thought? *Autism*, *21*(6), 733–737. http://doi.org/10.1177/1362361316682621

Ozonoff, S., Goodlin-Jones, B., & Solomon, M. (2005). Evidence-based assessment of autism spectrum disorders in children and adolescents. *Journal of Clinical Child and Adolescent Psychology*, *34*(3), 559–568. http://doi.org/10.1207/s15374424jccp3403

Ozonoff, S., Heung, K., Byrd, R., Hansen, R., & Hertz-Picciotto, I. (2008). The onset of autism: Patterns of symptom emergence in the first years of life. *Autism Research*, *1*(6), 320–328.

Pandolfi, V., & Magyar, C. I. (2016). Psychopathology. In J. Matson (Ed.). *Comorbid conditions among children with Autism Spectrum Disorder* (pp. 171–186). New York: Springer International.

Paul, R., Chawarska, K., Klin, A., & Volkmar, F. (2007). Dissociations in development of early communication in ASD. In R. Paul (Ed.), *Language disorders from a developmental perspective: Essays in honor of Robin Chapman* (pp. 163–194). Hillsdale, NJ: Lawrence Erlbaum Associates.

Paul, R., & Wilson, K. P. (2009). Assessing speech, language, and communication in autism spectrum disorders. In S. Goldstein, J. A. Nagliere, & S. Ozonoff (Eds.). *Assessment of autism spectrum disorders*. New York: Guilford Press.

Pearl, A. M., & Mayes, S. D. (2016). Methods and procedures for measuring comorbid disorders: Psychological. In J. Matson (Ed.). *Comorbid conditions among children with autism spectrum disorder* (pp. 45–63). New York: Springer International.

Perry, A., Condillac, R. A., Freeman, N. L., Dunn-Geier, J., & Belair, J. (2005). Multi-site study of the Childhood Autism Rating Scale (CARS) in five clinical groups of young children. *Journal of Autism and Developmental Disorders*, *35*(5), 625–634. http://doi.org/10.1007/s10803-005-0006-9

Rivet, T. T., & Matson, J. L. (2011). Review of gender differences in core symptomatology in autism spectrum disorders. *Research in Autism Spectrum Disorders*, *5*(3), 957–976. http://doi.org/10.1016/j.rasd.2010.12.003

Roid, G. H. (2003). *Stanford-Binet Intelligence Scales* (5th ed.). Torrance, CA: WPS Publishing.

Roid, G. H., Miller, L .J., Pomplun, M., & Koch, C. (2013). *Leiter international performance scale revised*. Torrance, CA: Western Psychological Services.

Rudra, A., Banerjee, S., Singhal, N., Barua, M., Mukerji, S., & Chakrabarti, B. (2014). Translation and usability of autism screening and diagnostic tools for autism spectrum conditions in India. *Autism Research*, 7(5), 598–607. http://doi.org/10.1002/aur.1404

Rutter, M., Bailey, A., & Lord, C. (2003). *Social Communication Questionnaire*. Los Angeles, CA: Western Psychological Services.

Rutter, M., Le Couteur, A., & Lord, C. (2003). *Autism Diagnostic Interview – Revised*. Los Angeles, CA: Western Psychological Services.

Saint-Georges, C., Cassel, R. S., Cohen, D., Chetouani, M., Laznik, M. C., Maestro, S., & Muratori, F. (2010). What studies of family home movies can teach us about autistic infants: A literature review. *Research in Autism Spectrum Disorders*, *4* (3), 355–366.

Sandercock, R. (2018). Assessing the convergence of self-report and informant measures for adults with Autism Spectrum Disorder. Master's thesis, University of North Carolina at Chapel Hill. (Available from ProQuest Dissertations and Theses A&I database [UMI No. 10790685].)

Schopler, E., Van Bourgondien, M. E., Wellman, G. J., & Love, S. R. (2010). *Childhood autism rating scale – 2nd Edition (CARS2)*. Torrance, CA: WPS Publishing.

Shalom, B. D., Mostofsky, S. H., Hazlett, R. L., Goldberg, M. C., Landa, R. J., Faran, Y., . . . & Hoehn-Saric, R. (2006). Normal physiological emotions but differences in expression of conscious feelings in children with high-functioning autism. *Journal of Autism and Developmental Disorders*, *36*(3), 395–400. http://doi.org/10.1007/s10803-006-0077-2

Shipley, K. G., & McAfee, J. G. (2015). *Assessment in speech-language pathology: A resource manual*. Toronto, ON: Nelson Education.

Silverman, W., Miezejeski, C., Ryan, R, Zigman, W., Krinsky-McHale, S., & Urv, T. (2010). Stanford-Binet and WAIS IQ differences and their implications for adults with intellectual disability (aka mental retardation). *Intelligence*, *38*(2), 242–248. https://doi.org/10.1016/j.intell.2009.12.005

Simonoff, E., Pickles, A., Charman, T., Chandler, S., Loucas, T., & Baird, G. (2008). Psychiatric disorders in children with autism spectrum disorders: Prevalence, comorbidity, and associated factors in a population-derived sample. *Journal of the American Academy of Child & Adolescent Psychiatry*, *47*(8), 921–929.

Smith, L.E., Maenner, M.J., Mailick Seltzer, M. (2012). Developmental trajectories in adolescents and adults with autism: The case of daily living skills. *Journal of the American Academy of Child and Adolescent Psychiatry*, *51(6)*, 622–631. https://doi.org/10.1016/j.jaac.2012.03.001

Smith, L., Malcolm-Smith, S., & de Vries, P. J. (2017). Translation and cultural appropriateness of the Autism Diagnostic Observation Schedule-2 in Afrikaans. *Autism*, *21*(5), 552–563. http://doi.org/10.1177/1362361316648469

Sparrow, S. S., Balla, D. A., & Cicchetti, D. V. (1984). *Vineland adaptive behavior scales (Expanded Form)*. Circle Pines, MN: American Guidance Service.

Sparrow, S. S., Cicchetti, D. V., & Balla, D. A. (2005). *Vineland Adaptive Behavior Scales* (2nd ed.). Livonia, MN: Pearson Assessments.

Sparrow, S. S., Cicchetti, D. V., & Saulnier, C. A. (2016). *Vineland adaptive behavior scales* (3rd ed.). Upper Saddle River, NJ: Pearson.

Stroop, J. R. (1935). Studies of interference in serial verbal reactions. *Journal of Experimental Psychology*, *18*(6), 643.

Suhr, J. A., Sullivan, B. K., & Rodriguez, J. L. (2011). The relationship of noncredible performance to continuous performance test scores in adults referred for attention-deficit/hyperactivity disorder evaluation. *Archives of Clinical Neuropsychology, 26* (1), 1–7. http://doi.org/10.1093/arclin/acq094

Taylor, J. L., & Seltzer, M. M. (2010). Changes in the autism behavioral phenotype during the transition to adulthood. *Journal of Autism and Developmental Disorders, 40*(12), 1431–1446. http://doi.org/10.1007/s10803-010–1005-z

Turner-Brown, L. M., Baranek, G. T., Reznick, J. S., Watson, L. R., & Crais, E. R. (2013). The First Year Inventory: A longitudinal follow-up of 12-month-old to 3-year-old children. *Autism, 17* (5), 527–540.

US Department of Health and Human Services. (2012). Child maltreatment 2012. US Department of Health and Human Services Administration on Children, Youth and Families, Children's Bureau. www.acf.hhs.gov/programs/cb/research-data-technology/statistics-research/child-maltreatment

Ventola, P. E., Kleinman, J., Pandey, J., Barton, M., Allen, S., Green, J., … & Fein, D. (2006). Agreement among four diagnostic instruments for autism spectrum disorders in toddlers. *Journal of Autism and Developmental Disorders, 36*(7), 839–847. http://doi.org/10.1007/s10803-006–0128-8

Vriezen, E. R., & Pigott, S. . (2010). The relationship between parental report on the BRIEF and performance-based measures of executive function in children with moderate to severe traumatic brain injury. *Child Neuropsychology : A Journal on Normal and Abnormal Development in Childhood and Adolescence, 8*(4), 296–303.

Wachtel, L. E., Jaffe, R., & Kellner, C. H. (2011). Electroconvulsive therapy for psychotropic-refractory bipolar affective disorder and severe self-injury and aggression in an 11-year-old autistic boy. *European Child and Adolescent Psychiatry, 20*(3), 147–152.

Watt, N., Wetherby, A. M., Barber, A., & Morgan, L. (2008). Repetitive and stereotyped behaviors in children with autism spectrum disorders in the second year of life. *Journal of Autism and Developmental Disorders, 38*(8), 1518–1533.

Wetherby, A. M., Woods, J., Allen, L., Cleary, J., Dickinson, H., & Lord, C. (2004). Early indicators of autism spectrum disorders in the second year of life. *Journal of Autism and Developmental Disorders, 34*(5), 473–493.

Wiggins, L. D., & Robins, D. L. (2008). Brief report: Excluding the ADI-R behavioral domain improves diagnostic agreement in toddlers. *Journal of Autism and Developmental Disorders, 38* (5), 972–976. http://doi.org/10.1007/s10803-007–0456-3

Woodbury-Smith, M., & Scherer, S.W. (2018). Progress in the genetics of autism spectrum disorder. *Developmental Medicine and Child Neurology, 60*(5), 445–451. https://doi.org/10.1111/dmcn.13717

Zwaigenbaum, L., Bryson, S. E., Szatmari, P., Brian, J., Smith, I. M., Roberts, W., … & Roncadin, C. (2012). Sex differences in children with autism spectrum disorder identified within a high-risk infant cohort. *Journal of Autism and Developmental Disorders, 42*(12), 2585–2596. http://doi.org/10.1007/s10803-012–1515-y

Zwaigenbaum, L., Thurm, A., Stone, W., Baranek, G., Bryson, S., Iverson, J., … & Rogers, S. (2007). Studying the emergence of autism spectrum disorders in high-risk infants: Methodological and practical issues. *Journal of Autism and Developmental Disorders, 37*(3), 466–480.

22 Assessment of Childhood Disruptive Behavior Disorders and Attention-Deficit/Hyperactivity Disorder

CHRISTOPHER T. BARRY, REBECCA A. LINDSEY, AND ALYSSA A. NEUMANN

The focus of this chapter is to provide an updated presentation of current evidence-based practices in the assessment of attention-deficit/hyperactivity disorder (ADHD) and disruptive behavior disorders (i.e., oppositional defiant disorder [ODD] and conduct disorder [CD]) in children and adolescents. In this chapter, the terms "disruptive behavior disorders" (DBDs) and "conduct problems" will be used interchangeably and are meant to reflect the array of behaviors associated with ODD and CD. Approaches to comprehensive, multi-informant, multimodal evaluations will be discussed, and some of the particular challenges in these evaluations and limitations of existing methods will also be described. We will first provide a current overview of principles of evidence-based assessment of ADHD, ODD, and CD. Issues to be addressed include assessment tools, informants, construct-relevant content, technological advances, and cultural factors. Finally, we will discuss directions for future research in this area as well as some of the practical implications of the issues presented in the chapter.

PRINCIPLES OF EVIDENCE-BASED ASSESSMENT OF ADHD AND CONDUCT PROBLEMS

At its core, evidence-based assessment is that which accounts for research on developmental psychopathology, including differences in manifestations of behavioral problems across childhood and adolescence, as well as issues involved in multimodal assessments that account for children's behavioral functioning in multiple settings (Mash & Hunsley, 2005). Furthermore, these assessments should provide a road map for intervention by accounting for a child's specific presentation of ADHD and/or conduct problems (Barry, Golmaryami et al., 2013). This discussion will center around the following principles: (1) the need to assess for the presence of a variety of symptoms/behaviors within the broad construct of externalizing behaviors to account for heterogeneous manifestations of ADHD, ODD, and CD (McMahon & Frick, 2005; Pelham, Fabiano, & Massetti, 2005); (2) the developmental context (e.g., onset, course, severity) of symptoms are crucial for diagnostic decisions and case conceptualization (Barry, Golmaryami et al., 2013); (3) in addition to core features of ADHD and DBDs, assessments should evaluate for the presence of co-occurring or comorbid difficulties; (4) assessment batteries should include tools that add incremental validity to the understanding of a child/adolescent's presentation (see Johnston & Murray, 2003); (5) the clinician should gather information connecting the child/adolescent's behavioral problems to academic, emotional, legal, or social impairment (Power et al., 2017); and (6) evidence-based assessment inherently involves a scientific approach whereby the accumulation of evidence about a case and relevant research inform the answer to the referral question and the resulting recommendations. Underlying each of these issues are considerations of which assessment tools to use, the sources from which to gather information, and the appropriateness of interpretations generated from the results of the assessment, all within ethical guidelines and potential practical constraints of the setting in which assessments are conducted.

As noted, one of the principal issues in the assessment of ADHD and conduct problems in youth is the need to assess for a wide array of symptoms and behaviors such that evaluations account for the heterogeneity of these constructs (Barry, Golmaryami et al., 2013; McMahon & Frick, 2005; Pelham et al., 2005). To do so, not only is knowledge of ADHD, ODD, and CD symptoms necessary but the clinician must also be aware of developmental influences on the manifestations of these symptoms and areas in which related impairment may be most pronounced. A crucial aspect of assessing ADHD and conduct problems both for diagnostic and for case conceptualization purposes is determining the age of onset of the symptoms. For ADHD, onset of symptoms before age twelve is necessary under the DSM-5 diagnostic criteria (American Psychiatric Association, 2013), whereas, for conduct problems, including diagnoses of ODD and CD, a wealth of evidence supports different etiological and prognostic implications for childhood onset vs. adolescent onset of problems (Frick & Viding, 2009; Moffitt, 1993).

Furthermore, these assessments should include information on important aspects of a child's psychosocial context, as situational or setting-specific factors may point to protective factors in a child's environments, issues that serve to maintain or exacerbate the child's functioning, and important targets for intervention.

Beyond assessing core symptomatology and contextual factors related to ADHD and DBDs, clinicians should be prepared to assess for the presence of a wide array of problems, including internalizing problems, as comorbidity in clinical child and adolescent populations is the rule rather than the exception (Frick, Barry, & Kamphaus, 2010). Indeed, the co-occurrence between symptoms of ADHD, ODD, and CD can be observed as early as the preschool years (Bendiksen et al., 2017). Moreover, the presence of additional problems has direct intervention implications. Research on the developmental psychopathology of ADHD and disruptive behaviors points to additional constructs that should be evaluated for a comprehensive picture of impairment. For example, ADHD has been associated with broad, pervasive executive functioning deficits that are connected with specific impairments at home and at school (Barkley, 2013). In the case of conduct problems, the presence of callous-unemotional (CU) traits, which are analogous to the characteristics of the Limited Prosocial Emotions Specifier in the DSM-5 criteria for CD (American Psychiatric Association, 2013), emerged as predicting the most severe and persistent behavioral problems in youth (see Frick et al., 2014).

Particularly from a cost-effectiveness standpoint, clinicians should strive to design assessment batteries wherein each component has incremental validity. That is, there should be limited redundancy in the assessment of symptoms and each assessment tool (e.g., interviews, behavioral observations, rating scales, neuropsychological testing) should provide unique information toward the answer of diagnostic or referral questions and for generating treatment recommendations. The concept of incremental validity as an additional consideration beyond traditional psychometric attributes of assessment measures is discussed further in the "General Issues in Selecting Measures" section.

If the result of a multimethod, multi-informant, evidence-based assessment suggests that a child or adolescent has significant problems with inattention, impulsivity/hyperactivity, oppositionality, and/or conduct problems, a diagnosis of ADHD, ODD, or CD may still not be appropriate. The clinician must first determine if the symptoms are atypical in their frequency or severity for the child's developmental level, as well as consider whether there are better, alternative explanations for the symptoms. At that point, the connection between apparent difficulties and functional impairment (e.g., academics, relationships) is needed to make a diagnosis. Perhaps more importantly, the evident impairments would highlight areas in which intervention is needed as well as potential specific interventions (e.g., effective command delivery if the child is persistently noncompliant with parent or teacher instructions). It should also be noted that a child or adolescent does not necessarily need diagnosis of ADHD or DBDs to benefit from available interventions, supports, or accommodations. As such, impairments in a child's daily life are still important to evaluate even if the child does not meet a diagnostic threshold for the number, frequency, or persistence of symptoms.

Lastly, an important element of evidence-based assessment is that, as more information regarding the depth and breadth of a client's symptomatology is gathered, the clinician should engage in a process of hypothesis testing, whereby all data from all sources are treated as information that helps to confirm or disconfirm hypotheses that address the referral question, including but not limited to diagnostic decisions (Barry, Frick, & Kamphaus, 2013). In this way, evidence-based assessment has been likened to the process of completing a scientific study in that hypotheses are developed based on background information, data are collected and interpreted, and conclusions are reached with an emphasis on the next steps to further address the problem (i.e., informing intervention; Frick et al., 2010). A central aspect of evidence-based assessment, though, is a careful consideration of the methods and informants used to gain a comprehensive view of the child's externalizing symptoms.

ASSESSMENT METHODS

General Issues in Selecting Measures

There is no evidence supporting a single measure or set of measures as the definitive approach to assessing ADHD or conduct problems. As noted, it is incumbent on a clinician to conduct an evaluation that will assess for a wide variety of behavioral issues associated with these constructs as well as potential comorbidities. To that end, clinical interviews, behavioral observations, and behavior rating scales may represent a parsimonious battery. Importantly, each of these methods provides incremental validity toward answering a referral question while still leaving an opportunity to use more specific tools if necessary.

Aside from selecting measures/methods that assess heterogeneous presentations of ADHD or conduct problems, it is also important for measures to appropriately reflect developmental context. For example, evaluations of preschool-age children should place more emphasis on assessing behavioral dysregulation (e.g., temper tantrums), whereas, for adolescents, conduct problems that reflect covert conduct problems (i.e., acts of opportunity) should be more central (Maughan et al., 2004; Ramtekkar et al., 2010). In the case of rating scales, there must be appropriate norms on which to base conclusions about the typicality/atypicality of a child's behavioral problems (Frick et al., 2010).

Psychometric features (e.g., reliability, validity, norm sample) are also important in selecting measures. However, because of the strengths of tools that are not norm-referenced (e.g., unstructured interviews, behavioral observations), there is no ground rule in the area of evidence-based assessment that states that a measure must pass a specific standard for inclusion in an assessment battery (Barry et al., 2013; Mash & Hunsley, 2005). Importantly, tests are not inherently reliable or valid. That is, one must consider the appropriateness of the conclusions drawn from a measure given its psychometric properties, content, and scope (Barry et al., 2013). For example, a rating scale that does not provide adequate coverage of symptoms of ADHD or DBDs (i.e., construct underrepresentation) should not be used as a basis for arriving at diagnostic decisions on these disorders.

In addition to reliability and validity, Mash and Hunsley (2005) emphasize clinical utility as another important consideration in evidence-based assessment (see also Hunsley & Allen, Chapter 2, this volume). Measures or methods with clinical utility "make a meaningful difference in relation to diagnostic accuracy, case formulation considerations, and treatment outcomes" (Mash & Hunsley, 2005, p. 365). Furthermore, as noted, incremental validity speaks to an assessment method's clinical utility in that it indicates the unique information provided by the measure (Johnston & Murray, 2003), thus aiding in decision-making and the design of interventions. In a practical sense, the assessment of ADHD and DBDs should include methods that provide adequate content coverage of the primary symptoms of these disorders, account for the symptoms across different settings, and recognize developmental differences in how the symptoms may manifest and link to impairment. To date, there remains limited data-driven consensus on the clinical utility of particular measures/methods. Therefore, clinicians must be aware of the relative strengths and limitations of methods such as interviews, behavioral observations, and rating scales and they should be prepared to design batteries that provide the most comprehensive and least redundant evaluation of a child's attention problems, behavioral issues, and co-occurring difficulties.

Clinical Interviews

Clinical interviews, particularly unstructured interviews that are tailored to the client, are indispensable in clinical assessment but are also inherently unreliable (Barry et al., 2013; Mash & Hunsley, 2005), as they are idiosyncratic to the case, interviewer, informant, and setting. Interviews provide important contextual information about the specific symptoms of ADHD and the disruptive behaviors exhibited by the child, their onset, the degree to which they are setting-specific, and numerous other risk and protective factors that may inform diagnostic decisions and treatment recommendations. Importantly, unstructured clinical interviews allow the clinician to gain information about the connection between the child/adolescent's symptomatology and functional impairments in important domains. A number of the tools described herein do not provide the flexibility needed to determine the extent to which problems with concentration, sustained attention or argumentativeness, for example, are related to academic or relational difficulties.

However, unstructured clinical interviews do not provide direct information about the extent to which the child's presentation is atypical for their age and the information is filtered through an informant who may have their own biases as to the significance of the child's symptoms. Importantly, there is no mechanism for unstructured clinical interviews to provide information about noncredible reporting, a limitation that is at least indirectly addressed by some rating scales, as discussed in "Behavior Rating Scales." In addition, because of their client-specificity, unstructured clinical interviews are inherently unreliable; thus, clinicians may also opt for structured diagnostic interviews to gain important information about symptom presentation in a consistent, reliable manner.

Structured interviews by nature are consistent and reliable, as the clinician is provided with the sequence and wording of questions that are presumably based directly on diagnostic criteria or core features of behavioral problems. In addition, there are clear procedures for scoring such interviews (Barry et al., 2013). Not surprisingly, structured interviews have far superior reliability to unstructured interviews, and structured interviews, if selected properly, have clear content validity in that they typically assess the diagnostic symptoms of interest directly (Frick et al., 2010). However, for the purposes of assessing ADHD and DBDs, structured interviews have limitations, including the amount of time required to conduct the interview, the potential for informants to present an inaccurately favorable or unfavorable view of the child/adolescent's behavior, and the lack of client-specific information that would lend itself to interventions (Frick et al., 2010). Therefore, structured diagnostic interviews may be most useful when clinicians are unable to make a diagnostic decision from information gleaned from the other tools discussed here. In that case, the specific, detailed assessment of diagnostic criteria offered by structured interviews would have clear incremental validity in assisting the clinician in answering a referral question related to ADHD or DBDs.

Behavioral Observations

Behavioral observations are unique in that they allow for direct data gathering of important behaviors of interest, often in a child's natural setting such as the classroom (Barry et al., 2013). Approaches to behavioral observations can vary in their structure and targets (see Frick et al., 2010). A unique strength of behavioral observations is the opportunity to observe and record consistent antecedents (e.g., extended periods of independent work) and consequences (e.g., teacher redirection) of a target behavior (e.g., becoming off-task, leaving one's seat). Indeed, objective behavioral observations of activity appear to outperform laboratory tasks designed to assess processes underlying ADHD in predictive validity (Hall et al., 2016). However, there is the potential for reactivity on the part of the child being observed, and there are important characteristics or behaviors that may not be directly observable in the selected situation (e.g., trouble concentrating, covert conduct problems). Despite these limitations, behavioral observations are necessary, though not sufficient, for drawing conclusions concerning the presence of ADHD and DBDs, as well as potential avenues for intervention.

Behavior Rating Scales

Behavior rating scales and symptom checklists have become a central part of assessment for a variety of child/adolescent problems as well as adaptive domains. Such measures stand out in terms of their efficiency and the availability of norm-referenced scores based on large, generally representative standardization samples. There are legitimate concerns about the lack of client-specific contextual information (e.g., antecedents, consequences of problem behaviors), as well as about potential noncredible reporting. The former points to the indispensability of clinical interviews to gain more information about the manifestation and developmental trajectory of a child's behavioral problems. The latter is addressed, in part, by the inclusion of validity scales in some behavior rating scale systems, such as the Behavior Assessment System for Children – Third Edition (BASC-3; Reynolds & Kamphaus, 2015) and Conners – Third Edition (Conners-3; Conners, 2008). Validity scales are geared toward noting a pattern of overly positive, overly negative, or inconsistent response patterns (Frick et al., 2010). However, noncredible reports could also be an artifact of reluctance to share information about negative behaviors, limited observation of a child by a particular informant, or alternatively a generally negative attitude regarding the child/adolescent's functioning that lends itself to negative reporting across psychological domains (Barry et al., 2013). Thus, knowledge of the relative strengths and weaknesses of different informants for child assessment and specific awareness of an informant's overall view of the child in question are essential for interpreting rating scale data.

The state-of-the-art rating scales in clinical child and adolescent assessments are broad-band (i.e., omnibus). These scales are efficient in that they assess a variety of domains (e.g., inattention, aggression, depression, social skills) in a relatively short format, include versions for different informants, and generally have strong, representative samples that are the basis of norm-referenced scores. A detailed review of these scales is not possible here but widely used rating scale systems, including the Achenbach System of Empirically Based Assessment (ASEBA; Achenbach & Rescorla, 2001), the BASC-3 (Reynolds & Kamphaus, 2015), and the Conners-3 (Conners, 2008), are summarized in Table 22.1.

Overall, omnibus rating scales, particularly those that cover theoretically relevant domains and have good psychometric properties, generally have the advantage of providing norm-referenced information in a reliable and cost-effective manner (Frick et al., 2010). However, information from rating scales is filtered through the perspective of an informant and they lack the depth of client-specific information necessary to ultimately arrive at an individualized case conceptualization. Knowledge of some of the potential pitfalls of using rating scales should greatly assist the clinician in selecting rating scales and in appropriately integrating their results with other available findings. Single-domain rating scales, often utilized in research, are also available for the assessment of attention or conduct problems, as well as related difficulties (e.g., executive dysfunction), and may be used to provide more in-depth coverage of the constructs of interest and the heterogeneity of symptom presentation but still present the potential issue of noncredible or biased reporting. However, to date, commonly used rating scales of these constructs do not include validity scales to aid in interpretation of potentially noncredible reporting.

In summary, it is important for a clinician to be familiar with the uses, strengths, and weaknesses of a variety of assessment methods to provide the most comprehensive evaluation of a child's problems. To do so, particularly in the assessment of children and adolescents, multiple sources or informants are routinely used. This multimethod, multi-informant approach has the unique advantage of gaining information about an individual's functioning in a variety of settings on a number of constructs without relying on a single informant or method that may be unreliable. However, that also means that a clinician must engage in the difficult process of carefully considering the use of different informants and deciding how to integrate data across different sources based on the available research (Achenbach, Ivanova, & Rescorla, Chapter 11, this volume).

INFORMANTS

Parent Informants

For multiple reasons, parents/caregivers are considered indispensable informants for assessments of children and adolescents. For children prior to adolescence, parents are thought to be the most useful informant (Frick et al., 2010). Parents are well-positioned to provide detailed developmental history and descriptions of behaviors for their children. Once the child reaches adolescence, a parent still can provide useful information regarding changes in functioning and, when combined

Table 22.1 Common rating scales used to assess ADHD, ODD, and CD

Measure Name	Type of Measure	Age Range	Informants	Number of Items	Relevant Subscales/ Symptom Count	Validity Scales	Overall Conclusions
Behavior Assessment System for Children – Third Edition Parent Rating Scale (BASC-PRS; Reynolds & Kamphaus, 2015)	Omnibus Rating Scale	2–5 (Preschool) 6–11 (Child) 12–21 (Adolescent)	Parent	132 (Preschool) 175 (Child) 173 (Adolescent)	Attention Problems, Hyperactivity, Aggression, Conduct Problems*	Yes	Normed based on current US Census population characteristics; adequate reliability and construct validity; assesses for comorbid disorders/ concerns
Behavior Assessment System for Children – Third Edition Teacher Rating Scale (BASC-TRS; Reynolds & Kamphaus, 2015)	Omnibus Rating Scale	2–5 (Preschool) 6–11 (Child) 12–21 (Adolescent)	Teacher	105 (Preschool) 156 (Child) 165 (Adolescent)	Attention Problems, Hyperactivity, Aggression, Conduct Problems*	Yes	Normed based on current US Census population characteristics; adequate reliability and construct validity; assesses for comorbid disorders/ concerns
Behavior Assessment System for Children – Third Edition Self Report of Personality (BASC; Reynolds & Kamphaus, 2015)	Omnibus Rating Scale	8–11 (Child) 12–21 (Adolescent)	Child	137 (Child) 189 (Adolescent)	Attention Problems, Hyperactivity	Yes	Normed based on current US Census population characteristics; adequate reliability and construct validity; assesses for comorbid disorders/ concerns
Child Behavior Checklist Parent Rating Scale (CBCL; Achebach & Rescorla, 2001)	Omnibus Rating Scale	1½ –5 (Preschool) 6–18 (Child)	Parent	100 (Preschool) 113 (Child)	Attention Problems, Aggressive Behavior,	No	Includes multicultural norms, adequate reliability and construct validity; assesses for comorbid disorders/ concerns
Child Behavior Checklist Teacher Rating Form (CBCL-TRF; Achenbach & Rescorla, 2001)	Omnibus Rating Scale	6–18	Teacher	113	Attention Problems, Aggressive Behavior, Rule-Breaking Behavior	No	Includes multicultural norms, adequate reliability and construct validity; assesses for comorbid disorders/ concerns
Child Behavior Checklist Youth Self Report (YSR; Achenbach & Rescorla, 2001)	Omnibus Rating Scale	11–18	Child	112	Attention Problems, Aggressive Behavior, Rule-Breaking Behavior	No	Includes multicultural norms, adequate reliability and construct validity; assesses for comorbid disorders/ concerns
Conners Rating Scales – 3 (Conners, 2008)	ADHD, ODD, CD	6–18 (Parent, Teacher) 8–18 (Child)	Parent, Teacher, Child	45 (Parent) 41 (Teacher) 41 (Child)	Inattention, Hyperactivity/ Impulsivity, Defiance/ Aggression, ADHD, ODD, CD Symptoms[a]	Yes	Normed based on current US Census population characteristics; adequate reliability and construct validity; assesses for comorbid disorders/ concerns

Note.
* Conduct Problems subscale is not on the Preschool Version of the BASC-3.

with adolescent self-reports, parent informants may shed light on the extent to which the adolescent engages in behavioral problems outside of the parent's awareness.

Some general principles regarding influences on parent reports should be kept in mind, particularly as they relate to assessment of ADHD and DBDs. For instance, parental psychopathology is associated with more negative views of the child's adjustment (see Frick et al., 2010), that is, parents experiencing their own distress may overreport their child's difficulties. De Los Reyes and Kazdin (2005) also noted that parents who view the child's problems as dispositional rather than situational are more likely to rate the child negatively. Such factors should be considered for case conceptualization but should not lead a clinician to eschew parental reports based on the central role parents play in a child's development/adjustment and in potential interventions.

Teacher Informants

By virtue of the amount of time that children spend in school, the opportunities available for socialization in that setting, and the potential for ADHD and conduct problems to translate to academic impairments, teacher informants play a valuable role in clinical assessments of children. As with parent informants, there are limitations in teacher reports that a clinician must consider. Teachers are thought to be particularly good at providing information on ADHD symptoms but they may not observe the full array of a child's problem behaviors (Barry et al., 2013). Furthermore, as the child gets older, teachers may be less useful, as an individual teacher likely spends less time with individual students and may also see more students in a number of classes throughout the day. Thus, their familiarity with a student receiving assessment should be expected to be lower than for teachers of young children. A unique strength of teacher informants is that they have professional knowledge of typical child development, can base their ratings of a given child on their understanding of behavioral expectations at a particular developmental level, and are also able to observe the child's classroom social functioning (Frick et al., 2010).

Child Informants

Although prior to approximately age eight or nine children are not considered reliable informants of their own attentional or behavioral difficulties, older children may be quite useful for gaining information on factors such as difficulty concentrating, feeling restless, and covert behavioral problems (Frick et al., 2010). It is reasonable to suggest that children or adolescents may underreport their own symptoms but there is no clear evidence that indicates a systematic tendency for youth informants to over- or underreport relative to parents (De Los Reyes & Kazdin, 2005). Thus, the clinician should be prepared to utilize youth self-report but make a determination as to whether the particular child or adolescent was sufficiently motivated to participate, was able to comprehend the assessment questions, and provided truthful information.

Peer Informants

Peer-referenced assessment is rarely used in routine assessments of ADHD and DBDs; yet, for some constructs (e.g., aggression, hostility toward others, classroom disruptions), peers may provide unique insights. In research contexts, classrooms have been one of the more commonly used contexts in which to conduct peer-referenced assessments and a common approach is to have children nominate a number of classmates on characteristics of interest (e.g., "fights most," "liked most," "is shy") and to determine the rate at which the child being assessed is nominated. Despite the unique information afforded by peer-referenced assessment, logistical and ethical concerns limit their use. If peer informants are desired, a professional must take steps to ensure confidentiality of the child who is the focus of the assessment and to limit the time required for children to complete the process so as to not disrupt their typical routine (Barry et al., 2013).

School/Institutional Records

Another source of relevant information for assessments of ADHD and DBDs include records from schools or other institutions (e.g., treatment facilities). Specifically, important information from these records may include academic grades, disciplinary citations or infractions, or positive achievements/awards. These records have the advantage of providing a more objective and ecologically valid account of the child's functioning. For example, instead of a parent simply reporting that a child is doing poorly in school, obtaining grades would aid the clinician in determining the degree of academic problems (if any) the child is experiencing and whether such problems are global or confined to certain subject areas. Unfortunately, there is no clear empirical evidence as to the validity or utility of such records or how these records should be integrated with data obtained through other means. The difficulty in arriving at clear guidelines for handling institutional records is based, at least in part, on the vast setting-specific ways in which child behavior and functioning are documented (Barry et al., 2013). At the very least, these records could provide indications of a child's impairments in important settings and thus might contribute unique information to case conceptualization and intervention planning.

Integration across Informants

Perhaps one of the most challenging aspects of conducting assessments with children and adolescents is the integration of information from multiple informants. Informant discrepancies should be expected based on factors such as situational specificity (Konold, Walthall, & Pianta, 2004) but also factors related to the informant and the measures used. These factors include the demographics (e.g., age, gender) of the child and attributions (e.g., purposeful, beyond their control) that the informant makes about the child's symptoms or behaviors (De Los Reyes & Kazdin, 2005). The clinician should be aware of these potential reasons for informant discrepancies, as well as factors that may be at play for a specific child.

To integrate and interpret findings, a process has been recommended in which all issues considered problematic by any informant are initially considered (see Barry et al., 2013; Frick et al., 2010). Areas of convergence (e.g., between parents and teachers) signal important concerns given their apparent pervasiveness across settings, whereas informant discrepancies may point to important considerations for intervention or issues in the assessment methods that warrant closer examination (see Kazak et al., 2010). From there, the clinician can conceptualize the primary and secondary concerns that need to be considered diagnostically and for treatment planning.

Pelham and colleagues (2005) discuss the concepts of positive predictive power and negative predictive power that may also prove useful in efficiently highlighting information that is diagnostically relevant. In brief, symptoms with negative predictive power are generally the core symptoms of a disorder (e.g., difficulty with sustained attention), the absence of which would help rule out the presence of a disorder (e.g., ADHD). Positive predictive power involves the unique symptoms of a disorder (e.g., fire setting for conduct disorder) that, if developmentally atypical, would increase the likelihood that the disorder is present. In the case of ADHD, Rosales and colleagues (2015) noted that each of the eighteen symptoms contributes unique information to the classification of ADHD but that symptoms involving losing or forgetting things, perhaps signifying positive predictive power, were indicative of the most severe presentations. Thus, if a clinician is preparing to conduct a comprehensive, multi-informant, multimethod assessment of ADHD and DBDs, an effective approach may be to first screen for core symptoms of the disorders of focus. From there, the lack of core symptoms would allow the clinician to focus on other issues, whereas their presence would signal to the clinician to then more carefully assess for other unique symptoms and the severity level of a disorder. More work is needed to further refine models of negative and positive predictive power across a number of clinical problems and across developmental levels.

The discussion herein has focused largely on interview and rating information obtained from informants such as parents, teachers, and children/adolescents. However, the field of clinical assessment has attempted for several decades to also develop presumably more objective, standardized tools that might provide important data on the child's functional impairments. Further advances in assessment may present useful models or algorithms for prioritizing and conceptualizing information in a clinically meaningful way.

TECHNOLOGICAL ADVANCES

Laboratory tasks represent an approach to assessment of externalizing problems that may have some intuitive appeal but they have mixed support in terms of validity and clinical utility. More specifically, laboratory tasks (e.g., Stroop, Continuous Performance Tests [CPTs], Lexical Decision Tests, Implicit Attitudes Tests) are presumed to tap into important processes that underlie the associated impairments of ADHD and conduct problems; yet the extent to which they do so in a reliable manner and with incremental validity is uncertain. Advances in the area of evidence-based assessment may eventually support the idea that a child's performance on an analogue task mimics their behavior in difficult, real-world situations. Such tasks would enjoy the advantage of not depending on the perspective of informant responses and may also have treatment implications (e.g., clear, consistent contingency management for children who demonstrate low responsiveness to punishment cues on a performance-based task).

Many of the well-known laboratory tasks have been in existence for a relatively long time. Generally, however, agreement between measures such as CPTs and informant reports has been only moderate to low. Recent research on preschoolers indicates that aspects of performance (e.g., omission and commission errors) correlate differently at different points in the test with teacher-reported ADHD symptoms, suggesting that performance on these tests is complex and multiply determined (Allan & Lonigan, 2015). It should be noted that laboratory tasks may have clinical utility for youth with behavioral problems insofar as task performance might highlight processes (e.g., reward dominance) connected to potential responsiveness to behavioral interventions (Frick & Loney, 2000; O'Brien & Frick, 1996). Nevertheless, there remains limited evidence that such tools are necessary or sufficient to make diagnostic and intervention decisions for youth with ADHD or DBDs.

An additional use of technology in assessment has been the online administration of rating scales and other measures, whereby the informant (and clinician) can access assessment materials outside of the typical clinical appointment. Such an approach has the potential advantage of increasing efficiency in the use of face-to-face time between the clinician, parents, and child/adolescent, as well as allow the clinician quicker access to ratings for scoring and interpretation purposes. Although there is limited evidence regarding the psychometric equivalence of online responses to standard assessment tools, initial findings indicate no differences in reliability in caregiver pencil-and-paper versus online ratings (Pritchard et al., 2017). Therefore, as the availability of online assessment tools (and, presumably, confidence in their security) increase, more clinicians may wish to utilize this resource.

DIVERSITY ISSUES

There is no evidence that cultural factors should result in qualitatively different approaches to assessment of ADHD and DBDs. However, aspects of evidence-based assessment described above should take into account a client/family's cultural background. For example, a systematic literature review found that white children were more likely to be diagnosed with ADHD compared to nonwhite children and that nonwhite children were more likely to be diagnosed with a DBD, suggesting that children's emotional and behavioral problems may be interpreted differently based on their racial/ethnic background and perhaps leading to an overrepresentation of minority children in diagnoses of DBDs (Liang, Matheson, & Douglas, 2016). A clinician may also choose to investigate a measure's psychometric properties relative to specific populations, as some measures have demonstrated acceptable reliability and validity in minority samples (Schmidt et al., 2017). This research, however, is still in relative infancy. Emerging psychometric research generally supports that the factor structures of ADHD- and DBD-related constructs (e.g., sluggish cognitive tempo, both ADHD subtypes, ODD) hold up in samples from Nepal (Khadka, Burns, & Becker, 2016), Spain (Servera et al., 2016), and Germany (Rodenacker et al., 2017). Other cultural issues, including the selection of measures, interpretation of findings, factors in how child behavior problems are viewed, and acceptability of treatment options, are also important and warrant more study.

FUTURE DIRECTIONS AND PRACTICAL IMPLICATIONS

In addition to being guided by the prevailing empirical evidence on the developmental trajectories of ADHD and conduct problems – and by sound assessment methods that adequately cover all relevant aspects of the constructs in question – it is also important that the assessments of these problems be conducted in a cost-effective manner. To be comprehensive means to account for heterogeneous presentations of ADHD and conduct problems, assess for co-occurring difficulties, address relevant aspects of the child's context for understanding symptom manifestation and potential approaches to intervention, and account for intrapersonal and contextual factors that might serve a risk or a protective role for the child's ongoing development. To be cost-effective includes efforts to address the central concern or referral question in a sound manner while using a parsimonious battery (Barry et al., 2013).

Further research is needed to delineate factors involved in increasing efficiency and cost-effectiveness of assessment of ADHD and conduct problems and in alternative modalities of service delivery. For example, preliminary evidence has suggested that assessments via videoconferencing may be comparable to face-to-face services (see Diamond & Bloch, 2010), and it is likely that clinicians have used variations of this approach for some aspects of assessment (e.g., teacher telephone interviews) for years. Nevertheless, such alternatives, particularly insofar as they increase efficiency and increase availability of services in rural areas, are in need of systematic empirical examination.

This discussion has attempted to briefly highlight research-supported principles of evidence-based assessment of ADHD and DBDs in children and adolescents. Foremost among these is a recognition of the heterogeneous ways in which youth may present with attention or conduct problems and the need to systematically consider evidence gathered through developmentally sensitive and incrementally valid tools that also document an individual child's specific impairments and contextual influences on their strengths and behavioral concerns. In this way, clinical assessment inherently uses population-based knowledge on developmental psychopathology to provide the best child-specific explanations for any difficulties and guidance as to the next steps for ameliorating those difficulties.

REFERENCES

Achenbach, T. M., & Rescorla, L. A. (2001). *Manual for the ASEBA*. Burlington: University of Vermont, Department of Psychiatry.

Allan, D. M., & Lonigan, C. J. (2015). Relations between response trajectories on the continuous performance test and teacher-rated problem behaviors in preschoolers. *Psychological Assessment, 27*, 678–88.

American Psychiatric Association. (2013). *Diagnostic and statistical manual of mental disorders* (5th ed.). Washington, DC: Author.

Barkley, R. A. (2013). Distinguishing sluggish cognitive tempo from ADHD in children adolescent: Executive functioning, impairment, and comorbidity. *Journal of Clinical Child and Adolescent Psychology, 42*, 161–173.

Barry, C. T., Frick, P. J., & Kamphaus, R. W. (2013). Psychological assessment in child mental health settings. In K. F. Geisinger, B. Bracken, J. Carlson, J. Hansen, N. Kucel, S. Reise, & M. Rodrequez (Eds.), *APA handbook of testing and assessment in psychology* (pp. 253–270). Washington, DC: American Psychological Association.

Barry, C. T., Golmaryami, F. N., Rivera-Hudson, N. J., & Frick, P. J. (2013). Evidence-based assessment of conduct disorder: Current considerations and preparation for DSM-5. *Professional Psychology: Research and Practice, 44*, 56–63.

Bendiksen, B., Svensson, E., Aase, H., Reichborn-Kjennerud, T., Friis, S., Myhre, A. M., & Zeiner, P. (2017). Co-occurrence of ODD and CD in preschool children with symptoms of ADHD. *Journal of Attention Disorders, 21*, 741–752.

Conners, C. K. (2008). *Conners* (3rd ed.). Toronto, ON: Multi-Health Systems.

De Los Reyes, A., & Kazdin, A. E. (2005). Informant discrepancies in the assessment of childhood psychopathology: A critical review, theoretical framework, and recommendations for further study. *Psychological Bulletin, 131*, 483–509.

Diamond, J. M., & Bloch, R. M. (2010). Telepsychiatry assessments of child or adolescent behavior disorders: A review of evidence and issues. *Telemedicine and e-Health, 16*, 712–716.

Frick, P. J., Barry, C. T., & Kamphaus, R. W. (2010). *Clinical assessment of child and adolescent personality and behavior* (3rd ed.). New York: Springer.

Frick, P. J., & Loney, B. R. (2000). The use of laboratory and performance-based measures in the assessment of children and adolescents with conduct disorders. *Journal of Clinical Child Psychology, 29*, 540–554.

Frick, P. J., Ray, J. V., Thornton, L. C., & Kahn, R. E. (2014). Can callous-unemotional traits enhance the understanding, diagnosis, and treatment of serious conduct problems in children and adolescents? A comprehensive review. *Psychological Bulletin, 140*, 1–57.

Frick, P. J., & Viding, E. (2009). Antisocial behavior from a developmental psychopathology perspective. *Development and Psychopathology, 21*, 1111–1131.

Hall, C. L., Valentine, A. Z., Groom, M. J., Walker, G. M., Sayal, K., Daley, D., & Hollis, C. (2016). The clinical utility of continuous performance tests and objective measures of activity for diagnosing and monitoring ADHD in children: A systematic review. *European Child and Adolescent Psychiatry, 25*, 677–699.

Johnston, C., & Murray, C. (2003). Incremental validity in the psychological assessment of children and adolescents. *Psychological Assessment, 15*, 496–507.

Kazak, A. E., Hoagwood, K., Weisz, J. R., Hood, K., Kratochwill, T. R., Vargas, L. A., & Banez, G. A. (2010). A meta-systems approach to evidence-based practice for children and adolescents. *American Psychologist, 65*, 85–97.

Khadka, G., Burns, G. L., & Becker, S. P. (2016). Internal and external validity of sluggish cognitive tempo and ADHD inattention dimensions with teacher ratings of Nepali children. *Journal of Psychopathology and Behavioral Assessment, 38*, 433–442.

Konold, T. R., Walthall, J. C., & Pianta, R. C. (2004). The behavior of child ratings: Measurement structure of the child behavior checklist across time, informants, and child gender. *Behavioral Disorders, 29*, 372–383.

Liang, J., Matheson, B. E., & Douglas, J. M. (2016). Mental health diagnostic considerations in racial/ethnic minority youth. *Journal of Child and Family Studies, 25*, 1926–1940.

Mash, E. J., & Hunsley, J. (2005). Evidence-based assessment of child and adolescent disorders: Issues and challenges. *Journal of Clinical Child and Adolescent Psychology, 34*, 362–379.

Maughan, B., Rowe, R., Messer, J., Goodman, R., & Meltzer, H. (2004). Conduct disorder and oppositional defiant disorder in a national sample: Developmental epidemiology. *Journal of Child Psychology and Psychiatry, 45*, 609–621.

McMahon, R. J., & Frick, P. J. (2005). Evidence-based assessment of conduct problems in children and adolescents. *Journal of Clinical Child and Adolescent Psychology, 34*, 477–505.

Moffitt, T. E. (1993). Adolescence-limited and life-course persistent anti-social behavior: A developmental taxonomy. *Psychological Reports, 100*, 674–701.

O'Brien, B. S., & Frick, P. J. (1996). Reward dominance: Associations with anxiety, conduct problems, and psychopathy in children. *Journal of Abnormal Child Psychology, 24*, 223–240.

Pelham, W. E., Fabiano, G. A., & Massetti, G. M. (2005). Evidence-based assessment of attention-deficit hyperactivity disorder in children and adolescents. *Journal of Clinical Child and Adolescent Psychology, 34*, 477–505.

Power, T. J., Watkins, M. W., Anastopolous, A. D., Reid, R., Lambert, M. C., & DuPaul, G. J. (2017). Multi-informant assessment of ADHD symptom-related impairments among children and adolescents. *Journal of Clinical Child & Adolescent Psychology, 46*, 661–674.

Pritchard, A. E., Stephan, C. M., Zabel, T. A., & Jacobson, L. A. (2017). Is this the wave of the future? Examining the psychometric properties of child behavior rating scales online. *Computers in Human Behavior, 70*, 518–522.

Ramtekkar, U. P., Reiersen, A. M., Todorov, A. A., & Todd, R. D. (2010). Sex and age differences in attention-deficit/hyperactivity disorder symptoms and diagnoses: Implications for DSM-V and ICD-11. *Journal of the American Academy of Child and Adolescent Psychiatry, 49*, 217–228.

Reynolds, C. R., & Kamphaus, R. W. (2015). *Behavior assessment system for children, 3rd edition (BASC-3)*. Circle Pines, MN: American Guidance Services.

Rodenacker, K., Hautmann, C., Gortz-Dorten, A., & Dopfner, M. (2017). The factor structure of ADHD – Different models, analyses and informants in a bifactor framework – testing the constructs in a German sample. *Journal of Psychopathology and Behavioral Assessment, 39*, 92–102.

Rosales, A. G., Vitoratou, S., Banaschewski, T., Asherson, P., Buitelaar, J., Oades, R. D., … & Chen, W. (2015). Are all the 18 DSM-IV and DSM-5 criteria equally useful for diagnosing ADHD and predicting comorbid conduct problems? *European Child and Adolescent Psychiatry, 24*, 1325–1337.

Schmidt, M., Reh, V., Hirsch, O., Rief, W., & Christiansen, H. (2017). Assessment of ADHD symptoms and the issue of cultural variation: Are Conners 3 rating scales applicable to children and parents with migration background? *Journal of Attention Disorders, 21*, 587–599.

Servera, M., Bernad, M. D., Carrillo, J. M., Collado, S., & Burns, G. L. (2016). Longitudinal correlates of sluggish cognitive tempo and ADHD-inattention symptom dimensions with Spanish children. *Journal of Clinical Child and Adolescent Psychology, 45*, 632–641.

23 Assessment of Depressive Disorders and Suicidality

RONALD R. HOLDEN AND G. CYNTHIA FEKKEN

The World Health Organization (WHO, 2017) describes depression as the single largest contributor to disability worldwide, defining it as a common mental disorder that affects mood, energy, pleasure, sleep, and appetite; it may interfere with a person's ability to meet their daily responsibilities; and it may contribute to suicide. The proportion of the global population with depression is estimated to be 4.4 percent for adults (WHO, 2017) and 2.6 percent for adolescents and children (Polanczyk et al., 2015). A large array of instruments has emerged over the last decades to assess: screening for depression; making a diagnosis of depression; deciding to prescribe treatment or assessing the success of a treatment; or performing psychological research. Assessment of suicide risk is of such profound relevance to depression and profound importance in its own right that we dedicate an entire section, labeled "Suicidality," to it in this chapter.

Despite common agreement that depression exists, there is no single agreed on definition of the depression construct. The *Diagnostic and Statistical Manual of Mental Disorders* (DSM) criteria have evolved over time, with adoption of a set of nine diagnostic criteria in DSM-IV-TR (American Psychiatric Association, 2000) for Major Depressive Disorder (MDD) that were again adopted in the DSM-5 (American Psychiatric Association, 2013). The definition of MDD in the latest version of the International Classification of Diseases (ICD-10-CM) offers a more elaborate description of the symptoms but specifies neither minimum symptom duration nor minimum number of symptoms, as the DSM-5 does. Indeed, the American ICD website specifically notes that potential discrepancies between its definition and international versions of the same ICD-10 diagnostic category may exist. One implication is that the different instruments that exist to measure MDD embody somewhat different conceptualizations of the depression construct. In addition, most definitions presume that depression is unidimensional and, hence, many instruments yield a single score to reflect depression severity. Conversely, a large-scale prospective study (Fried et al., 2016) found evidence for multidimensionality on four well-known depression scales as well as a lack of measurement invariance over retests at times ranging from six weeks to two years. Further, most common depression instruments have been factor analyzed and they reveal multiple factors, the number and interpretation of which do not appear to be stable across studies. The user of a depression measure needs to examine the definition of the depression construct embodied in particular instruments and ensure that the instrument selected is suited for the purpose of the assessment.

Instruments of depression have evolved over time for several other reasons. Instruments have been shortened to make them more suitable for persons who lack energy or have comorbid medical issues (Curran, Andrykowski, & Studts, 1995). However, the degree to which these shorter instruments retain the psychometric robustness of the original instrument needs careful review of the empirical data. Instrument versions have been improved in response to emerging psychometric data, a laudable goal, but, again, comparability of decisions made by the different instrument versions needs to be established empirically. Some disciplines have generated systematic reviews of the optimal instruments for their field (Nabbe et al., 2017), although such reviews are not common and must be continually updated. Clinicians and researchers alike should be aware that popular, well-known depression instruments are not necessarily interchangeable for multiple purposes.

Arguably, the gold standard for assessment should be a series of tests that include self-report and various types of objective reports, but self-report depression instruments are extremely popular for their practicality, cost-efficiency, and applicability in epidemiological studies. Nonetheless, noncredible responding exists as an issue for all self-report measures. None of the self-report scales detailed in this chapter contain explicit validity indices that are designed to identify careless, random, or dissimulated answering. Yet some at-risk individuals will conceal their negative feelings, ideations, and behaviors from others (D'Agata & Holden, 2018) and Shneidman (1994) has indicated that about 10 percent of persons who die by suicide may mislead, guard, mask, or fail to display their suicidal intentions. As such, sound clinical assessment practice demands that the interpretation of a specific individual's scale score not be done without the consideration of corroborating evidence from other sources (e.g., clinical interviews, other tests, significant others' reports).

There are few etic (i.e., universal or culture-general) measures sufficiently developed for fully meaningful clinical assessment application (Dana, 2000). The instruments described in this chapter are standard Anglo-American emic (i.e., culture-specific) instruments that are often used as if they were either etic or transferrable outside the population within which they were developed. Of course, clinical assessment, diagnosis, and intervention necessitate articulated knowledge of the specific culture in which these measures are being used. When moved from one population to another, the establishment of scale score norms, reliabilities, and validities, although meritorious, is not enough (Ziegler & Bensch, 2013). Rather, across languages, ethnicities, and other diversities, the establishment of measurement equivalence (Chen, 2008), operational equivalence (e.g., format), semantic equivalence (i.e., item meaning), and conceptual equivalence (is the construct the same?) is sound practice (Streiner, Norman, & Cairney, 2015).

Finally, the goal of this review is to provide up-to-date information on well-researched instruments for screening (see Tables 23.1 and 23.2). For both depression and suicidality, our focus is on multi-item screening instruments that are self-report. The merits of single-item instruments, full diagnostic assessment procedures, and non–self-report measures can be substantial but our aim is to address efficient screens that are applicable for both clinical and research purposes, have substantial psychometric strengths, and have popularity and longevity that attest to their merit for psychological assessment.

MEASURES OF DEPRESSIVE DISORDERS

Beck Depression Inventory – Second Edition

The Beck Depression Inventory – Second Edition (BDI-II; Beck, Steer, & Brown, 1996) is the latest in a series of psychological tests that Aaron Beck and his associates developed to assess severity of depression in clinical populations and to detect depression in nonclinical populations. The original measures evolved from being clinician-administered and focused on symptoms reported by patients diagnosed with depression to the

Table 23.1 Comparative features of scales of depression

Feature	Beck Depression Inventory – II	Center for Epidemiologic Studies Scale – Revised	Patient Health Questionnaire – 9	Profile of Mood States – POMS 2
Test Manual	Yes	No	No	Yes
Number of Items	21	20	9	Adults 65 or 35 Adolescents 60 or 35 Depression Scale 8
Response Format	Multiple choice/ Frequency ratings (4 options)	Multiple choice/ Frequency ratings (5 options)	Multiple choice/ Frequency ratings (4 options)	Intensity Ratings (5 options)
Completion Time	~ 5–10 minutes	~ 5–10 minutes	~ 3–5 minutes	~ 8–10 minutes (long) ~ 3 to 5 minutes (short) ~ 3 minutes (Depression)
Target Population	Clinical and nonclinical populations	Nonclinical populations	Primary and secondary care patients	Clinical and nonclinical populations
Minimum Respondent Age	13 years	13 to 17 years Adults	Adolescents Adults	Adolescents Adults
Scale to Detect Invalid Responding	No	No	No	No
Coefficient Alpha Reliability	Usually > 0.90	Usually > 0.90	Usually > 0.85	Usually > 0.95 Depression ~ 0.90
Validity Criteria	Diagnostic validity; Convergent validity	Diagnostic validity; Convergent validity	Diagnostic validity	Diagnostic validity Convergent validity

most recent BDI-II version, which is a self-report measure that embodies the definition of depression contained in the DSM-IV (American Psychiatric Association, 1994). According to a major review (Erford, Johnson, & Bardoshi, 2016), versions of the BDI have been translated into at least twenty-two languages.

The description from the manual indicates that the BDI-II is appropriate for use with adults and adolescents over the age of thirteen years. Although intended to be self-report, its twenty-one items may be read aloud by an examiner. According to the manual, the BDI-II requires approximately five to ten minutes to complete. The BDI-II is answered with respect to the previous two weeks, including the current day. The items are scored from 0 to 3; the two items related to Changes in Appetite or in Sleep have rating options to allow for either increases or decreases in appetite or sleep motivation. Also, responses to the specific items related to Pessimism or to Suicidal Thoughts or Wishes may have special clinical significance. A sample item related to worthlessness is "0 = I do not feel worthless; 3 = I feel utterly worthless." Based on the responses of 127 previously diagnosed patients, Beck and colleagues parsed total scores on the twenty-one items into four diagnostic categories derived from clinical ratings by constructing receiver operating characteristic curves with a goal of minimizing diagnostic false negatives. Thus, the BDI-II scoring is not norm referenced but criterion referenced: Raw scores above 29 are indicative of severe depression; 20 to 28 indicate moderate depression; 14 to 19 indicate mild depression; and raw scores 13 or below indicate minimal depression.

The BDI has been an enduring instrument and hundreds of studies have contributed evidence that bears on its psychometric adequacy (e.g., Wang & Gorenstein, 2013). Of particular interest is the meta-analysis of the English-language version of the BDI-II conducted by Erford and colleagues (2016) on 144 studies that met their inclusion criteria. For 99 studies with a combined sample size of 31,413 participants, scale score internal consistency reliability was reported to be close to 0.90, for both clinical and nonclinical samples, which is comparable to what is reported in the test manual by Beck and colleagues (1996) and supports the argument that the items form a unidimensional construct. The exact nature of this construct has been a source of debate: In a study by Osman and colleagues (2004), experienced expert clinical raters questioned the comprehensiveness of the items for measuring the full depression construct as defined in the DSM. Test-retest reliability for 1,562 participants from twelve studies that had a median time interval of six weeks yielded a mean coefficient of 0.75; when subdivided into clinical and nonclinical samples, clinical samples showed lower stabilities (0.68 versus 0.80), especially for intervals longer than one week. For a sample of eighty-four participants, Beck and colleagues reported a one-week stability coefficient of 0.84 between the BDI and the BDI-II. Overall, the test-retest reliability of the BDI-II is adequate for research purposes and for use of the BDI-II as a screening instrument over short intervals.

Although BDI-II items are almost always summed into a total score, Beck and colleagues (1996) proposed a two-factor structure based on analyses of 500 outpatients and replicated on the responses of 120 college students. They labeled their factors Cognitive-Affective, which includes items embodying thoughts related to self-dislike and suicide ideation and to feelings such as sadness and guilt; and Somatic, which reflects physical items related to fatigue and sleep or eating disruptions. Evidence for the stability of these two factors is weak: Erford and colleagues' (2016) meta-analysis reported on eighteen studies performing exploratory factor analyses that indicated one to five factors. As well, twenty-two studies performing confirmatory factor analyses generally supported a two-factor or, occasionally, a three-factor Cognitive-Affective-Somatic solution. Although the findings may in part result from the use of different factor analytic techniques across studies, it does bring into question the practical utility of factor-based subscales.

Erford and colleagues (2016) reported diagnostic accuracy from nine validity studies: They argued for a cut score of 13, which would yield a classification accuracy of 80 percent, with a median sensitivity of 0.83 and a median specificity of 0.76. However, mean scores are subject to inflation by somatic symptoms associated with medical problems (Thombs et al., 2010); moreover, there appear to be gender differences in mean scores (see Beck et al., 1996). Such influences may argue against a single cut score for the BDI-II. Indeed, several studies have reported evidence in favor of cut scores as low as 11 and as high as 18 (Erford et al., 2016). External validity calculated against forty-three other depression inventories yielded consistent and strong correlations, ranging from 0.45 to 0.88. This is similar to the correlations reported in the BDI-II manual. In two studies with adolescent patients, Osman and colleagues (2004) reported strong psychometric properties for the BDI-II for both boys and girls, arguing that the measure is appropriate for use with younger inpatient samples. Despite Beck's argument that the BDI-II is appropriate for use with adolescents, there remains a relative lack of research with this population at this time.

Center for Epidemiological Studies Depression Scale – Revised

The popular and widely used Center for Epidemiologic Studies Depression Scale (CESD) is a twenty-item measure that exists in the public domain (Eaton, Ybarra, & Schwab, 2012). It takes five to ten minutes to complete and was created for use in epidemiological research with nonclinical participants (Radloff, 1977). The original scale is atheoretical and was derived from other depression measures. Subsequently, the measure was revised (Center for Epidemiological Studies Depression Scale – Revised

[CESD-R; Eaton et al., 2004]) to align it with the DSM-IV criteria for MDD (Eaton et al., 2004) and to revise positively worded items to having uniformly depressed content. The CESD-R website describes nine subscales, each comprised of two or three items: Sadness, Loss of Interest, Appetite, Sleep, Thinking, Guilt, Fatigue, Movement, and Suicide. A sample item is "I felt sad" and the response categories are "Not at all or less than one day last week," "One or two days last week," "Three to four days last week," "Five to seven days last week," and "Nearly every day for two weeks." The CESD-R total score is the sum of responses to all twenty questions, where the first three response options are scored "0, 1, 2" and the last two are scored "3" to keep the range from 0 to 60, as in the original CESD. Radloff determined that a score above 16 indicates that a person is at risk for clinical depression. An algorithm based on DSM-IV criteria assigns respondents to categories labeled "subthreshold depression symptoms; possible major depressive episode; probable major depressive episode; and meets criteria for major depressive episode." Various short forms of the CESD and CESD-R exist. Notwithstanding a seven-item children's version of the CESD that is not recommended for use (Myers & Winters, 2002), a ten-item version of the CESD has been validated with older adults (Cheng & Chan, 2005; Cheng, Chan & Fung, 2006; Kohout et al., 1993) and a ten-item version of the CESD-R has been developed for adolescents (Haroz, Ybarra, & Eaton (2014). The CESD-R has been translated into most major European and Asian languages.

The psychometric robustness of the CESD has been established in many studies (e.g., Lewinson et al., 1997; Myers & Weissman, 1980); the CESD-R has been evaluated in relatively few studies. However, Eaton and colleagues (2004) report CESD-R scores correlated 0.88 with CESD scores, so generalizing from one version to the other seems appropriate. The internal consistency reliability of the CESD-R was initially reported by Eaton and his colleagues (2004) to be 0.93 for a sample of 868 female nursing assistants. A major psychometric study of the CESD-R was conducted by Van Dam and Earleywine (2011) on a sample of more than 7,000 American respondents to a survey for the National Organization for the Reformation of Marijuana Laws and on a smaller sample of 245 undergraduates – they also reported internal consistency reliabilities of 0.93 for each of their samples. In a study using two national samples of American youths (N = 3777; N = 1150), Haroz and colleagues (2014) reported internal consistencies of 0.91 for a ten-item CESD-R version. Thus, the construct measured by the CESD-R appears to be unidimensional and the size of the internal consistencies supports use of a single total score. Little attention is paid to the proposed nine subscales in the empirical literature; the nine subscales appear to be based on a "rational" analysis of the content of the items and, as yet, lack empirical support.

Test-retest coefficients are reported for the CESD by Radloff (1977) to range from 0.45 to 0.70 over intervals of two to fifty-two weeks. Likewise, Wong (2000) reports a retest correlation of 0.56 based on 430 homeless persons who were followed up three months to one year later as part of a larger study in California. These test-retest reliabilities suggest that the CESD-R has adequate reliability for research purposes; use of the CESD-R alone for clinical purposes, such as assessing treatment success, is not advisable.

Factor analytic studies of the CESD (Kohout et al., 1993; Radloff, 1977; Wong, 2000) have suggested that there may be four underlying factors: Depressed Affect; Positive Affect; Somatic Complaints; and Interpersonal Problems. For the CESD-R, Van Dam and Earlywine (2011) suggested two factors – labeled negative mood and functional impairment – might provide the best fit; however, these factors were highly correlated, leading them to recommend a one-factor solution. Haroz and her colleagues (2014) also argued for a single underlying factor for the ten-item CESD-R. Again, there is no evidence for the nine subscales and, indeed, the single score, especially for the shorter versions of the CESD-R, seems preferable to any number of subscales.

In their meta-analysis, Erford and colleagues (2016) reported a 0.72 correlation between the BDI-II and the CESD across eleven studies with a combined sample of N = 3209. Van Dam and Earleywine (2011) provided evidence for convergent and discriminant validity for theoretically similar constructs, although correlations around 0.7 between the CESD-R and the State Trait Inventory for Cognitive and Somatic Anxiety are arguably evidence for a lack of divergent validity (also see Brantley & Brantley, 2017). Haroz et al. (2014) argued that their ten-item CESD-R shows moderate evidence of construct validity when compared to measures of convenience, such as self-esteem, relationship with parents, and substance use. In a meta-analysis of twenty-eight studies representing 10,617 participants, Vilagut and colleagues (2016) reported a sensitivity of 0.87 and a specificity of 0.80 for a cut score of 16. They argued a cut score of 20 may offer a better trade-off between sensitivity (0.83) and specificity (0.78). Ideally, multiple measures of depression would be used to create a holistic picture of individuals but, in epidemiological research, the large scope of the projects makes intensive assessment extremely expensive. Epidemiologists would in particular want to strike a balance between under-identification of depressed individuals and overloading follow-up systems with false positives. The CESD-R would seem to be well suited for epidemiological research.

Patient Health Questionnaire

The Patient Health Questionnaire (PHQ-9; Kroenke, Spitzer, & Williams, 2001) is an instrument originally developed to screen for a possible diagnosis of depression in primary care patients. Its nine items were adopted from the longer Primary Care Evaluation of Mental Disorders measures (Spitzer et al., 1992) created in the 1990s to assess for five common mental disorders. Although the 1990 copyright is held by Pfizer, the items are widely available in the public domain (Kroenke et al., 2001) and embody the DSM-IV and DSM-5 diagnostic criteria for depression. Respondents indicate whether, over the last two weeks, they experienced symptoms such as "little interest or pleasure in doing things" "Not at all," "Several days," More than half the days," or "Nearly every day." Each of the nine items is scored 0 to 3. There is a linear scoring method in which item responses are summed and a score of 10 is set as the criterion for MDD depression. In the algorithmic method, scoring takes place in three steps. In Step 1, either Question 1 (little interest or pleasure) or Question 2 (feeling down, depressed, or hopeless) needs to be endorsed as "2" or "3." (Note: These two items comprise the PHQ-2 and have been separately validated as a screen for depression; Kroenke, Spitzer, & Williams, 2003). In Step 2, the remaining seven items are scored. In Step 3, a tenth question, which is not a part of the total score, must indicate that the problems identified by the respondent have made performing their daily activities at least "somewhat difficult." Finally, the total score is compared to a set of cut scores that suggest a provisional diagnosis. The Multicultural Mental Health website lists more than fifty (non-validated) different language versions of the PHQ-9. An adolescent version (PHQ A) has also been validated (PHQ A; Johnson et al., 2002).

The PHQ-9 was developed in two large validation studies that involved 6,000 primary care patients over eighteen years of age who were recruited from multiple sites (Kroenke et al., 2001). In this study, the PHQ-9 had internal consistency reliabilities of 0.86 to 0.89 and a forty-eight-hour test-retest stability of 0.84 for a sample of 580 patients. Wittkampf and colleagues (2007) reported similar reliability results across four separate studies that they reviewed. The PHQ-9 scale developers (Huang et al., 2006) demonstrated that the PHQ-9 items load a single factor for non-Hispanic white (N = 2,520), African American (N = 598), Chinese American (N = 941), and Latino (N = 974) primary care patients in support of a unidimensional construct and the use of a summed score. Although at least one study argues for a two-factor affective and somatic structure (Granillo, 2012), this model has not been embraced either in practice or in the literature and is not recommended.

The key focus for establishing the validity of the PHQ-9 has been on its diagnostic accuracy. In the original study, a cut-off score of 10 had a sensitivity of 88 percent and specificity of 88 percent for detecting MDD. Several recent meta-analyses of the PHQ-9 and its various scoring systems exist to examine diagnostic accuracy. Manea, Gilbody, and McMillan (2012) reported that, for eighteen studies conducted in clinical settings, the PHQ-9 had acceptable diagnostic properties at a range of cut scores from 8 to 11. They cautioned however, that the same cut score might not be appropriate in all settings, with higher scores resulting in more false positives in primary care and lower scores resulting in more false negatives in hospital settings. In a subsequent meta-analysis, this research team (Moriarty et al., 2015) reported on the diagnostic adequacy of the cut score of 10 for thirty-six studies that used industry standard instruments for the diagnosis of MDD. They reported that the PHQ-9 had a pooled sensitivity of 0.78 and a pooled specificity of 0.87 but concluded that the PHQ-9 is a better screener for primary care than secondary care settings. In a meta-analysis of twenty-seven studies that used the algorithmic scoring approach, Manea, Gilbody, and McMillan (2015) reported a pooled sensitivity of 0.58 and a specificity of 0.94. In thirteen studies, they were able to compare the algorithmic and summed scoring methods directly and concluded that, despite heterogeneity across studies, the summed scoring method provided far better sensitivity in both primary care and hospital settings. Mitchell and colleagues (2016) conducted a meta-analysis of forty studies and concluded that the PHQ-9 summed score and the PHQ-2 had similar diagnostic accuracy, with much higher specificities than the PHQ-9 algorithmic scoring method. Overall, the diagnostic accuracy of the PHQ-9 (summed) and PHQ-2 shows these measures are suitable for screening although they should not be used alone to confirm a diagnosis of MDD.

Profile of Mood States 2

The Profile of Mood States (POMS) was developed over several decades (McNair, Lorr, & Droppleman, 1992) as a screening measure for fluctuating mood states: Tension-Anxiety, Depression-Dejection, Anger-Hostility, Vigor-Activity, Fatigue-Inertia, and Confusion-Bewilderment. The POMS 2 (Heuchert & McNair, 2012) was created to modernize items; add more positive mood states; enhance normative data; and provide additional forms. The POMS 2 retains its original format, that is, respondents rate adjectives on five-point scales (0 = Not at all; 4 = Extremely) according to how they "have been feeling during the last week, including today" (Heuchert & McNair, 2012, p. 13). It is permissible to alter the time frame for responding. Sample items are "gloomy" and "exhausted." The POMS 2 has seven scales, the six noted above plus "Friendliness." The POMS 2 is available in sixty-five or sixty adjective versions for adults and adolescents, respectively, and in a thirty-five adjective short version for each group. All versions can be used to derive seven scale scores plus a Total Mood Disturbance score based on the original six scales. Administration takes eight to ten minutes for the full version and three to five minutes for the short version. Depression can be assessed directly using the Depression-Dejection scale or using the Total Mood Disturbance scale. The manual notes that the POMS (or POMS 2) has been translated into forty languages.

The POMS 2 manual (Heuchert & McNair, 2012) details the construction of norms based on 1,000 North American adults who were sampled using stratification that approximated the 2000 US Census. Adolescent norms were also tied to the 2000 US Census and based on sampling cohorts of 100 adolescents for each of the five age groupings. POMS scores are presented as *T*-scores. Although administration can be either paper or online, scoring and report generation can only be done via the publisher's online scoring system.

Reliability of the POMS 2 is thoroughly documented in the manual (Heuchert & McNair, 2012). Internal consistency reliability is provided for all four versions of the POMS 2 both for the normative samples and for two clinical samples. Total Mood Disturbance scores have internal consistency reliabilities above 0.95; 0.82 to 0.96 are reported for individual scales.

Test-retest stabilities for the POMS 2 range from 0.48 to 0.72 and from 0.45 to 0.75 for a one-week interval with full adult and adolescent versions, respectively; they range from 0.34 to 0.70 and from 0.02 to 0.59, respectively, after one month (Heuchert & McNair, 2012). Reliabilities are comparable to those for the original POMS (see McNair et al., 1992).

POMS 2 scale intercorrelations are moderate to high, ranging from -0.21 to 0.80 (Heuchert & McNair, 2012). In a series of confirmatory factor analyses performed on the six scales that comprise the Total Mood Disturbance score, Heuchert and McNair demonstrated that the individual adjectives load together on their appropriate scales and, further, that the scales load a single factor. Confirmatory factor analysis with a sample of 9,170 cancer patients supported the single-factor structure of the Depression-Dejection scale for both men and women (Kim & Smith, 2017). On the plus side, the demonstration of adequate internal structure for the Depression-Dejection scale supports its use to measure Depression-Dejection. On the other hand, the evidence that Depression-Dejection relates so robustly to a single Total Mood Disturbance calls into question its divergent validity.

The POMS 2 manual provides evidence of the ability of the POMS 2 to distinguish between normative samples and clinical populations diagnosed with either depression or anxiety for adults and for adolescents. Such findings build on a long history of evidence in support of the validity of the POMS. Patterson and colleagues (2006) demonstrated that the POMS Depression-Dejection scale has an overall hit rate of 80 percent, sensitivity of 55 percent, and specificity of 84 percent in detecting current MDD in 310 persons with HIV infection against the Structured Clinical Interview for DSM-IV (SCID) diagnosis of MDD. Further, they showed the POMS Depression-Dejection scale correlated significantly with the BDI-Cognitive Affective subscale ($r = 0.74$). The BDI-II total score and POMS Total Mood Disturbance score also correlated with one another for a sample of sixty-five men with HIV infection ($r = 0.85$; Gold et al., 2014). The manual provides evidence of the concurrent validity of the POMS 2 in terms of correlations with the Positive and Negative Affect Schedule, reporting correlations ranging from 0.57 to 0.84. Several sources noted that the current POMS literature includes about 4,000 studies (Boyle et al., 2015; Heuchert & McNair, 2012). A total of 212 studies on depression are reported in the POMS bibliographic database, suggesting that the POMS Depression Scale is a valid measure of depression for use with samples as varied as medical patients, persons with addictions, athletes, and the general population.

One of the challenges for the Depression-Dejection scale is lack of a robust demonstration of construct validity. This scale appears to be focused on the Cognitive-Affective aspects of depression and may be confounded with overall mood distress. Its conceptual and empirical relationship to the DSM is not well established, certainly not as well as with the other measures reviewed. Although there is no agreed on benchmark in the literature for sensitivity or specificity of depression measures, a rule of thumb might be that a good instrument would show both sensitivity and specificity above 0.80. The POMS Depression-Dejection scale may be useful in research but cannot be recommended for clinical assessment.

CRITIQUE OF CURRENT DEPRESSION MEASURES

Although an actual clinical diagnosis of MDD requires input from multiple assessments that encompass various types of information, self-report screening measures of depression remain extremely popular with clinicians and researchers alike for their efficiency. Each of the four depression scales reviewed here can be completed in less than ten minutes, although they were designed for somewhat different populations of adults and adolescents (see Table 23.1). The presence of a manual for the BDI-II and the POMS 2 is helpful, but the literatures for all four measures are so extensive that a conscientious user must read well beyond the manual to be adequately informed about any of these tests. Only the POMS 2 requires the use of a paid scoring service, which may make it less desirable for large-scale studies than the other three measures. None of the four measures includes a validity check so all measures remain vulnerable to undetected noncredible responding. Moreover, these self-report depression measures could be susceptible to other types of response biases, such as social desirability or acquiescence that cannot be detected unless external measures are added to the assessment. Another concern is that scores could be inflated due to symptoms (e.g., fatigue, appetite loss) related to the presence of physical illness. The PHQ-9 was developed for use with primary care patients and may be preferable for such populations although it too performs better psychometrically with primary than secondary care patients. Systematic sources of variance have implications for selecting cut scores. Meta-analyses on diagnostic accuracy exist for the BDI- II, the CESD, and, most extensively, for the PHQ-9. The POMS is not recommended for screening for a diagnosis of MDD but rather for research purposes.

Of final and significant consideration when selecting a screening measure of depression concerns the definition of the underlying construct. The PHQ-9 was aligned from its inception with the DSM criteria whereas the content of the BDI-II and the CESD-R were revised to align with the DSM. All have frequency ratings intended to match the two-week time frame associated with the DSM-IV/-5 criteria. When diagnostic schemes for depression other than the DSM are being used, none of these three measures would be ideal. In view of the high internal consistencies and the lack of stable replicability of factor structure across multiple studies, total scores are recommended for use.

SUICIDALITY

Across the world, 800,000 people die by suicide each year (WHO, 2014a). Suicide is one of the ten primary causes of death in the United States (National Institute of Mental Health, n.d.) and, among fifteen-to-twenty-nine-year-olds, suicide is the second leading cause of death globally (WHO, 2014b). As such, death by suicide represents a critical international public health issue. Identification of individuals at risk for death by suicide is an exceptionally difficult task. As a low base rate behavior, death by suicide presents a statistically challenging prediction issue that may require an intractable consideration of both false positive and false negative errors. It is further complicated in that a wealth of risk factors, warning signs, and protective factors have been identified, yet there is no individual assessment scale that can accurately predict, on an individual basis, who will die or attempt to die by suicide without producing a vexing number of false positive predictions (Fowler, 2012). A missed identification can result in tragic injury or death, while excessive identifications produce unnecessary hospitalizations or other interventions. Thus, in considering the merits of self-report measures of suicidality, it is essential to bear in mind that a single scale cannot, by itself, provide an accurate diagnosis but, nevertheless, it can be a useful implement that exists within a larger toolbox of assessment instruments.

A variety of tools for assessing suicide risk have been developed. These instruments often focus on suicidal actions or on other behaviors that are closely aligned with suicide risk. Short screening measures are particularly useful because they have the potential to efficiently screen in or screen out at-risk individuals in clinical and community samples. Brief clinician-administered measures have merit but are interview-based assessments and, consequently, are more costly than self-report instruments. Further, because single-item self-reports (e.g., Item 9 of the Beck Depression Inventory-II, Beck et al., 1996; Item 9 of the PHQ, Kroenke et al., 2001) may possess limited psychometric strengths (Hom, Joiner, & Bernert, 2016; Millner, Lee, & Nock, 2015), our focus here is on three commonly used, brief, multi-item, self-reports of suicidality. Summaries of some of the major features of each of the discussed scales are presented in Table 23.2.

In reviewing these three measures, a number of issues/caveats arise. First, none of the three reviewed measures contains validity checks. Because self-report scales are subject to the impact of various response

Table 23.2 Comparative features of scales of suicidality

Feature	Beck Scale for Suicide Ideation	The Suicidal Behaviors Questionnaire – Revised	Adult Suicidal Ideation Questionnaire
Test Manual	Yes	No	Yes
Number of Items	21	4	25
Response Format	Multiple choice / Frequency ratings (3–4 options)	Multiple choice / Frequency ratings (5–7 options)	Frequency ratings (7 options)
Completion Time	~ 5–10 minutes	~ 5 minutes	~ 10 minutes
Target Population	Suicide ideators	Suicide ideators and non-ideators	Suicide ideators and non-ideators
Minimum Respondent Age	17 years	14 years	Adult
Scale to Detect Invalid Responding	No	No	No
Coefficient Alpha Reliability	Usually > 0.80	Usually > 0.75	Usually > 0.95
Validity Criteria	Hospital admissions; suicide attempter status; death by suicide	Suicide ideation status; suicide attempter status	Suicide attempter status

styles and because the reporting of suicide ideation is not always candid and open (Busch, Fawcett, & Jacobs, 2003), the clinical use of self-report instruments requires corroborating evidence. Second, like most self-report measures of suicidality, normative data for these measures are based on clinical and nonclinical samples of convenience and not on representative sampling of the national population. As such, the use of normative data associated with the original scale development should be undertaken with appropriate caution, particularly when considering minority group individuals. It is also important to note that suicidal behavior is ethnically patterned (Stice & Canetto, 2008) with its antecedents and its manifestations being culturally scripted (Canetto & Lester, 1998). Third, the measures reviewed here are English-language scales developed in North America. Although some of the measures have been translated into other languages and are used outside the United States/Canada, the equivalence of these translated scales has not always been demonstrated. Further, normative data that are reported in these instruments' manuals or test development articles are now quite dated and require the confirmation of current appropriateness. In addition to these caveats, these measures also vary in terms of whether their availability is commercial or not – that is, whether or not they may be used without being purchased.

Beck Scale for Suicide Ideation

Beck and colleagues constructed a nineteen-item assessment of suicide ideation that exists as either the self-report Beck Scale for Suicide Ideation (BSS; Beck, Steer, & Ranieri, 1988; Beck & Steer, 1993) or the clinician-administered SSI (Scale for Suicide Ideation; Beck, Kovacs, & Weissman, 1979). The self-report version is more commonly used and has a test manual associated with it (Beck & Steer, 1993) and, here, we focus on the BSS. A sample BSS item is "Do you have any wish to die?"

The BSS is a measure designed to detect and quantify the extent of an individual's suicide ideation. The BSS is appropriate for persons aged seventeen to eighty years and, if necessary, may be administered orally. Although scored on nineteen items to yield an index of severity of suicide ideation, the BSS actually comprises twenty-one items. The additional (i.e., last) two items that inquire about the number of previous suicide attempts and the degree of intent associated with the most recent attempt are not used in computing the BSS total score. For the nineteen items generating the total BSS scale scores, individual items are scored from 0 to 2, yielding an overall total BSS score that can range from 0 to 38. The BSS requires five to ten minutes to complete. The first five BSS items act as a screen for suicide ideation and, if a respondent scores 0 on both Item 4 (desire to make an active attempt) and on Item 5 (avoidance of death), the administration of additional items is not necessary.

As normative data for individuals who are suicide ideators, the BSS manual (Beck & Steer, 1993) reports total scale mean scores of 15.63 (SD = 5.28) and 8.83 (SD = 4.58) for 126 inpatient ideator and 52 outpatient ideator samples, respectively. With a sample of fifty patients attending a psychiatric hospital crisis unit, Holden, Mendonca, and Mazmanian (1985) reported a mean scale score of 12.50 (SD = 5.93) for the clinician-administered version of the measure. For an online general community sample of 290 American adults, a BSS mean of 5.96 (SD = 5.50) has been found (Fekken, D'Agata, & Holden, 2016). In a sample of 683 first-year university students, Troister and colleagues (2013) indicated a mean scale score of 4.14 (SD = 3.68).

Attesting to the strong internal consistency reliability of BSS scale scores, coefficient alpha values of 0.90 and 0.87 are reported in the scale manual for inpatient and outpatient suicide ideator samples, respectively (Beck & Steer, 1993). Beck and colleagues (1988) indicated score alpha coefficients of 0.93 and 0.96 for psychiatric patient samples who completed paper-and-pencil and computerized versions of the BSS, respectively. For crisis unit psychiatric patients, Holden and colleagues (1985) reported a BSS scale score alpha coefficient of 0.84. With nonclinical respondents, scale alpha coefficients of 0.87 (Fekken et al., 2016) and 0.78 (Troister & Holden, 2012a) have been found in samples of community residents and first-year university students, respectively.

For test-retest reliability of total BSS scale scores, a correlation of 0.54 is reported for a one-week interval with a sample of sixty inpatients (Beck & Steer, 1993). For samples of general (N = 683) and elevated-risk (N = 262) first-year university students, Troister and colleagues (2013) found five-month test-retest reliabilities of 0.70 and 0.65, respectively. Using a two-year test-retest interval, Troister and Holden (2012b) reported a test-retest correlation of 0.53 for a sample of forty-one elevated-risk university students.

Factor analyses suggest that the BSS may be multidimensional. While the manual (Beck & Steer, 1993) reported five underlying dimensions (Intensity, Active Desire, Planning, Passive Desire, Concealment), other research has indicated the presence of three factors (Desire for Death, Preparation for Suicide, Active Suicidal Desire; Steer et al., 1993) or two factors (Motivation, Preparation; Holden & DeLisle, 2005). Given that there is not a consensus on the nature of this multidimensionality, only the use of a total score can be recommended at this time for clinical practice.

Validity evidence for the BSS has accumulated from a variety of sources. Beck and colleagues (1988) found that the correlation between patients' and clinician-rated forms of the BSS was 0.90 or greater for each of three psychiatric samples. Cochrane-Brink, Lofchy, and Sakinofsky (2000) reported that scores on the BSS predicted hospital admission based on suicidal concerns. In a twenty-year prospective study of 6,891 psychiatric patients, scores on the clinician-rated version of the BSS predicted eventual death by suicide, with a cut score of ≥ 3 identifying patients seven times more likely to die by suicide than those scoring less than 3.

Suicidal Behaviors Questionnaire-Revised

Osman and colleagues (2001) developed the Suicidal Behaviors Questionnaire-Revised (SBQ-R) – a four-item self-report questionnaire of past suicidal behaviors including ideation and attempts. The measure is based on the premise that previous suicidal behavior is a risk factor for future suicidal behavior. A sample item is "How often have you thought about killing yourself in the past year?" The origins of the SBQ-R trace back to Linehan's (1981) Suicidal Behaviors Questionnaire (SBQ), a thirty-four-item self-report measure of the frequency and severity of current and previous suicidal behaviors (Linehan & Addis, 1983). Linehan also developed a four-item version of the questionnaire (e.g., Linehan & Nielsen, 1981; Linehan et al., 1983). Subsequently, variations of the four-item SBQ evolved in the suicide literature – this proliferation indicates a widespread need for such a brief measure in the field of suicide research (Osman et al., 2001). With a lack of consensus on a psychometrically sound version of the SBQ for use with adolescents and adults in clinical and nonclinical settings, Osman and colleagues (2001) modified the SBQ to establish what is now known as the SBQ-R.

The SBQ-R was developed for individuals aged fourteen years and older and can be completed in approximately five minutes. Each item of the SBQ-R assesses a different facet of suicidality: lifetime suicide ideation and/or suicide attempt; suicide ideation frequency in the previous year; communication of a suicide intent; and self-reported future likelihood of a suicide attempt. Every SBQ-R item has a different set of response options and, after each item is scored, a total score for the SBQ-R can be generated by summing the scores of the four items.

No manual consolidating psychometric data for the SBQ-R exists. Osman and colleagues (2001) provide small-sample normative SBQ-R data at the individual item level. They also have reported total SBQ-R scale scores for suicidal (M = 11.33, SD = 3.27) and nonsuicidal (M = 3.95, SD = 1.48) high school, adolescent suicidal (M = 12.45, SD = 3.02) and nonsuicidal (M = 5.46, SD = 2.41) inpatient, undergraduate suicidal (M = 9.27, SD = 1.91) and nonsuicidal (M = 5.01, SD = 1.37), and adult suicidal (M = 11.18, SD = 3.99) and nonsuicidal (M = 5.19, SD = 1.94) groups. For a sample of deployed American military service members (Bryan et al., 2010), the mean scale score was 3.34 (SD = 1.26).

With regard to the reliability of total SBQ-R scores, Osman and colleagues' (2001) investigation of four different samples found coefficient alpha values in the range 0.76–0.87. For a sample of 342 university undergraduates, Gutierrez and colleagues (2001) calculated a scale score coefficient alpha of 0.83. In Portuguese samples drawn from the general community, coefficient alpha values of 0.83 (Campos & Holden, 2015) and of 0.77 and 0.69 (Campos & Holden, 2016) have been reported.

For test-retest reliability and for the factor structure of the SBQ-R, there is a paucity of published research. Campos and Holden (2018) reported a five-month test-retest reliability correlation of 0.65 for the total scale. Because there are only four items of the SBQ-R, the extraction of more than one factor is not feasible and, as such, there are no factor analytic reports regarding the SBQ-R item structure.

Validity for scores on the SBQ-R has been demonstrated by the ability of individual items and the total scale to distinguish between suicidal and nonsuicidal individuals in high school, adolescent inpatient, undergraduate, and adult inpatient samples (Osman et al., 2001). From this, total scale cut scores of 7 for nonsuicidal and 8 for clinical samples have been developed. Campos and Holden (2016) reported that the total SBQ-R scores distinguished with more than large effect sizes between suicide attempters and non-attempters and between suicide ideators and non-ideators. Gutierrez and colleagues (2001) found a correlation of 0.77 between SBQ-R scale scores and a measure of self-harming. Confirmatory support for the SBQ-R cut scores has also been demonstrated (Campos & Holden, 2016; Shakeri et al., 2015).

Adult Suicidal Ideation Questionnaire

Originally constructed as the thirty-item Suicidal Ideation Questionnaire (Reynolds, 1987) and, subsequently, refined as the twenty-five-item Adult Suicidal Ideation Questionnaire (ASIQ; Reynolds, 1991), this measure was developed to index the self-reported presence and frequency of suicidal thoughts in the previous month. A sample item is "I thought that people would be happier if I were not around." Designed for use with adults, the ASIQ is appropriate in both clinical and nonclinical settings and can be completed in approximately ten minutes. Items are responded to on 7-point frequency ratings that are scored from 0 to 6. In addition to computing an overall scale score by summing all scored items, there are six critical items that designate specific actual thoughts and plans for suicide.

The ASIQ manual (Reynolds, 1991) reports total scale norms (now quite dated) based on samples of 547 adults in the community and on 1,104 college students. Norms for these samples are presented both as mean scores (broken down by sex) and as percentiles. Normative data are also supplied for 361 psychiatric outpatients in total as well as broken down by diagnosis (major depression, anxiety disorders, other disorders). In addition, normative data for all these groups are provided at the individual item level.

Strong coefficient alpha reliability values above 0.95 have been reported for the ASIQ scale scores of samples of men and women in the community, male and female college students, male and female psychiatric outpatients, major depression and anxiety disorder patients, and college and outpatient suicide attempters (Reynolds, 1991). In a study of men from a psychiatrically hospitalized population, a coefficient alpha of 0.95 has been found for ASIQ scores (Horon et al., 2013). A coefficient alpha of 0.98 has been reported for a sample of consecutive admissions to state long-term care psychiatric inpatient units (Osman et al., 1999).

In examining test-retest reliability for ASIQ total scores, Reynolds (1991) reported a correlation of 0.86 for a two-week interval with a sample of sixty-two college students. He also found a correlation of 0.95 for a one-week interval in a mixed psychiatric and community adult sample ($N = 20$).

Factor analyses of the ASIQ items have yielded somewhat equivocal results that may be population specific. Whereas three factors have been reported in community adult and in college student samples, four factors have emerged in a psychiatric sample (Reynolds, 1991). Importantly, however, the existence of a large first unrotated principal component in all samples supports the scoring of items on a single scale. Osman and colleagues (1999) reported moderate to excellent fit for a one-factor model depending on whether individual items or item parcels of six or seven items were analyzed. Given the lack of consensus on the multidimensional nature of the ASIQ, only scoring of an overall total can be recommended.

The ASIQ manual (Reynolds, 1991) provides considerable evidence regarding scale validity. As well as substantial correlations with measures of depression, hopelessness, anxiety, and low self-esteem, correlations with a prior suicide attempt are 0.30 and 0.38 in samples of female and male college students, respectively. The corresponding correlation in a mixed psychiatric/community sample was 0.36. Other research (Horon et al., 2013) has demonstrated ASIQ scores are significantly higher in single time suicide attempters than non-attempters and that multiple time suicide attempters score significantly higher than single time attempters. In a three-month follow-up of psychiatric inpatients, Osman and colleagues (1999) demonstrated the validity of the ASIQ scores for predicting subsequent suicide attempts.

CRITIQUE OF CURRENT SUICIDALITY MEASURES

Although self-report scales of suicidal cognitions and behaviors have assessment merit, their ability to predict suicide in specific instances remains to be established (Fowler, 2012). The use of risk factors such as demographic variables (e.g., age, sex, education, ethnicity), psychiatric diagnoses (e.g., mood disorders, impulse disorders), personality variables (e.g., perceived burdensomeness, thwarted belongingness), risk-taking actions, and past suicidal behaviors, despite being relevant, produces high rates of false positive identifications because these markers are also found among persons who are not suicidal. As such, new approaches (e.g., implicit association tests; Randall et al., 2013) and technologies including genetic marking (e.g., the 5-HTT serotonin gene; Arango et al., 2003) and machine learning (Walsh, Ribeiro, & Franklin, 2017) are emerging for assessing suicide risk; however, their promise has yet to been fully tested or realized.

The three measures of suicidality reviewed here have both substantial strengths and also considerable limitations. First, all three measures are brief self-reports and two of them, the BSS and ASIQ, have test manuals whereas the SBQ-R does not. Second, the BSS and ASIQ emphasize the assessment of an individual client, whereas the SBQ-R has a more epidemiological focus. Third, the minimal respondent age for use varies from fourteen years (SBQ-R), to seventeen years (BSS), to adult (ASIQ). Fourth, in terms of psychometric properties, all three measures have scale scores with demonstrated acceptable reliabilities and validities for particular groups in particular contexts. That being said, the generalizability of these properties to other populations and contexts needs to be considered when using any of the measures. Further, the applicability to a new context of reported normative data and any cut scores, again, must be thoughtfully evaluated. Fifth, whereas the SBQ-R and ASIQ were constructed for assessing suicide ideators and non-ideators, the focus of the BSS development was primarily, if not exclusively, on suicide ideators. Sixth, while the BSS and SBQ-R measure both suicide ideation and suicide behavior, the ASIQ primarily focuses on suicide ideation. If choosing among the three measures, prudent clinicians and researchers must balance the relative merits and shortcomings of each of these instruments and how the measures fit with other aspects of the overall assessment context.

The availability of a brief, inexpensive, single scale with temporally and demographically relevant norms and a cut score that accurately identifies an individual who will subsequently either die by suicide or attempt to die by suicide may be the holy grail of suicidologists. However, it is an elusive goal. None of the scales reviewed here is capable of such an accomplishment. That being said, any of the three measures may provide useful information that, when combined with other clinical data, can assist the clinician in the evaluation of a client's suicidal risk.

CONCLUSION

Over the past fifty years, excellent screening measures for two major mental health issues, namely depression and suicide, have emerged in the literature. These instruments yield scores with strong psychometric properties and this supports the use of these measures for screening purposes in both clinical and research contexts. Test users (clinicians and researchers) have the opportunity to consider which measures might best fit their current needs. Of course, due caution always needs to be exercised in considering whether the respondent is willing and able to provide accurate self-report. Undoubtedly the measures reviewed here will continue to evolve as new research contributes to the improved understanding of depression and suicide.

REFERENCES

American Psychiatric Association (1994). *Diagnostic and statistical manual of mental disorders* (4th ed.). Washington, DC: Author.

American Psychiatric Association. (2000). *Diagnostic and statistical manual of mental disorders* (rev. 4th ed.). Washington, DC: Author.

American Psychiatric Association. (2013). *Diagnostic and statistical manual of mental disorders* (5th ed.). Arlington, VA: Author.

Arango, V., Huang, Y., Underwood, M. D., & Mann, J. J. (2003). Genetics of the serotonergic system in suicidal behavior. *Journal of Psychiatric Research, 37*, 375–386.

Beck, A. T., Kovacs, M., & Weissman, A. (1979). Assessment of suicidal intention: The Scale for Suicide Ideation. *Journal of Consulting and Clinical Psychology, 47*, 343–352.

Beck, A. T., & Steer, R. A. (1993). *Beck Scale for Suicide Ideation manual.* San Antonio, TX: Psychological Corporation.

Beck, A. T., Steer, R. A., & Brown, G. K. (1996). *Manual for the Beck Depression Inventory-II.* San Antonio, TX: Psychological Corporation.

Beck, A. T., Steer, R. A., & Ranieri, W. F. (1988). Scale for Suicide Ideation: Psychometric properties of a self-report version. *Journal of Clinical Psychology, 44*, 499–505.

Boyle, G. J., Helmes, E., Matthews G., & Izard, C. E. (2015). Measures of affect dimensions. In G. J. Boyle, D. H. Saklofske, & G. Matthews (Eds.), *Measures of personality and social psychological constructs* (pp. 190–224). New York: Elsevier.

Brantley, P. R., & Brantley, P. J. (2017). Screening for depression. In M. E. Maruish (Ed.), *Handbook of psychological assessment in primary care settings* (pp. 245–276). New York: Routledge.

Bryan, C. J., Cukrowicz, K. C., West, C. L., & Morrow, C. E. (2010). Combat experience and the acquired capability for suicide. *Journal of Clinical Psychology, 66*, 1044–1056.

Busch, K. A., Fawcett, J., & Jacobs, D. G. (2003). Clinical correlates of inpatient suicide. *Journal of Clinical Psychiatry, 64*, 14–19.

Campos, R. C., & Holden, R. R. (2015). Testing models relating rejection, depression, interpersonal needs and psychache to suicide risk in non-clinical individuals. *Journal of Clinical Psychology, 71*, 994–1003.

Campos, R. C., & Holden, R. R. (2016). Portuguese version of the Suicidal Behaviors Questionnaire – Revised: Validation data and the establishment of a cut-score for screening purposes. *European Journal of Psychological Assessment*. doi:10.1027/1015-5759/a000385

Canetto, S. S., & Lester, D. (1998). Gender, culture, and suicidal behavior. *Transcultural Psychiatry, 35*, 163–190.

Chen, F. F. (2008). What happens if we compare chopsticks with forks? The impact of making inappropriate comparisons in cross-cultural research. *Journal of Personality and Social Psychology, 95*, 1005–1018.

Cheng, S.-T., & Chan, A. C. M. (2005). The Center for Epidemiologic Studies Depression Scale in older Chinese: Thresholds for long and short forms. *International Journal of Geriatric Psychiatry, 20*, 465–470.

Cheng, S.-T., Chan, A. C. M., & Fung, H. H. (2006). Factorial structure of a short version of the Center for Epidemiologic Studies Depression Scale. *International Journal of Geriatric Psychiatry, 21*, 333–336.

Cochrane-Brink, K. A., Lofchy, J. S., & Sakinofsky, I. (2000). Clinical rating scales in suicide risk assessment. *General Hospital Psychiatry, 22*, 445–451.

Curran, S. L., Andrykowski, M. A., & Studts, J. L. (1995). Short form of the Profile of Mood States (POMS-SF): Psychometric information. *Psychological Assessment, 7*, 80–83.

D'Agata, M. T., & Holden, R. R. (2018). Self-concealment and perfectionistic self-presentation in the concealment of psychache and suicide ideation. *Personality and Individual Differences, 125*, 56–61.

Dana, R. H. (2000). An assessment-intervention model for research and practice with multicultural populations. In R. H. Dana (Ed.), *Handbook of cross-cultural and multicultural personality assessment* (pp. 5–16). Mahwah, NJ: Lawrence Erlbaum Associates.

Eaton, W. W., Smith, C., Ybarra, M., Muntaner, C., & Tien, A. (2004). Center for Epidemiologic Studies Depression Scale: Review and revision (CESD and CESD-R). In M. E. Maruish (Ed.), *The use of psychological testing for treatment planning and outcomes assessment: Instruments for adults* (pp. 363–377). Mahwah, NJ: Lawrence Erlbaum Associates.

Eaton, W. W., Ybarra, M., & Schwab, J. (2012). The CESD-R is available on the web. *Psychiatry Research, 196*, 161.

Erford, B. T., Johnson, E., & Bardoshi, G. (2016). Meta-analysis of the English version of the Beck Depression Inventory–Second Edition. *Measurement and Evaluation in Counseling and Development, 49*, 3–33.

Fekken, G. C., D'Agata, M. T., & Holden, R. R. (2016, July). *The role of psychological pain and physical dissociation for understanding suicidality*. Yokohama, International Congress of Psychology.

Fowler, J. C. (2012). Suicide risk assessment in clinical practice: Pragmatic guidelines for imperfect assessments. *Psychotherapy, 49*, 81–90.

Fried, E. I., van Borkulo, C. D., Epskamp, S., Schoevers, R. A., Tuerlinckx, F., & Borsboom, D. (2016). Measuring depression over time . . . Or not? Lack of unidimensionality and longitudinal measurement invariance in four common rating scales of depression. *Psychological Assessment, 28*, 1354–1367.

Gold, J. A., Grill, M., Peterson, J., Pilcher, C., Lee, E., Hecht, F. M., & Spudich, S. (2014). Longitudinal characterization of depression and mood states beginning in primary HIV infection. *AIDS and Behavior, 18*, 1124–1132.

Granillo, M. T. (2012). Structure and function of the Patient Health Questionnaire-9 among Latina and Non-Latina White female college students. *Journal of the Society for Social Work and Research 3*, 80–93.

Gutierrez, P. M., Osman, A., Barrios, F. X., & Kopper, B. A. (2001). Development and initial validation of the self-harm behavior questionnaire. *Journal of Personality Assessment, 77*, 475–490.

Haroz, E. E., Ybarra, M. L., & Eaton, W. W. (2014). Psychometric evaluation of a self-report scale to measure adolescent depression: The CESD-R-10 in two national adolescent samples in the United States. *Journal of Affective Disorders, 158*, 154–160.

Heuchert, J. P., & McNair, D. M. (2012). *The Profile of Mood States* (2nd ed.). North Tonawanda, NY: Multi-Health Systems.

Holden, R. R., & DeLisle, M. M. (2005). Factor analysis of the Beck Scale for Suicide Ideation with female suicide attempters. *Assessment, 12*, 231–238.

Holden, R. R., Mendonca, J. D., & Mazmanian, D. (1985). Relation of response set to observed suicide intent. *Canadian Journal of Behavioural Science, 17*, 359–368.

Hom, M. A., Joiner, T. E., & Bernert, R. A. (2016). Limitations of a single-item assessment of suicide attempt history: Implications for standardized suicide risk assessment. *Psychological Assessment, 28*, 1026–1030.

Horon, R., McManus, T., Schmollinger, J., Barr, T., & Jimenez, M. (2013). A study of the use and interpretation of standardized suicide risk assessment: Measures within a psychiatrically hospitalized correctional population. *Suicide and Life-Threatening Behavior, 43*, 17–38.

Huang, F. Y., Chung, H., Kroenke, K., Delucchi, K. L., & Spitzer, R. L. (2006). Using the Patient Health Questionnaire-9 to measure depression among racially and ethnically diverse primary care patients. *Journal of General Internal Medicine, 21*, 547–552.

Johnson, J. G., Harris, E. S., Spitzer, R. L., & Williams, J. B. W. (2002). The Patient Health Questionnaire for Adolescents: Validation of an instrument for the assessment of mental disorders among adolescent primary care patients. *Journal of Adolescent Health, 30*, 196–204.

Kim, J., & Smith, T. (2017). Exploring measurement invariance by gender in the profile of mood states depression subscale among cancer survivors. *Quality of Life Research, 26*, 171–175.

Kohout, F. J., Berkman, L. F., Evans, D. A., & Cornoni-Huntley, J. (1993). Two shorter forms of the CES-D Depression Symptoms Index. *Journal of Aging and Health, 5*, 179–193.

Kroenke, K., Spitzer, R. L., & Williams, J. B. W. (2001). The PHQ-9: Validity of a brief depression severity measure. *Journal of General Internal Medicine, 16*, 606–613.

Kroenke, K., Spitzer, R. L., & Williams, J. B. W. (2003). The Patient Health Questionnaire-2: Validity of a two-item depression screener. *Medical Care, 41*, 1284–1292.

Lewinsohn, P. M., Seeley, J. R., Roberts, R. E., & Allen, N. B. (1997). Center for Epidemiologic Studies Depression Scale (CES-D) as a screening instrument for depression among community-residing older adults. *Psychology and Aging, 12*, 277–287.

Linehan, M. M. (1981). The Suicidal Behaviors Questionnaire (SBQ). Unpublished instrument, University of Washington, Seattle, WA.

Linehan, M. M., & Addis, M. E. (1983). Screening for suicidal behaviors: The Suicidal Behaviors Questionnaire. Unpublished manuscript, University of Washington, Seattle, WA.

Linehan, M. M., Goodstein, L. J., Nielsen, S. L., & Chiles, J. A. (1983). Reasons for staying alive when you are thinking of killing yourself: The Reasons for Living Inventory. *Journal of Consulting and Clinical Psychology, 51*, 276–286.

Linehan, M. M., & Nielsen, S. L. (1981). Assessment of suicide ideation and parasuicide: Hopelessness and social desirability. *Journal of Consulting and Clinical Psychology, 49*, 773–775.

Manea, L., Gilbody, S., & McMillan, D. (2012). Optimal cut-off score for diagnosing depression with the Patient Health Questionnaire (PHQ-9): A meta-analysis. *Canadian Medical Association Journal, 184(3)*, E191–E196.

Manea, L., Gilbody, S., & McMillan, D. (2015). A diagnostic meta-analysis of the Patient Health Questionnaire-9 (PHQ-9) algorithm scoring method as a screen for depression. *General Hospital Psychiatry, 37*, 67–75.

McNair, D. M., Lorr, M., & Droppleman, L. F. (1992). *Profile of Mood States manual.* San Diego: Educational and Industrial Testing Service.

Millner, A., Lee, M. D., & Nock, M. K. (2015). Single-item measurement of suicidal behaviors: Validity and consequences of misclassification. *PLoS ONE, 10*, e0141606.

Mitchell, A. J., Yadegarfar, M., Gill, J., & Stubbs, B. (2016). Case finding and screening clinical utility of the Patient Health Questionnaire (PHQ-9 and PHQ-2) for depression in primary care: a diagnostic meta-analysis of 40 studies. *BJPsych Open, 2* (2), 127–138.

Moriarty, A. S., Gilbody, S., McMillan, D., & Manea, L. (2015). Screening and case finding for major depressive disorder using the Patient Health Questionnaire (PHQ-9): A meta-analysis. *General Hospital Psychiatry, 37*, 567–576.

Myers, J. K., & Weissman, M. M. (1980). Use of a self-report symptom scale to detect depression in a community sample. *American Journal of Psychiatry, 137*, 1081–1084.

Myers, K., & Winters, N. C. (2002). Ten-year review of rating scales. II. Scales for internalizing disorders. *Journal of the American Academy of Child & Adolescent Psychiatry, 41*, 634–659.

Nabbe, P., Le Reste, J. Y., Guillou-Landreat, M., Munoz Perez, M. A., Argyriadou, S., Claveria, A., ... & Van Royen, P. (2017). Which DSM validated tools for diagnosing depression are usable in primary care research? A systematic literature review. *European Psychiatry, 39*, 99–105.

National Institute of Mental Health (n.d.). *Suicide in the U.S.: Statistics and prevention.* www.nimh.nih.gov/health/publications/suicide-in-the-us-statistics-and-prevention/index.shtml

Osman, A., Bagge, C. L., Gutierrez, P. M., Konick, L. C., Kopper, B. A., & Barrios, F. X. (2001). The Suicidal Behaviors Questionnaire – Revised (SBQ-R): Validation with clinical and nonclinical samples. *Assessment, 8*, 443–454.

Osman, A., Kopper, B. A., Barrios, F., Gutierrez, P. M., & Bagge, C. L. (2004). Reliability and validity of the Beck Depression Inventory-II with adolescent psychiatric inpatients. *Psychological Assessment, 16*, 120–132.

Osman, A., Kopper, B. A., Linehan, M. M., Barrios, F. X., Gutierrez, P. M., & Bagge, C. L. (1999). Validation of the Adult Suicidal Ideation Questionnaire and the Reasons for Living Inventory in an adult psychiatric inpatient sample. *Psychological Assessment, 11*, 115–123.

Patterson, K., Young, C., Woods, S. P., Vigil, O., Grant, I., Atkinson, J. H., & HIV Neurobehavioral Research Center (HNRC) Group. (2006). Screening for major depression in persons with HIV infection: The concurrent predictive validity of the Profile of Mood States Depression-Dejection scale. *International Journal of Methods in Psychiatric Research, 15*, 75–82.

Polanczyk, G. V., Salum, G. A., Sugaya, L. S., Caye, A., & Rohde, L. A. (2015). Annual research review: A meta-analysis of the worldwide prevalence of mental disorders in children and adolescents. *Journal of Child Psychology and Psychiatry, 56*, 345–365.

Radloff L. S. (1977). The CES-D scale: A self-report depression scale for research in the general population. *Applied Psychological Measurement, 1*, 385–401.

Randall, J. R., Rowe, B. H., Dong, K. A., Nock, M. K., & Colman, I. (2013). Assessment of self-harm risk using implicit thoughts. *Psychological Assessment, 25*, 714–721.

Reynolds, W. M. (1987). *Suicidal Ideation Questionnaire.* Odessa, FL: Psychological Assessment Resources.

Reynolds, W. M. (1991). *Adult Suicidal Ideation Questionnaire.* Odessa, FL: Psychological Assessment Resources.

Shakeri, J., Farnia, V., Abdoli, N. Akrami, M. R., Arman, F., & Shakeri, H. (2015). The risk of repetition of attempted suicide among Iranian women with psychiatric disorders as quantified by the Suicide Behaviors Questionnaire. *Oman Medical Journal, 30*, 173–180.

Shneidman, E. S. (1994). Clues to suicide, reconsidered. *Suicide and Life-threatening Behavior, 24*, 395–397.

Spitzer, R. L., Williams, J. B. W., Gibbon, M., & First, M. B. (1992). The structured clinical interview for DSM-III-R (SCID). *Archives of General Psychiatry, 49*, 624–9.

Steer, R. A., Rissmiller, D. J., Ranieri, W. F., & Beck, A. T. (1993). Dimensions of suicidal ideation in psychiatric inpatients. *Behaviour Research and Therapy, 31*, 229–236.

Stice, B. D., & Canetto, S. S. (2008). Older adult suicide: Perceptions of precipitants and protective factors. *Clinical Gerontologist, 31*, 4–30.

Streiner, D. L., Norman, G. R., & Cairney, J. (2015). *Health measurement scales: A practical guide to their development and use* (5th ed.). New York: Oxford University Press.

Thombs, B., Ziegelstein, R., Pilote, L., Dozois, D., Beck, A., Dobson, K., ... & Abbey, S. (2010). Somatic symptom overlap in Beck Depression Inventory-II scores following myocardial infarction. *British Journal of Psychiatry, 197*, 61–65.

Troister, T., & Holden, R. R. (2012a). Suicide ideation in transitioning university undergraduates. Paper presented at the International Congress of Psychology, July, Cape Town, South Africa.

Troister, T., & Holden, R. R. (2012b). A two-year prospective study of psychache and its relationship to suicidality among high-risk undergraduates. *Journal of Clinical Psychology, 68*, 1019–1027.

Troister, T., Davis, M. P., Lowndes, A., & Holden, R. R. (2013). A five-month longitudinal study of psychache and suicide ideation: Replication in general and high-risk university students. *Suicide and Life-Threatening Behavior, 43*, 611–620.

Van Dam, N. T., & Earleywine, M. (2011). Validation of the Center for Epidemiologic Studies Depression Scale-Revised (CESD-R): Pragmatic depression assessment in the general population. *Psychiatry Research, 186*, 128–132.

Vilagut, G., Forero, C. G., Barbaglia, G., & Alonso, J. (2016). Screening for depression in the general population with the Center for Epidemiologic Studies Depression (CES-D): A systematic review with meta-analysis. *PLoS ONE, 11*(5), e0155431.

Walsh, C. G., Ribeiro, J. D., & Franklin, J. C. (2017). Predicting risk of suicide attempts over time through machine learning. *Clinical Psychological Science, 5*, 457–469.

Wang, Y. P., & Gorenstein, C. (2013). Assessment of depression in medical patients: A systematic review of the utility of the Beck Depression Inventory-II. *CLINICS (Sao Paulo), 68*(9), 1274–1287.

WHO (World Health Organization). (2014a). *Preventing suicide: A global imperative*. Geneva: Author.

WHO (World Health Organization. (2014b). *Global health estimates 2013: Deaths by cause, age, and sex, estimates for 2000–2012*. Geneva: Author.

WHO (World Health Organization). (2017). *Depression and other common mental disorders: Global health estimates*. Geneva: Author.

Wittkampf, K. A., Naeije, L., Schene, A. H., Huyser, J., & van Weert, H. C. (2007). Diagnostic accuracy of the mood module of the Patient Health Questionnaire: A systematic review. *General Hospital Psychiatry, 29*, 388–395.

Wong, Y.-L. I. (2000). Measurement properties of the Center for Epidemiologic Studies Depression Scale in a homeless population. *Psychological Assessment, 12*, 69–76. http://apps.who.int/iris/bitstream/10665/254610/1/WHO-MSD-MER-2017.2-eng.pdf

Ziegler, M., & Bensch, D. (2013). Lost in translation: Thoughts regarding the translation of existing psychological measures into other languages. *European Journal of Psychological Assessment, 29*, 81–83.

24 Assessment of Anxiety Disorders and Obsessive-Compulsive Disorder

LORNA PETERS, LAUREN F. MCLELLAN, AND KEILA BROCKVELD

Anxiety and anxiety-related disorders are prevalent (e.g., an estimate of current prevalence is 7.3 percent; Baxter et al., 2012) and impairing (e.g., Baxter et al., 2014) conditions that are often comorbid with other disorders, especially depression and substance use disorders (e.g., McEvoy, Grove, & Slade, 2011). This chapter restricts itself to coverage of the assessment of anxiety disorders in adults and in particular to Social Anxiety Disorder (SAD), Agoraphobia, Panic Disorder, Generalized Anxiety Disorder (GAD), and Obsessive-Compulsive Disorder (OCD). These disorders share features of excessive fear and anxiety that may lead to significant avoidance behaviors. They are differentiated from one another on the basis of the objects or situations that are associated with anxiety and avoidance and by the nature of the cognitions about the feared object or situation (American Psychiatric Association, 2013). The similarities between the disorders present an assessment challenge; however, evidence-based assessment tools are available to allow the clinician to make appropriate clinical decisions for these disorders.

In this chapter, we discuss assessment of anxiety disorders in adults for answering clinical questions about diagnosis and severity of the anxiety disorder; case formulation and treatment planning; monitoring of progress throughout treatment; and measurement of treatment outcome. Most available evidence on treatment efficacy in the anxiety disorders supports the use of cognitive behavioral therapy (CBT) for adult anxiety disorders (e.g., Hofmann & Smits, 2008). To date, most of the evidence-based treatments for anxiety disorders are focused on a single anxiety disorder.[1] Thus, assessment of diagnosis is important in order to allow selection of the appropriate evidence-based treatment for that disorder. Once an evidence-based treatment has been chosen, then assessment will focus on constructs proposed by the model underlying the treatment to maintain the disorder (case formulation), so that the evidence-based treatment can be tailored to the specific problems experienced by the individual. Specifically, in CBT the constructs to be assessed will be behaviors and cognitions proposed to maintain the anxiety disorder. Finally, assessment will focus on severity of the symptoms in order to allow monitoring of progress in treatment and to measure treatment outcome.

Evidence-based assessment of adult anxiety disorders includes use of semi-structured diagnostic interviews, self-report measures (questionnaires), clinician-rated measures, and behavioral assessment techniques. The current chapter necessarily reviews only the most prominent tools used for assessment of adult anxiety disorders. While it is recommended that assessment be multimodal, self-report measures are commonly used given their relative ease of use. One concern that clinicians may have in using self-report measures of anxiety disorders is the possibility that respondents are responding in a noncredible manner (e.g., exaggerating or underreporting symptoms or feigning disorder), particularly since none of the measures has validity indices that would reveal such responding. This is a question that has not been examined empirically for the majority of self-report measures reviewed in this chapter and, in fact, is a question that has not been addressed in general in the assessment of anxiety disorders. There is evidence, however, that participants instructed to feign an anxiety disorder when completing self-report measures are able to do so successfully (e.g., Rogers, Ornduff, & Sewell, 1993). For example, in an early study, 96.9 percent of participants instructed to feign a diagnosis of GAD when completing a self-report diagnostic checklist were able to do so (Lees-Haley & Dunn, 1994). In a more recent study, it was found that those instructed to simulate OCD were able to do so, although they did tend to have higher mean scores on a self-report measure of OCD than patients diagnosed with the disorder (Moritz et al., 2012). That participants can successfully complete self-report measures of anxiety so that they appear to be indistinguishable to those without a disorder is problematic, especially in settings where there might be motivation to fake an

[1] Note, however, that there is increasing evidence for a transdiagnostic approach to treating anxiety disorders (Pearl & Norton, 2017), which would decrease the emphasis on diagnosis of a particular anxiety disorder and make assessment of the severity and precipitating and maintaining factors more important in planning treatment.

anxiety disorder (e.g., to gain special accommodations in an educational or work setting or in a forensic setting). Clinicians should be aware that an inaccurate portrayal of symptoms may occur when self-report measures are used, so relying solely on that mode of assessment is not recommended: inclusion of clinician-rated tools and behavioral assessment will be important. More broadly, examination of noncredible responding on self-report measures of anxiety is a critical area for future research.

DIVERSITY AND CULTURAL CONSIDERATIONS

Prevalence rates of the anxiety disorders vary across ethnic and race groups. For example, for the disorders being addressed in this chapter, Asnaani and colleagues (2010) found that White Americans were more likely to be diagnosed with SAD, GAD, and Panic Disorder than African Americans, Hispanic Americans, and Asian Americans; and Asian Americans were less likely to meet criteria for GAD than Hispanic Americans and were less likely to meet criteria for SAD, GAD, and Panic Disorder than White Americans. In assessing anxiety disorders, then, we must pay attention to the racial or ethnic background of the person being assessed. In the case of diagnosis, the diagnostic criteria for the anxiety disorders include a recognition that the anxiety experienced is beyond that expected given the sociocultural context (American Psychiatric Association, 2013). For details on culturally bound expressions of anxiety disorders (e.g., Taijin kyofusho (TKS), a variant of SAD prevalent in Japan and Korea; trúng gió, ataque de nervios, and khyâl, variants of Panic Disorder prevalent in Vietnam, Latin America, and Cambodia, respectively), see the accompanying text for these diagnoses in the fifth edition of the *Diagnostic and Statistical Manual of Mental Disorders* (DSM-5; American Psychiatric Association, 2013).

Most of the self-report measures described in this chapter have been translated into different languages. Where translated versions have been created, there is usually an investigation of the psychometric properties of the instrument within the language group for which the translation was created. The mere fact of translation, however, will not always take into account cultural variations in expression of the disorder and resultant differences in scores; nor will use of an English language version in a cultural group where English is the spoken language necessarily mean that cultural variation is accounted for. However, where studies have examined cultural differences on self-report measures reviewed in this chapter by comparing the fit of factor analytically derived models to the data across cultural groups, for the most part, it appears that the structure of measurement is similar across cultural groups (e.g., Asnaani et al., 2015; Contreras et al., 2004; Oei et al., 2013; Wong et al., 2019 ; Zvolensky et al., 2003). Thus, it may be that the cultural differences in scores on self-report measures are a matter of degree rather than type. Nevertheless, careful attention will need to be paid to normative data gathered within a particular cultural group when interpreting scores on self-report measures.

DIAGNOSIS

One essential function of assessment in the anxiety disorders is differential diagnosis, an especially important task given the selection of an evidence-based treatment will be based on the diagnosis made and given the level of comorbidity with other disorders, particularly other anxiety disorders. The length of time taken to administer structured diagnostic interviews, often more than two hours, may impact the practicality of routine use in practice. Nevertheless, structured diagnostic interviews enhance the reliability and validity of diagnoses and are therefore recommended. The Anxiety and Related Disorders Interview Schedule for DSM-5 (ADIS-5; Brown & Barlow, 2014) and the Structured Clinical Interview for DSM-5 Disorders (SCID-5; First et al., 2016) are the most widely used structured interviews in the anxiety disorders.[2] The ADIS-5 and SCID-5 both aim to emulate the sort of questioning that a clinician would ordinarily use – there are some questions that are required to be asked but the clinician uses suggested follow-up questions that will elicit information to allow a clinical judgment about whether diagnostic criteria are met. Thus, structured diagnostic interviews ensure coverage of all of the relevant diagnostic criteria and provide a structure for making clinical decisions about diagnoses, thereby enhancing reliability of the diagnoses made.

The ADIS-5 is available in two versions – the adult version (ADIS-5), which provides current diagnoses, and the Lifetime version (ADIS-5L), which allows diagnosis of past episodes. The ADIS-5 is designed to allow differential diagnosis according to DSM-5 criteria of current anxiety, mood, obsessive-compulsive, and trauma disorders and includes diagnosis of other disorders commonly found to be comorbid with anxiety disorders, including somatic symptoms and substance use disorders. The ADIS-5 includes screening questions for a range of additional disorders (e.g., psychotic disorders). The anxiety disorders included are Panic Disorder, Agoraphobia, SAD, Separation Anxiety Disorder, GAD, and Specific Phobia. OCD is also covered. The interview begins with inquiry about demographic details and a description of the presenting problem and recent life events. Subsequent sections include questions relating to disorders. For each disorder, initial inquiry typically includes questions designed to assess the current and past occurrences of the key features of the disorder that can be answered yes or no. If it is clear from the initial inquiry that diagnostic

[2] The ADIS-5 and SCID-5 are updated versions to allow for diagnoses made according to DSM-5 criteria. The psychometric information for the interviews is for the versions that assessed DSM-IV. In both cases, however, the structure and procedure for administration of the interviews is similar between the DSM-IV and the DSM-5 versions, so the psychometric properties are likely to be similar.

Table 24.1 Reliability of Anxiety Disorder Interview Schedule (ADIS) and Structured Clinical Interview for DSM (SCID) diagnoses

Diagnosis	Any Diagnosis				
	ADIS-IV[a] (Current)	ADIS-IV[a] (Lifetime)	SCID-IV[b]	SCID-5[c] (Current)	SCID-5[c] (Lifetime)
Social Anxiety Disorder	κ = 0.77 (n = 152)	κ = 0.73 (n = 161)	κ = 0.25 (n = 17)	κ = 0.29 (n = 6)	κ = 0.18 (n = 13)
Panic Disorder	κ = 0.56 (n = 22)	κ = 0.58 (n = 30)	κ = 0.60 (n = 80)	–	κ = 0.46 (n = 9)
Panic Disorder with Agoraphobia/ Agoraphobia	κ = 0.81 (n = 102)	κ = 0.81 (n = 116)	–	–	–
Generalized Anxiety Disorders	κ = 0.65 (n = 113)	κ = 0.65 (n = 114)	κ = 0.45 (n = 17)	κ = 0.56 (n = 4)	κ = 0.77 (n = 7)
Obsessive-Compulsive Disorder	κ = 0.75 (n = 60)	κ = 0.75 (n = 73)	κ = 0.41 (n = 20)	κ = 0.64 (n = 4)	κ = 0.49 (n = 5)

Note. ADIS-IV – Anxiety Disorders Interview for DSM-IV; SCID-IV; Structured Clinical Interview for DSM-IV; SCID-5 – Structured Diagnostic Interview for DSM-5.

a. ADIS-IV information taken from Brown et al. (2001). Kappas represent reliability where participants (n = 362) received two independent ADIS-IV interviews an average of 10.60 (SD = 8.60) days apart.
b. SCID-IV information taken from Chmielewski et al. (2015). Kappas represent reliability where participants (n = 218) received two independent SCID-I/P interviews an average of 7.2 (SD = 1.44) days apart.
c. SCID-5 information taken from Shankman et al. (2018). Kappas represent reliability where participants (n = 51) received two independent SCID interviews an average of 8.51 (SD = 4.31) days apart. Note that the SCID-5 was a modified version and the data presented here should be interpreted with this caveat in mind.

criteria for that disorder cannot be met, then the remainder of the questions on that disorder are skipped; otherwise, questions are asked to allow rating of the symptoms of the disorder on a nine-point scale (e.g., 0 = never/none to 8 = constantly/very severe). This dimensional rating of symptoms is an advantage of the ADIS-5 over other structured diagnostic interviews. Finally, questions about the onset and remission of symptoms are asked. Table 24.1 presents inter-rater reliability for anxiety disorder diagnoses for the DSM-IV version of the ADIS. The kappa values indicate acceptable agreement ranging from 0.56 (for a current diagnosis of Panic Disorder) to 0.81 (for a current and lifetime diagnosis of Panic Disorder with Agoraphobia). To date, psychometric properties of the DSM-5 version have not been published. Similarly, while the DSM-IV version of the ADIS has been translated into several languages (e.g., German, Spanish, French), to our knowledge, apart from the German version (Schneider et al., 1992) there has been no published psychometric evaluation of these translated versions.

Where the clinician needs full coverage of diagnoses other than anxiety and related disorders, the SCID-5 may be used as an alternative to the ADIS-5. While the SCID-5 provides more detailed questioning than the ADIS-5 for mood disorders and full diagnostic coverage of other disorders such as psychotic disorders, this comes at the expense of less complete coverage of the anxiety disorders; for instance, the SCID-5 provides only screening questions for specific phobia and separation anxiety disorder. The SCID-5 is available in several versions, of which the SCID-5-Clinician Version (SCID-5-CV) is most likely to be useful in clinical practice. The SCID-5-CV allows for diagnosis of Panic Disorder, Agoraphobia, SAD, GAD, Anxiety Disorder Due to a Medical Condition, Substance/Medication-Induced Anxiety Disorder, and OCD. Similar to the ADIS-5, each section in the SCID-5-CV begins with questions about the main diagnostic features of the disorder, which, if answered such that it is clear diagnostic criteria for a disorder are not likely to be met, allows the interviewer to skip remaining questions. Table 24.1 presents inter-rater reliability for anxiety disorders diagnoses for the DSM-IV version of the SCID as well as for the SCID-5. The kappa values indicate acceptable, although not high, agreement for all disorders apart from SAD, where agreement is below the generally accepted kappa value of 0.40.

ASSESSMENT OF SEVERITY AND MONITORING OF PROGRESS THROUGH TREATMENT

Assessment of severity is useful for treatment planning and for monitoring progress throughout treatment by administration of brief measures at regular intervals throughout treatment. Some self-report measures can be used across the different anxiety disorders. For example, the Beck Anxiety Inventory (BAI; Beck et al., 1988) and the anxiety and stress subscales of the Depression Anxiety Stress Scales (DASS; Lovibond & Lovibond, 1995) all provide scores that quantify the distress experienced as a result of anxiety symptoms regardless of the type of anxiety disorder. These general measures of distress are useful as a measure of progress and outcome in settings where a single measure might be required across a number of anxiety disorders or where transdiagnostic treatment approaches are being used. However, these generic measures do not provide information about specific constructs that may be targeted in treatment for each disorder.

The BAI has twenty-one items designed to assess the severity of anxiety symptoms that are self-rated to indicate how much respondents have been bothered by each of the symptoms over the past week on a four-point scale (0 = not at all to 3 = severely, I could barely stand it). The score is a sum of the ratings on each item (in the range 0–63). Beck and colleagues (1988) report adequate reliability (internal consistency = 0.92 and test-retest = 0.75), convergent and discriminant validity (e.g., BAI scores correlated higher with a clinician rating of anxiety than with a clinician rating of depression and BAI scores differentiated patients with anxiety from patients with depression), and sensitivity to change. A meta-analysis of the psychometric properties of the English-language version of the BAI reported in 192 studies reported adequate internal consistency (α = 0.91) and test-retest reliability (r = 0.66) in clinical samples (Bardhoshi, Duncan, & Erford, 2016) and the convergent validity between the BAI and other anxiety measures ranged from 0.24 to 0.81 (Bardhoshi et al., 2016).

The DASS is a forty-two-item scale designed to distinguish between the states of anxiety, depression, and stress. There are fourteen items measuring each of those states rated on a scale of 0 (did not apply to me at all) to 3 (applied to me very much or most of the time) and ratings are summed to provide a total score for each state ranging from 0 to 42. The scores on the DASS have acceptable internal consistency, temporal stability over a two-week period, and construct validity (mood disorder groups had significantly higher scores on the depression scale than other disorder groups) (Brown et al., 1997). A short version (twenty-one-item version with seven items for each of depression, anxiety, and stress) is available and has adequate psychometrics in clinical samples (Antony et al., 1998).[3]

Social Anxiety Disorder

SAD is characterized by fear or anxiety about social situations (e.g., interacting with others, being observed, or performing in front of others) in which there is possible scrutiny by others. The individual fears that they will be embarrassed or humiliated (American Psychiatric Association, 2013). The Social Phobia Scale and the Social Interaction Anxiety Scale (SPS/SIAS) are a pair of self-report measures of the severity of SAD, designed to measure scrutiny fears (anxiety and fear about being observed by others) and concerns about interaction with others (Mattick & Clarke, 1998). See Table 24.2 for an overview. Although designed to be used together, it is common in the research literature to see the SIAS used as a stand-alone measure. Four research groups have developed short forms of the SIAS and SPS that, given their relative brevity, may be more useful in a clinical setting for screening for SAD and for monitoring progress throughout treatment. Carleton and colleagues (2014) conducted an empirical investigation of the four short forms in both undergraduate and clinical samples and concluded that the most robust psychometric support was for the Social Interaction and Phobia Scale (SIPS; Carleton et al., 2009) and the SPS-6 and SIAS-6 (Peters et al., 2012).

An issue that needs to be considered when assessing social anxiety severity is that items on questionnaires often assume heterosexuality (Shulman & Hope, 2016). For example, the SIAS has an item that refers to anxiety about interacting with those of the opposite sex ("I have difficulty talking to an attractive person of the opposite sex"). Using "opposite sex" in such items has at least two problems: first, the items are generally included to tap dating anxiety, yet use of "opposite sex" assumes that the person completing the measure will find those of the "opposite sex" attractive; and, second, use of "opposite sex" assumes that gender is binary. Weiss, Hope, and Capozzolo (2013) and Lindner and colleagues (2013) tested alternate, gender-neutral wording (e.g., "a potential romantic partner" and "persons of the sex/sexes that I am interested in") to replace terms like "opposite sex" in commonly used social anxiety measures including the SIAS and found that alternate wording did not alter the psychometric properties of the measure.

Generalized Anxiety Disorder

Generalized Anxiety Disorder (GAD) is characterized by excessive anxiety and worry about a number of domains. The individual finds it difficult to control the worry and experiences physical symptoms (e.g., restlessness, muscle tension) associated with the worry (American Psychiatric Association, 2013). The BAI can be used as a general measure of anxiety when assessing clients with GAD. Two additional tools designed to measure severity of GAD symptoms specifically might be considered. The Penn State Worry Questionnaire (PSWQ; Meyer, Miller, & Borkovec, 1990) is a sixteen-item questionnaire designed to measure the trait of worry. Items are specifically about worrying (e.g., Many situations make me worry) and therefore give a measure of the extent of worrying itself. To obtain a broader measure of severity of symptoms of GAD diagnosis, the PSWQ could be used alongside the Generalized Anxiety Disorder-7 (GAD-7; Spitzer et al., 2006). Although the PSWQ and GAD-7 scores are correlated, the correlation

[3] Both versions of the DASS are freely available to use (http://www2.psy.unsw.edu.au/dass/).

Table 24.2 Measures of severity in the anxiety disorders

Disorder Measure Source	Structure	Psychometric Properties
Social Anxiety Disorder		
Social Phobia Scale and Social Interaction Anxiety Scale (SPS/SIAS) Mattick & Clarke (1998)	– Self-report – Designed to measure scrutiny fears (anxiety and fear about being observed by others; SPS) and concerns about interaction with others (SIAS) – Each scale has 20 items rated from 0 (not at all characteristic or true of me) to 4 (extremely characteristic or true of me) – Total scores for each scale is the sum of ratings for the 20 items after appropriate reverse scoring	– Internal consistency (student sample): Cronbach's α for SPS = 0.8 and for SIAS = 0.93 – Test-retest reliability: 4 week (range 3–5) interval: SPS: $r = 0.91$ and SIAS = 0.92; 12 week (range 11–13) interval: SPS: $r = 0.93$ and SIAS: $r = 0.92$ – Convergent validity: SIAS and SPS scores have significant correlations with scores on scales that measure similar features of social phobia (Mattick & Clarke, 1998; Ries et al., 1998). – Discriminant validity: SIAS and SPS scores are higher in those diagnosed with SAD than in those without the disorder (Peters, 2000) – Sensitivity to change: SPS and SIAS scores show a significant decrease from before to after cognitive behavioral therapy when compared to a waitlist control group (Mattick & Peters, 1988; Mattick, Peters, & Clarke, 1989).
Generalized Anxiety Disorder		
Penn State Worry Questionnaire (PSWQ) Meyer, Miller, & Borkovec, 1990)	– Self-report – Designed to measure the trait of worry – 16 items are rated on a scale from 1 (not at all typical of me) to 5 (very typical of me) – Total score (ranging from 16 to 80) is obtained by summing the rating for each item	– Internal consistency: Cronbach's α = 0.93 (student sample); .93 (clinical sample: Brown et al., 1992) – Test-retest reliability (student sample): 8–10 week interval: $r = 0.92$ – Convergent and divergent validity: Significant correlation with scores on other measures of worry in a student sample (r's = 0.59 and 0.67); in a sample of GAD patients scores significantly correlated with a measure of tension ($r = 0.36$) and of emotional control ($r = -0.53$) but not with a measure of anxiety ($r = 0.11$) and a measure of depression ($r = 0.15$) (Brown et al., 1992) – Discriminant validity: Scores were significantly higher for those with a primary diagnosis of GAD than for those who met criteria for another anxiety disorder (Brown et al., 1992) – Sensitivity to change: scores decreased more for those who received cognitive therapy than for those who received a non-directive therapy.
Generalized Anxiety Disorder-7 (GAD-7) Spitzer et al. (2006)	– Self-report – Designed to measure GAD symptom severity – 7 items are rated for how much the stated symptom has bothered the respondent over the past two weeks on a 4-point scale (0 = not at all to 3 = nearly every day) – The total score (ranging from 0 to 21) is the sum of the ratings for each item	– Internal consistency: Cronbach's α = 0.92 – Test-retest reliability: one week interval: ICC = 0.83. – Convergent validity: increases in GAD-7 severity scores were associated with decreases in measures of general functioning; GAD-7 scores were significantly correlated with scores on measures of anxiety and depression (r's ranged from 0.64 to 0.77; Kertz, Bigda-Peyton, & Bjorgvinsson, 2013) – Sensitivity to change: scores decreased from pre- to posttreatment when treatment was a short intensive CBT program in an acute psychiatric sample (Kertz et al., 2013) and when treatment was an Internet-delivered CBT program for GAD (Dear et al., 2011)

Continued

Table 24.2 (cont.)

Disorder Measure Source	Structure	Psychometric Properties
Panic Disorder		
Panic Disorder Severity Scale (PDSS) Shear et al. (1997)	– Clinician-rated; structured interview – Designed to measure the severity of panic disorder symptoms as a whole – 7 items each tapping a symptom of panic disorder: frequency of panic attacks; distress during panic attacks; worry about future panic attacks (anticipatory anxiety); agoraphobic fear and avoidance; fear and avoidance of bodily sensations (interoceptive avoidance); impairment/interference in work functioning; and impairment/interference in social functioning – Items are rated for the severity of each of the symptoms over the past month on a 5-point scale ranging from 0 (none) to 4, with higher ratings indicating greater severity – The total score is calculated in two different ways in the published literature; either as an average of the ratings on the 7 items or as a sum of the ratings on the 7 items	– Internal consistency: Cronbach's $\alpha = 0.65$ – Inter-rater reliability: ICC = 0.88 – Convergent validity: significant correlations between the total score on the PDSS and ratings of frequency and fear of panic attacks made during the ADIS and between each item on the PDSS and a scale tapping a similar symptom – Divergent validity: lower correlations between each item on the PDSS and scales tapping different symptoms – Sensitivity to change: those independently classified as treatment responders had significantly lower total PDSS scores at posttreatment than at pre-treatment, while treatment non-responders did not show a decline in PDSS total scores between pre- and posttreatment
PDSS-SR Houck et al. (2002)	– Self-report – As for the PDSS	– Internal consistency: Cronbach's $\alpha = 0.917$ – Test-retest reliability: over two consecutive days: ICC = 0.83 – Sensitivity to change: a similar decrease in scores with treatment as that seen for the clinician-rated version of the scale
Agoraphobia		
Mobility Inventory for Agoraphobia (MIA) Chambless et al. (1985)	– Self-report – Designed to measure agoraphobic avoidance behavior and frequency of panic attacks – 28 situations (e.g., supermarkets, buses, being far away from home) are rated for degree of avoidance because of discomfort or anxiety on a scale from 1 (Never avoid) to 5 (Always avoid) under two circumstances, when the individual is alone and when the individual is accompanied by a trusted companion, providing two scores: the MIAAC (avoidance when accompanied) and MIAAL (avoidance when alone) – Scores are the sum of ratings for each item divided by the number of items; scores range from 1 (no avoidance) to 5 (always avoids)	– Internal consistency: Cronbach's $\alpha = 0.95$ for MIAAC; Cronbach's $\alpha = 0.96$ for MIAAL (Chambless et al., 2011) – Convergent and divergent validity: higher correlations with clinician-rated agoraphobia severity ratings ($r = 0.54$ for MIAAC and $r = 0.63$ for MIAAL) than with severity ratings of other anxiety disorders (r's ranged from 0.07 to 0.37 for MIAAC and from 0.10 to 0.29 for MIAAL) (Chambless et al., 2011)

Continued

Table 24.2 (cont.)

Disorder Measure Source	Structure	Psychometric Properties
Obsessive-Compulsive Disorder		
Yale-Brown Obsessive Compulsive Scale (Y-BOCS) Goodman et al. (1989a); Goodman et al. (1989b)	– Clinician-rated – Designed to provide a measure of severity of OCD symptoms that is not influenced by the number or type of obsessions and compulsions present – 10 items rated from 0 (no symptoms) to 4 (extreme symptoms) – 5 ratings made for each of obsessions and compulsions: time spent on obsessions/compulsions; interference from obsessions/compulsions; distress from obsessions/compulsions; resistance; control over obsessions/compulsions – Total Y-BOCS severity score is the sum of all 10 ratings; Obsessions severity score: sum of 5 ratings for obsessions; Compulsions severity score: sum of 5 ratings for compulsions	– Inter-rater reliability: $r = 0.98$ – Internal consistency: mean Cronbach's $\alpha = 0.89$ – Convergent validity: Significant correlations between Total Y-BOCS scores and scores on other measures of OCD (r's ranged between 0.53 and 0.74) – Divergent validity: Y-BOCS total scores had a moderate correlation with a measure of depression ($r = 0.38$) – Sensitivity to change: Patients receiving a drug treatment of OCD showed a significant decrease in scores from baseline as compared to a scores for patients who received a placebo (these patients showed no change in Y-BOCS scores).

Yale-Brown Obsessive Compulsive Scale – Second Edition (Y-BOCS-II)
Storch et al. (2010)
	– Clinician-rated
	– As for Y-BOCS with the following exceptions:
	  – Eliminates the resistance to obsession item replacing it with an item, assessing obsession-free intervals
	  – Ratings scale has 6 points
	  – Probes and anchor points added to capture active avoidance
	– Content and format of Y-BOCS-SC modified
		– Internal consistency: Cronbach's $\alpha = 0.89$ (total), 0.86 (obsessions), 0.84 (compulsions); Cronbach's $\alpha = 0.86$ (total), 0.83 (obsessions), 0.75 (compulsions) (Wu et al., 2016)
		– Inter-rater reliability: Total score ICC = 0.96; Total score ICC = 0.99 (Wu et al., 2016)
		– Test-retest reliability: 1-week interval ICC = 0.85; 1 to 2 week interval: $r = 0.81$ (Wu et al., 2016)
		– Convergent validity: Significant correlation between Y-BOCS-II total scores and scores on other measures of OCD (r's ranged between 0.22 and 0.85); $r = 0.84$ (Wu et al., 2016)
		– Divergent validity: Y-BOCS total scores had a moderate correlation with a measure of depression ($r = 0.35$) ; $r = 0.41$ (Wu et al., 2016)

Obsessive Compulsive Inventory Foa et al. (1998)	– Self-report – 42 items on 7 subscales: washing, checking, doubting, ordering, obsessing, hoarding, mental neutralizing – Items rated for their frequency (0 = never to 4 = almost always) and distress (0 = not at all to 4 = extremely) in the past month	– Internal consistency: Cronbach's $\alpha = 0.92$ (distress), 0.93 (frequency); subscales: Cronbach's α ranged from 0.72 for mental neutralizing frequency to 0.96 for washing frequency – Test-retest reliability: 2-week interval; distress ($r = 0.87$) and frequency ($r = 0.84$); subscales: r's ranged from 0.77 for ordering distress to $r =$ 0.97 washing distress – Discriminant validity: Distress and frequency total and subscale scores were higher for those with OCD than for those with another anxiety disorder or no diagnosis on all subscales apart from hoarding subscale, where the OCD participants did not differ from those with no diagnosis – Convergent validity: significant correlations with scores on other self-report measures of OCD: r's ranged from 0.65 to 0.75

Continued

Table 24.2 (cont.)

Disorder Measure Source	Structure	Psychometric Properties
		- Divergent validity: distress scores were found to significantly correlate with scores on a measure of depression ($r = 0.32$)
Obsessive Compulsive Inventory – Revised (OCI-R) Foa et al. (2002)	- Self-report - 18 items on 6 subscales: washing, checking, ordering, obsessing, hoarding, neutralizing - Items rated for their distress (0 = not at all to 4 = extremely) in the past month	- Internal consistency: total score $\alpha = 0.81$; α for the subscales ranged from 0.82 for obsessing to 0.90 for both hoarding and ordering - Test-retest reliability: over two weeks for a clinical sample was adequate (*r*'s ranged from 0.74 for checking to 0.91 for washing) - Convergent validity: significant correlations with scores on other measures of OCD (*r*'s ranged from 0.49 to 0.85) - Divergent validity: significant correlations with measures of depression ($r = 0.58$, $r = 0.70$)

Note. Table 24.2 is intended to provide examples of measures that are available to assist in assessing severity; it is not intended to be a comprehensive listing of all possible measures. Psychometric properties are taken from the source article unless an additional source is acknowledged. Where possible only studies examining psychometric properties in clinical samples are included.

is moderate ($r = 0.51$; Dear et al., 2011); thus they are likely to provide different information about severity. For the GAD-7, Spitzer and colleagues suggest that scores of 5–9 represent mild severity, 10–14 represent moderate severity, and 15–21 represent severe levels of anxiety. In a systematic review of the GAD-7's ability to identify anxiety disorders, Plummer and colleagues (2016) found that a score of 8 provided an acceptable cutoff score for identifying those with GAD, although scores of between 7 and 10 were also acceptable. Note, however, that these cutoff scores may not apply across all cultural groups. For instance, Parkerson and colleagues (2015) found that African American participants have lower GAD-7 scores at the same level of GAD severity than their White American counterparts. The brevity of the GAD-7 and its sensitivity to change with treatment make it a suitable tool for use across treatment to monitor progress.

Panic Disorder

Panic Disorder is characterized by recurrent, unexpected, abrupt surges of fear (i.e., panic attacks) involving physical (e.g., heart pounding, sweating, trembling) and cognitive (e.g., fear of losing control) symptoms that reach a peak within minutes. The individual is concerned persistently about additional attacks or changes their behavior (e.g., avoidance of situations that might lead to panic attacks) (American Psychiatric Association, 2013).

The Panic Disorder Severity Scale (PDSS; Shear et al., 1997) was originally developed as a clinician-rated scale to measure the severity of panic disorder symptoms as a whole. Furukawa and colleagues (2009) provide clinical descriptors for empirically derived ranges of summed scores on the PDSS: for those with agoraphobia scores from 3–7 indicate "borderline ill," 8–10 "slightly ill," 11–15 "moderately ill," and 16 and over "markedly ill." A self-report version of the PDSS (PDSS-SR; Houck et al., 2002) measuring severity over the past week has been developed. The self-report version may allow for a more cost-effective way of monitoring progress through treatment. A comparison of the PDSS and the PDSS-SR revealed similar psychometric properties and no difference between scores on the self-report and clinician-rated versions (Wuyek, Antony, & McCabe, 2011). However, it should be noted that Houcke and colleagues found that the mean total score on the self-report version was lower than on the clinician-rated version. Thus, users of the PDSS-SR should be aware that there may be underreporting of severity using this version of the scale.

Agoraphobia

Agoraphobia is characterized by anxiety about and avoidance of situations (e.g., using public transport, being in open spaces) because of concerns that escape might be difficult or help might not be available in the event of panic-like symptoms occurring (American Psychiatric Association, 2013). An important distinction needs to be made during assessment of Agoraphobia between avoidance of situations due to agoraphobic concerns versus avoidance of the same situations for fear of possible humiliation or embarrassment that occurs in SAD. Assessing the underlying fear (e.g., by using the ADIS-5) will help the clinician to distinguish between the two conditions.

The Mobility Inventory for Agoraphobia (MIA; Chambless et al., 1985) is a twenty-eight-item self-report scale designed to measure agoraphobic avoidance behavior and frequency of panic attacks. Twenty-eight situations (e.g., supermarkets, buses, being far away from home) are rated for degree of avoidance because of discomfort or anxiety on a scale from 1 (never avoid) to 5 (always avoid) under two circumstances, when the individual is alone and when the individual is accompanied by a trusted companion, providing two scores: the MIAAC is the avoidance when accompanied and MIAAL is the avoidance when alone. The scores are obtained by adding the rating for each item and dividing by the number of items so that scores range from 1 to 5, and can be interpreted using the scale where 1 indicates no avoidance and 5 indicates that the individual always avoids.

Obsessive-Compulsive Disorder

OCD is characterized by the presence of obsessions and compulsions. Obsessions are recurrent, persistent, unwanted, and intrusive thoughts, urges, or images (American Psychiatric Association, 2013) and compulsions are repetitive behaviors (e.g., washing, checking) or mental acts (e.g., praying silently) that are performed in response to an obsession and that the individual feels compelled to perform (American Psychiatric Association, 2013). There is heterogeneity in the content of obsessions and compulsions experienced by individuals diagnosed with OCD but, typically, obsessions and compulsions are focused on a limited set of themes: contamination and illness, responsibility for harming oneself or others, morality and religiosity, and symmetry (Abramowitz, 2018). Assessment of severity will require a good understanding of the specific obsessions and compulsions manifest in each client.

Clinician-rated and self-report measures are available to assess severity of obsessions and compulsions (see Table 24.2). The Yale-Brown Obsessive Compulsive Scale (Y-BOCS; Goodman et al., 1989b) and its revision, the Y-BOCS-II (Storch et al., 2010) provide a sound tool for clinician rating of severity of obsessions and compulsions after careful inquiry about the presence of a range of obsessions and compulsions. Administration of the measure follows a semi-structured interview and a manual provides guidance on the method of questioning and anchor points for each of the ratings to be made. The tool was designed to allow weekly ratings to be made throughout treatment. Given the finding that scores on the Y-BOCS and Y-BOCS-II have moderate to strong correlations with self-report measures of depression, a finding replicated by an independent researcher (Woody, Steketee, & Chambless, 1995), users of the tool should be aware that Y-BOCS scores might be impacted by the presence of depression. The Obsessive Compulsive Inventory (OCI; Foa et al., 1998) and its short form (OCI-R; Foa et al., 2002) provide sound self-report measures of the severity of OCD. They aim to assess the heterogeneity of obsessions and compulsions in OCD. Like the Y-BOCS, OCI scores have been found to significantly correlate with scores on measures of depression; so, again, users are cautioned to take into account levels of depression when interpreting scores on the OCI. It should also be noted that scores on the OCI-R have been found to be significantly higher among African American participants diagnosed with OCD as compared to the European American participants with OCD in the original validation sample, with the largest differences being seen for the hoarding and ordering subscales (Williams et al., 2013).

Assessment for Case Formulation and Treatment Planning

Case formulation is the process used by a clinician to describe the relationship between problems experienced by a client and to identify the etiological and maintaining mechanisms that will then be targeted in treatment (e.g., Persons, 2006, 2013). In the case of anxiety disorders, the most efficacious psychological treatment is CBT and thus assessment will focus on maintaining factors as described by cognitive behavioral models of the disorders in order to tailor the evidence-based CBT to the individual's specific concerns. Self-report measures can assist in the process of case formulation. Table 24.1 lists selected self-report measures of theoretical maintaining factors for each disorder that may be useful in case formulation. Table 24.3 is intended to provide examples of measures that are available to assist in case formulation; it is not intended to be a comprehensive listing of all possible measures.

Behavioral assessment is particularly informative in case formulation in the anxiety disorders. In behavioral assessment, the client is asked to engage in an activity that will allow for real-time measurement of cognitions and behaviors. An advantage of behavioral assessment is that it provides information that is idiosyncratic to the client's experience of their anxiety disorder, thus allowing for tailoring of the treatment to the individual's specific concerns. Two types of behavioral assessment are common in assessment of the anxiety disorders: self-monitoring, where the client is asked to monitor and record their anxiety, cognitions, and behaviors while in their own environment; and behavioral avoidance tasks, where a client engages in a task that is designed to emulate the situation that causes anxiety while in the presence of the clinician (e.g., a speech task for those with SAD). Self-monitoring allows for the client to record anxiety, thoughts, and behaviors as they occur in their own environment along with the associated triggers (e.g., details about the particular situation). Self-monitoring will be useful prior to treatment in order to allow for case formulation but will be particularly useful when used on an ongoing basis throughout treatment to monitor progress. However, compliance with instructions and accuracy of self-monitoring may be problematic (e.g., Barlow, Hayes,

Table 24.3 Measures of theoretical maintaining factors that are useful for case formulation in the anxiety disorders

Disorder Construct	Measure Source	Structure	Psychometric Properties
Social Anxiety Disorder			
Situational Avoidance	Liebowitz Social Anxiety Scale (LSAS) Liebowitz (1987)	– Clinician-rated – Two separate ratings (severity and frequency of avoidance) of 11 social interaction and 13 performance situations – Severity of fear rated on a 4-point scale: 0 = none to 3 = severe – Frequency of avoidance rated on a 4-point scale: 0 = never (0 percent) to 3 = usually (67–100 percent) – Six scores: fear of social interaction, fear of performance, total fear, avoidance of social interaction, avoidance of performance, total avoidance, and LSAS total (sum of total fear and total avoidance)	– Internal consistency: Cronbach's $\alpha = 0.81$ (Fear of performance) to k = 0.96 (LSAS total) – Convergent and divergent validity: significant correlations with scores on other measures of social anxiety and lower correlations with scores on measures of depression – Sensitive to change with treatment (Heimberg et al., 1999)
	Liebowitz Social Anxiety Scale –Self-Report (LSAS-SR)	– Self-report – Same as LSAS	– Internal consistency: Cronbach's $\alpha = 0.82$ (Fear of performance) to 0.95 (LSAS total) in a patient sample (Fresco et al., 2001) – Convergent validity: significant correlation between LSAS and LSAS-SR scores: 0.81 (Avoidance of performance) to 0.85 (Total score); significant correlations with scores on other measures of social anxiety and lower correlations scores on measures of depression (Fresco et al., 2001) – Test-retest reliability (12-week interval): $r = 0.83$ (Total score; Baker et al., 2002)
Safety Behaviors	Subtle Avoidance and Fear Evaluation (SAFE) Cuming et al. (2009)	– Self-report – 32 items rated for the frequency with which the listed behavior would be used if in a social situation – Ratings made on a 5-point scale: 0 = never to 4 = always; note that the original article used a 0–4 scale, while more recent articles (e.g., Piccirillo et al., 2016) describe a 1 (Never) to 5 (Always) scale	– Internal consistency: Cronbach's $\alpha = 0.91$ – Discriminant validity: scores are significantly higher for clinical than non-clinical participants – Convergent and divergent validity: Correlations with scores on social anxiety measures were highest; correlations with scores on measures of stress and depression were the lowest
Cognitions – Fear of Negative Evaluation	Brief Fear of Negative Evaluation Scale (BFNE) Leary (1983)	– Self-report – 12 items – Ratings made on a 5-point scale: 1 = not at all characteristic of me to 5 = extremely characteristic of me – Rodebaugh et al. (2011) suggest using only the 8 straightforwardly worded items and not reverse-scaled items (on the basis of IRT)	– Convergent validity: Correlation with original FNES scores: $r = 0.96$ – Test-retest reliability (Undergraduate sample; 4-week period): $r = 0.75$

Continued

Table 24.3 (cont.)

Disorder Construct	Measure Source	Structure	Psychometric Properties
Cognitions – Perception of Self	Social Thoughts and Beliefs Scale (STABS) Turner et al. (2003)	– Self-report – 21 items rated for the degree to which a particular thought or belief is typical when anticipating or participating in a social encounter – Ratings made on 5-point scale: 1 = never characteristic to 5 = always characteristic	– Internal consistency: Cronbach's $\alpha = 0.96$ – Test-retest reliability (over an average of 12 days): $r = 0.94$ – Discriminant validity: participants with SAD had significantly higher scores than participants with other anxiety disorders – Convergent and divergent validity: higher correlations with scores on measures of anxiety than with scores on measures of depression (Gros & Sarver, 2014) – Sensitive to change (Gros & Sarver, 2014)
Panic Disorder and Agoraphobia			
Cognitions-Misinterpretation of Anxiety	Agoraphobic Cognitions Questionnaire (ACQ) Chambless et al. (1984)	– Self-report – 14 items – Rated on a scale from 1 (the thought never occurs) to 5 (the thought always occurs)	– Internal consistency: $\alpha = 0.8$ – Test-retest reliability: $r = 0.86$ – Construct validity: correlations were as expected with measures of panic frequency, neuroticism, and depression. – Sensitive to change with treatment
Cognitions – Fear of Bodily Sensations	Body Sensations Questionnaire (BSQ) Chambless et al. (1984)	– Self-report – 17 items – 1 (not frightened or worried by this sensation) to 5 (extremely frightened by this sensation)	– Internal consistency: $\alpha = 0.87$ – Test-retest reliability: $r = 0.67$ – Construct validity: correlations were as expected with measures of panic frequency, neuroticism, and depression – Sensitive to change with treatment
Generalized Anxiety Disorder			
Positive and Negative Beliefs About worry	Meta-Cognitions Questionnaire – Short Form (MCQ-30) Wells & Cartwright-Hatton (2003)	– Self-report – 30 items – 5 subscales each with 6 items: positive beliefs; beliefs about uncontrollability and danger of thoughts; cognitive confidence in attention and memory; need to control thoughts; and cognitive self-consciousness (tendency to focus attention on thought processes) – Rated on a 1 (do not agree) to 4 (agree very much) scale – Subscale and total score are obtained by adding the ratings across items	– Internal consistency: α ranged from 0.72 to 0.93 – Test-retest reliability (nonclinical sample; 22 to 118 days): $r = 0.59$ to 0.87 – Convergent validity: significant correlations with other measures of worry – Construct validity: support for the five factor structure comes from factor analysis – Note that the psychometric properties were tested in a non-clinical sample
Intolerance of Uncertainty	Intolerance of Uncertainty Scale (IUS) Buhr & Dugas, 2002	– Self-report – 27 items – Rated on a 5-point scale: 1 = not at all characteristic of me to 5 = extremely characteristic of me – Total score is the sum of ratings	– Internal consistency (undergraduate sample; Buhr & Dugas); $\alpha = 0.94$; $\alpha = 0.93$ (mixed anxiety disorder sample; McEvoy & Mahoney, 2011)

Continued

Table 24.3 (cont.)

Disorder Construct	Measure Source	Structure	Psychometric Properties
			– Test-retest reliability (undergraduate sample; 5-week interval): $r = 0.74$ – Convergent validity: significant correlations with other measures of worry and anxiety (undergraduate sample; Buhr & Dugas); significant correlations with measures of other anxiety disorder and worry (mixed anxiety disorder sample; McEvoy & Mahoney, 2011) – Discriminant validity: significant differences between groups formed on the basis of severity of worry
Obsessive-Compulsive Disorder			
Dysfunctional Beliefs	Obsessive Beliefs Questionnaire OCCWG (2001)	– Self-report – Designed to assess obsessional beliefs – 87 items rated on a 7-point scale : 1 = disagree very much to 8 = agree very much – 6 subscales: control of thoughts, importance of thoughts, responsibility, intolerance of uncertainty, overestimation of threat, perfectionism – Subscale scores are the sum of ratings on items	– Internal consistency: Cronbach's α ranged from 0.88 (tolerance for uncertainty) to 0.93 (perfectionism) (OCCWG, 2003) – Test-retest reliability: Over an average interval of 65 days: r's ranged from 0.48 (control of thoughts) to $r = 0.83$ (responsibility), with all but control of thoughts having $r > 0.6$ (OCCWG, 2003) – Discriminant validity: Those with OCD had significantly higher scores than nonclinical participants in all 6 subscales; those with OCD had significantly higher scores on 3 (control of thoughts, importance of thoughts, responsibility) of 6 subscales than those with another anxiety disorder – Convergent validity: subscale scores correlated significantly with scores on a self-report measure of OCD severity (r's ranged from 0.32 to 0.55) and with scores on a measure of anxiety (r's ranged from 0.36 to 0.51) (OCCWG, 2003) – Divergent validity: scores correlated with scores on a self-report measure of depression (r's ranged from 0.32 to $r = 0.55$)

Note. Table 24.3 is intended to provide examples of measures that are available to assist in case formulation; it is not intended to be a comprehensive listing of all possible measures. Psychometric properties are taken from the source article unless an additional source is acknowledged. Where possible only studies examining psychometric properties in clinical samples are included.

& Nelson, 1984). That is, clients may not monitor thoughts and behaviors as they occur but rather complete self-monitoring sheets retrospectively, thus diluting the purpose of the assessment task (to capture anxiety, cognitions, and behaviors in real-time). It is in the area of self-monitoring that technological advances in assessment are most promising in that they allow for the client to be prompted at regular intervals to record relevant information, thus overcoming the issue of retrospective reporting (e.g., for a discussion of handheld devices in intensive assessment of psychopathological constructs, see Carlson et al., 2016). The behavioral avoidance task may also overcome issues of compliance that arise with self-monitoring and is a rich source of information that allows formulation and treatment planning. In a behavioral avoidance task, the clinician is able to prompt the client to provide a record of their anxiety and thoughts as the situation is occurring. Specific examples of behavioral avoidance tasks are provided for each anxiety disorder in the following subsections.

Social Anxiety

Prominent cognitive behavioral models (e.g., Clark & Wells, 1995; Rapee & Heimberg, 1997), on which evidence-based treatments for SAD are based, emphasize maladaptive avoidance behaviors (both overt avoidance of social situations and subtle avoidance or safety behaviors) and dysfunctional cognitions (especially distorted mental representation of the self and negative expectations about how others view the individual) as factors that maintain social anxiety. Stein and colleagues (2017) reviewed self-report measures of cognitive constructs in social anxiety and the strongest psychometric evidence was for the Social Thoughts and Beliefs Scale (STABS; Turner et al., 2003) as a measure of beliefs about the self in a social context and the Fear of Negative Evaluation Scale (FNES;[4] Watson & Friend, 1969) and its brief version (the Brief Fear of Negative Evaluation scale, BFNE; Leary, 1983) as measures of evaluation of threat (specifically negative evaluation) in social settings. In addition to self-report measures, assessment of maintaining factors can involve behavioral assessment. Self-monitoring will involve the client recording situations that are anxiety-provoking as they occur along with avoidance behaviors (overt avoidance of the situation and safety behaviors) and cognitions. A typical behavioral avoidance task that can be used for assessing social anxiety is a speech task. The client is asked to prepare a brief speech that they will then deliver while being video-recorded. This situation allows for the client to record, when prompted by the clinician, levels of anxiety and thoughts while anticipating the task, during the task, and after the task. In addition, the clinician can observe signs of anxiety (e.g., trembling, blushing).

[4] Given the FNES has been found not to discriminate between participants with SAD and those with other anxiety disorders (those with Agoraphobia, Panic Disorder, GAD; Turner, McCanna, & Beidel, 1987), only the BFNE is included in Table 24.3 and is recommended for use over the FNES.

Panic Disorder and Agoraphobia

Cognitive models of Panic Disorder with or without Agoraphobia include cognitive constructs (catastrophic misinterpretation of bodily sensations as more dangerous than they are; Clark, 1986) and fear of anxiety-related sensations (e.g., Anxiety Sensitivity; McNally, 2002). Agoraphobia is often viewed as a result of avoidance of situations in which panic attacks may occur, that is, avoidance as a consequence of the panic disorder results in Agoraphobia. In DSM-5, however, Agoraphobia is seen as a distinct disorder where the avoidance is due to fear that escape might not be possible or help may not be available if panic-like symptoms occur. Thus, assessment for the purposes of case formulation will focus on both cognitive and behavioral (specifically avoidance) constructs. Cognitive constructs can be assessed using self-report measures (see Table 24.3). While the Anxiety Sensitivity Index (Reiss et al., 1986; Taylor & Cox, 1998) is a measure of the disposition to fear anxiety-related sensations, anxiety sensitivity as a construct is not specific to panic disorder. Thus, the Body Sensations Questionnaire (Chambless et al., 1984), which was designed to measure fear of panic symptoms specifically, has been included as a measure of fear of bodily sensations in Table 24.3. A self-report measure of avoidance, the MIA, has been reviewed in Table 24.2. Avoidance may also be assessed using behavioral assessment. Self-monitoring in the case of Panic Disorder is particularly useful in providing information about the triggers for panic attacks (e.g., physical sensations, such as getting hot while exercising) as well as the physical sensations experienced during a panic attack and the cognitions associated with the panic attack. Self-monitoring can also provide information about the types of situations avoided. Behavioral assessment of panic disorder may include induction of panic-like symptoms in the clinician's office in order to allow for real-time recording of symptoms experienced. Antony and colleagues (2006) provide examples of the exercises that can be used in such panic induction. Behavioral avoidance tasks will be particularly useful in measuring agoraphobic avoidance. For example, for a housebound client, a behavioral avoidance task would involve asking them to walk as far away from their home as they are able. To be practical, the task will need to include situations that the clinician is able to observe readily in the course of the assessment (e.g., for a client who avoids shopping malls, the clinician will need to attend a shopping mall with the client).

Generalized Anxiety Disorder

Models of GAD (see Behar et al., 2009) have in common an emphasis on worry being used as a mechanism to avoid thoughts, beliefs, and emotions. The GAD models suggest various underlying mechanisms such as intolerance of uncertainty and negative and positive beliefs about worry (i.e., meta-worry) as maintaining factors. Selected self-report measures assessing these mechanisms are summarized in Table 24.1. Behavioral assessment of GAD is most likely to focus on self-monitoring of worry. Self-monitoring in the case of GAD may involve asking the client to record their level of anxiety at specific times of the day (rather than when a situation triggers anxiety as is the case in SAD and Agoraphobia) along with the content of their worry and the process of worry (e.g., how controllable they perceive the worry to be).

Obsessive-Compulsive Disorder

Cognitive behavioral models of OCD (see Taylor, Abramowitz, & McKay, 2007) propose that OCD is maintained by dysfunctional beliefs. Specifically, such models propose that obsessions are the result of normal intrusions being appraised as having serious consequences. The sorts of dysfunctional beliefs proposed to maintain OCD include beliefs about excessive responsibility, over importance of thoughts, need to control thoughts, overestimation of threat, perfectionism, and intolerance of uncertainty. In cognitive behavioral models of OCD, compulsions are seen as responses to the obsessions in order to control or reduce the unwanted thoughts. Compulsions are maintained by negative reinforcement, that is, compulsions reduce the distress associated with the obsessions. However, by engaging in the compulsion, the person with OCD does not learn that their appraisal of the obsession is unrealistic, thereby maintaining the compulsion. Although there are individual measures to assess different types of dysfunctional beliefs, the Obsessive Beliefs Questionnaire (OBQ) provides a single measure assessing a range of dysfunctional beliefs (see Table 24.3). A short form of the OBQ, which has forty-four as opposed to eighty-seven items, has been found to have adequate psychometric properties (Obsessive Compulsive Cognitions Working Group, 2005). Behavioral assessment of OCD might involve self-monitoring, where the client is asked to monitor situations that trigger the obsessions and compulsions as well as details of the behaviors – for example, the duration of compulsions and the amount of distress engendered by the obsessions. A behavioral task might be used, where the client is exposed to a trigger for their obsessions and cognitions (the obsessive thought itself and beliefs about it) and the desire to engage in rituals and ability to resist the rituals are recorded in real time.

PRACTICAL RECOMMENDATIONS AND CONCLUSION

Assessment in the anxiety disorders supports clinicians in making decisions about diagnosis, severity, case formulation, and monitoring of progress through treatment. This chapter has reviewed a number of evidence-based assessment methods. The challenge for the busy clinician is to select methods that will add to the reliability and validity of their decisions without unnecessarily consuming valuable time that can be spent on treatment. It is our position, however, that investing time in assessment will ultimately lead to better outcomes for clients with anxiety disorders. In particular, while structured diagnostic interviews may be perceived, on the surface, as time-intensive, they provide comprehensive assessments that facilitate clinically important differential diagnostic decisions. As a result, structured diagnostic interviews are likely to aid all aspects of treatment, from the correct selection of evidence-based treatment to early identification of cognitions and behaviors that inform case formulation and treatment progress/outcome monitoring. Their use is particularly important in the assessment of anxiety disorders, given disorder similarities and high rates of comorbidity. As such, we highly recommend their use in clinical practice. For each anxiety disorder discussed in this chapter, we recommend, then, an assessment battery that would include a structured diagnostic interview, a brief measure of severity that can be administered throughout treatment to monitor progress, and a selection of measures (e.g., a self-report measure and a behavioral assessment) that allows for case formulation and tailoring of evidence-based treatment to the client's individual needs.

REFERENCES

Abramowitz, J. S. (2018). Presidential address: Are the obsessive-compulsive related disorders related to obsessive-compulsive disorder? A critical look at DSM-5's new category. *Behavior Therapy, 49*, 1–11.

American Psychiatric Association. (2013). *Diagnostic and Statistical Manual of Mental Disorders* (5th ed.). Arlington, VA, American Psychiatric Association.

Antony, M. M., Bieling, P. J., Cox, B. J., Enns, M. W., & Swinson, R. P. (1998). Psychometric properties of the 42-item and 21-item versions of the Depression Anxiety Stress Scales (DASS) in clinical groups and a community sample. *Psychological Assessment, 10*, 176–181.

Antony, M. M., Ledley, D. R., Liss, A., & Swinson, R. P. (2006). Responses to symptom induction exercises in panic disorder. *Behaviour Research and Therapy, 44*, 85–98.

Asnaani, A., Aderka, I. M., Marques, L., Simon, N., Robinaugh, D. J., & Hofmann, S. G. (2015). The structure of feared social situations among race-ethnic minorities and Whites with social anxiety disorder in the United States. *Transcultural Psychiatry, 52*, 791–807.

Asnaani, A., Richey, J. A., Dimaite, R., Hinton, D. E., & Hofmann, S. G. (2010). A cross-ethnic comparison of lifetime prevalence rates of anxiety disorders. *The Journal of Nervous and Mental Disease, 198*, 551–555.

Baker, S. L., Heinrichs, N., Kim, H.-J., & Hofmann, S. G. (2002). The Liebowitz social anxiety scale as a self-report instrument: A preliminary psychometric analysis. *Behaviour Research and Therapy, 40(6)*, 701–715.

Bardhoshi, G., Duncan, K., & Erford, B.T. (2016). Psychometric meta-analysis of the English version of the Beck Anxiety Inventory. *Journal of Counseling and Development, 94*, 356–373.

Barlow, D. H., Hayes, S. C., & Nelson, R. O. (1984). *The scientist-practitioner: Research and accountability in clinical and educational settings*. Needham Heights, MA: Allyn & Bacon.

Baxter, A. J., Scott, K. M., Vos, T., & Whiteford, H. A. (2012). Global prevalence of anxiety disorders: a systematic review and meta-regression. *Psychological Medicine, 43*, 897–910.

Baxter, A. J., Vos, T., Scott, K. M., Ferrari, A. J., & Whiteford, H. A. (2014). The global burden of anxiety disorders in 2010. *Psychological Medicine, 44*, 2363–2374.

Beck, A. T., Epstein, N., Brown, G., & Steer, R. A. (1988). An inventory for measuring clinical anxiety: Psychometric properties. *Journal of Consulting and Clinical Psychology, 56*, 893–897.

Behar, E., DiMarco, I. D., Hekler, E. B., Mohlman, J., & Staples, A. M. (2009). Current theoretical models of generalized anxiety disorder (GAD): Conceptual review and treatment implications. *Journal of Anxiety Disorders, 23*, 1011–1023.

Brown, T. A., Antony, M. M., & Barlow, D. H. (1992). Psychometric properties of the Penn State Worry Questionnaire in a clinical anxiety disorders sample. *Behaviour Research and Therapy, 30*, 33–37.

Brown, T. A. & Barlow, D. H. (2014). *Anxiety and Related Disorders Interview Schedule for DSM-5 (ADIS-5) – Adults and Lifetime Version: Clinician Manual*. Oxford: Oxford University Press.

Brown, T. A., Chorpita, B. F., Korotitsch, W., & Barlow, D. H. (1997). Psychometric properties of the Depression Anxiety Stress Scales (DASS) in clinical samples. *Behaviour Research and Therapy, 35*, 79–89.

Brown, T. A., Di Nardo, P. A., Lehman, C. L., & Campbell, L. A. (2001). Reliability of DSM-IV anxiety and mood disorders: Implications for the classification of emotional disorders. *Journal of Abnormal Psychology, 110*, 49–58.

Buhr, K., & Dugas, M. J. (2002). The intolerance of uncertainty scale: Psychometric properties of the English version. *Behaviour Research and Therapy, 40*, 931–945.

Carleton, R. N., Collimore, K. C., Asmundson, G. J. G., McCabe, R. E., Rowa, K., & Antony, M. M. (2009). Refining and validating the Social Interaction Anxiety Scale and the Social Phobia Scale. *Depression and Anxiety, 26*, E71–E81.

Carleton, R. N., Thibodeau, M. A., Weeks, J. W., Sapach, M. J. N. T., McEvoy, P. M., Horswill, S. C., & Heimberg, R. G. (2014). Comparing short forms of the Social Interaction Anxiety Scale and the Social Phobia Scale. *Psychological Assessment, 26* (4), 1116–1126.

Carlson, E. B., Field, N. P., Ruzek, J. I., Bryant, R. A., Dalenberg, C. J., Keane, T. M., & Spain, D. A. (2016). Advantages and psychometric validation of proximal intensive assessments of patient-reported outcomes collected in daily life. *Quality of Life Research, 25*, 507–516.

Chambless, D. L., Caputo, G. C., Bright, P., & Gallagher. R. (1984). Assessment of fear of fear on agoraphobics: the body sensations questionnaire and the agoraphobic cognitions questionnaire. *Journal of Consulting and Clinical Psychology, 52*, 1090–1097.

Chambless, D. L., Caputo, G. C., Jasin, S. L., Gracely, E. I, & Williams, C. (1985). The mobility inventory for agoraphobia. *Behaviour Research and Therapy, 23*, 35–44.

Chambless, D. L., Sharpless, B. A., Rodriguez, D., McCarthy, K. S., Milrod, B. L., Khalsa, S. R., & Barber, J. P. (2011). Psychometric properties of the Mobility Inventory for Agoraphobia: Convergent, discriminant, and criterion-related validity. *Behavior Therapy, 42*, 689–699.

Chmielewski, M., Clark, L. A., Bagby, R. M., & Watson, D. (2015). Method matters: Understanding diagnostic reliability in DSM-IV and DSM-5. *Journal of Abnormal Psychology, 124*, 764–769.

Clark, D. M. (1986). A cognitive approach to panic. *Behaviour Research and Therapy, 24*, 461–470.

Clark, D. M., & Wells, A. (1995). A cognitive model of social phobia. In R. G. Heimberg, M. R. Liebowitz, D. A. Hope, & F. R. Schneier (Eds.), *Social Phobia: Diagnosis, assessment and treatment* (pp. 69–93). New York: Guilford Press.

Contreras, S., Fernandez, S., Malcarne, V. L., Ingram, R. E., Vaccarino, V. R. (2004). Reliability and validity of the Beck Depression and Anxiety Inventories in Caucasian Americans and Latinos. *Hispanic Journal of Behavioral Sciences, 26*, 446–462.

Cuming, S., Rapee, R. M., Kemp, N., Abbott, M. J., Peters, L., & Gaston, J. E. (2009). A self-report measure of subtle avoidance and safety behaviors relevant to social anxiety: Development and psychometric properties. *Journal of Anxiety Disorders, 23*, 879–883.

Dear, B. F., Titov, N., Sunderland, M., McMillan, D., Anderson, T., Lorian, C., & Robinson, E. (2011). Psychometric comparison of the Generalized Anxiety Disorder Scale-7 and the Penn State Worry Questionnaire for measuring response during treatment of Generalised Anxiety Disorder. *Cognitive Behaviour Therapy, 40*, 216–227.

First, M. B., Williams, J. B. W., Karg, R. S., & Spitzer, R. L. (2016). *Structured Clinical Interview for DSM-5 Disorders – Clinician Version (SCID-5-CV)*. Arlington, VA: American Psychiatric Association Publishing.

Foa, E. B., Huppert, J. D., Leiberg, S., Langner, R., Kichic, R., Hajcak, G., & Salkovskis, P. M. (2002). The Obsessive-Compulsive Inventory: Development and validation of a short version. *Psychological Assessment, 14*, 485–496.

Foa, E. B., Kozak, M. J., Salkovskis, P. M., Coles, M. E., & Amir, N. (1998) The validation of a new Obsessive-Compulsive Disorder scale: The Obsessive-Compulsive Inventory. *Psychological Assessment, 10*, 206–214.

Fresco, D. M., Coles, M. E., Heimberg, R. G., Liebowitz, M. R., Hami, S., Stein, M. B., & Goetz, D. (2001). The Liebowitz Social Anxiety Scale: A Comparison of the psychometric properties of self-report and clinician-administered formats. *Psychological Medicine, 31*, 1025–1035.

Furukawa, T. A., Shear, M. K., Barlow, D. H., Gorman, J. M., Woods, S. W., Money, R., Etschel, E., Engel, R. R., & Leucht, S. (2009). Evidence-based guidelines for interpretation of the Panic Disorder Severity Scale. *Depression and Anxiety, 26*, 922–929.

Goodman, W. K., Price, L. H., Rasmussen, S. A., Mazure, C., Delgado, P., Heninger, G. R., & Charney, D.S. (1989a). The Yale-Brown Obsessive Compulsive Scale: II. *Validity. Archives of General Psychiatry, 46*, 1012–1016.

Goodman, W. K., Price, L. H., Rasmussen, S. A., Mazure, C., Fleischmann, R. L., Hill, C. L., Heninger, G. R., & Charney, D. S. (1989b). The Yale-Brown Obsessive Compulsive Scale: I. Development, use, and reliability. *Archives of General Psychiatry, 46*, 1006–1011.

Gros, D. F., & Sarver, N. W. (2014). An investigation of the psychometric properties of the Social Thoughts and Beliefs Scale (STABS) and structure of cognitive symptoms in participants with social anxiety disorder and healthy controls. *Journal of Anxiety Disorders, 28*, 283–290.

Heimberg, R. G., Horner, K. J., Juster, H. R., Safren, S. A., Brown, E. J., Schneier, F. R., & Liebowitz, M. R. (1999).

Psychometric properties of the Liebowitz Social Anxiety Scale. *Psychological Medicine, 29*, 199–212.

Hofman, S. G., & Smits, J. A. J. (2008). Cognitive–behavioral therapy for adult anxiety disorders: A meta-analysis of randomized placebo-controlled trials. *The Journal of Clinical Psychiatry, 69*, 621–632.

Houck, P. R., Spiegel, D. A., Shear, M. K., & Rucci, P. (2002). Reliability of the self-report version of the Panic Disorder Severity Scale. *Depression and Anxiety, 15*, 183–185.

Kertz, S., Bigda-Peyton, J., Bjorgvinsson, T. (2013). Validity of the Generalised Anxiety Disorder-7 scale in an acute psychiatric sample. *Clinical Psychology and Psychotherapy, 20 (5)*, 456–464.

Leary, M. R. (1983). A brief version of the Fear of Negative Evaluation Scale. *Personality and Social Psychology Bulletin, 9*, 371–375.

Lees-Haley, P. R., & Dunn, J. T. (1994). The ability of naïve subjects to report symptoms of mild brain injury, post-traumatic stress disorders, major depression, and generalized anxiety disorder. *Journal of Clinical Psychology, 50*, 252–256.

Liebowitz, M. R. (1987). Social Phobia. *Modern Problems of Pharmacopsychiatry, 22*, 141–173.

Lindner, P., Martell, C., Bergström, J., Andersson, G., & Carlbring, P. (2013). Clinical validation of a non-heteronormative version of the Social Interaction Anxiety Scale (SIAS). *Health and Quality of Life Outcomes, 11*, 209.

Lovibond, P. F., & Lovibond, S. H. (1995). The structure of the negative emotional states: Comparison of the Depression Anxiety Stress Scales (DASS) with the Beck Depression and Anxiety Inventories. *Behaviour Research and Therapy, 33*, 335–343.

Mattick, R. P., & Clarke, J. C. (1998). Development and validation of measures of social phobia scrutiny fear and social interaction anxiety. *Behaviour Research and Therapy, 36*, 455–470.

Mattick, R. P., & Peters, L. (1988). Treatment of severe social phobia: Effects of guided exposure with and without cognitive restructuring. *Journal of Consulting and Clinical Psychology, 56*, 251–260.

Mattick, R. P., Peters, L., & Clarke, J. C. (1989). Exposure and cognitive restructuring for severe social phobia: A controlled study. *Behavior Therapy, 20*, 3–23.

McEvoy, P. M., Grove, R., & Slade, T. (2011). Epidemiology of anxiety disorders in the Australian general population: Findings of the 2007 Australian National Survey of Mental Health and Wellbeing. *Australian & New Zealand Journal of Psychiatry, 45*, 957–967.

McEvoy, P. M., & Mahoney, A. E. J. (2011). Achieving certainty about the structure of the intolerance of uncertainty in a treatment-seeking sample with anxiety and depression. *Journal of Anxiety Disorders, 25*, 112–122.

McNally, R. J. (2002). Anxiety sensitivity and panic disorder. *Biological Psychiatry, 52*,938–946.

Meyer, T. L., Miller. M. L., & Borkovec. T. D. (1990). Development and validation of the Penn State Worry Questionnaire. *Behaviour Research and Therapy, 28*, 487–495.

Moritz, S., Van Quaquebeke, N., Hauschildt, M., Jelinek, L., & Gonner, S. (2012). Good news for allegedly bad studies. Assessment of psychometric properties may help to elucidate deception in online studies on OCD. *Journal of Obsessive-Compulsive and Related Disorders, 1*, 331–335.

Obsessive Compulsive Cognitions Working Group. (2001). Development and initial validation of the obsessive beliefs questionnaire and the interpretation of intrusions inventory. *Behaviour Research and Therapy, 39*, 987–1006.

Obsessive Compulsive Cognitions Working Group. (2003). Psychometric validation of the Obsessive Beliefs Questionnaire and the Interpretation of Intrusions Inventory: Part 1. *Behaviour Research and Therapy, 41*, 863–878.

Obsessive Compulsive Cognitions Working Group. (2005). Psychometric validation of the Obsessive Beliefs Questionnaire and the Interpretation of Intrusions Inventory: Part 2: Factor analyses and testing of a brief version. *Behaviour Research and Therapy, 43*, 1527–1542.

Oei, T. P. S., Sawang, S., Goh, Y. W., & Mukhtar, F. (2013). Using the Depression Anxiety Stress Scale 21 (DASS-21) across cultures. *International Journal of Psychology, 48*, 1018–1029.

Parkerson, H. A., Thibodeau, M. A., Brandt, C. P., Zvolensky, M. J., & Asmundson, G. J. G. (2015). Cultural-based biases of the GAD-7. *Journal of Anxiety Disorders, 31*, 38–42.

Pearl, S. B., & Norton, P. J. (2017). Transdiagnostic versus diagnostic specific cognitive behavioural therapies for anxiety: A meta-analysis. *Journal of Anxiety Disorders, 46*, 11–24.

Persons, J. B. (2006). Case formulation-driven psychotherapy. *Clinical Psychology: Science and Practice, 13*(2), 167–170.

Persons, J. B. (2013). Who needs a case formulation and why: Clinicians use the case formulation to guide decision-making. *Pragmatic Case Studies in Psychotherapy, 9*(4), 448–156.

Peters, L. (2000). Discriminant validity of the Social Phobia and Anxiety Inventory (SPAI), the Social Phobia Scale (SPS) and the Social Inter- action Anxiety Scale (SIAS). *Behaviour Research and Therapy, 38*, 943–950.

Peters, L., Sunderland, M., Andrews, G., Rapee, R. M., & Mattick, R. P. (2012). Development of a Short Form Social Interaction Anxiety (SIAS) and Social Phobia Scale (SPS) using Nonparametric Item Response Theory: the SIAS-6 and the SPS-6. *Psychological Assessment, 24*(1), 66–76.

Piccirillo, M. L., Dryman, M. T., & Heimberg, R. G. (2016). Safety behaviors in adults with social anxiety: Review and future directions. *Behavior Therapy, 47*, 675–687.

Plummer, F., Manea, L., Trepel, D., & McMillan, D. (2016). Screening for anxiety disorders with the GAD-7 and GAD-2: a systematic review and diagnostic metaanalysis. *General Hospital Psychiatry, 39*, 24–31.

Rapee, R. M., & Heimberg, R. G. (1997). A cognitive-behavioral model of anxiety in social phobia. *Behaviour Research and Therapy, 35*, 741–756.

Reiss, S., Peterson, R. A., Gursky, D. M., & McNally, R. J. (1986). Anxiety sensitivity, anxiety frequency, and the prediction of fearfulness. *Behaviour Research and Therapy, 24*, 1–8.

Ries, B. J., McNeil, D. W., Boone, M. L., Turk, C. L., Carter, L. E., & Heimberg, R. G. (1998). Assessment of contemporary social phobia verbal report instruments. *Behaviour Research and Therapy, 36*, 983–994.

Rodebaugh, T. L., Heimberg, R. G., Brown, P. J., Fernandez, K. C., Blanco, C., Schneier, F. R., & Liebowitz, M. R. (2011). More reasons to be straightforward: Findings and norms for two scales relevant to social anxiety. *Journal of Anxiety Disorders, 25*, 623–630.

Rogers, R., Ornduff, S. R., & Sewell, K. W. (1993). Feigning specific disorders: A study of the Personality Assessment Inventory (PAI). *Journal of Personality Assessment, 60*, 554–560.

Schneider, S., Margraf, J., Spoerkel, H., & Franzen, U. (1992). Therapy-related diagnosis: Reliability of the Diagnostic

Interview for Mental Disorders (DIMD). *Diagnostica, 38*, 209–227.

Shankman, S. A., Funkhouser, C. J., Klein, D. N., Davila, J., Lerner, D., & Hee, D. (2018). Reliability and validity of severity dimensions of psychopathology assessed using the Structured Clinical Interview *for DSM-5*. International Journal of Methods in Psychiatric Research, *27*, e1590.

Shear, M. K., Brown, T. A., Barlow, D. H., Money, R., Sholomskas, D. E., Woods, S. W., Gorman, J. M., & Papp, L. A. (1997). Multicenter collaborative Panic Disorder Severity Scale. *American Journal of Psychiatry, 154*, 1571–1575.

Shulman, G. P., & Hope, D. A. (2016). Putting our multicultural training into practice: Assessing social anxiety disorder in sexual minorities. *The Behavior Therapist, 39*, 315–319.

Spitzer, R. L. Kroenke, K., Williams, J. B. W., & Löwe, B. (2006). A brief measure for assessing Generalised Anxiety Disorder: The GAD-7. *Archives of Internal Medicine, 166*, 1092–1097.

Stein, J., Modini, M., Hunt, C., & Abbott, M. J. (2017). A systematic review of the psychometric properties of trait cognitive self-report measures in social anxiety. *Journal of Psychopathology and Behavioural Assessment, 39*, 147–163.

Storch, E. A., Rasmussen, S. A., Price, L. H., Larson, M. J., Murphy, T. K., & Goodman, W. K. (2010). Development and psychometric evaluation of the Yale-Brown Obsessive-Compulsive Scale – Second edition. *Psychological Assessment, 22*, 223–232.

Taylor, S., Abramowitz, J. S., McKay, D. (2007). Cognitive-behavioural models of obsessive-compulsive disorder. In M. M. Antony, C. Purdon, & L. J. Summerfeldt (Eds.). *Psychological treatment of obsessive-compulsive disorder: Fundamentals and beyond* (pp. 9–29). Washington, DC: American Psychological Association.

Taylor, S., & Cox, B. J. (1998). An expanded Anxiety Sensitivity Index: Evidence for a hierarchic structure in a clinical sample. *Journal of Anxiety Disorders, 12*, 463–483.

Turner, S. M., Johnson, M. R., Beidel, D. C., Heiser, N. A., & Lydiard, R. B. (2003). The Social Thoughts and Beliefs Scale: A new inventory for assessing cognitions in social phobia. *Psychological Assessment, 15*, 384–391.

Turner, S. M., McCanna, M., & Beidel, D. C. (1987). Validity of the social avoidance and distress and fear of negative evaluation scales. *Behaviour Research and Therapy, 25*, 113–115.

Watson, D., & Friend, R. (1969). Measurement of social-evaluative anxiety. *Journal of Consulting and Clinical Psychology, 33*, 448–457.

Weiss, B. J., Hope, D. A., & Capozzolo, M. C. (2013). Heterocentric language in commonly used measures of social anxiety: Recommended alternate wording. *Behavior Therapy, 44*, 1–11.

Wells, A., & Cartwright-Hatton, S. (2003). A short form of the metacognitions questionnaire: Properties of the MCQ-30. *Behaviour Research and Therapy, 42*, 385–396.

Williams, M., Davis, D. M., Thibodeau, M. A., & Bach, N. (2013). Psychometric properties of the Obsessive-Compulsive Inventory revised in African Americans with and without obsessive-compulsive disorder. *Journal of Obsessive-Compulsive and Related Disorders, 2*, 399–405.

Woody, S. T., Steketee, G., & Chambless, D. L. (1995). Reliability and validity of the Yale-Brown Obsessive-Compulsive Scale. *Behaviour Research and Therapy, 33*, 597–605.

Wong, Q. J. J., Chen, J., Gregory, B., Baillie, A. J., Nagata, T., Furukawa, T. A., Kaiya, H., Peters, L., & Rapee, R. M. (2019). Measurement equivalence of the Social Interaction Anxiety Scale (SIAS) and the Social Phobia Scale (SPS) across individuals with social anxiety disorder from Japanese and Australian sociocultural contexts. *Journal of Affective Disorders, 243*, 165–174.

Wu, M. S., McGuire, J. F., Horng, B., Storch, E. A. (2016). Further psychometric properties of the Yale-Brown Obsessive Compulsive Scale – Second Edition. *Comprehensive Psychiatry, 66*, 96–103.

Wuyek, L. A., Antony, M. M., & McCabe, R. E. (2011). Psychometric properties of the Panic Disorder Severity Scale: Clinician-administered and self-report versions. *Clinical Psychology and Psychotherapy, 18*, 234–243.

Zvolensky, M. J., Arrindell, W. A., Taylor, S., Bouvard, M., Cox, B. J., Stewart, S. H., Sandin, B., Cardenas, S. J., & Eifert, G. H. (2003). Anxiety sensitivity in six countries. *Behaviour Research and Therapy, 41*, 841–859.

25 Assessment of Trauma- and Stressor-Related Disorders

DANIEL J. LEE, SARAH E. KLEIMAN, AND FRANK W. WEATHERS

Posttraumatic stress disorder (PTSD) is a serious mental disorder that develops in some individuals following exposure to severe psychological stressors such as combat, sexual assault, transportation accidents, natural disasters, and other life-threatening events. PTSD typically involves a complex clinical presentation, with a wide range of trauma-related symptoms; multiple comorbid problems such as depression and substance abuse; a chronic, unremitting course if left untreated; and extensive impairment in social or occupational functioning. Characteristic symptoms of PTSD, as reflected in the symptom criteria in the fifth edition of the *Diagnostic and Statistical Manual of Mental Disorders* (DSM-5; American Psychiatric Association, 2013), include emotionally painful reexperiencing of the traumatic event (e.g., distressing memories, nightmares, or dissociative flashbacks); deliberate avoidance of trauma-related thoughts, feelings, or situations; negative alterations in cognition and mood (e.g., exaggerated negative beliefs, diminished interest in usual activities, detachment or estrangement from others); and hyperarousal (e.g., verbal or physical aggression, hypervigilance, exaggerated startle). Further, DSM-5 PTSD criteria include two dissociative symptoms, depersonalization and derealization, which allow for specification of a dissociative subtype.

The PTSD criteria were substantially revised for DSM-5 (for a full discussion, see Weathers et al., 2014). Notable revisions include (1) narrowing the definition of a traumatic event in Criterion A, and removing Criterion A2, which required a peritraumatic emotional response of fear, helplessness, or horror; (2) dividing the avoidance and numbing symptom cluster into separate clusters of avoidance and negative alterations in cognition and mood (NACM); (3) adding three new symptoms and substantially revising others; (4) creating a dissociative subtype; and (5) creating separate criteria for preschool children. The most striking nosological revision, however, was moving PTSD from the anxiety disorders into a separate new chapter of trauma- and stressor-related disorders (TSRDs), where it is grouped with other disorders having a stressor as a diagnostic criterion, including reactive attachment disorder (RAD), disinhibited social engagement disorder (DSED), acute stress disorder (ASD), and adjustment disorder (AD).

PTSD poses a number of conceptual and logistical challenges for assessment due to its multifaceted nature and to a number of vigorously debated, still-unresolved theoretical issues in the field of traumatic stress (Weathers et al., 2014). Clinical investigators have addressed these challenges through the development of a wide range of psychometrically sound measures. The literature regarding the assessment of PTSD is extensive. Dozens of measures of trauma exposure and PTSD have been developed, including questionnaires, structured interviews, and physiological assessment protocols. Many of these have been extensively validated and have strong psychometric support for various clinical and research applications in a wide range of trauma populations.

In this chapter, we provide an overview of the conceptual issues, specific methods, and practical considerations in evidence-based assessment of PTSD. Owing to space limitations, we focus primarily on PTSD measures for adults (for a recent review of assessment issues and methods for PTSD in children, see Briggs, Nooner, & Amaya-Jackson, 2014). First, we outline the conceptual issues and practical components of a comprehensive assessment of PTSD. Second, we provide an overview of the most widely used self-rated and clinician-rated measures of trauma exposure and PTSD, comorbid disorders, and response bias. Third, we discuss cultural considerations in assessing PTSD. Fourth, we offer practical guidelines for conducting a clinically sensitive assessment of PTSD, highlighting some of the unique considerations in engaging trauma survivors in the assessment process and optimizing the information obtained. Last, in keeping with our focus on adult measures, we briefly summarize conceptual considerations and specific measures for ASD and AD, although not for RAD and DSED.

CONCEPTUAL AND METHODOLOGICAL CONSIDERATIONS IN PTSD ASSESSMENT

In this section, we describe a number of common conceptual and methodological challenges encountered in PTSD assessment, as well as practical considerations when deciding on an assessment approach, in order to facilitate case formulation, treatment planning, and evaluation of treatment progress.

Assessment of PTSD

There are a number of critical components in a comprehensive PTSD assessment. Establishing a DSM-5 diagnosis of PTSD requires determining that an individual has been exposed to a traumatic event (Criterion A), has the requisite number of symptoms from each cluster (Criteria B–E), has a symptom duration of at least one month (Criterion F), and experiences clinically significant distress or functional impairment (Criterion G). For DSM-5, a minimum of one intrusion symptom (Criterion B), one avoidance symptom (Criterion C), two negative alterations in cognition and mood symptoms (Criterion D), and two alterations in arousal and reactivity (Criterion E) symptoms related to the identified trauma must be present.

Trauma exposure. The first step in assessing PTSD is to evaluate trauma exposure. It is not uncommon for individuals to have experienced numerous stressful life experiences, only some of which satisfy the DSM-5 Criterion A definition of a traumatic event. Accordingly, assessment of trauma history requires careful attention. Although PTSD symptoms should be assessed in reference to specified "index" or most impactful event that satisfies the Criterion A definition as a trauma, a comprehensive history of exposure to potentially traumatic events can greatly inform assessment and case conceptualizing. First, understanding the full scope of trauma history is important in determining which event is the most impactful. Second, other traumatic events and even non–Criterion A stressors (e.g., parental abandonment, expected death of a loved one) often have major impacts on well-being (e.g., Bodkin et al., 2007) and may be important to consider when determining the impact of earlier or subsequent traumatic events. Likewise, a minority of individuals exposed to traumatic events develop PTSD (e.g., Hoge, Auchterlonie, & Milliken, 2006). Nonetheless, individuals exposed to trauma who do not meet full diagnostic criteria often struggle with substantial functional impairment (e.g., Marshall et al., 2001).

Criteria B-E symptoms. The next stage of PTSD assessment involves evaluating the twenty Criteria B–E symptoms in reference to the identified index trauma. If the sole desired outcome from assessment is determination of diagnostic status, each symptom can be rated using a measure that guides determination of the presence or absence of each symptom (e.g., Structured Diagnostic Interview for DSM-5 Disorders; First et al., 2015). However, if information regarding severity of each symptom, symptom cluster, and the disorder overall is of interest, measures that capture each symptom on a dimensional rating scale (e.g., Clinician-Administered PTSD Scale for DSM-5, Weathers, Blake, et al., 2013a) should be used.

Assessing Criteria B–E symptoms presents a number of challenges. Symptom presentations can be idiosyncratic and the level of insight into symptoms varies widely. For example, someone may avoid crowded or confined areas without realizing this circumstance is reminiscent of the traumatic event, or that doing so is abnormal. Likewise, symptoms overlap (e.g., nightmares and sleep disturbance) and can be difficult for clinicians to help respondents disentangle; this is also essential so as not to double count symptoms (i.e., mistakenly classify the same symptom as two separate symptoms). Additionally, several symptoms can be particularly challenging for both clinicians and respondents to understand. For example, dissociative amnesia can be challenging to distinguish from normal forgetting of events, particularly events that occurred many years earlier. Finally, many symptoms (e.g., difficulty experiencing positive emotions, sleep disturbance) are not inherently linked to the index event and require attribution. This task becomes particularly challenging in the case of co-occurring psychopathology (e.g., diminished interest in patients with major depressive disorder, concentration disturbance in patients in cannabis use disorder). Given these challenges, the clinician's functional understanding of the conceptual basis of PTSD symptoms is critical to accurate assessment.

Chronology. Symptom chronology is important to evaluating diagnostic status. According to DSM-5, symptom duration must be > 1 month (Criterion F). Further, understanding the temporal course of symptom onset can be helpful in case conceptualization and treatment planning. For example, identifying correlates of periods of symptom improvement such as medications, work environments, or relationships can help identify treatment targets and ideas for adjunctive intervention.

Related distress and impairment. Once B–E symptoms have been assessed and chronology has been established, the next step is to evaluate the degree to which identified symptoms cause clinically significant distress and/or impairment in social and occupational functioning (Criterion G). This task requires attributing the distress or impairment to B–E symptoms, which can be quite challenging, again often in the case of co-occurring psychopathology (e.g., substance use disorders, personality disorders) or when individuals experienced deficits in social or occupational functioning prior to trauma exposure. Care should be taken to carefully consider the temporal sequence in which impairment occurred relative to symptom onset or, in the case of preexisting deficits, the degree to which symptom onset exacerbated existing deficits.

Subtype. One revision in DSM-5 was the inclusion of the dissociative PTSD subtype. Assessment of dissociative symptoms is important for case conceptualization, both for understanding how dissociation interferes with social and occupational functioning and for planning treatment. Some initial research has suggested dissociation may help inform which specific intervention may benefit the client most (Resick et al., 2012). For interventions involving exposure (e.g., prolonged exposure therapy), the presence of dissociative features should warrant planning ahead of time to manage these symptoms while reacting to trauma reminders.

Other Assessment Considerations

Co-occurring psychopathology. The presence of co-occurring psychopathology among individuals with PTSD is the norm rather than the exception. Individuals with PTSD often struggle with co-occurring mood, substance use, and anxiety disorders (e.g., Keane & Kaloupek, 1997; Kessler et al., 1995). Presence of other psychological disorders is essential to assessment for several reasons. First, numerous PTSD symptoms overlap with other disorders (e.g., diminished interest, concentration disturbance, sleep disturbance). This overlap makes differential diagnosis from mood, anxiety, and other disorders particularly important. Second, co-occurring psychopathology is critical to a fully informed case conceptualization and treatment plan. PTSD may or may not be the primary diagnosis or the disorder for which the client has the most pressing need. Likewise, the client may prefer to seek treatment for other problems (e.g., substance use disorders) before engaging in PTSD treatment.

Assessment of response bias. Response bias is important to consider in every assessment context but warrants particular attention in contexts in which incentives could motivate biased responding (e.g., criminal forensic environments and disability evaluations). Although response bias tends to be thought of most often as negative impression management (i.e., overreporting symptoms), several other forms of response bias warrant consideration. Positive impression management (i.e., underreporting) is common in many populations and may be motivated by concerns that accurate reporting may have adverse consequences (e.g., active duty soldiers or law enforcement personnel). Likewise, social desirability can bias reporting of trauma history (e.g., engaging in unlawful events that satisfy DSM-5 Criterion A as traumatic) and symptom reporting (e.g., aggressive behavior, reckless or self-destructive behavior). Although several measures designed to assess response bias are described in "Measures of Assessment Validity," behavioral observations, corroborative reports, and multimodal assessment can each assist in evaluating response bias. Beyond individual symptoms or overall symptom severity, corroborative reports can be particularly helpful regarding the validity of index traumatic events (e.g., police reports, military discharge paperwork).

Context. Ideally, comprehensive assessment of PTSD would involve multimodal assessment of trauma exposure history, PTSD symptoms, co-occurring psychopathology, related features, and response bias using empirically supported measures. It is common practice to collect both clinician-administered and self-report questionnaire data of these domains. Likewise, this practice is not uncommon when comprehensive psychological assessments are conducted for complicated symptom presentations (for a discussion, see Weathers & Keane, 1999). However, this comprehensive assessment requires considerable time and resources that are unavailable in many settings. For example, many outpatient clinics administer an evidence-based questionnaire of PTSD symptoms (e.g., PTSD Checklist for DSM-5; Weathers, Litz et al., 2013), followed up with more time-intensive assessment (e.g., Clinician-Administered PTSD Scale for DSM-5; Weathers, Blake, et al., 2013b) for participants who self-report significant symptoms. Survey research, inherently limited to questionnaire data, may benefit from capturing breadth (i.e., inclusion of evidence-based self-report measures of trauma exposure history, PTSD symptoms, co-occurring psychopathology, related features, and response bias) to compensate for the depth of clinician-administered measures.

While it is not possible or practical to administer comprehensive assessments with all clients in many settings, explicit understanding of the sacrifices made in more narrow approaches is crucial to making informed clinical decisions. Multimeasure approaches (e.g., Kulka et al., 1991) provide the opportunity to combine information from multiple methods and ideally reduce assessment errors. Utilization of exclusively questionnaire data prohibits detailed differential diagnostic assessment, which is a common challenge in PTSD assessment. Although limited resources prevent multimeasure or even single modality approaches to assessment of all of these domains, clinicians should carefully weigh the cost-benefit ratio of including or excluding measurement of these areas against the sacrifices of excluding coverage.

ASSESSMENT MEASURES

This section provides a detailed overview of the most commonly used and psychometrically sound measures to assess PTSD and related features. Although detailed description of each measure is beyond the scope of this chapter, relevant references are provided and summaries of psychometric evaluation of each measure are provided in Table 25.1.

Trauma Exposure Measures

Careful assessment of trauma history is an important first step in assessing PTSD. Existing measures vary in

Table 25.1 Measures of trauma- and stressor-related disorders

Name	Domain(s)	Modality	Psychometric Properties
Life Events Checklist for DSM-5 (LEC-5)	Trauma exposure	Self-report	N/A – For the DSM-IV variant, strong test-retest reliability over 7 days (test-retest correlation r = 0.82) and strong association with the TLEQ (r =.55) among an undergraduate sample (N = 108; Gray et al., 2004)
Traumatic Life Events Questionnaire (TLEQ)	Trauma exposure	Self-report	Item endorsement on the TLEQ and an interview-administered version of the measure evidenced adequate agreement (κ ranged 0.30–1.00; > 0.40 for 15 of 16 items and > 0.60 for 13 items when administered on the same day) among an undergraduate student sample (N = 62; Kubany et al., 2000). Test-retest reliability varied by sample type (e.g., veterans vs. undergraduate students), traumatic event (e.g., κ ranged 0.60–0.79 for witnessing family violence but 0.27–0.59 for other accidents), and test-retest windows, which ranged from one week to two months by sample (Kubany et al., 2000)
Stressful Life Events Screening Questionnaire (SLESQ)	Trauma exposure	Self-report	Strong test-retest reliability over 14 days (test-retest correlation r = 0.89). Item endorsement on the SLESQ and a more detailed interview evidenced adequate agreement (κ ranged 0.26–0.90, median = 0.64) among an undergraduate sample (N = 140; Goodman et al., 1998)
Clinician-Administered PTSD Scale for DSM-5 (CAPS-5)	PTSD diagnostic status, symptom severity, dissociative subtype, related distress/ impairment, response validity, improvement since a previous assessment	Clinician-administered	Strong internal consistency (α = 0.88), inter-rater reliability (total score ICC = 0.91, diagnosis κ = 0.78), test-retest reliability over an average of 2.76 days (total score ICC = 0.78, diagnosis κ = 0.83), strong agreement with DSM-IV CAPS (diagnosis κ = 0.83), convergent associations with self-report PTSD measures (e.g., r = 0.66 with PCL-5) and nonsignificant association with a measure of psychopathy among a veteran sample (N = 167; Weathers et al., 2018)
PTSD Symptom Scale Interview for DSM-5 (PSSI-5)	PTSD diagnostic status, symptom severity, related distress and impairment	Clinician-administered	Strong internal consistency (α = 0.89), adequate test-retest reliability over an average of 6.23 days (total score r = 0.87; diagnosis κ = 0.65), strong inter-rater reliability (total score ICC = 0.98; diagnosis κ = 0.84), and theoretically consistent associations with self-report measures of PTSD (e.g., r = 0.85 with the PDS-5) and related symptoms (e.g., r = 0.73 with the BDI-II), but lower than anticipated agreement with the CAPS-5 (total score r = 0.72; diagnosis κ = 0.49) among undergraduate, community, and veteran samples (N = 242; Foa et al., 2016b)
Structured Clinical Interview for DSM-5 (SCID-5)	PTSD diagnostic status	Clinician-administered	N/A – For the DSM-IV SCID PTSD module, adequate inter-rater reliability (diagnosis κ = 0.88) and test-retest reliability over 10 days (diagnosis κ = 0.78) among adult outpatients

Continued

Table 25.1 (cont.)

Name	Domain(s)	Modality	Psychometric Properties
			(N = 17; Zanarini et al., 2000) and adequate inter-rater reliability (diagnosis κ = 0.77) among a mixed inpatient/outpatient sample (N = 151; Lobbestael, Leurgans, & Arntz, 2011)
Mini International Neuropsychiatric Interview (MINI)	PTSD diagnostic status	Clinician-administered	Adequate diagnostic agreement with the DSM-IV SCID PTSD module (diagnosis κ = 0.78) and test-retest reliability over 1–2 days (diagnosis κ = 0.73) among a community sample (N = 636; Sheehan et al., 1997)
PTSD Checklist for DSM-5 (PCL-5)	PTSD symptom severity	Self-report	Strong internal consistency (α = 0.96), test-retest reliability over an average of 31.02 days (r = 0.84), theoretically consistent associations with other self-report measures of PTSD (e.g., r = 0.87 with the PCL-C) and related symptoms (e.g., r = 0.74 with the PHQ-9), and good diagnostic utility relative to the CAPS-5 (total scores 31–33 provided the best sensitivity [0.88], specificity [0.69], and efficiency [0.58]) among a veteran sample (N = 468; Bovin et al., 2016). Strong internal consistency (α ranged 0.95–0.96), test-retest reliability over an average of 6.14 days (r = 0.82), and theoretically consistent associations with other self-report measures of PTSD (e.g., r = 0.85 with the PDS), related symptoms (e.g., r = 0.74 with the PHQ-9), and unrelated symptoms (e.g., r = 0.31 with the Personality Assessment Inventory [PAI] mania scale) among two large undergraduate samples (total N = 836; Blevins et al., 2015). Strong internal consistency (α = 0.96), theoretically consistent associations with other self-report measures of PTSD (e.g., r = 0.87 with the PCL-S), related symptoms (e.g., r = 0.64 with the BDI-II), and good diagnostic utility relative to the DSM-IV PSS-I (total score 42 provided the best sensitivity [0.77], specificity [0.68], and efficiency [0.45]) among an active duty military sample (N = 912; Wortmann et al., 2016)
Posttraumatic Diagnostic Scale for DSM-5 (PDS-5)	PTSD symptom severity	Self-report	Strong internal consistency (α = 0.96), test-retest reliability over an average of 6.23 days (r = 0.90), theoretically consistent associations with other self-report measures of PTSD (e.g., r = 0.90 with the PCL-S) and related symptoms (e.g., r = 0.77 with the BDI-II), and good diagnostic utility relative to the PSSI-5 (total scores ≥ 27.5 provided the best sensitivity [.79] and specificity [0.78]) among undergraduate, community, and veteran samples (N = 242; Foa et al., 2016a)
Mississippi Scale for Combat-Related PTSD (M-PTSD)	PTSD symptom severity	Self-report	Strong internal consistency (α = 0.94), test-retest reliability over one week (r = 0.97), and good diagnostic utility relative to a comprehensive diagnostic assessment (total

Continued

Table 25.1 (cont.)

Name	Domain(s)	Modality	Psychometric Properties
			scores ≥ 107 provided the best sensitivity [0.93] and specificity [0.89]) among a veteran sample (*N* = 431; Keane et al., 1988). Strong internal consistency (α = 0.96), diagnostic utility relative to the SCID (scores total scores ≥ 100 provided the best sensitivity [0.93] and specificity [0.88] in discriminating between participants with PTSD and participants with a substance use disorder without PTSD), and theoretically consistent associations with other self-report measures of PTSD (e.g., *r* = 0.66 with the MMPI PTSD scale) and related constructs (e.g., *r* = 0.58 with a measure of anger) among a veteran sample (*N* = 203; McFall et al., 1990)
Detailed Assessment of Posttraumatic Stress (DAPS)	PTSD symptom severity	Self-report	Strong internal consistency (α = 0.88–0.98) for all PTSD subscales and total scale in trauma-exposed normative sample (*N* = 446), clinical/community sample (*N* = 191), and university sample (*N* = 257); theoretically consistent associations between PTSD subscales and a variety of other self-report measures of trauma-related symptoms and PTSD (TSI, PCL, PDS, Civilian Mississippi Scale); good diagnostic utility against CAPS PTSD diagnosis (sensitivity = 0.88, specificity = 0.86, efficiency = 0.87, κ = 0.73) (Briere, 2001)
Trauma Symptom Inventory-2 (TSI-2)	PTSD symptom severity	Self-report	Strong internal consistency (α = 0.76–0.94) for all clinical scales and subscales in standardization sample (*N* = 678); strong test-retest reliability (approximately 1-week interval) for all clinical scales and subscales except suicidal behavior in subsample (*N* = 31; *r* = 0.76–0.93); theoretically consistent associations between scales and subscales and a variety of other self-report measures including IES-R and PCL; theoretically consistent factor structure and factorial invariance across three samples; good group discrimination between matched controls from standardization sample and several relevant clinical groups, including combat veteran, borderline personality disorder, sexual abuse, domestic violence, and incarcerated women groups (Briere, 2011)
Impact of Event Scale – Revised (IES-R)	PTSD symptom severity	Self-report	Strong internal consistency (α = 0.79–0.92), adequate test-retest reliability (*r* ranged 0.51–0.94) among first responders (total *N* = 626; Weiss & Marmar, 1997); strong internal consistency (α = 0.96), theoretically consistent association with the PCL-S (*r* = 0.84), and good diagnostic utility relative to PCL-S provisional diagnosis (total score of 1.5 [equivalent to a total score of 33] provided the best sensitivity [0.91], specificity [0.82]) among a mixed veteran and community sample (total N = 274; Creamer, Bell, & Failla, 2003)

important ways; care should be taken to determine the selected measure obtains the information of interest. Although the measures described here provide a detailed history of potentially traumatic event exposure, they typically do not comprehensively ensure event exposure satisfies DSM-5 Criterion A; clinicians should take care to determine the identified worst event meets this definition of a trauma.

The Life Events Checklist for DSM-5 (LEC-5; Weathers, Blake, et al., 2013b), a self-report measure of exposure to numerous potentially traumatic events, is a brief method of assessing lifetime trauma history. The LEC-5 is an update of the DSM-IV version (LEC; Gray et al., 2004). Respondents rate their degree of exposure (*Happened to me*; *Witnessed it*; *Learned about it*; *Part of my job*; *Not sure*; *Doesn't apply*) to a range of traumatic events (e.g., natural disaster, physical assault, sexual assault, combat). A clinician-administered format of this measure, the LEC-5 Interview (LEC5-I), is also available.

The Traumatic Life Events Questionnaire (TLEQ; Kubany et al., 2000) is a longer self-report measure of exposure to potentially traumatic events. Respondents rate often they were exposed to twenty-two categories of potentially traumatic events (e.g., natural disasters, assault, combat) on a seven-point scale ranging from *Never* to *More than 5 times*. Compared to the LEC-5, the TLEQ provides assessment of several additional features which could be of interest (e.g., relationship to perpetrator for assault, injury resulting from the event for some categories, peritraumatic emotional responding for some categories). One caution for using this measure is that, although the TLEQ provides good breadth of coverage in terms of potentially traumatic events, some events may not satisfy DSM-5 Criterion A (e.g., being physically punished while growing up, sexual harassment, being stalked). One limitation of the TLEQ is that, despite strong content validity, the measure has limited criterion-related validity evidence. Specifically, the measure was only validated against a clinician-administered version of the measure among a small undergraduate sample ($N = 62$; Kubany et al., 2000).

The Stressful Life Events Screening Questionnaire (SLESQ; Goodman et al., 1998) is another brief self-report trauma-exposure measure. Respondents report if they have ever been exposed to eleven categories of events (e.g., physical assault, life-threatening accident) on a dichotomous response ("yes" or "no"). Follow-up prompts for endorsed events are used to obtain additional information (e.g., types of injuries sustained during physical assault, relationship to perpetrator of sexual assault). Beyond the eleven main categories of events assessed, two general questions are used to screen for other potentially traumatic events not captured by the other categories. As with the TLEQ, the SLESQ has only been validated using an undergraduate sample (Goodman et al., 1998).

PTSD Measures

Clinician-administered measures. Whenever possible, it is recommended clinician-administered measures be used to assess PTSD rather than self-report questionnaires. Although there are numerous circumstances where doing so is either not practical or not possible, the advantages of clinician-administered measures are numerous (e.g., clarification of complex symptoms, differentiation between overlapping symptoms, differential diagnosis from co-occurring psychopathology) and warrant due consideration when selecting an assessment instrument.

The Clinician-Administered PTSD Scale for DSM-5 (CAPS-5; Weathers, Blake, et al., 2013a), a comprehensive measure of all PTSD criteria, is generally regarded as the "gold standard" for PTSD assessment (Briere, 2004). Previous versions of the CAPS have been extensively validated (Weathers, Keane, & Davidson, 2001) and widely used in research, clinical, and forensic applications (Elhai et al., 2005). The CAPS was recently revised for DSM-5. The new version, the CAPS-5, is psychometrically sound, more user-friendly, and backward compatible with the DSM-IV version (Weathers et al., 2018).

By including behaviorally anchored prompts and rating scales, separate assessment of symptom frequency and intensity, and assessment of trauma relatedness for symptoms not inherently linked to the trauma (e.g., diminished interest, concentration disturbance), the CAPS-5 provides a detailed assessment of each symptom and overall picture of syndrome severity. Clinicians rate each of the twenty core DSM-5 symptoms and the two dissociation symptoms on a five-point ordinal severity rating scale ranging from *0 = Absent* to *4 = Extreme/incapacitating*, using information about symptom frequency and intensity. These severity ratings can be used to provide both dichotomous (present/absent) and continuous ratings for individual symptoms and overall disorder severity. Thus, the CAPS-5 yields dichotomous PTSD diagnostic status, a continuous score reflecting PTSD symptom severity, and determination of the dissociative subtype. In addition to symptoms, clinicians rate related distress and impairment, response validity (based on clinical judgment), symptom severity, and improvement since a previous assessment. In initial psychometric research, the CAPS-5 demonstrated high test-retest and inter-rater reliability, good convergent and discriminant validity, and strong correspondence with the DSM-IV version among a veteran sample (Weathers et al., 2018).

The PTSD Symptom Scale Interview for DSM-5 (PSSI-5; Foa et al., 2016b) is another clinician-administered measure of PTSD. Like the CAPS-5, the PSSI-5 also provides both dichotomous and continuous ratings for individual symptoms and overall disorder severity. The PSSI-5 typically requires less time to administer than the CAPS-5. However, it also provides less detailed assessment of each symptom (e.g., no separate assessment of symptom frequency and intensity) and lacks assessment of related features (e.g., no ratings for response validity, improvement since a previous assessment, or assessment of the dissociative subtype). The PSSI-5 demonstrated good psychometric properties, including internal consistency, test-retest reliability, inter-rater reliability, and theoretically consistent associations with self-report measures of related constructs among a mixed undergraduate, community, and veteran sample (Foa et al., 2016b). However, diagnostic agreement with the CAPS-5 was somewhat lower than anticipated (diagnosis $\kappa = 0.49$).

In addition to the CAPS-5 and PSSI-5, several structured diagnostic interviews include assessment of PTSD within a comprehensive assessment of a wider range of disorders. The Structured Clinical Interview for DSM-5 (SCID-5; First et al., 2015) is perhaps the most widely used diagnostic interview. Past versions of the SCID have generally been regarded as "gold standard" diagnostic instruments and have been widely used in major clinical trials as well as the criterion measure for evaluating validity of self-report measures (e.g., Foa et al., 1997). The SCID-5 PTSD module includes a brief assessment of trauma history and identification of an index trauma. Interviewers rate each of the twenty DSM-5 PTSD symptoms on a three-point rating scale – *1 = Absent or false, 2 = Subthreshold, 3 = Threshold or true* – and also rate related distress and impairment.

The Mini International Neuropsychiatric Interview (MINI; Sheehan et al., 1997) is a brief diagnostic interview of DSM-5 disorders that emphasizes brevity over detailed assessment. This measure utilizes a brief screen of trauma history to identify an index event and clinicians make dichotomous ratings for symptoms. Although the MINI is an appropriate measure for determining diagnostic status, care should be taken to determine if the measure provides adequate content coverage. For example, the MINI uses a single dichotomous rating for all five Criterion B symptoms.

DSM-5 correspondent self-report measures. The PTSD Checklist for DSM-5 (PCL-5; Weathers, Litz, et al., 2013) is a twenty-item self-report measure of PTSD symptoms. Respondents use a five-point scale ranging from *Not at all* to *Extremely* to rate the degree to which they have been bothered by each of the twenty DSM-5 symptoms during the past month in reference to a specified event. Item scores can be summed to reflect individual cluster severity scores (e.g., items 1–5 for Cluster B) and overall symptom severity by summing all twenty items. Initial psychometric research suggests a PCL-5 total score cut-point score of 33 can be used to provide a provisional PTSD diagnosis among veterans (sensitivity = 0.88, specificity = 0.69; Bovin et al., 2015) but has yet to be replicated among other populations. The PCL-5 has demonstrated strong psychometric properties among numerous populations, including test-retest reliability and convergent and discriminant validity, structural validity, and diagnostic utility against the CAPS-5.

The Posttraumatic Diagnostic Scale for DSM-5 (PDS-5; Foa et al., 2016a) is a twenty-six-item self-report measure of PTSD symptom severity. Two items assess trauma exposure and identify the index event. Respondents then rate how often and how bothersome each of the twenty DSM-5 PTSD symptoms has been during the past month on a five-item scale ranging from *not at all* to *6 or more times a week/severe*. In addition, two items are used to rate related distress and impairment and two more items are used to establish symptom onset and duration. As with the PCL-5, PDS-5 items can be summed to total scores reflecting individual symptom cluster or overall disorder severity. Initial psychometric research suggests a cutoff score of 28 can be used to provide a provisional PTSD diagnosis (sensitivity = 0.79, specificity = 0.78; Foa et al., 2016a). The PDS-5 has demonstrated strong psychometric properties among a combined urban community, veteran, and undergraduate sample, including good test-retest reliability, convergent and discriminant validity, and criterion-related validity compared to the PSSI-5 (Foa et al., 2016a).

Other self-report measures. Several other self-report measures have yet to be adapted to DSM-5 but remain widely used; see Table 25.1 for psychometric evaluation. The Mississippi Scale for Combat-Related PTSD (M-PTSD; Keane, Caddell, & Taylor, 1988) is a thirty-five-item self-report measure of PTSD symptoms related to combat; a civilian version of the M-PTSD was developed for use in assessing PTSD in relation to traumatic events other than combat (Lauterbach et al., 1997). The Detailed Assessment of Posttraumatic Stress (DAPS; Briere, 2001) and Trauma Symptom Inventory-2 (TSI-2; Briere, 2011) are a 104- and 136-item self-report measure, respectively, of trauma exposure, DSM-IV PTSD symptoms, and related features. The Impact of Event Scale – Revised (IES-R; Weiss & Marmar, 1997) is a twenty-two-item self-report measure of trauma-related symptoms.

The M-PTSD is distinct from DSM-5 correspondent measures in that it incorporates assessment of depression, suicide risk, and substance use attributed to combat exposure as features of trauma-related sequalae. Also unlike DSM-5 correspondent measures, the IES-R only measures intrusion, avoidance, and hyperarousal symptoms. The lengthier but thorough DAPS and TSI-2 offer assessment of DSM-IV PTSD symptoms as well as additional areas of potential interest. Both the DAPS and the TSI-2 include assessment of validity and trauma-related impairment beyond what is included in DSM-5 criteria (e.g., somatization, suicidality). Further, the DAPS includes assessment of lifetime trauma exposure and identification of an index trauma.

Measures of Co-occurring Psychopathology

As noted, assessment of co-occurring psychopathology can greatly inform PTSD assessment. Understanding comorbid symptoms and their interaction with PTSD symptoms can provide a more nuanced understanding of all symptoms impacting a client, inform differential diagnosis, and guide both case conceptualization and treatment planning. Although assessment of psychopathology more broadly is beyond the scope of this chapter, several commonly administered instruments are described here.

Semi-structured diagnostic interviews are commonly used to assess co-occurring psychopathology in research settings (e.g., PTSD clinical trials) as well as comprehensive psychological assessment. The SCID-5 (First et al., 2015), ADIS-5 (Brown & Barlow, 2014), and MINI (Sheehan et al., 1997) are some of the most commonly used diagnostic interviews. As noted, these measures differ substantially in detail, brevity, and resulting ratings. Of particular note, these interviews vary in coverage of specific disorders. For example, the SCID-5 contains detailed assessment of DSM-5 psychotic disorders, whereas the ADIS-5 only includes a screener for psychotic symptoms. Likewise, the SCID-5 and MINI provide categorical ratings for presence or absence of disorders, whereas the ADIS-5 includes both categorical and dimensional ratings for each disorder.

Self-report measures of multiple domains of psychopathology are widely used in PTSD assessment. Two of the most common measures are the Minnesota Multiphasic Personality Inventory-2-Restructured Form (MMPI-2-RF; Ben-Porath & Tellegen, 2008) and the Personality Assessment Inventory (PAI; Morey, 1991). The MMPI-2-RF is a 338-item self-report measure of psychopathology and personality. The PAI is a widely used 344-item self-report measure of personality and psychopathology. Although each of these measures is long, both are well-validated and provide meaningful information about mental health symptoms, related features (e.g., suicide risk), personality, and response validity. For comprehensive review of these measures, see Chapters 16 and 17 of this volume.

Measures of Assessment Validity

Several measures already described in this chapter include integrated response bias scales. For example the DAPS, MMPI-2/MMPI-2-RF, and PAI each include measures of response validity to assess overreporting of psychopathology. In particular, the MMPI-2 and MMPI-2-RF validity scales have been subjected to strong empirical scrutiny in the assessment of PTSD with very promising results (e.g., Bagby et al., 2002; Goodwin, Sellbom, & Arbisi, 2013). One advantage to integrated validity measures is reduced opportunity for respondents to differentiate between measurement of symptoms and response bias.

Alternatively, a number of stand-alone response bias scales are available. The Marlowe-Crowne Social Desirability Scale (Crowne & Marlowe, 1960) is a thirty-three-item self-report measure of general tendency to be concerned with social approval. Regarding PTSD, this measure has been shown to be sensitive to symptom underreporting among combat veterans (Pitts et al., 2014). The Miller Forensic Assessment of Symptoms Test (M-FAST; Miller, 2005) is a twenty-five-item clinician-administered measure of several potential forms of misreporting (e.g., reported vs. observed symptoms, rare symptom combinations, suggestibility) that has been validated against other more time- and resource-intensive malingering measures. For contexts that permit greater time to assess validity, the Structured Interview of Reported Symptoms – Second Edition (SIRS-2; Rogers, Sewell, and Gillard, 2010) is a 172-item structured interview of malingering related to specific diagnoses. This measure has been validated in numerous settings and populations (e.g., Rogers et al., 2009) and provides measures of self-appraisal of honesty, defensiveness, and inconsistent responding.

Finally, one measure of PTSD-specific symptom malingering has been developed: the Morel Emotional Numbing Test for PTSD (MENT; Morel, 1998). This task involves instructing respondents that "some individuals with PTSD may have difficulty recognizing facial expressions" and then asking respondents to match displayed faces with corresponding emotion labels. Multiple studies have shown that more accurate matching of facial affect with emotion labels is associated with more accurate symptom reporting (Morel, 1998; Morel & Shephard, 2008). However, research on this measure has been constricted to combat-related PTSD to date.

CULTURAL CONSIDERATIONS IN PTSD ASSESSMENT

While there is substantial evidence of the cross-cultural validity of PTSD, there is notable cross-cultural variation in the expression of posttraumatic stress symptoms, particularly for avoidance symptoms, the interpretation of symptoms as being trauma-related, and the prevalence of somatic symptoms (Hinton & Lewis-Fernandez, 2011). Understanding the way in which these cultural factors affect PTSD symptom presentation and reporting style is paramount to an assessor's ability to conduct a valid PTSD assessment (e.g., Lewis-Fernandez, Hinton, & Marques, 2014). Therefore, an assessment of respondents' cultural backgrounds, including their race, ethnicity, gender identity, sexual orientation, religious affiliation, veteran status, disability status, and the intersectionality of multiple identities, should be included in every PTSD assessment. Doing so promotes an understanding of the cultural norms and stigmas associated with certain symptoms and an accurate interpretation of behaviors as either symptomatic or culturally normative. This consideration of cultural factors in turn prevents the under- or overdiagnosis of PTSD among diverse groups and can facilitate post-assessment treatment engagement.

The psychology literature includes an abundance of guidance for conducting culturally competent assessment (e.g., Hinton & Good, 2016; Murphy & Dillon, 2008; Sue & Sue, 2013). First, it is important for assessors to acknowledge culturally relevant barriers to seeking PTSD assessment. For example, due to the history of racist practices, severe mistreatment, and misdiagnosis of African Americans by the medical and mental health fields, distrust of health care fields and of Anglo-American mental health care providers is a significant barrier for many people of color (Suite et al., 2007). In addition, Hinton and Good (2016) warn of many potential errors that assessors can make when assessing a trauma-related disorder in another cultural context, such as decontextualizing (ignoring the ethnopsychology, ethnophysiology, and ethnospirituality as it relates to a presenting symptom).To build rapport and trust with a PTSD respondent and conduct a valid assessment, the assessor should ask about multiple aspects of the respondents' identities, be informed about relevant cultural considerations, acknowledge cultural differences between the assessor and respondent, invite discussion about these differences, and consult with colleagues who have expertise in the cultural background of a particular respondent.

It is also important to acknowledge the strengths and limitations of standard PTSD assessment instruments when used with diverse respondents. An obvious limitation is that many of validity studies of PTSD instruments were conducted with predominantly White participants who were relatively homogeneous demographically. However, replication studies increasingly seek to determine whether psychometric properties of the instruments generalize to diverse groups of participants and whether conceptual, semantic, and operational equivalence can be achieved when translating measures into languages other than English (e.g., Lima et al., 2016). Diagnostic interviews (e.g., CAPS-5), which allow for greater assurance of comprehension, applicability, and consideration of cultural context, may be more advantageous than self-report measures for diverse respondents.

PRACTICAL GUIDANCE FOR THE ADMINISTRATION OF PTSD ASSESSMENTS

Much more has been written about the psychometrics of PTSD assessment instruments than about the clinical skills and finesse involved in the administration of these instruments. Yet the validity and utility of a PTSD assessment rest on both the selection of appropriate assessment instruments *and* proper administration. Generalist foundational assessment skills (e.g., adhering to the standard scoring guidelines of an instrument) are essential for valid PTSD assessment. However, some aspects of PTSD symptom presentation that distinguish it from the clinical presentation of other mental disorders necessitate the use of specific clinical skills. The purpose of this section is to describe key clinical skills applicable to conducting PTSD assessments and how to apply these skills in challenging scenarios that routinely arise during PTSD assessments.

Maintaining a Supportive Presence and Building Rapport

It is imperative that PTSD assessors maintain a supportive, nonjudgmental presence and intentionally build and sustain rapport with the respondent. This empathic stance and rapport-building is critical because trauma survivors, especially those who have experienced interpersonal traumas, may be very reluctant to initiate or engage in a PTSD assessment for a number of reasons. The survivors may have negative schemas about the trustworthiness of others, trauma-related feelings of guilt or shame, fear of stigmatization or an invalidating response from the assessor, and discomfort with vulnerability. Even initiating contact with a mental health professional and showing up to the assessment session may be a significant hurdle for respondents, who may have strong anticipation anxiety and an entrenched pattern of avoidance behaviors. Therefore, to increase the likelihood of attending the assessment session, assessors should make a concerted effort to convey warmth, understanding, and transparency about the assessment process during the initial contact with the respondent. The physical environment for the session should be inviting and comfortable, with careful consideration of the seating arrangement, given that respondents with pronounced hypervigilant behaviors may not feel comfortable sitting with their back facing doors or windows, or in a confined space.

At the beginning of the assessment session, the assessor should briefly provide an overview of what the assessment will involve, as well as a discussion of what will happen if the respondent becomes upset. Respondents often experience PTSD assessments as emotionally triggering, as the assessment is essentially an exposure to the trauma memory and reminders. Normalization of initial anxiety during PTSD assessments can help reduce respondent's shame in response to distress that they may feel at the beginning of the assessment. Explicit encouragement from the assessor about the assessment process can help the respondent feel safe and prepared (e.g., "I know the topics we will be discussing today are difficult for a lot of trauma survivors to talk about. I want to make this experience as comfortable as I possibly can for you so please let me know if you would like to slow down and talk about how you are feeling, take a brief break."). Validation, empathy, and compassion are particularly critical to convey during the assessment of PTSD Criterion A (the index trauma). For many respondents, this may be one of the first times they are disclosing the trauma to others and therefore they may be particularly sensitive to perceived criticism, skepticism, or minimization of their experience.

Maintaining rapport and a supportive presence during the assessment can be accomplished through nonverbal communication of empathy (e.g., soft facial expressions, gentle tone of voice, reasonable pacing), occasional brief supportive sounds (e.g., "mm-hmm," "uh-huh," "I see"), and explicit statements of support (e.g., "That sounds like a horrific experience"; "It is very brave of you to be willing to talk about this"). Assessors should convey this empathy efficiently, while maintaining control over the interview and not engaging in tangential discussions that could prolong the assessment unnecessarily and that may serve an avoidance function for the respondent.

Appropriately Responding to Respondent Behavior

Given that it is not uncommon for respondents to engage in behaviors during PTSD assessments that may interfere with validity of the assessment, assessors should be aware of the potential for such behaviors, monitor for them during the assessment, and address them appropriately. Throughout the assessment, the assessor should informally or formally assess the respondent's mental status (e.g., sobriety, orientation to present, cognitive ability, distress). PTSD is highly comorbid with substance use and dependence, and substance use is a common method of coping with anticipated trauma-related distress. Therefore, assessors should be aware of potential for recent substance use and be prepared to assess current intoxication level. Emotional reactivity during the assessment may also interfere with the respondent's ability to provide valid data. While tearfulness, irritability, and mild physiological arousal are common, the assessor should monitor and provide containment if the emotional distress appears difficult for the respondent to tolerate or seems to be interfering with the assessment. For example, the assessor may make a behavioral observation and check in on how the respondent is feeling, provide active listening, and allow brief unstructured processing of the affect, offer a diaphragmatic breathing exercise, or allow the respondent to take a break from the assessment to stretch, walk around the room, or have a drink of water.

Several symptoms of PTSD, including concentration problems, avoidance of trauma reminders, flashbacks, and dissociation, may also occur during PTSD assessment sessions and should be addressed appropriately. Assessors should be prepared to repeat assessment prompts as needed and check over questionnaires to ensure completion. If respondents appear to be engaging in avoidance behaviors during the assessment (e.g., discussing the "easier" rather than worst trauma, tangential discussions of symptoms or stressors unrelated to PTSD), assessors should gently but firmly redirect the respondent and ensure that the assessment remains focused and on task. Assessors should be particularly vigilant for dissociative symptoms, such as flashbacks, derealization, or depersonalization, which may present as a blank stare, unresponsiveness, or responding to auditory or visual stimuli that are not present. If this occurs, the assessor should assist the respondent in the use of grounding techniques to reorient to the present and discuss potential adjustments to decrease the likelihood of another dissociative episode during the remaining portion of the assessment (e.g., holding a grounding object).

Effective Use of Clinical Judgment

The heterogeneity of PTSD symptom presentation, as well as variability in respondents' level of insight and reporting style, requires the use of clinical judgment while interpreting responses during PTSD assessments. Some respondents may minimize or exaggerate the manageability of their PTSD symptoms due to social desirability response bias or limited insight into the impact of their behavior. For example, a respondent may report that he is able to manage his anger by consuming nine drinks of alcohol or by driving 50mph over the speed limit, and therefore inaccurately describe his anger as manageable and "not a problem." Or, for example, a respondent's avoidance behaviors may be so chronic that they become an automatic habit that requires minimal effort, and therefore the respondent may deny or minimize the impact of the avoidance behaviors despite evidence of significant changes in behavior compared to pretrauma functioning. Respondents may not have insight into whether certain behaviors are trauma-related, or may not have the emotional vocabulary to describe their emotional experiences. Given that PTSD is highly comorbid with other mental disorders and medical conditions (e.g., Brady e al., 2000; Kessler et al., 1995), respondents' limited insight into their PTSD symptoms may also be exacerbated by co-occurring psychological distress or cognitive deficits. For these reasons, assessors should attend to not only what is being reported but also how it is being reported and whether behavioral observations during the assessment are congruent with reported symptoms.

Self-Awareness

Lastly, it is important for PTSD assessors to maintain self-awareness of their own beliefs, behaviors, and psychological well-being in order to ensure that they do not act in ways that bias the assessment. For example, assessors should be aware of any urges to collude with a respondent's avoidance behaviors by engaging in tangential discussions, or under-querying traumas or symptoms that are emotionally painful for the respondent to discuss or for the assessor to hear. Assessors should not provide evaluative responses that convey judgment in order to maintain neutrality and minimize their influence on the respondent's report of symptoms. Repeated exposure to the details of traumatic events can impact assessors over time in a variety of ways, including vicarious traumatization and desensitization (McCann & Pearlman, 1990). Given the heavy emotional content of PTSD assessments, PTSD assessors should attend to their own self-care, consult with their colleagues, and seek professional support as needed.

CONCLUSIONS

This chapter summarizes critical procedural, contextual, and methodological considerations for PTSD assessment. Additionally, this chapter provides a detailed overview of several of the most widely used clinician-administered and self-report measures of PTSD and related constructs. As noted in this chapter, care should be taken when selecting particular assessment instruments in order to facilitate case formulation, treatment planning, and evaluation of treatment progress. While assessment contexts (e.g., emergency room, outpatient clinic, survey study) inevitably impose limitations regarding assessment options, decisions should be weighed giving consideration to the psychometric evidence, quality of the assessment product, and setting needs.

REFERENCES

American Psychiatric Association. (2013). *Diagnostic and statistical manual of mental disorders* (5th ed.). Washington, DC: Author.

Bagby, R. M., Nicholson, R. A., Bacchiochi, J. R., Ryder, A. G., & Bury, A. S. (2002). The predictive capacity of the MMPI-2 and PAI validity scales and indexes to detect coached and uncoached feigning. *Journal of Personality Assessment, 78,* 69–86.

Ben-Porath, Y. S., & Tellegen, A. (2008). *Minnesota Multiphasic Personality Inventory—2 Restructured Form; Manual for administration, scoring, and interpretation.* Minneapolis: University of Minnesota Press.

Blevins, C. A., Weathers, F. W., Davis, M. T., Witte, T. K., & Domino, J. L. (2015). The Posttraumatic Stress Disorder Checklist for *DSM-5* (PCL-5): Development and initial psychometric evaluation. *Journal of Traumatic Stress, 28,* 489–498.

Bodkin, J. A., Pope, H. G., Detke, M. J., & Hudson, J. I. (2007). Is PTSD caused by traumatic stress?. *Journal of Anxiety Disorders, 21,* 176–182.

Bovin, M. J., Marx, B. P., Weathers, F. W., Gallagher, M. W., Rodriguez, P., Schnurr, P. P., & Keane, T. M. (2015). Psychometric properties of the PTSD Checklist for *Diagnostic and Statistical Manual of Mental Disorders-Fifth Edition* (PCL-5) in veterans. *Psychological Assessment, 28,* 1379–1391.

Brady, K. T., Killeen, T. K., Brewerton, T., & Lucerini, S. (2000). Comorbidity of psychiatric disorders and posttraumatic stress disorder. *The Journal of Clinical Psychiatry, 61(Suppl7),* 22–32.

Briere, J. (2001). *Detailed assessment of posttraumatic stress.* Odessa, FL: Psychological Assessment Resources.

Briere, J. (2004). *Psychological assessment of adult posttraumatic states: Phenomenology, diagnosis, and measurement* (2nd ed.). Washington, DC: American Psychological Association.

Briere, J. (2011). *Trauma Symptom Inventory, 2nd ed. (TSI-2) professional manual.* Odessa, FL: Psychological Assessment Resources.

Briggs, E. C., Nooner, K., & Amaya-Jackson, L. M. (2014). Assessment of childhood PTSD. In M. J. Friedman, T. M. Keane, & P. A. Resick (Eds.), *Handbook of PTSD: Science and practice* (2nd ed. pp. 391–405). New York: Guilford.

Brown, T. A., & Barlow, D. H. (2014). *Anxiety Disorders Interview Schedule for DSM-5 (ADIS-5).* New York: Oxford University Press.

Creamer, M., Bell, R., & Failla, S. (2003). Psychometric properties of the impact of event scale – revised. *Behaviour Research and Therapy, 41,* 1489–1496.

Crowne, D. P., & Marlowe, D. (1960). A new scale of social desirability independent of psychopathology. *Journal of Consulting Psychology, 24,* 349–354.

Elhai, J. D., Gray, M. J., Kashdan, T. B., & Franklin, C. L. (2005). Which instruments are most commonly used to assess traumatic event exposure and posttraumatic effects? A survey of traumatic stress professionals. *Journal of Traumatic Stress, 18,* 541–545.

First, M. B., Williams, J. B. W., Karg, R. S., & Spitzer, R. L. (2015). *Structured Clinical Interview for DSM-5 Disorders, Clinician Version (SCID-5-CV).* Arlington, VA: American Psychiatric Association.

Foa, E. B., Cashman, L., Jaycox, L., & Perry, K. (1997). The validation of a self-report measure of posttraumatic stress disorder: The Posttraumatic Diagnostic Scale. *Psychological Assessment, 9,* 445–451.

Foa, E. B., McLean, C. P., Zang, Y., Zhong, J., Powers, M. B., Kauffman, B. Y., ... & Knowles, K. (2016a). Psychometric properties of the posttraumatic diagnostic scale for *DSM-5* (PDS-5). *Psychological Assessment, 28,* 1166–1171.

Foa, E. B., McLean, C. P., Zang, Y., Zhong, J., Rauch, S., Porter, K., ... & Kauffman, B. Y. (2016b). Psychometric properties of the Posttraumatic Stress Disorder Symptom Scale Interview for *DSM–5* (PSSI–5). *Psychological Assessment, 28,* 1159–1165.

Goodman, L., Corcoran, C., Turner, K., Yuan, N., & Green, B. (1998). Assessing traumatic event exposure: General issues and preliminary findings for the Stressful Life Events Screening Questionnaire. *Journal of Traumatic Stress, 11,* 521–542.

Goodwin, B.E., Sellbom, M., & Arbisi, P.A. (2013). Post-traumatic stress disorder in veterans: The utility of the MMPI-2-RF validity scales in detecting over-reported symptoms. *Psychological Assessment, 25,* 671–678.

Gray, M., Litz, B., Hsu, J., & Lombardo, T. (2004). Psychometric properties of the Life Events Checklist. *Assessment, 11,* 330–341.

Hinton, D. E., & Good, B. J. (2016). The culturally sensitive assessment of trauma: Eleven analytic perspectives, a typology of errors, and the multiplex models of distress generation. In D. E. Hinton & B. J. Good (Eds.), *Culture and PTSD: Trauma in global and historical perspective* (pp. 50–113). Philadelphia: University of Pennsylvania Press.

Hinton, D. E., & Lewis-Fernandez, R. (2011). The cross-cultural validity of posttraumatic stress disorder: Implications for DSM-5. *Depression and Anxiety, 28,* 783–801.

Hoge, C. W., Auchterlonie, J. L., & Milliken, C. S. (2006). Mental health problems, use of mental health services, and attrition from military service after returning from deployment to Iraq or Afghanistan. *JAMA, 295,* 1023–1032.

Keane, T. M., Caddell, J. M., & Taylor, K. L. (1988). Mississippi Scale for Combat-Related Posttraumatic Stress Disorder: Three studies in reliability and validity. *Journal of Consulting and Clinical Psychology, 56,* 85–90.

Keane, T. M., & Kaloupek, D. G. (1997). Comorbid psychiatric disorders in PTSD: Implications for research. *Annals of the New York Academy of Sciences, 821,* 24–34.

Kessler, R. C., Sonnega, A., Bromet, E., Hughes, M., & Nelson, C. B. (1995). Posttraumatic stress disorder in the

National Comorbidity Survey. *Archives of General Psychiatry, 52*, 1048–1060.

Kubany, E. S., Leisen, M. B., Kaplan, A. S., Watson, S. B., Haynes, S. N., Owens, J. A., & Burns, K. (2000). Development and preliminary validation of a brief broad-spectrum measure of trauma exposure: The Traumatic Life Events Questionnaire. *Psychological Assessment, 12*, 210–224.

Kulka, R. A., Schlenger, W. E., Fairbank, J. A., Hough, R. L., Jordan, B. K., Marmar, C. R., & Weiss, D. S. (1991). Assessment of posttraumatic stress disorder in the community: Prospects and pitfalls from recent studies of Vietnam veterans. *Psychological Assessment, 3*, 547–560.

Lauterbach, D., Vrana, S. R., King, D. W., & King, L. A. (1997). Psychometric properties of the civilian version of the Mississippi PTSD Scale. *Journal of Traumatic Stress, 10*, 499–513.

Lewis-Fernandez, R., Hinton, D.E., & Marques, L. (2014). Culture and PTSD. In M. J. Friedman, T. M. Keane, & P. Resick (Eds.), *Handbook of PTSD: Science and practice* (pp. 522–539). New York: Guilford Press.

Lima, E. D. P., Vasconcelos, A. G., Berger, W., Kristensen, C. H., Nascimento, E. D., Figueira, I., & Mendlowicz, M. V. (2016). Cross-cultural adaptation of the Posttraumatic Stress Disorder Checklist 5 (PCL-5) and Life Events Checklist 5 (LEC-5) for the Brazilian context. *Trends in Psychiatry and Psychotherapy, 38*, 207–215.

Lobbestael, J., Leurgans, M., & Arntz, A. (2011). Inter-rater reliability of the Structured Clinical Interview for DSM-IV Axis I Disorders (SCID I) and Axis II Disorders (SCID II). *Clinical Psychology & Psychotherapy, 18*, 75–79.

Marshall, R. D., Olfson, M., Hellman, F., Blanco, C., Guardino, M., & Struening, E. L. (2001). Comorbidity, impairment, and suicidality in subthreshold PTSD. *American Journal of Psychiatry, 158*, 1467–1473.

McCann, I. L., & Pearlman, L. A. (1990). Vicarious traumatization: A framework for understanding the psychological effects of working with victims. *Journal of Traumatic Stress, 3*, 131–149.

McFall, M. E., Smith, D. E., Mackay, P. W., & Tarver, D. J. (1990). Reliability and validity of Mississippi Scale for Combat-Related Posttraumatic Stress Disorder. *Psychological Assessment, 2*, 114–121.

Miller, H. A. (2005). The Miller-Forensic Assessment of Symptoms Test (M-Fast) Test Generalizability and Utility across Race Literacy, and Clinical Opinion. *Criminal Justice and Behavior, 32*, 591–611.

Morel, K. R. (1998). Development and preliminary validation of a forced-choice test of response bias for Posttraumatic Stress Disorder. *Journal of Personality Assessment, 70*, 299–314.

Morel, K. R., & Shepherd, B. E. (2008). Meta-analysis of the Morel Emotional Numbing Test for PTSD: Comment on Singh, Avasthi, and Grover. *German Journal of Psychiatry, 11*, 128–131.

Morey, L. C. (1991). *The Personality Assessment Inventory professional manual*. Odessa, FL: Psychological Assessment Resources.

Murphy, B. C., & Dillon, C. (2008). *Interviewing in action in a multicultural world*. Belmont, CA: Brooks/Cole.

Pitts, B. L., Chapman, P., Safer, M. A., & Russell, D. W. (2014). Combat experiences predict postdeployment symptoms in US Army combat medics. *Military Behavioral Health, 2*, 343–350.

Resick, P. A., Suvak, M. K., Johnides, B. D., Mitchell, K. S., & Iverson, K. M. (2012). The impact of dissociation on PTSD treatment with cognitive processing therapy. *Depression and Anxiety, 29*, 718–730.

Rogers, R., Payne, J. W., Berry, D. T., & Granacher, R. P., Jr. (2009). Use of the SIRS in compensation cases: an examination of its validity and generalizability. *Law and Human Behavior, 33*, 213–224.

Rogers, R., Sewell, K. W., & Gillard, N. D. (2010). *SIRS: Structured Interview of Reported Symptoms* (2nd eds.). Odessa, FL: Psychological Assessment Resources.

Sheehan, D. V., Lecrubier, Y., Sheehan, K. H., Janavs, J., Weiller, E., Keskiner, A., . . . & Dunbar, G. C. (1997). The validity of the Mini International Neuropsychiatric Interview (MINI) according to the SCID-P and its reliability. *European Psychiatry, 12*, 232–241.

Sue, D. W., & Sue, D. (2013). *Counseling the culturally diverse: Theory and practice*. Hoboken, NJ: John Wiley & Sons.

Suite, D. H., La Bril, R., Primm, A., & Harrison-Ross, P. (2007) Beyond misdiagnosis, misunderstand, and mistrust: Relevance of the historical perspective in the medical and mental health treatment of people of color, *Journal of the National Medical Association, 99*, 1–7.

Weathers, F. W., Blake, D. D., Schnurr, P. P., Kaloupek, D. G., Marx, B. P., & Keane, T. M. (2013a). The Clinician-Administered PTSD Scale for *DSM-5* (CAPS-5). Interview available from the National Center for PTSD at www.ptsd.va.gov.

Weathers, F. W., Blake, D. D., Schnurr, P. P., Kaloupek, D. G., Marx, B. P., & Keane, T. M. (2013b). The Life Events Checklist for *DSM-5* (LEC-5). Instrument available from the National Center for PTSD at www.ptsd.va.gov

Weathers, F. W., Bovin, M. J., Lee, D. J., Sloan, D. M., Schnurr, P. P., Kaloupek, D. G., . . . & Marx, B. P. (2018). The Clinician-Administered PTSD Scale for DSM–5 (CAPS-5): Development and initial psychometric evaluation in military veterans. *Psychological Assessment, 30*, 383–395.

Weathers, F. W., & Keane, T. M. (1999). Psychological assessment of traumatized adults. In P. A. Saigh & J. D. Bremner (Eds.), *Posttraumatic stress disorder: A comprehensive text* (pp. 219–247). Needham Heights, MA: Allyn & Bacon.

Weathers, F. W., Keane, T. M., & Davidson, J. R. T. (2001). Clinician administered PTSD scale: A review of the first ten years of research. *Depression and Anxiety, 13*, 132–156.

Weathers, F. W., Litz, B. T., Keane, T. M., Palmieri, P. A., Marx, B. P., & Schnurr, P. P. (2013). The PTSD Checklist for *DSM-5* (PCL-5). National Center for PTSD. www.ptsd.va.gov/professional/assessment/adult-sr/ptsd-checklist.asp

Weathers, F. W., Marx, B. P., Friedman, M. J., & Schnurr, P. P. (2014). Posttraumatic stress disorder in *DSM-5*: New criteria, new measures, and implications for assessment. *Psychological Injury and Law, 7*, 93–107.

Weiss, D. S., & Marmar, C. R. (1997). The Impact of Event Scale – Revised. In J. Wilson & T. M. Keane (Eds.), *Assessing psychological trauma and PTSD* (pp. 399–411). New York: Guilford.

Wortmann, J. H., Jordan, A. H., Weathers, F. W., Resick, P. A., Dondanville, K. A., Hall-Clark, B., . . . & Litz, B. T. (2016). Psychometric analysis of the PTSD Checklist-5 (PCL-5) among treatment-seeking military service members. *Psychological Assessment, 28*, 1392–1403.

Zanarini, M. C., Skodol, A. E., Bender, D., Dolan, R., Sanislow, C., Schaefer, E., . . . & Gunderson, J. G. (2000). The collaborative longitudinal personality disorders study: Reliability of axis I and II diagnoses. *Journal of Personality Disorders, 14*, 291–299.

26 Assessment of People with Psychotic and Bipolar Disorders

RACHEL BRAND, GREG MURRAY, AND NEIL THOMAS

Carl is a thirty-four-year-old man who lives alone and volunteers two days a week in a shop. Carl regularly hears threatening voices that are only audible to him. The threats from these voices make Carl very anxious and he can sometimes struggle to leave the house. Carl also has periods when he is not able to sleep and he finds he is full of energy and his mind is racing. At these times, he begins to believe that God has sent him for some kind of special mission. When Carl was younger, he was diagnosed with bipolar disorder but, since the voices have become more persistent, Carl has been diagnosed with schizoaffective disorder.

As Carl's story shows, the symptoms and impact of psychotic and bipolar disorders can be wide-ranging and complex. Thus, the process of assessment may have different aims. We may want to *categorize* Carl's difficulties using diagnostic or other classification systems; or we may be seeking to *quantify* the severity of Carl's difficulties or progress that he makes. We may also want to understand Carl's difficulties fully in order to *formulate* a treatment plan. This chapter gives an overview of issues pertinent to each of these aims as well as outlining common assessment instruments for each. Readers are encouraged to source the original references for full details regarding the use of each instrument.

Psychotic and bipolar disorders are considered severe mental illnesses with a long-term course, fluctuating presentation, and considerable impact on functioning. They show significant symptom overlap, with both psychotic and mood features common in both. Owing to commonalities in assessment, we consider psychotic and bipolar disorders together in this chapter. However, while overlapping, psychotic and bipolar disorders fall into distinct categories in current diagnostic classification systems and many people will only experience symptoms associated with one of these syndromes. Psychotic disorders are particularly characterized by significant changes to beliefs, cognition, and perception and bipolar affective disorders by episodes of marked mood changes, including both periods of elevated mood and depressed mood. Where assessment instruments or issues are specific to either psychotic or bipolar disorders, this will be highlighted.

KEY ISSUES TO CONSIDER IN PREPARATION FOR AN ASSESSMENT

Prior to embarking on an assessment there are some key issues that should be considered. The fluctuating and episodic nature of symptoms requires a longitudinal approach to assessment. Consideration should be given to an individual's cultural context, since experiences deemed "unusual" in some cultures may be the norm in others (e.g., belief in black magic or djinns). Assessors also need to focus on engagement with the interviewee, since issues with mistrust (arising from paranoia, traumatic life histories, previous invalidating experiences with professionals, or histories of coercive treatment) can obstruct this. The differing explanatory models that many people with psychotic disorders and those in manic phases of bipolar disorders hold regarding their experiences (e.g., experiencing unusual beliefs as reality) may mean that assessment using purely a symptom or pathology-based model can be challenging. Therapeutic manuals (Fowler, Garety, & Kuipers, 1995; Morrison et al., 2003) provide resources to draw on in addressing the complexities of engaging this population.

ASSESSMENT TO CATEGORIZE

Differential Diagnosis

Kraepelin's (1898) distinction between schizophrenia-related and bipolar disorders is one of the oldest in psychiatry. Yet, in practice, psychotic and bipolar disorders are heterogeneous in their presentations and have much symptom overlap, including change between diagnoses over time. A common contemporary view is that the experiences of people with psychotic or bipolar disorders occur both on a continuum with each other (Craddock & Owen, 2010) and on continua with experiences in nonclinical populations (Johns & van Os, 2001). Indeed, the psychotic and bipolar disorders articulated in the fifth edition of the *Diagnostic and Statistical Manual of Mental Disorders* (DSM-5; American Psychiatric Association, 2013) and the International Classification of Diseases

(ICD-10; World Health Organization, 1992) may be better thought of as an overlapping spectrum of syndromes rather than distinct disease entities, with their boundaries defined in pragmatic but relatively arbitrary terms. As such, they provide categorizations of symptoms and their course that are primarily descriptive: useful for some purposes but not of major importance in treatment planning. In Carl's case, establishing a diagnosis of schizoaffective disorder highlights the presence of both psychotic and mood features but would not in itself provide much detail to help us develop a treatment plan.

Nonetheless, diagnostic assessment is often required in many clinical and research contexts. In clinical practice, diagnosis is usually based on a comprehensive psychiatric interview of symptoms and their course, with reference to DSM-5 or ICD-10. When a more robust approach is required, such as for research, structured clinical interviews are available. Widely used are the Structured Clinical Interview for DSM (SCID; First et al., 2015) and Mini International Neuropsychiatric Interview (MINI; Sheehan et al., 1998), with current versions (the SCID-5 and MINI 7.0) using DSM-5 criteria. In addition, there are diagnostic interviews that have a more specific focus on psychotic and bipolar disorders. The Schedule for Affective Disorders and Schizophrenia (Endicott & Spitzer, 1978) has a specific focus on the differential diagnosis of mood and psychotic disorders. The Diagnostic Interview for Psychotic Disorders (Castle et al., 2006) is a comprehensive interview schedule for the diagnosis of psychotic disorders.

The Identification and Categorization of Those at Risk of Developing Psychotic and Bipolar Disorders

Over the past two decades, there has been extensive interest in using the prodromal clinical syndrome to indicate increased risk of developing a psychotic disorder. Semi-structured interviews can assist in the classification of at risk mental states, the most commonly used being the Comprehensive Assessment of At Risk Mental States (Yung et al., 2005), the Structured Interview of Psychosis-Risk Syndromes (Miller et al., 2003), and the Schizophrenia Proneness Instrument – Adult version (Schultze-Lutter, Addington, & Ruhrmann, 2007). Assessors need to be clear about the rationale for using these instruments and potential adverse implications of being identified as "at risk" of psychosis, since approximately 70 percent of those identified as "at risk" will not go on to develop a psychotic disorder in the next three years (Fusar-Poli, Bonoldi, & Yung, 2012).

Noncredible Reporting

Although rare, noncredible reporting (feigning, exaggerating, or downplaying symptoms) can occur in response to external incentives (e.g., in forensic settings, disability or compensation claims and discharge planning from inpatient stays). Assessors should be aware of signs of noncredible reporting such as mismatches between reported symptoms and behavior, reporting of rare symptoms or symptom combinations, or indiscriminant symptom endorsement. In instances where noncredible reporting is suspected, schedules such as the Structured Interview of Reported Symptoms (SIRS; Rogers, Bagby, & Dickens, 1992) and scales of the extensively researched Minnesota Multiphasic Personality Inventory-2-Restructured Form (Ben-Porath & Tellegen, 2008/2011) can be utilized. The SIRS is generally considered to be the "gold standard" in assessing noncredible reporting, showing sensitivity of 0.74 and specificity of 0.89 (Green & Rosenfeld, 2011) and the revised SIRS-2 (Rogers, Sewell, & Gillard, 2010) showing higher specificity but decreased sensitivity (Green, Rosenfeld, & Belfi, 2013). Further research is needed into valid ways to formally assess noncredible reporting in this population.

ASSESSMENT TO QUANTIFY PROGRESS OR SEVERITY

There has been much debate around the conceptualization of meaningful outcomes for psychotic or bipolar disorders. Commonly, researchers and clinicians have focused on symptom remission or reduced severity as primary outcomes. Also of importance, however, is the impact of symptoms on an individual's ability to function and lead a meaningful and fulfilling life. The recovery movement, which has been informed by people with lived experience of severe mental health difficulties, has emphasized the importance of functional and personal recovery, in which the focus has shifted to the extent to which an individual is able to lead a contributing and meaningful life, despite any ongoing symptoms. In this section, we outline the most common outcomes of interest for psychotic and bipolar disorders, across both symptomatic outcomes (Table 26.1), and other indices of recovery (Table 26.2).

Measures of Overall Psychopathology

The most commonly used measures of overall symptom severity are the Positive and Negative Syndrome Scale (PANSS; Kay, Fiszbein, & Opler, 1987) and the Brief Psychiatric Rating Scale (BPRS; Lukoff, Nuechterlein, & Ventura, 1986). Although originally based on the classic "positive-negative" symptom distinction, factor analyses of the PANSS and BPRS have suggested that there is a more complex structure of psychotic disorders, with a five-factor solution providing the best fit: positive, negative, excited/activation, dysphoric/depressed, and disorganized (Marder, Davis, & Chouinard, 1997; Picardi et al., 2012). This dimensional approach has gained momentum as a model for measuring severity of symptoms in psychosis and extending conceptually from schizophrenia-related to mood disorders. As a result, there have also now been many measures developed that specifically measure these dimensions, or

Table 26.1 Common measures in the dimensional assessment of psychotic and bipolar disorders

Instrument	Overview	Comments
Measures of overall psychopathology		
Positive and Negative Symptom Scales (PANSS) (Kay et al., 1987)	30-item scale with a structured clinical interview (SCI-PANSS). Assesses positive and negative symptoms and general psychopathology in schizophrenia	40–50 minutes to administer. 14 PANSS items require input from an informant who is familiar with the interviewee. Consensus recommendations state that the PANSS negative factor derived from factor analyses be used over the original PANSS negative factor when measuring negative symptoms (Marder et al., 2011)
The Brief Psychiatric Rating Scales (BPRS) (Lukoff et al., 1986)	24-item scale with a semi-structured interview. Assesses symptom severity in people with serious psychiatric disorders, particularly schizophrenia	Briefer and easier to administer than the PANSS but yields less detailed information, particularly for negative symptoms. Predominantly used in psychosis populations, but has been used in populations with bipolar disorder (Picardi et al., 2008)
Positive symptoms (hallucinations and delusions)		
Scale for the Assessment of Positive Symptoms (SAPS) (Andreasen, 1984b)	34-item clinician-rated measure of presence and severity of positive symptoms. Items relate to hallucinations, delusions, bizarre behavior, and positive formal thought disorder	30 minutes to administer. Designed for use in conjunction with the SANS (see below)
The Psychotic Symptoms Rating Scale (PSYRATS) (Haddock et al., 1999)	Brief, clinician-administered scale. Quantifies the severity of empirically derived dimensions of hallucinations and delusions	Comprehensive, multidimensional measure of auditory hallucinations and delusions. Commonly used in trials of psychological therapies. Factor analysis suggests the PSYRATS rates the severity of four factors for auditory hallucinations and two factors for delusions (Woodward et al., 2014)
Questionnaire for Psychotic Experiences (QPE) (Still under development and validation; see qpeinterview.com)	Newly developed assessment tool. Assesses characteristics and severity of hallucinations and delusions	Assesses hallucinations in all sensory modalities
The Maudsley Assessment of Delusions Scale (MADS) (Buchanan et al., 1993)	Standardized interview assessing the phenomenology of delusional beliefs	Eight dimensions assessed: conviction, belief maintenance, affect, action, idiosyncrasy, preoccupation, systematization, and insight
The Mental Health Research Institute Unusual Perceptions Schedule (MUPS) (Carter et al., 1995)	Semi-structured interview assessing the respondent's experience of auditory hallucinations	In-depth focus on phenomenology
Negative symptoms (blunted affect, alogia, asociality, anhedonia, and avolition)		
Scale for the Assessment of Negative Symptoms (SANS) (Andreasen, 1984a)	25-item clinician-rated scale. Assesses negative symptoms. Items relate to: affective blunting, alogia, avolition, anhedonia, and attention	For use in conjunction with the SAPS (above). Includes items relating to cognitive functioning. Does not assess internal experiences
Negative Symptoms Assessment-16/4 (NAS-16/NSA-4) (Alphs et al., 1989)	16 item semi-structured interview. Assesses the negative syndrome of Schizophrenia. Includes: Communication, emotion/affect, social	Relies on behavioral markers and does not assess internal experiences. Measures reductions in sense of purpose and global severity of negative

Continued

Table 26.1 (cont.)

Instrument	Overview	Comments
	involvement, motivation and retardation. The NSA-4 is a shorter version	symptoms more adequately than the SANS or PANSS
Clinical Assessment Interview for Negative Symptoms (CAINS) (Kring et al., 2013)	13-item clinician-rated assessment. Provides an in-depth assessment of the five consensus negative symptom domains. Has two subscales: motivational/pleasure and expression	Developed following a National Institute of Mental Health consensus meeting and thought to address many of the shortcomings of the SANS, NSA-16 and PANSS
Brief Negative Symptom Scale (BNSS) (Kirkpatrick et al., 2011)	13-item clinician-rated instrument specifically for use in clinical trials. Concisely measures the five consensus negative symptom domains (plus distress)	As above. 15 minutes administration time
Disorganization (formal thought disorder)		
Communication Disturbances Index (CDI) (Docherty, DeRosa, & Andreasen, 1996)	Clinician-rated index of failures in communication of meaning from speaker to listener. Used to rate responses to a 10-minute open-ended interview	Differs from other measures of thought disorder due to specific focus on communication failures
Scale for the Assessment of Thought, Language, and Communication (TLC) (Andreasen, 1986)	Comprehensive rating scale for formal thought disorder based on a 45-minute open-ended interview. Defines and measures 18 types of thought disorder	Lengthy to administer. Does not include any rating of subjective experiences
Thought and Language Index (TLI) (Liddle et al., 2002)	Clinician-rated index of thought disorder based on eight 1-minute speech samples in response to eight pictures from the Thematic Apperception Test	Based on the Thought Disorder Index, but briefer to administer
Thought Disorder Index (TDI) (Johnston & Holzman, 1979)	Clinician-rated index of thought disorder. Assesses speech during two standardized tasks; Rorschach Inkblots and the Wechsler Adult Intelligence Scale. Includes 23 categories of thought disorder	Detects subtler differences than the TLC, but is time consuming to administer and requires significant training
Excitement/activation (mania)		
Young Mania Rating Scale (YMRS) (Young et al., 1978)	11-item scale for manic symptoms, rated by a trained clinician based on a semi-structured interview and observations during the interview	15–30 minute administration time. Widely used in treatment trials to measure mania. Covers core symptoms of a manic phase but not all DSM criteria for mania
Bech-Rafaelsen Mania Rating Scale (MAS) (Bech et al., 1979)	11-item clinician-rated measure of the severity of manic states. Covers the classic symptoms of mania	15–30 minute administration time. Widely used as an outcome measure for manic symptoms in treatment trials. Does not assess insight or appearance (as in YMRS)
Altman Self-Rating Mania Scale (ASRM) (Altman et al., 1997)	5-item self-report instrument. Measures mood, self-confidence, sleep disturbance, speech and activity levels	Brief to administer but less coverage of manic symptoms than other scales
Self-Report Manic Inventory (SRMI) (Braunig, Shugar, & Kruger, 1996)		May have limited use in inpatient settings due to item content

Continued

Table 26.1 (cont.)

Instrument	Overview	Comments
	47-item self-report measure designed as a diagnostic and severity scale for bipolar disorder	
Depression The Calgary Depression Scale for Schizophrenia (CDSS) (Addington et al., 1993)	9-item observer rated scale with a semi-structured interview. Assesses depressive symptoms separate from positive and negative symptoms, and extra-pyramidal medication side effects in people with schizophrenia	Addresses overlap between depression and negative symptoms/extra-pyramidal side effects
Bipolar Depression Rating Scale (BDRS) (Berk et al., 2007)	20-item clinician-administered scale. Measures the severity of depressive symptoms in bipolar depression	Rates symptoms characteristic of bipolar depression such as mixed features, hypersomnia, and increased appetite that are not picked up in standard depression measures

Table 26.2 Measures used in the assessment of other outcome domains

Instrument	Overview	Comments
Functioning UCSD Performance-Based Skills Assessment (UPSA) (Patterson et al., 2001)	Performance-based measure of capacity to perform everyday activities in people with severe mental health difficulties. Assesses household chores, communication, finance, transportation, and planning recreational activities	30 minutes administration time. Predictive of an individual's ability to live independently
Test of Adaptive Behavior in Schizophrenia (TABS) (Velligan et al., 2007)	Performance-based measure of adaptive functioning in populations with schizophrenia. Assesses shopping, work, and identifying products needed for daily functioning	Assesses initiation and problem identification, which may be particularly pertinent in schizophrenia populations
Independent Living Skills Survey (ILSS) (Wallace et al., 2000)	Informant (103 items) or self-rated (61 items) measure. Assesses performance of basic community living skills in those with severe mental health difficulties. Respondents are asked how often certain behaviors have occurred in the last month	Also has an interview format for people with literacy issues
Social Functioning Scale (SFS) (Birchwood et al., 1990)	Interview-based assessment for people with schizophrenia. Assesses seven areas of functioning: social engagement, interpersonal behavior, pro social activities, recreation, independence and employment	Frequently used in trials of psychosocial treatments for psychosis
Social Skills Performance Assessment (SSPA) (Patterson et al., 2001)	Brief role-play based assessment. Assesses social skills in people with schizophrenia	12-minute administration time

Continued

Table 26.2 (cont.)

Instrument	Overview	Comments
Quality of life		
Quality of Life in Bipolar Disorder (QoL.BD) (Michalak & Murray, 2010)	56-item measure of quality of life in bipolar disorder. Measures 12 domains	Also has a brief 12-item version. Cannot be used to compare quality of life across disorders
Manchester Short Assessment of Quality of Life (MANSA) (Priebe et al., 1999)	16-item interview focusing on subjective quality of life in people with severe mental health difficulties. Includes 12 life domains	15-minute administration time. Widely used in clinical trials in psychosis populations
Recovery		
Questionnaire about the Process of Recovery (QPR) (Neil et al., 2009)	22-item self-report measure of personal recovery. Includes two subscales: intrapersonal and interpersonal	Developed in collaboration with users of mental health services. Best aligned with domains of CHIME meta-synthesis of consumer views of recovery (Williams et al., 2015). Brief version has superior reliability.
Recovery Assessment Scale (RAS) (Corrigan et al., 1999)	41-item self-report measure assesses five domains: personal confidence and hope, willingness to ask for help, goal orientation, reliance on others, and domination by symptoms	Developed by users of mental health services through analysis of recovery stories. Widely used in mental health research

specific symptoms within each dimension. Table 26.1 outlines the most common measures used in each symptom dimension.

Positive Symptoms

Positive symptoms are generally assessed using interviewer-rated assessments. Issues of insight and engagement discussed under "Key Issues to Consider in Preparation for an Assessment" are particularly pertinent in assessing positive symptoms. Assessors need to have skill in gathering information in a way that provides enough information to make a rating but is also not invalidating of the person's experiences. Common measures of positive symptoms are shown in Table 26.1.

Negative Symptoms

The assessment and treatment of negative symptoms has been relatively neglected in comparison to positive symptoms; however, negative symptoms are strongly related to disability and functioning and are therefore an important treatment target and assessment domain. The robust assessment of negative symptoms is crucial to improving treatments.

A consensus review of measures of negative symptoms recommended the use of the Negative Symptoms Assessment-16 (Alphs et al., 1989), Scale for the Assessment of Negative Symptoms (Andreasen, 1984a), and subscales of the PANSS as the most reliable and valid measures of negative symptoms (Marder et al., 2011). Two newer measures, the Clinical Assessment Interview for Negative Symptoms (CAINS; Kring et al., 2013) and the Brief Negative Symptom Scale (BNSS; Kirkpatrick et al., 2011) have been developed in order to overcome some of the shortcomings of these earlier measures, improving the distinction between negative symptoms and other related constructs, such as neurocognitive dysfunction and disorganization, and focusing more on assessing internal experiences rather than behaviors. The BNSS and CAINS are also designed to reflect a two-factor conceptualization of negative symptoms (avolition/amotivation and expression) that has consistently emerged from research in the area.

Disorganization

Disorganization, characterized primarily by formal thought disorder (disorganized thinking evidenced by disruptions to the form or amount of speech), is a feature of both psychotic and bipolar disorders (generally more persistent and severe in psychotic disorders). Persisting thought disorder is a strong predictor of poor outcomes. In clinical practice, formal thought disorder can be assessed by engaging in open-ended conversation and observing responses. However, the presentation of formal thought disorder can be dependent on the content and form of a clinical interview; therefore a number of standardized assessments have been developed (see Table 26.1). The Scale for the Assessment of Thought, Language, and Communication has been most widely used and represents a comprehensive measure with good discriminant validity and reliability (Andreasen, 1986).

Mania

While many people experiencing elevated mood in the form of hypomania are aware of their changed mood, often those with full-blown mania lose touch with reality and are less able to reflect on their internal state. Many assessments therefore rely on clinician-rated interviews. The Young Mania Rating Scale in particular has been used extensively and shows good reliability and sensitivity to change (Young et al., 1978) Despite issues with insight, there are also some self-report measures with strong psychometric properties (see Table 26.1). The Altman Self-Rating Mania Scale (Altman et al., 1997) has been found to have superior psychometric properties, including good sensitivity to change and 93 percent sensitivity in identifying acute mania (Altman et al., 2001). An important consideration is the fluctuating nature of mania and hypomania. Assessment techniques that provide continuous monitoring are therefore useful to give a longitudinal picture of the pattern of symptoms over a period of time.

Depression

Depressive episodes are a core experience of bipolar disorder and there is evidence to suggest that there are symptomatic differences between people with unipolar depression and those with bipolar depression (Ghaemi et al., 2008). Those with bipolar depression are more likely to experience hypersomnia, increased appetite, psychomotor changes, psychotic symptoms or pathological guilt. General depression measures have been widely used in bipolar disorder populations; however, they can fail to capture these important "signature" aspects of bipolar depression. The Bipolar Depression Rating Scale is designed specifically to assess characteristic features of bipolar depression and has good internal and concurrent validity as well as moderate to high inter-rater reliability (Berk et al., 2007).

Depression is also common in psychotic disorders and is related to poor outcomes and increased risk of suicide. Generic measures of depression include items that overlap with negative symptoms and medication side effects (lack of energy, anhedonia, and psychomotor retardation). Specific measures of depression in psychotic disorders, such as the depression items in the PANSS and the Calgary Depression Scale for Schizophrenia (Addington et al., 1993), focus specifically on core symptoms of depression with less overlap.

Relapse

Psychotic and bipolar disorders have a fluctuating course, with symptoms and distress relapsing and remitting over periods of time. Treatments aim to reduce symptoms and distress but also to reduce future relapses of symptoms. As such, assessments tracking treatment outcomes will often be concerned with monitoring relapse rates. This can be done using diagnostic assessments (assessing whether the client's symptoms have reached diagnostic thresholds at certain time-points) or using symptom severity measures (with predetermined cutoffs to determine a relapse of symptoms).

Functioning

Psychotic and bipolar disorders can have a significant impact on people's ability to function. Though "normal" functioning is difficult to define, it is generally conceptualized as an individual's ability to perform daily activities required for maintaining themselves in the "real world" (encompassing daily living skills and social and occupational skills). Improvements in symptoms do not directly relate to improvements in functioning and therefore separate assessment of functioning is necessary to comprehensively capture treatment outcomes. Common measures of different areas of functioning are shown in Table 26.2.

Quality of Life

Quality of life has been an outcome of interest in psychiatric research for several decades; however, quality of life remains a relatively poorly defined construct. Broadly, quality of life as referred to in health literature is a multidimensional concept relating to the impact of a disease and treatment on domains of physical, psychological, and social functioning and the resulting degree of satisfaction with these areas. Generic measures of health-related quality of life have been used in populations with psychotic and bipolar disorders; however, there is some argument for the use of disorder-specific measures such as the Quality of Life in Bipolar Disorder (Michalak & Murray, 2010) and the Manchester Short Assessment of Quality of Life (Priebe, Huxley, Knight, & Evans, 1999) (shown in Table 26.2), both of which have adequate-to-good psychometric properties and are more sensitive to change in their specific target population than generic measures of quality of life.

PERSONAL RECOVERY

Increasing consumer involvement has led to an increased emphasis on outcomes that have personal meaning to people experiencing mental health difficulties. In this framework, symptom reduction or remission is not always central to recovery; rather, recovery is seen as a personal, unique process of living a meaningful and contributing life, regardless of symptoms and disability (Anthony, 1993). The "CHIME" framework for personal recovery (Leamy et al., 2011) provides a conceptual framework for personal recovery, identifying connectedness, hope, identity, meaning, and empowerment as central concepts. Measures developed to capture these constructs are shown in Table 26.2.

New Technologies in Symptom Measurement

Symptoms of psychotic and bipolar disorders are dynamic and show significant variability over time and within different contexts. People are generally poor at providing accurate retrospective estimates of internal experiences and this may be particularly challenging this population. Ecological Momentary Assessment (EMA) involves real-time sampling of a person's experiences or symptoms in the context of their daily life, providing ecological validity and reducing recall bias. Respondents are prompted several times a day for a number of days to report on their experiences. There are several smartphone applications that provide simple platforms for administering EMA assessments. Access to smartphones is widespread in this population and EMA is an acceptable and feasible assessment method (Bell et al., 2017).

New technologies, such as actigraphy (Bullock, Judd, & Murray, 2014) and voice monitoring (Faurholt-Jepsen et al., 2016) are also being developed to assess relapse in bipolar disorder; however, these are not yet ready for clinical use.

ASSESSMENT TO FORMULATE

The impact of psychotic and bipolar disorders is pervasive and complex. As can be seen from Carl's story, symptoms do not occur in isolation but impact on and are impacted by their intrapersonal, interpersonal, and environmental context. Diagnostic categories can miss this important information, which is key for engagement and providing an effective and meaningful intervention.

An assessment to guide a formulation will involve an in-depth exploration of an individual's strengths and difficulties and how these experiences have evolved over time and play out in the larger context of their everyday life. It is particularly important to assess the impact that symptoms are having on an individual's life in terms of the functional impact and the levels of distress experienced. In the case of bipolar and psychotic disorders, assessment for formulation is likely to include a full exploration of mood fluctuations and of common psychotic experiences. In addition, there are several assessment domains that are particularly pertinent.

Personal History (Including Trauma and Adversity)

Early childhood relationships have an impact on attachment styles, emotion regulation skills, and schematic beliefs, all of which are fundamental to understanding an individual's symptoms and how they relate to and cope with these experiences. Traumatic or adverse childhood experiences are common in people living with psychotic and bipolar disorders (Palmier-Claus et al., 2016; Varese et al., 2012). An assessment of trauma history can be undertaken using inventories used to assess trauma and childhood adversity in other populations. It is important to stress that information need only be given in as much detail as the person is comfortable and to have a plan or protocol in place to acknowledge and manage any disclosures.

Psychological Factors

Psychotic symptoms and mood fluctuations are inextricably linked to the psychological and behavioral context in which they occur. A few decades of research into psychological approaches to treating psychotic and bipolar disorders has highlighted the importance of beliefs about symptoms and patterns of responding to them.

Dynamic assessment of beliefs and behavioral responses can be conducted using classic cognitive behavioral therapy diaries to capture in-the-moment appraisals and responses to psychotic symptoms or mood changes (Fowler et al., 1995; Morrison et al., 2003).

There are also a number of more "static" measures of key beliefs and responses to symptoms. In the case of voice-hearing experiences (otherwise known as auditory verbal hallucinations), there are well-validated measures capturing key psychological constructs. For example, see the Beliefs about Voices Questionnaire – Revised (Chadwick, Lees, & Birchwood, 2000), the Voice Power Differential Scale (Birchwood et al., 2000) the Voice and You Scale (Hayward et al., 2008), and the Voices Acceptance and Action Scale (Shawyer et al., 2007).

Family and Social Context

The social networks of people living with psychotic and bipolar disorders influence quality of life and treatment outcomes. A review by Siette, Gulea, and Priebe (2015) found the Interview Schedule for Social Interaction (Henderson et al., 1980) and the Social Network Schedule (Dunn et al., 1990) to be the most commonly used measures in psychosis populations.

Family environment is also distinctly important. In particular, expressed emotion (EE) in the form of hostile or critical comments and emotional overinvolvement is associated with relapse and worse outcomes (Butzlaff & Hooley, 1998). The "gold standard" for measuring EE is the Camberwell Family Interview (Leff & Vaughn, 1985).

Biological Rhythms

Circadian rhythm and sleep disruptions are known to interact with mood states. In the case of bipolar disorders, these biological rhythms have a role in the etiology and maintenance of problematic mood fluctuations (Murray & Harvey, 2010). Sleep/wake patterns can be assessed through self-report sleep diaries. Actigraphy (measuring movement by wearable sensor) can provide an objective measurement of sleep/wake cycles.

Neurocognitive Assessment

Impairments in cognition are prominent in psychotic disorders and also present in bipolar disorders, though to a lesser degree (Bora, 2016). A wide range of cognitive domains are implicated, including impairments in attention, executive function, episodic memory, working memory, and processing speed. The MATRICS Consensus Cognitive Battery (Marder & Fenton, 2004) is a comprehensive assessment including key cognitive domains relevant to schizophrenia. Several briefer batteries are also widely used, including the Brief Assessment of Cognition in Schizophrenia/Affective Disorders (Keefe et al., 2004), and the Brief Cognitive Assessment (Velligan et al., 2004).

Risk

In some cases, people who experience psychotic and bipolar disorders can present elevated levels of risk to themselves and others. Usual approaches to risk assessment should be undertaken as part of any assessment. Of particular pertinence to this population are compliance with command hallucinations to harm self or others, intent to act on persecutory beliefs, risk-taking in the context of hypomanic or manic symptoms, and suicidal behaviors in the context of depressive symptoms.

CONCLUSION

An assessment of someone like Carl who may be experiencing symptoms of psychotic or bipolar disorders requires forethought and planning. Valid assessments are built on thoughtful and sensitive engagement with interviewees. Assessors need to be clear about the rationale, aims, and scope of their assessment in order to select appropriate assessment instruments. Generally, a holistic approach to assessment is likely to provide the most meaningful information.

REFERENCES

Addington, D., Addington, J., & Maticka-Tyndale, E. (1993). Assessing depression in schizophrenia: the Calgary Depression Scale. *British Journal of Psychiatry*(*22*), 39–44.

Alphs, L. D., Summerfelt, A., Lann, H., & Muller, R. J. (1989). The negative symptom assessment: A new instrument to assess negative symptoms of schizophrenia. *Psychopharmacology Bulletin*, *25*(2), 159–163.

Altman, E., Hedeker, D., Peterson, J. L., & Davis, J. M. (2001). A comparative evaluation of three self-rating scales for acute mania. *Biological Psychiatry*, *50*(6), 468–471.

Altman, E. G., Hedeker, D., Peterson, J. L., & Davis, J. M. (1997). The Altman Self-Rating Mania Scale. *Biological Psychiatry*, *42* (10), 948–955. doi:10.1016/S0006-3223(96)00548-3

American Psychiatric Association. (2013). *Diagnostic and statistical manual of mental disorders* (5th ed.). Arlington, VA: American Psychiatric Association.

Andreasen, N. C. (1984a). *Scale for the Assessment of Negative Symtoms (SANS)*. Iowa City: University of Iowa.

Andreasen, N. C. (1984b). *Scale for the Assessment of Positive Symptoms (SAPS)*. Iowa City: University of Iowa.

Andreasen, N. C. (1986). Scale for the assessment of thought, language, and communication (TLC). *Schizophrenia Bulletin*, *12*(3), 473–482.

Anthony, W. A. (1993). The guiding vision of the mental health service system in the 1990s. . *Psychosocial Rehabilitation*, *16*(4), 11.

Bech, P., Bolwig, T. G., Kramp, P., & Rafaelsen, O. J. (1979). The Bech-Rafaelsen Mania Scale and the Hamilton Depression Scale. *Acta Psychiatrica Scandinavia*, *59*(4), 420–430.

Bell, I. H., Lim, M. H., Rossell, S. L., & Thomas, N. (2017). Ecological momentary assessment and intervention in the treatment of psychotic disorders: A systematic review. *Psychiatric Services*, *68*(11), 1172–1181. doi:10.1176/appi.ps.201600523

Ben-Porath, Y. S., & Tellegen, A. M. (2008/2011). *MMPI-2-RF: Manual for administration, scoring and interpretation*. Minneapolis: University of Minnesota Press.

Berk, M., Malhi, G. S., Cahill, C., Carman, A. C., Hadzi-Pavlovic, D., Hawkins, M. T., ... & Mitchell, P. B. (2007). The Bipolar Depression Rating Scale (BDRS): Its development, validation and utility. *Bipolar Disorders*, *9*(6), 571–579. doi:10.1111/j.1399-5618.2007.00536.x

Birchwood, M., Meaden, A., Trower, P., Gilbert, P., & Plaistow, J. (2000). The power and omnipotence of voices: Subordination and entrapment by voices and significant others. *Psychological Medicine*, *30*(2), 337–344.

Birchwood, M., Smith, J., Cochrane, R., Wetton, S., & Copestake, S. (1990). The Social Functioning Scale: The development and validation of a new scale of social adjustment for use in family intervention programmes with schizophrenic patients. *British Journal of Psychiatry*, *157*, 853–859.

Bora, E. (2016). Differences in cognitive impairment between schizophrenia and bipolar disorder: Considering the role of heterogeneity. *Psychiatry and Clinical Neurosciences*, *70*(10), 424–433. doi:10.1111/pcn.12410

Braunig, P., Shugar, G., & Kruger, S. (1996). An investigation of the Self-Report Manic Inventory as a diagnostic and severity scale for mania. *Comprehensive Psychiatry*, *37*(1), 52–55.

Buchanan, A., Reed, A., Wessely, S., Garety, P., Taylor, P., Grubin, D., & Dunn, G. (1993). Acting on delusions. II: The phenomenological correlates of acting on delusions. *British Journal of Psychiatry*, *163*, 77–81.

Bullock, B., Judd, F. K., & Murray, G. (2014). *Using actigraphy to monitor sleep-wake patterns in bipolar disorder – A case study* (Vol. 253).

Butzlaff, R. L., & Hooley, J. M. (1998). Expressed emotion and psychiatric relapse: A meta-analysis. *Archives of General Psychiatry*, *55*(6), 547–552.

Carter, D. M., Mackinnon, A., Howard, S., Zeegers, T., & Copolov, D. L. (1995). The development and reliability of the Mental Health Research Institute Unusual Perceptions Schedule (MUPS): An instrument to record auditory hallucinatory experience. *Schizophrenia Research*, *16*(2), 157–165.

Castle, D. J., Jablensky, A., McGrath, J. J., Carr, V., Morgan, V., Waterreus, A., ... & Farmer, A. (2006). The diagnostic interview for psychoses (DIP): Development, reliability and applications. *Psychological Medicine*, *36*(1), 69–80. doi:10.1017/S0033291705005969

Chadwick, P., Lees, S., & Birchwood, M. A. X. (2000). The revised Beliefs About Voices Questionnaire (BAVQ-R). *The British Journal of Psychiatry*, *177*(3), 229.

Corrigan, P. W., Giffort, D., Rashid, F., Leary, M., & Okeke, I. (1999). Recovery as a psychological construct. *Community Mental Health Journal*, *35*(3), 231–239.

Craddock, N., & Owen, M. J. (2010). The Kraepelinian dichotomy – going, going ... but still not gone. *British Journal of Psychiatry*, *196*(2), 92–95. doi:10.1192/bjp.bp.109.073429

Docherty, N. M., DeRosa, M., & Andreasen, N. C. (1996). Communication disturbances in schizophrenia and mania. *Archives of General Psychiatry*, *53*(4), 358–364.

Dunn, M., O'Driscoll, C., Dayson, D., Wills, W., & Leff, J. (1990). The TAPS Project. 4: An observational study of the social life of long-stay patients. *British Journal of Psychiatry*, *157*, 842–848, 852.

Endicott, J., & Spitzer, R. L. (1978). A diagnostic interview: The schedule for affective disorders and schizophrenia. *Archives of General Psychiatry*, *35*(7), 837–844.

Faurholt-Jepsen, M., Busk, J., Frost, M., Vinberg, M., Christensen, E. M., Winther, O., ... & Kessing, L. V. (2016). Voice analysis as an objective state marker in bipolar disorder. *Translational Psychiatry*, *6*, e856. doi:10.1038/tp.2016.123

First, M. B., Williams, J. B. W., Karg, R. S., & Spitzer, R. L. (2015). *Structured Clinical Interview for DSM-5 (SCID for DSM-5)*. Arlington, VA: American Psychiatric Association.

Fowler, D., Garety, P., & Kuipers, E. (1995). *Cognitive-behaviour therapy for psychosis: Theory and practice*. Chichester: Wiley.

Fusar-Poli, P., Bonoldi, I., & Yung, A. R. (2012). Predicting psychosis: Meta-analysis of transition outcomes in individuals at high clinical risk. *Archives of General Psychiatry*, *69*(3), 220–229. doi:10.1001/archgenpsychiatry.2011.1472

Ghaemi, S. N., Bauer, M., Cassidy, F., Malhi, G. S., Mitchell, P., Phelps, J., ... & Force, I. D. G. T. (2008). Diagnostic guidelines for bipolar disorder: A summary of the International Society for Bipolar Disorders Diagnostic Guidelines Task Force Report. *Bipolar Disorders*, *10*(1 Pt 2), 117–128. doi:10.1111/j.1399-5618.2007.00556.x

Green, D., & Rosenfeld, B. (2011). Evaluating the gold standard: A review and meta-analysis of the Structured Interview of Reported Symptoms. *Psychological Assessment*, *23*(1), 95–107. doi:10.1037/a0021149

Green, D., Rosenfeld, B., & Belfi, B. (2013). New and improved? A comparison of the original and revised versions of the structured interview of reported symptoms. *Assessment*, *20*(2), 210–218. doi:10.1177/1073191112464389

Haddock, G., McCarron, J., Tarrier, N., & Faragher, E. B. (1999). Scales to measure dimensions of hallucinations and delusions: The psychotic symptom rating scales (PSYRATS). *Psychological Medicine*, *29*(4), 879–889.

Hayward, M., Denney, J., Vaughan, S., & Fowler, D. (2008). The voice and you: Development and psychometric evaluation of a measure of relationships with voices. *Clinical Psychology and Psychotherapy*, *15*(1), 45–52. doi:10.1002/cpp.561

Henderson, S., Duncan-Jones, P., Byrne, D. G., & Scott, R. (1980). Measuring social relationships: The Interview Schedule for Social Interaction. *Psychological Medicine*, *10*(4), 723–734.

Johns, L. C., & van Os, J. (2001). The continuity of psychotic experiences in the general population. *Clinical Psychology Review*, *21*(8), 1125–1141.

Johnston, M. H., & Holzman, P. S. (1979). *Assessing schizophrenic thinking*. San Francisco: Jossey-Bass.

Kay, S. R., Fiszbein, A., & Opler, L. A. (1987). The positive and negative syndrome scale (PANSS) for schizophrenia. *Schizophrenia Bulletin*, *13*(2), 261–276.

Keefe, R. S., Goldberg, T. E., Harvey, P. D., Gold, J. M., Poe, M. P., & Coughenour, L. (2004). The Brief Assessment of Cognition in Schizophrenia: reliability, sensitivity, and comparison with a standard neurocognitive battery. *Schizophrenia Research*, *68*(2–3), 283–297. doi:10.1016/j.schres.2003.09.011

Kirkpatrick, B., Strauss, G. P., Nguyen, L., Fischer, B. A., Daniel, D. G., Cienfuegos, A., & Marder, S. R. (2011). The brief negative symptom scale: Psychometric properties. *Schizophrenia Bulletin*, *37*(2), 300–305. doi:10.1093/schbul/sbq059

Kraepelin, E. (1989). *Diagnose und Prognose der Dementia Praecox*. Heidelberg.

Kring, A. M., Gur, R. E., Blanchard, J. J., Horan, W. P., & Reise, S. P. (2013). The Clinical Assessment Interview for Negative Symptoms (CAINS): Final development and validation. *American Journal of Psychiatry*, *170*(2), 165–172. doi:10.1176/appi.ajp.2012.12010109

Leamy, M., Bird, V., Le Boutillier, C., Williams, J., & Slade, M. (2011). Conceptual framework for personal recovery in mental health: Systematic review and narrative synthesis. *British Journal of Psychiatry*, *199*(6), 445–452. doi:10.1192/bjp.bp.110.083733

Leff, J., & Vaughn, C. E. (1985). *Expressed emotion in families*. New York: Guildford Press.

Liddle, P. F., Ngan, E. T., Caissie, S. L., Anderson, C. M., Bates, A. T., Quested, D. J., ... & Weg, R. (2002). Thought and Language Index: An instrument for assessing thought and language in schizophrenia. *British Journal of Psychiatry*, *181*, 326–330.

Lukoff, D., Nuechterlein, K. H., & Ventura, J. (1986). Manual for expanded Brief Psychiatric Rating Scale. *Schizophrenia Bulletin*, *12*, 594–602.

Marder, S. R., Daniel, D. G., Alphs, L., Awad, A. G., & Keefe, R. S. (2011). Methodological issues in negative symptom trials. *Schizophrenia Bulletin*, *37*(2), 250–254. doi:10.1093/schbul/sbq161

Marder, S. R., Davis, J. M., & Chouinard, G. (1997). The effects of risperidone on the five dimensions of schizophrenia derived by factor analysis: Combined results of the North American trials. *Journal of Clinical Psychiatry*, *58*(12), 538–546.

Marder, S. R., & Fenton, W. (2004). Measurement and Treatment Research to Improve Cognition in Schizophrenia: NIMH MATRICS initiative to support the development of agents for improving cognition in schizophrenia. *Schizophrenia Research*, *72*(1), 5–9. doi:10.1016/j.schres.2004.09.010

Michalak, E. E., & Murray, G. (2010). Development of the QoL.BD: A disorder-specific scale to assess quality of life in bipolar disorder. *Bipolar Disorders*, *12*(7), 727–740. doi:10.1111/j.1399-5618.2010.00865.x

Miller, T. J., McGlashan, T. H., Rosen, J. L., Cadenhead, K., Cannon, T., Ventura, J., ... & Woods, S. W. (2003). Prodromal assessment with the structured interview for prodromal syndromes and the scale of prodromal symptoms: Predictive validity, interrater reliability, and training to reliability. *Schizophrenia Bulletin*, *29*(4), 703–715.

Morrison, A. P., Renton, J. C., Dunn, H., Williams, S., & Bentall, R. P. (2003). *Cognitive Therapy for Psychosis: A Formulation-Based Approach*. London: Psychology Press.

Murray, G., & Harvey, A. (2010). Circadian rhythms and sleep in bipolar disorder. *Bipolar Disorders, 12*(5), 459–472. doi:10.1111/j.1399-5618.2010.00843.x

Neil, S. T., Kilbride, M., Pitt, L., Nothard, S., Welford, M., Sellwood, W., & Morrison, A. P. (2009). The questionnaire about the process of recovery (QPR): A measurement tool developed in collaboration with service users. *Psychosis, 1*(2), 145–155. doi:10.1080/17522430902913450

Palmier-Claus, J. E., Berry, K., Bucci, S., Mansell, W., & Varese, F. (2016). Relationship between childhood adversity and bipolar affective disorder: Systematic review and meta-analysis. *British Journal of Psychiatry, 209*(6), 454–459. doi:10.1192/bjp.bp.115.179655

Patterson, T. L., Goldman, S., McKibbin, C. L., Hughs, T., & Jeste, D. V. (2001). UCSD Performance-Based Skills Assessment: Development of a new measure of everyday functioning for severely mentally ill adults. *Schizophrenia Bulletin, 27*(2), 235–245.

Patterson, T. L., Moscona, S., McKibbin, C. L., Davidson, K., & Jeste, D. V. (2001). Social skills performance assessment among older patients with schizophrenia. *Schizophrenia Research, 48* (2–3), 351–360.

Picardi, A., Battisti, F., de Girolamo, G., Morosini, P., Norcio, B., Bracco, R., & Biondi, M. (2008). Symptom structure of acute mania: a factor study of the 24-item Brief Psychiatric Rating Scale in a national sample of patients hospitalized for a manic episode. *Journal of Affective Disorders, 108*(1–2), 183–189. doi:10.1016/j.jad.2007.09.010

Picardi, A., Viroli, C., Tarsitani, L., Miglio, R., de Girolamo, G., Dell'Acqua, G., & Biondi, M. (2012). Heterogeneity and symptom structure of schizophrenia. *Psychiatry Research, 198*(3), 386–394. doi:10.1016/j.psychres.2011.12.051

Priebe, S., Huxley, P., Knight, S., & Evans, S. (1999). Application and results of the Manchester Short Assessment of Quality of Life (MANSA). *International Journal of Social Psychiatry, 45*(1), 7–12. doi:10.1177/002076409904500102

Rogers, R., Bagby, R. M., & Dickens, S. E. (1992). *Structured Interview of reported symptoms*. Lutz, FL.

Rogers, R., Sewell, K. W., & Gillard, N. D. (2010). *SIRS-2: Structured Interview of Reported Symptoms: Professional manual*. Lutz, FL.

Schultze-Lutter, F., Addington, J., & Ruhrmann, S. (2007). *Schizophrenia Proneness Instrument, Adult Version (SPI-A)*. Rome: Fioriti.

Shawyer, F., Ratcliff, K., Mackinnon, A., Farhall, J., Hayes, S. C., & Copolov, D. (2007). The voices acceptance and action scale (VAAS): Pilot data. *Journal of Clinical Psychology, 63*(6), 593–606. doi:10.1002/jclp.20366

Sheehan, D. V., Lecrubier, Y., Sheehan, K. H., Amorim, P., Janavs, J., Weiller, E., ... Dunbar, G. C. (1998). The Mini-International Neuropsychiatric Interview (M.I.N.I.): The development and validation of a structured diagnostic psychiatric interview for DSM-IV and ICD-10. *Journal of Clinical Psychiatry, 59 Suppl 20*, 22–33;quiz 34–57.

Siette, J., Gulea, C., & Priebe, S. (2015). Assessing social networks in patients with psychotic disorders: A systematic review of instruments. *PLoS ONE, 10*(12), e0145250. doi:10.1371/journal.pone.0145250

Varese, F., Smeets, F., Drukker, M., Lieverse, R., Lataster, T., Viechtbauer, W., ... & Bentall, R. P. (2012). Childhood adversities increase the risk of psychosis: A meta-analysis of patient-control, prospective- and cross-sectional cohort studies. *Schizophrenia Bulletin, 38*(4), 661–671. doi:10.1093/schbul/sbs050

Velligan, D. I., Diamond, P., Glahn, D. C., Ritch, J., Maples, N., Castillo, D., & Miller, A. L. (2007). The reliability and validity of the Test of Adaptive Behavior in Schizophrenia (TABS). *Psychiatry Research, 151*(1–2), 55–66. doi:10.1016/j.psychres.2006.10.007

Velligan, D. I., DiCocco, M., Bow-Thomas, C. C., Cadle, C., Glahn, D. C., Miller, A. L., ... & Crismon, M. L. (2004). A brief cognitive assessment for use with schizophrenia patients in community clinics. *Schizophrenia Research, 71*(2–3), 273–283. doi:10.1016/j.schres.2004.02.027

Wallace, C. J., Liberman, R. P., Tauber, R., & Wallace, J. (2000). The independent living skills survey: A comprehensive measure of the community functioning of severely and persistently mentally ill individuals. *Schizophrenia Bulletin, 26*(3), 631–658.

Williams, J., Leamy, M., Pesola, F., Bird, V., Le Boutillier, C., & Slade, M. (2015). Psychometric evaluation of the Questionnaire about the Process of Recovery (QPR). *British Journal of Psychiatry, 207*(6), 551–555. doi:10.1192/bjp.bp.114.161695

Woodward, T. S., Jung, K., Hwang, H., Yin, J., Taylor, L., Menon, M., ... & Erickson, D. (2014). Symptom dimensions of the psychotic symptom rating scales in psychosis: A multisite study. *Schizophrenia Bulletin, 40(Suppl 4)*, S265–S274. doi:10.1093/schbul/sbu014

World Health Organization. (1992). *The ICD-10 classification of mental and behavioural disorders: Clinical descriptions and diagnostic guidelines*. Geneva: World Health Organization.

Young, R. C., Biggs, J. T., Ziegler, V. E., & Meyer, D. A. (1978). A rating scale for mania: Reliability, validity and sensitivity. *British Journal of Psychiatry, 133*, 429–435.

Yung, A. R., Yuen, H. P., McGorry, P. D., Phillips, L. J., Kelly, D., Dell'Olio, M., ... & Buckby, J. (2005). Mapping the onset of psychosis: The Comprehensive Assessment of At-Risk Mental States. *Australia and New Zealand Journal of Psychiatry, 39*(11–12), 964–971. doi:10.1080/j.1440-1614.2005.01714.x

27 Assessment of Eating Disorders

TRACEY WADE AND MIA PELLIZZER

Most if not all people with eating disorders have a degree of ambivalence in terms of readiness and motivation to change their eating disorder symptoms (Geller, Brown, & Srikameswaran, 2011). This ambivalence can translate to difficulty with respect to obtaining accurate and complete information in the assessment of eating disorders. A particular challenge is the assessment of anorexia nervosa, described as an ego-syntonic disorder because patients experience their symptoms as being congruent with their own values, for example self-control, mastery, and perfection (Vitousek, Watson, & Wilson, 1998). Accordingly, most patients with anorexia nervosa respond negatively to suggestions that they are ill and express ambivalence about their symptoms; this denial is more marked in patients with restricting-type anorexia nervosa, with 44 percent having impaired recognition of the illness compared with 25 percent of patients with the binge/purge type (Konstantakopoulos et al., 2011). In addition, across all eating disorders, patients experience shame (Duarte, Ferreira, & Pinto-Gouveia, 2016), which may account for the finding that eating disorder symptoms are more likely to be endorsed under conditions of anonymity (Lavender & Anderson, 2009), and that questionnaire and interview scores are more similar when interviews are conducted over the telephone rather than in person (Keel et al., 2002).

AIMS OF ASSESSMENT

In addressing the "where, why, what" questions in the psychological assessment of eating disorders (Anderson & Murray, 2010), this chapter focuses on the assessment of eating disorders for the purpose of deciding on appropriate treatment pathways. In order to increase the likelihood of accurate and informative reporting as well as the likelihood that the patient will move to treatment, the aims of assessment should include (1) the initiation and establishment of rapport and therapeutic alliance; (2) development of a collaborative understanding of the behaviors and cognitions that typify the eating disorder, where psychoeducational materials can be used to validate the patterns and cycles described (e.g., Waller et al., 2007); (3) development of an understanding of ambivalence and obstacles for change; and (4) a review of any comorbidity that may require resolution before treatment can commence for the eating disorder. Each of these aims are explored further in Table 27.1.

Establish Rapport

In order to establish rapport, we recommend assessment of eating disorders over two sessions where possible, with the first conducted in a semi-structured approach. Table 27.1 contains the information that can be sought in the first session. The use of a motivational enhancement style (Katzman et al., 2010; Miller & Rollnick, 2012) throughout assessment is recommended and is particularly critical if the assessment needs to be conducted in one session. This includes a respectful curiosity pertaining to the patient's perception of the problem, greater reliance on open than closed questions, consideration of the benefits of changing and the barriers to be overcome to change, and moving from the here and now to the future by envisioning key values and future goals.

The second session of assessment is focused on more structured assessment in order to develop a detailed description of specific symptoms, behaviors, and cognitions, a formulation and a diagnosis. We advise against the use of general psychiatric assessment tools that have skip rules (i.e., once a negative answer is obtained for a probe question, the remaining questions related to the diagnosis are not asked), such as the Composite International Diagnostic Interview (World Health Organization, 1993). These tools have been shown to underdiagnose eating disorders (Swanson et al., 2014; Thornton, Russell, & Hudson, 1998). More than one-third of people with an eating disorder endorse symptoms that would have been missed if skip rules had been used, and this uncaptured symptom pattern is associated with increased psychosocial impairment (Swanson et al., 2014). Instead, the use of eating disorder–specific assessment tools is recommended (summarized in Table 27.2).

Develop a Collaborative Understanding

Collaborative understanding of the vicious cycle and self-perpetuating nature of eating disorders is usually

Table 27.1 Unstructured assessment protocol for eating disorders

Aspect	Content
Understanding motivation for attendance	Some people come here under their own steam; others come because they feel pressured by others. Can you tell me if there is anything that troubles you about what is currently happening in your life? What would others who care about you (specify) be worried about?
Development of the eating disorder	Developmental review of eating and weight history (highest and lowest and current) and what else was happening in their life at that time; how coping skills and personality traits were helpful or exacerbated the disordered eating.
Previous treatment experience	Any previous treatment; what they thought they did in treatment; how they thought it helped or did not help.
Impairment resulting from the eating problem across the life domains	What has changed in your life since these things have been happening/since you have been at this lower weight? Address physical, psychological, family, work/education, friendships, getting on with life, social, romantic, being a good citizen, spiritual domains.
Psychiatric comorbidity	Any accompanying treatment (including medication), review previous such problems, and those in the family. Indicators of impulsive behavior (shop lifting, drug and alcohol, unprotected sex), mood intolerance (self-cutting).
Maintaining factors	Self-esteem and identity; sense of effectiveness, achievement, and control; perfectionism; emotion regulation; avoidance of responsibility, maturity, and intimacy.
Suicide risk	Frequency and intensity of any thoughts, specificity of plans, previous attempts (a contract for keeping safe should typically be agreed on at the end of assessment).
Interpersonal functioning	Who knows? Who offers support? Avoidance of social contact.
Attitude toward therapy	Assess ambivalence, pros and cons, fears of change, possible benefits of change; use of 100-point Visual Analogue Scales to assess importance of change, readiness to change, and self-efficacy (i.e., confidence in one's ability to change) especially with respect to being able to maintain nutritional health.

Table 27.2 Freely available diagnostic interview schedules specific to eating disorders

Name	Brief Description and Where It Can Be Found
Eating Disorder Examination (EDE) 17.0D	A semi-structured interview for DSM-5 eating disorder diagnoses www.credo-oxford.com/7.2.html
The Structured Inventory for Anorexic and Bulimic Eating Disorders (SIAB-EX)	A structured clinical interview for experts www.klinikum.uni-muenchen.de/Klinik-und-Poliklinik-fuer-Psychiatrie-und-Psychotherapie/de/forschung/forschungsfelder/essstoerungen/evaluation/index.html
The Eating Disorder Assessment for DSM-5 (EDA-5)	For feeding or eating disorders or related conditions according to DSM-5 criteria https://modeleda5.wordpress.com/

established at the end of assessment in some form of formulation or conceptualization. The form of this conceptualization is specific to the nature of the therapy to be used subsequently such as cognitive behavioral therapy (Fairburn, 2008; Waller et al., 2007); but across therapies many of the elements to be included are similar, including risk and maintenance factors (Startup et al., 2016). There is some indication that the use of formulation in eating disorders can promote greater retention and better outcome (Allen et al., 2016). If indications of rigid and detailed thinking styles are present, the use of neuropsychological testing can be helpful as part of developing this collaborative understanding, particularly measures of set shifting and central coherence, which can powerfully illustrate the problematic thinking patterns that can maintain disordered eating (Harrison et al., 2012).

Understanding Ambivalence

Most people being assessed for eating disorders typically have not experienced much understanding or sympathy about what is happening, with the most common response being akin to advice of the "just snap out of it" type. The assessment process offers opportunities to explore the functions of the eating disorder and the fears of change, balanced with explorations of the importance of change. Expectancies that thinness and control over weight, shape, and eating will provide overgeneralized life improvement, including intra- and interpersonal life functioning, are recognized risk factors for the development of bingeing and purging and disordered eating in adolescent girls (Pearson & Smith, 2015; Wilksch & Wade, 2010). The belief that control over eating and weight will make life better is captured in qualitative research with anorexia nervosa (Serpell et al., 1999; Sternheim et al., 2012), suggesting that the pursuit of low weight (whether successful or not) addresses a sense of ineffectiveness, makes the person feel safe, helps communicate distress related to possible rejection and abandonment, and moderates the experience of negative emotions. The Pros and Cons Eating Disorder Scale is a self-report measure that can usefully capture these expectancies (P-CED; Gale et al., 2006), as can the related Pros and Cons of Anorexia Nervosa Scale (P-CAN; Serpell et al., 1999). There is more evidence supporting the psychometrics of the P-CAN, with subscales having a Cronbach's α ranging from 0.68 to 0.89 and a test-retest reliability of 0.60–0.85 (Serpell et al., 2004), and good replication of the factor structure across two different samples (Serpell et al., 1999; Serpell et al., 2004).

Review of Medical Status, Comorbidity, and Other Issues

Assessment of medical functioning and comorbidities is essential across all eating disorders. Weight-based markers alone do not suffice to indicate medical risk and a multisystem assessment to measure mortality risk and resilience is required. Factors that can be incorporated into such assessments include, but are not limited to, rapid weight loss (especially in children), orthostatic hypotension, bradycardia or postural tachycardia, hypothermia, cardiac dysrhythmia and biochemical disturbance. Areas of medical assessment focus have been previously provided for both adults and children (Mitchell & Crow, 2006; Katzman, Kanbur, & Steinegger, 2010).

Suicidality is elevated for all eating disorders (Pisetsky et al., 2013). Individuals with eating disorders are at risk of taking their own lives, regardless of the presence of lifetime major depression, so it is imperative that suicidality be assessed routinely in clinical settings with eating disorder patients in order to ensure that appropriate support is provided (Wade et al., 2015) and an appropriate safety plan is agreed on between the patient and the therapist. Assessment of any comorbid psychiatric conditions is also required, with special attention paid to the temporal occurrence with respect to the emergence of the eating disorder. Some comorbidity, including personality disorders, can be expected to resolve with successful treatment of the eating disorder (Ames-Frankel et al., 1992).

When assessment is a precursor to treatment, this should also include a discussion about the treatment, expectations of treatment, and any nonnegotiables of therapy (e.g., in-session collaborative weighing, consequences for weight loss, regularity of attendance, completion of homework, and management of self-harm). An open discussion about the rationale for any nonnegotiables should be encouraged.

PSYCHOMETRICS OF ASSESSMENT TOOLS

The Eating Disorder Examination (EDE; Fairburn, Cooper, & O'Connor, 2014) is the oldest and most widely used eating disorder interview (Thomas, 2017), Test-retest reliability in clinical populations over two to seven days and six to fourteen days has ranged from 0.50 to 0.88 for the subscale scores, including 0.50–0.76 for shape concern and 0.52–0.71 for weight concern (Berg et al., 2012). Internal consistency for the shape and weight concern subscales has ranged from 0.68 to 0.85 and 0.51 to 0.76, respectively, and inter-rater reliability for these two subscales has ranged from 0.84 to 0.99 and 0.65 to 0.99 (Berg et al., 2012). The EDE has also been shown to satisfactorily distinguish between people with an eating disorder and controls (Berg et al., 2012). The EDE has been found to have good convergence with the subscale scores of the self-report version of the same instrument, the EDE-Questionnaire (EDE-Q; Berg et al., 2011). While temporal stability of the EDE over long periods has not been reported in community samples, the temporal stability of the EDE-Q in an Australian adult community sample aged eighteen to forty-five years over a median period of 315 days was 0.75 for shape concern and 0.73 for weight concern (Mond et al., 2004). Other psychometric properties of the EDE-Q are reported in Table 27.3.

There are numerous self-report instruments that can be used in assessment, depending on the aspects of the eating disorder that are to be targeted in treatment. A variety of more frequently used instruments is listed in Table 27.3. In addition to self-monitoring of eating, ongoing assessment of the associated behaviors and cognitions that are being targeted in therapy are useful to assess at regular intervals in order to chart progress and obstacles. In terms of supplements to the EDE-Q, it is worth considering the questionnaires that assess body checking, avoidance, and acceptance, given that lower weight and shape concern predicts better outcomes at the end of treatment (mean $r = 0.25$) and follow-up (mean $r = 0.16$) (Vall & Wade, 2015). In particular, the Body Image Acceptance & Action Questionnaire (BI-AAQ; Sandoz et al., 2013) has

Table 27.3 Frequently used self-report questionnaires for eating disorders

Assessment Tool and Function	Structure: Items, Response Scale, Factors	Psychometrics
Binge Eating Scale (BES; Gormally et al., 1982). Behavioral, cognitive, emotional features of objective binge eating in overweight/obese adults	16 items, 2 factors: 3- and 4-point Likert scales	See Cotter & Kelly, 2016; Kelly et al., 2012 Internal consistency (Cronbach's $\alpha > 0.8$) and test-retest reliability ($r = 0.87$) are adequate Demonstrated convergent validity for both male and female samples. A good indicator of severity of losing control while eating but inconsistent in successfully discriminating between subjective and objective binge eating. Factor structure replicated by Kelly et al. (2012). Sensitivity (84.8–97.8%) and specificity (20–74.6%) for binge eating disorder (BED) vary. Brazilian-Portuguese, Italian, Malaysian, and Spanish versions have been validated (Freitas et al., 2001; Partida, Garcia, & Cardenas, 2006; Ricca et al., 2000; Robert et al., 2013) and US samples have included participants who identify as Hispanic, Black, or Asian (Celio et al., 2004; Kelly et al., 2012; Mitchell & Mazzeo, 2004)
Body Checking Questionnaire (BCQ; Reas et al., 2002). Body checking behaviors	23 items, 3 factors: 5-point Likert scale	See Pellizzer et al., 2018 Internal consistency (Cronbach's $\alpha = 0.66$–0.96) and test-retest reliability ($r = 0.83$–0.94) vary across studies. Demonstrated convergent validity and higher scores in clinical and dieting samples. Inconsistent factor structure. Brazilian-Portuguese, Italian, and Norwegian versions have been validated (Calugi et al., 2006; Campana et al., 2013; Reas et al., 2009) and several US studies have included samples where 50–60% of participants identify as Asian American, African American, or Hispanic (Lydecker, Cotter, & Mazzeo, 2014; White et al., 2015; White & Warren, 2013).
Body Image Acceptance & Action Questionnaire (BI-AAQ; Sandoz et al., 2013). Body image flexibility	12 items, 1 factor: 7-point Likert scale	See Pellizzer et al., 2018 Internal consistency (Cronbach's $\alpha = 0.91$–0.95, Composite Reliability = 0.96), item-total reliability ($r = 0.50$–0.82), and test-retest reliability ($r = 0.80$–0.82) are consistent across studies Correlated with similar measures, discriminates between eating disorder, dieting, and healthy samples, and has been validated in diverse clinical and nonclinical samples. Factor structure consistent across studies. Validated with Brazilian-Portuguese and Portuguese versions (Ferreira et al., 2011; Lucena-Santos et al., 2017) and in a Hispanic sample and an ethnically diverse sample comprised of 70% African American, Hispanic, Native American, and other ethnicities (Kurz, Flynn, & Bordieri, 2016; Moore et al., 2014).
Body Image Avoidance Questionnaire (BIAQ; Rosen et al., 1991). Avoidance of body image–related situations	19 items, 4 factors/behavioral themes: 6-point Likert scale, higher scores indicated greater body image avoidance	See Pellizzer et al., 2018 Internal consistency (Cronbach's $\alpha = 0.64$–0.89, Composite Reliability = 0.92) and test-retest reliability ($r = 0.64$–0.87) vary. Demonstrated convergent validity and scores higher for participants with high levels of disordered eating and clinical samples compared to controls; scores decrease following CBT (Rosen et al., 1991). Varying factor structures found. Validated versions include Brazilian-Portuguese, German, French, Italian, and Polish (Brytek-Matera & Rogoza, 2016;

Continued

Table 27.3 (cont.)

Assessment Tool and Function	Structure: Items, Response Scale, Factors	Psychometrics
		Campana et al., 2009; Legenbauer, Vocks, & Schütt-Strömel, 2007; Maïano et al., 2009; Riva & Molinari, 1998). The BIAQ has also been validated in a sample of approximately 50% non-Caucasian participants, including Black, Asian, Hispanic, and Native Americans (Lydecker et al., 2014).
Body Shape Questionnaire (BSQ; Cooper et al., 1987). Concerns about body shape	34 items, 1 factor: 6-point Likert scale Two 16-item "alternative forms" (Evans & Dolan, 1993) and a 14-item version (Dowson & Henderson, 2001)	See Wade, 2016a Inter-item correlation ranging $r = 0.14–0.76$ and internal consistency $\alpha = 0.97$ (Evans & Dolan, 1993). Validated in other ethnic groups. Alternative versions have comparable internal consistency and are highly correlated with the original BSQ. Validated in diverse clinical and non-clinical populations and able to discriminate between eating disordered samples and healthy controls. Validated with Brazilian, Flemish, French, German, Norwegian, Persian, Spanish, Swedish, and Turkish populations (Akdemir et al., 2012; Ghaderi & Scott, 2004; Kapstad et al., 2015; Lentillon-Kaestner et al., 2014; Pook, Tuschen-Caffier, & Brähler, 2008; Probst, Pieters, & Vanderlinden, 2008; Sadeghi et al., 2014; Silva et al., 2016; Warren et al., 2008).
Bulimia Test Revised (BULIT-R; Thelen et al., 1991). DSM-III-R BN criteria and weight-control behaviors	28 scored items (DSM-III-R BN criteria), 8 unscored items (weight-control behaviors), 5 factors: 5-point Likert scale. The Binge Eating Disorder Test (BEDT; Vander Wal, Stein, & Blashill, 2011) is a subset of 23 BULIT-R items	See Thelen et al., 1991; Thelen et al., 1996 High internal consistency ($\alpha = 0.97–0.98$) and test-retest reliability ($r = 0.95$). Specificity, sensitivity, negative and positive predictive values range 0.61–0.98. Validated with clinical and non-clinical samples. Varying factor structures found: 1-, 4-, 5-, and 6- factor models all fit poorly using confirmatory factor analysis and exploratory factor analysis found differing solutions for American and Spanish samples (Berrios-Hernandez et al., 2007). A Korean version has been validated (Ryu et al., 1999) and the scale has been studied in a sample of 50% non-Caucasian participants, including African American, Asian American, and Latino American participants (Fernandez et al., 2006).
Clinical Impairment Assessment (CIA; Bohn & Fairburn, 2008). Impact of eating disorder psychopathology on psychosocial functioning	16 items, 1 factor: 4-point Likert scale. Provides a global impairment score (≥ 16 indicative of an eating disorder)	See Bohn & Fairburn, 2008 Internal consistency (Cronbach's $\alpha = 0.97$) and test-retest reliability ($r = 0.86$) are adequate Correlates well with the global EDE-Q score and clinician ratings of impairment, and discriminated between those with and without an eating disorder. 76% sensitivity and 86% specificity. Reliability and validity data have been replicated repeatedly (Bohn, 2015). Fijian, Norwegian, Spanish, and Swedish versions have been validated (Becker et al., 2010a; Martín et al., 2015; Reas et al., 2010; Welch et al., 2011).
Dutch Eating Behaviour Questionnaire (DEBQ; Van Strien et al., 1986). Eating behaviors that develop and maintain obesity	33 items, 3 subscales: 5-point Likert scale. A children's version (DEBQ-C) is also available (Van Strien & Oosterveld, 2008)	See Domoff, 2015 Good internal consistency ($\alpha = 0.79–0.97$) demonstrated and factor structure supported in translated versions. Mean differences in subscales discriminate between anorexia nervosa, bulimia nervosa, obese, and healthy samples. Mixed support for the emotional eating scale in nonclinical populations and further research is required

Continued

Table 27.3 (cont.)

Assessment Tool and Function	Structure: Items, Response Scale, Factors	Psychometrics
		to assess predictive and concurrent validity of all scales. English, French, German, Italian, Spanish, Swedish (with children), and Turkish versions have been validated (Bozan, Bas, & Asci, 2011; Cebolla et al., 2014; Dakanalis et al., 2013; Halvarsson & Sjödén, 1998; Lluch et al., 1996; Nagl et al., 2016; Wardle, 1987)
Eating Attitudes Test (EAT-26; Garner et al., 1982). Symptoms and concerns of eating disorders	Three sections: (1) height and weight to calculate BMI; (2) 26 items (3 subscales) assess engagement in specific behaviors using a 6-point Likert scale (scores ≥ 20 indicate follow-up assessment for an eating disorder is required; (3) 5 items assess eating disorder behaviors. Also available is the Children's version of the EAT (ChEAT; Smolak & Levine, 1994)	See Wade, 2016b Originally reported to have high internal consistency reliability (Cronbach's $\alpha = 0.90$ for those with anorexia nervosa) and strongly correlated with the original EAT-40. Discriminant validity has varied across studies, with some reporting significant differences between eating disorder groups and controls for adults (and others finding no significant differences in a sample of adolescents). Accuracy rate of 90%, 0.77 sensitivity, and 0.94 specificity; however, relatively low positive predictive value. Factor structure and item number are variable. Intercept invariance achieved across gender, age groups (i.e., early and late adolescence), ethnicities (European versus African origins), and weight categories (Maïano et al., 2013). Validated versions include Arabic, Brazilian-Portuguese, Chinese, Italian, Korean, Portuguese, Spanish, Turkish, Urdu, and Zulu (Al-Subaie et al., 1996; Choudry & Mumford, 1992; Dotti & Lazzari, 1998; Elal et al., 2000; Ko & Cohen, 1998; Lee et al., 2002; Nunes et al., 2005; Pereira et al., 2008; Rivas et al., 2004).
Eating Disorder Diagnostic Scale (EDDS; Stice, Telch, & Rizvi, 2000). Brief diagnostic tool for eating disorders	22 items: response formats include Likert, yes-no, frequency, and free-form. Scoring algorithms derive DSM-IV diagnosis for anorexia nervosa (AN), bulimia nervosa (BN), and binge eating disorder (BED). A symptom composite can also be derived (Bohon & Stice, 2015). A 23-item version of the EDDS using DSM 5 criteria is available: www.ori.org/stice measures/. OSFED diagnoses have been included	See Stice et al., 2000; Stice, Fisher, & Martinez, 2004 Good temporal reliability (mean $\kappa = 0.80$), test-retest reliability ($r = 0.87$) and internal consistency (mean $\alpha = 0.89$). Criterion validity with structured interview diagnoses (mean $\kappa = 0.83$), convergent validity with other eating disorder measures, and predictive validity with higher EDDS scores predicting response to an ED prevention program, likelihood of ED behaviors, and depression. Sensitive to intervention effects in an ED prevention intervention. Translated into several languages and psychometric studies in culturally diverse samples have found comparable reliability and validity (Bohon & Stice, 2015). Chinese, Dutch, and Icelandic versions have been validated (Lee et al., 2007; Krabbenborg et al., 2012; Thorsteinsdottir & Ulfarsdottir, 2008).
Eating Disorder Examination-Questionnaire (EDE-Q; Fairburn & Beglin, 2008). Cognitive and behavioral eating disorder symptoms during the past month	22 items: cognitive symptoms using 7-point Likert scale, higher scores indicate greater eating disorder psychopathology Four lower-order subscales and a higher-order global score. 6 items assess the frequency of behavioral symptoms. Algorithms are available to	See Berg et al., 2012; Berg, 2016 Internal consistency (Cronbach's $\alpha = 0.70$–0.93), test-retest reliability (short-term, over 1–14 days, $r = 0.66$–0.94), and temporal stability (long-term test-retest reliability, over 5–15 months, $r = 0.57$–0.82) for the four subscales are adequate. Test-retest reliability ($r = 0.51$–0.92) and temporal stability ($r = 0.28$–0.44) for behavioral items vary. Demonstrated convergent validity and scores successfully discriminate between eating disorder and control cases. Factor analyses have been variable. Validated versions include Dutch, Fijian,

Continued

Table 27.3 (cont.)

Assessment Tool and Function	Structure: Items, Response Scale, Factors	Psychometrics
	derive proxy DSM-IV and DSM-5 diagnoses	German, Greek, Italian, Mexican, Norwegian, Portuguese, Spanish, Swedish, and Turkish (Aardoom et al., 2012; Becker et al., 2010b; Calugi et al., 2016; Giovazolias, Tsaousis, & Vallianatou, 2013; Hilbert et al., 2007; Machado et al., 2014; Penelo et al., 2013; Rø, Reas, & Lask, 2010; Villarroel et al., 2011; Welch et al., 2011; Yucel et al., 2011)
Eating Disorder Inventory – 3 (EDI-3; Garner, 2004). Core eating disorder symptoms and psychopathology related to eating disorders	91 items, 3 eating disorder–specific subscales, 9 psychological scales, 6 composite scales, 3 validity scales: 6-point Likert scale. A symptom checklist (EDI-3-SC) and referral form (EDI-3-RF) are available to assess DSM-5 diagnostic criteria and identify at risk individuals	See Nyman-Carlsson & Garner, 2016 Most recent revision (EDI-3) has good internal consistency (majority of subscales and composites above 0.80) for adolescent and adult US samples. International samples have shown lower reliability for some subscales. Short-term test-retest reliability is considered excellent ($r = 0.93$–0.98) and factor structure is considered adequate. The EDI-3 successfully discriminates between eating disorder and control samples (in the United States and in cross-cultural samples) and has high sensitivity and specificity. Danish, Persian, Spanish, and Swedish versions of the EDI-3 have been validated (Clausen et al., 2011; Dadgostar et al., 2017; Elosua & López-Jáuregui, 2012; Nyman-Carlsson et al., 2015). Earlier validations of the EDI-1 and EDI-2 include Bulgarian, Chinese, Danish, Dutch, Korean, Portuguese, and Swedish (Boyadjieva & Steinhausen, 1996; Clausen, Rokkedal, & Rosenvinge, 2009; Lee et al., 1997; Machado et al., 2001; Nevonen, Clinton, & Norring, 2006; Ryu et al., 1999; van Strien & Ouwens, 2003)
Eating Disorder Questionnaire (EDQ; Mitchell et al., 1985). Demographic information, eating psychopathology, psychiatric, social, and medical history	16 sections with varying item numbers and response formats in each. Algorithms for DSM-IV diagnoses are available (Utzinger & Mitchell, 2016). DSM-5 algorithms have been proposed but have not yet been tested	Reliability has not been tested (Utzinger & Mitchell, 2016). DSM-IV algorithms have adequate agreement with structured ED interviews (kappa = 0.64; Keel et al., 2002) and scores are correlated with EDE and EDE-Q behavioral items and cognitive symptoms $r = 0.64$–0.66; Eddy et al., 2009). Has not been validated in other countries/languages
Night Eating Questionnaire (NEQ; Allison et al., 2008). Screens for Night Eating Syndrome (NES)	13 items, 4 subscales: 5-point Likert scale. One item is used to distinguish NES from sleep-related eating disorder and another item assesses duration of NES items. An additional two items assess distress and impairment (Allison, 2015). Related available measures include the Night Eating Syndrome History and Inventory (NESHI), the Night Eating Diagnostic Questionnaire (NEDQ) and the Night Eating Symptom Scale (NESS; Lundgren et al., 2012)	See Allison, 2015 Adequate internal consistency (Cronbach's $\alpha = 0.70$–0.79 total scale) and test-retest reliability ($r = 0.77$–0.86). In a bariatric sample, positive predictive value was low (40.7%) for a score of 25 and acceptable (72.7%) when using a score of 30. Good convergent validity, factor structure largely confirmed, and translated and validated in several languages with males and females. Validated versions include Arabic, Brazilian-Portuguese, French (children) German, Hebrew, Korean, Mandarin, Spanish, and Turkish (Atasoy et al., 2014; Dantas et al., 2012; Elsadek, Hamid, & Allison, 2014; Gallant et al., 2012; Kim, Kim, & Choi, 2016; Latzer et al., 2014; Meule, Allison, & Platte, 2014; Moizé et al., 2012; Tu et al., 2017). In addition, the scale has been used in an Indian study of Punjabi women (Randhawa et al., 2014)

shown robust factor structure across different populations and focuses on the development of psychological flexibility with respect to body image disturbance, which permits the development of constructive therapeutic goals. A useful and robust adjunct is the Eating Disorder Inventory, which assesses psychological dimensions of pertinence to eating disorders, such as *Drive for Thinness*, *Perfectionism*, *Ineffectiveness*, *Interpersonal Distrust*, *Interoceptive Awareness*, and *Maturity Fears*.

CAPTURING DIVERSITY

A common critique across most diagnostic tools in eating disorders is lack of validation with male samples and diverse racial/ethnic samples. Epidemiological studies indicate the presence of eating disorders in US Asian, Black, and Latino populations (Alegria et al., 2007; Taylor et al., 2007; Nicdao, Hong, & Takeuchi, 2007). While treatment seeking varies across different eating disorder and racial/ethnic groups, ranging from 20 percent to 50 percent, clinicians and health workers should not assume eating disorders to be a culture-bound phenomenon but should diligently screen for disordered eating behaviors (as opposed to diagnoses) across any population. For example, eating disorder symptoms are as frequent in Australian Aboriginal and Torres Strait Islander peoples as non-Indigenous Australians (Hay & Carriage, 2012), when using the diagnostic items modeled on those used in the EDE. As can be seen in Table 27.3, many of the self-report questionnaires have been validated across a variety of cultures, where the evidence seems to suggest that, if the questionnaire performs well in primarily English-speaking samples, it is also likely to perform well in other cultures.

Further, the advent of DSM-5 introduced a new and poorly understood category of feeding disorders, which includes Avoidant/Restrictive Food Intake Disorder (ARFID), and is most likely to be detected in children. There are currently no existing continuous measures of severity. Pilot testing is currently being conducted into a new tool, the Pica, ARFID (Avoidant/Restrictive Feeding Intake Disorder), and Rumination Disorder Interview (Thomas, 2017).

TECHNOLOGICAL ADVANCES

The gathering of ecologically, "real-time" data in the form of ecological momentary assessment (EMA) has been a feature of eating disorder assessment for some time. Data on negative affect and eating disorder behaviors suggest strong convergence between retrospective and EMA assessment methodologies (Wonderlich et al., 2015). Use of EMA has allowed the relationship between eating disorder behavior and affect to become increasingly clearer (Engel et al., 2016), showing that negative affect increases over time until the point at which eating disorder behavior occurs. However, what happens to negative affect after the eating disorder behavior occurs is somewhat unclear, with findings suggesting both an increase and a decrease in negative affect. EMA has become more affordable and easier as the technology of small devices has improved, and has the benefit of examining temporal association between moods and disordered eating but is more burdensome than traditional assessment methods given the ongoing nature of reporting.

ASSESSMENT OF NONCREDIBLE REPORTING

Noncredible reporting is a common occurrence with eating disorders, given high levels of ambivalence and shame. Matching self-reports of disordered eating with body mass index, changes in weight, and medical assessment are important to ensure that the full picture of the eating disorder emerges. With children and adolescents, it is particularly helpful to have multiple informants. Parents and adolescents have been found to be largely discordant on symptom reports, with parents generally less likely to report bulimic symptoms than the adolescent but more likely to report behaviors related to thinness (Swanson et al., 2014). Consultation with close others and carers of adults may also be useful in the assessment process. The use of motivational interviewing techniques can elicit more information than a series of closed questions (Price-Evans & Treasure, 2011). It is also important to keep in mind the cognitive impairment that can result from starvation and the need to frame questions and statements clearly and unambiguously.

COMMONLY MISUNDERSTOOD CONCEPTS

The most commonly misunderstood concepts in the assessment of eating disorders are objective binge episodes (OBE), the undue influence of body weight or shape on self-evaluation, and compulsive exercise. OBE require the presence of a large amount of food (i.e., unequivocally large given the circumstances) over a short (i.e., 2 hour) period of time accompanied by a sense of loss of control (i.e., unable to stop eating once started). Undue influence of body weight or shape on self-evaluation is best assessed by the impact that weight and shape have on evaluation of worth as a person compared to other issues that impact assessment of self-worth. Compulsive exercise assesses the extent that exercise is compulsive and driven and significantly interferes with day-to-day functioning such that it prevents attendance at social commitments or intrudes on work or exercising when it might do one harm. The EDE and EDE-Q provide clear definitions and direction for assessing these concepts and a recent review of exercise measures found that the Compulsive Exercise Test (Taranis, Touyz, & Meyer, 2011) explained the greatest variance in eating disorder psychopathology in patients with anorexia nervosa and demonstrated good-to-excellent reliability (Young et al., 2017).

PRACTICAL RECOMMENDATIONS

Based on many years of supervising trainees in the assessment of eating disorders (first author) and being trained in the assessment of eating disorders or the purpose of providing treatment (second author), we have developed clear ideas on what is required in the toolkit of a clinician who intends to assess eating disorders. To this end, we recommend the following components for such a toolkit:

1) A clear outline of the issues to cover in unstructured assessment
2) A checklist of medical aspects to be assessed that can be sent to a medical practitioner for completion and shared with the patient
3) A semi-structured assessment tool for eating disorders
4) Relevant psychoeducational material
5) A generic case formulation that can be personalized for the patient
6) A semi-structured assessment tool for comorbidity and suicidality
7) A safety plan template for self-harm and suicidality that can be personalized with the patient.[1]

Essentially, we encourage clinicians to use the assessment of eating disorders as an opportunity to maximize the discrepancy that the person is already experiencing, to some degree, about where they are and where they want to be heading in their life. The detailed information that can be collected as part of this process should be helpful for the person with the eating disorder as much as the clinician who is conducting the assessment.

REFERENCES

Aardoom, J. J., Dingemans, A. E., Slof Op't Landt, M. C., & Van Furth, E. F. (2012). Norms and discriminative validity of the Eating Disorder Examination Questionnaire (EDE-Q). *Eating Behaviors*, *13*(4), 305–309.

Akdemir, A., Inandi, T., Akbas, D., Karaoglan Kahilogullari, A., Eren, M., & Canpolat, B. I. (2012). Validity and reliability of a Turkish version of the body shape questionnaire among female high school students: Preliminary examination. *European Eating Disorders Review*, *20*(1), e114–115.

Alegria, M., Woo, M., Cao, Z., Torres, M., Meng, X., & Striegel-Moore, R. (2007). Prevalence and correlates of eating disorders in Latinos in the United States. *International Journal of Eating Disorders*, *40*, S15–S21.

Allen, K., O'Hara, C. B., Bartholdy, S., Renwicj, B., Keyes, A., Lose, A., ... & Schmidt U. (2016). Written case formulations in the treatment of anorexia nervosa: Evidence for therapeutic benefits. *International Journal of Eating Disorders*, *49*, 874–882.

Allison, K. C. (2015). Night eating syndrome history inventory (NESHI)/Night eating questionnaire (NEQ). In T. Wade (Ed.), *Encyclopedia of feeding and eating disorders*. Singapore: Springer. https://link.springer.com/referenceworkentry/10.1007/978-981-287-087-2_87-1

Allison, K. C., Lundgren, J. D., O'Reardon, J. P., Sarwer, D.B., Wadden, T.A., & Stunkard, A.J. (2008). The Night Eating Questionnaire (NEQ): Psychometric properties of a measure of severity of the Night Eating Syndrome. *Eating Behaviors*, *9* (1), 62–72.

Al-Subaie, A., Al-Shammari, S., Bamgboye, E., Al-Sabhan, K., Al-Shehri, S., & Bannah, A. R. (1996). Validity of the Arabic version of the Eating Attitude Test. *International Journal of Eating Disorders*, *20*(3), 321–324.

Ames-Frankel, J., Devlin, M. J., Walsh, B. T., Strasser, T. J., Sadik, C., Oldham, J. M., & Roose, S. P. (1992). Personality disorder diagnoses with bulimia nervosa: Clinical correlates and changes with treatment. *Journal of Clinical Psychiatry*, *53*, 90–96.

Anderson, D. A., & Murray, D. (2010). Psychological assessment of the eating disorders. In W. S. Agras (Ed.), *The Oxford handbook of eating disorders* (pp. 249–258). Oxford: Oxford University Press.

Atasoy, N., Saraçli, Ö., Konuk, N., Ankarali, H. Güriz, S. O., Akdemir, A., ... & Atik, L. (2014). Gece Yeme Anketi-Türkçe Formunun psikiyatrik ayaktan hasta popülasyonunda geçerlilik ve güvenilirlik çalışması. *Anatolian Journal of Psychiatry/Anadolu Psikiyatri Dergisi*, *15*(3), 328–247.

Becker, A. E., Thomas, J. J., Bainivualiku, A., Richards, L., Navara, K., Roberts, A. L., ... & Striegel-Moore, R. H. (2010a). Adaptation and evaluation of the Clinical Impairment Assessment to assess disordered eating related distress in an adolescent female ethnic Fijian population. *International Journal of Eating Disorders*, *43*(2), 179–186.

Becker, A. E., Thomas, J. J., Bainivualiku, A., Richards, L., Navara, K., Roberts, A. L., Gilman, S. E., & Striegel-Moore, R. H. (2010b). Validity and reliability of a Fijian translation and adaptation of the Eating Disorder Examination Questionnaire. *International Journal of Eating Disorders*, *43* (2), 171–178.

Berg, K. C. (2016). Eating disorder examination (EDE)(EDE-Q). In T. Wade (Ed.), *Encyclopedia of feeding and eating disorders*. Singapore: Springer. https://link.springer.com/referenceworkentry/10.1007/978-981-287-087-2_101-1

Berg, K. C., Peterson, C. B., Frazier, P., & Crow, S. J. (2011). Convergence scores on the interview and questionnaire versions of the Eating Disorder Examination: A meta-analytic review. *Psychological Assessment*, *23*, 714–724.

Berg, K. C., Peterson, C. B., Frazier, P., & Crow, S. J. (2012). Psychometric evaluation of the Eating Disorder Examination and Eating Disorder Examination-Questionnaire: A systematic review of the literature. *International Journal of Eating Disorders*, *45*(3), 428–438.

Berrios-Hernandez, M. N., Rodriguez-Ruiz, S., Perez, M., Gleaves, D. H., Maysonet, M., & Cepeda-Benito, A. (2007). Cross-cultural assessment of eating disorders: Psychometric properties of a Spanish version of the Bulimia Test-Revised. *European Eating Disorders Review*, *15*, 418–24.

Bohn, K. (2015). Clinical impairment assessment questionnaire (CIA). In T. Wade (Ed.), *Encyclopedia of feeding and eating disorders*. Singapore: Springer. https://link.springer.com/referenceworkentry/10.1007/978-981-287-087-2_85-1

Bohn, K., & Fairburn, C. G. (2008). Clinical Impairment Assessment Questionnaire (CIA 3.0). In C. G. Fairburn (Ed.), *Cognitive behavior therapy and eating disorders* (pp. 315–317). New York: Guilford Press.

Bohon, C., & Stice, E. (2015). Eating disorder diagnostic scale. In T. Wade (Ed.), *Encyclopedia of feeding and eating disorders*. Singapore: Springer. https://link.springer.com/referenceworkentry/10.1007/978-981-287-087-2_109-1

[1] There are a variety of websites that can assist in the collection of this material and we particularly recommend the National Eating Disorder Collaboration website (www.nedc.com.au/) and the Centre for Clinical Interventions website (www.cci.health.wa.gov.au).

Boyadjieva, S., & Steinhausen, H. C. (1996). The Eating Attitudes Test and the Eating Disorders Inventory in four Bulgarian clinical and nonclinical samples. *International Journal of Eating Disorders*, *19*(1), 93–98.

Bozan, N., Bas, M., & Asci, F. H. (2011). Psychometric properties of Turkish version of Dutch Eating Behaviour Questionnaire (DEBQ): A preliminary results. *Appetite*, *56*(3), 564–566.

Brytek-Matera, A., & Rogoza, R. (2016). The Polish version of the Body Image Avoidance Questionnaire: An exploratory structural equation modeling approach. *Eating and Weight Disorders-Studies on Anorexia, Bulimia and Obesity*, *21*(1), 65–72.

Calugi, S., Dalle Grave, R., Ghisi, R., & Sanavio, E. (2006). Validation of the body checking questionnaire in an eating disorders population. *Behavioural and Cognitive Psychotherapy*, *34*(2), 233–242.

Calugi, S., Milanese, C., Sartirana, M., El Ghoch, M., Sartori, F., Geccherle, E., ... & Dalle Grave, R. (2016). The eating disorder examination questionnaire: Reliability and validity of the Italian version. *Eating and Weight Disorders-Studies on Anorexia, Bulimia and Obesity*, *22*(3), 509–514.

Campana, A. N., da Consolacao, M., Tavares, G. C., da Silva, D., & Diogo, M. J. (2009). Translation and validation of the Body Image Avoidance Questionnaire (BIAQ) for the Portuguese language in Brazil. *Behavior Research Methods*, *41*(1), 236–243.

Campana, A. N. N. B., Swami, V., Onodera, C. M. K., da Silva, D., & Tavares, M. D. C. G. C. F. (2013). An initial psychometric evaluation and exploratory cross-sectional study of the body checking questionnaire among Brazilian women. *PLoS ONE*, *8*(9), e74649.

Cebolla, A., Barrada, J. R., Van Strien, T., Oliver, E., & Baños, R. (2014). Validation of the Dutch Eating Behavior Questionnaire (DEBQ) in a sample of Spanish women. *Appetite*, *73*, 58–64.

Celio, A. A., Wilfley, D. E., Crow, S. J., Mitchell, J., & Walsh, B. T. (2004). A comparison of the binge eating scale, questionnaire for eating and weight patterns-revised, and eating disorder examination questionnaire with instructions with the eating disorder examination in the assessment of binge eating disorder and its symptoms. *International Journal of Eating Disorders*, *36*(4), 434–444.

Choudry, I. Y., & Mumford, D. B. (1992). A pilot study of eating disorders in Mirpur (Pakistan) using an Urdu version of the Eating Attitudes Test. *International Journal of Eating Disorders*, *11*(3), 243–251.

Clausen, L., Rokkedal, K., & Rosenvinge, J. H. (2009). Validating the Eating Disorder Inventory (EDI-2) in two Danish samples: A comparison between female eating disorders patients and females from the general population. *European Eating Disorders Review*, *17*, 462–7.

Clausen, L., Rosenvinge, J. H., Friborg, O., & Rokkedal, K. (2011). Validating the Eating Disorder Inventory-3 (EDI-3): A comparison between 561 female eating disorders patients and 878 females from the general population. *Journal of Psychopathology and Behavioral Assessment*, *33*(1), 101–110.

Cooper, P., Taylor, M., Cooper, Z., & Fairburn, C. G. (1987). The development and validation of the Body Shape Questionnaire. *International Journal of Eating Disorders*, *6*(4), 485–494.

Cotter, E. W., & Kelly, N. R. (2016). Binge eating scale (BES). In T. Wade (Ed.), *Encyclopedia of feeding and eating disorders*. Singapore: Springer. https://link.springer.com/referenceworkentry/10.1007/978-981-287-087-2_9-2

Dadgostar, H., Nedjat, S., Dadgostar, E., & Soleimany, G. (2017). Translation and evaluation of the reliability and validity of Eating Disorder Inventory-3 Questionnaire among Iranian university students. *Asian Journal of Sports Medicine*, *8*(2), e13950.

Dakanalis, A., Zanetti, M. A., Clerici, M., Madeddu, F., Riva, G., & Caccialanza, R. (2013). Italian version of the Dutch Eating Behavior Questionnaire: Psychometric proprieties and measurement invariance across sex, BMI-status and age. *Appetite*, *71*, 187–195.

Dantas, G. M., Pinto, T. F., Pereira, E. D. B., Magalhã, R. M., Bruin, V. M. S. D., & Bruin, P. F. C. D. (2012). Validation of a new Brazilian version of the "Night Eating Questionnaire." *Sleep Science*, *5*(1), 7–13.

Domoff, S. E. (2015). Dutch eating behaviour questionnaire (DEBQ). In T. Wade (Ed.), *Encyclopedia of feeding and eating disorders*. Singapore: Springer. https://link.springer.com/referenceworkentry/10.1007/978-981-287-087-2_127-1

Dotti, A., & Lazzari, R. (1998). Validation and reliability of the Italian EAT-26: Eating and Weight Disorders-Studies on Anorexia. *Bulimia and Obesity*, *3*(4), 188–194.

Dowson, J., & Henderson, L. (2001). The validity of a short version of the Body Shape Questionnaire. *Psychiatry Research*, *102*(3), 263–271.

Duarte, C., Ferreira, C., & Pinto-Gouveia, J. (2016). At the core of eating disorders: Overvaluation, social rank, self-criticism, and shame in anorexia, bulimia, and binge-eating disorder. *Comprehensive Psychiatry*, *66*, 123–131.

Eddy, K. T., Crosby, R. D., Keel, P. K., Wonderlich, S. A., le Grange, D., Hill, L., Powers, P., & Mitchell, J. E. (2009). Empirical identification and validation of eating disorder phenotypes in a multisite clinical sample. *The Journal of Nervous and Mental Disease*, *197*(1), 41–49.

Elal, G., Altug, A., Slade, P., & Tekcan, A. (2000). Factor structure of the Eating Attitudes Test (EAT) in a Turkish university sample: Eating and Weight Disorders-Studies on Anorexia, *Bulimia and Obesity*, *5*(1), 46–50.

Elosua, P., & López-Jáuregui, A. (2012). Internal structure of the Spanish adaptation of the Eating Disorder Inventory-3. *European Journal of Psychological Assessment*, *28*(1), 25–31.

Elsadek, A. M., Hamid, M. S., & Allison, K. C. (2014). Psychometric characteristics of the Night Eating Questionnaire in a Middle East population. *International Journal of Eating Disorders*, *47*(6), 660–665.

Engel, S. G., Crosby, R. D., Thomas, G., Bond, D., Lavender, J. M., Mason, T., Steffan, K. J., Green, D. D., & Wonderlich, S. A. (2016). Ecological momentary assessment in eating disorder and obesity research: A review of the recent literature. *Current Psychiatry Reports*, *18*, 37.

Evans, C., & Dolan, B. (1993). Body Shape Questionnaire: Derivation of shortened alternate forms. *International Journal of Eating Disorders*, *13*(3), 315–321.

Fairburn, C. G. (2008). *Cognitive behaviour therapy and eating disorders*. New York: Guilford Press.

Fairburn, C. G., & Beglin, S. (2008). Eating Disorder Examination Questionnaire (EDE-Q 6.0). In C. G. Fairburn (Ed.), *Cognitive behavior therapy and eating disorders* (pp. 309–314). New York: Guilford Press.

Fairburn, C. G., Cooper, Z., & O'Connor, M. (2014). *Eating Disorder Examination 17.0D*. Oxford: Centre for Research on Dissemination at Oxford.

Fernandez, S., Malacrne, V. L., Wilfley, D. E., & McQuaid, J. (2006). Factor structure of the Bulimia Test-Revised in college women from four ethnic groups. *Cultural Diversity and Ethnic Minority Psychology*, *12*(3), 403.

Ferreira, C., Pinto-Gouveia, J., & Duarte, C. (2011). The validation of the Body Image Acceptance and Action Questionnaire: Exploring the moderator effect of acceptance on disordered eating. *International Journal of Psychology and Psychological Therapy*, *11*, 327–345.

Freitas, S., Lopes, C. S., Coutinho, W., & Appolinario, J. C. (2001). Tradução e adaptação para o português da Escala de Compulsão Alimentar Periódica. *Revista brasileira de psiquiatria*, *23*(4), 215–220.

Gale, C., Holliday, J., Troop, N. A., Serpell, L., & Treasure, J. (2006). The pros and cons of change in individuals with eating disorders: A broader perspective. *International Journal of Eating Disorders*, *39*(5), 394–403.

Gallant, A. R., Lundgren, J. D., Allison, K., Stunkard, A. J., Lambert, M., O'Loughlin, J., Lemieux, S., Tremblay, A., & Drapeau, V. (2012). Validity of the night eating questionnaire in children. *International Journal of Eating Disorders*, *45*, 861–865.

Garner, D. M. (2004). *Eating Disorder Inventory – 3: Professional manual*. Odessa, FL: Psychological Assessment Resources.

Garner, D. M., Olmsted, M. P., Bohr, Y., & Garfinkel, P. E. (1982). The Eating Attitudes Test: Psychometric features and clinical correlates. *Psychological Medicine*, *12*(4), 871–878.

Geller, J., Brown, K. E., & Srikameswaran, S. (2011). The efficacy of a brief motivational intervention for individuals with eating disorders: A randomized control trial. *International Journal of Eating Disorders*, *44(6)*, 497–505.

Ghaderi, A. T. A., & Scott, B. (2004). The reliability and validity of the Swedish version of the Body Shape Questionnaire. *Scandinavian Journal of Psychology*, *45*(4), 319–324.

Giovazolias, T., Tsaousis, I., & Vallianatou, C. (2013). The factor structure and psychometric properties of the Greek version of the Eating Disorders Examination Questionnaire (EDE-Q). *European Journal of Psychological Assessment*, *29*, 189–196.

Gormally, J., Black, S., Daston, S., & Rardin, D. (1982). The assessment of binge eating severity among obese persons. *Addictive Behaviors*, *7*(1), 47–55.

Halvarsson, K., & Sjödén, P. O. (1998). Psychometric properties of the Dutch Eating Behaviour Questionnaire (DEBQ) among 9–10-year-old Swedish girls. *European Eating Disorders Review*, *6*(2), 115–125.

Harrison, A., Tchanturia, K., Naumann, U., & Treasure, J. (2012). Social emotional functioning and cognitive styles in eating disorders. *British Journal of Clinical Psychology*, *51*(3), 261–279.

Hay, P. J., & Carriage, C. (2012). Eating disorder features in indigenous Australian and Torres Strait Islander Australian peoples. *BMC Public Health*, *12*, 233.

Hilbert, A., Tuschen-Caffier, B., Karwautz, A., Niederhofer, H., & Munsch, S. (2007). Eating disorder examination-questionnaire. *Diagnostica*, *53*(3), 144–154.

Kapstad, H., Nelson, M., Øverås, M., & Rø, Ø. (2015). Validation of the Norwegian short version of the Body Shape Questionnaire (BSQ-14). *Nordic Journal of Psychiatry*, *69*(7), 509–514.

Katzman, D. K., Kanbur, N. O., & Steinegger, C. M. (2010). Medical comorbidities of eating disorders. In W. S. Agras (Ed.), *The Oxford handbook of eating disorders* (pp. 267–291). Oxford: Oxford University Press.

Katzman, M. A., Bara-Carril, N., Rabe-Hesketh, S., Schmidt, U., Troop, N., & Treasure, J. (2010). A randomized controlled two-stage trial in the treatment of bulimia nervosa, comparing CBT versus motivational enhancement in phase 1 followed by group versus individual CBT in phase 2. *Psychosomatic Medicine*, *72(7)*, 656–663.

Keel, P. K., Crow, S., Davis, T. L., & Mitchell, J. E. (2002). Assessment of eating disorders: Comparison of interview and questionnaire data from a long-term follow-up study of bulimia nervosa. *Journal of Psychosomatic Research*, *53*(5), 1043–1047.

Kelly, N. R., Mitchell, K. S., Gow, R. W., Trace, S. E., Lydecker, J. A., Bair, C. E., & Mazzeo, S. (2012). An evaluation of the reliability and construct validity of eating disorder measures in white and black women. *Psychological Assessment*, *24* (3), 608.

Kim, B., Kim, I., & Choi, H. (2016). Psychometric Properties and Item Evaluation of Korean Version of Night Eating Questionnaire (KNEQ). *Journal of Korean Academy of Nursing*, *46*(1), 109–117.

Ko, C., & Cohen, H. (1998). Intraethnic comparison of eating attitudes in native Koreans and Korean Americans using a Korean translation of the eating attitudes test. *The Journal of Nervous and Mental Disease*, *186*(10), 631–636.

Konstantakopoulos, G., Tchanturia, K., Surguladze, S. A., & David, A. S. (2011). Insight in eating disorders: clinical and cognitive correlates. *Psychological Medicine*, *41*, 1951–61.

Krabbenborg, M. A. M., Danner, U. N., Larsen, J. K., van der Veer, N., van Elburg, A. A., de Ridder, D. T. D., ... & Engels, R. C. M. E. (2012). The eating disorder diagnostic scale: Psychometric features within a clinical population and a cut-off point to differentiate clinical patients from healthy controls. *European Eating Disorders Review: The Journal of the Eating Disorders Association*, *20*(4), 315–320.

Kurz, A. S., Flynn, M. K., & Bordieri, M. J. (2016). How Bayesian estimation might improve CBS measure development: A case study with body-image flexibility in Hispanic students. *Journal of Contextual Behavioral Science*, *5*(3), 146–153.

Latzer, Y., Tzischinsky, O., Hason, R. M., & Allison, K. (2014). Reliability and cross-validation of the Night Eating Questionnaire (NEQ): Hebrew version. *The Israel Journal of Psychiatry and Related Sciences*, *51*(1), 68–73.

Lavender, J. M., & Anderson, D.A. (2009). Effect of perceived anonymity in assessments of eating disordered behaviours and attitudes. *International Journal of Eating Disorders*, *42*, 546–551.

Lee, S., Kwok, K., Liau, C., & Leung, T. (2002). Screening Chinese patients with eating disorders using the Eating Attitudes Test in Hong Kong. *International Journal of Eating Disorders*, *32*(1), 91–97.

Lee, S., Lee, A. M., Leung, T., & Yu, H. (1997). Psychometric properties of the eating disorders inventory (EDI-1) in a nonclinical Chinese population in Hong Kong. *International Journal of Eating Disorders*, *21*(2), 187–194.

Lee, S. W., Stewart, S. M., Striegel-Moore, R. H., Lee, S., Ho, S., Lee, P. W. H., ... & Lam, T. (2007). Validation of the eating disorder diagnostic scale for use with Hong Kong adolescents. *The International Journal of Eating Disorders*, *40*(6), 569–574.

Legenbauer, T., Vocks, S., & Schütt-Strömel, S. (2007). Validierung einer deutschsprachigen Version des Body Image Avoidance Questionnaire BIAQ. *Diagnostica*, *53*, 218–225.

Lentillon-Kaestner, V., Berchtold, A., Rousseau, A., & Ferrand, C. (2014). Validity and reliability of the French versions of the Body Shape Questionnaire. *Journal of Personality Assessment*, *96*(4), 471–477.

Lluch, A., Kahn, J. P., Stricker-Krongrad, A., Ziegler, O., Drouin, P., & Méjean, L. (1996). Internal validation of a French version of the Dutch Eating Behaviour Questionnaire. *European Psychiatry*, *11*(4), 198–203.

Lucena-Santos, P., Carvalho, S. A., da Silva Oliveira, M., & Pinto-Gouveia, J. (2017). Body-Image Acceptance and Action Questionnaire: Its deleterious influence on binge eating and psychometric validation. *International Journal of Clinical and Health Psychology*, *17*(2), 151–160.

Lundgren, J. D., Allison, K. C., Vinai, P., & Gluck, M. E. (2012). Assessment instruments for night eating syndrome. In J. D. Lundgren, K. C. Allison, & A. J. Stunkard (Eds.), *Night eating syndrome: Research, assessment, and treatment* (pp. 197–217). New York: Guilford Press.

Lydecker, J. A., Cotter, E. W., & Mazzeo, S. E. (2014). Body checking and body image avoidance: Construct validity and norms for college women. *Eating Behaviors*, *15*(1), 13–16.

Machado, P. P., Gonçalves, S., Martins, C., & Soares, I. C. (2001). The Portuguese version of the eating disorders inventory: Evaluation of its psychometric properties. *European Eating Disorders Review*, *9*(1), 43–52.

Machado, P. P., Martins, C., Vaz, A. R., Conceição, E., Bastos, A. P., & Gonçalves, S. (2014). Eating disorder examination questionnaire: Psychometric properties and norms for the Portuguese population. *European Eating Disorders Review*, *22* (6), 448–453.

Maïano, C., Morin, A. J. S; Lanfranchi, M-C., & Therme, P. (2013). The Eating Attitudes Test-26 revisited using exploratory structural equation modeling. *Journal of Abnormal Child Psychology*, *41(5)*, 775–788.

Maïano, C., Morin, A. J., Monthuy-Blanc, J., & Garbarino, J. M. (2009). The Body Image Avoidance Questionnaire: Assessment of its construct validity in a community sample of French adolescents. *International Journal of Behavioral Medicine*, *16* (2), 125–135.

Martín, J., Padierna, A., Unzurrunzaga, A., González, N., Berjano, B., & Quintana, J. M. (2015). Adaptation and validation of the Spanish version of the Clinical Impairment Assessment Questionnaire. *Appetite*, *91*, 20–27.

Meule, A., Allison, K. C., & Platte, P. (2014). A German version of the Night Eating Questionnaire (NEQ): Psychometric properties and correlates in a student sample. *Eating Behaviors*, *15*(4), 523–527.

Miller, W. R., & Rollnick, S. (2012). *Motivational interviewing: Helping People Change* (3rd ed.). New York: Guilford Press.

Mitchell, J. E., & Crow, S. (2006). Medical complications of anorexia nervosa and bulimia nervosa. *Current Opinion in Psychiatry*, *19*, 438–443.

Mitchell, J. E., Hatsukami, D., Eckert, E., & Pyle, R. (1985). Eating disorders questionnaire. *Psychopharmacology Bulletin*, *21*(4), 1025–1043.

Mitchell, K. S., & Mazzeo, S. E. (2004). Binge eating and psychological distress in ethnically diverse undergraduate men and women. *Eating Behaviors*, *5*(2), 157–169.

Moizé, V., Gluck, M. E., Torres, F., Andreu, A., Vidal, J., & Allison, K. (2012). Transcultural adaptation of the Night Eating Questionnaire (NEQ) for its use in the Spanish population. *Eating Behaviors*, *13*(3), 260–263.

Mond, J. M., Hay, P. J., Rodgers, B., Owen, C., & Beumont, P. J. V. (2004). Validity of the Eating Disorders Questionnaire (EDE-Q) in screening for eating disorders in a community sample. *Behaviour Research and Therapy*, *42*, 551–567.

Moore, M., Masuda, A., Hill, M. L., & Goodnight, B. L. (2014). Body image flexibility moderates the association between disordered eating cognition and disordered eating behavior in a non-clinical sample of women: A cross-sectional investigation. *Eating behaviors*, *15*(4), 664–669.

Nagl, M., Hilbert, A., de Zwaan, M., Braehler, E., & Kersting, A. (2016). The German version of the Dutch eating behavior Questionnaire: Psychometric properties, measurement invariance, and population-based norms. *PloS ONE*, *11*(9), e0162510.

Nevonen, L., Clinton, D., & Norring, C. (2006). Validating the EDI-2 in three Swedish female samples: Eating disorders patients, psychiatric outpatients and normal controls. *Nordic Journal of Psychiatry*, *60*(1), 44–50.

Nicdao, E. G., Hong, S., & Takeuchi, D. T. (2007). Prevalence and correlates of eating disorders among Asian Americans: Results from the national Latino and Asian American study. *International Journal of Eating Disorders*, *40*, S22–S26.

Nunes, M. A., Camey, S., Olinto, M. T. A., & Mari, J. D. J. (2005). The validity and 4-year test-retest reliability of the Brazilian version of the Eating Attitudes Test-26. *Brazilian Journal of Medical and Biological Research*, *38*(11), 1655–1662.

Nyman-Carlsson, E., Engström, I., Norring, C., & Nevonen, L. (2015). Eating Disorder Inventory-3, validation in Swedish patients with eating disorders, psychiatric outpatients and a normal control sample. *Nordic Journal of Psychiatry*, *69*(2), 142–151.

Nyman-Carlsson, E., & Garner, D. M. (2016). Eating disorder inventory. In T. Wade (Ed.), *Encyclopedia of feeding and eating disorders*. Singapore: Springer. https://link.springer.com/referenceworkentry/10.1007/978-981-287-087-2_192-1

Partida, O. Z., Garcia, R. R., & Cardenas, A. R. (2006). Evaluation of the binge eating scale in Mexican population: Translation and psychometric properties of the Spanish version. *Psiquiatria*, *22*, 30–36.

Pearson, C., & Smith, G.T. (2015). Bulimic symptom onset in young girls: a longitudinal trajectory analysis. *Journal of Abnormal Psychology*, *124*, 1003–1013.

Pellizzer, M. L., Tiggemann, M., Waller, G., & Wade, T. D. (2018). Measures of body image: Confirmatory factor analysis and association with disordered eating. *Psychological Assessment*, *30*, 143–153. doi:10.1037/pas0000461

Penelo, E., Negrete, A., Portell, M., & Raich, R. M. (2013) Psychometric properties of the Eating Disorder Examination Questionnaire (EDE-Q) and norms for rural and urban adolescent males and females in Mexico. *PLoS ONE*, *8*(12), e83245.

Pereira, A. T., Maia, B., Bos, S., Soares, M. J., Marques, M., Macedo, A., & Azevedo, M. H. (2008). The Portuguese short form of the Eating Attitudes Test-40. *European Eating Disorders Review*, *16*(4), 319–325.

Pisetsky, E. M., Thornton, L. M., Lichtenstein, P., Pedersen, N. L., & Bulik, C. M. (2013). Suicide attempts in women with eating disorders. *Journal of Abnormal Psychology*, *122*, 1042–1056.

Pook, M., Tuschen-Caffier, B., & Brähler, E. (2008). Evaluation and comparison of different versions of the Body Shape Questionnaire. *Psychiatry research*, *158*(1), 67–73.

Price-Evans, K., & Treasure, J. (2011). The use of motivational interviewing in anorexia nervosa. *Child and Adolescent Mental Health*, *16*, 65–70.

Probst, M., Pieters, G., & Vanderlinden, J. (2008). Evaluation of body experience questionnaires in eating disorders in female patients (AN/BN) and nonclinical participants. *International Journal of Eating Disorders*, *41*(7), 657–665.

Randhawa, R., Kaur, J., Kaur, D., & Sidhu, S. (2014). Prevalence of night eating syndrome and obesity among urban adult females of Amritsar (Punjab). *International Journal of Research and Development of Health*, *2*, 70–74.

Reas, D. L., Rø, Ø., Kapstad, H., & Lask, B. (2010). Psychometric properties of the clinical impairment assessment: Norms for young adult women. *International Journal of Eating Disorders*, *43*(1), 72–76.

Reas, D. L., Von Soest, T., & Lask, B. (2009). Reliability and validity of the Norwegian version of the body checking questionnaire. *Tidsskrift for Norsk Psykologforening*, *46*(3), 260–262.

Reas, D. L., Whisenhunt, B. L., Netemeyer, R., & Williamson, D. A. (2002). Development of the body checking questionnaire: A self-report measure of body checking behaviors. *International Journal of Eating Disorders*, *31*(3), 324–333.

Ricca, V., Mannucci, E., Moretti, S., Di Bernardo, M., Zucchi, T., Cabras, P., & Rotella, C. (2000). Screening for binge eating disorder in obese outpatients. *Comprehensive Psychiatry*, *41* (2), 111–115.

Riva, G., & Molinari, E. (1998). Replicated factor analysis of the Italian version of the Body Image Avoidance Questionnaire. *Perceptual and Motor Skills*, *86*(3), 1071–1074.

Rivas, T., Franco, K., Bersabé, R., & Montiel, C. B. (2013). Spanish version of the eating attitudes test 40: Dimensionality, reliability, convergent and criterion validity. *The Spanish journal of psychology*, *16*, 1–11.

Rø, Ø., Reas, D. L., & Lask, B. (2010). Norms for the Eating Disorder Examination Questionnaire among female university students in Norway. *Nordic Journal of Psychiatry*, *64*(6), 428–432.

Robert, S. A., Rohana, A. G., Suehazlyn, Z., Maniam, T., Azhar, S. S., & Azmi, K. N. (2013). The validation of the Malay version of binge eating scale: A comparison with the structured clinical interview for the DSM-IV. *Journal of Eating Disorders*, *1* (1), 28.

Rosen, J. C., Srebnik, D., Saltzberg, E., & Wendt, S. (1991). Development of a Body Image Avoidance Questionnaire. *Psychological Assessment*, *3*(1), 32–37.

Ryu, H. R., Lyle, R. M., Galer-Unti, R. A., & Black, D. R. (1999). Cross-cultural assessment of eating disorders: Psychometric characteristics of a Korean version of the Eating Disorder Inventory-2 and the Bulimia Test-Revised. *Eating Disorders*, *7* (2), 109–122.

Sadeghi, K., Ahmadi, S. M., Rezaei, M., Veisy, F., Raeesi, F., & Shahverdi, J. (2014). Psychometric properties of the 34-item Body Shape Questionnaire in students. *Journal of Kermanshah University of Medical Sciences*, *18*(6), 316–322.

Sandoz, E. K., Wilson, K. G., Merwin, R. M., & Kellum, K. K. (2013). Assessment of body image flexibility: The Body Image-Acceptance and Action Questionnaire. *Journal of Contextual Behavioral Science*, *2*(1), 39–48.

Serpell, L., Teasdale, J., Troop, N., & Treasure, J. (2004). The development of the P-CAN: A scale to operationalise the pros and cons of anorexia nervosa. *International Journal of Eating Disorders*, *36*, 416–33.

Serpell, L., Treasure, J., Teasdale, J., & Sullivan, V. (1999). Anorexia nervosa: Friend or foe? *International Journal of Eating Disorders*, *25*, 177–86.

Silva, W. R., Costa, D., Pimenta, F., Maroco, J., & Campos, J. A. D. B. (2016). Psychometric evaluation of a unified Portuguese-language version of the Body Shape Questionnaire in female university students. *Cadernos de Saúde Pública*, *32*(7).

Smolak, L., & Levine, M.P. (1994). Psychometric properties of the Children's Eating Attitudes Test. *International Journal of Eating Disorders*, *16(3)*, 275–282.

Startup, H., Mountford, V., Lavender, A., & Schmidt, U. (2016). A cognitive behavioural case formulation in complex eating disorder. In N. Tarrier & J. Johnson (Eds.), *Case formulation in cognitive behaviour therapy: The treatment of challenging and complex cases* (pp. 239–264). London: Routledge.

Sternheim, L., Startup, H., Saeidi, S., Morgan, J., Hugo, P., Russell, A., & Schmidt, U. (2012). Understanding catastrophic worry in eating disorders: process and content characteristics. *Journal of Behavior Therapy and Experimental Psychiatry*, *43*, 1095–103.

Stice, E., Fisher, M., & Martinez, E. (2004). Eating disorder diagnostic scale: Additional evidence of reliability and validity. *Psychological Assessment*, *16*(1), 60–71.

Stice, E., Telch, C. F., & Rizvi, S. L. (2000). Development and validation of the eating disorder diagnostic scale: A brief self-report measure of anorexia, bulimia, and binge-eating disorder. *Psychological Assessment*, *12*(2), 123–131.

Swanson, S. A., Aloisio, K. M., Horton, N. J., Sonneville, K. R., Crosby, R. D., Eddy, K. T., Field, A. E., & Micali, N. (2014). Assessing eating disorder symptoms in adolescence: Is there a role for multiple informants? *International Journal of Eating Disorders*, *47*, 475–82.

Swanson, S. A., Brown, T. A., Crosby, R. D., & Keel, P. K. (2014). What are we missing? The costs versus benefits of skip rule designs. *International Journal of Methods and Psychiatric Research*, *23*, 474–85.

Szabo, C. P., & Allwood, C. W. (2004). Application of the Eating Attitudes Test (EAT-26) in a rural, Zulu speaking, adolescent population in South Africa. *World Psychiatry*, *3*(3), 169.

Taranis, L., Touyz, S., & Meyer, C. (2011). Disordered eating and exercise: Development and preliminary validation of the Compulsive Exercise Test. *European Eating Disorder Review*, *19*, 256–268.

Taylor, J. Y., Caldwell, C. H., Baser, R. E., Faison, N., & Jackson, J. S. (2007). Prevalence of eating disorders among blacks in the national survey of American life. *International Journal of Eating Disorders*, *40*, S10–S14.

Thelen, M. H., Farmer, J., Wonderlich, S., & Smith, M. (1991). A revision of the Bulimia Test: The BULIT-R. *Psychological Assessment*, *3*(1), 119–124.

Thelen, M. H., Mintz, L. B., Vander W., & Jillon, S. (1996). The Bulimia Test-Revised: Validation with DSM-IV criteria for bulimia nervosa. Psychological Assessment, *8*(2), 219–221.

Thomas, J. J. (2017). Assessment of feeding and eating disorders. In K. D. Brownell & B. T. Walsh (Eds.), *Eating disorders and obesity: A comprehensive handbook* (3rd ed., pp. 279–283). New York: Guilford Press.

Thornton, C., Russell, J., & Hudson, J. (1998). Does the Composite International Diagnostic Interview underdiagnose the eating disorders? *International Journal of Eating Disorders*, *23*, 341–5.

Thorsteinsdottir, G., & Ulfarsdottir, L. (2008). Eating disorders in college students in Iceland. *The European Journal of Psychiatry*, *22*(2), 107–115.

Tu, C. Y., Tseng, M. C. M., Chang, C. H., & Lin, C. C. (2017). Comparative validity of the Internet and paper-and-pencil versions of the Night Eating Questionnaire. *Comprehensive Psychiatry*, *75*, 53–61.

Utzinger, L. M., & Mitchell, J. E. (2016). Eating disorder questionnaire. In T. Wade (Ed.), *Encyclopedia of feeding and eating disorders*.Singapore: Springer. https://link.springer.com/referenceworkentry/10.1007/978-981-287-087-2_103-2

Vall, E., & Wade, T. D. (2015). Predictors of treatment outcome in individuals with eating disorders: A systematic review and meta-analysis. *International Journal of Eating Disorders, 48*, 946–71.

Van Strien, T., & Oosterveld, P. (2008). The children's DEBQ for assessment of restrained, emotional, and external eating in 7- to 12-year-old children. *International Journal of Eating Disorders, 41* (1), 72–81.

Van Strien, T., & Ouwens, M. (2003). Validation of the Dutch EDI-2 in one clinical and two nonclinical populations. *European Journal of Psychological Assessment, 19*(1), 66.

Van Strien, T., Frijters, J. E., Bergers, G., & Defares, P. B. (1986). The Dutch Eating Behavior Questionnaire (DEBQ) for assessment of restrained, emotional, and external eating behavior. *International Journal of Eating Disorders, 5*(2), 295–315.

Vander Wal, J.S., Stein, R.I., & Blashill, A.J. (2011). The EDE-Q, BULIT-R, and BEDT as self-report measures of binge eating disorder. *Eating Behaviours, 12*(4), 267–71.

Villarroel, A. M., Penelo, E., Portell, M., & Raich, R. M. (2011). Screening for eating disorders in undergraduate women: Norms and validity of the Spanish version of the Eating Disorder Examination Questionnaire (EDE-Q). *Journal of Psychopathology and Behavioral Assessment, 33*(1), 121–128.

Vitousek, K., Watson, S., & Wilson, G. T. (1998). Enhancing motivation for change in treatment-resistant eating disorders. *Clinical Psychology Review, 18*, 391–420.

Wade, T. (2016a). Body shape questionnaire. In T. Wade (Ed.), *Encyclopedia of feeding and eating disorders*. Singapore: Springer. https://link.springer.com/referenceworkentry/10.1007/978-981-287-087-2_212-1

Wade, T. (2016b). Eating attitudes test. In T. Wade (Ed.), *Encyclopedia of feeding and eating disorders*. Singapore: Springer. https://link.springer.com/referenceworkentry/10.1007/978-981-287-087-2_215-1

Wade, T. D., Fairweather-Schmidt, A. K., Zhu, G., Martin, N. G. (2015). Does shared genetic risk contribute to the co-occurrence of eating disorders and suicidality? *International Journal of Eating Disorders, 48*, 684–691.

Waller, G., Cordery, H., Corstorphine, E., Hinrichsen, H., Lawson, R., Mountford, V., & Russell, K. (2007). *Cognitive behavioural therapy for eating disorders. A comprehensive treatment guide*. Cambridge: Cambridge University Press.

Wardle, J. (1987). Eating style: A validation study of the Dutch eating behaviour questionnaire in normal subjects and women with eating disorders. *Journal of Psychosomatic Research, 31*, 161–169.

Warren, C. S., Cepeda-Benito, A., Gleaves, D. H., Moreno, S., Rodriguez, S., ... & Pearson, C. A. (2008). English and Spanish versions of the Body Shape Questionnaire: Measurement equivalence across ethnicity and clinical status. *International Journal of Eating Disorders, 41(3)*, 265–272.

Welch, E., Birgegård, A., Parling, T., & Ghaderi, A. (2011). Eating disorder examination questionnaire and clinical impairment assessment questionnaire: General population and clinical norms for young adult women in Sweden. *Behaviour Research and Therapy, 49*(2), 85–91.

White, E. K., Claudat, K., Jones, S. C., Barchard, K. A., & Warren, C. S. (2015). Psychometric properties of the body checking questionnaire in college women. *Body Image, 13*, 46–52.

White, E. K., & Warren, C. S. (2013). Body checking and avoidance in ethnically diverse female college students. *Body Image, 10*(4), 583–590.

Wilksch, S. M., & Wade, T. D. (2010). Risk factors for clinically significant importance of shape and weight in adolescent girls. *Journal Abnormal Psychology, 119*, 206–215.

Wonderlich, J. A., Lavender, J. M., Wonderlich, S. A., Peterson, C. B., Crow, S. J., Engel, S. G., Le Grange, D., Mitchell, J. E., & Crosby, R. D. (2015). Examining convergence of retrospective and ecological momentary assessment measures of negative affect and eating disorder behaviors. *International Journal of Eating Disorders, 48(3)*, 305–311.

World Health Organization. (1993). *Composite International Diagnostic Interview (CIDI) (Core Version 1.1): Interviewer manual*. New York: American Psychiatric Press.

Young, S., Touyz, S., Meyer, C., Arercelus, J., Rhodes, P., Madden, S., Pike, K., Attia, E., Crosby, R. D., Wales, J., & Hay, P. (2017). Validity of exercise measures in adults with anorexia nervosa: The EDE, compulsive exercise test, and other self-report scales. *International Journal of Eating Disorders, 50*, 533–541.

Yucel, B., Polat, A., Ikiz, T., Dusgor, B. P., & Yavuz, A. E. (2011). The Turkish version of the Eating Disorder Examination Questionnaire: Reliability and validity in adolescents. *European Eating Disorders Review, 19*(6), 509–511.

28 Assessment of Substance Use Disorders

JAMES LANGENBUCHER

Assessment and diagnosis are the necessary first steps in the effective treatment of addiction-related problems, yet few clinicians routinely screen their patients or know much about assessing an addiction-related problem that screening might uncover (Mitchell et al., 2012). Serious cases are regularly missed (O'Connor, Nyquist, & McLellan, 2011).

This chapter addresses important concepts and processes in the assessment of addictive illnesses. It reviews the types of information necessary for formal diagnostic criteria to be met and discusses additional, noncriterion constructs and assessment areas that must be examined if a given case is to be properly understood. Specific diagnostic instruments and enhancements are suggested in each section, one of which is focused on and briefly reviewed, with a preference for those that are more accessible, better tested, less burdensome, and lower in cost.

MAIN ASSESSMENT DOMAINS

Clinical History

Teaching the skill of clinical history-taking has been fundamental to psychiatry for more than a century and a half and is the reason grand rounds and case conferences continue to feature as crucial teaching aids today. History-taking requires, first, the development of a mutually respectful clinical relationship or "therapeutic alliance" (Gaume et al., 2009) within which to manage the denial, rationalization, and rebellion that are often the first qualities presented by new arrivals at the addictions clinic (Rinn et al., 2002). The means by which a therapeutic alliance can be fostered with members of this clinical group are well beyond the scope of this chapter, and even when a good alliance is formed there may still be significant underreporting of symptoms that will require a more searching examination, but there are many reviews and aids available (see Marsh et al., 2012; Meier, Barrowclough, & Donmall, 2015). While developing a good therapeutic alliance through cogent inquiry and frank feedback, the diagnostician maps, via history-taking, the signs and symptoms of addictive behaviors that the *Diagnostic and Statistical Manual of Mental Disorders* (*DSM*) requires, folds in other historical and contextual information, and arrives at a diagnosis, case formulation, and treatment plan that is shared with the patient.

The work-up must survey a number of elements in addition to diagnostic criteria. Chief among them are details about the current use pattern: (1) substances used, (2) typical quantity and frequency, (3) peak quantity and frequency, (4) subjective effects, (5) signs of physiological dependence, (6) route of administration, (7) setting and social aspects of use, (8) consequences of use, (9) benefits of use, (10) periods of abstinence, and (11) recent treatment attempts and relapses. Additionally, the substance use portion of the interview should address distal components including (12) family pattern, (13) age of onset, (14) reasons for initiation, (15) rapidity of symptom acquisition, (16) remote or other treatment history, (17) current chronicity, and others.

Suggested measures for clinical history. Most clinicians, of course, are daunted by the prospect of taking such a detailed history. Fortunately, a number of assessment and diagnostic enhancements are available to clinicians who are not used to taking detailed histories from alcohol and drug users. These include (1) structured and semi-structured interviews (e.g., Comprehensive Addictions and Psychological Evaluation [CAAPE; Hoffmann, 2000]), (2) rating scales (e.g., Addiction Severity Index [ASI; McLellan et al., 1992]), (3) self-administered questionnaires (e.g., Alcohol Use Inventory [AUI; Horn, Wanburg, & Foster, 1990]; Drug Abuse Screening Test [DAST; Skinner, 1982]), and (4) collateral reports (e.g., Drinker Inventory of Consequences [DrInC; Miller, Tonigan, & Longabaugh, 1995]). Many of these tools have specific strengths that can be exploited in particular contexts. It is important to note that study of all of these tools can be used to increase skill and accuracy in both clinical and research settings, whether the instruments themselves are formally administered, front to back, and scale scores are derived, or not. That is, the most skillful practitioners, through long familiarity with these measures, weave items from interviews like the SCID or PRISM, rating scales like the ASI, or questionnaires like the ADS into their interviews. Doing so, they both survey essential areas and produce unambiguous diagnostic results, while nevertheless maintaining a casual, flowing interrogatory style.

Focus on the Addiction Severity Index. The ASI, now in its sixth form, was originally fielded by McLellan and colleagues (1980) to explore "the big picture" of alcohol- and drug-troubled lives rather than diagnostic specifics per se. As such, it exemplifies better than most other measures the broad-ranging history-taking emphasized in this section. Downloadable on the Internet and available in more than eighteen languages (e.g., Japanese, French, German, Czech, Russian), the ASI is a modular, wide-ranging semi-structured interview that has become the go-to assessment instrument relied on by both public agencies and treatment providers (McLellan et al., 2006). Requiring some training in how to use the necessary hour or so of face-to-face interview time, the ASI queries lifetime and current status on seven functional domains – medical status, employment and finances, drug use, alcohol use, legal status and criminal background, family and social functioning, and psychiatric status. Scored by the interviewer, ASI results are available as lifetime severity scores, and computer-generated composite scores reflecting recent (thirty-day) functioning can also be derived. Most importantly, the assessment of multiple areas of functioning permits the interviewer to identify the most urgent problems for intervention, so that some areas that might otherwise be overlooked (e.g., legal or employment problems) can be prioritized in treatment planning.

The ASI was originally developed within a Veterans Administration inpatient system in Philadelphia, with original samples heavily weighted toward narcotics addiction and urban residence, with minority groups somewhat oversampled. Yet the ASI has since been the focus of scores of studies of its reliability and validity as its six versions evolved, applied to respondents as varied as prison inmates (Joyner, Wright, & Devine, 1996), homeless persons (Drake, McHugo, & Biesanz, 1995), and an addictions treatment center in the Netherlands (DeJong et al., 1995). Though usually reviewed in very positive and categorical terms – for example, "The ASI has been found to be reliable and valid across clients of varying demographic features and problems" (Wertz, Cleaveland, & Stephens, 1995) – meta-analysis (Makela, 2004) suggests that, in less than expert hands, only three of the instrument's seven domains – medical status, alcohol use, and psychiatric status – fare consistently well across an international body of studies when subjected to tests, say, of criterion validity (Alterman et al., 2001). Expert, often proprietary, training usually erases this deficit.

The ASI has been extensively normed, with Weisner, McLellan, and Hunkeler (2000), for example, publishing composite and subscale norms on more than 9,000 non-addict HMO enrollees and 327 cases with substance use disorders. Clinically significant cases are easily identified with the ASI in most clinical settings, and special versions applicable to specific demographic groups – for example, teenagers, Native American respondents – can be accessed. Its suggested use here as an enhancement of the kind of clinical history-taking necessary to adequately understand a case of alcohol or drug addiction is abundantly supported by the ASI's wide scope, by our nearly four decades of experience with it, and by its broad use in a variety of public and private service areas.

DSM Diagnosis

Rule-guided diagnosis is essential to all of mental health – clinical, research, and policy domains alike (Nathan, Skinstad, & Langenbucher, 1999). In America, diagnosis is governed by the current edition of the DSM, though assessment is a somewhat broader area, as we are seeing. In May 2013, the American Psychiatric Association released the manual's Fifth Edition (DSM-5; American Psychiatric Association, 2013). The DSM system is explicitly dimensional (Helzer, Bucholz, & Gossop, 2007), requiring that the case be assigned first to a diagnostic category – "Alcohol Use Disorder" or "Cannabis Use Disorder" – then graded for severity (Mild, Moderate, Severe). Severity in DSM-5 is measured by symptom count of 0–11 (though there are, as shown, other measures of severity). Common to all varieties of "Substance Use Disorder" (SUD) in DSM-5 is reference to a single set of eleven symptoms (Table 28.1) based in large part on the "alcohol dependence syndrome" (ADS) concept of Edwards and Gross (1976).

Suggested measures for DSM diagnosis. In the addictions clinic, enhancements based on structured and semi-structured interviews – instruments such as the Alcohol Use Disorder and Associated Disabilities Interview Schedule (AUDADIS-5; Grant et al., 2015), the Structured Clinical Interview for DSM-5 (SCID; First et al., 2016), or the Psychiatric Research Interview for Substance and Mental Disorders – IV (PRISM; Hasin et al., 2006) – are key to making quality diagnostic judgments. Research on interviews of these types shows them to be generally highly reliable, face-valid, with good external criterion validity (Rogers, 2018). The AUDADIS, for example, now in a fifth edition that maps on to DSM-5, has collected scores of reports on its reliability and validity as an interview, bragging kappa and test-retest reliabilities for SUD diagnoses that are uniformly good to excellent (Grant et al., 2015) and generally much higher than for diagnoses of other psychiatric disabilities (e.g., mood, anxiety, trauma, and stress-related concerns). Determining the clinical significance of a case is merely a matter of conducting the

Table 28.1 The dependence syndrome in DSM-5

Dependence Syndrome Construct	DSM-5 Criterion
Tolerance	Need for markedly increased amounts or markedly diminished effect with continued use of the same amount
Withdrawal	Withdrawal, as manifested by the characteristic withdrawal syndrome for the substance
Use to Avoid Withdrawal	Withdrawal, as manifested by the same (or a closely related) substance taken to relieve or avoid withdrawal symptoms
Subjective Compulsion	Continued substance use despite having persistent or recurrent social or interpersonal problems caused or exacerbated by the effects of the substance
	The substance use is continued despite knowledge of having a persistent or recurrent physical or psychological problem that is likely to have been caused or exacerbated by the substance
	The substance is often taken in larger amounts or over a longer period than was intended
	There is a persistent desire or unsuccessful efforts to cut down or control substance use
	Craving or a strong desire or urge to use a specific substance
Salience of Use	Recurrent substance use resulting in a failure to fulfill major role obligations at work, school, or home
	Recurrent substance use in situations in which it is physically hazardous
	A great deal of time is spent in activities necessary to obtain the substance, use the substance, or recover from its effects
	Important social, occupational, or recreational activities are given up or reduced because of substance use
Stereotyped Use Pattern	Not in DSM
Reinstatement of Addiction	

interview and observing which diagnoses are satisfied and at what severity levels. The well-tested interview item-stems, suggested probes, flow diagrams, embedded DSM text, and decision rules that we see in interviews like this are the factors responsible for the success of this kind of measure.

Focus on the PRISM. Designed originally as an enhancement of the SCID, the PRISM is a classic "three-column structured clinical interview," the middle column of each page presenting the actual DSM criterion, the left-hand column providing probes, paraphrases, and interview aids for querying that criterion, and the right-hand column providing checkboxes for whether the criterion was met, subthreshold, not met, or indeterminant. The instrument is also available in computer-administered versions that are easy to navigate and administer.

What makes the PRISM unique is the special steps taken to assess mood, anxiety, and some characterological symptoms in substance users, so as to discriminate legitimate, presumably enduring, illness states like severe anxiety or endogenous depression from more temporary intoxication and withdrawal effects. The diagnosis of comorbid psychiatric illnesses is fraught with difficulty in substance use cases, as pathologies that appear stable and perhaps even primary sometimes resolve and prove secondary and transient, the result of current or recent intoxication or withdrawal. It is for this reason that the PRISM is rated as the best diagnostic option in these cases, though other chapters in this volume may prefer other measures.

A general lifetime substance use screen begins the PRISM, which then assesses DSM symptoms for substance use disorders and for a fairly large number of common comorbidities, providing ample guidelines as these sections are covered for differentiating primary psychiatric symptoms (e.g., autonomic hyperactivity due to anxiety) from substance-induced phenomena (e.g., autonomic hyperactivity due to alcohol withdrawal). In this way, the PRISM is a preferred interview in many research and clinical settings, producing highly reliable diagnoses ($\kappa > 0.70$) for SUD diagnoses and significantly more reliable diagnoses of comorbid states than other interviews. It shows in addition strong associations (intraclass correlations > 0.70; Hasin et al., 2006) to independent measures of severity such as age of onset and chronicity. A further advantage is that the PRISM is fully modular, with users free to "pick and choose" which psychiatric illnesses will be interviewed for and which not. Though not as widely used as many other similar measures such as the SCID, the PRISM is clearly preferred in many settings.

Dependence Syndrome

As shown above, DSM-5 substance use disorders are described by a palette common to all SUDs, so that the diagnostic rules are roughly the same across substances. This was made possible by the elaboration over several decades of the "dependence syndrome" concept, originally termed the alcohol dependence syndrome or ADS and described by Edwards and Gross (1976). The ADS features seven elements (Table 28.1) from which the DSM symptoms are for the most part extracted, and has proven so heuristic that it provides the current framework for understanding even distant nondrug manifestations of appetitive dyscontrol.

DSM-III-R (American Psychiatric Association, 1987) introduced American psychiatry to a set of eleven criteria based in most respects on the ADS. These were carried over into DSM-IV (American Psychiatric Association, 1994), DSM-IV-TR (American Psychiatric Association, 2004) and, most recently, DSM-5, with only the substitution of the dependence syndrome construct of "craving" for the DSM-IV "recurrent legal problems resulting from substance use," which was shown to have important gender, socioeconomic, and cultural biases. While the ADS and the diagnostic criteria based on it arose in alcohol studies, their heuristic value is amply demonstrated in their transfer to other drugs of abuse (Feingold & Rounsaville, 1995; Kosten et al., 1987) and even to many nondrug forms of appetitive dyscontrol such as pathological gambling (Blume, 1997; Brown, 1988), eating disorder (Szmukler, 1987), addiction to exercise (Allegre et al., 2006), "internet addiction" (Cash et al., 2012) and others.

Suggested measures for the dependence syndrome. There is good evidence that the elements of the ADS are unidimensional (Langenbucher et al., 2004), arrayed along a single underlying dimension measurable by instruments or algorithms based on clinical features that the ADS describes. Well-developed instruments such as the Alcohol Use Disorders Identification Test (AUDIT; Babor et al., 2001), Severity of Alcohol Dependence Questionnaire (SADQ; Stockwell, Murphy, & Hodgson, 1983), and others are recommended to scale the severity of dependence in a given case.

Focus on the Alcohol Dependence Scale. The Alcohol Dependence Scale (Skinner & Horn, 1984) provides the best quantitative self-report of the strength of alcohol dependence, as operationalized by the model of Edwards and Gross. A twenty-five-item multiple-choice questionnaire available in paper-and-pencil, interview, or computer-administered form, and in shorter lengths (nine and twelve items) and many languages (e.g., Spanish, German, French, Portuguese, Italian), it contains items that probe such features of alcohol dependence as tolerance, withdrawal, impaired control, awareness of compulsion, and salience of drink-seeking. Thus, it provides a multifactorial assessment of dependence, scaling loss-of-control, obsessive drinking style, and withdrawal liability (Doyle & Donovan, 2009). Though it is a self-report instrument and contains no internal control for response bias (a limitation shared with the other self-report instruments discussed in this chapter), it is one of the most extensively researched questionnaires in the field, generating scores of supporting studies of its test-retest reliability, internal consistency, and its strong association with external severity indicators (Skinner & Horn, 1984) such as craving, chronicity, negative consequences, and others (Doyle & Donovan, 2009). It has been well-normed on various treatment samples: Any score above "0" indicates at least a nascent alcohol problem, while cutting scores of 13, 21, and 30 represent increasingly severe quartiles of alcohol dependence. The ADS requires less than five minutes of response time, is easily scored by the examiner, and is an important component of most good assessment strategies.

Impaired Volitional Control

An addictive process that clouds reason and degrades self-control was identified early by science and remains a feature that is thoroughly integrated in modern conceptualizations of the illness:

> Drug addiction ... is a chronic, relapsing disorder that has been characterized by a compulsion to seek and take drugs, loss of control over drug intake; and an emergence of a negative emotional state (e.g., dysphoria, anxiety and irritability) that defines a motivational withdrawal syndrome when access to the drug is prevented. (Edwards & Koob, 2010, p. 393)

Though by no means the entirety of the phenomenology of addiction, impairment in voluntary control over actions and appetites involving intoxicants or other foci of addictive behavior – a personality feature referred to in other areas of psychology as impulsivity, sensation-seeking, surplus behavioral activation, and so on – is close to the core of modern characterizations of substance dependence.

Suggested measures for impaired volitional control. At the center of the alcohol dependence syndrome and thus fundamental to the symptom palette for all recent versions of the DSM and ICD, the construct of impaired volitional control as it relates to substance use is directly tapped by several DSM-5 criteria – use in larger amounts or over a longer period of time than intended, repeated failures to quit or cut down, continued use despite knowledge of problems – and simply asking about them can prove a reliable guide to the degree of volitional impairment in a given case. Additional measures that can be applied to this dimension more generally include a host of self-reports, including the Barratt Impulsiveness Scale (BIS; Patton, Stanford, & Barratt, 1995), the Eysenck Impulsivity Questionnaire (I5Q; Eysenck et al., 1985), among others. Also available is a growing collection of lab-based, mostly computerized measures of brain processes that control sensitivity to reward delay and capacity to inhibit thought or action (e.g., Go/No-Go, Stop signal [Verbruggen & Logan, 2008], Immediate and Delayed

Memory Test [Dougherty, Marsh, & Mathias, 2002]) and others. Fortunately, there are many good alternatives available for use when assessing volitional control in the addictions clinic, with self-report measures being favored for feasibility and reliability in most applications.

Focus on the Barratt Impulsiveness Scale. The BIS, now in its eleventh iteration (BIS-11; Patton et al., 1995), is a thirty-item self-report measure of common impulsive behaviors and attitudes. In development for nearly fifty years, available in more than a dozen languages (e.g., Italian, German, Chinese, Arabic), widely normed on both American and foreign (e.g., Brazilian; Malloy-Diniz et al., 2015) clinical and normal samples, and probably the most often used and best-researched measure of this construct ever published (for a detailed review, see Stanford et al., 2009), the BIS-11 samples six first-order factors (attention, cognitive instability, motor, perseverance, self-control, and cognitive complexity) and three second-order domains (attentional, motor, and nonplanning) of volitional impairment. Spinella's (2007) detailed study of 700 community respondents developed data on BIS-11 norms adjustable by sex, age, and education. The measure's efficiency in SUD cases is quite impressive: BIS-11 total and some subscale scores predict level of cocaine and MDMA use, predict degree of nicotine dependence in alcoholics, and, among alcohol dependent cases, discriminate early from late onset cases (Dom et al., 2006). This efficiency adequately recommends it as a measure of impaired volitional control, as do its broad availability, deep research base, self-scoring feature, and low response burden.

Craving

Craving for a drug, or urge to use it, is a central feature of the ADS. "Subjective compulsion to use a drug" is related to the discussion on impaired control but it was never satisfactorily operationalized in DSM-III, DSM-III-R, or DSM-IV; none employed craving as a diagnostic criterion. This is surprising given that drug-craving is a well-understood and fairly well-measured feature of substance use (de Bruijn et al., 2005), one that can be identified at the phenomenological (urge to use), behavioral (cue-reactance), and even brain-visualization level (limbic activation). In alcohol research (Ludwig, Wikler, & Stark, 1974), craving is described as an appetitive urge similar to hunger for food or sex, triggered by both internal and external cues. Much of the most relevant and powerful research on craving emerges from the area of smoking cessation research (e.g., Pomerleau, Fertig, & Shanahan, 1983), as craving is a particularly common, enduring, and severe complication of tobacco abstinence that can be easily evoked in the smoking laboratory. Once craving is triggered, there follows a fairly reliable and well-understood cascade of brain and behavioral processes, particularly in severely dependent persons.

Added experimentally as an additional interview item to the existing DSM-IV alcohol dependence and abuse criteria for a survey of more than 18,000 drinkers in the National Longitudinal Alcohol Epidemiologic Survey (NLAES) dataset (Keyes et al., 2011), the experimental craving item distinguished itself as a high severity marker, being strongly associated with measures of prior alcohol dependence, depression, and age of onset. It so significantly increased the discriminatory capacity of Keyes and colleagues' experimental alcohol dependence algorithm compared with the stock DSM-IV algorithm that without much more ado "craving" was added as a criterion to the DSM-5 SUD algorithm, replacing "recurrent legal problems," which had been shown to be highly biased by gender and socioeconomic effects.

Suggested measures for craving. Though craving has been the subject of several hundred studies within the past decade alone, there is no generally accepted methodology for scaling it. It is usually assessed by a single face-valid item, for example "In your entire life, did you ever want a drink so badly that you couldn't think of anything else" (Keyes, 2011). A great deal of new neuroimaging research using various cue-reactivity paradigms is emerging that shows changes in brain areas controlling reward sensitivity, memory, executive control, and affect regulation when craving has presumably been induced in the lab. However, "the magnitude of the correlations between brain activity and craving report are, to date, not sufficiently or consistently robust to indicate that neuroimaging is ready to offer a clinically viable biomarker " (Tiffany & Wray, 2012, p. 412). Self-report measures, even single-items buried in a larger interview, are still preferred.

Focus on the Questionnaire of Smoking Urges. In contrast to using a single face-valid yes/no item as most researchers do, the Questionnaire of Smoking Urges (QSU; Tiffany & Drobes, 1991) permits the bidimensional analysis of tobacco craving – a desire and intention to smoke, and anticipated relief from negative affects – through the use of as few as ten items (Cox, Tiffany, & Christen, 2001). In this last-named study of the QSU-Brief, a ten-item version was found to be highly reliable (internal consistency α = 0.78–0.86), strongly correlated with the original thirty-two-item version of the QSU, and highly predictive of external measures of craving intensity (e.g., mood, smoking history, reasons for smoking, and others). As indicated above, single interview items are usually used to probe craving and are fairly reliable and valid when used in that way, but they are merely qualitative, while multi-item, multidimensional and quantitative measures like the QSU are to be preferred whenever available.

Neuroadaptation

Historically, in addiction studies, neuroadaptation is a *process* whereby the brain, perturbed by regular, sustained, and (usually) high-dose use of a substance, responds to the disturbance in homeostasis through an opponent process to bring the system back to set-point compliance. Most modern theories of alcohol and drug dependence (e.g., Koob & Kreek, 2007; Robinson & Berridge, 2008), however, posit gradual, progressive changes in an interrelated system of brain structures as patients transition from limited use of drugs, to frequent heavy use, to chronic, compulsive use. Most of this change occurs in the *reward* circuit, the *nucleus accumbens* and *the prefrontal cortex* at the level of neurotransmitter supply, receptor populations and sensitivity, second messenger processes, and even the topography itself of neuronal circuitry (Mamelli & Luscher, 2011). As the user transitions to more frequent and high-dose use, the reward circuit finally becomes fully "hijacked" (Lubman, Yücel, & Pantelis, 2004), with increased incentive salience of drug use and associated stimuli.

In the addictions clinic, neuroadaptation is usually encountered in two ways: (1) tolerance for higher doses of the drug to achieve the desired effect, or diminished effect at the same dose, after the body has learned to adapt to the drug, and (2) withdrawal effects, which occur after the regular use has been interrupted or attenuated. As such, neuroadaptation implies extensive, recent experience with a drug. It is usually referred to as physiological dependence and is generally considered a good proxy for case severity.

Suggested measures for neuroadaptation. As is often the case with craving, neuroadaptation is sometimes queried by one or two questions: "Did you find that you needed to drink a lot more in order to get the feeling you wanted than you did when you first started drinking?" "Did you have any withdrawal symptoms when you cut down or stopped drinking, like sweating or racing heart, hand shakes, [etc.]" – probes for tolerance and withdrawal, respectively, from the SCID for DSM-IVTR (First et al., 2007). Also like craving, neuroadaptation can often be assessed in the laboratory, by measurable changes in tolerance (such as body sway or standing steadiness; O'Malley & Maisto, 1984) or signs and symptoms of withdrawal.

Focus on the Clinical Institute Withdrawal Assessment. The Clinical Institute Withdrawal Assessment for Alcohol – Revised (CIWA-AR; Sullivan et al., 1989) is the best-researched measure of neuroadaptation in the form of substance-specific withdrawal. It has widespread application in the clinic, where it is used to guide benzodiazepine dosing and other management of acute alcohol withdrawal (Bayard et al., 2004). Administered as a rating scale by a clinician, the CIWA is the best available method for assessing neuroadaptation in the form of withdrawal liability by surveying ten symptom areas (nausea, tremor, sweating, anxiety, agitation, tactile disturbance, auditory disturbance, visual disturbance, headache, and clouding of sensorium) with carefully constructed and behaviorally anchored rating scales (BARS) scored 1–7 (1–4 for clouding of sensorium). Problem cases are readily identified by BARS score. Because of its many advantages – requiring less than a minute for a qualified professional to complete, use of a BARS response format, proven reliability in a variety of clinical settings (Sullivan et al., 1989), with strong associations with external criteria such as physician ratings (Shaw et al., 1981) – the CIWA is offered as an exceptional measure of this important construct, neuroadaptation.

Negative Consequences and Pathological Patterns

Physical deterioration, social impairment, and disease risk as a result of a pathological pattern of substance use were an early and abiding concern of alcohol and drug studies. We now understand the impairments from substance use to be even more broad (and with an earlier onset) than experts previously imagined, including deterioration in sensory, mobility, and metabolic function, cognitive ability, psychiatric status, employability and productivity, family and social functioning, and other important health dimensions. Key here was the work of E. M. Jellinek (1943, 1952, 1960) who used extensive experience with Alcoholics Anonymous (AA) attendees and adults in treatment to draw attention to many additional important consequences (e.g., frequent blackouts, chronic hangovers, loss of control, morning drinking, multiday benders).

Suggested measures for negative consequences and pathological patterns. Because the effects of alcohol and other drugs on functioning are so diverse, it is impossible to recognize single measures that tap the constructs adequately. There are, though, a number of questionnaires (such as the Michigan Alcoholism Screening Test; Selzer, 1971), screens (AUDIT; Babor et al., 2001), laboratory markers (e.g., elevated liver enzymes), and other measures that can be used to study and document negative consequences and pathological patterns.

Focus on the Drinker Inventory of Consequences. Developed in large part to provide a reliable assessment of problem severity for use in Project MATCH (a historical, multisite clinical trial of three different treatments for alcoholism), the cleverly acronymed "DrInC" (Miller et al., 1995) is a variable fifty-item questionnaire that provides total scores and subscores on five consequence dimensions (physical, interpersonal, intrapersonal, impulse control, and social responsibility). Actually a family of cloned measures, some of different length, it is available in parallel forms for drinkers (DrInC), drug users (the Inventory of Drug Use Consequences, InDUC), and as a "validity check" of the drinker's/user's veracity, significant others or collateral witnesses ratings of male (DrInC-SOm, InDUC-SOm) vs. female drinkers/users consequences (DrInC-SOf, InDUC-SOf), in "lifetime" (DrInC-2L) vs. recent (past three months; DrInC-2R) response frames, and in long (DrInC, InDUC) and short forms (Short Inventory of Problems [SIP-2L, SIP-2R]). Originally normed in its basic forms (DrInC-2L, DrInC-2R) on a sample of 1,728 alcohol in- and outpatients recruited nationally who were also administered a variety of other addiction severity measures, the DrInC was found to be highly reliable – "Subscale coefficients generally fall within the range (.70-.80) specified by Horn et al (1987) to be optimal for balancing scale fidelity and breadth of measurement" (Miller et al., 1995, p. 10) – with good criterion validity, correlating 0.40–0.64 with independent measures of consequences, such as the AUI Role Maladaptation scale, or the Social Behavior Scale of the Psychosocial Functioning Inventory (Feragne, Longabaugh & Stevenson, 1983). Extensive norming, high reliability and good validity, broad coverage of multiple consequences domains, the provision of parallel forms (e.g., DrInC-SOm) for witnesses of the subject's behavior, and good accessibility and low response burden (five minutes administration) make the DrInC family of measures the obvious choice for scaling severity and breadth of negative consequences, in most clinical and research settings.

Stage of Change

There are many important areas of assessment that could be included in this chapter – for example, genetic and early family vulnerability, marital dysfunction, medical consequences of substance use, social funneling, civil or criminal legal jeopardy, and suitability for nonabstinent treatment goals – but the last that will be mentioned here involves the patient's position on the construct of stage of change. Now with great currency in addiction studies, stage of change as both a determinant of treatment choice and a target of clinical intervention first emerged in the transtheoretical model of Prochaska and DiClemente (1983). Stage of change emphasizes variability in the level of intrinsic motivation to change personal behavior and develops a convincing model that behavior change does not happen in a single step but rather progresses through fairly recognizable, common stages, each with its own difficulties and resistances.

In the first stage, "Precontemplation," there is no problem awareness and no intention to change. As the substance user moves to the stage of "Contemplation," negative consequences have forced a gathering awareness of a problem but there is as yet no commitment to change. As the user moves toward "Preparation," there is intention to change and even small-scale stabs at it but the efforts are not disciplined, with frequent false-starts, failures, and brief successes. In "Action," where the bulk of effort is expended, there are overt behavioral changes – use of AA/NA, involvement in therapy, use of an adjuvant medication if indicated, and so on – and considerable commitment, though occasional failure. Finally, in "Maintenance," there is some relaxation of effort but work to consolidate gains and avert or minimize relapse continues. The stage of change model has held up well in application to diverse populations (Norcross, Krebs, & Prochaska, 2011), including alcoholism, anxiety, domestic violence, compulsive gambling, eating disorder, and more, and can be applied confidently when assessing and diagnosing persons suffering from these problems.

Suggested measures for stage of change. As was suggested for constructs such as neuroadaptation or craving, sometimes a single, face-valid query – "Are you contemplating reducing or eliminating your substance use in the near future, say, the next 6 months?" – can satisfactorily ascertain a patient's position on the stage-of-change trajectory. However, there are several well-researched quantitative measures to which the clinician can appeal to better gauge the patient's position, including the University of Rhode Island Change Assessment (URICA; McConnaughy, Prochaska, & Velicer, 1983) the Readiness to Change Questionnaire (RCQ; Heather, Gold, & Rollnick, 1991), among others.

Focus on the SOCRATES. The Stages of Change and Treatment Eagerness Scales (SOCRATES; Miller & Tonigan, 1996) are, somewhat like the DrInC cluster of measures, a family of parallel measures for measuring readiness to change in alcohol users (SOCRATES 8A) and drug users (SOCRATES 8D) and significant others of male vs. female alcohol users (SOCRATES 7A-SO-M and 7A-SO-F) and drug users (SOCRATES 7D-SO-M, 7D-SO-F). The forms used with alcohol and drug users themselves are in their eighth edition, are each composed of nineteen items, and yield total scores and subscores on three factorially derived scales – recognition, ambivalence, and taking steps – on which the SOCRATES is internally consistent and highly reliable. It shows good external validity and is able to predict quit attempts by smokers (DiClemente et al., 1991) and alcoholics (Zhang et al., 2004). Its predictive validity is particularly impressive: In an active-duty military sample of treatment-ready drinkers, SOCRATES scores were highly correlated with attitudes toward treatment, completion of treatment, and length of stay (Mitchell & Angelone, 2006). Detailed norms from the combined MATCH subject groups, along with interpretive guidelines, are in the original Miller and Tonigan (1996) monograph. Brevity, multiple parallel forms, a multifactorial structure, detailed norms, and a solid research base showing good concurrent and predictive validity recommend the SOCRATES as a measure of this important individual differences variable, stage of change.

CONCLUSIONS

Diagnosis and assessment have elements of both art and science (Birley, 1975). As this chapter has shown, the expert evaluation of cases of alcohol and drug addiction is a complex process, fraught with difficulties, and always a work-in-progress as new measures or technologies emerge, are tested, and are refined over time. In this chapter, we of course reviewed the formal diagnosis of substance use disorders through the use of a structured interview like the PRISM to insure that DSM-5 diagnostic criteria are in fact met, and we found that a number of other domains of inquiry – about clinical history, dependence syndrome, impaired volitional control, craving, neuroadaptation, negative consequences and pathological patterns, and stage of change – have themselves deep histories and a host of associated measures that can be useful in formulating the case.

The text of the chapter reviews exemplar and alternative measures in each of these important domains, with the information summarized in Table 28.2. The table in addition provides more descriptive information about exemplar measures and alternative measures, their validation and norming in diverse respondent groups, and whether each is able to assess for response bias. Because of their subject matter, assessment of these domains of substance use disorders relies predominantly on self-report questionnaires and interviews, underlining the importance of collateral reports and other sources of evidence, such as versions of the DrInC (Miller et al., 1995) completed by significant others (DrInC-SOm, DrInC-SOf). Also, users should be aware of the specific ethnic, gender, age, and other socioeconomic properties of the sample to which they wish to apply certain measures and should select them appropriately.

As noted at the outset of this chapter, rule-guided assessment and diagnosis are essential to all of mental health. In the clinic, well-developed systems for assessing and diagnosing patients allow practitioners from disparate backgrounds to communicate via a consensual nomenclature. They help identify patients at various levels of risk, validate effects (or failures) of treatments by providing a simple metric of symptom strength, and of course they confer on insurers the responsibility to honor charges for those treatments, a matter of increasing concern in an age of health care stress and uncertainty (Balsa et al., 2003).

For researchers, well-developed assessment practices are used to select some participants for inclusion in research samples while excluding others, thus protecting the homogeneity and integrity of human research samples. Well-developed assessment practices enable epidemiologists to find base rates, secular trends, and other patterns in the data, provide the key search terms by which research results are organized and archived, and serve numerous other scientific purposes. For policymakers, these diagnostic systems provide the tools to distribute clinical, research, professional training, and other resources fairly and wisely.

It was remarked at the outset that diagnosis and assessment are a truly "daunting task." Hopefully they are a task that, as this chapter lays out, is manifestly worth the effort.

Table 28.2 Favored and alternative measures

Assessment Domain	Measures
Clinical History	Favored: Addiction Severity Index (ASI; McLellan et al., 1980) – "Big picture" of troubled lives rather than diagnostic specifics per se – Modular, wide-ranging semi-structured, clinician-scored interview – Measures 7 functional domains – Scores of reliability and validity studies in varied respondent groups show high predictive and criterion validity when users are well-trained – Used by many public service providers to characterize their populations, the ASI has been extensively normed on clinical and service-seeking respondents of most racial/ethnic, gender, and age categories – Moderate response burden (60 minutes) – This is a clinician-administered rating scale Note also: Comprehensive Addictions and Psychological Evaluation (CAAPE-5; Hoffmann, 2000) – Queries and diagnoses all substance use disorders and comorbid illnesses – Moderate response burden (60 minutes)
DSM Diagnosis	Favored: Psychiatric Research Interview for Substance and Mental Disorders (PRISM; Hasin et al., 2006) – Classic three-column structured, interviewer-scored interview (computer-administered version also available) with item-stems, suggested probes, flow diagrams, embedded criterion text, and decision rules common to such structured interviews

Continued

Table 28.2 (cont.)

Assessment Domain	Measures
	– Queries and diagnoses all SUDs and common comorbid illnesses – Developed as an advanced version of the SCID to better assess common comorbidities of SUDs – Not widely used and so not widely tested but authors show high reliability and criterion validity in primarily urban, male samples – High response burden (> 120 minutes) – This is a clinician-administered interview Note also: Alcohol Use Disorder and Associated Disabilities Interview Schedule (AUDADIS-5; Grant et al., 2015), Comprehensive International Diagnostic Interview – Substance Abuse Module (CIDI-SAM; Cottler, Robins, & Helzer, 1989), Structured Clinical Interview for DSM-5 Disorders, Clinician Version (SCID-5-CV, First et al., 2016) and other similar instruments
Dependence Syndrome	Favored: Alcohol Dependence Scale (ADS; Skinner & Horn, 1984) – 25-item multiple-choice questionnaire (short forms available) – Paper-and-pencil questionnaire, interview or computer-administered – Available in many languages – Multifactorial assessment of dependence, scaling loss-of-control, obsessive drinking style, and withdrawal liability – Scores of studies supporting its test-retest reliability, internal consistency, and strong association with external severity indicators in various treatment samples including most racial/ethnic, gender, and age categories – Low response burden (< 5 minutes) – This is a self-report with no internal control for response bias Note also: AUDIT (Babor et al., 2001), SADQ (Stockwell et al1983), and other similar questionnaires These are measures very comparable to the ADS but generally not as widely applied or well-researched
Impaired Volitional Control	Favored: Barratt Impulsiveness Scale (BIS-11) (Patton et al., 1995) – 30-item self-report measure of common impulsive behaviors/attitudes – Samples from numerous first- and second-order domains of the impulsivity construct – Available in more than a dozen languages – Widely normed on both American and foreign clinical and normal samples, including subjects from most racial/ethnic, gender, and age categories – Very good reliability and good-to-excellent criterion validity – Low response burden (5 minutes) – This is a self-report with no internal control for response bias Note also: Eysenck Impulsivity Questionnaire (I5Q; Eysenck et al., 1985) and other similar self-reports Note also: Lab-based computerized measures (e.g., Go/No-Go, Stop signal [Verbruggen & Logan, 2008], Immediate and Delayed Memory Test [Dougherty et al., 2002]), which are intriguing and emerging but not at this time scientifically mature
Craving	Favored: Questionnaire of Smoking Urges (QSU; Tiffany & Drobes, 1991) – Variable length (10 to 32) self-report items – Yields bidimensional analysis of tobacco craving: desire/intention and anticipated relief – Well-normed on clinical samples of smokers, principally male and urban – Excellent reliability and criterion validity in clinical samples – Low response burden (5 minutes) – This is a self-report with no internal control for response bias Also: Single criterion items from any number of interviews or questionnaires (this is the typical assessment strategy) are sometimes used, e.g., ""In your entire life, did you ever want a drink so badly that you couldn't think of anything else?" (Grant, 1997). Potentially important neuroimaging methods based on cue-reactivity paradigms are emerging but none yet is of criterion quality
Neuroadaptation	Favored: Clinical Institute Withdrawal Assessment for Alcohol – Revised (Sullivan et al., 1989) – Scales neuroadaptation in the form of withdrawal liability – Clinician completes behaviorally anchored rating scales (BARS) for 10 symptom areas

Continued

Table 28.2 (cont.)

Assessment Domain	Measures
	– Highly reliable and strongly correlated with external criteria – Very low response burden (< 1 minute) – This is a clinician-administered rating scale Also note: Neuroadaptation is often queried by one or two direct questions about alcohol tolerance or withdrawal liability Also laboratory measures are available, such as measurable changes in body sway or standing steadiness (O'Malley & Maisto, 1984)
Negative Consequences and Pathological Patterns	Favored: Drinker Inventory of Consequences (Miller, Tonigan, & Longabaugh, 1995) – A family of variable 50-item questionnaires that provide total scores and subscores on 5 consequence dimensions (physical, interpersonal, intrapersonal, impulse control, and social responsibility) – Available in parallel forms for drinkers (DrInC), drug users (the Inventory of Drug Use Consequences, InDUC), and for significant others or collateral witnesses of both male vs. female drinkers/drug users. – Additional forms for lifetime vs. past 3 months problems – Highly reliable and with good criterion validity – Well-normed in its basic forms (DrInC-2L, DrInC-2R) on a sample of 1,728 alcohol in- and out-patients recruited nationally including most racial/ethnic, gender, and age categories – Low response burden (5 minutes) – This is a self-report with no internal control for response bias Also note: A number of highly correlated questionnaires (Michigan Alcoholism Screening Test [MAST]; Selzer, 1971), screens (Alcohol Use Disorders Identification Test [AUDIT]; Babor et al., 2001) are available Also, elevated liver enzymes and other laboratory markers can be used to study and document negative consequences and pathological patterns
Stage of Change	Favored: Stages of Change and Treatment Eagerness Scales (SOCRATES; Miller & Tonigan, 1996) – Similar to the DrInC cluster of measures, SOCRATES is a family of parallel measures for scaling readiness to change in alcohol users and drug users – Total scores and subscores on 3 subscales – recognition, ambivalence, and taking steps – Parallel forms for significant others of male vs. female alcohol vs. drug users are available – Internally consistent and highly reliable with good external and predictive validity – Well-normed in the original Miller and Tonigan (1996) monograph – Low response burden (10 minutes) – This is a self-report with no internal control for response bias Also note: Other well-researched measures include the University of Rhode Island Change Assessment (URICA; McConnaughy et al., 1983) and the Readiness to Change Questionnaire (RCQ; Heather, Gold & Rollnick, 1991) Also a single, face-valid query – "Are you contemplating reducing or eliminating your substance use in the near future, say, the next 6 months?" – can often satisfactorily ascertain a patient's position on the stage-of-change trajectory

REFERENCES

Allegre, B., Souville, M., Therme, P., & Griffiths, M. (2006). Definitions and measures of exercise dependence. *Addiction Research and Theory*, *14*, 631–646.

Alterman, A. I., Mulvaney, F. D., Cacciola, J. S., Cnaan, A., McDermott, P. A., & Brown, L. S., Jr. (2001). The validity of the interviewer severity rating in groups of ASI interviewers with varying training. *Addiction*, *96(9)*, 1297–1305.

American Psychiatric Association. (1987). *Diagnostic and statistical manual of mental disorders* (rev. 3rd ed.). Washington, DC: American Psychiatric Association.

American Psychiatric Association. (1994). *Diagnostic and statistical manual of mental disorders* (4th ed.). Washington, DC: American Psychiatric Association.

American Psychiatric Association. (2004). *Diagnostic and statistical manual of mental disorders* (rev. 4th ed.). Washington, DC: American Psychiatric Association.

American Psychiatric Association. (2013). *Diagnostic and statistical manual of mental disorders* (5th ed.). Washington, DC: American Psychiatric Association.

Babor, T. F., Higgins-Biddle, J. C., Saunders, J. B., & Monteiro, M. G. (2001). *The Alcohol Use Disorders Identification Test (AUDIT): Guidelines for use in primary care*. Geneva: World Health Organization.

Balsa, A. I., Seiler, N., McGuire, T. G., & Bloche, M. G. (2003). Clinical uncertainty and healthcare disparities. *American Journal of Law and Medicine*, *29*, 203–219.

Bayard, M., McIntyre, J., Hill, K. R., & Woodside, J., Jr. (2004). Alcohol withdrawal syndrome. *American Family Physician, 69(6)*, 1443–1450.

Birley, J. L. T. (1975). The history of psychiatry as the history of an art. *British Journal of Psychiatry, 127*, 393–400.

Blume, S. B. (1997). Pathological gambling: Addiction without a drug. In *Substance abuse: A comprehensive textbook* (3rd ed., pp. 330–337). Baltimore, MD: Williams and Wilkins.

Brown, R. I. F. (1988). Models of gambling and gambling addictions as perceptual filters. *Journal of Gambling Studies, 3*, 224–236.

Cash, H., Rae, C. D., Steel, A. H., & Winkler, A. (2012). Internet addiction: A brief summary of research and practice. *Current Psychiatry Review, 8(4)*, 292–298.

Cottler, L. B., Robins, L. N., & Helzer, J. E. (1989). The reliability of the SIDI-SAM: A comprehensive substance abuse interview. *British Journal of Addiction, 84(7)*, 801–814.

Cox, L. S., Tiffany, S. T., & Christen, A. G. (2001). Evaluation of the brief questionnaire of smoking urges (QSU-Brief) in laboratory and clinical settings. *Nicotine and Tobacco Research, 3(1)*, 7–16.

de Bruijn, C., van den Brink, W., de Graaf, R., & Vollebergh, W. A. (2005). The craving withdrawal model for alcoholism: Towards the DSM-V. Improving the discriminant validity of alcohol use disorder diagnosis. *Alcohol and Alcoholism, 40*, 314–22.

DeJong, C. A. J., Willems, J. C. E. W., Schippers, G. M., & Hendricks, V. M. (1995). The Addiction Severity Index: Reliability and validity in a Dutch alcoholic population. *International Journal of the Addictions, 30*, 605–616.

DiClemente, C. C., Prochaska, J. O., Fairhurst, S. K., Velicer, W. F., Velasquez, M. M., & Rossi, J. S. (1991). The process of smoking cessation: An analysis of precontemplation, contemplation, and preparation stages of change. *Journal of Consulting and Clinical Psychology, 59*, 295–304.

Dom, G., D'haene, P., Hulstijn, W., & Sabbe, B. (2006). Inpulsivity in abstinent early- and late-onset alcoholics: Differences in self-report measures and a discounting task. *Addiction, 101(1)*, 50–59.

Dougherty, D. M., Marsh, D. M., & Mathias, C. W. (2002). Immediate and delayed memory tasks: A computerized behavioral measure of memory, attention, and impulsivity. *Behavioral Research Methods: Instruments and Computers, 34*, 391–398.

Doyle, S. R., & Donovan, D. M. (2009). A validation study of the Alcohol Dependence Scale. *Journal of Studies on Alcohol and Drugs, 70(5)*, 689–699.

Drake, R. E., McHugo, G. J., & Biesanz, J. C. (1995). The test-retest reliability of standardized instruments among homeless persons with substance use disorders. *Journal of Studies on Alcohol, 56*, 161–167.

Edwards, G., & Gross, M. M. (1976). Alcohol dependence: Provisional description of a clinical syndrome. *British Medical Journal, 1*, 1058–1061.

Edwards, S., & Koob, G. F. (2010). Neurobiology of dysregulated motivational systems in drug addiction. *Future of Neurology, 5*, 393–401.

Eysenck, S. B. G, Pearson, P. R., Easting, G., & Allsopp, J. F. (1985). Age norms for impulsiveness, venturesomeness and empathy in adults. *Personality and Individual Differences, 6*, 613–619.

Feingold, A., & Rounsaville, B. (1995). Construct validity of the dependence syndrome as measured by DSM-IV for different psychoactive substances. *Addiction, 90*, 1661–1669.

Feragne, M., Longabaugh, R., & Stevenson, J. F. (1983). The Psychosocial Functioning Inventory. *Evaluation and Health Professions, 6*, 25–48.

First, M. B., Williams, J. B. W., Karg, R. S., & Spitzer, R. S. (2016). *Structured Clinical Interview for DSM-5 Disorders – Clinician version*. Washington, DC: American Psychiatric Association.

First, M. B., Williams, J. B. W., Spitzer, R. L., & Gibbons, M. (2007). *Structured Clinical Interview for DSM-IV-TR Axis I Disorders*. New York: Biometrics Research, New York State Psychiatric Institute.

Gaume, J., Gmel, G., Faouzi, M., & Daeppen, J. B. (2009). Counselor skill influences outcomes of brief motivational interventions. *Journal of Substance Abuse Treatment, 37*, 151–159.

Grant, B. F. (1997). Prevalence and correlates of alcohol use and DSM-IV alcohol dependence in the United States: Results of the National Longitudinal Alcohol Epidemiologic Survey. *Journal of Studies on Alcohol, 58*, 464–473.

Grant, B. F., Goldstein, R. B., Smith, S. M., Jung, J., Zhang, H., Chou, S. P. et al. (2015). The Alcohol Use Disorders and Associated Disabilities Interview Schedule – 5 (AUDADIS-5): Reliability of substance use and psychiatric disorder modules in a general population sample. *Drug and Alcohol Dependence, 148*, 27–33.

Hasin, D. S., Samet, S., Nunes, E., Meydan, J., Matseoane, K., & Waxman, R. (2006). Diagnosis of comorbid disorders in substance users: Psychiatric Research Interview for Substance and Mental Disorders (PRISM-IV): Reliability for substance abusers. *American Journal of Psychiatry, 163 (4)*, 689–696.

Heather, N., Gold, R., & Rollnick, S. (1991). *Readiness to Change Questionnaire: User's manual*. Sydney: National Drug and Alcohol Research Center and University of New South Wales

Helzer, J. E., Bucholz, K. K., & Gossop, M. (2007). A dimensional option for the diagnosis of substance dependence in DSM-V. *International Journal of Methods in Psychiatric Research, 16, Suppl 1*, S24–S33.

Hoffmann, N. G. (2000). *CAAPE (Comprehensive Addictions and Psychological Evaluation) manual*. Smithfield, RI: Evince Clinical Assessments

Horn, J., Wanberg, K. W., & Foster, F. M. (1990). *Alcohol Use Inventory*. San Antonio, TX: PsychCorp.

Jellinek, E. M. (1943). The alcohol problem: Formulations and attitudes. *Quarterly Journal of Studies on Alcohol, 4*, 446–461.

Jellinek, E. M. (1952). Phases of alcohol addiction. *Quarterly Journal of Studies on Alcohol, 13*, 673–684.

Jellinek E. M. (1960). *The disease concept of alcoholism*. Highland Park, NJ: Hillhouse Press.

Joyner, L. M., Wright, J. D., & Devine, J. A. (1996). Reliability and validity of the Addiction Severity Index among homeless substance misusers. *Substance Use and Misuse, 31*, 729–751.

Keyes, K. M., Krueger, R. F., Grant, B. F., & Hasin, D,S. (2011). Alcohol craving and the dimensionality of alcohol disorders. Psychological Medicine, *41*, 629–640.

Koob, G., & Kreek, M. J. (2007). Stress, dysregulation of drug reward pathways, and the transition to drug dependence. *American Journal of Psychiatry, 164*, 1149–1159.

Kosten, T. R., Rounsaville, B. J., Babor, T. F., Spitzer, R. L., & Williams, J. B. (1987). Substance-use disorders in DSM-III-R: Evidence for the dependence syndrome across different psychoactive substances. *British Journal of Psychiatry, 151*, 834–843.

Langenbucher, J., Labouvie, E., Sanjuan, P., Kirisci, L., Bavly, L., Martin, C., & Chung, T. (2004). An application of Item Response Theory analysis to alcohol, cannabis and cocaine criteria in DSM-IV. *Journal of Abnormal Psychology, 113(1)*, 72–80.

Lubman, D. I., Yucel, M., & Pantelis, C. (2004). Addiction, a condition of compulsive behavior? Neuroimaging and neuropsychological evidence of inhibitory dysregulation. *Addiction, 99*, 1491–1502.

Ludwig, A. M., Wikler, A., & Stark, L. H. (1974). The first drink: Psychobiological aspects of craving. *Archives of General Psychiatry, 30*, 539–547.

Makela, K. (2004). Studies of the reliability and validity of the Addiction Severity Index. *Addiction, 99*, 398–410.

Malloy-Diniz, L. F., de Paula, J. J., Vasconcelos, A. G., Almondes, K. M., Pessoa, R., Faria, L. et al. (2015). Normative data of the Barratt Impulsiveness Scale 11 (BIS-11) for Brazilian adults. *Brazilian Journal of Psychiatry, 37(3)*, 245–248.

Mamelli, M., & Luscher, C. (2011). Synaptic plasticity and addiction: Learning mechanisms gone awry. *Neuropsychopharmacology, 61(7)*, 1052–1059.

Marsh, J. C., Angell, B., Andrews, C. M., & Curry, A. (2012). Client-provider relationship and treatment outcome: A systematic review of substance abuse, child welfare, and mental health services research. *Journal of the Society of Social Work and Research, 3(4)*, 233–267.

McConnaughy, E. A., Prochaska, J. O., & Velicer, W. F. (1983). Stages of change in psychotherapy: Measurement and sample profiles. *Psychotherapy, 20*, 368–375.

McLellan, A. T., Cacciola, J. C., Alterman, A. I., Rikoon, S. H., & Carise, D. (2006). The Addiction Severity Index at 25: Origins, contributions and transitions. *American Journal on Addictions, 15*(2), 113–124.

McLellan, A. T., Kushner, H., Metzger, D., Peters, R., Smith, I., Grissom, G., Pettinati, H., & Argeriou, M. (1992). The fifth edition of the Addiction Severity Index. *Journal of Substance Abuse Treatment, 9*, 199–213.

McLellan, A. T., Luborsky, L, Woody, G. E., & O'Brien, C. P. (1980). An improved diagnostic evaluation instrument for substance abuse patients: The Addiction Severity Index. *Journal of Nervous and Mental Disease, 168*(1), 26–33.

Meier, P. S., Barrowclough, C., & Donmallo, M. C. (2015). The role of the therapeutic alliance in the treatment of substance misuse: A critical review of the literature. *Addiction, 100(3)*, 304–316.

Miller, W. R., & Tonigan, J. S. (1996). Assessing drinkers' motivation for change: The Stages of Change Readiness and Treatment Eagerness Scale (SOCRATES). *Psychology of Addictive Behaviors, 10*, 81–89.

Miller, W. R., Tonigan, J. S. & Longabaugh, R. (1995). *The Drinker Inventory of Consequences (DrInC): An instrument for assessing adverse consequences of alcohol abuse* (Project MATCH Monograph Series, Vol. *4*. DHHS Publication No. 95-3911.) Rockville, MD: National Institute on Alcohol Abuse and Alcoholism.

Mitchell, A. J., Meader, N., Bird, V., & Rizzo, M. (2012). Clinical recognition and recording of alcohol disorders by clinicians in primary and secondary care: Meta-analysis. *British Journal of Psychiatry, 201(2)*, 93–100.

Mitchell, D., & Angelone, D. J. (2006). Assessing the validity of the Stages of Change Readiness and Treatment Eagerness Scale with treatment-seeking military service member. *Military Medicine, 171*, 900–904.

Nathan, P. E., Skinstad, A. H., & Langenbucher, J. W. (1999). Substance abuse: Diagnosis, comorbidity, and psychopathology. In T. Millon, P. H. Blaney, & R. D. Davis (Eds.), *Oxford textbook of psychopathology* (pp. 227–248). New York: Oxford University Press.

Norcross, J. C., Krebs, P. M., & Prochaska, J. O. (2011). Stages of change. *Journal of Clinical Psychology, 67*, 143–154.

O'Connor, P. G., Nyquist, J. G., & McLellan, A. T. (2011). Integrating addiction medicine into graduate medical education in primary care: The time has come. *Annals of Internal Medicine, 154*, 56–9.

O'Malley, S. S., & Maisto, S. A. (1984). Factors affecting the perception of intoxication: Dose, tolerance, and setting. *Addictive Behaviors, 2*, 111–120.

Patton, J. H., Stanford, M. S., & Barratt, E. S. (1995). Factor structure of the Barratt Impulsiveness Scale. *Journal of Clinical Psychology, 51*, 768–774.

Pomerleau, O. F., Fertig, J. B., & Shanahan, S. O. (1983). Nicotine dependence in cigarette smoking: An empirically-based, multivariate model. *Pharmacology, Biochemistry and Behavior, 19*, 291–299.

Prochaska, J. O., & DiClemente, C. C. (1983). Stages and processes of self-change of smoking: Toward an integrative model of change. *Journal of Consulting and Clinical Psychology, 51*, 390–395.

Rinn, W., Desai, N., Rosenblatt, H., & Gastfriend, D. R. (2002). Addiction denial and cognitive dysfunction: A preliminary investigation. *Journal of Neuropsychiatry and Clinical Neuroscience, 14*, 52–7.

Robinson, T. E., & Berridge, K. C. (2008) Review. The incentive sensitization theory of addiction: Some current issues. *Philosophical Transactions of the Royal Society, London: B Biological Sciences, 363*, 3137–3146.

Rogers, R. (2018). *Handbook of Diagnostic and Structured Interviewing* (Amazon ePub RK–41182).

Selzer, M. I. (1971). The Michigan Alcoholism Screening Test (MAST): The quest for a new diagnostic instrument. *American Journal of Psychiatry, 127*, 1653–1658.

Shaw, J. M., Kolesar, G. S., Sellers, E. M., Kaplan, H. L., & Sandor, P. (1981). Development of optimal treatment tactics for alcohol withdrawal. I. Assessment and effectiveness of supportive care. *Journal of Clinical Psychopharmacology, 1*, 382–387.

Skinner, H. A. (1982). The Drug Abuse Screening Test. *Addictive Behaviors, 7*, 363–371.

Skinner, H. A., & Horn, J. L. (1984). *Alcohol Dependence Scale: User's guide*. Toronto: Addiction Research Foundation.

Spinella, M. (2007). Normative data and a short form of the Barratt Impulsiveness Scale. *International Journal of Neuroscience, 177*, 359–368.

Stanford, M. S., Mathias, C. W., Dougherty, D. M., Lake, S.L, Anderson, N.E., & Patton, J.H. (2009). Fifty years of the Barratt Impulsiveness Scale: An update and review. *Personality and Individual Differences, 47*, 385–395.

Stockwell, T., Murphy, D., & Hodgson, R. (1983). The severity of alcohol dependence questionnaire: Its use, reliability and validity. *British Journal of Addiction, 78(2)*, 145–156.

Sullivan, J. T., Sykora, K., Schneiderman, J., Naranjo, C. A., & Sellers, E. M. (1989). Assessment of alcohol withdrawal: The revised Clinical Institute Withdrawal Assessment for Alcohol scale (CIWA-Ar). *British Journal of Addiction, 84(11)*, 1153–1157.

Szmukler, G. I. (1987). Some comments on the link between anorexia nervosa and affective disorder. *International Journal of Eating Disorders*, *6*, 181–189.

Tiffany, S. T., & Drobes, D. J. (1991). The development and initial validation of a questionnaire on smoking urges. *British Journal of Addiction*, *86*, 1467–1476.

Tiffany, S. T., & Wray, J. M. (2012). The clinical significance of drug craving. *Annals of the New York Academy of Sciences*, *1248*, 1–17.

Verbruggen, F., & Logan, G. D. (2008). Response inhibition in the stop-signal paradigm. *Trends in Cognitive Science*, *12(11)*, 418–424.

Weisner, C., McLellan, A. T., & Hunkeler, M. A. (2000). Addiction Severity Index data from general membership and treatment samples of HMO members: One case of norming the ASI. *Journal of Substance Abuse Treatment*, *19 (2)*, 103–109.

Wertz, J. S., Cleaveland, B. I., & Stephens, R. S. (1995). Problems in the application of the Addiction Severity Index (ASI) in rural substance abuse services. *Journal of Substance Abuse*, *7*, 175–188.

Zhang, A. Y., Harmon, J. A., Werkner, J., & McCormick, R. A. (2004). Impacts of motivation for change on the severity of alcohol use by patients with severe and persistent mental illness. *Journal of Studies on Alcohol*, *65*(*3*), 392–397.

29 Assessment of Personality Disorder

LEONARD J. SIMMS, TREVOR F. WILLIAMS, AND CHLOE M. EVANS

The classification and assessment of personality disorder (PD) is a topic currently mired in confusion and controversy. Over the past decades, evidence has mounted showing the limitations of the traditional, categorical model of PD presented in our official diagnostic manuals, culminating in a significant effort to revise the official PD classification in the fifth edition of the *Diagnostic and Statistical Manual of Mental Disorders* (DSM-5; American Psychiatric Association, 2013). These efforts have led to a confusing state of affairs in which we have two distinct systems in place for classifying personality pathology: (1) the official categorical approach, presented in Section II of DSM-5, which essentially maintains the approach used to classify PDs since 1980, and (2) an alternative model of personality disorder (AMPD), presented in Section III of DSM-5, which was offered as a categorical-dimensional hybrid method for classifying PDs. Unfortunately, this diagnostic confusion has translated into a fractured assessment picture, with methods available for measuring PD rooted in more traditional syndromal accounts of PD or in trait-dimensional conceptualizations of personality pathology.

In this chapter, we describe the prominent methods available to assess PD from both traditions. Our review of traditional methods will take the form of a critical review, given the limitations of the DSM-based model underlying those measures. In contrast, our goal in presenting the measures rooted in the dimensional, AMPD tradition is to describe these measures and the future directions that are needed to improve their traction in applied settings. Notably, the scope of this chapter includes prominent models and measures and thus will not represent an exhaustive summary of all possible PD assessment methods. Rather, we focus on those methods that have gained traction in clinical or research settings, or that represent promising steps forward that need additional research and clinical translation efforts. Moreover, our review is focused on omnibus measures that present a relatively "complete" picture of personality pathology, rather than measures that focus on the features of only one or a limited set of PDs.

In addition, we will address two important topics relevant to PD assessment. First, we will discuss the cross-cultural PD assessment literature, which is characterized by a relative lack of strong cross-cultural research on the manifestation and measurement of PD. Second, we will address the glaring disconnect between research and applied measurement of PD.

TRADITIONAL CATEGORICAL MEASURES OF PD

Traditional PD classification systems, such as those based in the DSM and the International Classification of Diseases (ICD), describe PD using a medical model within which pathological syndromes are viewed as being either present or absent. However, although the inclusion of PDs on Axis II as an independent domain in DSM-III (American Psychiatric Association, 1980) was regarded as an important advance (e.g., reliability of PD diagnoses was supposed to improve relative to previous PD classifications), the categorical model used by that and subsequent editions of the DSM repeatedly has been shown to suffer from a number of problems that limit its usefulness, including high rates of diagnostic comorbidity (e.g., Clark, Watson, & Reynolds, 1995), within-disorder heterogeneity (e.g., Clark et al., 1995; Widiger, 1993), an arbitrary boundary between normal and abnormal personality traits (e.g., Clark et al., 1995; Livesley, Jang, & Vernon, 1998; Widiger & Clark, 2000), poor reliability (Dreessen & Arntz, 1998; Zanarini et al., 2000), and low convergent validity (see Clark, 2007, for a complete review of all of these issues).

These limitations led to a significant effort to revise the official PD classification in the run-up to the publication of DSM-5. Unfortunately, the efforts to update PD classification in a way that was responsive to the scientific literature were met with resistance from those within the American Psychiatric Association and, indeed, in other sectors of the mental health community (e.g., Krueger, 2013). Ultimately, the AMPD approach to PD classification – to be described in the "Dimensional Models and Measures" section of this chapter – was not approved by the American Psychiatric Association Board of Trustees, who instead agreed to publish it in Section III of DSM-5, presumably to spark much-needed research into this new model and the measures associated with it. The Section II PD classification, in contrast, essentially represents a copy and paste of the system that was presented in DSM-IV-TR (American Psychiatric Association, 2000).

Thus, the "official" PD classification in DSM-5 remains the same categorical approach that has been in place, in various forms, since 1980. In the current instantiation of this approach, ten purportedly distinct PDs are classified. Section II of DSM-5 includes the following ten PDs: Borderline PD, Antisocial PD, Narcissistic PD, Histrionic PD, Avoidant PD, Dependent PD, Obsessive-Compulsive PD, Schizotypal PD, Paranoid PD, and Schizoid PD. These disorders previously were nested within three "clusters" but that distinction was eliminated in DSM-5. Moreover, in addition to the previously described limitations regarding the categorical PD classification as a whole, it is worth noting that relatively few of the traditional PDs – notably Borderline, Antisocial, and, to a lesser extent, Schizotypal PD – account for the lion's share of research in the PD literature. That said, interest remains in measuring these traditional representations of personality pathology. DSM-based PD measures typically take the form of both self-report measures and interview-based methods. Self-report measures have the primary benefit of efficient and cost-effective administration, whereas interview methods are more labor-intensive. Moreover, some have argued that individuals with PDs sometimes lack enough insight into their personality problems to make reliable and valid reports of such, and thus interviews may be preferable because they permit clinical judgments of interviewers to clarify, refine, or confirm the diagnostic picture (e.g., McDermutt & Zimmerman, 2005). Although self-reports of PD symptoms have been shown to be reliable and valid, interview methods often are used in research and applied settings where diagnostic criteria are being assessed, presumably because of their greater attention to the exact PD criteria and their diagnostic thresholds.

In this section of the chapter, we will review DSM-based PD measures in several categories: (1) interview-based methods, (2) self-report methods solely focused on measuring PD, and (3) self-report methods embedded within broader omnibus psychopathology measures. In addition, we will briefly review several legacy methods for assessing personality pathology. All reviewed measures are summarized in Table 29.1 with respect to their basic features, aspects relevant to clinical translations, and our subjective evaluation of the overall quality of the reliability and validity evidence that is available.

Interview-Based Measures of Traditional PD Categories

Psychiatric interviews typically come in two basic varieties: fully structured and semi-structured. All prominent PD interviews are semi-structured, which means that they permit the interviewer some flexibility in terms of follow-up questions and other aspects of the interview. We briefly describe four semi-structured interviews developed to measure the official PDs found in DSM-IV-TR and, thus, in Section II of DSM-5: (1) the Structured Clinical Interview for DSM-IV Axis II Personality Disorders (SCID-II; First & Gibbon, 2004), (2) Structured Interview for DSM-IV Personality Disorders (SIDP-IV; Pfohl, Blum, & Zimmerman, 1997), (3) the Diagnostic Interview for DSM-IV Personality Disorders (DIPD-IV; Zanarini et al., 1996), and (4) the International Personality Disorder Examination (IPDE; Loranger, 1999). Notably, these interviews are quite similar in that they all are keyed to the official PD criteria as listed in DSM-IV/5. However, each also has unique features – that will be the focus of our discussion here – that differentiate them.

One way the interviews differ is in the attention they have been paid in the PD literature. The SCID-II clearly leads the pack in terms of research use. A search of PsycInfo with the keyword searches of "SCID-II," "IPDE," "SIDP," and "DIPD" yielded 716, 125, 99, and 15 published papers, respectively. Although these search results likely are not exhaustive (additional search terms might yield additional hits), the rank-ordering of these results is not likely to charge markedly from that presented here. Thus, the SCID-II is the predominant interview used to measure PDs keyed to DSM-IV/5 criteria. Notably, the SCID-II recently was updated for DSM-5 (SCID-5-PD; First et al., 2015). Although the PD criteria were unchanged in DSM-5, the website promoting the SCID-5-PD reports that "SCID-5-PD interview questions have been thoroughly reviewed and revised to optimally capture the construct embodied in the diagnostic criteria."[1] That said, only a single peer-reviewed study was evident on PsycInfo – using the search term "SCID-5-PD" – at the time of writing this chapter. Thus, more work clearly is needed to study this new version.

A second way the prominent PD interviews differ is whether they include an accompanying questionnaire that can be used either as a screening device or as an independent self-report measure of PD symptomatology. Of the four prominent measures reviewed here, only two – the SCID-II and IPDE – include such a questionnaire. A third way the PD interviews differ is in their ordering of questions. The SCID-II, IPDE, and DIPD-IV interviews present questions on a disorder-by-disorder basis, which may have the effect of alerting patients and research participants to the nature of the disorders being assessed. In contrast, the SIDP-IV arranges interview questions topically rather than by disorder. That is, SIDP-IV interview questions are presented within topical sections (e.g., "work activities" and "interests and activities"), which presumably guards against patients easily inferring the disorders being assessed. A final way the interviews differ is in

[1] See https://tinyurl.com/ya47dk6v

Table 29.1 Summary of personality disorder measures reviewed

Measure	Citation	Variables Measured	Validity Scales	Norm Samples	Related Measures	Languages	Quality of Reliability Evidence	Quality of Validity Evidence
				Interview/Clinician Measures Within The DSM Tradition				
Structured Interview for DSM-IV Personality Disorders (SIDP-IV)	Pfohl, Blum, & Zimmerman (1997)	DSM-IV PDs	None	criterion-referenced (DSM)	–	English	moderate	moderate
Structured Clinical Interview for DSM-IV Personality Disorders (SCID-II) (also a version for DSM-5)	First & Gibbon (2004); First et al. (2015)	DSM-IV PDs	None	criterion-referenced (DSM)	SCID-II-PQ	English, Mandarin, Korean, Danish, Dutch, French, German, Greek, Hebrew, Italian, Portuguese, Romanian, Spanish, Swedish, Turkish, Zulu	excellent	moderate
Diagnostic Interview for Personality Disorders (DIPD-IV)	Zanarini et al., 1996	DSM-IV PDs	None	criterion-referenced (DSM)		English, Spanish	moderate	moderate
International Personality Disorder Examination (IPDE)	Loranger (1999)	DSM-IV PDs	None	criterion-referenced (DSM)	screening questionnaire	English, Arabic	excellent	moderate
Shedler-Westen Assessment Procedure (SWAP-200)	Westen & Shedler (2007)	DSM PDs, alternative PDs, and traits	None	clinical PD sample (Westen & Shedler, 1999a, 1999b)	SWAP-II, SWAP-II-A (Adolescents)	English, German, French, Italian, Spanish, Portuguese, Dutch, Polish, Swedish, Norwegian, Russian, Hebrew, Persian, Japanese	excellent	moderate
				Standalone Self-Report DSM Measures				
Personality Diagnostic Questionnnaire-4 (PDQ-4)	Hyler (1994)	DSM-IV PDs	None	criterion-referenced (DSM)	–	English, Spanish, French, Chinese, Italian	fair	moderate
SCID-II Personality Questionnaire (SCID-II-PQ, plus the revised SCID-5-SPQ for DSM-5)	First & Gibbon (2004); First et al. (2016)	DSM-IV PDs	None	criterion-referenced (DSM)	SCID-II	English, Danish, Dutch, Greek, German, Italian, Korean, Polish, Romanian, Turkish	fair	moderate
Multi-Source Assessment of Personality Pathology (MAPP)	Oltmanns & Turkheimer (2006)	DSM-IV PDs	None	criterion-referenced (DSM)	self-report, other-report	English	moderate	moderate

Continued

Assessment of DSM-IV Personality Disorders (ADP-IV)	Schotte et al. (1998)	DSM-IV PDs	None	criterion-referenced (DSM)	–	English, German, Dutch	fair	moderate
DSM Measures Nested in Broader Measures								
SNAP-2 PD scales	Clark et al. (2002)	DSM-IV PDs + PD traits	Overreporting, underreporting, inconsistency scales	community adults, college students, clinical sample, military veterans (Calabrese et al., 2012)	SNAP-Youth, SNAP-Other Rating Form	English	moderate	moderate
OMNI-IV Personality Inventory	Loranger (2002)	DSM-IV PDs + personality traits	Inconsistency scale	community adults	OMNI	English	moderate	moderate
Coolidge Axis II Inventory (CATI)	Coolidge & Merwin (1992)	DSM-IV PDs, personality traits, other clinical syndromes	random responding, excessive denial, malingering scales	undergraduate sample	SCATI (Short Form)	English, Italian, Bulgarian	moderate	moderate
Minnesota Multiphasic Personality Inventory-2-Restructured Form PD scales	Sellbom, Waugh, & Hopwood (2018)	DSM-IV PDs, personality traits, other clinical syndromes	Overreporting, underreporting, inconsistency scales	community sample	MMPI-2	English, Bulgarian, Chinese, Croatian, Czech, Danish, Dutch, French-Canadian, German, Greek, Hebrew, Hmong, Hungarian, Italian, Korean, Norwegian, Polish, Romanian, Slovak, Spanish, Swedish, Ukrainian	moderate	moderate
PD similarity scores derived from the Revised NEO Personality Inventory (NEO PI-R/3)	Costa & McCrae (1992); Lynam & Widiger (2001)	DSM-IV PDs, personality traits	None	community sample			fair	moderate
Legacy Measures								
Millon Clinical Multiaxial Inventory-IV (MCMI-IV)	Millon, Grossman, & Millon, 2015)	DSM-IV and other PDs, personality traits, other clinical syndromes	Overreporting, underreporting, inconsistency scales	clinical sample (*N* = 600)	–	English, Spanish	excellent	moderate
Wisconsin Personality Disorders Inventory (WISPI-IV)	Klein et al. (1993)	DSM-IV PDs	None	criterion-referenced (DSM)	–	English, Spanish	excellent	fair
Non-AMPD Trait-Dimensional Measures								
Schedule for Nonadaptive and Adaptive Personality (SNAP-2)	Clark et al. (2002)	DSM-IV PDs + PD traits	Overreporting, underreporting, inconsistency scales	community sample	SNAP-Youth, SNAP-Informant Rating Form, Short Form	English	excellent	excellent

Continued

Table 29.1 (cont.)

Measure	Citation	Variables Measured	Validity Scales	Norm Samples	Related Measures	Languages	Quality of Reliability Evidence	Quality of Validity Evidence
Dimensional Assessment of Personality Pathology-Brief Questionnaire (DAPP-BQ)	Livesley & Jackson (2009)	PD traits	None	community and patient samples	DAPP-BQ-A (Adolescents), DAPP-BQ-SF (Short Form), DAPP-DQ (Differential Questionnaire)	English, French, Spanish, Portuguese	excellent	excellent
Personality Psychopathology Five (PSY-5) scales of the MMPI-2 and MMPI-2-RF	Butcher et al. (1989); Harkness, McNulty, & Ben-Porath (1995); Ben-Porath & Tellegen (2008)	PD traits	Overreporting, underreporting, inconsistency scales	community sample		English, Dutch, Chinese, Croatian, Spanish, Arabic, Farsi, French, Greek, Hebrew, Hmong, Icelandic, Italian, Japanese, Korean, Norwegian, Russian, Thai, Turkish, Vietnamese	excellent	excellent
NEO Personality Inventory-R/3 (NEO-PI-R/3)	Costa & McCrae (1992); McCrae, Costa, & Martin (2005)	Personality traits	None	community sample	self, observer forms	50+ languages	moderate	excellent
Structured Interview of the Five-Factor Model (SIFFM)	Trull & Widiger (1997)	Personality traits	None	clinical sample (Bagby et al., 2005)	–	English, French, German	moderate	excellent
				AMPD-Aligned Trait Measures				
Personality Inventory for DSM-5 (PID-5)	Krueger et al. (2012)	PD traits	No official validity scales	community and patient samples	Full, Short Forms (100 & 25 items), Informant, Child	English, Dutch, Norwegian, German, Arabic, Portuguese, French, Spanish	excellent	excellent
Personality Assessment Inventory (PAI) AMPD trait scoring	Busch, Morey, & Hopwood (2017)	PD traits + full range of other personality and clinical scales	Overreporting, underreporting, inconsistency scales	community and patient samples	Adult & Adolescent	English, Spanish	fair	moderate
Comprehensive Assessment of Traits relevant to Personality Disorder (CAT-PD)	Simms et al. (2011)	PD traits	Overreporting, underreporting, inconsistency scales	community and patient samples	Adaptive Form, Static Form, Informant Report, Interview	English, Dutch, Norwegian, Spanish	moderate	moderate
				PD Functioning Measures				
Levels of Personality Functioning Scale – Brief Form 2.0 (LPFS-BF 2.0)	Bach & Hutsebaut (2018)	PD functioning	None	outpatient, inpatient	–	English, Dutch	moderate	excellent

Continued

Level of Personality Functioning Scale – Self-Report (LPFS-SR)	Morey (2017)	PD functioning	None	MTurk (mechanical turk) sample	–	English	excellent	moderate
DSM-5 Levels of Personality Functioning Questionnaire (DLOPFQ)	Huprich et al. (2017)	PD functioning	None	psychiatric and medical outpatient sample	–	English	moderate	moderate
Severity Indices of Personality Problems (SIPP)	Verheul et al. (2008)	PD functioning	None	personality-disordered, psychiatric outpatient	Short Form (SIPP-SF 64 items)	English, Dutch, Norwegian, Argentinian, Italian	excellent	excellent
Measure of Disordered Personality Functioning Scale (MDPF)	Parker et al. (2004)	PD functioning	None	Italian community sample (Fossati et al., 2017)		English, Italian (Fossati et al., 2017)	moderate	fair
General Assessment of Personality Disorder (GAPD)	Livesley (2006)	PD functioning	None	Canadian community sample, Dutch clinical sample		English, Dutch, German	moderate	moderate
Inventory of Interpersonal Problems-Circumplex (IIP-C)	Alden, Wiggins, & Pincus (1990)	Interpersonal functioning	None	community sample	IIP-32 (short circumplex)	English, Finnish, Greek, Malay, Polish, Spanish	excellent	excellent

their cost, which is a nontrivial characteristic in many research and applied settings. The SCID-II, IPDE, and SIDP-IV interviews all include start-up costs and per-use charges to various degrees, whereas the DIPD-IV appears to be available for use simply by requesting it from the author.

Although not an interview in the strictest sense, an additional measure deserves mention in this section, given its reliance on clinician judgments of personality pathology. The Shedler-Westen Assessment Procedure 200 (SWAP-200; Westen & Shedler, 2007) is a measure of DSM-IV/5 PDs that is completed by clinicians after they have had sufficient experience with a given client (e.g., Shedler and Westen [2007] recommend that clinicians complete the SWAP-200 only after at least six hours of clinical contact with a given patient). For each SWAP-200 assessment, clinicians are required to sort 200 personality descriptive items – developed from a psychodynamic perspective on PD – into eight categories from most descriptive to least descriptive. A computer program then reports DSM-IV/5 PD diagnoses, personality diagnoses for alternative, empirically derived personality syndromes (Westen et al., 2012), and dimensional trait scores. Shedler and Westen (2007) report reliability and validity evidence. Notably, much of the research supportive of the SWAP-200 include one of the measure's authors. Independent research is much less common and has been decidedly more mixed regarding the measure's reliability and validity (e.g., Davidson et al., 2003; Smith, Hilsenroth, & Bornstein, 2009).

Notably, clinical utility is an important consideration for all of these interviews and the SWAP-200, for several reasons. First, given the mass of evidence mounting against categorical representations of PD symptomatology and the rise of dimensional alternatives, the long-term need for interviews keyed to DSM-IV/5 PD criteria is questionable. It is reasonable to argue that measures are only as valid as the model they purport to measure. Second, these interviews all are relatively time- and labor-intensive relative to their self-report counterparts, which can be administered and scored much more efficiently. Although lore in the research world drives many to argue for the superiority of interview methods over self-report methods (e.g., McDermutt & Zimmerman, 2005; Segal & Coolidge, 2007), there is no clear evidence for such relative superiority (Widiger & Boyd, 2009). Moreover, interviews have no control for the validity of the self-reports on which they are based.

Self-Report Measures of Traditional PD Categories

There are many self-report measures designed to measure the traditional PDs as represented in DSM-IV/5. These can be placed into several categories: (1) measures whose primary purpose is the assessment of the DSM PDs, (2) broader psychopathology measures that include scales measuring the DSM PDs, and (3) legacy measures of the DSM PDs that are rooted in specific theories of personality pathology rather than the specific PD criteria per se. Like the clinical interviews, a blanket critique about these self-report measures is that their validity is compromised to the extent that they adhere to a flawed PD classification system. Nonetheless, given the nature of the official PD classification in DSM-5, these measures remain relevant for research and applied practice and thus deserve mention in this section of the chapter.

Primary PD measures. Four prominent self-report measures are available whose primary purpose is the assessment of DSM-IV/5 PDs: (1) the Personality Diagnostic Questionnaire-4 (PDQ-4; Hyler, 1994), (2) the Structured Clinical Interview for DSM-IV PDs Personality Questionnaire (SCID-II-PQ; First & Gibbon, 2004), (3) the Multi-Source Assessment of Personality Pathology (MAPP; Oltmanns & Turkheimer, 2006), and (4) the Assessment of DSM-IV Personality Disorders (ADP-IV; Schotte et al., 1998). The PDQ-4 (Hyler, 1994) consists of ninety-nine items that measure all ten of the DSM-IV PDs. The measure has been widely used in research, is concise, and has shown evidence of reliability and convergent validity (e.g., Okada & Oltmanns, 2009). However, it also has been criticized for having a higher-than-ideal rate of false positive (i.e., high sensitivity and low specificity) PD diagnoses (e.g., Abdin et al., 2011). As such, the PDQ likely is best used as a screening instrument rather than a definitive diagnostic measure.

The SCID-II includes a personality questionnaire (i.e., the SCID-II-PQ) that can be used as a screening measure for the full SCID-II interview. In addition, many studies have opted to use this measure as a standalone measure of the ten primary PDs in DSM-IV. Notably, a version of this measure that has been updated for DSM-5 is now available (SCID-5-SPQ; First et al., 2016) but few data are available on how the revised version compares to the original version or to other measures of personality pathology. Interestingly, the name of this revised measure was changed from "personality questionnaire" to "screening personality questionnaire," presumably to make explicit that the measure is not intended to make diagnoses absent the full interview.

The MAPP (Oltmanns & Turkheimer, 2006) originally was developed for use in Oltmanns and Turkheimer's peer nomination studies of college students and air force recruits in the 1990s (e.g., Thomas, Turkheimer, & Oltmanns, 2003). The MAPP includes 105 items, 81 of which that refer to the features of the 10 DSM-IV PDs and 24 supplementary items that describe additional personality traits. The PD items were written to be lay translations of the PD criteria and to refer to others because it was developed to collect data from informants. Later, a self-report version of the MAPP was developed by revising the same items to refer to the self. Okada and Oltmanns (2009) compared the MAPP to the SCID-II-PQ and PDQ-4 with respect to convergent validity and diagnostic thresholds.

They reported evidence that the MAPP provides a more conservative threshold for diagnosing the DSM-IV PDs than the other two measures. Moreover, they reported only low to moderate agreement among these three measures, which replicates a general finding in this literature: Self-report and interview measures of PDs tend to correlate at rates lower than would be ideal given that they purport to be measuring the same PD constructs (see Clark, 2007, for a discussion of this and other problems in the PD assessment literature).

Finally, the ADP-IV (Schotte et al., 1998) is a ninety-four-item questionnaire that is designed to assess the ten primary DSM-IV PDs and two appendix diagnoses. The ADP-IV first investigates the self-rated typicality of each criterion by means of a seven-point *trait* scale. Next, for each criterion rated positively, the impairment associated with that criterion is assessed using a three-point *distress* scale. Thus, this measure attempts to distinguish between PD severity and style at the level of each criterion, something that is unique among self-report PD measures. Research has tended to support the convergent validity of the ADP-IV at levels roughly similar to that of other PD self-reports. For example, Schotte and colleagues (2004) found low to moderate correlations between ADP-IV PD ratings and those obtained using the full SCID-II interview in a sample of Flemish community participants and psychiatric patients.

Secondary PD measures. Five broader omnibus psychopathology and personality measures include scales designed to measure all ten traditional DSM-IV/5 PDs: (1) the Schedule for Nonadaptive and Adaptive Personality-2 (SNAP-2; Clark et al., 2002), (2) the OMNI-IV Personality Inventory (Loranger, 2002), (3) the Coolidge Axis II Inventory (CATI; Coolidge & Merwin, 1992), (4) the PD scales of the Minnesota Multiphasic Personality Inventory-2 (MMPI-2; Somwaru & Ben-Porath, 1995), and (5) PD similarity scores derived from the Revised NEO Personality Inventory (NEO PI-R, Costa & McCrae, 1992; Lynam & Widiger, 2001). Notably, these methods all are considerably longer than those measures whose sole purpose it is to measure the DSM-IV/5 PDs, with total items of 390, 375, 250, 567, and 240, respectively. Thus, these measures likely are less favorable in research or applied settings in which time is scarce and all that is desired is a tight measure of the DSM-IV/5 PDs.

That said, all of these measures, to various extents, include scales of more basic personality and/or PD traits that might be of interest to some users. For example, the SNAP-2 is a prominent measure of PD traits, and the NEO family of measures have been heavily studied with respect to their normal-range trait links to PD. Moreover, the MMPI-2 is the most heavily studied personality and psychopathology measure and includes a diverse array of validity scales, features that makes it particularly useful in high-stakes assessment contexts. Notably, PD "spectra scales" recently were developed using the item pool of the MMPI-2 Restructured Form (MMPI-2-RF; Tellegen & Ben-Porath, 2008), which is a compelling and efficient update (total items = 338) to the venerable MMPI-2. These scales (Sellbom, Waugh, & Hopwood, 2018) demonstrated evidence of construct validity in relation to external PD, trait, and chart data in a range of clinical, community, and forensic samples.

Legacy measures tied to specific theoretical models of PD. Finally, two measures are available that measure the ten traditional DSM PDs but do so from a particular theoretical perspective rather than as a strict representation of the DSM criteria. These include the Millon Clinical Multiaxial Inventory-IV (MCMI-IV; Millon, Grossman, & Millon, 2015) and the Wisconsin Personality Disorders Inventory (WISPI; Klein et al., 1993). The MCMI-IV is a 195-item true/false questionnaire that consists of 15 PD scales, 10 clinical syndrome scales, 5 validity scales, and 45 Grossman personality facet scales (3 per each PD scale). The primary characteristic that differentiates the MCMI-IV (and its earlier versions) from other mainstream PD measures is its theoretical foundation. The MCMI-IV is based on Millon's evolutionary theory of PD. This background likely has influenced the MCMI's convergent validity with respect to other PD measures, which has varied considerably across studies (e.g., Millon, Davis, & Millon; 1997; Retzlaff, 1996). The MCMI-IV is described in detail in Chapter 18 of this volume. The WISPI-IV (Klein et al., 1993) is a 204-item self-report measure of the DSM-IV/5 PDs. The WISPI-IV has its roots in object relations theory and Lorna Benjamin's Structural Analysis of Social Behavior model (SASB; Benjamin, 1996). Its validity against the SCID-II interview has been studied in psychiatric patients, showing poor convergence at the level of categorical diagnoses but better convergent and discriminant validity for five out of eleven WISPI-IV dimensional PD scales (Smith et al., 2011).

DIMENSIONAL MODELS AND MEASURES

In contrast to categorical systems of classification, a dimensional model conceptualizes psychopathology as lying on a continuum with normal psychological functioning, such that psychopathology is quantitatively, as opposed to qualitatively, different from psychological health. Furthermore, dimensional models are based on underlying theoretical models that have undergone empirical scrutiny (e.g., Harkness & McNulty, 1994; Widiger & Trull, 2007), as opposed to categorical models that derive their structure mainly from expert psychiatric opinion. Dimensional classification is especially relevant to the PD domain, for at least two reasons. First, there is extensive evidence that PD symptoms vary continuously between clinical samples and the general population, suggesting a shared, dimensional latent structure (e.g., Livesley et al., 1994). Second, a dimensional model would potentially ameliorate some of the well-documented limitations of the categorical model of PD in the various editions of the DSM (e.g., Clark, 2007). For example, categorical PD models have been roundly criticized for their excessive comorbidity. Dimensional trait models alleviate this concern to the extent that the seek to identify the underlying traits that arguably drive the co-occurrence of PDs that we see clinically.

In this section of the chapter, we review the prominent PD models and measures that are rooted in the dimensional approach. As noted, dimensional models recently have been formalized in the AMPD, which includes two primary components – Criterion A focused on personality functioning and Criterion B focused on personality traits – as well as a range of other inclusion and exclusion criteria that are similar to the traditional approach. To meet criteria for a PD using the AMPD, one must demonstrate both deficits in personality functioning and the presence of at least one maladaptive personality trait.[2] Thus, measures have been developed to measure each of these components. We organize this review into three subsections focused on (1) measures that predate the AMPD, (2) measures aligned with the traits presented in Criterion B of the AMPD, and (3) measures designed to represent PD-specific functioning (or impairment) that currently is represented in Criterion A of the AMPD.

Non-AMPD Dimensional Models and Measures

Schedule for Nonadaptive and Adaptive Personality-2. The SNAP-2 (Clark et al., 2002) provides a means for assessing trait dimensions relevant to PD. Clark initially developed the SNAP in the early 1990s based on the assumption that the problems associated with the DSM approach to PD classification (e.g., comorbidity, heterogeneity) were due to shared personality traits across the purportedly distinct DSM PDs. The SNAP-2 includes 390 items and measures three broad temperament dimensions corresponding to a Big Three personality model (i.e., negative temperament, positive temperament, and disinhibition vs. constraint), as well as twelve lower-order facets that were developed via an iterative bottom-up series of factor- and content-analytic procedures applied to PD diagnostic criteria and related features. The clinical utility of the measure is relatively strong, as it also includes a comprehensive set of validity scales and a set of scales keyed to the DSM-IV/5 PDs for clinicians who desire a bridge between categorical and trait-dimensional PD conceptualizations. Moreover, the measure has strong community and clinical norms and considerable evidence in support of its reliability and validity (e.g., see Simms & Clark, 2006).

The Dimensional Assessment of Personality Pathology – Basic Questionnaire (DAPP-BQ). The DAPP-BQ (Livesley & Jackson, 2009) is similar to the SNAP in that it was developed as an early attempt to represent and measure the traits underlying PD. The DAPP-BQ includes 290 items and measures eighteen lower-order traits nested within four higher-order dimensions – Emotional Dysregulation, Dissocial Behavior, Inhibition, and Compulsivity. Items were rationally written to capture the *DSM-III* PD criteria. All eighteen of the DAPP-BQ trait scales have documented evidence of internal consistency, test-retest reliability, and construct validity, and include strong clinical norms (e.g., Bagge & Trull, 2003; van Kampen, 2002).

MMPI-2-RF Personality Psychopathology Five Scales (PSY-5). The PSY-5 model (Harkness & McNulty, 1994) – which includes the five broad traits of Aggressiveness, Psychoticism, Constraint, Negative Emotionality, and Positive Emotionality – represents both a measure of broad traits thought to be relevant to adaptive and maladaptive personality and a model of such traits that has gained traction in recent years as a basis for the AMPD. The PSY-5 traits first appeared as a cohesive set of scales developed for the Minnesota Multiphasic Personality Inventory-2 (MMPI-2; Butcher et al., 1989; Harkness, McNulty, & Ben-Porath, 1995) and, later, as a refined set in the restructured form of the MMPI-2 (MMPI-2-RF; Ben-Porath & Tellegen, 2008). Items originally were chosen from the full MMPI-2 item pool via replicated rational selection procedures, followed by rational and psychometric pruning (Harkness et al., 1995). The scales have demonstrated good reliability, as well as convergent and discriminant validity with respect to the PID-5 and various external criteria (e.g., Harkness et al., 2013). However, the lack of integrated PSY-5 facet scales is a notable limitation of the PSY-5 model and scales (however, see Quilty & Bagby, 2007, for a post hoc set of PSY-5 facet scales).

Five-Factor Model Measures

Five-factor model (FFM) measures do not assess pathological traits per se; rather, they assume that extremely low or high levels of the FFM normal-range personality traits – neuroticism, extraversion, agreeableness, conscientiousness, and openness – constitute personality pathology and are associated with psychosocial impairment. The FFM has its roots in two distinct traditions. First, the FFM is rooted in the lexically based Big Five literature (e.g., Goldberg, 1993). That said, clinical applications of the FFM are rooted in the work of Costa and McCrae, who formalized the FFM in the NEO family of measures (Costa & McCrae, 1992; McCrae, Costa, & Martin, 2005) as the five broad traits listed above and their nested thirty lower-order facets. Although the NEO measures were designed to measure normal-range variants of personality, they have been the basis of a large literature linking FFM traits and PD (e.g., Widiger & Trull, 2007). Moreover, there now is good evidence that FFM traits represent normal-range

[2] Note that the AMPD also includes trait-based criteria for assessing six of the traditional PDs – Borderline, Antisocial, Schizotypal, Avoidant, Narcissistic, and Obsessive-Compulsive PDs.

variants of at least four of the five PSY-5 domains (e.g., Suzuki et al., 2015).

The full NEO-FFM model first emerged in the revised NEO Personality Inventory (NEO-PI-R; Costa & McCrae, 1992). A minor revision was published in 2005 (NEO-PI-3; McCrae, Costa, & Martin, 2005) but the NEO-FFM model has remained remarkably consistent for more than twenty-five years. Notably, the work of Tom Widiger and his colleagues and students has greatly enhanced our understanding of PD traits, using the FFM model as a foundation. The primary strength of the NEO measures is the strong research base documenting evidence of their psychometric features and links with PD. Limitations include the lack of integrated validity scales, a pay-per-use model, and a focus on normal-range variation in personality traits, which together make the NEO a tough sell in resource-poor clinical settings. However, a public domain parallel version of the NEO has been published in the International Personality Item Pool (Goldberg et al., 2006), which helps reduce costs associated with using the official NEO measures. However, clinical utility remains a concern.

Notably, Widiger and his colleagues have developed several FFM-based measures designed to explicitly extend the normal-range NEO traits into the maladaptive range, presumably making them more amenable to clinical-psychiatric research and practice. This work has moved in several directions. First, they have developed a series of short rating scale methods that attempt to explicitly model both adaptive and maladaptive variants of the FFM's thirty facets. The most recent of these, the Five Factor Form (FFF; Rojas & Widiger, 2014), consists of one item for each FFM facet, each rated on a five-point scale including the following anchors: 1 (*maladaptive low*), 2 (*normal low*), 3 (*neutral*), 4 (*normal high*), and 5 (*maladaptive high*). In addition, each item also includes exemplar descriptors of both the maladaptive and the normal-range options. For example, for the facet of Warmth, 1 = *"cold, distant"* and 2 = *"formal-reserved"* on the low end and 4 = *"affectionate, warm"* and 5 = *"intense attachments"* on the high end. Thus, options 1 and 5 reflect maladaptively low and high manifestations of warmth, respectively, whereas options 2 and 4 reflect normal-range variations in warmth. Although only limited research has been published on the FFF thus far, some early work has demonstrated evidence for its convergent and discriminant validity relative to a range of measures, including other FFM measures (e.g., Rojas & Widiger, 2018). That said, the explicit adaptive-maladaptive structure of the FFM has shown only mixed support thus far in the literature and deserves further scrutiny (Rojas, 2017).

Second, for FFM researchers and practitioners who desire a non–self-report assessment method, Trull and Widiger developed the Structured Interview for the Assessment of the Five-Factor Model of Personality (SIFFM; Trull & Widiger, 1997), which is a semi-structured interview measure of the thirty NEO-FFM facets. Finally, Widiger and his colleagues have embarked on an ambitious series of projects to develop FFM-inspired measures of the traits relevant to eight of the ten DSM-based PDs. These measures collectively represent the Five-Factor Model of Personality Disorder (FFM-PD). Each of these FFM-PD measures is limited to those facets of the FFM that have shown empirical relevance to a given PD based on extant research. Space constraints do not permit a full description of each FFM-PD measure; interested readers are referred to a recent special issue of *Psychological Assessment* that focuses on the measures within this collection (Bagby & Widiger, 2018). Although the early evidence is promising regarding these measures' reliability and validity, it is unclear how this collection of measures is meant to be used in clinical work, especially since these measures collectively include too many items and numerous overlapping scales to be efficiently used by practicing clinicians. Moreover, strong normative data are lacking. If the FFM-PD is to become a clinically useful measure, work is needed to integrate these eight measures into a single, efficient FFM-PD measure.

AMPD-Aligned Trait Measures

Personality Inventory for DSM-5 (PID-5). The PID-5 (Krueger et al., 2012) is the official measure of the AMPD as represented in Section III of DSM-5. It includes 220 self-report items that assess the twenty-five maladaptive traits of the AMPD. Traits are distributed across five higher-order domains that are isomorphic with the PSY-5 model: Negative Affectivity, Detachment, Antagonism, Disinhibition, and Psychoticism (Krueger et al., 2012). Items were conceptually generated by expert consensus and psychometrically pruned over two rounds of data collection. The PID-5 has demonstrated adequate to good convergent and discriminant validity with respect to normal-range trait measures, other maladaptive trait measures, and the traditional DSM-IV PD categories (e.g., Wright & Simms, 2014; Yam & Simms, 2014). Moreover, the measure has demonstrated adequate test-retest reliability and a replicable factor structure (e.g., Al-Dajani, Gralnick, & Bagby, 2016). The PID-5's status as the official measure of the AMPD and its large research base are features that improve its clinical utility; however, the lack of integrated validity scales limits its usefulness in high-stakes contexts. However, see papers by Bagby and Sellbom (2018) and Sellbom, Dhillon, and Bagby (2018) for reports of inconsistency and overreporting scales, respectively, that have been developed by other researchers, derived from the PID-5 item pool. In addition, the PID-5 now has two brief versions: a 25-item version (American Psychiatric Association, 2013) that permits users to assess only the five trait domains of the AMPD, and a 100-item short-form (Maples et al., 2015) of the full measure that permits scoring of the facets as well (albeit with compromised reliability). A final concern with the PID-5 is that strong, representative norms are not yet available (e.g., Al-Dajani et al., 2016)

Notably, the AMPD trait model also can be scored using the items of the Personality Assessment Inventory (PAI; Morey, 1991), which is a relatively popular self-report measure consisting of 344 items that assess a broad range of psychopathology constructs, including personality pathology. Busch, Morey, and Hopwood (2017) published a scoring algorithm by which the PAI scale scores can be used to assess the AMPD traits via regression estimated scales. These PAI-estimated AMPD traits were adequately correlated with PID-5–estimated AMPD trait profiles and reproduced the five factors of the AMPD with good fidelity (Busch et al., 2017). The primary advantage of using the PAI to estimate AMPD traits is that the PAI has a robust research literature and includes features that improve its clinical utility (e.g., strong norms and validity scales). Disadvantages include that these scales have yet to be cross-validated or validated against other measures by an independent group of researchers.

Comprehensive Assessment of Traits relevant to Personality Disorder-Static Form (CAT-PD-SF). The CAT-PD-SF (Simms et al., 2011) is a National Institute of Mental Health–funded measure that was developed to identify a comprehensive model and efficient measure of PD traits. Although developed independently, the CAT-PD facets are similar to those represented in the AMPD. The CAT-PD-SF is a brief measure drawn from the full CAT-PD item pool. The CAT-PD project yielded thirty-three facet scales measuring an integrative set of PD traits. These scales were formed following data collection through an iterative series of factor- and content-analytic procedures. The full CAT-PD scales are long by design (1,366 total items; *M* scale length = 44 items) so as to be amenable for computerized adaptive testing. However, a static form (CAT-PD-SF) was developed using a combination of statistical and content validity considerations to facilitate quick and standardized assessment across studies and in clinical settings. The static form measures all thirty-three traits using 216 items. In addition, a 246-item version exists that includes validity scales designed to detect inconsistent responding, overreporting, and underreporting.

The static scales demonstrate good internal consistency, test-retest reliability, and evidence of convergent and discriminant validity (e.g., Wright & Simms, 2014) and have been used in a growing number of PD trait studies. Notably, the CAT-PD has been shown to tap additional variance relevant to PD not directly assessed by the PID-5, such as self-harm and antisocial behavior (e.g., Evans & Simms; 2018; Yalch & Hopwood, 2016). Thus, the CAT-PD -SF is a promising measure of AMPD traits and offers an alternative representation of the PD trait space that should be useful as the field moves toward a consensual PD trait model. Moreover, its validity scales make it a strong option (as compared to the PID-5) for settings in which participants or patients might have some motivation to manipulate the test in some way. Notably, the CAT-PD offers psychiatric and community norms collected in Western New York; broader norms representative of the full US population would be desirable.

Personality Functioning Measures

As noted in the preceding sections, personality trait measurement in the PD literature dates back several decades. In contrast, assessment of "personality dysfunction" is a younger and less developed area of research (Ro & Clark, 2009). However, there has been an increased focus on conceptualizing and measuring personality dysfunction in recent years in the wake of the publication of DSM-5, particularly in response to AMPD's inclusion of a specific criterion requiring the presence of deficits in personality functioning, an attempt to codify PD impairments as something distinct from both personality traits and impairment due to other psychiatric conditions. Criterion A in the AMPD describes two broad areas of personality functioning – self and interpersonal functioning – each of which also are divided into two narrower domains of functioning. Taken together, the AMPD describes four aspects of personality functioning – intimacy, empathy, self-direction, and identity – as well as a prototype-based rating scale for measuring each (i.e., the Levels of Personality Functioning Scale [LPFS; American Psychiatric Association, 2013]).

In this section, we review the measures designed to measure personality functioning, both those based directly on the LPFS and those that predated the formal introduction of the LPFS. However, an important issue in this literature, one that goes beyond the scope of this chapter, is whether PD functioning and PD traits can be meaningfully differentiated. Indeed, evidence indicates that maladaptive personality trait measures tend to overlap substantially with a range of personality dysfunction measures (e.g., Hentschel & Pukrop, 2014; Berghuis, Kamphuis, & Verheul, 2014) and that such findings are consistent with conceptual overlap rather than measurement redundancy. Thus, despite the existence of separate measures to assess these constructs, recent literature has openly questioned whether PD traits and impairments are psychometrically differentiable (see Widiger et al., 2019, for a critical review).

LPFS-based measures. The LPFS is designed to be clinician-rated using a series of ordinally arranged prototypes provided in the AMPD. Its development was informed by extant clinician-rated personality dysfunction measures and secondary data analysis (Zimmerman et al., 2015). Research generally has supported the structural validity of the LPFS, with a handful of notable exceptions (e.g., see Zimmerman et al., 2015, for a strong example of this literature). Despite these challenges to the LPFS, interest has grown in developing efficient, self-report measures of these constructs. We will describe three such measures.

First, the Levels of Personality Functioning Scale – Brief Form 2.0 (LPFS-BF 2.0; Bach & Hutsebaut, 2018) was developed as a PD screen by a team of four clinicians and consists of twelve items corresponding to each of the twelve LPFS scoring criteria (Hutsebaut, Feenstra, & Kamphuis, 2016). Among its strengths are empirical support for its convergent validity with respect to similar measures of personality functioning and evidence that it empirically differentiates between those with versus without PDs in a clinical sample (e.g., Hutsebaut et al., 2016).

Second, the Level of Personality Functioning Scale – Self-Report (LPFS-SR; Morey, 2017) is an eighty-item measure of the LPFS constructs. The measure consists of one item per "information unit" in the LPFS scoring criteria. One unique aspect of this measure is that its scoring scheme weighs items according to the LPFS severity level to which they correspond, such that items that reflect moderate impairment are weighted +1.5, whereas items that reflect severe impairment are weighted +2.5 (Morey, 2017). This measure is relatively new on the scene but early evidence has provided good evidence of reliability and validity (e.g., Hopwood, Good, & Morey, 2018; Morey, 2017).

Finally, the DSM-5 Levels of Personality Functioning Questionnaire (DLOPFQ; Huprich et al., 2017) was developed from a larger pool of items written independently by experts to assess the constructs underlying the LPFS; the final sixty-six items were those agreed on by the experts as a team (Huprich et al., 2017). Each of the sixty-six items is asked twice: Respondents are asked to report how true each item is for them across the two distinct contexts of work/school and social relationships. Thus, the explicit consideration of cross-situational variability is a potential unique strength of the DLOPFQ; however, Huprich and colleagues (2017) failed to detect meaningful cross-situational differences in item responses in a mixed sample, calling into question the utility of this distinction. Notably, all of these LPFS measures lack validity scales and strong normative data, features that likely limit their usefulness in applied clinical settings.

Pre-LPFS measures. In addition to measures directly keyed to the LPFS constructs in the AMPD, several measures of personality functioning predated the AMPD's publication but nonetheless deserve mention here due, at least in part, to the similarity to and influence of the measured constructs to those now codified in the AMPD. First, the Inventory of Interpersonal Problems-Circumplex (IIP-64; Alden, Wiggins, & Pincus, 1990) directly assesses interpersonal problems that characterize personality dysfunction. It consists of two orthogonal higher-order dimensions (Dominance and Nurturance) and eight subordinate octant scales (Domineering, Vindictive, Cold, Socially Avoidant, Nonassertive, Exploitable, Overly Nurturant, and Intrusive) that together provide an elegant and conceptually strong way to understand and measure a broad range of interpersonal impairments. Second, the Measure of Disordered Personality Functioning Scale (MDPF; Parker et al., 2004) is not linked to any particular theory of personality functioning. Instead item development was informed by a comprehensive literature review (Parker et al., 2002) from which the research team identified seventeen constructs central to their definition of personality dysfunction. The resulting 141 items were factor analytically honed to twenty items loading onto two higher-order factors: Non-Coping and Non-Cooperativeness, which appear to correspond roughly to AMPD self and interpersonal dysfunction, respectively.

Third, the General Assessment of Personality Disorder (GAPD; Livesley, 2006) is an eighty-five-item self-report measure intended to assess the broad PD functioning domains of self and interpersonal pathology as defined by Livesley's adaptive failure model of PD (e.g., Livesley & Jang, 2000), which notably bear a strong resemblance to the similarly named functioning domains in the AMPD. The GAPD's structure is hierarchical, such that eight narrower facets are nested within these two broad functioning domains. The items for the GAPD were generated on the basis of both a literature review and therapy sessions with individuals with a PD; those that failed to differentiate between individuals with and without a PD were eliminated (Hentschel & Livesley, 2013).

Finally, the Severity Indices of Personality Problems (SIPP; Verheul et al., 2008) is a 118-item self-report measure developed using an expert-guided, rational-intuitive approach to measure five higher-order domains of personality functioning: Self-control, Identity Integration, Relational Capacities, Social Concordance, and Responsibility (Verheul et al., 2008), four of which appear to correspond neatly with the four LPFS components: Self-control with LPFS Self-direction, Identity Integration with LPFS Identity, Relational Capacities with LPFS Intimacy, and Social Concordance with LPFS Empathy. Verheul and colleagues (2008) described considerable evidence for the construct validity of the SIPP-118, including a replicated factor structure, test-retest reliability, internal consistency, and convergent and discriminant validity. These pre-LPFS measures also lack validity scales and strong normative data, features that limit their usefulness in applied clinical settings

SCID-AMPD: The First Complete Measure of the AMPD

None of the measures reviewed thus far provides a complete assessment of the full AMPD (i.e., both the trait and functioning criteria, as well as the revised criteria for the six retained PDs). Without such a complete measure, researchers and clinicians must pull together different measures if they wish to fully assess the AMPD, which can be cumbersome. A remedy to this problem recently was published: First and colleagues (2018) developed the Structured Clinical Interview for the DSM-5 Alternative Model for Personality Disorders (SCID-AMPD), which is a semi-structured diagnostic interview that guides assessment of the AMPD. As noted, the AMPD is a hybrid dimensional-categorical system that includes criteria requiring the presence of deficits in personality functioning (Criterion A) and the presence of one of more maladaptive personality traits (Criterion B). In addition, criteria are provided, based on combinations of specific personality impairments and traits, to diagnose the following six PDs: antisocial, avoidant, borderline, narcissistic, obsessive-compulsive, and schizotypal PDs.

The SCID-AMPD assesses all components of the model, in three separate modules that can be used separately or together. Module I is provided to assess the LPFS domains of self and interpersonal functioning. Module II assesses the traits of the AMPD at both the broad domain level as well as the nested twenty-five trait facets. Finally, Module III provides a complete assessment of each of the six PDs retained in the AMPD, as well as Personality Disorder–Trait-Specified, which is a residual category designed to capture personality pathology that falls outside the six classified PDs. The SCID-AMPD is a new measure and thus little has been written about its psychometric features other than what is included in the manual prepared by the authors. We could only find a single peer-reviewed paper about the SCID-AMPD. Christensen and colleagues (in press) reported positive findings regarding the inter-rater reliability of Module I ratings of the LPFS. Clearly much more research is needed on the AMPD and its component modules. Moreover, like other PD interviews, validity scales do not exist. We were fortunate enough to serve as a pilot testing site for the SCID-AMPD several years ago, and our feedback to the development team was that the measure, especially when all modules are used, was very cumbersome and time-consuming to administer. Now that the final version has been published, we clearly need studies to evaluate not only the reliability and validity of the measure but also its efficiency and clinical utility.

CURRENT TOPICS IN PD ASSESSMENT

Cross-Cultural Issues

The influence of culture, race, and ethnicity on the presentation and assessment of PD is understudied. Notably, both the categorical and the AMPD approaches to PD classification address culture in their PD definitions. For the official PD classification in DSM-5, PD is defined, in part, as "an enduring pattern of inner experience and behavior that *deviates from the expectations of the individual's culture*" (American Psychiatric Association, 2013, italics added). Similarly, in the AMPD approach, DSM-5 requires that impairments in personality functioning and the presence of maladaptive personality traits "are not better understood as normal for an individual's developmental stage or *sociocultural environment*" (American Psychiatric Association, 2013, italics added). Thus, regardless of approach, PD is defined such that individuals should not be diagnosed with a PD if their behavior is not considered problematic or impairing in the context of their sociocultural context.

Unfortunately, how exactly to account for such sociocultural variables is not spelled out in either set of PD criteria or in the measures reviewed in this chapter. In particular, several questions are relevant to this discussion. First, are some PD criteria or traits written such that they are more impairing in some cultural contexts relative to others? For example, Asian samples generally have been characterized as being more introverted and reserved relative to Western samples (e.g., McCrae & Terracciano, 2005). In this context, PDs associated with social withdrawal or detachment (e.g., Schizoid PD, Avoidant PD, AMPD traits related to Detachment) might be expected to be more heavily diagnosed in Asians despite the possibility that these features are more normative (and arguably, thus, less impairing) in such cultures. Research on this point is limited but a recent dissertation from our lab revealed (1) that the literature about such cultural differences in PD manifestation and impairment is quite limited and (2) that Asian samples do not differ in the ways predicted here with respect to disorders and traits related to social withdrawal (and for most PD straits, for that matter) (Yam, 2017). Much more work is needed to examine the impact of cultural differences as they relate to PD features, in particular whether such features differ in their associated impairment across cultures.

Interestingly, many of the measures reviewed in this chapter have been translated into one or more additional languages. This is an important step toward the cross-cultural application of these measures. For example, the PID-5 – the most visible measure of AMPD traits – already has been translated into Danish, Norwegian, Dutch, German, Arabic, Italian, Portuguese, French, and Spanish, and others undoubtedly are being developed. Similarly, the new SCID-5-PD already has versions in English as well as the following languages: Danish, Dutch, German, Greek, Italian, Korean, Polish, Romanian, and Turkish. Although development of translated versions of these (and other) PD measures is an important and necessary step, an additional question arises regarding the cross-cultural impact of PD features and traits: What should be used for norms for these translated PD scales? One might argue that these measures should collect comprehensive normative data within each new culture/language within which the measure is expected to be used and to use those within-group norms for diagnostic purposes. This would be relatively straightforward (although expensive and time-consuming) for trait scales such as the PID-5 and CAT-PD given the psychometric tradition underlying such measures. However, it is less clear how to explicitly account for cultural differences in structured interviews of PD criteria, where the criteria and thresholds are codified in the DSM and not usually interpreted with reference to local norms.

Thus, the PD field has much work to do in studying relative differences in PD symptoms and traits and the impact of such across cultures. These differences have important implications for our measures of PD, which – aside from offering translated versions of measures – generally have not articulated clear procedures for how to account for cultural differences in PD diagnoses. The problem applies equally to traditional and alternative models of PD but the solutions might vary across approaches.

Disconnect Between Research and Applied PD Assessment

Another task for the PD community to address is that of clinical utility, as currently there is a disconnect between research and clinical applications of PD measures. Features likely to improve the clinical utility of a measure include (1) the presence of norms representative of all populations within which the measure is designed to be used (e.g., community, psychiatric, different cultural and language groups); (2) validity scales designed to detect a range of problematic responding, including inconsistent responding, defensive responding, malingering, acquiescence, and denial; (3) scoring and interpretative manuals to aid practitioners use of these measures; (4) other training materials and seminars aimed to translate research findings into clinical practice; (5) theoretical models and treatment recommendations that help practitioners translate modern, dimensional PD measure into evidence-based treatments for their clients. Another factor that influences clinical utility is cost but this relationship is complex. On the one hand, costly measures are difficult to use in cost-sensitive research and applied settings. However, the features that serve to increase clinical utility often cost money to develop and implement and little grant money currently is available for measure development in the United States from traditional funding agencies (e.g., the National Institute of Mental Health). Thus, building clinical utility into PD measures is an uphill battle for many researchers unless they opt to commercialize their measures and use the profits to fund additional development and validation work.

The measures included in this chapter vary considerably in terms of whether they include features that improve their clinical utility. Measures attached to existing batteries, such as the MMPI-2/MMPI-2-RF, SNAP-2, and PAI, are in the best position to have immediate clinical impact, given that these measures already have enjoyed considerable traction in applied practice and include features such as validity scales, strong normative bases, and comprehensive interpretive and training materials. Conversely, more modern measures, such as the PID-5 and CAT-PD, appear to have a longer road to travel to become useful clinical instruments. All too often, researchers focus on developing research measures only and neglect adding the features that might make them more useful in clinical settings. This is true of some of the measures reviewed here, especially the measures of PD functioning/impairment, which largely lack adequate norms or clear interpretive guidelines.

Another factor that is important to note here is that clinical psychologists and related mental health practitioners often are relatively adherent to the measures on which they were trained in graduate school or initially elected to use in their clinical practice. For example, numerous reviews have documented that practicing clinicians continue to favor measures such as the MMPI-2, Rorschach Inkblot Method, and Thematic Apperception Test – which collectively represent seventy-, ninety-, and eighty-year-old assessment technologies, respectively – despite the information provided in reviews like this and the literature more broadly that more modern measures are available that provide more nuanced and evidence-based methods to assess personality pathology (e.g., Piotrowski, 1999). Why might this be? Although a full treatment of this question is beyond the scope of this chapter, it is clear that current PD researchers will need to do more than they are currently doing to counter this phenomenon. Adding features to tests to improve their clinical utility (e.g., strong norms, validity scales, interpretive materials, scoring services) is an important and necessary first step to improve the state of clinical PD assessment. However, more is probably needed, including efforts to interact directly with clinicians in workshops and continuing education activities, as well as to influence the methods emphasized in training programs for psychologists and allied mental health professionals.

SUMMARY, CONCLUSIONS, AND FUTURE DIRECTIONS

In this chapter, we have summarized the prominent categorical and dimensional measures related to PD. We reviewed the problems associated with traditional categorical approaches to PD classification and their associated measures, and we reported on the progress that has been made in the dimensional assessment of personality traits that are presumed to underlie PD. In addition, we discussed the challenges associated with classifying and measuring PD in a cross-culturally sensitive manner. Moreover, we discussed the ways that measure developers might improve the clinical utility of their PD measures and, thus, gain greater traction in research and applied settings in which PD assessment is desired. In sum, there is no shortage of ways to assess the features of personality pathology. Given the recent uptick in research examining the AMPD and related dimensional models, the future appears to be moving toward a dimensional PD classification. For example, Oltmanns and Widiger (2018) recently published a measure keyed to the new ICD-11 PD classification and thus research on that model and such measures is likely to grow in the coming years. Moreover, grassroots efforts currently are underway to integrate the classification of PD features in an evidence-based structural model of psychopathology (see the Hierarchical Taxonomy of Psychopathology [HiTOP] initiative; Kotov et al., 2017). Researchers in this domain would do well to work toward integration across models and build clinically useful measures of dimensional PD features.

REFERENCES

Abdin, E., Koh, K. G., Subramaniam, M., Guo, M. E., Leo, T., Teo, C., Tan, E. E., & Chong, S. A. (2011). Validity of the Personality Diagnostic Questionnaire-4 (PDQ-4+) among Mentally Ill Prison Inmates in Singapore. *Journal of Personality Disorders*, *25*, 834–841.

Al-Dajani, N., Gralnick, T. M., & Bagby, R. M. (2016). A psychometric review of the Personality Inventory for DSM-5 (PID-5): Current status and future directions. *Journal of Personality Assessment*, *98*(1), 62–81.

Alden, L. E., Wiggins, J. S., & Pincus, A. L. (1990). Construction of circumplex scales for the Inventory of Interpersonal Problems. *Journal of Personality Assessment*, *55*(3–4), 521–536.

American Psychiatric Association. (1980). *Diagnostic and statistical manual of mental disorders* (3rd ed.). Arlington, VA: American Psychiatric Publishing.

American Psychiatric Association. (2000). *Diagnostic and statistical manual of mental disorders* (rev. 4th ed.). Arlington, VA: American Psychiatric Publishing.

American Psychiatric Association. (2013). *Diagnostic and statistical manual of mental disorders* (5th ed.). Arlington, VA: American Psychiatric Publishing.

Bach, B., & Hutsebaut, J. (2018). Level of Personality Functioning Scale – Brief Form 2.0: Utility in capturing personality problems in psychiatric outpatients and incarcerated addicts. *Journal of Personality Assessment*. doi:10.1080/00223891.2018.1428984

Bagby, R. M., Costa, P. T., Widiger, T. A., Ryder, A. G., & Marshall, M. (2005). DSM-IV personality disorders and the Five-Factor Model of personality: A multi-method examination of domain- and facet-level predictions. *European Journal of Personality*, *19*, 307–324.

Bagby, R. M., & Sellbom, M. (2018). The validity and clinical utility of the Personality Inventory for DSM–5 Response Inconsistency Scale. *Journal of Personality Assessment*, *100*, 398–405.

Bagby, R. M., & Widiger, T. A. (2018). Five Factor Model personality disorder scales: An introduction to a special section on assessment of maladaptive variants of the five-factor model. *Psychological Assessment*, *30*(1), 1–9.

Bagge, C. L., & Trull, T. J. (2003). DAPP-BQ: Factor structure and relations to personality disorder symptoms in a non-clinical sample. *Journal of Personality Disorders*, *17*, 19–32.

Benjamin, L. S. (1996). *Interpersonal diagnosis and treatment of personality disorders* (2nd ed.). New York: Guilford.

Ben-Porath, Y. S., & Tellegen, A. (2008). *MMPI-2-RF: Manual for Administration, Scoring, and Interpretation*. Minneapolis: University of Minnesota Press.

Berghuis, H., Kamphuis, J. H., & Verheul., R. (2014). Specific personality traits and general personality dysfunction as predictors of the presence and severity of personality disorders in a clinical sample. *Journal of Personality Assessment*, *96*(4), 410–416.

Busch, A. J., Morey, L. C., & Hopwood, C. J. (2017). Exploring the assessment of the DSM-5 Alternative Model for Personality Disorders with the Personality Assessment Inventory. *Journal of Personality Assessment*, *99*(2), 211–218.

Butcher, J. N., Dahlstrom, W. G., Graham, J. R., Tellegen, A., & Kaemmer, B. (1989). *Minnesota Multiphasic Personality Inventory – 2 (MMPI-2): Manual for administration and scoring*. Minneapolis: University of Minnesota Press.

Calabrese, W. R., Rudick, M. M., Simms, L. J., & Clark, L. A. (2012). Development and validation of Big Four personality scales for the Schedule for Nonadaptive and Adaptive Personality-2nd Edition (SNAP-2). *Psychological Assessment*, *24*, 751–763.Christensen, T. B., Paap, M. C. S, Arnesen, M., Koritzinsky, K., Nysaeter, T., Eikenaes, I., et al. (in press). Interrater reliability of the Structured Clinical Interview for the DSM–5 Alternative Model of Personality Disorders Module I: Level of Personality Functioning Scale. *Journal of Personality Assessment*.

Clark, L. A. (2007). Assessment and diagnosis of personality disorder: Perennial issues and an emerging reconceptualization. *Annual Review of Clinical Psychology*, *58*, 227–257.

Clark, L. A., Simms, L. J., Wu, K. D., & Casillas, A. (2002). Schedule for Nonadaptive and Adaptive Personality (2nd ed.): Manual for administration, scoring, and interpretation. Unpublished test manual.

Clark, L. A., Watson, D., & Reynolds, S. (1995). Diagnosis and classification of psychopathology: Challenges to the current system and future directions. *Annual Review of Psychology*, *46*, 121–153.

Coolidge, F. L., & Merwin, M. M. (1992). Reliability and validity of the Coolidge Axis Two Inventory: A new inventory for the assessment of personality disorders. *Journal of Personality Assessment*, *59*, 223–238.

Costa, P. T., & McCrae, R. R. (1992). Normal personality assessment in clinical practice: The NEO Personality Inventory. *Psychological Assessment*, *4*(1), 5–13.

Davidson, K. M., Obonsawin, M. C., Seils, M., Patience, L. (2003). Patient and clinician agreement on personality using the SWAP-200. *Journal of Personality Disorders*, *17*, 208–218.

Dreessen, L., & Arntz, A. (1998). Short-interval test-retest interrater reliability of the Structured Clinical Interview for *DSM-III-R* Personality Disorders (SCID-II) in outpatients. *Journal of Personality Disorders*, *12*, 138–148.

Evans, C., & Simms, L. J. (2018). Assessing inter-model continuity between the Section II and Section III conceptualization of borderline personality disorder in DSM-5.*Personality Disorders: Theory, Research, and Treatment*, *9*, 290–296.

First, M. B., & Gibbon, M. (2004). The Structured Clinical Interview for DSM-IV Axis I Disorders (SCID-I) and the Structured Clinical Interview for DSM-IV Axis II Disorders (SCID-II). In M. J. Hilsenroth & D. L. Segal (Eds.), *Comprehensive handbook of psychological assessment, Vol. 2: Personality assessment* (pp. 134–143). Hoboken, NJ: John Wiley & Sons.

First, M. B., Skodol, A. E., Bender, D. S., & Oldham, J. M. (2018). *Structured Clinical Interview for the DSM-5 Alternative Model for*

Personality Disorders (SCID-AMPD). Arlington, VA: American Psychiatric Association.

First., M. B., Williams, J. B. W., Benjamin, L. S., Spitzer, R. L. (2015). *User's Guide for the SCID-5-PD (Structured Clinical Interview for DSM-5 Personality Disorder)*. Arlington, VA: American Psychiatric Association.

First, M. B., Williams, J. B. W., Benjamin, L. S., Spitzer, R. L. (2016). *Structured Clinical Interview for DSM-5 Screening Personality Questionnaire (SCID-5-SPQ)*. Arlington, VA: American Psychiatric Association.

Fossati, A., Somma, A., Borroni, S., & Miller, J. D. (2017). Assessing dimensions of pathological narcissism: Psychometric properties of the Short Form of the Five-Factor Narcissism Inventory in a sample of Italian university students. *Journal of Personality Assessment*, *100*, 250–258.

Goldberg, L. R. (1993). The structure of phenotypic personality traits. *American Psychologist*, *48*, 26–34.

Goldberg, L. R., Johnson, J. A., Eber, H. W., Hogan, R., Ashton, M. C., Cloninger, C. R., & Gough, H. G. (2006). The international personality item pool and the future of public-domain personality measures. *Journal of Research in Personality*, *40*, 84–96.

Harkness, A. R., & McNulty, J. L. (1994). The personality psychopathology five (PSY-5): Issues from the pages of a diagnostic manual instead of a dictionary. In S. Strack & M. Lorr (Eds.), *Differentiating normal and abnormal personality*. New York: Springer.

Harkness, A. R., McNulty, J. L., & Ben-Porath, Y. S. (1995). The Personality Psychopathology Five (PSY-5): Constructs and MMPI-2 Scales. *Psychological Assessment*, *7*(1), 104–114.

Harkness, A. R., McNulty, J. L., Finn, J. A., Reynolds, S. M., Shields, S. M., & Arbisi, P. (2013). The MMPI-2-RF Personality Psychopathology Five (PSY-5-RF) Scales: Development and validity research. *Journal of Personality Assessment*, *96*(2), 140–150.

Hentschel, A. G., & Livesley, W. J. (2013). The General Assessment of Personality Disorder (GAPD): Factor structure, incremental validity of self-pathology, and relations to *DSM-IV* personality disorders. *Journal of Personality Assessment*, *95*(5), 479–485.

Hentschel, A. G., & Pukrop, R. (2014). The essential features of personality disorder in DSM-5: The relationship between Criteria A and B. *Journal of Nervous and Mental Disease*, *202* (5), 412–418.

Hopwood, C. J., Good, E. W., & Morey, L. C. (2018). Validity of the DSM-5 Levels of Personality Functioning Scale-Self Report. *Journal of Personality Assessment*, *100*, 650–659.

Huprich, S. K., Nelson, S. M., Meehan. K. B., Siefert, C. J., Haggerty, G., Sexton, J., Baade, L. (2017). Introduction of the DSM-5 Levels of Personality Functioning Questionnaire. *Personality Disorders: Theory, Research, and Treatment*, *9*, 553–563.

Hutsebaut, J. Feenstra, D. J., & Kamphuis, J. H. (2016). Development and preliminary psychometric evaluation of a brief self-report questionnaire for the assessment of the *DSM-5* Level of Personality Functioning Scale: The LPFS Brief Form (LPFS-BF). *Personality Disorders: Theory, Research, and Treatment*, *7*(2), 192–197.

Hyler, S. E. (1994). *Personality Diagnostic Questionnaire-4 (PDQ-4)*. New York: New York State Psychiatric Institute.

Klein, M. H., Benjamin, L. S., Rosenfeld, R., Treece, C., Hsted, J., & Greist, J. H. (1993). The Wisconsin Personality Dis- orders Inventory. I: Development, Reliability, and Validity. *Journal of Personality Disorders, Supplement*, 18–33.

Kotov, R., Krueger, R. F., Watson, D., Achenbach, T. M., Althoff, R. R., Bagby, R. M., . . . & Zimmerman, M. (2017). The Hierarchical Taxonomy of Psychopathology (HiTOP): A dimensional alternative to traditional nosologies. *Journal of Abnormal Psychology*, *4*, 454–477.

Krueger, R. F. (2013). Personality disorders are the vanguard of the post-DSM-5.0 era. *Personality Disorders: Theory, Research, and Treatment*, *4*, 355–362.

Krueger, R. F., Derringer, J., Markon, K. E., Watson, D., & Skodol, A. E. (2012). Initial construction of a maladaptive personality trait model and inventory for *DSM-5*. *Psychological Medicine*, *42*, 1879–1890.

Livesley, W. K. (2006). The Dimensional Assessment of Personality Pathology (DAPP) approach to personality disorder. In S. Strack (Ed.), *Differentiating normal and abnormal personality* (pp. 401–429). New York: Springer.

Livesley, W. K., & Jackson, D. N. (2009). *Manual for the Dimensional Assessment of Personality Pathology-Basic Questionnaire (DAPP-BQ)*. Port Huron, MI: Sigma Assessment Systems.

Livesley, W. J., & Jang, K. L. (2000). Toward an empirically based classification of personality disorder. *Journal of Personality Disorders*, *14*, 137–151.

Livesley, W. J., Jang, K. L., & Vernon, P. A. (1998). The phenotypic and genetic structure of traits delineating personality disorder. *Archives of General Psychiatry*, *55*, 941–948.

Livesley, W. J., Schroeder, M. L., Jackson, D. N., & Jang, K. L. (1994). Categorical distinctions in the study of personality disorder: Implications for classification. *Journal of Abnormal Psychology*, *103*, 6–17.

Loranger, A. W. (1999). *International Personality Disorder Examination (IPDE)*. Odessa, FL: Psychological Assessment Resources.

Loranger, A. W. (2002). *OMNI Personality Inventory and OMNI-IV Personality Disorder Inventory manual*. Odessa, FL: Psychological Assessment Resources.

Lynam, D. R., & Widiger, T. A. (2001). Using the five-factor model to represent the DSM-IV personality disorders: An expert consensus approach. *Journal of Abnormal Psychology*, *110*, 401–412.

Maples, J. L., Carter, N. T., Few, L. R., Crego, C., Gore, W., Samuel, D. B., . . . & Miller, J. D. (2015). Testing whether the DSM-5 personality disorder trait model can be measured with a reduced set of items: An item response theory investigation of the Personality Inventory for DSM-5. *Psychological Assessment*, *27*, 1–16.

McCrae, R. R., Costa, P. T., Jr., & Martin, T. A. (2005). The NEO-PI-3: A more readable Revised NEO Personality Inventory. *Journal of Personality Assessment*, *84*(3), 261–270.

McCrae, R. R., & Terracciano, A. (2005). Personality profiles of cultures: Aggregate personality traits. *Journal of Personality and Social Psychology*, *89*, 407–425.

McDermutt, W., & Zimmerman, M. (2005). Assessment instruments and standardized evaluation. In J. M. Oldham, A. E. Skodol, & D. S. Bender (Eds.), *Textbook of personality disorders* (pp. 89–101). Washington, DC: American Psychiatric Association Press.

Millon, T., Davis, R., & Millon, C. (1997). *MCMI-III manual* (2nd ed.). Minneapolis, MN: National Computer Systems.

Millon, T., Grossman, S., & Millon, C. (2015). *MCMI-IV: Millon Clinical Multiaxial Inventory manual* (1st ed.). Bloomington, MN: NCS Pearson.

Morey, L. C. (1991). *Professional manual for the Personality Assessment Inventory*. Odessa, FL: Psychological Assessment Resources.

Morey, L. C. (2017). Development and initial evaluation of a self-report form of the DSM-5 Level of Personality Functioning Scale. *Psychological Assessment*, *29*, 1302–1308.

Okada, M., & Oltmanns, T. F. (2009). Comparison of three self-report measures of personality pathology. *Journal of Psychopathology and Behavioral Assessment*, *31*, 358–367.

Oltmanns, J. R., & Widiger, T. A. (2018). A self-report measure for the ICD-11 dimensional trait model proposal: The Personality Inventory for ICD-11. *Psychological Assessment*, *30*, 154–169.

Oltmanns, T. F., & Turkheimer E. (2006). Perceptions of self and others regarding pathological personality traits. In R. F. Krueger & J. L. Tackett (Eds.), *Personality and psychopathology* (pp. 71–111). New York: Guilford.

Parker, G., Both, L., Olley, A., Hadzi-Pavlovic, D., Irvine, P., & Jacobs, G. (2002). Defining disordered personality functioning. *Journal of Personality Disorders*, *16*(6), 503–522.

Parker, G., Hadzi-Pavlovic, D., Both, L., Kumar, S., Wilhelm, K., & Olley, A. (2004). Measuring disordered personality functioning: To love and to work reprised. *Acta Psychiatrica Scandinavica*, *110*(3), 230–239.

Pfohl, B., Blum, N., & Zimmerman, M. (1997). *Structured Interview for DSM-IV Personality*. Washington, DC: American Psychiatric Press.

Piotrowski, C. (1999). Assessment practices in the era of managed care: Current status and future directions. *Journal of Clinical Psychology*, *55*(7), 787–796.

Quilty, L. C., & Bagby, R. M. (2007). Psychometric and Structural Analysis of the MMPI-2 Personality Psychopathology Five (PSY-5) Facet Subscales. *Assessment*, *14*, 375–384.

Retzlaff, P. (1996). MCMI-III diagnostic validity: Bad test or bad validity study. *Journal of Personality Assessment*, *66*(2), 431–437.

Ro, E., & Clark. L. A. (2009). Psychosocial functioning in the context of diagnosis: Assessment and theoretical issues. *Psychological Assessment*, *21*(3), 313–324.

Rojas, S. L. (2017). Dismantling the Five Factor Form. Unpublished doctoral dissertation, University of Kentucky.

Rojas, S. L., & Widiger, T. A. (2014). Convergent and discriminant validity of the Five Factor Form. *Assessment*, *21*(2), 143–157.

Rojas, S. L., & Widiger, T. A. (2018). Convergent and discriminant validity of the Five Factor Form and the Sliderbar Inventory. *Assessment*, *25*(2), 222–234.

Schotte, C. K. W, De Doncker, D. A. M., Dmitruk, D., Mulders, I. V ., D'Haenen, H., & Cosyns, P. (2004). The ADP-IV Questionnaire: Differential validity and concordance with the semi-structured Interview. *Journal of Personality Disorders*, *18*, 405–419.

Schotte, C. K. W., De Doncker, D., Vankerckhoven, C., Vertommen, H., & Cosyns, P. (1998). Self-report assessment of the DSM-IV personality disorders. Measurement of trait and distress characteristics: The ADP-IV. *Psychological Medicine*, *28*, 1179–1188.

Segal, D. L., & Coolidge, F. L. (2007). Structured and semi-structured interviews for differential diagnosis: Issues and application. In M. Hersen, S. M. Turner, & D. C. Beidel (Eds.), *Adult psychopathology and diagnosis* (5th ed., pp. 72–103). New York: John Wiley & Sons.

Sellbom, M., Dhillon, S., & Bagby, R. M. (2018). Development and validation of an Overreporting Scale for the Personality Inventory for DSM–5 (PID-5). *Psychological Assessment*, *30*, 582–593.

Sellbom, M., Waugh, M. H., & Hopwood, C. J. (2018) Development and validation of personality disorder spectra scales for the MMPI–2–RF. *Journal of Personality Assessment*, *100*, 406–420.

Shedler, J., & Westen, D. (2007). The Shedler-Westen Assessment Procedure (SWAP): Making personality diagnosis clinically meaningful. *Journal of Personality Assessment*, *89*, 41–55.

Simms, L. J., & Clark, L. A. (2006). The Schedule for Nonadaptive and Adaptive Personality (SNAP): A dimensional measure of traits relevant to personality and personality pathology. In S. Strack (Ed.), *Differentiating Normal and Abnormal Personality* (2nd ed., pp. 431–450). New York: Springer.

Simms, L. J., Goldberg, L. R., Roberts, J. E., Watson, D., Welte, J., & Rotterman, J. H. (2011). Computerized Adaptive Assessment of Personality Disorder: Introducing the CAT-PD Project. *Journal of Personality Assessment*, *93*, 380–389.

Smith, S. W., Hilsenroth, M. J., & Bornstein, R. F. (2009). Convergent validity of the SWAP-200 Dependency Scales. *Journal of Nervous and Mental Disease*, *197*, 613–618.

Smith, T. L., Klein, M. H., Alonson, C., Salazar-Fraile, J., Felipe-Castano, E., Moreno, C. L. et al. (2011). The Spanish Version of the Wisconsin personality Disorders Inventory-IV (WISPI-IV): Tests of Validity and Reliability. *Journal of Personality Disorders*, *25*, 813–833.

Somwaru, D. P., & Ben-Porath, Y. S. (1995). Development and reliability of MMPI-2 based personality disorder scales. Paper presented at the 30th Annual Workshop and Symposium on Recent Developments in Use of the MMPI-2 & MMPI-A. St. Petersburg Beach, Florida.

Suzuki, T., Samuel, D. B., Pahlen, S., & Krueger, R. F. (2015). DSM-5 alternative personality disorder model traits as maladaptive extreme variants of the five-factor model: An item-response theory analysis. *Journal of Abnormal Psychology*, *124*, 343–354.

Tellegen, A., Ben-Porath, Y. S., McNulty, J. L., Arbisi, P. A., Graham, J. R., & Kaemmer, B. (2003). *The MMPI-2-RF Restructured Clinical Scales: Development, validation, and interpretation*. Minneapolis: University of Minnesota Press.

Thomas C., Turkheimer E., & Oltmanns T. F. (2003). Factorial structure of pathological personality traits as evaluated by peers. *Journal of Abnormal Psychology*, *112*, 1–12.

Trull, T. J., & Widiger, T. A. (1997). *Structured Interview for the Five-Factor Model of Personality (SIFFM): Professional manual*. Odessa, FL: Psychological Assessment Resources.

van Kampen, D. (2002). The DAPP-BQ in the Netherlands: Factor structure and relationship with basic personality dimensions. *Journal of Personality Disorders*, *16*(3), 235–254.

Verheul, R., Andrea, H., Berghout, C. C., Dolan, C., Busschbach, J. J. V., van der Kroft, P. J. A. et al. (2008). Severity Indices of Personality Problems (SIPP-118): Development, factor structure, reliability, and validity. *Psychological Assessment*, *20*(2), 23–34.

Westen, D., & Shedler, J. (1999a). Revising and assessing Axis II, Part 1: Developing a clinically and empirically valid assessment method. *American Journal of Psychiatry*, *156*, 258–272.

Westen, D., & Shedler, J. (1999b). Revising and assessing Axis II, Part 2: Toward an empirically based and clinically useful classification of personality disorders. *American Journal of Psychiatry*, *156*, 273–285.

Westen, D., & Shedler, J. (2007). Personality diagnosis with the Shedler-Westen Assessment Procedure (SWAP): Integrating clinical and statistical measurement and prediction. *Journal of Abnormal Psychology*, *116*, 810–822.

Westen, D., Shedler, J., Bradley, B., & DeFife, J. (2012). An empirically derived taxonomy for personality diagnosis: Bridging science and practice in conceptualizing personality. *American Journal of Psychiatry*, *169*, 273–284.

Widiger, T. A. (1993). The *DSM-III-R* categorical personality disorder diagnoses: A critique and an alternative. *Psychological Inquiry*, *4*, 75–90.

Widiger, T. A., Bach, B., Chmielewski, M. S., Clark, L. A., DeYoung, C. G., Hopwood, C. J., et al. (in press). Criterion A of the AMPD in HiTOP. *Journal of Personality Assessment*.

Widiger, T. A., & Boyd, S. (2009). Personality disorders assessment instruments. In J. N. Butcher (Ed.), *Oxford handbook of personality assessment* (pp. 336–363). New York: Oxford University Press.

Widiger, T. A., & Clark, L. A. (2000). Toward *DSM-V* and the classification of psychopathology. *Psychological Bulletin*, *126*, 946–963.

Widiger, T. A., Sellbom, M., Chmielewski, M., Clark, L. A., DeYoung, C. G., Kotov, R. et al. (2019). Personality in a Hierarchical Model of Psychopathology. *Clinical Psychological Science*, *7*(1), 77–92.Widiger, T. A., & Trull, T. J. (2007). Plate tectonics in the classification of personality disorder: Shifting to a dimensional model. *American Psychologist*, *62*(2), 71–83.

Wright, A. G. C., & Simms, L. J. (2014). On the structure of personality disorder traits: Conjoint analyses of the CAT-PD, PID-5, and NEO-PI-3 trait models. *Personality Disorders: Theory, Research, and Treatment*, *5*, 43–54.

Yalch, M. M., & Hopwood, C. J. (2016). Convergent, discriminant, and criterion validity of *DSM-5* traits. *Personality Disorders: Theory, Research, and Treatment*, *7*, 394–404.

Yam, W. H. (2017). Examination of personality pathology across cultures: Comparisons among White, Chinese, and Indian Individuals in the United States. Unpublished doctoral dissertation, University at Buffalo.

Yam, W. H., & Simms, L. J. (2014). Comparing criterion- and trait-based personality disorder diagnoses in DSM-5. *Journal of Abnormal Psychology*, *123*, 802–808.

Zanarini, M. C., Frankenburg, F. R., Sickel, A. E., & Yong, L. (1996). *The Diagnostic Interview for DSM-IV Personality Disorders (DIPD-IV)*. Belmont, MA: McLean Hospital.

Zanarini, M. C., Skodol, A. E., Bender, D., Dolan, R., Sanislow, C., Schaefer, E. et al. (2000). The Collaborative Longitudinal Personality Disorders Study: Reliability of Axis I and II diagnoses. *Journal of Personality Disorders*, *14*, 291–299.

Zimmerman, J., Bohnke, J. R., Eschstruth, R., Mathews, A., Wenzel, K., & Leising, D. (2015). The latent structure of personality functioning: Investigating Criterion A from the Alternative Model for Personality Disorders in DSM-5*Journal of Abnormal Psychology*, *124*, 532–548.

30 Neuropsychological Assessment of Dementia

DAVID P. SALMON

Dementia is a syndrome of acquired cognitive impairment that is severe enough to clearly interfere with usual activities of daily living (also known as Major Neurocognitive Disorder; American Psychiatric Association, 2013). The diagnosis requires evidence of significant decline from a previous level of performance in one or more cognitive domains (i.e., complex attention, executive function, learning and memory, language, perceptual-motor, or social cognition) based on subjective report of the individual (or clinician or a knowledgeable informant) and/or objective evidence from standardized neuropsychological testing or quantified clinical assessment. The cognitive deficits must be due to brain dysfunction and cannot be better explained by another mental disorder (e.g., major depressive disorder, schizophrenia) or occur exclusively in the context of a delirium.

Neuropsychological assessment of dementia has grown in importance over the past several decades with the emergence of Alzheimer's disease (AD), the major cause of dementia, as a significant public health issue (Larson et al., 1992). AD currently affects approximately 5.2 million Americans and is one of the leading causes of death in the United States. The prevalence of AD is expected to increase to 13.8 million Americans by the year 2050 (Alzheimer's Association, 2018). The need for early, accurate detection and monitoring of progression of dementia has led to extensive clinical and experimental neuropsychological research to better characterize cognitive deficits associated with AD throughout its course and to identify patterns of deficits that might help distinguish between AD and other neurodegenerative diseases that give rise to a dementia syndrome. Findings from this research not only provide a clearer picture of the AD dementia syndrome but also identify unique patterns of cognitive deficits associated with neurodegenerative diseases that primarily affect subcortical brain structures (e.g., Huntington's disease, dementia with Lewy bodies) or circumscribed regions of frontal and/or temporal cortex (e.g., frontotemporal dementia) or that arise from vascular disease (e.g., vascular cognitive impairment or vascular dementia).

The preparation of this chapter was supported by the Shiley-Marcos Alzheimer's Disease Research Center (NIA AG-05131) and the Helen A. Jarrett Chair for Alzheimer's Disease Research.

Thus, the neuropsychological assessment of dementia has evolved beyond simple documentation of cognitive impairment to identification and quantification of deficits in specific cognitive processes and their relationship to deterioration in specific brain structures in the va"rious dementing disorders.

The present chapter will review these advances with a focus on clinical and prodromal stages of AD, the impact of cultural background on the assessment of AD, and how cognitive deficits differ across various age-related neurodegenerative diseases with distinct etiologies and neuropathology. The implications of these findings for differential diagnosis, prognosis, and our understanding of the neurocognitive architecture of the brain will be discussed.

NEUROPSYCHOLOGICAL FEATURES OF ALZHEIMER'S DISEASE

AD is an age-related neurodegenerative disease characterized by the abnormal extracellular accumulation of amyloid plaques, the abnormal formation of tau-protein positive neurofibrillary tangles in neurons, cortical atrophy with associated neuron and synapse loss, and alterations in neurogenesis (Crews & Masliah, 2010; Masliah & Salmon, 1999). These neuropathological changes usually occur first in medial temporal lobe structures such as the entorhinal cortex and hippocampus and then advance to anterior and lateral cortical areas such as the basal forebrain and frontal and temporal lobe association cortices. Eventually, the pathology occurs in association cortices in the parietal and occipital lobes (Braak & Braak, 1991). Primary sensory and motor cortex usually remains relatively free of AD pathology, with the exception of olfactory cortex (Pearson et al., 1985). Subcortical structures (e.g., thalamus, basal ganglia) and cerebellum are also relatively spared, making AD a classic form of diffuse cortical dementia (Terry & Katzman, 1983).

The extensive pathology that occurs in medial temporal lobe structures and cortical association areas in AD gives rise to a dementia syndrome characterized by severe memory impairment and additional "cortical" deficits in language and semantic knowledge, "executive" functions (i.e., goal formulation, planning, and the execution of goal-directed plans), and constructional and visuospatial abilities. Because primary sensory and motor cortices and most subcortical structures (e.g., the basal ganglia) are relatively preserved, a number of cognitive abilities such as visual and auditory discrimination and the ability to learn and retain motor skills are unaffected until later stages of the disease.

The most prominent clinical feature of AD is a deficit in the ability to learn, retain, and retrieve information that is newly acquired through personal experience (i.e., episodic memory). This episodic memory deficit affects both verbal and visual information and occurs in the context of normal attentional processes. Abnormally rapid forgetting of initially acquired information is a prominent feature of the memory impairment (e.g., Butters et al., 1988; Locascio et al., 1995; Welsh et al., 1991). A number of studies have shown that measures of rapid forgetting expressed as absolute delayed recall scores or "savings" scores (i.e., amount recalled after the delay divided by the amount recalled on the immediate learning trial) can differentiate mildly demented AD patients from healthy older adults with approximately 85 to 90 percent accuracy (Butters et al., 1988; Flicker et al., 1991; Knopman & Ryberg, 1989; Morris et al., 1991; Tröster et al., 1993; Welsh et al., 1991).

Abnormally rapid forgetting suggests that the memory impairment exhibited by patients with AD may be due to ineffective consolidation of information. This possibility is supported by studies that show to-be-remembered information is not accessible after a delay even if retrieval demands are reduced by the use of recognition testing (e.g., Delis et al., 1991). In addition, patients with AD have an attenuation of the primacy effect (i.e., recall of words from the beginning of a list) in list learning tasks, suggesting that they cannot effectively transfer information from primary memory (i.e., a passive, time-dependent, limited capacity store that allows the most recent items to be better recalled than other items) to secondary memory (an actively accessed, long-lasting store that allows early list items that received the greatest amount of processing to be better recalled than other items), and/or cannot maintain information in secondary memory after its successful transfer (Bayley et al., 2000; Capitani et al., 1992; Carlesimo et al., 1995; Delis et al., 1991; Greene et al., 1996; Massman et al., 1993; Miller, 1971; Pepin & Eslinger, 1989; Spinnler et al., 1988; Wilson et al., 1983). This deficit has been targeted by several widely used clinical tests of memory that can distinguish between primary (or short-term) and secondary (or long-term) memory such as the Buschke Selective Reminding Test (Buschke, 1973; Buschke & Fuld, 1974).

A deficient ability in initially encoding information may also adversely affect AD patients' performance on episodic memory tasks. The use of semantic encoding procedures (Buschke et al., 1997; Dalla Barba & Goldblum, 1996; Goldblum et al., 1998; Grober et al., 1997) or information that can be semantically organized in a learning task (Backman & Herlitz, 1996; Backman & Small, 1998) is less effective in improving the performance of patients with AD than in improving the performance of healthy older adults. Clinical memory tests that utilize semantic information to improve encoding (e.g., Free and Cued Selective Reminding Test; Grober et al., 1997) are quite effective in detecting early AD.

Another prominent feature of the memory deficit of patients with AD is an enhanced tendency to produce intrusion errors (i.e., when previously learned information is produced during the attempt to recall new material) on both verbal and nonverbal memory tests (Butters et al., 1987; Delis et al., 1991; Jacobs et al., 1990). The abnormal production of intrusion errors has been interpreted as increased sensitivity to interference and/or decreased inhibitory processes in patients with AD. Although intrusion errors are not a pathognomonic sign of AD (Jacobs et al., 1990), their prevalence can be a useful adjunct to other memory measures (e.g., total recall, recognition memory, rate of forgetting) in developing clinical algorithms for differentiating AD from other types of dementia (Delis et al., 1991; Massman et al., 1992).

Increased sensitivity to interference in patients with AD is effectively assessed by the Loewenstein-Acevedo Scales of Semantic Interference and Learning (LASSI-L). The LASSI-L is a cued-recall paradigm that allows proactive and retroactive interference effects to be evaluated while controlling for global memory impairment (Crocco et al., 2014). Two trials of free and cued recall of fifteen common words that are members of three semantic categories are carried out, followed by two trials of free and cued recall of fifteen different words from the same three semantic categories. Finally, free and cued recall of the original fifteen words is carried out. A recent study using this procedure with patients with amnestic Mild Cognitive Impairment (MCI) with or without evidence of AD pathology on amyloid PET imaging showed that both patient groups had much greater proactive and retroactive interference effects than healthy older adults, even after controlling for overall memory impairment. LASSI-L indices had high levels of sensitivity and specificity for distinguishing MCI from NC, with an overall correct classification rate of 90 percent, and could differentiate between those with or without biomarker evidence of amyloid in their brain (Loewenstein et al., 2018).

Semantic memory that underlies conceptual knowledge and language is often disturbed relatively early in the course of AD (for reviews, see Bayles & Kaszniak, 1987; Hodges & Patterson, 1995; Nebes, 1989; Salmon & Chan, 1994). This disturbance is evident in AD patients' reduced ability to recall overlearned facts (e.g., the number of days in a year) and in their impairment on tests of confrontation naming (Bayles & Tomoeda, 1983; Bowles et al., 1987;

Hodges et al., 1991; Huff et al., 1986; Martin & Fedio, 1983) and verbal fluency (Butters et al., 1987; Martin & Fedio, 1983; Monsch et al., 1994).

There is evidence to suggest that the semantic memory deficit of patients with AD reflects the loss of knowledge for particular items or concepts. When knowledge of various concepts is probed across different modes of access and output (e.g., fluency, confrontation naming, sorting, word-to-picture matching, definition generation) there is item-to-item correspondence so that when a particular stimulus item is missed (or correctly identified) in one task, it is likely to be missed (or correctly identified) in other tasks that attempt to access the information in a different way (Chertkow & Bub, 1990; Hodges et al., 1992). There is also a progressive decline in semantic knowledge in mildly demented patients with AD evident on a test of general knowledge that has minimal language demands (Norton et al., 1997) and a high degree of consistency in the individual items missed across annual longitudinal administrations of the test. This consistency suggests a true loss of knowledge (rather than deficient retrieval) over the course of the disease (also see Salmon et al., 1999). Consistent with a gradual loss of semantics, the spontaneous speech of patients with AD frequently becomes vague, empty of content words, and filled with indefinite phrases and circumlocutions (Nicholas et al., 1985).

Deficits in "executive" functions responsible for concurrent mental manipulation of information, concept formation, problem-solving, and cue-directed behavior occur early in the course of AD (for review, see Perry & Hodges, 1999). The ability to perform concurrent manipulation of information appears to be particularly vulnerable, as a study by Lefleche and Albert (1995) demonstrated that mildly demented patients with AD were significantly impaired relative to healthy older adults on tests that required set-shifting, self-monitoring, or sequencing but not on tests that required cue-directed attention or verbal problem-solving. Bondi and colleagues (1993) found that the number of categories achieved on a modified version of the Wisconsin Card Sorting Task, a test that assesses set-shifting and self-monitoring, provided excellent sensitivity (94 percent) and specificity (87 percent) for differentiating between mildly demented patients with AD and healthy older adults. Patients with AD have also been shown to be impaired on difficult problem-solving tests (e.g., Tower of London puzzle; Lange et al., 1995) and on various other clinical neuropsychological tests that involve executive functions, such as the Porteus Maze Task, Part B of the Trail Making Test, and Raven's Progressive Matrices Task (Grady et al., 1988). Deficits are also apparent on dual-processing tasks, tasks that require the disengagement and shifting of attention, and working memory tasks that are dependent on the control of attentional resources (for reviews, see Parasuraman & Haxby, 1993; Perry & Hodges, 1999). However, the ability to focus and sustain attention is usually only affected in later stages of the disease (Butters et al., 1988).

Patients with AD exhibit impaired performance on tests of constructional praxis such as the Block Design Test (Larrabee et al., 1985; La Rue & Jarvik, 1987; Mohr et al., 1990; Pandovani et al., 1995; Villardita, 1993), the Clock Drawing Test (for review, see Freedman et al., 1994), and drawing complex figures (Locascio et al., 1995; Mohr et al., 1990; Pandovani et al., 1995; Villardita, 1993). They are also impaired on tasks that require visual perception and orientation such as the Judgment of Line Orientation Test (Ska et al., 1990), the Left-Right Orientation Test (Fischer et al., 1990), the Money Road Map Test (Flicker et al., 1988; Liu et al., 1991; Locascio et al., 1995), and tests of mental rotation (Lineweaver et al., 2005). These visuospatial deficits are usually not as prominent as memory, language, and executive function deficits early in the course of disease but there are rare variants of AD when they are the earliest and most prominent cognitive deficit. This variant of AD is characterized by a posterior cortical distribution of atrophy and neuritic plaque and neurofibrillary tangle pathology and is known as Posterior Cortical Atrophy (Crutch et al., 2017).

Characterization of the nature and extent of cognitive deficits associated with AD through experimental neuropsychological research has fostered the development of effective clinical neuropsychological assessment methods for the detection of mild AD dementia. Salmon and colleagues (2002), for example, used Receiver Operating Characteristic (ROC) curve analyses to show that a number of individual neuropsychological tests that incorporated these principles provided excellent sensitivity and specificity for differentiating very mild AD (i.e., Mini-Mental State Exam (MMSE) $\geq$ 24) from cognitively normal individuals: Mattis Dementia Rating Scale (sensitivity: 96 percent, specificity: 92 percent), learning and delayed recall measures from the California Verbal Learning Test (CVLT) (sensitivity: 95–98 percent, specificity: 88–89 percent), delayed recall from the Wechsler Memory Sale – Revised (WMS-R) Logical Memory Test (sensitivity: 87 percent, specificity: 89 percent), delayed recall from the WMS Visual Reproduction Test (sensitivity: 87 percent, specificity: 86 percent), Category Fluency Test (sensitivity: 96 percent, specificity: 88 percent), and Part B of the Trail Making Test (sensitivity: 85 percent, specificity: 83 percent). The Block Design Test was an effective measure from the visuospatial domain (sensitivity: 78 percent, specificity: 79 percent). Performance on a combination of these cognitive measures (i.e., Visual Reproduction Recall, Category Fluency) determined by a nonparametric recursive partitioning procedure called Classification Tree analysis accurately classified 96 percent of the patients with AD and 93 percent of the older adult controls, a level of accuracy higher than achieved with any individual cognitive measure.

In light of findings such as these, neuropsychological assessment has assumed an important role in current diagnostic schemes. When a patient meets DSM-5 criteria for Major Neurocognitive Disorder (i.e., dementia), "probable" AD can be specified when the patient demonstrates impairment in learning and memory as one of two cognitive domains affected, the course is characterized by gradual decline with no extended plateaus, and there is no evidence of mixed etiology for the cognitive decline (i.e., other neurological, mental, or systemic disorder) or of a causative genetic mutation (via family history or genetic testing). If another potentially contributing etiology for the cognitive decline is present, the diagnosis is specified as "possible" AD (American Psychiatric Association, 2013). The criteria largely overlap with those of the National Institute on Aging – Alzheimer's Association (NIA-AA; McKhann et al., 2011), although these criteria allow for a non-amnestic presentation (i.e., deficits primarily in the domain of language, visuospatial abilities, or executive function) and incorporate the use of biomarkers (e.g., positron-emission tomography [PET] amyloid imaging, cerebrospinal fluid [CSF] levels of Aβ and/or tau) to increase certainty that the clinical dementia syndrome is due to AD pathophysiology (McKhann et al., 2011). Biomarker verification is particularly important in identifying "atypical" presentations of AD (Galton et al., 2000; Koedam et al., 2010; Licht et al., 2007; Mendez et al., 2012).

Cultural Factors in the Neuropsychological Detection of Alzheimer's Disease

The growing prevalence of AD in the United States is occurring in conjunction with a growing older Hispanic population (United States Census Bureau, 2017). As AD increases in this population, consideration must be given to how culturally related demographic (e.g., bilingualism and education) and health (e.g., high vascular risk) factors impact current clinical and neuropsychological assessment of dementia and AD. There are almost no studies, unfortunately, that have examined the relationship between these factors and cognitive deficit profiles in Hispanic patients with (eventually) autopsy-confirmed AD.

One exception is a recent study by Weissberger and colleagues (2019) that retrospectively compared cognitive deficit profiles in Hispanic (mostly of Mexican descent from the southwestern United States) and non-Hispanic White patients with autopsy-confirmed AD after test scores were z-transformed relative to respective culturally appropriate normal control groups. The patient and controls groups were similar in age and education, and the patient groups were similar in global mental status and severity of functional decline (falling in the mildly-to-moderately demented range). Results showed that Hispanic patients with AD were significantly less impaired than non-Hispanic White patients with AD across memory, attention, and executive function domains. Furthermore, the groups had different profiles of deficits. Hispanic patients exhibited a greater deficit in memory than in other domains – a profile typical of early AD (Salmon et al., 2002; Weintraub et al., 2012). In contrast, non-Hispanic White patients had a less severe deficit in visuospatial abilities than in other domains but the other domains did not differ from each other– a profile typical of more moderate disease stages when cognitive domains beyond episodic memory become significantly affected (Weintraub et al., 2012). It is notable that, with the exception of memory, average domain scores of Hispanic patients with AD were less than or equal to 1 standard deviation below normal performance, a level that is not usually considered clinically impaired. In contrast, average domain scores of non-Hispanic White patients (other than attention) were more than 1.5 standard deviations below normal performance. These differences in severity and profiles of neuropsychological deficits occurred despite comparable global markers of disease (global mental status, functional decline, test-death interval) at the time of testing.

The apparently milder deficits in Hispanic than non-Hispanic patients with AD may be related to differences in the performance of the cognitively healthy older adult groups to whom the patients were compared. The Hispanic and non-Hispanic White patients with AD performed comparably on virtually all cognitive measures. In contrast, the Hispanic NC group performed significantly worse than the non-Hispanic White NC group on key measures from several cognitive domains, including the WAIS-R Vocabulary test, the WAIS-R Digit Symbol Substitution test, Part B of the Trail Making Test, and the WAIS-R Digit Span test. This disadvantage on neuropsychological tests is consistent with previous findings (LaRue et al., 1999; Pedraza & Mungas, 2008; Weissberger et al., 2013) and may reflect differences in quality of past educational experiences for majority vs. minority populations (e.g., Manly & Echemendia, 2007) or incomplete and inappropriate cultural and linguistic adaptation of cognitive tests (Ardila, 2018; Fortuny et al., 2005; Pena, 2007; see also Nell, 2000, for a discussion of these issues in a broader context).

Despite differences in the severity and pattern of their cognitive deficits, the Hispanic and non-Hispanic White patients had comparable levels of AD pathology (i.e., Braak stage and counts of neuritic plaques and neurofibrillary tangles) at the time of death. Hispanics with AD did, however, have a greater degree of small parenchymal arteriolar disease and amyloid angiopathy. This potential shift in balance between neurovascular and AD pathology may have altered specific aspects of cognition (Lo et al., 2012) so that the profile of cognitive impairment that typifies the mild-to-moderate stage of AD becomes less salient in Hispanics with AD. Overall, these results suggest that cultural factors, linguistic history, and vascular contributions to neuropathology may alter the profile of cognitive deficits exhibited by Hispanics with AD and impact the sensitivity and specificity of cognitive tests used to diagnose dementia. Further research is clearly needed to improve the ability to effectively detect and characterize cognitive impairment in this growing population.

Another factor that may come into play during the assessment of dementia in Hispanic individuals is the impact of bilingualism on the manifestation of cognitive deficits. Many Hispanics in the United States speak both Spanish and English. Recent research suggests that bilingualism may delay the onset of first symptoms of AD by up to four or five years (Bialystok et al., 2007; Craik et al., 2010; Gollan et al., 2011). This effect is particularly evident in immigrant bilinguals when compared with immigrants who remained monolingual (Chertkow et al., 2010). A possible mechanism for this protective effect is that bilingualism enhances executive function (for review, see Bialystok et al., 2009) and thereby confers a degree of "cognitive reserve" (Stern, 2009) that allows the bilingual individual to better withstand the gradual development of AD pathology.

Bilingualism can also be used to develop novel ways to probe cognition in Hispanic individuals. Gollan and colleagues (2017) investigated the effects of AD on production of bilingual speech errors in a paragraph reading task in which subjects read aloud eight paragraphs in four conditions: (1) English-only, (2) Spanish-only, (3) English-mixed (mostly English with six Spanish words), and (4) Spanish-mixed (mostly Spanish with six English words). Bilingual patients with AD produced more *cross-language intrusion* errors (e.g., saying *la* instead of *the*) and *within-language* errors (e.g., saying *their* instead of *the*) than bilingual normal control subjects. These differences were most salient in the dominant language. The production of intrusion errors effectively differentiated between patients and controls, suggesting that patients with AD are impaired in a variety of linguistic and executive control mechanisms needed to mix languages fluently. Thus, intrusion errors elicited in just four minutes of reading aloud provided a highly robust means of discriminating bilingual patients with AD from cognitively normal bilinguals.

Neuropsychological Detection of "Prodromal" Alzheimer's Disease

Longitudinal studies with nondemented older adults who eventually develop AD have shown that a subtle decline in episodic memory and other cognitive functions often occurs prior to the emergence of the obvious cognitive and behavioral changes required for a clinical diagnosis of dementia (for review, see Twamley et al., 2006). This prodromal stage of disease is known as Mild Cognitive Impairment (MCI; Peterson et al., 1995). MCI was initially identified as an amnestic condition in which an individual met the following diagnostic criteria: (1) a subjective memory complaint, (2) objective memory impairment for age, (3) relatively preserved general cognition, (4) essentially intact activities of daily living, and (5) not clinically demented (Petersen et al., 1999). This classification scheme was later modified to distinguish between "amnestic MCI" and "non-amnestic MCI" with "single domain" and "multiple domain" classifications to indicate the number of cognitive domains affected (Petersen, 2004; Winblad et al., 2004). A 2011 update changed subjective memory complaint to "concern regarding a change in cognition" (rather than just memory) and now accepts mild problems in performing complex instrumental activities of daily living (Albert et al., 2011). Although MCI (also known as Minor Neurocognitive Disorder; American Psychiatric Association, 2013) has many etiologies, the usual cause is prodromal AD, with about 45 percent of those with MCI subsequently developing AD dementia within a five-year period (Grundman et al., 1996). AD can be identified as the likely cause of MCI if comprehensive medical and neuropsychological assessment rules out other systemic or brain diseases that might cause cognitive decline. The presence of AD can be supported by positive AD biomarkers (e.g., CSF β-amyloid and tau or amyloid PET imaging).

Studies over the past ten to fifteen years have examined memory processes (e.g., encoding, retrieval, associative "binding") and types of memory (e.g., recognition, prospective memory) that might differ in healthy older adults and patients with amnestic MCI. These studies have shown that the episodic memory deficit in MCI is usually characterized by abnormally rapid forgetting on tests of delayed recall (Libon et al., 2011; Manes et al., 2008; Perri et al., 2007) and comparable levels of impairment on tests of free recall and recognition (Libon et al., 2011). The recognition memory deficit appears to involve poor recollection (i.e., the conscious reexperience of a recent event) in the face of relatively preserved familiarity (i.e., the feeling of having previously encountered an event with no associated contextual information) (Anderson et al., 2008; Bennett et al., 2006; Hudon et al., 2009; Serra et al., 2010; Westerberg et al., 2006; but see Ally et al., 2009; Wolk et al., 2008). Patients with amnestic MCI fail to benefit in a normal fashion from deep semantic encoding (Hudon et al., 2011) and have an enhanced tendency to produce prototypical intrusion errors during free recall (Libon et al., 2011). They have a deficit in associative memory (i.e., the ability to remember relationships between two or more items or between an item and its context) for simple geometric forms and their spatial location (Troyer et al., 2008), symbols and the digits with which they were paired (Troyer et al., 2008), or verbal-verbal (de Rover et al., 2011; Pike et al., 2008) or face-name paired-associates (Rentz et al., 2011). They are also impaired on prospective memory tasks that require them to remember a delayed intention to act at a certain time (time-based) or when some external event occurs (event-based) (Costa et al., 2010; Karantzoulis et al., 2009; Schmitter-Edgecombe et al., 2009; Thompson et al., 2010; Troyer & Murphy 2007). Taken together, this pattern of memory deficits in MCI is virtually identical to that of AD dementia and is generally attributed to ineffective encoding and consolidation of new information due to damage in medial temporal lobe structures (Salmon & Squire, 2009) that are typically the site of the earliest pathological changes of AD (Braak & Braak, 1991).

Although memory is typically impaired prior to development of AD dementia, recent reviews suggest that cognitive decline during this prodromal period is largely nonspecific (Backman et al., 2004; Backman et al., 2005; Twamley et al., 2006). For example, patients with "amnestic" MCI are often impaired on tests of language such as semantically demanding confrontation naming tasks that require production of names of famous people or buildings (Adlam et al., 2006; Ahmed et al., 2008; Borg et al., 2010; Joubert et al., 2010; Seidenberg et al., 2009). They are also often impaired when required to generate exemplars from a specific semantic category (e.g., "animals") but not when required to rapidly generate words beginning with a particular letter (e.g., F, A, or S) (Adlam et al., 2006; Biundo et al., 2011; Brandt & Manning, 2009; Murphy et al., 2006; Nutter-Upham et al., 2008). This is the same pattern exhibited by patients with mild AD dementia and is thought to reflect a loss of semantic knowledge (Butters et al., 1987).

Deficits in executive functions, attention, and working memory have been reported in preclinical AD ("cognitively normal" individuals with positive AD biomarkers; Sperling et al., 2011) and amnestic MCI. Composite executive function measures decline significantly several years prior to the diagnosis of dementia (Mickes et al., 2007) and accurately predict AD dementia onset (Albert et al., 2007). Executive function deficits are greater in those with multidomain MCI compared to those with amnestic MCI, suggesting that the former are at higher risk for imminent onset of dementia (Brandt & Manning, 2009). There is a decline in inhibition and attentional control in preclinical AD shown by an abnormal number of errors on the noncongruent trials of a Stroop test (i.e., naming the color of the ink of noncongruent color words) and an increased Stroop effect (i.e., difference between congruent and noncongruent trial reaction times) (Balota et al., 2010). Patients with amnestic MCI are also impaired on expectancy violation tasks (Davie et al., 2004), cognitive set switching tasks (Sinai et al., 2010), and tasks that require production of a nondominant response (Belanger & Belleville, 2009). Deficits in working memory occur but are usually limited to mild central executive dysfunction and poor attentional control (Darby et al., 2002; Gagnon & Belleville, 2011; Grober et al., 2008; Rapp & Reischies, 2005; Saunders & Summers, 2011; Sinai et al., 2010).

Diagnostic rigor for MCI can be dramatically improved through an actuarial neuropsychological diagnostic method (Bondi et al., 2014; Clark et al., 2013; Dawes et al., 1989; Jak et al., 2009, 2016). This method assigns a diagnosis of MCI based simply on scores on multiple objective neuropsychological tests that assess a range of cognitive domains. Actuarial diagnosis leads to greater diagnostic stability (Jak et al., 2009) and stronger relationships between cognition, biomarkers, and development of dementia (Bondi et al., 2014), compared to MCI diagnosed in the conventional manner by subjective report, poor performance on a single memory test, and clinical judgment. Furthermore, with actuarial methods statistical techniques (e.g., cluster analysis, latent class analysis) can be used to identify various cognitive subtypes beyond the standard amnestic/non-amnestic distinction (Clark et al., 2013; Delano-Wood et al., 2009; Edmonds et al., 2015; Libon et al., 2011, 2014). Using these techniques with Alzheimer's Disease Neuroimaging Initiative (ADNI) data, Edmonds and colleagues (2015) found that approximately one-third of patients with conventionally diagnosed MCI performed within normal limits on more extensive cognitive testing, had normal cerebrospinal fluid AD biomarker levels, overreported subjective cognitive complaints, and had a low rate of progression to AD. Thus, the conventional method was highly susceptible to false-positive diagnostic errors that would not have been made by the actuarial approach to MCI diagnosis.

Neuropsychological Contributions to Differential Diagnosis of Dementia Disorders

Although AD is the leading cause of dementia in older adults, it has been known for some time that dementia can arise from a wide variety of etiologically and neuropathologically distinct disorders that give rise to somewhat different patterns of relatively preserved and impaired cognitive abilities (for review, see Weintraub et al., 2012). This is quite evident in differences observed between dementia syndromes associated with neurodegenerative diseases that primarily involve regions of the cerebral cortex (e.g., AD and frontotemporal dementia) and those that have their primary locus in subcortical brain structures (e.g., Huntington's disease). This heuristic classification does not, of course, fully reflect the distribution of pathology in each disease since some degree of cortical and subcortical pathology that can impact cognition occurs in almost all of these diseases. However, knowledge of similarities and differences in cognitive deficit profiles can aid in differential diagnosis and lead to better understanding of the neurobiological basis of various cognitive disorders.

Huntington's disease (HD) is an inherited neurodegenerative disease that causes deterioration of the neostriatum (caudate nucleus and putamen) (Vonsattel et al., 1985) and disruption of fronto-striatal circuits (Alexander et al., 1986). The dementia syndrome of HD is characterized by mild deficits in memory retrieval and prominent deficits in attention, working memory, and executive functions, a pattern consistent with fronto-striatal dysfunction.

Dementia with Lewy bodies (DLB) is a clinicopathologic condition characterized by the presence of Lewy bodies (i.e., α-synuclein inclusions) in subcortical regions usually affected in Parkinson's disease and in limbic and neocortical regions. AD pathology is also often present in DLB (McKeith et al., 2017). Given this overlapping pathology, the cognitive deficits in DLB are similar to those in AD but there is greater executive dysfunction that may reflect its more extensive subcortical involvement, and greater visuospatial impairment that may be related to occipital cortex dysfunction (Minoshima et al. 2001).

Vascular dementia is often characterized by prominent subcortical ischemic pathology (Pantoni et al., 2010) and white matter pathology that interrupts frontal-subcortical circuits (Mathias & Burke, 2009). This leads to a pattern of cognitive deficits with prominent executive dysfunction and a mild memory retrieval deficit similar to HD (for review, see Wetzel & Kramer, 2008). Concomitant AD pathology is often present in subcortical ischemic vascular dementia, which impacts the cognitive profile (Reed et al., 2007). Vascular dementia due to multiple or strategically placed infarcts may mimic a variety of dementia syndromes because infarction can occur in nearly any cortical region and totally ablate the associated cognitive ability.

Behavioral variant of frontotemporal dementia (bvFTD) is characterized by pathology and cortical atrophy that is relatively restricted to frontal and anterior temporal lobes of the brain. Although changes in behavior, personality, and social understanding occur earlier than obvious cognitive deficits in bvFTD, the cognitive deficits that develop include alterations in judgment, problem-solving, concept formation, and executive functions, often with relative sparing of visuospatial abilities and episodic memory (Miller et al., 1997; Rascovsky et al., 2002, 2007, 2011; Snowden et al., 2001).

Similarities and differences in cognitive deficits among AD and these other causes of dementia are summarized by cognitive domain in Table 30.1.

Noncredible Responding in the Assessment of Dementia

Although purposeful feigning or exaggeration of cognitive impairment for personal gain (i.e., malingering) is rarely observed during the assessment of dementia (particularly for a suspected neurodegenerative disease), it is important to determine whether or not the patient is putting forth adequate effort so that the results of cognitive testing are a valid reflection of their cognitive abilities. Therefore, various performance validity tests have been developed and used as freestanding measures of effort or as measures of effort built into existing memory or other cognitive tests. These performance validity measures often consist of a two-alternative, forced-choice recognition memory test that can be performed at a very high level of accuracy by individuals with mild cognitive deficits so that poor performance most likely reflects poor effort rather than true cognitive impairment.

One example of a freestanding test that uses this procedure is the Test of Memory Malingering (TOMM; Tombaugh, 1997). Patients with mild cognitive deficits generally score above 95 percent accuracy on the TOMM (i.e., correctly identify more than forty-seven of fifty drawings of objects) and scoring below that level is considered evidence of poor effort or malingering. However, patients with mild dementia averaged only 92 percent accuracy on the TOMM in the initial study in which it was used, and those with moderate dementia often fell below the proposed cutoff (Tombaugh, 1997). In subsequent studies, only 20 to 80 percent of mildly demented patients scored above the proposed cutoff on the TOMM (Dean et al., 2009; Merten et al., 2007; Teichner & Wagner, 2004; Walter et al., 2014) indicating that the test produces an unacceptably high rate of false-positive diagnoses of poor effort or malingering in this population. It may, however, be effective in detecting poor effort in patients with MCI (Walter et al., 2014).

The two-alternative, forced-choice recognition memory format is also used as a measure of effort in several standardized tests of memory that are often used in the dementia evaluation. A forced-choice recognition trial in the second edition of the California Verbal Learning Test (CVLT-II) was found to have excellent sensitivity for detecting poor effort in patients with traumatic brain injury (Connor et al., 1997) or MCI (Clark et al., 2012) using a cutoff of less than 15/16 correct. However, 12 percent of patients with mild AD dementia and 71 percent of patients with moderate AD dementia fell below the cutoff (i.e., "failed") (Clark et al., 2012). A similar result was found with the Recognition Discrimination Index from the Hopkins Verbal Learning Test (HVLT), which showed relatively good sensitivity and specificity in distinguishing between nondemented older adults with or without invalid responding on an independent measure of effort (Sawyer et al., 2017).

Other embedded measures of performance validity attempt to identify invalid responding by detecting discrepancies in performance across various components of tests widely used in the assessment of dementia. For example, an effort scale was developed for the Repeatable Battery for the Assessment of Neuropsychological Status (RBANS) that largely examines the discrepancy in performance on the word list recognition item and several measures of free recall (e.g., word recall, story recall, digit span). This scale reliably identified valid from invalid responders (based on the TOMM) in an older adults sample with mild cognitive deficits (Paulson et al., 2015).

Table 30.1 Similarities and differences in cognitive deficits among Alzheimer's disease (AD) and other causes of dementia

	Memory	Language and Semantic Knowledge	Attention, Working Memory, and Executive Function	Visuospatial Function
Alzheimer's Disease	Rapid forgetting Equally impaired recall and recognition Prominent encoding and consolidation deficit	Word finding deficits and impaired confrontation naming (i.e., anomia) Semantic fluency deficit greater than letter fluency deficit Semantic knowledge degradation	Mild attention deficit in early stages Deficits in some aspects of working memory (i.e., information manipulation) Deficits in planning, problem-solving, goal-directed behavior, cognitive flexibility	Mild constructional apraxia and visuoperceptual deficits in early stage Worse Clock Drawing than Clock Copy due to loss of semantic attributes Decline in extrapersonal spatial orientation
Huntington's Disease	Near normal rate of forgetting Less impaired recognition than free recall Prominent retrieval deficit	Slow and reduced speech output with dysarthria Relatively normal confrontation naming Equivalent semantic and letter fluency deficits Relatively preserved semantic knowledge	Prominent deficit in attention in early stages Deficits in all aspects of working memory Prominent deficits in planning, problem-solving, goal-directed behavior, cognitive flexibility	Mild constructional apraxia and visuoperceptual deficits in early stage Poor Clock Drawing and Clock Copy due to planning and motor dysfunction Decline in personal spatial orientation
Dementia with Lewy Bodies	Rapid forgetting, but relatively < AD Slightly worse recall than recognition deficit Encoding, consolidation and retrieval deficit	Deficits similar to AD Word finding deficits and impaired confrontation naming (i.e., anomia) Semantic fluency deficit greater than letter fluency deficit Semantic knowledge degradation	Prominent deficit in attention in early stages Prominent deficits in planning, problem-solving, goal-directed behavior, cognitive flexibility Recognition span that requires integration of episodic and working memory worse in DLB than AD	Disproportionately severe deficits compared to other cognitive domains Prominent constructional apraxia and visuoperceptual deficits in early stages Impaired detection of direction of moving stimuli Impaired visual integration of object components
Frontotemporal Dementia (behavioral variant)	Near normal rate of forgetting Normal recognition, but impaired free recall Primary retrieval deficit	Relatively normal confrontation naming Preserved semantic knowledge Prominent and equivalent semantic and letter fluency deficits due to impaired strategic retrieval	Prominent deficit in attention in early stages Prominent deficits in judgment, planning, problem-solving, goal-directed behavior, cognitive flexibility Deficits in all aspects of working memory	Normal constructional and visuoperceptual abilities in mild-to-moderate stages
Vascular Dementia (subcortical ischemic small vessel disease)	Near normal rate of forgetting Less impaired recognition than free recall Prominent retrieval deficit	Relatively normal confrontation naming Equivalent semantic and letter fluency deficits Relatively preserved semantic knowledge	Prominent deficit in attention and working memory in early stages Prominent deficits in planning, problem-solving, goal-directed behavior, cognitive flexibility Disproportionately severe deficits compared to other cognitive domains	Mild constructional apraxia and visuoperceptual deficits in early stage Poor Clock Drawing and Clock Copy due to planning dysfunction

However, the RBANS effort scale had an unacceptably high "false-positive" rate in patients with dementia (Bortnick et al., 2013; Sieck et al., 2013). An embedded measure of valid responding has also been developed for the Digit Span test on the assumption that this test assesses attention rather than memory and is relatively insensitive to change in neurologically compromised individuals. A measure of Reliable Digit Span derived from the Digit Span test (i.e., the sum of the longest string of digits correctly repeated under forward and backward conditions; cutoff $\leq$ 7) was effective in identifying poor effort (or malingering) in nondemented individuals or those with mild dementia (Kiewel et al., 2012) but not in those with more severe dementia (Dean et al., 2009; Heinly et al., 2005; Merten et al., 2007).

Summary and Conclusions

Neuropsychological assessment plays an important role in detecting and characterizing the dementia syndrome associated with neurodegenerative disease. Comprehensive cognitive assessment can detect the cognitive deficits that typically occur in AD and differentiate them from those that occur in other neurodegenerative disorders such as HD, DLB, bvFTD, and vascular dementia. The distinct cognitive profiles associated with these various disorders reflect different distributions of brain pathology; thus, they provide a useful model for understanding brain-behavior relationships that mediate the affected cognitive abilities. Early detection of dementia due to AD or other neurodegenerative diseases has improved greatly over the years and has moved into the prodromal (e.g., MCI) and even preclinical stages of disease. Unbiased actuarial neuropsychological methods may become particularly important as the field increasingly focuses on early disease states where the boundary between normal aging and prodromal AD is unclear. Finally, it must be recognized that cognitive deficits that are prominent in non-Hispanic White patients with AD may be less salient in Hispanic patients due to culturally related demographic factors (e.g., bilingualism), social disadvantages (e.g., quality of the educational experience), distinct health factors (e.g., high vascular risk), or incomplete and inappropriate cultural and linguistic adaptation of cognitive tests. Further research is necessary to improve the ability to effectively detect subtle cognitive impairment in this and other underrepresented populations.

REFERENCES

Adlam, A. L., Bozeat, S., Arnold, R., Watson, P., & Hodges, J. R. (2006). Semantic knowledge in mild cognitive impairment and mild Alzheimer's disease. *Cortex, 42*, 675–684.

Ahmed, S., Arnold, R., Thompson, S. A., Graham, K. S., & Hodges, J. R. (2008). Naming of objects, faces and buildings in mild cognitive impairment. *Cortex, 44*, 746–752.

Albert, M. S., Blacker, D., Moss, M. B., Tanzi, R., & McArdle, J. J. (2007). Longitudinal change in cognitive performance among individuals with mild cognitive impairment. *Neuropsychology, 21*, 158–169.

Albert, M. S., DeKosky, S. T., Dickson, D., Dubois, B., Feldman, H. H., Fox, N. C., & Phelps, C. H. (2011). The diagnosis of mild cognitive impairment due to Alzheimer's disease: Recommendations from the National Institute on Aging-Alzheimer's Association workgroups on diagnostic guidelines for Alzheimer's disease. *Alzheimer's and Dementia, 7*, 270–279.

Alexander, G. E., DeLong, M. R., & Strick, P. L. (1986). Parallel organization of functionally segregated circuits linking basal ganglia and cortex. *Annual Review of Neuroscience, 9*, 357–381.

Ally, B. A., McKeever, J. D., Waring, J. D., & Budson, A. E. (2009). Preserved frontal memorial processing for pictures in patients with mild cognitive impairment. *Neuropsychologia, 47*, 2044–2055.

Alzheimer's Association. (2018). 2018 Alzheimer's disease facts and figures. *Alzheimer's and Dementia, 14*, 367–429.

American Psychiatric Association. (2013). *Diagnostic and statistical manual of mental disorders* (5th ed.). Arlington, VA: American Psychiatric Publishing.

Anderson, N. D., Ebert, P. L., Jennings, J. M., Grady, C. L., Cabezza, R., & Graham, S. (2008). Recollection- and familiarity-based memory in healthy aging and amnestic mild cognitive impairment. *Neuropsychology, 22*, 177–187.

Ardila, A. (2018). *Historical development of human cognition* (pp. 135–159).New York: Springer.

Backman, L., & Herlitz, A. (1996). Knowledge and memory in Alzheimer's disease: A relationship that exists. In R. G. Morris (Ed.), *The cognitive neuropsychology of Alzheimer's disease* (pp. 89–104). Oxford: Oxford University Press.

Backman, L., Jones, S., Berger, A. K., Laukka, E. J., & Small, B. J. (2004). Multiple cognitive deficits during the transition to Alzheimer's disease. *Journal of Internal Medicine, 256*, 195–204.

Backman, L., Jones, S., Berger, A. K., Laukka, E. J., & Small, B. J. (2005). Cognitive impairment in preclinical Alzheimer's disease: A meta-analysis. *Neuropsychology, 19*, 520–531.

Backman, L., & Small, B. J. (1998). Influences of cognitive support on episodic remembering: Tracing the process of loss from normal aging to Alzheimer's disease. *Psychology and Aging, 13*, 267–276.

Balota, D. A., Tse, C., Hutchison, K. A., Spieler, D. H., Duchek, J. M., & Morris, J. C. (2010). Predicting conversion to dementia of the Alzheimer's type in a healthy control sample: The power of errors in Stroop color naming. *Psychology and Aging, 25*, 208–218.

Bayles, K. A., & Kaszniak, A. W. (1987). *Communication and cognition in normal aging and dementia*. Boston: College-Hill /Little, Brown and Company.

Bayles, K. A., & Tomoeda, C. K. (1983). Confrontation naming impairment in dementia. *Brain and Language, 19*, 98–114.

Bayley, P. J., Salmon, D. P., Bondi, M. W., Bui, B. K., Olichney, J., Delis, D. C., Thomas, R. G., & Thal, L. J. (2000). Comparison of the serial position effect in very mild Alzheimer's disease, mild Alzheimer's disease, and amnesia associated with electroconvulsive therapy. *Journal of the International Neuropsychological Society*, *6*, 290–298.

Belanger, S., & Belleville, S. (2009). Semantic inhibition impairment in mild cognitive impairment: A distinctive feature of upcoming cognitive decline? *Neuropsychology*, *23*, 592–606.

Bennett, I. J., Golob, E. J., Parker, E. S., & Starr, A. (2006). Memory evaluation in mild cognitive impairment using recall and recognition tests. *Journal of Clinical and Experimental Neuropsychology*, *28*, 1408–1422.

Bialystok, E., Craik, F. I. M., & Freedman, M. (2007). Bilingualism as a protection against the onset of symptoms of dementia. *Neuropsychologia*, *45*, 459–464.

Bialystok, E., Craik, F. I. M., Green, D. W., & Gollan, T. H. (2009). Bilingual minds. *Psychological Science in the Public Interest*, *10*, 89–129.

Biundo, R., Gardini, S., Caffarra, P., Concari, L., Martorana, D., Neri, T. M., Shanks, M. F., & Venneri, A. (2011). Influence of APOE status on lexical-semantic skills in mild cognitive impairment. *Journal of the International Neuropsychological Society*, *17*, 423–430.

Bondi, M. W., Edmonds E. C., Jak, A. J., Clark, L. R., Delano-Wood L., McDonald C. R., & Salmon, D. P. (2014). Neuropsychological criteria for mild cognitive impairment improves diagnostic precision, biomarker associations, and prediction of progression. *Journal of Alzheimer's Disease*, *42*, 275–289.

Bondi, M. W., Monsch, A. U., Butters, N., Salmon, D. P., & Paulsen, J. S. (1993). Utility of a modified version of the Wisconsin Card Sorting Test in the detection of dementia of the Alzheimer type. *Clinical Neuropsychologist*, *7*, 161–170.

Borg, C., Thomas-Atherion, C., Bogey, S., Davier, K., & Laurent, B. (2010). Visual imagery processing and knowledge of famous names in Alzheimer's disease and MCI. *Aging, Neuropsychology and Cognition*, *17*, 603–614.

Bowles, N. L., Obler, L. K., & Albert, M. L. (1987). Naming errors in healthy aging and dementia of the Alzheimer type. *Cortex*, *23*, 519–524.

Braak, H., & Braak, E. (1991). Neuropathological staging of Alzheimer-related changes. *Acta Neuropathologica*, *82*, 239–259.

Brandt, J., & Manning, K. J. (2009). Patterns of word-list generation in mild cognitive impairment and Alzheimer's disease. *Clinical Neuropsychologist*, *23*, 870–879.

Buschke, H. (1973). Selective reminding for analysis of memory and learning. *Journal of Verbal Learning and Verbal Behavior*, *12*, 543–550.

Buschke, H., & Fuld, P. A. (1974). Evaluating storage, retention, and retrieval in disordered memory and learning. *Neurology*, *24*, 1019–1025.

Buschke, H., Sliwinski, M. J., Kuslansky, G., & Lipton, R. B. (1997). Diagnosis of early dementia by the double memory test. *Neurology*, *48*, 989–997.

Butters, N., Granholm, E., Salmon, D. P., Grant, I., & Wolfe, J. (1987). Episodic and semantic memory: A comparison of amnesic and demented patients. *Journal of Clinical and Experimental Neuropsychology*, *9*, 479–497.

Butters, N., Salmon, D. P., Cullum, C. M., Cairns, P., Troster, A. I., Jacobs, D., Moss, M., & Cermak, L. S. (1988). Differentiation of amnesic and demented patients with the Wechsler memory scale – revised. *Clinical Neuropsychologist*, *2*, 133–148.

Capitani, E., Della Sala, S., Logie, R., & Spinnler, H. (1992). Recency, primacy, and memory: Reappraising and standardising the serial position curve. *Cortex*, *28*, 315–342.

Carlesimo, G. A., Sabbadini, M., Fadda, L., & Caltagirone, C. (1995). Different components in word-list forgetting of pure amnesics, degenerative demented and healthy subjects. *Cortex*, *31*, 735–745.

Chertkow, H., & Bub, D. (1990). Semantic memory loss in dementia of Alzheimer's type. *Brain*, *113*, 397–417.

Chertkow, H., Whitehead, V., Phillips, N., Wolfson, C., Atherton, J., & Bergman, H. (2010). Multilingualism (but not always bilingualism) delays the onset of Alzheimer disease: Evidence from a bilingual community. *Alzheimer Disease and Associated Disorders*, *24*, 118–125.

Clark, L. R., Delano-Wood, L., Libon, D. J., McDonald, C. R., Nation, D. A., Bangen, K. J., ... & Bondi, M. W. (2013). Are empirically derived subtypes of mild cognitive impairment consistent with conventional subtypes? *Journal of the International Neuropsychological Society*, *19*, 1–11.

Clark, L. R., Stricker, N. H., Libon, D. J., Delano-Wood, L., Salmon, D. P., Delis, D. C., & Bondi, M. W. (2012). Yes/No forced choice recognition memory in mild cognitive impairment and Alzheimer's disease: Patterns of impairment and associations with dementia severity. *Clinical Neuropsychology*, *26*, 1201–1216.

Connor, D. J., Drake, A. I., Bondi, M. W., & Delis, D. C. (1997). Detection of feigned cognitive impairments in patients with a history of mild to severe closed head injury. Paper presented at the American Academy of Neurology, Boston.

Costa, A., Perri, R., Serra, L., Barban, F., Gatto, I., Zabberoni, S., Caltagirone, C., & Carlesimo, G. A. (2010). Prospective memory functioning in mild cognitive impairment. *Neuropsychology*, *24*, 327–335.

Craik, F. I. M., Bialystok, E., & Freedman, M. (2010). Delaying the onset of Alzheimer disease: Bilingualism as a form of cognitive reserve. *Neurology*, *75*, 1726–1729.

Crews, L., & Masliah, E. (2010). Molecular mechanisms of neurodegeneration in Alzheimer's disease. *Human Molecular Genetic*, *19*, R12–R20.

Crocco, E., Curiel, R. E., Acevedo, A., Czaja, S. J., & Loewenstein, D. A. (2014). An evaluation of deficits in semantic cueing and proactive and retroactive interference as early features of Alzheimer's disease. *American Journal of Geriatric Psychiatry*, *22*, 889–897.

Crutch, S. J., Schott, J. M., Rabinovici, G. D., Murray, M., Snowden, J. S., van der Flier, W. M., et al. (2017). Consensus classification of posterior cortical atrophy. *Alzheimer's and Dementia*, *13*, 870–884.

Dalla Barba, G., & Goldblum, M. (1996). The influence of semantic encoding on recognition memory in Alzheimer's disease. *Neuropsychologia*, *34*, 1181–1186.

Darby, D., Maruff, P., Collie, A., & McStephen, M. (2002). Mild cognitive impairment can be detected by multiple assessments in a single day. *Neurology*, *59*, 1042–1046.

Davie, J. E., Azuma, T., Goldinger, S. D., Connor, D. J., Sabbagh, M. N., & Silverberg, N. B. (2004). Sensitivity to expectancy violations in healthy aging and mild cognitive impairment. *Neuropsychology*, *18*, 269–275.

Dawes, R. M., Faust, D., & Meehl, P. E. (1989). Clinical versus actuarial judgment. *Science,243*, 1668–1674.

Dean, A. C., Victor, T. L., Boone, K. B., Philpott, L. M., & Hess, R. A. (2009). Dementia and effort test performance. *The Clinical Neuropsychologist, 23*, 133–152.

Delano-Wood, L., Bondi, M. W., Sacco, J., Abeles, N., Jak, A. J., Libon, D. J., & Bozoki, A.(2009). Heterogeneity in mild cognitive impairment: Differences in neuropsychological profile and associated white matter lesion pathology. *Journal of the International Neuropsychological Society, 15*, 906–914.

Delis, D. C., Massman, P. J., Butters, N., Salmon, D. P., Cermak, L. S., & Kramer, J. H. (1991). Profiles of demented and amnesic patients on the California verbal learning test: Implications for the assessment of memory disorders. *Psychological Assessment, 3*, 19–26.

de Rover, M., Pironti, V. A., McCabe, J. A., Acosta-Cabronero, J., Arana, F. S., Morein-Zamir S. et al. (2011). Hippocampal dysfunction in patients with mild cognitive impairment: A functional neuroimaging study of a visuospatial paired associates learning task. *Neuropsychologia, 49*, 2060–2070.

Edmonds, E. C., Delano-Wood, L., Clark, L. R. Jak, A. J., Nation, D. A., McDonald, C. R., & Bondi, M. W. (2015). Susceptibility of the conventional criteria for mild cognitive impairment to false-positive diagnostic errors. *Alzheimer's and Dementia, 11*, 415–424.

Fischer, P., Marterer, A., & Danialczyk, W. (1990). Right-left disorientation in dementia of the Alzheimer type. *Neurology, 40*, 1619–1620.

Flicker, C., Ferris, S. H., Crook, T., Reisberg, B., & Bartus, R. T. (1988). Equivalent spatial-rotation deficits in normal aging and Alzheimer's disease. *Journal of Clinical and Experimental Neuropsychology, 10*, 387–399.

Flicker, C., Ferris, S. H., & Reisberg, B. (1991). Mild cognitive impairment in the elderly: Predictors of dementia. *Neurology, 41*, 1006–1009.

Fortuny, L. A. I., Garolera, M., Romo, D. H., Feldman, E., Barillas, H. F., Keefe, R. et al. (2005). Research with Spanish-speaking populations in the United States: Lost in the translation a commentary and a plea. *Journal of Clinical and Experimental Neuropsychology, 27*, 555–564.

Freedman, M., Leach, L., Kaplan, E., Winocur, G., Shulman, K. I., & Delis, D. C. (1994). *Clock drawing: A neuropsychological analysis*. New York: Oxford University Press.

Gagnon, L. G., & Belleville, S. (2011). Working memory in mild cognitive impairment and Alzheimer's disease: Contribution of forgetting and predictive value of complex span tasks. *Neuropsychology, 25*, 226–236.

Galton, C. J., Patterson, K., Xuereb, J. H., & Hodges, J. R. (2000). Atypical and typical presentations of Alzheimer's disease: A clinical, neuropsychological, neuroimaging and pathological study of 13 cases. *Brain, 123*, 484–498.

Goldblum, M., Gomez, C., Dalla Barba, G., Boller, F., Deweer, B., Hahn, V., & Dubois, B. (1998). The influence of semantic and perceptual encoding on recognition memory in Alzheimer's disease. *Neuropsychologia, 36*, 717–729.

Gollan, T. H., Salmon, D. P., Montoyoa, R. I., & Galasko, D. R. (2011). Degree of bilingualism predicts age of diagnosis of Alzheimer's disease in low-education but not in highly-educated Hispanics. *Neuropsychologia, 49*, 3826–3830.

Gollan, T. H., Stasenko, A., Li, C., & Salmon, D. P. (2017). Bilingual language intrusions and other speech errors in Alzheimer's disease. *Brain and Cognition, 118*, 27–44.

Grady, C. L., Haxby, J. V., Horwitz, B., Sundaram, M., Berg, G., Schapiro, M., Friedland, R. P., & Rappaport, S. I. (1988). Longitudinal study of the early neuropsychological and cerebral metabolic changes in dementia of the Alzheimer type. *Journal of Clinical and Experimental Neuropsychology, 10*, 576–596.

Greene, J. D. W., Baddeley, A. D., & Hodges, J. R. (1996). Analysis of the episodic memory deficit in early Alzheimer's disease: evidence from the doors and people test. *Neuropsychologia, 34*, 537–551.

Grober, E., Hall, C. B., Lipton, R. B., Zonderman, A. B., Resnick, S. M., & Kawas, C. (2008). Memory impairment, executive dysfunction, and intellectual decline in preclinical Alzheimer's disease. *Journal of the International Neuropsychological Society, 14*, 266–278.

Grober, E., Merling, A., Heimlich, T., & Lipton, R. B. (1997). Comparison of selective reminding and free and cued recall reminding in the elderly. *Journal of Clinical and Experimental Neuropsychology, 19*, 643–654.

Grundman, M., Petersen, R. C., Morris, J. C., Ferris, S., Sano, M., Farlow, M. et al. (1996). Rate of dementia of Alzheimer type (DAT) in subjects with mild cognitive impairment: The Alzheimer's Disease Cooperative Study [abstract]. *Neurology, 46*, A403.

Heinly, M. T., Greve, K. W., Bianchini, K. J., Love, J. M., & Brennan, A. (2005). WAIS Digit Span-based indicators of malingered neurocognitive dysfunction: Classification accuracy in traumatic brain injury. *Assessment, 12*, 429–444.

Hodges, J. R., & Patterson, K. (1995). Is semantic memory consistently impaired early in the course of Alzheimer's disease? Neuroanatomical and diagnostic implications. *Neuropsychologia, 33*, 441–459.

Hodges, J. R., Salmon, D. P., & Butters, N. (1991). The nature of the naming deficit in Alzheimer's and Huntington's disease. *Brain, 114*, 1547–1558.

Hodges, J. R., Salmon, D. P., & Butters, N. (1992). Semantic memory impairment in Alzheimer's disease: Failure of access or degraded knowledge? *Neuropsychologia, 30*, 301–314.

Hudon, C., Belleville, S., & Gauthier, S. (2009). The assessment of recognition memory using the remember/know procedure in amnestic mild cognitive impairment and probable Alzheimer's disease. *Brain and Cognition, 70*, 171–179.

Hudon, C., Villeneuve, S., & Belleville, S. (2011). The effect of orientation at encoding on free-recall performance in amnestic mild cognitive impairment and probable Alzheimer's disease. *Journal of Clinical and Experimental Neuropsychology, 33*, 631–638.

Huff, F. J., Corkin, S., & Growdon, J. H. (1986). Semantic impairment and anomia in Alzheimer's disease. *Brain and Language, 28*, 235–249.

Jacobs, D., Salmon, D. P., Tröster, A. I., & Butters, N. (1990). Intrusion errors in the figural memory of patients with Alzheimer's and Huntington's disease. *Archives of Clinical Neuropsychology, 5*, 49–57.

Jak, A. J., Bondi, M. W., Delano-Wood, L., Wierenga, C., Corey-Bloom, J., ... & Delis, D.C.(2009). Quantification of five neuropsychological approaches to defining mild cognitive impairment. *American Journal of Geriatric Psychiatry, 17*, 368–375.

Jak, A. J., Preis, S. R., Beiser, A. S., Seshadri, S., Wolf, P. A., Bondi, M. W., & Au, R. (2016). Neuropsychological criteria for mild cognitive impairment and dementia risk in the

Framingham Heart Study. *Journal of the International Neuropsychological Society*,*22*, 937–943.

Joubert, S., Brambati, S. M., Ansado, J., Barbeau, E. J., Felician, O., Didac, M. et al. (2010). The cognitive and neural expression of semantic memory impairment in mild cognitive impairment and early Alzheimer's disease. *Neuropsychologia*, *48*, 978–988.

Karantzoulis, S., Troyer, A. K., & Rich, J. B. (2009). Prospective memory in amnestic mild cognitive impairment. *Journal of the International Neuropsychological Society*, *15*, 407–415.

Kiewel, N. A., Wisdom, N. M., Bradshaw, M. R., Pastorek, N. J., & Strutt, A. M. (2012). A retrospective review of digit span-related effort indicators in probable Alzheimer's disease patients. *The Clinical Neuropsychologist*, *26*, 965–974.

Knopman, D. S., & Ryberg, S. (1989). A verbal memory test with high predictive accuracy for dementia of the Alzheimer type. *Archives of Neurology*, *46*, 141–145.

Koedam, E. L., Lauffer, V., van der Viles, A. E., van der Flier, W. M., Scheltens, P., & Pijnenburg, Y. A. (2010). Early-versus late-onset Alzheimer's disease: More than age alone. *Journal of Alzheimer's Disease*, *19*, 1401–1408.

Lange, K. W., Sahakian, B. J., Quinn, N. P., Marsden, C. D., & Robbins, T. W. (1995). Comparison of executive and visuospatial memory function in Huntington's disease and dementia of Alzheimer type matched for degree of dementia. *Journal of Neurology, Neurosurgery and Psychiatry*, *58*, 598–606.

Larrabee, G. L., Largen, J. W., & Levin, H. S. (1985). Sensitivity of age-decline resistant ("Hold") WAIS subtests to Alzheimer's disease. *Journal of Clinical and Experimental Neuropsychology*, *7*, 497–504.

Larson, E. B., Kukull, W. A., & Katzman, R. (1992). Cognitive impairment: Dementia and Alzheimer's disease. *Annual Review of Public Health*, *13*, 431–449.

La Rue, A., & Jarvik, L. R. (1987). Cognitive function and prediction of dementia in old age. *International Journal of Aging and Human Development*, *25*, 79–89.

La Rue, A., Romero, L. J., Ortiz, I. E., Chi Lang, H., & Lindeman, R. D. (1999). Neuropsychological performance of Hispanic and non-Hispanic older adults: An epidemiologic survey. *Clinical Neuropsychologist*, *13*, 474–486.

Lefleche, G., & Albert, M. S. (1995). Executive function deficits in mild Alzheimer's disease. *Neuropsychology*, *9*, 313–320.

Libon, D. J., Bondi, M. W., Price, C. C., Lamar, M., Joel, E., Wambach, D. M., ... & Penney, D. L.(2011). Verbal serial list learning in mild cognitive impairment: A profile analysis of interference, forgetting, and errors. *Journal of the International Neuropsychological Society*, *17*, 905–914.

Libon, D. J., Drabick, D. A., Giovannetti, T., Price, C. C., Bondi, M. W., Eppig, J., ... & Swenson, R. (2014). Neuropsychological syndromes associated with Alzheimer's/vascular dementia: a latent class analysis. *Journal of Alzheimer's Disease*, *42*, 999–1014.

Licht, E. A., McMurtray, A. M., Saul, R. E., & Mendez, M. F. (2007). Cognitive differences between early- and late-onset Alzheimer's disease. *American Journal of Alzheimer's Disease and Other Dementias*, *22*, 218–222.

Lineweaver,T. T., Salmon, D. P., Bondi, M. W., & Corey-Bloom, J. (2005). Distinct effects of Alzheimer's disease and Huntington's disease on performance of mental rotation. *Journal of the International Neuropsychological Society*, *11*, 30–39.

Liu, L., Gauthier, L., & Gauthier, S. (1991). Spatial disorientation in persons with early senile dementia of the Alzheimer's type. *American Journal of Occupational Therapy*, *45*, 67–74.

Locascio, J. J., Growdon, J. H., & Corkin, S. (1995). Cognitive test performance in detecting, staging, and tracking Alzheimer's disease. *Archives of Neurology*, *52*, 1087–1099.

Loewenstein, D. A., Curiel, R. E., DeKosky, S., Bauer, R. M., Rosselli, M. ... & Duara, R. (2018). Utilizing semantic intrusions to identify amyloid positivity in mild cognitive impairment. *Neurology*, *91*, e976–e984.

Manes, F., Serrano, C., Calcagno, M. L., Cardozo, J., & Hodges, J. R. (2008). Accelerated forgetting in subjects with memory complaints. *Journal of Neurology*, *255*, 1067–1070.

Manly, J. J., & Echemendia, R. J. (2007). Race-specific norms: Using the model of hypertension to understand issues of race, culture, and education in neuropsychology. *Archives of Clinical Neuropsychology*, *22*, 319–325.

Martin, A., & Fedio, P. (1983). Word production and comprehension in Alzheimer's disease: The breakdown of semantic knowledge. *Brain and Language*, *19*, 124–141.

Masliah, E., & Salmon, D. (1999). Neuropathological correlates of dementia in Alzheimer's disease. In A. Peters & J. Morrison (Eds.), *Cerebral cortex*, Vol. *14* (pp. 513–551). New York: Kluwer Academic/Plenum Publishers.

Massman, P. J., Delis, D. C., & Butters, N. (1993). Does impaired primacy recall equal impaired long-term storage?: Serial position effects in Huntington's disease and Alzheimer's disease. *Developmental Neuropsychology*, *9*, 1–15.

Massman, P. J., Delis, D. C., Butters, N., Dupont, R. M., & Gillin, J. C. (1992). The subcortical dysfunction hypothesis of memory deficits in depression: Neuropsychological validation in a subgroup of patients. *Journal of Clinical and Experimental Neuropsychology*, *14*, 687–706.

Mathias, J. L., & Burke, J. (2009). Cognitive functioning in Alzheimer's and vascular dementia: a meta-analysis. [Meta-Analysis]. *Neuropsychology*, *23*(4), 411–423.

McKeith, I. G., Boeve, B. F., Dickson, D. W., Halliday, G., Taylor, J. P., ... & Kosaka, K. (2017). Diagnosis and management of dementia with Lewy bodies 4th consensus report of the DLB consortium. *Neurology*, *89*, 88–100.

McKhann, G. M., Knopman, D. S., Chertkow, H., Hyman, B. T., Jack, C. R., Jr., Kawas, C. H., ... & Phelps, C. H. (2011). The diagnosis of dementia due to Alzheimer's disease: Recommendations from the National Institute on Aging-Alzheimer's Association workgroups on diagnostic guidelines for Alzheimer's disease. *Alzheimer's and Dementia*, *7*, 263–269.

Mendez, M. F., Lee, A. S., Joshi, A., & Shapira, J. S. (2012). Nonamnestic presentation of early-onset Alzheimer's disease. *American Journal of Alzheimer's Disease and other Dementia*, *27*, 413–420.

Merten, T., Bossink, L., & Schmand, B. (2007). On the limits of effort testing: Symptom validity tests and severity of neurocognitive symptoms in nonlitigant patients. *Journal of Clinical and Experimental Neuropsychology*, *29*, 308–318.

Mickes, L., Wixted, J. T., Fennema-Notestine, C., Galasko, D., Bondi, M. W., Thal, L. J., & Salmon, D. P. (2007). Progressive impairment on neuropsychological tasks in a longitudinal study of preclinical Alzheimer's disease. *Neuropsychology*, *21*, 696–705.

Miller, E. (1971). On the nature of memory disorder in presenile dementia. *Neuropsychologia*, *9*, 75–78.

Miller, B. L., Ikonte, C., Ponton, M., Levy, M., Boone, K., Darby, A., Berman, N., Mena, I., & Cummings, J. L. (1997). A study of the Lund-Manchester research criteria for frontotemporal dementia: clinical and single-photon emission CT correlations. *Neurology, 48*, 937–942.

Minoshima, S., Foster, N. L., Sima, A., Frey, K. A., Albin, R. L., & Kuhl, D. E. (2001). Alzheimer's disease versus dementia with Lewy bodies: Cerebral metabolic distinction with autopsy confirmation. *Annals of Neurology, 50*, 358–65.

Mohr, E., Litvan, I., Williams, J., Fedio, P., & Chase, T. N. (1990). Selective deficits in Alzheimer and Parkinson dementia: Visuospatial function. *Canadian Journal of Neurological Science, 17*, 292–297.

Monsch, A. U., Bondi, M. W., Butters, N, Paulsen, J. S., Salmon, D. P., Brugger, P., & Swenson, M. (1994). A comparison of category and letter fluency in Alzheimer's disease and Huntington's disease. *Neuropsychology, 8*, 25–30.

Morris, J. C., McKeel, D. W., Storandt, M., Rubin, E. H., Price, J. L., Grant, E. A., Ball, M. J., & Berg, L. (1991). Very mild Alzheimer's disease: Informant-based clinical, psychometric, and pathologic distinction from normal aging. *Neurology, 41*, 469–478.

Murphy, K. J., Rich, J. B., & Troyer, A. K. (2006). Verbal fluency patterns in amnestic mild cognitive impairment are characteristic of Alzheimer's type dementia. *Journal of the International Neuropsychological Society, 12*, 570–574.

Nebes, R. (1989). Semantic memory in Alzheimer's disease. *Psychological Bulletin, 106*, 377–394.

Nell, V. (2000). *Cross-cultural neuropsychological assessment: Theory and practice*. Mahwah, NJ: Lawrence Erlbaum Associates.

Nicholas, M., Obler, L., Albert, M., & Helm-Estabrooks, N. (1985). Empty speech in Alzheimer's disease and fluent aphasia. *Journal of Speech and Hearing Research, 28*, 405–410.

Norton, L. E., Bondi, M. W., Salmon, D. P., & Goodglass, H. (1997). Deterioration of generic knowledge in patients with Alzheimer's disease: Evidence from the Number Information Test. *Journal of Clinical and Experimental Neuropsychology, 19*, 857–866.

Nutter-Upham, K. E., Saykin, A. J., Rabin, L. A., Roth, R. M., Wishart, H. A., Pare, N., & Flashman, L. A. (2008). Verbal fluency performance in amnestic MCI and older adults with cognitive complaints. *Archives of Clinical Neuropsychology, 23*, 229–241.

Pandovani, A., Di Piero, V., Bragoni, M., Iacoboni, M., Gualdi, G. G., & Lenzi, G. L. (1995). Patterns of neuropsychological impairment in mild dementia: A comparison between Alzheimer's disease and multi-infarct dementia. *Acta Neurologica Scandinavica, 92*, 433–442.

Pantoni, L. (2010). Cerebral small vessel disease: from pathogenesis and clinical characteristics to therapeutic challenges. [Review]. *Lancet Neurology, 9*, 689–701.

Parasuraman, R., & Haxby, J. V. (1993). Attention and brain function in Alzheimer's disease. *Neuropsychology, 7*, 242–272.

Paulson, D., Horner, M. D., & Bachman, D. (2015). A comparison of four embedded validity indices for the RBANS in a memory disorders clinic. *Archives of Clinical Neuropsychology, 30*, 207–216.

Pearson, R. C., Esiri, M. M., Hiorns, R. W., Wilcock, G. K., & Powell, T. P. (1985). Anatomical correlates of the distribution of the pathological changes in the neocortex in Alzheimer disease. *Proceeding of the National Academy of Sciences of the USA, 82*, 4531–4534.

Pedraza, O., & Mungas, D. (2008). Measurement in cross-cultural neuropsychology. *Neuropsychology Review, 18*, 184–193.

Peña, E. D. (2007). Lost in translation: Methodological considerations in cross-cultural research. *Child Development, 78*, 1255–1264.

Pepin, E. P., & Eslinger, P. J. (1989). Verbal memory decline in Alzheimer's disease: A multiple-processes deficit. *Neurology, 39*, 1477–1482.

Perri, R., Serra, L., Carlesimo, G. A., & Caltagirone, C. (2007). Amnestic mild cognitive impairment: difference of memory profile in subjects who converted or did not convert to Alzheimer's disease. *Neuropsychology, 21*, 549–558.

Perry, R. J., & Hodges, J. R. (1999). Attention and executive deficits in Alzheimer's disease: A critical review. *Brain, 122*, 383–404.

Petersen, R.C. (2004). Mild cognitive impairment as a diagnostic entity. *Journal of Internal Medicine, 256*, 183–194.

Petersen, R. C., Smith, G. E., Waring, S. C., Ivnik, R. J., Tangalos, E. G., & Kokmen E. (1999). Mild cognitive impairment: Clinical characterization and outcome. *Archives of Neurology, 56*, 303–308.

Pike, K. E., Rowe, C. C., Moss, S. A., & Savage, G. (2008). Memory profiling with paired associate learning in Alzheimer's disease, mild cognitive impairment, and healthy aging. *Neuropsychology, 22*, 718–728.

Rapp, M. A., & Reischies, F. M. (2005). Attention and executive control predict Alzheimer's disease in late life: results from the Berlin aging study (BASE). *American Journal of Geriatric Psychiatry, 13*, 134–141.

Rascovsky, K., Hodges, J. R., Kipps, C. M., Johnson, J. K., Seeley, W. W., Mendez, M. F., Knopman, D., ... & Miller, B. L. (2007). Diagnostic criteria for the behavioral variant of frontotemporal dementia (bvFTD): Current limitations and future directions. *Alzheimer Disease and Associated Disorders, 21*, S14–18.

Rascovsky, K., Hodges, J. R., Knopman, D., Mendez, M. F., Kramer, J. H., Neuhaus, J. et al. (2011). Sensitivity of revised diagnostic criteria for the behavioral variant of frontotemporal dementia. *Brain, 134*, 2456–2477.

Rascovsky, K., Salmon, D. P., Ho, G. J., Galasko, D., Peavy, G. M., Hansen, L. A., & Thal, L. J. (2002). Cognitive profiles differ in autopsy-confirmed frontotemporal dementia and AD. *Neurology, 58*, 1801–1808

Reed, B. R., Mungas, D. M., Kramer, J. H., Ellis, W., Vinters, H. V., Zarow, C., Jagust, W. J., & Chui, H. C. (2007). Profiles of neuropsychological impairment in autopsy-defined Alzheimer's disease and cerebrovascular disease. *Brain, 130*, 731–739.

Rentz, D. M., Amariglio, R. E., Becker, J. A., Frey, M., Olson, L. E., Frishe, K. et al. (2011). Face-name associative memory performance is related to amyloid burden in normal elderly. *Neuropsychologia, 49*, 2776–2783.

Salmon, D. P., & Chan, A. S. (1994). Semantic memory deficits associated with Alzheimer's disease. In L. S. Cermak (Ed.), *Neuropsychological explorations of memory and cognition: Essays in honor of Nelson Butters* (pp. 61–76). New York: Plenum Press.

Salmon, D. P., Heindel, W. C., & Lange, K. L. (1999). Differential decline in word generation from phonemic and semantic categories during the course of Alzheimer's disease: Implications for the integrity of semantic memory. *Journal of the International Neuropsychological Society, 5*, 692–703.

Salmon, D. P., & Squire, L. R. (2009). The neuropsychology of memory dysfunction and its assessment. In I. Grant & K. Adams (Eds.), *Neuropsychological assessment of neuropsychiatric and neuromedical disorders* (3rd ed., pp. 560–594). New York: Oxford University Press.

Salmon, D. P., Thomas, R. G., Pay, M. M., Booth, A., Hofstetter, C. R., Thal, L. J., & Katzman, R. (2002). Alzheimer's disease can be accurately diagnosed in very mildly impaired individuals. *Neurology*, *59*, 1022–1028.

Saunders, N. L. J., & Summers, M. J. (2011). Longitudinal deficits to attention, executive, and working memory in subtypes of mild cognitive impairment. *Neuropsychology*, *25*, 237–248.

Sawyer, R. J., Testa, S. M., & Dux, M. (2017). Embedded performance validity tests within the Hopkins Verbal Learning Tests-Revised and the Brief Visuospatial Memory Test-Revised. *The Clinical Neuropsychologist*, *31*, 207–218.

Schmitter-Edgecombe, M., Woo, E., & Greeley, D. R. (2009). Characterizing multiple memory deficits and their relation to everyday functioning in individuals with mild cognitive impairment. *Neuropsychology*, *23*, 168–177.

Seidenberg, M., Guidotti, L., Nielson, K. A., Woodard, J. L., Durgerian, S., Zhang, Q., Gander, A., Antuono, P., & Rao, S. M. (2009). Semantic knowledge for famous names in mild cognitive impairment. *Journal of the International Neuropsychological Society*, *15*, 9–18.

Serra, L., Bozzali, M., Cercignani, M., Perri, R., Fadda, L., Caltagirone, C., & Carlesimo, G. A. (2010). Recollection and familiarity in amnestic mild cognitive impairment. *Neuropsychology*, *24*, 316–326.

Sieck, B. C., Smith, M. M., Duff, K., Paulsen, J. S., & Beglinger, L. J. (2013). Symptom validity test performance in the Huntington disease clinic. *Archives of Clinical Neuropsychology*, *28*, 135–143.

Sinai, M., Phillips, N. A., Chertkow, H., & Kabani, N. J. (2010). Task switching performance reveals heterogeneity amongst patients with mild cognitive impairment. *Neuropsychology*, *24*, 757–774.

Ska, B., Poissant, A., & Joanette, Y. (1990). Line orientation judgement in normal elderly and subjects with dementia of Alzheimer's type. *Journal of Clinical and Experimental Neuropsychology*, *12*, 695–702.

Snowden, J. S., Bathgate, D., Varma, A., Blackshaw, A., Gibbons, Z. C., & Neary, D. (2001). Distinct behavioural profiles in frontotemporal dementia and semantic dementia. *Journal of Neurology, Neurosurgery and Psychiatry*, *70*, 323–332.

Sperling, R. A., Aisen, P. S., Beckett, L. A., Bennett, D. A., Craft, S., Fagan, A. M., Iwatsubo, T., ... & Phelps, C. H. (2011). Toward defining the preclinical stages of Alzheimer's disease: Recommendations from the National Institute on Aging-Alzheimer's Association workgroups on diagnostic guidelines for Alzheimer's disease. *Alzheimer's and Dementia*, *7*, 280–292.

Spinnler, H., Della Sala, S., Bandera, R., & Baddeley, A. (1988). Dementia, aging, and the structure of human memory. *Cognitive Neuropsychology*, *5*, 193–211.

Stern, Y. (2009). Cognitive reserve. *Neuropsychologia*, *47*, 2015–2028.

Teichner, G., & Wagner, M. T. (2004). The Test of Memory Malingering (TOMM): Normative data from cognitively intact, cognitively impaired, and elderly patients with dementia. *Archives of Clinical Neuropsychology*, *19*, 455–464.

Terry, R. D., & Katzman, R. (1983). Senile dementia of the Alzheimer type. *Annals of Neurology*, *14*, 497–506.

Thompson, C., Henry, J. D., Rendell, P. G., Withall, A., & Brodaty, H. (2010). Prospective memory function in mild cognitive impairment. *Journal of the International Neuropsychological Society*, *16*, 318–325.

Tombaugh, T. N. (1997). The Test of Memory Malingering (TOMM): Normative data from cognitively intact and cognitively impaired individuals. *Psychological Assessment*, *9*, 260–268.

Troyer, A. K., & Murphy, K. J. (2007). Memory for intentions in amnestic mild cognitive impairment: Time- and event-based prospective memory. *Journal of the International Neuropsychological Society*, *13*, 365–369.

Troyer, A. K., Murphy, K. J., Anderson, N. D., Hayman-Abello, B. A., Craik, F. I. M., & Moscovitch, M. (2008). Item and associative memory in amnestic mild cognitive impairment: performance on standardized memory tests. *Neuropsychology*, *22*, 10–16.

Twamley, E. W., Ropacki, S. A. L., & Bondi, M. W. (2006). Neuropsychological and neuroimaging changes in preclinical Alzheimer's disease. *Journal of the International Neuropsychological Society*, *12*, 707–735.

United States Census Bureau. (2017). Facts for Features: Hispanic Heritage Month 2017.

Villardita, C. (1993). Alzheimer's disease compared with cerebrovascular dementia. *Acta Neurologica Scandinavica*, *87*, 299–308.

Vonsattel, J. P., Myers, R. H., Stevens, T. J., Ferrante, R. J., Bird, E. D., & Richardson, E. P. (1985). Neuropathological classification of Huntington's disease. *Journal of Neuropathology and Experimental Neurology*, *44*, 559–577.

Walter, J., Morris, J., Swier-Vosnos, A., & Pliskin, N. (2014). Effects of severity of dementia on a symptom validity measure. *The Clinical Neuropsychologist*, *28*, 1197–1208.

Weintraub, S., Wickland, A. H., & Salmon, D. P. (2012). The neuropsychological profile of Alzheimer's disease. In D. Selkoe, D. Holtzman, & E. Mandelkow (Eds.), *The biology of Alzheimer's disease* (pp. 25–42.) Cold Spring Harbor, NY: Cold Spring Harbor Laboratory Press.

Weissberger, G. H., Gollan, T. H., Bondi, M. W., Nation, D. A., Hansen, L. A., Galasko, D., & Salmon, D. P. (2019). Neuropsychological deficit profiles, vascular risk factors, and neuropathological findings in Hispanic older adults with autopsy-confirmed Alzheimer's disease. *Journal of Alzheimer's Disease*, *67*, 291–302.

Weissberger, G. H., Salmon, D. P., Bondi, M. W., & Gollan, T. H. (2013). Which neuropsychological tests predict progression to Alzheimer's disease in Hispanics? *Neuropsychology*, *27*, 343–355.

Welsh, K., Butters, N., Hughes, J., Mohs, R., & Heyman, A. (1991). Detection of abnormal memory decline in mild cases of Alzheimer's disease using CERAD neuropsychological measures. *Archives of Neurology*, *48*, 278–281.

Westerberg, C. E., Paller, K. A., Weintraub, S., Mesulam, M., Holdstock, J. S., Mayes, A. R., & Reber, P. J. (2006). When memory does not fail: Familiarity-based recognition in mild cognitive impairment and Alzheimer's disease. *Neuropsychology*, *20*, 193–205.

Wetzel, M. E., & Kramer, J. H. (2008). The neuropsychology of vascular dementia. *Handbook of Clinical Neurology*, *88*, 567–583.

Wilson, R. S., Bacon, L. D., Fox, J. H., & Kaszniak, A. W. (1983). Primary and secondary memory in dementia of the Alzheimer type. *Journal of Clinical Neuropsychology*, *5*, 337–344.

Winblad, B., Palmer, K., Kivipelto, M., Jelic, V., Fratiglioni, L., Wahlund, L. O., … & Petersen, R. C. (2004). Mild cognitive impairment – beyond controversies, towards a consensus: Report of the International Working Group on Mild Cognitive Impairment. *Journal of Internal Medicine*, *256*, 240–246.

Wolk, D. A., Signoff, E. D., & Dekosky, S. T. (2008). Recollection and familiarity in amnestic mild cognitive impairment: A global decline in recognition memory. *Neuropsychologia*, *46*, 1965–1978.

31 Assessment of Traumatic Brain Injuries

LILIAN SALINAS AND WILLIAM BARR

Brain injuries are typically associated with a wide range of acute and chronic impairments to cognition, behavior, and psychological well-being. As such, adequate assessment and identification of these impairments is vital for determining appropriate short- and long-term treatment interventions in the acute and chronic stages of recovery.

Accurate assessment of traumatic brain injury (TBI) patients has become increasingly important as awareness and interest in brain injury has increased over the last several years. According to the Center for Disease Control (CDC), there were approximately 2.8 million emergency department visits, 282,000 hospitalizations, and 56,000 deaths related to TBI between 2007 and 2013 (Taylor et al., 2017). These increases in emergency visits and hospitalizations may be representative of greater public awareness of the effects of TBI due to media coverage of sports-related injuries.

DEFINITION OF TBI

While one might have an intuitive sense of what constitutes a TBI, it has been defined in a variety of ways by different medical, research, and public policy organizations. For instance, the CDC defines TBI as "an occurrence of injury to the head that is documented in a medical record with one of the following conditions attributed to head injury: observed or self-reported decreased level of consciousness, amnesia, skull fracture, or objective neurological or neuropsychological abnormality or diagnosed intracranial lesion" (Marr, 2004). Another definition put forth by the Department of Veterans Affairs and Department of Defense specifies that the TBI is associated with new onset or worsening of at least one of the following: decreased level of consciousness, loss of memory for events before or after the injury, altered mental status, neurological deficits, and intracranial lesion (VA/DoD, 2009).

CLASSIFICATION OF TBI

In addition to differences in the definition of TBI, there is also variability in the classification of brain injuries as mild, moderate, or severe (ACRM, 1993; Stein & Ross, 1992; Teasdale & Jennett, 1974). Most of these systems focus on the duration and depth of loss of consciousness (LOC), presence and extent of post-traumatic amnesia (PTA), mental status alteration, and structural imaging results. In particular, the Glasgow Coma Scale (GCS) score and PTA have been found to be predictive of long-term outcomes in TBI (Dikmen et al., 2003; Dikmen et al., 1995; Ellenberg, Levin, & Saydjari, 1996; Sherer et al., 2014).

Severe TBIs are defined by GCS scores of less than 8, LOC longer than twenty-four hours, PTA longer than one week, altered mental status, and positive neuroimaging findings (Malec et al., 2007; Teasdale & Jennett, 1974). Moderate TBIs are associated with a GCS score of 9–12, LOC between thirty minutes and twenty-four hours, PTA longer than twenty-four hours and less than one week, altered mental status, and positive neuroimaging findings (Malec et al., 2007; Stein & Ross, 1992; Teasdale & Jennett, 1974). Of the three classification categories, the mild TBI (MTBI) has been the most challenging to describe for clinicians and the scientific community. MTBI is defined by a GCS score of 13–15, LOC less than thirty minutes, and PTA less than twenty-four hours (ACRM, 1993; Malec et al., 2007). Although neuroimaging studies are typically normal, abnormalities are seen among those whose injuries are complicated by an intracranial bleed or lesion, otherwise referred to as complicated MTBIs.

Unfortunately, individuals often have heterogeneous presentations and they may not exactly fit into these categories and cutoffs. For example, moderate TBI may present with significant initial impairments that are difficult to distinguish from those with severe TBI. Similarly, complicated MTBI may be erroneously classified as a moderate injury. To complicate the issue of definition and classification further, the measures typically used to determine injury severity (i.e., GCS and PTA) may not be entirely reliably and validly measured in all instances. For example, often a GCS score may not be readily available or recorded until a significant amount of time after the injury (Tator, 2009), especially in MTBI cases. Other injury-related factors (e.g., physical wounds, pain, alcohol/substance intoxication) may also influence initial GCS score (Ricker, 2010). Relying solely on the initial GCS score for individuals presenting with rapidly progressing subdural or epidural hematomas may also lead to an underestimation of the injury's severity (Ricker, 2010). PTA assessments may also not be as reliable in assessing injury severity, as initial confusion and/or agitation may preclude an individual from accurately describing memories around the event (Esselman & Uomoto, 1995; Ricker, 2010).

COGNITIVE, BEHAVIORAL, AND AFFECTIVE IMPAIRMENTS IN TBI

Pervasive cognitive and neurobehavioral symptoms are seen in those with moderate to severe TBIs. Common cognitive deficits include poor immediate and complex attention, slowed processing speed, executive dysfunction, and disrupted learning and memory (Fork et al., 2005; Mathias & Wheaton, 2007). These impairments are prominent within the first month after injury, experience a steep recovery between one and six months after the injury, continued recovery up to one to two years post-injury, and a more gradual decrease in recovery between two and five years after the injury (Christensen et al., 2008).

Millis and colleagues (2001) found that rates of improvement within individual cognitive domains might vary, with more simple abilities improving prior to more complex ones. Those with severe TBI have worse cognitive and functional outcomes than moderate or MTBI patients (Novack et al., 2000; Novack et al., 2001). Long-lasting deficits in cognition and functional activities have been seen more than ten years post-injury among those with severe injuries (Draper & Ponsford, 2008). Neuropsychological results, age, education, and pre-injury work history have been found to be the strongest predictors of return to work and independent living following a moderate to severe TBI (Dikmen et al., 1995).

MTBIs are associated with short-term difficulties in recall, slow processing speed, reduced attention, depression, anxiety, and/or irritability following the injury, which typically resolve within seven to ten days and persist no longer than three months (Belanger & Vanderploeg, 2005; McCrea et al., 2003). When symptoms persist longer than three months, they are attributed to post-concussion syndrome (PCS) (Boake et al., 2005; Erlanger et al., 2003; Malec et al., 2007). PCS symptoms are not related to the injury itself but influenced by premorbid and current psychological factors (McCrea et al., 2003; McCrea et al., 2009). Individuals with MTBI typically have good functional outcomes, except for those in which psychological factors or litigation factors play a role in development of PCS symptoms and affect recovery. Complicated TBI has been associated with a greater level of disability and worse cognitive and functional outcomes one year post-injury (Kashluba et al., 2008).

Behaviorally and emotionally, individuals across all three TBI groups present with a range of problems, including irritability, agitation, disinhibition, restlessness, depression, anxiety, apathy, among others (McKinley, 1999). Typically, those with severe TBI exhibit worse symptoms but presentation and severity are heavily influenced by other factors like premorbid personality, psychiatric history, substance use, social support, and reaction/adjustment to injury (Whelan-Goodinson et al., 2010; Whelan et al., 2009). Depression and anxiety are common among those with TBI (Dikmen et al., 2003; Hart et al., 2012; Van Reekum et al., 1996; van Reekum, Cohen, & Wong, 2000). PTSD is most common among those who experienced acute stress disorder shortly after their injury or have a history of trauma (Bryant & Harvey, 1998; Hiott & Labbate, 2002). Substance abuse disorders may also exist prior to or may develop after the injury (Whelan-Goodinson et al., 2010)

Neuropsychological Assessment in TBI

Within the acute and subacute stages of recovery, neuropsychologists are called on to administer brief, repeatable measures to assess alterations in level of consciousness and general mental status, evaluate readiness to engage in rehabilitation therapies, and to provide education and support to family members. (Boake et al., 2001; Sherer et al., 2014). As individuals progress into outpatient rehabilitation settings and the chronic/long-term phase of recovery, neuropsychologists conduct more comprehensive assessments, with particular focus on attention, processing speed, executive functioning, and memory, which are commonly affected in TBI populations, in order to assess cognition and predict outcomes (e.g., level of independence and activity, ability to return to work) (Boake et al., 2001; Millis et al., 2001; Sherer et al., 2014; Sherer & Novack, 2003; Sherer et al., 2002).

A comprehensive neuropsychological evaluation typically includes:

1. Medical record review
2. Clinical interview with the patient and/or collateral sources about injury details; changes in cognition, behavior, or mood; medical history; psychiatric history (e.g., mood disorder, substance abuse/dependence); social history (e.g., education, employment); family medical and psychiatric history; and treatment goals and expectations
3. Neuropsychological assessment, including symptom and performance validity testing, and self-report measures of emotional and behavioral functioning

Once the neuropsychological assessment results are interpreted and documented, clinicians can use them to assist the treatment team and family members in determining the need for ongoing supervision versus return to work and independent living, as well as devising individualized interventions, including referrals for individual and group cognitive remediation therapy, individual and family therapy, and medication management (Boake et al., 2001; Cicerone et al., 2005; Hart et al., 2003; Novack et al., 2000; Novack et al., 2001).

Assessment Interpretation in TBI

Throughout the assessment process, neuropsychologists go beyond concrete interpretations of test data by incorporating neurological, psychiatric, and sociocultural variables into their understanding of patients' level of cognitive, behavioral, and affective functioning throughout acute and chronic stages of recovery from TBI. This is achieved by taking a biopsychosocial approach to understanding and assessing functioning following a brain injury.

One model that has been used in TBI rehabilitation settings to understand the effects of structural neurological damage on cognitive and behavioral functioning following TBI and how this may impact an individual's ability to return to daily activities within home, school, and work environments is the World Health Organization's International Classification of Functioning, Disability, and Health (ICF; WHO, 2001) model (Bilbao et al., 2003; Laxe et al., 2012; Laxe et al., 2014).

The ICF model looks at TBI sequelae in terms of the injury's effect on the following areas:

1. Body structures and functions (structural brain changes and cognitive and emotional functioning)
2. Activities or tasks performed within home, school, and work environments
3. Participation in daily activities and societal roles (e.g., academic or vocational)
4. Environmental factors that can facilitate or hinder functioning and recovery
5. Personal factors (e.g., age, gender, education, habits, prior history)

Conducting a neuropsychological evaluation that is informed by a biopsychosocial model, like ICF, can contribute to adequate assessment of an individual's functioning, education/support for the individual and their caretakers, and identification of adequate interventions aimed at improving cognitive, behavioral, and affective functioning and promoting greater independence and reintegration into home and community activities. Unfortunately, the heterogeneity in assessment and interpretation approaches does not always allow for the use of a biopsychosocial model and integration of its components into TBI diagnostic and treatment considerations.

Limitations in Neuropsychological Assessment of TBI

Although neuropsychologists are well-equipped to evaluate cognitive, behavioral, and affective symptoms in TBI patients, our assessment measures and practices are not devoid of their own limitations, which can further complicate result interpretation and translation into adequate treatment options.

First, the functions that are typically most affected in TBI, such as attention, processing speed, and memory, are often the least reliable ones to measure or ones that can be impacted by disruption to several processes rather than a single area. This makes it difficult to accurately track change throughout the different phases of recovery. Second, some of the measures that are widely used in assessing individuals with TBIs have not been developed for specific use in this population, which may affect their sensitivity to detect impairments and changes over time. Therefore, several factors like practice effects, methodological limitations (e.g., unreliable or unavailable reliable change index scores, statistical regression to the mean), environmental differences (e.g., inpatient versus outpatient contexts), and individual differences (e.g., motivation, litigation proceedings, demographic variables) should be considered when evaluating changes in scores throughout recovery (Heilbronner et al., 2010).

Third, although this issue is not specific to TBI assessment, most neuropsychological measures have been in use for long periods of time without much change and some may even be outdated. Therefore, neuropsychologists must weigh the pros and cons of utilizing older or newer measures in their assessments of TBI patients, taking into consideration ethical principles and availability of proper validity/reliability data (Bush et al., 2018; Loring & Bauer, 2010; Loring et al., 2016).

Fourth, there are inconsistencies among practitioners in the interpretation of neuropsychological testing data. These discrepancies may lead to erroneous interpretations of abnormalities within some neuropsychological measures as indicative of organic "brain damage," if not considered within the appropriate biopsychosocial context for the examinee (e.g., demographic background, past medical and psychiatric history).

Fifth, motivation and effort may affect the accuracy of testing procedures and results' interpretation, especially in cases where secondary gain factors (e.g., litigation, disability payments, release of service) have the potential to influence motivation and engagement (Larrabee, 2003, 2012; Meyers & Diep, 2000; Meyers & Volbrecht, 2003). Although performance and symptoms validity measures are not universally used by practicing neuropsychologists (Rabin, Barr, & Burton, 2005), it is important to include several performance validity (PVT) and symptom validity (SVT) measures in neuropsychological batteries to allow for appropriate interpretation of results (Boone, 2009; Heilbronner et al., 2009; Lippa, 2018; Lippa et al., 2014; Lippa et al., 2017; Miller et al., 2017). Neuropsychologists should also show caution in their interpretation of PVT and SVT results and consider factors, such as low intellectual functioning, dementia, low education, race/ethnicity, and English-as-a-Second-Language status, that have been found to affect their specificity and sensitivity (Dean et al., 2008; Dean et al., 2009; Loring et al., 2016; Marshall & Happe, 2007; Robles et al., 2015; Salazar et al., 2007; Strutt et al., 2011; Vilar-López et al., 2008; Vilar-López et al., 2007).

Lastly, the neuropsychology field struggles with the assessment of ethnically and culturally diverse individuals due to a lack of appropriate measures and normative data. This is particularly relevant in TBI because ethnic and minority status have been linked to greater risk for TBI occurrence and poorer outcomes (Arango-Lasprilla et al., 2008; Arango-Lasprilla et al., 2007; Gary, Arango-Lasprilla, & Stevens, 2009; Sherer et al., 2008). In addition to the lack of measures and normative data, interpretation of findings is often challenging due to other factors, such as language and cultural confounds, limited education, low socioeconomic status, and low acculturation (Arango-Lasprilla et al., 2007; Rosenthal et al., 1996; Sander et al., 2009).

Proper evaluation and interpretation of the cognitive, behavioral, and affective symptoms related to TBI requires a comprehensive, flexible, empirically based, and culturally minded assessment approach. This chapter focuses on reviewing assessment practices utilized to evaluate individuals with mild, moderate, and severe TBIs.

Assessment of Moderate and Severe TBI

The complexities involved in assessing, predicting, and tracking the neurocognitive and neurobehavioral recovery of individuals with moderate and severe TBI require comprehensive evaluations of cognitive, behavioral, and affective functioning at the different stages of recovery.

Acute Stage of Recovery

Within the early recovery period, individuals may not be able to complete comprehensive assessments. Therefore, brief evaluations that primarily assess for arousal, orientation, level of awareness, PTA, confusion, general cognition, and affective/behavioral functioning and can be administered quickly (e.g., within less than thirty minutes) and repeated over time are recommended.

Specifically, at this stage, clinicians assess emergence from coma, vegetative, minimally conscious, and confusion states using brief measures such as the Disability Rating Scale (Gouvier et al., 1987), Coma/Near Coma Scale (Rappaport, 2005; Rappaport, Dougherty, & Kelting, 1992), Rancho Los Amigos Scale (Gouvier et al., 1987), and Coma Recovery Scale-Revised (Giacino, Kalmar, & Whyte, 2004). Later, the focus changes to tracking recovery of orientation with measures like the Galveston Orientation and Amnesia Test (Levin, O'Donnell, & Grossman, 1979) and O-Log (Jackson, Novack, & Dowler, 1998).

Subacute Stage of Recovery

Generally, more comprehensive measures can be administered once individuals emerge from PTA. At this stage, cognitive functioning is assessed using brief cognitive screening measures like Montreal Cognitive Assessment (Nasreddine et al., 2005) and the Cognistat (Kiernan et al., 1987; Schwamm et al., 1987). Assessment of emotional and behavioral functioning involves a clinical interview with the patient and collateral sources, clinical observations, and brief standardized measures like Patient Health Questionnaire-9 (Kroenke, Spitzer, & Williams, 2001), Generalized Anxiety Disorder-7 (Spitzer et al., 2006), and Hospital Anxiety and Depression Scale (Zigmond & Snaith, 1983).

Long-Term Stage of Recovery

Following inpatient rehabilitation discharge, individuals are typically referred to outpatient settings to receive more long-term rehabilitation treatment. In-depth neuropsychological evaluations are typically conducted at the beginning of this long-term treatment and periodically thereafter. The goals of assessment during this chronic stage of recovery include providing information about functioning, recovery, prognosis, need for supervision, and reintegration to home, academic, and work settings (Sherer & Novack, 2003).

As seen in Table 31.1, a neuropsychological test battery used by the authors and their colleagues at NYU Langone Health includes an assessment of premorbid functioning, general intellectual functioning, individual cognitive domains (i.e., attention, working memory, processing speed, executive functions, language, visuospatial, motor), and new onset or exacerbation of affective and behavioral symptoms. It also includes freestanding and embedded PVTs and symptom validity scales.

Assessment of MTBI

Neuropsychological assessment of an individual following MTBI requires a much different approach than those sustaining moderate- or severe-level injuries. Evidence supporting the diagnosis of more severe brain injuries is commonly provided by neuroimaging and other diagnostic methods. In contrast, the evidence supporting the presence of an MTBI is based on an integration of the patient's symptom reporting with the available clinical history, making neuropsychological testing, in most cases, the primary method for documentation of the injury's effects. It is important to remember that neuropsychological testing is not used to diagnose MTBI but rather to provide useful, objective information in the context of other clinical observations and findings.

The scientific literature on MTBI supports a functional rather than structural etiology (McCrory et al., 2017). The pathophysiology of concussion in its acute stage is often conceptualized as a multilayered neurometabolic cascade, involving a complex of interwoven cellular and vascular changes that develop rather acutely and are commonly clear within days to weeks afterwards (Giza & Hovda, 2014). This initial stage of injury can be followed by

Table 31.1 Neuropsychological test battery for assessment of moderate to severe TBI – NYU Langone Health

Name	Reference
• Test of Premorbid Functioning (TOPF)	Pearson, 2009
• Wechsler Adult Intelligence Scale (WAIS-IV)	Wechsler, 2008
• Trail Making Test (TMT)	Reitan, 1955
• Stroop Color Word Test (SCWT)	Golden, 1978
• Wisconsin Card Sorting Test-64 (WCST-64)	Heaton et al., 1993
• Controlled Oral Word Association Test (COWAT)	Borkowski et al., 1967
• Boston Naming Test (BNT)	Kaplan, Goodglass, & Weintraub, 1983
• Grooved Pegboard Test (GPT)	Heaton, Grant, & Matthews, 1991
• Wechsler Memory Scale (WMS-IV)	Wechsler, 2008
• California Verbal Learning Test-2 (CVLT-2)	Delis, 2000
• Rey Complex Figure Test (RCFT)	Rey, 1941
• Test of Memory Malingering (TOMM)	Tombaugh, 1996
• Reliable Digit Span (RDS)	Greiffenstein, Baker, & Gola, 1994
• CVLT-2 Forced Choice Recognition	Delis, 2000
• Symptom Evaluation (SCAT-5)	Echemendia et al., 2017
• Beck Depression Inventory (BDI-II)	Beck, Steer, & Brown, 1996; Gunstad & Suhr, 2001
• Beck Anxiety Inventory (BAI)	Beck & Steer, 1993
• Minnesota Multiphasic Personality Inventory (MMPI-2; MMPI-2-RF)	Ben-Porath & Tellegen, 2011

a subacute period where the brain is continuing to recover, in spite of the fact that most clinical symptoms have resolved. Based on results from imaging and electrophysiological studies, there is no reason to believe that this second period of recovery persists beyond a period of two to three months (Nelson, Janecek, & McCrea, 2013). Individuals reporting symptoms extending beyond that time period (>3 months) are viewed as having PCS, which represents the crossover point where the potential for any persisting physiological effects of the injury becomes unlikely and psychological factors begin to predominate.

A neuropsychological test battery designed for individuals following MTBI will naturally focus on assessment of cognitive functioning. There also needs to be a means to evaluate symptom reporting with the use of standardized instruments, as well as a means to evaluate the validity of the reported deficits and symptoms. In the age of health care reform and efforts to reduce costs and increase efficiency, neuropsychologists should be in a position to assess all of these areas in an efficient manner, using a relatively brief and focused test battery. The scope and breadth of the test battery and choice of instruments will ultimately depend on whether the assessment is performed in the acute, subacute, or long-term stage of recovery.

Acute Stage of Recovery

With the exception of sport settings, neuropsychological assessment is rarely conducted in the acute stage. However, when neuropsychologists do encounter patients within a week or two following the injury, the primary aim is to utilize standardized assessment instruments, in conjunction with other information, to establish or confirm a diagnosis of MTBI and to assist with recommendations for return to school, work, or athletic competition.

One of the major goals of the clinical evaluation is to provide a means to supplement the patient's subjective report of symptoms with results from more objective testing. This has been a major challenge in the study of MTBI, as biomarkers from neuroimaging and blood-based studies are lacking. Instead, brief methods have been developed for screening of the "objective" clinical signs of MTBI, including impairments in cognition, balance, or oculomotor functioning. The Standardized Assessment of Concussion (SAC; Echemendia et al., 2017), a thirty-point measure including orientation, memory, and concentration items, remains the premier method for screening cognition during the early stage of concussion (McCrea et al., 1997). The Balance Error Scoring System (BESS; Echemendia et al., 2017) is a standardized and rapid method for assessing balance (Guskiewicz, Ross, & Marshall, 2001). More recent studies have demonstrated the value of oculomotor testing during the early stage of MTBI recovery, with the King-Devick Test (KD) and Vestibular/Ocular-Motor Screening (VOMS) emerging as the most studied measures (Kontos et al., 2017).

There has been some controversy on the topic of whether a formal neuropsychological test battery is useful for clinical purposes during the early stage of MTBI recovery (McCrea et al., 2005). Therefore, a number of computerized test batteries have been developed and used in studies of athletes, soldiers, and civilians presenting to emergency departments (Alsalaheen et al., 2017; Resch, McCrea, & Cullum, 2013). The results of a recent head-to-head comparison of these instruments demonstrate that none of them outperformed the use of a symptom checklist (SCAT), in terms of sensitivity to identification of injured subjects from controls (Nelson et al., 2018; Nelson et al., 2013). While many of the computerized measures of neurocognitive functioning have been marketed aggressively to the public and to health care providers, their sensitivity, reliability, and overall value for assessment of acute MTBI symptoms remain questionable and they are not recommended for routine clinical use (McCrory et al., 2017; Resch et al., 2013).

With regard to post-concussion symptom reporting, the most commonly used measures have been developed in applied settings, with results demonstrating rather good validity and sensitivity to MTBI effects in comparison to controls (McLeod & Leach, 2012).

The Post-Concussion Scale – Revised (PCS-R; Lovell et al., 2006) and Sports Concussion Assessment Tool (SCAT-5; Echemendia et al., 2017) are two commonly used symptom measures developed primarily for use with athletes, which have shown the ability to distinguish between injured and noninjured athletes in prospective studies (McCrea et al., 2003; Nelson et al., 2016). There are also recent studies demonstrating some efficacy in using SCAT with nonathletes in more diverse urban emergency department samples (Bin Zahid et al., 2018; Nelson et al., 2018). The Neurobehavioral Symptom Inventory (NSI) has also been studied extensively and validated for assessment of symptoms in deployment-related MTBI among veterans (Meterko et al., 2012). The Rivermead Post-Concussion Symptom Questionnaire (RPSQ; King et al., 1995) is another measure that has been widely used for symptom assessment across the spectrum of recovery (King et al., 1995).

Assessing symptom reporting is a very complex task for the clinician, especially during the earliest stage of recovery from MTBI. For example, in the sports setting, while it is acknowledged that some athletes will not be entirely forthcoming about reporting symptoms following concussion, there are studies demonstrating that self-report measures provide the most sensitive means for tracking acute symptoms (McCrea et al., 2005; McCrea et al., 2004; Nelson et al., 2016). In addition, while most of these methods demonstrate adequate sensitivity when used within the first few days of recovery, longitudinal studies demonstrate that scores from the vast majority of subjects return to baseline thereafter, making them less effective for assessing or tracking symptoms over the full course of recovery (Karr, Areshenkoff, & Garcia-Barrera, 2014). They are also less effective in terms of their test-retest reliability in the acute stage, their ability to disentangle reporting of post-concussion symptoms, and their ability to control for symptom under- or overreporting, in comparison to those arising from comorbid emotional or somatic conditions.

Subacute Stage of Recovery

Encountering a patient in the subacute stage of recovery from MTBI means, by definition, that they are continuing to experience symptoms beyond the time point by which the vast majority have recovered. While there is some evidence that the brain is continuing to recover during that period, there is a possibility that extended symptom reporting arises from a range of possible psychosocial and emotional effects related to the injury and other independent factors. In any case, a neuropsychological evaluation can be extremely valuable to aid in making a decision to refer for rehabilitative and/or psychotherapeutic treatment with the goal of fostering recovery and preventing the patient from developing features of persistent post-concussive symptoms. In other cases, assessment findings can assist in answering remaining questions about return to work or school, providing assurance in the event of negative findings that there are no residual cognitive deficits that would interfere with that process.

At this stage of recovery, the clinician will need to conduct more than a screening of cognitive functioning in the form of a focused neuropsychological test battery. While there are a number of standardized batteries, such as the RBANS (Randolph et al., 1998), that could suffice for this purpose, most neuropsychologists tend to use a brief fixed/flexible battery of individual paper-and-pencil tests (Volbrecht, Meyers, & Kaster-Bundgaard, 2000). At this stage of recovery, one wants to ensure that the reported symptoms are not influenced by a range of psychological and/or motivational factors, creating a need to include self-report questionnaires of mood and pain and some method of evaluating validity of test performance and symptom reporting.

The contents of a brief test battery used by the authors and their colleagues at the Concussion Center at NYU Langone Health are listed in Table 31.2. The test battery includes a brief assessment of general intellectual functioning to obtain a context to interpret other test indices, since there is no evidence that MTBI affects intelligence in any manner that would lead directly to a decline in intellectual functioning. It also includes several tests designed to assess functions most commonly affected in patients following MTBI like attention, processing speed, and memory (Belanger & Vanderploeg, 2005). All of the measures included in the test battery have moderate-to-good levels of reliability and have been demonstrated to be sensitive to the effects of MTBI. The test battery is relatively brief by other standards, with the goal of being economical and trying to reduce the probability of making a Type I statistical error secondary to a positive finding on an isolated test arising by "chance." It also includes a combination of freestanding and embedded PVTs to aid in determining any possible effects of psychological and/or motivational factors.

While continued use of brief measures of post-concussion symptoms can provide a valuable method for measuring the degree of distress reported by an individual patient and for tracking recovery, they tell us very little about the specificity of the symptoms, as many similar symptoms are known to occur in association with other

Table 31.2 Neuropsychological test battery for assessment of MTBI – NYU Health Concussion Center

Name	Reference
General Functioning	
• Test of Premorbid Functioning (TOPF)	Pearson, 2009
• Wechsler Abbreviated Scale of Intelligence-II (WASI-II)	Wechsler, 2011
Attention and Executive Functioning	
• Wechsler Adult Intelligence Scale (WAIS-IV)	
Digit Span	Wechsler, 2008
Coding	Wechsler, 2008
• Trail Making Test (TMT)	Reitan, 1955
• Delis Kaplan Executive Function System	Delis et al., 2001
Color Word Interference Test	Delis et al., 2001
Verbal Fluency	Delis et al., 2001
Learning and Memory	
• California Verbal Learning Test - 2 (CVLT-2)	Delis, 2000
Performance Validity	
• Test of Memory Malingering (TOMM)	Tombaugh, 1996
• Reliable Digit Span (RDS)	Greiffenstein, Baker, & Gola, 1994
• CVLT-2 Forced Choice Recognition	Delis, 2000
Self-Report and Symptom Validity	
• Symptom Evaluation (SCAT-5)	Echemendia et al., 2017
• Beck Depression Inventory (BDI-II)	Beck, Steer, & Brown, 1996
• Beck Anxiety Inventory (BAI)	Beck & Steer, 1993
• Minnesota Multiphasic Personality Inventory (MMPI-2; MMPI-2-RF)	Ben-Porath & Tellegen, 2011

clinical conditions like chronic pain and mood disorder, both of which are frequently comorbid conditions in patients following MTBI. For that reason, the inclusion of additional brief measures of mood, chronic pain, or PTSD symptoms are recommended as a useful adjunct to symptom assessment, although none of these measures provides a means of determining the presence of symptom magnification. A more comprehensive assessment of symptom reporting is recommended for MTBI patients using a larger scale self-report instrument such as the Minnesota Multiphasic Personality Inventory-2-Restructured Form (MMPI-2-RF; Ben-Porath & Tellegen, 2008) or the Personality Assessment Inventory (PAI; Morey, 2007). These measures contain well-validated measures of symptom validity, in particular the MMPI-2-RF that can help to identify cases where patients might be overreporting symptoms as a result of somatization or externally based motivational factors.

Long-Term Recovery

Patients reporting symptoms of MTBI extending for more than three months post-injury are often classified as having PCS. The exact number of these individuals remains controversial. While some have described a "miserable minority" of approximately 15 percent of MTBI victims (Alexander, 1995; Pertab, James, & Bigler, 2009), more rigorous studies, using prospective methods and meta-analyses, indicate that the number is more likely to be closer to 3 percent (Rohling, Meyers, & Millis, 2003).

There is no scientific evidence indicating that PCS symptoms are the result of any direct physiologic effects of brain injury. The World Health Organization (WHO) task force on MTBI concluded that symptoms extending beyond the typical window of recovery are attributable to a number of "noninjury" factors, such as depression, PTSD, chronic pain, life stress, or secondary gain (Carroll et al., 2004). There have been a number of excellent studies that have sought to describe and analyze psychological factors (e.g., misattribution, nocebo effect, "good-old-days" phenomena) underlying the tendency to report persisting symptoms, providing further evidence that these symptoms are the result of nonphysiological effects (Gunstad & Suhr, 2001; Mittenberg et al., 1992).

Additional controversy surrounding long-term effects of MTBI has developed following reports of symptoms and neuropathological changes associated with dementia appearing in a small number of contact sport athletes exposed to repetitive head injury (McKee et al., 2009). While there has been much media coverage on the topic, the existing evidence indicates that development of chronic traumatic encephalopathy (CTE) does not appear to be related to single MTBI but rather the cumulative effects of repeated "sub-concussive" blows to the head (McKee et al., 2009). At this point, there is no evidence that clinicians evaluating nonathlete patients with persisting MTBI symptoms should be on any alert for their patients to develop neurodegenerative effects as a result of that injury.

Based on the combination of presenting problems, neuropsychologists are, by virtue of their training and use of empirically based assessment methods, uniquely qualified among health care professionals to assess the complex display of symptoms seen in individuals presenting with persisting symptoms. The aim of the neuropsychological evaluation is to tease apart the nature of the symptoms and the presence of comorbid conditions to make recommendations for treatment. In many cases, a battery of tests similar to what is presented in Table 31.2 will suffice. In other cases, particularly those requiring more extensive documentation (i.e., for disability assessment or forensic purposes), a more extensive test battery will be needed, similar to what was described in Table 31.1.

Testing of cognitive functioning will often begin with a brief assessment of intellectual functioning to obtain a context to interpret other test indices, since there is no evidence that MTBI affects intelligence in any manner that would lead directly to a decline in intellectual functioning. This might include the use of a combined reading and demographic index of premorbid functioning, such as the Test of Premorbid Functioning (TOPF; Pearson, 2009) and a brief measure of current intellectual functioning such as the two-subtest version of the Wechsler Abbreviated Scale of Intelligence (WASI-2; Wechsler, 2011). However, use of the full IQ test might be required in certain forensic applications or when evaluating the need for accommodations in the workplace or school.

Formal assessment of attention in patients following MTBI will include measures of attention span, processing speed, and more complex attentional control, including the Wechsler scales Digit Span and Coding, Symbol Digits Modalities Test (SDMT; Smith, 1982), Trail Making Test (TMT; Reitan, 1958), Stroop Color Word Test (SCWT; Golden, 1978), and Controlled Oral Word Association Test (COWAT; Borkowski, Benton, & Spreen, 1967).

Comprehensive evaluations of memory are clearly warranted in patients following MTBI and are usually performed most efficiently with any one of a number of verbal list-learning measures, such as the California Verbal Learning Test (CVLT-2; Delis, 2000), Rey Auditory Verbal Learning Test (RAVLT; Schmidt, 1996), and Hopkins Verbal Learning Test (HVLT; Brandt, 1991), that provide the clinician with a means to evaluate various stages of memory processing. Those exhibiting restrictions during initial learning trials, in combination with low scores on other attention measures, will be identified as having memory encoding difficulties. Low scores on delayed recall trials, in combination with higher levels of performance on yes/no recognition, will signal the presence of a retrieval deficit. Further information regarding memory can be provided through assessment of the patient's ability to recall more contextually based material through the Wechsler Memory Scale – Fourth Edition (WMS-IV) Logical Memory subtest (Wechsler, 2008) and nonverbal memory tests like the Brief Visuospatial Memory Test – Revised (BVMT; Benedict, 1997) and Rey Complex Figure Test (RCFT; Rey, 1941), although it is debatable whether that measure adds any significant information to the evaluation of MTBI.

From a theoretical perspective, there is no evidence that higher-order executive functions, language, visuospatial, and academic skills are affected directly or persistently through any known physiological effects of MTBI. In fact, reports of impairments in these areas may be related to secondary effects of attentional issues stemming from anxiety and/or distractions from somatic symptoms, such as headache or pain. Therefore, inclusion of a few of these measures is dictated by whether these symptoms are emphasized by the patient during the interview. Neuropsychologists should use caution when including these measures, as their addition may serve to increase the probability of finding "impairment" by chance as a result of committing a Type I statistical error (Binder, Iverson, & Brooks, 2009; Schretlen et al., 2008) and cause the patient and treatment team to believe that these are acquired deficits indicating the presence of chronic brain dysfunction.

A formal evaluation of validity and response bias is critical in any test battery, particularly in MTBI. It is important to note that these measures are not only used for detection of malingering, which is known to be seen at relatively high rates in patients alleging MTBI in forensic contexts, but are also useful in helping to identify the influence that somatization, mood, and other psychological disorders are having on the individual's ability to maintain the level of effort that is necessary to obtain valid results on neuropsychological testing. As a result, the neuropsychological test battery should include at least one freestanding PVT using forced-choice methodology, such as the Word Memory Test (WMT; Green, 2003) or the Test of Memory Malingering (TOMM; Tombaugh, 1996), in addition to other embedded PVTs.

Assessment of symptom reporting continues to be an essential element of the clinical evaluation of patients with persisting symptoms following MTBI through the use of brief instruments and comprehensive psychological inventories. The authors prefer to use the Minnesota Multiphasic Personality Inventory (MMPI-2-RF; Ben-Porath & Tellegen, 2008) with this population as a result of its brevity and the growing literature supporting its use for assessing the validity and range of factors underlying symptom reporting in MTBI. To date, the MMPI-2-RF has been shown to be sensitive to detecting symptom magnification in MTBI using standard validity indices such as F-r, Symptom Validity Scale (FBS-r), and Response Bias Scale (RBS) (Nelson et al., 2010; Wygant et al., 2010). It also has a number of scales that are useful in identifying patients with features of somatization (RC1) and a high level of cognitive complaints (COG) (Youngjohn et al., 2011). Results from this instrument are effective for identifying patients who might be malingering the effects of neurological illness, in addition to helping identify those who are likely to be helped by psychological intervention.

Summary and Conclusions

TBI is one of the more prevalent neurological disorders, with a varied set of physical, cognitive, and emotional effects. Whether it is the assessment of cognition among mild or severe TBIs, neuropsychologists are uniquely trained to integrate information from an individual's sociocultural, educational, occupational, medical, and psychiatric background with neuropsychological evaluation results to obtain a full account of the factors affecting the road to recovery and help design more specific, tailored, and effective interventions to improve cognitive and functional outcomes for TBI patients.

Neuropsychologists assess cognitive, behavioral, and affective functioning throughout the acute, subacute, and chronic/long-term stages of recovery from mild, moderate, and severe TBI. These evaluations are typically tailored to include appropriate measures that can assess functioning at each specific time point, with short, repeatable measures used during acute recovery and more comprehensive batteries used in later stages of recovery.

MTBI has gained notoriety as a health concern in the scientific and public community in recent years. The majority of individuals sustaining a MTBI exhibit a full recovery within a relatively brief period of time, while others experience persistent symptoms. Thus, the end result of the neuropsychological evaluation in MTBI is to provide an explanation on factors other than the physiological effects of "brain damage" that are likely to be playing a role in the maintenance of symptoms and how those factors can be addressed through appropriate psychological intervention or other forms of rehabilitation.

REFERENCES

ACRM (American Congress of Rehabilitation Medicine). (1993). Definition of mild traumatic brain injury. *Journal of Head Trauma Rehabilitation*, *8*(3), 86–87.

Alexander, M. P. (1995). Mild traumatic brain injury: Pathophysiology, natural history, and clinical management. *Neurology*, *45*(7), 1253–1260.

Alsalaheen, B., Stockdale, K., Pechumer, D., Giessing, A., He, X., & Broglio, S. P. (2017). Cumulative effects of concussion history on baseline computerized neurocognitive test scores: Systematic review and meta-analysis. *Sports Health*, *9*(4), 324–332.

Arango-Lasprilla, J. C., Ketchum, J. M., Williams, K., Kreutzer, J. S., Marquez de la Plata, C. D., O'Neil-Pirozzi, T. M., & Wehman, P. (2008). Racial differences in employment outcomes after traumatic brain injury. *Archives of Physical Medicine and Rehabilitation*, *89*(5), 988–995.

Arango-Lasprilla, J. C., Rosenthal, M., Deluca, J., Komaroff, E., Sherer, M., Cifu, D., & Hanks, R. (2007). Traumatic brain injury and functional outcomes: Does minority status matter? *Brain Injury*, *21*(7), 701–708.

Beck, A. T., & Steer, R. A. (1993). *Beck Anxiety Inventory manual*. San Antonio, TX: Psychological Corporation.

Beck, A. T., Steer, R. A., & Brown, G. K. (1996). *Beck Depression Inventory manual* (2nd ed.). San Antonio, TX: Psychological Corporation.

Belanger, H. G., & Vanderploeg, R. D. (2005). The neuropsychological impact of sports-related concussion: A meta-analysis. *Journal of the International Neuropsychological Society*, *11*(4), 345–357.

Ben-Porath, Y., & Tellegen, A. (2011). *MMPI-2 RF (Minnesota Multiphasic Personality Inventory-2 Restructured Form): Manual for administration, scoring, and interpretation*. Minneapolis: University of Minnesota Press.

Bilbao, A., Kennedy, C., Chatterji, S., Ustun, B., Barquero, J. L., & Barth, J. T. (2003). The ICF: Applications of the WHO model of functioning, disability and health to brain injury rehabilitation. *NeuroRehabilitation*, *18*(3), 239–250.

Bin Zahid, A., Hubbard, M. E., Dammavalam, V. M., Balser, D. Y., Pierre, G., Kim, A., Samadani, U. (2018). Assessment of acute head injury in an emergency department population using Sport Concussion Assessment Tool – 3rd edition. *Applied Neuropsychology: Adult*, *25*(2), 110–119.

Binder, L. M., Iverson, G. L., & Brooks, B. L. (2009). To err is human: "Abnormal" neuropsychological scores and variability are common in healthy adults. *Archives of Clinical Neuropsychology*, *24*(1), 31–46.

Boake, C., McCauley, S. R., Levin, H. S., Pedroza, C., Contant, C. F., Song, J. X., ... & Diaz-Marchan, P. J. (2005). Diagnostic criteria for postconcussional syndrome after mild to moderate traumatic brain injury. *Journal of Neuropsychiatry and Clinical Neurosciences*, *17*(3), 350–356.

Boake, C., Millis, S. R., High, W. M., Jr., Delmonico, R. L., Kreutzer, J. S., Rosenthal, M., ... & Ivanhoe, C. B. (2001). Using early neuropsychologic testing to predict long-term productivity outcome from traumatic brain injury. *Archives of Physical Medicine and Rehabilitation*, *82*(6), 761–768.

Boone, K. B. (2009). The need for continuous and comprehensive sampling of effort/response bias during neuropsychological examinations. *Clinical Neuropsychologist*, *23*(4), 729–741.

Borkowski, J. G., Benton, A. L., & Spreen, O. (1967). Word fluency and brain damage. *Neuropsychologia*, *5*(2), 135–140.

Brandt, J. (1991). The hopkins verbal learning test: Development of a new memory test with six equivalent forms. *Clinical Neuropsychologist*, *5*(2), 125–142.

Broglio, S. P., Katz, B. P., Zhao, S., McCrea, M., & McAllister, T. (2018). Test-Retest Reliability and Interpretation of Common Concussion Assessment Tools: Findings from the NCAA-DoD CARE Consortium. *Sports Med*, *48*(5), 1255–1268.

Bryant, R. A., & Harvey, A. G. (1998). Relationship between acute stress disorder and posttraumatic stress disorder following mild traumatic brain injury. *Am J Psychiatry*, *155*(5), 625–629.

Bush, S. S., Sweet, J. J., Bianchini, K. J., Johnson-Greene, D., Dean, P. M., & Schoenberg, M. R. (2018). Deciding to adopt revised and new psychological and neuropsychological tests: an inter-organizational position paper. *Clinical Neuropsychologist*, *32*(3), 319–325.

Carroll, L. J., Cassidy, J. D., Peloso, P. M., Borg, J., von Holst, H., Holm, L., ... & Pepin, M. (2004). Prognosis for mild traumatic brain injury: Results of the WHO Collaborating Centre Task Force on Mild Traumatic Brain Injury. *Journal of Rehabilitation Medicine* (43 Suppl), 84–105.

Christensen, B. K., Colella, B., Inness, E., Hebert, D., Monette, G., Bayley, M., & Green, R. E. (2008). Recovery of cognitive function after traumatic brain injury: A multilevel modeling analysis of Canadian outcomes. *Archives of Physical Medicine and Rehabilitation*, *89*(12), S3–S15.

Cicerone, K. D., Dahlberg, C., Malec, J. F., Langenbahn, D. M., Felicetti, T., Kneipp, S., ... & Catanese, J. (2005). Evidence-based cognitive rehabilitation: Updated review of the literature from 1998 through 2002. *Archives of Physical Medicine and Rehabilitation*, *86*(8), 1681–1692.

Dean, A. C., Victor, T. L., Boone, K. B., & Arnold, G. (2008). The relationship of IQ to effort test performance. *Clinical Neuropsychologist*, *22*(4), 705–722.

Dean, A. C., Victor, T. L., Boone, K. B., Philpott, L. M., & Hess, R. A. (2009). Dementia and effort test performance. *Clinical Neuropsychologist*, *23*(1), 133–152.

Delis, D. C. (2000). *California Verbal Learning Test – Adult Version. Manual*. San Antonio, TX: Psychological Corporation.

Delis, D. C., Kaplan, E., & Kramer, J. H. (2001). *Delis-Kaplan executive function system: Examiner's manual*. San Antonio, TX: Psychological Corporation.

Dikmen, S. S., Machamer, J. E., Powell, J. M., & Temkin, N. R. (2003). Outcome 3 to 5 years after moderate to severe traumatic brain injury. *Archives of Physical Medicine and Rehabilitation*, *84*(10), 1449–1457.

Dikmen, S. S., Machamer, J. E., Winn, H. R., & Temkin, N. R. (1995). Neuropsychological outcome at 1-year post head injury. *Neuropsychology*, *9*(1), 80–90.

Draper, K., & Ponsford, J. (2008). Cognitive functioning ten years following traumatic brain injury and rehabilitation. *Neuropsychology*, *22*(5), 618–625.

Echemendia, R. J., Meeuwisse, W., McCrory, P., Davis, G. A., Putukian, M., Leddy, J., ... & Herring, S. (2017). The Sport Concussion Assessment Tool 5th Edition (SCAT5): Background and rationale. *British Journal of Sports Medicine*, *51*(11), 848–850.

Ellenberg, J. H., Levin, H. S., & Saydjari, C. (1996). Posttraumatic Amnesia as a predictor of outcome after severe closed head injury: Prospective assessment. *Archives of Neurology*, *53*(8), 782–791.

Erlanger, D., Feldman, D., Kutner, K., Kaushik, T., Kroger, H., Festa, J., ... & Broshek, D. (2003). Development and validation of a web-based neuropsychological test protocol for sports-related return-to-play decision-making. *Archives of Clinical Neuropsychology*, *18*(3), 293–316.

Esselman, P. C., & Uomoto, J. M. (1995). Classification of the spectrum of mild traumatic brain injury. *Brain Injury*, *9*(4), 417–424.

Fork, M., Bartels, C., Ebert, A. D., Grubich, C., Synowitz, H., & Wallesch, C. W. (2005). Neuropsychological sequelae of diffuse traumatic brain injury. *Brain Inj*, *19*(2), 101–108.

Garcia, G. P., Broglio, S. P., Lavieri, M. S., McCrea, M., & McAllister, T. (2018). Quantifying the value of multidimensional assessment models for acute concussion: An analysis of data from the NCAA-DoD Care Consortium. *Sports Medicine*, *48* (7), 1739–1749.

Gary, K. W., Arango-Lasprilla, J. C., & Stevens, L. F. (2009). Do racial/ethnic differences exist in post-injury outcomes after TBI? A comprehensive review of the literature. *Brain Inj*, *23* (10), 775–789.

Giacino, J. T., Kalmar, K., & Whyte, J. (2004). The JFK Coma Recovery Scale-Revised: measurement characteristics and diagnostic utility. *Archives of Physical Medicine and Rehabilitation*, *85*(12), 2020–2029.

Giza, C. C., & Hovda, D. A. (2014). The new neurometabolic cascade of concussion. *Neurosurgery*, *75*(0 4), S24–S33.

Golden, C. J. (1978). *Stroop Color and Word Test: A Manual for Clinical and Experimental Uses*. Wood Dale, IL: Stoelting Company.

Gouvier, W. D., Blanton, P. D., LaPorte, K. K., & Nepomuceno, C. (1987). Reliability and validity of the Disability Rating Scale and the Levels of Cognitive Functioning Scale in monitoring recovery from severe head injury. *Archives of Physical Medicine and Rehabilitation*, *68*(2), 94–97.

Green, P. (2003). *Word memory test for windows: User's manual and program*. Edmonton: Green's Publishing.

Greiffenstein, M. F., Baker, W. J., & Gola, T. (1994). Validation of malingered amnesia measures with a large clinical sample. *Psychological Assessment*, *6*(3), 218–224.

Gunstad, J., & Suhr, J. A. (2001). "Expectation as etiology" versus "the good old days": Postconcussion syndrome symptom reporting in athletes, headache sufferers, and depressed individuals. *Journal of the International Neuropsychological Society*, *7* (3), 323–333.

Guskiewicz, K. M., Ross, S. E., & Marshall, S. W. (2001). Postural stability and neuropsychological deficits after concussion in collegiate athletes. *Journal of Athletic Training*, *36*(3), 263–273.

Hart, T., Hoffman, J. M., Pretz, C., Kennedy, R., Clark, A. N., & Brenner, L. A. (2012). A longitudinal study of major and minor depression following traumatic brain injury. *Archives of Physical Medicine and Rehabilitation*, *93*(8), 1343–1349.

Hart, T., Millis, S., Novack, T., Englander, J., Fidler-Sheppard, R., & Bell, K. R. (2003). The relationship between neuropsychologic function and level of caregiver supervision at 1 year after traumatic brain injury. *Archives of Physical Medicine and Rehabilitation*, *84*(2), 221–230.

Heaton, R. K., Grant, I., & Matthews, C. (1991). *Comprehensive norms for an expanded Halstead-Reitan neuropsychological battery: Demographic corrections, research findings, and clinical applications*. Odessa, FL: Psychological Assessment Resources.

Heaton, S. K., Chelune, G.J., Talley, J.L., Kay, G.G., & Curtiss, G. (1993). *Wisconsin Card Sorting Test manual: Revised and expanded*. Odessa, FL: Psychological Assessment Resources.

Heilbronner, R. L., Sweet, J. J., Attix, D. K., Krull, K. R., Henry, G. K., & Hart, R. P. (2010). Official position of the American academy of clinical neuropsychology on serial neuropsychological assessments: The utility and challenges of repeat test administrations in clinical and forensic contexts. *Clinical Neuropsychologist*, *24*(8), 1267–1278.

Heilbronner, R. L., Sweet, J. J., Morgan, J. E., Larrabee, G. J., & Millis, S. R. (2009). American Academy of Clinical Neuropsychology Consensus Conference Statement on the neuropsychological assessment of effort, response bias, and malingering. *Clinical Neuropsychologist*, *23*(7), 1093–1129.

Hiott, D. W., & Labbate, L. (2002). Anxiety disorders associated with traumatic brain injuries. *NeuroRehabilitation*, *17*(4), 345–355.

Jackson, W. T., Novack, T. A., & Dowler, R. N. (1998). Effective serial measurement of cognitive orientation in rehabilitation: The Orientation Log. *Archives of Physical Medicine and Rehabilitation*, *79*(6), 718–720.

Kaplan, E., Goodglass, H., & Weintrab, S. (1983). *The Boston naming test*. Philadelphia: Lea & Febiger.

Karr, J. E., Areshenkoff, C. N., & Garcia-Barrera, M. A. (2014). The neuropsychological outcomes of concussion: A systematic review of meta-analyses on the cognitive sequelae of mild traumatic brain injury. *Neuropsychology*, *28*(3), 321–336.

Kashluba, S., Hanks, R. A., Casey, J. E., & Millis, S. R. (2008). Neuropsychologic and functional outcome after complicated mild traumatic brain injury. *Archives of Physical Medicine and Rehabilitation*, *89*(5), 904–911.

Kiernan, R. J., Mueller, J., Langston, J. W., & Van Dyke, C. (1987). The Neurobehavioral Cognitive Status Examination: A brief but quantitative approach to cognitive assessment. *Annals of Internal Medicine*, *107*(4), 481–485.

King, N. S., Crawford, S., Wenden, F. J., Moss, N. E., & Wade, D. T. (1995). The Rivermead Post Concussion Symptoms Questionnaire: A measure of symptoms commonly experienced after head injury and its reliability. *J Neurol*, *242* (9), 587–592.

Kontos, A. P., Deitrick, J. M., Collins, M. W., & Mucha, A. (2017). Review of vestibular and oculomotor screening and concussion rehabilitation. *Journal of Athletic Training*, *52*(3), 256–261.

Kroenke, K., Spitzer, R. L., & Williams, J. B. (2001). The PHQ-9: Validity of a brief depression severity measure. *J Gen Intern Med*, *16*(9), 606–613.

Larrabee, G. J. (2003). Detection of malingering using atypical performance patterns on standard neuropsychological tests. *Clinical Neuropsychologist*, *17*(3), 410–425.

Larrabee, G. J. (2012). Performance validity and symptom validity in neuropsychological assessment. *Journal of the International Neuropsychological Society*, *18*(4), 625–630.

Laxe, S., Tschiesner, U., Zasler, N., López-Blazquez, R., Tormos, J. M., & Bernabeu, M. (2012). What domains of the International Classification of Functioning, Disability and Health are covered by the most commonly used measurement instruments in traumatic brain injury research? *Clinical Neurology and Neurosurgery*, *114*(6), 645–650.

Laxe, S., Zasler, N., Robles, V., López-Blázquez, R., Tormos, J. M., & Bernabeu, M. (2014). ICF profiling of patients with traumatic brain injury: an international professional survey. *Disability and Rehabilitation*, *36*(1), 82–88.

Levin, H. S., O'Donnell, V. M., & Grossman, R. G. (1979). The Galveston Orientation and Amnesia Test: A practical scale to assess cognition after head injury. *J Nerv Ment Dis*, *167*(11), 675–684.

Lippa, S. M. (2018). Performance validity testing in neuropsychology: A clinical guide, critical review, and update on a rapidly evolving literature. *Clinical Neuropsychologist*, *32* (3), 391–421.

Lippa, S. M., Agbayani, K. A., Hawes, S., Jokic, E., & Caroselli, J. S. (2014). Effort in acute traumatic brain injury: Considering more than pass/fail. *Rehabilitation Psychology*, *59* (3), 306–312.

Lippa, S. M., Lange, R. T., French, L. M., & Iverson, G. L. (2017). Performance Validity, Neurocognitive Disorder, and Post-concussion Symptom Reporting in Service Members with a History of Mild Traumatic Brain Injury. *Archives of Clinical Neuropsychology*, *33*(5), 1–13.

Loring, D. W., & Bauer, R. M. (2010). Testing the limits: Cautions and concerns regarding the new Wechsler IQ and Memory scales. *Neurology*, *74*(8), 685–690.

Loring, D. W., Goldstein, F. C., Chen, C., Drane, D. L., Lah, J. J., Zhao, L., & Larrabee, G. J. (2016). False-positive error rates for reliable digit span and auditory verbal learning test performance validity measures in amnestic mild cognitive impairment and early Alzheimer disease. *Archives of Clinical Neuropsychology*, *31*(4), 313–331.

Lovell, M. R., Iverson, G. L., Collins, M. W., Podell, K., Johnston, K. M., Pardini, D., ... & Maroon, J. C. (2006). Measurement of symptoms following sports-related concussion: Reliability and normative data for the post-concussion scale. *Applied Neuropsychology*, *13*(3), 166–174.

Malec, J. F., Brown, A. W., Leibson, C. L., Flaada, J. T., Mandrekar, J. N., Diehl, N. N., & Perkins, P. K. (2007). The mayo classification system for traumatic brain injury severity. *Journal of Neurotrauma*, *24*(9), 1417–1424.

Marr, A. C. V. (2004). *Central Nervous System Injury Surveillance: Annual Data Submission Standards for the Year 2002*. Atlanta: U.S. Department of Health and Human Services, CDC, National Center for Injury Prevention and Control.

Marshall, P., & Happe, M. (2007). The performance of individuals with mental retardation on cognitive tests assessing effort and motivation. *Clinical Neuropsychologist*, *21*(5), 826–840.

Mathias, J. L., & Wheaton, P. (2007). Changes in attention and information-processing speed following severe traumatic brain injury: A meta-analytic review. *Neuropsychology*, *21*(2), 212–223.

McCrea, M., Barr, W. B., Guskiewicz, K., Randolph, C., Marshall, S. W., Cantu, R., ... & Kelly, J. P. (2005). Standard regression-based methods for measuring recovery after sport-related concussion. *Journal of the International Neuropsychological Society*, *11*(1), 58–69.

McCrea, M., Guskiewicz, K. M., Marshall, S. W., Barr, W., Randolph, C., Cantu, R. C., ... & Kelly, J. P. (2003). Acute effects and recovery time following concussion in collegiate football players: The NCAA Concussion Study. *Jama*, *290*(19), 2556–2563.

McCrea, M., Hammeke, T., Olsen, G., Leo, P., & Guskiewicz, K. (2004). Unreported concussion in high school football players: Implications for prevention. *Clin J Sport Med*, *14*(1), 13–17.

McCrea, M., Iverson, G. L., McAllister, T. W., Hammeke, T. A., Powell, M. R., Barr, W. B., & Kelly, J. P. (2009). An integrated review of recovery after mild traumatic brain injury (MTBI): Implications for clinical management. *Clinical Neuropsychologist*, *23*(8), 1368–1390.

McCrea, M., Kelly, J. P., Kluge, J., Ackley, B., & Randolph, C. (1997). Standardized assessment of concussion in football players. *Neurology*, *48*(3), 586–588.

McCrory, P., Meeuwisse, W., Dvorak, J., Aubry, M., Bailes, J., Broglio, S., ... & Vos, P. E. (2017). Consensus statement on concussion in sport-the 5(th) international conference on concussion in sport held in Berlin, October 2016. *British Journal of Sports Medicine*, *51*(11), 838–847.

McKee, A. C., Cantu, R. C., Nowinski, C. J., Hedley-Whyte, E. T., Gavett, B. E., Budson, A. E., ... & Stern, R. A. (2009). Chronic traumatic encephalopathy in athletes: Progressive tauopathy after repetitive head injury. *Journal of Neuropathology and Experimental Neurology*, *68*(7), 709–735.

McKinley, W. (1999). Cognitive and behavioral effects of brain injury. In M. Rosenthal (Ed.), *Rehabilitation of the adult and child with traumatic brain injury* (pp. 74–86). Philadelphia:FA Davis Co.

McLeod, T. C., & Leach, C. (2012). Psychometric properties of self-report concussion scales and checklists. *Journal of Athletic Training*, *47*(2), 221–223.

Meterko, M., Baker, E., Stolzmann, K. L., Hendricks, A. M., Cicerone, K. D., & Lew, H. L. (2012). Psychometric assessment of the Neurobehavioral Symptom Inventory-22: The structure of persistent postconcussive symptoms following deployment-related mild traumatic brain injury among veterans. *Journal of Head Trauma Rehabilitation*, *27*(1), 55–62.

Meyers, J. E., & Diep, A. (2000). Assessment of malingering in chronic pain patients using neuropsychological tests. *Applied Neuropsychology*, *7*(3), 133–139.

Meyers, J. E., & Volbrecht, M. E. (2003). A validation of multiple malingering detection methods in a large clinical sample. *Archives of Clinical Neuropsychology*, *18*(3), 261–276.

Miller, J. B., Axelrod, B. N., Schutte, C., & Davis, J. J. (2017). Symptom and performance validity assessment in forensic neuropsychology. In S. S. Bush, G. J. Demakis, & M. L. Rohling (Eds.). *APA handbook of forensic neuropsychology* (pp. 67–109). Washington, DC: American Psychological Association.

Millis, S. R., Rosenthal, M., Novack, T. A., Sherer, M., Nick, T. G., Kreutzer, J. S., ... & Ricker, J. H. (2001). Long-term neuropsychological outcome after traumatic brain injury. *Journal of Head Trauma Rehabilitation*, *16*(4), 343–355.

Mittenberg, W., DiGiulio, D. V., Perrin, S., & Bass, A. E. (1992). Symptoms following mild head injury: Expectation as aetiology. *Journal of Neurology, Neurosurgery, and Psychiatry*, *55*(3), 200–204.

Morey, L. C. (2007). *Personality Assessment Inventory (PAI): Professional manual*. Odessa, FL: Psychological Assessment Resources.

Nasreddine, Z. S., Phillips, N. A., Bedirian, V., Charbonneau, S., Whitehead, V., Collin, I., ... & Chertkow, H. (2005). The Montreal Cognitive Assessment, MoCA: A brief screening tool for mild cognitive impairment. *Journal of the American Geriatrics Society*, *53*(4), 695–699.

Nelson, L. D., Furger, R. E., Ranson, J., Tarima, S., Hammeke, T. A., Randolph, C., ... & McCrea, M. A. (2018). Acute clinical predictors of symptom recovery in emergency department patients with uncomplicated mild traumatic brain injury or non-traumatic brain injuries. *Journal of Neurotrauma*, *35*(2), 249–259.

Nelson, L. D., Janecek, J. K., & McCrea, M. A. (2013). Acute clinical recovery from sport-related concussion. *Neuropsychology Review*, *23*(4), 285–299.

Nelson, L. D., LaRoche, A. A., Pfaller, A. Y., Lerner, E. B., Hammeke, T. A., Randolph, C., ... & McCrea, M. A. (2016). Prospective, head-to-head study of three Computerized Neurocognitive Assessment Tools (CNTs): Reliability and validity for the assessment of sport-related concussion. *Journal of the International Neuropsychological Society*, *22*(1), 24–37.

Nelson, N. W., Hoelzle, J. B., Sweet, J. J., Arbisi, P. A., & Demakis, G. J. (2010). Updated meta-analysis of the MMPI-2 symptom validity scale (FBS): Verified utility in forensic practice. *Clinical Neuropsychologist*, *24*(4), 701–724.

Novack, T. A., Alderson, A. L., Bush, B. A., Meythaler, J. M., & Canupp, K. (2000). Cognitive and functional recovery at 6 and 12 months post-TBI. *Brain Injury*, *14*(11), 987–996.

Novack, T. A., Bush, B. A., Meythaler, J. M., & Canupp, K. (2001). Outcome after traumatic brain injury: Pathway analysis of contributions from premorbid, injury severity, and recovery variables. *Archives of Physical Medicine and Rehabilitation*, *82* (3), 300–305.

Pearson. (2009). *Test of Premorbid Functioning (TOPF)*. San Antonio, TX: NCS Pearson.

Pertab, J. L., James, K. M., & Bigler, E. D. (2009). Limitations of mild traumatic brain injury meta-analyses. *Brain Injury*, *23*(6), 498–508.

Rabin, L. A., Barr, W. B., & Burton, L. A. (2005). Assessment practices of clinical neuropsychologists in the United States and Canada: A survey of INS, NAN, and APA Division 40 members. *Archives of Clinical Neuropsychology*, *20*(1), 33–65.

Randolph, C., Tierney, M. C., Mohr, E., & Chase, T. N. (1998). The Repeatable Battery for the Assessment of Neuropsychological Status (RBANS): Preliminary clinical validity. *Journal of Clinical and Experimental Neuropsychology*, *20*(3), 310–319.

Rappaport, M. (2005). The Disability Rating and Coma/Near-Coma scales in evaluating severe head injury. *Neuropsychological Rehabilitation*, *15*(3–4), 442–453.

Rappaport, M., Dougherty, A. M., & Kelting, D. L. (1992). Evaluation of coma and vegetative states. *Archives of Physical Medicine and Rehabilitation*, *73*(7), 628–634.

Reitan, R. M. (1955). The relation of the trail making test to organic brain damage. *Journal of Consulting Psychology*, *19*, 393–394.

Reitan, R. M. (1958). Validity of the Trail Making Test as an indicator of organic brain damage. *Perceptual and Motor Skills*, *8*(3), 271–276.

Reitan, R. M., & Wolfson, D. (1995). Category test and trail making test as measures of frontal lobe functions. *Clinical Neuropsychologist*, *9*(1), 50–56.

Resch, J. E., McCrea, M. A., & Cullum, C. M. (2013). Computerized neurocognitive testing in the management of sport-related concussion: an update. *Neuropsychology Review*, *23*(4), 335–349.

Rey, A. (1941). L'examen psychologique dans les cas d'encephalopathie traumtique. *Archives of Psychology*, *28*, 286–340.

Ricker, J. H. (2010). Traumatic brain injury in adults. In Frank, R. G., Rosenthal, M., & Caplan, B. (Eds.) *Handbook of rehabilitation psychology* (2nd ed., pp. 43–62). Washington, DC: American Psychological Association.

Robles, L., Lopez, E., Salazar, X., Boone, K. B., & Glaser, D. F. (2015). Specificity data for the b Test, Dot Counting Test, Rey-15 Item Plus Recognition, and Rey Word Recognition Test in monolingual Spanish-speakers. *Journal of Clinical and Experimental Neuropsychology*, *37*(6), 614–621.

Rohling, M. L., Meyers, J. E., & Millis, S. R. (2003). Neuropsychological impairment following traumatic brain injury: A dose-response analysis. *Clinical Neuropsychologist*, *17*(3), 289–302.

Rosenthal, M., Dljkers, M., Harrison-Felix, C., Nabors, N., Witol, A. D., Young, M. E., & Englander, J. S. (1996). Impact of minority status on functional outcome and community integration following traumatic brain injury. *Journal of Head Trauma Rehabilitation*, *11*(5), 40–57.

Salazar, X. F., Lu, P. H., Wen, J., & Boone, K. B. (2007). The use of effort tests in ethnic minorities and in non-English-speaking and English as a second language populations. In K. B. Boone (Ed.) *Assessment of feigned cognitive impairment: A neuropsychological perspective* (pp. 405–427). New York: Guilford Press.

Sander, A. M., Pappadis, M. R., Davis, L. C., Clark, A. N., Evans, G., Struchen, M. A., & Mazzei, D. M. (2009). Relationship of race/ethnicity and income to community integration following traumatic brain injury: Investigation in a non-rehabilitation trauma sample. *NeuroRehabilitation*, *24*(1), 15–27.

Schmidt, M. (1996). *Rey auditory verbal learning test: A handbook*. Los Angeles: Western Psychological Services.

Schretlen, D. J., Testa, S. M., Winicki, J. M., Pearlson, G. D., & Gordon, B. (2008). Frequency and bases of abnormal performance by healthy adults on neuropsychological testing. *Journal of the International Neuropsychological Society*, *14*(3), 436–445.

Schwamm, L. H., Van Dyke, C., Kiernan, R. J., Merrin, E. L., & Mueller, J. (1987). The Neurobehavioral Cognitive Status Examination: Comparison with the Cognitive Capacity Screening Examination and the Mini-Mental State Examination in a neurosurgical population. *Annals of Internal Medicine*, *107*(4), 486–491.

Sherer, M., Giacino, J. T., Doiron, M. J., LaRussa, A., & Taylor, S. R. (2014). Bedside evaluations. In M. Sherer & A. M. Sander (Eds.), *Handbook on the neuropsychology of traumatic brain injury* (pp. 49–75). New York: Springer.

Sherer, M., & Novack, T. A. (2003). Neuropsychological assessment after brain injury. In G. Prigatano, & N. Pliskin (Ed.), *Clinical neuropsychology and cost outcome research: A beginning* (pp. 39–60). New York: Psychology Press.

Sherer, M., Novack, T. A., Sander, A. M., Struchen, M. A., Alderson, A., & Thompson, R. N. (2002). Neuropsychological assessment and employment outcome after traumatic brain injury: A review. *Clinical Neuropsychologist*, *16*(2), 157–178.

Sherer, M., Yablon, S. A., Nakase-Richardson, R., & Nick, T. G. (2008). Effect of severity of post-traumatic confusion and its constituent symptoms on outcome after traumatic brain injury. *Archives of Physical Medicine and Rehabilitation*, *89*(1), 42–47.

Smith, A. (1982). *Symbol Digit Modalities Test (SDMT): Manual (revised)*. Los Angeles: Western Psychological Services.

Spitzer, R. L., Kroenke, K., Williams, J. B., & Lowe, B. (2006). A brief measure for assessing generalized anxiety disorder: The GAD-7. *Archives of Internal Medicine*, *166*(10), 1092–1097.

Stein, S. C., & Ross, S. E. (1992). Moderate head injury: A guide to initial management. *Journal of Neurosurgery*, *77*(4), 562–564.

Strutt, A. M., Scott, B. M., Shrestha, S., & York, M. K. (2011). The Rey 15-item memory test and Spanish-speaking older adults. *Clinical Neuropsychologist*, *25*(7), 1253–1265.

Tator, C. H. (2009). Let's standardize the definition of concussion and get reliable incidence data. *Canadian Journal of Neurological Sciences*, *36*(4), 405–406.

Taylor, Bell, J. M., Breiding, M. J., & Xu, L. (2017). Traumatic brain injury-related emergency department visits, hospitalizations, and deaths – United States, 2007 and 2013. *MMWR Surveillance Summaries*, *66*(9), 1–16.

Teasdale, G., & Jennett, B. (1974). Assessment of coma and impaired consciousness: A practical scale. *Lancet*, *2*(7872), 81–84.

Tombaugh, T. N. (1996). *TOMM, Test of Memory Malingering*. North Tonawanda: Multi-Health Systems.

VA/DoD (Department of Veterans Affairs, Department of Defense). (2009). VA/DoD Clinical Practice Guideline for Management of Concussion/Mild Traumatic Brain Injury. *Journal of Rehabilitation Research and Development*, *46*(6), 1–68.

Van Reekum, R., Bolago, I., Finlayson, M. A. J., Garner, S., & Links, P. S. (1996). Psychiatric disorders after traumatic brain injury. *Brain Injury*, *10*(5), 319–328.

van Reekum, R., Cohen, T., & Wong, J. (2000). Can traumatic brain injury cause psychiatric disorders? *Journal of Neuropsychiatry and Clinical Neurosciences*, *12*(3), 316–327.

Vilar-López, R., Gomez-Rio, M., Caracuel, A., Llamas-Elvira, J., & Perez-Garcia, M. (2008). Use of specific malingering measures in a Spanish sample. *Journal of Clinical and Experimental Neuropsychology*, *30*(6), 710–722.

Vilar-López, R., Santiago-Ramajo, S., Gomez-Rio, M., Verdejo-García, A. M., Llamas, J., & Perez-Garcia, M. (2007). Detection of malingering in a Spanish population using three specific malingering tests. *Archives of Clinical Neuropsychology*, *22*(3), 379–388.

Volbrecht, M. E., Meyers, J. E., & Kaster-Bundgaard, J. (2000). Neuropsychological outcome of head injury using a short battery. *Archives of Clinical Neuropsychology*, *15*(3), 251–265.

Wechsler, D. (2008). *Wechsler Memory Scale – fourth edition (WMS-IV)*. San Antonio, TX: NCS Pearson.

Wechsler, D. (2011). *Wechsler Abbreviated Scale of Intelligence – second edition (WASI-II)*. San Antonio, TX: NCS Pearson.

Whelan-Goodinson, R., Ponsford, J. L., Schonberger, M., & Johnston, L. (2010). Predictors of psychiatric disorders following traumatic brain injury. *Journal of Head Trauma Rehabilitation*, *25*(5), 320–329.

Whelan, R., Ponsford, J., Johnston, L., & Grant, F. (2009). Psychiatric disorders following traumatic brain injury. *Journal of Head Trauma Rehabilitation*, *24* (5), 324–332.

WHO (World Health Organization). (2001). International Classification of Functioning, Disability and Health. www3.who.int/icf/icftemplate.cfm

Wygant, D. B., Sellbom, M., Gervais, R. O., Ben-Porath, Y. S., Stafford, K. P., Freeman, D. B., & Heilbronner, R. L. (2010). Further validation of the MMPI-2 and MMPI-2-RF Response Bias Scale: Findings from disability and criminal forensic settings. *Psychological Assessment*, *22* (4), 745–756.

Youngjohn, J. R., Wershba, R., Stevenson, M., Sturgeon, J., & Thomas, M. L. (2011). Independent validation of the MMPI-2-RF Somatic/Cognitive and Validity scales in TBI Litigants tested for effort. *Clinical Neuropsychologist*, *25*(3), 463–476.

Zigmond, A. S., & Snaith, R. P. (1983). The hospital anxiety and depression scale. *Acta Psychiatrica Scandinavica*, *67*(6), 361–370.

PART IV

CLINICAL ASSESSMENT IN SPECIFIC SETTINGS

32 Screening and Assessment in Integrated Primary Care Settings

JEFFREY L. GOODIE AND KEVIN WILFONG

INTEGRATED PRIMARY CARE AND THE ROLE OF PSYCHOLOGISTS

Behavioral health services, including assessment, are a growing critical component of primary care services (Hunter, Dobmeyer, & Reiter, 2018). Systemic changes in the health care system, including the implementation of the patient-centered medical home (PCMH; Baird et al., 2014), the focus of policymakers and providers on the Triple and Quadruple Aim (Berwick, Nolan, & Whittington, 2008; Bodenheimer & Sinsky, 2014), and the passage of the Patient Protection and Affordable Care Act (Public Law No: 111–148, 111th Congress: Patient Protection and Affordable Care Act, 2010) have all contributed to increased behavioral health provider integration in primary care.

Historically, assessing and managing the behavioral health needs of patients in primary care was largely done by medical providers with no or limited training in psychological assessment. Over the past twenty years, large health care systems (e.g., Department of Defense, Federally Qualified Health Systems, Veterans Affairs) and other community health organizations and settings (e.g., Cherokee Health Systems, university health clinics, homeless clinics; Reiter, Dobmeyer, & Hunter, 2018) have placed an increasing number of behavioral health providers into primary care clinics. The growing importance of psychologists in primary care settings is reflected in the publication of competencies for psychologists practicing in primary care by the American Psychological Association (APA; McDaniel et al., 2014), the development of training material for teaching those who will practice in primary care settings,[1] and the development of a curriculum for an interprofessional seminar on integrated primary care (APA, 2016).

The opinions and assertions expressed herein are those of the authors and do not necessarily reflect the official policy or position of the Uniformed Services University, Department of Defense, Department of Health and Human Services, or their agencies.

[1] See https://societyforhealthpsychology.org/training/integrated-primary-care-psychology/

Models of Integrated Primary Care

It is beyond the scope of this chapter to describe the full range of methods used to integrate behavioral health in primary care; however, it is important to distinguish between co-locating a specialty behavioral health clinic in or near a primary care clinic versus integrating behavioral health providers into the primary care system. Readers who seek a more complete description of models and terms within the field of behavioral health in integrated primary care may be interested in the Peek and the National Integration Academy Council (2013) publication focusing on the lexicon for behavioral health and primary care integration.

Co-located specialty behavioral health. To improve behavioral health care, some systems co-locate behavioral health clinics near or within primary care. In these cases, the behavioral health clinic operates similarly to a traditional behavioral health clinic (e.g., fifty-minute follow-up appointments, separate records from the primary care team, care is independent of medical care). There are multiple benefits to co-locating these clinics, including improving the communication between a patient's medical and behavioral health teams as well as improving access to behavioral health treatment. Co-location does not improve the capacity to see more patients (i.e., the same number of patients with behavioral health problems are seen) because the amount of time spent with each patient does not change. The assessment measures described throughout this book that are intended for traditional behavioral health clinics could be administered within a primary care co-located behavioral health clinic without concerns about whether the validity or reliability of those measures are compromised.

Primary care behavioral health. An integration model that dramatically changes how behavioral health providers assess and intervene with patients, while increasing the number of individuals in the population who have access to a behavioral health clinician, is the Primary Care Behavioral Health (PCBH) model (Hunter et al., 2017; Reiter et al., 2018; Robinson & Reiter, 2015). In this model, psychologists serve as behavioral health consultants (BHCs) for the primary care team. The BHC helps the team and patients target a range of general behavioral health (e.g., anxiety, depression, partner discord), health behaviors (e.g., substance misuse, physical activity), and disease processes with a significant biopsychosocial component (e.g., diabetes, chronic pain, obesity). In the PCBH model, patients are seen typically one to four times for twenty-to-thirty-minute appointments, notes are entered in the medical record, and the patient's primary care provider receives direct feedback about the plan for the patient. If patients do not improve after four appointments, it is likely that they would be referred for specialty care (e.g., outpatient mental health clinic). In some cases, BHCs may see patients for more than four appointments to help the primary care team and patient manage chronic medical (e.g., diabetes, obesity) or behavioral health concerns.

BHCs can work in the full range of primary care clinics, including Family Medicine, Internal Medicine, Pediatrics, and Obstetrics and Gynecological clinics. Particularly in Family Medicine clinics, BHCs must be prepared to see individuals from across the lifespan, as these clinics provide care from cradle to grave. Therefore, BHCs working in Family Medicine clinics must be familiar with screening and assessment measures appropriate not only for a broad range of problems but also for a diverse age range. The screening and assessment measures described in this chapter cover a broad range of behavioral health conditions seen in adults and are appropriate for use in the PCBH model.

ROLE OF SCREENING AND ASSESSMENT IN INTEGRATED PRIMARY CARE

Standardized measures administered in primary care settings are typically used for screening, assessing the functional impact of interventions, and symptom monitoring. Measures are never interpreted in isolation but are placed in context of the interview with the patient. Screening helps to identify individuals who may need further assessment and might benefit from integrated behavioral health services (Derogatis, 2017). Primary care clinics and health providers vary in how and when screening measures are used. In some cases, there are standard screening measures that are used for all patients when they are seen at the clinic (e.g., the PHQ-2 to screen for depression); in other cases, screening measures are targeted based on the patient's presenting problems. Regardless of the screening measures used, the results of the screening help to direct the functional assessment of the presenting problem.

Given the time constraints within primary care, most functional assessments are conducted through a targeted clinical interview, with brief measures supplementing these assessments. The functional assessment focuses on the specific reason the patient was referred to the BHC and includes defining the problem symptoms; the onset, duration, frequency of symptoms; factors that improve and worsen symptoms; and the functional impact (e.g., work, school, home, relationships, enjoyable activities). Functional assessments also focus on health behaviors (e.g., alcohol use, medication adherence, physical activity, sleep behaviors, substance use), social support systems, and relevant medical conditions.

In addition to screening at the initial appointment, symptoms may be monitored over time using measures assessing global functioning or specific problems. In the same way that standard vital signs (e.g., blood pressure, temperature, pain level) are assessed at most primary care appointments, regardless of the presenting problem, a standard global functioning measure administered at every BHC visit allows the BHC to monitor changes and differences within and between patients. Targeted measures for a specific problem often require more coordination or time out of the scheduled appointment.

The process of selecting and administering assessments in primary care settings requires an understanding of the potential benefits and limitations of these assessments. Competencies for conducting assessments in primary care have been developed by the APA (McDaniel et al., 2014, pp. 420–421). The competencies for psychologists conducting assessments in primary care settings include:

1. Selecting and implementing screening methods using evidence-based assessment measures to identify patients at risk or in need of specialized services.
2. Ensuring that psychological assessments for the PC setting are utilized, administered, and interpreted in a manner that maintains test integrity.
3. Using assessment questions and measures geared toward current functioning, while simultaneously incorporating psychological, behavioral, and physical components of health and well-being.
4. Identifying patient's needs and rationale for appointment rapidly.
5. Assessing pertinent behavioral risk factors.
6. Involving input of significant others in the assessment process as indicated.
7. Evaluating and using intrapersonal, family and community strengths, resilience, and wellness to inform understanding of a patient's needs and to promote health.
8. Monitoring patients longitudinally to identify changes in presenting problems and effectiveness of recommended interventions.

It is critical that any behavioral health provider who is conducting screenings and assessments within primary care develops these competencies and employs the skills to conduct assessments and screenings effectively.

Pros and Cons of Screening

The collection of actionable information that ensures the efficiency and efficacy of health service delivery requires that providers carefully consider of the pros and cons of screening and assessment measures. By necessity of the time constraints in primary care, any measure that is administered must be brief with a method for quickly scoring responses. Although screening measures aid clinicians in identifying the functional impact of behavioral, cognitive, and emotional concerns, it is necessary to consider the benefits within the limitations of screening in the context of primary care. Broad guidelines regarding the risk-benefit ratio of screening procedures have been published by the World Health Organization (Derogatis, 2017); however, there are several specific concerns that should be considered by BHCs.

One of the primary concerns is the amount of time required for screening. Providers must consider the amount of time required to complete, score, and interpret the responses a screening measure. The time constraints of primary care often require that measures can be administered and scored in less than five minutes. A second concern is that, if a problem is detected using a screening measure (e.g., depression), it may be necessary to develop a care pathway for a concern (e.g., suicidal ideation) that was not the initial purpose of the consult. A third concern is whether the measures being used are appropriate for administration within the context of primary care. Many measures are developed and tested in the context of specialty behavioral health clinics. When introducing one of these measures into the primary care environment, it is important to consider whether the measure is valid for the environment and populations seen in primary care.

It may be possible to reduce some of the barriers associated with the administration of screening measures through the use of technology. Using kiosks, electronic tablets (e.g., iPads), or other electronic devices that allow the measures to be automatically scored and incorporated into the electronic health record can reduce the time required for the administration of measures and increase the utility of using such measures in primary care (Ranallo et al., 2016). However, it is important to consider that some patients (e.g., older adults, socioeconomically disadvantaged) may have less experience using electronic devices, interfering with rapid assessments.

In specialty behavioral health care settings, providers may focus on the validity of symptom presentations, and therefore use assessment strategies designed to assess for the validity of particular patient presentations (e.g., validity scales on the MMPI-2-RF; see Ben-Porath, Sellbom, & Suhr, Chapter 16, this volume). In integrated primary care settings, screening and assessment measures are designed to guide the brief interventions and treatment strategies used by the entire primary care team given how a patient is presenting in the context of primary care. If the interventions within primary care do not result in improved functioning or there are larger questions about whether a patient's symptom presentation is valid, then a referral to specialized behavioral health care services would be appropriate. Similarly, if there were concerns about misusing or diverting medications (e.g., opioids, stimulants), the BHC may ask questions to assess for inconsistencies between the patient and PCP, review the medical record for documented concerns regarding medication use, and listen for aberrant medication-related behaviors (e.g., requesting early refills, medications misuse; Robinson & Reiter, 2015). When working with specific populations, such as those with chronic pain, screeners such as the Screener and Opioid Assessment for Patients with Pain- Revised (SOAPP-R; Butler et al., 2008) and the Brief Risk Questionnaire (Jones, Lookatch, & Moore, 2015) may help identify patients at greater risk for misusing their medications.

Misuse and Misunderstanding of Assessment in Integrated Primary Care

When evaluating assessment results in integrated primary care settings, there may be tendencies to both underestimate and overestimate the values of these results. Providers who have worked in traditional behavioral health clinics may be accustomed to prolonged interviews and extensive assessment batteries for making diagnoses and developing treatment plans. The assessment efforts and strategies used in primary care may be considered rudimentary and insufficient in comparison to the extensive assessment efforts completed within traditional behavioral health clinics. However, such comparisons undervalue the impact of conducting evidence-based, or at least evidence-informed, assessment screening within the context of primary care. A more appropriate comparison would be to consider what assessment, if any, was being done in primary care before the integration of behavioral health providers. Most behavioral health diagnoses (e.g., depression, anxiety, and insomnia) are made and treated in primary care (Croghan & Brown, 2010). Integrating behavioral health providers within the primary care environment may help to better inform these assessments and treatments; however, more research is needed to examine what assessment methods will work best in this setting.

At the same time, most models of integrated primary care are not substitutes for traditional behavioral health care assessment and treatment. There will always be individuals who need the complex assessment strategies and treatments offered within specialty behavioral health clinics. Such an approach to behavioral health care is similar to the way patients with hypertension are assessed and treated. The vast majority of these patients are managed in primary care but complicated presentations of hypertension may be managed by a specialist (e.g., cardiologist, nephrologist). It is helpful to think of integrated behavioral health care as an important part of a stepped-care system (Bower & Gilbody, 2005). The assessment strategies need to be appropriate for where this care exists within the larger system.

Role of Diversity and Cultural Issues

One significant benefit of embedding behavioral health providers into primary care is the reduction of barriers such as access and stigma (Richmond & Jackson, 2018;

Sanchez et al., 2012; Scott et al., 2015). Specifically, cultural stigma around seeking behavioral health care is reduced by incorporating BHCs into traditional medical care settings, making access easier and a more regular component of their overall health care (Sanchez et al., 2012). In a primary care clinic serving a low-income, primarily Latino population, 61 percent of respondents who reported high satisfaction with their BHC encounter indicated that they would "definitely not" or "probably not" attend a traditional behavioral health appointment (Ogbeide et al., 2018). Additionally, Bridges and colleagues (2014) showed that integrated behavioral health care reduced mental health disparities among Latinos. Together these findings suggest that many individuals from diverse backgrounds, who may benefit from psychological screenings and assessments may be unlikely to present to traditional behavioral health care clinics but are willing to be seen by behavioral health in primary care. Incorporating systematic screenings and assessments by behavioral health providers in primary care clinics may enhance the likelihood that these individuals are assessed.

Despite the potential value of screenings and assessments in primary care, often there are limited data related to the psychometrics of these screenings and assessments specific to diverse populations. Richmond and Jackson (2018) suggest that, to provide culturally competent care, behavioral health providers integrated into primary care need to demonstrate cultural sensitivity, cultural congruency, and health literacy. Health equity may be improved by behavioral health providers using culturally informed screening and assessment strategies; however, whether a particular measure or strategy is appropriate in primary care for a given ethnic or cultural group is seldom evaluated (Richmond & Jackson, 2018). As we describe measures in the following section, we include psychometric information about diverse populations when available, but it is a frequent limitation of measures that this information is not available, particularly when used in primary care settings.

COMMON PROBLEMS AND SCREENING MEASURES

Providers in primary care need to be prepared to assess and develop a plan with a full range of presenting concerns. The US Preventive Services Task Force (USPSTF),[2] which is comprised of members from preventive medicine and primary care, including behavioral health, makes recommendations for clinical preventive services in primary care settings. The USPSTF encourages screening for alcohol misuse, depression, and tobacco. In this section, we describe measures that help screen for alcohol misuse and depression as well as other common presenting problems in primary care. Although it is critical to assess for and target tobacco use in primary care, patterns of tobacco use are typically found through brief questions rather than with standardized measures and therefore are not addressed in this chapter. The focus of assessment in primary care, particularly within the PCBH model, is not typically on comprehensive diagnosis; therefore, the measures presented are used for identifying potential behavioral health concerns and monitoring functional changes. We provide brief descriptions, and sensitivity and specificity (i.e., when available), for these measures. In Table 32.1, we provide a brief description of each measure, the primary reference, and where the measure can be obtained. The purpose of this chapter is to highlight common measures that have been found to be useful and appropriate for primary care settings; we do not intend to provide a systematic review of all measures and psychometrics for all conditions that may be appropriate for primary care settings.

Diagnostic Measures and Global Functioning

Measuring treatment outcomes in psychotherapy has become increasingly important to more precisely tailor the level and type of care to the needs of the patient. Specifically, monitoring systems that provide comprehensive feedback on patient responsiveness to an intervention allow providers to better inform evidence-based treatment (Lambert, 2010). The following are global outcome measures that capture a holistic perspective of patient functioning.

Behavioral Health Measure – 20 (BHM-20). The BHM-20 is a treatment outcome measure designed for repeated measure of global psychological distress and a wide range of mental health syndromes, using a structure consistent with the phase model of psychotherapy outcomes (Bryan et al., 2014; Kopta & Lowry, 2002). The BHM-20 consists of twenty self-report items on a five-point (0–4) Likert scale, which can be administered electronically in approximately ninety seconds (Kopta, Owen, & Budge, 2015). All twenty items make up a Global Mental Health scale, where higher scores are representative of higher levels of health. The BHM-20 also contains three subscales: Well-Being (three items), Psychological Symptoms (thirteen items), and Life Functioning (four items; Kopta & Lowry, 2002). The Well-Being scale evaluates emotional distress, life satisfaction, and level of motivation and energy. The Psychological Symptoms scale identifies symptoms of anxiety, depression, panic, bipolar mood swings, eating problems, suicidal ideation, homicidal ideation, and alcohol or drug use problems. The Life Functioning scale measures perceived functioning in intimate relationships, social relationships, work or school, and life enjoyment (Kopta et al., 2015). Measures of internal consistency have revealed good reliability for the Global Mental Health scales (0.89 to 0.90) and adequate reliability for the subscales (Well-Being, 0.65 to 0.74; Symptoms, 0.85 to 0.86; and Life Functioning, 0.72 to 0.77); the sensitivity to pathology, sensitivity to change, and correlation with similar measures support the

[2] See www.uspreventiveservicestaskforce.org

Table 32.1 Integrated primary care assessment measures

Domain	Assessment Tool or Measure	Description/Format	Primary References (Website Location)
Health Outcomes and Functioning			
	BHM-20	Treatment outcome measure for global psychological distress; 20-item; electronic admin and scoring	Kopta & Lowry, 2002; Kopta et al., 2015 (celesthealth.com)
	Duke Health Profile	Quality of life measure targeting health and dysfunction; 17-item; 10 individual scales without a general health outcome measure	Parkerson et al., 1990 (cfm.duke.edu/research/duke-health-measures)
	Quick Psychodiagnostic Panel	Automated screener for 11 mental disorders using advanced branching to reduce item count; electronic administration and scoring in less than 10 minutes	Shedler, 2017 (qpdpanel.com)
Depression			
	PHQ-9	Screens for depression; 9-item; self-report; cutoff score 10	Kroenke et al., 2001 Moriarty et al., 2015 (phqscreeners.com)
	PHQ-2	Ultra-brief screen for depression; 2-item; cutoff score 2	Kroenke et al., 2003 Arroll et al., 2010 (phqscreeners.com)
	BDI-PC	Screens for depression; 7-item; self-report; cutoff score 4	Beck et al., 1997 Steer et al., 1999
	EPDS	Screens for postnatal depression; 10-item; cutoff score 13	Cox et al., 1987 Eberhard-Gran et al., 2001 (fresno.ucsf.edu/pediatrics/downloads/edinburghscale.pdf)
Anxiety			
	GAD-7	Screens for anxiety; 7-item; self-report; cutoff score 10	Spitzer et al., 2006 (phqscreeners.com)
	GAD-2	Ultra-brief screen for anxiety; 2-item; cutoff score 3	Kroenke et al., 2007 (phqscreeners.com)
	SHAI	Screens for health anxiety and health concerns; 18-item	Salkovskis et al., 2002 (available at end of article)
PTSD			
	PC-PTSD-5	Screens for PTSD; 6-item; self-report; cutoff score 3	Prins et al., 2016 (ptsd.va.gov/professional/assessment/screens/pc-ptsd.asp)
	PCL-5	Screens for PTSD; 20-item; self-report; cutoff score 33	Weathers et al., 2013 Wortmann et al., 2016 (ptsd.va.gov/professional/assessment/adult-sr/ptsd-checklist.asp)
Alcohol Misuse			
	Alcohol Use Disorders Identification Test (AUDIT)	Screens for alcohol misuse; 10-items, clinician- or self-administered; cutoff score 8	Saunders et al., 1993 Gomez et al., 2005 (drugabuse.gov/sites/default/files/files/AUDIT.pdf)
	AUDIT-C	Screens for alcohol misuse; 3-items; clinician- or self-administered; cutoff score 3	Gomez et al., 2005 (integration.samhsa.gov/images/res/tool_auditc.pdf)
	Single Question	Screens for alcohol misuse 1-item; cutoff score 1 or more times per year	Moyer, 2013 Smith et al., 2009

Continued

Table 32.1 (cont.)

Domain	Assessment Tool or Measure	Description/Format	Primary References (Website Location)
Illicit Substance Misuse			
	Drug Abuse Screening Test-10 (DAST-10)	Screens for illicit substance and medication misuse; 10-item; yes/no responses	Smith et al., 2010 (bu.edu/bniart/files/2012/04/DAST-10_Institute.pdf)
	Single Question	Screens for illicit substance and medication misuse 1-item; cutoff 1 or more	Smith et al., 2010
Insomnia			
	Insomnia Severity Index (ISI)	Screens for insomnia; 7-item; self-report; cutoff score 14	Bastien et al., 2001 Gagnon et al., 2013 (ons.org/sites/default/files/InsomniaSeverityIndex_ISI.pdf)
	Berlin Questionnaire	Screens for OSA; 10-item; self-report; Meeting criteria for 2 or more categories suggests risk for OSA	Netzer et al., 1999 Senaratna et al., 2017 (sleepapnea.org/assets/files/pdf/berlin-questionnaire.pdf)
	STOP-Bang Questionnaire	Screens for OSA; 8-item; self-report; cutoff score 3	Chung et al., 2008 Chiu et al., 2017 (sleepmedicine.com/files/files/StopBang_Questionnaire.pdf)
Dementia			
	Mini-Mental State Examination (MMSE)	Measure of cognitive functioning; 30-item	Folstein et al., 1975 (minimental.com/)
	Clock Drawing Test	Measure of executive functioning; use circle to draw clock face, set time to 10 minutes past 11	Shulman, 2000 Lin et al., 2013 (alz.org/documents_custom/141209-CognitiveAssessmentToo-kit-final.pdf)
	Montreal Cognitive Assessment (MoCA)	Measure of cognitive functioning; 30-item	Nasreddine et al., 2005 (mocatest.org)
Chronic Pain			
	Pain intensity, Enjoyment and General Activity (PEG)	Pain outcome measure assessing pain intensity, interference with life enjoyment and general activity; 3-item	Krebs et al., 2009 (available in article)
	Oswestry Disability Index (ODI)	Measure of pain-related functional impairment (% disability); 10-item	Fairbank & Pynsent, 2000 (rehab.msu.edu/_files/_docs/Oswestry_Low_Back_Disability.pdf)

construct validity and concurrent validity of the BHM-20 (Kopta & Lowry, 2002). The factor structure for the BHM-20 has been validated among diverse samples in primary care settings (Bryan et al., 2014); although these authors suggest that a seventeen-item version of the BHM resulted in improved psychometric properties. The validity and reliability for specific diverse samples in primary care remain unclear.

Duke Health Profile (DUKE). The DUKE is a broad health functioning measure, designed for primary care, consisting of seventeen self-report items (Parkerson, Broadhead, & Tse, 1990). The items of the DUKE evaluate six health measures (physical, mental, social, general, perceived health, and self-esteem) and four dysfunction measures (anxiety, depression, pain, and disability; Parkerson et al., 1990). Physical, mental, and social health are each assessed using five independent items to target the major dimensions of health identified by the World Health Organization; these also make up the fifteen-item general health measure. The remaining two items assess perceived health and disability individually. Measures of anxiety (six items), depression (five items), pain (one item), and self-esteem (five items) are a recombination of the seventeen items (Parkerson et al., 1990). Each item is rated on a three-point Likert scale. The items are calculated into their respective measures and standardized on a 0 to 100 scale, with 100 representative of good health for health measures and poor health for dysfunction measures (Parkerson et al., 1990). There is no general scale utilizing all seventeen items of the DUKE. Studies assessing the psychometrics of the DUKE reveal adequate reliability ($r = 0.30–0.78$), good construct validity, and good concurrent validity (e.g., DUKE depression and anxiety scores correlated with measure of depression $r = 0.68$) and across a broad range of populations (e.g., Parkerson et al., 1990, Perret-Guillaume et al., 2009; Tran et al., 2015). Most recently, Tran et al. (2015) found that, within a sample of patients in Vietnam who had suffered a stroke, constructs measured by the DUKE were more highly correlated with similar constructs (e.g., $r = 0.53–0.66$) compared to dissimilar constructs ($r = 0.11–0.43$). Specific psychometric data for diverse populations are limited.

Quick Psychodiagnostic Panel (QPD Panel). The QPD Panel is a fully automated mental health assessment that screens for eleven mental disorders, as defined by the DSM-5, in less than ten minutes. Patients complete a series of true/false questions presented at a fifth-grade reading level to screen for major depressive, persistent depressive, bipolar, generalized anxiety, panic, obsessive-compulsive, post-traumatic stress, substance use, binge-eating, bulimia nervosa, and somatic symptom disorders (Shedler, 2017). To reduce administration time, the QPD Panel employs advanced branching techniques to determine which items to present based on previous responses. The responses are compiled into a brief report of symptoms endorsed by the patient and their respective diagnostic label (Shedler, 2017). In a primary care setting, the QPD Panel was found to have a sensitivity and specificity of 0.81 and 0.96 for Major Depression, 0.79 and 0.90 for Generalized Anxiety Disorder, 0.71 and 0.97 for Panic Disorder, and 0.69 and 0.97 for Obsessive-Compulsive Disorder (Shedler, Beck, & Bensen, 2000). Reliability and validity were established using a clinical sample under the DSM-IV criteria, which could limit generalizability to a primary care and diverse populations (Boardman, 2001; Shedler et al., 2000).

Depression

The twelve-month prevalence rate for depression in the US adult population is 9.4 percent (Kessler et al., 2012), with one-half of individuals diagnosed with depression presenting in a primary care setting (CDC, 2014). Studies indicate that providers have difficulty recognizing depression in almost half of cases, especially those in geriatric populations (Mitchell, Rao, & Vaze, 2010). Screening for depression in primary care can provide a means for more effective detection and treatment. El-Den and colleagues (2017) provide a systematic review of primary care screening measures for depression; we highlight several of the most commonly used measures in the sections that follow.

Patient Health Questionnaire – 9 (PHQ-9). A systematic review of the psychometric properties of depression screening tools used in primary care settings found that the PHQ-9 was the most extensively evaluated tool in this setting (El-Den et al., 2017). Derived from the larger Patient Health Questionnaire, the PHQ-9 is a screener targeting symptoms of major depressive disorder. This sixty-second self-report measure consists of nine items scored as 0 (*not at all*), 1 (*several days*), 2 (*more than half the days*), or 3 (*nearly every day*) over the last two weeks (Kroenke, Spitzer, & Williams, 2001). The summed total ranges from 0 to 27, with severity categories including *minimal* (0–4), *mild* (5–9), *moderate* (10–14), *moderately severe* (15–19), and *severe* (20–27; Kroenke et al., 2001). Although there is some question as to the optimal score for maximizing sensitivity and specificity, studies suggest a clinical cutoff score of 10 provides sensitivity of 78 percent and specificity of 87 percent (Moriarty et al., 2015). Item 9 assesses for suicidal ideation and has been found to predict increased risk of a suicide attempt or death (Simon et al., 2013). When the PHQ-9 is used with this item, it is critical for the clinic to have care pathways established to further assess and address suicidal risk. The PHQ-9 is considered reliable and valid for screening depressive symptoms (Kroenke et al., 2001; Moriarty et al., 2015). Studies suggest psychometric properties are maintained across age and gender (Phelan et al., 2010; Thibodeau & Asmundson, 2014), as well as across diverse population samples (e.g., African Americans, Chinese Americans, and Latinos [Huang et al., 2006]).

Patient Health Questionnaire – 2 (PHQ-2). The PHQ-2 consists of the first two items of the PHQ-9 targeting anhedonia and depressed mood. This ultra-brief screener for depressive symptoms is used in some settings as a precursor to administering the entire PHQ-9 (Arroll et al., 2010); it is also combined with the GAD-2 to create the PHQ-4, a screener for anxiety and depression (Kroenke et al., 2009). The two items are scored from 0 (*not at all*) to 3 (*nearly every day*) over the last two weeks (Kroenke et al., 2009). At a clinical cutoff score of 2, the PHQ-2 provides a sensitivity of 86 percent and specificity of 78 percent in a primary care setting (Arroll et al., 2010).

Beck Depression Inventory for Primary Care (BDI-PC). The BDI-PC is a seven-item self-report measure for depression, derived from the fourteen items of the Beck Depression Inventory – II (Beck et al., 1997). The BDI-PC takes less than five minutes and identifies symptoms of major depressive disorder under the DSM-IV through items related to *sadness, pessimism, past failure, loss of pleasure, self-dislike, self-criticalness*, and *suicidal thoughts or wishes* (Steer et al., 1999). Patients pick a statement from each item that best describes their experience over the past two weeks. The statements are ordered by increasing severity using a four-point scale from 0 to 3, with higher scores indicating greater distress. At a clinical cutoff score of 4, the BDI-PC provides a sensitivity of 82 to 99 percent and specificity of 94 to 99 percent in a primary care setting (Steer et al., 1999). How these findings change among diverse populations in primary care settings is unclear.

Edinburgh Postnatal Depression Scale (EPDS). The EPDS is a five-minute self-report screener for postnatal depression in women (Cox, Holden, & Sagovsky, 1987). The EPDS focuses on cognitive and emotional symptoms and excludes somatic symptoms that are common during and after pregnancy (Boyd, Le, & Somberg, 2005). Each item provides a statement with four related responses regarding their experiences over the last week; the items are scored from "0" to "3," with a maximum score of 30. For example, item 10 assesses suicidal ideation stating, "*The thought of harming myself has occurred to me: (3) Yes, quite often (2) Sometimes (1) Hardly ever (0) Never*." The EPDS also provides an example item to assist the patient in understanding the directions. A review of eighteen different studies with cutoff scores from 8.5 to 12.5 suggests further research is needed to determine an optimal clinical cutoff (Eberhard-Gran et al., 2001). O'Connor and colleagues (2016) reviewed eight studies that examined the accuracy of the English version of the EPDS compared to a diagnostic interview. The authors found that when using a cutoff score of 13 for identifying MDD, the sensitivity ranged from 0.67 to 1.00, while the specificity was 0.87 or greater. Sensitivity for detecting major or minor depression using 10 as the cutoff score was between 0.63 and 0.84, while specificity ranged from 0.79 to 0.90. Among low-income African American women, the sensitivity was 0.84 and specificity was 0.81 for major or minor depression (O'Connor et al., 2016). Non-English versions, which have been used with a large range of diverse populations (e.g., Spanish, French, Italian, Japanese), also found high levels of sensitivity (i.e., most studies between 0.67 to 0.90) and specificity (i.e., most studies between 0.86 and 1.00) for major and minor depressive symptoms using 10 or 13 as cutoff scores (Boyd et al., 2005; O'Connor et al., 2016).

Anxiety

The twelve-month prevalence rate for anxiety in the US adult population is 22.2 percent (Kessler et al., 2012), with four in ten individuals diagnosed with an anxiety disorder presenting in a primary care setting (CDC, 2014). In 2013, personal health care spending on anxiety in the United States was approximately $29.7 billion in total; primary care spending accounted for 71.4 percent of that total cost (Dieleman et al., 2016). Screening for anxiety in primary care can provide a means for more effective detection and treatment (Kroenke et al., 2007).

Generalized Anxiety Disorder – 7 (GAD-7). The GAD-7 is a sixty-second self-report screener intended to capture symptoms of anxiety over the last two weeks. This seven-item measure asks patients to report the frequency of symptoms such as "trouble relaxing" and is scored from 0 (*not at all*) to 3 (*nearly every day*). In addition to the seven primary items, there is an optional assessment of perceived functional difficulty created by the endorsed symptoms (Spitzer et al., 2006). The summed total ranges from 0 to 21, with severity categories including *minimal* (0–4), *mild* (5–9), *moderate* (10–14), and *severe* (15–21). A recommended clinical cutoff score of 10 provides a sensitivity of 89 percent and a specificity of 82 percent for diagnosis of a generalized anxiety disorder (Spitzer et al., 2006). This measure has shown good reliability (e.g., rho = 0.85) and validity (e.g., convergent validity *rs* = 0.52 to 0.68; divergent validity *rs* = 0.42 and 0.47; Rutter & Brown, 2017) in both a primary care setting and the general population (Rutter & Brown, 2017; Spitzer et al., 2006).

Generalized Anxiety Disorder – 2 (GAD-2). The GAD-2 consists of the first two items of the GAD-7 targeting anxious feeling and uncontrollable worry (Kroenke et al., 2007). This ultra-brief screener for anxiety symptoms is used in some settings as a precursor to administering the entire GAD-7; it is also combined with the PHQ-2 to create the PHQ-4, a screener for anxiety and depression (Kroenke et al., 2009). The two items are scored from 0 (*not at all*) to 3 (*nearly every day*) over the last two weeks (Kroenke et al., 2007). At a clinical cutoff score of 3, the GAD-2 provides a sensitivity of 88 percent and specificity of 83 percent for diagnosis of a generalized anxiety disorder in a primary care setting (Kroenke et al., 2007). Recent psychometric analyses using item response theory continue to validate the use of the GAD-2 as an ultra-brief screener for moderate to severe levels of anxiety (Jordan et al., 2017).

Short Health Anxiety Inventory (SHAI). The SHAI is an eighteen-item self-report measure targeting health anxiety, the presence of current health concerns, and perceived consequences of a serious medical condition (Salkovskis et al., 2002). The first fourteen items most directly correlate with health anxiety or hypochondriasis. The last four items prompt the patient to imagine having a serious illness and assesses perceived negative consequences of becoming seriously ill. Each item consists of four statements describing increasingly obsessive or distressing tendencies regarding health; patients pick a statement from each item that best describes their experience over the past six months (Salkovskis et al., 2002). A meta-analysis of the literature suggests the SHAI is psychometrically sound regarding internal consistency in addition to convergent, divergent, criterion, and factorial validity; still, further research is needed to determine clinically relevant cutoff scores, test-retest reliability, and incremental validity (Alberts et al., 2013).

Post-Traumatic Stress Disorder

PTSD is estimated to present in 10 percent to 20 percent of primary care patients, with veteran, urban, female, minority, and treatment-seeking populations reporting two to three times higher rates (Freedy et al., 2010; Prins et al., 2016). Additionally, there is an estimated 6 percent to 36 percent lifetime prevalence of PTSD in primary care (Freedy et al., 2010). Currently, primary care settings demonstrate poor recognition and improper treatment of PTSD, resulting in continued symptomology and exacerbation of associated health issues (Freedy et al., 2010).

Primary Care PTSD Screen for DSM-5 (PC-PTSD-5). The PC-PTSD-5 is a brief screener adapted from the MINI-International Neuropsychiatric Interview to identify probable symptoms of PTSD in a primary care setting (Prins et al., 2016). This screener consists of six yes/no items and takes less than two minutes to complete. The first is a qualifying item, which asks whether patients have experienced any of a list of potentially traumatic events. The remaining five items are symptoms of PTSD as defined by the DSM-5 (Prins et al., 2016). The PC-PTSD-5 demonstrates good diagnostic accuracy; however, there is little additional research on the psychometric properties of the PC-PTSD-5 since its adaptation from the PC-PTSD for DSM-IV. It is recommended that patients endorsing three or more items be further assessed for PTSD; the cutoff score of 3 provides a sensitivity of 95 percent and specificity of 85 percent (Prins et al., 2016).

PTSD Checklist – 5 (PCL-5). The PCL-5 is a twenty-item self-report measure that corresponds with the symptoms of PTSD as defined by DSM-5 (Weathers et al., 2013). The questionnaire takes less than five minutes and asks patients how much they were bothered by each symptom in the last month. Responses are rated on a five-point scale from 0 (*Not at all*) to 4 (*Extremely*), with a maximum score of 80 indicating the greatest level of distress (Bovin et al., 2016). The PCL-5 demonstrated strong internal consistency, test-retest reliability, and convergent and discriminant validity in both civilian and military samples (Blevins et al., 2015; Bovin et al., 2016). A clinical cutoff score of 33 is recommended, providing a sensitivity of 93 percent and specificity of 72 percent (Wortmann et al., 2016).

Alcohol Misuse

Among patients seen in primary care settings, 21.3 percent engage in risky drinking behaviors (Vinson et al., 2010). The National Institute on Alcohol Abuse and Alcoholism (NIAAA) recommends that women consume no more than three alcoholic drinks per day and no more than seven drinks per week; for men, they recommend no more than four drinks per day and fourteen drinks per week (NIAAA, 2010). Screening adults eighteen and over in primary care for alcohol misuse is recommended by the US Preventive Services Task Force (USPSTF; Moyer, 2013).

Alcohol Use Disorders Identification Test (AUDIT). The AUDIT (Saunders et al., 1993) is a ten-item measure that may be clinician- or self-administered. It takes approximately three minutes to administer. For the best balance of sensitivity and specificity in primary care a cutoff score of 4 or 5 or more is recommended; higher cutoff points increase specificity but decrease sensitivity for detecting alcohol misuse (Moyer, 2013). The AUDIT-C, which consists of the first three questions of the AUDIT, also has good sensitivity (83 percent) and specificity (91 percent) for alcohol misuse using 3 or 4 as a cutoff score (Moyer, 2013). Although commonly used in primary care settings, the CAGE (Cut Down, Annoyed, Guilty, and Eye Opener) questions are not recommended for alcohol misuse screening (Moyer, 2013).

Single Question Alcohol Screening Test. After a patient says "yes" to the question "Do you sometimes drink alcohol beverages?," asking the question "How many times in the past year have you had (four for women, five for men) or more drinks in a day?" can be an effective screening method for alcohol misuse (Smith et al., 2009). Using a cutoff of 1 or more times in a year yields a sensitivity of 81.8 percent and specificity of 79.3 percent for alcohol misuse; gender, ethnicity, education, and primary language do not meaningfully change these estimates (Smith et al., 2009).

Illicit Substance and Opioid Medication Misuse

In contrast to alcohol screening, at this time, the USPSTF suggests that there is insufficient evidence to determine whether to recommend screening for illicit drug use in primary care settings (Polen et al., 2008). In a sample of 2,000 adults, across five diverse primary care practices, 8.9 percent of patients met criteria for a substance use disorder, not including alcohol or marijuana use (Wu et al., 2017).

Drug Abuse Screening Test-10 (DAST-10). The DAST-10 is a ten-item self-report screening measure that takes approximately five minutes to administer. Individuals respond "yes" or "no" to each of the items. The DAST-10 was derived from the original twenty-eight-item DAST (Skinner, 1982). In a primary care setting, the DAST-10 sensitivity was 100 percent, with 77 percent specificity for illicit substance and medication misuse (Smith et al., 2010).

Single Question Screening Test for Drug Use in Primary Care. A single question, "How many times in the past year have you used an illegal drug or used a prescription medication for non-medical reasons?" where a response of one or more is considered positive, has been shown to be an effective screening method for drug misuse (Smith et al., 2010). The single question was compared with the DAST-10 and was 100 percent sensitive and 73.5 percent specific for detecting current drug use disorder and 92.9 percent sensitive and 94.1 percent specific for detecting current drug use (Smith et al., 2010).

Insomnia

Sleep problems have been estimated to present in up to 49 percent of primary care patients and commonly remain undiagnosed by physicians or unrecognized as a treatment concern by patients. Additionally, 10–15 percent of patient report chronic insomnia and 4.2 percent report obstructive sleep apnea; however, far more report symptoms of sleep problems that may be related to more severe sleep conditions (Ram et al., 2010). Chronic sleep problems are strongly associated with functional impairment, medical conditions, quality of life, and other psychological concern (Gagnon et al., 2013).

Insomnia Severity Index (ISI). The ISI is a seven-item self-report screener for insomnia targeting the subjective severity and distress created by related symptoms (Bastien, Ballieres, & Morin, 2001). This screener is rated on a 0–4 scale for a maximum score of 28, with higher scores indicating greater severity of insomnia. The ISI takes less than five minutes and can be completed by both the patient and to collect collateral information. Items assess sleep-onset, sleep maintenance, sleep satisfaction, noticeability of interference in daily life, perceived distress, and severity of interference with daily functioning (Bastien et al., 2001). The ISI has been validated in a primary care setting with a suggested cutoff score of 14 for detecting clinical insomnia; this cutoff provides a sensitivity of 82.4 percent and specificity of 82.1 percent (Gagnon et al., 2013). It is unclear whether the psychometric properties of the ISI change for specific diverse populations.

Berlin Questionnaire. The Berlin is a ten-item plus body mass index (BMI) self-report screener developed to detect obstructive sleep apnea (OSA) in primary care populations (Netzer et al., 1999). The ten items and BMI are broken down into three categories: snoring and cessation of breathing (five items), symptoms of daytime sleepiness (four items), and BMI and hypertension (two items; Senaratna et al., 2017). Each item has specified positive responses that contribute to thresholds for each category; risk of OSA is identified if two or more categories meet the threshold of positive responses (Netzer et al., 1999). A meta-analysis of the Berlin Questionnaire revealed it provides a pooled sensitivity of 69–89 percent and a pooled specificity of 22–70 percent for moderate to severe OSA (Senaratna et al., 2017).

STOP-Bang Questionnaire. The STOP-Bang is an eight-item self-report screener developed to detect OSA in surgery patient populations. STOP-Bang is a mnemonic that parallels the eight items of the screener: *S*noring, daytime *T*iredness, *O*bserved apnea, high blood *P*ressure, *B*ody mass index, *A*ge, *N*eck circumference, and *G*ender (Chung et al., 2008). Each item is forced-choice (yes/no). The first four items are adapted from the Berlin Sleep Questionnaire and can be administered as an abbreviated STOP questionnaire (Chung et al., 2008). Patients endorsing three or more items from the STOP-Bang are considered high risk for OSA (Chung et al., 2012). A meta-analysis of the STOP-Bang revealed it provides a pooled sensitivity of 88 percent and a pooled specificity of 42 percent for moderate to severe OSA (Chiu et al., 2017). Although the STOP-Bang was developed for detecting OSA in surgical patients, it has been identified as the superior tool for detecting mild, moderate, and severe OSA across settings (Chiu et al., 2017).

Dementia

Concern about dementia among older adults is common in primary care; however, between 26 and 76 percent of cases go undiagnosed (Holsinger et al., 2007). The goal for many behavioral health providers working in primary care is to determine whether there is a significant cognitive impairment that needs further assessment in a specialty clinic by a neuropsychologist, neurologist, or geriatrician.

Mini-Mental State Examination (MMSE). The MMSE (Folstein, Folstein, & McHugh, 1975) consists of thirty questions assessing orientation, registration, attention and calculation, recall, and language. It is one of the most widely used measures for screening for cognitive functioning in older adults. The MMSE is brief (i.e., it takes approximately five to ten minutes to administer) and has been extensively researched. Overall studies have shown the MMSE to have a sensitivity of 88.3 percent and specificity of 86.2 percent using cut points of 23/24 or 24/25 for detecting dementia (Lin et al., 2013). Although the MMSE is widely used, age, schooling, social class, and gender have been found to impact performance (e.g., Moraes et al., 2010).

Clock Drawing Test. The Clock Drawing Test measures executive functioning (e.g., how well an individual can plan behaviors) and is useful for assessing cognitive functioning. The Clock Drawing Test includes the following steps (Shulman, 2000): (1) hand the patient a predrawn 4-inch diameter circle; (2) state, "This circle represents a clock face. Please put in the numbers so that it looks like a clock and then set the time to 10 minutes past 11."

The Clock Drawing Test produces a wide range of sensitivity (67–98 percent) and specificity (69–94 percent) estimates for dementia (Lin et al., 2013). Scoring methods for the Clock Drawing Test vary. One quick scoring method is to divide the clock into four quadrants by drawing a line between the 12 and 6, then a perpendicular line to divide the circle into four equal quadrants. Errors in the first through third quadrant are assigned a 1, and an error in the fourth quadrant is assigned a four. Scores 4 and higher are considered clinically significant and indicate that more extensive testing should be performed. Essentially, a clock drawing with any significant abnormalities is a cue that more testing is needed.

In primary care settings, it may be particularly useful to administer the MMSE and the Clock Drawing Test together. The combined results of these measures results in high sensitivity (100 percent) and specificity (91 percent) estimates (Harvan & Cotter, 2006).

Montreal Cognitive Assessment (MoCA). The MoCA assesses visuospatial/executive functioning, naming, memory, attention, language, abstraction, delayed recall, and orientation domains; one of the tasks is a version of the clock drawing test (Nasreddine et al., 2005). Scores of 26 or higher out of 30 are considered normal; the test takes ten minutes to administer and is available for free on the MoCA website in a variety of languages, including versions for the blind.[3] Systematic reviews of the evidence related to the MoCA confirm that it has high sensitivity (e.g., 90 percent) for detecting Alzheimer's and other dementias but lower rates of specificity (e.g., 60 percent; Davis et al., 2015; Ozer et al., 2016). Concerns have been raised about the use of 26 as the cutoff score for older adults and those with a lower education levels; in a meta-analysis, a cutoff score of 23 has been shown to decrease the false positive rate and improve diagnostic accuracy (Carson, Leach, & Murphy, 2018). According to the website, a brief version of the MoCA (i.e., a five-minute version) is in development, which may be of particular value for primary care settings. The website also allows the provider to administer the test using an electronic tablet (e.g., an iPad). The evidence is growing for the value of the MoCA as a valid and reliable screening measure for cognitive impairment and, given that it is free, it may be preferable over the MMSE.

Chronic Pain

According to the Institute of Medicine (2011), 116 million US adults suffer from chronic pain. Most individuals first report pain to a health care provider (Dobkin & Boothroyd, 2008) and an estimated 52 percent of chronic pain treatment is provided in primary care (Breuer, Cruciani, & Portenoy, 2010). Given that most chronic pain interventions are focused on functional improvement, it is important for measurement-based care to be able to track those functional changes. Two measures useful in primary care settings for monitoring these functional changes are the Pain intensity, Enjoyment and General Activity measure and the Oswestry Disability Index.

Pain intensity, Enjoyment and General Activity (PEG). The PEG is a three-item outcome measure for pain that assesses *P*ain intensity (P), interference with *E*njoyment of life (E), and interference with *G*eneral activity (G). Each item asks the respondent to rate the item on a 0 (No pain) to 10 (Pain as bad as you can image) scale. The PEG can help to monitor changes in functioning for those experiencing chronic pain and has shown good construct validity for pain assessment compared to other pain-specific measures (i.e., construct validity comparable to the Brief Pain Inventory; Krebs et al., 2009). For example, the PEG has demonstrated sensitivity to change in primary care and veteran patients over six months (Krebs et al., 2009). It is unclear how the PEG performs across diverse populations in primary care.

Oswestry Disability Index (ODI). This self-report scale, originally developed by Fairbank and colleagues (1980), evaluates pain-related functional impairment. It consists of ten questions, with response for each scored from 0 to 5 (higher scores indicating greater impairment). A total sum score is derived from adding all of the item scores, which is multiplied by 2 for a final score ranging from 0–100. This final score represents the respondent's percent of disability. The ODI generally takes about five minutes to complete and is available in the public domain for free use (Fairbank & Pynsent, 2000). This measure is sensitive to change in time frames as brief as three weeks (Gatchel et al., 2009). Additionally, its emphasis on function is highly aligned with primary care priorities. The ODI has been shown to maintain reliability (e.g., mean test-retest reliability intraclass correlation coefficient 0.94) and construct validity (e.g., $r = 0.73$) when tested in diverse populations (Sheahan, Nelson-Wong, & Fischer, 2015).

SUMMARY

Primary care remains an important environment for psychologists and other behavioral health providers to offer behavioral health services. A single chapter is not sufficient to cover all existing measures appropriate for primary care environments. Further, new measures will be developed to enhance the speed and accuracy with which individuals who could benefit from behavioral health care are identified. When choosing measures to using in primary care, it is important to ensure they are appropriate for the setting and provide information that accurately informs care. Measures that can be scored and interpreted quickly, as well as easily incorporated into the electronic medical record, will add the most value to medical and behavioral health providers in primary care.

REFERENCES

Alberts, N. M., Hadjistavropoulos, H. D., Jones, S. L., & Sharpe, D. (2013). The short health anxiety inventory: A systematic review and meta-analysis. *Journal of Anxiety Disorders*, *27*(1), 68–78. doi:10.1016/j.janxdis.2012.10.009

[3] See www.mocatest.org

APA (American Psychological Association). (2016). *A Curriculum for an Interprofessional Seminar on Integrated Primary Care*. APA Interprofessional Seminar on Integrated Primary Care Work Group. www.apa.org/education/grad/curriculum-seminar.aspx

Arroll, B., Goodyear-Smith, F., Crengle, S., Gunn, J., Kerse, N., Fishman, T., ... & Hatcher, S. (2010). Validation of PHQ-2 and PHQ-9 to screen for major depression in the primary care population. *Annals of Family Medicine*, *8*(4), 348–353. doi:10.1370/afm.1139

Baird, M., Blount, A., Brungardt, S., Dickinson, P., Dietrich, A., Epperly, T., & deGruy, F. (2014). Joint principles: Integrating behavioral health care into the patient-centered medical home. *Annals of Family Medicine*, *12*(2), 183–185. doi:10.1370/afm.1634

Bastien, C. H., Vallières, A., & Morin, C. M. (2001). Validation of the Insomnia Severity Index as an outcome measure for insomnia research. *Sleep Medicine*, *2*(4), 297–307. doi:10.1016/S1389-9457(00)00065-4

Beck, A. T., Guth, D., Steer, R. A., & Ball, R. (1997). Screening for major depression disorders in medical inpatients with the beck depression inventory for primary care. *Behaviour Research and Therapy*, *35*(8), 785–791. doi:10.1016/S0005-7967(97)00025-9

Berwick, D. M., Nolan, T. W., & Whittington, J. (2008). The triple aim: Care, health, and cost. *Health Affairs*, *27*(3), 759–769. doi:10.1377/hlthaff.27.3.759

Blevins, C. A., Weathers, F. W., Davis, M. T., Witte, T. K., & Domino, J. L. (2015). The Posttraumatic Stress Disorder Checklist for DSM-5 (PCL-5): Development and initial psychometric evaluation. *Journal of Traumatic Stress*, *28*(6), 489–498. doi:10.1002/jts.22059

Boardman, J. (2001). The Quick PsychoDiagnostics Panel was accurate for identifying psychiatric disorders in primary care. *Evidence-Based Mental Health*, *4*(1), 26–26. doi:10.1136/ebmh.4.1.26

Bodenheimer, T., & Sinsky, C. (2014). From triple to quadruple aim: Care of the patient requires care of the provider. *The Annals of Family Medicine*, *12*(6), 573–576. doi:10.1370/afm.1713

Bovin, M. J., Marx, B. P., Weathers, F. W., Gallagher, M. W., Rodriguez, P., Schnurr, P. P., & Keane, T. M. (2016). Psychometric properties of the PTSD Checklist for Diagnostic and Statistical Manual of Mental Disorders–Fifth Edition (PCL-5) in veterans. *Psychological Assessment*, *28*(11), 1379–1391. doi:10.1037/pas0000254

Bower, P., & Gilbody, S. (2005). Stepped care in psychological therapies: Access, effectiveness and efficiency: narrative literature review. *The British Journal of Psychiatry*, *186*(1), 11–17. doi:10.1192/bjp.186.1.11

Boyd, R. C., Le, H. N., & Somberg, R. (2005). Review of screening instruments for postpartum depression. *Archives of Women's Mental Health*, *8*(3), 141–153. doi:10.1007/s00737-005-0096-6

Breuer, B., Cruciani, R., & Portenoy, R. K. (2010). Pain management by primary care physicians, pain physicians, chiropractors, and acupuncturists: A national survey. *Southern Medical Journal*, *103*(8), 738–747.

Bridges, A. J., Andrews III, A. R., Villalobos, B. T., Pastrana, F. A., Cavell, T. A., & Gomez, D. (2014). Does integrated behavioral health care reduce mental health disparities for Latinos? Initial findings. *Journal of Latina/o Psychology*, *2*(1), 37–53. doi:10.1037/lat0000009

Bryan, C. J., Blount, T., Kanzler, K. A., Morrow, C. E., Corso, K. A., Corso, M. A., & Ray-Sannerud, B. (2014). Reliability and normative data for the behavioral health measure (BHM) in primary care behavioral health settings. *Families, Systems and Health : The Journal of Collaborative Family Healthcare*, *32*(1), 89–100. doi:10.1037/fsh0000014

Butler, S. F., Fernandez, K., Benoit, C., Budman, S. H., & Jamison, R. N. (2008). Validation of the revised Screener and Opioid Assessment for Patients with Pain (SOAPP-R). *The Journal of Pain*, *9*(4), 360–372.

Carson, N., Leach, L., & Murphy, K. J. (2018). A re-examination of Montreal Cognitive Assessment (MoCA) cutoff scores. *International Journal of Geriatric Psychiatry*, *33*, 379–388.

CDC (Centers for Disease Control and Prevention). (2014). *Annual number and percent distribution of ambulatory care visits by setting type according to diagnosis group, United States 2009–2010*. www.cdc.gov/nchs/data/ahcd/combined_tables/2009–2010_combined_web_table01.pdf

Chiu, H. Y., Chen, P. Y., Chuang, L. P., Chen, N. H., Tu, Y. K., Hsieh, Y. J., ... & Guilleminault, C. (2017). Diagnostic accuracy of the Berlin Questionnaire, STOP-BANG, STOP, and Epworth Sleepiness Scale in detecting obstructive sleep apnea: A bivariate meta-analysis. *Sleep Medicine Reviews*, *36*, 57–70. doi:10.1016/j.smrv.2016.10.004

Chung, F., Subramanyam, R., Liao, P., Sasaki, E., Shapiro, C., & Sun, Y. (2012). High STOP-Bang score indicates a high probability of obstructive sleep apnea. *British Journal of Anesthesia*, *108*(5), 768–775. doi:10.1093/bja/aes022

Chung, F., Yegneswaran, B., Liao, P., Chung, S. A., Vairavanathan, S., Islam, S., ... & Shapiro, C. M. (2008). STOP Questionnaire: A tool to screen patients for obstructive sleep apnea. *Anesthesiology: The Journal of the American Society of Anesthesiologists*, *108*(5), 812–821. doi:10.1097/ALN.0b013e31816d83e4

Cox, J. L., Holden, J. M., & Sagovsky, R. (1987). Detection of postnatal depression. *British Journal of Psychiatry*, *150*(06), 782–786. https://doi.org/10.1192/bjp.150.6.782

Croghan, T. W., & Brown, J. D. (2010). *Integrating mental health treatment into the patient centered medical home* (AHRQ Publication No. 10–0084-EF). Rockville, MD: Agency for Healthcare Research and Quality.

Davis, D. H., Creavin, S. T., Yip, J. L., Noel-Storr, A. H., Brayne, C., & Cullum, S. (2015). Montreal Cognitive Assessment for the diagnosis of Alzheimer's disease and other dementias. *Cochrane Database of Systematic Reviews 2015*(10), 1–50. doi:10.1002/14651858.CD010775.pub2

Derogatis, L. R. (2017). Screening for psychiatric disorders in primary care settings. In M. E. Maruish (Ed.), *Handbook of psychological assessment in primary care settings* (2nd ed., pp. 167–192). New York: Routledge.

Dieleman, J. L., Baral, R., Birger, M., Bui, A. L., Bulchis, A., Chapin, A., ... & Murray, C. J. L. (2016). US Spending on Personal Health Care and Public Health, 1996–2013. *JAMA*, *316*(24), 2627. https://doi.org/10.1001/jama.2016.16885

Dobkin, P. L., & Boothroyd, L. J. (2008). Organizing health services for patients with chronic pain: When there is a will there is a way. *Pain Medicine*, *9*(7), 881–889.

Eberhard-Gran, M., Eskild, A., Tambs, K., Opjordsmoen, S., & Ove Samuelsen, S. (2001). Review of validation studies of the Edinburgh Postnatal Depression Scale. *Acta Psychiatrica Scandinavica*, *104*(4), 243–249. doi:10.1034/j.1600-0447.2001.00187.x

El-Den, S., Chen, T. F., Gan, M. Y. L., Wong, M. E., & O'Reilly, C. L. (2017). The psychometric properties of depression screening tools in primary healthcare settings: A systematic review. *Journal of Affective Disorders, 225*, 503–522.

Fairbank, J. C., Couper, J., Davies, J. B., & O'Brien, J. P. (1980). The Oswestry low back pain disability questionnaire. *Physiotherapy, 66*(8), 271–273.

Fairbank, J. C., & Pynsent, P. B. (2000). The Oswestry Disability Index. *Spine, 25*(22), 2940–2953.

Folstein, M. F., Folstein, S. E., & McHugh, P. R. (1975). Mini-mental state: A practical guide for grading the cognitive state of patients for the clinician. *Journal of Psychiatric Research, 12*, 189–198.

Freedy, J. R., Steenkamp, M. M., Magruder, K. M., Yeager, D. E., Zoller, J. S., Hueston, W. J., & Carek, P. J. (2010). Posttraumatic stress disorder screening test performance in civilian primary care. *Family Practice, 27*(6), 615–624. doi:10.1093/fampra/cmq049

Gagnon, C., Bélanger, L., Ivers, H., & Morin, C. M. (2013). Validation of the insomnia severity index in primary care. *Journal of the American Board of Family Medicine, 26*(6), 701–710. doi:10.3122/jabfm.2013.06.130064

Gatchel, R. J., McGeary, D. D., Peterson, A., Moore, M., LeRoy, K., Isler, W. C., & ... Edell, T. (2009). Preliminary findings of a randomized controlled trial of an interdisciplinary military pain program. *Military Medicine, 174*(3), 270–277. doi:10.7205/MILMED-D-03-1607

Harvan, J. R., & Cotter, V. T. (2006). An evaluation of dementia screening in the primary care setting. *Journal of the American Academy of Nurse Practitioners, 18*, 351–360. doi:10.1111/j.1745-7599.2006.00137.x

Holsinger, T., Deveau, J., Boustani, M., & Williams, J. W. (2007). Does this patient have dementia? *The Journal of the American Medical Association, 297*, 2391–2404. doi:10.1001/jama.297.21.2391

Huang, F. Y., Chung, H., Kroenke, K., Delucchi, K. L., & Spitzer, R. L. (2006). Using the patient health questionnaire-9 to measure depression among racially and ethnically diverse primary care patients. *Journal of General Internal Medicine, 21*(6), 547–552.

Hunter, C. L., Dobmeyer, A. C., & Reiter, J. T. (2018). Integrating behavioral health services into primary care: Spotlight on the primary care behavioral health (PCBH) model of service delivery. *Journal of Clinical Psychology in Medical Settings, 25*, 105–108. doi:10.1007/s10880-017-9534-7

Hunter, C. L., Goodie, J. L., Oordt, M., & Dobmeyer, A. C. (2017). *Integrated Behavioral Health in Primary Care: Step-by-Step Guidance for Assessment and Intervention* (2nd ed.). Washington, DC: American Psychological Association.

Institute of Medicine. (2011). *Relieving pain in America: A blueprint for transforming prevention, care, education, and research*. Washington, DC: The National Academies Press.

Jones, T., Lookatch, S., & Moore, T. (2015). Validation of a new risk assessment tool: The Brief Risk Questionnaire. *Journal of Opioid Management, 11*(2), 171–183.

Jordan, P., Shedden-Mora, M. C., & Löwe, B. (2017). Psychometric analysis of the generalized anxiety disorder scale (GAD-7) in primary care using modern item response theory. *PLoS ONE, 12*(8), e0182162. doi:10.1371/journal.pone.0182162

Kessler, R. C., Petukhova, M., Sampson, N. A., Zaslavsky, A. M., & Wittchen, H. U. (2012). Twelve-month and lifetime prevalence and lifetime morbid risk of anxiety and mood disorders in the United States. *International Journal of Methods in Psychiatric Research, 21*(3), 169–184. doi:10.1002/mpr.1359

Kopta, S. M., & Lowry, J. L. (2002). Psychometric evaluation of the behavioral health questionnaire-20: A brief instrument for assessing global mental health and the three phases of psychotherapy outcome. *Psychotherapy Research, 12*(4), 413–426. doi:10.1093/ptr/12.4.413

Kopta, M., Owen, J., & Budge, S. (2015). Measuring psychotherapy outcomes with the behavioral health measure-20: Efficient and comprehensive. *Psychotherapy (Chicago, Ill.), 52*(4), 442–448. doi:10.1037/pst0000035

Krebs, E. E., Lorenz, K. A., Bair, M. J., Damush, T. M., Jingwei, W., Sutherland, J. M., ... & Kroenke, K. (2009). Development and initial validation of the PEG, a three-item scale assessing pain intensity and interference. *Journal of General Internal Medicine, 24*(6), 733–738. doi:10.1007/s11606-009-0981-1

Kroenke, K., Spitzer, R. L., & Williams, J. B. W. (2001). The PHQ-9: Validity of a brief depression severity measure. *Journal of General Internal Medicine, 16*(9), 606–613. doi:10.1046/j.1525-1497.2001.016009606.x

Kroenke, K., Spitzer, R. L., Williams, J. B., & Löwe, B. (2009). An ultra-brief screening scale for anxiety and depression: The PHQ–4. *Psychosomatics, 50*(6), 613–621. doi:10.1016/S0033-3182(09)70864-3

Kroenke, K., Spitzer, R. L., Williams, J. B., Monahan, P. O., & Löwe, B. (2007). Anxiety disorders in primary care: Prevalence, impairment, comorbidity, and detection. *Annals of Internal medicine, 146*(5), 317–325.

Lambert M. J. (2010). *Prevention of treatment failure*. Washington, DC: American Psychological Association.

Lin, J. S., O'Connor, E., Rossom, R. C., Perdue, L. A., Burda, B. U., Thompson, M., & Eckstrom, E. (2013). *Screening for cognitive impairment in older adults: An evidence update for the US Preventive Services Task Force*. Rockville, MD: Agency for Healthcare Research and Quality. www.ncbi.nlm.nih.gov/books/NBK174643

McDaniel, S. H., Grus, C. L., Cubic, B. A., Hunter, C. L., Kearney, L. K., Schuman, C. C., ... & Miller, B. F. (2014). Competencies for psychology practice in primary care. *American Psychologist, 69*(4), 409–429. doi:10.1037/a0036072

Mitchell, A. J., Rao, S., & Vaze, A. (2010). Do primary care physicians have particular difficulty identifying late-life depression? A meta-analysis stratified by age. *Psychotherapy and Psychosomatics, 79*(5), 285–294. doi:10.1159/000318295

Moraes, C., Pinto, J. A., Lopes, M. A., Litvoc, J., & Bottino, C. M. (2010). Impact of sociodemographic and health variables on mini-mental state examination in a community-based sample of older people. *European Archives of Psychiatry and Clinical Neuroscience, 260*(7), 535–542.

Moriarty, A. S., Gilbody, S., McMillan, D., & Manea, L. (2015). Screening and case finding for major depressive disorder using the Patient Health Questionnaire (PHQ-9): A meta-analysis. *General Hospital Psychiatry, 37*(6), 567–576. doi:10.1016/j.genhosppsych.2015.06.012

Moyer, V. A. (2013). Screening and behavioral counseling interventions in primary care to reduce alcohol misuse: US preventive services task force recommendation statement. *Annals of Internal Medicine, 159*(3), 210–218. doi:10.7326/0003-4819-159-3-201308060-00652

Nasreddine, Z. S., Phillips, N. A., Bédirian, V., Charbonneau, S., Whitehead, V., Collin, I., ... & Chertkow, H. (2005). The

Montreal Cognitive Assessment, MoCA: A brief screening tool for mild cognitive impairment. *Journal of the American Geriatrics Society, 53*(4), 695–699. doi:10.1111/j.1532-5415.2005.53221.x

Netzer, N. C., Stoohs, R. A., Netzer, C. M., Clark, K., & Strohl, K. P. (1999). Using the Berlin questionnaire to identify patients at risk for the sleep apnea syndrome. *Annals of Internal Medicine, 131*(7), 485–491. doi:10.7326/0003-4819-131-7-199910050-00002

NIAAA (National Institute on Alcohol Abuse and Alcoholism). (2010). *Rethinking drinking: Alcohol and your health.* https://pubs.niaaa.nih.gov/publications/RethinkingDrinking/Rethinking_Drinking.pdf

O'Connor, E., Rossom, R. C., Henninger, M., Groom, H. C., & Burda, B. U. (2016). Primary care screening for and treatment of depression in pregnant and postpartum women: Evidence report and systematic review for the US Preventive Services Task Force. *The Journal of the American Medical Association, 315*, 388–406.

Ogbeide, S. A., Landoll, R. R., Nielsen, M. K., & Kanzler, K. E. (2018). To go or not go: Patient preference in seeking specialty mental health versus behavioral consultation within the primary care behavioral health consultation model. *Families, Systems, and Health, 36*(4), 513–517. https://doi.org/10.1037/fsh0000374

Ozer, S., Young, J., Champ, C., & Burke, M. (2016). A systematic review of the diagnostic test accuracy of brief cognitive tests to detect amnestic mild cognitive impairment. *International Journal of Geriatric Psychiatry, 31*(11), 1139–1150. doi:10.1002/gps.4444

Parkerson G. R., Jr., Broadhead, W. E., & Tse, C. J. (1990). The Duke Health Profile: A 17-item measure of health and dysfunction. *Medical Care, 28*(11), 1056–1072. doi:10.1097/00005650-199011000-00007

Peek, C. J. and the National Integration Academy Council. (2013). *Lexicon for behavioral health and primary care integration: Concepts and definitions developed by expert consensus* (AHRQ Publication No.13-IP001-EF). Rockville, MD: Agency for Healthcare Research and Quality. http://integrationacademy.ahrq.gov/sites/default/files/Lexicon.pdf.

Perret-Guillaume, C., Briancon, S., Guillemin, F., Wahl, D., Empereur, F., & Nguyen Thi, P. L. (2009). Which generic health related quality of life questionnaire should be used in older inpatients: Comparison of the duke health profile and the MOS short-form SF-36? *Journal of Nutrition, Health and Aging, 14*(4), 325–331. doi:10.1007/s12603-010-0074-1

Phelan, E., Williams, B., Meeker, K., Bonn, K., Frederick, J., LoGerfo, J., & Snowden, M. (2010). A study of the diagnostic accuracy of the PHQ-9 in primary care elderly. *BMC Family Practice, 11*(1), 63–63. doi:10.1186/1471-2296-11-63

Polen, M. R., Whitlock, E. P., Wisdom, J. P., Nygren, P., & Bougatsos, C. (2008). *Screening in primary care settings for illicit drug use: Staged systematic review for the United States Preventive Services Task Force* (AHRQ Publication No. 08--05108-EF-s). Rockville, MD: Agency for Healthcare Research and Quality.

Prins, A., Bovin, M. J., Smolenski, D. J., Marx, B. P., Kimerling, R., Jenkins-Guarnieri, M. A., Tiet, Q. Q. (2016). The primary care PTSD screen for DSM-5 (PC-PTSD-5): Development and evaluation within a veteran primary care sample. *Journal of General Internal Medicine, 31*(10), 1206–1211. doi:10.1007/s11606-016-3703-5

Public Law No: 111–148, 111th Congress: Patient Protection and Affordable Care Act. (2010). 124 STAT. 119. www.gpo.gov/fdsys/pkg/PLAW-111publ148/pdf/PLAW-111publ148.pdf.

Ram, S., Seirawan, H., Kumar, S. K., & Clark, G. T. (2010). Prevalence and impact of sleep disorders and sleep habits in the United States. *Sleep and Breathing, 14*(1), 63–70. doi:10.1007/s11325-009-0281-3

Ranallo, P. A., Kilbourne, A. M., Whatley, A. S., & Pincus, H. A. (2016). Behavioral health information technology: From chaos to clarity. *Health Affairs, 35*(6), 1106–1113. doi:10.1377/hlthaff.2016.0013

Reiter, J. T., Dobmeyer, A. C., & Hunter, C. (2018). The primary care behavioral health (PCBH) model: an overview and operational definition. *Journal of Clinical Psychology in Medical Settings, 25*, 109–126. doi:10.1007/s10880-017-9531-x

Richmond, A., & Jackson, J. (2018). Cultural considerations for psychologists in primary care. *Journal of Clinical Psychology in Medical Settings, 3*, 305–315.

Robinson, P. J., & Reiter, J. D. (2015). *Behavioral consultation and primary care: A guide to integrating services* (2nd ed.). New York: Springer.

Rutter, L. A., & Brown, T. A. (2017). Psychometric properties of the generalized anxiety disorder scale-7 (GAD-7) in outpatients with anxiety and mood disorders. *Journal of Psychopathology and Behavioral Assessment, 39*, 140–146.

Salkovskis, P. M., Rimes, K. A., Warwick, H. M. C., & Clark, D. M. (2002). The Health Anxiety Inventory: Development and validation of scales for the measurement of health anxiety and hypochondriasis. *Psychological Medicine, 32*(5), 843–853. doi:10.1017/S0033291702005822

Sanchez, K., Chapa, T., Ybarra, R., & Martienez, O. N. Jr. (2012). *Eliminating disparities through the integration of behavioral health and primary care services for racial and ethnic minority populations, including individuals with limited English proficiency: A literature report.* US Department of Health and Human Services Office of Minority Health and Hogg Foundation for Mental Health.

Saunders, J. B., Aasland, O. G., Babor, T. F., De la Fuente, J. R., & Grant, M. (1993). Development of the alcohol use disorders identification test (AUDIT): WHO collaborative project on early detection of persons with harmful alcohol consumption-II. *Addiction, 88*(6), 791–804. doi:10.1111/j.1360-0443.1993.tb02093.x

Scott, E. D., Gil, K., King, B. C., & Piatt, E. (2015). Clinical outcomes in a primary care practice within a center for health equity. *Journal of Primary Care and Community Health, 6*, 239–242.

Senaratna, C. V., Perret, J. L., Matheson, M. C., Lodge, C. J., Lowe, A. J., Cassim, R., ... & Dharmage, S. C. (2017). Validity of the Berlin questionnaire in detecting obstructive sleep apnea: A systematic review and meta-analysis. *Sleep Medicine Reviews, 36*, 116–124. doi:10.1016/j.smrv.2017.04.001

Sheahan, P. J., Nelson-Wong, E. J., & Fischer, S. L. (2015). A review of culturally adapted versions of the Oswestry Disability Index: The adaptation process, construct validity, test–retest reliability and internal consistency. *Disability and Rehabilitation, 37*, 2367–2374.

Shedler, J. (2017). Automated mental health assessment for integrated care. In R. E. Feinstein, J. V. Connely, & M. S. Feinstein (Eds.) *Integrating behavioral health and primary care* (pp. 134–145). New York: Oxford University Press.

Shedler, J., Beck, A., & Bensen, S. (2000). Practical mental health assessment in primary care. *Journal of Family Practice*, *49*(7), 614–622.

Shulman, K. I. (2000). Clock-drawing: Is it the ideal cognitive screening test? *International Journal of Geriatric Psychiatry*, *15*, 548–561. doi:10.1002/1099-1166(200006)15:6<548::aid-gps242>3.0.CO;2-U

Simon, G. E., Rutter, C. M., Peterson, D., Oliver, M., Whiteside, U., Operskalski, B., & Ludman, E. J. (2013). Does response on the PHQ-9 depression questionnaire predict subsequent suicide attempt or suicide death? *Psychiatric Services*, *64*(12), 1195–1202. doi:10.1176/appi.ps.201200587

Skinner, H. A. (1982). The drug abuse screening test. *Addictive Behaviors*, *7*, 363–371.

Smith, P. C., Schmidt, S. M., Allensworth-Davies, D., & Saitz, R. (2009). Primary care validation of a single-question alcohol screening test. *Journal of General Internal Medicine*, *24*, 783–788. doi:10.1007/s11606-009-0928-6

Smith, P. C., Schmidt, S. M., Allensworth-Davies, D., & Saitz, R. (2010). A single-question screening test for drug use in primary care. *Archives of Internal Medicine*, *170*(13), 1155–1160. doi:10.1001/archinternmed.2010.140

Spitzer, R. L., Kroenke, K., Williams, J. B., & Löwe, B. (2006). A brief measure for assessing generalized anxiety disorder: The GAD-7. *Archives of Internal Medicine*, *166*(10), 1092–1097.

Steer, R. A., Cavalieri, T. A., Leonard, D. M., & Beck, A. T. (1999). Use of the Beck Depression Inventory for Primary Care to screen for major depression disorders. *General Hospital Psychiatry*, *21*(2), 106–111. doi:10.1016/S0163-8343(98)00070-X

Thibodeau, M. A., & Asmundson, G. J. (2014). The PHQ-9 assesses depression similarly in men and women from the general population. *Personality and Individual Differences*, *56*(1), 149–153. doi:10.1016/j.paid.2013.08.039

Tran, P. L., Blizzard, C. L., Srikanth, V., Hanh, V. T., Lien, N. T., Thang, N. H., & Gall, S. L. (2015). Health-related quality of life after stroke: Reliability and validity of the Duke Health Profile for use in Vietnam. *Quality of Life Research*, *24*(11), 2807–2814.

Vinson, D. C., Manning, B. K., Galliher, J. M., Dickinson, L. M., Pace, W. D., & Turner, B. J. (2010). Alcohol and sleep problems in primary care patients: A report from the AAFP National Research Network. *The Annals of Family Medicine*, *8*(6), 484–492. doi:10.1370/afm.1175

Weathers, F. W., Litz, B. T., Keane, T. M., Palmieri, P. A., Marx, B. P., & Schnurr, P. P. (2013). *The PTSD Checklist for DSM–5 (PCL-5)*. Boston, MA: National Center for PTSD.

Wortmann, J. H., Jordan, A. H., Weathers, F. W., Resick, P. A., Dondanville, K. A., Hall-Clark, B., ... & Mintz, J. (2016). Psychometric analysis of the PTSD Checklist-5 (PCL-5) among treatment-seeking military service members. *Psychological Assessment*, *28*(11), 1392. doi:10.1037/pas0000260

Wu, L. T., McNeely, J., Subramaniam, G. A., Brady, K. T., Sharma, G., VanVeldhuisen, P., ... & Schwartz, R. P. (2017). DSM-5 substance use disorders among adult primary care patients: Results from a multisite study. *Drug and Alcohol Dependence*, *179*, 42–46. doi:10.1016/j.drugalcdep.2017.05.048

33 Psychological Assessment in Forensic Settings

PATRICIA A. ZAPF, AMANDA BELTRANI, AND AMANDA L. REED

Psychological assessments are conducted to evaluate an individual's cognitive, social, and/or emotional functioning. The scope is typically broad and the aim is to generate a formulation that will assist in treatment planning to improve one or more aspects of an individual's functioning. Forensic mental health assessments (FMHA) are a particular category of psychological assessment that are conducted to assess an individual's functioning in relation to a specific legal question and with the intention of assisting a legal decision maker (Heilbrun, 2001). The focus in a forensic assessment is on an individual's functional impairments and *how those might affect* relevant legal capacities, differing from traditional therapeutic assessments, which are geared toward *what to do* about an individual's impairments.

FMHA differ from therapeutic psychological assessments in several important ways (see Heilbrun, Grisso, & Goldstein, 2009 for a detailed discussion). Whereas in traditional psychological assessments the client is the person being evaluated, in FMHA the client is the party that retains the evaluator or that requests the evaluation (e.g., an attorney, a court, an employer) and not the subject of the evaluation (i.e., the defendant, plaintiff, claimant, etc.). This has important implications for whether and how a forensic evaluator communicates the results of the FMHA. In addition, whereas therapeutic psychological assessments rely primarily on the perspective and self-report of the individual being evaluated, in FMHA the evaluator relies heavily on third-party and collateral information sources, with the intention of attempting to corroborate the self-report of the evaluee. Specialized testing and evaluation procedures to assess the response style of the evaluee figure prominently in FMHA, as every evaluator must consider the degree to which an evaluee's presentation has impacted the validity of the evaluation results. Furthermore, some forensic assessments, including court-ordered evaluations, do not require informed consent from the subject of the evaluation (although professional ethics require that an evaluee be provided with notification of the nature and purpose of the evaluation as well as other relevant details). Thus, whereas participation of the evaluee in the assessment process is paramount to traditional psychological assessment, FMHA does not *require* participation by the subject of the evaluation. These and other distinctions between traditional psychological assessments and forensic assessments underscore the importance of specialized knowledge, training, and experience for forensic evaluation and the use of methods and procedures that allow for scrutiny by legal decision makers.

FMHA may be categorized in various ways, including the focus of the time frame for which an individual's mental state or functioning is in question (i.e., retrospective, current, future) or the legal domain for which the evaluation is sought (i.e., criminal, civil, family/juvenile court). In this chapter, we will begin with a discussion of the nature and method of psychological assessment in forensic settings, delineating some of the common features of all forensic evaluations. We then describe some of the most common types of evaluations that are conducted in criminal, civil, and family/juvenile court contexts and highlight specific assessment instruments and tools that have been developed for use in each domain. We end with a brief discussion of the nature and format of the written forensic evaluation report.

NATURE AND METHOD OF FORENSIC ASSESSMENT

Forensic mental health assessment is a specialized field of assessment that has achieved significant advances in the past several decades (see Heilbrun et al., 2009 for a review of the history of FMHA). Heilbrun (2001) was instrumental in setting out principles of forensic mental health assessment that have since been further developed and applied to various specific domains of FMHA (see DeMatteo et al., 2016; Heilbrun, DeMatteo, & Marczyk, 2004; Heilbrun et al., 2008). In this section, we provide a brief overview of the common aspects regarding the nature and method of forensic assessment that apply across forensic domains.

Referral Question

In forensic mental health assessment, the referral question is of primary importance, forming the basis for the evaluation to be conducted. The evaluator must be careful to understand the referral question, clarifying an ambiguous referral with the retaining party when necessary to obtain a clear sense of the legal issue at hand and the scope of the evaluation being requested. In some instances, forensic evaluators are asked to assess only one aspect of a larger legal issue (e.g., a defendant's risk for violence as part of a broader evaluation of mitigation), whereas, in others, the evaluator may be tasked with a thorough evaluation of all relevant aspects of the legal issue. The nature and scope of the referral question dictate the scope and focus of the evaluation.

Data Sources

Three types of data typically form the basis for FMHA: third-party and collateral information sources, an interview with the subject of the evaluation, and forensic/psychological test data. The evaluator is tasked with identifying and collecting relevant information about the subject of the evaluation, reviewing the information in detail, determining what hypotheses need to be tested (and obtaining additional information, as appropriate, to test), and then consolidating the data (giving appropriate weight to data sources on the basis of relevance and reliability) to arrive at an opinion about the referral question that provides the most parsimonious explanation of the data.

Third-party/collateral information. Third-party and collateral information sources are perhaps the most important category of data to collect in a forensic assessment. These data include official accounts surrounding the issue in question (e.g., police reports and discovery materials for criminal offenses; incident reports or witness accounts related to personal injury claims; child welfare reports related to parenting capacity concerns) as well as records and other documents or files that provide relevant details about the current and previous functioning of the subject of the evaluation. Medical, mental health, school, and correctional records are all common types of third-party information that might be considered in a forensic evaluation, but the evaluator should also remain aware of other potential third-party records that might be relevant/requested for an evaluee. Mental health records (or the complete lack thereof) can be helpful in establishing the possibility (or not) of mental illness at the time of the offense. In addition, medical and other treatment records can be helpful in developing an understanding of the evaluee's functioning, both prior to as well as after an incident. In addition to records and documents, collateral information sources also include people, that is, collateral interviews with individuals who have knowledge of and can speak about the behavior or functioning of the person being evaluated (see Achenbach, Ivanova, & Rescorla, Chapter 11, this volume).

The forensic evaluator works with the referral source to request and collect relevant sources of third-party and collateral information, which is typically reviewed prior to conducting an interview with the individual being evaluated. The evaluator will seek out additional information sources as necessary and is tasked with determining how much weight to place on each source of data considered, with more weight being given to credible, reliable sources without an interest in the outcome of the evaluation and less weight being given to those information sources, such as family members or co-accused, who might have a vested interest in the outcome. Thus, the evaluator is careful to consider the validity and reliability of all information collected, especially from collateral informants.

Third-party and collateral information is an important component of the forensic evaluation, as this information provides the necessary background for the evaluator to both develop specific questions to be asked in interview and ascertain the validity of self-reported information provided by the evaluee. The evaluator will pay close attention to any discrepancies that arise between third-party/collateral data and that provided by the evaluee in the interview and will confront the evaluee about these discrepancies as necessary.

Interview. Although it is not always possible to interview the subject of a forensic assessment (and, in some cases, such as in psychological autopsies, is impossible), it is considered a professional best practice to do so and evaluators who do not conduct an interview as part of their evaluation must be clear about the limits of their opinions as a result. An interview with the subject of the evaluation is both necessary and important when the evaluator is expected to give an opinion regarding the mental health or other functioning of the evaluee. In that small proportion of evaluations where it is not possible to interview the evaluee, the evaluator should be explicit about this limitation in the written report and should be cautious about offering opinions regarding the evaluee's functioning.

Forensic interviews are more akin to investigative interviews as direct questioning and confrontations regarding inconsistent information are typical. The forensic interview is used to gain specific information that is relevant to the referral question being evaluated and to provide an opportunity for the evaluator to assess the response style of the evaluee. The degree to which the self-report of the interviewee appears to be consistent with or in opposition to third-party and collateral information, the consistency of the presentation of the interviewee throughout the interview or from one interview to another, and the degree of consistency between behaviors reported by the interviewee and those observed by the evaluator should be considered by the evaluator in making a determination about the response style. The evaluator will use these observations to make a determination regarding whether additional testing is required to evaluate the response style of the interviewee.

In addition to allowing for the assessment of an evaluee's response style, the interview also provides the evaluator with the opportunity to assess the evaluee's current mental state, to make clinical observations, and to ask questions that will assist the evaluator in arriving at a formulation about the referral question being addressed. Detailed and specific inquiries will be made regarding the legal issue in question and structured inquiries for relevant aspects of the legal issue provide increased reliability and reduced bias in the evaluation process (see Grisso, 2003).

Testing. Test data in forensic assessment can be of three different types: psychological test data, forensically relevant test data, and data from forensic assessment instruments (see Heilbrun, Rogers, & Otto, 2002). Psychological tests provide information about the general cognitive, clinical, or personality functioning of an individual, whereas forensically relevant tests provide information about some aspect of functioning that has specific relevance to the forensic context (such as response style/malingering). The data that these types of tests provide, although not specific to the legal issue being evaluated, may be relevant for providing information about an area of functioning that is implicated by the referral question (e.g., intelligence testing can provide information about cognitive functioning that may be relevant to the issue of competence to stand trial). The evaluator is tasked with making a determination about the relevance of data from psychological or forensically relevant tests to the specific issue being evaluated (see Wygant, Burchett, & Harp, Chapter 6, this volume).

Forensic assessment instruments (FAIs), on the other hand, are tests that have been developed for the purpose of assessing relevant aspects of functioning related to a specific legal question. FAIs provide a structure for legally related inquiries that serves to standardize the evaluation process, improve communication between the evaluator and the legal decision maker, increase reliability, and decrease bias (Grisso, 2003). Although FAIs have not been developed for every domain of forensic evaluation, they are an important component of the forensic evaluations for which they have been developed and evaluators are encouraged to incorporate relevant FAIs into their forensic evaluations (Heilbrun et al., 2009). The vast majority of FAIs have been developed for psycho-legal questions as they have been framed in the United States. While other countries may have similar standards for some of these psycho-legal issues, evaluators should be cautious about adopting these instruments for use in other jurisdictions and should be clear about the potential limitations of such. We will highlight those domains for which FAIs have been developed in the next three sections of this chapter.

Forensic evaluators must consider which tests might provide relevant information for the legal question being addressed and select tests/instruments with appropriate psychometric properties and relevant validation samples (see Hunsley & Allan, Chapter 2, this volume). In addition, the background of the evaluee must be taken into consideration along with any relevant cultural considerations in selecting tests and evaluation techniques. In those cases where no test data are collected, the evaluator should be prepared to describe why test data are not relevant to the evaluation.

Hypothesis testing. As the evaluator is collecting and considering the evaluation data, they are formulating a number of hypotheses that are specific and relevant to the legal issue being evaluated. The goal is for the evaluator to consider relevant and competing hypotheses and to make a determination regarding those that can be ruled out and those that appear valid. It will often be the case that the evaluator will seek additional information to assist in confirming or ruling out various hypotheses as they work through the case formulation.

We now move to a discussion of some of the most common types of forensic evaluations in each of three domains: criminal, civil, and juvenile/family.

Criminal Forensic Assessments

Forensic assessments for the criminal courts typically address any of a number of psycho-legal issues relevant to a criminal case. Each type of evaluation is predicated on a specific legal principle, which forms the basis for the referral question (Heilbrun & LaDuke, 2015). Legal decision makers rely on forensic mental health professionals to inform their decisions related to psychological factors that might impact an individual's ability to participate in the trial process, to be held accountable for a criminal offense, to be released from custody, or other case-specific legal questions. Here, we briefly review three common types of evaluations that occur within the criminal context: adjudicative competence, mental state at the time of the offense, and violence risk assessment.

Adjudicative competence. The most frequently requested criminal forensic assessment is that of a defendant's adjudicative competence (Bonnie & Grisso, 2000), commonly referred to as competency to stand trial but referring to a defendant's participation at any stage of criminal proceedings from arrest and arraignment through trial and sentencing (adjudicative competence is an umbrella term that encompasses competence to stand trial as well as competence to waive Miranda, to confess, to waive the right to counsel, to be sentenced, and to be executed). The issue of a defendant's competence to proceed can be raised by any party to the proceedings (defense, prosecution, court) once a bona fide doubt as to the defendant's competency arises. A low threshold exists for ensuring that a defendant's due process is not violated, which means that, once the issue of competency has been raised, it typically must be formally considered by having an evaluator conduct an assessment of the defendant's competence-related abilities. The interested reader is referred to additional sources for more information on conducting evaluations of adjudicative competence (see Goldstein & Goldstein, 2010; Grisso, 2003; Kruh & Grisso, 2009; Zapf & Roesch, 2009).

Competency assessments require that an evaluator examine the *current* mental state of a defendant to identify whether they can demonstrate the necessary capacities to understand the court process and assist in their own defense. The standard for competence to stand trial was established in *Dusky v. United States* (1960). *Dusky* delineated that to be competent to proceed a defendant must have (1) sufficient present ability to consult with counsel with a reasonable degree of rational understanding (e.g., communicate their version of the offense, assist counsel in formulating a legal strategy, make rational decisions regarding trial strategy) and (2) the ability to rationally and factually understand the proceedings against them (e.g., understand the nature of the charges, the available pleas, the likely outcome).

Several assessment instruments have been developed to assist in the evaluation of a defendant's competence to stand trial. These instruments can be divided into two different categories: idiographic – instruments that guide evaluators through an assessment of various competence-related abilities but are not scored and provide no normative information – and nomothetic – instruments that use standardized administration and criterion-based scoring and that provide an indication of how a specific defendant compares to groups of competent and/or incompetent defendants. The MacArthur Competence Assessment Tool – Criminal Adjudication (MacCAT-CA; Poythress et al., 1999) and the Evaluation of Competency to Stand Trial – Revised (ECST-R; Rogers, Tillbrook, & Sewell, 2004) are two well-established nomothetic competence assessment instruments whereas the Fitness Interview Test – Revised (FIT-R; Roesch, Zapf, & Eaves, 2006) and the Interdisciplinary Fitness Interview – Revised (IFI-R; Golding, 1993) are examples of idiographic assessment instruments for competence. Grisso (2003) provides a detailed review of most instruments that have been developed to assist in the assessment of a defendant's competence. These instruments are useful in that they are typically structured to reflect the criteria set out in *Dusky* and they provide a means of standardizing the evaluation of a defendant's competence-related abilities, resulting in increased reliability and decreased opportunity for bias to impact the evaluation (Grisso, 2003). While the majority of these instruments do not include a formal means of assessing an evaluee's response style, the ECST-R has incorporated various scales to be used as a screen for response style.

Mental state at the time of the offense. Assessment of a defendant's mental state at the time of the offense is another common forensic assessment in the criminal context. Mental state at the time of the offense is a retrospective evaluation, wherein the evaluator is tasked with assembling data in an attempt to reconstruct the defendant's mental state at some earlier point in time to assess whether and how this could have impacted the defendant's cognition or behavior during and around the time of the offense. Most evaluations of mental state at the time of the offense are to address the issue of a defendant's criminal responsibility; however, other related issues include various mens rea defenses, such as extreme emotional disturbance, diminished capacity, duress, and provocation. We focus here on criminal responsibility and suggest that interested readers consult Packer (2009) and Melton et al. (2007) for more in-depth discussions of mental state at the time of the offense.

Evaluations of criminal responsibility, commonly referred to as insanity evaluations, focus on the retrospective evaluation of a defendant's mental state to determine the extent to which mental disease or defect might have impacted the defendant's criminal responsibility or accountability for the offense in question. The insanity defense in the United States has its roots in English Common Law and nearly every state has an insanity statute that allows for certain defendants to be found Not Guilty by Reason of Insanity (NGRI). The two most commonly used standards for an insanity defense are the M'Naghten standard and the American Law Institute standard. The M'Naghten standard requires that a defendant, because of mental disease or defect, lacks an understanding of (1) the nature and quality of his actions or (2) the wrongfulness of those actions. The American Law Institute standard incorporates a volitional prong and requires that a defendant show substantial impairment in the ability to (1) appreciate the nature, quality, and wrongfulness of the act or (2) conform their conduct to the requirements of the law. Various other insanity standards are used in a minority of jurisdictions; but, regardless of the specific standard used, a causal connection between the defendant's mental disease or defect and their criminal behavior must be established for a successful insanity defense.

Given the retrospective nature of this type of assessment, collection of and reliance on third-party and collateral information are of paramount importance. The evaluator must attempt to collect data that will assist in reconstructing the defendant's mental state and functioning at the time the offense occurred. In interview with the defendant, the evaluator will attempt to ascertain the defendant's explanation of and motivation for the criminal behavior. Careful questioning regarding the defendant's thoughts, feelings, beliefs, and perceptions – including an accounting and description of what was occurring with respect to each of the defendant's five senses – is undertaken during the interview. Criminal responsibility evaluations are investigative in nature, with the forensic evaluator attempting to obtain as much information about the defendant as possible to arrive at an opinion regarding whether and how the defendant's mental state might have impacted their thoughts and behaviors at the time of the crime. Two instruments have been developed to assist in the assessment of mental state at the time of the offense – the Mental State at the Time of the Offense Screening Evaluation (MSE; Slobogin, Melton, & Showalter, 1984) and the Rogers Criminal Responsibility Assessment Scales (R-CRAS; Rogers, 1984) – although it appears that the MSE is not used with any frequency (Lally, 2003). The R-CRAS provides areas of inquiry and a structure for the evaluation that lead evaluators through a decision tree model for determining whether the defendant appears to meet criteria for various insanity standards (e.g., M'Naghten, American Law Institute [ALI]). This tool is helpful for assisting the evaluator in considering relevant details and formulating the case in a manner consistent with the legal test for insanity in those jurisdictions that use either the ALI or M'Naghten standard but does not provide any formal assessment of response style.

Violence risk assessment. Similar to adjudicative competence and mental state at the time of the offense, violence risk assessment encompasses a breadth of various types of assessments of an individual's risk for some future behavior (e.g., violence, sexual violence, intimate partner violence). The assessment of risk for violence focuses on actual, attempted, or threatened physical harm that is deliberate and nonconsenting (Kropp, Hart, & Belfrage, 2005). The context for violence risk assessments varies and can include release from correctional facilities (e.g., probation and parole decisions), civil commitment proceedings (e.g., sexually violent predators, dangerous offenders), transfer hearings (e.g., adjudicating juvenile offenders in criminal court), and custody placement decisions (e.g., determining the level of supervision required in custody). Indeed, the landmark case of *Kansas v. Hendricks* (1997) expanded the scope of violence risk assessment from the criminal to the civil domain with the decision that sexually violent predators could be indefinitely committed after serving a prison term should they be considered mentally ill and dangerous. The repercussions of risk assessments are broad, with lasting implications for individuals and society, ranging from forced medication to indefinite confinement, to capital punishment (Guy, Douglas, & Hart, 2015). Thus, it is imperative that forensic evaluators identify factors that both increase (risk factors) and decrease (protective factors) an individual's risk for violence, in addition to making determinations about the severity and immediacy of violence.

Several tools for violence risk have been developed, falling into two broad categories reflecting structured approaches to risk assessment: actuarial and structured professional judgment (SPJ). Actuarial tools, such as the Violence Risk Appraisal Guide (VRAG: Rice, Harris, & Lang, 2013) and the Static-99 Revised (Static-99 R; Helmus et al., 2012) use statistical methods to assess a particular variable using empirically known outcomes to predict an individual's risk for future violence. SPJ tools were created to guide an evaluator's decision-making process, as opposed to simply tallying factors that are identified as present or absent, and to provide a structured format for evaluators to consider various scenarios in arriving at a formulation of an individual's risk as well as strategies for managing that risk. The HCR-20 (Douglas et al., 2013; Webster et al., 1997) is the most widely used SPJ risk assessment tool (Singh, Grann, & Fazel, 2011) and focuses on general violence, but other SPJ tools have also been developed to evaluate other types of violence, such as sexual violence (e.g., RSVP: Hart et al., 2003; ERASOR: Worling & Curwen, 2001), intimate partner violence (e.g., SARA: Kropp & Hart, 2015), stalking (e.g., SAM: Kropp, Hart, & Lyon, 2008), honor-based violence (e.g., PATRIARCH: Kropp, Belfrage, & Hart, 2013), violence in youth (START:AV: Viljoen et al., 2014; SAVRY: Borum, Bartel, & Forth, 2006), and workplace violence (WAVR-21 Version 2: White & Meloy, 2010). Given the vast literature on violence risk assessment and the numerous tools that have been developed for use in these evaluations, the interested reader is referred to several additional resources for more information (e.g., Conroy & Murrie, 2007; Guy, Douglas, & Hart, 2015; Mills, Kroner, & Morgan, 2007; Otto & Douglas, 2010).

Risk factors can also be categorized into two broad categories: static and dynamic. Static risk factors are those factors that are generally unchangeable – such as offense history, family background, gender – and that are associated with an elevated level of risk. Many actuarial risk assessment instruments take into account multiple static risk factors in making a determination about level of risk. Dynamic risk factors are those factors that are changeable – such as mental health functioning, substance use, and treatment compliance – and therefore offer the opportunity for intervention. SPJ risk assessment instruments take into account these changeable factors in determining level of risk and management of risk. Protective factors are those that are associated with a reduction in one's level of risk and include social support, insight, and strong relationships with non-deviant peers. Risk management often relies on strategies to increase protective factors and decrease risk factors.

Similar to the aforementioned criminal forensic assessments, the referral question and applicable legal standards determine the trajectory of a risk assessment. It is important that the evaluator clarify the referral question to determine what type of risk is being evaluated, which will guide the collection of relevant data – including the administration or scoring of relevant risk assessment tools – and the communication of findings to the legal decision maker. An extensive legal history is beyond the scope of this chapter but we refer interested readers to Guy and colleagues (2015) and Heilbrun (2009).

Civil Forensic Assessments

Civil forensic assessments primarily involve issues in civil litigation and lawsuits that center on "damages" or monetary awards. Civil litigation rules vary by jurisdiction and competent civil forensic evaluators must be well versed in the laws and civil statutes of the jurisdictions in which they practice. As in criminal forensic assessments, forensic psychologists may be called on to conduct several different types of assessments in the civil context, with the focus of each typically being the nature and degree of psychological harm and distress that a plaintiff is experiencing and the resulting limitations on that plaintiff's functioning. We briefly describe two of the more common forensic evaluations conducted in the civil forensic context.

Personal injury. In the event of physical and/or emotional damage of one individual by another, whether it be intentional or the result of negligence, the individual seeking redress files a tort claim for a civil wrong. Civil forensic assessments are conducted to determine whether and to what extent the individual bringing the tort action (plaintiff) was harmed by the alleged conduct of the defendant (Foote & Lareau, 2013). It is essential to determine whether the plaintiff was actually harmed, whether the defendant caused the plaintiff's harm, in what capacity has the plaintiff been impaired since the onset of the harm, and what intervention/treatment would be needed for the plaintiff to return to their prior level of functioning (Wygant & Lareau 2015). Personal injury and tort damage claims involve a comprehensive assessment that must consider the plaintiff's life both prior to and after the alleged conduct of the defendant. Psychological testing can be useful in assessing the nature and degree of harm and distress as well as for gauging the credibility of the claims of symptoms endorsed by the plaintiff. Thus, both psychological assessment instruments and forensically relevant instruments are typically used in personal injury evaluations, whereas FAIs (developed specifically for the purpose of evaluating a specific legal issue) have not been developed for this purpose given the general focus on an individual's functioning and well-being. The interested reader is referred to Kane and Dvoskin (2011) for a detailed discussion of personal injury evaluations.

Disability and worker's compensation cases. Private disability insurance, social security disability, and worker's compensation each compensate individuals who are unable to work or to continue their usual employment as a result of physical and/or emotional injuries. In most disability cases, forensic assessments are conducted to determine the presence of a disability, the degree of impairment, and the length of time that the disability may prevent an individual from performing their job duties. In contrast to personal injury evaluations, the extent of an individual's disability is more relevant than the source of the disability in disability and worker's compensation evaluations (Wygant & Lareau, 2015) and decisions regarding entitlement to disability benefits are based on relevant legal policy, statutes, regulations, and case law (see Piechowski, 2011 for a review). Forensic mental health professionals evaluate the clinical aspects of a claimant's condition and provide relevant psychological information to assist the adjudicator in rendering a decision about disability benefits. Disability and worker's compensation evaluations are complex, and evaluators must incorporate multiple pieces of data from multiple information sources to develop a complete and objective understanding of the individual's functioning and capacity. Forensic evaluators typically utilize data from psychological and neuropsychological tests in these assessments; but there is no standardized approach for evaluating disability claims and evaluators are tasked with selecting appropriate psychological tests and forensically relevant instruments to evaluate both the nature and the extent of the disability as well as the validity of the disability claim. The interested reader is referred to Piechowski (2011) for a detailed discussion of workplace disability evaluation.

Family/Juvenile Court Assessments

Forensic assessments are also required with respect to issues that arise in family and juvenile courts. Many of the referral questions discussed earlier with respect to criminal court proceedings (e.g., competency to stand trial, risk assessments) can also be applicable to juveniles, either within the juvenile justice system or for those juveniles who are transferred/waived from the juvenile justice system to the criminal court system. However, there are also forensic evaluations that specifically pertain to family court issues, such as evaluations for child custody and those for the termination of parental rights. A detailed discussion of family and juvenile court evaluations is beyond the scope of this chapter but the interested reader is referred to Grisso (2013) and Salekin (2015) for more information on juvenile forensic assessment and to Stahl (2011) and Drozd, Saini, and Olesen (2016) for more information on family court evaluations.

Parenting capacity. One type of evaluation conducted in the area of family law is the evaluation of parenting capacity. Here the central question is related to the welfare of the child with a focus on family preservation (Choate, 2009). Parenting capacity evaluations may be requested if there is suspected abuse or neglect of a child. The evaluation considers the current needs of the child, the barriers to providing care for the parents, the strengths of the parents, and the effects of terminating parental rights on the child (Budd, Clark, & Connell, 2011). In these evaluations, the burden is on the State to show "clear and convincing" evidence in favor of terminating parental rights, a higher standard than in other evaluations or proceedings, because the legal precedent dictates that the primary objective is to keep the children in the care of the parents (*Santosky v. Kramer*, 1982). Evaluations in this area follow the Best Interests of the Child standard adopted in all US jurisdictions. The evaluator will consider factors such as the age and health of the child, the age, health, and lifestyle related factors for the parents, the emotional bond between the child and the parents, the parents' abilities to provide for the basic needs of the child including medical care, and the effect termination would have on the child. In addition, the child's preference may also be taken into consideration (Budd, Clark, & Connell, 2011). As with most evaluations concerning children, an evaluator will typically interview both parents and the child(ren) in order to best assess the totality of the relationship among the family members. Evaluators may also conduct collateral interviews with service providers, coaches, teachers, and other adults with knowledge of the family dynamic. For more comprehensive information about the process of conducting a parenting capacity evaluation, see Budd, Clark, and Connell (2011).

Child custody. Child custody evaluations are a common forensic assessment conducted within the context of family court. The focus of these evaluations is on understanding the psychological best interests of the child and the suitability of the parents to act as caregivers (Fuhrmann & Zibbell, 2012). These evaluations are often requested after an amicable agreement between parents could not be reached and, as such, are often contentious and difficult evaluations to perform. It is not uncommon for all parties involved in the evaluation to be suspicious of the forensic evaluator and wary of the assessment process (Ackerman & Gould, 2015). This affects not only the approach taken for the evaluation but also the use and interpretation of psychological testing.

Each state has its own statutes to guide child custody determinations. However, the foundational principle for all of these statutes is that the needs of the child are paramount to the needs of the parents and the court is to act in the best interest of the child (Ackerman & Gould, 2015), a principle affirmed by the US Supreme Court in both *Ford v. Ford* (1962) and *Palmore v. Sidoti* (1984). Similar to other Court decisions there is ambiguity in the language of the ruling and consequential debate about what the *best interest of the child* means. However, within the field of forensic psychology it is generally accepted that the psychological needs of the child outweigh other considerations including economic, educational, or medical (Emery, Otto, & O'Donahue, 2005). As such, the assessment and resulting recommendations of the evaluator are of particular value to child custody proceedings.

When conducting child custody evaluations, forensic mental health professionals should reference the recent literature regarding the impact of factors pertinent to the case on the child's well-being. The *guidelines for child custody evaluations in family law proceedings* established by the American Psychological Association (APA, 2010) emphasize the importance of using multiple data points to make recommendations regarding custody. In conducting the assessment, mental health professionals may conduct multiple interviews with the child, the parents, and other collateral parties (e.g., coaches, teachers, doctors) as well as obtain third-party records from those sources. Direct observation of the interactions between each parent and child is paramount in understanding the dynamic of these relationships, the attachment the child has with each parent, and for identifying overtly problematic interaction styles. The evaluator may also conduct psychological testing, using established measures of personality and psychopathology for parents (e.g., the Minnesota Multiphasic Personality Inventory-2-Restructured Form [MMPI-2-RF]; Ben-Porath & Tellegen, 2008) and behavioral rating scales for children (e.g., Achenbach Child Behavior Checklist; Achenbach, 2001). The use of embedded scales in personality assessment instruments such as the MMPI-2-RF are especially useful for assessing response styles, including "faking good," which can be helpful as underreporting of symptoms is common in this context. Some specialized measures for child custody evaluations have been developed (e.g., Ackerman-Schoendorf Scales for Parent Evaluation of Custody ASPECT; Ackerman & Schoendorf, 1992; and the Bricklin Perceptual Scales: BPS; Bricklin, 1990), but the available literature on these instruments indicates little empirical support for their use in child custody evaluation (see Otto & Edens, 2003 for a review).

Juvenile waiver/transfer to criminal court. Another domain of assessment involves the decision whether to treat a justice-involved juvenile as an adult for criminal court proceedings. Typically, individuals below the age of eighteen are tried in juvenile or family court settings where the focus is on rehabilitation, not punishment. However, in some cases, a determination is made that the individual should be held to the same standard as adults and sentenced according to the same guidelines (i.e., waived/transferred to criminal court). While the Supreme Court has ruled against the use of the death penalty for juveniles (*Roper v. Simmons,* 2005) and against the sentence of life without the possibility of parole (*Miller v. Alabama,* 2012 & *Graham v. Florida*, 2010), juveniles can be given any other sentence proportionate with an adult sentence. The decision to transfer a juvenile to criminal court is based on principles established in *Kent v. United States* (1966), including the juvenile's risk for future violence or reoffending, developmental maturity, and potential for rehabilitation (see Salekin, 2015 for a detailed discussion).

Many of the considerations for treating juvenile offenders differently than adults arise from the scientific literature examining juvenile decision-making capacities and brain development (Woolard, Vidal, & Fountain, 2015). The Court's decisions in *Roper v. Simmons*, *Miller v. Alabama*, and *Graham v. Florida* were based on scientific evidence that juvenile brains are still developing and are, therefore, different from adult brains and different from the brains they, themselves, will have as adults. Therefore, forensic mental health professionals are called on to conduct assessments related to the principles outlined in *Kent v. United States* in an effort to evaluate for the effectiveness of treatment or rehabilitation of the individual adolescent. The evaluator is tasked with collecting all relevant data, including an interview with the juvenile and any collateral data sources. Assessment instruments, such as the Risk-Sophistication-Treatment Inventory (Salekin, 2004) may be helpful for assessing the *Kent v. United States* criteria. In addition, evaluators may also choose to use instruments to evaluate risk for general violence (e.g., Structured Assessment of Violence Risk in Youth; Borum, Bartel, & Forth, 2006) and psychopathy as it relates to risk for violence (e.g., the Psychopathy Checklist-Youth Version; Forth, Kosson, & Hare, 2003). As with all assessment measures, evaluators are expected to choose instruments that match the referral question and the specific details of the case, including diversity and cultural considerations.

WRITTEN FORENSIC EVALUATION REPORTS

We end this chapter with a brief overview of the written forensic evaluation report. Unlike psychological evaluations that are conducted in a therapeutic context, forensic evaluation reports are targeted at a legal decision maker and serve the specific function of documenting the evaluation methods and procedures, the data considered, and the rationale for the interpretations and opinions reached on the basis of those data. Forensic evaluation reports should be written in a clear, jargon-free manner, with a specific focus on the psycho-legal issue being evaluated. The evaluator should describe the nature and purpose of any testing that was conducted as well as any psychological constructs that were addressed as well as any hypothesis that were tested.

There is an expectation that forensic evaluation reports will document the data that the evaluator considered, describe the assumptions and inferences that the evaluator made on the basis of those data, and delineate the reasoning used by the evaluator in arriving at their opinion regarding the psycho-legal issue being evaluated. The data are to be presented in a logical and organized way and any inferences that are offered should be distinguishable from the data on which they were based, making for a clear and transparent report. The evaluator is required by the *Specialty Guidelines for Forensic Psychology* (APA, 2013) to attribute data to their source as well as to give relevant weight to each source according to its reliability.

In addition, evaluators are required to keep the scope of the evaluation report to the issue being evaluated, without including superfluous information that is not relevant to the issue or that might violate the privacy of the individual being evaluated. It is important that for the evaluator to have specifically defined the referral question and purpose of the evaluation prior to commencing the evaluation. By doing so, the evaluator is able to focus data collection and report writing to include only information pertinent to the specific issue (referral question) being addressed in the evaluation. Evaluators must ensure that all information included in a report will assist the court in understanding the basis for the opinion being presented regarding the specific legal question. Grisso (2003) recommends using a problem-focused approach to report writing, wherein only information that serves as an important basis for the reasoning used by the evaluator is included in the evaluation report.

Including irrelevant information in a report can be potentially biasing and evaluators are tasked with assessing the relevance of the information they review. Evaluators are cautioned against including incriminating information in the evaluation report and should take care to reflect the process, rather than the content, of (potentially) incriminating information offered by the evaluee. Regarding data that are contrary to or inconsistent with the opinion being offered, it is important that the evaluator consider this information by formulating and testing alternate hypotheses that might account for these data. Disconfirming data should be noted and the evaluator should take care to outline the reasons why these data were considered less relevant to the opinion presented. Excluding relevant information from an evaluation report could call the validity of that report's conclusions into question more so than a careful evaluation of the impact of that data on the proffered opinion of the evaluator.

A well-written report will not leave the reader surprised by the final opinion; the reader should be able to follow the connections made between the data considered, the inferences made on the basis of those data, and the opinions reached by the evaluator. Since the evaluation report will serve as the basis for testimony by the evaluator, it is prudent for the evaluator to be clear, direct, and careful to delineate all relevant data, analyses, and opinions while ensuring that incriminating information is kept out of the written report. The interested reader is referred to Otto, DeMier, and Boccaccini (2014) for detailed information on forensic report writing and testimony.

REFERENCES

Achenbach, T. M. (2001). *Child behavior checklist*. Burlington: University of Vermont.

Ackerman, M. J., & Gould, J. W. (2015). Child custody and access. In B. L. Cutler & P. A. Zapf (Eds.), *APA handbook of forensic psychology, Vol. 1: Individual and situational influences in criminal and civil contexts* (pp. 425–469). Washington, DC: American Psychological Association. doi:10.1037/14461-013

Ackerman, M. J., & Schoendorf, K. (1992). *ASPECT Ackerman-Schoendorf Scales for Parent Evaluation of Custody*. Los Angeles: Western Psychological Services.

APA (American Psychological Association). (2010). Guidelines for child custody evaluations in family law proceedings. *American Psychologist*, *65*(9), 863–867. doi:10.1037/a0021250

APA (American Psychological Association). (2013). *Specialty guidelines for forensic psychology*. American Psychologist, *68*, 7–19.

Ben-Porath, Y., & Tellegen, A. (2008). *The Minnesota Multiphasic Personality Inventory – 2 – Restructured Form (MMPI-2-RF) manual for administration and scoring*. Minneapolis, MN: University of Minnesota Press.

Bonnie, R. J., & Grisso, T. (2000). Adjudicative competence and youthful offenders. In T. Grisso & R. G. Schwartz (Eds.), *Youth on trial: A developmental perspective on juvenile justice* (pp. 73–103). Chicago: University of Chicago Press.

Borum, R., Bartel, P., & Forth, A. (2006). *Manual for the Structured Assessment of Violence Risk in Youth (SAVRY), version 1.1*. Tampa, FL: University of South-Florida.

Bricklin, B. (1990). *Bricklin Perceptual Scales manual*. Furlong, PA: Village Publishing.

Budd, K. S., Clark, J., & Connell, M. A. (2011). *Evaluation of parenting capacity in child protection*. New York: Oxford University Press.

Choate, P. W. (2009). Parenting capacity assessments in child protection cases. *The Forensic Examiner, 18*(1), 52–59.

Conroy, M. A., & Murrie, D. C. (2007). *Forensic assessment of violence risk: A guide for risk assessment and risk management*. Hoboken, NJ: Wiley.

DeMatteo, D.,Burl, J., Filone, S., & Heilbrun, K. (2016). Training in forensic assessment and intervention: Implications for principle-based models. In R. Jackson & R. Roesch (Eds.), *Learning forensic assessment: Research and practice* (pp. 3–31). New York: Routledge.

Douglas, K. S., Hart, S. D., Webster, C. D., & Belfrage, H. (2013). *HCR-20^{V3}: Assessing risk for violence – User guide*. Burnaby, BC: Mental Health, Law, and Policy Institute, Simon Fraser University.

Drozd, L., Saini, M., & Olesen, N. (2016). *Parenting plan evaluations: Applied research for the family court* (2nd ed.). New York: Oxford University Press.

Emery, R. E., Otto, R. K., & O'Donahue, W. T. (2005). A critical assessment of child custody evaluations: Limited science and a flawed system. *Psychological Science in the Public Interest, 6* (1), 1–29. doi:10.1111/ j.1529–1006.2005.00020.x

Foote, W. E., & Lareau, C. R. (2013). Psychological evaluation of emotional damages in tort cases. In R. K. Otto, I. B. Weiner, R. K. Otto, & I. B. Weiner (Eds.), *Handbook of psychology: Forensic psychology* (pp. 172–200). Hoboken, NJ: John Wiley & Sons.

Forth, A. E., Kosson, D. S., & Hare, R. (2003). *The Hare Psychopathy Checklist: Youth version*. New York: Multi-Health Systems.

Fuhrmann, G. S. W., & Zibbell, R. A. (2012). *Evaluation for child custody*. New York: Oxford University Press.

Golding, S. L. (1993). *Interdisciplinary Fitness Interview-Revised: Training manual*. Salt Lake City: University of Utah.

Grisso, T. (2003). *Evaluating competencies: Forensic assessments and instruments* (2nd ed.). New York: Kluwer/Plenum.

Grisso, T. (2013). *Forensic evaluation of juveniles*. Sarasota, FL, US: Professional Resource Press.

Goldstein, A., & Goldstein, N. E. S. (2010). *Evaluating capacity to waive Miranda rights*. New York: Oxford.

Guy, L. S., Douglas, K. S., & Hart, S. D. (2015). Risk assessment and communication. In B. L. Cutler & P. A. Zapf (Eds.), *APA handbook of forensic psychology*, Vol. *1* (pp. 35–86). Washington, DC: American Psychological Association. doi:10.1037/14461-003.

Hart, S. D., Kropp, P. R., Laws, D. R., Klaver, J., Logan, C., & Watt, K. A. (2003). *The Risk for Sexual Violence Protocol (RSVP): Structured professional guidelines for assessing risk of sexual violence*. Burnaby, BC: Mental Health Law and Policy Institute, Simon Fraser University.

Heilbrun, K. (2001). *Principles of forensic mental health assessment*. New York: Kluwer Academic/Plenum.

Heilbrun, K. (2009). *Evaluation for risk of violence in adults*. New York: Oxford University Press. doi:10.1093/med:psych/ 9780195369816.001.0001

Heilbrun, K., DeMatteo, D., & Marczyk, J. (2004). Pragmatic psychology, forensic mental health assessment, and the case of Thomas Johnson: Applying principles to promote quality. *Psychology, Public Policy, and Law, 10*, 31–70.

Heilbrun, K., DeMatteo, D., Marczyk, J., & Goldstein, A. M. (2008). Standards and practice and care in forensic mental health assessment: Legal, professional, and principles-based consideration. *Psychology, Public Policy, and Law, 14*, 1–26.

Heilbrun, K., Grisso, T., & Goldstein, A. (2009). *Foundations of forensic mental health assessment*. New York: Oxford University Press.

Heilbrun, K., & LaDuke, C. (2015). Foundational aspects of forensic mental health assessment. In B. L. Cutler & P. A. Zapf (Eds.), *APA handbook of forensic psychology* (*1*), 3–18. Washington, DC: American Psychological Association. doi:10.1037/14461-001

Heilbrun, K., Rogers, R., & Otto, R. K. (2002). Forensic assessment: Current status and future directions. In J. R. P. Ogloff (Ed.), *Taking psychology and law into the 21st century*. New York: Kluwer/Plenum.

Helmus, L., Thornton, D., Hanson, R. K., & Babchishin, K. M. (2012). Improving the predictive accuracy of Static-99 and Static-2002 with older sex offenders: Revised age weights. *Sexual Abuse: A Journal of Research and Treatment, 24*, 64–101. doi:10.1177/1079063211409951.

Kane, A. W., & Dvoskin, J. A. (2011). *Evaluation for personal injury claims*. New York: Oxford University Press.

Kropp, P. R., Belfrage, H., & Hart, S. D. (2013). *Assessment of risk for honor-based violence (PATRIARCH): User manual*. Vancouver: ProActive ReSolutions.

Kropp, P. R., & Hart, S. D. (2015). *SARA-V3: User manual for Version 3 of the Spousal Assault Risk Assessment guide*. Vancouver: ProActive ReSolutions.

Kropp, P. R., Hart, S. D., & Belfrage, H. (2005). Structuring judgments about spousal violence risk and lethality: A decision support tool for criminal justice professionals. *JustResearch, 13*, 22–27.

Kropp, P. R., Hart, S. D., & Lyon. D. R. (2008). *The Stalking Assessment and Management guidelines (SAM): User manual*. Vancouver: ProActive ReSolutions.

Kruh, I., & Grisso, T. (2009). *Evaluation of juveniles' competence to stand trial*. New York: Oxford University Press.

Lally, S. J. (2003). What tests are acceptable for use in forensic evaluations? A survey of experts. *Professional Psychology: Research and Practice, 34*, 491–498.

Melton, G. B., Petrila, J., Poythress, N. G., & Slobogin, C. (2007). *Psychological evaluations for the courts: A handbook for mental health professionals and lawyers* (3rd ed.). New York: Guilford Press.

Mills, J. F., Kroner, D. G., & Morgan, R. D. (2007). *Clinician's guide to violence risk assessment*. New York: Guilford.

Otto, R. K., DeMier, R. L., & Boccaccini, M. T. (2014). *Forensic reports and testimony: A guide to effective communication for psychologists and psychiatrists*. Hoboken, NJ: Wiley.

Otto, R. K., & Douglas, K. D. (2010). *Handbook of violence risk assessment*. New York: Routledge.

Otto, R., & Edens, J. (2003). Parenting capacity. In T. Grisso (Ed.), *Evaluating competencies: Forensic assessments and instruments* (2nd ed., pp. 229–307). New York: Springer.

Packer, I. K. (2009). *Evaluation of criminal responsibility*. New York: Oxford University Press.

Piechowski, L. D. (2011). *Evaluation of workplace disability*. New York: Oxford University Press.

Poythress, N. G., Nicholson, R., Otto, R. K., Edens, J. F., Bonnie, R. J., Monahan, J., & Hoge, S. K. (1999). *The MacArthur Competence Assessment Tool – Criminal Adjudication (MacCAT-CA): Professional Manual*. Lutz, FL: Psychological Assessment Resources.

Roesch, R., Zapf, P. A., & Eaves, D. (2006). *FIT-R: Fitness Interview Test-Revised. A structured interview for assessing competency to stand trial*. Sarasota, FL: Professional Resource Press/Professional Resource Exchange.

Rice, M. E., Harris, G. T., & Lang, C. (2013). Validation of and revision to the VRAG and SORAG: The violence risk appraisal guide-revised (VRAG-R). *Psychological Assessment, 25*, 951–965. doi:10.1037/a0032878.

Rogers, R. (1984). *Rogers criminal responsibility assessment scales (R-CRAS) and test manual*. Odessa, FL: Psychological Assessment Resources.

Rogers, R., Tillbrook, C. E., & Sewell, K. W. (2004). *Evaluation of Competency to Stand Trial – Revised professional manual*. Lutz, FL: Psychological Assessment Resources.

Salekin, R. T. (2004). *Risk-Sophistication-Treatment Inventory*. Lutz, FL: Psychological Assessment Resources.

Salekin, R. T. (2015). *Forensic evaluation and treatment of juveniles: Innovation and best practice*. Washington, DC: American Psychological Association. doi:10.1037/14595 000

Singh, J. P., Grann, M., & Fazel, S. (2011). A comparative study of violence risk assessment tools: A systematic review and metaregression analysis of 68 studies involving 25, 980 participants. *Clinical Psychology Review, 31*, 499–513. doi:10.1016/j.cpr.2010.11.009

Slobogin, C., Melton, G. B., & Showalter, C. R. (1984). The feasibility of a brief evaluation of mental state at the time of offense. *Law and Human Behavior, 8*, 305–321. doi:10.1007/BF01044698

Stahl, P. M. (2011). *Conducting child custody evaluations: From basic to complex issues*. Thousand Oaks, CA: Sage.

Viljoen, J. L., Nicholls, T. L., Cruise, K. R., Desmarais, S. L., & Webster, C. D. (2014). *Short-Term Assessment of Risk and Treatability: Adolescent Version (START:AV) – User guide*. Burnaby, BC: Mental Health, Law, and Policy Institute.

Webster, C. D., Douglas, K., Eaves, D., & Hart, S. (1997). *HCR-20: Assessing risk for violence: Version 2*. Burnaby, BC: Simon Fraser University.

White, S. G., & Meloy, J. R. (2010). *WAVR-21: A structured professional guide for the Workplace Assessment of Violence Risk* (2nd ed.). San Diego, CA: Specialized Training Services.

Wygant, D. B., & Lareau, C. R. (2015). Civil and criminal forensic psychological assessment: Similarities and unique challenges. *Psychological injury and law, 8*, 11–26. doi:10.1007/s12207-015-9220-8

Woolard, J. L., Vidal, S., & Fountain, E. (2015). Juvenile offenders. In B. L. Cutler & P. A. Zapf (Eds.), *APA handbook of forensic psychology, Vol. 2: Criminal investigation, adjudication, and sentencing outcomes* (pp. 33–58). Washington, DC: American Psychological Association. doi:10.1037/14462-002

Worling, J. R., & Curwen, T. (2001). *Estimate of Risk of Adolescent Sexual Offense Recidivism (ERASOR): Version 2.0*. Toronto: SAFE-T Program, Thistletown Regional Centre, Ontario Ministry of Community and Social Services.

Zapf, P. A., & Roesch, R. (2009). *Evaluation of competence to stand trial*. New York: Oxford University Press.

34 Assessment Issues within Neuropsychological Settings

F. TAYLOR AGATE AND MAURICIO A. GARCIA-BARRERA

The practice of neuropsychological assessment is supported by substantial specialized training, due not only to the amount of cumulative knowledge neuropsychologists must acquire but also to the number of issues that we encounter in practice and research in neuropsychological settings. This chapter focuses on a handful of assessment issues that are quite relevant to us. To start, we will discuss the recommended model of training in neuropsychology, embedded within a bio-psycho-social approach to neuropsychological assessment. To give the reader a sense of the current context of neuropsychological assessment, we also describe the most typical work settings, populations, and instruments used in our field. We then discuss some issues and accommodations clinicians frequently consider in their assessment process, as well as some common challenges to our clinical and research practice, such as the assessment of practice effects, effort, assessment of individuals from diverse cultural and linguistic backgrounds, and general validity issues that we need to consider when conducting assessments in neuropsychological settings. Finally, we end this chapter with a brief discussion of the future of neuropsychological assessment and how technology plays a relevant role in shaping the activities and settings of our practice.

BECOMING A CLINICAL NEUROPSYCHOLOGIST IN NORTH AMERICA

Clinical neuropsychology is a growing and ever-changing field. During the past decades, clinicians and researchers have witnessed great advancement in test development, assessment techniques, integration of online services into test administration, and refinement of psychometric approaches to evaluate reliability and validity of the test scores produced by a range of instruments. Given such progress, the scientist-practitioner approach to our specialized training, adopted since the Houston Conference (Hannay et al., 1998), remains the cornerstone of our field. The guidelines provided by the members of the Houston Conference recommend that, to perform assessment in neuropsychological settings, psychologists should acquire broad knowledge in generic and specialized areas during their graduate training, including *general psychology* topics (statistics and methodology; learning, cognition, and perception; social psychology and personality; biological basis of behavior; life span development; history; and cultural and individual differences and diversity), *general clinical psychology* topics (psychopathology; psychometric theory and norming issues; interview and assessment techniques; intervention techniques; and professional ethics), *foundations for the study of brain-behavior relationships* (functional neuroanatomy, neurological, and related disorders including their etiology, pathology, course and treatment; non-neurologic conditions affecting central nervous system functioning; neuroimaging and other neurodiagnostic techniques; neurochemistry of behavior and psychopharmacology; and neuropsychology of behavior), and *foundations for the practice of clinical neuropsychology* (specialized neuropsychological assessment techniques; specialized neuropsychological intervention techniques; research design and analysis in neuropsychology; professional issues and ethics in neuropsychology; and practical implications of neuropsychological conditions).

The Houston Conference defined a clinical neuropsychologist as:

> A professional psychologist trained in the science of brain-behavior relationships. The clinical neuropsychologist specializes in the application of assessment and intervention principles based on the scientific study of human behavior across the lifespan as it relates to normal and abnormal functioning of the central nervous system. (Hannay et al., 1998, p. 161)

Most American and Canadian Psychological Association (APA, CPA) accredited graduate training programs include the curriculum required to acquire these foundations, in addition to program-approved short-term practicum rotations and a one-year full-time internship devoted in large part to clinical neuropsychology-based activities (Hebben & Milberg, 2002). This combination of specialized coursework and applied experience offers opportunities for trainees to develop a range of skills, including assessment, treatment and intervention techniques, consultation,

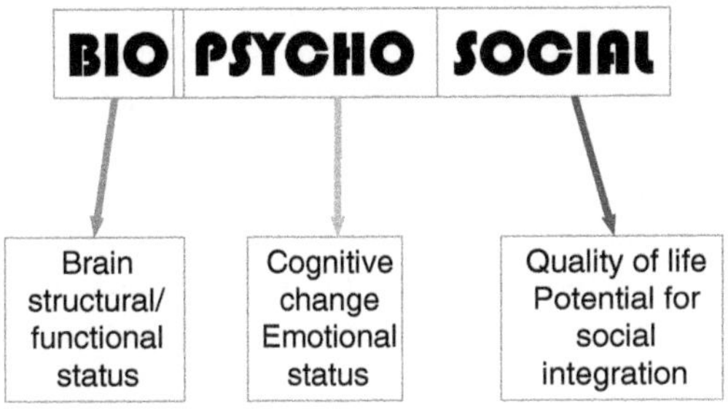

Figure 34.1 The Bio-Psycho-Social Framework in neuropsychology

neuropsychological research, teaching, and supervision. Altogether, the range of topics covered in these curricular and didactic experiences equips neuropsychologists with the basic knowledge to approach clinical practice under a bio-psycho-social framework (Figure 34.1), that is, understanding the brain structural/functional status of the patient (bio), having the ability to identify cognitive change and evaluate emotional status (psycho), and considering issues affecting the patient's quality of life and social functioning, as well as evaluating the potential for social reintegration (social).

PURPOSES OF THE ASSESSMENT IN NEUROPSYCHOLOGY

Lezak and colleagues (2012) propose six main purposes of neuropsychological assessment: (1) It can serve as a *diagnostic tool*, helping in the differentiation between neurological conditions, or between neurological and psychiatric presentations, as well as aiding diagnosis of brain damage that is not easily identifiable by neuroimaging techniques (e.g., neurotoxicity-related damage), neurodevelopmental disorder cases, or in situations where an early detection or prediction of degenerative disorders may be indicated. In a recent survey of common neuropsychological tools and practice activities conducted by Rabin, Paolillo, and Barr (2016), determination of diagnosis emerged as the most common referral question. (2) Beyond diagnosis, neuropsychologists are often asked "What is the nature and extent of cognitive impairment?"; "What are the practical consequences of cognitive impairment?"; and "How are an individual's mood and behavior affected by brain dysfunction?" (Evans, 2010). Neuropsychological assessment can be of great utility in describing the current areas of cognitive, behavioral, and emotional strengths and weaknesses needed to make informed decisions about a given patient's capacity for self-care, ability to participate in daily living activities (including work and leisure), as well as planning of treatment and accommodations. In fact, (3) rehabilitation and treatment planning has become the second most common reason for referrals to neuropsychological evaluations (Rabin et al., 2016), and the field is shifting from an early focus on assessment activities to directing much effort in the development of evidence-based interventions (Lezak et al., 2012). Assessment to inform rehabilitation emphasizes a patient's employability, how well they respond to the intervention, and the identification of any potential environmental support mechanisms to help them recover everyday function and independence (Groth-Marnat, 2000). Indeed, the goal of rehabilitation is to enhance the patient's independence by helping them to cope with, or compensate for, their deficits (Evans, 2010). (4) After a treatment has been implemented (e.g., rehabilitation, neurosurgical procedures, chemotherapy, pharmacological regimen), follow-up neuropsychological assessment is quite useful in determining its efficacy, answering questions such as how might cognitive functioning be affected by rehabilitation, neurosurgery, medication, and so on (Evans, 2010). Even in the absence of an intervention, follow-up assessment can be helpful in identifying indicators of recovery, fluctuation, and rate of change over time. (5) At the root of the definition of neuropsychology, we aim to understand brain and behavior relationships; data provided by systematic neuropsychological assessment have been the primary source of our knowledge of such relationships, aiding the interpretation of neuroimaging research. In addition, research on neuropsychological assessment has been pivotal for psychometric and technological developments such as computer-assisted assessment, narrow-band specialized assessment batteries, and detection of malingering and other forms of noncredible reporting. With increased technological advancement for cognitive and behavioral testing, repeated testing has become more accessible and effective in helping our understanding of disease trajectory over time. Further, determination of the ecological validity of neuropsychological assessment outcomes has been a driving force for research in our field; and, more consistently, research has shown the robust predictive accuracy of our neuropsychological data. Finally, (6) neuropsychological assessment has become a regular contributor to court decisions and legal proceedings, particularly in cases where there is a need to clarify the cognitive status of the claimant or defendant when there is a suspicion of brain damage involvement. Loss of earnings, cost of care, reduced capacity to work, and overall stress due to cognitive and behavioral changes after brain damage are often in the list of issues considered in civil cases, particularly when assessing for capacity and when calculating compensation by determining liability and quantum (amount) of damages (McKinlay, McGowan, & Russell, 2010). Rabin and colleagues (2016) noted that forensic assessment is among the top ten most common reasons for referrals to clinical neuropsychologists in North America.

NEUROPSYCHOLOGICAL WORK SETTINGS AND POPULATIONS ASSESSED

Clinical neuropsychologists work in a variety of settings, including both inpatient and outpatient. Based on the recent survey data collected by Rabin and colleagues (2016), the most common work setting for psychologists practicing neuropsychology was a private or group practice, with 59.8 percent reporting working in either. The next most common setting was a medical hospital (32.2 percent), followed by a rehabilitation facility (14.7 percent), Veterans Affairs (VA) hospital (10 percent), psychiatric hospital (6.5 percent), community mental health center (2.9 percent), college/university counseling center (2.2 percent), state prison/correctional facility (2.2 percent), and business/industry (0.8 percent); 11.6 percent of neuropsychologists reported working in a different setting, such as a school or outpatient clinic. This distribution of work settings generally did not differ from ten years prior; but, notably, the percentage who worked in a VA hospital did double over this time span compared to the 5 percent in 2001 (Rabin, Barr, & Burton, 2005).

Neuropsychologists also assess a wide range of patient populations. The most commonly assessed population in 2011 was head injury, as the majority of clinicians (54.8 percent) saw these patients. Dementia was the second most common neuropsychology population (48.6 percent), followed by attention-deficit/hyperactivity disorder (ADHD; 37.5 percent), learning disabilities (24.9 percent), mood disorders (18.7 percent), stroke/vascular diseases (17.7 percent), and seizure disorders (13.5 percent). This distribution was generally similar to that in 2001 (Rabin et al., 2016).

Patient populations, along with several aspects of assessment, can vary greatly among neuropsychology settings. The literature, particularly recent, seems limited in discussing the unique aspects of specific settings. The following is a very brief discussion of issues and characteristics within a range of settings, including private practice, hospitals/university-affiliated medical centers, rehabilitation centers, forensic settings, and psychiatric settings.

Private Practice

Despite variation between cohorts, types of surveyed membership, and study authorships, practicing in private or group practice seems to be a common setting for neuropsychologists (Sweet, Moberg, & Suchy, 2000; Sweet et al., 2015; Rabin et al., 2016). Results demonstrate that about half of the neuropsychologists completing the surveys have affiliation to a private practice; in some cases, they may work on a combination of private and institutional practice. In an earlier survey, the majority (78 percent) of private practice neuropsychologists reported devoting at least 80 percent of their time to full-time clinical services, including a larger portion of their time in the provision of treatment than their peers with institutional affiliations (Sweet et al., 2000). The patient populations examined in private practice settings can vary. However, the most common referral sources are neurologists, followed by attorneys, primary care physicians, pediatricians, and self-referrals (Sweet et al., 2015). As indicated by the prevalence of referring attorneys, it is common for neuropsychologists in private settings to see patients who require forensic assessment, which will be discussed in more detail in the "Forensic Assessment" section. While it is more common to work individually in a private setting than in other settings, it is typical to work with other neuropsychologists, psychologists, or professionals outside of psychology, such as physicians. In addition to carrying out neuropsychological assessment work, clinicians in private settings have administrative responsibilities that are inherent in conducting a business. Interestingly, recent data have shown that, despite a growing trend of having female neuropsychologists in private practice, women are more likely to be affiliated with an institution than to work in an independent setting (Sweet et al., 2018).

Hospitals and University-Affiliated Centers

In hospital settings and university-affiliated medical centers, there tends to be a greater diversity of patient populations whom neuropsychologists assess. Most referrals come internally (within the institution) or externally (from the community). Referrals are requested by physicians from a multitude of fields, with neurology being the most common, followed by primary care medicine, physiatry, psychiatry, and pediatrics (Sweet et al., 2015). As in group private settings, neuropsychologists in hospitals commonly work in teams with other neuropsychologists. However, they are likely to have additional personnel, such as technicians/psychometrists, practicum students, students on internship, and postdoctoral fellows (Torres & Pliskin, 2003). In this way, neuropsychologists working in these settings tend to be more involved in training. Additionally, there may be more opportunities for involvement in research.

In addition to working with others within the neuropsychology sector, clinicians in these public settings are often part of a multidisciplinary integrated care team. Such a team, which is comprised of physicians and potentially other psychologists, usually aims to treat a particular patient population, such as individuals with epilepsy who are considering surgery (Torres & Pliskin, 2003). Roles of neuropsychologists may vary from team to team. In some circumstances, their role might be comprehensive and diagnostic; in some settings, they may carry administrative roles such as directing the team. Some neuropsychologists may have minor involvement, contributing with roles such as consultation and program evaluation. According to a 2014 survey of neuropsychologists, 64 percent reported being a part of at least one such integrated care unit (Kubu et al., 2016). Out of these neuropsychologists, 72 percent endorsed working in a neurology/neurosurgery clinic, which was the most common integrated care setting. To maximize the effectiveness of neuropsychologists in these teams, Kubu and colleagues (2016) recommend that neuropsychologists strongly advocate for their role, collaborate with other team members by adjusting their work to enhance efficiency (i.e., shortening protocols and reports), and communicate the principles of the bio-psycho-social model to other team members in order to ultimately improve patient satisfaction, compliance, and health outcomes.

Neuropsychologists working in hospitals or university-affiliated centers usually carry out a blend of outpatient and inpatient assessments, which can differ from one another. Compared to outpatient assessments, inpatient assessments typically address a more specific referral question that requires less comprehensive examination and more qualitative bedside techniques (e.g., neurobehavioral examinations), as standardized measures are often less practical or appropriate. Moreover, inpatient assessment requires more flexibility, due to the priority of other medical services. Lastly, there is generally less turnaround time for reports, such that verbal feedback is usually given the same day, and written reports are finalized within one or two days. Thus, efficient and synthetic report writing is made a priority, which minimizes jargon and maximizes readability (Baum et al., 2018). In a survey by Sweet and colleagues (2015), clinical neuropsychologists reported spending generally less time on inpatient referrals than they did on outpatient referrals (for example, they reported spending less than half the time to determine diagnosis).

Rehabilitation

In rehabilitation settings, neuropsychologists predominantly assess traumatic brain injury (TBI) populations. In contrast to those in other settings, referral questions here usually do not ask for a diagnosis, because it has typically already been determined prior to rehabilitation (Stringer & Nadolne, 2000). Rather, assessment calls for an overall focus on independent daily functioning, as measured by instrumental activities of daily living (IADLs) and the way in which the injury has impacted these through cognitive and behavioral impairments. General steps of this type of neuropsychological assessment include an initial determination of premorbid ability in order to establish goals of interventions, followed by an impairments and strengths profile. This neuropsychological profile data help a rehabilitation team recommend a therapy plan and accommodations. Neuropsychologists in rehabilitation settings are also typically involved in carrying out recommended cognitive treatment plans that help patients regain cognitive abilities or compensate for them with certain strategies. As in medical institutions, neuropsychologists typically work as part of a multidisciplinary team that consists of other professionals, such as speech-language pathologists and occupational therapists (Ricker, 2003).

Forensic Assessment

In forensic assessment, a field of work that continues to be dominated by males (Sweet et al., 2018), neuropsychologists predominantly see individuals who have experienced a TBI, particularly in the context of a motor vehicle accident (Stringer & Nadolne, 2000), as well as those exposed to neurotoxins (Sweet, Ecklund-Johnson, & Malina, 2008). The majority of referrals come from attorneys working in personal injury, criminal, or competency hearings. In civil cases, referring lawyers are most interested in the likelihood that the injury in question, as opposed to other factors, has caused or contributed to the presenting problems. Therefore, neuropsychologists in these settings consider the nature and extent of neuropsychological impairment, along with the proposed causality and contributions of the injury to such impairment. Moreover, neuropsychologists also consider long-term trajectories of impairments and their impact on functional behavior, as well as any further necessary interventions (McKinlay et al., 2010). In criminal cases, especially those involving capital murder, neuropsychological assessment is used to help determine culpability, by way of insanity and/or diminished capacity/competency to stand trial – in the United States, this determination often means the difference between the death penalty and a life sentence (Stringer & Nadolne, 2000). For competency hearings, neuropsychologists are asked to determine patient capacity (cognitive, behavioral, and emotional), such as their ability to make medical-related decisions, consent to treatment (informed consent), refuse medications, drive, and manage finances (Sweet et al., 2008).

In addition to working in civil and criminal cases, neuropsychologists may be asked by third parties, such as insurance companies, to provide independent medical evaluations (IMEs). In an IME, the neuropsychologist gives their professional, objective opinion on the diagnosis, status, and/or prognosis of a patient. Here, the neuropsychologist's goal is to provide an objective assessment of relevant contributors to a claimant's functioning. Their report goes directly to the third party, who acts as the primary client, with the claimant potentially never seeing it. Owing to this dynamic, potential ethical conflicts may arise surrounding privacy and confidentiality. Neuropsychologists involved in these situations tend to be meticulous about their assessment protocols, following appropriate ethical guidelines, such as informing the claimant up front (i.e., during the consent process) about limitations to privacy and confidentiality.

Psychiatric Settings

In psychiatric settings, neuropsychologists are predominantly called on by psychiatrists to assess individuals who present with mood, or otherwise psychiatric, disorders/symptoms. In these cases, the primary role of the neuropsychologist is to disentangle psychiatric versus neurologic etiologies of abnormal behavior (Stringer & Nadolne, 2000). In most cases, where both etiologies are at play, neuropsychologists help determine their respective contributions to the presentation.

Table 34.1 Most commonly administered neuropsychological instruments

Rank 2001	2011	Instrument	Domain(s) Assessed	Percentage of Clinicians Who Use It 2001	2011
1	1	WAIS-IV or prior version	Intelligence	63.1	64.9
2	2	WMS-IV of prior version	Memory	42.7	27.4
3	3	Trail Making Test	Executive Functions	17.6	26.4
4	4	CVLT-II	Memory	17.3	21.5
5	5	WISC-IV or prior version	Intelligence	15.9	20.5
	6	D-KEFS*	Executive Functions		10.1
23	7	RBANS	Memory	2.1	9.9
8	8	RCFT	Memory, Visuospatial perception	10.4	7.3
11	8	NEPSY-II or prior version	Overall neurocognitive functioning	4.4	7.3
6	10	HRNB/HRB	Overall neurocognitive functioning	15.5	5.3

*D-KEFS was not developed until 2001 Adapted from Rabin et al. (2016)WAIS-IV = Wechsler Adult Intelligence Scale – Fourth Edition; WMS-IV = Wechsler Memory Scale – Fourth Edition; CVLT-II = California Verbal Learning Test – Second Edition; WISC-IV = Wechsler Intelligence Scale for Children – Fourth Edition; D-KEFS = Delis-Kaplan Executive Function System; RBANS = Repeatable Battery for the Assessment of Neuropsychological Status; RCFT = Rey-Osterrieth Complex Figure Test; HRNB/HRB = Halstead-Reitan Neuropsychological Test Battery/Halstead-Reitan Test Battery

Veterans Affairs Settings

In VA settings, neuropsychologists see a variety of veterans who are experiencing some neurological or psychological difficulty. With primary care physicians being the most common referral source, referrals questions typically involve distinction between dementia and depression, identification of secondary deficits to a known disorder (e.g., head trauma), differential diagnosis (e.g., psychiatric versus neurological process), and opinions concerning the prognosis of a condition (e.g., dementia) with or without intervention (Delaney, 2003). In addition to clinical assessment work, neuropsychologists in VA settings spend much of their time training student clinicians in clinical or counseling psychology programs. While VAs serve as practicum sites, they are a particularly popular setting for internships in clinical and counseling psychology, being the second most common type of setting (Stedman, 2006).

NEUROPSYCHOLOGICAL INSTRUMENT USAGE

Clinicians have turned to a variety of instruments to measure neuropsychological functioning. These tools assess cognition, as well as psychological areas like personality and mood. Table 34.1 displays the ten most commonly used neuropsychological measures, as reported by neuropsychologists in 2011 (Rabin et al., 2016). The most commonly administered assessment instrument was the Wechsler Adult Intelligence Scale – Fourth Edition (WAIS-IV; Wechsler, 2008) or prior version, used by 64.9 percent of surveyed clinicians. This is followed by the Wechsler Memory Scale – Fourth Edition (WMS-IV; Wechsler, 2009; 27.4 percent), Trail Making Test (Reitan, 1958; 26.4 percent), California Verbal Learning Test – Second Edition (CVLT-II; Delis et al., 2000; 21.5 percent), and Wechsler Intelligence Scale for Children – Fourth Edition (WISC-IV; Wechsler, 2003; 20.5 percent). Of note, these same instruments, or prior versions of them, were also the most utilized in 2001 (Rabin et al., 2005). The most commonly used instrument to assess memory was the WMS-IV or prior version, with almost two-thirds (62.4 percent) of clinicians reported using it. The other most popular tests that measured their respective domain were the Digit Span subtest of the WAIS or WMS (37.1 percent) for attention and working memory; the Wisconsin Card Sorting Test (WCST; Heaton et al., 1993; 63.1 percent) for executive functioning; the WAIS-IV or prior version (92.9 percent) for intelligence and achievement; the Boston Naming Test (Kaplan, Goodglass, & Weintraub, 1983; 61.0 percent) for language; the Rey-Osterrieth Complex Figure Test (RCFT; Meyers & Meyers, 1995; 66.5 percent) for visuospatial/visuoconstruction measurement; the Grooved Pegboard Test (GPT; Kløve, 1963; 70.6 percent) for sensory/motor functioning; the Mini-

Mental State Examination (MMSE; Folstein, Folstein, & McHugh, 1975; 53.5 percent) for overall mental status/global cognition; and the Minnesota Multiphasic Personality Inventory-2 (MMPI-2; Butcher et al., 1989), MMPI-2-RF or prior version (60 percent) for mood and personality (Rabin et al., 2016). See Suhr and Angers, Chapter 15, this volume on neuropsychological assessment for a more detailed discussion of commonly used neuropsychological instruments.

It is important to note that numerous neuropsychological instruments have been developed since 2011 when the survey by Rabin and colleagues (2016) was distributed. For instance, some prominent updated instruments include the Wechsler Abbreviated Scale of Intelligence – Second Edition (WASI-II; Wechsler, 2011), Repeatable Battery for the Assessment of Neuropsychological Status Update (RBANS Update; Randolph, 2012), and the Wechsler Intelligence Scale for Children – Fifth Edition (WISC-V; Wechsler, 2014), Behavior Rating Inventory of Executive Function – Second Edition (BRIEF-2; Gioia et al., 2015), Behavior Assessment System for Children – Third Edition (BASC-3; Reynolds & Kamphaus, 2015), and the Behavioral and Emotional Screening System (BESS-3; Kamphaus & Reynolds, 2015). Test updates typically include changes in subtests, as well as more user-friendly administration procedures and visually appealing test stimuli, while updated questionnaires more accurately reflect modern theories of behavioral constructs such as executive behavior. In addition, recent instruments, particularly questionnaires, often include online formats so that clients can complete them remotely.

SPECIAL CONSIDERATIONS IN NEUROPSYCHOLOGICAL ASSESSMENT

Test Selection

The specific tests that are included in a neuropsychological assessment tend to vary from patient to patient. Some clinicians may endorse the use of a core fixed battery approach for all assessments, making a few adjustments according to the patient's capacities (e.g., limited language ability) or the assessment context (e.g., follow-up assessment), while others may prefer to sort out a specific test battery for each patient, certainly within the constraints of testing time and a clinician's access to test materials. In making an efficacious test selection, neuropsychologists have several variables in mind, including the examination goals and referral questions, the hypotheses generated from the clinical interview, the patient's demographic characteristics (e.g., age, primary language, and fluency in the language used for testing, sensory, and motor deficits), and the psychometric properties of the tests selected (e.g., quality of norms, validity, reliability, sensitivity and specificity, predictive value; Lezak et al., 2012). In addition, clinicians consider the patient's stamina and level of motivation for testing and make accommodations to the test selection to ensure that patients are given an opportunity to demonstrate their strengths as much as their relative difficulties.

Once the tests are selected, clinicians often sequence the tests in an order that allows them to best use peak times of alertness while avoiding the cumulative effects of fatigue (e.g., testing for attention and memory early during the session, grip strength and motor control later on, and ending with self-rating questionnaires). In addition, the test order may be influenced by the characteristics of the task (e.g., several verbal memory tasks in a sequence can elicit interference effects on delayed recall accuracy) or the characteristics of the patient and need for continued rapport (e.g., less threatening tasks early on or allowing a difficult task to be followed by a task that is easier for the patient). Recognizing these considerations, several cognitive test batteries are already designed with built-in time delays and prompters for alternating between sets. One of the issues that remains largely untested is the effectiveness of the most typical sequences of test arrays clinicians use in their assessment practices (Hebben & Milberg, 2002). Finally, test selection can also be influenced by practical issues such as limitations to assessment billing and administration time; particularly, clinicians may avoid expensive tests or delay adoption of newer versions of tests to avoid assuming higher cost. A recent position paper by Bush and colleagues (2018) offers a practical set of recommendations to guide the decision of when to adopt a new version of an old test or a new test altogether.

Use of Psychometrists

The use of psychological technicians, also known as psychometrists, dates back to the early ages of psychology. William Hunt in the late 1930s and Ward C. Halstead and Ralph M. Reitan in the 1940s are credited with regularly employing technicians in their psychological assessment laboratories, and this practice influenced neuropsychological assessment as well (Malek-Ahmadi et al., 2012). To date, it continues to be common practice in the United States and Canada to allow psychometrists to administer and score standardized objective psychological and neuropsychological tests; according to the interpretation of the scope of practice law, technicians are required to hold a bachelor's degree in psychology or a related field, and their practice must be supervised by a licensed psychologist. There are recommended guidelines for the use of psychometrists in testing (AACN, 1999; Division 40 Task Force on Education Accreditation Credentialing, 1991; Puente et al., 2006). Supporting the assessment process with the collaboration of a psychometrist is not only a growing trend but also an established tradition in the field (Malek-Ahmandi et al., 2012).

Factors Affecting Test Performance

Patients undergoing neuropsychological evaluation often present with sensory and motor difficulties, reduction in language capacity (fluency, comprehension), slow processing speed, and attentional deficits that are likely going to interfere with testing outcomes in other areas of cognition, becoming an important consideration when interpreting the assessment results. In addition, several brain disorders tend to create heightened fatigue levels, increasing the need for strenuous mental effort during tasks and, in turn, further affecting processing speed and attention. Secondary effects of medication intake is yet another variable that can affect test performance, behavior, and emotional regulation. There is a large amount of literature concerning this issue, and neuropsychologists are mindful in collecting detailed information about the patient's prescribed and over-the-counter medication intake. Chemotherapy has been associated with cognitive difficulties experienced during treatment and even a few weeks after. Patients may also present with both acute and chronic pain issues, affecting their performance during testing, particularly in regards to their capacity to sustain attention and avoid distractors, and speed of mental and psychomotor processing.

CHALLENGES IN NEUROPSYCHOLOGY ASSESSMENT

Test Validity and Other Psychometric Issues

Clinical neuropsychologists have expressed concerns over certain challenges associated with neuropsychology assessment, including the lack of neuropsychological measures with ecological or predictive validity, a lack of large, demographically representative normative samples, and the heterogeneity of normative data across measures in a flexible battery. These challenges are discussed in detail in Chapter 15.

A particular challenge worth discussing is the fact that culture and language affect performance on neuropsychological testing. Unfortunately, despite the significant growth of our field beyond the United States and Europe (Ponsford, 2017), neuropsychologists from ethnic/racial minorities remain underrepresented in our field (Elbulok-Charcape et al., 2014). Ardila (2007) suggests five cultural aspects that clinicians should have in mind when interpreting test performance: (1) patterns of abilities: "Culture prescribes what should be learned, at what age, and by which gender. Consequently, different cultural environments lead to the development of different patterns of abilities" (p. 27); (2) cultural values: "A culture provides specific models for ways of thinking, acting and feeling" (p. 27), "the rationale and the procedures used in cognitive testing rely on a whole array of cultural values that in no way can be regarded as universal values" (p. 29); (3) familiarity with the elements used in testing (including their cultural relevance) and with the testing environment; (4) language: differences in phonology, lexicon, grammar, pragmatics, and reading systems can affect test performance; and (5) education: "Education plays a double role in test performance: School, on the one hand, provides some contents frequently included in cognitive tests; and on the other hand, trains some learning strategies and develops positive attitudes toward intellectual matters and intellectual testing" (p. 30). Furthermore, Ardila (2007) suggests that members of cultural groups evaluated outside their cultural environments and language (minority members) may present with characteristics such as paranoia, decreased self-esteem, isolation, cultural solitude, frustration, anger, depression, homesickness, and feelings of failure (or success), which can affect their mental health and well-being and likely have an impact on their performance and clinical presentation.

Despite the growing interest in cross-cultural neuropsychology, including several guidelines for the ethical assessment of minority members' diverse ethnic, cultural, and linguistic backgrounds (e.g., Harris, 2002), there continues to be a scarcity of test adaptations, research regarding the development of norms, validity, and reliability of tests in other languages, and examination of local versions and translations of tests to support cross-cultural and minority assessment (Duggan et al., 2018; Elbulok-Charcape et al., 2014; Poreh, 2002; Suzuki, & Ponterotto, 2007). More worrisome are the results of a recent survey by Elbulok-Charcape and colleagues (2014) demonstrating that multicultural training remains unavailable for some neuropsychologists and that some colleagues are conducting assessments in foreign languages despite being unqualified due to limited proficiency. Neuropsychological assessment of Hispanics, especially those located in the United States, is one particular area in which more research is needed (Puente et al., 2015).

Furthermore, given the goals of assessment in neuropsychological settings, clinicians face some specific challenges associated with the validity of performance data, as it can be affected by exaggeration, perseveration, non-credible effort, response bias, and feigned cognitive impairment (or malingering). As it is of utmost relevance, the literature on the topic is vast (e.g., Boone, 2007; Larrabee, 2007; Sweet, 1999), and it is imperative for neuropsychologists to be informed of several sources of information and specific tests that provide data on effort and validity (Bush et al., 2005). Chapters 6 and 15 in this volume discuss these issues in great detail.

Intra-individual Variability and Base Rates

Although a term that originated in research studies, clinicians are increasingly interested in identifying reliable ways of assessing for intra-individual variability (IIV), with analysis of inconsistency and dispersion standing as the two most common and informative methods. Inconsistency of response times or accuracy on trial-to-trial outcome quantifies the variability in within-task performance. Dispersion refers to the within-subject variability within a battery of neuropsychological tests, calculated as the intra-individual standard deviation of standardized performance scores across multiple cognitive tasks (e.g., Hilborn et al., 2009). IIV has become a relevant indicator of "a compromised central nervous system struggling to maintain optimal and consistent performance" (Hill & Rohling, 2011, p. 164), and, as such, neuropsychologists are starting to translate its implementation from the lab to the clinical setting. For instance, cumulative evidence has demonstrated an association between IIV indicators in relation to neuropsychological impairment following TBI (Stuss et al., 1994), in ADHD, autism spectrum disorders, and Tourette's syndrome (Geurts et al., 2008), Mild Cognitive Impairment (MCI) and Alzheimer's disease (Gorus et al., 2008), Parkinson's disease (de Frias et al., 2007), post-concussive syndrome (PCS) following sports concussions (Rabinowitz, & Arnett, 2013), among others. It also holds promise as a potential indicator of malingering (Strauss et al., 2002). Examination of the neural substrates of IIV has shown multiple executive-related neurological structures and functions overlapping with IIV (MacDonald, Nyberg, & Bäckman, 2006). Consistent with these findings, heightened IIV has been identified in cases of frontal lobe lesions (Stuss et al., 2003) and in older adults presenting with executive functioning decline (Halliday et al., 2018). However, meta-analytical evidence has also shown increased IIV in healthy older adults (sixty plus years of age) when compared to younger (twenty to thirty-nine) and middle-aged (forty to fifty-nine) adults (Dykiert et al., 2012). Therefore, increased IIV should not be associated just to instances of brain injury. One way to examine IIV in the clinical context involves analysis of accuracy rates scatter (the distribution of patterns of successes and failures; Lezak et al., 2012). Neuropsychologists can look at performance patterns within a test (intra-test scatter) or between tests (inter-test scatter).

Analysis of performance scatter and IIV is also informed by base rates: the probability of obtaining a low score when multiple tests are administered and interpreted based on the number of individuals within the normative sample, with one or more low scores when commonly used clinical cutoffs are applied (Karr et al., 2016, 2017). Low scores are actually common among healthy individuals completing any battery of tests and vary as a function of the intelligence and demographic characteristics of participants and clients.

Estimation of Premorbid Cognitive Abilities

The estimation of premorbid cognitive abilities is an area of great contention in neuropsychological assessment. As discussed in the previous section, when a battery of tests is administered, there is evidence of large IIV across tests performance, making it difficult to estimate the level of cognitive functioning prior to a brain insult based on only one measure (e.g., word reading or a vocabulary test). Yet, and unfortunately, this is the most common method used due to its parsimony and in the absence of available records or prior (e.g., baseline) assessments. This method relies on the finding that subtests of crystallized intelligence such as Vocabulary from the Wechsler family of tests or word reading tests such as the National Adult Reading Test (NART, Nelson, 1982; and revised NART, Blair & Spreen, 1989), the Wechsler Test of Adult Reading (WTAR; Psychological Corporation, 2001), among others, tend to be resistant to brain injury. Vanderploeg and Schinka (2004) call them the "hold approaches," and they tend to produce adequate estimates of verbal intelligence but fall short in prediction of nonverbal (fluid) aspects of cognitive functioning, including memory. As also discussed by Vanderploeg and Schinka (2004), there are several other approaches, all offering their own caveats. One of them includes the use of educational and occupational levels to predict intelligence based on their correlations but this tends to produce estimated Full Scale IQ (FSIQ) within a range of 24–30 IQ points when a band error of 1 standard deviation is applied. Another approach involves the best performance method that estimates premorbid levels based on best current performance on a test or historical reports but this tends to produce overestimated premorbid functioning. Population-specific norms can illustrate how a patient's performance compares to what would have been expected based on normative data but they tend to be limited to only a few demographic considerations. Finally, regression methods can be used to predict IQ scores using richer demographic data such as age, gender, race, education level, occupation, and place of residence. However, they tend to make the best predictions when the actual IQ falls within the average range (see Schinka & Vanderploeg, 2000 or Vanderploeg & Schinka, 2004 for some detailed recommended guidelines and alternatives to combine these methods).

PRESENT AND FUTURE: TECHNOLOGICAL ADVANCEMENT IN NEUROPSYCHOLOGY ASSESSMENT

Computerized and Mobile Assessment Tools

Although computerized tests have been around for many years, they are not being used nearly as often as traditional paper-and-pencil instruments. In their survey of clinicians practicing neuropsychology, Rabin and colleagues (2014) found that almost half of all clinicians (45.5 percent) reported never using computerized tests. This lack of usage has been attributed to several factors, including concerns over lack of familiarity in using such technology, diminished roles of examiners and clinicians, data security, and the loss of qualitative behavioral data (Miller & Barr, 2017).

However, newer computerized testing tools utilizing tablets are beginning to address some of these issues, while also offering several advantages over traditional tests. In addition to offering the usual benefits inherent in computerized testing, such as less administration time, self-administration, high accessibility, and automated data storage and analysis (Collie, Darby, & Maruff, 2001), tablets offer data on extremely nuanced behavior that could not otherwise be detected, allowing for more sensitive detection of abnormalities. Moreover, computerized assessment with tablets is user-friendly, with individuals showing preference for the touchscreen nature of tablets compared to mouse clicking that is involved in other computerized testing (Canini et al., 2014).

Examples of two popular neuropsychological instruments currently digitalized into tablet versions are the Clock Drawing Test and the Trail Making Test. Davis and Penney (2014) recently created a digital version of the Clock Drawing Test that uses a digitized pen to record its position on the page with detailed spatial and temporal accuracy. For older adults, there is evidence that, because of its sensitivity to every nuanced behavior involved in the process of the drawing, this test may help in the early detection of cognitive impairment (Souillard-Mandar et al., 2016). Similarly, Fellows and colleagues (2017) have developed a digital version of the Trail Making Test that measures several "process-related" aspects of performance in addition to the typical recordings of total time to completion and number of errors. These secondary measures, which include the number and duration of pauses and pen lifts, as well as time to draw in between circles, were shown to be predicted by performance on other tests measuring processing speed, inhibitory control, and visual/spatial sequencing (Fellows et al., 2017).

Similarly, advances in the digitization of test materials have facilitated the implementation of even smaller and everyday mobile technology, such as smartphones. With promising results from Moore, Swendsen, and Depp (2017), other studies have started to investigate the feasibility and psychometric properties of cognitive testing scores obtained from personal devices, such as mobile phones. In particular, researchers are interested in the longitudinal examination of cognitive change in geriatric research and the effect of clinical interventions in older adults (Brouillette et al., 2013; Brown et al., 2017; Schweitzer et al., 2017) and brain-injured patients (Resnick & Lathan, 2016), among other populations (Moore et al., 2017). As Au, Piers, and Devine (2017) explain, the ability for such technology to detect preclinical abnormalities carries enormous implications, such as disease prevention, economic relief regarding health care costs, and a shift in cognitive assessment to incorporate algorithms that integrate multisensory information.

Virtual Reality

Virtual reality (VR) can be defined as an advanced human-computer interface in which users interact with, and immerse themselves in, a virtual environment (Schultheis & Rizzo, 2001). Designed to feel more natural and realistic, VR-based measures have been implemented in clinical neuropsychology for both assessment and rehabilitation. For the purposes of this chapter, we will very briefly address their use in assessment.

VR offers a potentially sensitive and ecologically valid measure of cognitive processes. A recent meta-analysis by Negut and colleagues (2016) examined the sensitivity of VR-based measures of cognition for healthy and clinical populations. Using data from eighteen studies comparing performance between clinical and healthy control groups, they found that VR-based measures were moderately sensitive to cognitive impairment, with healthy groups outperforming clinical groups overall, and in each examined cognitive domain: visuospatial ability, memory, and executive functions. The magnitude of this sensitivity was similar to that of traditional neuropsychological measures. Furthermore, VR-based measures tended to be a more sensitive assessment tool for cases involving brain injury, ADHD, schizophrenia, and special populations such as older adults. High sensitivity has been associated with decreased task difficulty and virtual environments that do not contain distractors.

Regarding VR's utility for ADHD populations, a virtual version of the Conners Continuous Performance Test (CPT), a common measure of attention, has shown to be an effective tool for assessing attention in children and adolescents, using a virtual classroom environment (Nolin et al., 2016). For both individuals with Alzheimer's disease and those who have sustained a TBI, VR instruments examining IADLs appear to be particularly useful (Allain et al., 2014; Besnard et al., 2016). Similarly, assessment of IADLs in people with schizophrenia has also benefited from VR tools, which have elicited and captured behaviors that are comparable to those in a natural environment (Aubin, Béliveau, & Klinger, 2018). Fueled by an accelerating public interest in immersive technology, and no longer hampered by high costs, difficulty in use, and clinician unfamiliarity, VR is expected to become an indispensable tool in psychological research and practice (Rizzo & Koenig, 2017).

Teleneuropsychology

Long-distance neuropsychological assessment, called teleneuropsychology, offers an avenue for providing services to individuals living in remote, rural, or otherwise underserved areas. Falling under the larger umbrella of telepsychology, teleneuropsychology most often occurs via video teleconference (VTC) communication. A major benefit of teleneuropsychology is its affordability. Particularly in cases where the client lives in a rural community, teleneuropsychology has shown to be approximately 19 percent less expensive for the client compared to in-person assessment (Schopp, Johnstone, & Merrell, 2000). Furthermore, compared to the costs of a neuropsychologist traveling to a remote area for assessment, teleneuropsychology was found to be 72 percent cheaper.

In regard to psychometric quality, teleneuropsychology assessment has demonstrated sound validity and reliability compared to equivalent in-person testing. For instance, Cullum and colleagues (2014) compared results of neuropsychological testing that was administered in-person versus via VTC, finding that performance was similar between conditions. Strongest correlations came for a global test of cognition (MMSE), while the lowest correlation occurred for a verbal learning and memory test (HVLT-R). These results lend support to the psychometric quality of teleneuropsychology assessment but further research is needed to examine psychometric integrity in more populations and using larger batteries.

Teleneuropsychology has shown to have varying effects on overall satisfaction of its use. In a survey by Schopp and colleagues (2000), there were no differences found between teleneuropsychology and in-person groups regarding client ratings of global satisfaction, ease of communication, level of relaxation, or perceived "caring" by the psychologist. Furthermore, clients who underwent teleneuropsychology endorsed a higher likelihood to repeat the experience. Conversely, neuropsychologists endorsed less overall satisfaction for the use of teleneuropsychology citing concern around the confidentiality of communications, along with technological difficulties of the equipment.

Recommendations for the Use of Teleneuropsychology

Considering the novelty of and concerns about teleneuropsychology, efforts have been made to create guidelines for its use. Grosch, Gottlieb, and Cullum (2011) addressed this in the context of VTC, examining topics relevant to telepsychology in general but also those specific to teleneuropsychology. As in general telepsychology practices, neuropsychologists should go to great lengths in protecting and securing private health information, which becomes more vulnerable from digitization. Additionally, neuropsychologists should ensure that such concerns surrounding privacy and confidentiality are understood and permitted when obtaining informed consent. Regarding issues that are particularly relevant for teleneuropsychology, any employed psychometrists, not just clinicians, must be competent in carrying out teleneuropsychology assessment, having undergone sufficient training. Additionally, it is paramount to ensure test integrity by maintaining and upholding the same rigorous standards used for in-person test administration and scoring. Clinicians should also, whenever practical, use measures that have been empirically supported as valid teleneuropsychology tests. In their reports, clinicians should also mention any limitations from teleneuropsychology assessments, pertaining to both administration and scoring. As neuropsychological testing relies heavily upon the quality of stimuli, predominantly visual or auditory, technological equipment used in teleneuropsychology should work properly with limited interruptions. To assist with any technical difficulties, on-site assistants should be available, but they should otherwise not be in the room during testing. Lastly, in considering possible sensory impairment in elderly populations, extra care should be taken to ensure that these clients are able to communicate and receive information via VTC.

SUMMARY

Neuropsychology offers a unique yet multidimensional approach to clinical assessment, with its emphasis of the bio-psycho-social model regarding neurological conditions. Neuropsychologists undergo years of extensive training as scientist-practitioners, during which they acquire knowledge in areas of general psychology, general clinical psychology, brain-behavior relationships, and the practice of clinical neuropsychology. There can be numerous functions of a neuropsychological assessment, such as serving as a diagnostic tool, delineating a client's cognitive strengths and weaknesses, informing a plan for rehabilitation or intervention and determining its efficacy, helping understand overall brain-behavior relationships and disease trajectory, and aiding in legal proceedings like those involving brain injury. Clinical neuropsychologists work in a variety of settings, which come with their own set of unique issues and demands, and see a diversity of clinical populations. In doing so, they use a myriad of instruments to assess all domains of cognition in addition to psychological factors. When determining test batteries to administer, neuropsychologists consider the selection of the tests themselves, their order, and the duration of the battery. When making interpretations of information collected in an assessment, neuropsychologists take many variables into account, such as those directly impacting test performance (e.g., fatigue), and factors that impact test validity, such as cultural and language differences, poor effort, and particular psychometric properties of the tests. Other challenges to neuropsychological assessment include repeated assessment, IIV and base rates, and estimation of premorbid cognitive abilities. Although gradual, the shift away from traditional paper-and-pencil assessment methods toward those of computerized and mobile assessment, and VR, is growing, and it is likely that such innovative techniques will continue to permeate the practice of neuropsychology in the future. Along with teleneuropsychology, these advances in the field carry incredibly promising implications and possibilities for assessing neurological conditions, but clinicians must be mindful of using them responsibly and ethically, following appropriate guidelines.

REFERENCES

AACN (American Academy of Clinical Neuropsychology). (1999). American Academy of Clinical Neuropsychology policy on the use of nondoctoral personnel in conducting clinical neuropsychological evaluations. *The Clinical Neuropsychologist*, *13*(4), 385. https://doi.org/10.1076/1385-4046(199911)13:04;1-Y;FT385.

Allain, P., Foloppe, D. A., Besnard, J., Yamaguchi, T., Etcharry-Bouyx, F., Le Gall, D., . . . & Richard, P. (2014). Detecting everyday action deficits in Alzheimer's disease using a nonimmersive virtual reality kitchen. *Journal of the International Neuropsychological Society*, *20*(5), 468–477.

Au, R., Piers, R. J., & Devine, S. (2017). How technology is reshaping cognitive assessment: Lessons from the Framingham Heart

Study. *Neuropsychology, 31*(8), 846–861. doi:10.1037/neu0000411.

Aubin, G., Béliveau, M. F., & Klinger, E. (2018). An exploration of the ecological validity of the Virtual Action Planning–Supermarket (VAP-S) with people with schizophrenia. *Neuropsychological rehabilitation, 28*(5), 689–708.

Ardila, A. (2007). The impact of culture on neuropsychological test performance. In B. P. Uzzell, M. Ponton, & A. Ardila (Eds.), *International handbook of cross-cultural neuropsychology* (pp. 23–44). Hillsdale, NJ: Lawrence Erlbaum Associates.

Baum, K.T., von Thomsen, C., Elam, M., Murphy, C., Gerstle, M., Austin, C.A., & Beebe, D. W. (2018). Communication is key: The utility of a revised neuropsychological report format. *The Clinical Neuropsychologist, 32*(3), 345–367. doi:10.1080/13854046.2017.1413208

Besnard, J., Richard, P., Banville, F., Nolin, P., Aubin, G., Le Gall, D., . . . & Allain, P. (2016). Virtual reality and neuropsychological assessment: The reliability of a virtual kitchen to assess daily-life activities in victims of traumatic brain injury. *Applied Neuropsychology: Adult, 23*(3), 223–235.

Blair, J. R., & Spreen, O. (1989). Predicting premorbid IQ: A revision of the National Adult Reading Test. *The Clinical Neuropsychologist, 3*, 129–136.

Boone, K. B. (2007). *Assessment of feigned cognitive impairment: A neuropsychological perspective*. New York: Guilford Press.

Brouillette, R. M., Foil, H., Fontenot, S., Correro, A., Allen, R., Martin, C. K., . . . & Keller, J. N. (2013). Feasibility, reliability, and validity of a smartphone based application for the assessment of cognitive function in the elderly. *PloS ONE, 8*(6), e65925.

Brown, E. L., Ruggiano, N., Li, J., Clarke, P. J., Kay, E. S., & Hristidis, V. (2017). Smartphone-based health technologies for dementia care: Opportunities, challenges, and current practices. *Journal of Applied Gerontology, 38*(1), 73–91. doi:10.1177/0733464817723088

Bush, S. S., Ruff, R. M., Tröster, A. I., Barth, J. T., Koffler, S. P., Pliskin, N. H., . . . & Silver, C. H. (2005). Symptom validity assessment: Practice issues and medical necessity NAN Policy & Planning Committee. *Archives of Clinical Neuropsychology, 20*(4), 419–426. http://dx.doi.org/10.1016/j.acn.2005.02.002

Bush, S. S., Sweet, J. J., Bianchini, K. J., Johnson-Greene, D., Dean, P. M., & Schoenberg, M. R. (2018). Deciding to adopt revised and new psychological and neuropsychological tests: An inter-organizational position paper. *The Clinical Neuropsychologist, 32*(3), 319–325. doi:10.1080/13854046.2017.1422277

Butcher, J. N., Dahlstrom, W. G., Graham, J. R., Tellegen, A., & Kaemmer, B. (1989). *MMPI-2:Manual for administration and scoring*. Minneapolis: University of Minnesota Press.

Canini, M., Battista, P., Della Rosa, P. A., Catricalà, E., Salvatore, C., Gilardi, M. C., & Castiglioni, I. (2014). Computerized neuropsychological assessment in aging: testing efficacy and clinical ecology of different interfaces. *Computational and Mathematical Methods in Medicine*. doi:10.1155/2014/804723

Collie, A., Darby, D., & Maruff, P. (2001). Computerised cognitive assessment of athletes with sports related head injury. *British Journal of Sports Medicine, 35*(5), 297–302. doi:10.1136/bjsm.35.5.297.

Cullum, C. M., Hynan, L. S., Grosch, M., Parikh, M., & Weiner, M. F. (2014). Teleneuropsychology: Evidence for video teleconference-based neuropsychological assessment. *Journal of the International Neuropsychological Society, 20*(10), 1028–1033. doi:10.1017/S1355617714000873

Davis, R., & Penney, D. L. (2014). U.S. Patent No. 8,740,819. Washington, DC: U.S. Patent and Trademark Office.

de Frias, C. M., Dixon, R. A., Fisher, N., & Camicioli, R. (2007). Intraindividual variability in neurocognitive speed: A comparison of Parkinson's disease and normal older adults. *Neuropsychologia, 45*(11), 2499–2507. doi:10.1016/j.neuropsychologia.2007.03.022

Delaney, R. C. (2003). The practice of clinical neuropsychology in a VA setting. In G. J. Lamberty, J. C. Courtney, & R. L. Heilbronner (Eds.), *The practice of clinical neuropsychology* (pp. 267–279). Leiden: Swets & Zeitlinger.

Delis, D. C., Kramer, J. H., Kaplan, E., & Ober, B. A. (2000). *The California Verbal Learning Test – Second Edition: Adult version manual*. San Antonio, TX: The Psychological Corporation.

Division 40 Task Force on Education Accreditation Credentialing. (1991). Recommendations for the education and training of nondoctoral personnel in clinical neuropsychology. *The Clinical Neuropsychologist, 3*(1), 23–24. https://doi.org/10.1080/13854049108401838

Duggan, E. C., Awakon, L. M., Loaiza, C. C., & Garcia-Barrera, M. A. (2018). Contributing towards a cultural neuropsychology assessment decision-making framework: comparison of WAIS-IV norms from Colombia, Chile, Mexico, Spain, United States, and Canada. *Archives of Clinical Neuropsychology, 34*(5), 657–681. http://dx.doi.org/10.1093/arclin/acy074

Dykiert, D., Der, G., Starr, J. M., & Deary, I. J. (2012). Age differences in intra-individual variability in simple and choice reaction time: systematic review and meta-analysis. *PLoS ONE, 7* (10). doi:10.1371/journal.pone.0045759.

Elbulok-Charcape, M. M., Rabin, L. A., Spadaccini, A. T., & Barr, W. B. (2014). Trends in the neuropsychological assessment of ethnic/racial minorities: A survey of clinical neuropsychologists in the United States and Canada. *Cultural Diversity and Ethnic Minority Psychology, 20*(3), 353–361. doi:10.1037/a0035023.

Evans, J. J. (2010). Basic concepts and principles of neuropsychological assessment. In J. M. Gurd, U. Kischka, & J. C. Marshall (Eds.), *Handbook of clinical neuropsychology* (pp. 15–27). New York: Oxford University Press.

Fellows, R. P., Dahmen, J., Cook, D., & Schmitter-Edgecombe, M. (2017). Multicomponent analysis of a digital Trail Making Test. *The Clinical Neuropsychologist, 31*(1), 154–167.

Folstein, M. F., Folstein, S. E., & McHugh, P. R. (1975). "Mini-mental state": A practical method for grading the cognitive state of patients for the clinician. *Journal of psychiatric research, 12*(3), 189–198.

Geurts, H. M., Grasman, R. P., Verté, S., Oosterlaan, J., Roeyers, H., van Kammen, S. M., & Sergeant, J. A. (2008). Intra-individual variability in ADHD, autism spectrum disorders and Tourette's syndrome. *Neuropsychologia, 46*(13), 3030–3041. doi:10.1016/j.neuropsychologia.2008.06.013.

Gioia, G. A., Isquith, P. K., Guy, S. C., & Kenworthy, L. (2015). *BRIEF-2: Behavior Rating Inventory of Executive Function*. Lutz, FL: Psychological Assessment Resources.

Gorus, E., De Raedt, R., Lambert, M., Lemper, J. C., & Mets, T. (2008). Reaction times and performance variability in normal aging, mild cognitive impairment, and Alzheimer's disease. *Journal of Geriatric Psychiatry and Neurology, 21*(3), 204–218. doi:10.1177/0891988708320973.

Grosch, M. C., Gottlieb, M. C., & Cullum, C. M. (2011). Initial practice recommendations for teleneuropsychology. *The*

Clinical Neuropsychologist, *25*(7), 1119–1133. doi:10.1080/13854046.2011.609840.

Groth-Marnat, G. E. (2000). *Neuropsychological assessment in clinical practice: A guide to test interpretation and integration*. New York: John Wiley & Sons.

Halliday, D. W. R., Mulligan, B. P., Garrett, D. D., Schmidt, S., Hundza, S. R., Garcia-Barrera, M. A., Stawski, R. S., & MacDonald, S. W. S. (2018). Mean and variability in functional brain activations differentially predict executive function in older adults: An investigation employing functional near-infrared spectroscopy, *Neurophotonics 5*(1), 011013. doi:10.1117/1.NPh.5.1.011013.

Hannay, J., Bieliauskas, L., Crosson, B., Hammeke, T., Hamsher, K., & Koffler, S. (1998). Proceedings of the Houston Conference on Specialty Education and Training in Clinical Neuropsychology. *Archives of Clinical Neuropsychology*, *13*, 157–250.

Harris, J. G. (2002). Ethical decision making with individuals of diverse ethnic, cultural, and linguistic backgrounds. In S. S. Bush & M. L. Drexler (Eds.), *Ethical issues in clinical neuropsychology* (pp. 223–241). Leiden: Swets & Zeitlinger.

Heaton, R. K., Chelune, G. J., Talley, J. L., Kay, C. G., & Curtiss, G. (1993). *Wisconsin Card Sorting Test manual*. Odessa, FL: Psychological Assessment Resources.

Hebben N & Milberg, W. (2002). *Essentials of neuropsychological assessment*. New York: John Wiley & Sons.

Hilborn, J. V., Strauss, E., Hultsch, D. F., & Hunter, M. A. (2009). Intraindividual variability across cognitive domains: Investigation of dispersion levels and performance profiles in older adults. *Journal of Clinical and Experimental Neuropsychology*, *31*(4), 412–424.

Hill, B. D., & Rohling, M. L. (2011). Diagnostic utility of measures of variability in patients suffering from traumatic brain injury: Intra-individual variability as an indicator of validity and pathology. In K. S. Baker & N. C. Edwards (Eds.), *Brain injuries: New research* (pp. 159–174). Hauppauge, NY: Nova Science.

Kamphaus, R. W., & Reynolds, C. R. (2015). *Behavior Assessment System for Children – Third Edition (BASC-3): Behavioral and emotional screening system (BESS)*. Bloomington, MN: Pearson.

Kaplan, E.F., Goodglass, H., & Weintraub, S. (1983). *The Boston Naming Test – Second Edition*. Philadelphia: Lea & Febiger.

Karr, J. E., Garcia-Barrera, M. A., Holdnack, J. A., & Iverson, G. L. (2016). Using multivariate base rates to interpret low scores on an abbreviated battery of the Delis–Kaplan Executive Function System. *Archives of Clinical Neuropsychology*, *32*(3), 297–305. doi:10.1093/arclin/acw105.

Karr, J. E., Garcia-Barrera, M. A., Holdnack, J. A., & Iverson, G. L. (2017). Advanced clinical interpretation of the Delis-Kaplan Executive Function System: Multivariate base rates of low scores. *The Clinical Neuropsychologist*, *32*(1), 1–12. doi:10.1080/13854046.2017.1334828.

Kløve, H. (1963). *Grooved pegboard*. Lafayette, IN: Lafayette Instruments.

Kubu, C. S., Ready, R. E., Festa, J. R., Roper, B. L., & Pliskin, N. H. (2016). The times they are a changin': Neuropsychology and integrated care teams. *The Clinical Neuropsychologist*, *30*(1), 51–65.

Larrabee, G. J. (2007). *Assessment of malingered neuropsychological deficits*. New York: Oxford University Press

Lezak, M. D., Howieson, D. B., Bigler, E. D., & Tranel, D. (2012). *Neuropsychological assessment* (5th ed.). New York: Oxford University Press.

MacDonald, S. W., Nyberg, L., & Bäckman, L. (2006). Intra-individual variability in behavior: Links to brain structure, neurotransmission and neuronal activity. *Trends in Neurosciences*, *29*(8), 474–480.

Malek-Ahmadi, M., Erickson, T., Puente, A. E., Pliskin, N., & Rock, R. (2012). The use of psychometrists in clinical neuropsychology: History, current status, and future directions. *Applied Neuropsychology: Adult*, *19*(1), 26–31.

McKinlay, W. W., McGowan, M., & Russell, J. V. (2010). Forensic issues in neuropsychology. In J. M. Gurd, U. Kischka, & J. C. Marshall (Eds.), *Handbook of clinical neuropsychology* (pp. 741–761). New York: Oxford University Press.

Meyers, J. E., & Meyers, K. R. (1995). *Rey Complex Figure Test and recognition trial: Professional manual*. Odessa, TX: Psychological Assessment Resources.

Miller, J. B., & Barr, W. B. (2017). The technology crisis in neuropsychology. *Archives of Clinical Neuropsychology*, *32*(5), 541–554.

Moore, R. C., Swendsen, J., & Depp, C. A. (2017). Applications for self-administered mobile cognitive assessments in clinical research: A systematic review. *International Journal of Methods in Psychiatric Research*, *26*(4), e1562.

Neguț, A., Matu, S. A., Sava, F. A., & David, D. (2016). Virtual reality measures in neuropsychological assessment: A meta-analytic review. *The Clinical Neuropsychologist*, *30*(2), 165–184. https://doi.org/10.1080/13854046.2016.1144793.

Nelson, H. E. (1982). *National Adult reading test (NART): Test manual*. Windsor, UK: NFER-Nelson.

Nolin, P., Stipanicic, A., Henry, M., Lachapelle, Y., Lussier-Desrochers, D., & Allain, P. (2016). ClinicaVR: Classroom-CPT: A virtual reality tool for assessing attention and inhibition in children and adolescents. *Computers in Human Behavior*, *59*, 327–333.

Ponsford, J. (2017). International growth of neuropsychology. *Neuropsychology*, *31*(8), 921–933. doi:10.1037/neu0000415.

Poreh, A. (2002). Neuropsychological and psychological issues associated with cross-cultural and minority assessment. In F. R. Ferraro (Ed.), *Minority and cross-cultural aspects of neuropsychological assessment* (pp. 329–343). Leiden: Swets & Zeitlinger.

Psychological Corporation. (2001). *The Wechsler Test of Adult Reading (WTAR)*. San Antonio, TX: Psychological Corporation.

Puente, A. E., Adams, R., Barr, W., Bush, S. S., & NAN Policy and Planning Committee. (2006). The use, education, training, and supervision of neuropsychological test technicians (psychometrists) in clinical practice: Official statement of the National Academy of Neuropsychology. *Archives of Clinical Neuropsychology*, *21*(8), 837–839. doi:10.1016/j.acn.2006.08.011.

Puente, A. E., Ojeda, C., Zink, D., Portillo Reyes, V. (2015). Neuropsychological testing of Spanish speakers. In K. F. Geisinger (Ed.), *Psychological testing of Hispanics* (pp. 135–152). Washington, DC: American Psychological Association.

Rabin, L. A., Barr, W. B., & Burton, L. A. (2005). Assessment practices of clinical neuropsychologists in the United States and Canada: A survey of INS, NAN, and APA Division 40 members. *Archives of Clinical Neuropsychology*, *20*(1), 33–65. doi:10.1016/j.acn.2004.02.005.

Rabin, L. A., Paolillo, E., & Barr, W. B. (2016). Stability in test-usage practices of clinical neuropsychologists in the United States and Canada over a 10-year period: A follow-up survey of INS and NAN members. *Archives of Clinical Neuropsychology*, *31*(3), 206–230. doi:10.1093/arclin/acw007.

Rabin, L. A., Spadaccini, A. T., Brodale, D. L., Grant, K. S., Elbulok-Charcape, M. M., & Barr, W. B. (2014). Utilization rates of computerized tests and test batteries among clinical neuropsychologists in the United States and Canada. *Professional Psychology: Research and Practice*, *45*(5), 368–377. doi:10.1037/a0037987.

Rabinowitz, A. R., & Arnett, P. A. (2013). Intraindividual cognitive variability before and after sports-related concussion. *Neuropsychology*, *27*(4), 481–490. doi:10.1037/a0033023.

Randolph, C. (2012). *RBANS update: Repeatable battery for the assessment of neuropsychological status*. Bloomington, MN: NCS Pearson.

Reitan, R. M. (1958). Validity of the Trail Making test as an indicator of organic brain damage. *Perceptual and Motor Skills*, *8*, 271–276.

Resnick, H. E., & Lathan, C. E. (2016). From battlefield to home: A mobile platform for assessing brain health. *Mhealth*, *2*(30), 1–6.

Reynolds, C. R., & Kamphaus, R. W. (2015). *Behavior assessment system for children—third edition (BASC-3)*. Bloomington, MN: Pearson.

Ricker, J. H. (2003). Neuropsychological practice in medical rehabilitation. In G. J. Lamberty, J. C. Courtney, and R. L. Heilbronner (Eds.), *The practice of clinical neuropsychology* (pp. 305–317). Leiden: Swets & Zeitlinger.

Rizzo, A., & Koenig, S. T. (2017). Is clinical virtual reality ready for primetime?. *Neuropsychology*, *31*(8), 877–899. doi:10.1037/neu0000405.

Schinka, J. A., & Vanderploeg, R. D (2000). Estimating premorbid level of functioning. In: R. D. Vanderploeg (Ed.), *Clinician's guide to neuropsychological assessment* (2nd ed., pp. 39–67). Hillsdale, NJ: Lawrence Erlbaum Associates.

Schopp, L., Johnstone, B., & Merrell, D. (2000). Telehealth and neuropsychological assessment: New opportunities for psychologists. *Professional Psychology: Research and Practice*, *31*(2), 179–183. doi:10.1037//0735-7028.31.2.179,

Schultheis, M. T., & Rizzo, A. A. (2001). The application of virtual reality technology in rehabilitation. *Rehabilitation psychology*, *46*(3), 296–311. doi:10.1037/0090–5550.46.3.296.

Schweitzer, P., Husky, M., Allard, M., Amieva, H., Pérès, K., Foubert-Samier, A., ... & Swendsen, J. (2017). Feasibility and validity of mobile cognitive testing in the investigation of age-related cognitive decline. *International Journal of Methods in Psychiatric Research*, *26*(3), e1521.

Souillard-Mandar, W., Davis, R., Rudin, C., Au, R., Libon, D. J., Swenson, R., ... & Penney, D. L. (2016). Learning classification models of cognitive conditions from subtle behaviors in the digital clock drawing test. *Machine learning*, *102*(3), 393–441. doi:10.1007/s10994-015-5529-5.

Stedman, J. M. (2006). What we know about predoctoral internship training: A review. *Training and Education in Professional Psychology*, *S*(2), 80–95.

Strauss, E., Slick, D. J., Levy-Bencheton, J., Hunter, M., MacDonald, S. W., & Hultsch, D. F. (2002). Intraindividual variability as an indicator of malingering in head injury. *Archives of Clinical Neuropsychology*, *17*(5), 423–444. https://doi.org/10.1016/S0887–6177(01)00126–3.

Stringer, A. Y., & Nadolne, M. J. (2000). Neuropsychological assessment: Contexts for contemporary clinical practice. In G. Groth-Marnat (Ed.), *Neuropsychological assessment in clinical practice* (pp. 26–47). John Wiley & Sons.

Stuss, D. T., Murphy, K. J., Binns, M. A., & Alexander, M. P. (2003). Staying on the job: The frontal lobes control individual performance variability. *Brain*, *126* (11), 2363–2380.

Stuss, D. T., Pogue, J., Buckle, L., & Bondar, J. (1994). Characterization of stability of performance in patients with traumatic brain injury: variability and consistency on reaction time tests. *Neuropsychology*, *8*(3), 316. https://doi.org/10.1037/0894–4105.8.3.316.

Suzuki, L. A., & Ponterotto, J. G. (Eds.). (2007). *Handbook of multicultural assessment: Clinical, psychological, and educational applications*. John Wiley & Sons.

Sweet, J. J. (1999). Malingering: differential diagnosis. In J. J. Sweet, *Forensic Neuropsychology: Fundamentals and practice* (pp. 255–285). Leiden: Sets & Zeitlinger.

Sweet, J. J., Benson, L. M., Nelson, N. W., & Moberg, P. J. (2015). The American Academy of Clinical Neuropsychology, National Academy of Neuropsychology, and Society for Clinical Neuropsychology (APA Division 40) 2015 TCN professional practice and 'salary survey': Professional practices, beliefs, and incomes of US neuropsychologists. *The Clinical Neuropsychologist*, *29*(8), 1069–1162.

Sweet, J. J., Ecklund-Johnson, E., & Malina, A. (2008). Forensic neuropsychology: An overview of issues and directions. In J. E. Morgan and J. H. Ricker (Eds.), *Textbook of clinical neuropsychology* (pp. 869–890). New York: Taylor & Francis Group.

Sweet, J. J., Lee, C., Guidotti Breting, L. M., & Benson, L. M. (2018). Gender in clinical neuropsychology: Practice survey trends and comparisons outside the specialty. *The Clinical Neuropsychologist*, *32*(2), 186–216. doi:10.1080/13854046.2017.1365932

Sweet, J. J., Moberg, P. J., & Suchy, Y. (2000). Ten-year follow-up survey of clinical neuropsychologists: Part I. Practices and beliefs. *The Clinical Neuropsychologist*, *14*(1), 18–37.

Torres, I. J., & Pliskin, N. H. (2003). Adult practice in a university-affiliated medical center. In G. J. Lamberty, J. C. Courtney, and R. L. Heilbronner (Eds.), *The practice of clinical neuropsychology* (pp. 213–225). Leiden: Swets & Zeitlinger.

Vanderploeg, R. D., & Schinka, J. A. (2004). Estimation of premorbid cognitive abilities: Issues and approaches. In J. H. Ricker (Ed.), *Differential diagnosis in adult neuropsychological assessment* (pp. 27–65). New York: Springer.

Wechsler, D. (2003). *Wechsler Intelligence Scale for Children – Fourth Edition (WISC-IV)*. San Antonio, TX: The Psychological Corporation.

Wechsler, D. (2008). *Wechsler Adult Intelligence Scale – Fourth Edition (WAIS–IV)*. San Antonio, TX: The Psychological Corporation.

Wechsler, D. (2009). *Wechsler Memory Scale – Fourth Edition (WMS-IV)*. San Antonio, TX: The Psychological Corporation.

Wechsler, D. (2011). *Wechsler Abbreviated Scale of Intelligence – Second Edition (WASI-II)*. San Antonio, TX: NCS Pearson.

Wechsler, D. (2014). *Wechsler Intelligence Scale for Children – Fifth Edition (WISC-V)*. San Antonio, TX: NCS Pearson.

35 Assessment in Educational Settings

BENJAMIN J. LOVETT AND JASON M. NELSON

Consider the following situations:

- Should Sophia be given an individualized education program (IEP) for her problems with anxiety or would an accommodation plan be sufficient?
- Jeremy has attention-deficit/hyperactivity disorder (ADHD), but does this mean that he should be provided with additional time when taking college admissions tests?
- Kaylee received services for a learning disability in mathematics last year but her family just moved to a new state. Is she still eligible for services?
- Lucas's parents are unhappy with the special education evaluation that a school conducted; are you able to provide an independent educational evaluation (IEE)?

Topics like these are not typically given substantial attention in clinical or counseling psychology training programs but they arise frequently when working with children, adolescents, and families. Private practitioners are often given evaluation reports from schools and, in some states, private practitioners conduct evaluations in the schools. In addition, psychotherapists and counselors often serve students who are eligible for school-based interventions, accommodations, or other services that can enhance clinical outcomes. For these reasons, among others, any clinical professional who works with young people or families should be familiar with the basic features of assessment procedures in educational settings.

In this chapter, we start by discussing general features of those procedures, focusing on the steps by which students with educationally relevant disabilities are identified and their service needs are determined. We then discuss three specific assessment topics that arise frequently in the schools: the identification of learning disabilities (the most common special education classification), the provision of testing accommodations to students with disabilities, and the influences of motivation and effort on children's test performance.

ASSESSMENT PROCEDURES IN SCHOOLS

Students are being assessed almost constantly in school. Most school days consist of classwork and homework assignments, quizzes, tests, and other teacher-designed assessment tools that aim to increase and measure academic skills. Report cards summarize all students' skill development several times a year, including nonacademic skills such as attention and conduct; and, famously, students complete district- and state-wide tests annually to assess the individual students themselves as well as their teachers and schools.

Other assessment procedures are given only to particular students. Students who are not making adequate academic progress may be given more frequent assessments in a particular subject area (e.g., reading) so that instructional methods can be adjusted as needed. Similarly, students exhibiting problem behavior may be given daily behavior report cards (e.g., Volpe & Fabiano, 2013) that are sent home to a parent in the hopes that such feedback – perhaps along with other interventions – will reduce the problem behavior.

This distinction between universal assessment procedures and targeted procedures has recently been formalized in the concept of Multi-Tiered Systems of Support (MTSS; Burns et al., 2016). The first "tier" of support involves providing all students with research-based instructional techniques – an effective academic curriculum and effective classroom management/discipline strategies. Students' academic skills and social-emotional behaviors are monitored frequently by teachers, and students who are falling behind in any area are provided with supplemental or remedial instruction and/or behavioral support, as needed. Targeted assessments then determine if the additional instruction/support is working, during what are sometimes called the second and third tiers of support (second-tier supports are less intensive and less individualized approaches than third-tier supports). When multiple targeted supports have been implemented, and targeted assessments have failed to show significant improvement in a student's problems, the formal process of evaluating for an educationally relevant disability begins.

The Legal Framework for Special Education Identification

For students in US public schools, covered by the Individuals with Disabilities Education Act (IDEA; Heward, 2013), the evaluation procedure for identifying special education needs can be divided into several steps, and the first step has just been described. Sometimes called "prereferral intervention," this step involves trying out multiple targeted supports to a student before considering an educational disability label. Although supports should be chosen thoughtfully and data should be collected on the effectiveness of these supports, the process at this step is rather informal in many schools. Typically, a teacher brings a concern about a student to a small group of fellow teachers and other professionals who discuss the problem and suggest trying out interventions that are relatively easy to implement. The teacher then reports back regarding how well the interventions worked.

When these interventions have failed, the school conducts a "multifactored evaluation," in which any area of suspected disability is assessed by a relevant professional. The evaluation team often includes a psychologist who measures the student's intellectual abilities and symptoms of any emotional/behavioral disorders, as well as other professionals, such as a speech-language pathologist, a special education teacher (who may give diagnostic achievement measures instead of the psychologist), and an occupational therapist (if the student has fine motor or other relevant concerns). In most states, school psychologists are employed full-time by schools to participate in the evaluations (and often to coordinate the evaluations as case managers as well); however, in some states and school districts, clinical psychologists are hired to conduct specific components of the evaluations.

After the various professionals complete their assessment procedures, a team (composed largely of the same professionals) meets to determine if, based on the assessment data, the student qualifies as having an educationally relevant disability. IDEA defines thirteen disability categories (e.g., specific learning disability, emotional disturbance, blindness), and US federal and state regulations further define the criteria for each category (Heward, 2013). The team members review the assessment data to determine if the student meets the full criteria for any of the IDEA categories and, if so, whether the student requires special education and/or related services (e.g., counseling, transportation) to receive an appropriate education. If parents are unhappy with the evaluation, they may request an IEE at the school district's expense; if the district refuses, a hearing is held to adjudicate the dispute.

If special education and/or related services are needed for a student who fulfills the criteria for one or more of IDEA's categories, an IEP is developed for the student, specifying their current levels of achievement or behavior, along with measurable goals and objectives for improvement. The IEP specifies how the objectives will be measured, who will be responsible for providing services, and where the services will be provided. That final issue constitutes a separate step in the special education process: determining the "least restrictive environment" (LRE) in which educational services can be provided. IDEA requires that, to the maximum extent possible, students with disabilities be educated along with their nondisabled peers rather than in separate settings. For each student, the LRE will be different, since students with more severe disabilities may need to be in separate settings for a larger part of the school day. In practice, an individual student's needs interact with a particular school district's educational options and the most appropriate placement is determined.

The final steps in the special education process involve implementing the IEP and following up to measure the student's progress after implementation. Progress is measured at time points specified in each student's IEP, and more formal follow-ups typically occur (1) once a year during an *annual review*, when parents are invited to a meeting with team members to review progress and set new goals and objectives that adjust to a student's new skill levels, and (2) every three years during a *triennial reevaluation* in which the student completes a new multifactored evaluation to determine if the criteria for an educational disability are still met.

The summary above pertains to students who may be eligible for services under IDEA. However, there is a second law, Section 504 of the Rehabilitation Act (RA) of 1973, which prohibits discrimination against individuals with disabilities by any entity receiving federal funding (as public schools typically do). A third law, the Americans with Disabilities Act (ADA), has provisions similar to Section 504 but extends to all entities regardless of funding status, and so it covers private schools as well. The ADA/RA definition of a disability is different from that of IDEA (ADA and RA require that a student have a condition that substantially limits one or more major life activities). Generally, students who meet this definition – often through documentation provided by an outside professional such as a physician or clinical psychologist – receive accommodations (such as additional time on tests or special seating in a classroom) but not specialized instruction.

Trends and Emerging Practices

Although the basics of the legal framework for identifying students with disabilities have not changed substantially in the past few decades, there has been a major shift in the way that schools apply that framework. Briefly, more emphasis has been placed on the prereferral intervention process, attempting to solve problems before formally labeling a student with a disability. Sometimes referred to as MTSS, and sometimes as Response-to-Intervention (RTI), this approach blurs the distinction between general education and special education (Fuchs, Fuchs, & Stecker, 2010). Interventions that were once reserved for special education students can be used before a comprehensive evaluation is even performed. More generally, when a student is showing a lag in academic skill development or exhibiting problem behavior, the MTSS/RTI perspective tends to see this as being due to a limitation of the instructional or behavior management approach rather than due to the student possessing an internal dysfunction (a disability condition) per se.

In practice, the MTSS/RTI perspective has led to new types of assessment for all students as part of Tier 1 procedures. With regard to academic skill development, many elementary schools now use brief, curriculum-based probes of reading, writing, and math skills that can be given frequently (e.g., weekly), by teachers, aides, or even fellow students. Each probe only takes one to three minutes to administer, and, given the frequency of assessment, each student's progress can be monitored to ensure appropriate rates of skill development. With regard to problem behavior, some schools administer standardized screeners of socioemotional symptoms to all students (via teacher ratings), to identify students who may need a Tier 2 intervention/support in that area of functioning.

Psychologists who practice in the schools increasingly see data from these new types of assessments and must learn how to interpret them and integrate them with traditional assessment tools when making decisions about diagnoses and treatment planning. In general, the new types of assessment emphasize behavioral conceptions of students' traits. For instance, a student's performance on curriculum-based academic skill probes is interpreted as a sample of the student's behavior that is likely to generalize to performance on similar tasks rather than being interpreted as a sign of a latent trait such as dyslexia. Similarly, a teacher's ratings of a student's inattention symptoms are viewed as an average of behavioral observations over time, indicating a student's typical response to a particular environment rather than the presence or absence of a latent condition such as ADHD. Such interpretations can be helpful in inhibiting psychologists from rushing to diagnostic judgments and directing them to focus on the various stimulus factors that affect student behavior and performance (cf. Ysseldyke, 2001). In addition, behavioral interpretations require less tendentious inferences – such "low inference" techniques emphasize clear relations between students' observed responses and similar responses that the student is likely to exhibit in the future (Eckert & Lovett, 2013). In contrast, using an IQ score to predict growth in reading skills or using a projective personality measure to judge a student's character structure requires "high inference" and such inferences are more likely to be wrong.

The trends toward MTSS/RTI systems of service delivery, and toward behavioral-style assessments, have occurred unevenly across schools, school districts, and states, and they have not occurred without controversy (e.g., Gersten, Jayanthi, & Dimino, 2017). Even sympathetic commentators have noted that selecting and implementing research-based supports and interventions is easier said than done and that, if not everyone in a school is "on board" with the new service delivery model, it is not likely to succeed. Even staff who are "on board" may not be sufficiently trained in the delivery of evidence-based interventions. In addition, requiring multiple failed interventions prior to a formal evaluation has been criticized as delaying a thorough understanding of a student's individual profile of deficits and needs, forcing a student and their teacher to endure months of ineffective interventions while falling further behind peers or while showing worsening behaviors (for more on the conflict between RTI and the need for timely evaluation, see Yell, Katsiyannis, & Collins, 2010). Finally, some of the behavioral-style assessments fail to meet traditional standards for reliability and validity evidence, and determining whether a student has made adequate progress at Tier 1 (e.g., calculating a growth curve based on data from curriculum-based reading probes) raises its own psychometric problems. These issues notwithstanding, there are also significant benefits to adopting more recent approaches to assessment and service delivery; and, in any case, psychologists who work with youth should be aware of these shifts.

A Continuing Controversy: Disproportionality

As with any area of clinical practice, psychologists who work in educational settings must be sensitive to issues of diversity, including the influence of students' racial and ethnic backgrounds. As we have discussed, special education assessment practices have changed significantly in recent years, but one of the diversity issues that has remained controversial relates to whether students from minority racial/ethnic groups are identified (through assessment) as having special education needs at a disproportionally high rate due to bias or other untoward influences. In the United States, a far higher proportion of African American students are identified than White students; for instance, Sullivan and Bal (2013) found the percentages of those two groups identified by one large urban school district were 25 percent and 13 percent, respectively.

Skiba and colleagues (2008) noted that disproportionality may be due to factors that include tests that are biased against minority children, teachers who are more likely to identify a child with a particular profile of traits as needing special education if the child is from a minority group, and a mismatch between minority students' cultural norms and values and those of schools. However, these scholars also admitted that the research evidence is mixed and often indirect, making conclusions about causes of disproportionality difficult to draw. Other scholars have been less circumspect; for instance, Blanchett (2006) argued that "white privilege" and racism cause disproportionality, although even she acknowledged that "additional research is needed to clearly document *the ways in which*" these factors exert their purported influence (p. 27, emphasis added).

The disproportionality debate has taken a surprising turn in the past several years, as a small group of scholars have argued that minority students are actually *underrepresented* rather than overrepresented in special education (e.g., Morgan et al., 2012; Morgan et al., 2015). These scholars have conducted more sophisticated analyses of disproportionality in which other child background factors that raise the risk of disability (e.g., poverty, low birth weight) are statistically controlled. With these controls, minority students are actually found to be less likely than *similar White students* to be placed in special education. Of course, this could be taken as evidence that minority students are being inappropriately denied the benefits of specialized instruction and supports to which they have a right (Morgan et al., 2015). As that argument suggests, general claims of bias against minority students may be unfalsifiable, if statistical discrepancies in either of two directions (i.e., underidentification *or* overidentification) could be used to support the claim of bias in the same direction. In any case, the disproportionality issue suggests a need for psychologists working in school settings to be aware of possible biases as well as the sociopolitical consequences of their assessment work.

ASSESSMENT OF SPECIFIC LEARNING DISABILITIES

In the United States, specific learning disability (SLD) has long been the largest disability category under IDEA (Heward, 2013). Although SLD has detailed *clinical* diagnostic criteria found in the fifth edition of the *Diagnostic and Statistical Manual of Mental Disorders* (DSM-5; American Psychiatric Association, 2013), federal and state special education regulations define the category as well. Different jurisdictions use different definitions and there is even more variability in methods of assessment (Maki, Floyd, & Roberson, 2015). In this section, we describe four different assessment models and each serves as a different operational definition of SLD. Each model has its own advantages and disadvantages and clinicians should be aware of these when selecting a model, keeping in mind that public schools will follow their own state's regulations when qualifying a student for special education under IDEA.

IQ-Achievement Discrepancy

Although research on isolated academic skill deficits goes back over a century, the modern concept of SLD was developed in the 1960s (see e.g., Kirk, 1962). The first widely accepted assessment model for SLD was proposed around the same time (Bateman, 1965): a discrepancy between a student's intellectual potential and their academic performance. The idea behind the discrepancy approach is simple and intuitive: Intelligence establishes a potential for achievement in academic areas and, if a student fails to live up to their academic potential, this underachievement may be due to SLD. Over time, the discrepancy approach came to be operationalized by giving a student an IQ test and an achievement battery; if there was a "severe discrepancy" between IQ and achievement in some academic area, the student was said to have SLD in the academic area. For instance, if a student's full-scale IQ (or similar overall intelligence estimate) was 108, and their score on a diagnostic reading test was 82, this might be considered as evidence supporting the presence of SLD in reading.

Until about a decade ago, most states required that students show an IQ-achievement discrepancy to be classified as SLD (Reschly & Hosp, 2004), and the approach continues to be popular in many schools as well as by many psychologists practicing in clinical settings. This is especially true when working with populations of children with above-average IQs; some of these students have very high IQs but "only" average academic skills and are said to be both gifted and learning disabled, or "twice-exceptional" (for discussion, see Lovett & Lewandowski, 2006). However, researchers generally take a dim view of discrepancy approaches (e.g., Scanlon, 2013; Stanovich, 2005; Sternberg & Grigorenko, 2002); and even twenty years ago, one researcher was already prepared to write an obituary for the approach (Aaron, 1997), certain that it would not last much longer. Critiques of the approach are numerous and varied, and actual arguments in favor of the approach are rare today, making its continued use unfortunate.

One critique of the approach has to do with the unreliability of discrepancies. When a difference is calculated between scores on two different tests, the reliability of the difference score is always less than the reliabilities of either of the two initial scores, each of which already has imperfect reliability. Moreover, as the correlation between the two initial scores increases, the reliability of the difference score actually *decreases*. This may sound counterintuitive, but consider that, if two scores are highly correlated, a large difference between them is more likely to be due to measurement error rather than a genuine discrepancy in the skills being measured. More sophisticated discrepancy formulas have been developed to address issues with reliability and related statistical issues (e.g., regression to the mean), but they cannot meet other objections

A second critique notes that the relationship between IQ and achievement is far from perfect in the general population (Hunt, 2011), and so it should not be surprising that a student shows a gap between IQ and an achievement score. Rather than some kind of innate potential, IQ is, after all, itself a score based on demonstration of skills that have been developed through learning and other environmental factors. Therefore, we should not view IQ as a birthright that entitles students to score in the same range for all academic areas, and we should expect that discrepancies between IQ and achievement scores will naturally occur in both directions, not due to disabilities but due to the known imperfect relationship between intelligence and achievement.

Still other critiques of the discrepancy approach include that discrepancies do not predict a student's benefit from interventions (i.e., discrepancies lack *treatment validity*; Vellutino, Scanlon, & Lyon, 2000) and there is no agreement over the exact procedures for calculating a discrepancy (e.g., whether full-scale IQ should be used, how large the discrepancy should be). In addition, requiring a certain size of discrepancy can delay needed intervention in young children while we wait for a discrepancy to grow over time, as it often does. Finally, discrepancy approaches will lead to false-positive diagnoses in students who have average academic skills (and therefore are not in need of intervention), if the students have a sufficiently high IQ.

Response-to-Intervention

We have already mentioned RTI as a general approach to monitoring and supporting student development, but it actually originated as a method for identifying students with learning disabilities (Berninger & Abbott, 1994; Gresham, 2002; for a contemporary RTI model of SLD assessment, see Kovaleski, VanDerHeyden, & Shapiro, 2013). This method starts with providing effective instruction to all students (Tier 1) while continually monitoring academic skill development. Tier I in RTI is analogous to "primary prevention" strategies for public health such as water fluoridation; *everyone* gets the intervention and then students are monitored (screened) for problems, knowing that some students will develop problems even with instructional strategies that have been shown to be effective. The goal at this point is to *prevent* deficits in academic skills, and good Tier 1 instruction is generally thought to be sufficient to keep 80–85 percent of students developing academic skills appropriately. In schools that practice RTI in the most formal ways, each student is essentially a research participant whose data are tracked continually using curriculum-based probes and the student's rate of progress in academic skill development is judged against an expected rate (typically the upward slope of a line on a graph measuring skills over time).

A minority of students will fail to respond sufficiently to Tier 1 instruction, and those students will be moved up to Tier 2. Sometimes, Tier 2 functions as a "Plan B" back-up instructional program; for instance, if one evidence-based reading program fails to work for a small group of students at Tier 1, those students are automatically placed into a second reading program. This is called the "standard protocol" approach to Tier 2. Alternatively, a small team can select an individualized Tier 2 program, matched to what appear to be each particular student's needs; this "problem-solving" approach to Tier 2 is more time-consuming up front but it may save time in the long run if it keeps ineffective Tier 2 interventions from being attempted. Whether the standard protocol or problem-solving approach is used, students' academic skill development continues to be monitored frequently, in the hopes of detecting improvement, which would allow a student to drop back down to Tier 1.

A small number of students (perhaps 5 percent) will fail to respond to either Tier 1 or Tier 2 instruction/intervention. These students are moved up to Tier 3, at which point they receive the most intensive, individualized interventions and their progress is monitored especially closely so as to make adjustments to the intervention as needed. Only when Tier 3 has failed is a student referred for the multifactored evaluation for formal labeling and placement. In essence, RTI considers the student to have a learning disability only when the student has truly been unable to learn academic skills at an appropriate level despite exposure to several types of increasingly intensive attempts at instruction/intervention.

As might be expected, criticisms of RTI have generally been very different from the criticisms of the discrepancy approach. Some critics have noted RTI's lack of integration with (or even interest in) the cognitive and neurological bases of SLD (see chapters in Fletcher-Janzen & Reynolds, 2008), although RTI proponents would likely label this a *virtue* of the approach! More persuasive criticisms of RTI concern its implementation. For instance, as RTI proponents have acknowledged at times (e.g., Burns, 2007), to be successful, an RTI system must place primary emphasis on Tier 1, providing instruction that has been proven to be effective for the vast majority of students. Unfortunately, many districts have officially switched to "RTI" without choosing genuinely effective instructional programs and then providing adequate training to staff. More generally, RTI is not an especially compelling *diagnostic* approach to SLD (or anything else) since it eschews formal diagnostic labels whenever possible and avoids discussion of exactly what diagnostic assessments should be done if interventions fail to work. In addition, psychometric concerns have been raised about the specific operationalizations of a student's responsiveness to intervention; different operational definitions (e.g., a particular steepness of the progress slope) often contradict each other regarding whether a student is making adequate progress (Barth et al., 2008), and some indices of responsiveness have disappointing low reliability (Ardoin & Christ, 2009).

Given the focus of the present handbook, we add a final limitation of the RTI approach: It cannot be executed by a clinician conducting a diagnostic evaluation at a single point in time. Obviously, if a school refers a student for evaluation and asks if the student has SLD, there is no time to implement and monitor the effectiveness of multiple interventions. RTI is best viewed as a general approach to delivering education, including the building of academic skills and the individualization of instruction when needed. When implemented well, it is an excellent approach to instruction, and it helps to rule out poor instruction as a cause of a student's problems. However, as a *diagnostic* method per se, it is insufficient, for the reasons discussed here.

Pattern of Strengths and Weaknesses

One interesting feature of the RTI approach to SLD assessment is that it makes intelligence testing unnecessary. Indeed, the cognitive abilities that are thought to underlie academic achievement are mostly ignored. A third approach to SLD assessment is instead centered around the relationship between cognitive abilities and academic skills and has come to be called the Pattern of Strengths and Weaknesses (PSW) approach. Unlike the IQ-achievement discrepancy approach, which typically uses intelligence tests to arrive at a global, overall estimate of general cognitive ability (from which academic skills may be discrepantly low), the PSW approach looks for a meaningful pattern of one or more deficits in academic skills, one or more deficits in relevant cognitive abilities, and evidence that the student's other, unrelated skills and abilities are higher. For instance, consider a student with a low score in writing and a low score on a test of working memory. Working memory has been shown to relate to writing skills (Flanagan, Alfonso, & Mascolo, 2011), and so the two low scores have a logical relationship; the student's deficit in working memory may be causally related to the poor writing skills. If the student's other abilities and academic skills are average or better, this would be taken as strong evidence of a SLD in written expression.

Several PSW assessment models have been proposed; all are similar, requiring an academic weakness, a related cognitive weaknesses, and higher scores on other measures. One issue the models vary on is which theory of cognitive abilities (i.e., intelligence) the model is linked to. Dawn Flanagan and her colleagues (2011) have proposed what is sometimes called the Cross-Battery Assessment (XBA) model, in which the specific cognitive abilities are interpreted through the framework of the Cattell-Horn-Carroll (CHC) model of cognitive abilities (Schneider & McGrew, 2012). Jack Naglieri (e.g., Naglieri, 2011) has proposed the Discrepancy/Consistency model, which is instead based on the PASS (planning, attention, simultaneous processing, and successive processing) model of cognitive abilities. Finally, Brad Hale and his colleagues (e.g., Hale, Wycoff, & Fiorello, 2011) have proposed what is known as the Concordance-Discordance Model (CDM), which is not linked to a particular model of cognitive abilities.

PSW models appear to best address the conception of learning disabilities as neuropsychological disorders with disturbances in the cognitive processes that would typically allow normal acquisition and growth in academic skills. Use of these models helps psychologists, teachers, and parents to feel as though they understand *why* a student is having difficulty learning. However, PSW models have a number of limitations as well. First, what counts as a "relevant" cognitive deficit underlying an achievement deficit is not entirely clear. Many cognitive abilities are domain-general (i.e., used to process a variety of types of stimuli) and so are linked to many different academic skills. Since the chance of having one or more low cognitive scores is actually quite high in the general population of schoolchildren (Brooks, 2011), it is important to clearly define which cognitive deficits are relevant. Second, several recent research studies have found that PSW models have low sensitivity (failing to detect most cases of students with academic skill deficits) and low agreement with each other (for review, see McGill et al., 2016). Finally, different PSW profiles do not appear to be associated with differential benefit from academic skills interventions (Miciak et al., 2016), undermining the practical utility of the approach.

Low Achievement Models

At this point, after we have reviewed the problems with discrepancy, RTI, and PSW models, the reader may be wondering if there is any alternative. In fact, there is a final model that has received increased attention and research support. Simply put, such a model makes low academic skills and educational impairment (as indexed by below-average scores on standardized diagnostic achievement tests and poor performance in school) the central feature of SLD, and the rest of the diagnostic process involves excluding other likely causes (e.g., low effort, sensory impairments, intellectual disability; see Lovett & Kilpatrick, 2018). Such a model has been endorsed by scholars (e.g., Dombrowski, Kamphaus, & Reynolds, 2004) and is actually similar to what is found in the DSM-5 (American Psychiatric Association, 2013), whose criteria for "Specific Learning Disorder" require that someone have academic skills that "are substantially and quantifiably below those expected for the individual's chronological age" (p. 67), that the skill deficits cause impairment in real-world (e.g., educational or occupational) settings, and that other causes for the skill deficits are ruled out. This is a practical model for clinically trained psychologists who practice privately or in schools to use, especially after routine back-up instructional approaches and simple interventions have failed.

Does the low achievement model have any limitations? Like any non-RTI approach, the assessment only takes place in one point in time, and so careful attention should be given to the reliability of the tests used (Fletcher, Denton, & Francis, 2005) and as we discuss below, the effort of the student during the psychoeducation evaluation. In addition, there is no one perfect threshold at which point academic skills become "below average." The DSM-5 (American Psychiatric Association, 2013) recommends that skills be at least 1.5 standard deviations below the mean for the greatest diagnostic confidence and suggests that 1 standard deviation below the mean should be the bare minimum even when other data are supportive of the diagnosis. In some cases, we might relax that a bit further, but relevant achievement test scores should consistently be below the 25th percentile compared to age peers, and educational outcomes should generally meet that standard as well, at least for initial diagnosis (before accommodations or other services are provided). A final limitation is less easily addressed: The low achievement model ignores traditional conceptions of learning disabilities as internal dysfunctions that are *detected* rather than *defined* by diagnostic test scores. Therefore, the low achievement model provides a pragmatic operational definition for identifying students with SLD but may not provide users with a sense of having *explained* the student's low achievement.

DETERMINATION OF TESTING ACCOMMODATION NEEDS

A second "special topic" that arises frequently when conducting assessments in educational settings involves making recommendations about testing accommodations. Here, we are not discussing accommodations on diagnostic tests but accommodations for the tests (both teacher-made and standardized) that students will take as part of their general educational program.

A testing accommodation involves altering the administration procedure for a test without altering its content (Lovett & Lewandowski, 2015). Accommodations are typically grouped into categories such as *timing/scheduling accommodations* (e.g., being permitted to take more time to complete a test, altering the time of day when the test is given, spreading a lengthy exam across multiple, briefer testing sessions), *response format accommodations* (e.g., dictating answers to a scribe, being permitted to mark answers in a test booklet rather than on a bubble sheet), *setting* accommodations (e.g., taking an exam in a separate location with fewer distractions, altering the lighting or furniture set-up of the location), and *presentation* accommodations (e.g., enlarging the font of the exam text, reading a test aloud to a student, providing clarification of directions). The examples we have noted are only a small subset of the accommodations that have been provided in educational settings (for more examples, see Thurlow, Elliott, & Ysseldyke, 2003).

The goal of testing accommodations is to increase the validity of a student's test scores (or, more technically, the validity of interpretations made on the basis of students' test scores). Consider a blind student who is given a typical paper-and-pencil test in math class. If the student is unable to see the items, the resulting test score will not reflect the student's actual math skills, just their visual acuity. If a presentation accommodation (e.g., large print, Braille) is provided, the student's test score is more likely to reflect the skills that the test was designed to measure, thus increasing validity. The logic of accommodations is easiest to see in cases of physical or sensory disabilities (such as blindness), and common sense can be used to make many accommodations decisions in these cases. Final decisions about testing accommodations are made by a school-based team, but psychologists often serve in a critical role in these decisions, either as a member of that team (e.g., a school psychologist) or as an external professional making recommendations that the team considers.

Of course, psychologists are typically involved with cases of students whose disabilities are not as clear-cut as blindness and where it is far more difficult to determine which accommodations are truly needed to access tests. Consider a student with an anxiety disorder who feels more comfortable taking a test when no one else is present; would this make a private testing room an appropriate accommodation? What about a student with ADHD who reports feeling pressed for time on state-wide exams; should this student receive an extended time accommodation? When should students with reading disabilities have tests read aloud to them? In cases of learning, cognitive, and psychiatric disabilities (i.e., the types of disabilities that psychologists diagnose and are expected to have expertise in managing), the diagnostic standards often vary from psychologist to psychologist, and it is harder to say whether a student is actually unable to take a test under standard administration conditions.

To assist in difficult cases, Phillips (1994) proposed five questions that should be asked before an accommodation is granted. More than twenty years later, her questions remain very important, and much research has examined them in the interim. The five questions are presented here, in a somewhat modified form, but reflecting Phillips's concepts:

1. Are the psychometric properties of the test scores maintained when an accommodation is given? (For instance, does the reliability of the scores stay approximately the same?)
2. Are the test's tasks comparable when the accommodation is provided or does the accommodation fundamentally change the test so that it no longer measures everything that it is supposed to measure?
3. Are the benefits of the accommodation specific to individuals with relevant disabilities or would other students also benefit from the accommodation? (Does the accommodation function as an unfair advantage?)
4. Can students with disabilities adapt to standard test administration conditions? That is, are the accommodations being given due to a genuine *need* or could the students adjust to standard conditions if necessary?
5. Is the accommodations decision made using procedures that themselves have adequate reliability and validity?

For psychologists conducting diagnostic evaluations and making general recommendations about accommodations for a student, perhaps the most important question is the fourth one: What accommodations, if any, does the student truly need? Accommodations should not be given merely to make a student more comfortable or to make tests more enjoyable. Instead, there should be credible, objective, direct evidence that the student is deficient in skills that are needed to access an exam. Such "access skills" are not what the exams are designed to measure but what the student needs to fully participate in the exam and obtain a valid score. For instance, if a student with a learning disability has significantly below-average levels of reading fluency, extended time accommodations would often be appropriate on written tests (i.e., tests where the items need to be read by the student) so long as the exam is not designed to be at all speeded. Similarly, if a student has significantly below-average levels of decoding skills, a read-aloud (or similar) accommodation would generally be appropriate, so long as the exam is not designed to measure reading skills. In contrast, most students with anxiety and mood disorders are able to access tests under standard conditions, even if the student would find an accommodation to be comforting. Note that most diagnostic categories have tremendous internal heterogeneity with regard to students' accommodation needs. For instance, some students with ADHD may be deficient in skills needed to access timed tests but many others are not (Lewandowski et al., 2013), making extended time accommodations unnecessary and inappropriate for those students.

School-based teams should consider all of Phillips's questions carefully when making decisions. For instance, the second question, concerning whether an accommodation would fundamentally alter a test so that the test no longer measures everything that it is designed to measure, is often ignored but quite vital. An increasing number of states are permitting students with reading disabilities to have *reading* tests read aloud to them (e.g., Infante-Green, 2016), which turns reading tests into listening tests and keeps students' resulting scores from informing score users (e.g., parents, teachers) about students' actual levels of reading skills. Similarly, allowing a student to use a calculator on a math test, as an accommodation, would compromise the ability of a test to measure calculation skills, although the accommodation may be appropriate on some tests designed to measure math *reasoning* where calculation is merely a skill needed to access the test. When making accommodations recommendations in an evaluation report, psychologists should address this issue by specifying when an accommodation would be appropriate and when it would not be, or by at least acknowledging that the accommodation would only be appropriate when it does not fundamentally alter a test.

THE INFLUENCES OF MOTIVATION AND EFFORT ON CHILDREN'S TEST PERFORMANCE

Finally, we consider a frequently overlooked factor when psychologists conduct evaluations to aid in determining eligibility for special education or other education-related services: children's motivation and effort during the evaluation. In this section, we discuss the necessity of good effort in producing valid testing results; potential reasons for children's noncredible performance during psychological evaluations; and methods for identifying noncredible performance, with a special emphasis on SLD evaluations.

Because psychologists make impactful inferences about children based on testing results, it is essential that the validity of these inferences be well supported. Of course, many psychologists are careful to use tests that have adequate psychometric properties, but many factors beyond the test's properties affect the validity of the inferences made from test scores, with substantial implications for the accuracy of diagnostic and management decisions. Student motivation or effort during psychoeducational evaluations is one such factor. Indeed, the *Standards for Educational and Psychological Testing* highlight "students' motivation to perform well on the test" (AERA, APA, & NCME, 2014, p. 189) as a key factor influencing the validity of test results.

Although some children may give their best effort in nearly all situations, many children do not. If optimal test effort were universal among children, then their test performance would be the same regardless of situational conditions. In fact, however, those conditions are substantially associated with student effort and subsequent performance. For instance, students who believe their test scores will affect their grades or their teacher's employment status due to state accountability standards earn higher scores than do students whose test performance has no such attached stakes (Rutkowski & Wild, 2015). Similarly, when students believe that their test performance has consequences for high school graduation, they earn substantially higher average scores and pass rates compared to students taking the same test without these known consequences (Steedle & Grochowalksi, 2017). Material incentives (e.g., candy) have also been shown to significantly increase students' test scores, with large effects even on intelligence tests. Duckworth and colleagues (2011) found especially large effects when children had below-average baseline IQ. When these children were provided a material incentive, they increased their IQ scores by nearly a full standard deviation. Furthermore, Duckworth and colleagues (2011) found a dose-response relationship, with large material incentives increasing IQ scores by more than 1.5 standard deviations. Clearly, the stakes of tests matter to children, and some children's effort levels appear to fluctuate significantly based on the value they attribute to tests. Therefore, it cannot be assumed that all children put forth optimal effort during psychological evaluations, the nature of which many children do not understand (Carone, 2015).

Children may put forth low effort during psychoeducational evaluations for a variety of reasons. Some children may simply avoid engagement in tasks that they do not value or that they find frustrating (Adelman et al., 1989), while others may have specific incentives for intentionally performing poorly. Whereas external incentives for adults to put forth poor effort during evaluations are often clear (e.g., college students attempting to obtain stimulant medication or to receive testing accommodations), the incentives for children may be less obvious, requiring a close examination of incentives that matter to the individual child (Sherman, 2015). Many examples of incentives for children to give noncredible effort during evaluations have been provided in the literature, such as attempts to avoid school for various reasons (e.g., academic stress and bullying) and to avoid returning to a sport the child does not want to play (see Kirkwood, 2015, and Kirkwood et al., 2010 for additional examples). Cases of children putting forth noncredible effort due to parental pressure because of parental external incentive (referred to as malingering by proxy) have also been reported in the literature (see, e.g., Chafetz & Prentowski, 2011; Walker, 2011). These case examples illustrate the diversity of motivations behind poor effort, some of which are likely subconscious rather than conscious, leading to an even more challenging situation for psychologists.

To meet this challenge, performance validity tests (PVTs) – very easy tests that can be passed by even individuals with significant neurological impairment or intellectual disability as long as they put forth good effort – have been developed to identify noncredible presentations during psychoeducational evaluations. These tests are designed based on the "principle of insensitivity to actual impairment" (Green & Flaro, 2003, p. 191), meaning that they are created to be unrelated to ability and ability-related influences (e.g., age). Two types of PVTs have been developed: *freestanding PVTs* specifically designed to measure only effort and *embedded PVTs* created based on scores from actual ability measures. Although originally developed for use with adults, PVTs and their adult cutoffs have generally been found to be effective in detecting noncredible presentations in children (DeRight & Carone, 2015; Kirkwood, 2015), with some exceptions (a topic we return to). Many psychologists may believe that they are able to detect noncredible effort using their clinical judgment. This is true for obvious cases (e.g., a student who defiantly refuses to engage in the evaluation process), but, in other cases, psychologists are generally unable to detect noncredible presentations using their clinical judgment (Guilmette, 2013), necessitating the use of PVTs to assess effort in a credible and objective manner.

PVTs are particularly important during child SLD evaluations because the various models of SLD identification require the assessment of academic functioning, and some models (IQ-achievement discrepancy and PSW models) require the assessment of cognitive functioning. Test score profiles consistent with these various conceptualizations of SLD are easily produced by individuals who do not have SLD but who have been directed to feign SLD during simulation studies; these profiles are generally indistinguishable from the profiles of those with genuine SLD (Harrison, Edwards, & Parker, 2008; Lindstrom et al., 2009). Not only is SLD easily feigned but there is also evidence that a sizable minority of individuals being evaluated for SLD (approximately 15 percent) do not put forth sufficient effort during these evaluations (Harrison & Edwards, 2010; Sullivan, May, & Galbally, 2007). These base rates of noncredible effort are based on college students; base rates from SLD evaluations of school-age children have yet to be empirically investigated, although case examples have been presented in the literature (see, e.g., Harrison, Green, & Flaro, 2012).

Fortunately, PVTs have been found to be highly sensitive to detecting individuals who have been instructed to feign SLD during simulation studies. Again, these studies used college students as participants rather than school-age children, but the studies' results likely apply to younger children, given the mounting evidence that adult cutoffs for PVTs are appropriate for children (Kirkwood, 2015). Both general-global and domain-specific PVTs have been shown to be effective in detecting noncredible presentations during SLD evaluations. General-global PVTs are tasks that do not incorporate stimuli specific to the layperson's knowledge of a specific disorder, whereas domain-specific PVTs incorporate this specific type of stimuli (Osmon et al., 2006). For instance, a domain-specific PVT for dyslexia may include words with letter reversals, given the lay public's belief that dyslexia involves reading words backwards. In contrast, a general-global PVT is designed to be a task requiring general effort (e.g., a simple memory task) that is sensitive to broad effort issues across disorders. Regarding general-global memory-based PVTs, Lindstrom and colleagues (2009) found that both the Test of Mental Malingering (TOMM; Tombaugh, 1996) and the Word Memory Test (WMT; Green, 2003) had excellent specificity (> 0.90) when used to detect simulated SLD but the WMT was shown to have better sensitivity (> 0.90) than the TOMM (0.68). Similarly, Frazier and colleagues (2008) found the Victoria Symptom Validity Test (Slick et al., 1997) to identify accurately more than 90 percent of simulated SLD cases. The Word Reading Test (WRT; Osmon et al., 2006) and the Dyslexia Assessment of Simulation and Honesty (DASH; Harrison et al., 2008) are domain-specific PVTs that use reading-related stimuli to detect feigned SLD in reading. Both the WRT and the DASH have been shown to demonstrate excellent accuracy in detecting simulated SLD in reading (Harrison et al., 2008; Harrison et al., 2010; Osmon et al., 2006). These results using college-age samples are promising, but further research is needed to determine their generalizability to school-age individuals, specifically in the context of SLD evaluations.

Because the stimuli of some PVTs require some reading, it is important to establish that children with bona fide SLD in reading can pass these tests if they put forth adequate effort. Although only a paucity of studies have examined PVTs with children with SLD, results from two studies have been promising. In one study, Harrison and Armstrong (2014) investigated the classification accuracy of various embedded performance validity measures when used with adolescents with confirmed SLD. They found that Reliable Digit Span of the Wechsler Intelligence Scale for Children – Fourth Edition (WISC-IV) had excellent classification accuracy, whereas other WISC-IV embedded performance validity measures (i.e., cutoff score on Digit Span and Vocabulary–Digit Span difference score) did not. In the other study, Larochette and Harrison (2012) administered the WMT to a sample of adolescents with confirmed SLD and no external incentive for noncredible presentations (i.e., they had already been determined eligible for disability-related services). They found that more than 90 percent of the entire sample passed the effort measures of the WMT and that 100 percent of the sample with a third-grade reading level or higher passed. The few participants who failed the WMT had severely impaired reading skills (e.g., mean standard score of 48.5 on a norm-referenced word reading measure), and the researchers concluded that these participants failed because of impaired reading skills rather than noncredible effort. Thus, the WMT may not be well suited for use with children with severe SLD in reading, although there are special administration instructions that can be used with this group (i.e., the words can be read to them; Green, 2003) and additional analyses (i.e., Advanced Interpretation Program; Green, 2009) can be conducted to distinguish possible noncredible presentations from severe reading impairment. Further research is needed to determine the validity of using the WMT with very young children and those with below-third-grade reading levels. In the meantime, using a nonverbal PVT (e.g., TOMM) with this population is likely more appropriate (DeRight & Carone, 2015).

Finally, although space prevents a full discussion regarding the use of PVTs with children evaluated for SLD, one additional issue having to do with use of the term "malingering" is important to highlight. Malingering refers to the *intentional* feigning of symptoms when motivated by external incentive (American Psychiatric Association, 2013). Failure on PVTs does not necessarily indicate malingering because PVTs only measure behavior, not intention (Kirkwood et al., 2010). Although detailed criteria for determining malingering have been proposed (e.g., see Slick, Sherman, & Iverson, 1999), malingering remains difficult to determine because its identification continues to be based substantially on the clinician's subjective judgment (Kirkwood et al., 2010). Some psychologists may equate PVTs only with malingering identification and therefore may be reluctant to use them, knowing that the diagnosis of malingering is difficult to make and creates potentially contentious relationships with some clients. This reluctance is unfortunate because psychologists who regularly use PVTs find them to be valuable beyond malingering identification, and most do not diagnose malingering even if PVTs are failed (Martin, Schroeder, & Odland, 2015). The larger importance of PVTs rests on their ability to ensure that evaluations results are credible, regardless of the specific reasons for noncredible presentations. As we have discussed psychologists are not adept at making this determination on their own and it cannot be assumed that children will always put forth credible effort. Without evaluation data that accurately represent examinees' actual skills and abilities, psychologists cannot make accurate decisions about children's functioning, decisions that in schools may substantially affect children's educational placement and future.

CONCLUSIONS

As we hope this chapter has shown, assessment in educational settings brings a variety of unique challenges. The regulations governing school-based evaluations are sometimes very different from what clinicians in private practice operate under. Different methods of assessing learning problems each have their own advantages and disadvantages. Determining a student's need for testing accommodations can be a complex, multifaceted process; and formally monitoring student motivation and effort during an evaluation is paramount but often neglected. These challenges can be off-putting but they are also what makes the work so exciting. Given the importance of valid assessment practices in this context, we hope that clinicians are motivated to surmount these challenges and perform evaluations that yield accurate information about children and adolescents, leading to thoughtful and evidence-based decisions about diagnoses, accommodations, and interventions for struggling youth.

REFERENCES

Aaron, P. G. (1997). The impending demise of the discrepancy formula. *Review of Educational Research*, *67*(4), 461–502.

Adelman, H. S., Lauber, B. A., Nelson, P., & Smith, D. C. (1989). Toward a procedure for minimizing and detecting false positive diagnoses of learning disability. *Journal of Learning Disabilities*, *22*(4), 234–244.

AERA (American Educational Research Association), APA (American Psychological Association), & NCME (National Council on Measurement in Education). (2014). *Standards for educational and psychological testing*. Washington, DC: American Educational Research Association.

American Psychiatric Association. (2013). *Diagnostic and statistical manual of mental disorders* (5th ed.). Arlington, VA: American Psychiatric Publishing.

Ardoin, S. P., & Christ, T. J. (2009). Curriculum-based measurement of oral reading: Standard errors associated with progress monitoring outcomes from DIBELS, AIMSweb, and an experimental passage set. *School Psychology Review*, *38*(2), 266–284.

Barth, A. E., Stuebing, K. K., Anthony, J. L., Denton, C. A., Mathes, P. G., Fletcher, J. M., & Francis, D. J. (2008). Agreement among response to intervention criteria for identifying responder status. *Learning and Individual Differences*, *18* (3), 296–307.

Bateman, B. D. (1965). An educator's view of a diagnostic approach to learning disorders. In J. Hellmuth (Ed.), *Learning disorders* (pp. 219–239). Seattle, WA: Special Child Publications.

Berninger, V. W., & Abbott, R. D. (1994). Redefining learning disabilities: Moving beyond aptitude–achievement discrepancies to failure to respond to validated treatment protocols. In G. R. Lyon (Ed.), *Frames of reference for the assessment of learning disabilities* (pp. 163–183). Baltimore, MD: Brookes.

Blanchett, W. J. (2006). Disproportionate representation of African American students in special education: Acknowledging the role of white privilege and racism. *Educational Researcher, 35*(6), 24–28.

Brooks, B. L. (2011). A study of low scores in Canadian children and adolescents on the Wechsler Intelligence Scale for Children, (WISC-IV). *Child Neuropsychology, 17*(3), 281–289.

Burns, M. K. (2007). RTI will fail, unless ... *NASP Communiqué, 35*(5), 38–40.

Burns, M. K., Jimerson, S. R., VanDerHeyden, A. M., & Deno, S. L. (2016). Toward a unified response-to-intervention model: Multi-tiered systems of support. In S. R. Jimerson, M. K. Burns, & A. M. VanDerHeyden (Eds.), *Handbook of response to intervention* (2nd ed., pp. 719–732). New York: Springer.

Carone, D. A. (2015). Clinical strategies to assess the credibility of presentations in children. In M. W. Kirkwood (Ed.), *Validity testing in child and adolescent assessment: Evaluating exaggeration, feigning, and noncredible effort* (pp. 107–124). New York: Guilford.

Chafetz, M., & Prentkowski, E. (2011). A case of malingering by proxy in a Social Security Disability psychological consultative examination. *Applied Neuropsychology, 18*, 143–149. doi:10.1080/09084282.2011.570619

DeRight, J., & Carone, D. A. (2015). Assessment of effort in children: A systematic review. *Child Neuropsychology, 21*(1), 1–24. doi:10.1080/09297049.2013.864383

Dombrowski, S. C., Kamphaus, R. W., & Reynolds, C. R. (2004). After the demise of the discrepancy. *Professional Psychology: Research and Practice, 35*(4), 364–372.

Duckworth, A. L., Quinn, P. D., Lynam, D. R., Loeber, R., Stouthamer-Loeber, M., & Smith, E. E. (2011). Role of test motivation in intelligence testing. *Proceedings of the National Academy of Sciences of the United States of America, 108*(19), 7716–7720. doi:10.1073/pnas.10118601108/-/DCSupplemental

Eckert, T. L., & Lovett, B. J. (2013). Principles of behavioral assessment. In D. H. Saklofske, C. R. Reynolds, & V. L. Schwean (Eds.), *Oxford Handbook of Child Psychological Assessment* (pp. 366–384). New York: Oxford University Press.

Flanagan, D. P., Alfonso, V. C., & Mascolo, J. T. (2011). A CHC-based operational definition of SLD: Integrating multiple data sources and multiple data-gathering methods. In D. P. Flanagan & V. C. Alfonso (Eds.), *Essentials of specific learning disability identification* (pp. 233–298). Hoboken, NJ: Wiley.

Fletcher, J. M., Denton, C., & Francis, D. J. (2005). Validity of alternative approaches for the identification of learning disabilities: Operationalizing unexpected underachievement. *Journal of Learning Disabilities, 38*(6), 545–552.

Fletcher-Janzen, E., & Reynolds, C. R. (Eds.). (2008). *Neuropsychological perspectives on learning disabilities in the era of RTI: Recommendations for diagnosis and intervention.* Hoboken, NJ: Wiley.

Frazier, T. W., Frazier, A. R., Busch, R. M., Kerwood, M. A., & Demaree, H. A. (2008). Detection of simulated ADHD and reading disorder using symptom validity measures. *Archives of Clinical Neuropsychology, 23*, 501–509. doi:10.1016/j.acn.2008.04.001

Fuchs, D., Fuchs, L. S., & Stecker, P. M. (2010). The "blurring" of special education in a new continuum of general education placements and services. *Exceptional Children, 76*(3), 301–323.

Gersten, R., Jayanthi, M., & Dimino, J. (2017). Too much, too soon? Unanswered questions from national Response to Intervention evaluation. *Exceptional Children, 83*(3), 244–254.

Green, P. (2003). *Word Memory Test*. Edmonton: Green's Publishing.

Green, P. (2009). *The Advanced Interpretation Program*. Edmonton: Green's Publishing.

Green, P., & Flaro, L. (2003). Word Memory Test performance in children. *Child Neuropsychology, 9*(3), 189–207. doi:10.1076/chin.9.3.189.16460

Gresham, F. M. (2002). Responsiveness to intervention: An alternative approach to the identification of learning disabilities. In R. Bradley, L. Danielson, & D. P. Hallahan (Eds.), *Identification of learning disabilities: Research to practice* (pp. 467–519). Mahwah, NJ: Erlbaum.

Guilmette, T. J. (2013). The role of clinical judgment in symptom validity assessment. In D. Carone & S. Bush (Eds.), *Mild traumatic brain injury: Symptom validity assessment and malingering* (pp. 31–45). New York: Springer.

Hale, J. B., Wycoff, K. L., & Fiorello, C. A. (2011). RTI and cognitive hypothesis testing for identification and intervention of specific learning disabilities: The best of both worlds. In D. P. Flanagan & V. C. Alfonso (Eds.), *Essentials of specific learning disability identification* (pp. 173–202). Hoboken, NJ: Wiley.

Harrison, A. G., & Armstrong, I. (2014). WISC-IV unusual digit span performance in a sample of adolescents with learning disabilities. *Applied Neuropsychology: Child, 3*(2), 152–160. doi:10.1080/21622965.2012.753570

Harrison, A. G., & Edwards, M. J. (2010). Symptom exaggeration in post-secondary students: Preliminary base rates in a Canadian sample. *Applied Neuropsychology, 17*, 135–143. doi:10.1080/09084281003715642

Harrison, A. G., Edwards, M. J., Armstrong, I., & Parker, K. C. H. (2010) An investigation of methods to detect feigned reading disabilities. *Archives of Clinical Neuropsychology, 25*, 89–98. doi:10.1093/arclin/acp104

Harrison, A. G., Edwards, M. J., & Parker, K. C. H. (2008). Identifying students feigning dyslexia: Preliminary findings and strategies for detection. *Dyslexia, 14*, 228–246. doi:10.1002/dys.366

Harrison, A. G., Green, P., & Flaro, L. (2012). The importance of symptom validity testing in adolescents and young adults undergoing assessments for learning or attention difficulties. *Canadian Journal of School Psychology, 27*(1), 98–112. doi:10.1177/0829573512437024

Heward, W. L. (2013). *Exceptional children* (10th ed.). Boston: Pearson.

Hunt, E. (2011). *Human intelligence*. New York: Cambridge University Press.

Infante-Green, A. (2016). Changes in allowable testing accommodations on the Grades 3–8 New York State English Language Arts Assessments. www.p12.nysed.gov/specialed/publications/testing-accommodations-ela-grades-3-8.htm

Kirk, S. A. (1962). *Educating exceptional children*. Boston: Houghton Mifflin.

Kirkwood, M. W. (2015). Review of pediatric performance and symptoms validity tests. In M. W. Kirkwood (Ed.), *Validity testing in child and adolescent assessment: Evaluating exaggeration, feigning, and noncredible effort* (pp. 79–106) New York: Guilford.

Kirkwood, M. W., Kirk, J. W., Blaha, R. Z., & Wilson, P. (2010). Noncredible effort during pediatric neuropsychological evaluations: A case series and literature review. *Child Neuropsychology, 16*, 604–618. doi:10.1080/09297049.2010.495059

Kovaleski, J. F., VanDerHeyden, A. M., & Shapiro, E. S. (2013). *The RTI approach to evaluating learning disabilities*. New York: Guilford.

Larochette, A., & Harrison, A. G. (2012). Word Memory Test performance in Canadian adolescents with learning disabilities: A preliminary study. *Applied Neuropsychology: Child, 1*, 38–47. doi:10.1080/21622965.2012.665777

Lewandowski, L., Gathje, R. A., Lovett, B. J., & Gordon, M. (2013). Test-taking skills in college students with and without ADHD. *Journal of Psychoeducational Assessment, 31*(1), 41–52.

Lindstrom, W. A., Lindstrom, J. H., Coleman, C., Nelson, J., & Gregg, N. (2009). The diagnostic accuracy of symptom validity tests when used with postsecondary students with learning disabilities: A preliminary investigation. *Archives of Clinical Neuropsychology, 24*, 659–669. doi:10.1093/arclin/acp071

Lovett, B. J., & Kilpatrick, D. A. (2018). Differential diagnosis of SLD versus other difficulties. In D. P. Flanagan & V. C. Alfonso (Eds.), *Essentials of specific learning disability assessment* (2nd ed., pp. 549–571). Hoboken, NJ: Wiley.

Lovett, B. J., & Lewandowski, L. J. (2006). Gifted students with learning disabilities: Who are they? *Journal of Learning Disabilities, 39*(6), 515–527.

Lovett, B. J., & Lewandowski, L. J. (2015). *Testing accommodations for students with disabilities: Research-based practice*. Washington, DC: American Psychological Association.

Maki, K. E., Floyd, R. G., & Roberson, T. (2015). State learning disability eligibility criteria: A comprehensive review. *School Psychology Quarterly, 30*(4), 457–469. doi:10.1037/spq0000109

Martin, P. K., Schroeder, R. W., & Odland, A. P. (2015). Neuropsychologists' validity testing beliefs and practices: A survey of North American professionals. *The Clinical Neuropsychologist, 29*(6), 741–776. doi:10.1080/13854046.2015.1087597

McGill, R. J., Styck, K. M., Palomares, R. S., & Hass, M. R. (2016). Critical issues in specific learning disability identification: What we need to know about the PSW model. *Learning Disability Quarterly, 39*(3), 159–170.

Miciak, J., Williams, J. L., Taylor, W. P., Cirino, P. T., Fletcher, J. M., & Vaughn, S. (2016). Do processing patterns of strengths and weaknesses predict differential treatment response? *Journal of Educational Psychology, 108*(6), 898–909.

Morgan, P. L., Farkas, G., Hillemeier, M. M., & Maczuga, S. (2012). Are minority children disproportionately represented in early intervention and early childhood special education? *Educational Researcher, 41*(9), 339–351.

Morgan, P. L., Farkas, G., Hillemeier, M. M., Mattison, R., Maczuga, S., Li, H., & Cook, M. (2015). Minorities are disproportionately underrepresented in special education: Longitudinal evidence across five disability conditions. *Educational Researcher, 44*(5), 278–292.

Naglieri, J. A. (2011). The discrepancy/consistency approach to SLD identification using the PASS theory. In D. P. Flanagan & V. C. Alfonso (Eds.), *Essentials of specific learning disability identification* (pp. 145–172). Hoboken, NJ: Wiley.

Osmon, D. C., Plambeck, E., Klein, L., & Mano, Q. (2006). The Word Reading Test of effort in adult learning disability: A simulation study. *The Clinical Neuropsycholgist, 20*, 315–324. doi:10.1080/13854040590947434

Phillips, S. E. (1994). High-stakes testing accommodations: Validity versus disabled rights. *Applied Measurement in Education, 7*(2), 93–120.

Reschly, D. J., & Hosp, J. L. (2004). State SLD identification policies and practices. *Learning Disability Quarterly, 27*(4), 197–213.

Rutkowski, D., & Wild, J. (2015). Stakes matter: Student motivation and the validity of student assessments for teacher evaluation. *Educational Assessment, 20*(3), 165–179. doi:10.1080/10627197.2015.1059273

Scanlon, D. (2013). Specific learning disability and its newest definition: Which is comprehensive? And which is insufficient? *Journal of Learning Disabilities, 46*, 26–33.

Schneider, W.J. , & McGrew, K. S. (2012). The Cattell-Horn-Carroll model of intelligence. In D. Flanagan & P. Harrison (Eds.), *Contemporary intellectual assessment: Theories, tests, and issues* (3rd ed., pp. 99–144). New York: Guilford.

Sherman, E. M. S. (2015). Terminology and diagnostic concepts. In M. W. Kirkwood (Ed.), *Validity testing in child and adolescent assessment: Evaluating exaggeration, feigning, and noncredible effort* (pp. 22–41). New York: Guilford.

Skiba, R. J., Simmons, A. B., Ritter, S., Gibb, A. C., Rausch, M. K., Cuadrado, J., & Chung, C. G. (2008). Achieving equity in special education: History, status, and current challenges. *Exceptional Children, 74*(3), 264–288.

Slick, D., Hopp, G., Strauss, E., & Thompson, G. B. (1997). *Victoria Symptom Validity Test*. Odessa, FL: Psychological Assessment Resources.

Slick, D. J., Sherman, E. M. S., & Iverson, G. L. (1999). Diagnostic criteria for malingered neurocognitive dysfunction: Proposed standards for clinical practice and research. *The Clinical Neuropsychologist, 13*(4), 545–561. doi:10.1076/1385-4046-(199911)13:041-Y; FT545

Stanovich, K. E. (2005). The future of a mistake: Will discrepancy measurement continue to make the learning disabilities field a pseudoscience? *Learning Disability Quarterly, 28*(2), 103–106.

Steedle, J. T., & Grochowalkski, J. (2017). The effects of stakes on accountability test scores and pass rates. *Educational Assessment, 22*(2), 11–123. doi:10.1080/10627197.2017.1309276

Sternberg, R. J., & Grigorenko, E. L. (2002). Difference scores in the identification of children with learning disabilities: It's time to use a different method. *Journal of School Psychology, 40*(1), 65–83.

Sullivan, A. L., & Bal, A. (2013). Disproportionality in special education: Effects of individual and school variables on disability risk. *Exceptional Children, 79*(4), 475–494.

Sullivan, B. K., May, K., & Galbally, L. (2007). Symptom exaggeration by college adults in attention-deficit hyperactivity and learning disorder assessments. *Applied Neuropsychology, 14*(3), 189–207. doi:10.1080/09084280701509083

Thurlow, M. L., Elliott, J. L., & Ysseldyke, J. E. (2003). *Testing students with disabilities: Practical strategies for complying with district and state requirements*. Thousand Oaks, CA: Corwin.

Tombaugh, T. N. (1996). *Test of Memory Malingering*. Toronto: Multi-Health Systems.

Vellutino, F. R., Scanlon, D. M., & Lyon, G. R. (2000). Differentiating between difficult-to-remediate and readily remediated poor readers: More evidence against the IQ-achievement discrepancy definition of reading disability. *Journal of Learning Disabilities*, *33*(3), 223–238.

Volpe, R. J., & Fabiano, G. A. (2013). *Daily behavior report cards*. New York: Guilford.

Walker, J. S. (2011). Malingering in children: Fibs and faking. *Child and Adolescent Psychiatric Clinics of North America*, *20*, 547–556. doi:10.1016/j.chc.2011.03.13

Yell, M. L., Katsiyannis, A., & Collins, J. C. (2010). Compton Unified School District v. Starvenia Addison: Child find activities and response to intervention. *Journal of Disability Policy Studies*, *21*(2), 67–69.

Ysseldyke, J. (2001). Reflections on a research career: Generalizations from 25 years of research on assessment and instructional decision making. *Exceptional Children*, *67*(3), 295–309.

Index

For EU product safety concerns, contact us at Calle de José Abascal, 56–1°,
28003 Madrid, Spain or eugpsr@cambridge.org.

www.ingramcontent.com/pod-product-compliance
Ingram Content Group UK Ltd.
Pitfield, Milton Keynes, MK11 3LW, UK
UKHW051118290926
15471UKWH00010B/1751